Dictionary of World Biography

The Ancient World

Dictionary of World Biography

Dictionary of World Biography

Volume 1
The Ancient World

Frank N. Magill, *editor*

Christina J. Moose, *managing editor*

Alison Aves, *researcher and bibliographer*

Mark Rehn, *acquisitions editor*

FITZROY DEARBORN PUBLISHERS
CHICAGO • LONDON

SALEM PRESS
PASADENA • ENGLEWOOD CLIFFS

Dictionary of World Biography is a copublication of Salem Press, Inc. and Fitzroy Dearborn Publishers Ltd.

For information, write to:

SALEM PRESS, INC.
P.O. Box 50062
Pasadena, California 91115

or

FITZROY DEARBORN PUBLISHERS
70 East Walton Street
Chicago, Illinois 60611
USA

or

FITZROY DEARBORN PUBLISHERS
11 Rathbone Place
London W1P 1DE
England

∞ The paper used in this volume conforms to the American National Standard for Permanence of Paper for Printed Library Materials, Z39.48-1992.

Library of Congress Cataloging-in-Publication Data
Dictionary of world biography / editor, Frank N. Magill ; managing editor, Christina J. Moose ; researcher and bibliographer, Alison Aves ; acquisitions editor, Mark Rehn.
      v. cm.
      A revision and reordering, with new entries added, of the material in the thirty vols. comprising the various subsets designated "series" published under the collective title: Great lives from history, 1987-1995.
      Includes bibliographical references and indexes.
      Contents: v.1. The ancient world.
      ISBN 0-89356-313-7 (v. 1 : alk. paper)
      ISBN 0-89356-273-4 (set : alk paper)
      1. Biography. 2. World history. I. Magill, Frank Northen, 1907-1997. II. Moose, Christina J., 1952- . III. Aves, Alison. IV. Great lives from history.
CT104.D54 1998
920.02—dc21
                                                     97-51154
                                                       CIP

British Library Cataloguing-in-Publication Data is available.
Fitzroy Dearborn ISBN 1-57958-040-8

First Published in the U.K. and U.S., 1998
Printed by Braun-Brumfield, Inc.

Cover design by Peter Aristedes.

First Printing

CONTENTS

PUBLISHERS' NOTE

The *Dictionary of World Biography, Volume I: The Ancient World* is the first installment in a projected ten-volume series covering the lives of important personages from "The Ancient World" through the twentieth century. This new series is a revision and reordering of Salem Press's thirty-volume *Great Lives from History* series. The contents of the various *Great Lives from History* sets have been integrated then rearranged from a geographical perspective into a chronological one, combining important people from all over the world into a single title covering an era. The existing essays are enhanced by the addition of new entries, updated bibliographies, a new page design, and illustrations.

The Ancient World, volume 1 of the dictionary, gathers 218 essays from the *Great Lives from History: Ancient and Medieval* series (1988) and adds 43 new biographies, creating a total of 261 essays covering 263 important figures. The date of A.D. 450 was selected, by the editors, as the cutoff between the ancient world and the middle ages. Those lives falling on the cusp were moved into the period that most encompassed their life's work or major accomplishments.

The articles in this series range from two- to three-thousand words in length and follow a standard format. Each article begins with ready-reference listings, including a brief statement summarizing the individual's contribution to his or her society and later ages. The body of the article is divided into three parts. "Early Life," the first section, provides facts about the individual's upbringing and the environment in which he or she was reared, setting the stage for the heart of the article, the section entitled "Life's Work." This section consists of a straightforward account of the period during which the individual's most significant achievements were made. The concluding section, the "Summary," is not a recapitulation of what has been discussed but rather an overview of the individual's place in history. Each essay is supplemented by an annotated, evaluative bibliography, a starting point for further research.

The temporal and geographical scope of *The Ancient World* volume is broad. Represented here are figures as ancient as the Egyptian king Zoser (fl. twenty-seventh century B.C.) and as late as the Jute chief Hengist (A.D. 420-488), spanning the Eastern and Western hemispheres. The editors have sought to provide coverage that is broad in area of achievement as well as geography, while at the same time including the recognized shapers of history essential in any liberal arts curriculum. Major world leaders appear here—pharaohs, emperors, conquerors, kings, and khans—as well as giants of religious faith: Buddha, Moses, Zoroaster, Jesus Christ, and the priests and saints who left their imprint on our political as well as spiritual institutions. Also included are scholars, philosophers, scientists, explorers, and artists—all of them architects of today's civilization.

While each volume in the *Dictionary of World Biography* has its distinctive qualities, several features distinguish this series as a whole from other biographical reference works. The articles combine breadth of coverage with a format that offers the user quick access to the particular information needed. For convenience of reference, this volume is indexed by area of achievement, by geographical location, as well as by name. The tenth volume of the series will provide a comprehensive index to all previous volumes, allowing users access to all the figures covered from the ancient world through the twentieth century.

We would like to extend our appreciation to all those involved in development and production of this series. Each essay has been written by an academician who specializes in the area of discussion, and without his or her expert contribution, a project of this nature would not be possible. A full list of contributors and their affiliations appears in the front matter of this volume.

CONTRIBUTING ESSAYISTS

Linda Perry Abrams
Bob Jones University, South Carolina

Patrick Adcock
Henderson State University, Arkansas

Amy Allison
Toluca Lake, California

J. Stewart Alverson
University of Tennessee at Chattanooga

James A. Arieti
Hampden-Sydney College, Virginia

Mike Ashley
Chatham, Kent

Bryan Aubrey
Maharishi International University, Iowa

Richard Badessa
University of Louisville, Kentucky

S. P. Baeza
Oakland, California

Iraj Bashiri
University of Minnesota, Twin Cities Campus

Michael E. Bauman
Hillsdale College, Michigan

Albert A. Bell, Jr.
Hope College, Michigan

Richard P. Benton
Trinity College, Connecticut

Milton Berman
University of Rochester, New York

Terry D. Bilhartz
Sam Houston State University, Texas

Cynthia A. Bily
Adrian College, Michigan

Nicholas Birns
The New School for Social Research, New York

Edward Bleiberg
Memphis State University, Tennessee

Gerhard Brand
California State University at Los Angeles

William S. Brockington, Jr.
University of South Carolina at Aiken

W. R. Brookman
North Central Bible College, Minnesota

David D. Buck
University of Wisconsin at Milwaukee

Jeffrey L. Buller
Loras College, Iowa

Edmund M. Burke
Coe College, Iowa

William H. Burnside
John Brown University, Arkansas

Edmund J. Campion
University of Tennessee

Rosemary M. Canfield-Reisman
Troy State University, Alabama

Joan E. Carr
Washington University, Missouri

Gilbert T. Cave
Lakeland Community College, Ohio

James T. Chambers
Texas Christian University

Mark W. Chavalas
University of Wisconsin at La Crosse

Victor W. Chen
Chabot College, California

Pei-kai Cheng
Pace University, New York

Key Ray Chong
Texas Tech University

Patricia Cook
Emory University, Georgia

Owen C. Cramer
University of Chicago, Illinois

Frank Day
Clemson University, South Carolina

Bruce L. Edwards
Bowling Green State University, Ohio

Michael M. Eisman
Temple University, Pennsylvania

Robert P. Ellis
Worcester State College, Massachusetts

Thomas L. Erskine
Salisbury State College, Maryland

Randall Fegley
Pennsylvania State University

Gary B. Ferngren
Oregon State University

John W. Fiero
University of Southwestern Louisiana

R. Leon Fitts
Dickinson College, Pennsylvania

Michael S. Fitzgerald
Purdue University, West Lafayette, Indiana

Edwin D. Floyd
University of Pittsburgh, Pennsylvania

Robert J. Forman
Saint John's University, New York

Douglas A. Foster
David Lipscomb College, Tennessee

Rita E. Freed
Memphis State University, Tennessee

Richard N. Frye
Harvard University, Massachusetts

Keith Garebian
Mississauga, Ontario

Daniel H. Garrison
Northwestern University, Illinois

Donald S. Gochberg
Michigan State University

Hans Goedicke
Johns Hopkins University, Maryland

Leonard J. Greenspoon
Clemson University, South Carolina

William S. Greenwalt
Santa Clara University, California

Christopher E. Guthrie
Tarleton University, Texas

Thomas Halton
Catholic University of America, D.C.

Gavin R. G. Hambly
University of Texas at Dallas

J. S. Hamilton
Old Dominion University, Virginia

Sandra Hanby Harris
Tidewater Community College, Virginia

Paul B. Harvey, Jr.
Pennsylvania State University

Peter B. Heller
Manhattan College, New York

Diane Andrews Henningfeld
Adrian College, Michigan

Michael Hernon
University of Tennessee at Martin

Charles W. Holcombe
Northeast Missouri State University

James P. Holoka
Eastern Michigan University

Tonya Huber
Wichita State University, Kansas

J. Donald Hughes
University of Denver, Colorado

Shakuntala Jayaswal
University of New Haven, Connecticut

Cynthia Lee Katona
Ohlone College, California

Robert B. Kebric
University of Louisville, Kentucky

Kenneth F. Kitchell, Jr.
Louisiana State University and A&M College

Wilbur R. Knorr
Stanford University, California

Donald G. Kyle
University of Texas at Arlington

Eugene S. Larson
Los Angeles Pierce College, California

John M. Lawrence
Faulkner University, Alabama

Daniel B. Levine
University of Arkansas, Fayetteville

Leon Lewis
Appalachian State University, North Carolina

Thomas T. Lewis
St. Cloud, Minnesota

Winston W. Lo
Florida State University

Rita E. Loos
Framingham State College, Massachusetts

Reinhart Lutz
University of California at Santa Barbara

Ruth van der Maas
Michigan State University

Peter F. Macaluso
Montclair State College, New Jersey

Murray C. McClellan
Emory University, Georgia

C. Thomas McCullough
Centre College, Kentucky

Michelle C. K. McKowen
New York, New York

Kerrie L. MacPherson
University of Hong Kong

John D. Madden
University of Montana

Paul Madden
Hardin-Simmons University, Texas

Paolo Mancuso
Stanford University, California

Ralph W. Mathisen
University of South Carolina

James M. May
Saint Olaf College, Minnesota

Lysle E. Meyer
Moorhead State University, Minnesota

Ian Morris
University of Chicago, Illinois

Terry R. Morris
Shorter College, Georgia

Terence R. Murphy
American University, D.C.

B. Keith Murphy
Fort Valley State University, Georgia

Carolyn Nelson
University of Kansas

Frances Stickney Newman
University of Illinois at Urbana-Champaign

Steven M. Oberhelman
Texas A&M University

Glenn W. Olsen
University of Utah

Robert M. Otten
Assumption College, Massachusetts

Lisa Paddock
Cape May Court House, New Jersey

Robert J. Paradowski
Rochester Institute of Technology, New York

William E. Pemberton
University of Wisconsin, La Crosse

Mark Pestana
City College of Chicago-Richard J. Daley College

Nis Petersen
Jersey City State College, New Jersey

John R. Phillips
Purdue University Calumet, Indiana

Linda J. Piper
University of Georgia

Clifton W. Potter, Jr.
Lynchburg College, Virginia

David Potter
University of Michigan

Dorothy T. Potter
Lynchburg College, Virginia

David Powell
Western New Mexico University

Thomas Rankin
Walnut Creek, California

Abe C. Ravitz
California State University at Dominguez Hills

John D. Raymer
South Bend, Indiana

Clark G. Reynolds
College of Charleston, South Carolina

Edward A. Riedinger
Columbus, Ohio

Francesca Rochberg-Halton
University of Notre Dame, Indiana

Carl Rollyson
*Bernard M. Baruch College
City University of New York*

Joseph Rosenblum
University of North Carolina at Greensboro

Susan Rusinko
Bloomsburg University of Pennsylvania

Thomas Ryba
Michigan State University

Stephen Satris
Clemson University, South Carolina

Daniel C. Scavone
University of Southern Indiana

Thomas C. Schunk
Bellevue College, Nebraska

Victoria Scott
Lick Observatory, California

John C. Sherwood
University of Oregon

H. J. Shey
University of Wisconsin at Milwaukee

T. A. Shippey
University of Texas at Austin

R. Baird Shuman
University of Illinois at Urbana-Champaign

Thomas J. Sienkewicz
Monmouth College, Illinois

Donald C. Simmons, Jr.
Mississippi Humanities Council

Donna Addkison Simmons
Jackson, Mississippi

Andrew C. Skinner
Metropolitan State College, Colorado

Ralph Smiley
Bloomsburg University of Pennsylvania

Clyde Curry Smith
University of Wisconsin at River Falls

Ronald F. Smith
Massachusetts Maritime Academy

Norman Sobiesk
Winona State University, Minnesota

C. Fitzhugh Spragins
Arkansas College

Heinrich von Staden
Yale University, Connecticut

David L. Sterling
University of Cincinnati, Ohio

Leslie A. Stricker
Park College/WPAFB, Ohio

Paul Stuewe
Toronto

Susan A. Stussy
Kansas City, Kansas

Bruce M. Sullivan
Northern Arizona University

James Sullivan
California State University at Los Angeles

Roy Arthur Swanson
University of Wisconsin at Milwaukee

Shelley A. Thrasher
Lamar University-Orange, Texas

Greg Tomko-Pavia
Los Angeles

Antonía Tripolitis
Rutgers University New Brunswick, New Jersey

Marlin Timothy Tucker
David Lipscomb College, Tennessee

Larry W. Usilton
University of North Carolina at Wilmington

George W. Van Devender
Hardin-Simmons University, Texas

Peter L. Viscusi
Central Missouri State University

William T. Walker
Philadelphia College of Pharmacy and Science

John Walsh
Hofstra University, New York

Thomas H. Watkins
Western Illinois University

Ronald J. Weber
University of Texas at El Paso

Winifred Whelan
St. Bonaventure, New York

Thomas Willard
University of Arizona

Julie A. Williams
Lehigh University, Pennsylvania

John F. Wilson
University of Hawaii at Manoa

John D. Windhausen
Saint Anslem College, New Hampshire

Johnny Wink
Ouachita Baptist University, Arkansas

Michael Witkoski
South Carolina House of Representatives

Robert W. Yarbrough
Wheaton College, Illinois

Clifton K. Yearley
State University of New York at Buffalo

William M. Zanella
Hawaii Loa College

LIST OF ENTRANTS

AARON

Born: c. 1395 B.C.; Egypt
Died: c. 1272 B.C.; Moserah or Mount Hor, Sinai
Area of Achievement: Religion
Contribution: The founder of the Jewish priesthood, Aaron serves as the prototype of the ideal religious leader.

Early Life

Aaron remains a figure surrounded by mystery and seeming contradiction. Even his name is questioned. Is it of Egyptian origin? Does it derive from the Hebrew word for the ark of the covenant (*arōn*) located in the Holy of Holies, that inner sanctum closed to all but the high priest? Or is it the phrase his mother, Jochebed, uttered at his birth as she lamented bearing a son: "A, harōn" (woe, alas)? (Only a few months before Aaron's birth Pharaoh had issued his decree condemning to death all male children born to the Hebrews in Egypt.)

Yet his parents seem to have made no effort to hide Aaron, as they would three years later with his brother, Moses, when he was born. Indeed, tradition maintains that Aaron's father, Amram, was one of Pharaoh's councillors and that the boy himself grew up in the palace before filling his father's post. Aaron was also emerging as a leader of his enslaved people, urging them to remain faithful to the God of Abraham and to hope for delivery from bondage. His marriage to Elisheba, daughter of Amminadab, allied Aaron with a distinguished family from the powerful tribe of Judah—his brother-in-law, Nahshon, was that tribe's leader—and so enhanced his already prominent position.

Consequently, when God instructed Moses to return from his self-imposed exile in Midian and lead the Jews out of Egypt, Moses urged that Aaron be assigned this task instead. Here, after all, was someone familiar with the Egyptian court and trusted by his own people, whereas Moses, having lived in another country for forty years, was a stranger. Moreover, Moses regarded his brother as the better orator. Although Moses finally accepted the primary responsibility, Aaron, too, would play a large role in the Exodus.

Life's Work

Just as God appeared to Moses and told him to return to Egypt, so He informed Aaron of his brother's imminent return and instructed him to meet Moses at the border of Midian. Together they appeared before the leaders of the Hebrews, Aaron speaking and performing signs to establish the legitimacy of their mission. Together also they appeared before Pharaoh to demand the release of the Jews. Once again, Aaron offered a sign of their divine ministry: He threw his rod onto the floor of the palace, and the stick turned into a snake. Pharaoh's magicians duplicated this feat, but Aaron bested them when his rod devoured theirs. Pharaoh remained unmoved, though, and the ten plagues began with Aaron's stretching his hand over the waters of Egypt, turning them to blood. Aaron would bring on the next two plagues—frogs and lice—as well, and with Moses he created the sixth, boils.

After the Exodus, the eighty-three-year-old Aaron seems to have become one of the triumvirate of leaders, sharing power with Moses and Hur. When the Amalekites attacked the Hebrews at Rephidim, Aaron stood on one side of Moses, Hur on the other, to hold up Moses' hands and so ensure the victory for Joshua and his troops. When Moses ascended Mount Sinai to receive the Ten Commandments, Aaron and Hur remained behind to govern.

The strangest episode of Aaron's life occurred about this time. Moses' lengthy absence—he would be gone forty days—persuaded the Hebrews that their leader was dead, so they demanded an idol to replace him. Hur refused to comply and was killed, as were the elders opposing this wish. Alone and unsupported, Aaron instructed the people to bring him all of their gold. Was he hoping that they would be unwilling to part with their treasure? If so, he was disappointed, for they readily complied. According to the account in certain rabbinical commentaries, he cast the gold into a furnace, apparently intending only to melt it, yet a golden calf emerged, seemingly of itself. The Hebrews responded by acclaiming the calf as the god that had led them out of Egypt. Perhaps to delay any worship of this idol, Aaron declared that the next day would be a festival for the graven image; by the time Moses returned, though, the celebration had already begun.

According to some accounts, only the intervention of Moses saved Aaron's life from divine retribution. Yet shortly afterward, Aaron was designated high priest. Was he being rewarded for his efforts to delay the idolatrous worship? Might the

1

golden calf, in fact, have represented a deity worshipped by the Hebrews in Egypt? Was Aaron's role in its creation the cause of his elevation to the priesthood? In later Jewish worship, the temple altar had two horns, and after the division of Israel into two kingdoms, Jeroboam erected golden calves at Bethel and Dan to compete with the Temple in Jerusalem. The choice of this animal suggests lingering loyalty to a bull as deity, or at least as representative of the deity.

The consecration of Aaron to the priesthood, whatever its cause, divorced religious leadership from the secular and placed priests under the power of the latter. God was to appear only to Moses in the desert, never to the high priest, and it was Moses who dictated the laws and rituals that Aaron and his sons were to follow. This subordination would become even more pronounced as political power passed from the tribe of Levi (to which both Aaron and Moses belonged) to Benjamin and then Judah, after the conquest of Canaan and the establishment of the monarchy. That elevation to the post of high priest removed Aaron from political leadership did not escape his notice; with Miriam, his older sister, Aaron protested against Moses' emergence as sole leader. For her criticism, Miriam was afflicted with leprosy for seven days; Aaron escaped with a divine rebuke.

A more serious challenge came from Korah, a kinsman of Moses and Aaron. Organizing many of the tribal leaders, he attacked the brothers for assuming undue power, but this rebellion was quickly suppressed by an earthquake that destroyed the ringleaders and a plague that killed more than fourteen thousand others. The toll would have been higher had Aaron not taken his censer and arrested the plague by standing between the living and the dead.

To reinforce the message that Aaron was the divine choice for the priesthood, Moses instructed each tribal elder to bring his staff to the tabernacle (the tent of worship), and Aaron placed his own among them. The next morning they found that Aaron's staff had flowered and had produced almonds. The others removed their rods, while Aaron's remained in the tent as a warning against further rebellions.

Despite such challenges, it is clear that Aaron was popular—more popular, in fact, than the sometimes stern and irascible Moses. Aaron must have been an impressive figure in the camp—his flowing white beard, his priestly garments, and the breast-plate of twelve precious stones commanding reverence. He was not only respected but also loved. The famous Jewish rabbi Hillel urged his students to imitate Aaron, "loving peace and pursuing peace, loving one's fellow men and bringing them nigh to the Torah."

Freed from the role of judge and lawgiver, Aaron could devote himself to teaching and making peace. Legend says that he would go from tent to tent to instruct those unfamiliar with the law. In a similar way, when he heard that two people had quarreled, he would go to one and say, "The person you argued with deeply regrets his hasty words and actions and seeks your forgiveness." Then he would go to the other party and say the same thing, thereby effecting a reconciliation. He was famous for reuniting feuding husbands and wives, who generally named their next child for him. The eighty thousand Hebrews bearing the name of Aaron attest his success as a marriage counselor.

Throughout the forty years that the Jews wandered in the desert, Aaron served as high priest, assisted by his two younger sons, Eleazar and Ithamar; his two older sons, Nadab and Avihu, had died when they offered "strange fire"—apparently some form of idolatry—in the sacred tent. Like his brother Moses and his sister Miriam, Aaron was not, however, destined to enter the Promised Land.

According to certain Jewish commentaries, it was, in fact, the death of Miriam at the beginning of the fortieth year of wandering that indirectly led to the punishment and death of both her brothers. Tradition holds that during Miriam's life a well had followed the Hebrews from camp to camp; as soon as she died, the well vanished. Lacking water at Meribah in the Wilderness of Zin, the Hebrews criticized Moses and Aaron for leading them into a wasteland. God commanded the two men to assemble the people and then speak to a rock, which would bring forth water. Distracted and angered by the threats and complaints of the people, Moses struck the rock instead, thus disobeying the divine order and diminishing the greatness of the miracle. For this failing, both men were condemned to die outside Canaan.

Aaron's death followed Miriam's by four months. Unwilling to reveal to his brother that God had decreed Aaron's death, Moses summoned Aaron and Eleazar to accompany him up Mount Hor. There they found a cave. Aaron removed his priestly garments and gave them to his son; the high priest then entered the cave, lay down on a couch, and died—as the story goes—by a kiss from the Shekinah, the Holy Spirit (c. 1272 B.C.).

The people's reaction to Aaron's disappearance again reveals his popularity. When Moses and Eleazar returned, the Hebrews suspected that they had murdered Aaron out of jealousy. Tradition maintains that to save the two from being stoned, God showed Aaron lying dead in the cave, proving that he had died naturally, not violently. For thirty days all Israel mourned Aaron's passing; when Moses died eight months later the sense of loss was not so universally shared.

Summary

As the first high priest and founder of the priestly caste, Aaron has served as the model of the religious leader. Christian theologians saw him as the prototype of Jesus Christ, differing only in the fact that Aaron sacrificed animals, whereas Christ offered himself to be killed. Though Aaron is less popular as an artistic subject than Moses, the French painter Jean Fouquet and the English painter John Everett Millais produced idealized portraits of him.

Nineteenth and twentieth century biblical scholars have been less kind, questioning his priestly role and, indeed, challenging his very existence. Whether he was the creation of some late biblical redactor or indeed Moses' brother, whom God chose to preside over the holy tabernacle, Aaron has assumed an important role in the Judeo-Christian tradition and has become inextricably associated with the early development of the Jewish religion.

Bibliography

Aberbach, Moses, and Leivy Smolar. "Aaron, Jeroboam, and the Golden Calves." *Journal of Biblical Literature* 86 (1967): 129-140. Points out the similarities between the biblical description of Aaron and that of Jeroboam and suggests that either the latter consciously imitated the former in the construction of the golden calves at Bethel and Dan or the story in Exodus was written by members of a non-Aaronite priesthood in Jerusalem to discredit the northern kingdom. Offers a careful examination of Aaron's role in the creation of the golden calf.

Ginzberg, Louis. *The Legends of the Jews.* Translated by Henrietta Szold and Paul Radin. 7 vols. Philadelphia: Jewish Publication Society of America, 1909-1938. Draws together biblical, Talmudic, and post-Talmudic sources to create a coherent narrative of Jewish history from the Creation to the time of Esther. Aaron receives extensive coverage in volumes 2 and 3, which treat life in Egypt, the Exodus, and the wanderings in the desert.

Kaufmann, Yehezkel. *The Religion of Israel.* Translated by Moshe Greenberg. New York: Schocken Books, and London: Allen and Unwin, 1960. Originally published in eight volumes in Hebrew between 1937 and 1956. The English version, condensed and translated by Greenberg, discusses the growth of Judaism and, inter alia, examines the role that Aaron and the priesthood played in the process.

Kennett, R. H. "The Origin of the Aaronite Priesthood." *The Journal of Theological Studies* 6 (January, 1905): 161-186. Seeks to reveal the character of Aaron and trace the development of his personality—and of the Jewish priesthood—through the various versions of the Pentateuch and prophetic books.

Meek, Theophile James. "Aaronites and Zadokites." *The American Journal of Semitic Languages and Literatures* 45 (April, 1920): 149-166. Maintains that two rival priestly traditions existed in early Judaism and considers the way this conflict affected the biblical portrayal of Aaron, who in places seems saintly and elsewhere idolatrous.

———. *Hebrew Origins.* Rev. ed. New York: Harper and Brothers, 1950. In the fourth chapter of this work, Meek discusses the rise of the Jewish priesthood. Challenging the orthodox religious view, Meek maintains that Aaron "is clearly a supernumerary who was later introduced into the [biblical] narrative as Israelite and Judean sagas became fused with the union of the two people."

Joseph Rosenblum

ABRAHAM

Born: c. 2050 B.C.; Ur, Chaldea

Died: c. 1950 B.C.; Macpelah, Mesopotamia

Area of Achievement: Religion

Contribution: According to Hebrew tradition and biblical record, Abraham is the ancient ancestor of the people of Israel to whom God first promised territory, nationhood, and spiritual blessing. He is therefore the key patriarch in the history of Judaism and of extreme importance as well to the development of both Christianity and Islam.

Early Life

The only historical record of the life of Abraham is found in the Pentateuch, the first five books of the Old Testament, one of the two divisions of the Bible whose composition is traditionally attributed to Moses. The full story of Abraham's life is contained in Genesis 11:27-25:11, though there are references to Abraham's life scattered throughout the rest of the Bible. The dating of Abraham's birth and early life is primarily informed guesswork, but archaeological consensus is that Abraham was born sometime around the twentieth century B.C. His father is identified as Terah in the biblical genealogy (Genesis 11:27); evidently, Terah was a wealthy man who owned property and livestock and who worshipped the pagan gods of Chaldea. Chaldea, the ancient name for Babylonia, was a center of advanced culture and commerce in antiquity, and it is quite likely that Abraham was a highly educated, cosmopolitan citizen of this society, himself no doubt wealthy. Some archaeologists contend that it is possible that Abraham left written records of his journey to the ancient Near East that were incorporated into the Pentateuch. Most modern scholars accept the substantial historicity of these narratives.

The biblical record introduces Abraham as "Abram," which means "father" in Hebrew; later in the narrative, Abram will be renamed as the better known "Abraham," which means "father of many." Abram is called by God to leave his father's house in Ur to journey to a land that God promises to him and his descendants. There is no indication in the narrative that Abram had been chosen for any particular merit or religious devotion, though later Old and New Testament writings present him as the archetypal man of faith, who serves as an example to all of the power of belief in God's sovereignty. Accompanying him on the journey are his wife, Sarah, and nephew Lot, and their families.

Most startling in this sequence of events is Abraham's willingness to abandon the pagan deities of his family to embrace a seemingly new God—and thus become a declared monotheist in a decidedly polytheistic and pagan antiquity. The next episodes reported in the life of Abram trace his growing acceptance of this unique belief and center on his journey to Canaan, the land promised to him. His path takes him and his traveling companions through Egypt and the surrounding nations. In Egypt, Abram fears that his beautiful wife will be taken from him, so he claims that she is his sister and thus attempts to deceive Pharaoh and his princes. When God reveals her true identity to the Egyptian monarch, Pharaoh orders Abram and his entourage to leave. Upon leaving Egypt, Abram and his nephew decide to go their separate ways, Lot choosing the fertile land of Sodom and Gomorrah for settlement and Abram the northern country of Hebron. These choices become fateful in the lineage of both men.

Life's Work

The life of Abraham as it unfolds in the book of Genesis encompasses the fulfillment of the promises God had announced to him before he left Ur. Important in the light of the birth of modern Israel is the fact that the land promised to Abraham is quite explicitly identified in the biblical record: God promises Abraham and his descendants possession of the whole land from the Euphrates River southwestward, an area, in fact, larger than the land area occupied by Israel since World War II.

The three most important episodes recounted in Genesis involve Abraham's attempt to secure an heir to receive the inheritance of God's promises, the institution of the covenant between God and Abraham sealed with the act of circumcision, and the judgment and destruction of the cities of Sodom and Gomorrah—Lot's new homeland—because of their rampant rebellion and decadence. It is in these episodes that the character of Abraham as a man of faith as well as of action is established and becomes the pattern for later biblical and traditional portraits of his heroism and trust.

Soon after he and Lot part company, Abram is called upon to rescue Lot; in so doing he proves himself both a good military strategist and also a

offspring will be as numerous as the stars in the sky and that the land and nation promised to him will indeed come to his descendants if he will only continue to trust. Thereafter, Abram is called Abraham by God, indicating the surety of His promises that he will be the father of many nations. Reluctant to wait for God's timing, Abram proceeds to father a son by Hagar, his maidservant. This son, named Ishmael, is rejected by God; Abraham is instead exhorted to await the rightful heir with patience and confidence. In Genesis 17, the covenant between God and Abraham is proclaimed once more and God asks Abraham and all the males of his household to be circumcised as a sign of their commitment to the covenant. The act of circumcision is ever after a peculiar sign of God's presence with the Hebrew people, not merely a hygienic practice but a religious symbol of dramatic proportion to every Hebrew family of God's blessing as well.

In the midst of Abraham's tribulations, he receives word that Lot's city, Sodom, will be destroyed along with Gomorrah because of its wickedness. In a famous conversation, Abraham bargains with God over the city, pleading with Him to spare the cities if He can find even ten righteous men. He cannot, and the cities are destroyed, with Lot and his family spared. On their way out of the destruction, however, Lot's wife—against the direct command of God—looks back at the fallen cities and is turned into a pillar of salt.

Because of their faith and righteousness, Abraham and Sarah are blessed with the birth of a son, Isaac—whose name meant "laughter," a reference to Sarah's incredulity at becoming pregnant at the age of one hundred. Some years later, Abraham faces the final test of faith in his life when God calls upon him to sacrifice his son. Obedient to the end, Abraham and Isaac make the long trek to an altar far from their camp where Abraham once sacrificed animals. As he prepares to offer his son, he ties Isaac down and raises his knife, about to end the boy's life. Just before the knife is plunged into Abraham's only heir, God calls upon Abraham to stop for his faith has been shown to be full and unyielding. Because of his obedient heart, God promises him once more that he will have descendants as numerous as the sand at the seashore.

Abraham eventually outlives Sarah and is blessed to see Isaac's marriage to Rebekah. Isaac and Rebekah later become the parents of Jacob and Esau, and the historical saga of Israel's develop-

devout, unselfish believer. Lot has found himself the captive of rival kings who have plundered the cities of Sodom and Gomorrah. Abram raises an army and, in saving Lot, also manages to recover all of his lost possessions and captured kinsmen. In returning from these exploits, Abram encounters the mysterious King of Salem, Melchizadek, who pronounces a blessing upon Abram for his faith and his canny defeat of the treacherous armies in the land about him. Melchizadek is also a priest of "the God Most High," or "Yahweh," the same God who has called Abraham out of Ur to a special blessing. Abram pays a tithe to Melchizadek, and, when the King of Salem praises him, Abram defers the praise to God, who had blessed him with victory.

The promises to Abraham in Genesis 12 were intended to foreshadow the tapestry of events in his life and in Genesis 15 God reiterates them as Abram continues his quest for the land. He becomes skeptical and impatient of the likelihood of their fulfillment, however, given that he is still childless because of Sarah's barrenness. Nevertheless, God renews His promise to Abram that his ment as a nation under the governance of God is initiated, a fulfillment of a divine promise to the itinerant man from Ur.

Summary

It is difficult to overestimate the impact of the life of Abraham on Hebrew culture both in the ancient and medieval world and in the modern world. His acceptance of belief in one, true God, and its implications, sets him apart in the history of religions common to his time and place. It is the name of this God (Yahweh) that Moses, the champion of Israel's flight from Egyptian captivity, invokes in confronting Pharaoh and in leading his people from bondage. Further, the promises made by the God of the Old Testament to Abraham have remained a part of the political and social history of the land of Israel even to this day and have played an essential part in the formation of modern Israel after World War II. To be a Jew is to trace one's ancestry back to Abraham and his sons, Isaac and Jacob. To adherents of Judaism, Abraham is the quintessential man of success, faith, and loyalty whose stature overshadows nearly every other ancient Hebrew notable except Moses.

Further, Abraham's character as a man of trust and perseverance has heavily influenced both Christianity and Islam to the extent that both faiths regard the biblical record of Abraham as the starting point for their own systems of doctrine. Jesus Christ, according to the New Testament, claimed to be a descendant of Abraham—basing His teaching on the authority that this heritage bestowed upon Him—while at the same time claiming that His own life, as the eternal Son of God, is in fulfillment of God's promise to Abraham that He would bless all nations through him and his descendants. Paul, the Christian convert who wrote most of the letters of the New Testament, cites Abraham as the man who exemplifies commitment and truth for Christianity, a man who was counted "righteous" not because of his works but because of his faith. Muhammad, the prophet of Islam, claimed Abraham as his forerunner as well, proclaiming that he and his message stood in the same historical and intellectual genealogy as Abraham's.

The story of Abraham's willingness to sacrifice his own son in response to the call of God has long interested artists and storytellers; in the modern age, it has come to be emblematic of the piercing moment of destiny and decision-making in an individual's life when he must make a choice that will set the pattern for the rest of his life. Abraham thus comes to represent to Jew and non-Jew alike the epitome of the "righteous man," one who takes a stand in the midst of turmoil, doubt, and confusion for the side of justice, equality, and fairness. His covenant with God and his faithfulness animate inhabitants of both Western and Eastern cultures in their quest for security and hope in a troubled world.

Bibliography

Albright, W. F. *The Archaeology of Palestine*. Rev. ed. London and Baltimore: Penguin Books, 1954. This is a standard work on the archaeology of the ancient world that remains the most comprehensive and informed overview of the historical data gleaned from the ancient world. Overall, it provides the reader with an authentic sense of the world from which Abraham came and the one to which he traveled.

Alexander, David, and Pat Alexander, eds. *Eerdmans' Handbook to the Bible*. Rev. ed. Grand Rapids, Mich.: Eerdmans, 1973. This is a comprehensive handbook to biblical history and geography with helpful charts and maps that trace Abraham's journey and illuminate the specific episodes in his life drawn from the biblical text for the lay reader.

Bright, John. *A History of Israel*. 3d ed. Philadelphia: Westminster Press, and London: SCM Press, 1981. Bright's study is probably the most thorough and compelling nontheological treatment of the history of Israel in print. Includes sections on the world of the patriarchs, ancient Chaldea, Egypt, and Israel that enlighten the story of Abraham and sustain the interest of both the common reader and the scholar with helpful "anecdotal" commentary on life in ancient times.

Harrison, R. K. *An Introduction to the Old Testament*. Grand Rapids, Mich.: Eerdmans, 1969; London: Tyndale, 1970. Harrison provides a complete overview of the origin, message, and impact of each book of the Old Testament which speaks directly and comprehensively to the issues of the chronology, authenticity, and influence of the life of Abraham. A comprehensive scholarly work with extensive documentation.

Kidner, Derek. *Genesis*. Downers Grove, Ill. and Leicester: Inter-Varsity Press, 1967. A helpful one-volume commentary on the key biblical book containing the narratives regarding Abraham, this volume provides useful insights into what might be called the "psychology" of Abraham's call and journey to Canaan.

Kitchen, K. A. *Ancient Orient and Old Testament.* Chicago: Inter-Varsity Press, and London: Tyndale, 1966. An insider's look at the world of archaeology and how it functions in validating ancient records and narratives, this work is particularly helpful in its extensive tracing of the various stops in the journey of Abraham to the promised land against the backdrop of the patriarchal age.

Schultz, Samuel J. *The Old Testament Speaks.* 4th ed. San Francisco: Harper, 1990. Written for the lay reader, this cogent and lucid volume presents an objective, historical analysis of the lives of the patriarchs—including a major section on Abraham—and other characters in the evolution of ancient Israel and suggests their relevance to the study of both Christianity and Islam.

Thompson, J. A. *Handbook to Life in Bible Times.* Downers Grove, Ill. and Leicester: Inter-Varsity Press, 1986. A colorful, lavishly illustrated reference tool with key sections on the domestic life, travel, family customs, and cultural preoccupations of the biblical world; this work illuminates the life and times of a person living in twentieth century B.C. and thus is a helpful contextualizing volume for a study of Abraham.

Bruce L. Edwards

AESCHYLUS

Born: 525-524 B.C.; Eleusis, Greece
Died: 456-455 B.C.; Gela, Sicily
Areas of Achievement: Theater and drama
Contribution: Aeschylus' dramaturgy marks a major stage in the development of Western theater, especially tragedy.

Early Life

Knowledge of the life of Aeschylus is limited by minimal and unreliable sources. A Hellenistic biography surviving in the manuscript tradition of Aeschylus' plays is filled with ancient gossip, conjecture, and elaboration. The only extant portraits of the dramatist are probably not authentic.

Aeschylus was born about 525-524 B.C. in Eleusis, an Attic town about fourteen miles northwest of Athens. His father, Euphorion, a Eupatrid or wealthy aristocrat, had several children: at least two other sons, Cynegirus and Ameinias, and a daughter whose name is not recorded.

As a Eupatrid, Aeschylus belonged to one of the ancient and powerful landed families who had controlled Greece for generations but whose political power deteriorated in Aeschylus' own lifetime, especially in Attica. Aeschylus' birthplace was an ancient city which had retained a sense of local pride despite its incorporation into the city-state of Athens many years before. While it is uncertain whether Aeschylus was ever initiated into the famous cult of Demeter at Eleusis, he certainly grew up within its shadow. Later in life, Aeschylus is said to have been prosecuted for revealing a mystery of Demeter in one of his plays but to have been exonerated on the grounds that he had done so unwittingly.

The young Aeschylus, benefiting from the wealth and prestige of his aristocratic family, undoubtedly received a good education, founded upon the poetry of Homer. With such learning, Aeschylus developed a strong sense of a Eupatrid's civic responsibility and authority and was exposed to the traditional poetry, myths, and music upon which his tragedies were later based.

If ancient tradition can be trusted, Aeschylus began composing plays as a teenager. His early dramatic career is poorly documented. Sometime between 499 and 496, he entered the Athenian dramatic competition at the Greater Dionysia with an unknown group of plays but did not receive first prize. There is no record of how many contests he entered before his first victory in 484, again with unknown plays.

As an Athenian citizen, the young Aeschylus lived through some of the most exciting years in that city's history. In the tightly knit aristocratic society of late sixth century Athens, Aeschylus would have observed at first hand the turmoil associated with the murder of the Athenian prince Hipparchus in 514, the expulsion of his brother Hippias in 510, and the constitutional reforms of democratic Cleisthenes in 508. The progression from tyranny to democracy in Athens inevitably meant less power for the Eupatrid class. While the political position of Aeschylus and his family in this period is uncertain, these events undoubtedly encouraged the cautious conservatism which Aeschylus exhibited in later years.

The young playwright was also a soldier. In the first decade of the fifth century, the Persian Empire ruthlessly suppressed a revolt by Ionian Greek cities along the coast of modern Turkey and then invaded the mainland of Greece in retaliation for

support of the Ionians. In 490, the Persian king Darius the Great was soundly defeated by united Greek forces at the battle of Marathon, where Aeschylus fought and where his brother Cynegirus died. Ten years later, during a second Persian invasion of Greece by Darius' son, Xerxes I, Aeschylus also participated in the naval battle of Salamis, at which the Athenians defeated the Persian fleet against great odds. Accounts of Aeschylus' participation in other battles, especially at Plataea in 479, must be dismissed as examples of biographical exaggeration. These victories permanently curtailed the threat of Persian domination of the Greek mainland and brought about the period of Athenian political hegemony during which Aeschylus produced all of his extant plays.

Life's Work

While the titles of at least eighty Aeschylean plays are known, only seven tragedies survive in the Aeschylean corpus. Since entries in the Greater Dionysia always consisted of three tragedies plus one satyr play, about three-quarters of Aeschylus' plays were tragedies. Plots for these plays were generally connected with the Trojan War or with the myths of Thebes and Argos. At the height of his dramatic career, Aeschylus, who acted in his own plays, was extremely successful. Of the twenty-odd productions attributed to his name, he was victorious at least thirteen times, maybe more; in addition, several of his plays were produced after his death.

Aeschylus' earliest extant work, *Persai* (472 B.C.; *The Persians*), was first performed in Athens in 472 together with the lost plays *Phineus* and *Glaucus Potnieus*. This production, which won first prize, commemorated the Athenian victory at Salamis and includes Aeschylus' own eyewitness account, placed in the mouth of a messenger. In choosing historical rather than mythical subject matter for this play, Aeschylus followed a contemporary, Phrynichus, who had earlier composed two historical plays. Aeschylus' producer for his plays of 472 was Pericles, but the playwright's association with this great Athenian statesman and champion of democracy is not necessarily an indication of Aeschylus' political inclinations, for producers were assigned by the state, not chosen by the playwright.

Shortly after 472, at the invitation of the tyrant Hieron, Aeschylus traveled to Syracuse in Sicily, where *The Persians* was reproduced. Hieron, a great patron of the arts, attracted to his court not only Aeschylus but also the philosopher Xenophanes and the poets Pindar, Bacchylides, and Simonides. During his stay in Sicily, which may have lasted several years, Aeschylus also produced another play, *Aetnae*, now lost. Since this play celebrated Hieron's founding of the city of Aetna in 476, a visit by Aeschylus to Sicily prior to 472 was once considered to have been likely, but most scholars now believe that *Aetnae* was produced sometime shortly after 472. Aeschylus' long stay in Sicily left a permanent mark on the playwright's work, which is filled with Sicilian words and expressions.

Aeschylus was certainly back in Athens by 468, for his unknown production of that year was defeated when Sophocles won his first victory at the Greater Dionysia. In the following year, Aeschylus won the competition with a group including the lost *Laius* and *Oedipus* and the extant *Hepta epi Thēbas* (*Seven Against Thebes*).

Sometime between 467 and 458, Aeschylus produced the so-called Danaid trilogy, composed of the extant *Hiketides* (463 B.C.?; *The Suppliants*, also as *Suppliant Women*) and the lost *Egyptians* and *Danaids*. For stylistic reasons, *The Suppliants* used to be considered Aeschylus' earliest extant play, until the twentieth century publication of a papyrus fragment containing part of an ancient production notice for the play. This new evidence makes it likely that Aeschylus competed in 463 with the Danaid trilogy and was victorious over Sophocles.

In 458, Aeschylus directed his last Athenian production, which included the extant *Agamemnōn* (*Agamemnon*), *Choēphoroi* (*Libation Bearers*), and *Eumenides* and the lost satyr play *Proteus*. Together, these three tragedies, known as the *Oresteia*, make up the only surviving connected trilogy. The *Eumenides* is filled with allusions to such events as the recent Athenian alliance with Argos and the reform of the ancient court of Areopagus by the democrat Ephialtes. This evidence has been interpreted to suggest both that Aeschylus supported and that he opposed the political agenda of Athens in the middle of the fifth century.

Shortly after this production, which won first prize, Aeschylus left Athens for Sicily, never to return. Ancients conjectured that the playwright left Athens because of political dissatisfaction or professional disappointment. None of the evidence is certain, however, and the reasons for Aeschylus' second journey to Sicily remain obscure.

Some scholars believe that the seventh play surviving in the Aeschylus corpus, *Prometheus desmōtēs* (*Prometheus Bound*), was composed during Aeschylus' second stay in Sicily. Others deny that the play was written by Aeschylus at all.

The playwright also wrote epigrams and elegies. Fragments of Aeschylus' elegy composed in honor of the dead at Marathon were discovered in the Athenian agora in 1933. This poem is said to have been written for a competition, at an unknown date, which Aeschylus lost to the poet Simonides.

Aeschylus died in Gela, Sicily, in 456 or 455. An ancient biography recounts the following version of Aeschylus' death: An eagle flying overhead with a tortoise in its beak mistook Aeschylus' bald head for a rock upon which to shatter the shell of its prey and thus killed the poet. The Gelans erected this inscription over the poet's tomb:

> This memorial hides the Athenian Aeschylus,
>   Euphorion's son,
>   Who died in wheat-bearing Gela.
> The sacred battlefield of Marathon may tell of his
>   great valor.
>   So, too, can the long-haired Mede, who knows it
>   well.

By tradition, Aeschylus himself is said to have requested that he be remembered only as a patriotic Athenian and not as a great playwright.

Aeschylus had at least two sons, Euphorion and Euaeon, both of whom wrote plays. In 431, Euphorion defeated both Sophocles and Euripides. A few years later, Sophocles, competing with his masterpiece, *Oidipous Tyrannos* (c. 429 B.C.; *Oedipus Tyrannus*), was defeated by Aeschylus' nephew Philocles. After Aeschylus' death, a special decree was passed to permit revivals of his plays, which won several victories in subsequent years. In 405, the comic poet Aristophanes produced *Batrachoi* (*The Frogs*), in which the dead Aeschylus and Euripides debate about the quality of each other's tragedies.

Summary

Aeschylus is rightly considered the "father of Western tragedy." His works, coming at a strategic time, helped mold Greek tragedy into a great literary form. While Aristotle's statement in *De poetica* (c. 334-323 B.C.; *Poetics*) that Aeschylus "first introduced a second actor to tragedy and lessened the role of the chorus and made dialogue take the lead" cannot be proved, Aeschylus' extant plays do illustrate a skilled use of dialogue which made possible the agons, or great debates between characters so important in later Greek tragedy.

Whether Aeschylus himself introduced the second actor, he almost certainly invented the connected trilogy/tetralogy. As a rule, the group of three tragedies and one satyr play which a playwright produced at the festival were not connected thematically. It was Aeschylus who first saw the brilliant potential of linking the plays together. While his first extant play, *The Persians,* was not part of a connected group, all of his other surviving plays were. No other Greek playwright was able to make use of the trilogy form as successfully as Aeschylus did.

In *The Suppliants,* Aeschylus also experimented with the use of the chorus as dramatic protagonist. Traditionally a reflective and nondramatic element in the tragedy, the chorus became in this play the central character. Similarly, in *Eumenides* the chorus played a significant role as the prosecutor of the matricide Orestes.

Aeschylus' dramatic skills are particularly apparent in his handling of spectacular stage techniques. His plays, frequently making dramatic use of such stage trappings as altars, tombs, ghosts, and the *eccyclema,* a wheeled vehicle employed to show the interior, thus confirm Aeschylus as a master playwright who established for his successors a high standard of dramatic skill and power.

Bibliography

Goldhill, Simon. *Aeschylus: The Oresteia.* From *Landmarks of World Literature.* Cambridge and New York: Cambridge University Press, 1992. A concise, reliable introduction to Aeschylus' most frequently read plays. The first chapter provides historical background to tragedy and its function at Athens, the second discusses a variety of topics within the plays, and the third sketches some of the history of *The Oresteia*'s influence.

Herington, C.J. *Aeschylus.* New Haven, Conn.: Yale University Press, 1986. An excellent introduction to Aeschylus for the general reader. One chapter is devoted to biography with a short annotated bibliography and a table of dates.

————. "Aeschylus in Sicily." *Journal of Hellenic Studies* 87 (1967): 74-85. This discussion of the evidence for Aeschylus' trips to Sicily gives a chronology as well as a citation of the ancient evidence in Greek.

Lefkowitz, Mary. *The Lives of the Greek Poets.* London: Duckworth, and Baltimore, Md.: Johns Hopkins University Press, 1981. A translation and analysis of the Hellenistic biography of Aeschylus, otherwise unavailable in English, can be found in this book, which also includes a bibliography.

Lesky, Albin. *Greek Tragedy.* Translated by H. A. Frankfort. 3d ed. London: Benn, and New York: Barnes and Noble Books, 1979. A scholarly introduction to Aeschylus' dramaturgy, with a brief summary of his life. A bibliography is included.

———. *A History of Greek Literature.* Translated by James Willis and Cornelis de Heer. New York: Thomas Y. Crowell, and London: Methuen, 1966. Aeschylus' place in the literature of ancient Greece can be traced in this standard history, which includes biographical information and a bibliography.

Murray, Gilbert. *Aeschylus: The Creator of Tragedy.* Oxford: Clarendon Press, 1940; Westport, Conn.: Greenwood Press, 1978. Written by one of the most important scholars of Greek tragedy in the twentieth century, this book begins with a biography of the poet but does not include the revision to Aeschylus' chronology required by the papyrus find.

Podlecki, Anthony J. *The Political Background of Aeschylean Tragedy.* Ann Arbor: University of Michigan Press, 1966. This book contains an excellent life of Aeschylus in the first chapter and an interesting appendix on Aeschylus' description of the battle of Salamis.

Rosenmeyer, Thomas G. *The Art of Aeschylus.* Berkeley: University of California Press, 1982. Primarily a literary study, this work contains a short but good appendix on the life and times of Aeschylus. There is also an excellent "comparative table of dates and events" as well as a select bibliography.

Smyth, Herbert Weir. Introduction to *Aeschylus: Plays and Plays and Fragments with an English Translation.* 2 vols. Cambridge, Mass.: Harvard University Press, and London: Heinemann, 1922. Smyth's biography of Aeschylus, found in the introduction to volume 1, is still excellent despite being published prior to the discovery of the papyrus redating *The Suppliants.*

Spatz, Lois. *Aeschylus.* Boston: Twayne Publishers, 1982. Written for the general reader, this book includes a biography and an annotated bibliography.

Thomas J. Sienkewicz

AESOP

Born: Probably early sixth century B.C.; Thrace, Greece

Died: Probably sixth century B.C.; Delphi, Greece

Area of Achievement: Literature

Contribution: Aesop is reputed to have been a prolific inventor of fables, in which animals are endowed with human speech, for the purpose of illustrating a moral (or immoral) lesson. He probably wrote nothing himself but was rather a famous teller of tales that were later set down. As other fables were invented and collected, the authority of his name became attached to them.

Early Life

Although some scholars claim that he is purely a legendary figure, the following assertions are most often accepted as historically true in the ancient sources pertaining to Aesop: He originally came from Thrace; he was for a time a slave on the Greek island of Samos, off the coast of Asia Minor, in the service of a man named Iadmon, who later freed him; he was a contemporary of the poet Sappho in the early sixth century B.C.; and he was famed as a maker and teller of prose stories.

Later documents add details, of varying degrees of credibility, to Aesop's biography. For example, *The Life of Aesop,* apparently written by a Greek-speaking Egyptian in the first century A.D., states that he was very ugly, worthless as a servant, pot-bellied, misshapen of head, snub-nosed, swarthy, dwarfish, bandy-legged, short-armed, squint-eyed, and liver-lipped. The sources for this late biography may go back as far as the fifth century B.C., but that, of course, does not guarantee its authenticity. Indeed, its cumulative details relating to Aesop's life are typically as fanciful and entertaining as the fables attributed to him.

In that entertaining first century biography, Aesop is portrayed as mute until the Egyptian goddess Isis gives him speech in thanks for guiding one of her lost priestesses. Isis and the nine muses, the patron goddesses of the arts in Greek myth, also give him the power to conceive stories and the ability to elaborate tales in Greek that would make him famous. Aesop's sharp wit and inventive imagination contrast greatly to his grotesque appearance and to the dullness of those about him, both his master and his fellow slaves. Rejected because of his superior intellect and inferior exterior, Aesop soon becomes the property of a slave dealer, who sells him promptly and cheaply to the pompous philosopher Xanthus on the island of Samos.

Aesop outwits his master and mistress at every opportunity, usually through his verbal dexterity. There is even an episode in which Aesop has sex ten times with his master's wife, as a form of revenge. (There is a general mistrust of women's fidelity throughout the narrative.) Eventually, Xanthus is forced to grant freedom to his troublesome slave, who is the only one able to interpret an omen in which an eagle flies away with the city's official seal. Aesop interprets the omen as an indication that powerful King Croesus of Lydia will subjugate the island. The treacherous people of Samos then surrender Aesop to Croesus, but Aesop's skillful telling of fables so pleases the king that, at Aesop's request, he does not attack Samos. Aesop then writes down all the stories and fables that will be attached to his name and deposits them in the king's library. When he returns to the island, he is richly rewarded for having saved it from invasion. His first act in his newly exalted position on Samos is to erect a shrine to his patron goddesses—the

Muses and their mother, Mnemosyne, goddess of memory—thereby insulting the Olympian god Apollo by not honoring him as leader of the Muses.

After many prosperous years in Samos, Aesop sets off to see the world. Arriving in Babylon, Aesop wins him the position of chamberlain to King Lycurgus of Babylon. He enables Lycurgus to win many contests of wit with other monarchs and thereby to expand his kingdom; the most notable of these contests is with King Nectanabo of Egypt. Lycurgus is so grateful that he orders the erection of a golden statue of Aesop and holds a great celebration in honor of Aesop's wisdom.

Life's Work

Late in his life, Aesop wishes to go to Delphi, the Greek city that contains the sacred oracle of Apollo. After having sworn to return to Babylon, he journeys to other cities and gives demonstrations of his wisdom and learning. When he comes to Delphi, its people enjoy hearing him at first, but they give him nothing. After he insults the people of Delphi by pointing out that they are the descendants of slaves, they plot to kill him for damaging their reputation. Their stratagem is to hide a golden cup from Apollo's temple in Aesop's baggage and then to convict him of theft from a sacred place, a capital offense. Despite Aesop's pleas of innocence and his recitation of fables indicating that the Delphians would be harmed by executing him, they stand him on the edge of the cliff at Delphi. Aesop curses them, calls on the Muses to witness that his death is unjust, and throws himself over the cliff. Later, according to the first century biography, when the Delphians are afflicted with a famine, they receive an oracle from Zeus, king of the gods, that they should expiate the death of Aesop. *The Life of Aesop* goes on to say that the peoples of Greece, Babylon, and Samos avenged Aesop's death, although the mode of vengeance is not specified.

There are several other ancient references to Aesop's brutal fate at Delphi. For example, the Greek "father of history," Herodotus (c. 490-425 B.C.), states that Aesop was by birth a Thracian, "the slave of Iadmon, son of Hephaestopolis of Samos. . . . When the Delphians, in obedience to the oracle's command, repeatedly advertised for someone to claim compensation for Aesop's murder, the only person to come forward was the grandson of Iadmon." The greatest fifth century

B.C. comic playwright, Aristophanes, in his *Wasps* refers to the Delphians' falsely charging Aesop with theft. Perhaps the most memorably moving ancient Greek reference to Aesop occurs in the *Phaedo* by the philosopher Plato. Aesop is describing the last day in the life of his beloved teacher Socrates in 399 B.C. The Athenians had sentenced Socrates to death for his critical ideas. Socrates had been spending his last hours before execution turning Aesop's fables into verse. Since no written collection of short fables would have then been available, they must have been part of the common person's memorized cultural stock. When his friends come to visit Socrates, he wonders if Aesop had ever invented a fable about the connection of pleasure and pain. The second century A.D. Greek historian Plutarch, in his series of short *Lives*, makes many references to Aesop's fables when they are relevant to the fates of his biographical subjects. Thus, whether legend or reality, the character of Aesop has been an enduring literary inspiration.

Aesop's *Fables* represents the literature of the common person, in striking contrast to the aristocratic heroic mode of the dominant Homeric epics, *The Iliad* and *The Odyssey*. The *Fables* are part of that tradition of folk wisdom carried by the spoken word from generation to generation through such genres as parables and proverbs, as well as fables. The form of the Aesopic fable is that of a brief anecdote focused on a single event and designed to teach some principle of successful living. The characters in the *Fables* are typically animals endowed with human speech and personal qualities. Each quality fits the stereotype for that creature; for example, the fox is untrustworthy, the ass stupid, the lamb naïve and helpless, the wolf cruel, the lion noble, the ant industrious. These animals, as well as the people in the *Fables*, become easily recognized images of human types. The concluding moral of each story, often tagged onto the text centuries later, is drawn from common human experience and, therefore, makes an easily understood lesson.

Although Aesop's language is spare and simple, the ancients did not consider the *Fables* as intended only for children. Their point of view is really adult, often satirical, and never sentimental. Aesop, for example, is reputed to have told to the Athenians the story of "The Frogs Who Asked for a King" when they expressed discontent with their ruler. The story tells of some frogs who, bothered at not having a ruler, ask Zeus to send them a king. Realizing their stupidity, Zeus drops a log into their pool. At first, the frogs are frightened and dive to the bottom. Later, when the log floats quietly, they become contemptuous of it and climb over it. Indignant at having such an inactive ruler, the frogs bother Zeus again, asking for a change of rulers. Zeus, now angry with the frogs, this time sends a water snake who catches and eats them. "Better no rule than cruel rule," says the moral tag. The Aesopic fables are thus typical of that sort of folk literature in which people shrewdly examine their own lives, with abrasive honesty, and thus come to a better understanding of their own follies.

Summary

Many phrases derived from Aesop's *Fables* are common expressions in the folk heritage of the English language: "Sour grapes," "the boy who cried 'wolf,'" "the wolf in sheep's clothing," "fishing in muddy waters," "out of the frying pan into the fire," "the dog in the manger," "the ant and the grasshopper," "the tortoise and the hare," and "the goose that laid the golden egg" are only some of the better-known examples.

The Greek tradition of telling fables goes back at least as far as Hesiod's *Works and Days*, from the eighth century B.C. Hesiod recounts a brief episode in which a hawk carries off a whimpering nightingale in its cruel claws. The powerful hawk tells the complaining and usually proud nightingale that "I will make a meal of you if I choose, or I will let you go. Foolish is he who would match himself against those who are stronger. . . ." Hesiod's fable is told as if its content and form are already well known; there were Mesopotamian fables even older than those of the Greeks. Indeed, Aristotle, the great fourth century B.C. Greek philosopher, says in his *Rhetoric*, "Fables are suited to popular oratory and have this advantage that, while historical parallels are hard to find, it is comparatively easy to find fables."

The first written collection of fables in Greek attributed to Aesop is recorded as having been made by Demetrius of Phalerum in the fifth century B.C. Unfortunately, that collection has not survived. The oldest existing collection is a Latin version in verse done by the freedman Phaedrus in the first century A.D. The Latin verse of Phaedrus became the basis for the great seventeenth century French verse fables of Jean de La Fontaine, whose satirical verses are familiar to many generations of French schoolchildren. In the late second century A.D., Babrius made a version in Greek verse, thereby completing the task conceived by Socrates. Prose versions, however, have also survived the ages, dating from at least as far back as the first three centuries of the Christian era, with their roots perhaps extending to Aesop in the sixth century B.C. These prose fables are the primary basis of most modern English versions. The fabulist tradition has remained alive in the twentieth century United States, with such fable-spinners as James Thurber and Woody Allen reinforcing the Aesopic tradition of satirical folk wisdom.

Bibliography

Aesop. *Fables of Aesop*. Stanley A. Handford, trans. London and Boston: Penguin, 1954. A lean translation that preserves Aesop's satirical, cynical edge.

Aesop. *The Fables of Aesop: Selected, Told Anew, and Their History Traced*. Joseph Jacobs, ed. London: Macmillan, 1894; New York: Macmillan, 1925. Reprint. Ann Arbor, Mich.: University Microfilms, 1966. Skillfull retellings with excellent illustrations and source notes.

Babrius, Valerius. *Aesop's Fables: Told by Valerius Babrius*. Denison B. Hull, ed. Chicago: University of Chicago Press, 1960. A rhyming translation in iambic tetrameter couplets of Babrius' iambic Greek version.

Daly, Lloyd W. *Aesop Without Morals: The Famous Fables, and a Life of Aesop*. New York and London: Thomas Yoseloff, 1961. The only English translation of the *Fables* to include a translation of the first century A.D. *Life of Aesop*.

Perry, Ben Edwin. *Babrius and Phaedrus*. London: Heinemann, and Cambridge, Mass.: Harvard University Press, 1965. A scholarly edition of the Greek and Latin texts, together with facing prose translations.

Donald S. Gochberg

AGESILAUS II

Born: c. 444 B.C.; Sparta
Died: c. 360 B.C.; Cyrene, Libya
Areas of Achievement: Government and warfare
Contribution: By common consent the most powerful and illustrious Greek leader of his day, Agesilaus took Sparta to its peak of influence. Unfortunately, his policies led to a devastating defeat at Leuctra in 371, and at his death he left an impoverished and weakened kingdom that would never again play a dominant role in Greek affairs.

Early Life

When Eupolia, the young second wife of the aging Spartan king Archidamus II, gave birth to Agesilaus in 444, her son's prospects must have seemed quite limited. Archidamus already had an heir apparent, Agis, by his first wife. Worse, Agesilaus was born lame, an egregious liability in militaristic, fitness-minded Sparta. Indeed, his very survival is remarkable, given the official inspection and possible infanticide to which the Spartan authorities subjected every infant. That he passed their scrutiny may be attributed to Sparta's growing manpower shortage, a problem that would become acute in Agesilaus' lifetime.

Because he was not considered an heir to the throne, from age seven to eighteen the boy underwent the normal Spartan training—the *agoge*. Royal heirs were normally spared this rigorous, competitive, and often-violent regimen, designed to produce the bravest, most disciplined soldiers possible. Despite his lameness and small stature, Agesilaus excelled in the *agoge*. He was the first to jest at his deformity and deliberately sought out the most difficult tasks to prove that his weak leg was no real hindrance. If the young man displayed any weakness, it was excessive loyalty and favoritism to family and friends.

At some point in his youth, Agesilaus formed a relationship that would change the course of his life. It was customary that a Spartan youth cultivate a special friendship with a mature man who would guide him and advance his career. Agesilaus had the good fortune to become the special friend of Lysander, the honored and influential general who spearheaded Sparta's victory over Athens in the Peloponnesian War. Before his extreme ambition and egotism brought him discredit and demotion in 403, Lysander had initiated an aggressive style of Spartan imperialism, and he would remain a powerful advocate of Spartan expansion.

At his death in 400, after a reign of twenty-seven years, King Agis left a son and presumptive successor, Leotychides. Nevertheless, Agesilaus asserted his own claim to the throne. His participation in the *agoge* had given him a strong following among average Spartan citizens. There was also some question as to the legitimacy of Leotychides, and Agesilaus made the most of it. When supporters of Leotychides recalled that an oracle had warned Spartans against the "lame kingship," Agesilaus countered that the warning was against a king of nonroyal blood. Perhaps the decisive factor in this contest was the intervention of Lysander on behalf of Agesilaus. Unable to serve as king himself, Lysander championed the claim of his friend. Leotychides lost not only the kingship but also his inheritance, and Agesilaus assumed the throne in 400, when he was about forty-four years old.

Because Sparta had a curious double monarchy with two royal houses, a Spartan king had to share his royal authority with a colleague—and potential rival. During the forty-year reign of Agesilaus, exile and premature death from disease or combat brought him five comparatively short-reigned and weak colleagues in the kingship. As a result, despite some factional disputes at home, Agesilaus had an unusually free hand to lead Sparta as he saw fit.

Life's Work

Agesilaus inherited a kingdom politically and militarily supreme in Greece, but that very fact of supremacy presented potentially dangerous temptations and challenges. Specifically, Agesilaus would have to decide whether to limit Sparta's hegemony to its traditional area of dominance, southern Greece, or extend it to include central Greece or even regions beyond. He would also have to reckon with the ambitions of a former ally in central Greece, Thebes. The Thebans wanted to unify the district of Boeotia in a federal state headed by Thebes. Agesilaus could attempt to prevent this, or he could accept it and at the same time compensate by encouraging the traditional rivalry between Thebes and its neighbor Athens.

At home, Sparta had certain long-standing internal weaknesses which needed attention, most notably the decline in the number of Spartan citizens.

The gradual concentration of slave-worked land in the hands of wealthy families meant that fewer Spartans could afford to pay the dues required of all citizens. Accelerated by casualties in war and natural disasters, this trend had reduced the Spartan community to no more than three thousand male citizens at the accession of Agesilaus. His performance as king must be judged by his responses to these challenges and problems.

In his first year on the throne, Agesilaus had to deal with the revolutionary conspiracy of Cinadon, a crisis that revealed the precarious position of the dwindling Spartan citizen body. Cinadon was an "inferior," one of a sizable and growing body of Spartans who had lost their citizen status because of poverty. He based his revolutionary hopes on the fact that the Spartans were dangerously outnumbered by their subjects: the free *perioikoi*, who lived in semiautonomous villages around Sparta, and the servile Helots, who lived primarily in Messenia, west of Sparta. Cinadon boasted that his supporters—Helots, freed Helots, inferiors, and *perioikoi*—hated the Spartans so much that they would be glad to eat them raw. Because of an in-

formant, who betrayed the plot in its early stages, Agesilaus and the other Spartan authorities were able to suppress the conspiracy, but they took no steps to correct the conditions that had engendered it.

Instead, in 396, Agesilaus undertook his first military campaign to distant Asia Minor, where he challenged the power of Persia. Agesilaus may have presented this expedition as a Panhellenic crusade on behalf of the Asiatic Greeks, but others saw it as an attempt to extend Spartan hegemony. Both Athens and Thebes refused to take part, and the Thebans further offended Agesilaus by disrupting his parting sacrifices at Aulis in Boeotia. After several victories against the Persians, Agesilaus received joint command of both land and sea forces, an honor unprecedented in Spartan history. The Asian campaign won fame for Agesilaus and much treasure for Sparta, but his victories accomplished little in the military sense. Moreover, his poor choice of an incompetent brother-in-law, Peisandros, as admiral resulted in a disastrous naval defeat in 394, which seriously weakened Sparta's position overseas. How Agesilaus might have responded to this setback is uncertain, since he had already been recalled home to help Sparta face a hostile alliance of major Greek states in the so-called Corinthian War (395-386 B.C.).

Primarily instigated by Thebes, this war challenged Sparta's domination of central Greece and had already produced the death of the reckless Lysander and the banishment of King Pausanias, Agesilaus' first comonarch. Victory in a major battle at Coronea secured Agesilaus' safe passage through Boeotia to Sparta, but it failed to reestablish Spartan preeminence in central Greece. His vengeful frontal assault on the Theban force, moreover, needlessly risked his men and produced severe casualties, including several wounds to Agesilaus himself. In subsequent engagements, Agesilaus generally got the upper hand, although one of his companies was decimated by a tactically innovative, lightly armed force near Corinth in 390. As the war became a stalemate, Agesilaus formed an alliance with his erstwhile enemy, the Persian king. By the terms of the "King's Peace" of 386, the Asiatic Greeks were abandoned to Persian domination. In return, the Persian king promised to make war on any Greek state that violated the accord and backed Sparta as overseer and arbiter of a general peace in Greece.

By a just and conciliatory administration of the King's Peace, Agesilaus might have maintained Sparta's security and hegemony indefinitely. Instead, he intervened in the affairs of other Greek states in order to install governments friendly to Sparta. Above all, he indulged his obsessive hatred of Thebes, and he condoned—if he did not instigate—the unlawful military occupation of Thebes in 382. This act more than any other outraged Greek opinion and helped the Thebans to establish an alliance with their natural rivals, the Athenians. After Thebes expelled the Spartan garrison, Agesilaus twice led invasions of Boeotia in vain attempts to recapture the city. Despite serious injuries in 377 that kept him out of military action until 370, Agesilaus continued to reject the claims of Thebes to represent all of Boeotia. He presided at a peace conference in 371, and, after a bitter exchange with the Theban leader Epaminondas, he excluded Thebes from the general peace. Then, against the advice of other Spartans, Agesilaus urged an immediate invasion of Boeotia. A momentous battle duly ensued at Leuctra, where the Spartans suffered a devastating defeat at the hands of the more tactically advanced Thebans. King Cleombrotus

and four hundred of his fellow Spartans died in this conflict, the worst defeat in Spartan history.

Sparta never recovered from the setback at Leuctra. The battle itself inflicted heavy casualties on an already dangerously small Spartan citizen body and shattered the myth of Spartan invincibility. The ensuing Theban invasion of southern Greece permanently sundered Sparta's regional alliance and prompted defections among the long subordinate *perioikoi* and Helots who surrounded Sparta. In the face of the Theban advance, many Spartans panicked, while others plotted revolution. Only the energetic emergency measures of Agesilaus, who was then in his early seventies, saved the city from destruction. Worst of all in the long run, the Thebans liberated Messenia and thereby deprived Sparta of its richest agricultural district with its large number of Helot slaves.

Agesilaus refused to accept the loss of Messenia, and in the last decade of his life he pursued its recovery with a stubbornness that equaled his earlier opposition to Thebes. Unfortunately, he now ruled a weakened and impoverished Sparta with a citizen population of only one thousand. In the end, he was forced to undertake foreign mercenary service in order to finance his efforts to regain Messenia. Such was the military reputation of the aging king that rebellious Persian governors in Asia Minor and Egypt paid handsomely for his skills. In 360, after completing his final campaign in Egypt, Agesilaus set sail for home but died en route in Libya at about age eighty-four.

Summary

For more than two decades, Agesilaus II was, in effect, King of Greece. Nevertheless, his reign must be seen as a failure. A general of unquestioned talent and bravery, Agesilaus shared in the Spartans' failure to keep up with the military innovations of that time. The resulting tactical backwardness of the Spartan army helps explain the defeat at Leuctra. As a statesman, Agesilaus pursued unwise policies. The attempt to extend Sparta's hegemony was unrealistic in the light of Sparta's declining manpower, while his flagrantly aggressive administration of the King's Peace needlessly alienated other Greek states and made allies for Thebes. Above all, his relentless hatred of Thebes caused a breakdown of the common peace and led directly to the disastrous confrontation at Leuctra.

Agesilaus cannot be held responsible for the structural ills of the Spartan system, but he seems to have been blind to its most glaring problem, the decline in Spartan manpower. During his reign, the number of Spartan male citizens dropped by two-thirds to a mere one thousand. He left his son a feeble kingdom that would never again play a major role in Greek affairs.

A Spartan's Spartan, a product of the *agoge*, Agesilaus sadly exemplifies Aristotle's famous critique of the Spartans: Because their whole system was directed to securing only a part of virtue, military prowess, they did well at war but failed at the higher art of peace.

Bibliography

Cartledge, Paul. *Agesilaos and the Crisis of Sparta.* London: Duckworth, and Baltimore, Md.: Johns Hopkins University Press, 1987. This exhaustive study from a Marxist perspective is now the starting point for serious study of Agesilaus. More than a mere biography, it places Agesilaus in the context of fourth century Greek history and provides an outstanding introduction to the whole political and social system of Sparta. Includes a very helpful chronological table.

Cawkwell, G. L. "Agesilaus and Sparta." *The Classical Quarterly* 26 (1976): 62-84. Perhaps the most favorable of the recent treatments of Agesilaus, this article argues that his aggressive policy toward Thebes was warranted. Cawkwell attributes Sparta's decline not to Agesilaus' foreign policy but to the Spartans' inability to adapt their army to the new military demands of the fourth century.

David, Ephraim. *Sparta Between Empire and Revolution (404-243 B.C.): Internal Problems and Their Impact on Contemporary Greek Consciousness.* New York: Arno Press, 1981. An excellent study of the internal problems of Sparta, this book deals with the period of Agesilaus' rule in chapters 1 through 3.

Forrest, W. G. *A History of Sparta, 950-192 B.C.* 2d ed. London: Duckworth, 1980. A brief introduction to ancient Sparta. Chapters 13 and 14 cover the period of Agesilaus' rule.

Hamilton, Charles D. *Agesilaus and the Failure of Spartan Hegemony.* Ithaca, N.Y.: Cornell University Press, 1991. This book situates Agesilaus in the wider history of 4th century B.C. Sparta and uses a "psychohistorical" approach to argue that Agesilaus' personal obsession with Thebes caused him to adopt ill-considered policies. The study is notable for its meticulous discussions of the ancient sources for Agesilaus' reign.

————. *Sparta's Bitter Victories: Politics and Diplomacy in the Corinthian War.* Ithaca, N.Y.: Cornell University Press, 1979. An excellent detailed study of Greek international affairs in the period 405-386 B.C., this book is especially good in presenting the policies of Agesilaus and Lysander in the context of Spartan factional politics.

Plutarch. *Agesilaus.* In *Plutarch's Lives,* translated by Bernadotte Perrin, 11 vols. London and Cambridge, Mass.: Harvard University Press, 1959-1967. This brief biography is the most balanced ancient source for the career of Agesilaus.

Wylie, Graham, "Agesilaus and the Battle of Sardis." *Klio* 74 (1992): 118-130. A reconstruction of Agesilaus' Asian campaign and a discussion of his political goals.

Xenophon. *A History of My Times (Hellenica).* Translated by George Cawkwell. Harmondsworth, England and Boston: Penguin Books, 1966. In this work, the Athenian soldier-historian provides a contemporary narrative of the whole period of Agesilaus' rule, the only such account to survive complete. A personal friend of Agesilaus, he participated in many of the events he describes and provides many revealing details. Unfortunately, he is biased in favor of Agesilaus and omits several very important events.

James T. Chambers

MARCUS VIPSANIUS AGRIPPA

Born: c. 63 B.C.; place unknown
Died: March, 12 B.C.; Rome
Areas of Achievement: Government and warfare
Contribution: Agrippa's military genius, on both land and sea, provided Augustus with the support he needed to establish the Roman principate. His gift for planning and building contributed to the improvement of Rome's roads, water supply, and major public buildings.

Early Life

Marcus Vipsanius Agrippa seems linked with Octavian (as Augustus was called before 27 B.C.) almost from birth. They were born into politically insignificant families in about the same year. Agrippa's equestrian (middle-class) family was obscure, and the family name (Vipsanius) was so unaristocratic that in later life he preferred not to use it at all. He and Octavian were friends from childhood and attended school together, according to the emperor's court biographer.

Nothing certain is known of Agrippa's life before 44 B.C. It seems safe to assume that he performed the military service which young men of his class were expected to undertake at that stage of their lives. At the time of Julius Caesar's assassination, Agrippa was with Octavian, Caesar's grandnephew, in Greece, where they had been sent to study. Agrippa seems to have been chosen by Caesar as a suitable companion for Octavian, along with Gaius Maecenas and several other solid, if unspectacular, young men. When Octavian decided to return to Rome, claim his inheritance from Caesar, and become embroiled in the political and military struggle which had been ravaging the Mediterranean world for almost a century, Agrippa accompanied him.

In spite of his youth, Agrippa helped raise an army to oppose Caesar's assassins and to give Octavian leverage against Marc Antony, who had impounded Caesar's papers and money and hoped to assume the dead dictator's place. Although Antony and Octavian reached an accord in order to pursue Caesar's assassins, relations between them soon soured. In 41, with Antony in the east, his brother Lucius revolted against Octavian's authority and in opposition to his efforts to provide land for Caesar's retiring veteran soldiers. Agrippa forced Lucius to surrender early in 40, the first of his many victories on Octavian's behalf.

Life's Work

Agrippa proved how indispensable he was to Octavian by filling several important offices during the following few years. As governor of Gaul, he suppressed a revolt in the strategic southern district of Aquitania. In 37, he was Octavian's colleague in the consulship and built up the navy to oppose Sextus, who was attacking Roman shipping from bases in Sicily in a final act of opposition to the Caesarean faction's takeover of the state. This campaign brought Agrippa's engineering abilities to the fore, as he linked Lake Avernus with the Bay of Naples to create a harbor where the new fleet could be trained. His improved grappling equipment played a significant role in Sextus' defeat.

Augustus liked to boast that he had found Rome brick and left it marble, but Agrippa's buildings were as much responsible for that accomplishment as anything the emperor did. Agrippa began making his mark by repairing and upgrading the city's aqueducts during his time as an aedile in 33, a responsibility which he kept in his own hands for the rest of his life. The first of his aqueducts bore the

name of the Julian family, into which Octavian had been adopted by Caesar's will. Agrippa's major building contributions were the Pantheon, one of the largest domed structures erected in antiquity, and the baths which bore his name. The Pantheon, which visitors to Rome still admire, bears Agrippa's name on the frieze, but it was rebuilt by Hadrian circa A.D. 133. How much of Agrippa's original design remains is a disputed question. Also to Agrippa's credit were a granary and a new bridge over the Tiber River. He constructed buildings and roads in the provinces as well.

If he had any political ambitions, Agrippa subordinated them to Octavian's needs. He contributed significant victories over frontier tribes in Illyria in 35 and 34 and should be credited with defeating Antony and Cleopatra VII at the Battle of Actium in 31. That victory removed Octavian's last rival and made him the undisputed ruler of Rome.

Rome had been rent by bloody civil strife since 133, because the empire had outgrown the republican constitution under which it had functioned since the overthrow of the last Etruscan king in 509. Annually elected magistrates who shared their power and could veto one another's actions could not effectively govern an empire stretching from Spain to Syria. As Julius Caesar had found, however, the Romans would not tolerate a monarch. He had taken the illegal position of dictator for life, a stopgap measure that probably crystalized the resentment against him into a fatal conspiracy.

Octavian's problem was the same as Caesar's: to find a way for one man to govern the Roman Empire while preserving the appearance of the old republic. Between 31 and 27, Octavian relied on holding the consulship, with Agrippa as his colleague in 28 and 27. While Octavian was away from Rome trying to stabilize affairs in the urbanized, Greek-speaking east (which resented its domination by the agricultural and Latin west), Agrippa directed governmental affairs in Italy and the west with the aid of Maecenas.

These two men seem to have been most influential in helping Octavian solve the dilemma of governing Rome. The historian Dio Cassius records a debate among the three of them, with speeches by Maecenas and Agrippa advocating, respectively, that Octavian become a constitutional monarch or restore the republic. The speeches summarize the two philosophical points of view, but they probably have no historical validity. The settlement which

Octavian worked out with the senate in 27 appeared on the surface to gratify the Romans' desire to see their republic restored, but it actually granted to Octavian (by that time called Augustus) all the civilian and military powers necessary to make him an effective ruler.

This subtle monarchy, called the principate, had one flaw. Since it was not technically a legal magistracy or a hereditary monarchy, it could not be passed on to a successor designated by the princeps, the head of state. In 23, Augustus was taken ill and almost died. In the depths of his illness, he gave his signet ring, which served as his signature and the symbol of his power, to Agrippa, perhaps indicating his desire that his loyal friend succeed him. Upon his recovery, Augustus gave Agrippa proconsular power similar to his own.

In spite of his respect for Agrippa, Augustus soon realized that the aristocratic senate would never accept him as princeps because of his plebeian origins. Augustus hoped to groom some member of his own family to succeed him, but he had difficulty finding anyone suitable. He had only one child, a daughter Julia, so he promoted the career of his nephew Marcellus by sharing the consulship with him and marrying him to Julia.

The attention showered on Marcellus provoked the first strain between Agrippa and Augustus. It was said of Agrippa that, while he did not want to be the first man in the empire, he would be second to only one man. His departure to govern the eastern provinces, though touted as a promotion, seems to have been regarded by Agrippa as a kind of exile. He did not return to Rome until after Marcellus' untimely death in 22. In 20 and 19, Agrippa put down minor revolts in Gaul and Spain. His policy in dealing with the provinces was to defend, not expand, the borders. Soon after Agrippa's death, Augustus began listening to other advice, and Rome suffered two of its worst defeats ever in Germany.

Not all Agrippa's service to Augustus was military. In 28, he married Octavian's niece Marcella; in 21, with Augustus' approval, he divorced her to marry the widow Julia, who was then about sixteen. Augustus may have taken him as his son-in-law because Agrippa had become so powerful and so popular that he had to be taken into the imperial family or suppressed like an enemy. By Julia, Agrippa fathered two daughters and three sons, two of whom Augustus adopted and promoted as possible successors.

Augustus continued to honor Agrippa and to associate him in the imperial power. In 18, Agrippa was given tribunician power, one of the basic grants on which Augustus' position rested. The holder of this power could veto the actions of any other Roman magistrate. The grant was renewed in 13. By March of the next year, Agrippa had quieted a revolt in Pannonia (in modern Yugoslavia) and returned to Rome ill. He died by the end of the month, and his ashes were laid in the Julian family mausoleum.

Summary

Marcus Vipsanius Agrippa was a remarkable man, willing to subordinate his military and engineering genius to the service of a friend who was less talented than himself. Writers such as Suetonius and Cornelius Tacitus, who could find some hint of scandal to besmirch any reputation, report nothing of the kind about Agrippa. In an age when treachery and shifting alliances were common in politics, Agrippa displayed unswerving loyalty to Augustus for more than thirty years. His support enabled Augustus to defeat his rivals and assume power in the first place. His buildings and public works—many of them financed out of his personal funds—contributed to the well-being and happiness of the populace of Rome. This general good feeling was an essential element in maintaining the stability of the principate. It is extremely doubtful that Augustus could have taken power in the first place or held it for long without Agrippa's assistance.

Not only did Agrippa have a profound impact on the course of events in the first century B.C. and for some time after that, but also he contributed directly as the progenitor of two later emperors. His daughter Agrippina the Elder was the mother of Caligula and the grandmother (through her daughter) of Nero. While his descendants may not have been popular leaders, Agrippa cannot be blamed for all of their flaws. Through a complex web of imperial marriages, they also carried the genes of Augustus and Marc Antony.

Agrippa would be better known if his autobiography and his geographical commentary had survived. The latter was used to make a map which was prominently displayed in Rome and was an important source for Strabo, Pliny the Elder, and other writers with geographic or ethnographic interests. The opinion of antiquity, that he was the noblest Roman of his day, has not been revised by later historians.

Bibliography

Badian, E. "Notes on the *Laudatio* of Agrippa." *Classical Journal* 76 (1981): 97-109. This article discusses a recently discovered papyrus containing a portion of Augustus' funeral oration for Agrippa.

Buchan, J. *Augustus*. Boston: Houghton Mifflin Co., and London: Hodder and Stoughton, 1937. This slightly romantic biography of the first Roman emperor covers in detail Agrippa's contribution to his success.

Evans, H. B. "Agrippa's Water Plan." *American Journal of Archeology* 86 (1982): 401-411. The best analysis available of Agrippa's contribution to Rome's system of aqueducts, which provided more water per person in Augustus' day than does the system of modern Rome.

Firth, J. B. *Augustus Caesar and the Organization of the Empire of Rome*. New York: G. P. Putnam's Sons, 1903. Helpful references to Agrippa throughout, and an insightful chapter on Maecenas and Agrippa.

Gray, E. W. "The Imperium of M. Agrippa: A Note on P. Colon. Inv. No. 4701." *Zeitschrift für Papyrologie und Epigraphik* 6 (1970): 227-238. This article discusses the precise dates when grants of power were given to Agrippa.

McKechnie, P. "Cassius Dio's Speech of Agrippa: A Realistic Alternative to Imperial Government?" *Greece and Rome* 28 (October, 1981): 150-155. Agrippa's speech is a set piece, not truly reflecting his views on democracy. In other passages, Dio describes Agrippa as an ardent supporter of monarchy.

Reinhold, M. *Marcus Agrippa*. Geneva, N.Y.: W. F. Humphrey Press, 1933. Despite some traces of hero worship, this volume is still the most thorough study of Agrippa available in English. It follows his career and characterizes him as a self-made man, lacking in the subtle intellect of Augustus or Maecenas but a master of practical matters of organization.

Shipley, Frederick W. *Agrippa's Building Activities in Rome*. St. Louis, Mo.: Washington University, 1933. This short book studies Agrippa's building activity by location in various districts of Rome. It also discusses the problem of determining exactly where some of the buildings were. Shipley argues that the Pantheon as Hadrian rebuilt it bears little resemblance to Agrippa's original plan.

Albert A. Bell, Jr.

AKHENATON
Amenhotep IV

Born: c. 1390 B.C.; Egypt
Died: c. 1360 B.C.; Akhetaton (modern Tel el Amarna), Egypt
Areas of Achievement: Government and religion
Contribution: Akhenaton is credited with the establishment of monotheism in Egypt; he built a new capital, Akhetaton, in honor of Aton, the sun god.

Early Life

Born Amenhotep IV and also known as Amenophis IV, Akhenaton (or Ikhnaton) was the son and successor of Amenhotep III (also known as Amenophis III) of the Twenty-eighth Dynasty. Akhenaton's life and accomplishments need to be seen in the context of his family and of Egyptian history in general. Egyptian history is conventionally divided into thirty-one dynasties, which stretched from about 3100 B.C. to 332 B.C., and were succeeded by the Greek Ptolemies from 332 until 30 and the Roman emperors from 30 B.C. to A.D. 395. These dynasties are clumped together in groups under various designations, with the period of Akhenaton falling into the group of dynasties known as the New Kingdom, approximately in the middle of ancient Egyptian history.

The New Kingdom in the fifteenth century B.C. covered an area almost two thousand miles from north to south, most of it centered on the Nile River. The architects of this kingdom were Thutmose I (1525-1514), Thutmose III (1503-1450), and Amenhotep II (1453-1426). By the time of Amenhotep II, the northern city of Memphis had been in effect displaced by Thebes as the center of royal power. Three hundred miles upriver from Memphis, Thebes was the home of the royal family, and the rulers of the Twenty-eighth Dynasty began building tombs for themselves in the desolate region west of Thebes known as the Valley of the Kings. There are sixty-two tombs in the Valley, and the sixty-second one, that of the famous King Tutankhamon, was discovered in 1922 by the English Egyptologist Howard Carter.

One consequence of Thebes's rise to power was an increase in the influence of the god Amon, whose large temple was at nearby Karnak. Amon was a powerful sun god whose name is embedded in such proper names as Tutankhamon and Amenhotep. As a result of Amon's dominance at Thebes, the city became the center of religious celebrations.

Akhenaton's father, whose reign was roughly from 1416 to 1377, controlled Egypt at the peak of its power. He married, when quite young, a general's daughter named Tiy, but as was common, he had numerous concubines from Syria and other regions. Only the six children—two boys and four girls—of his marriage to Tiy, however, had royal significance. The second son, who became Amenhotep IV, was born around 1390.

Amenhotep III was an impressive man who achieved a reputation as a bold hunter and a gifted diplomat. He publicized his reign in a series of innovative scarab seals, each inscribed with a brief account of some historic event. Amenhotep III was also an ambitious builder; although early in his reign he continued to maintain a royal household in Memphis, he later moved to Thebes and spent the last ten years of his life directing construction projects in that city. At the same time, he had built the temple of Amon (in modern Luxor) near Karnak on the Nile River. The costs were enormous: The temple at Montu alone used two and one-half tons of gold and 1,250 pounds of lapis lazuli.

During these last ten years in Thebes, Amenhotep III hosted three opulent jubilees in his palace. The sybaritic life took its toll. Amenhotep III's mummy presents a fat, bald man with rotten teeth; the king died at about the age of thirty-eight and was succeeded by his second son, Amenhotep IV, or Akhenaton, as he soon came to call himself.

Life's Work

His older brother apparently having died young, Amenhotep IV ascended the throne in about 1377. One peculiarity of the new king's background is his failure to appear on his father's monuments, suggesting that for some reason his existence had deliberately been downplayed. The depictions of him show a deformed body that may have been an embarrassment to his family. His sagging belly, elongated face and neck, and feminine hips all point to a pituitary condition now known as Frölich's syndrome. Although Frölich's syndrome usually results in eunuchoidism, Amenhotep IV mar-

ried Nefertiti and they had several children. Unfortunately, nothing is known about Nefertiti—she may have been Amenhotep's cousin—and it is not even certain that Amenhotep was the natural father of the children she bore.

For the first year of his reign, Amenhotep continued the building projects of his father. He then embarked on his own distinctive projects. He soon planned a spectacular jubilee, a surprising departure from the usual practice of hosting them only after a reign of thirty years; this jubilee was marked by the building of four large temples at nearby Karnak.

The historical record at this point is extremely sketchy for two reasons: When he erected his new city of Akhetaton, Amenhotep thoroughly eradicated the memorials to Amon and the other sun gods, and after his death, one of his successors, Horemheb, destroyed the four temples at Karnak, whose remains, in the form of blocks known as *talatat*, scholars have recently been painstakingly fitting together.

The reconstructed reliefs on these temple remains have produced several surprises for scholars.

The *talatat* reveal, for example, that Amenhotep maintained a heavy military presence around himself at all times, a practice that implies insecurity. The *talatat* reliefs also celebrate Nefertiti in diverse depictions—especially surprising since Amenhotep himself appears nowhere in the decorations of his structures. No firm conclusions can be drawn, but it is impossible not to speculate on the possibility that Nefertiti played a much greater role in the royal planning than that evinced by the scanty evidence available before the *talatat* reconstructions.

After about five years at Thebes, Amenhotep suddenly abandoned that city and built a new capital farther north down the Nile River. This new capital was named Akhetaton, or "horizon of the Disc." At the same time, Amenhotep changed his name to Akhenaton (he who is useful to the Sundisc). In keeping with his new name and devotion, Akhenaton declared Amon, the old sun god, anathema. He had Amon's name plastered over on all of the royal cartouches (an oblong figure enclosing a royal name or epithet) and the name Aton was then inscribed on them. Throughout the kingdom, the name Amon was also at this time desecrated wherever it appeared on such objects as walls and tombs. Akhetaton was built on what is today called Tel el Amarna, and the period of Akhetaton's dominance is designated the "Amarna Age."

Akhenaton's new city was a hastily constructed affair, probably of inferior workmanship, stretching out for seven miles along the east bank of the Nile in Middle Egypt. Akhenaton's own residence was a large village at the city's north end. An unusual walled enclosure designated *Maru-aton* dominated the southern part of the city; with its pools and gardens, it was probably a site for cult observances.

Akhenaton's mother, Queen Tiy, was part of the entourage that moved to Akhetaton, and it now appears that a second wife, known as Queen Kiya, also accompanied him to the new home, although her role and status are unclear. The military guard continued as strong around Akhenaton at Akhetaton as at Thebes, but there was a complete shuffle in the important personnel at the court. The other cities, especially Thebes and Memphis, were allowed to fend for themselves; the old elite believed that they had been snubbed by the heretic king and his parvenus in the new center of the kingdom.

In about the eleventh year of Akhenaton's rule, the royal family began dying, perhaps as a result of a plague in the region. Thus by the fourteenth year, Queen Tiy, Kiya, and four of Akhenaton's six daughters were all dead. With their passing, and the king's aging, his daughter Meretaton rose in power and esteem, and by year fifteen, she was being depicted in statuary with her husband, Smenkhkare (he whom the spirit of Re has ennobled). The epithets devoted to Smenkhkare indicate that he probably acted as the king's coregent. It is an open question whether Smenkhkare ever actually ruled by himself or whether the throne went directly to Tutankhamon upon Akhenaton's death around the year 1360.

What happened to Nefertiti during these last years of Akhenaton's reign is not known. The fact that she seems to have disappeared at about the same time that Smenkhkare came on the scene has inspired scholarly conjecture that they were the same person, but the theory is burdened by too many improbabilities to be convincing. As far as is known, she survived these final years at Akhetaton but with greatly reduced royal influence.

Tutankhamon, possibly Akhenaton's son by Kiya, moved back to Thebes after three years, and the power in the kingdom was concentrated largely in the capable hands of one of Akhenaton's top officials, Aya, who himself ruled for about four years after Tutankhamon's death. Aya's successor, Horemheb, destroyed Akhenaton's temples at Karnak, and the work and innovations of the heretic king were concluded.

Summary

Recent scholarship challenges the old romantic picture of a humanist Akhenaton, a pioneering champion of monotheism in whose steps Moses followed. The king was an insecure ruler, physically unattractive, thrust into a role that surrounded him with figures from his father's establishment whom he feared. His vacillation weakened Egypt's control of its northern provinces, and he left the administration of his kingdom to his military advisers. Donald Redford characterizes Akhenaton as a dreamy soul devoted to cultic reforms that he did not really understand. By not replacing Amon with a significant mythology, Akhenaton was actually propagating atheism. The Sun-disc, Redford says, could never be seen as "god," and Redford spells out his conception of the real focus of Akhenaton's worship:

What it was Akhenaton tells us plainly enough: the Disc was his father, the universal king. Significant, it seems to me, is the fact that, on the eve of Amenophis III's passing, the king who sat upon Egypt's throne bore as his most popular sobriquet the title "The Dazzling Sun-disc"; on the morrow of the "revolution" the only object of veneration in the supernal realm is King Sun-disc, exalted in the heavens and ubiquitously termed by Akhenaton "my father."

Redford's contemptuous verdict on Akhenaton is that the king was an effete and slothful leader of an "aggregation of voluptuaries." Moreover, Akhenaton appears to Redford as the worst kind of totalitarian, one who demanded "universal submission" from everyone. It is a harsh verdict that Redford submits, and one that more sympathetic scholars will surely challenge as they continue to study the meager evidence of the life and accomplishments of this elusive king.

Bibliography

Aldred, Cyril. *Akhenaten and Nefertiti*. New York: Viking Press, and London: Thames and Hudson, 1973. This catalog of an exhibition at the Brooklyn Institute of Arts and Sciences, written by one of the period's most eminent scholars, is an invaluable study of the art of Akhenaton's reign. Includes illustrations, many in color, and an extensive bibliography. Fully annotated.

———. *Akhenaten, King of Egypt*. New York: Thames and Hudson, 1988; London: Thames and Hudson, 1991. The author draws heavily on archaeological evidence to piece together an account of Akhenaton's reign and his religious innovations. A good introduction to the current state of research.

———. *The Egyptians*. Rev. ed. London and New York: Thames and Hudson, 1984. Aldred provides an excellent general history of the region, with many black-and-white and color illustrations. Includes a bibliography and indexes.

Baines, John, and Jaromir Málek. *Atlas of Ancient Egypt*. New York: Facts on File, and Oxford: Phaidon, 1980. Baines and Málek provide an especially full and detailed reference book, replete with excellent tables, summaries of the ancient hieroglyphic writing system, maps, and timelines.

Drury, Allen. *A God Against the Gods*. Garden City, N.Y.: Doubleday, and London: Joseph, 1976. This work, along with its sequel, *Return to*

Thebes (1977), provides a highly fictionalized account of the life of Akhenaton and its aftermath. Includes a bibliography, extensive notes from the editors, and illustrations.

Redford, Donald B. *Akhenaten: The Heretic King.* Princeton, N.J.: Princeton University Press, 1984. A detailed scholarly analysis of Akhenaton and his accomplishments by the man who directed the Akhenaten Temple Project. Professor Redford's account is one of the standard studies. Includes an index, bibliography, and illustrations.

Frank Day

AKIBA BEN JOSEPH

Born: c. A.D. 40; probably near Lydda (modern Lod), Palestine
Died: c. A.D. 135; Caesaria, Palestine
Areas of Achievement: Religion and politics
Contribution: The most influential rabbi in the formation of Jewish legal tradition and Mishnah, Akiba is the one scholar most often quoted in the text. He espoused the unsuccessful cause of Simeon Bar Kokhba and died a martyr. The legends about Akiba have been almost as influential as his teachings and life.

Early Life

Akiba (also transliterated Aqiba) ben Joseph was born to humble parents. His father's name was Joseph, but tradition has no other information about him. Akiba worked as an unschooled shepherd. He was part of the lower class designated as the *am-ha-aretz* (people of the land), a term of common abuse. While working for a wealthy man of Jerusalem whose name is sometimes given as Johanan ben Joshua, Akiba fell in love with his daughter, Rachel, who returned his love.

This period of Akiba's life has been variously treated in exaggerated fashion by legendary accounts. Based on the historically most reliable traditions from the Mishnah, it appears reasonably certain that Rachel, agreeing to marry him, was disinherited by her father, and the couple lived in poor circumstances. It was only after his marriage and the birth of a son (probably at about age thirty-five) that Akiba began learning how to read. After learning the basics, Akiba (probably now age forty) left both home and occupation to attend the rabbinic academy at Yavneh, in southwestern Judaea.

In the generation after the destruction of the temple (c. 80-100), the rabbinic assembly at Yavneh was presided over by Rabbi Gamaliel II (an aristocrat) as *Nasi* (Ethnarch) and Rabbi Joshua ben Hananiah (a nonaristocrat) as *Ab Bet Din* (head of the rabbinic court). It was to the latter that Akiba went for instruction, but Hananiah directed him first to Rabbi Tarfon, who was in turn his teacher, friend, and then follower. Later, Akiba studied with Rabbi Nahum of Gimzo and then Hananiah himself. Thus by birth, training, and temperament, Akiba was aligned with the more liberal antiaristocratic wing of the academy, which traced its roots back to Rabbi Hillel. Finally, Akiba studied under Rabbi Eliezer ben Hyrcanus, a leading figure of the aris-

tocratic wing, whose tradition went back to Rabbi Shammai. Akiba's formal training came to a conclusion at Yavneh when in public debate Hananiah was defeated by Eliezer on the primacy of sacrificial duties over Sabbath rest. As the debate was being concluded, the relatively unknown Akiba entered the debate and carried the day against Eliezer. At this point, Akiba was recognized as a rabbi. He began to teach, and pupils began to seek him out.

During this thirteen-year period of study, Akiba must have spent long periods of time away from home. He was encouraged and supported by his wife. While popular legend has undoubtedly exaggerated this aspect of Akiba's life, there is an underlying truth to the material, and, more important, his love and appreciation for Rachel are reflected in his teaching.

Life's Work

In the beginning, Akiba began to teach in Yavneh and spent most of his time actively engaging in the disputes of the rabbinical assembly. These must have been vigorous, for tradition indicates that there were punishments meted out to Akiba on several occasions for his lack of respect for procedure and that at one point he left the assembly and retired to Zifron in Galilee. Akiba was later invited to return to Yavneh by Gamaliel.

Akiba was a tall man, bald, muscular from years of outdoor work. He had transformed himself into a gentle scholar who stressed the value of polite behavior and tact. This emphasis on courtesy, however, did not stop him from entering into debates and arguing passionately for his convictions. As part of his philosophy, he upheld the authority of the *Nasi*, even when he was arguing strongly against the specific ideas that the *Nasi* held.

While he was never entrusted with either of the chief offices of the assembly, he was an important member of the inner circle. When Gamaliel was removed from office because of his arrogance, it was Akiba who was chosen to inform Gamaliel. Eleazar ben Arariah was made *Nasi* in his place, but he was a figurehead, and real leadership rested with Hananiah and Akiba. Having secured dominance of the assembly, Akiba and Hananiah brought the number of the assembly members up from 32 to 72, seating younger scholars to whom Gamaliel had refused admission because of their positions, which were similar to those of Akiba. Akiba seems also to have played an important part in the restoration of Gamaliel to the position of *Nasi*. Direction of the assembly was in the hands of Gamaliel, Eleazar, Hananiah, and Akiba. At that time, he was appointed overseer for the poor. In that capacity, he traveled widely in the area, raising funds. He traveled throughout Judaea, Cappadocia, Arabia, and Egypt.

In the fall of 95, Akiba, Gamaliel, Hananiah, and Eleazar were sent as an embassy to the Emperor Domitian to calm the imperial displeasure over the fact that a member of the imperial family, Flavius Clemens, had converted to Judaism. During this visit, the rabbis probably consulted the Jewish historian and imperial freedman, Flavius Josephus, for advice on imperial protocol and influence for their petition. Before this could be done, however, Domitian died, and Nerva was appointed emperor. Although there is no written record of what was done, it would have been unthinkable for the embassy not to have given the new emperor the formal greetings of the Jewish community and to have made expressions of loyalty. Nerva was seen as opening up a new era in Jewish-Roman relations.

At this point (c. 97), Akiba was between fifty and sixty years of age. He established his own school at Bene-Berak (near modern Tel Aviv). It was during this time that Akiba's most enduring work was accomplished. In his teaching, he used a combination of demanding logic, rules of interpretation, and homely parables to put forth his ideas and ideals. He set the basic organization of what was to become the Mishnah into its six parts, and developed his ideas of interpretation of the Law based on the mystic significance of the text. In addition to a passion for social justice, he developed his unique positions on women, marriage, and other issues. None of these positions was achieved without extensive debate and discussion in Akiba's own school and in the assembly in Yavneh. There, the new leading opponent of Akiba was Rabbi Ishmael ben Elisha. Many of the teachings of these men were later arranged into opposing debates, even when it can be shown that no such discussion took place. The two men had great respect for each other and were cordial in their relations, but they were not friends.

The first generation of Akiba's disciples—Elisha ben Abuyah, Simeon ben Azzai, and Simeon ben Zoma—did not fare well. Elisha became an apostate, Simeon ben Azzai became mad, and Simeon ben Zoma lost his life. The second generation of scholars taught by Akiba, however, provided the rabbinic leadership of the next generation. Of these, Rabbi Meir and Aquila deserve special attention. Meir, who had studied with Elisha ben Abuyah and Ishmael before coming to Akiba, was responsible for continuing the arrangement of the Mishnah following the principles of Akiba. He wrote down many of the sayings of Akiba, often giving the opposing view of Ishmael. Aquila was a Greek who converted to Judaism and studied with Akiba. With Akiba's encouragement, he made a new (or made revisions to the) Greek translation of the Hebrew scriptures. For a time, Aquila seems to have been in the confidence of both the Jews and the Roman officials.

The last phase of Akiba's life is a matter of considerable debate among scholars. Relations with Rome, never good under the best of circumstances, went through a series of radical shifts. There is no clear understanding of these years since the sources (Jewish Talmudic and Roman writers) preserve the misunderstandings of the principals. What part, if any, Akiba played in the formulation of Jewish positions is not clear until the very end of the conflict. Some indicate that he used his position as overseer of the poor to travel throughout the land and ferment revolt. Others suggest that his position was essentially nonpolitical and that he did not resist until religious practices, including prayer and study, were forbidden. There is no evidence that Akiba was active in politics or any other capacity during the troubles at the end of Trajan's reign through the beginning years of Hadrian.

In about 130, to ease some of the existing tension, Hadrian sought to rebuild the temple but insisted on placing a statue of himself in it and dedicating the temple to Jupiter Capitolinus. The implications of this position for the Jews clearly was not understood by Hadrian. There is a tradition, not in itself improbable, that the rabbis selected the now-aged Akiba to lead a delegation to Hadrian to reverse this stand. It is not known whether they reached the emperor, but their efforts, for whatever reason, were unsuccessful. Open and widespread rebellion broke out, which required five years and some of Hadrian's best military talent to quell.

Of Akiba's activities during that period, only a few events are clear. The Talmudic evidence shows that Akiba was a firm supporter of living within the restrictions of 125 that forbade circumcision and severely restricted the rights of Jewish legal courts and synagogue practices. At some point in the rebellion, Akiba joined other rabbis, including Ishmael, and gave his endorsement to Simeon Bar Kokhba. Bar Kokhba (meaning son of a star), the name taken by Simeon Bar Kosiba, carried messianic implications; it was Akiba who applied the verse from Numbers 24:17, "The star rises from Jacob," to him. This stance was not without opposition. The Midrash records that "when Rabbi Akiba beheld Bar Kosiba he exclaimed, 'This is the king Messiah!' Rabbi Johanan ben Tortha retorted: 'Akiba, grass will grow in your cheeks and he will still not have come!'" (*Lamentations* 2:2). Thus, at least in the last stages, Akiba gave his support to Bar Kokhba, who claimed to be the *Nasi*, superceding the rabbinical *Nasi* at Yavneh; Akiba hailed him as Savior (Messiah).

Sometime after 130, and possibly as late as 134, Akiba was arrested and imprisoned by the consular legate, Tineius Rufus. For a while, he was allowed to have visitors and continued to teach. There is a strong element of folktale about these circumstances, and the possibility of the sources imitating the classical model of Socrates cannot be ignored. Akiba's final act of scholarship was to bring the religious calendar into order. Whether these activities were too much for the Romans to allow or whether Akiba's support of Bar Kokhba made him a symbol of resistance, Rufus brought him to trial in Caesaria and ordered his execution.

Summary

Akiba ben Joseph's most significant contributions were made to the organization of the Mishnah and the teachings in the Talmud. Akiba took the many rabbinic decisions and arranged them under these major headings: Zeraim (Seeds, on agriculture), Mo'ed (Seasons, on holidays), Nashim (Women, on marriage and divorce), Kodashim (Sanctities, on offerings), and Teharoth (Purities, on defilement and purification). These headings with their tractates (subheadings) were continued by Rabbi Meir and then codified by Rabbi Judah ha-Nasi around 200. There are more than twenty-four hundred citations of Akiba in the Talmud; he is the most frequently cited authority.

Akiba championed a special method of interpretation of the text which he learned from Rabbi Nahum of Gimzo and which he retained even though the latter abandoned it. Akiba saw hidden significance in every aspect of the received text, whether it was an unusual wording, a special grammatical form, or an aberrant spelling. He was opposed on that count by Ishmael, who declared that the Torah was written in the language of men (with its possibility of error). Akiba made his points by Ishmael's method and then would extend the argument with his method. Akiba was fond of using parable to explain ethical points.

Akiba's area of special concern was marriage, where he championed attractiveness for women as a means of holding their husbands' affections and divorce for loveless matches. He opposed polygamy, which was still permitted and practiced by the aristocrats. As an extension of this stance, he fought for and gained the acceptance of the Song of Songs (*Shir ha-Shirim*) in the biblical canon, against heavy opposition.

As important as Akiba's work was, the stories about his life have exerted an equal influence on Judaism. Many of them are gross exaggerations and many are probably apocryphal, but the points which they make are consistent with the known teachings of Akiba.

Bibliography

Aleksandrov, G. S. "The Role of Aqiba in the Bar Kochba Rebellion." In *Eliezer ben Hyrcanus*, vol. 2, by Jacob Neusner. Leiden, Netherlands: E. J. Brill, 1973. Aleksandrov refutes the position that Akiba was active in the Bar Kokhba rebellion but admits that he could have given the rebellion moral support. The volume is part of the Studies in Judaism in Late Antiquity series.

Finkelstein, Louis. *Akiba: Scholar, Saint, and Martyr*. New York: Covici, Friede, 1936. The only book-length study of Akiba's life and thought in English. Finkelstein re-creates Akiba's life by taking a mildly critical look at the biographical sources and then placing the teachings of Akiba where they most easily fit into Akiba's life. Finkelstein sees Akiba representing the popular party against the aristocrats. He also sees Akiba as a pacifist to the end. Both positions are overstated and are generally not accepted by other scholars.

Ginzberg, Louis. "Akiba." In *Jewish Encyclopedia*, vol. 1. New York: Funk and Wagnalls, 1912. This brief article, although old, is extremely well reasoned and lucidly written.

Goldin, Judah. "Toward a Profile of a *Tanna*, Aqiba ben Joseph." *Journal of the American Oriental Society* 96 (1976): 38-56. An important scholarly article which demonstrates that much of the biographical material about Akiba may be accepted as historical. Goldin's emphasis is on Akiba's marriage and his teachings regarding marriage, love, and divorce.

Marks, Richard G. *The Image of Bar Kokhba in Traditional Jewish Literature: False Messiah and National Hero.* University Park: Pennsylvania State University Press, 1994. Traces the judgments that have been passed on the Jewish rebel Bar Kokhba from antiquity to the early modern period. The first chapter discusses Akiba's role in proclaiming Bar Kokhba the Messiah.

Neusner, Jacob. *Judaism, The Evidence of the Mishnah.* 2d ed. Atlanta, Ga.: Scholars Press, 1988. A distillation of Neusner's work and that of his students. He leads the critical school which rejects much of the traditional information about the rabbis' lives and questions the attribution of many teachings to specific rabbis.

―――, ed. *Studies in Judaism in Late Antiquity.* Vol. 20, *The Jews Under Roman Rule: From Pompey to Diocletian*, by E. Mary Smallwood. Leiden, Netherlands: E. J. Brill, 1976. Solid scholarly work which should be used to update Schürer. The study is concerned almost exclusively with the political aspects of the problem. Good background; understandably little on Akiba.

Schürer, Emil. *A History of the Jewish People in the Time of Jesus Christ.* New York: Scribner, 1891. While the bibliography of secondary sources is obsolete, that is the only unusable part of this excellent study. Schürer has an absolute command of the classical and talmudic sources and gives more detail about the Jewish problems of Trajan and Hadrian than one will find elsewhere.

Strack, Hermann L. *Introduction to the Talmud and Midrash.* Philadelphia: Jewish Publication Society of America, 1931. There are many guides to the Talmud, but this is still the best short guide.

Michael M. Eisman

ALCIBIADES

Born: c. 450 B.C.; Athens?, Greece
Died: 404 B.C.; Phrygia, Asia Minor
Areas of Achievement: Government and warfare
Contribution: Although it might be argued that Alcibiades was a demagogue, a traitor, a heretic, and morally dissolute, he was a gifted politician and military leader—and certainly one of the most romantic figures of the Peloponnesian War.

Early Life

Alcibiades was born around 450 B.C. the son of Cleinias, a wealthy aristocrat and participant in the Battle of Artemisium. His mother, Deinomache, was a member of the Alcmaeonid clan and a cousin of Pericles, in whose house the youth was reared after the death of his father in 447. Unfortunately, Alcibiades proved to be a difficult boy and failed to acquire any of his guardian's noble qualities—except, perhaps, some political ambition. Even so, according to Plutarch Alcibiades was uniquely equipped for success. He was tall, handsome, wealthy, charming, imaginative, and one of the best orators of the day; clearly, he had qualities which endeared him to the masses. At the same time, he was impious, insolent, and incurably egocentric. He could, perhaps, have become another Themistocles or Pericles were it not for the fact that he had no interest in Athenian democracy. His political affinities were probably much closer to those of Peisistratus and the other Greek tyrants.

Alcibiades' military training began at the outset of the Peloponnesian War, which forced the youth into action quickly. He served with distinction in battles at Potidaea (432 B.C.) and Delium (424 B.C.), and, as a result, Alcibiades became quite popular in Athens and elsewhere. He acquired numerous admirers—among whom was the great philosopher Socrates, who saved the youth's life in battle and then later had the favor returned. A lasting friendship was formed, although Socrates must have found his protégé's rapacious life-style intolerable at times. It was during this period that Alcibiades took a wife, a certain Hipparete of the house of Hipponius, who, after an unsuccessful attempt at divorce, closed her eyes to his infidelity and proved a dutiful wife. Together they had a son named Axiochus, who apparently acquired some of the father's less desirable traits.

Life's Work

Alcibiades began his political career in 420, when he was elected one of the ten generals of the state, a position of great importance. Unlike Pericles, who had served on the same board for more than thirty years, Alcibiades was less devoted to Athens than to himself. Realizing that war with Sparta was the quickest route to fame and fortune, he cast his lot with the radicals of the state. This political decision placed him at odds with Nicias, the leader of the conservative faction, who had effected a peace treaty with the Spartans in 421. Displeased with the lull in fighting, Alcibiades formed an alliance with Argos, Elis, and Mantinea against Sparta. He was successful and was reelected in 419 to his seat on the board of generals. Yet his moment of glory was brief. When the alliance with Argos eventually failed, Alcibiades' popularity suffered, and he lost his generalship. It was only through a brief political *amicitia* with his enemy Nicias that he narrowly averted ostracism.

His political demise did not last long. In 416, another opportunity presented itself when a delega-

tion from the city of Egesta in Sicily appealed to Alcibiades and the radicals in Athens for assistance in war against the neighboring state of Selinus, which was supported by Syracuse. The promise of wealth and the possibility of a western empire struck a responsive chord in Alcibiades. Under his influence and over the strenuous objections of Nicias, Athens prepared to send a large amphibious force against Syracuse.

Unfortunately, the expedition was doomed from the start. Alcibiades, selected as one of the leaders, was accused by his detractors of impiety; the likelihood of his acquittal, however, prompted the opposition to postpone the trial, and Alcibiades was free, for the moment, to resume his position within the triumvirate of leadership designated for the Sicilian campaign. One of those with whom he would rule was Nicias, his former political adversary. It is not surprising that their inability to agree on strategy hindered field operations. Moreover, the siege had just begun when Athens dispatched a galley to bring Alcibiades back for his trial. Although he offered no resistance, the possibility of a death sentence in Athens led Alcibiades to escape at Thurii. From Thurii he made his way to Sparta, where he would remain for two years. While there, he earned the admiration of the Spartans with abstemious behavior. He plunged immediately into politics, urging the Spartans to assist Syracuse in its war with Athens. He also convinced the Spartans to fortify Decelea, from which they could strike into Attica. Alcibiades was determined to have his revenge.

Although Alcibiades adapted to the Spartan way and rendered valuable services, he had not abandoned all the vices of earlier years. He seduced the Spartan queen while her husband, King Agis, was away at Decelea. The queen became pregnant and gave birth to a son. By the summer of 412, it was clear that Alcibiades could no longer remain in Sparta. From there, he fled to the court of the Persian satrap of Sardis, Tissaphernes, who, like others before him, was very impressed with his peripatetic guest. Alcibiades worked hard to effect an alliance with Tissaphernes and Persia which would prove injurious to Sparta and enable him to return to power in Athens. First the democracy must be overthrown and an oligarchy established in its place, he reasoned. In the deliberations which followed, many Athenians were receptive to the plan, and in 411 an oligarchic faction took control of the government. Unfortunately, the satrap's demands were too great, and the oligarchy quickly lost faith in Alcibiades. Even so, a number of generals remained loyal to Alcibiades, who continued to control the bulk of Athens' military forces on the island of Samos.

The threat of a Spartan invasion, however, soon threw Athens into chaos; the oligarchy was toppled, and Alcibiades was recalled. Yet he did not return immediately, choosing instead to remain in the eastern Aegean Sea area, where he achieved significant victories at Cynossema and Cyzicus. In the latter engagement, all Spartan ships were either destroyed or captured, and a Spartan admiral was killed. Between 410 and 408, Alcibiades enjoyed other successes—in the Bosporus Thracius, the Hellespontus, the area neighboring the Propontis Sea, and the area north of the Aegean Sea—as he struggled to keep Athenian food supplies flowing from the Black Sea area.

By the autumn of 408, Alcibiades was supreme in the Aegean area and was now ready to return triumphant to Athens. He reached the city in the following year and was given ultimate authority over Athenian military forces. It was at this time, during the peak of his power, that he probably intended to establish a tyranny. The Spartan commander Lysander, however, turned the tide of battle in the Aegean again, with a victory at Notium over one of Alcibiades' subordinates. Even though Alcibiades was not wholly responsible for the defeat, the capricious Athenians could not forgive him. Deprived of his command, Alcibiades went into exile in Thrace. Ignored by his former countrymen and hounded by his enemies, he fled to Phrygia, where, at the insistence of Lysander, he was assassinated in 404.

Summary

When Pericles died in 429, a void was left in Athenian leadership. Into this void stepped Alcibiades. Endowed with the physical and intellectual requisites for greatness, he might have been the leader—indeed, the hero—for whom Athens was looking. Certainly Alcibiades was a great general whose judgment in military matters carried him from victory to victory and earned for him the admiration of Spartans, Athenians, and Persians. It might be argued that his superior generalship in the eastern Aegean prolonged the Peloponnesian War for the Athenians and, if the Athenian leadership had accepted his advice from exile in Thrace, Athens might not have lost the Battle of Aegospotami in 405.

Yet military victories alone are not always sufficient to attain greatness. In the opinion of most scholars, Alcibiades, although a gifted individual, was a traitor, a heretic, and an opportunist. In all arenas, he was determined to win, regardless of the cost. In the Olympic Games of 416, he entered seven four-horse teams in the chariot race and came away with all the top prizes. He was a demagogue who tempted Athens into costly schemes—such as the Syracusan expedition of 415, which resulted in the loss of about fifty thousand men and more than two hundred triremes. He also conspired to overthrow the democracy and dreamed of the day when he might become a dictator. Alcibiades was all these things and more, yet he remains one of the most colorful and interesting figures of classical Greece.

Bibliography

Benson, E. F. *The Life of Alcibiades.* New York: D. Appleton Co., and London: Benn, 1929. The standard biography of Alcibiades, old but still very useful. Written in large part from primary materials, especially Thucydides and Plutarch. A sympathetic study which, at times, reads like a novel. Should appeal to scholars and students alike.

Bury, J. B., and Russell Meiggs. *A History of Greece.* 4th ed. New York: St. Martin's Press, and London: Macmillan, 1975. The best one-volume survey of Greek history to the time of Alexander the Great. The main events of Alcibiades' life are treated in the chapter "The Decline and Downfall of the Athenian Empire." Maps, illustrations, and copious bibliographical notes enhance the value of this volume.

Bury, J. B., S. A. Cook, and F. E. Adcock, eds. *The Cambridge Ancient History.* Vol. 5. New York: Macmillan, and London: Cambridge University Press, 1927. In four chapters covering the Peloponnesian War, from "Sparta and the Peloponnese" to "The Athenian Expedition to Sicily," W. S. Ferguson recounts the war and gives valuable insight into Alcibiades' role in it. Especially useful to the more advanced student of Greek history.

Ellis, W. M. *Alcibiades.* Classical Lives. London and New York: Routledge, 1989. Less a biography of Alcibiades than a survey of late 5th-century history with Alcibiades as the organizing figure. Useful as a general overview.

Forde, Steven. *The Ambition to Rule: Alcibiades and the Politics of Imperialism in Thucydides.* Ithaca, NY: Cornell University Press, 1989. This book treats Thucydides' portrayal of Alcibiades as a key to explicating some of the historian's larger concerns, such as the relationship between the individual and the polity. Less interested in the historical Alcibiades than in what Thucydides makes of him.

Henderson, Bernard W. *The Great War Between Athens and Sparta: A Companion to the Military History of Thucydides.* London: Macmillan, 1927; New York: Arno, 1973. Excellent study of the Peloponnesian War. One of the better sources for the life of Alcibiades. A sympathetic survey from boyhood to death. Written in large part from primary materials. Should appeal to both scholars and students.

Meiggs, Russell. *The Athenian Empire.* Oxford: Clarendon Press, 1972; New York: Oxford University Press, 1979. Excellent political and military history of the fifth century B.C. Athens. Treats the more important events in Alcibiades' career. Includes a good bibliography.

Plutarch. *The Rise and Fall of Athens: Nine Greek Lives.* Translated by I. Scott-Kilvert. Baltimore and London: Penguin Books, 1960. Plutarch was a first century A.D. Greek historian whose biographies of Greek and Roman heroes are an indispensable resource. This edition contains nine of those biographies, including that of Alcibiades. Especially useful for getting a sense of Alcibiades' character.

Starr, Chester G. *A History of the Ancient World.* 4th ed. New York: Oxford University Press, 1991. Good one-volume survey of ancient world from man's beginnings to fifth century A.D. Excellent bibliographical essays at the end of each chapter. Brief survey of chief events of Alcibiades' life in a chapter entitled "End of the Golden Age."

Thucydides. *The Peloponnesian War.* Rev. ed. London and Baltimore: Penguin Books, 1972. Written by a famous Greek historian of the fifth century B.C., this book is the most valuable source of information on the Peloponnesian War. Considered a model of objectivity and accuracy. Chronicles the main events of Alcibiades' life in scattered references, from his role in the alliance with Argos to the Athenian victory at Cynossema in 411. Most secondary accounts of Alcibiades begin with Thucydides and Plutarch.

Larry W. Usilton

ALCMAEON

Born: c. 510 B.C.; Croton, Magna Graecia (southern Italy)

Died: c. 430 B.C.; place unknown

Areas of Achievement: Medicine and philosophy

Contribution: Alcmaeon was one of the earliest Greeks known to have written on medicine and the first to have practiced scientific dissection. He held that the brain is the central organ of sensation and that health is the result of an equilibrium of qualities or forces in the body.

Early Life

Of Alcmaeon's early life almost nothing is known, except that his father's name was Peirithous and that he was a native of Croton (Greek Crotona), a coastal town inside the "toe" of Italy. Even Alcmaeon's dates are uncertain. According to Aristotle, he lived during the old age of the philosopher Pythagoras, whose life spanned much of the sixth century B.C. and who died about 490 or later. It was once assumed that, as a younger contemporary of Pythagoras, Alcmaeon probably should be placed in the sixth century. It is now widely held, however, largely from the evidence of his ideas, that he probably lived in the fifth century. The evidence at the disposal of modern scholars is not sufficient to fix the date of his lifetime more precisely.

Croton was a Greek city founded by Achaeans from mainland Greece in 710 B.C. It had a fine harbor and enjoyed extensive commerce. As a result, it became the wealthiest and most powerful city in Magna Graecia (the Greek name for southern Italy), especially after its forces defeated and completely destroyed its enemy, the neighboring city of Sybaris, in 510. It boasted the most splended temple in southern Italy, the temple of Hera Lacinia, which drew large numbers of Greeks to a great annual religious assembly. Croton was renowned for its devotion to gymnastics; one of its citizens, Milon, became the most famous athlete in Greece, having won the victory in wrestling at Olympia six times. Croton is said to have produced more Olympic victors than any other city.

Croton was also the home of a well-known school of medicine, which was perhaps the earliest in Greece and which long retained its reputation. The city enjoyed the distinction of producing the finest physicians in Greece, of whom the most prominent was Democedes, regarded as the best physician of his day (the latter half of the sixth century B.C.). His fame carried him to Aegina, Athens, and Samos, where he was employed by the tyrant Polycrates, and to Persia (as a prisoner), where he cured both King Darius the Great and his wife, Atossa, before he escaped, returning to Croton to marry the daughter of Milon.

Croton was also known as the home of the philosopher Pythagoras and his followers. Born in Samos, Pythagoras emigrated to Croton about 530, where he formed a religious brotherhood composed of about three hundred young men. Pythagoras quickly gained influence over the political affairs of the city, but growing opposition to his order led to his retirement from Croton. In the latter half of the fifth century, a democratic revolution resulted in a massacre of nearly all the members of the order. Alcmaeon is said by some ancient authors to have been a disciple of Pythagoras, but it is likely that this belief was based only on inferences from the similarities of some of his doctrines to those of the Pythagoreans. Aristotle compares his theory of

opposites with that of the Pythagoreans but says that Alcmaeon either borrowed this idea from them or they took it from him. There is, in fact, no definitive evidence that associates Alcmaeon with the Pythagoreans. He lived during the period in which the Pythagorean brotherhood flourished at Croton, and he probably knew of the Pythagoreans and their beliefs. His precise relationship to them, however, is not known. Diogenes Laertius reports that Alcmaeon wrote mostly on medicine, and it has been inferred from this statement that he was a physician. Given Croton's reputation as a medical center, it is not unlikely. He wrote on physics and astronomy as well, however, and in this respect he resembles the Ionian philosophers, some of whom were interested in medicine. He was certainly a natural philosopher, interested in science and medicine; he may or may not have been a physician.

Life's Work

Alcmaeon lived in the pre-Socratic period, when the study of physiology was merely a part of philosophy. Only later did Hippocrates separate medicine from philosophy. Greek medical theory, in fact, grew out of philosophical speculation rather than the practice of medicine. Alcmaeon's contributions include both cosmological conjecture and anatomical research. He was credited in antiquity with having written the first treatise on natural philosophy. The book is no longer extant, but some idea of its contents can be gleaned from portions that were summarized by later writers. In the opening sentence of the work, Alcmaeon declared that the gods alone have certain knowledge, while for men only inference from things seen is possible. Thus, he eschewed all-encompassing, oversimplified hypotheses in favor of careful observation as the basis of understanding nature.

Nevertheless, Alcmaeon shared with the Ionian philosophers an interest in natural speculation. Thus, he posited a microcosmic-macrocosmic relationship between man and the universe. He believed that the human soul was immortal because it was continuously in motion like the heavenly bodies, which he thought divine and immortal because they moved continuously and eternally in circles. While the heavenly bodies are immortal, however, men perish because "they cannot join the beginning to the end." Alcmaeon seems to mean by this that human life is not circular but linear and thus is not eternally renewed but runs down and dies when its motion ceases.

Alcmaeon developed a theory of opposites, according to which human beings have within them pairs of opposing forces, such as black and white, bitter and sweet, good and bad, large and small. He may well have been indebted to the Pythagoreans, who posited pairs of contrary qualities on mathematical lines (or they may have borrowed the notion from him). Alcmaeon, however, applied his theory particularly to health and disease. He defined health as a balance or equilibrium (*isonomia*) of opposing forces in the body (for example, warm and cold, bitter and sweet, wet and dry). He explained disease as the excess or predominance (*monarchia*) of one of these qualities or pairs of opposites that upsets the balance. This predominance could be caused by an excess or deficiency of food or by such external factors as climate, locality, fatigue, or exertion. Alcmaeon probably based this theory on his observation of factional struggles in Greek city-states, and he may have been influenced by the growth of democratic political ideas. Of all Alcmaeon's theories, this concept of opposites was to be the most influential in later Greek thought. The Hippocratic treatise *Peri archaies ietrikes* (c. 430-400 B.C.; *Ancient Medicine*) defends and elaborates this explanation.

Alcmaeon's theoretical speculation was balanced by a notable empirical tendency. It is this mixture of theory and observation that gives his work a distinctive and even pioneering nature. Alcmaeon, like many pre-Socratic philosophers, was interested in physiology, but he appears to have been the first to test his theories by examination of the body. In a celebrated case, he cut out the eye of an animal (whether dead or alive is uncertain). He was apparently interested in observing the substances of which the eye was composed. Whether he dissected the eye itself is not known. He also discovered (or inferred the existence of) the channels that connect the eye to the brain (probably the optic nerves).

There is no evidence that Alcmaeon ever dissected human corpses, and it is unlikely that he did so. He believed that the eye contained fire (which could be seen when the eye was hit) and water (which dissection revealed to have come from the brain). He concluded that there were similar passages connecting the other sense organs to the brain, and he described the passages connecting the brain to the mouth, nose, and ears (and quite possibly was the first to discover the Eustachian tubes). He thought that these channels were hollow and carried *pneuma* (air). Alcmaeon concluded that the brain provided the sensations of sight, hearing, smell, and taste, for he noticed that when a concussion occurred, the senses were affected. Similarly, when the passages were blocked, communication between the brain and the sense organs was cut off. Plato followed Alcmaeon in holding that the brain is the central organ of thought and feeling, but Aristotle and many other philosophers continued to attribute that function to the heart. Alcmaeon also differed from most contemporary philosophers in distinguishing between sensation and thought. He observed that sensation is common to all animals, while only man possesses intelligence.

According to Alcmaeon, whether the body was awake or asleep had to do with the amount of blood in the veins. Sleep was caused by the blood retiring to the larger blood vessels, while waking was the result of the blood being rediffused throughout the body. Alcmaeon was also interested in embryology, and he opened birds' eggs and examined the development of the embryo. He believed that the head, not the heart, was the first to develop. He resorted to speculation rather than observation in holding that human semen has its origin in the brain. He explained the sterility of mules by the theory that the seed produced by the male was too fine and cold, while the womb of the female did not open, and hence conception was prevented.

Summary

Alcmaeon is recognized as an important figure in the development of the biological sciences in ancient Greece. Although his date is uncertain and few details regarding either his career or his scientific methods are known, it is clear that he exercised considerable influence on subsequent Greek writers in the fields of medicine and biology. He introduced ideas that were later elaborated by Empedocles, Democritus, several Hippocratic writers, Plato, and Aristotle, among others. His idea that health is a balance of opposing forces in the body, although later modified, was accepted for many hundreds of years. Alcmaeon has often been called the father of embryology, anatomy, physiology, and experimental psychology. While such titles may be unwarranted, in each of these areas Alcmaeon did make significant contributions.

Regardless of whether Alcmaeon was a physician, he was one of the earliest Greeks to formulate medical theories. Many of his ideas were speculative and borrowed from earlier philosophers. Although influenced by the Pythagoreans, he avoided their mysticism, and he recognized the limitations of scientific inference. His medical theory did not grow out of medical practice but always retained a close affinity with philosophy; such theories tended to have little influence on the general practice of Greek medicine. Still, Alcmaeon's anatomical investigation (particularly his dissection of the eye) and his recognition that the senses are connected with the brain established him as a genuine pioneer in the development of Greek medical science.

Bibliography

Codellas, P.S. "Alcmaeon of Croton: His Life, Work, and Fragments." *Proceedings of the Royal Society of Medicine* 25 (1931/1932): 1041-1046. A brief but comprehensive discussion of Alcmaeon's life and contributions, published by the Royal Society of Medicine's Section on the History of Medicine.

Guthrie, W.K.C. *A History of Greek Philosophy.* Vol. 1. Cambridge: Cambridge University Press, 1962; New York: Cambridge University Press, 1981. A discussion of the evidence for Alcmaeon's dates and an examination of his medical, physiological, and cosmological theories (particularly his doctrine of the soul) by a leading expert on Greek philosophy.

Jones, W.H.S. *Philosophy and Medicine in Ancient Greece.* New York: Arno Press, 1979. Provides translations of the most important sources for Alcmaeon's life and doctrines, and discusses Alcmaeon's relationship to Plato and Aristotle.

Lloyd, Geoffrey. "Alcmaeon and the Early History of Dissection." *Sudhoffs Archiv* 59 (1975): 113-147. A detailed examination of the evidence for Alcmaeon's use of dissection, which Lloyd believes Alcmaeon to have practiced in a very limited manner rather than systematically. Explores as well the history of early Greek dissection after Alcmaeon.

Longrigg, James. *Greek Rational Medicine: Philosophy and Medicine from Alcmaeon to the Alexandrians.* London and New York: Routledge, 1993. An investigation of the relationship between philosophical and medical ideas in classical greece. The author argues that while natural philosophy liberated medicine from a superstitious belief in divine causes of illness, over-reliance on philosophical concepts retarded the use of experiment until the Hellenistic Age. Major figures in medical history are discussed, with copious translated citations from the ancient texts.

Sigerist, Henry E., ed. *A History of Medicine*. Vol. 2, *Early Greek, Hindu, and Persian Medicine*. New York: Oxford University Press, 1961. A general discussion of Alcmaeon and his work in the context of early Greek medicine and philosophy. Valuable for its general treatment of Greek medicine and its background.

Gary B. Ferngren

ALEXANDER THE GREAT

Born: 356 B.C.; Pella, Macedonia

Died: June 13, 323 B.C.; Babylon

Areas of Achievement: Government and conquest

Contribution: By military genius, political acumen, and cultural vision, Alexander unified and Hellenized most of the civilized ancient world and in so doing became a legendary figure in subsequent ages.

Early Life

Born into royalty of King Philip II of Macedonia and Olympias, daughter of King Neoptolemus of Epirus, Alexander was educated during his early teenage years by the Greek philosopher Aristotle. Although tutor and pupil later differed on political matters such as Alexander's decision to downgrade the importance of the city-state, Aristotle performed his assigned task of preparing his young charge for undertaking campaigns against the Persian Empire as well as inculcating in him a love of learning so vital to Hellenic (that is, Greek) culture.

In 340, at age sixteen, Alexander's formal training ended with his appointment to administer Macedonia while Philip was absent on a campaign. Young Alexander won his first battle against a force of Thracians and in 338 distinguished himself as commander of the left wing during Philip's crushing victory over the combined Greek army at Chaeronea. A break with his father over the latter's divorce and remarriage led Alexander to flee with his mother to Epirus. Although father and son reaffirmed their ties, Alexander feared for his status as successor. Philip's assassination in 336, along with the army's support of Alexander, eliminated all doubt of his kingship, and he had the assassins and all of his apparent enemies executed.

Life's Work

At the age of twenty, Alexander proceeded to fulfill Philip's planned attack on Persia and thereby to free Greeks living under Persian rule in Asia Minor (Turkey). Soon, however, he determined to place himself on the throne of Persia. Anxious to represent all Greece at the head of a Panhellenic union, he first received the approval and military support of the Greek League at Corinth and the endorsement of the oracle at Delphi as invincible. (The Romans later called him "the Great.")

In order to consolidate his rear guard in Europe before crossing into Asia, he spent the year 335 subduing restive peoples north and west of Macedonia and crushing an Athenian-endorsed revolt of Thebes by taking and razing the city of Thebes, killing six thousand and selling the rest as slaves. His harsh policy had the desired effect of discouraging further attempts by the Greeks to undermine his authority. Alexander therefore had no need to punish Athens, center of Hellenic culture, source of the largest navy available to him, and vital to the financial administration of the territories he would conquer. Nevertheless, he remained sufficiently suspicious of the Athenians to decline employing their fleet against Persia. The only Greek city-state openly disloyal to Alexander was Sparta, but it was isolated and later brought into line by Alexander's governor of Greece.

Alexander crossed the Hellespont (Dardanelles) into Asia Minor with his army of thirty-five thousand Macedonians and Greeks in the spring of 334 intent on humbling the Persian army and gaining spoils adequate to restore the strained Macedonian treasury. The army was a superbly balanced force of all arms, based on the highly disciplined maneuvers of the Macedonian phalanx and cavalry. With its offensive wing on the right, the infantry phalanxes would advance steadily, using their longer spears and supported by light-armed archers and javelin throwers. That was in reality a holding force, however, for while it moved forward, the cavalry attacked the enemy's flank and rear. If that did not succeed, then the infantry would institute a skillful fighting withdrawal to open a gap in the enemy's line and to gain the higher ground. This difficult maneuver thus created a flank, upon which Alexander's men would then rush. The key to success was timing, and Alexander's great ability was knowing where and when to strike decisively. Then he pursued the retreating enemy, who could not regroup. Alexander's tactical skills triumphed almost immediately when he met and crushed a Persian army at the river Granicus, largely as a result of his realization that victory was possible only after an interceding river was crossed.

No less a genius as a strategist, Alexander neutralized the Persian fleet by marching down the coasts of the Eastern Mediterranean, taking the enemy's seaports by land. To establish himself as a liberator, he dealt harshly only with those cities

which opposed his advance, and he installed Greek-style democracies in those which yielded without a fight. Indeed, he retained local governors, customs, and taxes, insisting only upon loyalty to himself instead of to King Darius III of Persia. This political policy had the additional logistical benefit of making available supplies crucial to keeping his army in the field. To provide balanced governments of occupation, however, as at Sardis, he appointed a Macedonian governor with troops, a local militia officer as fortress commander, and an Athenian overseer of monies. Also, the fact that the army was accompanied by scientists, engineers, and historians is evidence that he planned a long campaign to conquer all Persia and to gather new knowledge as inspired by Aristotle.

The conquest of Asia Minor was completed in the autumn of 333 when Alexander crushed Darius' army at Issus on the Syrian frontier, then advanced down the coast, receiving the submission of all the Phoenician cities except Tyre. Enraged by its defiance, he besieged Tyre for seven months, building a long mole (causeway) with siege towers and finally assaulting the city in July, 332. Tyre suffered the same fate as Thebes, and the rest of the coast lay open to Alexander, save for a two-month standoff at Gaza. Then Egypt welcomed him as a deliverer, whereupon he established the port city of Alexandria there. Returning to Syria, he advanced into Mesopotamia, where he routed the Grand Army of Darius at Arbela (or Gaugamela) in mid-331. One year later, Darius was killed by a rival as Alexander advanced eastward, the same year that Alexander burned down the Persian royal palace at Persepolis.

Alexander's vision of empire changed from 331 to 330 to that of a union of Macedonians and Persians under his kingship. He began to wear Persian dress, married the first of two Persian princesses after conquering the eastern provinces in 328, and later prevailed upon the Macedonian troops to do the same. As his men increasingly resisted such alien practices, Alexander ordered the execution of some of the most vocal critics, notably his second in command, Parmenio, his late father's intimate counselor, who was the spokesman for the older opponents of assimilation. In spite of such excesses, the army remained loyal and followed Alexander into India to his last great victory—one over local rulers at the Hydaspes River in June, 326, using native troops and methods, as well as elephants. Now his Macedonian troops, however,

tired and homesick, refused to go on, and he had no choice but to end his offensive. His engineers thereupon built a fleet of more than eight hundred vessels which ferried and accompanied the army downriver to the Indus, then to the Indian Ocean and west again to Persia. Heavy fighting, severe desert terrain, and unfavorable weather inflicted much suffering and heavy losses on his forces.

By the time he reached Susa, administrative capital of the Persian Empire, in 324, Alexander had indeed fashioned a sprawling empire. He had established numerous cities bearing his name and had infused Asia with the dynamic Hellenic culture which would influence the region for centuries to come. In addition, he now attempted greater racial intermixing, which led to another near-complete break with his fellow Macedonians. Alexander, ever more megalomaniacal, pronounced himself a god and had more of his subordinates put to death, usually during drunken sprees. These were so frequent in his last seven years that there is every reason to believe he had become a chronic alcoholic. As a result of one binge at Babylon in 323, he became ill and died ten days later; he was thirty-three years old. His empire was quickly divided among his successor generals, who eliminated his wives and two children.

Summary

Inculcated by Aristotle with the superiority of high Greek culture, Alexander the Great undertook the political unification of the Greek world along Panhellenic lines, followed by its extension over the vast but internally weak Persian Empire. His tools were the superb Macedonian army inherited from his father and his own genius at command. As one success followed another, however, his horizons became broader. He identified himself with the religion and deities of each land he conquered, especially Egypt, and ultimately seems to have concluded that it was his destiny to merge most of the known world under common rule. That vision possibly included Carthage and the Western Mediterranean, though death denied him further territorial acquisitions.

Alexander's shrewd administrative skills enabled him to succeed in the five major facets of statehood. In religion, he began with the Greek pantheon but then recognized all faiths, with himself as the common godhead. Hellenic culture was also the intellectual power which drove his social ambitions and which prevailed in spite of his attempts to amalgamate it with Persian ways, leaving a predominantly Hellenistic world in his wake. In the economic sphere, he followed the Greek practices of silver-based coinage, which with Persian gold brought about common commercial practices and general prosperity. As one of the greatest generals in history, Alexander obtained victory with skillful tactics, flexibility, a keen sense of logistics, and superior leadership, followed by an effective system of garrisons with divided commands. His charismatic personality and vision combined all these elements into the final one—firm, dynamic, political rule. Once Alexander passed from the scene, however, the system could not be sustained. Nevertheless, his example of continental empire contributed to the eventual rise of the Roman Empire and the expansion of Christianity.

Bibliography

Arrian. *The Life of Alexander the Great*. Translated by Aubrey de Sélincourt. London: Penguin Books, 1958. The best and most reliable of the ancient works on Alexander, actually entitled the *Anabasis,* though preoccupied with the military aspects. For the most part, it takes the form of straight narrative.

Badian, Ernst. "Alexander the Great and the Unity of Mankind." *Historia* 7 (1958): 425-444. A rejection of other scholars' attempts to idealize the man, viewing him instead as merely pragmatic and thus reflecting the ongoing debate about Alexander's true motives.

Bosworth, A. B. *Conquest and Empire: The Reign of Alexander the Great*. Cambridge and New York: Cambridge University Press, 1988. Bosworth states that his book should not be considered a biography but rather a larger historical study of Alexander's impact. Alexander himself is neither overly praised nor openly scorned. In the latter half of the book much attention is given to the governmental structures of Alexander's new empire.

Burn, A. R. *Alexander the Great and the Hellenistic Empire*. 2d ed. London: English Universities Press, 1951; New York: Collier, 1962. An almost complete rejection of Alexander as a heroic figure, denying the impact ascribed to him by most other writers.

Engels, Donald W. *Alexander the Great and the Logistics of the Macedonian Army*. Berkeley: University of California Press, 1978. A masterful use of mathematics to ascertain the four-day carrying load of Alexander's soldiers and the means by which these considerations influenced his strategy and movements.

Fox, Robin Lane. *Alexander the Great*. London: Allen Lane, and New York: Dial Press, 1973. A direct, no-nonsense use of the sources to fashion a serious examination of Alexander, scholarly in every way except exhaustive citations and virtually ignoring Tarn's thesis, which Fox rejects.

Fuller, J. F. C. *The Generalship of Alexander the Great*. London: Eyre and Spottiswoode, 1958; Birmingham, Ala.: 1960. The best work on Alexander's military achievements, complete with campaign maps and battle diagrams; by a retired British general and leading military pundit of the twentieth century.

Green, Peter. *Alexander the Great*. Rev. ed. Oxford and Berkeley: University of California Press, 1991. A judicious biography, replete with illustrations of the territory that Alexander traversed, which rejects the "brotherhood of man" ascribed to Alexander's motives by others and includes many surviving legends.

Hammond, N. G. L. *Alexander the Great: King, Commander, and Statesman*. 3d ed. London: Bristol, 1994. A good overview with an appendix on the question of Alexander's drinking and possible alcoholism.

———. *The Genius of Alexander the Great*. Chapel Hill: University of North Carolina Press, and London: Duckworth, 1997. A straight biographical account by an expert in the field. Hammond subscribes to the "great man" theory of history and holds a generally positive view of Alexander's character and accomplishments. One chapter deals with the reliability of the ancient sources.

M'Crindle, J. W. *The Invasion of India by Alexander the Great as Described by Arrian, Q. Curtius, Diodorus, Plutarch, and Justin*. New ed. Westminster: Archibald Constable and Co., 1896; New York: Barnes and Noble Books, 1969. A specialized treatment of Alexander's Indian foray, reprinted from the original 1893 edition, which includes the verbatim accounts of the ancient authorities Arrian, Quintus Curtius Rufus, Plutarch, Diodoros Siculus, and Justin (useful for comparisons) and an informative biographical appendix.

O'Brien, John Maxwell. *Alexander the Great: The Invisible Enemy*. London and New York: Routledge, 1992. This book, by the author of two previous articles on Alexander's alcoholism, largely dispenses with detailed, specialist argumentation and provides a lively, anecdotal account of Alexander's life, focusing particularly on Alexander's relationship to the god Dionysus and his emulation of heroic men and deeds from Greece's mythical past.

Roisman, Joseph, ed. *Alexander the Great: Ancient and Modern Perspectives*. Problems in European Civilization Series. Lexington, Mass. and Toronto: D. C. Heath, 1995. A useful compilation of ancient sources and some important modern scholarly opinions about various aspects of Alexander's background and career.

Savill, Agnes. *Alexander the Great and His Time*. 3d ed. London: Barrie and Rockliff, 1959; New York: Citadel Press, 1966. A sound volume for the general reader which draws on most ancient and modern scholarship.

Stewart, Andrew. *Hellenistic Culture and Society*. Vol. 11, *Faces of Power: Alexander's Image and Hellenistic Politics*. Berkeley: University of California Press, 1993. A learned investigation of the surviving ancient art dealing with Alexander. The images reveal Alexander's complexity and the many-sidedness of his reputation. Includes a discussion of the famous Alexander Mosaic in the archaeological museum at Naples.

Stoneman, Richard. *Alexander the Great*. Lancaster Pamphlets. London and New York: Routledge, 1997. A short, useful introduction to the life and impact of Alexander, as well as to the nature and problems of the ancient sources. Directed toward the beginning student or interested layperson.

Tarn, W. W. *Alexander the Great*. 2 vols. Cambridge: Cambridge University Press, and Boston: Beacon, 1948. A complete and sympathetic biography—the most influential one in English, by a leading Hellenistic historian who views Alexander as having sought the brotherhood of man; especially useful for its in-depth review of all the ancient authorities.

Wilcken, Ulrich. *Alexander the Great*. Translated by G. C. Richards. New York: Dial Press, and London: Chatto and Windus, 1932. An excellent, balanced treatment of Alexander's life and achievements, introduced by lengthy discussions of the Greek world in the fourth century B.C. and of his father, Philip II. This translated reprint of the 1931 work includes a useful historiographical overview by Eugene N. Borza.

Clark G. Reynolds

SAINT AMBROSE

Born: 339; Augusta Treverorum, Gaul
Died: April 4, 397; Milan, Italy
Areas of Achievement: Religion and government
Contribution: By the practical application of Roman virtue and Christian ethics Ambrose established the Nicene Creed as the orthodox doctrine of Christianity and asserted the spiritual authority of the church over the state.

Early Life

Ambrose is a good example of why Christianity replaced traditional paganism as the official religion of the Roman Empire. The son of one of the highest civilian officials in the Roman hierarchy, he was educated in the best Roman tradition and reared in a devout Christian family. When Ambrose was born, his father, Aurelius Ambrosius, was Praetorian Prefect of Gaul and could offer Ambrose every advantage of Roman life. Ambrosius died when Ambrose was still an infant, and thus it was left to his mother, whose name is unknown, to rear the young Ambrose, his sister Marcellina, and his brother Satyrus. Almost immediately the family returned to Rome. Little is known about this time in Rome except that Ambrose and his brother attended the usual Roman schools, where they learned grammar and composition by reading and reciting the works of the Roman masters. Ambrose stated that he most enjoyed Cicero, Vergil, and Sallust. Later both brothers studied rhetoric and prepared for careers in the civil service.

Christianity seems to have been established within the family well before Ambrose's birth. The family boasted of a holy ancestor, a great-aunt Soteris, who had suffered martyrdom in 304 during the persecutions propagated by Diocletian. The depth of this belief first appeared on the feast of the Epiphany in 353, when Marcellina, in the presence of Pope Liberius, dedicated her virginity to God and committed herself to the practice of an ascetic life. Afterward, Marcellina continued to live in her mother's house and with her mother formed the core for one of the first groups of patrician women who renounced the world and gave themselves up to Christian study, prayer, and good works.

The effects of a Christian life were not immediately obvious in Ambrose's own life. In 365, Emperor Valentinian I appointed him and Satyrus legal advocates in Sirmium at the tribunal of the Praetorian Prefect of Italy, Africa, and Illyria. Both men impressed successive prefects with their eloquence and intelligence and advanced quickly. As a result, in 370 both received provincial governorships. Ambrose became governor of Aemilia-Liguria in northern Italy. Since the capital of the province was at Milan, then the principal seat of the Imperial Government in the West, Ambrose became known to the most important people of the time. An anecdote in the biography written after his death by his secretary Paulinus indicates how popular a governor he was. In 373, when Bishop Auxentius died, governor Ambrose, in an effort to keep the peace, addressed the bickering factions of orthodox and Arian Christians. From the crowd a child's voice was heard to call "Bishop Ambrose." It was enough to start a public outcry for his consecration as the next Bishop of Milan.

Life's Work

Ambrose's whole career as Bishop of Milan was directed toward defending what he called the "cause of God," which included the advocacy of an

orthodox Christian doctrine, the defining of Church authority, and the disestablishment of pagan state religion. From the time of his consecration, Bishop Ambrose had made known his opposition to the Arian heresy, but he was unable to influence the Emperor Valentinian I. To maintain public order, Valentinian followed a policy of neutrality toward the different religions of the empire, even though he himself was a Christian. Ambrose's first successes were in shaping the attitudes and programs of the Emperor Gratian. His strongly worded statement against Arianism, *De fide* (380), used extensive scriptural quotations to present the argument that orthodoxy provided a physical protection for the empire. Ambrose pointed out that the Goths had devastated the Arian provinces of the Balkan Peninsula but that the provinces defended by the orthodox Gratian were spared. Convinced by the argument, Gratian enlisted Ambrose as an adviser and teacher. It was probably Ambrose who inspired Gratian's firm stands against heresy and his decree for the removal of the Altar of Victory from the Senate House in 382. The Altar of Victory to the people of the time was a symbol of the ancient association of paganism and the Roman government.

Ambrose's relationship with Gratian proved his powers of persuasion, but it established no real authority for the Church. Since the time of Constantine the Great, emperors had freely interfered in Church affairs as a legitimate function of their office. After Gratian's death in 383, Justina and her son Valentinian II represented the imperial family in Milan. They favored Arian doctrine. At the beginning of 385 Justina ordered Ambrose to assign a church for Arian worship. Ambrose refused, saying that sacred things were not subject to the power of the emperor. He was unwilling to allow the gains made against heresy to be lost as the result of changes in the religious preference of the civil authorities. For more than a year, Ambrose resisted the queen mother's demands and the pressures of the emperor. At times he physically obstructed troops trying to occupy Christian churches. In the end he was successful for several reasons. First, Ambrose's popularity ensured broad public support for his stand. Second, while excavating for the construction of the new basilica, workmen discovered the skeletal remains of two large men. Ambrose interpreted the finds as the remains of the martyred saints Gervasius and Protasius, a sign from Heaven on the correctness of his position.

The emperor found it difficult to combat a sign from God. Third, in 387 the usurper Magnus Maximus moved his armies toward Milan, and Valentinian and Justina fled. Circumstances left Ambrose in control in Milan.

The prestige which Ambrose achieved as the result of his successful resistance to Justina and Valentinian was the basis for future success in asserting Church authority over the authority of the soldier emperor Theodosius the Great. In late 388, at the instigation of the local bishop, a mob looted and burned a Jewish synagogue at Callinicum in Syria. The news of the event reached Milan in a report that also told of monks destroying a chapel of a Gnostic sect. In the interest of public order, Theodosius ordered reparations. In particular he ordered the bishop to rebuild the synagogue at his own expense and to see to the restoration of the stolen articles. The offending monks were to be punished. Ambrose was appalled. In a letter written to Theodosius, he took the position that if the bishop rebuilt the place of worship for the enemies of Christ he would be guilty of apostasy. It would be better for the bishop to refuse and become a martyr for not obeying the emperor. Ambrose's position was that the maintenance of civil law is secondary to religious interests. Even Theodosius' amended order that the state rebuild the synagogue would not satisfy Ambrose. A bold sermon, delivered while Theodosius was in the congregation, demanded that there be no reparation of any kind. In the past, Ambrose stated, gross breaches of public order by pagans and Jews against Christians had gone unpunished. He had in mind the violence that had occurred during the reign of the Emperor Julian. It was perverse reasoning, but it was effective. Theodosius yielded, not because he accepted Ambrose's argument but because politically he could not afford to alienate the popular bishop. In the dispute with Justina, Ambrose had proved his ability to arouse public sentiment. Unfortunately, Ambrose's stance provided a justification for anti-Semitism throughout the Middle Ages.

This public humiliation of the emperor had a chilling effect upon Ambrose's relationship with the imperial court, and for a time Theodosius preferred the advice of others. One result was Theodosius' cruel response to a violent outburst by the citizens of the Greek city of Thessalonica. During the summer of 390, the Thessalonians became upset over the quartering of barbarian troops within the city. When Botheric, the barbarian commandant, ordered the imprisonment of a popular charioteer and refused to allow him to participate in the upcoming public games, riots erupted. An angry mob savagely attacked Botheric, killed him, and dragged his body through the streets. Theodosius was furious and yielded to counsel that he punish the city. He soon repented his anger, but too late to stop a general massacre. Enticed to attend a gala exhibition in the circus, the citizens filled the arena. At a signal the gates were shut and armed soldiers rushed in, attacking and killing indiscriminately anyone they found. For three hours, no distinctions were made between citizens and visitors, guilty and not guilty, young and old. In all, at least seven thousand people died.

Ambrose's response, after a judicious delay, was to excommunicate the emperor. Tradition has it that the proclamation was made publicly and that the emperor was ordered to undergo public penance, which would have increased Theodosius' humiliation before Ambrose. Yet the letter in which Ambrose refused the Sacraments to the emperor is a model of tact and restraint. Ambrose acts the part of the concerned confessor and moral guardian. His position is the sanctity of divine law over a man who has sinned grievously against God and humanity. Thus, while Theodosius again had to yield to the bishop's authority, he submitted to spiritual and not secular authority. In effect, Theodosius recognized the Church's right to preserve the fundamental principles of religion and morality over princes and people alike. The affair actually brought Ambrose and Theodosius closer together. Thereafter, Ambrose was Theodosius' chief spiritual adviser and confidant. They were truly partners in establishing the Nicene ideals in the Western church. Together, they defined the Nicene Creed as the orthodox religion. Ambrose outlived Theodosius by only three years. He died on the Vigil of Easter.

Summary

Ambrose is best known for asserting the dominance of Church authority over the Emperor Theodosius. Through his example, future ministers of the Gospel confidently claimed the right to judge, condemn, punish, and pardon princes. Ambrose was not motivated by any personal desire to demonstrate priestly power over the sovereign. Even in the episode of Callinicum, which was so little to his credit, he acted according to what he saw as the interests of the Church. In his mind, church and state were dominant in two separate but mutually dependent spheres. It was the function of the church to pray for the state and to act as its spiritual leader, while the state was the secular arm of society, which facilitated the spiritual purpose of the church. His confrontations with Theodosius and other secular leaders arose from the conviction that they had crossed the line separating church and state and were interfering in spiritual affairs. These became the principles which guided both civil and papal law in the Middle Ages.

This approach was a direct result of Ambrose's Roman, Stoic upbringing. In a very practical way, he was able to use what was best of Roman values as the foundation of everyday Christian virtue. Ambrose was convinced that because of the tremendous gulf between God and humankind, the day-to-day adherence to faith was the issue of greatest importance. He was not an original thinker, preferring to use his tremendous gift for oratory as a tool for education. Concern with the details of Scripture as they applied to life situations prompted him to rely on allegory, especially in his discussions of the Old Testament. The result was a dynamic body of doctrine and a devout core of converts, the most famous of whom was Saint Augustine. Typically, as one practical way to increase the involvement of women and children in church services, Ambrose advocated a greater use of music in religious services. Although not the first to use music in the liturgy, he is considered the father of liturgical music.

Bibliography

Campenhausen, Hans von. *Men Who Shaped the Western Church*. Translated by Manfred Hoffman. New York: Harper and Row, Publishers, 1964. A collection of short analytical biographies for seven of the best-known men in Latin Christianity, the aim of this book is to depict how personality contributed to the differences between the Greek and Latin churches. The biography of Ambrose highlights his contribution to the practical legalism of Western Christianity.

Deferrari, Roy J., ed. *The Fathers of the Church*. Vols. 26, 42, 44, 65. New York: Fathers of the Church, 1954-1972. A collection of significant pieces of Ambrose's writings. Volume 26 contains ninety-one of his letters and is the most useful biographical source.

Dudden, F. Homes. *The Life and Times of St. Ambrose*. 2 vols. Oxford: Clarendon Press, 1935.

The standard, most thorough treatment of Ambrose's life. It combines biographical detail with insightful analysis and source criticism and corrects many of the mistaken ideas about Ambrose. Contains an extensive bibliography.

Gilliard, Frank D. "Senatorial Bishops in the Fourth Century." *Harvard Theological Review* 77, no. 2 (1984): 153-175. In an examination of the class origins of prominent fourth century bishops, Gilliard seeks to determine if social class aided those who attained high church office, and whether that affected the conversion of the Roman aristocracy.

King, N. Q. *The Emperor Theodosius and the Establishment of Christianity.* Philadelphia: Westminster Press, 1960; London: SCM Press, 1961. A useful account of the secular leadership in the fight for Christian orthodoxy. It addresses the obstacles of conscience and civil disorder which concerned Theodosius in his support of Ambrose. The view is through the eyes of Theodosius, Christian and emperor.

McLynn, Neil B. *Ambrose of Milan: Church and Court in a Christian Capital.* Vol. 22, *The Transformation of the Classical Heritage.* Berkeley: University of California Press, 1994. This study places Ambrose in the larger context of late antique history and society and portrays him as a skilled player in a game of high political stakes, willing to use every opportunity at hand to increase his prestige. Central to the author's argument is the claim that previous views of Ambrose have been distorted by reliance on the carefully-crafted image that the saint himself created for public consumption.

Paredi, Angelo. *Saint Ambrose: His Life and Times.* Translated by Joseph Costelloe. Notre Dame, Ind.: University of Notre Dame Press, 1964. A history of the period in which Ambrose lived, not a biography. Religious in its outlook, it is more accepting of the legends and less critical of the sources than are most scholarly treatments.

Paulinus. *Life of St. Ambrose by Paulinus.* Translated by John A. Lacy. New York: Fathers of the Church, 1952. Paulinus' biography is the basic source for information about the life of Ambrose. Paulinus was enamored of Ambrose and considered him a saint. He retells fantastic events as truth.

Ronald J. Weber

ANAXAGORAS

Born: c. 500 B.C.; Clazomenae, Anatolia

Died: c. 428 B.C.; Lampsacus

Areas of Achievement: Philosophy, natural history, and science

Contribution: By devising a philosophical system to explain the origins and nature of the physical universe which overcame the paradoxes and inconsistencies of earlier systems, Anaxagoras provided an indispensable bridge between the pre-Socratic philosophers of the archaic period of Greek history and the full flowering of philosophy during the Golden Age of Greece.

Early Life

Virtually nothing is known of Anaxagoras' parents, his childhood, his adolescence, or his education. Born into a wealthy family in an Ionian Greek city, he almost certainly was exposed to the attempts by Ionian philosophers, especially Parmenides, to explain the physical universe by postulating that everything is made from a single primordial substance. Anaxagoras apparently realized even before he was twenty years of age that such an assumption could not explain the phenomena of movement and change, and he began to devise a more satisfactory system.

He grew to adulthood during the turbulent years of the wars of the Greek city-states against the Persian Empire. His own city, Clazomenae, forced to acknowledge the suzerainty of Darius the Great in 514, joined the Athenian-aided Ionian revolt against Persia in 498. That revolt was ultimately suppressed in 493. Anaxagoras' childhood was spent during a time when the echoes of Athens' great victory over Darius at Marathon in 490 were reverberating throughout the Hellenic world.

According to tradition, Anaxagoras became a resident of Athens in 480. That a young scholar should be attracted to the intellectual and artistic center of Greek civilization is not surprising, but it is doubtful that this change of residence took place in 480. Xerxes I chose that year to attempt to realize Darius' dream of conquering the Greek polis. His plans were frustrated and his great host scattered at the battles of Salamis and Plataea during that same year. The next year, the Ionian cities of Asia Minor again rose in rebellion against Persia, and in 477, joined with Athens in the Delian League. The League succeeded in expelling the Persians from the Greek states of Asia Minor. It

seems more likely that the young Anaxagoras came to Athens after the alliance between the Ionian cities and the Athenians.

While in Athens, Anaxagoras became friends with the young Pericles and apparently influenced him considerably. Several classical scholars have concluded that Anaxagoras' later trial was engineered by Pericles' political rivals, in order to deprive Pericles of a trusted friend. Convicted of impiety after admitting that he thought the sun was a huge mass of "hot rock," Anaxagoras went into exile at Lampsacus, where many young Greeks came to study with him before his death, probably in 428.

Life's Work

Sometime in or shortly after 467, Anaxagoras published his only written work, apparently entitled Nature. Of this work, only seventeen fragments totaling around twelve hundred words have survived, all recorded as quotations in the works of later generations of philosophers. That so few words could have inspired the more than fifty books and articles written about him in the twentieth century alone is ample testimony to Anaxagoras' importance in the evolution of Greek philosophy and natural science.

Anaxagoras' book was an ambitious attempt to explain the origins and nature of the universe without recourse (or so it seemed to many of his contemporaries) to any supernatural agents. Other Ionian philosophers, notably Parmenides, had preceded Anaxagoras in this endeavor, but their systems were logically unable to explain the multiplicity of "things" in the universe or to explain physical and biological change in those things because they had postulated that all things are made from the same basic "stuff." Anaxagoras overcame the logical inconsistencies of this argument by postulating an infinite variety of substances that make up the whole of the universe. Anaxagoras argued that there is something of everything in everything. By this he meant that, for example, water contains a part of every other thing in the universe, from blood to rock to air. The reason that it is perceived to be water is that most of its parts are water. A hair also contains parts of every other thing, but most of its parts are hair.

In the beginning, according to the first fragment of Anaxagoras' book, infinitely small parts of everything in equal proportions were together in a sort of primal soup. In fragment 3, he proposes a primitive version of the law of the conservation of energy, by saying that anything, no matter how small, can be divided infinitely, because it is not possible for something to become nonexistent through dividing. This idea of infinite divisibility is unique to the Anaxagorean system; no philosopher before or since has proposed it.

This universal mixture of all things acquired form and substance, according to fragment 12, through the actions of nous, or "Mind." Mind, Anaxagoras argues, is not part of everything (though it is a part of some things), nor is a part of everything found in Mind (though parts of some things are found in Mind). Mind set the primal soup into rotation and the different things began to "separate off," thus forming the universe. The rotation of the primal mixture not only separated everything according to its kind (but not perfectly, since everything still contains parts of every other thing) but also supplied heat, through friction. Among other things, friction ignited the sun and the stars. Considerable disagreement over the exact meaning Anaxagoras was trying to convey with the term "Mind" has colored scholarly works on his book since Aristotle and continues to be a controversial issue.

Anaxagoras' system not only enabled him and his students to describe all existing objects, but it also permitted the explanation of physical and biological change. It was the introduction of the idea of Mind and its action as a formative agent in the creation of the universe for which Anaxagoras became famous and which rejuvenated Socrates' interest and faith in philosophy.

Sometime after 467, Anaxagoras was accused of and tried for impiety (denying the gods) and "medism" (sympathizing with the Persians). The actual date of his trial and subsequent banishment from Athens is still hotly debated among classical scholars. The traditional date accepted by most historians is 450, but this seems unlikely for several reasons. By 450, the charge of medism could hardly have been a serious one, since the Persian wars were long since over. Also, had he been in Athens in 450, the young Socrates would almost certainly have met him personally, but Socrates' own words indicate that he knew Anaxagoras only through his book. Finally, Anaxagoras' friend Pericles would have been fully able to protect his mentor from political opponents in 450. An earlier date for his exile from Athens seems likely. Some scholars have

attempted to solve this problem by postulating that Anaxagoras visited Athens one or more times after being exiled shortly after the publication of his book. This seems the most reasonable explanation to reconcile the dispute, especially since several ancient sources place him in Athens as late as 437.

One of Anaxagoras' most notable achievements during his stay in Athens was to postulate the correct explanation for a solar eclipse. Anaxagoras was apparently the first to argue that an eclipse occurs when the moon (which he said was a large mass of cold rocks) passes between the Earth and the sun (which he said was a larger mass of hot rocks). He may have reached this conclusion after the fall of a large meteorite near Aegypotomi in 467, which excited wide discussion throughout the Hellenic world.

After leaving Athens, Anaxagoras spent his remaining years as the head of a flourishing school at Lampsacus. How his philosophical system may have changed over the years between the publication of his book and the end of his life is unknown. He died at Lampsacus, probably in 428.

Summary

The thesis that Anaxagoras greatly influenced Socrates and Aristotle is easily proved by their elaborate discussions of his system in their own words. Through those two most influential of all Greek thinkers, he has had a profound impact on all subsequent generations of philosophers and natural scientists in the Western world. Some of Anaxagoras' critics, both ancient and modern, accuse him of merely substituting the word "Mind" for "God" or "the gods." Thus in their estimation his philosophy becomes merely a humanistic religion. Other critics have dismissed Anaxagoras' teachings as simplistic and unworthy of serious consideration. His supporters, from Aristotle to the present, have defended him as a pioneering thinker who provided much of the inspiration for the flowering of post-Socratic philosophy during the Golden Age of Greece and the Hellenistic world.

Early critics and supporters alike may have missed an important point in the Anaxagoras fragments. Late twentieth century work on Anaxagoras points out that his concept of Mind giving form to the universe is not far removed from the position of some modern physicists who argue that our perception of the universe is determined by our own senses, which provide an imperfect understanding at best. Anaxagoras may well have been trying to express this same concept (that without cognitive perception there is no form or substance to the universe) without possessing the technical language to do so.

Bibliography

Davison, J. A. "Protagoras, Democritus, and Anaxagoras." *Classical Quarterly*, N.s. 3 (1953): 33-45. Establishes Anaxagoras' position vis-à-vis other Greek philosophers and shows his influence on the "atomist" school that succeeded him. Also contains some information on his early life not available elsewhere in English and argues for an early date for his exile from Athens.

Gershenson, Daniel E., and Daniel A. Greenberg. *Anaxagoras and the Birth of Physics*. New York: Blaisdell Publishing Co., 1964. This controversial work suggests that the Anaxagoras fragments are not really the words of Anaxagoras, but rather his words as interpreted by later philosophers, notably Simplicius, who succeeded him. Contains a good, if somewhat theoretical, explanation of Anaxagoras' system.

Guthrie, W. K. C. *A History of Greek Philosophy*. Vol. 2. Cambridge: Cambridge University Press, 1962; New York: Cambridge University Press, 1978. Contains the most complete account available of Anaxagoras' life. Puts his life and teachings in the context of his times.

Kirk, G. S., and J. E. Raven. *The Presocratic Philosophers: A Critical History with a Selection of Texts*. 2d ed. Cambridge and New York: Cambridge University Press, 1983. A very readable account of Anaxagoras' life and works and of his place in the history of philosophy.

Mansfield, J. "The Chronology of Anaxagoras' Athenian Period and the Date of His Trial." *Mnemosyne* 33 (1980): 17-95. Offers the most convincing arguments concerning Anaxagoras' arrival in Athens, his trial, and his banishment.

Also contains references to Anaxagoras' relationship with Pericles and the political motives behind the former's exile.

Sandywell, Barry. *Presocratic Reflexivity: The Construction of Philosophical Discourse, c. 600-450 B.C.* Volume 3. London and New York: Routledge, 1996. A difficult, wide-ranging book that attempts to evaluate pre-Socratic thinkers in terms of the "cultural discourse" in which they participated and to which they in turn contributed. Chapter 8 deals with Anaxagoras.

Schofield, Malcolm. *An Essay on Anaxagoras*. Cambridge and New York: Cambridge University Press, 1980. A clear, witty exposition of the philosophy of Anaxagoras and his importance in the history of philosophy. Perhaps the best work on Anaxagoras' system and its meaning available in English.

Taylor, A. E. "On the Date of the Trial of Anaxagoras." *Classical Quarterly* 11 (1917): 81-87. A good discussion of the backdrop against which Anaxagoras' sojourn in Athens was played and the political and intellectual milieu during which his book was written.

Teodorsson, Sven-Tage. *Anaxagoras' Theory of Matter*. Göteborg, Sweden: Acta Universitatis Gothoburgensis, 1982. Although this book is too difficult for the average reader (its author includes quotations throughout the text in six different languages), it is valuable because it contains the best English translation of the Anaxagoras fragments.

Wright, M. R. *Cosmology in Antiquity*. London and New York: Routledge, 1995. A general account, designed for the non-specialist reader, of ancient cosmology. Extensive coverage given to the pre-Socratics. Arrangement is not chronological but topical.

Paul Madden

ANAXIMANDER

Born: c. 610 B.C.; Miletus, Greek Asia Minor
Died: c. 547 B.C.; probably Miletus
Areas of Achievement: Natural history, astronomy, and geography
Contribution: Anaximander realized that no ordinary physical element could be the source of the world's diversity; instead, he saw that the fundamental stuff much be an eternal, unlimited reservoir of qualities and change.

Early Life

Anaximander was a fellow citizen and student of Thales, the Milesian usually credited with having inaugurated Western philosophy. Thales, some forty years older than his protégé, put none of his philosophical thought in writing and maintained no formal pedagogical associations with pupils. Yet Thales' cosmological views (as reconstructed by historians) doubtless inspired Anaximander, and Anaximander finally expanded on Thales' ideas with innovative leaps in conceptual abstraction.

Anaximander was known in his day for his practical achievements and his astronomical discoveries. Anaximander is said to have been chosen by the Milesians as the leader for a new colony in Apollonia on the Black Sea. He traveled widely and was the first Greek to publish a "geographical tablet," a map of the world. The map was circular, and it was centered on the city of Delphi, since Delphi was the location of the *omphalos*, or "navel" stone, that was thought to be the center of Earth. Anaximander is also said to have designed a celestial map and to have specified the proportions of stellar orbits. In addition to the celestial map, he built a spherical model of the stars and planets, with Earth located at the center and represented as a disk or cylinder whose height was one third its diameter. The heavenly bodies were rings of hollow pipe of different sizes that were placed on circling wheels in ratios of three to six to nine, in proportion to the magnitude of Earth. This model was dynamic; the wheels could be moved at different speeds, making it possible to visualize patterns of planetary motion. Anaximander is also credited with inventing the sundial, or gnomon, and with having discovered the zodiac.

All these eclectic interests and discoveries illustrate, with elegance, Anaximander's particular genius, namely, his rational view of the world. This way of thinking was quite an innovation at a time

when both scientific and protophilosophical thought took their content from the mythical and literary traditions, and thus were marked by vagueness and mystery. Anaximander viewed the world as steadily legible; he had the expectation of its rational intelligibility. His map of the world and his model of the heavens show his anticipation of symmetry and order. Earth, he argued, remained at rest in the center of the cosmos by reason of its equidistance at all points to the celestial circumference; it had no reason to be pulled in one direction in preference to any other. He projected the celestial orbits in perfect and pleasing proportions, and he anticipated regular motions.

Anaximander's mapping and modeling techniques themselves were products of his rationalistic thinking. Models and maps relocate some set of unified phenomena into a new level of abstraction. Implicit in map and model design is the assumption that the abstractions will preserve the intelligible relationships present in the world that they reproduce. Thus Anaximander's introduction of models and maps represents a tremendous and utterly original conceptual leap from the world "seen" to the world's operations understood and faithfully reproduced by the abstracting human mind.

Life's Work

Anaximander's rational view of the world received its fullest and most innovative expression in his philosophy of nature. Here one finds the first unified and all-encompassing picture of the world of human experience in history that is based on rational deduction and explanation of all phenomena.

In order to understand Anaximander properly, his terminology must be put into its historical context. What Anaximander (and Thales as well) understood by "nature" is not quite the same as its modern sense. In Ionian Greece, *physis* denoted the process of growth and emergence. It also denoted something's origin, or source, that from which the thing is constantly renewed. Nature, in the Ionian sense of *physis*, had nothing to do with matter; even Aristotle was mistaken in thinking that it did. In fact, no word for matter even existed in Anaximander's day. It is also important to note that Anaximander's thought is reconstructed entirely from ancient secondary sources. The one extant fragment of Anaximander's own words is the quotation of an ancient historian. Thus, any explication of Anaximander's thought is to some extent conjectural and interpretive.

Anaximander's philosophy of nature arose in part as a response to Thales' ideas on nature. Thales held that Water was the nature of everything. This meant, in the light of the ancient idea of *physis*, that Water was the origin of everything, that everything was sustained by, and constantly renewed from, Water. This notion does not have any allegorical or mythical connotations in Thales' formulation. Water is the ordinary physical stuff in the world, not some engendering god such as the Oceanus of Thales' predecessors. That is the reason Thales is the first philosopher: He had a theory about the origin of things that competed with ancient creation myths.

Anaximander agreed with Thales that the origin of the things of the world was some common stuff, but he thought that the stuff could not be some ordinary element. He rejected Thales' conception on purely logical grounds, and his reasoning was quite interesting. How could any manifestly singular stuff ever give rise to qualities that pertained to things differently constituted, such as earth and fire? What is more, if Water were the source of things, would not drying destroy them? Thus, reasoned Anaximander, the thing with which the world begins cannot be identical with any of the ordinary stuff with which humans are acquainted, but it must be capable of giving rise to the wide multiplicity of things and their pairs of contrary qualities. What therefore distinguishes the source from the world is that the source itself is "unbounded": It can have no definite shape or quality of its own but must be a reservoir from which every sort or characteristic in the world may be spawned. So Anaximander called the source of things this very name: *apeiron*, Boundlessness, or the Boundless. Anaximander designated the Boundless an *arche*, a beginning, but he did not mean a temporal beginning. The Boundless can have no beginning, nor can it pass away, for it can have no bounds, including temporal ones.

Thus the eternal source, the Boundless, functions as a storehouse of the world's qualities, such that the qualities that constitute some present state of the world have been separated out of the stock, and when their contrary qualities become manifest, they will, in turn, be reabsorbed into the reservoir. When Earth is hot, heat will come forth from the Boundless; when Earth cools, cold will come forth

and heat will go back. For Anaximander, this process continued in never-ending cycles.

The cause of the alternating manifestations of contrary qualities is the subject of the single existing fragment of Anaximander's own words, the only remains of the first philosophy ever written. Out of the Boundless, Anaximander explains, the worlds arise, but

> from whatever things is the genesis of the things that are, into these they must pass away according to necessity; for they must pay the penalty and make atonement to one another for their injustice according to the ordering of Time.

History has produced no consensus of interpretation for this passage and its picturesque philosophical metaphor for the rationale of the world. Anaximander was probably thinking of a courtroom image. Each existing thing is in a state of "having-too-much," so that during the time it exists it "commits injustice" against its opposite by preventing it from existing. In retribution, the existing thing must cede its overt existence for its opposite to enjoy and pay the penalty of returning to the submerged place in the great Boundless reservoir. This cycling, he added, is how Time is ordered or measured. Time is the change, the alternating manifestation of opposites.

Here is the apotheosis of Anaximander's rational worldview. The world's workings are not simply visible and perspicuous, but neither are they whimsical and mysterious. The hidden workings of things may be revealed in the abstractions of the human mind. The world works, and is the way that it is, according to an eternal and intelligible principle. What is more, this world and its workings are unified, indeed form a cosmos. The cosmos, in turn, can be understood and explained by analogy with the human world; the justice sought in the city's courts is the same justice that sustains everything that human perception finds in the universe.

Summary

Classical antiquity credited Thales with having pioneered philosophy. Anaximander, with his scientific curiosity and his genius for abstract insight, poised philosophical inquiry for new vistas of exploration; his new philosophical approach inaugurated penetrating, objective analysis. His principle of the eternal Boundless as the source of the world's multifarious qualities and change forms the conceptual backdrop against which twenty-five centuries of science and natural philosophy have developed.

Two particular innovations of Anaximander have never been abandoned. First, his extension of the concept of law from human society to the physical world continues to dictate the scientific worldview. The received view in Anaximander's time—that nature was capricious and anarchic—has never again taken hold. Second, Anaximander's invention of the use of models and maps revolutionized science and navigation and continues to be indispensable, even in people's daily lives. All scientific experiments are models of a sort: They are laboratory-scale contrivances of events or circumstances in the world at large. Purely visual three-dimensional models continue to be crucial in scientific discoveries: the so-called Bohr model of the atom played a crucial role in physics; the double-helical model was important to the discovery of the structure and function of DNA. Maps are taken for granted now, but if human beings had relied on verbal descriptions of spatial localities, civilization would not have proceeded very far.

Thus, Anaximander's innovations and influence persist. Indeed, it is difficult to imagine a world without his contributions. Anaximander himself could hardly have seen all the implications of his discoveries, for even now one can only guess at the future direction of abstract thought.

Bibliography

Brumbaugh, Robert S. *The Philosophers of Greece*. New York: Thomas Y. Crowell, 1964; London: Allen and Unwin, 1966. This volume contains a short, digested chapter on Anaximander's life and accomplishments. Emphasizes cartography and engineering. Includes a reproduction of the first map designed by Anaximander.

Burnet, John. *Early Greek Philosophy*. 4th ed. London: Black, and New York: Barnes and Noble Books, 1930. A detailed scholarly analysis of Anaximander's thought in the context of comparisons with, and influences on, other pre-Socratic philosophers.

Guthrie, W. K. C. *A History of Greek Philosophy*. Vol. 1, *The Earlier Presocratics and the Pythagoreans*. Cambridge: Cambridge University Press, 1962; New York: Cambridge University Press, 1978. Contains a chapter on Anaximander's cosmology. Focuses in a very close analysis on the concepts of *apeiron* and *apeiron* as *arche*.

Kahn, Charles H. *Anaximander and the Origins of Greek Cosmology*. New York: Columbia University Press, 1960. Surveys the documentary evidence for Anaximander's views, reconstructs a detailed cosmology from documentary texts, and devotes an entire chapter to analysis and interpretation of Anaximander's fragment.

Kirk, Geoffrey S., and John E. Raven. *The Presocratic Philosophers*. 2d ed. Cambridge and New York: Cambridge University Press, 1983. Contains a chapter on Anaximander and a close formal analysis of textual testimony on Anaximander's thought.

Sandywell, Barry. *Presocratic Reflexivity: The Construction of Philosophical Discourse, c. 600-450 B.C.* Volume 3. London and New York: Routledge, 1996. A difficult, wide-ranging book that tries to evaluate pre-Socratic thinkers in terms of the "cultural discourse" in which they participated and to which they in turn contributed. Chapter 3 deals with Anaximander.

Seligman, Paul. *The "Apeiron" of Anaximander*. London: Athlone Press, 1962; Westport, Conn.: Greenwood Press, 1974. A detailed analysis of the *apeiron* as a linguistic concept and as a metaphysical entity.

Wheelwright, Philip, ed. *The Presocratics*. New York and London: Macmillan, 1966. A primary source. Contains the Anaximander fragment in translation. Also contains testimonies from Aristotle and other Greek and Latin sources who read and commented on Anaximander's treatise.

Wright, M. R. *Cosmology in Antiquity*. London and New York: Routledge, 1995. A general account, designed for the non-specialist reader, of ancient cosmology. Extensive coverage given to the pre-Socratics. Arrangement is not chronological but topical.

Patricia Cook

ANAXIMENES OF MILETUS

Born: Early sixth century B.C.; probably Miletus
Died: Second half of the sixth century B.C.; place unknown
Areas of Achievement: Philosophy and science
Contribution: Anaximenes was the last of the great early pre-Socratic thinkers from Miletus and the first, apparently, to attribute the nature of matter entirely to physical rather than moral laws. Thus, his ideas provided a necessary step from the generalized ideas of Thales to the specific physical ideas of the Atomists of the fifth century.

Early Life

The writings of Anaximenes of Miletus no longer exist. Thus, knowledge of Anaximenes is based on a few statements made by Aristotle and later writers on the history of Greek philosophy, some of whom quote earlier writers whose work is now lost. A few of these earlier writers show that they had access to Anaximenes' writings, but it is difficult to determine the veracity of any of their statements. Thus, scholars have almost no reliable information about Anaximenes' life; not even his dates can be accurately ascertained, and only the most general of assumptions can be made. These biographical assumptions are usually applied to Thales and Anaximander as well as Anaximenes. These men were the most famous thinkers from Miletus, then the largest and most prosperous Greek city on the west coast of Asia Minor.

While they are known only for their philosophical work, it is believed that all three were financially secure and that philosophical thought was for them an avocation. Apparently, Anaximenes was the youngest of the three. Some sources suggest that Anaximenes was the pupil of Anaximander, while others suggest that he was a fellow student and friend. Most scholars place the work of Anaximenes after the fall of Sardis to Cyrus the Great (c. 545 B.C.) and before the fall of Miletus (494 B.C.).

Life's Work

Anaximenes' work must be viewed against the background of sixth century Miletus and the work of his predecessors. Miletus in the sixth century was a flourishing center between the eastern kingdoms and the mainland of Greece. The city was ruled by a ruthless tyrant, Thrasybulus, whose methods of control were to do away with anyone who looked threatening.

It has been suggested that the emergence of tyranny in Miletus was the crucial factor in the emergence of philosophy, that the need to overthrow the existing myth-centered system of values was behind philosophical speculation. It has also been said that the emergence of philosophy coincides with the emergence of participatory forms of government, the development of written codes of law, and the expansion of the role of nonaristocrats in government through oratory, which encouraged logical argument and objective reasoning. As attractive as these theories may be, they overlook the fact that Miletus itself was under the rule of a tyrant who discouraged participatory democracy absolutely.

It seems more logical to conclude that philosophy became a means of escaping the brutality of the immediate, political world. Travel brought Milesians in contact with Egypt and Phoenicia—and eventually Mesopotamia. Milesians developed an independence of thought that led them to use their knowledge of the pragmatic world gained through observation to see the contradictions in the mythologies of different peoples and to make the leap to a nonmythologaical explanation of causation and the nature of matter.

The work of Anaximenes was summarized in a single book whose title is unknown. In the fourth century, Theophrastus, Aristotle's successor, is said to have noted its "simple and economical Ionic style." One supposes that this comment refers to the shift from writing in poetry to writing in prose. Clearly, Anaximenes was more concerned with content than with the conventions of poetical expression.

Anaximenes wrote that "air" was the original substance of matter. Scholars of ancient history agree, however, that the exact meaning of this statement is unclear. To take the position that all other matter was derived from air, Anaximenes must have believed that air was a changeable substance which, by rarefaction and condensation, was able to take other forms. When rarefied, it became fire; when condensed, it became wind, clouds, water, earth, and finally stones. Thus, Anaximenes had modified Thales' idea that water was the original substance and contradicted Anaximander's thesis of unchanging infinity while still staying within the Milesian monist tradition.

Having determined the nature of air and its properties, Anaximenes apparently developed other ideas by extension. Topics which he addressed include the nature of hot and cold as expressions of rarefaction and condensation, the divine nature of air, the motion of air, cosmogony, and cosmological problems. Under the latter heading he seems to have commented on the nature of Earth, which he saw as flat and riding on a cushion of air, and the nature of heavenly bodies. In his consideration of meteorological phenomena, Anaximenes seems to have followed Anaximander rather closely. Anaximenes' description of air also resembles Hesiod's description of Chaos. Both Chaos and air surround Earth, persist within the developed world, and can be characterized by darkness, internal motion, divinity, immense size, and probable homogeneity.

Anaximenes, like his two predecessors, challenged the mythological world of Homer and Hesiod by introducing free and rational speculation. Anaximenes also presented a challenge by writing in prose. Prior to this, poetry had been the preferred form for serious expression—not only in literature but also in politics. By writing in prose, the early philosophers moved, in part, from the world of the aristocrat to that of the new man of Greece: the hoplite, the merchant, the small, free farmer. While this new method of thought was not accepted by the average Greek (nor even, one suspects, the average Milesian), it did gain respect and placed philosophical speculation on an elevated footing.

For Anaximenes, unlike his predecessors, however, the differences that could be observed in matter were not qualitative but quantitative. Thus it is that he was the first to suggest a consistent picture of the world as a mechanism.

Summary

Any account of Anaximenes' life and ideas must by virtue of scant evidence be unsatisfactory. Yet in spite of a lack of information about him and his ideas, his place in and contribution to intellectual development are clear. Anaximenes' methods were far more influential than his specific theories on matter. Together with Thales and Anaximander, he was the first to free speculative thought from mythology and mythological terms. The methods of these three thinkers are the foundation for all modern scientific and philosophical thought. They began with intellectual curiosity about the nature of matter and combined this curiosity with keen observation of the world around them—with little regard to prior religious explanations.

At first glance, Anaximenes' ideas about air seem regressive. When, however, the idea is seen as a more general concept—as the first theory to explain a single substance capable of changing its form—its sophistication can be appreciated. Most ancient thinkers agreed that Anaximenes provided a better explanation of natural phenomena.

It is a small step from Anaximenes' ideas of rarefaction and condensation to Empedocles' definition of matter and the atomic theories of Heraclitus of Ephesus and Democritus. Clearly, no one in the modern world would take these ideas at face value, but with a small shift in the translation of Anaximeneian terms, one approaches the modern concepts of states of matter and the relationship between energy and matter. Thus, Anaximenes is an important figure in the development of Western philosophical and scientific thought.

Bibliography

Barnes, Jonathan. *The Presocratic Philosophers.* Rev. ed. London and Boston: Routledge, 1982. Contains a section on Anaximenes as well as scattered comments on his ideas. Barnes is most at home with philosophical discourse and relates ancient philosophical concepts to more modern thinkers. With bibliography and concordances of ancient sources.

Burnet, John. *Early Greek Philosophy.* 4th ed. London: Black, and New York: Barnes and Noble Books, 1930. The major ancient texts are translated and the ideas of Anaximenes discussed in this excellent work.

Guthrie, W. K. C. *A History of Greek Philosophy.* Vol. 1, *The Earlier Presocratics and the Pythagoreans.* Cambridge: Cambridge University Press, 1962; New York: Cambridge University Press, 1978. Contains an extended section on Anaximenes which is judicial and well balanced. Guthrie's account is used as the standard by historians. With good bibliographies and concordances of ancient sources.

Hurwit, Jeffrey M. *The Art and Culture of Early Greece, 1100-480 B.C.* Ithaca, N.Y.: Cornell University Press, 1985. An exciting analysis of Greek life that integrates studies of literature, philosophy, and art.

Kirk, G. S., and J. E. Raven. *The Presocratic Philosophers.* 2d ed. Cambridge and New York:

Cambridge University Press, 1983. The most extensive attempt to reconstruct Anaximenes by examining all of the relevant ancient references with detailed discussions of each text. The relevant Greek and Latin texts are given, with translations provided in the notes. Includes interpretation based on the texts but little or no reference to other modern scholarly ideas. Contains concordances of ancient texts.

Sandywell, Barry. *Presocratic Reflexivity: The Construction of Philosophical Discourse, c. 600-450 B.C.* Volume 3. London and New York: Routledge, 1996. A difficult, wide-ranging book that tries to evaluate pre-Socratic thinkers in terms of the "cultural discourse" in which they participated and to which they in turn contributed. Chapter 4 deals with Anaximenes.

Stokes, M. C. *The One and Many in Presocratic Philosophy.* Washington, D.C.: Center for Hellenic Studies with Harvard University Press, 1971. While this book is not about Anaximenes, he looms large in the investigation, and Stokes's ideas about him are important. Stokes investigates the relationship between Anaximander's and Anaximenes' ideas, as well as the relationship of Anaximenes to ancient Near Eastern thought and Hesiod.

Sweeney, Leo. *Infinity in the Presocratics: A Bibliographical and Philosophical Study.* The Hague: Martinus Nijhoff, 1972. Each of the pre-Socratics is discussed in terms of his contribution to this specific topic. Important discussions on the usability of each ancient source for Anaximenes are included.

Wright, M. R. *Cosmology in Antiquity.* London and New York: Routledge, 1995. A general account, designed for the non-specialist reader, of ancient cosmology. Extensive coverage given to the pre-Socratics. Arrangement is not chronological but topical.

Michael M. Eisman

SAINT ANTHONY OF EGYPT

Born: c. 251; Coma, near Memphis, Egypt
Died: Probably January 17, 356; Mount Kolzim, near the Red Sea
Areas of Achievement: Religion and monasticism
Contribution: A Christian hermit renowned for his ascetic labors and Gospel teachings, Anthony became celebrated within Christendom as the founder of the eremitic movement and the father of monasticism.

Early Life

Saint Anthony of Egypt was born about the year 251 in the village of Coma (the modern Queman el Aroune) in Upper Egypt. The only son of wealthy Coptic Christian parents, Anthony spent his childhood along the Nile working on the family farm and attending the village church with his pious sister and parents. Because his father feared the worldly learning of Greek academies, Anthony never attended school and did not learn to read or write. His religious training, therefore, was limited to the instructions he received from his parents and from the local priest, who read from the Coptic Bible. While not interested in questions of theology, Anthony was deeply sensitive to spiritual matters. Even as a child he preferred spending time alone in prayer and meditation to playing games with his friends.

At about age twenty, Anthony suffered the death of both his father and mother. Though a young man of considerable inherited wealth, Anthony became depressed and overburdened with the responsibilities of administrating his 130-acre estate and caring for his young sister. In church, Anthony heard the priest read the Gospel story of a rich young man who asked Jesus what he must do to inherit eternal life. Jesus' reply, "If thou wilt be perfect, go, sell that thou hast and give to the poor, and thou shalt have treasure in heaven; and come, follow me" (Matthew 19:21), haunted Anthony, for he (like the protagonist in the story) was rich, had from birth followed all the commandments of the law, and yet still lacked spiritual maturity. That day Anthony decided to respond literally to the Gospel command. He gave his personal possessions to the inhabitants of Coma, sold his estate, and gave the proceeds to the poor, reserving only a small sum for the benefit of his sister.

Soon after that event, upon hearing the reading of another scriptural command, "Take therefore no thought for the morrow: for the morrow shall take thought for the things of itself" (Matthew 6:34), Anthony determined to make a complete break with his former life. Taking his sister to a convent to be educated for a religious life, Anthony moved to a hut at the edge of the village and sought direction from a hermit on how to live a holy life. Clothed only in a camel's hair garment, Anthony studied how to resist worldly temptations by prayer, fasting, mortification, and manual labor.

Life's Work

Anthony, for all of his asceticism, did not achieve sanctification without a struggle. Despite his renunciation of all earthly pleasures, memories of his former life and possessions as well as erotic visions disrupted his quest for spiritual fullness. According to his biographer Saint Athanasius, the Devil "raised up in [Anthony's] mind a great dust-cloud of arguments, intending to make him abandon his set purpose." Anthony persevered and gradually learned to overcome the temptations of his thoughts.

After years of self-conquest on the borders of the village, Anthony was ready to attack the Devil in his own territory. Anthony left his arbor hut and moved farther into the desert, into the mortuary chamber of an Egyptian tomb. Permitting the visits of only one friend, who brought him bread and water at infrequent intervals, Anthony challenged the forces of Satan by entering the dark burial cell which Egyptians believed was haunted by demons. In closing the door behind him, Anthony symbolically severed himself from the world of the living.

The modern mind can only interpret the accounts of Anthony's struggles with the Devil in the tomb as fantasies conjured by his excessive fasting. For contemporaries of Anthony, however, his confrontation with Satan—which included battling demons disguised as bulls, serpents, scorpions, and wolves—was perceived as physical and real. When he emerged after sixteen years in the subterranean tomb, Anthony was widely renowned as a warrior of God who had fought and conquered the powers of darkness.

Anthony's thirst for solitude, which first prompted him to withdraw to the outskirts of the village and then to the burial chamber on the fringe of the desert, finally drove him into the depths of the desert. He withdrew to Mount Pispir, near the Nile.

Anthony at first lived in total seclusion—praying, fasting, and weaving mats from palm leaves. Disciples brought him supplies of bread occasionally, but he fasted for days at a time. As news of Anthony's disappearance into desert isolation spread, a train of visitors followed him into the wilderness. Some went simply out of curiosity; others sought spiritual guidance. Although at first Anthony attempted to avoid the visitors, in time he acquiesced and assumed pastoral responsibilities: praying for the sick, driving out demons, offering instructions for holy living, and training seekers in the path of asceticism.

Pispir became a monastery, and in or near 313, Anthony moved still farther away, settling in a cave on Mount Kolzim near the Red Sea. He remained in this remote setting, receiving some visitors, for the rest of his life.

Anthony's teachings generally emphasized one's interior development. Unimpressed with mere human knowledge, Anthony reminded his followers that the mind created letters, not letters the mind, and that therefore "one whose mind is sound has no need of letters." Rather than coveting worldly wisdom, Anthony urged his disciples to live every day as if it were their last, always remembering that "the whole of earth is a very little thing compared with the whole of heaven." He warned them against taking pride in their own accomplishments or in thinking that in giving up worldly pleasures they were making great sacrifices. He urged his followers constantly to inspect their spiritual progress, not worrying about things that do not last, but gathering those "that we can take with us: prudence, justice, temperance, fortitude, understanding, charity, love of the poor, faith in Christ, graciousness, hospitality." For Anthony, asceticism was not an end in itself, but a necessary means to spiritual maturity.

On one occasion, probably in the year 311, Anthony visited the city of Alexandria, where he offered encouragement to Christians being persecuted under the edict of the emperor Maximinus Daia. A short time later, after Constantine emerged as head of Rome, Anthony received a letter from the newly converted Christian emperor seeking spiritual guidance. Although unable either to read the message or to pen a response, Anthony dictated for the Roman emperor the following reply: "Practice humility and contempt of the world, and remember that on the day of judgment you will have to account for all your deeds." In 338, Anthony again

left his retreat for Alexandria, allegedly to help the orthodox bishop Athanasius in his theological struggle with the Arian Christians, who denied that Christ was equal in essence with the Father. As Saint Athanasius, this church leader would write the biography of Anthony. Such contact with the outside world—with people of power—was rare. Anthony much preferred the simplicity of desert life, which did not distract him from concentrating on spiritual matters.

Saint Jerome told a story about a visit in 341 between Anthony and the 113-year-old Saint Paul of Thebes, a hermit who allegedly had not seen either man or woman for more than ninety years. While this story is no doubt apocryphal, the legend was celebrated by Christians for centuries and served as an inspiration for numerous artists, including the master of Dutch Renaissance art, Lucas van Leyden.

In the year 356, Anthony—knowing that he was about to die—invited his closest followers to come to his desert hermitage in order to give them a parting farewell. To his surprise, thousands responded to the invitation. Anthony walked among this throng of pilgrims, blessed them, and asked them to persevere in their devotion to God. According to tradition, Anthony died on January 17, 356, at the age of 105.

Summary

It is ironic that Saint Anthony of Egypt—an unassuming, deeply private, illiterate man, who refused to pander to crowds and who renounced the efforts of the establishment to reconcile Christianity with culture—became the celebrated founder of the eremitic movement and the father of monasticism. As a result of his ascetic example and teachings, during his lifetime and for a hundred years following his death, hermitages sprang up and the deserts of Egypt became cluttered with the cells of anchorites. Stories of his desert retreat, circulated by Saint Athanasius' *The Life of Saint Anthony the Hermit*, spread across the empire to Rome, Palestine, Gaul, and Spain. Constantine and his sons wrote to him. Saint John Chrysostom in his homilies designated Anthony as the greatest man Egypt had produced since the time of the Apostles. During the third and fourth centuries, thousands of pilgrims followed Anthony's example and flocked to the desert. The exodus was so great that a traveler through Egypt and Palestine about 394 reported that the dwellers in the desert equaled the population living in the towns.

For fifteen hundred years, the temptations of Anthony have captured the imagination of artists, who have delighted especially in picturing the more dramatic episodes of devils in hideous and alluring disguises tempting, frightening, and beating the desert saint. From Saint Athanasius to Gustave Flaubert and Anatole France, Anthony has been portrayed as the prototype of a man who suffers temptation and through the power of renunciation, overcomes it.

In an age filled with Christological problems and theological hairsplitting, Anthony and the desert fathers proclaimed a message of righteous living and simplicity of life. His teaching—"No one of us is judged by what he does not know, and no one is called blessed because of what he has learned and knows; no, the judgment that awaits each asks this: whether he has kept the faith and faithfully observed the commandments"—offered a corrective to the tendency at the time to define Christianity in purely philosophical or religious terms. Anthony's ascetic labors and simple teachings introduced themes that would run throughout the history of the monastic movement.

Bibliography

Athanasius, Saint. *The Life of Saint Antony.* Translated and annotated by Robert T. Meyer. Westminster, Md.: Newman Press, 1950. Saint Athanasius' biography is the single most important primary source on the life of Anthony.

Chadwick, Henry. *The Early Church.* Rev. ed. London and New York: Penguin Books, 1993. The best single-volume introduction to the history of the Christian church during the first through fourth centuries.

Fülöp-Miller, René. *The Saints That Moved the World: Anthony, Augustine, Francis, Ignatius, Theresa.* Translated by Alexander Gode and Erika Fülöp-Miller. New York: Thomas Y. Crowell, and London: Hutchinson, 1945. Contains an eighty-page chapter on Anthony, bibliography, and index.

Nigg, Walter. *Warriors of God: The Great Religious Orders and Their Founders.* Translated and edited by Mary Ilford. London: Secker and Warburg, and New York: Alfred A. Knopf, 1959. The opening chapter provides a scholarly treatment of Anthony and his impact upon the monastic movement.

Queffelec, Henri. *Saint Anthony of the Desert.* Translated by James Whitall. New York: E. P. Dutton, 1954. An entertaining biography based on Saint Athanasius' account.

Rubenson, Samuel. *The Letters of St. Antony: Monasticism and the Making of a Saint.* Minneapolis, Minn.: Fortress Press, 1995. A re-examination of the so-called "Letters of St. Anthony" that first attempts to demonstrate their authenticity, then analyzes the theological views contained in them. The evidence of the letters, augmented by a consideration of Anthony's background and environment, suggests that Anthony and his monks were more intellectually active and sophisticated than has been previously thought.

Waddell, Helen. *The Desert Fathers.* New York: Henry Holt, and London: Constable, 1936. A translation from the Latin of the writings of the desert fathers. Includes many of the sayings attributed to Anthony.

Ward, Maisie. *Saints Who Made History: The First Five Centuries.* New York: Sheed and Ward, 1959. A lively, nonscholarly account of the lives of early saints of the Church. Includes a fourteen-page treatment on Anthony.

Terry D. Bilhartz

ANTIGONUS I MONOPHTHALMOS

Born: 382 B.C.; probably Macedonia
Died: 301 B.C.; Ipsus, Phrygia, Asia Minor
Areas of Achievement: Government and warfare
Contribution: Though Antigonus failed to unify Macedonian conquests after Alexander the Great's death in 323 B.C., he did establish an eponymous dynasty (Antigonid), which was to rule Macedonia and exert a great influence on Greek affairs elsewhere until the Roman victory at the Battle of Pydna in 168 B.C.

Early Life

Antigonus' father was an aristocrat named Philip. Beyond this fact, nothing of significance is known about Antigonus' life before his service in Alexander's army and his appointment to the governorship of Phrygia in 333 B.C. at the age of forty-nine.

Antigonus is known to have been a tall man; his appellation, Monophthalmos (One-Eyed), or Cyclops, referred to his having lost an eye. It is not known whether this blinding occurred in battle or by some other means. To conceal the handicap, Apelles, the famous artist at the Macedonian court, departed from custom and painted a portrait of Antigonus in profile.

Life's Work

Before attention is turned to the course of Antigonus' life and work, it is helpful to survey the situation immediately following the death of Alexander the Great in 323 B.C. Alexander left no arrangement for succession. The assembly of the Macedonian army determined that rule be given to Alexander's half brother, Philip III, and his unborn son, Alexander IV, but the real control of Alexander's empire lay in the hands of Antipater, in Greece, and Perdiccas, in Asia. In the struggle for power which ensued (in the year 321), Antigonus sided with Antipater against Perdiccas. After Perdiccas was assassinated, Antigonus was given command of Antipater's army in Asia and continued the war against Perdiccas' brother, Alcetas, and Eumenes, Satrap of Cappadocia. Antipater died in 319. Antigonus continued fighting against Eumenes until 316, when, through intrigues and deceit, he managed to have him executed. Eumenes' remains were cremated, placed in a vessel, and returned to his wife and children. Among Alexander's successors, Antigonus was now in the strongest position to reunite the lands conquered by Alexander.

Antigonus was unquestionably desirous of sole rule, and his ambition was immediately recognized by his regal adversaries, Ptolemy, Lysimachus, Cassander, and Seleucus, all of whom allied themselves against Antigonus in a war lasting from 315 to 311. The war had no clear resolution; its temporary end came after Antigonus' son, Demetrius Poliorcetes, was defeated by Seleucus and Ptolemy at the Battle of Gaza in 312. Peace was made between Antigonus and all of his adversaries except Seleucus. Still, the ambitions of all involved could not be suppressed, and war broke out again one year later and lasted until Antigonus' death in 301.

In the first war, most of the fighting had taken place in Asia Minor; in the war of 310-301, the final resolution would be reached in Asia Minor at the Battle of Ipsus in Phrygia, but mainland Greece was the scene of many of the most important battles. Antigonus came to recognize, perhaps a bit too late, the importance of support from the Greek cities on the mainland. In 307, Antigonus' son, Demetrius Poliorcetes, took control of Athens from Cassander's representative, Demetrius of Phaleron, and a democratic constitution was reestablished in Athens. As an expression of gratitude, the Athenians granted divine honors to Antigonus and Demetrius. Antigonus' intervention on behalf of the Athenian democracy impressed many other Greek city-states, and by 302 most of mainland Greece had rallied in his support. Highlights of the war on mainland Greece are vividly recounted by Plutarch in his "Life of Demetrius," written in the early second century A.D. In spite of some major military and naval successes in Asia Minor, the war on that front was, for Antigonus, indecisive. It was his successes against Cassander on mainland Greece, more than anything, that forced his opponents to realize that their positions would be secure only with the elderly Antigonus out of the way. Attacks on Antigonus' positions in Asia came from all sides, and the situation became so serious that he recalled Demetrius, together with his army, from mainland Greece to stand with him. The decisive battle was fought at Ipsus in 301, and Antigonus, now about eighty years of age, died in this battle. Thus, at the time of his death this great general was pursuing the same course that he had pursued throughout his life: a military resolution to a political problem.

Summary

Antigonus fell between two worlds. Born and educated amid the fragmented politics of competing Greek city-states, he could have had no idea, even as a mature man, of the profound changes Alexander was to bring about. In this new world, the only exemplar of success available was Alexander's, and that was primarily military and not political. Alexander's early death prevented him from demonstrating whether his political leadership was as adept as his military.

Antigonus was not alone in following Alexander's lead; all the *diadochoi* (successors to Alexander) were as quick as Antigonus to rely on the sword as the means of obtaining the power that they sought. It was Antigonus, however, who had the means to consolidate Macedonian conquests, for he was the most successful of Alexander's successors militarily. His ultimate failure to unite Alexander's conquests through force, in spite of his most advantageous situation, should have shown the futility of such an approach in the face of a coalition of equally determined, although individually less powerful, dynasts. This lesson was not learned, and the result was almost constant warfare among Hellenistic monarchs who continued to present themselves as Alexander's rightful successor until Rome's final victory in the Greek East at the Battle of Actium in 31 B.C. Thus, it was the ambitions and methods of Antigonus, almost as much as those of Alexander, that served for some two hundred years as an example for those who sought to control the Greek world.

Bibliography

Austin, M. M. *The Hellenistic World from Alexander to the Roman Conquest: A Selection of Ancient Sources in Translation*. Cambridge and New York: Cambridge University Press, 1981. Offers translations of and introductions to many important documentary sources, primarily epigraphical, which are not generally available. This collection of primary source material contains a number of documents which bear directly on Antigonus' attempts to unify Alexander's conquests.

Bar-Kochva, B. *The Seleucid Army*. Cambridge and New York: Cambridge University Press, 1976. Describes and interprets the changes in the strategy and tactics of land warfare that led to Antigonus' military successes and the continuing domination of the Macedonians over the art of warfare until Rome's victory at Pydna in 168 B.C.

Billows, Richard A. *Antigonos the One-Eyed and the Creation of the Hellenistic State*. Berkeley: University of California Press, 1990. A full and careful biographical and historical account, especially interested in Antigonus' achievement as a political organizer and critical of the ancient sources' portrayal of him as arrogant and power-hungry.

De Ste. Croix, G. E. M. *The Class Struggle in the Ancient Greek World: From the Archaic Age to the Arab Conquests*. Ithaca, N.Y.: Cornell University Press, and London: Duckworth, 1981. Presents a Marxist view of the decline of Greek democracies. This volume is the masterpiece of a very distinguished ancient historian; it is particularly valuable for its focus on the role of political factions in Antigonus' struggle for the support of city-states on mainland Greece and Asia.

Gardner, Jane F. *Leadership and the Cult of Personality*. London: Dent, 1974. Emphasizes the importance of controlling armies and populations through the projection of a royal personality. It discusses both leadership theory and the concrete ways in which Alexander and those who followed him manipulated regal propaganda.

Gruen, Erich S. *The Hellenistic World and the Coming of Rome*. 2 vols. Berkeley: University of California Press, 1984. A revisionist interpretation of the course of Roman expansion in the Greek East. Gruen presents a view of Roman imperialism that is more sympathetic to the Roman position than the position taken by most scholars. This volume contains a good review of the battle among Alexander's successors. Includes a helpful bibliography.

Simpson, R. H. "Antigonus the One-Eyed and the Greeks." *Historia* 8 (1959): 385-409. This article presents a detailed account of the relations between Antigonus and the city-states on the Greek mainland, alliances that played a decisive role in convincing Antigonus' opponents to unify against him.

Smith, R. R. R. *Hellenistic Royal Portraits*. Oxford: Clarendon, and New York: Oxford University Press, 1988. An account of the visual image of kingship which Hellenistic dynasts chose to present. This study is lavishly illustrated. Includes reproductions of portraits in varied media (including coins and marble). A valuable archaeological complement to the literary and documentary evidence.

Tarn, W. W. *Hellenistic Civilization*. 3d ed. New York: New American Library, 1952; Cambridge: Cambridge University Press, 1960. A standard, but somewhat dated, survey of the Hellenistic world. Includes chapters on the social, economic, and cultural history of the period.

Walbank, R. W. *The Hellenistic World*. Cambridge, Mass.: Harvard University Press, 1981. The best general account of the period, by a scholar who devoted his life to its study. It combines a narrative account of military and political events with sections on the rich and varied cultural life of the Hellenistic world.

John Walsh

ANTIOCHUS THE GREAT

Born: 242 B.C.; possibly Antioch

Died: 187 B.C.; Elymais, near Susa

Areas of Achievement: Warfare and conquest

Contribution: Antiochus went the furthest of any of the successors of Alexander the Great toward reuniting what had once been the vast Alexandrian empire.

Early Life

Antiochus, who was probably born in Antioch, the capital city of the Seleucid empire, was the younger son of Seleucus II and Laodice II. Nothing is known about his early life. When his father died in 226, his older brother, Seleucus III, fell heir to the empire and all of its problems, not the least of which was Asia Minor, formerly held by the Seleucids but now controlled by Attalus of Pergamum. One unsuccessful attempt had already been made to regain this territory. During the second, in 223, Seleucus was assassinated by two of his own generals. Since he had no heirs, his younger brother Antiochus succeeded him.

Antiochus was eighteen years old at his brother's death and living in Babylon—possibly as regent of the east since that was the usual Seleucid practice—but many thought him too young for the throne. His cousin Achaeus, who had punished Seleucus' murderers, was popular with the army, but he remained loyal to the ruling house. Finally, Antiochus was recognized as successor under the tutelage of Seleucus' former adviser, Hermias, Achaeus was given control of military affairs in Asia Minor, and two brothers, Molon and Alexander, were sent as governors (satraps) to Media and Persia respectively. Trouble began almost immediately: Although Achaeus remained loyal for some time and even regained much of Asia Minor from Attalus, Hermias became excessively arrogant, and, in 221, the brothers in the east rebelled against Seleucid authority. These actions marked the beginning of an almost constant state of war which would continue throughout the reign of Antiochus.

In 221, with Achaeus operating successfully in Asia Minor, the first priority for the Seleucid government was the rebellion of Molon. Hermias, who was still in control, appointed Xenon and Theodotus as commanders against Molon, while convincing the king to make war against Ptolemy IV of Egypt for possession of Coele-Syria, but when Molon easily defeated his opponents and Antiochus' southern campaign proved futile, the king turned to the recovery of his eastern territories. In early spring of 220, Antiochus held a council to plan his campaign. There were two important results of this meeting: Antiochus proved himself able to choose the best strategy—the immediate crossing of the Tigris River—and in crossing the river he, for the first time, split his army in three parts, initiating what would become his standard policy for advancing his forces. The majority of Molon's army, refusing to fight a Seleucid king, surrendered to Antiochus at the first opportunity. The two rebel brothers committed suicide; Antiochus was now in full command in the east.

Three problems remained: Hermias; Achaeus, now the self-proclaimed king of Asia Minor; and the subjection of Coele-Syria. Antiochus ordered the assassination of Hermias, ignored Achaeus, whose men also refused to fight a Seleucid ruler, and marched his army south, where he was at first successful. His youthful inexperience, however, led him to delay battle against a Ptolemaic army until his opponent had the advantage, and in 217 he suffered a humiliating defeat at Raphia. Ptolemy fortunately agreed to a peace treaty, thus ending the war.

Life's Work

Antiochus gained the title of "the Great" because through successful military strategy and shrewd diplomacy he managed to reunite most of the territory which had been assigned to Seleucus I after the death of Alexander the Great. His prestige had suffered a blow at Raphia, but he redeemed himself by defeating Achaeus and regaining Seleucid Asia Minor. After a long siege, the capital city of Sardis fell in 214, and the citadel was betrayed a year later. Achaeus was first mutilated and then beheaded. Some sort of understanding with Attalus of Pergamum, his other rival in Asia Minor, seems to have been reached, since by 212 Antiochus had turned his back on the west in order to attempt the restoration of his eastern dominions. The Greek historian Polybius (c. 200-118) gives a fairly comprehensive account of Antiochus' movements up to this time, although most of the war against Achaeus is missing. Now, unfortunately, the detailed history of Antiochus ends, just as he begins his eastern campaigns.

By 212, Antiochus was in Armenia, where he settled affairs by arranging the marriage of his sister Antiochis to King Xerxes. Two years later, he had arrived at the Euphrates River and in the next year reached the limits of the Seleucid empire in Media. He could have stopped there, but Parthia and Bactria, once part of the empire, had seceded in 250, and his plan was to regain all the lost territories, a very expensive endeavor. It was in Ecbatana, the old summer capital of the Persian kings, that Antiochus for the first time robbed a temple treasury, an act that was to become a policy for both him and his successors.

Although the Parthians put up a stiff resistance, by 209 they had been defeated and had agreed to an alliance. Bactria was invaded in the next year; peace came two years later with another alliance. Antiochus then continued on to India to renew Seleucid relations with the new border king, from whom he received 150 elephants. He had thought of invading Arabia, but after sailing down the Arabian coast, he abandoned the idea. He was back in Syria by 204, with a reputation second only to that of Alexander. From this time on, he would be called Antiochus the Great.

Now that the king had experience and maturity, he made his final attempt to gain Coele-Syria, this time backed by an alliance with Philip V of Macedonia. Appian (c. 160 A.D.) gives the terms of the agreement, but the sources are uniformly silent on this war, the Fifth Syrian War. Ptolemy V was still a child, but his general, Scopas, moved an army across the Sinai Peninsula. The two forces met at Panion in 200 in a battle in which Antiochus' elephants played an important role in gaining for him a decisive victory. After winning the complete submission of Palestine, including Jerusalem, Antiochus decided against an invasion of Egypt and returned to Asia Minor. Ptolemy had agreed to a treaty in which he ceded Coele-Syria to the Seleucid empire. The war finally ended in 195, when Ptolemy promised to marry Antiochus' daughter Cleopatra.

Meanwhile, Philip V had been courting disaster in the north. Rhodes and Pergamum had allied against him and called on Rome for help. The Romans declared war on Philip in 200, but also sent an embassy to Antiochus warning him that Egypt was under Roman protection, a threat he could hardly take seriously. The embassy arrived shortly after his success at Panion. By the spring of 197, the Seleucid army was in Asia Minor, along with a navy of three hundred ships just off the southern coast. The navy was stopped for a while by a Rhodian ultimatum, but after news of Philip's defeat by the Romans in 196 arrived, the Rhodians withdrew, leaving Antiochus free to take the western coast of Asia Minor to the Troas, his original plan. The city of Lampsacus appealed to Rome, but the Seleucid army was in Thrace before the Roman ambassadors caught up with it. Antiochus' answer to Roman charges of aggression was that he did not meddle in Italian affairs and Rome had no business in Asia. Shortly after that, the king lost almost his entire fleet in a storm off the coast of Syria.

Antiochus was now at the height of his power; unfortunately, he did not know when to stop. The Aetolians, unhappy over Rome's settlement with Philip, convinced Antiochus to join an anti-Rome coalition which never materialized. In the latter part of 192, a small Seleucid army arrived, the forerunner of a much larger contingent, at Demetrias. The Aetolians, who had promised the king their full support, were distressed by the size of his force, and both Philip and the Achaen League to the south had decided to ally with Rome. In 191 a joint Roman-Macedonian army faced the Seleucid forces at Thermopylae. Antiochus' reinforcements had not arrived and the promised Aetolian aid proved illusory. When it became evident that he could not win, Antiochus fled, losing most of his army in what was more a skirmish than a battle.

Antiochus' loss was the result not so much of Aetolian deceit as of the failure of his officers back in Asia to send him the necessary reinforcements. Even then, as was proved by Philip's earlier losses, the clumsy phalanx was no match for the Roman legion. Antiochus discovered that for himself when the Romans invaded Asia Minor. The Roman historian Livy (c. 59 B.C.-A.D. 17) claims that the king, once he had escaped from Greece, believed that he had nothing more to fear from the Romans, that they would not follow him to Asia. If so, he had badly misjudged Roman determination to end the Seleucid threat forever. The Romans were also well aware that Antiochus had welcomed Hannibal, their most feared enemy, to his court. A Roman fleet first cleared the Aegean Sea of Seleucid ships, and by either late 190 or early 189 (historians do not agree on the date) Antiochus fought his last major battle in the field outside Magnesia and lost. He could do nothing more than ask for and accept whatever terms the Romans offered.

Even before Antiochus' final defeat, his eastern dominions had begun to break away. After Magnesia, the Seleucid army was no longer a threat and the empire dissolved. As soon as the peace was signed, Antiochus appointed his son Seleucus as joint king to rule Syria, which was all the Romans had left him, while he turned again to the east. A year later, Antiochus was dead, killed while attempting to loot a temple in the Elymaean hills. His son succeeded as Seleucus IV.

Summary

With the defeat of Antiochus by the Romans, the Eastern world was lost to Western culture. The Seleucid empire crumbled, and Rome could hold only the areas bordering the Mediterranean Sea. These were so systematically exploited by Roman policy that they almost gladly welcomed the Muslim armies of the seventh century A.D.

Antiochus was perhaps not a great king or a great general. He made the same mistake of pressing too hard with his right wing at Magnesia that he had made at Raphia, and he was very unwise in antagonizing the Romans by invading Greece. He had been reared on stories of Alexander, however, and he came closer than anyone else in his attempt to restore the empire to its original size. He could be cruel when necessary, as he was with Achaeus, but his eastern campaigns were marked by leniency and diplomacy, and he refused to hand over Hannibal when the Romans demanded it. There is no record of any domestic rebellion during his long reign. The worst charge against him is the one that led to his death. Ancient temples were also treasuries, and Antiochus was constantly in need of money. It is a sad commentary on his priorities that his last act was one of sacrilege.

Bibliography

Bar-Kochva, B. *The Seleucid Army: Organization and Tactics in the Great Campaigns.* Cambridge and New York: Cambridge University Press, 1976. This work contains several chapters giving the details from ancient sources on the major battles fought by Antiochus. Includes maps of the battlefields and interesting analyses of strategy.

Bevan, Edwyn Robert. *The House of Seleucus.* 2 vols. London: Edward Arnolds, 1902; New York: Barnes and Noble, 1966. Still the only comprehensive work on the Seleucids in English. Gives a full, although dated, account of the reign of Antiochus.

Cook, S. A., F. E. Adcock, and M. P. Charlesworth, eds. *The Cambridge Ancient History.* Vols. 7 and 8. New York: Macmillan, 1928, 1930. Includes a scholarly analysis of motives behind Antiochus' actions not contained in new edition of *The Cambridge Ancient History.* Indexes, maps, and chronological tables.

Grabbe, Lester L. *Judaism from Cyrus to Hadrian.* 2 vols. Minneapolis, Minn.: Fortress Press, 1992; London: SCM Press, 1994. A reference handbook that provides bibliographies, historiographical discussion of sources, and summary accounts of important events in Jewish history, including Jewish relations with Antiochus.

Kincaid, C. A. *Successors of Alexander the Great.* London: Pasmore and Co., 1930; Chicago: Argonaut, 1969. Kincaid presents brief sketches of four successors, concluding with Antiochus. A good summary of the campaigns and policies, but excuses the weaknesses of the king.

Livy. *Rome and the Mediterranean.* Translated by H. Bettenson. London: Penguin Books, 1976. An excellent translation of the part of Livy's history concerning Rome's move toward the East. A Roman interpretation of Antiochus' actions. Includes an introduction by A. H. McDonald.

Rawlings, Hunter R. "Antiochus the Great and Rhodes, 197-191 B.C." *American Journal of Ancient History* 1 (1976): 2-28. An analysis of Rhodes's inconsistent policy concerning Antiochus and the Aegean Sea. Rawlings claims that Rhodes cooperated with Antiochus after Rome defeated Philip but deserted him after his naval defeat in 191.

Sherwin-White, Susan and Amélie Kuhrt. *From Samarkhand to Sardis: A New Approach to the Seleucid Empire.* London: Duckworth, and Berkeley: University of California Press, 1993. The authors argue that the Seleucid Empire, far from being a weak state poorly ruled by a thin upperstratum of Greeks, was a relatively efficient empire that drew on the support of local elites.

Linda J. Piper

ANTISTHENES

Born: c. 444 B.C.; Athens, Greece
Died: c. 365 B.C.; Athens, Greece
Area of Achievement: Philosophy
Contribution: Founder of the philosophical school of classical Cynicism, Antisthenes regarded virtue as the sole basis of happiness and viewed self-control and rejection of materialism as the only means of achieving virtue.

Early Life

Antisthenes was the son of an Athenian citizen, also named Antisthenes; his mother was a Thracian slave. Because both parents were not Athenian citizens, Antisthenes was not entitled to citizenship under a law passed by Pericles in 451 B.C., and he could not take part in Athenian politics or hold public office. He probably attended the Cynosarges gymnasium, located outside the gates of Athens and reserved for children of illegitimate unions (gymnasia were the central institutions of Greek mental as well as physical education). Antisthenes bitterly resented Athenian boasts of superiority; when Athenians asserted that they had always resided in Attica, having been born of its soil, he responded that snails and wingless locusts could make the same claim. Although not a citizen, he served in the Athenian army; Socrates congratulated him on his brave conduct at the battle of Tanagra in 426 B.C. during the Peloponnesian War.

Despite any disadvantage Antisthenes experienced as a consequence of his outsider status, he remained in Athens his entire life and was a major participant in the vibrant intellectual and cultural activity of the city. When the Sophist Gorgias lectured on rhetoric and logic in Athens, the young Antisthenes attended, and he adopted the Sophist approach, writing and offering lectures on these topics himself. After Antisthenes met Socrates, however, he abandoned his own teaching to follow his new mentor, walking five miles every day from his house at the Piraeus to listen and join in the dialogues through which Socrates taught.

Although he did not live in poverty—his father had left him enough property to provide an adequate income—Antisthenes disdained luxury and prided himself on his austere lifestyle. Socrates joked that he could see Antisthenes' love of fame peeping through the holes in his cloak. Plato records that Antisthenes was one of the close friends of Socrates who attended him during his execution. After the death of Socrates in 399 B.C., Antisthenes returned to teaching at the Cynosarges gymnasium and developed the philosophical approach that came to be known as Classical Cynicism, radicalizing and exaggerating the ideas and attitudes he had learned from Socrates.

Life's Work

Few statements can be made about Antisthenes' ideas and actions that are not contradicted by one scholar or another. During his lifetime, he reportedly produced sixty-two dialogues, orations, and essays that were collected in ten volumes; however, only brief fragments of these survive, mostly in quotations and paraphrases by later Greek and Roman authors, many of whom were critical of Antisthenes. The quotations were frequently chosen for their wit and reflect Antisthenes' liking for paradoxes that challenged accepted ideas and customs. As a result, the fragments are sufficiently ambiguous to support widely varying interpretations.

Even the origin of the name "Cynicism" is disputed. The word "cynic" derives directly from the Greek word *cunikos*, meaning "doglike." Some claim it was applied to the philosophy because of the name of the gymnasium where Antisthenes taught, interpreting the name "Cynosarges" as "Agile Dog" or "White Dog." Others say it came from Antisthenes' Greek nickname (which translates as "Absolute Dog"), given him derisively because of his desire to live life as a dog might, free of human restraints and conventions. This appellation was accepted by Antisthenes and his successors as an appropriate label. Another version credits the origins of the name to his follower, Diogenes of Sinope. When some men eating at a feast threw bones at him and called him a dog, Diogenes approached the men in doglike fashion and urinated upon them.

From Socrates, Antisthenes had learned that virtue was the only good worth striving for and that virtue could be taught. In contrast, wealth, fame, pleasure, and power were worthless. Life should be devoted to reason, self-control, and self-sufficiency. Language should be used only to express the truth. Antisthenes proceeded to expand and exaggerate the ideas learned from Socrates and to illustrate his concepts through his manner of living. To demonstrate his self-sufficiency and contempt for materialism, he reduced his possessions to the bare minimum, walking about Athens supporting himself by a strong stick, his hair and beard uncombed, in what became the Cynic uniform: a threadbare cloak and a leather knapsack containing a few necessities.

The Cynics believed that they needed to shun what others considered desirable—possessions, wealth, honors, and position. For Antisthenes, pleasure, especially, was to be avoided; it produced the illusion of happiness, thus preventing realization of true contentment, which was obtainable only through the practice of virtue. To emphasize this point, Antisthenes expressed his view with characteristic extremism, saying he would rather be mad than feel pleasure. When he heard luxury praised, Antisthenes retorted that luxury was something to wish upon the sons of one's enemy. The true Cynic should be totally self-sufficient and self-governing, owing nothing to anyone, needing nothing from anyone, and being under the control of no one.

Antisthenes constantly ridiculed and expressed his contempt for the democratic political ideas and practices of Athens. He told its citizens they might as well vote to call donkeys "horses" as to believe that they could create leaders and generals by using the ballot. A true king or leader, he said, would act well and have a bad repute—that is, he would do what was right even though it was certain to be unpopular. Like many of Socrates' followers, he admired the disciplined lifestyle of Sparta, finding it a more rational way to produce leaders and followers than democratic practices—yet even Sparta was far from perfect. The political world as a whole, with its factions, greed, cruelty, and wars, was irrational and undesirable; no country and few political practices met his standards. The wise man would be guided in his public acts not by established laws but by the laws of virtue.

Nor did the speculations of the philosophers and scientists of his day please Antisthenes. He dismissed their theories as linguistic games that failed to meet the Socratic standard of absolute truthfulness. Antisthenes' focus was on practical ethics; anything beyond that he considered an illusion. He was especially scornful of the Platonic theory that ideal forms had a concrete existence outside the world of sense perception and were the unchanging reality that lay behind the world of appearances. Antisthenes is reported to have told Plato that while his horse could be seen, "equinity" (the idea of a horse) could not be seen.

Antisthenes carefully distinguished between customs created by humans and what was natural and true. Everywhere he looked, he found illusions and practices that failed to meet his test of what was natural and rational. Antisthenes liked to interpret the story of Heracles—the hero who succeeded at apparently impossible labors and whose temple abutted the Cynosarges gymnasium— allegorically, as an example of the moral virtues of hard work and perseverance. However, Antisthenes did not consider the Greek epics to be serious religious tracts. At times, he came close to espousing monotheism, arguing that "according to custom there are many gods, but in nature there is only one." He rejected the anthropomorphic approach of Greek mythology, claiming that God resembled nothing and no one. God could not be seen with the eyes and therefore could not be understood through imagery. When a priest who was celebrating the Orphic Mysteries boasted about how wonderfully he and the initiates of the Mysteries would be treated in the afterlife, Antisthenes sarcastically asked the priest why he was still alive.

Antisthenes, viewing Greek society through the eyes of an outsider, questioned and criticized many of the accepted customs and values of his day. He rejected the idea that Greeks were by nature superior to the rest of humankind. He deplored the extreme parochialism and nationalism that dominated Greek city-states and led to endless internecine warfare. He was scornful of the widely held notion that work was demeaning and that craftsmen were of lower value than intellectual workers. Instead, he viewed hard labor and perseverance as a means of achieving true virtue. Women were not necessarily inferior to men. Since virtue could be taught to both sexes, men and women were virtuous or vicious depending on how they had been educated. By rejecting the distinction between Greek and barbarian, Antisthenes challenged the Greek justification of slavery as a status befitting inferior human beings.

Summary

Antisthenes the Cynic was far removed from today's cynic, whom the dictionary defines as a person who believes that humankind is motivated wholly by self-interest and who expects the worst from human conduct and motives. Antisthenes' philosophy stressed virtue as the true aim of all men and women. Ascetic self-control and independence of thought were the means of achieving true happiness. His ideas and practices were admired and adopted by a series of Cynics who persisted through the whole of classical antiquity.

His immediate successor, Diogenes of Sinope, became the best known of the Cynics. Although many anecdotes describe Diogenes as learning directly from Antisthenes, it is unclear whether the two actually met. In any case, Diogenes' ideas obviously derive from those of his predecessor, and his activities represent an extreme and exaggerated image of what Antisthenes had taught. Diogenes, adopting the Cynic uniform that Antisthenes had pioneered, went further; he limited his possessions to what he could carry in his leather knapsack, and he slept outdoors in a barrel to demonstrate still greater freedom from material possessions. He was even more vitriolic than Antisthenes in his condemnation of custom and society. Diogenes' successor, Crates of Thebes, continued the practice of asceticism and the public flouting of human customs of his predecessors, while avoiding the sarcastic insults that Diogenes employed.

Zeno of Citium, the founder of Stoicism, began as a Cynic follower of Crates, but by 300 B.C. he had begun to diverge and create his own school of philosophy. Zeno stressed the self-reliant and independent strain of Antisthenes' philosophy while eliminating the challenges to the status quo that had characterized the earlier Cynics. Of the three philosophical traditions descending from Socrates, the two deriving from Plato and Aristotle are more significant for their impact on the modern world than that pioneered by Antisthenes. In the ancient world, however, the two schools of practical morality that derive from Antisthenes, Classical Cynicism and Stoicism, were of major significance in teaching people how to criticize and yet manage to live in an imperfect society.

Bibliography

Branham, R. Bracht, and Marie-Odile Goulet-Cazé, eds. *The Cynics: The Cynic Movement in Antiquity and Its Legacy.* Berkeley and London: University of California Press, 1996. A collection of fifteen scholarly articles on the impact of Antisthenes and his followers on Western culture from classical antiquity to the present. Footnotes and selective annotated bibliography.

Dudley, Donald R. *A History of Cynicism: From Diogenes to the Sixth Century A.D.* London: Methuen, 1937; New York: Gordon Press, 1974. Chapter 1, on Antisthenes, argues that he was not the original founder of Cynicism, reserving that title for Diogenes of Sinope. Footnotes.

Guthrie, William Keith Chambers. *A History of Greek Philosophy.* Vol. 3. *The Fifth-Century Enlightenment.* London: Cambridge University Press, 1969. The standard work on its topic discusses Antisthenes in three separate sections, describing how his ideas relate to the philosophical developments in fifth century Athens. Footnotes and bibliography.

Navia, Luis E. *Classical Cynicism: A Critical Study.* Westport, Conn.: Greenwood Press, 1996. Chapter 2 is the single most informative discussion of the life and ideas of Antisthenes. Footnotes and bibliography.

———.*The Philosophy of Cynicism: An Annotated Bibliography.* Westport, Conn.: Greenwood Press, 1995. Provides lengthy summaries of books and articles dealing with Cynicism, including works in French, German, and Italian. The chapter on Antisthenes contains 139 items.

Rankin, H. D. *Sophists, Socratics, and Cynics.* London: Croom Helm, and Totowa, N.J.: Barnes & Noble, 1983. Devotes a chapter to Antisthenes, arguing that he was particularly influenced by the Sophistic movement, especially by the ideas of Gorgias. Brief bibliography.

Sayre, Farrand. "Antisthenes the Socratic." *The Classical Journal* 43 (1948): 237-244. Questions whether Antisthenes should be considered a true Cynic, arguing that he is best regarded as a Socratic philosopher expanding on the ideas of his teacher. Footnotes to classical sources.

Milton Berman

MARC ANTONY

Born: c. 82 B.C.; place unknown

Died: 30 B.C.; Alexandria, Egypt

Areas of Achievement: Politics, warfare, and government

Contribution: The military and political defeat of Antony by Octavian (later known as Augustus) resulted in the demise of the republican form of government in Rome and the creation of the Roman Empire, which would rule much of the known world for some five hundred years.

Early Life

Marcus Antonius (called Marc Antony in English) was born into a distinguished Roman family around 82 B.C. His grandfather, also named Marcus Antonius, had attained the highest offices of Roman public life. Antony's father, Marcus Antonius Creticus (died c. 72 B.C.), however, did not equal his father's distinction. More important for Antony's future, on his mother's side he was related to Julius Caesar. Until he was about twenty-five, Antony, not unlike many of his contemporaries, was a profligate: His moral failings and excesses were detailed by Cicero, his enemy, in a series of attacks known as *Philippicae* (44-43 B.C.; *Philippics*, 1926), and his energy was no doubt wasted, as Plutarch stated, "in drinking bouts, love-affairs, and excessive spending." He studied rhetoric in Athens and from there turned his attention to a military career and public life. By that time, many of the characteristics (both good and bad) which constituted Antony's personality had developed: his bawdy and often self-deprecating sense of humor, his familiarity with the men under his command, his liberality, and his attraction to the Greek way of life. Antony's family claimed descent from the Greek hero Hercules, and his Roman nose and other features encouraged positive comparisons between Antony and images of Hercules. Antony also cultivated a forceful and powerful appearance in figure, dress, and demeanor at public functions.

Life's Work

It is true that in the end Antony lost the struggle against Octavian for control of the Roman world, but this should not negate the accomplishments of a truly remarkable Roman who had a long and successful military and political career. Antony's failure was the result not of his character or tactics, as some of his critics believe, but of his opposition to

Octavian, the most successful of all Roman politicians and one of the most astute and imposing political figures of all time. Antony's early political career was bound closely to that of Julius Caesar. In 51, he served as a junior officer under Caesar's command, and under Caesar's patronage he rose very quickly to a position only second in importance in the Caesarean forces. After this, there is some evidence of a rift between Caesar and Antony, who seems not to have participated in Caesar's final victories over Pompey the Great. Nevertheless, Caesar and Antony were sufficiently close politically that Antony was a colleague in the consulship of 44, the year of Caesar's assassination. Antony's intentions after Caesar's death are impossible to determine. His inflammatory and dramatic reading of Caesar's will may be seen as an attempt to seize control of Rome. On the other hand, such funerary demonstrations were well within the traditionally accepted bounds of political and familial behavior in the Roman Republic. Antony's attitude toward Caesar's assassins was at first ambivalent and conciliatory, but ultimately tensions between Antony and Marcus Junius Brutus, one of Caesar's assassins, led to hostilities.

At this point, Octavian, Caesar's adopted son, entered the political and military scene; he defeated Antony at Mutina in 43. This defeat did not destroy Antony's position—his support was too strong. The Second Triumvirate, an arrangement lasting five years, was created; the three members, Marcus Aemilius Lepidus, Antony, and Octavian, were assigned with the task of "establishing the form of republican government." The Roman world was split among the triumvirs, while at Rome a reign of terror resulted, and thousands of Romans perished as the triumvirs persecuted their enemies. The most notable casualty of this reign of terror was Antony's particular adversary and critic, Cicero. Having accomplished his goals in Rome, Antony turned his attention to the East. For all of their significant differences, Antony and Octavian shared a common purpose. It was to the advantage of both to move against the republican forces led by Caesar's assassins; after the victory at the Battle of Philippi (42 B.C.), the only opposition to the triumvirate left was Pompey the Younger, the son of Pompey the Great.

After Philippi, Antony remained in the East to restore order to the provinces. His first step was to

set up Herod and his brother, Phasael, over Judaea. Antony then met with Cleopatra VII at Tarsus in 41. (Cleopatra's spectacular arrival in her golden barge was recorded by Plutarch and later portrayed by William Shakespeare in *Antony and Cleopatra*, c. 1606-1607.) The political significance of this meeting was underscored by the establishment of a personal relationship which would capture the imagination of subsequent generations. Antony visited Cleopatra in the winter of 41-40, and twins were born after his departure. The relationship continued until Antony's death, and his connection with Cleopatra was in large measure responsible for his ultimate defeat.

Antony was separated from Cleopatra from 40 to 37 as a result of a serious threat from an old Roman enemy from the east, the Parthians. In 53, a Roman army under Marcus Licinius Crassus had been defeated at Carrhae, and revenge was never far from the Romans' minds. In 40, the Parthians moved as far west as Syria and Antony was determined to repulse this attack. A crisis in the west intervened, and Antony was forced to return to Italy to mediate a struggle between Octavian and Antony's wife and brother. Hostilities were averted when Octavian

and Antony reached an agreement at Brundisium in 40. In the meantime, Antony's wife, Fulvia, had died; Antony strengthened his ties to Octavian through the time-honored Roman tradition of an arranged marriage with Octavian's sister, Octavia. Antony returned to Athens with Octavia, and a daughter, Antonia, was born to them. Soon after, Antony was again forced to return to Italy and his arrangement with Octavian was formally renewed at Brundisium for another five years. During all of this, Octavia proved a loyal and helpful wife and on occasion supported Antony against her brother.

Antony and Octavia returned to Athens, but not long after the birth of a second daughter, Octavia was sent back to Italy. Once matters at Rome were settled, Antony once again turned his attention to the campaign against the Parthians. After initial Roman victories, he decided to launch a full-scale expedition into the Parthian homeland. In preparation for this very risky enterprise, Antony sought support from the rulers of Roman client-states in the Near East. Among these rulers was Cleopatra. Their personal relationship resumed and a son, Ptolemy Philadelphus, was born in 36. There was now no retreating from their personal and political alliance: Politics and love became one. Antony's first full campaign in 36 against the Parthians was a disaster; it was only with great difficulty that the remaining members of the Roman force were able to escape complete destruction. A second campaign in 33 was more successful, but it fell short of complete victory. Nevertheless, Antony felt confident enough to assign dominion over much territory under Roman influence to Cleopatra and her children in a settlement known as the "Alexandrian Donations." Thus, on three fronts Antony lost whatever support he may have had at Rome: military failure against the Parthians, individualistic settlement of territories under Roman influence, and rejection of Octavian's sister as his Roman wife.

Antony's independent actions in the East, together with Octavian's aggressive behavior at Rome, led to a final confrontation. Octavian sensed the weakness of Antony's position at Rome, and he made public the supposed conditions of Antony's will. Its exact text remains unknown, but the effect of its publication is certain. War followed, and Antony and Cleopatra were defeated by Octavian in a naval battle at Actium in September of 31. They fled to Egypt, where, about a year later, Antony, under the mistaken impression that Cleopatra had already killed herself, committed suicide and died in her arms. Some time after this, Cleopatra did the same; according to tradition, she used the poison of an asp.

Summary

Literary sources present a very negative picture of Marc Antony's personality and achievements, probably because Octavian won, and much of history has been written under the direct influence of winners. Antony's youthful excesses made it easy for critics to claim that his failure was the result of a life devoted to pleasure and self-gratification; although there is some truth to this, it nevertheless offers a one-sided view. He was an excellent general whose soldiers responded with devotion and loyalty. His administration of the Greek East was efficient and without many of the failings of his predecessors. Antony was politically astute, but he failed to appreciate sufficiently the impact of his image at Rome as a Hellenistic potentate. His enduring relationship with Cleopatra did great harm to his standing, and some even began to believe that Antony's devotion to her led to his considering moving the seat of imperial power from Rome to Alexandria. Octavian, a master propagandist, took advantage of this situation by contrasting his traditional Roman values with Antony's Eastern way of life.

Antony's person and career highlight the tensions present in Roman society during the last century of the Republic between conservative Roman values and the more attractive Hellenistic way of life. As Augustus, Octavian based his rule on a return to the old Roman values, but most of the autocrats who succeeded him followed Antony's style more closely. Indeed, the division of the Roman Empire between East and West, which Antony may have seen as inevitable, eventually became reality. The history of the Roman Empire has shown that Antony's vision and style would become the rule rather than the exception.

Bibliography

Charlesworth, M. P., and W. W. Tarn. *Octavian, Antony, and Cleopatra*. Cambridge: Cambridge University Press, 1965; as *From Republic to Empire: The Roman Civil War, 44 B.C.-27 B.C.* New York: Barnes and Noble, 1996. This is an abridged, but detailed and valuable, account of the relations among these three in the years between 44 and 30 B.C. Originally published in volumes 9 and 10 of *The Cambridge Ancient History* (1934).

Cicero, Marcus Tullius. *Philippics*. Translated by Walter C. A. Ker. Cambridge, Mass.: Harvard University Press, and London: Heinemann, 1926. These orations, composed in 44 or 43 B.C., provide graphically detailed and scathingly personal attacks on Antony's moral character. Their tone is so hostile, however, that they cannot be taken at face value.

Gowing, Alain M. *The Triumviral Narratives of Appian and Cassius Dio*. Michigan Monographs in Classical Antiquity. Ann Arbor: University of Michigan Press, 1992. Provides a comparison of the two major sources for the triumviral period, organized according to the topics they cover. Chapter 7 deals with the portrayal of Antony.

Huzar, Eleanor G. *Mark Antony: A Biography*. Minneapolis: University of Minnesota Press, 1978; London: Croom Helm, 1986. A readable account of Antony's life. Well documented, it attempts to provide a more balanced view of Antony's career by separating negative propaganda from fact.

Kent, J. P. C. *Roman Coins*. Rev. ed. New York: Harry N. Abrams, and London: Thames and Hudson, 1978. A lavishly illustrated collection of numismatic evidence; contains material important for understanding the ways in which Antony wished to present his image to the public.

Plutarch. *Life of Antony*. New York: P. F. Collier and Son, 1909. Written early in the second century A.D., this biography provides the most complete and engaging narrative account of Antony's life. Much of it is overtly hostile to Antony, and Plutarch chose to emphasize his subject's vices. The account of the love affair which led to Antony's and Cleopatra's suicides is among the most stirring stories of antiquity and formed the basis for Shakespeare's *Antony and Cleopatra*.

Syme, R. *The Roman Revolution*. Oxford: Clarendon, 1939; New York: Oxford University Press, 1951. An eminent historian's masterful interpretive account of the reasons for the collapse of the Republic. Syme uses prosopographical analysis to explain the ways in which relations among aristocratic Romans led to Octavian's victory.

Toynbee, Jocelyn Mary Catherine. *Roman Historical Portraits*. London: Thames and Hudson, and Ithaca, N.Y.: Cornell University Press, 1978. This study effectively combines visual and literary evidence in an exploration of the historical tradition in which the portraits of Antony and Octavian must be understood.

John Walsh

APOLLONIUS OF PERGA

Born: c. 262 B.C.; Perga, Asia Minor
Died: c. 190 B.C.; Alexandria, Egypt
Areas of Achievement: Mathematics and astronomy
Contribution: One of the ablest geometers in antiquity, Apollonius systematized the theory of conic sections in a treatise that remained the definitive introduction to this field until modern times. His study of circular motion established the foundation for Greek geometric astronomy.

Early Life

Information on Apollonius' life is meager. Born at Perga after the middle of the third century B.C., he studied mathematics with the successors of Euclid at Alexandria. His activity falls near the time of Archimedes (287-212 B.C.), but links between their work are indirect. In his surviving work, Apollonius once mentions the Alexandria-based geometer Conon of Samos, but his principal correspondents and colleagues (Eudemus, Philonides, Dionysodorus, Attalus I) were active at Pergamum and other centers in Asia Minor. It appears that this circle benefited from the cultural ambitions of the new Attalid dynasty during the late third and the second centuries B.C.

Life's Work

Apollonius' main achievement lies in his study of the conic sections. Two properties of these curves can be distinguished as basic for their conception: First, they are specified as the locus of points whose distances x, y from given lines satisfy certain second-order relations: When $x^2 = ay$ (for a constant line segment a) the curve of the locus is a parabola, when $x^2 = ay - ay^2/b$ the curve is an ellipse (it becomes a circle when $b = a$), and when $x^2 = ay + ay^2/b$ it is a hyperbola. The same curves can be produced when a plane intersects the surface of a cone: When the plane is parallel to the side of the cone, there results a parabola (a single open, or infinitely extending, curve); when the plane is not parallel to the side of the cone, but cuts through only one of its two sheets, there results an ellipse (a single closed curve); and when it cuts through both sheets of the cone, there results a hyperbola (a curve consisting of two separate branches, each extending indefinitely).

The curves were already known in the fourth century B.C., for the geometer Menaechmus introduced the locus forms of two parabolas and a hyperbola in order to solve the problem of doubling the cube. By the time of Euclid (c. 300 B.C.), the formation of the curves as solid sections was well understood. Euclid himself produced a major treatise on the conics, as had a geometer named Aristaeus somewhat earlier. Since Archimedes often assumes theorems on conics, one supposes that his basic reference source (which he sometimes cites as the "Conic Elements") was the Euclidean or Aristaean textbook. Also in the third century, Eratosthenes of Cyrene and Conon pursued studies in the conics (these works no longer survive), as did Diocles in his writing on burning mirrors (extant in an Arabic translation).

Apollonius thus drew from more than a century of research on conics. In the eight books of his treatise, *Kōnica* (*Treatise on Conic Sections*, 1896; best known as *Conics*), he systematized the elements of this field and contributed many new findings of his own. Only the first four books survive in Greek, in the edition prepared by Eutocius of Ascalon (active at Alexandria in the early sixth century A.D.), but all of its books except for the eighth exist in an Arabic translation from the ninth century.

Among the topics that Apollonius covers are these: book I, the principal constructions and properties of the three types of conics, their tangents, conjugate diameters, and transformation of axes; book II, properties of hyperbolas, such as their relation to their asymptotes (the straight lines they indefinitely approach, but never meet); book III, properties of intersecting chords and secants drawn to conics; book IV, how conics intersect one another; book V, on the drawing of normal lines to conics (lines defined as the minimal distance between a curve and given points); book VI, on similar conics; book VII, properties of the conjugate diameters and principal axes of conics; book VIII (lost), problems solved via the theorems of book VII.

As Apollonius states in the prefaces to the books of his treatise, the chief application of conics is to geometric problems—that is, propositions seeking the construction of a figure satisfying specified conditions. Apollonius includes only a few examples in the *Conics:* for example, to find a cone whose section produces a conic curve of specified parameters (I 52-56), or to draw tangents and normals to given conics (II 49-53 and V 55-63). Much

of the content of the *Conics,* however, deals not with problems but with theorems auxiliary to problems. This is the case with book III, for example, which Apollonius says is especially useful for problem solving, but which actually contains no problems. In his preface, he explicitly mentions the problem of the "locus relative to three (or four) lines," all cases of which, Apollonius proudly asserts, can be worked out by means of his book III, whereas Euclid's earlier effort was incomplete.

The significance of problem solving for the Greek geometric tradition is evident in works such as Euclid's *Stoicheia* (*Elements*) and *Ta dedomena* (*Data*). In more advanced fields such as conic theory, however, the surviving evidence is only barely representative of the richness of this ancient activity. A notable exception is the *Synagogē* (*Collection*), a massive anthology of geometry by Pappus of Alexandria (fourth century A.D.), which preserves many examples of problems. Indeed, the whole of its book VII amounts to an extended commentary on the problem solving tradition—what Pappus calls the "analytic corpus" (*topos analyomenos*), a group of twelve treatises by Euclid,

Apollonius, and others. Of the works taken from Apollonius, two are extant—*Conics* and *Logou apotomē* (*On Cutting Off a Ratio,* 1987)—while another five are lost—*Chōriou apotomē* (cutting off an area), *Diōrismenē tomē* (determinate section), *Epaphai* (tangencies), *Neyseis* (vergings), and *Topoi epipedoi* (plane loci). Pappus' summaries and technical notes preserve the best evidence available regarding the content of these lost works. Thus it is known that in *Epaphai,* for example, Apollonius covered all possible ways of constructing a circle so as to touch any combination of three given elements (points, lines, or circles); in *Neyseis* he sought the position of a line verging toward a given point and such that a marked segment of it lies exactly between given lines or circles; in *Topoi epipedoi* circles were produced as loci satisfying stated conditions, several of these being equivalent to expressions now familiar in analytic geometry.

It is significant that these last three works were restricted to planar constructions—that is, ones requiring only circles and straight lines. Pappus classifies problems in three categories: In addition to the planar, he names the solid (solvable by conics)

and the linear (solvable by special curves, such as certain curves of third order, or others, such as spirals, now termed "transcendental," composed of coordinated circular and rectilinear motions). For Pappus, this scheme is normative; a planar solution, if known, is preferable to a solid one, and, similarly, a solid solution to a linear. For example, the problems of circle quadrature, cube duplication, and angle trisection can be solved by linear curves, but the last two can also be solved by conics and so are classed as solid. Historians often misinterpret this classification as a restriction on solutions, as if the ancients accepted only the planar constructions. To the contrary, geometers throughout antiquity so fully explored all forms of construction as to belie any such restriction. Presumably, in his three books on planar constructions, Apollonius sought to specify as completely as possible the domain of such constructions rather than to eliminate those of the solid or linear type. In any event, from works before Apollonius there is no evidence at all of a normative conception of problem-solving methods.

There survive isolated reports of Apollonian studies bearing on the regular solids, the cylindrical spiral, irrationals, circle measurement, the arithmetic of large numbers, and other topics. For the most part, little is known of these efforts, and their significance was slight in comparison with his treatises on geometric constructions.

Ptolemy reports in *Mathēmatikē suntaxis* (c. A.D. 150; *Almagest*) that Apollonius made a significant contribution to astronomical theory by establishing the geometric condition for a planet to appear stationary relative to the fixed stars. Since, according to Ptolemy, he proved this condition for both the epicyclic and the eccentric models of planetary motion, Apollonius seems to have had some major responsibility for the introduction of these basic models. Apollonius studied only the geometric properties of these models, however, for the project of adapting them to actual planetary data became a concern only for astronomers such as Hipparchus a few decades later in the second century B.C.

Summary

If Apollonius of Perga did indeed institute the eccentric and epicyclic models for planetary motion, as seems likely, he merits the appellation assigned to him by historian Otto Neugebauer: "the founder of Greek mathematical astronomy." These geometric devices, when adjusted to observational data and made suitable for numerical computation, became the basis of the sophisticated Greek system of astronomy. Through its codification by Ptolemy in the *Almagest*, this system flourished among Arabic and Hindu astronomers in the Middle Ages and Latin astronomers in the West through the sixteenth century. Although Nicolaus Copernicus (1473-1543) made the significant change of replacing Ptolemy's geocentric arrangement with a heliocentric one, even he retained the basic geometric methods of the older system. Only with Johannes Kepler (1571-1630), who was first to substitute elliptical orbits for the configurations of circles in the Ptolemaic-Copernican scheme, can one speak of a clear break with the mathematical methods of ancient astronomy.

Apollonius' work in geometry fared quite differently. The fields of conics and advanced geometric constructions he so fully explored came to a virtual dead end soon after his time. The complexity of this subject, proliferating in special cases and lacking convenient notations (such as the algebraic forms, for example, of modern analytic geometry that first appeared only with François Viète, René Descartes, and Pierre de Fermat in the late sixteenth and the seventeenth centuries), must have discouraged further research among geometers in the second century B.C.

In later antiquity, interest in Apollonius' work revived: Pappus and Hypatia of Alexandria (fourth to early fifth century A.D.) and Eutocius (sixth century) produced commentaries on the *Conics*. Their work did not extend the field in any significant way beyond what Apollonius had done, but it proved critical for the later history of conic theory, by ensuring the survival of Apollonius' writing. When the *Conics* was translated into Arabic in the ninth century, Arabic geometers entered this field; they approached the study of Apollonius with considerable inventiveness, often devising new forms of proofs, or contributing new results where the texts at their disposal were incomplete. Alhazen (early eleventh century), for example, attempted a restoration of Apollonius' lost book VIII.

In the early modern period, after the publication of the translations of Apollonius and Pappus by Federigo Commandino in 1588-1589, the study of advanced geometry received new impetus in the West. Several distinguished mathematicians in this period (François Viète, Willebrord Snel, Pierre de Fermat, Edmond Halley, and others) tried their hand at restoring lost analytic works of Apollonius.

The entirely new field of projective geometry emerged from the conic researches of Gérard Desargues and Blaise Pascal in the seventeenth century. Thus, the creation of the modern field of geometry owes much to the stimulus of the *Conics* and the associated treatises of Apollonius.

Bibliography

Alhazen. Translated by J.P. Hogendijk. *Ibn al-Haytham's Completion of the "Conics."* New York: Springer Verlag, 1985. This edition of the Arabic text of Alhazen's restoration of the lost book VIII of the *Conics* is accompanied by a literal English translation, a mathematical summary in modern notation, and discussions of the Greek and Arabic traditions of Apollonius' work. See also Hogemdijk's "Arabic Traces of Lost Works of Apollonius" in *Archive for History of Exact Sciences* 35 (1986): 187-253, which represents an edition, with English translation, of medieval Arabic documents revealing knowledge of certain works of Apollonius.

Apollonius. *On Cutting Off a Ratio*. Translated by Edward Macierowski. Rev. ed. Fairfield, Conn.: Golden Hind Press, 1988. This translation is literal and provisional; a full critical edition is being prepared by Macierowski.

———. *Treatise on Conic Sections*. Translated and edited by Thomas Little Heath. Cambridge: Cambridge University Press, 1896; Ann Arbor, Mich.: Edwards Brothers, 1938. Translation in modern notation, with extensive commentary. Heath surveys the older history of conics, including efforts by Euclid and Archimedes, and then summarizes the characteristic terminology and methods used by Apollonius. A synopsis appears in Heath's *History of Greek Mathematics* (Oxford: Clarendon Press, 1921), together with ample discussions of the lost Apollonian treatises described by Pappus.

Knorr, W. R. *Ancient Tradition of Geometric Problems*. Cambridge, Mass.: Birkhauser Boston, 1986. A survey of Greek geometric methods from the pre-Euclidean period to late antiquity.

Chapter 7 is devoted to the work of Apollonius, including his *Conics* and lost analytic writings.

Neugebauer, Otto. *A History of Ancient Mathematical Astronomy*. New York: Springer-Verlag, 1975. The section on Apollonius in this work provides a detailed technical account of his contributions to ancient astronomy.

Pappus of Alexandria. *Book 7 of the "Collection."* Translated by A. Jones. New York: Springer-Verlag, 1986. A critical edition of Pappus' Greek text (collated with the former edition of F. Hultsch in volume 2 of *Pappi Collectionis Quae Supersunt*, 1877), with English translation and commentary. Pappus' book preserves highly valuable information on Apollonius' lost works on geometric construction. Jones surveys in detail Pappus' evidence of the lost works and modern efforts to reconstruct them.

Toomer, G. J. "Apollonius of Perga." In *Dictionary of Scientific Biography*, vol. 1. Charles C. Gillispie, ed. New York: Scribner, 1970. What is known of Apollonius' life and work is here summarized, with an extensive bibliography. For a discussion of the earlier field of conics, see also Toomer's translation of Diocles' *Peri pyreiōn: Diocles on Burning Mirrors* (New York: Springer-Verlag, 1976).

van der Waerden, Bartel Leendert. *Science Awakening*. Translated by Arnold Dresden. 4th ed. Leyden: Noordhoff, 1975; Princeton Junction, N.J.: Scholar's Bookshelf, 1988. In this highly readable survey of ancient mathematics, van der Waerden includes a useful synopsis of the geometric work of Apollonius.

Zeuthen, H. G. *Die Lehre von den Kegelschnitten im Altertum*. Copenhagen: Höst and Sohn, 1886. The definitive modern study of Apollonius' work in the conics, with detailed discussions also of the earlier history of the conics and of Apollonius' lost works. Zeuthen's principal theses are discussed by Heath, Toomer, Jones, and Knorr (see above).

Wilbur R. Knorr

ARCHIMEDES

Born: 287 B.C.; Syracuse, Sicily

Died: 212 B.C.; Syracuse, Sicily

Areas of Achievement: Science, mathematics, and engineering

Contribution: The greatest mathematician of antiquity, Archimedes did his best work in geometry and also founded the disciplines of statics and hydrostatics.

Early Life

Few details are certain about the life of Archimedes. His birth in 287 B.C. was established from a report, about fourteen hundred years after the fact, that he was seventy-five years old at his death in 212 B.C. Ancient writers agree in calling him a Syracusan by birth, and he himself provides the information that his father was the astronomer Pheidias, the author of a treatise on the diameters of the sun and moon. His father's profession suggests an explanation for the son's early interest in astronomy and mathematics. Some scholars have characterized Archimedes as an aristocrat who actively participated in the Syracusan court and who may have been related to King Hieron II, the ruler of Syracuse. He certainly was friendly with Hieron and Hieron's son Gelon, to whom he dedicated one of his works. (Original titles of Archimedes' works are not known, but most of his books were first translated into English in 1897 in the volume *Works*.)

Archimedes traveled to Egypt to study in Alexandria, then the center of the scientific world. Some of his teachers had, in their youth, been students of Euclid. He made two close friends in Alexandria: Conon of Samos, a gifted mathematician, and Eratosthenes of Cyrene, also a good mathematician. From the prefaces to his works, it is clear that Archimedes maintained friendly relations with several Alexandrian scholars, and he played an active role in developing the mathematical traditions of this intellectual center. It is possible that he visited Spain before returning to Syracuse, and a return trip to Egypt is also a possibility. This second visit would have been the occasion for his construction of dikes and bridges reported in some Arabian sources.

In Syracuse, Archimedes spent his time working on mathematical and mechanical problems. Although he was a remarkably ingenious inventor, his inventions were, according to Plutarch, merely di-

versions, the work of a geometer at play. He possessed such a lofty intellect that he considered these inventions of much less worth than his mathematical creations. Plutarch may have exaggerated Archimedes' distaste for engineering, because there is evidence that he was fascinated by mechanical problems from a practical as well as theoretical point of view.

In the stories that multiplied about him, Archimedes became a symbol of the learned man—absentminded and unconcerned with food, clothing, and the other necessities of life. In images created long after his death, he is depicted as the quintessential sage, with a heavily bearded face, massive forehead, and contemplative mien. He had a good sense of humor. For example, he often sent his theorems to Alexandria, but to play a trick on some conceited mathematicians there, he once slipped in a few false propositions, so that these individuals, who pretended to have discovered everything by themselves, would fall into the trap of proposing theorems that were impossible.

Life's Work

The range of Archimedes' interest was wide, encompassing statics, hydrostatics, optics, astronomy, and engineering, in addition to geometry and arithmetic. It is natural that stories should tell more about his engineering inventiveness than his mathematical ability, for clever machines appealed to the average mind more than abstract mathematical theorems. Unfortunately, many of these stories are doubtful. For example, Archimedes is supposed to have invented a hollow, helical cylinder that, when rotated, could serve as a water pump, but this device, now called the Archimedean screw, antedates its supposed inventor.

In another well-known story, Archimedes boasted to King Hieron that, if he had a place on which to stand, he could move the earth. Hieron urged him to make good this boast by hauling ashore a fully loaded three-masted merchantman of the royal fleet. Using a compound pulley, Archimedes, with modest effort, pulled the ship out of the harbor and onto the shore. The compound pulley may have been Archimedes' invention, but the story, told by Plutarch, is probably a legend.

The most famous story about Archimedes is attributed to Vitruvius, a Roman architect under Emperor Augustus. King Hieron, grateful for the suc-

cess of one of his ventures, wanted to thank the gods by consecrating a golden wreath. Upon delivery, the wreath had the weight of the gold supplied for it, but Hieron suspected that it had been adulterated with silver. Unable to make the goldsmith confess, Hieron asked Archimedes to devise some way of testing the wreath. Since it was a consecrated object, Archimedes could not subject it to chemical analysis. He pondered the problem without success until one day, when he entered a full bath, he noticed that the deeper he descended into the tub, the more water flowed over the edge. This suggested to him that the amount of overflowed water was equal in volume to the portion of his body submerged in the bath. This observation gave him a way of solving the problem, and he was so overjoyed that he leapt out of the tub and ran home naked through the streets, shouting: "Eureka! Eureka!" Vitruvius then goes on to explain how Archimedes made use of his newly gained insight. By putting the wreath into water, he could tell by the rise in water level the volume of the wreath. He also dipped into water lumps of gold and silver, each having the same weight as the wreath. He found that the wreath caused more water to overflow than the gold and less than the silver. From this experiment, he determined the amount of silver admixed with the gold in the wreath.

As amusing and instructive as these legends are, much more reliable and interesting to modern historians of science are Archimedes' mathematical works. These treatises can be divided into three groups: studies of figures bounded by curved lines and surfaces, works on the geometrical analysis of statical and hydrostatical problems, and arithmetical works. The form in which these treatises have survived is not the form in which they left Archimedes' hand: They have all undergone transformations and emendations. Nevertheless, one still finds the spirit of Archimedes in the intricacy of the questions and the lucidity of the explanations.

In finding the areas of plane figures bounded by curved lines and the volumes of solid figures bounded by curved surfaces, Archimedes used a method originated by Eudoxus of Cnidus, unhappily called the "method of exhaustion." This indirect proof involves inscribing and circumscribing polygons to approach a length, area, or volume. The name "exhaustion" is based on the idea that, for example, a circle would finally be exhausted by inscribed polygons with a growing number of sides.

In *On the Sphere and Cylinder*, Archimedes compares perimeters of inscribed and circumscribed polygons to prove that the volume of a sphere is two-thirds the volume of its circumscribed cylinder. He also proves that the surface of any sphere is four times the area of its greatest circle.

Having successfully applied this method to the sphere and cylinder, Archimedes went on to use the technique for many other figures, including spheroids, spirals, and parabolas. *On Conoids and Spheroids* treats the figures of revolution generated by conics. His spheroids are what are now called oblate and prolate spheroids, which are figures of revolution generated by ellipses. Archimedes' object in this work was the determination of volumes of segments cut off by planes from these conoidal and spheroidal solids. In *On Spirals,* Archimedes studies the area enclosed between successive whorls of a spiral. He also defines a figure, now called Archimedes' spiral: If a ray from a central point rotates uniformly about this point, like the hand of a clock, and if another point moves uniformly along this line (marked by the clock hand), starting at the central point, then this linearly moving and rotating point will trace Archimedes' spiral.

Quadrature of the Parabola is not Archimedes' original title for the treatise, since "parabola" was not used in the sense of a conic section in the third century B.C. On the other hand, quadrature is an ancient term: It denotes the process of constructing a square equal in area to a given surface, in this case a parabolic segment. Archimedes, in this treatise, proves the theorem that the area of a parabolic segment is four-thirds the area of its greatest inscribed triangle. He is so fond of this theorem that he gives different proofs for it. One proof uses a method of exhaustion in which the parabolic segment is "exhausted" by a series of triangles. The other consists of establishing the quadrature of the parabola by mechanically balancing elements of the unknown area against elements of a known area. This latter method gives an insight into how Archimedes discovered theorems to be proved. His most recently discovered work, *Method of Mechanical Theorems* (translated in 1912), provides other examples of how Archimedes mathematically balanced geometrical figures as if they were on a weighing balance. He did not consider that this mechanical method constituted a demonstration, but it allowed him to find interesting theorems, which he then proved by more rigorous geometrical methods.

Archimedes also applied geometry to statics and hydrostatics successfully. In his *The Equilibrium of Planes,* he proves the law of the lever geometrically and then puts it to use in finding the centers of gravity of several thin sheets of different shapes. By center of gravity, Archimedes meant the point at which the object can be supported so as to be in equilibrium under the pull of gravity. Earlier Greek mathematicians had made use of the principle of the lever in showing that a small weight at a large distance from a fulcrum would balance a large weight near the fulcrum, but Archimedes worked this principle out in mathematical detail. In his proof, the weights become geometrical magnitudes acting perpendicularly to the balance beam, which itself is conceived as a weightless geometrical line. In this way, he reduced statics to a rigorous discipline comparable to what Euclid had done for geometry.

Archimedes once more emphasizes geometrical analysis in *On Floating Bodies.* The cool logic of this treatise contrasts with his emotional discovery of the buoyancy principle. In this work, he proves that solids lighter than a fluid will, when placed in the fluid, sink to the depth where the weight of the solid will be equal to the weight of the fluid displaced. Solids heavier than the fluid will, when placed in the fluid, sink to the bottom, and they will be lighter by the weight of the displaced fluid.

Although Archimedes' investigations were primarily in geometry and mechanics, he did perform some interesting studies in numerical calculation. For example, in *Measurement of the Circle* he calculated, based on mathematical principles rather than direct measurement, a value for the ratio of the circumference of a circle to its diameter (this ratio was not called pi until much later). By inscribing and circumscribing regular polygons of more and more sides within and around a circle, Archimedes found that the ratio was between $223/71$ and $220/71$, the best value for π (pi) ever obtained in the classical world.

In *The Sand-Reckoner,* Archimedes devises a notation suitable for writing very large numbers. To put this new notation to a test, he sets down a number equal to the number of grains of sand it would take to fill the entire universe. Large numbers are also involved in his treatise concerned with the famous "Cattle Problem." White, black, yellow, and dappled cows and bulls are grazing on the island of Sicily. The numbers of these cows and bulls have to satisfy several conditions. The problem is to find the number of bulls and cows of each of the four colors. It is unlikely that Archimedes ever completely solved this problem in indeterminate analysis.

Toward the end of his life, Archimedes became part of a worsening political situation. His friend Hieron II had a treaty of alliance with Rome and remained faithful to it, even after the Second Punic War began. After his death, however, his grandson Hieronymus, who became king, was so impressed by Hannibal's victories in Italy that he switched sides to Carthage. Hieronymus was then assassinated, but Sicily remained allied with Carthage. Consequently, the Romans sent a fleet under the command of Marcellus to capture Syracuse. According to traditional stories, Archimedes invented devices for warding off the Roman enemy. He is supposed to have constructed large lenses to set the fleet on fire and mechanical cranes to turn ships upside down. He devised so many ingenious war machines that the Romans would flee if so much as a piece of rope appeared above a wall. These stories are grossly exaggerated if not totally fabricated, but Archimedes may have helped in the defense of his city, and he certainly provided the Romans with a face-saving explanation for their frustratingly long siege of Syracuse.

Because of treachery by a cabal of nobles, among other things, Syracuse eventually fell. Marcellus ordered that the city be sacked, but he made it clear that his soldiers were to spare the house and person of Archimedes. Amid the confusion of the sack, however, Archimedes, while puzzling over a geometrical diagram drawn on sand in a tray, was killed by a Roman soldier. During his lifetime he had expressed the wish that upon his tomb should be placed a cylinder circumscribing a sphere, together with an inscription giving the ratio between the volumes of these two bodies, a discovery of which he was especially proud. Marcellus, who was distressed by the great mathematician's death, had Archimedes' wish carried out. More than a century later, when Cicero was in Sicily, he found this tomb, overgrown with brush but with the figure of the sphere and cylinder still visible.

Summary

Some scholars rank Archimedes with Sir Isaac Newton and Carl Friedrich Gauss as one of the three greatest mathematicians who ever lived, and historians of mathematics agree that the theorems Archimedes discovered raised Greek mathematics to a new level of understanding. He tackled very difficult and original problems and solved them through boldness and vision. His skill in using mechanical ideas in mathematics was paralleled by his ingenious use of mathematics in mechanics.

The Latin West received its knowledge of Archimedes from two sources: Byzantium and Islam. His works were translated from the Greek and Arabic into Latin in the twelfth century and played an important role in stimulating the work of medieval natural philosophers. Knowledge of Archimedes' ideas multiplied during the Renaissance, and by the seventeenth century his insights had been almost completely absorbed into European thought and had deeply influenced the birth of modern science. For example, Galileo was inspired by Archimedes and tried to do for dynamics what Archimedes had done for statics. More than any other ancient scientist, Archimedes observed the world in a way that modern scientists from Galileo to Albert Einstein admired and sought to emulate.

Bibliography

Aaboe, Asger. *Episodes from the Early History of Mathematics.* New York: Random House, 1964. After a brief account of Archimedes' life and a survey of his works, the third chapter of this book presents three samples of Archimedean mathematics: the trisection of an angle, the construction of a regular heptagon, and the determination of a sphere's volume and surface area.

Bell, E. T. *Men of Mathematics.* New York: Simon and Schuster, and London: Gollancz, 1937. A widely available popular collection of biographical essays on the world's greatest mathematicians. Bell discusses Archimedes, along with Zeno of Elea and Eudoxus, in an early chapter on "Modern Minds in Ancient Bodies."

Clagett, Marshall. "Archimedes." In *Dictionary of Scientific Biography,* vol. 1. Charles Couston Gillispie, ed. New York: Scribner, 1970. Clagett is an eminent scholar of Archimedes, and in his five-volume work, *Archimedes in the Middle Ages* (1964-1984), he has traced the medieval Latin tradition of Archimedes' works. This article makes his major insights on Archimedes available to the general reader.

Dijksterhuis, E. J. *Archimedes.* New York: Humanities Press, 1957. This edition of the best survey in English of Archimedes' life and work also contains a valuable bibliographical essay by Wilbur R. Knorr.

Finley, Moses I. *A History of Sicily.* Vol. 1, *Ancient Sicily.* New York: Viking Press, and London: Chatto and Windus, 1968. Finley's account of the history of Sicily from antiquity to the Arab conquest has a section explaining how the politics of the Second Punic War led to Archimedes' death.

Heath, T. L. *A History of Greek Mathematics.* 2 vols. Oxford: Clarendon Press, 1921; New York: Dover, 1981. A good general survey of ancient Greek mathematics that contains, in volume 2, a detailed account of the works of Archimedes. This book and the author's *Works of Archimedes* (1897, with supplement 1912) unfortunately use modern notation, which risks misrepresenting the thrust of Archimedes' proofs.

Kline, Morris. *Mathematical Thought from Ancient to Modern Times.* New York: Oxford University Press, 1972. Kline's aim is to present the chief ideas that have shaped the history of mathematics rather than the people involved. Consequently, his treatment of Archimedes emphasizes the themes of his work rather than the events of his life.

Lloyd, G. E. R. *Greek Science After Aristotle.* New York: Norton, and London: Chatto and Windus, 1973. Lloyd's book, intended for the general reader, centers on the interaction of Hellenistic science and mathematics with religion, philosophy, and technology. It contains a brief but good account of the life and work of Archimedes in this larger intellectual context.

van der Waerden, B. L. *Science Awakening.* 4th ed. Leyden: Noordhoff, 1975; Princeton Junction, N.J.: Scholar's Bookshelf, 1988. A survey of ancient Egyptian, Babylonian, and Greek mathematics. The chapter on the Alexandrian era (330-220 B.C.) contains a detailed account of Archimedes' life, legends, and mathematical accomplishments.

Robert J. Paradowski

ARETAEUS OF CAPPADOCIA

Born: Probably second century A.D.; Cappadocia, Roman Empire

Died: Date unknown; place unknown

Area of Achievement: Medicine

Contribution: Considered by many the greatest ancient physician after Hippocrates, Aretaeus wrote the best and most accurate descriptions of many diseases and made landmark studies of diabetes and neurological and mental disorders.

Early Life

Not even the exact century of Aretaeus of Cappadocia's birth is known; most scholars agree on the second century A.D., although a few offer the first or third century. Aretaeus' epithet is "Cappadocian," implying that he was born in that most eastern of Roman provinces. No other information about his life is certain. Scholars conjecture, however, that he studied in Egypt at Alexandria, founded in 331 B.C. as the major center for medical study, research, and teaching. Aretaeus mentions Egypt in his works and describes its geography and some diseases and therapeutics unique to that country. Some scholars also believe that Aretaeus practiced medicine in Rome; he prescribed wines known to second century Rome—namely, Falernian, Fundian, Sequine, and Surrentine.

Aretaeus was an Eclectic by practice and a Pneumatist by training. After Hippocrates in the fifth century B.C. there was little advance in the knowledge of disease and its treatment, although there were significant gains at Alexandria in the area of anatomy because of the dissections of human bodies. Instead, post-Hippocratic physicians tended to theorize about medicine as a philosophy and to develop various schools of medicine. Dogmatism and Empiricism were the first schools. The Dogmatists employed theoretical principles; they believed that reason and systematic studies of anatomy and physiology were necessary for the physician. The Empiricists, on the other hand, rejected theory and anatomy; they stressed experience and observation. The "tripod" of the Empiricists' knowledge was personal observation, researched historical observation, and use of analogy in analyzing unknown cases.

Two schools developed in reaction to the Dogmatists and Empiricists. Methodism, founded in the late first century B.C., rejected the theory of the humors so prevalent in Hippocratic medicine and advocated an atomic stance. The Methodists considered disease an interference of the normal position and motion of the atoms in the human body; treatments were prescribed to restore the proper order of the atoms—relaxants to counteract excessive tension, astringents to counteract excessive looseness.

The Pneumatic school, established around A.D. 50 by Athenaeus of Attaleia, stressed *pneuma,* meaning "vital air" or "breath." The beliefs of the Pneumatists were a combination of the Stoic philosophy, with its emphasis on primordial matter, the *pneuma,* from which all life comes, and Hippocratic pathology. Disease occurs when an imbalance of the four humors (blood, phlegm, black bile, and yellow bile) disturbs the *pneuma* in the human body.

Each of these various schools had both strengths and glaring weaknesses in their theories and practices. The knowledge of these weaknesses, coupled with Roman common sense, which rejected the Greek love of theory, led most Roman physicians,

beginning with Archigenes (who flourished around A.D. 100), to pick and choose among the various doctrines and ideas of the four schools. Such physicians were called Eclectics. That Aretaeus was an Eclectic is obvious from his work: For example, although he followed Pneumatism in its concept of the vital breath and its relation to the four humors, Aretaeus pursued anatomy and physiology avidly, as the Dogmatists did, yet he also relied heavily on observation and experience in the manner of an Empiricist; his emphasis on simple regimens and treatments recalls the Methodist school as well as Hippocrates.

Life's Work

Aretaeus refused to be dogmatic and speculative. He attempted to describe diseases in clear, scientific, and rational terms, and his writings bear the marks of careful thought and extensive clinical experience. Aretaeus wrote seven works, two of which survive: *Peri aition kai semeion oxeon kai chronion pathon* (*On the Causes and Symptoms of Acute and Chronic Diseases,* 1856) and *Oxeon kai chronion nouson therapeutikon biblion* (*Book on the Treatment of Acute and Chronic Diseases,* 1856). The lost works discussed fevers, surgery, pharmacology, gynecology, and prophylaxis. Aretaeus wrote in Ionic Greek, a dialect which had not been in use for centuries; he chose the Ionic style to imitate Hippocrates, who also wrote in that dialect.

Aretaeus followed the Methodist classification of diseases into chronic and acute; the distinction was made on the course of the disease, that is, whether the disease lasted over a long period of time or was of a short duration and reached a "crisis" (the point in the progress of the disease when the patient recovered or died). Chronic diseases include paralysis, migraine headaches, and insanity, while examples of acute diseases are pneumonia, pleurisy, tetanus, and diphtheria. Aretaeus' descriptions of these and other diseases show him to be an accurate observer who was concerned more for the patient than for theory itself. His accounts, so important in the history of medicine, may be summarized in the following categories: anatomy and physiology, symptomatology (physical description of diseases such as diabetes, leprosy, and ulcers), neurology and psychiatry, surgery, and therapeutics.

Aretaeus devoted more attention to anatomy and physiology than most ancient physicians. As stated earlier, Aretaeus followed the Pneumatist doctrine: He believed that the body is composed of the four humors and of spirit (*pneuma*), and the proper mixture and interplay of these elements constitutes health. Blood is formed in the liver from food; phlegm is secreted by the brain into the other organs; yellow bile comes from the liver, black bile from the spleen. The most important organ is the heart, since the heart is the site of heat and *pneuma*. The heart draws the *pneuma* from the lungs, which are stimulated by it. Respiration itself depends upon the movement of the thorax and diaphragm and also upon the lungs' contraction and expansion. Regarding the nervous system, nerves originate in the brain; this idea was based on the perception that the spinal cord was a prolongation of the brain. All nerves cross between their origin in the brain and their final termination in the body; Aretaeus based this belief on his startling observation that a cerebral lesion caused paralysis on the opposite side of the body.

Aretaeus knew much about circulation. The aorta, he stated, comes from the heart and is located to the left of the vena cava; the aorta carries the *pneuma* to the other organs. The veins, which originate in the liver, bring the blood to all the body. Aretaeus asserted that the content of the arteries was light-colored, that of the veins dark. The liver itself is composed mostly of blood and produces blood and bile; if it becomes inflamed, jaundice results. Aretaeus wrote remarkable accounts of the kidneys and the bile ducts. He thought of the kidneys as cavities which acted like sieves for collecting urine and were connected to the bladder by two tubes, one from each kidney. Digestion of food occurs not only in the stomach but also in the intestines. The portal vein takes the food after digestion to the liver, where it is taken out as blood by the vena cava to the heart. This scheme shows that Aretaeus was aware of nearly all circulatory processes and the direction of blood flow in the veins.

One of Aretaeus' greatest accomplishments was his practice of physical diagnosis. He used anatomical inspection, distinguishing the appearances of ulcers in the small and large bowels, for example. Also, before he discussed a disease, Aretaeus prefixed an anatomical and physiological introduction concerning the part(s) of the body afflicted by the disease (this is the method used in many modern medical textbooks). In his physical examinations, Aretaeus employed auscultation of the heart, palpitation of the body (to check for enlargement of the liver and spleen), and percussion of the abdomen. Aretaeus always noted carefully the patient's symptoms: temperature, breathing, pulse, secretions, color of skin, and condition of the pupils. In the tradition of Hippocrates, Aretaeus related diseases to foods eaten by the patient and to climate, time of year, and environment.

Aretaeus' symptomatology is considered excellent by medical historians and, in some instances, not improved upon even by contemporary medicine. Especially praiseworthy are Aretaeus' accounts of hematemesis, jaundice, dropsy, tuberculosis, tetanus, epilepsy, and cardiac syncope. Aretaeus distinguished between pneumonia and pleurisy and is credited with the initial descriptions of diphtheria and asthma. He was the first European to write a symptomatic account of diabetes, and he gave the disease its name. Aretaeus correctly thought of diabetes as a progressive form of dropsy with polyuria and excessive thirst that results in emaciation of flesh. Finally, Aretaeus' accounts of leprosy are invaluable. He offered useful distinctions between the types of leprosy: elephantiasis (the tuberous form of leprosy) and the maculo-anesthetic form, which involves mutilation of the body; he also provided the first recorded instance of isolating lepers and distinguished between conveyance of disease by actual contact (contagion) and transmission of disease at a distance (infection).

Aretaeus' discussions of neurological and mental diseases are important. He divided such illnesses into acute and chronic classes. The acute diseases, as he described them, are phrenitis (a febrile delirium or, at times, meningitis); lethargy (a comatose state, or encephalitis); marasmus (atrophy); apoplexy (an acute form of paralysis); tetanus; and epileptic paroxysm. Chronic diseases include cephalaea (migraine headache), vertigo (chronic paralysis), and all forms of insanity. Especially important are Aretaeus' astute distinctions between apoplexy, paraplegia, paresis, and paralysis; the basis of division was the extent of loss of movement and sensation. Aretaeus was the first to distinguish between spinal and cerebral paralysis: When the paralysis is spinal, it occurs on the same side as the lesion; when cerebral, the paralysis occurs on the opposite side (crossed paralysis).

Aretaeus' clear and full discussion of the different kinds of insanity has remained unsurpassed. He noted the stages by which intermittent insanity (manic depression) can become a senile melancholia that does not remit. While the former may be treated by phlebotomy, wormwood, and black hellebore (a plant that produces violent shocks to the nervous system similar to those in modern electric shock treatment), senile melancholia is incurable.

Aretaeus' book on surgery has been lost; he did, however, refer to surgery throughout his extant writings. Aretaeus recommended craniotomy (trepanning) for epilepsy and for cephalalgia and cephalaea (acute and chronic headache, respectively). He used catheters for urological diseases and mentioned surgery to remove kidney stones. It should be noted that surgery was not commonly practiced in antiquity, but when it was deemed necessary, the practicing physician usually performed it.

Aretaeus' treatments of disease are conservative. As in his discussions of the causes and forms of diseases, Aretaeus relied on experience and common sense, not abstract theory. He rejected tracheotomy and pleaded for extreme caution in the application of phlebotomy, venesection, cupping, and leeches: Aretaeus argued that only in severe cases should much blood be removed. Instead, he used purgatives, emetics, suppositories, laxatives, ointments, and poultices. Aretaeus also stressed exercise, massages, baths, temperate life-styles, and a healthy diet including milk, fruits, vegetables, and foods without starch and fat. It is interesting that Aretaeus also prescribed opium for people afflicted with feverish delirium.

Summary

No ancient medical writer, except perhaps Hippocrates, surpassed Aretaeus of Cappadocia for vividness and clarity in the description of diseases. Aretaeus' descriptions of diabetes, tetanus, diphtheria, leprosy, asthma, and mental and neurological disorders are especially valuable and are landmarks in medical history. Aretaeus tried his best to put his symptomatology on a sound anatomical basis; for every disease, he supplied splendid accounts of anatomy. He gave therapeutics and cures for every disease, acute and chronic; his treatments are simple and rational. In his writings, Aretaeus was perhaps the most unbiased physician in antiquity, rejecting dogmatic thought, theory, and superstition. Finally, Aretaeus was unique in refusing to abandon the patient who was incurable; while even Hippocrates recommended turning away hopeless cases, Aretaeus ordered all measures to be taken, and, when those failed, he offered support and sympathy.

Bibliography

Allbutt, Sir Thomas. *Greek Medicine in Rome.* London: Macmillan, 1921; New York: Blom, 1970. Still one of the best textbooks on the medical schools and the practice of medicine in the Roman Empire. Chapter 11 ("Some Pneumatist and Eclectic Physicians") discusses Aretaeus and is superb in providing background information to the Eclectic and his writings.

Aretaeus of Cappadocia. *The Extant Works of Aretaeus the Cappadocian.* Francis Adams, ed. London: Sydenham Society, and Boston: Milford, 1856. The only available translation of Aretaeus' work. The introduction to Aretaeus, his background, and his work is somewhat difficult for the nonspecialist, and the antiquated English of the translation is forbidding.

Cordell, E. F. "Aretaeus of Cappadocia." *Bulletin of The Johns Hopkins Hospital* 20 (1909): 371-377. This volume provides a very useful discussion of the physiology, symptomatology, and therapy in Aretaeus' works. Intended for a knowledgeable but general audience.

Leopold, Eugene. "Aretaeus the Cappadocian: His Contribution to Diabetes Mellitus." *Annals of Medical History* 2 (1930): 424-435. An excellent, straightforward account of Aretaeus' life and writings. Especially good is the discussion of Aretaeus' place in the history of medicine and diabetes. Very readable.

Mettler, Cecilia. *History of Medicine.* Philadelphia: Blakiston, 1947. Mettler offers an exhaustive survey of Aretaeus' discussions and treatments of diseases. One must use the index, however, as the accounts are scattered throughout the text according to typology of disease.

Neuburger, Max. *History of Medicine.* Translated by Ernest Playfair. London: Frowde, 1910; as *Essays on the History of Medicine.* New York: Medical Life Press, 1930. This classic text has useful chapters on the Pneumatists and Eclectics and Aretaeus, in particular. With invaluable discussions of the various medical schools of Aretaeus' time.

Robinson, Victor. *Pathfinders in Medicine.* New York: Medical Life Press, 1929. This volume includes an essay on Aretaeus designed for lay readers. It is excellent as a general introduction to Aretaeus, although it lacks references and notes.

Stannard, J. "Materia Medica and Philosophic Theory in Aretaeus." *Sudhoffs Archiv für Geschichte der Medizin und der Naturwissenschaften* 48 (March, 1964): 27-53. Contains extensive discussion of the therapeutics, especially dietetics, of Aretaeus. Invaluable for information on Aretaeus and his relation to Pneumatism.

Steven M. Oberhelman

ARISTIPPUS

Born: c. 435 B.C.; Cyrene, Cyrenaica (present-day Libya)
Died: 365 B.C.; Athens, Greece
Area of Achievement: Philosophy
Contribution: Departing from the Sophism to which he was exposed as Socrates' student, Aristippus founded the Cyrenaic School of philosophy, the hallmark of which was hedonism.

Early Life

Because Aristippus left no writings for posterity, what is known about him is derived from secondary sources, the most notable of which is Xenophon's Memorabilia (c. 381-355). From these scant and distant sources, it appears that Aristippus was born in North Africa in the city of Cyrene in what is currently Libya but was then Cyrenaica. His family was reputed to have had considerable influence and to have been sufficiently rich to support the young Aristippus in his travels and studies. Cyrene was at the height of its prosperity and influence during Aristippus's early life.

From all accounts, Aristippus experienced life with an ebullient enthusiasm. He was affable and had a winning personality and disposition. He was also remarkably intelligent, quick to learn and eager to share his learning with others. He had a legendary sense of humor and was considered a *bon vivant* whose chief aim during his early days was to seek pleasure, broadly defined.

The existing sources agree that Aristippus went to Athens and studied under Socrates in the *agora* and that he also journeyed to Sicily, where he was a part of the court of Dionysius I at Syracuse. Scholars are at odds in suggesting the order in which these two occurrences took place. The *Memorabilia* suggests that Aristippus went first to Athens, then left to go to Syracuse after Socrates' death, whereas other sources suggest the opposite sequence. In the absence of hard evidence, it is impossible to know which interpretation is accurate.

It is known that Aristippus studied with Socrates, attracted to this pivotal Athenian philosopher by his obvious humanity, his fun-loving qualities, his cordiality, and, most important of all, his indisputable intellectual superiority. Aristippus spent considerable time in Athens during its golden age, its most significant period of intellectual influence.

Because Socrates died in 399 B.C., it is known that Aristippus probably spent part of his late twen-

ties and early thirties in Athens. It is also known that he was in Athens in his later life, because he died there thirty-four years after Socrates' death.

Aristippus also went to Syracuse, where he taught rhetoric and was associated with the court of Dionysius, all ill-tempered, often rude tyrant. Once, when Aristippus invoked Dionysius' wrath, the tyrant spat in his face. Aristippus, demonstrating his ready wit, took this indignity in stride, observing that one who is landing a big fish must expect to be splashed.

After Aristippus had taught for some time in Syracuse, he returned to his native Cyrene to begin a school of philosophy. It seems logical that the correct sequence of events is that he studied first in Athens with Socrates, that he then went to Syracuse, well equipped to teach through his studies in Athens, and that he then returned to Cyrene, where he remained for several years until his ultimate return to Athens, where he spent the remainder of his life.

Life's Work

In modern philosophical terminology, Aristippus would likely be classified as a relativist. Schooled in Sophism by Socrates, the great master of the Sophist philosophy based on dialogue and structured argument, Aristippus had been exposed continually to the prevailing Socratic theory of innate ideas—to the notion that ideal forms exist, while the objects of the "real" world are mere imitations of the ideal forms (the word "idea" is derived from a Greek word meaning "shape" or "form").

Aristippus early questioned this notion, believing rather that all individuals experience and perceive things around them in unique and individual ways. One cannot, for example, speak of a universal "red." To begin with, there are many reds; the red of human blood is not the exact red of an apple, of the sun at sunset, or of a red cabbage. Further, what is red to one person might be grey-green to someone who is color blind but who has been conditioned to the notion that apples, human blood, and some cabbages are red.

Similarly, according to Aristippus, the nominalist concept that words such as "chair," "wheel," or "bottle" evoke a universal image is flawed, because all individuals necessarily filter their concepts of words through their own experience and consciousness, each arriving perhaps at a totally different image. In other words, for Aristippus, no physical object (table, chair), quality (blue), or concept (goodness) in the real world possesses generalized qualities detached from the specific object, quality, or concept. To him, perception, which is wholly individual and idiosyncratic, determines what any object or concept communicates to any single individual.

These notions led Aristippus to the conclusion that there exists no explicit, objective, and absolute world identically perceived by all people. He further posited that it is impossible accurately to compare the experiences of different people, because all individuals can know are their own perceptions and reactions. Aristippus further contended that, from birth, all living humans seek pleasure and avoid pain. In Aristippus's view, therefore, pleasure and pain become polar opposites in the lives of most humans, pleasure being associated with good, pain with evil.

As Socrates' student, Aristippus surely knew that his teacher explained virtue in terms of the pleasure it brings to the virtuous, as opposed to the pain that vice brings. This was at the heart of Socrates' moral philosophy, as shown particularly in his death dialogues. Aristippus, on the other hand, contended that life must be lived in pursuit of pleasure.

His one caveat was that pleasure must be defined by all people for themselves, that there is no universal pleasure. Some people, therefore, find the greatest pleasure in leading law-abiding, virtuous lives, whereas others find it in raucous, drunken revelry. Aristippus did not make moral judgments about where individuals sought and found their pleasures.

Using the formal logic that his background in rhetoric had instilled in him, Aristippus denied that there was any universal standard of pleasurableness. Drawing on his conclusion that it is impossible to compare concepts between or among individuals, he argued that it is futile to say that some pleasures are better than others or that they possess a greater good.

Aristippus also argued that the source of pleasure is always the body—which, he was quick to point out, includes the mind. For him, pleasures were most fully and satisfactorily experienced in the present. Memories of pleasures past or the contemplation of pleasures promised at some future date are weak semblances of pleasures that are immediately enjoyable.

The school of philosophy that Aristippus founded at Cyrene, based on concepts such as these, was designated the Hedonistic School, "hedonistic" being derived from the Greek word for "pleasure." Hedonism was closely akin in many ways to the Cynicism of Antisthenes, who, like Aristippus, questioned the existence of universals, claiming that the so-called universals were nothing more than names. Together, Antisthenes and Aristippus formulated the Nominalist theory of universals, which flew in the face of Socrates' and Plato's realism.

For Aristippus, the moral good dwells in the immediate, intense pleasures of the moment. These pleasures are experienced through the senses. Aristippus considered them the best and greatest pleasures, the ends toward which all moral activity is directed.

This philosophy, however, proved unworkable over time. The Cyrenaics quickly realized that considerable pain is involved in the attainment of some pleasures and that anyone who would judge the intensity and, ultimately, the moral good of that pleasure must consider as well the pain involved in achieving it.

The Cyrenaics also questioned the absoluteness with which Aristippus linked pain to evil. They came to understand that pain that in the end results in the achievement of pleasure can in itself be viewed as a good. They contended that the truly good person will do nothing evil or antisocial because of the punishments or disapproval that might accompany such actions (the avoidance of pain). Unlike Aristippus, they began to view the mental and bodily pleasures as dichotomous.

Finally, those who sought to refine Aristippus's theories arrived at the realization that the understanding of pleasure and of the pleasure/pain dichotomy required an outside, objective judge. They found such a judge in reason and wisdom, which led them to the inevitable conclusion that intelligence is a determining and indispensable component of virtue. Without this element, true happiness is impossible. Indeed, this turn in their reasoning took them back into proximity with Socrates' notions of virtue and of pleasure.

Summary

Perhaps Aristippus's greatest contribution to western thought came in his questioning of Socrates' theory of ideas. In disputing these theories, he focused on individual differences and arrived at a philosophy infinitely more relativistic than the prevailing philosophies of his day.

In a sense, Aristippus took the earliest tentative steps in a march of insurgent ideas that led inevitably to the Reformation of the sixteenth century, in which Martin Luther demanded that all people be their own priests when it came to interpreting Scripture. This movement, along with the invention of the printing press in the preceding century, much stimulated the move toward universal literacy in the western world.

If the Cynics under the leadership of Antisthenes represented the school of apathy in the ancient world, the Cyrenaics, following the lead of Aristippus, represented the school of happiness. These ideas ran counter to the prevailing philosophy emerging from Athens and were considered both exotic and quixotic by the most influential thinkers of the day.

As Athens skulked into defeat and steady decline, however, many of its citizenry found Hedonism—and Epicurus's refinement of it, Epicureanism—quite to their liking. Among the Cyrenaics who introduced new concepts into Aristippus's earlier philosophy was Theodorus, who did not accept categorically that pleasure is good and pain is bad. He looked to wisdom as the true source of happiness and contentment, but not as a means of procuring pleasures.

Hegesias was essentially similar to Theodorus in his view that wisdom could not procure pleasure, but he recommended the avoidance of pain as a step toward achieving happiness. He advised people to regard dispassionately such dichotomies as wealth and poverty, slavery and freedom, life and death.

Anniceris reinstituted some of the earlier teachings of Aristippus into his version of the older Hedonist philosophy and was a closer advocate of the founder of the movement than were Theodorus and Hegesias. Ultimately, Epicurus adopted many of the ethical views of the Hedonists into Epicureanism.

Bibliography

Durant, Will. *The Story of Philosophy.* 2d ed. New York: Simon & Schuster, 1967. In this reader-friendly history of philosophy, Durant demonstrates the relationships between Aristippus's Hedonism and that of his later followers. He also places it in the context of other prevailing philosophical movements of its day such as Epicureanism, Sophism, Stoicism, and Cynicism.

Fuller, Benjamin A. G. *A History of Ancient and Medieval Philosophy.* Rev. ed. New York: Holt, 1955. This comprehensive history of ancient and medieval philosophy offers the most extensive treatment in print of Aristippus. The presentation is clear and easily understandable to the general reader.

Hamlyn, D. W. *A History of Western Philosophy.* London and New York: Viking, 1987. Hamlyn deals briefly with the Cyrenaic school of philosophy and with Aristippus's founding of that school, placing it in its context within the prevalent Sophist philosophy of fifth century Athens.

Kenny, Anthony, ed. *The Oxford History of Western Philosophy.* Oxford and New York: Oxford University Press, 1994. Although the presentation on Aristippus is brief, it covers the high points of his philosophy well and accurately. Places Aristippus's philosophy in sharp contrast to the philosophical outlooks that prevailed in Athens during his lifetime.

Renault, Mary. *The Last of the Wine.* London: Allen Lane, and New York: Pantheon, 1956. Renault captures better than any contemporary writer the essence of Sophism and the atmosphere of ancient Greece.

R. Baird Shuman

ARISTOPHANES

Born: c. 450 B.C.; Athens, Greece
Died: c. 385 B.C.; Athens, Greece
Areas of Achievement: Theater and drama
Contribution: Aristophanes' highly entertaining
plays provide the only extant examples of Old
Comedy, and his last works anticipate the shift to
the New Comedy of Menander, Terence, and
Plautus. His writings reveal much about not only
dramaturgy in late fifth century B.C. Athens but
also the social, political, and economic conditions of the time.

Early Life

The son of Philippos, who may have been a landowner in Aegina, Greece, Aristophanes was born in
Athens about 450 B.C. Though little is known about
his early life, he was clearly well educated, for his
plays quote or allude to many sources. These
works also suggest a deep interest in public affairs,
and Aristophanes was to serve as representative of
his district on the Athenian Council.

His literary ability became apparent quite early:
When he was between seventeen and twenty-three
years old he began participating in Athens' annual
dramatic competitions. The Lenaian Dionysia, or
Lenaia, held in Gamelion (January-February), was
devoted largely to comedies, whereas the Great, or
City, Dionysia, established in 536 B.C. and celebrated in Elaphebalion (March), presented tragedies but also offered three comic plays. Both festivals were religious as well as literary, honoring
Dionysus, the god of wine, and associated with agriculture in general.

The comedies derived both their name and purpose from the ancient komos, or procession of rejoicing in the vital forces of nature, which supposedly drove away evil spirits and guaranteed
continued fertility of the land and its inhabitants.
Bawdy jokes and costumes that include large phalluses constitute part of the ritual, as does the gamos, or sexual union, that frequently concludes the
plays. Similarly, the mockery of prominent political or cultural figures serves as a liberating force
that temporarily allows free rein to irrational and
suppressed urges; such antics are connected with
the madness of intoxication.

To these satiric and sexual elements, Aristophanes added a lyricism rivaling that of any other
Hellenic poet. An excellent example appears in the
parabasis (choral interlude) of *Ornithes* (c. 414;

The Birds), which begins with a summoning of the
nightingale:

> Musician of the Birds
> Come and sing
>   honey-throated one!
> Come, O love,
>   flutist of the Spring,
> accompany our song.

The Chorus then presents a myth of the creation of
the world through the power of Love, all told in
lyrical anapests.

Only a fragment survives of Aristophanes' first
play, *Daitalēis* (banqueters), which won second
prize at the Lenaia of 427, yet the remains suggest
that the dramatist already was treating an issue
which would become important in his more mature
writing. Though still a young man himself, he attacks Athenian youth and their new ways, especially modern modes of education. An old man sends
one son to the city, while the other remains in the
country. The former learns only to eat, drink, and
sing bawdy songs; his body is no better trained
than his mind. When he returns home he is too
weak to work and no longer cares whether he does.

Babylōnioi (Babylonians), another lost play, was
produced at the Great Dionysia of 426 and won
first prize. Cleon, the Athenian demogogue then in
power, had undertaken a policy of mass terror to
force Athens' allies to support its military efforts
against Sparta in the Peloponnesian War. As a believer in peace and pan-Hellenism, Aristophanes
attacked Cleon's measures. Cleon responded by
taking Aristophanes to court. Despite the playwright's claim in his next comedy that during the
proceedings he almost "gave up the ghost," he does
not seem to have been punished severely, if at all.
As is evident from his next plays, he was unde-
terred from speaking out against war and against
Cleon.

Life's Work

Acharnēs (*The Acharnians*), which in 425 won first
prize at the Lenaia (a major dramatic competition
devoted largely to comedies), continues to attack
Cleon's war policy. When the demigod Amphitheus raises the question of peace in the Athenian
assembly, he is ejected. Dikaiopolis (which means
Honest Citizen or Just City), a refugee farmer
whose land has been ravaged by war, supports this

pacific plea and sends Amphitheus to Sparta to negotiate a separate peace for himself. When the demigod returns with a thirty-year treaty, the Acharnians attack him. These old men, represented by the Chorus, have suffered in the war, but they want revenge, not peace. Dikaiopolis must defend his views while he rests his head on a chopping block, so that if he fails to persuade the Chorus that his policy is best, they can kill him at once. His speech divides the old men, who resolve to summon Lamachos, a general, to argue the matter further. The agon, or debate, ensues, allowing Aristophanes to present further arguments against the war. The Chorus finally sides with Dikaiopolis, but Lamachos leaves vowing eternal resistance.

The farmer now sets up a market. While the play shows him prospering through peace, it also reveals the hardships of war. For example, a Megarian has become so impoverished that he is willing to sell his daughters for a pittance. The final scenes highlight the contrast between the policies of Cleon and Aristophanes: Lamachos returns from war wounded just as Dikaiopolis, victorious in a drinking bout, appears with two young women to celebrate wine and fertility, the gifts of Dionysus and peace.

In *Hippēs* (424; *The Knights*), which took first prize at the Lenaia, Aristophanes again attacks Cleon. A lost play, *Holkades*, presented at the next Lenaia, is still another attack on Cleon. Then, at the Great Dionysia, Aristophanes turned his attention to a different subject in *Nephelai* (423; *The Clouds*). Strepsiades (Twisterson) has fallen deeply in debt because of the extravagance of his wife and the gambling of his horse-loving son, Pheidippides. To cheat his creditors, Strepsiades resolves to send the youth to the Phrontisterion (Thinkery), the local academy run by Socrates, who can make the weaker side appear the stronger. When Pheidippides refuses to attend, his father enrolls instead. Despite his best efforts, the father cannot grasp the new learning, and at length his son agrees to enter the academy.

Now Pheidippides must choose a mentor; Dikaios Logos (Just Cause) and Adikos Logos (Unjust Cause) offer themselves, and to help Pheidippides choose they engage in a debate, or agon. Dikaios Logos speaks for the old morality and simple life, but when Adikos Logos advocates skepticism and amorality, even Dikaios Logos is converted. Pheidippides becomes certified as an adept at the new philosophy and even teaches his father

enough to allow Strepsiades to outwit two of his creditors.

The old man's triumph is, however, short-lived. When Strepsiades reproves his son for singing an obscene song by Euripides, Pheidippides beats him. The father appeals to the Clouds, those symbols of obscurity and form without substance that are the deities and patrons of Socrates' school. They, however, side with the son, who has used his new skill to argue that, because Strepsiades, when he was stronger, would beat Pheidippides, Pheidippides may now beat his father. Enraged, Strepsiades heeds the advice of Hermes and burns down the Phrontisterion.

In 399, *The Clouds* was used as evidence against Socrates, yet Aristophanes' attitude toward the philosopher may be more sympathetic than the play suggests. During its performance, Socrates is supposed to have stood up in the stadium to point out how closely the actor's mask resembled him, and Plato later included Aristophanes in the *Symposium*, where he is treated kindly. Perhaps, in fact, Socrates was among the few who actually enjoyed the piece, for it received only the third prize at the festival; Aristophanes blamed its failure on its being too intellectual for the masses.

Sphēkes (*The Wasps*), which won second prize at the Lenaia of 422, returns to political issues, as Aristophanes once more criticizes Cleon as well as the litigious nature of the Athenians. In the autumn of 422, Cleon died, and ten days after the Great Dionysia of 421 Athens concluded a peace treaty with Sparta. Aristophanes' *Eirēnē* (*Peace*), which won second prize that year, celebrates the end of the fighting, as Trygaios rides to heaven on a giant dung-beetle to rescue Eirēnē from the clutches of Polemos (War). He also saves Opora (Harvest) and Theoria (Ceremony), the private and public benefits of peace. The former becomes his wife; the latter he gives to the Athenian Council. As the play ends, Trygaios regains his youth and is guaranteed perpetual fertility through his union with the goddess.

None of Aristophanes' plays from the next several years has survived, though he apparently returned to the theme of regeneration in *Geras* (c. 421) and *Amphiaraus* (c. 414). His next extant piece, *The Birds*, dates from the Great Dionysia of 414, at which it won second prize. Pisthetairos (Trusty) and Euelpides (Son of Good Hope) have tired of the corruption, fast-paced life, and litigious habits of their fellow Athenians and so resolve to find a pastoral retreat among the birds. Aristophanes demonstrates that though one can leave Athens, one cannot suppress the Athenian *polupragmosunē*, that energy, daring, curiosity, restlessness, and desire for ever-expanding empire.

Instead of basking in rural retirement, Pisthetairos and Euelpides create Nephelokokkugia (Cloudcuckooland), which chooses Athena as its patroness, builds a wall like that surrounding the Acropolis, and undertakes a blockade to keep the smoke of burnt offerings from reaching the gods. In short, these refugees from Athens create a city very much like the one they have fled, except that they are now rulers instead of subjects. Nephelokokkugia does differ from its earthly counterpart in some respects, though, for Pisthetairos expels informers, oracle-mongers, and lawyers, while he treats poets well. In other words, he eliminates those elements whom Aristophanes regarded as preying on their fellow Athenians. In the final scenes, the blockade of the gods succeeds: The Olympians surrender to the birds, Pisthetairos becomes a deity, and he marries the divine Basileia.

The success of the blockade marks another difference between Nephelokokkugia and Athens. As spectators watched *The Birds*, the Athenian fleet was sailing toward disaster in Sicily. In 413, the Peloponnesian War resumed, and, as a result, so did Aristophanes' criticism of the fighting. In the Lenaia of 411, he offered his solution to end the conflict. Women in Athens were virtually powerless, but in *Lysistratē* (*Lysistrata*), they become the architects of peace by refusing to sleep with their husbands until the fighting ends. In a display of pan-Hellenism, they also recruit women from all of Greece to join the sexual embargo.

The results of this effort are soon apparent in the enlarged phalluses of the husbands. Naturally, this tumidity is comical, and the large phallus is ritualistic as well. In another sense, though, it represents all the thwarted desires of Greece: the yearning for peace, prosperity, normalcy. It also links Spartan and Athenian by showing their common humanity, a point Aristophanes emphasizes further by showing that Greeks have cooperated before and can again. The Dionysian power of sex achieves peace between the warring parties as the play ends in a reconciliatory *gamos*.

Thesmophoriazousai (411; *Thesmophoriazusae*) dates from about the same time as *Lysistrata* and was performed either at the Great Dionsia of 411 or during the Lenaia of the following year. The piece has little political significance; instead, it satirizes several tragedies by Euripides, who had already been a comic target of Aristophanes in several of his earlier pieces. Yet, as *The Clouds* does not imply that the dramatist disliked Socrates, so *Thesmophoriazusae* should not be read as a true condemnation of Euripides.

In fact, *Batrachoi* (405; *The Frogs*), Aristophanes' next surviving comedy and the last surviving work of Old Comedy, suggests that Aristophanes admired his fellow playwright. As the piece opens, Dionysus is preparing to go to Hades to resurrect Euripides, who had died in 406 (as had Sophocles). The god arrives just in time to judge a debate between Aeschylus and Euripides, each of whom claims to be the better writer. The succeeding agon reveals Aristophanes' keen critical sense. Euripides points out that he used common language so that the audience would understand him; Aeschylus replies that his own language is dignified and elevated to encourage spectators to aspire to lofty ideals. Euripides explains that his characters are drawn from real life; Aeschylus maintains that heroic figures are more appropriate for tragedy because ordinary people cannot serve as good examples.

Although Dionysus admires both writers, he finally decides to resurrect Aeschylus, for the older dramatist represents the values Aristophanes himself admired. Aeschylus had fought in the Battle of Marathon (490) and revered the customs and gods of Athens, whereas Euripides was modern and skeptical, embracing values Aristophanes had repeatedly attacked.

Thirteen years separate *The Frogs* and Aristophanes' next play, *Ekklesiazousai* (c. 392; *Ecclesiazusae*). As in *Lysistrata*, women here seize control of events to create a Utopian society. Peace is no longer an issue, because in 404 Sparta defeated Athens and tore down the vanquished city's walls. The new philosophy is no concern, either; in 399, Socrates had been executed. Although Athens was beginning to recover from a decade of economic, political, and social turmoil—in 395, it rebuilt its walls, for example—the play reflects a new mood and new conditions. Both here and in *Ploutos* (388; *Plutus*) the role of the chorus is greatly diminished, perhaps because the city could not afford to pay for one. Gone, too, is the sharp personal satire, as is criticism of contemporary events. Instead, the plays are escapist fantasies, one promising a communistic paradise, the other a society in which all receive their just desserts.

Aristophanes died shortly after the performance of *Plutus* but left two plays that his son Araros produced. *Aiolosikōn* was presumably a parody of one of Euripides' plays which is not extant, and *Kōkalos* seems to be based on the myth of a Sicilian king, who is the hero of one of Sophocles' lost plays. *Kōkalos*, which, like *Aiolosikōn*, was produced about 385, introduces a love story involving Daedalus and one of the king's daughters, and it presents a recognition scene of some sort; both features were to become standard in New Comedy.

Summary

Aristophanes, the advocate of the old order, helped to create a new kind of play. Crafty servants such as Cario in *Plutus*, lovers thwarted by their elders such as those in *Ecclesiazusae*, intrigue, disguise, and recognition scenes such as the ones believed to be in *Kōkalos* became hallmarks of New Comedy. By the first century A.D., Plutarch in his *Moralia* (c. 75; *The Philosophie, Commonly Called the Morals*) would condemn the coarseness of Old Comedy, characterizing Aristophanes' plays as resembling "a harlot who has passed her prime."

Aristophanes' plays remain historically important. Not only do they provide the only surviving record of the form and content of Old Comedy, but also they reveal much about daily life in late fifth century Athens. "Great, charming, and eloquent," Quintilian called Aristophanes' works, and the 150 extant manuscripts of *Plutus* alone attest his enduring popularity in antiquity. Modern productions, unencumbered by prudery, have demonstrated the vitality and beauty of his comedies, which, though written for a particular time and place, continue to speak to people everywhere.

Bibliography

Bowie, A. M. *Aristophanes: Myth, Ritual and Comedy.* Cambridge and New York: Cambridge University Press, 1993. This study focuses less on Aristophanes as an individual author than on the relationship between comedy and Greek rituals and myths. In Bowie's view comedy functions not as a vehicle for sharp, reformist political commentary but as an essentially conservative reinforcer of pre-existing social and religious values.

Croiset, Maurice. *Aristophanes and the Political Parties at Athens.* Translated by James Loeb. London: Macmillan, 1909; New York: Arno Press, 1973. As the title suggests, Croiset focuses on the political implications of Aristophanes' plays. He offers a good discussion of the military, political, social, and economic milieu of Aristophanes' Athens.

David, Ephraim. *Aristophanes and Athenian Society of the Early Fourth Century B.C.* Leiden, Netherlands: Brill, 1984. Seeks to fill a gap in studies of Aristophanes, which concentrate on his contributions to Old Comedy and his comments on Athens during the Peloponnesian War. David instead examines the two extant plays dating from the 300's, giving special attention to the economic situation they address.

Konstan, David. *Greek Comedy and Ideology.* New York and London: Oxford University Press, 1995. Contains essays on *Wasps, Birds, Lysistrata, Frogs,* and *Plutus* organized around the perceived interaction between the world of comedy and that of civic ideology.

MacDowell, Douglas M. *Aristophanes and Athens: An Introduction to the Plays.* Oxford and New York: Oxford University Press, 1995. An introductory work that discusses the background of Athenian dramatic festivals and then considers in turn each of Aristophanes' eleven surviving plays. Particular attention is paid ot the contemporary political events that lie behind parts of the plays.

Murray, Gilbert. *Aristophanes: A Study.* Oxford and New York: Oxford University Press, 1933. Although Murray claims in the preface that the book contains little research, it reflects decades of study. Murray had published a chapter on Aristophanes almost forty years earlier and in the interim had taught and translated the comedies. He concentrates on analyzing the plays and their revelation of Aristophanes' attitudes, but he also gives useful information about dramatic conventions and historical events that influence the plays.

Reckford, Kenneth J. *Aristophanes' Old-and-New Comedy: Six Essays in Perspective.* Chapel Hill: University of North Carolina Press, 1987. Aimed at nonspecialists who want to gain more familiarity with Aristophanes, as well as students and teachers of the playwright. Examines Aristophanes and his world from six perspectives: religious, psychological, theatrical, poetic, political, and literary-historical.

Spatz, Lois. *Aristophanes.* Boston: Twayne Publishers, 1978. After an introductory chapter on the nature of Old Comedy, Spatz presents a roughly chronological discussion of Aristophanes' contributions to this genre, focusing especially on the lesser-known works. Includes a helpful annotated bibliography.

Taaffe, L. K. *Aristophanes and Women*. London and New York: Routledge, 1993. The author contends that Aristophanes' representations of women should be seen not as liberating or "feminist" but as dependent on traditional images of women as sly deceivers. Male authority is always ultimately affirmed.

Ussher, Robert Glenn. *Aristophanes*. Oxford: Clarendon Press, and New York: Oxford University Press, 1979. Part of the New Surveys in the Classics series, this work offers an excellent brief introduction to the poet and his plays. Includes a chronology of the surviving comedies and discusses them in terms of structure, theme, character, language, staging, and performance. Contains a good bibliography of primary and secondary sources.

Joseph Rosenblum

ARISTOTLE

Born: 384 B.C.; Stagirus, Chalcidice, Greece
Died: 322 B.C.; Chalcis, Euboea, Greece
Areas of Achievement: Philosophy, ethics, natural
  history, and science
Contribution: Building on Plato's dialogical approach, Aristotle developed what is known as the
  scientific method. In addition, he founded the
  Lyceum, the second university-type institution
  (after Plato's Academy), which, with its vast collections of biological specimens and manuscripts of verse and prose, housed the first
  research library.

Early Life

Aristotle was born in the town of Stagirus, located
on the northeast coast of the Chalcidice Peninsula
in Greece, most likely in 384 B.C. His father, Nicomachus, was a physician and a member of the clan,
or guild, of the Asclepiadae, as had been his ancestors; the family probably had migrated from Messenia in the eighth or seventh century B.C. Aristotle's
mother was from Chalcis, the place where he
sought refuge during the last year of his life. Both
parents died while Aristotle was very young.

Aristotle was adopted and reared by Proxenus,
court physician to Amyntas II of Macedonia (an
occasional source suggests that Nicomachus also
held this position, but others disagree); it is likely,
therefore, that young Aristotle lived part of his
youth at Pella, the royal seat. He may even have
learned and practiced surgery during this time.

Aristotle's early environmental influences
helped determine his outlook: his detached, objective way of looking at a subject, his interest in biological science, and his universality. In his early
life, Aristotle was surrounded by physicians and
princes, not philosophers. When he was eighteen,
he was sent to Athens for training in the best
school available, Plato's Academy, where he would
spend the next twenty years. Thus ended the first of
the four phases of Aristotle's life.

Life's Work

Aristotle's career divides itself naturally into three
periods: the twenty (some say nineteen) years at
Plato's Academy, from 368 to 348; the thirteen
years of travel, from 348 to 335; and the return to
Athens, or the years in the Lyceum, from 335 to
323.

When young Aristotle arrived at the Academy,
Plato was away on a second journey to Syracuse.
When the master returned the following year, however, Aristotle became his prize student and ardent
friend. Although most of Aristotle's earlier works
have been preserved only in fragments, usually in
quotations within works by later scholars of the
Peripatetic School, several are attributed to this period and the one that followed.

As Plato's method was dialogue, Aristotle, like
other students at the Academy, began writing in dialogue. Aristotle was influenced by Plato about the
time the master altered his own form, moving toward dialogues other than those with Socrates as
questioner and main speaker. Aristotle, in turn,
made himself the main speaker in his own dialogues.

Some scholars consider *De anima* the best of Aristotle's works from this period. Translated as *On
the Soul,* this work treats the soul and immortality,
and is imitative of Plato's *Phaedo,* which was written circa 388-366 B.C. (Critic Werner Jaeger believes that each of Aristotle's early dialogues was

influenced by a particular Platonic dialogue, that the student was still dependent on the master as far as metaphysics was concerned but independent in the areas of methodology and logic.) Aristotle's *Protrepticus* (*Protreptics*) is named for a term designating a letter written in defense of philosophy; the method employed in this work (questions and answers by teacher and student) is from Plato, but the protreptic form is borrowed from the philosopher Isocrates, who was also at Athens during this time. In the year 348 (or 347), two events influenced Aristotle's future: the death of Plato (and possibly the choice of a new leader of the Academy), which caused Aristotle to leave Athens, and Philip II's destruction of Stagirus, which caused the philosopher to look elsewhere for a new home.

With a fellow Academic, Xenocrates, Aristotle left Athens for Mysia (modern Turkey), accepting the invitation of Hermeias, a former fellow student at the Academy who had risen from slavery to become ruler of Atarneus and Assos. Aristotle presided over his host's small Platonic circle, making of it a school modeled after the Academy. He married Pythias, niece and adopted daughter of Hermeias, after the ruler's death; they had a daughter, also named Pythias. His wife lived until late in Aristotle's so-called second Athenian period. After three years came another move, this time to Mytilene on the nearby island of Lesbos; it is possible that Theophrastus found him a suitable place of residence there. Having begun research in marine biology at Assos, Aristotle continued this work at Mytilene. During these years, he probably wrote *De philosophia* (*On Philosophy*), *Ethica Eudemia* (*Eudemian Ethics*), and early portions of *Physica* (*Physics*), *Metaphysica* (*Metaphysics*), and *Politica* (*Politics*).

In 343, Aristotle accepted Philip's invitation to move to Pella and become tutor to his thirteen-year-old, Alexander (the Great). The tutoring lasted until Alexander became regent in 340. It is uncertain whether Aristotle remained in Pella or moved to Stagira, which had been rebuilt by Philip in honor of Aristotle. With the assassination of Philip in 335 and the resultant accession of Alexander, Aristotle returned to Athens.

This time Aristotle's purpose was not to attend the Academy but to found its greatest competitor. The Lyceum was situated on rented property just outside the city, since an outsider could not own Athenian land. In addition to the marine specimens Aristotle himself had collected, the school housed

many more. It is said that Alexander became his old teacher's benefactor, donating eight hundred talents and instructing all under his command throughout the world to preserve for Aristotle any unusual biological specimens. The site was probably to the northeast of the city, where lay a grave sacred to Apollo Lyceius and the Muses, a place where Socrates had enjoyed walking.

In addition to specimens, the Lyceum housed hundreds of manuscripts and numerous maps. The objects in the museum were used to illustrate Aristotle's lectures and discussions. In the mornings, he utilized the peripatetic (walking) method by strolling through the trees, discussing with more advanced students difficult (esoteric) subjects; in the evenings, he would lecture to larger groups on popular (exoteric) subjects. Logic, physics, and metaphysics were discussed; lectures included rhetoric, sophistic, and politics. In turn, Aristotle seems to have prepared and made available two types of notes: preliminary ones, from which he lectured, and more polished treatises, based on the discussions. Many of these have survived as his later, published works. They are in the form of treatises rather than dialogues.

With the death of Alexander and the rise of feelings in Athens against Macedonians, especially those who had been close to Alexander, Aristotle left Athens for his mother's birthplace of Chalcis, where he died a year later of a disease that had afflicted him for some time.

In his later years at Athens, Aristotle is described as well-dressed, enjoying the easy life of self-indulgence; he was bald and thin-legged with small eyes; he spoke with a lisp and had a mocking disposition and a ready wit. After the death of his wife, he lived with a mistress, Herpyllis, in a permanent but nonlegal relationship. Together, they had a son, whom Aristotle named Nicomachus, after his father.

Summary

Aristotle developed through the earliest stage for about seventeen or eighteen years, moving in circles with doctors and princes. He then spent the next twenty years at the Academy with Plato, both imitating and growing away from his great master. Aristotle learned the method of dialogue while he moved toward his own method; he respected and loved Plato but questioned some Platonic thought, such as the theory of forms (dualistic being). During the next thirteen or fourteen years in Asia Minor, he established a smaller academy and did biological research, continuing the writing of dialogues as he had done at Athens but developing his own method of writing treatises. For three years he was tutor to Alexander, becoming lifelong friends with the future conqueror and ruler of the Mediterranean world but failing to impart his own political views to his student.

When Aristotle returned to Athens to found and preside over the Lyceum, he perfected his scientific method of examining specimens and establishing logical systems of substantiation before arriving at tentative conclusions, a method that has continued to modern times. Through his teaching, he influenced a few advanced students and the large public groups who heard his lectures. Through the Peripatetic School, his work continued for centuries and many of his writings were preserved to influence even later centuries. He learned from and utilized the thought of Greek philosophers from Thales to Plato, extending their ideas and synthesizing them. He perfected the method of Socrates (who had intended such an extension himself) by reaching conclusions rather than probing endlessly. Plato and Aristotle have been more influential than all other Western philosophers, advancing Greek philosophy to its greatest height.

Bibliography

Ackrill, J. L. *Aristotle the Philosopher.* Oxford and New York: Oxford University Press, 1981. According to this interesting guidebook, "What really characterizes Aristotle as a philosopher is not the number and weight of his conclusions (his 'doctrines'), but the number and power and subtlety of his arguments and ideas and analyses."

Aristotle. *The Works of Aristotle Translated into English Under the Editorship of W.D. Ross.* 12 vols. Oxford: Clarendon Press, 1908-1952. This multivolume text of Aristotle's works, translated over many years, is the recommended version for English-reading students.

Barnes, Jonathan, ed. *The Cambridge Companion to Aristotle.* Cambridge and New York: Cambridge University Press, 1995. This collection of essays focuses on Aristotle's philosophy, examined from a philosophical (i.e. not a historical or literary) standpoint. The essays are intended for readers new to Aristotle's thought and, following an introduction on the philosopher's life and works, go on to discuss metaphysics, rhetoric, poetics, logic, science, psychology, ethics, and politics.

Brumbaugh, Robert S. *The Philosophers of Greece.* New York: Crowell, 1964; London: Allen and Unwin, 1966. This introductory volume traces Greek philosophy from Thales to Socrates, Plato, and Aristotle. Focusing on three important regions—Ionia, southern Italy/Sicily, and Athens—Brumbaugh reviews three questions asked by the Greeks: What is being (what is real)? What am I? and Is there one world or many?

Cantor, Norman F., and Peter L. Klein, eds. *Ancient Thought: Plato and Aristotle.* Vol. 1, *Monuments of Western Thought.* Waltham, Mass.: Blaisdell Publishing Co., 1969. In this volume, contrasts between the two great philosophers are noted.

Ferguson, John. *Aristotle.* New York: Twayne Publishers, 1972. Assisting the general reader in the study of Aristotle's works, this book presents chapters such as "Life and Times," "The Lost Dialogues," "Philosophy of Nature," "Psychology," and "The Legacy of Aristotle." Part of Twayne's World Authors series.

Fuller, B.A.G. *History of Greek Philosophy.* Vol. 3, *Aristotle.* London: Cape, 1923; New York: Henry Holt, 1931. Chapter 1 tells of Aristotle's life, while chapters 2 through 11 treat the various phases of his philosophical thought from metaphysics to form and matter, including Aristotelian physics, concern for the unmoved mover, logic, ethics, political thought, rhetoric, and poetics. The final chapter provides a useful review.

Irwin, Terence. *Aristotle's First Principles.* Oxford: Clarendon Press, and New York: Oxford University Press, 1988. Explores the nature of Aristotle's dialectical reasoning and traces the philosopher's efforts to find a way of establishing valid first principles.

Jaeger, Werner. *Aristotle: Fundamentals of the History of His Development.* Translated by Richard Robinson. 2d ed. Oxford: Clarendon Press, 1948. A translation from the German, this volume attempts to show that Aristotle's views were not static. Jaeger traces Aristotle's development through three life stages—"The Academy," "Travels," and "Maturity"—and treats both biographical data and the works. Here, Aristotle is approached according to the Aristotelian developmental method. A highly recommended source.

Kiernan, Thomas P., ed. *Aristotle Dictionary.* New York: Philosophical Library, 1962. This useful dictionary of Aristotelian terms is preceded by a 157-page introduction outlining the philosopher's life and works. Well-organized and readable.

McKeon, Richard. *Introduction to Aristotle.* 2d ed. Chicago: University of Chicago Press, 1973. The general introduction is divided into treatments, including the life and times, scientific method in the philosophy, theoretical and practical sciences, and influence. Works and their respective introductions are treated in sections entitled "Logic," "Physics," "Psychology and Biology," "Ethics," "Politics," and "Rhetoric and Poetics."

Plato. *The Worlds of Plato and Aristotle.* Harold Joseph Allen and James B. Wilbur, eds. Buffalo: Prometheus Books, 1979. This volume treats the philosophies of the two men "as whole perspectives of life and the world by utilizing the actual writings." Plato is the subject of the first half, Aristotle the second. The general introduction to the latter discusses the two men, then Aristotle's method. Numerous selections from the works are discussed and cited under six topics and many subtopics.

Ross, Sir David. *Aristotle.* 6th ed. London and New York: Routledge, 1995. Following a very detailed overview of the life and works, this source treats the works under the same headings as does McKeon. Much attention is given to whether a work is authentic, Ross often ruling that it is not. This approach contrasts with that of Jaeger, who tends to regard many works as authentic. Includes detailed data regarding Aristotle's successors, citers, and commentators in the main text and in a chronology at the end.

George W. Van Devender

ARISTOXENUS

Born: 375-360 B.C.; Tarentum
Died: Date unknown; probably Athens
Area of Achievement: Music
Contribution: The theoretical writings on music by Aristoxenus established a foundation upon which modern theory is based.

Early Life

Aristoxenus, born in Tarentum, was a Greek philosopher and music theorist who flourished during the fourth century B.C. He received his earliest musical training at the hands of his father, Spintharus, who enjoyed some reputation as a musician. He later studied with Lamprus of Erythrae, of whom little is known. In time Aristoxenus moved to Athens, where he studied with the Pythagorean Xenophilus—important in view of the position he was to take in his theoretical treatises. He also studied at the Lyceum with Aristotle. Because Aristoxenus later competed, although unsuccessfully, with Theophrastus, a colleague, for headship of the Lyceum around 322, it may be assumed that Aristoxenus was a superior student and respected in scholarly circles.

Life's Work

Aristoxenus was apparently a prolific writer, with one source attributing more than 450 works to him, although only a few Aristoxenus fragments have survived. The writings, which cover a variety of topics, including works on music, biography, history, and philosophy, reflect the diversity of his studies. All the fragments are of interest, but the most important of the extant fragments pertain to music: Aristoxenus made his truly original contribution as he challenged the way that theorists, past and contemporary with him, had studied and written about music. So great was his influence that theorists and philosophers on music who followed him were compelled to address his arguments.

Numbering among the music fragments that survive are parts of three books entitled *Harmonika stoicheia* (*The Harmonics,* 1902), the contents of which are believed to have been derived from Aristoxenus' earlier writings on the subject. Much of what is known about ancient Greek theory comes from his writings and the writings of later men, such as Plutarch, Cleonides, and Aristides, who expounded upon Aristoxenus' principles.

In addition to *The Harmonics,* there is a fragment on rhythm, consisting of approximately 250 lines, which was treated by Aristides several centuries later. While Aristoxenus' work reveals a man who could be rather pompous and contentious, his writings are clearly the product of a first-rate mind.

Aristoxenian theory was about melody and articulated a system that addressed the issues of pitch, intervals, genera, systems, modes, and modulation as they applied to melody. The smallest consonant interval recognized in his system was a perfect fourth, which also formed the fixed outer boundary of a four-note unit called a tetrachord. The tetrachord was a kind of building block which, in combination with other tetrachords, formed larger structures. The tetrachord could belong to one of three types, or genera: diatonic, enharmonic, or chromatic. This system was determined according to the placement of the two inner notes that fell within the boundary of the fixed interval of the fourth, which was formed by the two outer notes of the tetrachord. The varied placements of the two inner notes of the tetrachord were known as shadings, or colors. Aristoxenus recognized two alternative positions of the inner notes in the diatonic genus and three in the chromatic, although he accepted that the variety of shadings was theoretically infinite.

The tetrachords could be combined, either sharing a common note and called conjunct or, if a whole step separated the two tetrachords, called disjunct. The combining of the tetrachords produced three important larger theoretical structures known as the Greater Perfect System, the Lesser Perfect System, and the Immutable System. The Greater Perfect System consisted of two pairs of conjunct tetrachords with an added note, or, in modern terminology, it can be seen in its diatonic form as a two-octave scale ranging from A to a' as seen on the piano keyboard. The range most used for the writing of Greek melodies, however, appears to have been the octave e' to e, and the Greater Perfect System was probably regarded as a central octave from e' to e lying within the A to a' range previously noted and with a conjunct tetrachord on either end and an added note on the bottom. The Greater Perfect System produced seven different species of the octave, since a different intervallic sequence would occur for the octave scale built on each of the seven different pitches represented in the system as it is brought within the central octave of e' to e.

The Lesser Perfect System consisted of three conjunct tetrachords with an added note that, using the piano keyboard for purposes of illustration, had the range of A to d'. The Lesser Perfect System is believed to have assisted in the function of change, or modulation, from one species to another.

The Immutable System was a combination of the Lesser Perfect and Greater Perfect systems and could be performed at various pitch levels. Such a structure was called a *tonos*. Aristoxenus identified thirteen different *tonoi*. The term is not without ambiguity, and scholars are not exactly sure what the term meant to Aristoxenus. It is, however, generally believed that the octave species and the *tonos* were one and the same during the time of Aristoxenus.

Aristoxenus' approach to the theory of music, conceived around 320, was unique for his time. A superior student of Aristotelian logic who was familiar with the "new math," geometry, Aristoxenus turned both logic and geometry to his advantage as he defined the way subsequent theorists were to look at the discipline of music. His treatise was not simply an exercise in abstract logic. He elevated the musician's "ear" to a level equal with the intellect. By doing so, he recognized the value and importance of the commonsense judgment of the practicing musician.

Aristoxenus' writings clearly challenged both the teachings of Pythagoras, who flourished around 530 B.C. and whose reputation and writings were legendary by the time of Aristoxenus, and those of a group known as the Harmonists.

The supporters of Pythagoras' theories about music were scientists and mathematicians who were not interested in explanations or observations about the interplay of musical elements or about the science of music itself. They believed that understanding numbers was central to understanding the universe, and, therefore, it was quite logical to express musical intervals, of key importance to the Pythagoreans, in terms of mathematical ratios.

The Harmonists, criticized by Aristoxenus for failing to establish a rigorous system, were interested in the practical and empirical aspects of music theory but fell short of articulating an acceptable system. They were preoccupied with the identification and measurement of microintervals, which emphasized the study of certain scales to the exclusion of others.

A key factor in Aristoxenus' approach was his description of sound as a continuum, or line, along which the pitch could come to rest at any point, permitting him the freedom to create intervals of varying sizes without regard to whether the interval could be expressed using rational numbers. While abstract mathematical expression of a musical interval had become most important to the Pythagoreans and the Harmonists, Aristoxenus focused instead on the development of a system which would afford him the freedom and flexibility to identify subtleties of scalar structure. He based his system on judgments made by the ear and then represented it through geometric application.

Summary

Aristoxenus was the earliest writer on music theory known to address practical musical concerns. When he took the unique position that the ear along with the intellect should be used in the study of music, he established a precedent that ultimately altered the course of music theory. In effect, he redefined what music theory was, taking it out of the hands of the scientists and mathematicians and creating a new discipline which focused only on the interrelationship of musical elements. His arguments, which owed much to Aristotelian influence and methodology, enabled him to produce a clearly defined and organized system of music theory.

Bibliography

Aristoxenus. *Aristoxenus: Elementa Rhythmica: The Fragment of Book II and the Additional Evidence for Aristoxenean Rhythmic Theory.* Translated and edited by Lionel Pearson. Oxford: Clarendon Press, and New York: Oxford University Press, 1990. This volume includes a translation of all Aristoxenus' surviving writings on rhythm, an introduction to Greek rhythmic theory, and a commentary on the text.

Aristoxenus. *"The Harmonics" of Aristoxenus.* Translated by Henry Macran. Oxford: Clarendon Press, 1902; New York: Olms, 1974. The only English translation of Aristoxenus' main work, it also contains some commentary and some biographical material. Invaluable for the reader who is restricted to English.

Barker, Andrew. *"Hoi Kaloumenoi harmonikoi:* The Predecessors of Aristoxenus." *Proceedings of the Cambridge Philological Society* 24 (1978): 1-21. Discusses the issues of Aristoxenian theory as perceived by Aristoxenus with respect to his predecessors. Compares the different positions.

―――. "Music and Perception: A Study in Aristoxenus." *Journal of Hellenic Studies* 98 (1978): 9-16. Examines Aristoxenus' approach to music theory through an attempt to clarify the exact role the ear plays in relation to the intellect and also with respect to mathematics.

Crocker, Richard. "Aristoxenus and Greek Mathematics." In *Aspects of Medieval and Renaissance Music,* edited by Jan LaRue. New York: W. W. Norton and Co., 1966. An excellent article that discusses the key aspects of Aristoxenus' theories on music. Compares and explains Pythagorean arithmetic with Aristoxenus' use of geometric principles to illustrate and explain his new theories on music.

Henderson, Isobel. "Ancient Greek Music." In *The New Oxford History of Music.* Vol. 1, *Ancient and Oriental Music,* edited by Egon Wellesz. London and New York: Oxford University Press, 1957. An excellent study of ancient Greek music with considerable treatment of Aristoxenus. There is a brief discussion of the Harmonists and the Pythagoreans. The history, issues, and elements of Greek music are all discussed.

Levin, Flora. "Synesis in Aristoxenian Theory." *American Philological Transactions* 103 (1972): 211-234. Asserts that Aristoxenus established a new science that used only materials that belonged to music. Makes the case that Aristoxenus' system goes beyond cold facts and dry rules in an attempt to identify what is music.

Lippman, Edward. *Musical Thought in Ancient Greece.* New York: Columbia University Press, 1964. It is not necessary to be a practicing musician or theorist to appreciate or understand this book. There is an excellent treatment of Greek ethics, philosophy, and aesthetics of music.

Rowell, Lewis. "Aristoxenus on Rhythm." *Journal of Music Theory* 23 (Spring, 1979): 63-79. Provides a translation of Aristoxenus' fragment on rhythm. Rowell identifies the fragment as being in an Aristotelian format and discusses Aristoxenus' concept of rhythm.

Winnington-Ingram, R. P. "Aristoxenus." In *New Grove Dictionary of Music and Musicians,* edited by Stanley Sadie, vol. 1. London: Macmillan, and Washington, D.C.: Grove's Dictionaries of Music, 1980. The article contains important biographical material. The author discusses the philosophical differences between Aristoxenus and the Pythagoreans. He also provides a summary of Aristoxenus' contribution to theory. There is a short but important bibliography at the end of the article.

Michael Hernon

ASCLEPIADES OF BITHYNIA

Born: 124 B.C.; Prusa (Cios), Bithynia
Died: c. 44 B.C.; Rome
Area of Achievement: Medicine
Contribution: Asclepiades was the first physician to establish Greek medicine in Rome.

Early Life

Asclepiades, whose father was probably Andreas, a noted physiologist of the time, was born in Prusa, also called Cios, in Bithynia, Asia Minor. A widely read man, he seems to have had a liberal education in his youth. Apparently, there was enough money for him to be able to travel and study.

After studying rhetoric and medicine in Athens and Alexandria, he practiced medicine, first in Parion, a town on the Hellespont (Dardanelles), and later in Athens. After extensive traveling, in the year 91 he settled in Rome, where he may have become a Roman citizen. A man of amiable manners, good fortune, and worldly prosperity, Asclepiades formed friendships with such prominent individuals as Cicero and Marc Antony.

Preferring the freedom of a solitary life in a suburban villa, Asclepiades refused the invitation of King Mithradates of Pontus to join his court. Though he did not participate in public debates, he was not afraid to disagree with others. He condemned all those who thought that anatomy and physiology were the foundation of medicine. He was responsible for introducing Democritus' atomistic philosophy to Rome.

His daily routine included three basic activities: visiting and treating the sick throughout the city, giving written advice, and writing books. Although he was a voluminous author, little remains of the twenty or more treatises he prepared. Specific dates of his works are not known; the fragments that remain have been assigned English titles according to their subject matter. He wrote one book of definitions, one commentary on some of the short and obscure works of Hippocrates, one treatise on fevers, and three on febrile, inflammatory, and acute diseases. He also wrote *Concerning Common Aids,* a precursor of modern guides to healthy living; *Enemata,* which was frequently quoted by Aulus Cornelius Celsus in *De medicina* (c. A.D. 30; English translation, 1830); and *Method of Giving Wine in Sickness.*

Asclepiades also offered public lectures on medicine and had a large number of students. Applying many of his principles, these students, led by Themison of Laodicea, later founded the Methodist school, which emphasized diet and exercise in the treatment of illness.

By the age of thirty, Asclepiades was already famous. Some of that fame had grown from a story about him which circulated in Rome. According to this story, one day Asclepiades encountered a funeral procession. Just as the corpse was placed upon the pyre and the fire was about to be lit, he ordered the ceremony stopped, had the body taken down and delivered to his home, administered restoratives, and soon revived the man.

A statue excavated in Rome in 1700 was assumed to be a correct likeness of Asclepiades. From this it would appear that he was a man of slender stature who possessed a rather tranquil countenance.

Life's Work

Asclepiades was one of the foremost physicians of his century, exhibiting rich practical and philosophical attainments, versatility of mind, and an ability to make rapid diagnoses. Opposing the Hippocratic idea that morbid conditions resulted from a disturbance of the humors of the body, he held that nothing happened without a cause and that the causes of events were always mechanical—that is, dependent upon matter and motion.

The medical practice that Asclepiades founded was based on a modification of the atomic, or corpuscular, theory of Democritus, the Greek philosopher, according to which disease resulted from an irregular or inharmonious motion of the corpuscles of the body. Asclepiades believed that these masses were in continual motion, splitting into fragments of different shapes and sizes which then re-formed to create perceptible bodies. These particles were separated by invisible gaps, or pores. Friction between the particles created normal body heat; jamming the pores, or obstruction, was the cause of fever and inflammatory disorders. Fainting, lethargy, weakness, and similar complaints were attributed to an abnormal relaxation of the pores. Since disease was attributed to either constricted or relaxed conditions of the

body's solid particles, Asclepiades founded his therapy on the efficacy of systematic interference as opposed to the healing power of nature. The regimens that he prescribed incorporated such therapies as fresh air, light, appropriate diet, hydrotherapy, massage, clysters or enemas, local applications, and, occasionally, very small amounts of medication.

For those complaints which he believed to be caused by obstruction, he proposed various kinds of exercise to relax the pores; in this way, the free transmission of the interrupted atoms or molecules would be facilitated. For pain, localized venesection might be cautiously practiced, but only for instant relief, because bleeding tended to draw off the finer, more vital atoms first and leave the coarser atoms behind. Rigor, or rigidity of the body, might result.

He believed that dropsy, an excessive accumulation of fluid in the tissues, resulted from an infinite number of small holes in the flesh that converted all the food received into water. How such a conversion might occur, however, he did not explain. To illustrate that the brain was the seat of the finest

atoms, he performed decapitation experiments on animals such as eels, tortoises, and goats.

Asclepiades condemned purgatives, emetics, and drugs. Instead, he relied greatly on changes in diet, accompanied by friction, bathing, and exercise. He paid special attention to the patient's pulse. His remedies were directed to the restoration of harmony, based on the fundamental principle that treatments should be given promptly, safety, and pleasantly. For relaxants, he used wine and massage; to stimulate patients, he used wine, cold water, vinegar, and narcotics. He taught that patients tolerated diseases differently. Exercise, in his view, was unnecessary for healthy people. In cases of dropsy, he recommended making small cuts near the ankles to release the fluid. He advised that, when tapping was done to remove fluid, the opening be made as small as possible.

Asclepiades was particularly interested in psychiatric cases. He placed these patients in brightly lit, well-ventilated rooms, used occupational therapy, prescribed exercises for improving the memory and increasing attention, soothed them with music, and used wine to induce sleep.

According to Pliny the Elder, the Roman naturalist and writer, Asclepiades had three principal modes of cure. The early stages of illness often called for "gestation," which consisted of being transported in some way such as a boat or litter to exhaust the patient's strength and cause fever. Asclepiades also used suspended beds that could be rocked, as well as hanging baths and other forms of hydrotherapy. He firmly believed and taught that one fever was to be cured by another. The second mode was friction or massage. The third mode was wine, which he gave to febrile patients and used as a stimulant in cases of lethargy. He believed that it was necessary to force a patient to endure thirst. All patients were required to fast during the first three days of illness. In later stages, wine and moderate amounts of food were allowed.

Asclepiades showed great accuracy in distinguishing between various diseases, describing and dividing them into acute and chronic classes. For example, he gave a correct description of malaria; he also observed the psychic complications that occurred in cases of pneumonia and pleurisy. His special attention was devoted to chronic diseases, conditions which had been somewhat neglected by Hippocrates.

Asclepiades wagered that he would never die of disease; indeed, he is not known to have ever fallen ill. His death, at an advanced age, was the result of an accidental fall down a flight of stairs.

Summary

Asclepiades of Bithynia may be ranked as the first physician to introduce Greek medicine to Rome. A full assessment of his merits cannot be made because most of his writings have been lost. The fragments of them which have surfaced in later literature deal with subjects such as the pulse, respiration, heart disease, ulcers, climate, drugs, and the preparation of remedies.

By the fourth century, Asclepiades was almost forgotten. His critics had characterized him as a man of natural talents acquainted with human nature and possessed of considerable shrewdness but little scientific or professional skill. Galen strongly opposed him because Asclepiades had been the first to attack and repudiate the humoral teachings of Hippocrates. Pliny also disliked him and regarded him as a charlatan.

On the other hand, Celsus, the first compiler of medical history and procedures, admitted that he learned much from Asclepiades. Galen grudgingly credited Asclepiades as having pioneered two surgical procedures, laryngectomy and tracheotomy. As has been noted, his ideas were influential in the development of the Methodist school, with its emphasis on diet and exercise. Furthermore, Asclepiades was a pioneer in the humane treatment of mental patients.

Bibliography

Allbutt, Sir Thomas C. *Greek Medicine in Rome: The Fitzpatrick Lectures on the History of Medicine Delivered at the Royal College of Physicians of London in 1909-10.* London: Macmillan, 1921; New York: Blom, 1970. This series of lectures addressed to interested physicians and others with a strong medical background may be too abstract for the general reader. It is a complete medical history of the period with extensive commentary on all major figures, but only one brief chapter on Asclepiades. Excellent illustrations, bibliography, and additional chronology.

Cumston, Charles Greene. *An Introduction to the History of Medicine: From the Time of the Pharaohs to the End of the Nineteenth Century.* New York: Alfred A. Knopf, and London: Paul, Trench, Trubner, 1926. This volume, which contains only one brief chapter on Asclepiades, is a compilation of numerous essential contributions to the general subject of a history of medicine. Written for the general reader and as an introduction for students of medicine, it is a lengthy work containing many illustrations but limited bibliographical material.

Gordon, Benjamin Lee. *Medicine Throughout Antiquity.* Philadelphia: F. A. Davis Co., 1949. Gordon's book contains only a very brief section on Asclepiades, along with scattered page references. The author makes mention of a wide-ranging array of facts that are not ordinarily accessible to a busy practitioner or to lay people interested in medical history. There are brief reference notes and a few illustrations but no chronology or bibliography.

Green, Robert M., ed. and trans. *Asclepiades, His Life and Writings: A Translation of Cocchi's "Life of Asclepiades" and Gumpert's "Fragments of Asclepiades."* New Haven, Conn.: Elizabeth Licht, 1955. Green has prepared a complete translation of *Discorso primo di Antonio Cocchi sopra Asclepiade* (c. 1740) and of selections from Christian Gumpert's *Fragmenta* (1794), a compilation of extant writings of Asclepiades. This volume contains the most detailed information available in English for the general reader, although it lacks reference notes and a bibliography.

Major, Ralph. "Medicine in the Roman Empire." In *A History of Medicine.* Springfield, Ill.: Charles C Thomas, 1954. This chapter includes a brief section on Asclepiades. There is no presumption of background knowledge about medical history. Very limited information is presented and few illustrations are given. There is no chronology and only a limited bibliography.

Rawson, Elizabeth. "The Life and Death of Asclepiades of Bithynia." *Classical Quarterly* 32, no. 2 (1982): 358-370. Rawson presents a critical analysis of the information known about Asclepiades. A scholarly approach utilizing much research in Latin and Greek sources, but no translations of the numerous quotes are given. It presumes extensive background knowledge concerning Asclepiades as well as the period in which he lived.

Vallance, J. T. *The Lost Theory of Asclepiades of Bithynia.* Oxford: Clarendon Press, and New York: Oxford University Press, 1990. An attempt to reconstruct Asclepiades' medical theories, dealing especially with the question of whether Asclepiades adopted Epicurean atomist ideas and, more generally, with the influence (which Vallance attempts to minimize) of philosophy on medicine.

Rita E. Loos

ASHURBANIPAL

Born: c. 685 B.C.; Nineveh, Assyria

Died: 627 B.C.; Nineveh, Assyria

Areas of Achievement: Government, architecture, art, and literature

Contribution: The last great king of ancient Assyria, Ashurbanipal lived within a generation of its total annihilation. Inside his exquisitely decorated palace complex at Nineveh, he brought together a magnificent library of cuneiform writing upon clay tablets, which included materials from twenty-five hundred years of achievement by Sumerians, Akkadians, Babylonians, and Assyrians.

Early Life

Ashurbanipal was born toward the end of a fifteen-hundred-year period of Assyrian ascendancy. His name in Assyrian is Ashur-bani-apli (the god Ashur has made a[nother] son), affirming that he was not intended to stand in the line of royal accession.

His father, Esarhaddon, youngest son of Sennacherib, had become heir when the crown prince, Ashur-nadin-shumi, was deposed by rebels from his position as vassal for Babylon. Esarhaddon was not the son of Sennacherib's queen, Tashmetum-sharrat, but of the West Semitic "palace woman" Zakutu, known by her native name Naqi'a. The only queen known for Esarhaddon was Ashur-hamat, who died in 672.

Ashurbanipal grew up in the small palace called *bit reduti* (house of succession), built by Sennacherib when he was crown prince in the northern quadrant of Nineveh. In 694, Sennacherib had completed the "Palace Without Rival" at the southwest corner of the acropolis, obliterating most of the older structures. The "House of Succession" had become the palace of Esarhaddon, the crown prince. In this house, Ashurbanipal's grandfather was assassinated by uncles identified only from the biblical account as Adrammelek and Sharezer. From this conspiracy, Esarhaddon emerged as king in 681. He proceeded to rebuild as his residence the *bit masharti* (weapons house, or arsenal). The "House of Succession" was left to his mother and the younger children, including Ashurbanipal.

The names of five brothers and one sister are known. Sin-iddin-apli, the intended crown prince, died prior to 672. Not having been expected to become heir to the throne, Ashurbanipal was trained in scholarly pursuits as well as the usual horseman-ship, hunting, chariotry, soldierliness, craftsmanship, and royal decorum. In a unique autobiographical statement, Ashurbanipal specified his youthful scholarly pursuits as having included oil divination, mathematics, and reading and writing. Ashurbanipal was the only Assyrian king who learned how to read and write.

In 672, upon the death of his queen, Esarhaddon reorganized the line of succession at the instigation of his mother. He used the submission of Median chieftains to draft a treaty. The chieftains swore that if Esarhaddon died while his sons were still minors, they and their descendants would guarantee the succession of Ashurbanipal as king of Assyria and Shamash-shum-ukin as king of Babylon. A monumental stela set up two years later in a northwestern province portrays Esarhaddon in high relief upon its face and each of the sons on a side. These portraits, the earliest dated for Ashurbanipal and his brother, show both with the full beard of maturity.

The princes pursued diverse educations thereafter. Extant letters from Shamash-shum-ukin offer his father reports of the situation in Babylon; Ashurbanipal at home received letters as crown prince. The situation came to an immediate crisis in 669, when Esarhaddon, on campaign to Egypt, died suddenly. Ashurbanipal did not accede to the kingship of Assyria until late in the year. His grandmother required all to support his sole claim to the throne. The official ceremonies of coronation came in the second month of the new year, and within the same year (668), Ashurbanipal installed his brother as king of Babylon. The transition took place smoothly, and the dual monarchy of the youthful brothers began. Texts describe their relationship as if they were twins. It was clear, however, that Ashurbanipal, as king of Assyria, like his fathers before him, was also "king of the universe."

Life's Work

One of the first challenges that Ashurbanipal had to face was a rebellion in a region of Egypt over which Esarhaddon had established Assyrian sovereignty. In 667, the ousted king Taharqa came as far north as Memphis, which he recaptured. The Assyrian army rushed south to defeat him, but he again fled. Ashurbanipal enlisted new troops from Syria and followed, capturing Thebes. Three vassals were found guilty of plotting against Assyria,

and they were sent to Nineveh. One of them, Necho, convinced Ashurbanipal of his personal loyalty and was returned to his position in Sais in the Delta.

After Taharqa's death, Tanutamon tried to drive out the Assyrians. He captured Memphis and drove the Assyrian vassals into the Delta. With the return of Ashurbanipal and the Assyrian army, Tanutamon fled back to Thebes, which again fell to the Assyrians. In the course of this war, Necho had fallen, and his son Psammetichus I was installed as vassal at Sais; he became king of all Egypt upon the death of Tanutamon.

These events in Egypt, and Ashurbanipal's success in maintaining his position, made a considerable impression on the contemporary world. The Phoenician states, such as Sidon, quieted down. In Anatolia, Gyges, King of Lydia, sought Ashurbanipal's help against the Cimmerians, offering to acknowledge Assyrian suzerainty. There was a similar gesture from the Urartian king. Ashurbanipal did not, however, succumb to the temptation to get entangled in an impossible war with the mountainous Cimmerians.

Rather, he turned against the Elamites. In the campaign against their capital at Susa, the Elamite army was routed and their king, Tept-Humban (Teumman), was killed. This event was portrayed afterward in a chamber of Sennacherib's "Palace Without Rival," which had become Ashurbanipal's residence upon accession. In Teumman's place, a prince, Ummannish, who had earlier fled to the Assyrian court, became king.

The Assyrian empire stretched from Egypt to Urartu, from Lydia to Susa, along the full extent of both the Tigris and the Euphrates. Shamash-shumukin could not help feeling overshadowed by his brother, who, though technically his equal, treated him as another vassal. Messengers went out secretly from Babylon to other discontented states; in 651, Shamash-shum-ukin initiated full revolt, together with Gyges of Lydia, Ummanigash of Elam, Arabians, and others. Ashurbanipal implored the gods to save him. The chronicle of his inscriptions reflects the new situation created by the revolt; the one who had been called his "full brother" became the "faithless, hostile brother."

The army from Arabia was delayed, so that Shamash-shum-ukin had to face the entire Assyrian army alone. He withdrew into the fortified cities in Babylonia. The Assyrians proceeded to lay siege to one after another. In 648, realizing that all was lost, Shamash-shum-ukin threw himself into the fire which consumed his palace at Babylon. For the remainder of Ashurbanipal's reign, Babylon was held directly by Assyria. The official in charge, according to all subsequent Babylonian sources, was named Kandalanu; he is impossible to identify further, unless the name is a Babylonian throne name for Ashurbanipal. Kandalanu disappeared in the same year in which Ashurbanipal died.

Ashurbanipal undertook several more campaigns between 648 and 642, including at least two against Elam. He penetrated to Susa and sacked it thoroughly. There was one final campaign against the Arabs, fought as a running battle between his cavalry and the Arabs' mounted camel corps. Ashurbanipal returned from these forays with ample spoils to finance the construction of his grand new palace on the site of the old "House of Succession."

In decorating the walls of this palace, Ashurbanipal repeated the artistic narration of the earlier defeat of Teumman, giving thereby a second version to that in Sennacherib's palace. The most intriguing detail is the final celebration of the victory, in which Ashurbanipal with his queen are served a repast outdoors under some grapevines within which hangs the severed head of the disobedient vassal. Fully illustrated are the victories over Shamash-shum-ukin in 648, the Elamites in 642, and the Arabians. More noteworthy are the extensive scenes of a rather boyish Ashurbanipal hunting—none more exquisitely rendered than the one in which he single-handedly slaughters a pride of lions. Visitors to his palace got a clear impression that this king of Assyria was not merely a great king, but indeed "king of the universe."

From any later perspective, the destructive events of the 640's may be judged as contributory to the final end of Assyria. Yet the last fifteen years of reign appear so quiescent that Ashurbanipal went to his grave assured of the permanence of the land of Ashur that had been his inheritance.

Summary

Ashurbanipal left behind an impressive legacy in architecture, in artistic decoration, and in the collection of the literary treasures of the past, which he greatly enjoyed personally. This is borne out not merely by inscriptional claim, but also by lengthy colophons which he personally added to a wide variety of texts, gathered for the library at Nineveh from all parts of Mesopotamia and from all periods of time, going beyond the Babylonia of Hammurabi to what Ashurbanipal called the "obscure Akkadian and even more difficult Sumerian" on tablets he thought to have come "from before the Flood."

The letters he wrote to request manuscripts indicate that he knew where older collections existed and what they contained: the scholarly apparatus for reading and writing the cuneiform script, including multilingual dictionaries; collections of omens, essential for prognostication of every element of the royal life; and cycles of conjurations, incantations, and prayers, often with interlinear translation of the original Sumerian. To these essentials were added epics of gods or heroes, including previous kings; collections of fables, proverbial wisdom, and unusual tales, some humorous; and a miscellany reflecting the operations of the scribal school and its scholarship, especially in law.

Ashur-etil-ilani and Sin-shar-ishkun, two of his sons, succeeded him, but immediately faced increasing pressure from many opponents. The last Assyrian ruler was an army general, Ashur-uballit II, who held off as long as he could the final destruction of the Assyrian state by retreating to Harran, after the capitals fell to the combined strength of the Medes and Babylonians.

The biblical tradition recalled Ashurbanipal as "the great and noble Asnappar" who had "deported and settled, in the cities of Samaria and in the rest of the province called 'Beyond-the-River,'" various conquered peoples from Babylonia and Elam. The Greek tradition conflated Ashurbanipal with his brother Shamash-shum-ukin into a cowardly, effeminate "Sardanapalus" who presided over Assyria's destruction and committed suicide. Sardanapalus became well known through George Gordon, Lord Byron's verse drama of 1821 and Eugène Delacroix's 1827 painting. Neither of these is characterized by historical veracity, since they were both products of the Romantic era, which immediately preceded the archaeological rediscovery of the real Ashurbanipal.

Bibliography

Barnett, R.D. *Sculptures from the North Palace of Ashurbanipal at Nineveh (668-627).* London: British Museum, 1976. The history of the excavations and of the reconstruction of the plans of the palace is covered, with an explanation of the location within the chambers of all known sculpted slabs. Photographs and drawings are laid out to illustrate the slabs in their discovered configuration in this massive folio.

Grayson, A.K. "The Chronology of the Reign of Ashurbanipal." *Zeitschrift für Assyriologie* 70 (1980): 227-245. This study serves as a guide to the texts, historiographically evaluated, and to the correlation of detail within the various text editions to the actual events and their dates. It does not address the problems of the conclusion of the reign.

Luckenbill, Daniel David, trans. *Ancient Records of Assyria and Babylonia.* Vol. 2, *From Sargon to the End.* Chicago: University of Chicago Press, 1926; London: Histories and Mysteries of Man, 1989. An English translation of the inscriptions of the kings of Assyria. This volume covers Ashurbanipal and his three predecessors, Sargon II, Sennacherib, and Esarhaddon.

Oates, J. "Assyrian Chronology, 631-612 B.C." *Iraq* 27 (1965): 135-159. This effort to identify the sources and define the issues related to the conclusion of Ashurbanipal's reign judiciously sifts the conflict of opinion which has dominated Assyriology. Extensive bibliographical notes and internal catalogs of data guide the reader.

Olmstead, A.T. *History of Assyria*. New York and London: Scribner, 1923. Written in the immediate wake of World War I, this comprehensive history was selected for reprinting for its mastery of Assyrian materials and their critical evaluation. Ashurbanipal and his capital receive extensive treatment in chapters 30-47.

Reade, J.E. "Assyrian Architectural Decoration." *Baghdader Milleilungen* 10/11 (1979/1980): 17-110, 71-87. This series of articles provides a comprehensive and comparative study of the four major Assyrian palaces excavated since the mid-nineteenth century, with reference to techniques and subject matter, narrative composition, the immense scale of the art, and the architectural context.

Russell, John Malcolm. *Sennacherib's Palace without Rival at Nineveh*. Chicago and London: University of Chicago Press, 1991. This thorough study draws on physical remains and literary evidence in a full discussion of the building, design, and decoration of Sennacherib's Palace. Ashurbanipal's later work on the palace is occasionally treated.

Smith, C. C. "Some Observations on the Assyrians and History." *Encounter* 30 (1969): 340-353. This methodological essay on the nature of source materials coming from ancient Assyria and its kings indicates what they knew, how, and why, as well as the significance of that information to them. The Assyrian Royal Tradition is given focus, while the bibliographical notes provide an introduction to the subject. (Readers, please note: This *Encounter* is published by the Christian Theological Seminary in Indianapolis; it is not to be confused with the British journal of the same name.)

Clyde Curry Smith

ASHURNASIRPAL II

Born: c. 915 B.C.; Ashur, Assyria

Died: 859 B.C.; Kalhu, Assyria

Areas of Achievement: Warfare, government, architecture, and art

Contribution: Ashurnasirpal II created the Neo-Assyrian empire, expanding its boundaries to the Mediterranean coast and into the mountainous regions north and west of the Tigris homeland. At Kalhu, he built an enormous fortress capped by his magnificent palace, which featured the first extensive use of decorated bas-relief.

Early Life

The royal name Ashur-nasir-apli means "the god Ashur protects the son (as heir)." On each decorative slab in his palace, Ashurnasirpal II noted the names of his father, Tukulti-Ninurta II, and his grandfather, Adad-nirari II, along with a summary of his military and architectural achievements. He knew that his great-grandfather Ashur-dan II had "freed cities and founded temples," setting in motion the process of reorganizing and expanding the Assyrian empire which had been reduced to the capital area.

Adad-nirari II had made the first Assyrian attack to the east, into the Tigris' tributary basin. South of the Diyala River, he had defeated the Babylonian king, precipitating a revolution in Babylon and ensuring the perpetuation of the peace treaty by intermarriage. By treaty renewal during a period of eighty years, from the reign of Tukulti-Ninurta II through that of Ashurnasirpal's grandson, Shamshi-Adad V, parity was maintained by Assyria and Babylonia, which secured Assyria's southern front.

Adad-nirari II told of making new plows throughout Ashur-land, heaping up grain, and increasing the breed and quantity of horses. Tukulti-Ninurta II had continued this economic development, which served as a base for serious expansion.

The Nairi states to the north were fragmented remains of the Hurrian kingdom, which had been demolished by royal Assyrian predecessors five centuries earlier. These states were related to the territory known as Hanigalbat and to the important Urartian mountain kingdom around Lake Van. To the northwest were Aramaean tribal states, related to peoples beyond the Euphrates. It was against these states that Tukulti-Ninurta had begun campaigning when his reign prematurely ended.

Life's Work

Ashurnasirpal II came relatively young to the throne, but continued the expansion begun by his grandfather and father with unparalleled energy. The army was reorganized, with cavalry units introduced for the first time to supplement infantry, which were accompanied by chariotry. The latter afforded mobility during long treks. The bas-relief art of Ashurnasirpal portrays improved vehicles of six-spoked wheels pulled by four horses, with three men standing upon the armored platform. Ashurnasirpal fired bow and arrow from such a chariot, and the increased firepower was a significant development for his military strategy and tactics. The army was furnished with battering rams and other siege machines. The former appear as a kind of pointed-nosed tank with four wheels, propelled against city gates by the strength of the many men who could be sheltered under its armored top and sides. It was during Ashurnasirpal's reign that elephants were first employed by a king on campaign.

With Ashurnasirpal came an advanced art of beleaguering cities, and few were prepared to withstand his attack. Sculptures show these sieges, the prodigious amounts of tribute garnered, and a propagandistic expression of the requisite levels of brutality. In his inscriptions, Ashurnasirpal claimed to have employed this brutality so that conquered domains would not again rebel by withholding tribute. Minor princes saw the better part of valor in paying the requisite tribute before the siege and annually thereafter.

Ashurnasirpal's army employed its innovative tactics in continuous campaigns throughout his reign, although specific details are fully documented only for his initial years, from 883 to 878. Some scattered, undated events of the following decade and a half can be identified, but during this later period, the main energy of the king was given over to architectural construction and artistic enterprises recording the events of the first years.

Of the surrounding lands, only Babylonia in the south was not invaded during Ashurnasirpal's reign. The most significant results of Ashurnasirpal's campaigns were in the north and northwest. The land of Nairi (later Armenia) and the Habur region were secured. He forced the ruler of Bit-Adini on the Euphrates to pay tribute and thus secured a bridgehead across that river, allowing not merely his army but also his merchant envoys to pass without duty. Later campaigns took him as far as the Mediterranean, where in a traditional gesture he dipped his weapon into the sea to symbolize its incorporation within his empire.

The methods of drawing conquered peoples into the Assyrian empire were redefined. Adopting the words of an ancient predecessor Tukulti-apal-Esharra I (also called Tiglath-pileser), Ashurnasirpal affirmed, "To Ashur's land I added land, to Ashur's people I added people." His annexation proceeded in three ways. First, peripheral states were assumed to owe lavish tribute, which was collected whenever the Assyrian army was at their borders. Second, interim states submitting directly to Assyria paid yearly, nonruinous tribute and retained native rulers and almost complete self-government. The Assyrian official who remained to see that tribute was sent regularly to the capital could call on the army to enforce compliance. Third, conquered neighboring states became direct provinces, receiving an appointed governor supported by a military garrison. These states were under the same administrative system as Assyria itself and were required to pay the same taxes in goods or in conscripted labor and military service.

To control an empire conceived in these new ways with enlarged levels of displayed military power required not only a new capital city but also a revised conception of its fortresslike structure. The new capital at Kalhu was laid out by Ashurnasirpal on the east bank of the Tigris, nineteen miles north of its junction with the Greater Zab; its walls enclosed an irregular rectangle some seven thousand feet east to west by fifty-five hundred feet north to south, an area of 884 acres.

Two citadels formed the southeast and southwest corners within the walls which Ashurnasirpal completed. The *ekal masharti*, or arsenal, occupied the somewhat lower southeast citadel, but it was not fully completed until the days of his son Shalmaneser III (named for Shalmaneser I, whom Ashurnasirpal knew to have begun the original fortifications on the site of Kalhu).

On a height some sixty-five feet above the plain, the original acropolis of the southwest citadel formed an irregular rectangle because of the abutment of its western edge along the original bed of the Tigris. In the northwest corner, the remains of the ziqqurat rose to a conical peak one hundred feet high; at its base Ashurnasirpal built the temple for the war god Ninurta.

To the south of the ziqqurat and accompanying temple, a huge palace complex occupied six and a half acres; upon its rediscovery in the mid-nineteenth century it was dubbed the "Northwest Palace of Ashurnasirpal II." At its northern end was the administrative wing, with a variety of bureaucratic chambers, including a records repository, surrounding a great open court area which was used for ceremonial and reception functions. At the southern end were the domestic suites, including harem quarters. In neither of these wings were the walls decorated with bas-relief slabs.

Beginning from the south side of the great open court of the northern administrative wing, stretching southward to the southern domestic wing, was a central ceremonial block, which opened impressively off the southern side of the great courtyard through two massive, magnificently decorated gateways leading to the largest room of the palace, the throne room. With the exception of one built by Sennacherib at Ninua (Nineveh), the room is the largest within any Assyrian palace, measuring 154 feet by 33 feet. Tribute bearers from all parts of the empire were led into this room, as the bas-relief slabs of the entrance document, with details such as the type of tribute borne and the garments worn by the divergent ethnic representatives.

On the south side of the throne room lay an inner courtyard. Beyond, through a series of gateways, was a further maze of chambers, many of them decorated, like the throne room, with huge bas-relief slabs standing at least seven feet high from floor level. Only the throne room walls portray the fury of the king as hunter of lions and destroyer of cities. Another nine rooms have slabs with a single large relief, cut across the middle by a band of inscription right over the figures. Each room shows minor variations in lines of text or exact detail of royal campaigns during the first six years, reflecting the sequence in the construction process. In one corridor leading to the throne room, an inscribed stela of 864, with a relief portraying the king, records a celebration of the completion of the great palace and an exotic arboretum—a banquet at which 69,574 people from the extent of the empire, including the sixteen thousand inhabitants of Kalhu and fifteen hundred palace officials, were in attendance. The menu was varied and prodigious, and the feast lasted ten days.

When Ashurnasirpal died, in 859, his body was laid to rest in a gigantic sarcophagus made from a single block of diorite weighing eighteen tons, at the old capital of Ashur, the source of the Assyrian royal tradition. His inscribed memorial stela was placed in the row with his predecessors'.

Summary

Numerous portraits of the king came from the sculptured rooms. Sections of this bas-relief have been excavated and sent to many parts of the world, making Ashurnasirpal's face the best-known of all Assyrian kings'. A variety of quasi-human, quasi-divine creatures are shown accompanying the king in the performance of ritual duties. The inner core of the ceremonial midsection of the palace was the setting for a peculiar mix of propagandistically displayed belligerence, formally arranged processionals, and mysterious rites of purification. The effect was that the farther the king and his advisers penetrated into the inner chambers, the more they perceived the need for exorcism. Fearful things of humans and gods surrounded Ashurnasirpal II. Empire was an awesome matter, even for its creator.

He was succeeded by his son Shalmaneser III, grandson Shamshi-Adad V, and great-grandson Adad-nirari III, who attempted to match the achievements of their distinguished predecessor. At a later date, Sargon II remodeled a section of the great palace for his own use, leaving inscriptional tribute to his ancestor. Esarhaddon rebuilt the *ekal masharti* and the canal which provided water from the Zab, but was at his death in the process of dismantling the "Northwest Palace" so that he might use the reverse of its wall slabs in the decoration of a palace which he had only begun to construct. Ashurbanipal reconstructed the Ehulhul Temple at Harran, which Ashurnasirpal II had founded, and honored the earlier king's work. Then began that silence from which his memory was not disinterred until A.H. Layard began excavations at Kalhu on November 9, 1845, and brought to light the remarkable bas-reliefs, the inscriptions, and the monumental buildings of Ashurnasirpal II.

Bibliography

Brinkman, J.A. *A Political History of Post-Kassite Babylonia, 1158-722 B.C.* Rome: Pontificium Institutum Biblicum, 1968. This standard of historiographic excellence mines all material pertinent to the period with enormous bibliographic detail in its extensive notes.

Grayson, A.K. *Assyrian Royal Inscriptions.* Vol. 2, *From Tiglath-pileser I to Ashur-nasir-apli II.* Wiesbaden, West Germany: Otto Harrassowitz, 1972. A complete reediting in English translation of all source materials is the intention of this series. A consideration of Ashurnasirpal II occupies about half of this volume.

Mallowan, M.E.L. *Nimrud and Its Remains.* 3 vols. London: Collins, and New York: Dodd, Mead, 1966. Sir Max Mallowan reexcavated the principal features of Kalhu between 1949 and 1962. These volumes, the third of which contains maps and plans, detail the history of the site, the previous excavations, and the materials found in the remains of Ashurnasirpal's "Northwest Palace."

Paley, S.M. *King of the World: Ashur-nasir-pal II of Assyria 883-859 B.C.* Brooklyn, N.Y.: Brooklyn Museum, 1976. Many museums around the world received examples of the bas-relief slabs from the "Northwest Palace." The Brooklyn Museum used the occasion of publishing its own holdings to reconstruct the plan of the palace and identify the original location of all known examples.

Reade, J.E. "Assyrian Architectural Decoration." *Baghdader Mitteilungen* 10/11 (1979/1980): 17-110, 71-87. This series of articles provides a comprehensive comparative study of the four major Assyrian palaces excavated since the mid-nineteenth century, with reference to techniques and subject matter, narrative composition, the immense scale of the art, and the architectural context.

Stearns, J.B. *Reliefs from the Palace of Ashurnasirpal II.* Graz, Austria: Ernst F. Weidner, 1961. John Barker Stearns began the effort to identify all surviving examples of Ashurnasirpal palace relief slabs held in museum collections around the world and to classify their types and functions.

Clyde Curry Smith

AŚOKA THE GREAT

Born: c. 302 B.C.; probably near Pataliputra, Magadha, India

Died: c. 232 B.C.; place unknown

Areas of Achievement: Government and religion

Contribution: Through energetic and enlightened administration of his kingdom, Aśoka spread the Buddhist faith in all directions and, by means of his Rock, Pillar, and Cave edicts, provided India, the districts surrounding India, and, ultimately, the entire world with an example of regal compassion that is as admirable as it is rare.

Early Life

What can be known of the life of Aśoka derives from two primary sources: first, the legends that sprang up during and after his death (and which are often suspected of helping to grind certain zealous religious axes); second, Aśoka's own "sermons in stone," the thirty-five edicts which he began issuing in 260 and which were inscribed on rocks, pillars hewn from sandstone, and the walls of caves in the Barabar Hills of ancient Magadha. Therefore, only a very fragmentary early life can be pieced together. There is much to be left to conjecture and little to be known with certainty.

Aśoka was the son of Bindusara and the grandson of Chandragupta Maurya, the founder of the Mauryan dynasty and consolidator of a great empire that included all northern India as far west as the Hindu Kush. A charming legend is told of the naming of Aśoka. His mother, who may have been named Subhadrangi, was supposedly kept away from the king's bed by party politics; finally gaining access to the bed, she bore the king a son and said thereafter, "I am without sorrow," which is to say, in Sanskrit, "Aśoka."

Aśoka is reputed to have been ungainly in appearance and, perhaps, to have been disliked by his father. In his early manhood, however, he was called upon by Bindusara to put down a revolt in Taxila and from there to proceed to Ujjain to act as a viceroy. Aśoka appears to have had numerous brothers and sisters, and, if certain Ceylonese legends are accepted, he was most cruel to his brothers in the process of jockeying for the succession to the throne, murdering ninety-nine of them before becoming king. Such an account, however, may well be part of the tradition of Chandasoka (Black Aśoka), the epithet intended to indicate that, before his conversion to Buddhism, he was a man whose ruthlessness and cruelty knew no bounds. That there was a struggle for the throne is supported by the fact that Aśoka's accession to it (c. 274) occurred four years before his coronation. That blood might have been shed in the process of Aśoka's becoming king seems not unlikely. Hsuan Tsang, a Chinese Buddhist pilgrim who traveled in India in the seventh century A.D., reports having seen a high pillar which commemorated the site of what had been called "Aśoka's Hell," a prison which housed a series of elaborate torture chambers. According to one of the legends, Aśoka's enlightenment came about when he beheld a Buddhist holy man whose imperviousness to torture moved him to become aware in a painful way of his cruelty, destroy the prison, and relax the laws against criminals. Solider evidence, however, indicates that Aśoka's conversion may well have been the consequence of his beholding, not the indestructibility of a holy man, but rather the extreme destructibility of the Kalinga people in southeastern India. In 262, Aśoka fought and won a war against the Kalingas; in Rock Edict 13, referring to himself as "Priyadarsi, Beloved of the Gods," he chronicled his conversion, noting that 150,000 persons were captured, 100,000 were slain, and many times that number had died from the general effects of the war. The havoc that the war had wreaked had caused Aśoka to become intensely devoted to the study, love, and inculcation of *dharma*. This intense devotion, coupled with his sorrow and regret, had led him to desire "security, self-control, impartiality, and cheerfulness for all living creatures." He went on in the edict to announce a radical new program for his empire: He would abandon military conquest and would try to effect moral conquest in and among people.

Life's Work

In 260, Aśoka issued the first of the Rock Edicts and made his first "pious tour." Both edict and tour were part of his plan to endow his people with *dharma*. The concept of *dharma* is a complex one generally, and it becomes no simpler in Aśoka's use of it. For him, it had to do both with his Buddhist underpinnings and with morality and righteousness in general. *Dharma* was something he did out of Buddhist piety; it was also a complex of responses to life available to non-Buddhists. It was a kind of ecosystem, a recognition that one's well-being was closely and eternally connected with the well-being of everyone else. Aśoka's attempt to promulgate this understanding represents a tremendous evolution in the moral development of mankind.

Aśoka had the edict written in the languages of the districts where they were to be placed. Monumental Prakrit, a kind of lingua franca for India at the time, was the primary language of the edicts, but on the western frontier of the kingdom, edicts written in Greek and Aramaic have been found. Noting that in past times rulers had made great pleasure trips through the land, Aśoka determined to embark upon another series of tours, during which he would talk to people about *dharma*, visit the aged, and give gifts and money to those in need.

In 257, Aśoka appointed the first *dharma-mahamatras*, the officers of an institution charged with traveling about the kingdom and helping to spread *dharma*. Interestingly, these men were responsible for spreading the Aśokan notion of *dharma* through all sects; they were not supposed to attempt sectarian conversions but were rather to supervise the distribution of various gifts and to help promote conformity to the ideals of compassion, liberality, truthfulness, purity, gentleness, and goodness. Aśoka worried about the almost reflexive tendency of people dedicated to a particular religion to quarrel over dogma, and some of his sternest statements in the edicts address this problem; in one inscription, he baldly proclaims that dissident nuns and monks must be expelled from their order. Aśoka recognized two ways in which people could advance in *dharma*: moral prescription and meditation. The teachers of any religious sect, be it Buddhist, Christian, Islamic, or any other, are always ready to provide moral prescription. So, in fact, was Aśoka, and he did so in the edicts. In Pillar Edict 7, however, he acknowledged that people make greater progress in *dharma* through practicing meditation than through heeding moral prescription.

There has been considerable argument concerning the precise nature of Aśoka's religion. The edicts have little to say of doctrinaire Buddhism. Aśoka's tolerance of other religions is declared clearly and eloquently in the inscriptions. He often spoke of *svarga* (Heaven) and the possibility of obtaining it through *dharma*. He had nothing to say on stone or pillar of *nirvana*, a veritable plank in the Buddhist platform. Some scholars have been led by these facts to suggest that Aśoka was—as

Akbar was to be almost two thousand years later—a practitioner of some sort of universal religion. In many other ways, however, Aśoka strongly supported and promoted *dharma* as revealed in and through Buddhism, and his religion's spread through western Asia during his reign was certainly in part a result of those tremendous administrative energies that helped further his humanitarian purposes.

Throughout the 250's, Aśoka made moral tours, erected Buddhist shrines, and commissioned edicts. In 258-257, he issued in one body the fourteen Major Rock Edicts and granted cave dwellings to the Ajivikas, an order of Buddhist monks. In 250, he made a pilgrimage to Lumbinī Garden, the birthplace of the Buddha, and erected there a commemorative pillar. In 243-242, he issued the Pillar Edicts.

According to one account of Aśoka's last days, by 232 he had lost his power to the high officials of the court. In his old age, Aśoka supposedly nominated as his successor Samprati, one of his grandsons. Under the influence of the usurping officers, Samprati proceeded to abuse his grandfather, reducing Aśoka's allowances so drastically that, finally, for dinner the aging king would be sent only half an amalaka fruit on an earthen plate. How or where Aśoka died remains a matter of conjecture, but that he died in straitened circumstances seems likely.

Summary

That might makes right is an idea that has been taken for granted by such historical leaders as Alexander the Great, Julius Caesar, and Genghis Khan. What made Aśoka great was his grasping another truth and giving it life in third century India. In Rock Edict 13, he asserted that "the chiefest conquest is the conquest of Right and not of Might," and he went on to make his deeds commensurate with his rock-inscribed words. He abolished war within his empire immediately after he had subdued the Kalingas. He never fought another one. That he desired to civilize both his people and neighboring peoples is made clear by the testimony of the edicts; the usual formula, however, the one that equates civilization of a people with subjugation, did not apply. Aśoka did not give up entirely the idea that chastisement may on occasion be necessary, though, for he reminded the forest people who had come under his sway that they must grow in *dharma*, and he reserved the right to exercise punishment, despite having repented of his violent ways, in order to make them cease their criminal behavior. The edicts of Aśoka reveal a fascinating blend of the practical and the ideal, the proud and the humble; they record the workings of a complex mind.

Writing of Aśoka in *The Outline of History* (1921), H. G. Wells judged:

> Amidst the tens of thousands of names of monarchs that crowd the columns of history, their majesties and graciousnesses and serenities and royal highnesses and the like, the name of Aśoka shines, and shines almost alone, a star. From the Volga to Japan his name is still honoured. China, Tibet, and even India, though it has left his doctrine, preserve the tradition of his greatness. More living men cherish his memory to-day than have ever heard the names of Constantine or Charlemagne.

The high-flown rhetoric of this passage ought not to bias one against the beauty of its vision. If most people do not today cherish the memory of Aśoka above the memories of Constantine the Great and Charlemagne, that fact is perhaps a measure of the twentieth century's bad taste in heroes.

Bibliography

Ahir, D. C. *Aśoka the Great*. Delhi: B. R. Publishing, 1995. A general and laudatory biography that includes background on the rise of Buddhism and the founding of the Mauryan empire. The author traces Aśoka's career and posthumous reputation down to the 20th century and modern India. An appendix contains translations of Aśoka's major edicts.

Bhandarkar, D. R. *Aśoka*. 4th ed. Calcutta, India: Calcutta University Press, 1969. A spirited and at times combative rehearsal of Aśoka's life and works, dealing especially well with the Aśokan concept of *dharma* and according Aśoka a high place in history. Contains translations of the Rock and Pillar Edicts accompanied by detailed notes.

Campbell, Joseph. *The Masks of God: Oriental Mythology*. New York: Viking Press, 1959; London: Penguin Books, 1976. This volume contains a brief, but luminous, discussion of Aśoka, comparing the destiny of Buddhism under Aśoka to that of Christianity under Constantine the Great and noting the absence from the Rock Edicts of certain fundamental Buddhist doctrines.

Durant, Will. *Our Oriental Heritage*. New York: Simon and Schuster, 1935. Durant presents a respectful but slightly skeptical account of the life of Aśoka, seeing the seeds of the downfall of the Mauryas in the very piety of Aśoka that is so admired. Provides an especially vivid description, by way of Hsuan Tsang, of "Aśoka's Hell."

Mookerji, Radhakumud. *Aśoka*. 3d ed. Delhi: Motilal Banarsidas, 1962. A scholarly biography which, like Bhandarkar's book, accords Aśoka a high place in the moral annals of humankind. It contains copiously annotated translations of the Rock and Pillar Edicts and three cave inscriptions as well as appendices concerning the chronology of the edicts and the scripts, dialects, and grammar of the texts.

Nikam, N. A., and Richard McKeon. *The Edicts of Aśoka*. Chicago: University of Chicago Press, 1959. This handy translation of all the edicts except for the Queen's Edict and some variants of the minor edicts also features a brief introduction that makes interesting comparisons between Aśoka and other great world figures such as Hammurabi, Charlemagne, Akbar, and Marcus Aurelius.

Thapar, Romila. *Aśoka and the Decline of the Mauryas*. Rev. ed. New York: Oxford University Press, 1997. A thoroughgoing study of the life and times of Aśoka featuring an account of the disrepair into which his empire fell after his death. Includes numerous valuable appendices concerning the historical record of Aśoka's period based on pottery and coins, the geographical locations of the edicts, and the titles of Aśoka. A translation of the edicts is also provided.

Wells, H. G. *The Outline of History*. 4th ed. London: Cassell, and New York: Doubleday, 1961. A vivid and highly laudatory account of Aśoka, allotting him a more significant place in history than that of Alexander the Great and arguing that the epithet "great" is more properly applied to Aśoka.

Johnny Wink

ASPASIA

Born: c. 475 B.C.; Miletus, Asia Minor (modern Turkey)

Died: After 428 B.C.; probably Athens, Greece

Areas of Achievement: Government and politics; philosophy

Contribution: Aspasia's role as companion to the Athenian statesman Pericles made her the target of contemporary abuse and criticism; that same status and her reputation for skill in rhetoric made her a philosophic and historical ideal of the independent, educated, influential woman.

Early Life

Aspasia was born in the ancient Greek city of Miletus. Her father was named Axiochus; her mother's name is unknown. Located on the southwest coast of Asia Minor (modern Turkey), Miletus enjoyed a reputation for wealth based on extensive seaborne trade and for philosophic inquiry into the nature of the universe.

The city suffered severely in a Persian attack of 494 B.C. It is therefore not surprising that Miletus in 479 B.C. joined the Athenian-led league against Persia. The political and military relationship of Miletus with Athens was, however, problematic. For some years after 450 B.C., an Athenian garrison occupied the city, and toward the end (after 411 B.C.) of the long-term war of Athens with Sparta, Miletus was suspected of collusion with Athens' enemies. Nevertheless, during this same period, several Milesians left their home city to achieve prominence in Athens. Those emigrants included the city planner Hippodamus, the poet and musician Timotheus, and the most famous woman of fifth century Athens, Aspasia.

Life's Work

The surviving ancient sources for fifth century Athenian history do not permit a connected biography of Aspasia. The most reliable sources are a few notices in contemporary Athenian comic literature and several references to Aspasia by Socrates' pupils (including Plato). Many details are offered by the Greek biographer Plutarch in his *Life of Pericles*, but that brief account was written about A.D. 100, more than five hundred years after Aspasia's lifetime.

Aspasia must have come from Miletus to Athens before c. 450 B.C. She first appears in the historical record about 445 B.C., when the prominent Athenian politician and military leader Pericles (c. 495-429 B.C.) divorced—under, it was asserted, amicable circumstances—the mother of his two sons. Soon thereafter, Pericles began living and appearing in public with Aspasia. Ancient sources consistently identify her as a *hetaera*, a Greek term literally meaning "female companion" and used of women (often of slave or freedwoman status and usually of foreign origin) who were sexual, social, and occasionally intellectual nonmarital companions of prominent Athenian men.

Because of her status as a foreign-born, intelligent, articulate companion of Pericles, Aspasia was, throughout Pericles' later political career, consistently attacked as a malign influence on his public policies and his political and military leadership. She was, for example, viewed by Pericles' enemies as responsible for his leadership in a war Athens fought with the island of Samos, a traditional rival of Miletus. The Athenian comic poet Aristophanes, in his play *Acharnians* (425 B.C.), which amusingly, but quite seriously, expressed the Athenian longing for a peaceful resolution to military conflicts, represented Aspasia as partially responsible for provoking the Peloponnesian War between Athens and Sparta. Another Athenian comic poet, Aristophanes' peer Cratinus, referred to Aspasia on the stage as nothing but a shameless prostitute who influenced Pericles with her sex. A third Athenian comedian, Hermippus, also abused Aspasia publicly and was said to have prosecuted her for impiety in an Athenian court; Pericles, in turn, reportedly offered in court an emotional, tearful defense of his mistress. These legal episodes, however, are almost certainly apocryphal, prompted by later generations' overly-literal readings of Hermippus's comedies.

All these accusations simply reflect the perceived influence of a woman of independent judgment, education, intelligence, and resourcefulness. She may well have been, as were other *hetaerae*, the owner and operator of a brothel. She was certainly Pericles' mistress, but other prominent Athenian men of the time also enjoyed relationships with similar "companions." For example, Pericles' political opponent, the great Cimon—whose own sister, Elpinice, had once been the object of Pericles' attention—reportedly had liaisons with two *hetaerae*. In a later generation, the Athenian rheto-

rician Isocrates was reported to have had a similar female "companion".

More significant than the political abuse she attracted as Pericles' partner is the strong tradition that Aspasia was skilled at oratorical composition, instruction, and philosophic conversation. Pericles himself is recorded as praising her wisdom and sense of politics. Thus, several ancient authorities imply or allege that Aspasia advised Pericles on his own acclaimed public speeches (including the famous funeral oration of 430 B.C., reported in the works of Thucydides), and several sources state that she participated actively in philosophic argument with Socrates.

Aspasia had a child by Pericles. The son's irregular status had been defined by Pericles' own law denying Athenian citizenship to anyone who did not have two Athenian citizens as parents. Pericles' eldest son by his wife, Xanthippus (with whom his relationship was said to be tense), died in the great plague that struck Athens in 429 B.C.. Before Pericles' own death later that year, therefore, the Athenian democracy bestowed a special exemption so that his son born of Aspasia could become a Athenian citizen. Pericles the Younger, as he was called, grew to maturity and served the Athenian democracy as a general at the naval victory of Arginusae in 406 B.C.. Soon thereafter, however, he was among the generals executed by the Athenians for having failed to rescue naval crews after the battle.

After Pericles' death, Aspasia virtually disappears from the historical record. A single reference mentions that she became the companion of another rising politician, a man named Lysicles, who died in 428 B.C..

Summary

In his philosophic dialogue *Menexenos*, written after 387 B.C. and therefore after the life and prominence of its characters, Plato portrayed Socrates as praising Aspasia's literary and oratorical skills. Indeed, Plato presented Socrates as reciting a brief funeral oration claimed as Aspasia's own composition. Plato's depiction of Aspasia in this dialogue is sarcastic—Aspasia is said to have composed speeches well, for a woman—and typical. For Plato manifestly enjoyed pretending that some aspects of his master Socrates' knowledge were derived from sources other Athenians would have thought unlikely. Thus, in his dialogue *Symposium*, composed before 378 B.C., Plato asserted that Socrates learned the philosophic basis for and logical consequences of love from Diotima, a probably fictitious woman identified as coming from a rural Greek setting. Plato's mention of Aspasia, and the rhetorical exercise he attributed to her—along with the tradition about Aspasia maintained by other contemporaries in the circle of Socrates—turned her memory into a rhetorical commonplace: She became the ideal philosophic woman, one who could influence statesmen and converse on equal terms with philosophers.

This process of idealization began with Socrates' students Antisthenes and Aeschines, both of whom wrote philosophic dialogues entitled "Aspasia." The process continued in Greek philosophical and rhetorical schools down through the fourth century A.D. Aspasia's likeness adorned Roman gardens; much later, in the nineteenth century, she became the idealized figure of an educated ancient Greek woman and was represented in numerous academic paintings and historical novels. More recently, she has become a symbol of independence for the North American feminist movement; for example, Aspasia is prominently depicted in artist Judy Chicago's multimedia work *The Dinner Party* (1979).

Bibliography

De Ste. Croix, G. E. M. *The Origins of the Peloponnesian War*. London: Duckworth, and Ithaca, N.Y.: Cornell University Press, 1972. A scholarly, detailed, and convincing discussion of the issues that led to the Peloponnesian War. The policies and personality of Pericles are treated prominently throughout. The accusations made against Aspasia regarding her influence on Pericles are discussed in pages 235-243.

Dover, K. J. "The Freedom of the Intellectual in Greek Society." In *Greeks and Their Legacy*. Oxford and New York: Blackwell, 1988. A critical examination of the tradition of Aspasia's trial for impiety. Pays full attention to social context and to the ancient evidence.

Ehrenberg, Victor. *The People of Aristophanes*. 3d ed. New York: Schocken, 1962. A classic introduction to Athenian society and social history in the age of Aspasia and Pericles. Ehrenberg provides (especially in pages 177-181) a reliable, lively treatment of what is known of the *hetaera* in Athenian society, and he discusses throughout what the Greek comic dramatists of fifth century Athens can—and cannot—tell modern readers about the realities of Greek life.

Henry, Madeleine M. *Prisoner of History: Aspasia of Miletus and Her Biographical Tradition.* New York: Oxford University Press, 1995. A rare attempt at writing the biography of an ancient woman for whom the sources are far from satisfactory. The first several chapters provide a scholarly account of Aspasia, with a critical review of the evidence for reconstructing her biography. The remainder of the book is an entertaining introduction to how Aspasia has been represented by primarily male interpreters in the literary, philosophic, and pictorial traditions of Western European society.

Kebric, Robert B. *Greek People.* 2d ed. Mountain View, Calif.: Mayfield, 1997. A reliable account of classical Greek history presented in terms of biographical portraits. Chapter 6 offers a highly readable, nuanced, but very traditional perception of Aspasia as a participant in fifth century aristocratic Athenian society.

Richter, Gisela M. A. *The Portraits of the Greeks.* Rev. ed. Oxford: Phaidon, and Ithaca, N.Y.: Cornell University Press, 1984. Pages 99-100 show a Roman portrait of Aspasia. The accompanying discussion is an important supplement to Henry's work.

Stadter, Philip A. *Commentary on Plutarch's Pericles.* Chapel Hill: University of North Carolina Press, 1989. Stadter's commentary is the best available introduction to the historical and historiographic issues surrounding Plutarch's presentation of Pericles and Aspasia.

Paul B. Harvey, Jr.

SAINT ATHANASIUS

Born: c. 293; Alexandria, Egypt

Died: May 2, 373; Alexandria, Egypt

Areas of Achievement: Religion and historiography

Contribution: For half a century, Athanasius helped to maintain Christian orthodoxy in the Eastern church from his position as Bishop of Alexandria. His defense of the doctrine of the Trinity was influential in the formulation of the Nicene Creed.

Early Life

Athanasius was born about A.D. 293 in Alexandria, one of the leading cities of Egypt. Since its founding in 332 B.C. by Alexander the Great, Alexandria had been a focal point of the Greco-Roman world. Its beautiful harbor served as a center for extensive trade with all parts of the Mediterranean. The native flax of Egypt was woven into linen which was shipped as far away as Britain, and Alexandria enjoyed a world monopoly on the papyrus plant and its products—not only writing materials but also sails, mats, and sandals.

With a population of a million or more in Athanasius' time, Alexandria was not only a commercial and administrative center but also one of the greatest centers of learning in the ancient world. The Alexandrian library preserved documents from all parts of the ancient Near East and accommodated scholars from the entire Mediterranean area. It was here that the Greek Old Testament, the Septuagint, had been translated from the original Hebrew by Jewish scholars. Alexandria was a cosmopolitan city with large populations of Egyptians, Jews, Greeks, and Romans. Its array of palaces and public buildings, gardens and groves, pagan temples and Christian churches, made Alexandria one of the wonders of the Roman Empire.

Athanasius' parents, who were moderately wealthy, provided him with a liberal education, typical of the Greek culture in which he lived. He learned Greek, Latin, Egyptian antiquities, philosophy, and religion, but it was the Holy Scriptures that impressed him most. Alexandria was a focal point of intense persecution of Christians during the reign of Diocletian and Galerius, and several of Athanasius' teachers, along with many church leaders, suffered martyrdom. Athanasius well understood the seriousness of converting to the Christian faith.

Athanasius was an earnest and diligent young man who early came to the attention of Alexander, the Bishop of Alexandria from 312 to 328. The bishop helped in the boy's education, and eventually Athanasius became his secretary and a presbyter under his supervision.

Athanasius was very small of stature, rather stooped, and somewhat emaciated in appearance. He had a forceful personality and sharpness of intellect. Though he was gentle and meek of spirit, he was driven by a determination to keep the orthodox Christian faith no matter what the cost, no matter how many opposed him. His inner intensity made him quick of movement and constantly active. He was known for his deep faith in God, and he manifested an ability to inspire steadfast loyalty in the congregations he served, despite persecution, exile, and denunciations.

Life's Work

The fierce persecution of the Church abruptly changed when Constantine became emperor and began to favor Christianity throughout the Empire. Such a sudden change must have been difficult for Athanasius and his fellow Christians to comprehend. The amazement and incredulity that they experienced is reflected in Eusebius of Caesarea's description of a church council:

> No bishop was absent from the table of the emperor. Bodyguards and soldiers stood guard, with sharp swords drawn, around the outer court of the palace, but among them the men of God could walk fearlessly and enter the deepest parts of the palace. At dinner [they ate with the emperor.] Easily one could imagine this to be the kingdom of Christ or regard it as a dream rather than reality.

Some of those who enjoyed Constantine's favor bore scars from the Diocletian era, such as Bishop Paphnutius from Egypt, who had lost an eye in that persecution, and Paul of Caesarea, who had been tortured with a red-hot iron under Licinius and was crippled in both hands. A disadvantage of Constantine's patronage of the Church, however, was that the power of the state would be used to enforce church discipline, as Athanasius learned later when he was exiled by Constantine to the Rhineland region of Germany.

The Roman emperor called the first ecumenical council of the Church, which met at Nicaea, in

Asia Minor, in 325. ("Ecumenical" literally means "of the empire.") Constantine himself presided over the beginning sessions of this great assembly of the leadership of the Church and in so doing set an important precedent of involvement between church and state that lasted throughout the European Middle Ages and into modern times: Decisions of church councils were to be enforced by political authorities. For many years there had been local and regional synods or councils, but the idea of bringing together the entire Church, East and West, was new.

The Nicene Council met only twenty miles from the imperial palace of Nicomedia, easily accessible by sea and land from all parts of the Roman Empire. Some three hundred bishops and more than a thousand presbyters and laymen assembled in an effort to bring unity to the Church. Most of these people were from the Eastern church; only seven came from Europe. At least one, a Persian bishop, was from outside the Roman Empire. The council met from mid-June to the end of July, discussing theology and matters ecclesiastical in Latin and translating speeches into Greek.

Athanasius, a young archdeacon at the time, accompanied his bishop, Alexander, and spoke often at the council, demonstrating a brilliant intellect and impressive eloquence. Though only twenty-seven at the time, Athanasius set forth an influential defense of the orthodox position that Christ was God from all eternity, uncreated and equal to God the Father. The result was the Nicene Creed, recited by millions of Christians worldwide in their liturgy:

> We believe in One God, the Father Almighty,
> Maker of all things visible and invisible,
> and in one Lord Jesus Christ, the Son of God, . . .
> begotten not made, One in essence with the Father,
> by Whom all things were made, both things in Heaven
> and things in Earth. . . .

The Nicene Creed is acknowledged by Eastern Orthodox, Roman Catholic, and Protestant churches alike. The Greek Orthodox Church annually observes (on the Sunday before Pentecost) a special feast in memory of the Council of Nicaea.

In 328, Athanasius succeeded Alexander as Bishop of Alexandria and remained in that position, except for five exiles, for forty-six years. As a defender of the orthodox faith, he was popular in the Alexandrian church where he ministered. He was, however, opposed by the Arians, those who thought of Christ as a great teacher, but less than God Himself. The Emperor Constantine, more interested in unity than in truth, thought the matter merely one of theological semantics. Hoping to have more uniformity and less discord in the Church, he removed Athanasius from his office and banished him from Alexandria.

When Constantine died in 337, Athanasius returned, but soon he was exiled a second time for seven years, which he spent in Rome, where the orthodox position was strongly affirmed. The sons of Constantine, acting on the suggestion of Julius, Bishop of Rome, convened another church council at Sardica in 343. There Athanasius was reinstated as bishop.

Before long it became apparent that the differences between the Arian bishops and the orthodox leaders were more than doctrinal. The Arians gained support from the Roman Emperor Constantius because of their belief that the Church should submit to the emperor in doctrinal as well as administrative matters. Arguing from Scripture, Athanasius insisted on the independence of the Church in doctrine. As a result, Athanasius in 356 was again sent into exile, this time for six years in the Egyptian desert, where he became a close acquaintance of the famed Anthony, who helped begin the Western system of monasteries.

In 361, the pagan Emperor Julian recalled banished bishops on both sides of the controversy. By diligent and wise administration, Athanasius restored harmony to his diocese, but Julian exiled him for a fourth time and sent two hired assassins to kill him on board an imperial ship. Athanasius, however, managed to escape from the ship while it was sailing up the Nile River.

Athanasius returned to Alexandria after Julian's death, but endured yet a fifth and final brief exile under the Emperor Valens. He spent the last seven years of his life mostly undisturbed in his diocese. He continued writing, content to see the vindication of the orthodox position in the Church. He died in 373; his epitaph, "Athanasius contra mundum" (Athanasius against the world), reflected the steadfastness with which he had stood his ground against all opposition.

Throughout his tumultuous life, Athanasius was a prolific writer. He was noted for his theological depth, intellectual precision, and clarity of style; he wrote to make his meaning plain, not to embellish or entertain. He incisively demolished his opponents' arguments and methodically built a logical structure for his own position. Most of his works were written in response to some pressing matter or in defense of an action or position. Though he wrote in Greek, his works are now known solely by their Latin titles.

Athanasius' writings fall into several categories. For example, he produced apologetical works in defense of Christianity, such as *De incarnatione Verbi Dei* (before 325; *On the Incarnation of the Word of God*). Many of his theological works were written to defend the orthodox Nicene faith. For example, he wrote a letter in this regard to the bishops of Egypt and Libya (356) and a commentary on the decrees of the Council of Nicaea (352), *Contra Arianos* (350; *An Apology Against the Arians*) and *Apologia ad Constantinum* (356; *An Apology to Constantius*). Athanasius also wrote exegetical works interpreting Scripture; in his commentary on the Psalms, he followed the allegorizing style of the Alexandrian school in identifying in these Hebrew worship songs many types of Christ and the Church. Also in this category is his synopsis of the Bible. Of his devotional works, his *Epistolae festales* (*The Festal Epistles*) are most interesting. During the Easter season, these letters were read in the churches to edify and exhort the congregations.

Summary

Athanasius was not a historian, but many of his writings provide important primary source materials for historians. His *Historia Arianorum* (*History of the Arians*) is a good example, as is *An Apology Against the Arians*. Athanasius is noted for his great accuracy and his practice of documenting his assertions. Thus, later generations were indebted to him not only for his histories but also for the compilation of many documents of the fourth century.

Athanasius' biography of Saint Anthony helped to extend the monastic system into Europe. Anthony, a native of Upper Egypt, lived a completely solitary life for a time in the Egyptian desert. Others who followed his example became known as monks, from the Greek word *monachoi* (people who live alone). Athanasius was impressed by Anthony's deep spirituality, and it was through Athanasius that Anthony began to realize that he needed to take more interest in the welfare of the Church. When Athanasius visited Rome in 340, during his second exile, he explained to the Roman Christians the life-style of the Egyptian monks and thus introduced monasticism into the Western church.

Because of the early period in which he lived, Athanasius' listing of the canon of Scripture has been of great interest to later theologians. His thirty-ninth Festal Epistle of Easter, 367, made mention of all the books now included in the New Testament, but in the older order of the Gospels, Acts, the General Epistles, Paul's Epistles (including Hebrews), and the Apocalypse. His Old Testament canon comprised twenty-two books, as in the Alexandrian Jewish system, not the older Talmudic listing of twenty-four. The Apocrypha, accepted by the later Roman Catholic church, was not included in Athanasius' list.

Throughout his long life, Athanasius demonstrated a remarkable lack of self-interest and ambition. Though he held one of the great bishoprics of the Eastern church, he never compromised what he was convinced to be the truth. His manner was humble and conciliatory, but for him, truth was not subject to political compromise. His contemporaries were strengthened by his stability, consistency, and courage in the midst of tribulation, and the later Church is indebted to him for the clarity of his theology.

Bibliography

Arnold, Duane W. H. *The Early Episcopal Career of Athanasius of Alexandria*. Notre Dame: University of Notre Dame Press, 1991. The author concentrates on the first seven years of Athanasius' episcopate in Alexandria. Dense and primarily concerned with reporting and adjudicating scholarly debates. Arnold argues for a positive assessment of the bishop's character, refuting those who see him as "violent and duplicitous."

Athanasius. *The Life of Saint Antony*. Westminster, Md.: Newman Press, 1950. Translated with notes by Robert T. Meyer. This brief volume brings insight into the thinking of a man who had a great influence upon Athanasius: the Egyptian monk Saint Anthony.

Barnes, Timothy D. *Athanasius and Constantius: Theology and Politics in the Constantinian Empire*. Cambridge, Mass.: Harvard University Press, 1993. Barnes provides a scrupulously researched account of Athanasius' career (though he is more concerned with political occurences than with exploring Athanasius' mind and personality). Barnes argues that the ecclesiastical and civil governments affected and influenced one another profoundly.

Brakke, David. *Athanasius and the Politics of Asceticism.* Oxford: Clarendon Press, and New York: Oxford University Press, 1995. The author pays close attention to Athanasius' writings on asceticism and argues that they represent a reinterpretation of ascetic practice as a way to unify Christians into a "heavenly polity." Athanasius wished to move the image of sanctity away from "intellectual contemplation of God" (something open to only a few) and toward "control of the body's passions" (an ideal open to all, in varying degrees).

Bruce, F.F. *The Spreading Flame: The Rise and Progress of Christianity from Its First Beginnings to the Conversion of the English.* Grand Rapids, Mich.: Wm. B. Eerdmans Publishing Co., 1953; London: Paternoster, 1958. An excellent detailed history of the early Church. There are many references to Athanasius, but the principal value of this book is in providing the historical context in which Athanasius lived. The author is an outstanding expert in his field.

Frend, W.H.C. *The Rise of Christianity.* Philadelphia, Pa.: Fortress Press, and London: Darton, Longman, and Todd, 1984. A useful introduction to church history. Includes a seventy-five-page chart which gives a synopsis of events in three categories from 63 B.C. to A.D. 615. Also includes five unusual maps which shed light on the text. Frend makes many references to Athanasius.

Latourette, Kenneth Scott. *A History of Christianity.* 7th ed. New York and London: Harper, 1945. The first three hundred pages of this classic fifteen-hundred-page history of Christianity are useful in interpreting Athanasius' role in the early Church and later Roman Empire.

Pettersen, Alvyn. *Athanasius.* Harrisburg, Penn.: Morehouse, and London: Geoffrey Chapman, 1995. This book treats Athanasius' thought and trinitarian theology rather than the outward course of his life. A good introduction to the subject that contains numerous quotations from Athanasius' writings.

Schaff, Philip. *History of the Christian Church.* Vol. 3, *Nicene and Post-Nicene Christianity, A.D. 311-600.* 3d ed. Peabody, Mass.: Hendrickson, 1996. The most exhaustive church history available in the English language. The section on Athanasius, Constantine, and the Nicene Council are absolutely indispensable for an understanding of the life and influence of Athanasius. Schaff is noted for the thoroughness of his history and the detailed precision of his narrative.

A Select Library of Nicene and Post-Nicene Fathers of the Christian Church. Vol. 4., *Athanasius: Select Works and Letters.* New York: Scribner, 1889. This six-hundred-page book is indispensable for understanding Athanasius. It contains a detailed account of his extant writings, with helpful editorial notes. Contains index, tables, and appendix.

Shelley, Bruce. *Church History in Plain Language.* 2d ed. Dallas, Tex.: Word Books, 1995. Though this volume is rather sparse on Athanasius, it is valuable for its accessibility. Recommended for those with little background in church history. Makes clear what the conversion of Constantine meant to the Church.

William H. Burnside

ATTILA

Born: 406?; Pannonia?

Died: 453; probably Jazberin

Areas of Achievement: Government and conquest

Contribution: By uniting all the Hunnic tribes from the northern Caucasus to the upper Danube River, rendering the Romans a tributary state, Attila fashioned the most powerful empire of the West in the fifth century.

Early Life

The movement of the Huns from Asia westward through the steppes in the fourth century caused the Great Migration of Germans and Alans into Europe. By 420, the Huns had found a home in Pannonia, the seat of the main body of the nation, which was divided into three ulus, each ruled by a khan. Here was a strategic base for later operations in Italy and the Balkans. The Huns' superior cavalry tactics were well publicized, and the Romans of the East and West soon realized the need to appease them.

When Khan Roila died in 433 or 434, two of his nephews, Attila and his brother Bleda, were elected as joint rulers. Nothing is known of the early life of Attila or of his grandparents and mother. He was the son of Mundjuk, brother of Roila and Oktar. Mundjuk may have been a co-khan with Roila, but the evidence is unclear. What is certain is that Mundjuk and Oktar died before Roila did and that Attila became the chief khan, subordinating his older brother from the start.

The Roman statesman and writer Cassiodorus described Attila as Asian in appearance, beardless, flat-nosed, and swarthy. His body was short and square, with broad shoulders. He was adept at terrorizing enemies with the use of his deep-set eyes. Edward Gibbon, in *History of the Decline and Fall of the Roman Empire,* says that he was feared as much for his magic as for his militarism.

Life's Work

The death of Roila brought relief to Constantinople since the late king of the Huns was planning an invasion of Eastern Rome. Bishops attributed his death to the intervention of God. Attila quickly exhibited a genius for leadership and statesmanship. His first task was to settle the disputes with the Romans at Constantinople, demanding an end to the use of Huns in their service. Attila and Bleda met Roman envoys from both empires at the River

Morava to sign a treaty in 434. Negotiating from horseback, as was the Hunnic custom, they secured from Emperor Theodosius II the promise to end the use of Hunnish warriors, the return of those in his service, free access to border towns for Hunnish merchants, and the doubling of the annual tribute of gold from 350 to 700 pounds. Two of the fugitives handed back to the Huns were young boys, Mama and Atakam, relatives of the khans who summarily were crucified. The Roman Flavius Aetius continued to use Huns and Alans against Germans in the West.

After this treaty of Margus with Theodosius, Attila and Bleda devoted their efforts to consolidating the eastern possessions. Striving to unite all the ulus under their rule, the khans forged an empire from the northern Caucasus to central Europe. Within five years this objective was reached, and the brothers divided their administration into two sections.

Meanwhile Persians attacked Roman Armenia in 438 in a war that lasted fifteen years, and the Romans were hoping to recover Carthage in North Africa from the Vandals, who posed a danger to Roman shipping. Partly because of other problems, the Roman emperor neglected payments to the Hun and was preparing new operations against the Vandal Gaiseric and the Sassanian shah in Persia, allies of Attila. With the opportunity at hand, Attila launched an invasion of the Eastern Roman Empire in 441. Gibbon says that this move was prompted by Gaiseric. In any case, Attila's forces moved rapidly across the Morava, seizing Margus, Constantia, Singidunum (Belgrade), and Sirmium, the key to the defense of the Danube. A puzzling one-year truce followed, enabling the Romans to prepare for defense. An angry Attila launched a new offensive in 443, destroying Ratiaria and Naissus, birthplace of Constantine, and Sardica (Sophia), thus opening the highway to the capital. Roman armies led by Aspar, an Alan, contested the Huns but were no match for the swiftly moving forces of Attila. Although Constantinople was well defended by troops and terrain, Theodosius decided to sue for peace and so paid six thousand pounds of gold to Attila to make up for his arrears of tribute. The treaty of Anatolius was signed on August 27, 443.

Within two years, Bleda was officially removed from power and soon after was killed by Attila himself. No details exist about the power struggle

between the brothers. Attila was master of the entire Hunnic world empire and would have no more rivals.

The location of Attila's court is only educated conjecture. Hungarians argue that it was located about thirty-six miles west of Buda, at Jazberin. Others suggest that the location was at Tokay or Agria, all in the plains of upper Hungary. This court included a wooden palace on a hill, as well as another for his chief wife, Queen Cerca, houses for his adjutants, storehouses, service buildings, and even a stone bathhouse. All were enclosed by a wooden wall. At table, Attila ate only meat, used wooden utensils, and never tasted bread. Inside the spacious palace were servants of many nationalities: Alans, Greeks, Germans, Romans, and Slavs.

The same international character prevailed within the Hunnish borders, as Attila's policy of no taxation attracted many settlers. Taxation was unnecessary, owing to the large tribute from Constantinople and annual collections of booty from warfare. Even the army comprised other nationalities. Persian engineers from the shah and deserters from the Romans helped Attila's forces pre-

pare for siege warfare against stone walls. Slavs, taught the methods of warfare by the Huns, formed special detachments in the khan's armies, evidenced by references to the troops drinking kvas.

The Huns invaded Rome again in 447, but there are no sources indicating the motive—perhaps Attila needed more plunder. The Eastern Romans were besieged by famine and plagues and not likely to provoke the Huns. Nevertheless, Attila invaded with armies of subject peoples augmenting his Huns. In the midst of the campaign, a fierce earthquake struck the Eastern Roman world, destroying sections of the walls around Constantinople. The people summoned the determination to rebuild the fortifications hastily and even constructed another, outer wall to ward off the Huns. West of the capital a pitched battle took place at Utus. Although the Huns won the battle, it was fought so energetically by the Romans that the Huns suffered serious losses. Choosing to bypass the capital, Attila contented himself with enormous plunder in the Balkans. This would be his last victory over Roman forces.

That same year, the khan received news of a renegade Hunnic nation in Scythia. The Acatziri were corresponding with the emperor at Constantinople, posing a danger to Attila's rearguard position. Consequently, Attila's forces crushed the rebels, and Ellac, Attila's son, was sent to rule over them. There followed the second peace of Anatolius, in 448.

Attila found it necessary to construct an intelligence network to combat Roman espionage. At one point his German agent, Edecon, was drawn into a scheme to assassinate Attila in 448. Sent to Constantinople on business, he was "bribed" by a Roman official of the emperor, the eunuch Chrysaphius, to join the plot. Loyal to Attila, Edecon feigned acceptance and exposed the affair to the khan, who then exploited the matter to obtain more tribute from Constantinople.

Attila next considered a plan to marry Honoria, the sister of Emperor Valentinian III. The Roman princess herself initiated the idea, perhaps in bitterness after having been placed in confinement by her mother for many years following a teenage pregnancy, or to avoid marrying an old Roman courtier and friend of her brother. The khan saw an opportunity to demand one-half of the imperial lands as dowry for the marriage. When the emperor's expected refusal arrived, Attila prepared for war. Honoria was sent to Ravenna, Italy, by Valentinian, who called upon Aetius to defend the imperial borders. Both sides sought allies as Aetius gained the support of Visigoths, Burgundians, and most of the Franks; Attila won the support of the younger of the two Frankish brother-rulers, as well as the Ostrogoths, Vandals, and Alans.

The Alans of Gaul were compelled to accede to Aetius, and the great battle of the nations occurred at Châlons in June, 451. The Huns were disheartened for failure to capture the city of Orléans and then weakened by guerrilla tactics as they made their way to plains more suited to their cavalry. Attila delivered an inspiring address to his soldiers on the eve of battle, but the opposing armies were strong. The coalitions fought a bloody encounter but the result was indecisive. Attila led his forces back to the Danube and the Visigoths retreated to Toulouse. His plan to take the Western Empire failed, so Attila prepared to invade Italy. Aetius found it more difficult to defend this region, since he feared the consequences of bringing Visigoths to Italy. In 452, Attila invaded across the Alps, coming to Milan, where he met Pope Leo (the Great) and two Roman senators, who convinced him to turn back. It was unlikely that idealism was the issue; rather, the epidemic of dysentery among his troops and the imminent arrival of Aetius' forces via Ravenna more likely encouraged the retreat. It is also probable that Leo gave ransom for the release of prominent prisoners. Nevertheless, the Huns devastated the plains of Lombardy, forcing many to flee to the lagoons of the Adriatic Sea, where the Venetian republic arose. Returning home, Attila wished instead to strike at Byzantium.

Once back in the Danubian country, however, the khan, who had numerous wives, married again, this time to a German named Ildico. After the usual wedding party, Attila lay down to rest and was later found dead in his bed (453). Despite rumors that he was stabbed or poisoned by Ildico (who was found at his bedside), it is more likely that he simply choked to death on vomit or blood from a hemorrhage. Hunnic warriors immediately cut off part of their own hair and disfigured their own faces with deep wounds, as was their mourning custom.

The khanate was divided among Attila's three sons: Dengizik, Ernack, and Ellac. The latter was killed the next year, when a rebellion occurred; the other two brothers took their ulus to Dacia and Bessarabia for a time. Other bands of Huns penetrated the right bank of the Danube, settling in the Roman world as allies. Most of the Alans supported the Byzantines when the forces of Dengizik were crushed in a war of 468-469. The Great Bulgarian nation of the Huns disintegrated in the East as well, as some joined Slavs to find their way to the southern Balkans to a land that bears their Hunnic name. Other Bulgar descendants of the Huns settled for a while on the upper Volga River until they were absorbed into the nomad empire of the Khazars.

Summary

Attila was never a divine-right monarch in the sense of a Persian shah or even the Macedonian Alexander the Great. He never posed as a god before his people but, rather, wore simple clothing without jewelry, mixing with his people—often without bodyguards. Attila did not create a permanent administrative structure for the Hunnic nation; his influence, while truly awesome, was temporary for the Huns. He seemed to profit little from cultural contacts with the Romans of the East or West; most artistic objects traced to Hunnish origins have been discovered in the Ukraine or Volga River regions, not from the Danubian plains. Nor did Attila's Huns adopt the Roman proclivity for the plow, as some eastern Huns did.

Attila's empire helped to hasten the fall of the Roman Empire in the West. Although his forces did not destroy the Roman imperial structure, they weakened the mystique of Rome by their continuous exactions of tribute. In the steppelands of the East, they destroyed the German and Iranian control of the Russian world, preparing the way for the next nomad empire, that of the Khazars, and even teaching the hitherto peaceful Slavs how to defend themselves from future invaders.

Ironically, by 451 the Roman tribute had ceased and the aura of Attila's invincibility had vanished. His armies had failed at Châlons, he could no longer intimidate subject nations, and his resources were quickly disappearing. Then, when the Italian campaign was cut short, his allies grew restive without the gold and booty of former days. Perhaps his timely death preserved his historical reputation.

Bibliography

Gibbon, Edward. *History of the Decline and Fall of the Roman Empire*. New York: Modern Library, 1932. A vivid picture of Attila's personality and his court is presented by this master eighteenth century historian, who has culled a wealth of detail from limited sources.

Gordon, G. D. *The Age of Attila: Fifth-Century Byzantium and the Barbarians*. Ann Arbor: University of Michigan Press, 1960. This valuable work cleverly arranges selections of primary sources to relate the history of Attila's age.

Jones, A. H. M. *The Decline of the Ancient World*. New York: Holt, Rinehart and Winston, and London: Longman, 1966. Jones's work includes a short but useful presentation of the relationships among Attila, Aetius, and Theodosius.

Macartney, C. A. "The End of the Huns." *Journal of Hellenic Studies* 10 (1934): 106-114. This article attempts to locate the various branches of the Huns following the death of Attila.

Mänchen-Helfen, Otto J. *The World of the Huns: Studies in Their History and Culture*. Edited by Max Knight. Berkeley: University of California Press, 1973. The most scholarly treatment of the subject, by a recognized authority who died before completing the manuscript. It is replete with excellent linguistic analysis of the sources.

Thompson, E. A. *A History of Attila and the Huns*. Oxford: Clarendon, 1948; Westport, Conn.: Greenwood Press, 1975. Still the most readable and clear presentation of the life of Attila. Its scholarly treatment holds up well under later academic scrutiny.

Vernadsky, George. *Ancient Russia*. New Haven, Conn.: Yale University Press, 1943. The chapter on the Huns is a short but remarkably complete story that is not limited to the settlements in Southern Russia. The author was the leading authority on Russian history in America for many years.

John D. Windhausen

SAINT AUGUSTINE

Born: November 13, 354; Tagaste, Numidia
Died: August 28, 430; Hippo Regius, Numidia
Areas of Achievement: Religion and philosophy
Contribution: Renowned for his original interpretations of Scripture and extensive writings—in particular, his *Confessions*—Augustine was the greatest Christian theologian of the ancient world.

Early Life

Aurelius Augustinus was born of middle-class parents, Patricius and Monica, in the Roman province of Numidia (now Algeria). His pious mother imbued him with a reverence for Christ, but as he excelled in school he found the Church's teachings and practices unsatisfactory. As he studied at nearby Madauros and then Carthage, he was swayed by various philosophies. From 370 to 383, with the exception of one year in Tagaste, he taught rhetoric in Carthage. Part of these early years were wasted (he later regretted) on womanizing, but this experience created in him a lifelong sensitivity to overcoming the desires of the flesh. Upon the birth of an illegitimate son, Adeodatus, in 373, Augustine identified himself with the prophet Mani, who had preached a belief in the spiritual forces of light and darkness which also included Christ as the Redeemer. Hoping to explore the tension in this dualism, Augustine was disappointed by the shallow intellect of the Manichaean bishop Faustus and became disillusioned with that faith.

Desirous of a fresh outlook and a better teaching position, Augustine sailed to Rome in 383 and the next year began teaching rhetoric in Milan. There he was awakened to the potential of Christian theology by the sermons of Saint Ambrose and, in particular, the Neoplatonism of Plotinus. In this philosophy—the beliefs of Plato adapted to Christianity by Plotinus—the individual can only know true existence and the one God by searching within to attain unity with God's love. Only spiritual faith, and not reason or physical appearances, could provide the ultimate answers. At first a skeptic, Augustine began his inner search and in 386 had a mystical experience in which he believed he had discovered God. Resigning his teaching position, Augustine converted completely to Christianity and was baptized by Ambrose at Milan in the spring of 387.

Life's Work

Augustine plunged into the cause of discovering and articulating God's will as a Christian philosopher. He did so with such zeal that a steady stream of treatises flowed from his pen. He returned to Numidia in 389 and established a monastery at Hippo, intending to live there quietly and write. He was ordained as a priest in 391, and he became Bishop of Hippo in 396. Thus, instead of developing his theological ideas systematically, Augustine revealed them in sermons, letters in reply to queries for guidance, tracts against separatists, and books. In addition, he wrote a lengthy autobiography of his early life, *Confessiones* (397-400; *Confessions*).

God, in Augustine's view, is at the center of all events and explanations. Such a theocentric philosophy depends on Holy Scripture; for Augustine, the Psalms, Genesis, and the First Letter of John were especially important. His commentaries on the first two sources are famous treatises, along with *De Trinitate* (c. 419; *On the Trinity*) and *De civitate Dei* (412-427; *The City of God*).

God, as "the author of all existences" and "the illuminator of all truth," is Wisdom itself and therefore the highest level of reality. The second level is the human soul, which includes memory, understanding, and will. By looking to God, the individual discovers the true knowledge that God has already bestowed upon him. All things emanate from that ultimate authority; through faith, one gains truth, the use of reason being only secondary. The third and lowest level of reality is the human body, whose greatest ethical happiness can only be realized by aspiring to God's love. Human beings are endowed with the free choice to do good or evil, but God by divine grace may bestow the greater freedom of enabling a person to escape an attraction to evil. Similarly, revelation frees the mind from skepticism. By grappling with the elusive problem of evil, Augustine managed to bring better focus to an issue of universal concern to all religions.

Also a practical thinker, Augustine was an acute observer of the natural universe. By focusing on God in nature, however, and believing that true knowledge came only through spiritual introspection, he came to regard physical things as least important and science as having little utility. Faith rather than reason provides the ultimate truth. By the same token, Augustine viewed history optimistically; humankind was saved by Christ's sacrifice on the Cross, the premier event of the past.

The collapse of Roman hegemony to barbarian invasions, even as Augustine preached his sermons on faith, caused many doubters to blame Christianity for Rome's decline. Augustine refuted this accusation in *The City of God*. He envisioned two cities, the heavenly City of God and the other one an earthly entity, patterned respectively after the biblical examples of Jerusalem—which means "Vision of Peace"—and Babylon, permeated with evil. Whereas perfection is the hallmark of the City of God, Augustine offered important guidelines for the conduct of human cities. Earthly "peace" he defined as harmonious order, a condition whereby a person, a community, or a state operates by the ideals of felicity (good intentions) and virtue (good acts) without suffering under or imposing dominion. No pacifist, Augustine believed that a nation might go to war, but only on the authority of God and then to achieve a "peace of the just." "Good men undertake wars," he wrote to Faustus the Manichaean in 398, to oppose evil enemies: "The real evils in war are love of violence, revengeful cruel-ty, fierce and implacable enmity, wild resistance, and the lust of power."

The greatest challenge to Augustine's teachings centered on the issue of how the individual might escape the evils of the flesh—whether by one's own choice or by the initiative of God through divine grace. Augustine insisted on the latter and regarded the Pelagians as heretics for arguing the former view. As Saint Paul taught, each person is guilty of Original Sin, must admit it, and can only accept salvation from God's grace through the Holy Spirit. Indeed, Augustine concluded early in his episcopate that God decides which elected souls will receive divine grace—a clear belief in the predestination of each individual. The barbarian army of the Vandals was at the gates of Hippo when Augustine died.

Summary
Saint Augustine was, by any measure, a genius of Christian philosophy and has been so venerated since his death. That all subsequent Christian thinkers owe him an immense debt is evident from the continuous outpouring of reprints of his vast works and discussions concerning his ideas. He brought focus to the major issues which continue to challenge the Church to the present day, and he motivated key figures to adopt aspects of his thinking outright. In the early Middle Ages, Charlemagne founded the Holy Roman Empire in the mistaken belief that Augustine's *The City of God* had been written as a blueprint for a divine kingdom on earth. Saint Thomas Aquinas accepted Augustine's notions of predestination for the later Middle Ages, as did John Calvin during the Protestant Reformation. The power of Augustine's theology has remained undiminished through the ages.

Bibliography
Ancient Christian Writers: The Works of the Fathers in Translation. Rev. ed. New York: Newman Press, 1978. A major English-language multivolume collection of the early theological thinkers. Eight volumes have been published on Augustine.

Augustine, Saint. *The Essential Augustine*. Vernon Joseph Bourke, ed. 2d ed. Indianapolis: Hackett, 1974. An excellent collection of excerpts from Augustine's principal writings, introduced topically by this Thomist writer. Includes a bibliography. Still useful as an introduction is Bourke's *Augustine's Quest of Wisdom* (Milwaukee:

Bruce, 1945), augmented by Bourke's anthology of his own essays, *Wisdom from St. Augustine* (Houston: Center for Thomistic Studies, 1984).

Brown, Peter. *Augustine of Hippo.* Berkeley: University of California Press, and London: Faber, 1967. One of the best biographical accounts of Augustine, which uses the chronological approach to show Augustine's writings as they evolved during his lifetime. Heavily annotated. Complemented by Brown's volume which places Augustine in context: *Religion and Society in the Age of St. Augustine* (New York: Harper and Row, Publishers, 1972).

Chadwick, Henry. *Augustine.* Oxford and New York: Oxford University Press, 1986. This volume in the Past Masters series provides a concise introduction to Augustine's thought.

Deane, Herbert A. *The Political and Social Ideas of St. Augustine.* New York: Columbia University Press, 1963. A treatment of the theology and psychology behind Augustine's notion of "Fallen Man." Focuses on morality and justice, the state and order, war and relations among states, the church, state, heresy, and Augustine's view of history.

Gilson, Etienne. *The Christian Philosophy of St. Augustine.* Translated by L.E.M. Lynch. New York: Random House, 1960; London: Gollancz, 1961. Perhaps the best and most scholarly work on Augustine's philosophy. A translation of the 1943 version in French, more than half of which is annotations. Gilson regards Augustinianism as the discovery of humility, built upon charity.

Lawless, George P. *Augustine of Hippo and His Monastic Rule.* Oxford: Clarendon Press, and New York: Oxford University Press, 1987. An excellent summary of the lifetime work of the late Luc Verbraken, tracing the monastic orientation of Augustine's life and showing how his love of friends in a community setting established the monastic tradition in the Christian West.

LeMoine, Fannie, and Christopher Kleinhenz, eds. Garland Medieval Casebooks. Vol. 9, *Saint Augustine the Bishop: A Book of Essays.* New York: Garland, 1994. Proceedings of a conference held to commemorate Augustine's ordination as bishop of Hippo. Seven essays on such topics as "Augustine of Hippo as Preacher" (G. P. Lawless), "Augustine on the Resurrection" (G. O'Collins), "Augustine on History, the Church, and the Flesh" (C. P. Fredriksen).

McWilliam, Joanne. *Augustine: From Rhetor to Theologian.* Waterloo, Ontario: Wilfred Laurier University Press, 1992. A collection of 15 essays on Augustine's life and thought.

Markus, R.A., ed. *Augustine: A Collection of Critical Essays.* Garden City, N.Y.: Anchor, 1972. An anthology of in-depth essays by prominent interpreters of Augustine, extensive in its coverage of his various interests.

Nash, Ronald H. *The Light of the Mind: St. Augustine's Theory of Knowledge.* Lexington: University Press of Kentucky, 1969. Contests Augustine's illumination of knowledge as interpreted by Bourke, Gilson, and other Thomist writers.

Oates, Whitney J., ed. *Basic Writings of St. Augustine.* 2 vols. New York: Random House, 1948. Volume 1 includes the *Confessions,* volume 2 *The City of God* and *On the Trinity,* with introductions by Oates. Random House's Modern Library published the *Confessions* in 1949, translated by Edward B. Pusey with an introduction by Fulton J. Sheen, and *The City of God* in 1950, translated by Marcus Dods with an introduction by Thomas Merton.

O'Daly, Gerard. *Augustine's Philosophy of the Mind.* Berkeley: University of California Press, and London: Duckworth, 1987. The first monograph in more than a century to analyze Augustine's arguments about the mind.

O'Donnell, James J. *Augustine: Confessions.* 3 vols. Oxford: Clarendon Press, 1992. This is the only modern English commentary on the *Confessions,* and although it is suitable only for the relatively advanced student, it must be mentioned. The introductory sections contains a useful account of the history of Augustinian scholarship over the past century.

Starnes, Colin. *Augustine's Conversion: A Guide to the Arguments of Confessions I-IX.* Waterloo, Ontario: Wilfred Laurier University Press, 1990. An analytical account of the argument in the *Confessions* that considers Augustine's intellectual relationship to the Manichaeans, the neo-Platonists, the Stoics, and others.

Stock, Brian. *Augustine the Reader: Meditation, Self-Knowledge and the Ethics of Interpretation.* Cambridge, Mass.: Harvard University Press, and London: Belknap, 1996. An interesting but dense examination of Augustine's attitudes toward reading and interpretation, which the author shows to be intimately linked with the rest of his philosophy. Several chapters on the *Confessions* as well as discussion of other works.

van der Meer, F.G.L. *Augustine the Bishop*. London and New York: Sheed and Ward, 1961. Reviews Augustine's adult life after becoming Bishop of Hippo. Augmented by archaeological information from North African digs.

Clark G. Reynolds

AUGUSTUS
Gaius Octavius

Born: September 23, 63 B.C.; Rome

Died: August 19, A.D. 14; Nola

Area of Achievement: Government

Contribution: Through his political skill and intelligence, Augustus transformed the chaos that followed the assassination of Julius Caesar into the long-lasting Roman Empire.

Early Life

The first emperor of Rome was born Gaius Octavius, and during his youth he was known to history as Octavian. His family was an old and wealthy one from the small town of Velitrae (Velletri), about twenty miles southeast of Rome. The Octavii were not, however, a noble family; they were of the equestrian order, which meant that they did not sit in the Roman senate and thus could not hold the higher offices of the state. Octavian's father, a supporter of Julius Caesar, was the first of the family to achieve those distinctions; he died when Octavian was four.

Octavian's great-uncle was that same Julius Caesar whom he so admired, and Caesar discerned in the young man possibilities of future greatness. At sixteen, Octavian planned to accompany Caesar to Spain in his campaign against the forces of Pompey the Great, Caesar's enemy in the civil wars. Delayed by illness, Octavian followed Caesar, risking considerable hardship along the way, including a shipwreck from which he narrowly escaped. Although he arrived after the hostilities had ended, his daring and initiative greatly impressed Caesar.

In 44 B.C., while Caesar was preparing his campaign against the Parthian empire in the east, Octavian went on ahead, intending to join the army en route. He was in Apollonia, in the Adriatic coast, when he learned that Caesar had been assassinated in Rome on the ides of March (March 15). Along with this shocking news, he soon learned that in his will Caesar had named him heir to the bulk of the dictator's vast estate and, much more significantly, had adopted him. Although it was impossible to transmit political office or power through inheritance, Caesar had clearly signaled his choice of successor. Octavian, in turn, indicated his determination to claim his rights by an immediate return to Italy and by taking the name Gaius Julius Caesar.

At eighteen he was prepared to contest control of the Roman world.

Portrait busts, statues, and the writings of historians have left a clear picture of the first emperor. He was of average height and wore lifts in his sandals to appear taller. His hair was blondish, and his teeth were small and widely spaced. The ancient historian Suetonius describes Octavian as handsome, and other writers have remarked on his calm, quiet expression. He had clear, bright eyes and liked to believe that a certain divine radiance could be seen in them. Throughout his life he was bothered by a number of illnesses, some of them quite serious; perhaps because of his poor health he was temperate in his habits, drinking little and eating lightly. Although a conscientious administrator, he hated to rise early, and his chief pastime was gambling with his friends. More than anything else, his actions and achievements clearly indicate that he was a man of great ambition and clear intelligence with a profound perception of the qualities of others.

Life's Work

When Octavian returned to Italy, he had two immediate goals: to claim his inheritance from Caesar and to avenge his adoptive father's death. He first tried to establish an alliance with Marc Antony, a close associate and colleague of Caesar, but Antony took a harsh attitude toward the much younger man and even blocked the implementation of Caesar's will. As a result, Octavian went over to the side of the senate, which was attempting to regain control of the state. With the help of Octavian and an army raised largely from Caesar's veterans, the senatorial forces defeated Antony at Mutina (Modena, northern Italy) in 43 B.C. Octavian quickly realized, however, that the senate planned to use him to remove Antony as a threat and then discard him. The orator Cicero summed up their plan for Octavian: "The young man is to be praised, honored, and exalted." In Latin the last word can be understood as a pun for "removed."

Sensing this design, Octavian arranged a meeting with Antony and Marcus Aemilius Lepidus, another associate of Caesar. The three formed the Second Triumvirate, patterned on the earlier alliance of Caesar, Marcus Licinius Crassus, and Pompey. Both triumvirates became the effective power of the Roman world, largely because of their command of military forces. The Second Triumvirate was sealed by marriage: Octavian wed the daughter of Antony's wife; later, Antony would marry Octavian's sister.

The triumvirs quickly had themselves voted unlimited powers and began to eradicate their opposition, especially those associated with the murder of Caesar. A proscription was proclaimed, and hundreds of Romans, including Cicero, were put to death. Octavian and Antony then confronted the army of Marcus Junius Brutus and Gaius Cassius Longinus, the leaders of the conspiracy against Caesar. In the Battles of Philippi in Greece (October 23 and November 14, 42 B.C.), the last forces capable of restoring the republic were smashed.

Octavian and Antony divided the Roman world between them, Octavian taking the west, Antony the east. Lepidus was shunted aside and sank into obscurity, eventually ending his life under house arrest. Relations between the two major partners steadily deteriorated. The alliance was patched up by marriage, and in 36 B.C. the two cooperated in the defeat of Sextus Pompeius (son of Pompey the Great) in Sicily. Developments after that, however, led to inevitable conflict.

While in the east, Antony formed a close liaison with Cleopatra, Queen of Egypt and former lover of Caesar. Antony granted her territories once held by Egypt but now subject to Rome, and he displayed signs of establishing an independent monarchy in Asia. Octavian skillfully exploited the antiforeign sentiments that these actions aroused, and in 32 B.C. Rome declared war on Antony and Cleopatra.

Octavian gathered a fleet and an army and moved east. Under his friend Marcus Vipsanius Agrippa, the Roman forces defeated those of Antony and Cleopatra at the naval battle of Actium, off the Greek coast, on September 2, 31 B.C. The two lovers escaped to Egypt, but when surrounded by Octavian's forces, they committed suicide. Octavian annexed Egypt as a Roman province; he was now sole ruler of the Roman state.

His position was still precarious, however, and for the rest of his life he had to balance the reality of his power carefully with the appearance of a restored republic. Although briefly considering a true return to the republic, Octavian realized that it was impossible, since it would lead to bloody civil war.

Instead of claiming or accepting offices of overt power—such as the dictatorship—which had brought about the death of Caesar, Octavian was content to serve in more traditional ways, such as consul (thirteen times in all) or tribune. His most frequently used title was an innovation: *princeps* (short for *princeps civitatis,* "first citizen"); this appellation was vague enough not to offend, yet sufficient to preserve his authority.

In 27 B.C., Octavian was granted the title Augustus by the senate, indicating the religious aspect of his position; throughout his reign, Augustus artfully underscored the moral need for a strong ruler to end centuries of internecine bloodshed. It is as Augustus that he is best known to history.

As ruler, Augustus' major concerns were internal reform and external defense. In Rome, he revised the senate roll, striking off many who were unfit to serve. He vigorously enforced laws against immorality, even sending his own daughter into exile for her numerous and blatant adulteries. His own life was less circumscribed. He stole his wife, Livia, from her first husband and was married to her while she was pregnant; he was known later for his many affairs, showing a particular preference for young virgins.

Nevertheless, he was careful in his observance of ancient Roman religious rituals and in A.D. 12 was elected *pontifex maximus,* or head priest. Whenever possible, he revived old customs and mores, attempting to strengthen patriotism and social order. His many building projects, especially in Rome, repaired years of neglect and greatly improved life in the city.

Along the borders, Augustus was content to maintain existing boundaries for most of the empire. In Germany, he made an effort to extend the limits of Roman rule to the Elbe. These attempts were abruptly ended in A.D. 6, when German tribes ambushed and massacred three legions under the command of Publius Quintilius Varus. The disaster caused Augustus to fix the boundaries at the Rhine; for a long time after he could be heard crying out in his palace, "Varus, give me back my legions!"

As he grew older, Augustus attempted to fix the succession of power, realizing that he must provide for an orderly transition lest his accomplishments be destroyed in another round of civil war. When his three grandsons either died or proved unfit, he was forced to turn to Tiberius, Livia's son by her first husband. Tiberius had long served Augustus in civil and military posts and had been advanced as heir on several occasions, only to be set aside for a candidate more suitable to Augustus' needs. At last, however, he was adopted by Augustus and served as his colleague and virtual coemperor until Augustus' death.

Augustus died in A.D. 14 and the fact that Tiberius succeeded him without a renewal of internal strife and disastrous civil war is perhaps the best indication of Augustus' success in creating a new and lasting political order—the Roman Empire.

Summary

One of the sayings attributed to Augustus is that he found Rome a city of brick and left it one of marble. This is literally true: His extensive renovation and construction transformed Rome from top to bottom—from its temples to its sewer system. A similar transformation was wrought by Augustus in the whole of the Roman world.

He found a state that was wracked by internal unrest, one that was seemingly incapable of ruling itself without resorting to self-destructive civil war. Through patience, tact, and, when necessary, force, he translated the ruins of the republic into the edifice of the empire. So difficult a task, to refound the Roman state, was made all the harder by the need to disguise its true nature. Throughout his reign, Augustus carefully retained the forms and procedures of a republic, deferring to the senate, refusing extravagant titles, and being careful to allow others a measure of honor and prestige—although never enough to threaten his preeminent position.

Augustus' major accomplishments were to establish the Roman Empire and to become its first emperor, almost without public notice. While all knew that power had shifted into the hands of one man, the shift had been accomplished in such a gradual, subtle fashion, and with such positive results, that few openly complained. Most Romans probably approved of the changes made by Augustus. There was security, increasing prosperity, and, above all, peace. The arts flourished, and the golden age of Roman literature under Augustus produced such lasting writers as Horace, Ovid, Livy, and Vergil.

Augustus restored peace to a society that badly needed it. Conflicts continued on the borders, but internal warfare came to an end. In one of his most significant acts, Augustus closed the gates to the temple of Janus, an act done only when Rome was formally at peace. Before his time, the gates had been shut only twice in Rome's long history. More than anything else it was this peace, this Pax Romana and the blessings it brought, that caused a grateful senate to accord Augustus the title *pater patriae*—father of his country.

Bibliography

Buchan, John. *Augustus.* Boston: Houghton Mifflin Co., and London: Hodder and Stoughton, 1937. A popular history by a well-known novelist who uses his skills to present a briskly moving but informative narrative. While Buchan's work has been dated in some respects by more recent scholarly studies and findings, it remains a good starting point for the student.

Grant, Michael. *The Roman Emperors: A Biographical Guide to the Rulers of Imperial Rome, 31 B.C.-A.D. 476.* London: Weidenfeld and Nicolson, and New York: Charles Scribner's Sons, 1985. A lucid, compressed review of the life and times of Augustus, placing him within the context of his society. Once again, Grant demonstrates his ability as a historian to unearth new and interesting insights from well-known material.

————. *The Twelve Caesars*. Rev. ed. London and New York: Penguin Books, 1979. This volume takes the ancient biographer Suetonius as its starting point but goes far beyond him in its exploration and explanation of the difficulties and accomplishments of Augustus. Grant is especially good in delineating the agonizingly careful line Augustus had to trace in establishing an empire on the ruins of a fallen, but still potent, republic.

Jones, A. H. *Augustus*. Edited by M. I. Finley. New York: Norton, and London: Chatto and Windus, 1970. A well-researched and well-presented overview of Augustus' life and career, giving equal attention to both. Jones is particularly good in considering the various aspects of the new empire both in chronological terms and in separate, in-depth considerations, offering the reader either a broad or concentrated treatment depending on his needs.

Massie, Allan. *The Caesars*. London: Secker and Warburg, 1983; New York: Franklin Watts, 1984. A popular biography of Rome's imperial rulers, and a good place to start a study of Augustus. The section on the first emperor is well done and provides several interesting views of his task in setting up the imperial system.

Raaflaub, Kurt A., and Mark Toher. *Between Republic and Empire: Interpretations of Augustus and His Principate*. Berkeley and Oxford: University of California Press, 1990. A substantial collection of scholarly essays concerned with various aspects (historical, literary, artistic) of Augustus' reign. The book is billed as a revision of Sir Ronald Syme's *Roman Revolution* and is therefore a good summary of the course of scholarly discussion on Augustus as it has developed in the years since Syme's book appeared in 1939.

Shotter, D. C. A. *Augustus Caesar*. Lancaster Pamphlets. London and New York: Routledge, 1991. Shotter provides an introductory overview and a positive assessment of Augustus.

Suetonius, Gaius Tranquillus. *Lives of the Twelve Caesars*. Edited by Joseph Gavorse. New York: Modern Library, 1931. Suetonius is long on incident and short on evaluation, but his lively portrait of Augustus has never been surpassed. While other, later authors have given more facts about the founder of the empire, Suetonius presents him as a human being. This work certainly deserves its reputation as a classic.

Michael Witkoski

BOADICCA

Born: First century A.D.; Britain
Died: A.D. 60; Central Britain
Area of Achievement: Warfare and conquest
Contribution: Having endured flogging and the violation of her daughters, Boadicca led a rebellion of the Britons against the Roman invaders. Although the Romans were caught by surprise and lost three cities burned by the rebels, the uprising was quelled, and Boadicca herself died by taking poison.

Early Life

Boadicca was born and grew up in iron-age Britain, which was in the process of subjugation and colonization by imperial Rome. Her place and date of birth and her parentage are not known; nor in fact are any details of her early life except that she married Prasutagus, who was allowed by the Romans to rule his tribe, the Iceni, as a client king. By him, she had two daughters who were probably teenagers by A.D. 60. It seems likely that Boadicca was born circa A.D. 20 to A.D. 30. Two classical authors provide the known extended written accounts of Boadicca: The *Agricola* and *Annals* (c. A.D. 100) of Tacitus, and the *History of Rome* by Dio Cassius (late second century A.D). Many archaeological finds have tended to confirm the written accounts: coins, pottery, and ruins of forts and buildings. Tacitus is generally accepted as the more reliable historian, because he wrote only forty years after the events and because his father-in-law, Julius Agricola, was a high official in the colonial administration at the time of Boadicca's revolt. Also, the work of Dio Cassius has survived only in the form of a summary, or "epitome," made by the monk Xiphilinus of Trapezus in the eleventh century.

The first Roman military adventure in Britain was that of Julius Caesar in 55 B.C. After several skirmishes with the Britons in which the Romans were largely victorious, Caesar withdrew, only to return again the next year with additional troops and cavalry. Some Britons, fearing destruction, made peace and agreed to pay tribute to Rome; others in more remote regions held out fiercely. Distracted by signs of trouble in Gaul, Caesar withdrew again, leaving further conquests to others in the reign of the emperor Claudius, more than a hundred years later.

In A.D. 43, Roman legions led by Aulus Plautius landed in Britain and campaigned against the many tribes of the island in order to bring them under Roman rule. In awe of Roman might, and seeking advantage over other tribes, some leaders made deals with Rome and were allowed to rule as client kings. Others withdrew to the west into Wales to wage guerrilla warfare.

The most effective leader of resistance against the Romans was Caratacus, who continued to rally support for his cause even after a decisive Roman victory near the river Medway. These events occurred during the girlhood and young womanhood of Boadicca. Her husband Prasutagus was allowed to rule his tribe, the Iceni, as a client king, a sort of intermediary between the Romans, who were the real rulers, and the people.

When Aulus Plautius retired, he was replaced by the experienced and stern general Publius Ostorius Scapula, who arrived in Britain just in time to confront serious uprisings in the West, led by Caratacus. In order to prevent an attack from behind while chasing Caratacus, Scapula ordered all the British tribes to be disarmed, and he established a colony of retired military men at Camulodunum (modern Colchester) that he hoped would be a stabilizing influence. These measures were resented by the Britons, more so because the Romans of the colony lorded it over them, taking their property and treating them as slaves. Eventually, Caratacus fled to the north and was betrayed to the Romans by Queen Cartimandua, who needed to curry Roman favor in return for protection against other tribes. In A.D. 51, Caratacus was taken to Rome in chains. About this time, Scapula died and was succeeded by Didius Gallus, who remained as governor until A.D. 58.

Gallus had to deal with uprisings in the north and with continual trouble with the Silures, a tribe in Wales. Upon the death of Emperor Claudius, Gallus retired in favor of Veranius, who died within a year, but not before waging a vigorous campaign against the Silures. His efforts were continued and expanded by the next governor, Suetonius Paulinus, who had served with distinction in North Africa and who was a specialist in mountain warfare. The death of Prasutagus in A.D. 59 brought on the events for which his widow Boadicca has become famous.

Life's Work

Prasutagus had become wealthy and knew of the Romans' greed and contempt for the rights of the Britons. He made a will leaving half of his estate to the Emperor Nero, thinking thus to protect the enforcement of the will and to preserve some of the estate for his wife and daughters. Nevertheless, the local Roman officials, under command of the procurator Catus Decianus, sought to plunder the estate for their own benefit. Boadicca's objections were met with brutality; she herself was scourged, and her daughters were raped.

Far from the quietus they had sought, the Romans soon found they had stirred a hornet's nest. The Iceni and their allies gathered in a horde that may have numbered in the tens of thousands. They descended on the hated encampment of Camulodunum, where a huge temple to the recently deified Claudius was under construction, built with British taxes and British slave labor. In spite of the arrival of two hundred Roman troops, the defenders of Camulodunum were driven into the temple of Claudius and annihilated, their whole town burned and looted. A legion commanded by Petillius Cere-

alis marched to the relief of Camulodunum but was ambushed and suffered severe losses, Cerealis barely escaping with his life.

The Britons, excited by victory and looting, approached London, which was little more than a village with few defenses. Meanwhile, Suetonius Paulinus had been in the far west on the island of Mona (Anglesey), where his forces had destroyed a druid stronghold and cut down the sacred groves of the cult. He sped to London to see what could be done, but he decided that the city had to be abandoned to the rebels. Catus Decianus fled to Gaul to save himself from the common fate.

Boadicca and her forces burned London to the ground and slew everyone they found there, including Britons they regarded as turncoats. Even today, there is a layer of ashes about seventeen feet beneath the surface in London testifying to the holocaust. The rebels then turned to Verulamium (St. Albans) and sacked it, massacring the occupants, mostly Britons who had befriended the Romans.

Meanwhile, Suetonius Paulinus withdrew to the west and north of London because he needed time to gather provisions. He also sought reinforcements from the legion commanded by Poenius Posthumus stationed near Exeter. Preparing for the approach of the Britons, Paulinus moved his forces to a carefully chosen battlefield in a canyon with a forest behind it. The exact location is unknown, but it may have been near Mancetter, where the horde of Britons confronted the ordered ranks of the Romans. So confident were the Britons that all their families were drawn up behind them in wagons to watch the battle. Boadicca rode on a chariot with her daughters and exhorted the men and women of her army, reciting her grievances against the Romans and urging the Britons to fight for freedom.

Tall and serious in mien, Boadicca was an impressive figure, with fair, waist-long hair and dressed in a multicolored tunic and long cloak. Suetonius Paulinus told his men to ignore the cries of the attacking savages and to press on with their spears and swords, forgetting thoughts of plunder but intent on victory and the glory it would bring.

The Britons attacked with wild, warlike shouting and trumpet blasts, brandishing their yard-long swords, some of them naked with their skins painted with intricate designs in blue. The Romans waited in orderly ranks, wearing armor of steel and leather strips and equipped with shields, spears, and short, thick swords.

The Romans carried the day by superior discipline and benefit of the terrain. After showering the rebels with spears, the Roman phalanx drove ahead, forcing the Britons back into their wagons. In the rout that followed, the Romans put to death anyone they could catch, including the pack animals. Boadicca took poison and died rather than accept capture and humiliation. The Roman reinforcements from Exeter failed to arrive in time for the battle, depriving them and their commander Poenius Posthumus from a share in the glory of victory. It is not known whether Posthumus delayed because he feared being ambushed on the way or because he was involved in other military actions. In any event, he felt sufficient shame that he killed himself by falling on his sword. It is asserted that eighty thousand people died in the battle.

In revenge for the uprising, Paulinus and his army swept through the lands of the Iceni, burning crops, looting, and killing anyone they suspected of aiding the rebels. Boadicca was reportedly buried in a magnificent tomb, which has never been found.

Summary

Boadicca's rebellion and its aftermath were probably the bloodiest events ever to occur on British soil. The Romans were forced to the realization that their terror tactics had led to unacceptable losses and that a more diplomatic policy was needed. Many more years were required for the pacification of Britain, and the Caledonians in the north were never completely subdued. Increased trade and the wealth it brought to cooperative Britons was a major factor in pacification.

The memory of Boadicca turned to the stuff of legend, and she became the symbol of freedom and independence for the British. Her story was retold many times in literature by such authors as Ben Jonson, William Cowper, Alfred, Lord Tennyson, and others. An opera has also been written by Gillian Carcas.

Queen Elizabeth I and Queen Victoria were both compared with Boadicca, and it is thought that the name "Boadicca" (also spelled Boudicca, Boadicea, and Boudica) probably means "victory" in the Celtic language. A statue of Boadicca in London made by Thomas Thornycroft was placed near the Houses of Parliament in 1902. It depicts the heroine and her daughters on a huge chariot quite unlike the small Celtic war chariots described by Julius Caesar.

Bibliography

Cassius Dio Cocceianus. *Dio's Roman History.* E. Cary, trans. London: Heinemann, and Cambridge, Mass.: Harvard University Press, 1914-1927. Boadicca's revolt is discussed in volume 8.

Dudley, Donald R., and Graham Webster. *The Rebellion of Boudicca.* London: Routledge, and New York: Barnes & Noble, 1962. This and Webster's 1978 book (cited below) are major works devoted solely to Boadicca. Legends and traditions are covered as well as history. Portions of Tacitus' *Annals* and *Agricola* describing the rebellion are quoted at length in an appendix, both in the original Latin and in translation.

Fraser, Antonia. *The Warrior Queens.* London: Weidenfeld and Nicolson, 1988; New York: Knopf, 1989. Interesting account of women who assumed roles of power usually reserved for men. Boadicca is considered the archetypal "warrior queen" and is discussed alongside Cleopatra, Golda Meir, Margaret Thatcher, and others.

Ireland, S. *Roman Britain: A Sourcebook*. 2d ed. London and New York: Routledge, 1996. Translations are provided for selections from Tacitus and Dio Cassius.

Salway, Peter. *Roman Britain*. Oxford: Clarendon Press, and New York: Oxford University Press, 1981. Part of the *Oxford History of England* series. Scholarly account of history (55 B.C. to A.D. 449), culture, economy, and religion. Extensive bibliography and maps.

Tacitus, Cornelius. *Tacitus on Britain and Germany*. H. Mattingly, trans. London and Baltimore: Penguin, 1948. Pages 64-67 treat the revolt of Boadicca.

————. *The Annals of Imperial Rome*. Translated by M. Grant. Rev. ed. London and New York: Penguin, 1989. Pages 317-321 provide the most reliable classical source for Boadicca's revolt.

Webster, Graham. *Boudica*. Totowa, N.J.: Rowman and Littlefield, 1978. The 1962 book by Webster and Dudley cited above has been updated to incorporate extensive new archaeological findings from excavations at London, Verulamium, and Colchester. Includes photographs of coins, inscriptions, and other artifacts and views of sites observed from aircraft.

John R. Phillips

MARCUS JUNIUS BRUTUS

Born: 85 B.C.; probably Rome
Died: October 23, 42 B.C.; Philippi, Greece
Area of Achievement: Government and politics; warfare and conquest
Contribution: As leader and conscience of the conspiracy that assassinated the dictator Julius Caesar, Brutus attempted to restore the Roman Republic but instead ushered in the Empire.

Early Life

According to his family's traditions, Marcus Junius Brutus was a descendent of the legendary Lucius Junius Brutus who had founded the Roman Republic. According to these accounts, in 509 B.C., Lucius Brutus expelled the last of the early Roman kings, Tarquinius Superbus (Tarquin the Proud) and established the Republic, serving as its first consul. So devoted to liberty and the new republic was Junius Brutus, according to Plutarch and other biographers, that he condemned to death his own sons when they plotted to restore Tarquinius and the monarchy. The family line continued, Plutarch explained, because only the two older sons were condemned; an innocent younger brother survived to be the ancestor of Marcus Brutus.

The Junii family continued an active role in Roman life. Marcus Junius's father, of the same name, was an adherent of Gaius Marius during the civil wars with Cornelius Sulla. At the siege of Mutina, in 77 B.C., the elder Brutus surrendered to the Sullustian general Gaius Pompeius (better known as Pompey Magnus, or Pompey the Great) and was put to death in cold blood. Despite this, in later years Brutus' son would be allied with Pompey against Julius Caesar, believing Pompey to be a champion of the Republic.

Marcus Brutus was connected with other famous republican figures of Roman history. Through the family of his mother, Servilia, he was related to Servilius Ahala, who had killed a potential tyrant in fifth century Rome. His uncle on his mother's side was the famous Cato Uticensis (Cato of Utica), who was one of the most notable of the opponents of Julius Caesar and who committed suicide amid the ruins of Utica following the collapse of the republic. Following the death of her first husband, Servilia married D. Junius Silanus and had three daughters. The eldest of them, Junia, married M. Aemilius Lepidus, who became a member of the Second Triumvirate with Gaius Octavian (later

the emperor Augustus Caesar) and Marc Anthony. A second daughter, Junia Tertia, married Cassius Longinus, along with Brutus a key conspirator in the plot against Julius Caesar; thus, Brutus and Cassius were brothers-in-law.

Marcus Brutus followed the traditional course of studies for an aristocratic Roman. He was well educated in Greek literature and philosophy and in Latin rhetoric. He continued his schooling in Athens, where his teacher, Pammenes, was described by the famous orator Marcus Tullius Cicero as the most eloquent man in Greece. While in Athens, Brutus was exposed to the philosophical schools of the Stoics and the Platonists; the latter had an especially profound influence on him.

Life's Work

His education complete, Brutus returned to Rome to pursue the *cursus honorum* (literally, the "course of honor"), which took members of the patrician class such as Brutus through a series of public offices and duties to the highest rank of all, the consulship. Among his earlier offices, Brutus was in charge of the mint—where, significantly, he issued coins with the head of Liberty on one side and a portrait of his ancestor Lucius Brutus on the other. He was a quaestor for the province of Cilicia in Asia Minor, and he became increasingly known as a successful advocate in the Roman law courts. In 54 B.C., he married Claudia, daughter of Appius Claudius; he divorced her in 45 B.C. and married his cousin Porcia, daughter of Cato.

In this marriage and in his public life, Brutus had positioned himself with the opponents of Julius Caesar. When the antagonism between Caesar and Pompey erupted into outright civil war, Brutus sided with Pompey as being the defender, such as he was, of the traditional republic. He fought in Pompey's army at the decisive battle of Pharsalus in 48 B.C., but after that defeat he quickly settled with Caesar and received a pardon.

Despite his Pompeian associations and his family's traditional hostility, Brutus was highly regarded by Caesar, who arranged for his continued advance, including service in 46 B.C. as proconsul of Cisalpine Gaul, one of Rome's most important strategic provinces. In 44 B.C., Caesar appointed Brutus *praetor urbanus*, the highest official in Rome itself.

It was during this period that the conspiracy against Caesar was taking shape. Following the defeat and death of Pompey and the destruction of his remaining forces, Julius Caesar had become preeminent in the Roman world. In February of 44 B.C., he was appointed dictator for life, an unprecedented step. Along with this came outward marks of almost monarchical dignity, including a statue among the Roman kings, a special seat at the theater, a raised throne in the senate house, religious rites associated with him, and the naming of a month, July, in his honor. All these struck at the traditional liberties of Rome; perhaps worse for men such as Brutus and Cassius, they destroyed their prospects for advancing on the *cursus honorum.*

According to the historians Plutarch and Appian, Cassius was the leader of the conspiracy against Caesar and pressured Brutus into joining, knowing that Brutus' reputation for honesty and virtue was essential. The writer Dio Cassius, on the other hand, says that Brutus himself took the lead from the beginning, inspired largely by the memory of his family's active opposition to tyranny.

Eventually there were some sixty conspirators involved; their motives were mixed and their goals uncertain. Brutus and Cassius seem to have thought that once Caesar was dead, the traditional republic would naturally return. In this, they ignored more than half a century of vicious civil war, first between Marius and Sulla and then between Caesar and Pompey. When the conspirators struck on the Ides of March in 44 B.C., they succeeded in killing Julius Caesar, but they signally failed to kill caesarism.

For several months following the assassination, Brutus remained on his estates outside Rome. During this time, Marc Anthony and Gaius Octavian, Caesar's grand-nephew, who had been adopted in the dictator's will and who therefore styled himself as Gaius Caesar, began to forge an alliance against the conspirators. In 43 B.C. Brutus and Cassius left Italy for the eastern provinces, Brutus going to Athens and Cassius to Syria. Moving with considerable speed, Brutus raised an army and took effective control of the provinces of Greece, Illyria, and Macedonia. He was soon joined by Cassius with additional troops from Asia Minor.

In Italy, Anthony, after an initial defeat, had linked with Octavian, and the two had consolidated their hold over Rome. Joining with Lepidus, Brutus' brother-in-law and Caesar's former master of

the horse (second in command), they formed the Second Triumvirate. It was about this time, according to Plutarch and other writers, that Brutus' wife Porcia committed suicide, either by swallowing live coals or from breathing charcoal fumes until she was overcome. Her suicide, and Brutus' calm acceptance of it, became famous examples of traditional Roman stoicism in the face of great personal adversity.

In the spring of 42 B.C., both the republicans under Brutus and Cassius and the triumvirs Anthony and Octavian had moved armies into Macedonia. In October, after months of maneuvering, the opposing forces met near the town of Philippi. According to his biographers, on the march there Brutus had been awakened in his tent by an apparition. Some claimed it was the ghost of Caesar, others, Brutus' evil genius. All agreed the specter warned Brutus, "I will see you again at Philippi."

There were two battles at Philippi, both marked by confusion. In the first battle, Brutus' forces defeated the troops under command of Octavian and captured his camp, although Octavian escaped. At the same time, however, Anthony's troops had overwhelmed those of Cassius, who, unaware of Brutus' victory, retreated into the hills and killed himself rather than be captured. As the fighting died away, Brutus collected the republican forces and held his position.

The second and decisive battle of Philippi came relatively shortly thereafter. The joint army of Anthony and Octavian appeared to be in a bad situation, short of supplies and suffering from the bad weather. After three weeks, Brutus, urged on by his lieutenants and the ardor of his troops, launched an attack that was initially successful but that could not be sustained. By the end of the day, the forces of Anthony and Octavian had completely routed the republicans. Fleeing from the battlefield, Brutus escaped from the vengeance of the triumvirs by committing suicide by falling upon his sword.

In a scene made famous by William Shakespeare's play *Julius Caesar* (160), Anthony and Octavian praised Brutus as "the noblest Roman of them all" and promised an honorable funeral. According to Plutarch, this is indeed what happened, and the assassin's ashes were carried back to his mother Servilia. The historian Suetonius, however, asserts that Octavian had Brutus' head sent back to Rome to be thrown at the feet of a statue of Julius Caesar. Dio Cassius further embroiders this tale by adding that the head never reached Rome: During a storm, the superstitious sailors in the vessel carrying the head cast it overboard, fearing it was bringing them bad luck. Whatever the ultimate fate of Brutus' body, with his death came the effective end of the Roman Republic.

Summary

Marcus Junius Brutus is one of the most ambiguous figures of classical antiquity. During his lifetime, he was acclaimed by many, Cicero among them, as one of the most noble figures of the dying republic, and he was seen as representing one of its last, best hopes for revival. Yet he was unable to transform his commitment to those historic principles into effective action. His role in the assassination of Caesar could be seen as either a selfless action to restore the old and proper order or as the result of a self-centered and selfish vision of a member of the patrician order intent only upon personal and family honor. In later years, Brutus would be honored by the French Revolution as the first of the champions of humankind. Centuries earlier, Dante Alighieri in *The Inferno* had placed Brutus and Cassius along with Judas Iscariot in the mouth of Satan as among the foremost sinners and ingrates of all creation for the murder of Julius Caesar, the divinely ordained founder of the Roman Empire.

Whatever Brutus' reputation, the immediate and enduring impact of his deed was undeniable: the assassination of Julius Caesar ended the danger a single individual posed to the republic, but it also revealed how corrupt and weakened the republic had become and made its fall inevitable. Where Caesar had openly asserted his desire for power and prominence, his nephew and successor Octavian, later the first emperor, Caesar Augustus, was more circumspect and more successful. Where Caesar had flirted with the hated title of king, Augustus was content with the more modest "princeps," or first among equals. This pretense of republican forms masking the reality of imperial rule was the most lasting and certainly the most unintended legacy of Marcus Junius Brutus.

Bibliography

Clarke, M. L. *The Noblest Roman*. London: Thames and Hudson, and Ithaca, N.Y.: Cornell University Press, 1981. A volume in the "Aspects of Greek and Roman Life" series, this small but highly informative work provides an outstanding brief biography of Brutus the man and a survey of his reputation over the centuries.

Grant, Michael. *Caesar*. London: Weidenfeld and Nicolson, and New York: McGraw-Hill, 1969. An excellent introduction both to the lives of Caesar, Brutus, and other major figures and to the milieu of the late Republic itself. Copiously and carefully illustrated.

Heitland, W. E. *The Roman Republic*. Cambridge: Cambridge University Press, 1909; New York: Putnam, 1911. The chapters on the efforts of Brutus, Cassius, and others to restore the Roman Republic after the assassination of Caesar are of considerable help in understanding the fundamental changes that swept the Roman world and led, eventually, from republic to empire.

Plutarch. *Lives*. Arthur H. Clough, ed. London and New York: Dutton, 1910. The classic account of the life, deeds, and death of Brutus. This brief biography gives the modern reader a sense of what Brutus's contemporaries thought of him and how they viewed their world.

Syme, Ronald. *The Roman Revolution*. Oxford: Oxford University Press, 1939; New York: Oxford University Press, 1951. The fundamental modern study of the transformation of the state and society of Rome between 60 B.C. and A.D. 14. Does an excellent job of placing Brutus within the context of his time.

Wistrand, Erik. *The Policy of Brutus the Tyrannicide*. Goteborg, Sweden: Kungl, 1981. An in-depth examination of Brutus's motives and expectations in the assassination of Julius Caesar; especially good in its study of the relationship between Brutus and Cicero.

Michael Witkoski

BUDDHA
Siddhārtha Gautama

Born: c. 566 B.C.; Lumbinī, Nepal
Died: c. 486 B.C.; Kuśinagara, India
Areas of Achievement: Religion, philosophy, and monasticism
Contribution: By his own example and teaching, Buddha showed that all people can attain an enlightened state of mind by cultivating a combination of compassion (loving-kindness toward all beings without exception) and wisdom (seeing things as they really are).

Early Life

The historical Buddha—known variously as Gautama, Siddhārtha, and Śākyamuni—was born in Lumbinī, in the Himālayan foothills of what is now Nepal. His father, Śuddhodana, was king of nearby Kapilavastu, a town whose archaeological remains have yet to be found. His mother, Māyā, died seven days after giving birth to the young prince; Śuddhodana then married her sister, who brought up the boy.

According to legend, the infant's conception and birth were accompanied by unusual signs, and he walked and talked at birth. Legend also has it that an ancient sage prophesied that the young prince would become either a Buddha (an enlightened one) or a universal monarch. Śuddhodana, determined on the latter career, kept his son confined within the palace walls to prevent him from seeing unpleasant sights that might cause him to renounce the world and take up the religious life of a wandering mendicant.

The Buddha's given name was Siddhārtha ("he who has achieved his goal"). Later, he was called Śākyamuni (Sage of the Śākyas), because his family was part of the warrior (*kṣatriya*) Śākya clan, which also used the Brahman clan name Gautama (descendant of the sage Gotama). He is described as a handsome, black-haired boy.

The oldest Buddhist canon is in the Pali language and was transmitted orally for several hundred years after the Buddha's death; it was then written down on palm leaves. The Pali canon records few details about Siddhārtha's early years, but it does mention that he spontaneously entered a state of meditation while sitting under a tree watching his father plowing. It also recounts his becoming aware of the inevitability of old age, illness, and death, supposedly by seeing his first old man, ill man, and corpse on clandestine trips outside the palace gates.

When he came of age, Siddhārtha was married to Yaśodharā. They had a son who was named Rāhula (the fetter), perhaps because Siddhārtha was already turning away from householder life. Indeed, at the age of twenty-nine, he left home forever to seek enlightenment, initially with two teachers, then through extended fasting and other austerities, in which he was joined by five other ascetics. At the age of thirty-five, having failed to attain his goal, he ate enough to regain strength and sat under a tree (later known as the Bodhi Tree) at Uruvelā, near Benares, vowing to stay there until he reached enlightenment.

The Pali canon includes several different descriptions of the enlightenment that followed, "as though one were to describe a tree from above, from below and from various sides, or a journey by land, by water and by air" (Ñāṇamoli, *Life of the Buddha According to the Pali Canon,* 1972). What these accounts have in common is Śākyamuni's claim of having attained direct knowledge of the final nature of mind itself.

Examining the mind via meditation, Śākyamuni found it empty of independent existence. In combination with compassion (an altruistic attitude toward everyone, especially one's "enemies"), this knowledge led to Buddhahood. It was this discovery that Gautama Buddha would spend the rest of his life setting forth to those who came to listen to him teach.

Life's Work

The newly enlightened Buddha's first impulse was not to disseminate the truth that he had worked so diligently to uncover. He realized that every human being had the potential to attain enlightenment, just as he himself had done, but he also knew that enlightenment could not be bestowed by anyone else; each person had to reach it himself. Thus the Buddha is said to have hesitated to propagate his Dharma ("truth" or "law"), thinking that it would be too difficult for beings still deluded by craving to understand. Only his compassion for the suffering of all beings eventually convinced him to do so.

Accordingly, the Buddha set out to find the five ascetics with whom he had practiced austerities. They were not immediately convinced of his enlightenment, so he elucidated the Middle Way of avoiding both sensual and ascetic extremes. At this point the Buddha is said to have first taught the Four Noble Truths—namely, that life inevitably involves suffering or woefulness (*dukkha*), that the cause of suffering is craving or grasping, that there is a way for craving to cease, and that the way consists of the Eightfold Path of right view, right intention, right speech, right action, right livelihood, right effort, right mindfulness, and right concentration.

During this talk, which took place four miles north of Benares, in the Deer Park at Isipatana, one of the five ascetics realized that all conditioned (interdependent) things are impermanent, and he became enlightened. The remaining four soon followed suit; other wanderers and householders from all walks of life, including Rāhula and Śākyamuni's stepmother/aunt, did the same.

The formula that distinguishes a Buddhist from a non-Buddhist evolved during this time. The Buddha taught that "oneself is one's own refuge" and that all beings are, ultimately, manifestations of Buddha nature or enlightened mind. Thus Buddhists take refuge in what is called the Three Jewels or Triple Gem: the Buddha as a representation of enlightenment; the Dharma, or teaching of how to attain enlightenment; and the Sangha, the community of fellow aspirants on the path.

The Buddha continued to teach for the next forty-five years, which he spent journeying around the central Gangetic plain, giving discourses (*sūtras*), establishing monastic guidelines (*vinaya*) as the need arose for them, and answering any questions put to him.

Śākyamuni was not concerned with metaphysical questions about the origins of the world, explaining that a man with an arrow in his chest is more sensible to address himself to removing it than to ask how it got there. The Buddha had found a way to end man's mental and physical suffering, by developing inner clarity and peace; to him, questions of how and why were not useful in progressing toward that goal.

According to the law of Karma (the law of cause and effect), to which the Buddha subscribed, wholesome actions eventually lead to good results, while unwholesome or harmful deeds result in suffering, in this or a future life. By cultivating whole-some actions of body, speech, and mind, the Buddha maintained that anyone can experience enlightenment. To do this, the Buddha advocated dissolving the obstacles of craving, anger, and ignorance by cultivating ethical conduct, moral discipline, and wisdom.

The Buddha was not immune to death, but he remained fearless and lucid when the time came. Having become ill in his eightieth year, he told one of his foremost disciples, his cousin Ananda, that he would soon die. He then asked the assembled monks three times whether they had any doubts or questions, but they remained silent. The Buddha's last words summarized his teaching: "Conditioned things are perishable by nature. Diligently seek realization." He died in meditation.

Summary

Śākyamuni elucidated seminal ideas and methods whose effect can only be compared to the teachings of Moses, Jesus, and Muhammad. He rejected some key elements of the Hindu worldview of his era—notably the caste system, the idea of a permanent self (*ātman*), and the practice of austerities—but retained the notions of Karma and rebirth. To these he added his unique insight into what is worthwhile: an altruistic aspiration to enlightenment for the sake of all beings.

Although Buddhism declined and eventually disappeared in India (where it is experiencing a revival today), it spread to Southeast and Central Asia, China, Korea, and Japan. Today there are many different schools of Buddhism, whose styles range from the baroque iconography of Tibetan tantrism to the stark simplicity of Zen. All recognize subsequent adepts on the Buddhist path and reflect the different cultures in which they have developed. All Buddhist traditions, however, trace their lineage and the common essence of their teaching to Śākyamuni, the man who, in recorded history, first became an enlightened one, a Buddha.

Bibliography

Anderson, Walt. *Open Secrets: A Western Guide to Tibetan Buddhism*. New York: Viking Press, 1979. A straightforward introduction to the form Buddhism took in Tibet.

[Gyatso, Tenzin] Bstan-dzin-rgya-mtsho (the fourteenth Dalai Lama). *Kindness, Clarity, and Insight*. Edited by Jeffrey Hopkins and Elizabeth Napper. Ithaca, N.Y.: Snow Lion Publications, 1984. Twenty talks ranging from succinct discussions of the nature of Karma and the role of compassion in global politics to technical explanations of various methods for attaining enlightenment.

Ñāṇamoli, Bhikku, comp. *The Life of the Buddha According to the Pali Canon.* 3d ed. Kandy, Sri Lanka: Buddhist Publication Society, 1992. A biography translated from the oldest authentic records and supplemented with historical notes, by an eminent English scholar-monk.

Rahula, Walpola. *What the Buddha Taught.* 2d ed. New York: Grove Press, 1974; London: Fraser, 1978. A reliable introduction to the complexities of Buddhism. Includes a selection of texts from the Pali canon translated by the author, who is a Buddhist monk and scholar.

Reps, Paul, and Nyogen Senzaki, comps. *Zen Flesh, Zen Bones: A Collection of Zen and Pre-Zen Writings.* New York: Doubleday, 1957; London: Penguin Books, 1971. A classic introduction to Zen, including the quintessential parable of the Ten Bulls and the koan (paradox for meditation) of the "sound of one hand."

Robinson, Richard H., Willard L. Johnson, Sandra A. Wawrytko, and Geoffrey DeGraff. *The Buddhist Religion: A Historical Introduction.* 4th ed. Belmont, Calif.: Wadsworth Publishing Co., 1996. An overview that traces the antecedents of Buddhism, describes the Buddha's life, and explains the development of Buddhism both in India and in Southeast Asia, Tibet, East Asia, and the West. Includes a glossary of key Sanskrit terms, an essay on meditation, and a list of selected readings.

Senzaki, Nyogen, and Ruth Strout McCandless. *Buddhism and Zen.* Foreword by Robert Aitken. New York: Philosophical Library, 1953. Collection of talks, notes, and translations by one of the earliest and most accomplished Zen teachers in the West.

Victoria Scott

JULIUS CAESAR

Born: July 12/13, 100 B.C.; Rome

Died: March 15, 44 B.C.; Rome

Areas of Achievement: Government, warfare, and literature

Contribution: With his conquest of Gaul, Caesar expanded Roman rule into northern Europe. He then won a desperate civil war to establish himself as sole ruler of the Roman world, ending the republic and preparing the stage for the empire.

Early Life

The family of Gaius Julius Caesar was of great antiquity and nobility in Roman history; Caesar was to claim descent not only from the ancient kings of the city but also from Aeneas, its legendary founder, and his mother, the goddess Venus. In actual life, however, the Julian clan had more history than money and tended to favor the cause of the common people rather than the aristocrats. The twin pressures of finance and popular politics were the dominant forces that shaped the life and career of Julius Caesar.

During the first century B.C., the city-state of Rome had become the dominant power in the Mediterranean world, and with this expansion had come enormous wealth, immense military strength, and a gradual but unmistakable decline in the old republic. By the time of Caesar's birth, the political factions in Rome had coalesced into two major camps. The *populares* were led by Gaius Marius, who was married to Caesar's aunt Julia; this group championed the cause of the middle and lower classes. Their opponents, the *optimates,* favored the upper classes and the traditional rule of the senate; they found their leader in Lucius Cornelius Sulla. The bloody civil war between the two sides ended with Sulla's victory and assumption of the dictatorship.

In 84, Caesar married Cornelia, the daughter of a leading follower of Marius. This action so angered Sulla that Caesar found it prudent to secure a diplomatic post at the court of Nicomedes, the King of Bithynia in northeastern Asia Minor. Caesar did not return to Rome until after Sulla's death.

Once back, he embarked upon a daring and ambitious course of bringing charges against the leading members of the *optimates,* in the hope of winning renown and establishing his support among the followers of Marius. Unsuccessful in these attempts, Caesar journeyed to Rhodes to study orato-ry—an art essential to any successful Roman politician. On the voyage, Caesar was captured by pirates and held for ransom. Insulted by the small amount they demanded, Caesar had them increase it and promised that when he was freed he would return to crucify them. He was good to his word, but according to his biographer Suetonius, Caesar mercifully cut the throats of the pirates before crucifixion.

In 70, Caesar fully entered public life with his funeral oration for his aunt Julia. It was in this speech that he traced his family ancestry to the goddess Venus; more important, he launched a searing attack on the conservative party in Rome, announcing his intent to challenge their rule. The rest of his life would be spent in making good that challenge.

According to ancient writers, Caesar was tall and fair-complexioned, with a full face and keen black eyes. He enjoyed excellent health until the last years of his life, when he was subject to fainting fits which may have been epileptic. He was bald early and quite vain about it; Suetonius says that of all the honors granted him, the one Caesar used most was the privilege of wearing a laurel wreath at all times.

In his private life, Caesar was noted for his incessant womanizing; even amid the somewhat lax morality of the late republic, his escapades were cause for widespread comment. He was also exceedingly avaricious, but this may have been less a character flaw than a political necessity.

Caesar's main characteristic was his amazing energy, both physical and mental. He endured the dangers and fatigues of military campaigns without complaint or distress, and he composed his lucid, fast-moving *De bello Gallico* (52-51 B.C.; *The Gallic Wars*) and *De bello civili* (45 B.C.; *The Civil Wars*) almost before his battles were ended. He was so brilliant, in so many areas, that his contemporaries were dazzled—and historians continue to be fascinated—by him.

Life's Work

It is impossible to tell if Caesar wished to destroy the last remnants of the old republic and replace it with a formal autocracy, or whether he merely intended to become the leading citizen—although one without rivals—in the Roman world. In the

end, the result was the same, for Caesar for a brief time did become supreme ruler, and the republic was destroyed. Although it was Caesar's nephew and heir Octavian (later known as Augustus) who became the first Roman emperor, it was Caesar who made the empire possible.

Following a term as quaestor (a junior military officer) in Spain in 69, Caesar returned to Rome and allied himself with Marcus Licinius Crassus and Pompey the Great; the first was the richest man in Rome, the second its leading general. Together, these three formed the First Triumvirate, which was to become the real power in the Roman world.

In 61, Caesar was appointed governor of Farther Spain and honored with a triumph for his military campaigns there. The next year, he was elected as one of the two consuls who headed the Roman government; his term of office began in 59. The rest of Caesar's career stems, directly or indirectly, from this consulship.

As one of two consuls, Caesar had to deal with his colleague, a conservative opponent. Impatient with this and other obstructions, Caesar initiated numerous highly irregular, sometimes illegal, actions. These were designed to benefit Pompey's discharged veterans, increase the wealth of Crassus, and advance the general aims of the Triumvirate. So blatant, however, were the offenses—including violence against officials whose positions made them virtually sacred—that Caesar knew that his enemies would not rest until he had been prosecuted, convicted, and condemned.

His only recourse was to remain in office, since then he would be immune from trial. He secured the provinces of Cisalpine Gaul (now northern Italy) and Illyricum (the coast of modern Yugoslavia), and soon added Transalpine Gaul (southern France), which bordered on lands unconquered by Rome.

Caesar wasted no time in finding an excuse to wage war against the Gauls, and for the next eight years he was embroiled in the Gallic Wars, which are vividly recounted in his commentaries. During his campaigns, he crossed the Rhine to drive back the German tribes and twice launched an invasion of Britain. Although his attempts on the island were unsuccessful, his second fleet numbered eight hundred ships—the largest channel invasion armada until the Normandy invasion in World War II.

In 52, the recently subdued Gauls revolted against the Romans and, led by Vercingetorix, came close to undoing Caesar's great conquests.

By brilliant generalship and extraordinary efforts, Caesar pinned the Gauls in their fortress town of Alesia (Aliese-Sainte-Reine) and destroyed their army, finally ending the Gallic Wars. According to Caesar, he had fought thirty battles, captured eight hundred towns, and defeated three million enemies, of whom almost a million had been slain, another million captured. Although these figures are surely exaggerated, they do illustrate the extent of Caesar's victory. Its long-lasting effect was the opening of northern Europe to the influence of Greek and Roman culture and the rich heritage of the Mediterranean civilization.

Caesar's Gallic victories, however, had not secured his position in Rome. The Triumvirate had drifted apart, and Pompey was now allied with the senate and the conservatives. They demanded that Caesar give up his governorship and return to Rome. Knowing that such a move would be fatal, Caesar instead attacked his opponents. In January, 49, he led his troops across the Rubicon, the narrow stream that marked the border of his province. He took this irrevocable step with a gambler's daring, remarking, "Jacta alea est" (the die is cast).

Pompey and the senatorial forces were caught by surprise, and within three months they had been driven from Italy to Greece. Caesar turned west and seized Sicily to secure Rome's grain supply, then attacked Pompey's supporters in Spain. He trapped their army near the Ebro River at Ilerda (now Lerida), and when they surrendered, he showed considerable clemency in pardoning them, in marked contrast to his earlier harsh treatment of the Gauls.

Returning to Rome, Caesar became dictator for the first time and proceeded to deal with numerous social problems, especially that of widespread debt, caused by the breakdown of the republic. In 48, he daringly crossed the Adriatic in winter and besieged Pompey's larger forces at their base of Dyrrachium (Durazzo). Forced to retire into Thessaly, Caesar turned and defeated Pompey at the battle of Pharsalus, destroying his army. Pompey fled to Egypt, hoping to rally support, but instead was murdered; the whole Roman world was in Caesar's grasp.

Following Pompey to Egypt, Caesar intervened in a power struggle between Cleopatra and her younger brother. In this, the Alexandrine War, Caesar narrowly escaped death on several occasions, but was successful in placing Cleopatra upon the throne. There followed an intense affair between the young queen and Caesar, and the son born in September, 48, was named Caesarion.

After more campaigns against foreign states in the east and the remnants of Pompey's supporters, Caesar returned to Rome in 46 to celebrate four triumphs: over Gaul, Egypt, Pontus, and Africa. Cleopatra arrived soon after to take up residence in the city; perhaps along with her came the eminent Egyptian astronomer Sosigenes of Alexandria, who aided Caesar in his reform of the calendar. This Julian calendar is the basis of the modern system.

Caesar was active in other areas. He settled many of his veterans in colonies throughout the empire, and with them many of the poor and unemployed of Rome, thus reducing the strain on the public economy. Numerous other civic reforms were instituted, many of them laudable, but most of them giving increased power to Caesar alone. Although he publicly rejected the offer of kingship, he did accept the dictatorship for life in February, 44.

This action brought together a group of about sixty conspirators, led by Gaius Cassius Longinus and Marcus Junius Brutus. Brutus may have been Caesar's son; certainly he was an avowed, almost fanatic devotee of the republic who thought it his duty to kill Caesar.

Realizing that Caesar planned to depart on March 18 for a lengthy campaign against the Parthian Empire in the east, the conspirators decided to strike. On March 15, the ides of March, they attacked Caesar as he entered the Theater of Pompey for a meeting of the senate. As he fell, mortally wounded, his last words are reported to have been either "Et tu, Brute?" (and you too, Brutus?) or, in Greek, "And you too, my child?"

Summary

"Veni, vidi, vinci"—I came, I saw, I conquered—is one of the most famous military dispatches of all time, and totally characteristic of Julius Caesar. He sent it to Rome after his defeat of King Pharnaces of Pontus in 47, a campaign that added greatly to Rome's eastern power, but which represented almost an interlude between Caesar's victories in Egypt and his final triumph in the civil war. The message captures the essence of Caesar, that almost superhuman mix of energy, ability, and ambition.

This mixture fascinated his contemporaries and has enthralled the world ever since. Caesar was ambitious, but so were others, Pompey among them; he was bold, but many other bold Romans had their schemes come to nothing; he was certainly able, but the Roman world was full of men of ability.

It was Caesar, however, who united all these qualities, and had them in so much fuller measure than his contemporaries that he was unique. As a writer or speaker, he could easily hold his own against acknowledged masters such as Cicero; in statesmanship and politics, he was unsurpassed; in military skill, he had no peer. When all of these qualities were brought together, they amounted to an almost transcendent genius that seemed to give Julius Caesar powers and abilities far beyond those of mortal men.

The central question, in 44 and today, is to what use—good or bad—did Caesar put those qualities and abilities? Clearly, Brutus, Cassius, and the other conspirators believed that he had perverted his qualities and subverted the state and thus must be destroyed. In later years, the term "Caesarism" has been applied to those who wished to gain supreme power for themselves, disregarding the laws and careless of the rights of others. Viewed from this perspective, Caesar destroyed the last remnants of the Roman Republic and thus stamped out what liberty and freedom remained.

From another view, he was the creator, or at least the forerunner, of a new and better system, the empire, which brought order from chaos, peace from endless civil war. The ancient republic had already disappeared in all but name, had become empty form without real substance, and it was for the general good that it finally disappeared. This is the view of Caesar as archetypal ruler and dispenser of order, the view which made his very name a title of monarchs—the Caesars of Rome, the kaisers of Germany, the czars of Russia.

In the end, a sensible view of Caesar must combine a mixture of these two perspectives, seeing both his faults and virtues. He accomplished much during his lifetime, and his achievements have endured for millennia after his assassination. Even in death, Caesar is best described in the words of Shakespeare: "He doth bestride this narrow world like a colossus."

Bibliography

Caesar, Gaius Julius. *Commentaries*. Translated by Rex Warner. London: Macmillan, 1914; New York: New American Library, 1961. Caesar's own version of his conquest of Gaul and struggle in the civil war against Pompey. One of the masterpieces of classical literature, this work gives a vivid and exciting view of truly world-changing events by the major actor of his time. Indispensable for a full understanding of the period.

Fuller, J. F. C. *Julius Caesar: Man, Soldier, and Tyrant*. London: Eyre and Spottiswoode, and New Brunswick, N.J.: Rutgers University Press, 1965. Written by a distinguished soldier and military theorist, this work concentrates on Caesar's achievements on the battlefield, and why he was such an outstanding and innovative commander. The study, which is generally free of technical obscurities and military jargon, helps the reader understand the difficulties of Caesar's triumphs.

Grant, Michael. *Caesar*. London: Weidenfeld and Nicolson, and New York: McGraw-Hill, 1969. A well-written, well-researched biography of the man and his time, careful to place Caesar within the context of the fall of the Roman Republic. Caesar's accomplishments become even more impressive when viewed as part of a larger whole, and this Grant does extremely well. The volume is well illustrated.

———. *The Roman Emperors: A Biographical Guide to the Rulers of Imperial Rome*. New York: Charles Scribner's Sons, 1985. A brief introductory sketch of Caesar can be found in this volume. Although relatively short, it provides all the necessary information to begin an investigation of the man's life and accomplishments.

———. *The Twelve Caesars*. Rev. ed. London and New York: Penguin Books, 1979. Grant is one of the outstanding modern historians of ancient Rome, and this book is both a continuation of Suetonius' classical biography and a commentary upon it. Gives the reader a thorough understanding of what Caesar accomplished and an insight into why and how those accomplishments occurred.

Meier, Christian. *Caesar*. London and New York: BasicBooks/HarperCollins, 1995. A full biography of Julius Caesar that fills in gaps in evidence by extensive consideration of the environment of the late Republic. Meier views Caesar as a prodigiously talented "outsider" who found himself unable to fulfill his ambitions within the old (and decaying) republican framework.

Suetonius. *The Lives of the Twelve Caesars*. Edited by Joseph Gavorse. New York: Modern Library, 1931. Suetonius' work is the essential starting point for any study of the early Roman emperors. His biography of Caesar may lack historical rigor and objectivity, but it is a fascinating source of anecdotes and character traits. The content and style (even in translation) makes *The Lives of the Twelve Caesars* a good starting place for the beginning student.

Michael Witkoski

CALIGULA
Gaius Julius Caesar

Born: August 31, A.D. 12; probably Antium (Anzio), Italy

Died: January, A.D. 41; Rome

Area of Achievement: Government and politics; Roman Caesars

Contribution: The third ruler of the Julio-Claudian dynasty, Caligula did much during his short reign to transform the position of Roman emperor into an institution of absolute monarchy.

Early Life

Gaius Julius Caesar was born in the resort town of Antium (modern Anzio) on August 31, A.D. 12, the third son of Germanicus Caesar, nephew of the future emperor Tiberius, and his wife Agrippina the Elder, granddaughter of the current emperor Augustus. As a toddler, Gaius spent time in northern Europe and Syria, accompanying his father during his various military and diplomatic assignments. In fact, it was during a stay at a military installation near the Rhine River that Gaius received the nickname "Caligula" from his father's soldiers. Agrippina often dressed her young son up as a legionnaire, and the nickname came from the small version of soldier's hob-nailed boots (*caliga*) that he wore. "Caligula" means "little boots."

Imperial politics at this time were unsettled and volatile. Augustus, after his victory at the Battle of Actium in 31 B.C., had emerged as the undisputed master of Rome, but he accepted only the title of *princeps* (which implied that he was the first official among equals) and preferred to exercise power in an indirect fashion by exploiting existing republican offices and institutions. He employed this cautious method of governing because he feared that a too blatant disregard for Roman republican traditions might offend the sensibilities of his subjects and thereby jeopardize the stability of the empire.

In keeping with this fiction, Augustus hesitated to set up a clear-cut succession system that would pass on power in a hereditary fashion. Therefore, when Augustus died in A.D. 41, his designated successor, his stepson Tiberius, had to accept the position from the Senate and secure the support of the army and Praetorian Guard (the ruler's personal bodyguard) before he could assume power. For a long time, Tiberius hesitated to designate his choice as successor. Caligula's father, Germanicus, was the most likely candidate because of his general popularity and the fact that he was the grandson of Augustus. Tiberius, however, appears to have been jealous of his nephew's fame and kept him out of Rome on various military and diplomatic missions. It was on one such mission to the Middle East that Germanicus died in A.D. 19, under suspicious circumstances. His widow, Agrippina, was convinced that her husband had been poisoned by the governor of Syria on the orders of Tiberius. While no hard evidence has ever appeared to link Tiberius with the death of Germanicus, from that point forward Agrippina became the emperor's bitter enemy.

With the death of Germanicus, Tiberius began to groom the latter's two eldest sons, Nero and Drusus, for power. Yet both young men, as well as their mother, fell victim to the plots of Lucius Aelius Sejanus, Tiberius' evil prefect of the Praetorian Guard, who wanted to eliminate the family of Germanicus in order to strengthen his power over the emperor. He fabricated evidence that charged both Nero and Agrippina with involvement in plots against the emperor's life, and both were banished to remote islands where they subsequently died. Sejanus then accused Drusus of various sexual crimes and, as a result, he was imprisoned in a cell below the palace (where he also would die in A.D. 33)

After the banishment of his mother in A.D. 27, Caligula lived first with Livia, his great-grandmother and the widow of Augustus; after her death in A.D. 29, he lived with Antonia, the sister of Augustus, Caligula's paternal grandmother. Although he had originally been too young to warrant the attention of Sejanus, the elimination of his two older brothers made Caligula the next target for the prefect's machinations. Fortunately for the young man, Sejanus fell from power and was executed in A.D. 31. Tiberius then took Caligula into his household (the emperor now lived on the island of Capri) and began to groom him as his successor.

Life's Work

The Roman historian Suetonius argues that Tiberius took Caligula under his wing because the boy's

interests, which were already depraved, coincided with his own. Other historians, however, have offered less sensationalistic explanations for the decision. Tiberius had promised Augustus to promote the interests of the children of Germanicus and, if possible, to name one as his successor, and Tiberius, despite his other possible faults, was a man who kept his word. In addition, the new prefect of the Praetorian Guard, Naevius Cordus Sutorius Macro, saw a brilliant future for himself with the ascension of Caligula and actively campaigned for his official designation as heir. As the engineer of the fall of Sejanus, Macro already had the emperor's ear. He strengthened his relationship with Caligula by flattering the young man and even encouraging him to have an affair with his wife.

Tiberius was also intelligent enough to recognize Caligula's weaknesses. This was the most likely reason for his final decision regarding the succession. He named Caligula as co-heir along with his young grandson, Tiberius Gemellus. Thus when the old emperor finally died in A.D. 37 (Suetonius recorded that Macro and Caligula smothered him with a pillow on his sickbed), the twenty-six-year-

old Caligula and his ten-year-old cousin assumed power in Rome.

Caligula never had any intention of sharing power with Gemellus. With the skillful aid of Macro, he moved rapidly to consolidate his position at his cousin's expense. Two days after the death of Tiberius, the Senate hailed Caligula as "Imperator" and granted him, in one block, all the powers that both Augustus and Tiberius had only gradually assumed. Gemellus was left isolated and powerless.

At the time that he assumed power, Caligula was, by most accounts, an unattractive man. He was very tall, with thin legs and a pasty complexion. He had small, deep-set eyes and a broad forehead. His hair was thin, and he already had a large bald spot at the back of his head. Suetonius reports that he was so self-conscious of his baldness that he made it a crime punishable by death to look at him from above. He had married Junia Claudilla in A.D. 33, but he engaged in numerous affairs with other women and with men. It was rumored that he routinely committed incest with his sister Drusilla, and he may have also done so with his other two sisters. An inveterate gambler on chariot races,

Caligula developed such a fondness for his favorite horse, Incitatus, that he had the animal attend Senate meetings and even wanted to make him a consul.

At the beginning of his reign, however, Caligula made an effort to be a popular ruler. He treated the Senate with respect, put on lavish entertainments for the Roman populace, abolished the crime of *maiestas*, or speaking or acting against the *princeps*, which Tiberius had used to punish personal enemies, and destroyed incriminating records that Tiberius had kept on many notable Romans. In late September, A.D. 37, however, Caligula fell ill, and when he recovered in late October, his reign took a dramatic turn for the worse.

Caligula emerged from his illness convinced that there was a conspiracy against him. Determined to eliminate it, he ordered the deaths of Gemellus and his father-in-law, Junius Silanus. He then divorced his wife and married Livia Orestilla. This marriage also ended in divorce within a year, whereupon he married Lollia Paulina. His third marriage lasted less than a year. Upon his divorce from Lollia in A.D. 39, Caligula married Caesonia, who was already pregnant by him. She gave birth to a daughter, Drusilla, a month after the wedding.

Meanwhile, Caligula continued to go after his real and imagined enemies. The emperor forced the devious Macro and his wife to commit suicide in early A.D. 38. He accused his former best friend and lover, Marcus Lepidus, of conspiring against him with the military commander Gaetulicus and had them both executed in A.D. 39. He reintroduced the crime of *maiestas* that same year, thereby opening the door to many more executions of prominent Romans. He even went as far as to accuse his two surviving sisters, Agrippina and Livilla (Drusilla had died in A.D. 38), of trying to overthrow him and had them both banished from Rome. During this same period, Caligula also began to claim that he was a god. He ordered statues erected to him throughout the empire and even demanded that one be placed in the main Jewish synagogue in Jerusalem (this order does not seem to have been carried out). Once, on a military expedition in northern Europe, Caligula claimed to have been offended by the god Neptune and declared war on him. He reportedly ordered his troops to march into the English Channel and flay the water with their swords. He then declared victory and had his men collect seashells along the shore as tribute from the defeated god.

Caligula was also extravagant in his spending. Even though he inherited a budget surplus from Tiberius of approximately 2,500 million *sesterces*, he managed to spend it all in less than a year. To gain additional revenue, he forced all rich Romans to name him as their heir and then often found reasons to have them executed. He imposed a number of new direct taxes and, according to several sources, even opened a brothel in his palace staffed by the daughters and wives of noble Romans.

Caligula's increasingly erratic and bizarre behavior finally did give rise to the conspiracy he so feared. Organized by several prominent senators and an officer in the Praetorian Guard, Cassius Chaerea, the assassins separated Caligula from his German bodyguards as he left the games celebrating the holiday of Ludi Palatini in A.D. 41. Caligula was stabbed at least thirty times, and the assassins killed his wife and daughter shortly thereafter. After a brief period of confusion, the Praetorian Guard named Caligula's uncle Claudius the new emperor, and the Senate ratified the selection the next day.

Summary

Augustus, the first *princeps*, pretended not to be a monarch, even though he was one in reality. Tiberius had more or less continued this tradition. During his short reign, Caligula, through his blatantly excessive and autocratic behavior, destroyed the last remnants of the fiction surrounding the position. Although he was not a good ruler in many important respects, Caligula nevertheless clearly demonstrated to the Roman people that the Republic was over and that a new era of imperial monarchy had begun.

Bibliography

Balsdon, V. D. *The Emperor Gaius*. Oxford: Clarendon Press, 1934; New York: AMS Press, 1976. Until the 1990 publication of the Anthony Barret book discussed below, this work was the standard treatment in English on Caligula. Although the author uncritically repeats many negative stories from Suetonius and others, he also argues that the Roman Senate was as guilty as the emperor himself for many of the abuses committed during Caligula's reign.

Barrett, Anthony. *Agrippina: Sex, Power, and Politics in the Early Empire*. New Haven, Conn.: Yale University Press, 1996. Although its subject is Caligula's sister, Agrippina the Younger, this volume provides an excellent examination of Caligula's reign, his relationship with his family, and the question of whether or not he committed incest with his sisters.

————. *Caligula: The Corruption of Power.* London: Batsford, 1988; New Haven, Conn.: Yale University Press, 1990. A biography of Caligula that argues that although the emperor was morally irresponsible, insufferably arrogant, and emotionally unequipped to rule, he was not the psychotic maniac of popular imagination.

Sandison, A. T. "The Madness of the Emperor Caligula." *Medical History* 2 (1958): 202-209. Discusses the various possible causes for Caligula's illness in A.D. 37 and examines whether the experience caused his mind to snap.

Suetonius, Gaius (Tranquillus). *The Twelve Caesars.* London and Baltimore: Penguin Books, 1957. Chapter 5 deals with the life of Caligula and is the source of many of the most bizarre stories about the emperor. Given the biases of the author, however, many of these stories should not be taken at face value.

Wells, Colin. *The Roman Empire.* 2d ed. Cambridge, Mass.: Harvard University Press, and London: Fontana, 1992. An excellent examination of the institution of Roman emperor as it evolved from Augustus to Diocletian. The author's treatment of Caligula is balanced and perceptive.

Christopher E. Guthrie

CALLIMACHUS

Born: c. 305 B.C.; Cyrene, Libya
Died: c. 240 B.C.; Alexandria, Egypt
Area of Achievement: Literature
Contribution: Although most of Callimachus' work has been lost, his hymns and epigrams—incorporating drama, sophistication, and a sense of history—survive as masterpieces of their kind. He set an ideal of tone and content which has influenced poets for centuries.

Early Life

The world into which Callimachus was born was a very different one from the world of the great poets and prose writers of fifth century Greece. Alexander the Great's empire had eclipsed and absorbed the old city-states and in turn had been divided into smaller warring empires after his death. Egypt had become the center of a new Greek state ruled by the Greek Ptolemies, and Alexandria had become not only a major political and commercial center and royal capital but also the center of a new and flourishing Greek culture, as rich as the old but somewhat diffident about its ability to live up to the glories of the past. Callimachus himself came from the Greek colony of Cyrene in Libya, a somewhat uneasy vassal of the Ptolemies. Although he was of a distinguished family which claimed Cyrene's founder Battus as an ancestor, it was natural for Callimachus to be drawn to Alexandria, with its promise of literary friends and royal patronage.

Callimachus began as a teacher of grammar in the suburb of Eleusis, but at length he attracted royal notice and received an appointment in the great library, which with the museum, a sort of "university complex" with lecture halls and roofed walks, was the center for the literary and scientific life of the city. Euclid and Archimedes flourished there. Not much is known of Callimachus' duties—only that he never became chief librarian and that he regarded a big book as a big evil—but the list of his lost prose works ("Catalog of Writers Eminent in All Fields of Literature," "Local Names of Months," "Rivers of the World," and so on) suggests an industrious cataloger. Compliments scattered through his work indicate royal patronage throughout his life.

Life's Work

The scanty evidence in his poems suggests that, once secure of royal patronage, Callimachus led a long, agreeable, and productive life in Alexandria. Symposia must have been frequent, although Callimachus prided himself on being a moderate drinker. It might be noted that only one of his erotic poems was written to a woman, and he was almost certainly a bachelor. He valued the didactic poet Aratus for sharing his preference for brevity and craftsmanship. He may have been ambivalent toward Apollonius Rhodius, a former pupil, for attempting a full-scale epic on the Argonauts. He wrote a romantic poem to one Theocritus, who is believed to be the inventor of pastoral poetry.

It is said that Callimachus wrote poems in every meter and that his books amounted to eight hundred (although this sum probably means counting parts of books as individual works). Callimachus sometimes brought together his shorter works under a loose framework—hence his most notable work, the *Aetia* (causes), in which a whole series of local rituals are described and explained, somewhat in the manner of Ovid's *Metamorphoses* (C.A.D. 8), which indeed it influenced.

The *Aetia* shows Callimachus' cataloging zeal, as well as his interest in religious matters and in local affairs. The revised version begins with an apology in the manner of Alexander Pope in which Callimachus satirizes the works of his Rhodian critics, including Apollonius, who bray like donkeys while his own Muse chirps like the cicada. The *Aetia*, which must have been a lengthy collection, included stories of the Graces, Hercules, the Argonauts, Ariadne, and much else. Only two episodes survive in substantial form: the charming love story of Acontius and Cydippe and a court poem which is the remote inspiration of Pope's *The Rape of the Lock* (1712, 1714), *The Lock of Berenice* (Berenice was a real queen and a native of Cyrene).

Callimachus wrote a transitional poem to lead from the *Aetia* into his other great collection, the *Iambi*, a collection of which only tantalizing fragments exist. Written in Greek iambic—a conversational meter used not only for drama but also for fables and lampoons—Callimachus' *Iambi* sounds as much like Pope's *The Dunciad* (1728-1743) as anything else. It included an Aesopian fable about the origin of language, a quarrel between the Laurel and the Olive, a satire on a pederastic schoolmaster, a poem in honor of a victor in the jar race, a serious poem honoring a friend's daughter, and finally an answer to those who criticized Callimachus for failing to specialize. There was another invective poem, the "Ibis," possibly directed at Apollonius, but of this little remains.

The *Aetia* and the *Iambi* were Callimachus' longest poems. He was also a practitioner of the *epyllion*, or little epic, which differed from the full-scale epic not only in length but also in subject matter: The central episode might indeed be heroic, but the emphasis might be on some unheroic character. Thus, in *Hecale* the ostensible subject is Theseus' taming the bull of Marathon, but most of the poem told how Theseus sheltered in the hut of an old peasant woman, Hecale.

Of all Callimachus' works, the least frustrating are the hymns—to Zeus, Apollo, Artemis, Delos, the Bath of Pallas, and Demeter—which are nearly intact. There seems no reason to doubt that these were designed to be performed as part of religious ceremonies and that they embody genuine religious feeling, as well as a feeling for nature and Callimachus' usual curiosity about local customs and traditions. *The Bath of Pallas* and *To Delos* are particularly striking.

Callimachus' epigrams, of which a fair number have survived in anthologies and other sources, including a Roman wall, contain epitaphs, votive dedications, love lyrics, and other miscellaneous short poems. Many seem to be occasional poems written as a favor to friends or patrons and have the limited appeal of occasional poetry, such as the following lament for the poet Heraclitus:

> They told me, Heraclitus, they told me you were dead;
> They brought me bitter news to hear and bitter tears to shed.
> I wept, as I remember'd how often you and I
> Had tired the sun with talking and sent him down the sky.
> And now that thou art lying, my dear old Carian guest,
> A handful of grey ashes, long, long ago at rest,
> Still are thy pleasant voices, thy nightingales, awake,
> For Death, he taketh all away, but them he cannot take.

William Cory's translation, published in 1858, lacks the conciseness which was Callimachus' ideal but is otherwise worthy of the original. Some of the epitaphs have grace and dignity which rise above the immediate occasion:

> Shipwrecked stranger, Leóntikhos found your
> Anonymous corpse and gave you burial
> On the seabeach here. His tears, though, were for

His own mortality. Restless sailor,
He beats over the sea like a flashing gull.

Because most of Callimachus' work is lost, his epigrams are prized. With any other poet, these occasional poems would be treated as an appendix rather than a central portion of the lifework. Scholarly editions of Callimachus, however, include dozens of isolated quotations, often mere phrases quoted in a dictionary, for the sake of preserving a rare word from this master.

Summary

Callimachus was a far greater poet than the surviving fragments would indicate; in the Greek and Roman world, which knew his work in its entirety, his prestige was enormous. When a modern scholar pieces together what is left of Callimachus' work, he can conjure up the ghosts of the *Hecale*, the *Aetia*, and the *Iambi*. He can prove how great these poems were and even give something of their flavor, but in the end he can only point to how much of Callimachus' distinguished poetry is lost. (On the other hand, if the prose works had survived, perhaps they would have only a historical interest.)

The hymns are impressive even in translation and would have been even more impressive in their liturgical setting. The epigrams, however, seldom translate well and too often depend on some figure or allusion which must be elaborately footnoted. A reader who knows Greek literature thoroughly and who can work with the available parallel editions (original Greek and English translation on facing pages) has a better chance of enjoying Callimachus; for others, there is still hope. Every so often papyruses containing fragments of Callimachus' work are found in Egypt, and perhaps a less fragmentary manuscript of the *Hecale* or the *Aetia* will surface. If that happens, Callimachus will be read as much as his rival Apollonius.

Bibliography

Callimachus. *Aetia, Iambi, Lyric Poems, Hecale, Minor Epic and Elegiac Poems, and Other Fragments.* Translated by C. A. Trypanis. Cambridge, Mass. and London: Harvard University Press, 1958. Provides a Greek text, a serviceable prose translation, and excellent notes.

Cameron, Alan. *Callimachus and His Critics.* Princeton, NJ: Princeton University Press, 1995. This controversial but formidably learned and carefully argued book re-examines all the ancient evidence about the life and career of Callimachus. Cameron places the poet in the context of Alexandrian literary and social practices, makes some adjustments in the chronology of his life, and argues that he was not, contrary to the prevailing modern opinion, opposed to the writing of epic. All future studies of Callimachus will be affected by this work.

de Romilly, Jaqueline. *A Short History of Greek Literature*. Translated by Lillian Doherty. Chicago: University of Chicago Press, 1985. Includes excellent impressionistic accounts of Callimachus and Apollonius. De Romilly doubts that Callimachus shared the "simple faith" of the Homeric hymns.

Ferguson, John. *Callimachus*. Boston: Twayne Publishers, 1980. A general survey of Callimachus, this work is interesting and thorough. Ferguson pieces together fragments of gossip to make a coherent life of Callimachus, and he includes the fragments of the poems. Callimachus' social and cultural background is treated. Ferguson compares Callimachus with T. S. Eliot. Contains an excellent bibliography.

Fraser, P. M. *Ptolemaic Alexandria*. Oxford: Clarendon Press, 1972. Gives an especially useful account of the library and museum and of Alexandrian scholars and science generally, as well as the commercial and social life of the city. Contains a chapter on Callimachus.

Harder, M. A., R. F. Regtuit, and G. C. Wakker, eds. *Hellenistica Groningana*. Vol. 1, *Callimachus*. Groningen: Egbert Forsten, 1993. A collection of 13 papers on various aspects of Callimachus' oeuvre, concentrating primarily on the *Hymns* and the *Aetia*. Most of the papers portray the poet as an acutely self-conscious literary artist, determined to adapt genres and traditions to his own unique ends.

Hutchinson, G. O. *Hellenistic Poetry*. Oxford and New York: Clarendon Press, 1988. An introduction to the aesthetics of Callimachus and others. The author argues that their salient literary quality is a "piquant combination of the serious and the unserious."

Lane Fox, Robin. "Hellenistic Culture and Literature." In *The Oxford History of the Classical World*, edited by John Boardman, Jasper Griffin, and Oswyn Murray. New York: Oxford University Press, 1986. An excellent survey of the cultural background, with some interesting comments on Callimachus. Includes a good treatment of literary patronage and comparisons to other Hellenistic figures. Lane Fox compares Callimachus with the Wordsworth of the River Duddon sonnets.

John C. Sherwood

CASSIUS
Gaius Cassius Longinus

Born: Date unknown; probably Rome

Died: 44 B.C.; Philippi

Areas of Achievement: Government and politics; warfare and conquest

Contribution: As a diehard republican, Cassius distrusted Julius Caesar's ambition to control the Roman government. With his brother-in-law Marcus Brutus and others, Cassius organized Caesar's assassination on the Ides of March in 44 B.C.

Early Life

Little is known about the early life of Cassius. Since he was born into a family long prominent in Roman history, Cassius almost certainly received the traditional education of a late Roman republican aristocrat and slaveowner. Plutarch credited Cassius with a fluent command of the Greek language, which was employed by most Roman aristocrats during the Hellenistic Age for all important cultural and scholarly activities. Cassius would later correspond with the gifted lawyer and rhetorician Marcus Tullius Cicero, since both men wished to preserve the republican form of government and prevent the concentration of power in the hands of a dictator or oligarchical group.

Cassius apparently displayed an opposition to privilege at an early age. As a schoolboy, Cassius fought Faustus, son of a dictator, when Faustus attempted to use his father's position to intimidate other youths. Pompey refused to allow the relatives of Faustus to bring legal action against Cassius.

Before he became an assassin, Cassius held several important positions in the Roman government and significant military commands fighting against the Parthians. In 49 B.C., Cassius was tribune when civil war broke out between Caesar and Pompey, and he supported Pompey. Cassius surrendered to Caesar after Pompey lost the battle of Pharsallus in 48 B.C. Given Caesar's strong position, he generously pardoned Cassius, who still harbored a smoldering resentment against him as a possible would-be king of Rome.

Life's Work

Cassius was a respected military leader. He first achieved public recognition in 53 B.C. while serving under Marcus Crassus in his campaign against the Parthians. After surviving the Roman defeat at Carrhae, he was able to secure Syria against the Parthians by 51 B.C. After receiving the pardon from Caesar, Cassius enjoyed a respected public position despite the fact that Caesar and others continued to question his motives.

Despite the generosity of Caesar, Cassius was alarmed as Caesar acquired more and more governmental power. In addition, Caesar appropriated some lions that Cassius had donated to the city of Megara, and Cassius may have held a long-term grudge over this issue. For whatever reasons, Cassius organized the assassination of Caesar on March 15, 44 B.C., and he recruited Marcus Junius Brutus in order to give moral credibility to the plot. Although Cassius may have resented the fact that Caesar had given an important praetorship to Brutus instead of to him, Cassius subordinated his own personal concerns to the political end he wished to achieve, despite the fact that even Caesar had said that Cassius had been the better-qualified candidate. Members of the conspiracy included Casca, one of two contemporaries named Cinna, Decimus Brutus, and Tullius Cimber. Some sources say that as many as sixty individuals were involved in the assassination plot.

Initially, the conspirators had reason to believe that they had been successful in the goals they had set in the assassination of Caesar. Plutarch indicates that the Cnidian teacher Artemidorus may have unsuccessfully tried to warn Caesar on the day of Caesar's death, and Caesar may have held an unread written warning in his hands as he died.

After Caesar died, Brutus gave a successful speech explaining the reasons behind the assassination. Initially, it appeared as though the conspiracy would have the political impact Cassius and his allies had desired. Although the Senate promptly recognized Caesar as a god to help appease the military veterans of his campaigns, a general amnesty was declared, and Brutus and Cassius both initially received honors and politically and militarily significant posts.

While Cassius needed to have Brutus involved in the assassination plot in order to give it more credibility, Brutus lacked Cassius' ability to plan ahead for Roman government after the death of Caesar. Brutus foolishly insisted that the conspirators spare

Marc Antony, whose funeral oration for Caesar turned the bulk of public opinion against the conspirators, particularly when the crowds learned that Caesar's will had left a bequest to every Roman citizen. Popular anger led to the murder of the Cinna who had not been involved in the conspiracy.

The conspirators thus found themselves increasingly isolated in Italy. As a result, Brutus departed for Macedonia and Cassius for Syria, where he had earlier successful experience as a Roman general and hoped to rally support. Cassius put his military prowess to efficient use, and in 43 B.C. he defeated an army led by Dolabella, whom Marc Antony had sent East to oppose him.

Despite his initial military successes and the addition to his army of troops brought by Brutus, who joined him, Cassius found himself in a difficult situation in 42 B.C., when Marc Antony and Caesar's great-nephew Octavian marched east to oppose Brutus and Cassius. Cassius attempted to confront the military test he faced at the battle of Philippi with courage. As a convinced Epicurean, Cassius apparently distrusted the influence of the senses, especially when individuals were under stress. According to Plutarch's account, the more rational Cassius reassured Brutus when Brutus claimed to have seen an evil spirit that threatened to meet him at Philippi. Unlike Brutus, Cassius did not believe in spirits, or at least doubted their power to affect the living and take on a human appearance.

At Philippi, Anthony and Octavian had twenty-eight legions to oppose nineteen legions under the command of the co-conspirators. Brutus and Cassius faced a difficult military situation, and Cassius wished to postpone battle in order to take advantage of his troops' superior supplies. Yet Brutus and Cassius did not consider their situation hopeless when they parted to assume their respective battle commands, although they decided that they would commit suicide if they were defeated. Miscalculation played a large role in the fact that Cassius lay dead at the end of the battle, having committed suicide by running on the sword he had used to kill Caesar. For many years, Cassius's Parthian freedman Pindarus had been pledged to assist in Cassius' suicide if requested, and Cassius decided to die when he thought, erroneously, that the initial battle had gone as badly for Brutus as it had for him.

Since he survived Cassius, Brutus performed the last rites for his co-conspirator, having his body wrapped and sent to Thaos for burial. A somber Brutus mourned Cassius as a man whose like would not be seen again, and Cassius' death probably marked a dramatic turning point in Roman history. The republican form of government, which had followed the overthrow of the early monarchy by a purported ancestor of Brutus, gave way to a more efficient imperial form of government. While no verifiable statement survives of the political ideals that brought Cassius to Philippi, a speech attributed by Appian to Cassius does. In the speech, Cassius reviewed the events of the past three years and honored the bond between soldiers and their leaders. Cassius claimed that the tyrannicides held no personal enmity for Caesar but possessed a justified concern for the preservation of Roman republican institutions.

Summary

In modern terms, Cassius might be compared to senators who aspire to the presidency and never quite achieve their goal. He sincerely believed in the traditional republican ideals that had governed the Roman Republic for centuries, despite the fact that the acquisition of an empire logically necessitated changes in Rome's governmental structure to govern unruly subject peoples. With Cassius' suicide, the old Roman Republic was doomed. His ally Brutus died three weeks later, as Brutus followed Cassius' example in taking his own life. Despite the fact that Octavian, later Augustus, represented the future of Rome, Cassius was not forgotten. Among the ancient historians, however, only Appian showed respect for him as a political as well as a military leader.

Cassius' namesake descendent in the following century, who became a noted legal scholar, was exiled from Rome by Nero for his devotion to outmoded republican ideals, although he managed to die peacefully in Rome under the more moderate Vespasian. In later centuries, those seeking to justify assassination often turned to the example of Brutus and Cassius, although Cassius never obtained the respect widely granted Brutus. William Shakespeare's fictional description of Cassius as a "lean and hungry" man has remained the characteristic view of Cassius held by later generations.

Bibliography

Cassius Dio Cocceianus. *The Roman History: The Reign of Augustus.* Translated by Ian Scott-Kilvert. London and New York: Penguin Books,

1987. In this history, Cassius Dio covers the period immediately after the deaths of Brutus and Cassius. Dio claims that Agrippa threatened Octavian (Augustus) with the fate of Julius Caesar unless he proceeded toward monarchy. Agrippa warned Octavian that he would find his own Brutus and Cassius unless he moved resolutely to consolidate power.

Cicero, Marcus Tullius. *Selected Letters*. Translated with an introduction by D. R. H. Shackleton Bailey. London and New York: Penguin Books, 1986. Cassius and his co-conspirator Marcus Brutus corresponded with Cicero. They shared a similar devotion to traditional Roman republican ideals and an aversion to Julius Caesar. Cicero approved of the assassination of Caesar; he did, however, regret that Caesar's assassins had left the apparatus necessary to create a monarchy intact. A January 45 B.C. letter from Cassius to Cicero reveals the former's basic philosophical convictions. In a cogent expression of Epicurean philosophy, Cassius holds that one cannot attain pleasure without living rightly and justly.

Gowing, Alain M. "Appian and Cassius' Speech Before Philippi." *Bella Civilia* 490: 100. Gowing concentrates on strengthening the reputation of Appian as a historian and proving that Appian did more than copy earlier sources. To show Appian's craft, Gowing focuses on Appian's version of Cassius' final speech to his men at Philippi, a battle that would end in Cassius' suicide. Appian viewed Cassius more favorably than most ancient historians. For Appian, Cassius was a credible military leader who acted out of sincere belief that the Roman republican tradition, which had endured since the overthrow of the early monarchs, should not be discarded.

Plutarch. *Fall of the Roman Republic: Six Lives*. Rex Warner, trans. Rev. ed. London and New York: Penguin Books, 1972. Plutarch discusses Cassius in his life of Julius Caesar. In this selection, Plutarch has Caesar describe both Brutus and Cassius as "pale and thin." In his sketch of Caesar, Plutarch refers his readers to his "Life of Brutus." He also stresses that Cassius employed the dagger he had used against Caesar to kill himself and discusses the many supernatural signs that purportedly surrounded the death of Caesar.

———. *Makers of Rome: Nine Lives by Plutarch*. Translated, with an introduction, by Ian Scott-Kilvert. London and Baltimore: Penguin Books, 1965. This selection includes the life of Brutus, the respected co-conspirator Cassius recruited to assassinate Caesar. According to Plutarch's account, Brutus hated the concentration of power in Caesar's hands, and Cassius hated Caesar. Plutarch also describes Cassius' suicide at Philippi and how it may have been prompted by poor eyesight and error.

Shakespeare, William. *The Tragedy of Julius Caesar*. Edited by Lawrence Mason. New Haven, Conn.: Yale University Press, 1919. A dramatic portrayal of Caesar's assassination. Shakespeare's account was based on Plutarch and perhaps on Appian. In addition, Shakespeare may have consulted portrayals of the same events by other Elizabethan dramatists. Shakespeare presents Brutus as noble in his motivations for tyrannicide but implies that Cassius was correctly described by Caesar as "lean and hungry" (act 1, scene 2, line 193) motivated by ambition.

Susan A. Stussy

CATO THE CENSOR

Born: 234 B.C.; Tusculum, Italy
Died: 149 B.C.; Rome, Italy
Area of Achievement: Government
Contribution: Through his personal example, public service, and writings, Cato advocated an ideal of a powerful, prosperous state populated with self-reliant, active citizens.

Early Life

Marcus Porcius Cato was born in Tusculum, about fifteen miles from Rome. Little is known about his family, except that his father, Marcus, and great-grandfather Cato were well-respected soldiers. The name Cato, meaning "accomplished," was given to a *novus homo* (new man) who came to public attention by his own achievements rather than by connection to a distinguished family. Young Cato spent his youth on an estate in the Sabine territory, where he learned farming, viticulture, and other agricultural skills.

When Cato was seventeen, the Carthaginian general Hannibal invaded Italy and defeated several Roman armies, inflicting huge losses (more than fifty thousand Romans died at the Battle of Cannae in 216 B.C.). Cato enlisted soon after Cannae and served with distinction for more than a decade. He fought in major battles in Sicily and Italy, including the siege of Syracuse and the defeat of Hasdrubal (Hannibal's brother) at Metaurus in 207. By the time Hannibal fled Italy and Carthage surrendered, around 201, Cato's personality and career had been shaped. He had proved heroic and fearless in combat. He carried an implacable hatred for Carthage. He displayed leadership, being elected a military tribune responsible for the soldiers' welfare in and out of battle.

Cato now entered public life and held a series of elective offices. In 204 he became quaestor, the official charged with watching over public expenditures. In this capacity he accompanied the army of Scipio Africanus in its attack on Carthaginian soil. In 199 Cato became a plebeian aedile, one who administered public buildings, streets, temples, and the marketplace. A year later, Cato was one of four praetors chosen; praetor was a more significant post that included the power to dispense justice and to command an army. Cato spent his praetorship as Governor of Sardinia, where he gained a reputation for honest and frugal administration.

Important patrons as well as ordinary voters were attracted to Cato and readily supported his advancing career. The Greek historian Plutarch described Cato at this time as a man with ruddy complexion, gray eyes, and unusual public speaking skills. Cato's quick mind—his knack for striking analogies and turns of phrase—and fearless attitude made him a successful orator, valued as an ally and feared as an opponent.

Life's Work

Cato's election as consul in 195 began a period of forty-six years during which he exerted significant influence in both domestic politics and foreign affairs. Cato's leadership coincided with a period of profound change in Roman manners at home and in Roman policies toward other world powers. By the time of Cato's death, Rome had defeated its imperial rivals, conquering Greece and Macedonia and destroying Carthage, burning the city to the ground. Military and political supremacy brought

Rome economic supremacy, and great wealth poured into a country where simplicity and austerity were traditional. Wealth became the basis of a leisured culture that looked to Greece for social values—a culture more intellectual, aesthetic, and self-indulgent than the Roman heritage. None of these changes occurred quickly or without dispute. Cato participated in the major controversies of the era. Could Rome dominate other nations without exploiting them? Could Romans maintain a work ethic amid unprecedented luxury? Would Greek attitudes supplant Roman ones?

Cato served as one of the two consuls appointed annually. Consuls were the senior Roman magistrates who executed the senate's will in political and military affairs. Soon after he took office, Cato went to Spain to lead the effort to subdue several tribes in rebellion since 197. Drilling inexperienced troops rigorously, Cato prepared them so effectively that they routed a veteran Spanish force at Emporiae. Cato showed mercy to the survivors and successfully induced other rebel groups and cities to surrender. Upon his return to a triumph in Rome, Cato boasted that he had captured more towns than he had spent days in Spain. Soon afterward he married a senator's daughter, a sign that a *novus homo* was now acceptable to the aristocracy.

Four years later, Cato went to Greece as military tribune with the army advancing against Antiochus, Rome's chief threat in Greece and Hannibal's protector. The army's march was blocked at the pass of Thermopylae (where three centuries before Spartan troops had held off invading Persians) until Cato led a cohort over rocks and crags to take the enemy rearguard by surprise. Cato claimed as much credit as Glabrio, the Roman commander, for the successful campaign. For years afterward, the two were political rivals.

In 189, Cato ran for the office of censor but was defeated. A censor ranked just below consul: He oversaw public morals, carried out the census, selected new members for the senate, expelled unfit senators, and conducted religious services. Previously, Cato had involved himself in important public debates about morality and ethics, such as the controversies surrounding the Oppian Law and the Junian Law. In the first, Cato argued for continuing a ban on ostentatious displays of wealth; in the second, he opposed repealing interest-rate limits. Already he was known as a champion of austerity and self-discipline in financial matters, both for the individual and for the state.

At the next election for censor in 184, Cato triumphed. Immediately he implemented the stern, rigorous platform on which he had campaigned. Though his program involved him in lawsuits for years to come, his supporters regarded his censorship as a landmark effort to reverse a perceived laxness in public standards. Cato and his cocensor expelled seven senators for unfitness, imposed a heavy tax on luxury goods, demolished private buildings encroaching on government property, fined those who neglected farms or vineyards, and renegotiated state contracts with private suppliers to reach better deals. Though contemporaries stressed the stringency of his actions, it is important to note that he executed his duties meticulously; he was careful to respect the letter as well as the spirit of the laws. For Cato, the primary goal was to see Rome thrive and prosper. Unlike many aristocratic Romans, Cato believed that public prosperity did not result from exploiting individuals—and he also believed that individuals ought not to thrive at public expense.

Certain individuals resented Cato's stern censorship and became enemies. Before his death he fought at least forty-four indictments and suits filed against him; none is recorded as successful. Each accusation became an occasion for Cato to display his well-honed oratorical skills, thereby leaving a rich rhetorical legacy for later generations. Cato took the unusual and self-confident step of publishing his speeches.

Though never elected censor again, Cato used his position in the senate to defend high standards and accountability for public officials. He prosecuted a provincial governor in 171 for manipulating corn prices; twenty years later, while in his eighties, Cato spoke against a special envoy and another governor who used their posts for profit. In 169, Cato led the supporters of the Voconian Law to keep inheritances concentrated rather than wastefully fragmented. In the same year, he argued against a triumph for a general whose troops complained of cruel treatment. In 153, Cato supported a proposal to prevent a consul from serving a second term, lest a man find public office too profitable to do without.

Cato exercised leadership in the senate through his oratory and among the educated class through his writings. Some scholars call Cato the father of Latin prose literature because of the volume and influence of his writing. The major works, which exist only in fragments (except for the treatise on agriculture), are *Ad filium*, a compendium of precepts on practical issues written for his son; *De re militari*, a manual of military training; *De agri cultura (On Agriculture*, 1913), a how-to guide for managing a prosperous farm; and *Origines*, a seven-book history of Rome. They are didactic works, displaying common sense rather than imagination. They suggest, however, that Cato possessed a reflective side to complement his pragmatic side: He addressed what to do and why it was worth doing. His literary works embody the moral vision of his censorship and his oratory: Knowledgeable, self-reliant individuals best lead the austere, just state.

In foreign policy, Cato seems to have advocated the restrained display of Rome's unchallenged military power. After victory in the Third Macedonian War (168), Cato sided with those anxious to see Macedonia a free ally rather than a subjugated client state. He consistently argued that smaller competitor nations and reluctant allies be treated leniently. The one exception to Cato's usual moderation made him legendary. All of his life Cato feared the resurgence of Carthage. Leading a senatorial delegation to Africa in 152, Cato saw signs of economic and military recovery. Henceforward, Cato argued that Rome must destroy her ancient rival before it grew powerful. "Carthago delenda est" ("Carthage must be destroyed") became the injunction repeatedly brought to the senate. War broke out in 149; Carthage was razed in 146. Cato died soon after the declaration of war, relieved that this time war's devastation would occur on enemy soil.

Summary

Because Cato the Censor's insistence that Carthage be destroyed dominated his last years, it has often been seen as the climactic event of his career. Without a doubt Cato was influential in securing war, and without a doubt that war changed the course of Roman history by extending Rome's dominion into northern Africa. Remembering Cato as a spokesman of steely, merciless national self-interest was easy for subsequent generations. It was—and is—too narrow an estimate of the man.

Cato's memorable reign as censor was also easy to recall, so easy that it gave the name by which history calls him. Rome reigned supreme for nearly six hundred years after Cato's death. Its life span as a great state encompassed extensive conquest, civil war, the transition from republic to empire, the acquisition of incalculable wealth, and profound social change. In times of crisis, many citizens remembered Cato. He was an emblem of personal self-control and public austerity. He knew the difference between public good and private welfare, between national prosperity and enervating materialism, between commonsensical good and rationalized failings. In subsequent neoclassical periods—Italy in the sixteenth century, England in the late seventeenth century, France and the United States in the late eighteenth century—Cato the Censor was a model of political leadership. He represented the highest civic virtue, the leader who rallied citizens by example and by eloquence to identify the public good with wise, orderly, and restrained government.

As dramatic as Cato's censorship was in combating obvious abuses, his time in office was one brief episode in a career. One must remember his lifetime of service to a civic ideal. He was not like the Old Testament prophets, men who lived obscurely until some crisis called them from obscurity to lead their people from darkness into light. His was not a lonely voice crying in the wilderness. He provided constant leadership in articulating a vision of the good state which, for the span of his life, most Romans held in common.

Bibliography

Astin, Alan E. *Cato the Censor*. Oxford: Clarendon Press, and New York: Oxford University Press, 1978. This is the definitive study in English. It analyzes Cato as soldier, politician, orator, and writer. Astin admires his subject's rugged individualism and active public service. Astin disputes the image of Cato as a puritanical traditionalist and asserts that he is important for much more than his final act of destroying Carthage.

Cicero, Marcus Tullius. "On Old Age." In *Letters and Treatises of Cicero and Pliny*, translated by E. S. Shuckburgh. New York: P. F. Collier and Son, 1909. Part of the Harvard Classics Series. Cato at age eighty-four is the hero of this philosophic dialogue. His conversation embodies Cicero's idea that in advancing years men should turn their thoughts from physical prowess to spiritual ideals in preparation for death. Cicero's wise, patient, transcendent Cato is attractive but fictitious. Cicero's essay shows some of the values Cato embodied for subsequent generations.

Livy, Titus. *The History of Rome from Its Foundation*. Translated by Henry Betterson. London and Baltimore: Penguin Books, 1960. The section of Livy's landmark history called "Rome and the Mediterranean" describes Rome's competition with Macedonia after the Second Punic War with Carthage. It covers the period from 210 to 167, during which Cato was consul, censor, and senator. Working from Cato's own writings, now lost, Livy presents vivid accounts of Cato's campaign in Spain, his support for the Oppian Law, and his term as censor.

Plutarch. *The Lives of the Noble Grecians and Romans*. Translated by John Dryden. London: Nutt, and New York: AMS Press, 1895. Writing as a moralist, rather than a biographer, Plutarch analyzes the strengths and weaknesses of Cato's character. The moralist praises Cato for old-fashioned virtues of temperance, public service, and frank speaking but faults him for avariciousness. By selling aging slaves and urging others to farm for profit, Plutarch charges, Cato dehumanized the social fabric he tried to save.

Scullard, H. H. *Roman Politics, 220-150 B.C.* 2d ed. Oxford: Clarendon Press, 1973; Westport, Conn.: Greenwood Press, 1981. This scholarly study documents the competition for political power between the son of an aristocratic family, such as Scipio Africanus, and the *novus homo*, such as Cato. Scullard provides detailed information about Cato's duties as censor, consul, and senator. He makes clear who supported Cato's policies, who opposed them, and why contemporaries took one side or the other.

Smith, R. E. "Cato Censorius," in *Greece and Rome* 9 (1940): 150-165. Smith analyzes the literary portraits of Cato offered by Cicero and Plutarch. He warns that Plutarch's account especially is an exaggerated version that pits "antique morality" against "modern morality." Smith himself judges that Cato held typical rather than reactionary opinions on wealth and empire. He concludes that Cato shaped, not stunted, Roman expansion.

Robert M. Otten

CATO THE YOUNGER

Born: 95 B.C. Rome, Italy

Died: 46 B.C. Utica, Africa

Areas of Achievement: Government and politics; philosophy

Contribution: Cato the Younger was a Stoic philosopher who represented the conservative Senatorial Party in Roman politics. He sought to preserve the dying Roman Republic at a time of rising military dictatorships.

Early Life

Cato the Younger, also known as "Cato Uticensis" from the place of his death, was born in Rome in 95 B.C. He was the great-grandson of Cato the Censor, who remained an inspiration for the younger Cato throughout his life. Cato the Younger was orphaned at an early age and grew up in the household of his maternal uncle Marcus Livius Drusus. Cato idealized the early Republic. He cultivated the old Roman virtues of simplicity and frugality in contrast to the materialism of his own day. He studied the philosophy of Stoicism, from which he came to believe that true freedom comes from within. According to the Stoics, the human body was merely a shell, and whatever happened to it was without consequence in the great world order.

Cato was known for the austerity of his life. He accustomed his body to labor and hard exercise. He traveled on foot everywhere. In taking journeys with friends who rode on horseback, he would remain on foot, conversing with one, then another, along the way. He bore illnesses with patience. He seldom laughed. He learned the art of oratory and spoke in a deep, full voice without refinements.

Cato first saw military service in 72 B.C. serving in the ranks against the slave revolt led by Spartacus. He distinguished himself to the extent that his commander wished to bestow a prize upon him, but he refused, saying that he did no more than others. In 67-66 B.C. Cato served as a military tribune in Macedonia. As commander of a legion, he shared the hardships with his troops. He ate the same food, wore the same clothing, and marched on foot with the soldiers in the ranks, even when his staff rode on horseback. After completing his term of military service, Cato traveled through the cities of Asia and brought back the Stoic philosopher Athenodorus with him when he returned to Rome.

Life's Work

At the outset of his political career, Cato was elected to the office of *quaestor*, or finance minister, in 64 B.C. During his year in office, he kept exact records of accounts, collected old debts, and dismissed and prosecuted clerks in the treasury who for years had been stealing from the public funds. The following year, Cato won the election for tribune. As tribune-elect, he made a powerful speech in the Senate denouncing the Catilinarian conspirators, whose plot to overthrow the government had been uncovered by the consul Marcus Tullius Cicero. Cato's speech, which called for the death penalty for the conspirators, carried the day despite a plea by Julius Caesar for a lesser punishment. In the same year, Cato prosecuted the consul-elect Lucinius Murena for bribery in winning the election to the consulship for 62 B.C., but Murena was acquitted.

In subsequent years, Cato became the leader of the conservative senatorial faction that opposed any threat to the established order. When Pompey the Great returned from the east at the end of 62 B.C. seeking ratification for his treaties and land for his veterans, Cato rigidly opposed Pompey's requests. Cato also prevented the passage of a bill that would have revised the tax codes for Asia. In opposing this measure, Cato antagonized both the equestrian class that stood to profit by the new tax revisions as well as Marcus Licinius Crassus, who had invested heavily in the publican tax companies. The equestrians withdrew their support from the Senatorial Party, and Cicero's hope that the equestrian class would act in harmony with the Senatorial Party was destroyed.

When Caesar returned from Spain in 60 B.C. seeking a triumph, he asked permission to run for the consulship in absentia while he remained with the army outside of the city. The Senate refused, with Cato speaking all day to prevent approval. Caesar gave up his triumph and entered the city as an ordinary citizen to stand for the consulship. Pompey, Caesar, and Crassus now joined forces, and the First Triumvirate was born. The three men agreed to work together toward their common goals.

With the support of Pompey and Crassus, Caesar won the consulship for the year 59 B.C. Caesar soon paid off his political debts with proposals for the ratification of Pompey's treaties in the east, a land-distribution bill for Pompey's veterans and some of the poor in Rome, and a revision of the tax codes for Asia. Cato vigorously opposed all these measures but was unable to block their passage in the Assembly. When the Assembly passed a bill giving Caesar the military command of Cisalpine Gaul and Illyricum for five years, Cato protested so strongly that Caesar had him arrested for a brief time.

In 58 B.C., the Triumvirate decided to rid themselves of Cato by securing his appointment as commissioner to oversee the annexation of Cyprus and to reconcile two opposing factions in Byzantium. At the time, Cyprus was ruled as a client state of Rome by King Ptolemy, the brother of Ptolemy XII, pharaoh of Egypt. Cato realized that he was being relegated to the backwaters of Roman politics but accepted the assignment out of a sense of duty. He was given only two secretaries and neither a ship nor money for the undertaking. Cato first traveled to Byzantium, where he brought about a peaceful settlement between conflicting parties. At Cyprus, the problem was resolved when King Ptolemy committed suicide. Cato supervised the inventory of the royal treasures and sent a precious cargo worth seven thousand talents of silver back to Rome.

Cato returned to Rome in 56 B.C. In the years that followed, he continued to oppose the political ambitions of the Triumvirate but with little success. In 54 B.C., Cato was elected to the office of *praetor*, or judge. During his one-year term, he rendered his decisions from the praetor's bench with fairness and integrity. In 51 B.C., he stood for the consulship but was unsuccessful; he refused to resort to bribery or other corrupt practices that had become part of Roman politics.

When the civil war between Pompey and Caesar began in 49 B.C., Cato sided with Pompey as the best hope for saving the republic. Pompey had been moving closer to the Senate since the death of Crassus during an unsuccessful invasion of Parthia in 53 B.C. Cato now viewed Pompey as a counterforce to the growing power of Caesar in Gaul. As Caesar swept down the Italian peninsula, Pompey and the senatorial forces retreated to Greece. Cato was entrusted with the defense of Sicily but was forced to withdraw from the island after the arrival of Caesarean forces. Cato joined Pompey in Greece and was with him at the Battle of Dyrrhachium in western Greece, where Caesar's forces were repulsed.

Pompey followed Caesar into the interior of Greece but was defeated at the Battle of Pharsalus in 48 B.C. Cato was not present at Pharsalus. He was given command of fifteen cohorts and garrisoned Dyrrhachium, which held Pompey's weapons and stores as well as the civilians in Pompey's camp.

When news of Pompey's defeat reached Cato, he brought his forces to the island of Corcyra, where he joined Pompey's fleet. Correctly surmising that Pompey had fled to North Africa, Cato sailed with ten thousand troops and landed at Cyrene only to learn of Pompey's death in Egypt. Cato now marched his troops westward through the Libyan deserts and eventually reached Utica, where he joined forces with other remnants of Pompey's army under Metellus Scipio, Titus Labienus, and King Juba of Numidia. As proconsul, Metellus Scipio was given command of the Pompeian forces. While Cato commanded the camp at Utica, Scipio met Caesar at the Battle of Thapsus in 46 B.C. and suffered a severe defeat.

Cato remained unperturbed when the news of Scipio's defeat reached Utica. He readied ships in the harbor and made certain that those who might wish to flee would be able to do so. With Caesar and his army only a day's march away, Cato spent the evening at dinner engaging in philosophic discussions with his friends. After dinner, he retired to his room and read Plato's *Phaedo*, on the immortality of the soul. When he saw that his sword had been removed from its usual place near his bed, he called his servants and ordered that it be returned. Cato then slept for a few hours. In the early hours, before dawn he rose and suddenly stabbed himself with his sword in the abdomen. His servants heard him fall; entering the room, they found him still alive, lying in blood with his intestines protruding from his stomach. A physician pushed back the intestines, which were not pierced, and bandaged the wound. When left alone again, Cato removed the bandages, pulled open his wound, and died soon afterward; he was forty-eight years old. When Caesar arrived the next day, he grieved that Cato had deprived him of the glory of granting a pardon to his defeated adversary.

Summary

Cato is remembered as a man of principle whose honesty and integrity was unquestioned in an age conspicuous for its political corruption and opportunism. He idealized the virtues of the early republic and dedicated his life to preserving those traditions and values upon which the republic was founded. Like the ancient fathers of the early republic, he found monarchy to be an abomination. Ironically, Cato's uncompromising opposition to the early demands of Pompey, Crassus, and Caesar had the effect of driving the three of them together to form the First Triumvirate. In the years that followed, Cato remained an obstructionist but could no longer control the sequence of events. When Cato died at Utica, the Republic died with him. Julius Caesar emerged as the sole power of the Roman world, but Cato's life and the manner of his death became an inspiration for later generations of republicans.

Bibliography

Gruen, Erich S. *The Last Generation of the Roman Republic*. Berkeley: University of California Press, 1974. A highly interpretive study that seeks to show the continuity of Roman political institutions into the age of Cicero. Valuable insights on the life of Cato the Younger in the context of the historical background. Useful notes and bibliography.

Oman, C. W. *Seven Roman Statesmen of the Late Republic*. London: Edward Arnold, and New York: Longmans, 1902. Biographical sketches of the outstanding political figures of the late republic. The chapter on Cato the Younger provides a detailed and sympathetic account of Cato's efforts to preserve the republic amid the corruption and power politics of the age.

Plutarch. *Lives of the Noble Grecians and Romans*. Translated by John Dryden. New York: The Modern Library, 1932. The indispensable primary source for the study of Cato the Younger. Plutarch's life of Cato provides a detailed narrative on Cato's life. Plutarch includes numerous anecdotes that serve to highlight Cato's character.

Scullard, H. H. *From the Gracchi to Nero*. 5th ed. London and New York: Methuen, 1982. Useful for the background of the last century of the Roman Republic. Highly readable and assembled with sound scholarly judgment. Numerous references to Cato the Younger and his role in Roman politics. Extensive notes, with references for additional study.

Syme, Ronald. *The Roman Revolution*. Oxford: Oxford University Press, 1939; New York: Oxford University Press, 1951. The classic study of the transformation of Roman government from an oligarchy to one-man rule. Covers the years from 60 B.C. to 14 A.D. Contains details of Cato's political career as the leader of the Senatorial Party.

Norman Sobiesk

CATULLUS

Born: c. 85 B.C.; Verona, Cisalpine Gaul
Died: c. 54 B.C.; probably Rome
Area of Achievement: Literature
Contribution: Catullus was the leader of a group of poets, the *novi poetae*, who created a more native idiom for Roman poetry. Intensely personal, epigrammatic, and more colloquial than epic or dramatic, this style of poetry prepared the way and set the standards for the literary achievements of the Augustan Age.

Early Life

Like most figures of Greek and Roman antiquity, Catullus provides little information about his early life, and the ancient sources add few additional facts. His family was prominent in Verona, which was then a part of the province of Cisalpine Gaul. They also owned a villa on the peninsula of Sirmio (modern Sermione) in the Lago di Garda, about twenty miles east of Verona. Catullus' later references to this country home reveal his deep attachment to the family seat. Suetonius' biography of Julius Caesar records that Catullus' father was prominent enough to entertain Caesar during the latter's governorship of that province in the early 50's B.C.

Although his views about family ties were firmly traditional, Catullus makes no reference to either of his parents. An emotional tribute to his brother, who died near Troy, is the only mention of a relative, but it strengthens the inference that Catullus' family was closely knit.

The usual education of a wealthy and talented provincial is likely to have included study in Athens, and although there is no record of an educational sojourn in Greece, Catullus' poetry is that of a young man thoroughly imbued with Greek poetry from Homer to Callimachus. Yet his many attachments to friends from northern Italy, including several of the *novi poetae*, suggest that unlike the Augustans Vergil and Horace, Catullus did not completely detach himself from his provincial origins to become a Hellenized Roman. The demotic, vernacular coloring of his poetry is symptomatic of a mind that resisted imitation of the accepted Greco-Roman literary canons.

Life's Work

Catullus' reputation as one of the greatest poets of all Roman literature is even more remarkable because it is based on a collection of poems smaller than a fourth of Vergil's *Aeneid* (c. 29-19 B.C.) and because this collection survived antiquity in only a single copy. The 113 poems range in length from epigrams of two lines to a miniature epic of 408 lines. The near extinction of this great poet is attributable to the audacious and racy subject matter of some of his poems, which made them unsuitable for use in the schools.

It is impossible to reconstruct a dependable chronology of Catullus' poetic career on the basis of the poems themselves, and, as previously noted, the ancient sources provide little additional information. Clearly, the shortness of his life means that his oeuvre represents the work of a young poet, but nothing in it could be described as juvenilia. The poems appear to have been selected by him for publication. Poem 1 of the collection now extant refers to a "slim volume" (*libellus*) which he is dedicating to his friend the historian Cornelius Nepos, but there is no evidence that this slim volume is the same as the extant collection. There exists a scrap of another dedication also, apparently part of another collection.

The existing collection is divided into three parts on purely formal grounds. The first group, poems 1 through 60, are in a variety of meters; hence, they are called the polymetric poems. The favorite meter of this group is the hendecasyllabic, or Phalaecian, an eleven-syllable line of Greek origin that lends itself well to the colloquial tone of his work. The second group consists of eight long poems in various meters, two of them the dactylic hexameter familiar to epic poetry. The third group is written in elegiac couplets, a meter which had become popular in Hellenistic epigrams but was on its way to becoming the medium of the Latin love elegy. Yet not all Catullus' elegiac poems are on love. He wrote a poem to his dead brother, as well as a number of purely satirical pieces. Judging from what has survived, scholars agree that the elegiac couplet was Catullus' favorite medium. Within the three sections of the now-canonical collection, there is evidence of design in the ordering of the poems. The collection is not organized chronologically or by subject matter, but it betrays a subtly designed miscellany of moods and subjects, each poem contrasting with or corresponding to its neighbors in ways that sustain the reader's interest.

Because there is no known chronology, one good way to perceive the work of Catullus is through the people about whom and to whom he wrote his poems. The social character of his poetry, much of which is addressed to somebody specific, is also well served by this approach. The most visible and intense of the poet's personal relationships is with a woman he calls Lesbia, mentioned in some twenty-five of Catullus' love poems. Lucius Apuleius wrote that her real name was Clodia, and it is generally believed that she was a married woman ten years older than the poet. If Apuleius' testimony is correct, Clodia was the sister of Cicero's enemy P. Clodius Pulcher and wife (later the widow) of Q. Metellus Celer, who governed Cisalpine Gaul between 64 and 62 B.C. For her, the affair she had with Catullus was casual, one of many. For Catullus, it was the cause of both euphoria and anguish, with little middle ground. This stormy relationship lasted about six years, from perhaps 58 or 59 (before the death of Metellus in 59) to 55 or 54. The Lesbia poems are the best known of Catullus' work.

A second episode in Catullus' life, one whose dates are known more definitely, was his year of public service on the staff of C. Memmius, the Roman governor of Bithynia. Such tours of duty were a normal part of the life of young Romans of rank, and although Catullus complains loudly in his poems about Memmius' tightfisted policies and writes eloquently of the pleasure of returning home, this year of furlough (from 57 to 56 B.C.) from the stresses of his affair with Lesbia/Clodia and the high life of Rome may have contributed much to Catullus' achievement as a poet. It is a reasonable inference that the job itself was not demanding and that in his enforced isolation on the southern shore of the Black Sea Catullus had ample opportunity to study, write, and revise.

A significant part of Catullus' poetry may be described as occasional verse, that which commemorates an event of no great objective importance in such a way as to bring out its humor, irony, or emotional significance. The Greek tradition in which he chose to write was satirical, and a large number of the poems of the collection expand on the foibles of people whom the poet wished to embarrass. Some of these were amatory rivals, some were social climbers or nuisances (such as Asinius Marrucinus, the napkin thief of poem 12). Others, including the orator Cicero, the politician Julius Caesar, and Caesar's protégé Mamurra, were public figures. In spite of attacks of varying intensity (in poems 29, 57, and 93), Caesar remained an admirer of Catullus; according to Suetonius, Catullus eventually apologized for his attacks (in one of which he accuses Caesar of sexually molesting little girls) and was invited to dine with Caesar the same day.

Traditional serious poetry also exerted its attraction for Catullus. In the course of what might be viewed as a licentious life of pleasure and scandal, Catullus composed three long wedding hymns (poems 61, 62, and 63) which show every sign of a deep belief in the institution of marriage. In addition, there is an impressive long poem about the religious frenzy of a legendary young Greek named Attis, who emasculates himself in order to serve the Asiatic goddess Cybele. Notwithstanding the emphasis of the Neoterics on short poetry

C: VAL: CATVLLVS.

in a native poetic idiom, epic remained the medium of choice for the highest achievement. Catullus' effort in this genre, the miniature epic or epyllion on the wedding of Peleus and Thetis, with its digression on Theseus' abandonment of Ariadne (poem 64), ranks with his best work. Parts of it, such as Ariadne's lament, are unsurpassed in Latin literature.

Summary

Although it remains the slimmest volume on a bookshelf of classical works, the poetry of Catullus is a unique testament to the power of a young poet working in a still-raw language. As Cicero, writing a decade later, found Latin a poor vehicle for philosophy, poets of Catullus' generation had none of the vocabulary and native traditions which Greek had developed over the course of seven centuries. Instead of borrowing Greek vocabulary, themes, and genres wholesale to produce feeble imitations, Catullus set out to create a genuinely Latin poetry. The only Roman model of significant use to him was the comedian Plautus, the Umbrian stagehand-turned-playwright, who transformed Greek comedies into lively shows for untutored audiences. Though inevitably indebted to Greek inspiration for most of what he wrote, Catullus put Latin poetry on a more independent course and set the agenda for Augustan poetry: to write what Horace was to call a *Latinum carmen*, or Latin song.

Specifically, this agenda meant adapting Greek poetic rhetoric to the more subjective taste of a Roman audience, reducing the dependence on words borrowed from the Greek, modifying the rigid syntactic structure of formal Latin to gain the flexibility which Greek had long enjoyed, and broadening the range of subjects which were acceptable for poets to essay. By succeeding as conspicuously as he did in these tasks, Catullus opened the way for Latin poetry to become a worthy successor to Greek rather than a mere imitator.

Ultimately more interesting to the average reader than his place in the history of Roman poetry is the vibrant and colorful picture Catullus gives of private life in the Rome of Cicero and Caesar. As it happens, Catullus wrote for all time, but his poetry is an intimate portrait of life in his own time, written with an art which few successors dared imitate.

Bibliography

Catullus, Gaius Valerius. *Catullus: A Commentary.* C. J. Fordyce, ed. Oxford: Clarendon Press, 1961; New York: Oxford University Press, 1990. An extensive and illuminating commentary in English on the Latin text, flawed by the author's refusal to print or discuss some thirty-two poems "which do not lend themselves to comment in English."

Gaisser, Julia Haig. *Catullus and His Renaissance Readers.* Oxford: Clarendon Press, and New York: Oxford University Press, 1993. This wide-ranging study follows the reception of Catullus through his fame in antiquity, obscurity in the Middle Ages, and rediscovery in the Renaissance. Gaisser provides extensive detail on the activities of Renaissance scholars and poets who encountered Catullus and argues that critical views about him were often shaped more by personal and scholarly controversies than by careful readers of the poems themselves.

Martin, Charles. *Catullus.* New Haven, Conn. and London: Yale University Press, 1992. An introduction designed for the general reader, combining literary history with some analysis of the poems themselves.

Quinn, Kenneth, ed. *Catullus: The Poems.* 2d ed. London: Macmillan, and New York: St. Martin's Press, 1973. A good commentary, somewhat idiosyncratic but suitable for college-level readers and beyond. Latin text of all poems, with introduction and commentary in English. A short bibliographical guide for further study of each of the poems is included.

Small, Stuart G. P. *Catullus: A Reader's Guide to the Poems.* Lanham, Md.: University Press of America, 1983. A running narrative, not of the poet's life but of his poetic achievement. Divided by topic, with sane judgments on matters of literary and scholarly controversy. Small supplements a reading of the poems by giving topical overviews. With bibliography.

Thomson, Douglas F. S. *Catullus.* Toronto and Buffalo: University of Toronto Press, 1997. The most recent edition, providing a new text of the poems. The commentary is primarily concerned with questions of language and structure and is directed toward the student of Latin. The introduction contains a brief survey of Catullus' life and milieu.

Wilder, Thornton. *The Ides of March*. New York: Harper and Row, and London: Longmans, 1948. The classic historical novel on the Rome of Cicero, Catullus, Clodius, and his sister—and Caesar, the emperor whose life ended on the title day in 44 B.C.

Wiseman, Timothy Peter. *Catullus and His World*. Cambridge and New York: Cambridge University Press, 1985. A highly readable reconstruction of the social and political context, informative not only about Catullus but also about late republican Rome and its personalities. Richly documented, with eight pages of bibliography.

Daniel H. Garrison

AULUS CORNELIUS CELSUS

Born: c. 25 B.C.; possibly near Narbonne on the Mediterranean coast of France

Died: c. A.D. 50; probably Rome

Areas of Achievement: Historiography and medicine

Contribution: Celsus wrote the first complete history of medicine and the first comprehensive account of medical and surgical procedures.

Early Life

Aulus Cornelius Celsus probably lived during the Augustan Age and the reign of Tiberius. He is thought to have been a member of the patrician family of Cornelius. Patricians were the ruling class of Rome, nobles of wealth and influence, and they considered the practice of medicine beneath their dignity. Consequently, it is highly unlikely that Celsus was a practicing physician. Still, some knowledge of medicine was customary among the educated men of Rome. The head of the household usually practiced domestic medicine on the family, slaves, and livestock. Celsus may have followed this custom.

He was an avid reader and certainly knew both Greek and Latin. Records for the years A.D. 25 and 26 clearly indicate that he lived in Rome. Quintilian, the Roman rhetorician and critic, and Gaius Pliny, or Pliny the Elder, the Roman naturalist and writer, mention Celsus with considerable praise.

Celsus was never referred to as a physician, only as an author or compiler. His literary interests were apparently comprehensive in scope and resulted in an encyclopedia called *De artibus* (A.D. 25-35). There is no clear idea of the contents and arrangement of *De artibus*. It is certain, however, that there were five books on agriculture and also sections of unknown length on military science, rhetoric, history, philosophy, government, and law.

The only portion of this encyclopedia to survive is *De medicina* (c. A.D. 30; *The Eight Books of Medicine,* 1830; better known as *De medicina,* 1935-1938). It was a compilation from various sources such as Hippocrates' *Corpus Hippocraticum* (written during the fifth century B.C.) and from the lost works of Asclepiades of Bithynia, Heracleides Ponticus, Erasistratus, and others.

Life's Work

De medicina was intended primarily for practitioners. Celsus set down a guiding principle for phy-

sicians in any age: that an accurate diagnosis must precede treatment. Celsus noted the errors of both Empiricists and Methodists. He rejected the inflexible doctrines of the Empiricists, who advocated the use of drugs, and the Methodists, who stressed diet and exercise. He was influenced by Asclepiades, who established Greek medicine in Rome, and adopted many of the physiological concepts of the Alexandrian School.

The introduction to *De medicina* constitutes a first attempt at a history of medicine and includes references to eighty medical authors, some of whom are known only through this book. Celsus gave an account of the Alexandrian school, the part played by Hippocrates, and the contributions of Asclepiades.

The book, actually eight books in one, is divided into three parts. Section 1 contains a general introduction on the efficacy of diet and hygiene. Two main chapters consider the subject of general and local diseases governed by diet. Section 2 considers diseases treated with drugs. Discussed at length

are different remedies, divided into various groups according to their effects: purgatives, diaphoretics, diuretics, emetics, and narcotics. There is also an examination of those diseases which require immediate treatment, diseases presenting acute or chronic manifestations, accidental or traumatic manifestations, and diseases with external symptoms. Section 3 is devoted to surgical diseases. One division concentrates on the organs, the other on orthopedics, or bones.

Celsus held strictly to the teachings of Hippocrates concerning pathological concepts and etiology, or the study of the causes of disease. He took into consideration the influence of the seasons, the weather, the patient's age and constitution, and any sudden weight changes, increases and decreases.

Diseases of the stomach are considered at length. Treatment generally consisted of diet, massage, and baths. Celsus believed that it was better to keep the bowels open by diet rather than by purgatives. Where diarrhea and fever existed, fast was the prescription. Celsus believed in the doctrine of critical days for diseases, that is, the disease would peak within a certain number of days and then the patient would begin to recover.

In *De medicina,* Celsus addressed pneumonia, arthritis, dysentery, tonsilitis, cancer, kidney and liver diseases, tuberculosis, hemorrhoids, and diabetes. Symptoms were accurately reported for a number of diseases, such as epilepsy, and mental illnesses, such as paranoia, a form of insanity characterized by delusions. He clearly pictured the way in which malaria attacks occurred, giving a very detailed and highly accurate account of malarial fever. According to Celsus, the fever was an effort to eliminate morbid material from the body. He was the first to name the four cardinal signs of inflammation: heat, pain, swelling, and redness.

The arguments of Celsus against taking the pulse of the patient as a criterion in the identification of disease are interesting. He regarded the pulse as an uncertain indication of the health of a person, because its frequency varied considerably with the sex, age, and constitution of the patient. The pulse also varied because of the patient's nervousness when in the presence of the doctor. For these reasons, the pulse was not to be examined on the doctor's first visit.

In Celsus' time, surgery was performed on all parts of the body: goiters, fistulas, tonsils, and gallstones. Cancerous growths of lips and breasts were removed. He described ulcers, tumors, amputation, and trepanation, or the removal of part of the skull, which he regarded as a treatment of last resort.

Celsus carefully reported on plastic surgery for the repair of the nose, lips, and ears and described some dental surgery, including the wiring of teeth. He also suggested lithotomy, an operation for crushing stones in the bladder, discussed ligature, or how to tie off an artery, and presented methods for stopping hemorrhages. He was very much aware of the dangers of gangrene.

Celsus was concerned with the treatment of wounds, necrosis (decaying tissues), fractures, and dislocations. His book contains an excellent account of the treatment of various fractures and dislocations. For fractures, he recommended wooden splints held in place by wax and advocated exercise after the fracture healed. Thus, he was a forerunner to modern rehabilitative therapy. In addition, Celsus described the widely used painkillers, such as opium, and anesthetics, such as the root of the mandragora plant. The root of the plant, which contained narcotics such as scopolamine, was soaked in wine, and the wine was given to the patient to induce a deep sleep.

Celsus paid particular attention to headaches, which he regarded as coming from various sources, and approved the treatment of insomnia by oil massage, which he credited directly to Asclepiades. Celsus recommended removing snake poison from a wound by sucking and correctly claimed that the venom was lethal only when absorbed into the wound, not when swallowed.

Celsus clearly recognized the importance of anatomy in medicine. He attended autopsies, and his anatomical descriptions are brief but clear, including information which shows that he knew about sutures of the cranium. He distinguished between veins and arteries and favored dissection as a means to discovering more about internal organs.

In short, Celsus taught that diagnosis and prognosis must precede treatment. In so doing, he confirmed the sound doctrine of the Hippocratic school. Celsus also advocated different types of baths, massage, hygiene, and dietary rules. He relied somewhat on drugs for treatment but emphasized the benefits of sports, such as hunting, fishing, and sailing.

Summary

Galen, a Greek philosopher and writer, prepared a medical encyclopedia which remained the standard authority until the sixteenth century. When Pope

Nicholas V discovered Aulus Cornelius Celsus' work in the Vatican Library, he arranged to have it published in 1478. Thus, *De medicina* was the first classical book on medicine to be printed. It was also the first translation of Greek medical terms into Latin. The Latin nomenclature used in the book has dominated Western medicine for two thousand years.

The book is of interest for two reasons: its literary skill and the techniques presented. From a literary point of view, his work is outstanding. Celsus ranks as Rome's most important master of the encyclopedic literary form. As the first comprehensive account of surgical procedures by a Roman writer, *De medicina* provides much useful information on medicine of the Hellenistic period and on Alexandrian surgery. It includes a careful description of more than one hundred different types of surgical instruments.

Celsus' ideas on malaria, the treatment of fractures, and plastic surgery were ahead of his time. He was a disciple of Asclepiades, but unlike Asclepiades, Celsus was a great admirer of Hippocrates and was among the first to introduce Hippocrates' teaching to the Romans. During the first century, it was typical for medicine and other sciences to draw upon many sources. Celsus followed this custom and can thus be regarded as a true eclectic.

Bibliography

Allbutt, Sir Thomas C. *Greek Medicine in Rome*. London: Macmillan, 1921; New York: Blom, 1970. A series of lectures addressed to interested physicians and others with a good medical background. Perhaps too abstract for the general reader, this volume is a complete medical history of the period, with extensive commentary on all major figures but only one brief chapter on Celsus. Excellent illustrations, bibliography, and chronology.

Castiglioni, Arturo. *A History of Medicine*. Translated by E. B. Krumbhaar. 2d ed. New York: Alfred A. Knopf, 1947. Considered a classic reference for the period, this volume contains a full translation of Castiglioni's work. Included are numerous illustrations, a full chronology, and a bibliography for each chapter. Designed for the general reader, it contains information relating to the content of *De medicina*.

Celsus, Aulus Cornelius. *De medicina*. Translated by W. G. Spencer. 3 vols. Cambridge, Mass.: Harvard University Press, 1935; London: Heinemann, 1938. This work includes both the original Latin text and a full translation of Celsus' work. It is a major source of information about the history of medicine, as well as medical and surgical procedures for the Hellenistic period.

Gordon, Benjamin Lee. *Medicine Throughout Antiquity*. Philadelphia: F. A. Davis Co., 1949. Contains only a very brief section on Celsus, along with scattered page references. The author cites facts from widely scattered fields that are not ordinarily accessible to a busy practitioner or to lay people interested in medical history. With brief reference notes and a handful of illustrations but no chronology or bibliography.

Jackson, Ralph. *Doctors and Diseases in the Roman Empire*. London: British Museum Publications, and Norman: University of Oklahoma Press, 1988. A survey of medical thought in the Roman empire that includes translated selections from the major medical writers.

Lipsett, W. G. "Celsus, First Medical Historian." *Science Digest* 48 (October, 1960): 83-87. Gives very complete information about the various divisions of *De medicina* but concentrates on the surgical chapters. A very brief article which is perhaps too simplistic in language and approach, it does have appeal to the general reader.

Rita E. Loos

CH'IN SHIH HUANG-TI

Born: 259 B.C.; Handan, State of Chao, China

Died: 210 B.C.; North China

Area of Achievement: Government and politics

Contribution: Ch'in Shih Huang-ti established the first unified empire that ruled China. His empire functioned through appointed officials managing administrative districts rather than feudal lords who were granted territories. The word "China" derives from the name his state, "Ch'in." In 221 B.C., after defeating all the other kings, the man who was first known as King Cheng of Ch'in assumed a new title, Shih Huang-ti (the "First Emperor"). His short-lived Ch'in dynasty was marked by uniform laws, harsh justice, massive public works, and the ruler's elevation into an almost divine figure. Ch'in Shih Huang-ti redefined the Chinese notion of the state, and his conduct established a model that all later Chinese emperors attempted to emulate, modify, or avoid.

Early Life

The future Ch'in Shih Huang-ti was born into the family of a secondary prince of the state of Ch'in in 259. China was divided into a number of feudal states, and Ch'in was a formidable power with a strong army, an efficient administration, and an excellent geographical location in the Wei River valley, west of the center of Chinese civilization on the North China plain. The future First Emperor's father, Prince Tzu-ch'u, lived as a hostage in the state of Chao. He was a living pledge that Ch'in would uphold its agreements with the ruler of Chao.

Prince Tzu-ch'u had no male heirs, but after acquiring a concubine from his confidant, the merchant Lu Pu-wei, she bore him the son who was to become Shih Huang-ti. After his son's birth, Tzu-ch'u made the child's mother his proper first wife.

Both Prince Tzu-ch'u and his son grew up in an era known as the "Warring States," which was marked by almost continuous warfare that eliminated small feudal territories, leaving seven large states ruled by kings. In spite of the lack of peace, ideas and technology flourished. The state of Ch'in's importance grew in the fourth and third centuries B.C. because of its assocation with a school of thinkers called Legalists, who emphasized simple administration, harsh justice, and mobilization of the state's subjects to enhance the

kingdom's power. This Legalist approach contrasted with Confucianism, which stressed that the ruler and his officials must be good men of high moral character who sought peace, prosperity, and justice for the common people. The Legalist style, so named for an emphasis on rules rather than good men, appeared more than a century before Shih Huang-ti's birth but reached its height during his rule. It has thus been associated with him ever since.

Prince Tzu-ch'u's chief supporter, Lu Pu-wei, returned to Ch'in, where he spent his wealth freely to gain advantage for the prince and himself. Lu Pu-wei managed to have Tzu-ch'u placed in direct line of succession for the Ch'in throne. In 251, Tzu-ch'u's grandfather died, and the throne passed to his adoptive father (actually his paternal uncle), who ruled for less than a year. Tzu-ch'u then ascended to the kingship, but for only four years (250-246). Upon his death, Lu Pu-wei ensured that the future Shih Huang-ti, then a boy of thirteen, would be crowned King Cheng of Ch'in.

For nine years, Lu Pu-wei continued as King Cheng's chief minister, but in 237 a scandal linked him to a plot to overthrow his young charge. The historian Ssu-ma Ch'ien (c. 145-86) produced an account of these events that has shaped the contemporary view of Shih Huang-ti as a morally bad man. Ssu-ma Ch'ien, an advocate of Confucianism and an opponent of Legalism, wrote that Lu Pu-wei was Shih Huang-ti's biological father because, when he had given the concubine to Prince Tzu-ch'u, she was already pregnant. Ssu-ma Ch'ien further tarred the First Emperor's parentage by claiming that his mother, after the death of her spouse Tzu-ch'u, resumed sexual relations with Lu Pu-wei. Unable to satisfy her, he provided a highly virile but uncouth partner named Lao Ai, who fathered children with her. She is said to have plotted with Lao Ai to remove her illegitimately conceived son from the throne and substitute one of their children as king of Ch'in.

These lurid tales paint Ch'in Shih Huang-ti as the bastard son of a déclassé merchant and loose woman who was so base that she could join a plot to kill her own first-born son. Such behavior violated the prevailing moral standards of the time, which stressed the importance of proper blood descent for rulers, the strong ties between parents and children, and the propriety of female chastity, especialy for widows. Ssu-ma Ch'ien, as the official historian of the succeeding Han dynasty, surely meant to defame Ch'in Shih Huang-ti with this account.

Life's Work

Whatever the truth of these stories, the events of 237 mark the beginning of King Cheng's active rulership. First, he ordered the deaths of Li Ao and his family, required his mother to return to live in the Ch'in court under supervision, and banished Lu Pu-wei, who, fearing further punishment, committed suicide. For the next sixteen years, King Cheng of Ch'in focused on defeating his rivals. He relied on civilian ministers to run his kingdom and on generals to fight his wars, while living in grand style. His most important adviser was a former protégé of Lu Pu-wei, Li Ssu, whom many historians have seen as a Legalist genius for his role in creating the Empire. Li Ssu became chief minister after the Ch'in empire was established in 221 and served in that post until 208, two years after the First Emperor's death.

Beginning in 230, Ch'in conquered all six of its rival states. These states, realizing the ambitions of Ch'in, had attempted alliances, but these always failed. Ch'in won a reputation of being as ferocious as a wolf or tiger. In 221, the last of these states, Ch'i, located in China's present-day eastern coastal Shantung province, fell, and King Cheng declared himself a new kind of ruler, an emperor, with the title "Shih Huang-ti."

Over the next eleven years, Ch'in Shih Huang-ti fashioned a remarkable new political order by applying the Legalist approach to governing, which had worked in Ch'in, to the whole of China. He divided the empire into a hierarchy of territorial administrative units: thirty-six commandaries and one thousand counties. Appointed officials serving at the emperor's pleasure, administered the law, meted out justice, and collected revenue. In Legalist fashion, the Ch'in worked through simple but oppressive statutes applied to common people with uniform harshness.

During the Warring States era, different practices had grown up in the feudal states, but, under Shih Huang-ti, the Ch'in ways became the standard through the empire. He established one set of weights and measures, one coinage, one standard way of writing Chinese characters, and one standard width for cart axles.

The First Emperor required the wealthy and powerful families from the east—meaning the survivors in the six defeated rival states—to reside in his capital of Hsien-yang (near the modern city of Hsi-an in Shansi province). He let them live privileged lives but forestalled their participation in plots of rebellion in their old homelands. He confiscated weapons from around the empire and brought them to Hsien-yang, where they were melted down into twelve great statues. He also ordered the burning of the archives in the former rival states, thereby destroying many philosophical works of ancient China and acquiring a reputation as an anti-intellectual tyrant.

At Hsien-yang, as a reflection of his own megalomania, he began work on an enormous palace and a huge tomb of unprecedented size and magnificence. It is said that 700,000 workers were employed at the tomb site alone. The First Emperor seemed to care nothing for the cost and the sacrifices his subjects made for these extravagances.

Among his most remarkable achievements were a series of great public works undertaken by huge armies of corvée laborers and tens of thousands of families uprooted and relocated as colonists at the First Emperor's whim. Impressive roads connected Hsien-yang with the territory of the empire that extended east, north, and south of the original state of Ch'in. Newly dug canals moved grain to the capitol, where it was used to feed its large population or dispatched to armies and workers. In the Warring States period, the rival states had raised walls and earthen dikes for defensive purposes. Shih Huang-ti had some of these removed but ordered the walls along the northern border of the Empire, meant to protect against the Turkish people called Hsiung-nu, linked together into the Great Wall, which remains one of the best-known features of ancient China.

Shih Huang-ti thought himself omniscient and ruled in a highly autocratic manner. Following a challenge from a Confucian in 212, he ordered four hundred Confucian scholars killed. It was this, along with the burning of Confucian texts on the advice of Li Ssu, that earned him the undying enmity of Confucianists for the next two thousand years.

Shih Huang-ti undertook imperial tours to the far reaches of his newly won empire. These trips served to unify his control and acquaint him with the various parts of his great state. On these journeys, he visited mountain temples associated with local gods for whom he conducted proper ceremonies, thus fulfilling a key responsibility of the rulers he had defeated and replaced.

Shih Huang-ti had great personal interest in the Taoist theories of nature. These notions embodied both proto-scientific ideas and superstitious occult beliefs centered around yin-yang dualism, which saw the world in terms of an unceasing alteration of forces operating through five elements or powers (*wu-hsing*). Shih Huang-ti delighted in the elaborate systems of correspondence developed by devotees of this approach and, during his imperial tours, sought out those claiming to be able to prolong life or to unlock the secret of immortality.

Returning from one of these trips in 210, Shih Huang-ti became ill and died at Sha-ch'iu, on the North China plain, some distance from his capital at Hsien-yang. Shih Huang-ti intended for his eldest son to succeed him, but his chief traveling companions—a favorite younger son named Hu Hao, the chief minister Li Ssu, and a court eunuch named Chao Kao—attempted to hide the First Emperor's death until they could return to Hsien-yang and put Hu Hao on the throne. By the crude but effective ruse of loading the imperial entourage with dead fish to cover the odor of the putrefying First Emperor's corpse, the plotters managed to make the court think the First Emperor was still alive and that he had declared Hu-hai to be his successor before his own death.

The First Emperor was buried in his vast and splendid tomb along with many palace women, who were to accompany him in the afterlife, and the chief builders of the tomb, who died so they could not reveal its secrets. In the 1970's, Chinese farmers digging a well accidentally revealed portions of a huge army of terra cotta soldiers ranged in front of the tomb. The main tomb mound itself remained unexcavated, but the newly opened sections yielded a major attraction for Chinese and foreign tourists alike at Hsi-an.

As Erh Huang-ti (Second Emperor), Hu-hai aped the style of his father and murdered several of his brothers on the recommendation of the eunuch Chao Kao, who thus won a place in history as the first of a long series of notorious eunuchs who have harmed various Chinese ruling houses. Revolts broke out around the Empire, the most important led by commoners drafted for corvée service. At the Ch'in court, the Chao Kao became chief minister and engineered an attack on the Second Emperor, who commited suicide. One of Shih Huang'ti's

surviving sons succeeded to the Ch'in throne, but with the title of king (*wang*), not emperor. This ruler quickly surrendered to Liu Pang in late 207. Liu Pang went on to consolidate his power and established the Han dynasty, which endured for four centuries.

Summary

Ch'in Shih Huang-ti is the most famous and best-known of all China's emperors. Some features of his rule became generally accepted by Confucianist rulers and scholars, including appointed officials administering territorial units organized in a hierarchical fashion, uniform laws throughout the society, canal for grain transportation, wall construction to mark China's northern boundary, extravagent magnificence at court, and grand imperial tours around the empire. Still, later Confucians always added condemnation of his ruthlessness, his anti-intellectualism, and his lack of concern over the common people's suffering. Nevertheless, many dynamic rulers in China, Korea, Japan, and Vietnam emulated the style and substance of the First Emperor in their own careers. Ch'in Shih Huang-ti's influence lasted into the twentieth century when, in the 1970's, Mao Tse-tung accepted comparisons of his own attempts to revolutionize China with those of the First Emperor.

Bibliography

Bodde, Derk. "The State and Empire of Ch'in." In *The Cambridge History of China, Volume 1: The Ch'in and Han Empires 221 B.C.-A.D. 220*. Edited by Denis Twitchett and Michael Loewe. Cambridge and New York: Cambridge University Press, 1986. The best summary of Ch'in Shih Huang-ti's life in English.

Cotterell, Arthur. *The First Emperor of China*. London: Macmillan, and New York: Holt, Rinehart, 1981. A well-illustrated volume emphasizing early excavations at the First Emperor's tomb. Contains a long section summarizing the Ch'in conquest and Ch'in Shih Huang-ti's life.

Guisso, R. W. L., Catherine Pagani, and David Miller. *The First Emperor of China*. New York: Birch Lane, and London: Sidgwick and Jackson, 1989. A book to accompany the National Film Board of Canada's docudrama film *The First Emperor of China*. Lavishly illustrated, but the text is somewhat disjointed.

Li, Yu-ning, ed. *The First Emperor of China: The Politics of Historiography*. White Plains, N.Y.:

International Arts and Sciences, 1975. Emphasizes Chinese fascination with Ch'in Shih Huang-ti during the Maoist era in China (1949-1976). Contains a translation of Hung Shih-ti's popular biography of Ch'in Shih Huang-ti, which was first published in Chinese in 1972.

Records of the Grand Historian: The Qin Dynasty. Translated by Burton Watson. New York and London: Columbia University Press, 1961. Contains translation of thirteen sections of Sima's (Ssu-ma Ch'ien) famous first century B.C. work *Shih Chi*, which include his accounts relating to Ch'in Shih Huang-ti. Extracts from the *Shih Chi* dealing with Ch'in Shih Huang-ti are frequently included in various anthologies concerning Chinese history and literature, but this is the best.

David D. Buck

SAINT CHRISTOPHER

Born: place and date unknown; possibly third century Asia Minor

Died: c. 250 A.D.; possibly Lycia

Area of Achievement: Religion and saints

Contribution: Although a legendary figure, Saint Christopher has long been a popular Christian saint, known as the patron of travelers and ferrymen.

Early Life

Virtually nothing is known about the early life of Saint Christopher. Indeed, the historical documentation for his life is so scant that some scholars question whether he actually even lived. The stories of Saint Christopher's life belong to a genre known as *vitae*, or "saints' lives." The purpose of a *vita* is to present the life of a saint in such a way that it will inspire believers and persuade nonbelievers.

Saint Christopher belongs to a group of very early saints known as "martyrs." During the Roman persecution of early Christians, martyrs gave their lives for their faith. The early Christian church kept records of those who died as a result of the persecution. There is evidence to suggest that as early as the second century, the church commemorated and venerated martyrs by memorializing the dates of their deaths.

Saint Christopher's name appears on early lists of martyrs known as "martyrologies." As early as 452 A.D., a church in Bithnyia was dedicated to him. Saint Christopher's cult is ancient in both the West and the East.

The stories of Saint Christopher's life are internally inconsistent and offer no insight as to his birth or his childhood. In an early Greek *vita*, Saint Christopher was described as a monster with a dog's head who ate people. His name before his baptism was listed as "Reprobus" in some sources and "Offeros" in others. By all accounts, Saint Christopher was a very large man, or even a giant, with a fearsome face. In addition, most sources suggest that he was descended from the Canaanites.

Life's Work

Most accounts of Saint Christopher available in English are retellings of William Caxton's *The Golden Legend.* Caxton, the first printer in England, translated *The Golden Legend* from Jacobus de Voragine's *Legenda Aurea*, one of the most popular of all medieval books. Caxton completed this work in 1483.

Like most saints' lives, Caxton's life of Saint Christopher follows a predictable pattern. First, there is a description of Saint Christopher's early pagan life, followed by the details of his conversion. Next, the writer describes with great flourish the miracles of the saint and his ability to convert others. Finally, the persecution and martyrdom of the saint at the hands of a temporal king and by a description of posthumous miracles closes the account.

According to *The Golden Legend*, Saint Christopher, known as either "Reprobus" or "Offeros," was in the service of a great Christian king. It was Christopher's desire to serve the most powerful of all kings. When the name of the Devil was spoken, however, the king crossed himself. Christopher, discovering that there was someone whom the powerful king feared, went in search of the Devil.

When Christopher found the Devil, he pledged himself to his service. However, one day the Devil demonstrated his fear of a cross by the side of the road. Christopher demanded to know why the Devil was afraid, and the Devil admitted, "There was a man called Christ which was hanged on the cross, and when I see His sign I am sore afraid and flee from it wheresoever I see it." When Christopher heard this, he vowed to find Christ and serve him, since any man who gave the Devil fear must be stronger than the Devil himself.

In his search for Christ, according to *The Golden Legend*, Christopher met a hermit. The hermit preached to Christopher about Christ, telling him that he should fast and pray upon awakening. Christopher replied that he could not fast, because it would cause him to lose his great strength. In addition, Christopher said he did not know how to pray. Therefore, the hermit told Christopher to go to a dangerous river and there carry people across the river as his service to Christ.

Certainly the most famous of all stories about Saint Christopher is connected to his service as a ferryman. *The Golden Legend* recounts that one night while Christopher slept, he heard a voice that awoke him, asking him for passage across the river. When he went outside, he found no one. This happened a second and a third time. On the third entreaty, Christopher once again went outside, where

he found a child who wanted to be carried across the river. He put the child on his shoulders and started across the river. It was a difficult passage that grew more dangerous with each step. As he walked, the river swelled. The child grew heavier and heavier, and Christopher feared for his life. When he reached the other side, he told the child that he was the greatest burden that he had ever carried. The child responded that he was the Christ child and that he was so heavy because he carried the weight of the whole world on his shoulders.

As a result of this legend, medieval and renaissance artists painted Saint Christopher with a staff in one hand and a child on his shoulders. The image of Saint Christopher and the child has been a popular one since the Middle Ages, and many paintings and artworks survive, including a famous woodcut of this event by the artist Albrecht Dürer. The name "Christopher" means "Christ-bearer," and thus it is thought that this incident gave rise to his name. However, it is equally possible that the saint's name gave rise to the legend.

Saints' lives also usually include stories of the saint's ability to convert people to the Christian faith. Saint Christopher was reputed to have converted more than eight thousand people. In addition, saints' lives usually include a description of some sort of contest between the saint and a temporal, or earthly, king. In this case, Saint Christopher was arrested by a king called Dagnus and subjected to many temptations and persecutions. One temptation included two women, Nicaea and Aquilina, who were sent by the king to seduce Saint Christopher. He did not waver in his faith, however. He converted both of the women, who were subsequently tortured and killed.

The king then began his torture of Saint Christopher, but to no avail; Saint Christopher could not be injured, even by arrows aimed at him by soldiers. One of the arrows turned back on the king and blinded him. Christopher said to the king, "Tyrant, I shall die tomorrow. Make a little clay, mixed with my blood, and anoint therewith thine eye, and thou shalt receive health." On the next day, the king had Saint Christopher beheaded. As Saint Christopher predicted before his death, his own blood mixed with mud healed the king's eyes. Because of this miracle, the king converted to Christianity.

Although *The Golden Legend* calls the king who persecuted Saint Christopher "Dagnus," the Roman martyrologies report that Saint Christopher suffered at the hands of Decius. The Roman emperor Decius did in fact start a wave of persecution in 250 A.D., the traditional year of Saint Christopher's death. Other scholars attribute Saint Christopher's martyrdom to the emperor Diocletian.

Summary

The stories of Saint Christopher were well known throughout the Christian West and East. Out of these stories grew the belief that Saint Christopher was the patron saint of travelers and ferryman. His name was invoked as protection against water hazards, storms, and plagues. There was also the belief that anyone who looked at an image of the saint would not be injured or hurt on that day. Many churches erected large statues or frescoes of Saint Christopher so that their parishioners would be protected. This belief, and the general popularity of Saint Christopher's cult, resulted in the many paintings and drawings of the saint made throughout the Middle Ages and Renaissance.

Further, as travel became increasingly possible through the years, Saint Christopher's popularity grew. Many Catholics wore Saint Christopher medals and placed statues of Saint Christopher on the dashboards of their cars.

The Catholic church, however, in an effort to honor only those saints for whom they could establish a historical basis for sainthood, removed Saint Christopher's Feast Day (July 25) from the liturgical calendar in 1969. The removal caused an uproar among Catholics, and many Catholics continued to honor the saint by wearing medallions and maintaining statues in their vehicles. The significance of this veneration is striking and demonstrates an important point about popular sainthood. Regardless of official church rulings, and regardless of historical documentation, believers continue to believe and pray for intercession in times of need. The importance of Saint Christopher is not in whatever life he may or may not have led in the distant past, but rather in what Christians have chosen to believe about him through the centuries.

Bibliography

Bouquet, John A. *A People's Book of Saints*. London and New York: Longmans, Green, 1930. Includes a chapter on Saint Christopher that contains a retelling of the popular stories about the saint. Also included is a photograph of a famous woodcut, "Saint Christopher, the Bearer of the Christ Child," by Dürer.

Butler, Alban. *Butler's Lives of the Saints*. Edited, revised, and supplemented by Herbert J. Thurston and Donald Attwater. 4 vols. New York: Kenedy, and London: Burns and Oates, 1956. Updated version of Butler's early eighteenth century work. Contains index, bibliography, and liturgical calendar. A standard source for lives of the saints.

Cunningham, Lawrence. *The Meaning of Saints*. San Francisco: Harper & Row, 1980. An excellent general introduction to the idea of sainthood, demonstrating the way historical reality can be transformed into popular belief. Includes some interesting summary statements on Saint Christopher and a useful bibliography.

De Voragine, Jacobus. *The Golden Legend: Readings on the Saints*, edited by William Ryan Granger. London and New York: Longmans, Green, 1941. A new edition of the English version of *The Golden Legend*. Provides index and bibliography.

"The Heavenly Jobless." *Time*, June 20, 1969, 70-71. A contemporary account of the furor that arose over the demotion of a number of popular saints, including Saint Christopher.

Hodges, Margaret. *Saint Christopher*. Grand Rapids, Mich.: Eerdmans, 1997. An illustrated adaptation of Caxton's version of the life of Saint Christopher found in *The Golden Legend*. Although a juvenile work, a good starting place for the student looking for the basics of the Saint Christopher legend.

New Catholic Encyclopedia. 18 vols. New York: McGraw-Hill, 1967. This reference volume provides the most accessible and complete source for any student beginning a study of saints' lives. Most useful are the articles "Devotion to the Saints;" "Iconography of the Saints;" and "Intercession of the Saints," all located in volume 12 in a general section about sainthood. Also included are a number of iconographic images of Saint Christopher.

Weinstein, Donald, and Rudolph M. Bell. *Saints and Society: The Two Worlds of Western Christendom*. Chicago: University of Chicago Press, 1982. A classic scholarly discussion of the role of sainthood in medieval society. Includes both statistical detail and thorough analysis useful for providing a cultural context for the idea of sainthood.

White, Helen. *Tudor Books of Saints and Martyrs*. Madison: University of Wisconsin Press, 1963. Opens with a description of the saint's life as a literary type. Includes a comprehensive chapter-length discussion of the history and impact of Caxton's *The Golden Legend* and a long bibliography of both primary and secondary sources.

Wilson, Stephen, ed. *Saints and Their Cults: Studies in Religious Sociology, Folklore, and History*. Cambridge and New York: Cambridge University Press, 1983. A collection of essays written by major scholars on sainthood. Most useful is a chapter by Evelyne Patlagean, "Ancient Byzantine Hagiography and Social History," which she analyzes the genre of the saint's life in the Eastern tradition. Also useful is the long annotated bibliography provided by Wilson.

Diane Andrews Henningfeld

SAINT JOHN CHRYSOSTOM

Born: c. A.D. 354; Antioch, Syria
Died: September 14, A.D. 407; Comana, Pontus
Areas of Achievement: Religion and oratory
Contribution: Chrysostom, the greatest homiletic preacher of the Greek church, later became the patron saint of preachers.

Early Life

John Chrysostom (which means golden mouth) was born around A.D. 354 in Antioch and was reared by a devout mother, Anthousa, who had been widowed at the age of twenty. He received a first-rate education, especially in rhetoric, and his teachers are supposed to have included the renowned orator Libanius and the philosopher Andragathius. Libanius, when asked on his deathbed who should succeed him as head of his school of rhetoric, is said to have replied: "John, if the Christians had not stolen him from us." John's theological studies were undertaken at the renowned exegetical school of Antioch under one of the most illustrious scholars of the period, Diodore of Tarsus. The school favored literal rather than allegorical interpretation of the Bible.

Life's Work

According to Palladius' *Dialogus de vita S. Joannis Chrysostomi* (c. 408; *Dialogue on the Life of St. John Chrysostom,* 1921), "when [John] was eighteen, a mere boy in years, he revolted against the sophists of word-mongering, for he had arrived at man's estate and thirsted for living knowledge." Like many early Christians Chrysostom did not receive baptism until he was about twenty years old. He became a deacon in 381 under Bishop Meletius, a native of Armenia, whose protégé Chrysostom quickly became. To this period of deaconship (381-386) probably belongs his six-book *De sacerdotio* (*On the Priesthood,* 1728), a classic on the subject and one of the jewels of patristic literature. Book 5 is of particular interest because, like book 4 of Saint Augustine's *De doctrina Christiana* (426; *On Christian Instruction*), it constitutes a veritable monograph on the art and science of preaching. Book 6 is also of interest in that it contrasts the active with the contemplative life. Chrysostom had already been attracted to the rigors of the latter; he had spent four years in the mountains sharing ascetic life with an old hermit. This ascetic interlude is reflected in several treatises he wrote on monastic life, including two exhortations to his friend Theodore, later Bishop of Mopsuestia, who was growing tired of the monastic way of life, and the three-book *Adversus subintroductas,* which defended monasticism. In the sixth book of *On the Priesthood,* however, Chrysostom spoke out in favor of the active life, arguing that saving the souls of others demands more effort and generosity than merely saving one's own. He was ordained to the priesthood in 386 and remained in Antioch until 398; most of his great homilies belong to this period. They include more than seventy homilies on Genesis, six on Isaiah, and a particularly fine commentary on fifty-eight selected psalms. Also surviving are ninety homilies on the Gospel of Matthew, eighty-eight on the Gospel of John, fifty-five on the Acts of the Apostles, and thirty-two on Romans, this latter the finest of all his works. Almost half his surviving homilies are expositions of the Epistles of Saint Paul, his lifelong model. A series of seven homilies in praise of Paul survive among his many panegyrics on the saints of the Old and New Testaments.

S. CHRYSOSTOM.

Chrysostom's reputation as a pulpit orator became so widespread during his Antioch years that he was chosen to succeed Nectarius, Archbishop of Constantinople, upon the latter's death; he was consecrated on February 26, 398, by Theophilus, Bishop of Alexandria. According to Palladius, Theophilus disliked John, "for his custom all along was not to ordain good and shrewd men lest he make a mistake. He wished to have them all weak-willed men whom he could influence."

Despite this ominous installation, Chrysostom entered on a comprehensive program of reform of church officials and church revenues; he even criticized abuses in the imperial court. He used church revenues to set up hospitals and to aid the poor, leading a life of great simplicity himself. He was particularly critical of the luxury and wealth of the upper classes. His outspokenness soon incurred the wrath of the Empress Eudoxia, to whom Chrysostom's enemies suggested that she was the real target of his strictures.

After a synod in Ephesus in 401, when Chrysostom had six simoniac bishops deposed, some neighboring bishops made an alliance with Theophilus in a bid to unseat the archbishop. At the Oak Synod in 403, attended by thirty-six bishops, Chrysostom was deposed and sentenced to exile by order of the emperor. He was recalled the following day because of riots in his support in Constantinople, but after an uneasy peace of a few months, the emperor banished him to Cucusus in Lesser Armenia. To his three-year period there belong more than two hundred extant letters, which testify to his continuing pastoral zeal and interest in reform. This continued "meddling" proved unacceptable to his enemies, who had him transferred to the more distant Pityus, a city on the eastern shore of the Black Sea. Worn out, John Chrysostom died on his way there, at Comana in Pontus, on September 14, 407.

Summary

John Chrysostom is considered one of the four great fathers of the Eastern church and one of the three ecumenical doctors of the church. He has always been regarded as the most outstanding preacher of the Greek church and one of its greatest exegetes; his eloquence had already earned for him the title "Golden Mouth" in the sixth century. He shares with Origen the reputation of being the most prolific writer of the East. His surviving works extend through eighteen volumes of J.-P. Migne's great *Patrologia Graeca* (1842-1853), and there are still others, notably a work translated as *On Vainglory and the Right Way for Parents to Bring Up Children* (1951). Chrysostom's recently discovered baptismal homilies add to church historians' knowledge of practices surrounding Christian rites of initiation in the end of the fourth century. His homilies are interesting more for their rhetorical brilliance than for any philosophical or theological profundity; they reflect the simple faith of his audience more than the contemporary struggles with Arianism and Apollinarianism. *On the Priesthood* is deservedly a classic, setting forth the most exacting standards for the clerical life. John Chrysostom's own life is eloquent proof that he practiced what he preached.

Bibliography

Attwater, Donald. *St. John Chrysostom: The Voice of Gold*. London: Harvill, and Milwaukee, Wis.: Bruce Publishing Co., 1939. A short, accessible account of the great preacher's life, illustrating both the genius and the humility of Chrysostom. Designed for the general reader.

Baur, Chrysostomus. *John Chrysostom and His Times*. Translated by M. Gonzaga. 2 vols. 2d ed. London: Sands, and Westminster, Md.: Newman Press, 1959. This work by a German priest is still the most detailed biography, but its style and content are both somewhat antiquated. In need of updating or replacement. Includes a bibliography.

Chrysostom, John. *Apologist*. Translated by Margaret A. Schatkin and Paul W. Harkins. Washington, D.C.: Catholic University of America Press, 1985. Contains first translations of two works, one extolling the martyred Babylas and one upholding the divinity of Christ. These renderings by two seasoned Chrysostom scholars are generally reliable. Succinct notes and helpful bibliographies.

———. *Homilies on Genesis*. Translated by Robert C. Hill. Washington, D.C.: Catholic University of America Press, 1986. Contains the first seventeen of the homilies that together make up a complete commentary on Genesis. The introduction deals with Chrysostom's exegetical works, the homilist and his congregation in Antioch, the structure of the homilies, and the use of Scripture in them. Select bibliography.

————. *On Marriage and Family Life.* Translated by Catharine P. Roth and David Anderson. Crestwood, N.Y.: St. Vladimir's Seminary Press, 1986. Includes two hitherto untranslated homilies, with a good introduction showing that Chrysostom, who has often been accused of misogyny, had a better theology of marriage than has been commonly thought.

Kelly, J. N. D. *Golden Mouth: The Story of John Chrysostom, Ascetic, Preacher, Bishop.* London: Duckworth, and Ithaca, N.Y.: Cornell University Press, 1995. The most recent biography of the saint, containing a full narrative of his life and based as much as possible on the primary evidence. Some attention given to Chrysostom's larger milieu.

Lim, Richard. *Public Disputation, Power, and Social Order in Late Antiquity.* Berkeley: University of California Press, 1995. This study of the meaning of public debate in late antique Christianity deals, in its fifth chapter, with Gregory Nazianzus and John Chrysostom, who in their sermons (Lim claims) attempted to stem the tide of excessive theological disputation by mystifying and "obfuscating" contentious questions about divine nature.

Palladius. *Dialogue on the Life of St. John Chrysostom.* Translated and edited by Robert T. Meyer. New York: Newman Press, 1985. Though clearly partial to Chrysostom, this work has value for having been written by a contemporary who was actually present at the Synod of the Oak. Vivid descriptions of the intrigues and violence of Constantinople that led to Chrysostom's downfall and exile.

Wilken, Robert. *John Chrysostom and the Jews: Rhetoric and Reality in the Late Fourth Century.* Berkeley: University of California Press, 1983. Particularly useful in its attempt to separate rhetoric from reality in Chrysostom's *Adversus Iudaeos* (c. 386; *Homilies Against the Jews,* 1889). These were aimed at Judaizing Christians in his congregation who were still attracted to meetings in the synagogue. Chrysostom is seen as a master of invective, and Judaism emerges as a continuing social and religious force in Antioch.

Thomas Halton

CH'Ü YÜAN

Born: c. 343 B.C.; Ch'u, China
Died: 278 B.C.; in the Mi-lo River, China
Areas of Achievement: Government and literature
Contribution: A skilled statesman who always tried to speak the truth no matter what the cost, Ch'ü Yüan exemplified the Confucian ideal of the virtuous official; his country's first widely known poet, he became one of the founding fathers of Chinese literature.

Early Life

Ch'ü Yüan was born about 343 B.C. in the southern Chinese state of Ch'u, which was centered in what is the modern province of Hubei. The Warring States period (which extended from 481 to 221 B.C.) was characterized by China's fragmentation into a multitude of rival kingdoms, of which Ch'u was one of the major powers. Although little is known of Ch'ü Yüan's childhood, tradition holds that his father's name was Po-yung and that he was related to Ch'u's royal family. Ch'ü Yüan is also reputed to have achieved great distinction as a student and to have been marked for high government service from an early age.

In his late twenties, Ch'ü Yüan was appointed to the important post of *tsotu,* or "left counselor," in his country's bureaucracy. He became the most influential confidant of the reigning King Huai Wang, and his advice was sought on all significant matters of both foreign and domestic policy. As a young man who believed in the ethical ideals inculcated by Confucianism, Ch'ü Yüan tried to convince the king that he should look for these qualities in his new officials and cease the automatic preferment of the nobly born which had been the traditional way of doing things.

The king's son, Tse Lan, successfully argued that to do so was obviously not in the interest of the aristocracy; Ch'ü Yüan fell out of favor, his counsels were disregarded, and eventually, he was banished to a remote area in Ch'u's northern hinterlands. In the years to come, Ch'ü Yüan's star would rise and fall several times as his country changed rulers and policies, but he never again would wield the kind of influence he had with Huai Wang. It was the disappointment of these youthful hopes for thorough reform that turned Ch'ü Yüan toward literature, in which he was destined for far greater fame than he could ever have achieved in his homeland's civil service.

Life's Work

Ch'ü Yüan's political aspirations had received a crushing blow, but his profoundly idealistic nature was not much affected by his being sent away from court. His poem "In Praise of the Orange Tree," which was written about this time, articulated his confidence in what the future would have to say about his unwillingness to play partisan politics with his country's future:

> Oh, your young resolution has something different from the rest.
> Alone and unmoving you stand. How can one not admire you!
> Deep-rooted, hard to shift: truly you have no peer!

The rural region north of the Han River to which Ch'ü Yüan was banished proved to be a rich source of myths and folktales, many of them related to the shamanistic cults which still flourished in the area. A set of poems known as *Chiu ko* (third century B.C.; *The Nine Songs*, 1955), thought to be among his earliest literary works, includes many references to such deities as the River God and the Mountain Spirit, and it is possible that the songs were originally sacred hymns that Ch'ü Yüan used as a basis for poetic composition.

Whatever their origin, *The Nine Songs* combined religious and romantic impulses in a manner completely new to Chinese poetry. Just as Homer described a world in which gods and men were akin in terms of psychology if not in their respective powers, so Ch'ü Yüan envisaged crossing the barriers that divided humanity from the deities it worshipped. This excerpt from "The Princess of the Hsiang" depicts a god waiting for his human lover:

> I look for my queen, but she comes not yet:
> Of Whom do I think as I play my reed-pipes?
> North I go, drawn by flying dragons . . .
> And over the great River waft my spirit:
> Waft, but my spirit does not reach her;
> And the maiden many a sigh heaves for me.

The Nine Songs immediately established Ch'ü Yüan as the foremost literary figure of his time.

During the first of what would prove to be several periods of banishment for Ch'ü Yüan, Huai Wang was murdered in 297 while participating in a supposed peace conference—which Ch'ü Yüan had warned him against attending—in the neighboring state of Ch'in. This shocking event sparked one of Ch'ü Yüan's most fervently emotional poems, "Great Summons"; the refrain "O soul, come back!" expresses both general fear of death and specific anxiety as to what would now become of the poet. For the moment, however, his fortunes took a turn for the better: The new King of Ch'u, Ching Hsiang, remembering that Ch'ü Yüan had argued against the visit to Ch'in, recalled him to the court and at first followed his adviser's policy of breaking off relations with those who had executed his father. For the next two or three years, Ch'ü Yüan was once again his country's most respected political adviser.

Despite this esteem, Chiang Hsiang's younger brother Tse Lan, who had engineered Ch'ü Yüan's first downfall, worked unremittingly to bring about his second. The crisis came when Ch'in attacked and subdued one of Ch'u's neighbors in 293 and threatened to invade Ch'u unless normal relations were restored. Ch'ü Yüan counseled against this, but Tse Lan's opposing faction won the day: Chiang Hsiang married a Ch'in princess, Ch'u and Ch'in reestablished diplomatic contact, and Ch'ü Yüan was once more banished, this time to another remote province south of the Yangtze River.

In the remaining fifteen years of his life, Ch'ü Yüan was several times recalled to court when Ch'in aggression seemed imminent, but his refusal to compromise with Tse Lan's pro-Ch'in faction led to his swift dismissal each time. After one of these disappointments, he considered emigrating to some other country but finally decided that it was his destiny to set an example for those who would come after him. He now wrote the autobiographical poem that is considered his finest achievement: *Li Sao* (c. 293-278 B.C.; *The Li Sao*, 1895), literally "encountering sorrow," offers a moving account of the agonies and ecstasies of his turbulent career as poet and politician.

The Li Sao opens with the birth of Ch'ü Yüan, who is given the names "True Exemplar" and "Divine Balance" by his father. His youthful enthusiasm is soon quenched by a sobering dash of political reality: He learns that "All others press forward in greed and gluttony" while he alone seems to care about leaving behind "an enduring name." His greatest disappointment comes when he learns that even the king is subject to an all-too-human inconstancy of mind, but Ch'ü Yüan is nevertheless determined to continue campaigning for what he believes is right:

But I would rather quickly die and meet dissolution
Before I ever would consent to ape their behaviour.

Ch'ü Yüan presents his love of beauty and poetry as a kind of contrapuntal relief from his political misfortunes, and it is these passages which make *The Li Sao* such a landmark in Chinese verse. Just as he had combined religion and romanticism in his early poetry, so this later work merges the conduct of contemporary affairs with the more permanent consolations offered by aesthetic accomplishment and appreciation. In a world where most people are too busy seeking power to care about either art or morality, Ch'ü Yüan argues that a sensitive soul must protect its natural heritage of grace and good conduct against the constant temptation to conform.

The implications of the conclusion of *The Li Sao*, which announces that the author intends to "go and join P'eng Hsien in the place where he abides," are still a matter of some disagreement among students of Chinese literature. The statement has been interpreted as a decision to become a hermit as well as a desire to commit suicide; since nothing is known about P'eng Hsien, it seems unlikely that the issue will ever be resolved. This ongoing debate demonstrates how timelessly relevant *The Li Sao* is to questions of individual and social morality and of the artist's role in the world, and it helps to explain why Ch'ü Yüan is so important a figure in Chinese literature.

After years of gradual encroachment, the Ch'in armies sacked Ch'u's capital in 278 and threw the country into turmoil. This final disaster was too much for Ch'ü Yüan to bear: He drowned himself in the Mi-lo River, a tributary of the Yangtze, shortly thereafter. Nevertheless, his name lived on as a symbol of selfless dedication to both the highest standards of morality and the good of his country; in addition, he was commemorated by a national holiday. On the day of the annual Dragon Boat Festival, small boats are raced as an expression of the desire to rescue him from drowning, while specially prepared rice balls are thrown into the water so that his spirit will not go hungry.

Summary

Very few people have been accorded the degree of respect given to Ch'ü Yüan in traditional Chinese culture. He exemplified the ideal Confucian official, so loyal to the state that he would not compromise his opinions even when aware that they would be negatively received; his development of his literary talents exemplified the Renaissance-man wholeness that Confucius had advocated but which was often neglected by bureaucrats who found it easier to conform to tradition than attempt to expand it.

Even the People's Republic of China, which has discouraged the respect paid to many traditional historical figures on the grounds that they were reactionary influences, considers Ch'ü Yüan's exemplary loyalty to the state a model of correct social behavior. This esteem has had the important incidental effect of maintaining his status as one of the founding fathers of Chinese literature, and his work has thus been preserved as an important element of his country's cultural heritage. Many poets of subsequent generations, among them Sung Yü, T'ao Ch'ien, and Li Po, were deeply affected by Ch'ü Yüan's energetic defense of the highest ethical and aesthetic standards. Even today he is often acknowledged as an influence by writers striving for a balance between imaginative idealism and moral realism. Wherever Chinese is spoken, his name remains synonymous with personal integrity above and beyond worldly success.

Bibliography

Hawkes, David, trans. *Ch'u tz'u: The Songs of the South, an Ancient Chinese Anthology.* Oxford: Clarendon Press, and Boston: Beacon, 1959. The only complete English translation of Ch'ü Yüan's poetry (which was first collected with that of other writers in an anthology entitled *Ch'u tz'u*). Hawkes's versions of the poems, which are accompanied by excellent notes, are somewhat different from those of earlier translators and are generally considered more accurate by his fellow scholars.

———. "The Quest of the Goddess." In *Studies in Chinese Literary Genres*, edited by Cyril Birch. Berkeley: University of California Press, 1974. This article places Ch'ü Yüan's work in its cultural perspective, compares it with that of his predecessors and successors, and argues that he represents the victory of a written, secular approach to literature over earlier oral and religious modes of expression. A seminal discussion by Ch'ü Yüan's foremost modern interpreter.

Schneider, Laurence A. *A Madman of Ch'u: The Chinese Myth of Loyalty and Dissent.* Berkeley: University of California Press, 1980. A well-researched account of the development of Ch'ü Yüan's reputation into a synonym for political rectitude. The treatment is basically historical and culminates in a convincing demonstration of how he became the patron saint of modern Chinese intellectuals. The poetry is used merely as thematic evidence, but even those more interested in Ch'ü Yüan as a poet will find the book a useful source for social and cultural insights.

Ssu-ma Ch'ien. *Records of the Grand Historian of China.* Burton Watson, trans. 2 vols. Rev. ed. New York: Columbia University Press, 1993. Includes the original historical evidence upon which all subsequent research about Ch'ü Yüan is based. Its biographies of his era's political contemporaries provide a vivid sense of what life was like during the Warring States period.

Waley, Arthur. *The Nine Songs: A Study of Shamanism in Ancient China.* London: Allen and Unwin, 1955; San Francisco: City Lights Books, 1973. Waley stresses the religious origins of Ch'ü Yüan's verse, suggesting that its depth of feeling may be an indication of the author's madness. Although his grasp of the historical context is second to none and makes the book still worth consulting, Waley was not a very sophisticated literary critic; his diagnosis has been disregarded by most subsequent commentators.

Watson, Burton. *Early Chinese Literature.* New York: Columbia University Press, 1962. Includes a detailed discussion of Ch'ü Yüan's work in its historical and textual aspects. A descriptive rather than interpretive approach that occasionally ventures opinions regarding symbolic or thematic significances; a good introduction for the general reader.

Paul Stuewe

CHUANG-TZU

Born: c. 365 B.C.; Mêng, Kingdom of Sung, China
Died: c. 290 B.C.; Nan-hua Hill, Ts'ao-chou, Kingdom of Ch'i, China
Areas of Achievement: Philosophy, monasticism, and literature
Contribution: Chuang-tzu was the greatest thinker of the Chinese Taoist school of philosophy. He went much beyond its founder, Lao-tzu, in constructing an apolitical, transcendental philosophy designed to promote an individual's spiritual freedom.

Early Life

Chuang-tzu was born sometime around 365 B.C.; according to his biographer, Ssu-ma Ch'ien, the philosopher was a native of the town of Mêng in the Kingdom of Sung. His personal name was Chou. Beyond this, little is known regarding Chuang-tzu's life and career. He was born into a time known as the Warring States period, during which China had become divided into many small, fiercely competitive states as a result of the collapse of the Chou Dynasty. Thus, Chuang-tzu was a contemporary of the famous Confucian philosopher Mencius.

For a brief time, Chuang-tzu served as a government official in Ch'i-yuan, not far from his birthplace. He soon tired of public life, however, and resolved to pursue philosophical meditation and writing. Thereupon, he retired to the state of Ch'i, where he took up residence on Nan-hua Hill, in the prefecture of Ts'ao-chou. Here he spent the remainder of his life.

Chuang-tzu's disillusionment with law and politics is apparent in an anecdote recorded in chapter 17 of the *Chuang-tzu:*

> Once, when Chuang Tzu was fishing in the P'u River, the king of Ch'u sent two officials to go and announce to him: "I would like to trouble you with the administration of my realm."
> Chuang Tzu held on to the fishing pole and, without turning his head, said, "I have heard that there is a sacred tortoise in Ch'u that has been dead for three thousand years. The king keeps it wrapped in cloth and boxed, and stores it in the ancestral temple. Now would this tortoise rather be dead and have its bones left behind and honored? Or would it rather be alive and dragging its tail in the mud?"
> "It would rather be alive and dragging its tail in the mud," said the two officials.

Chuang Tzu said, "Go away! I'll drag my tail in the mud!"

A portrait of this stubbornly independent thinker has been preserved in Taipei's National Palace Museum. It shows a rather short, slightly built man with sparse hair and penetrating eyes. He stands with his hands clasped over his chest, a pose that conveys dignity and serenity.

Life's Work

The Taoism of Chuang-tzu's time derived from the *I Ching (Book of Changes)*, the ancient manual of divination based on the concept that the world and the laws of change are an ordered, interdependent unit, and from Lao-tzu's *Tao-te Ching*, which described the workings of the Tao (the Way), the primordial generative principle that is the mother of all things. Tao was interpreted as "the Way of Heaven," or natural law, and the Taoists explained natural phenomena and the social order in reference to this principle. Proper human behavior consisted of not interfering with the Tao but living in harmony with it. Thus, the Taoists taught the doctrine of *wu-wei* (not doing), or, more explicitly, *wei-wu-wei* (doing by not doing). This standard did not imply absolute quietism but rather acting intuitively, spontaneously, and effortlessly in imitation of the Tao, which manages to accomplish everything naturally. Although some Taoists retired entirely from the world and lived as hermits, Taoism was not designed for the hermit but for the Sage king, who, though not withdrawing from the world, seeks to avoid interfering with it.

For the Taoists, then, the best government was the least government. Indeed, they reasoned, if all men acted in harmony with the Tao, government as an institution would be unnecessary. Government by law and even the notions of good and evil were regarded by the Taoists as deviations from the Tao and unwarranted interference with it. Such an attitude gave Taoists considerable independence in regard to politics and worldly affairs generally.

It is evident that Chuang-tzu's decision to withdraw from political entanglements was amply supported by Taoist teachings. His interpretations of this and other doctrines have been passed down in the *Chuang-tzu*, an imaginative compilation of anecdote and dialogue. In the words of a modern scholar, in the *Chuang-tzu* "animals speak, natural forces are personified, and dialogues which begin in soberness unexpectedly veer into humor, fantasy, and absurdity."

Where the *Tao-te Ching* of Lao-tzu sets forth the universal Tao as a political and social ideal, the *Chuang-tzu* is mostly concerned with the individual and his or her intellectual and spiritual freedom. Unlike Lao-tzu's work, which is addressed to rulers, the *Chuang-tzu* addresses anyone, ruler or private person, who wishes to become a member of the spiritual elite. To achieve this goal, the seeker must begin by achieving an awareness of the existence and workings of the universal Tao and of his or her own relation to the scheme of things.

The Tao is nameless; the name assigned to it is merely a convenient label. Though it is preexistent, formless, and imperceptible, it latently contains all forms, entities, and forces; it permeates all things. All Being issues from it and returns to it. The life and death of human beings take part in this transformation from Non-being into Being and back again to Non-being.

After accepting this metaphysical scheme, the seeker faces the second step on the ladder of knowledge: the realization of the importance of making full and free use of his natural ability. Whatever ability he possesses stems from his tê, the power within him that comes directly from the Tao. The individuated forms of things come from their tê, which confers on them their natural properties and abilities. Things differ both in their nature and in their natural abilities. One kind of bird can fly a thousand miles; another kind has difficulty flying from one tree to another. It is no use for a man to discuss the ocean with a frog that has lived its whole life in a well.

It is important for the seeker to distinguish between what is heavenly—that is, of nature—and what is entirely human. What is heavenly is internal; what is human is external. The human is all that is artificial: the artifacts of man; his institutions of government, education, and religion; his cultural codes of etiquette, law, and morals. All these artificialities involve restrictions on man's independence and freedom. To the extent that a person can exercise his natural abilities independently of or in spite of the restrictions imposed on him, he ought to do so. In so doing, he will achieve a measure of happiness, although it will be a relative, not an absolute, happiness. Interference with nature should be avoided, according to Chuang-tzu's teachings. Government that seeks to rule people by strict laws and strong institutions is pictured as putting a halter around a horse's neck or a cord through an ox's nose. The use of violence by governments is like trying to lengthen the short legs of a duck or to shorten the long legs of a crane.

Relative happiness, then, can be attained by making good use of one's natural ability; yet, other factors such as avoiding injury and disease and overcoming fear of death are also necessary to happiness. If the seeker gains a proper understanding of the nature of things, he can greatly mitigate his anxiety regarding death as well as the grief he may feel when a loved one dies. Chapter 18 of the *Chuang-tzu*, "Perfect Happiness," records an anecdote that illustrates this notion. Chuang-tzu's wife had died, and Hui-tzu had gone to pay his condolences to the philosopher. Upon entering his house, Hui-tzu was amazed to find the master "sitting with his legs sprawled, pounding on a tub and singing." Scandalized, Hui-tzu hastened to remind Chuang-tzu that he had lived with his wife a long time, that she had borne and reared his children, and that she had grown old along with him. Hui-tzu reproached his friend: "It should be enough simply not to weep at her death. But pounding on a tub and singing— this is going too far, isn't it?" Chuang-tzu replied:

> You're wrong. When she first died, do you think I didn't grieve like anyone else? But I looked back to her beginning and the time before she was born. Not only the time before she was born, but the time before she had a body. Not only the time before she had a body, but the time before she had a spirit. In the midst of the jumble of wonder and mystery a change took place and she had a spirit. Another change and she had a body. Another change and she was born. Now there's been another change and she's dead. It's just like the progression of the four seasons, spring, summer, fall, winter.
>
> Now she's going to lie down peacefully in a vast room. If I were to follow after her bawling and sobbing, it would show that I don't understand anything about fate. So I stopped.

Thus, death is simply a phase in the turning of the wheel of fortune that is the Tao. The turning of the wheel voids the identity and disintegrates the material body of the dead person. From the standpoint of the Tao, however, no state of being is more desirable than another. As a natural event in the cycle of human life, death is neither to be feared nor to be sorrowed over.

How does the seeker reach the third and last rung of his upward way? To answer this question, Chuang-tzu proposed an epistemology, a theory of knowledge. Knowledge, he said, is of two kinds: lower and higher. The lower involves sense perception, reason, and language; it depends on relativity, finitude, and memory. Higher knowledge involves suprasensible perception, intuition, and silence; it depends on the unity of opposites, infinitude, and forgetfulness. Lower knowledge lacks understanding. Higher knowledge is filled with understanding, a condition in which everything is illuminated by "the light of Heaven."

To achieve higher knowledge, the seeker must forget the knowledge that he has acquired. He must transcend all relativity, finitude, and apparent contradictions implied in conventional opposites such as right and wrong, great and small, life and death. The seeker can transcend such distinctions when he realizes that the Tao makes them all one. Once he has attained this realization, he has no use for categories. Where "ordinary men discriminate and parade their discriminations before others," the enlightened man "embraces things." Thus, forgetfulness and "no-knowledge" constitute the highest wisdom.

The lower level of knowledge permits the use of speech. Good language is dispassionate and calm; bad language is "shrill and quarrelsome." At the higher level of knowledge, however, language is inadequate: "The Great Way is not named; Great Discriminations are not spoken. . . . If discriminations are put into words, they do not suffice." The holy man does not speak, for him silence reigns supreme. Content within himself because he has forgotten self and the world, he may be said to have entered Heaven. He has achieved absolute happiness.

Summary

If the real Chuang-tzu is a barely perceptible shadow cast by the dim light of history, he is brightly visible in the pages of the *Chuang-tzu*. Here he emerges as a living, breathing, dynamic human being, radiant of mind, wide-ranging in imagination, full of wit and humor. The *Chuang-tzu* is a monumental book and a great classic of Chinese literature. Its style is brilliant, full of clever rhetorical devices, satire, fantasy, metaphor, jokes, dreams, and parody. Although it is a work of philosophy, it may also be termed "protofictional." It not only uses historical characters, such as Confucius, fictionally, but also creates fictional characters as foils for its protagonist. In this way, the *Chuang-tzu*

contributed to the development of later Chinese fictional genres such as *hsiao-shuo* and *chih-kuai*.

Philosophically, Chuang-tzu went beyond Lao-tzu in offering a clear alternative to the philosophies of his age. He emphasized the personal ideal of the emancipation of the individual for his own sake in place of the social ideal of the harmonious society ruled by the Sage king. Although the *Chuang-tzu* never gained the popularity and influence of the *Tao-te Ching*, it continued to command the interest and admiration of Chinese rulers and philosophers. The Neo-Taoist philosophers Hsiang Hsiu (c. A.D. 221-c. 300) and Kuo Hsiang (who died around A.D. 312) both wrote commentaries on the *Chuang-tzu*, seeking to reconcile the social ideal of Confucius with the private ideal of Chuang-tzu. Despite their criticism of Chuang-tzu, they performed the important service of transmitting his work and preserving it for posterity.

In the West, the *Chuang-tzu* has made a decided impression on numerous prominent thinkers, beginning perhaps with the great German philosopher G. W. F. Hegel, who in 1816 lectured at the University of Heidelberg on Taoism and Confucianism, based on the *Book of Changes* and the *Chuang-tzu*. His concept of the Absolute as a process rather than a source and his description of the dialectical process (thesis and antithesis merging into a synthesis) are reminiscent of Chuang-tzu's concept of the Tao and the underlying unity of opposites. Later thinkers such as Pierre Teilhard de Chardin, Carl Jung, Jacques Maritain, Jacques Lacan, and Thomas Merton all show evidence in their writing of an intimate acquaintance with Taoism and the thought of Chuang-tzu.

Bibliography

Chan, Wing-tsit, trans. and comp. *A Source Book in Chinese Philosophy*. Princeton, N.J.: Princeton and University Press, 1963. Readable translations of the basic texts of Chinese philosophy, including the *Chuang-tzu*. The early texts, however, follow Neo-Confucian interpretations. Some dubious translations of important terms: *ch'êng* is translated "sincerity" in places where it means something else; *tê* is translated "character" rather than "virtue" or "power."

Chang, Chung-yuan. *Creativity and Taoism: A Study of Chinese Philosophy, Art, and Poetry*. New York: Julian Press, 1963; London: Wildwood House, 1975. Shows the important part

Taoism has played in Chinese artistic and intellectual activity.

Chuang-tzu. *Chuang-tzu: The Seven Inner Chapters and Other Writings from the Book of Chuang-tzu*. Translated by A. C. Graham. London and Boston: Allen and Unwin, 1981. This volume offers more than a new translation. Graham attempts to resolve major textual problems and edits the texts in terms of new categories. Lucid and interesting. Highly recommended.

————. *The Complete Works of Chuang Tzu*. Translated by Burton Watson. New York: Columbia University Press, 1968. The translation of the extant thirty-three-chapter version of the *Chuang-tzu*. It incorporates the modern research of Japanese scholars. It is perhaps the best translation available.

Creel, H. G. *Chinese Thought from Confucius to Mao Tsê-tung*. Chicago: University of Chicago Press, 1953; London: Eyre and Spottiswoode, 1954. Good general survey of Chinese thought except that the philosophies most prominent from the fourth century through the seventeenth century—Buddhism, Neo-Taoism, and Neo-Confucianism—are not given adequate coverage.

————. *What Is Taoism? And Other Studies in Chinese Cultural History*. Chicago: University of Chicago Press, 1970; London: University of Chicago Press, 1977. A collection of essays well worth reading. Includes Creel's notable essay "The Great Clod: A Taoist Conception of the Universe."

Durrant, Stephen. "*Chu-tzu pai-chia* (The Various Masters and the Hundred Schools)." In *The Indiana Companion to Traditional Chinese Literature*, edited by William H. Nienhauser, Jr. Bloomington: Indiana University Press, 1986. A relatively brief but nevertheless excellent survey of its topic.

Merton, Thomas. *The Way of Chuang Tzu*. Rev. ed. London: Burns and Oates, 1995. The author was a poet, prose writer, mystic, and Trappist monk. Knowing no Chinese, he made an effort here to capture his intuitive sense of Chuang-tzu's spirit on the basis of translations in Western languages. He succeeds as well as the translators.

Watson, Burton. *Early Chinese Literature*. New York: Columbia University Press, 1962. A history of Chinese literature—"literature" meaning history, philosophy, and poetry—from the Chou Dynasty to the middle of the Later Han Dynasty. An informative and enjoyable volume. The translations are readable and generally accurate, with only a few minor errors.

Richard P. Benton

CICERO

Born: January 3, 106 B.C.; Arpinum, Latium

Died: December 7, 43 B.C.; Formiae, Latium

Areas of Achievement: Government, law, oratory, philosophy, and literature

Contribution: With courageous and principled statesmanship, Cicero guided Rome through a series of severe crises. While he was not able to save the Republic, he transmitted its political and cultural values in speeches and treatises that became models of style for posterity.

Early Life

Marcus Tullius Cicero, the elder son of Marcus Tullius Cicero and Helvia, was born a few miles from Arpinum, a small town in Latium, southeast of Rome. Long established in the district, his family had, like many other Roman families, a rather undignified source for its name: *Cicer* is Latin for chickpea, or garbanzo. According to one story, "Cicero" originated as the nickname of a wart-nosed ancestor. The Tullius clan was of equestrian, or knightly, rank—that is, they were well-to-do but their members had never served in the senate. Cicero was to be the first in the family to attain nobility as a magistrate.

Centuries earlier, Arpinum had been a stronghold of the Volscians in their unsuccessful struggle to avoid subjugation by Rome. For nearly one hundred years before Cicero's birth, however, the people of Arpinum had enjoyed full Roman citizenship. Cicero took pride in his local origins as well as in his Roman citizenship, and he sometimes referred to his "two fatherlands." His description in *Cato Maior de Senectute* (44 B.C.; *On Old Age*, 1481) of the slow, well-regulated growth of Arpinum's figs and grapes suggests the influence of his birthplace on his politics at Rome: He was a lifelong defender of order and gradual change, an enemy of both mob violence and aristocratic privilege.

Cicero's first exposure to learning came through the papyrus scrolls in his father's library at Arpinum. While still very young, both Cicero and his brother, Quintus, showed such zeal to study philosophy and oratory that their father took them to Rome to seek the best instruction available. This move to Carinae Street in the capital, coinciding with his father's retirement from active life, presented young Cicero with an opportunity to excel academically and advance socially.

Latin literature had yet to come into its own. Early Roman poets such as Livius Andronicus and Quintus Ennius simply did not compare well with Homer, and the educators of the day made heavy use of Greek poetic works to teach elocution and rhetoric. One of Cicero's teachers was the Greek poet Aulus Licinius Archias, who himself had come to Rome in 102 B.C. and whom Cicero afterwards credited with having sparked his interest in literature. Cicero adapted the cadences of Greek and Latin poetry to his original orations, developing a complex but supple rhetorical and literary style that became a standard for his own time and for the Renaissance, fifteen hundred years later. In retrospect, however, Cicero faulted the education of his youth for not teaching how to obtain practical results through rhetoric—a problem he set himself to solve through legal studies.

In 89 B.C., at age seventeen, he interrupted these studies to serve on Rome's side in the Social War, a rebellion by Rome's Italian allies. His brief role in this disastrous ten-year conflict aroused in him a lifelong hatred of military service. He became more convinced than ever that his success would lie in progressing through the prescribed sequence of public offices, as it had for his models at the time, the orators Lucius Licinius Crassus and Marcus Antonius Creticus (grandfather of Marc Antony). He continued to study rhetoric and also resumed his legal studies under Quintus Mucius Scaevola, the augur (priest of the state religion), who had been consul some twenty-eight years previously.

Life's Work

Among Cicero's important achievements was a series of celebrated orations in connection with legal cases. His oratorical skills aided him in the pursuit of public office and helped secure his place in history as the savior of Rome.

Cicero launched his career as an orator and advocate in 81 B.C., during the dictatorship of Lucius Cornelius Sulla. Under that regime no one's life was safe; to become conspicuous through forensics was especially dangerous. Not only did Cicero confront this risk, but from his earliest cases onward he also often bravely opposed the established leaders. *Pro Quinctio* (81 B.C.), his first speech in a court of law, had little importance in itself; in taking on this case, however, Cicero pitted himself against the leading advocate of the day, Quintus Hortensius Hortalus.

The following year, in *Pro Roscio Amerino,* Cicero defended a young man accused of parricide by Chrysogonus, a favorite of Sulla's. After the father of Roscius was murdered, Chrysogonus had fabricated a charge to get the dead man's name on Sulla's list of proscribed citizens—those banished from Rome for certain offenses. By law the property of a proscribed person, dead or alive, was put up at auction; Chrysogonus wanted to buy the dead father's property cheaply. He later conspired to make Roscius appear responsible for the murder. It was a bold and dangerous step to reveal in a public speech this evil scheme of Sulla's favorite. Yet Cicero resolutely undertook the defense of Roscius and carried it off so effectively that his reputation was immediately established. Suddenly his services as advocate were in great demand, and Cicero sought to capitalize on this trend by publishing some of his forensic speeches.

Apparently Sulla bore Cicero no ill will; in any case, the dictator abdicated in 79 B.C. The next two years, however, Cicero spent away from Rome, studying philosophy and oratory in Greece and Rhodes under Molo, who had also taught Julius Caesar. During this period, Cicero regained his health; it was also during this time that he formed the great friendship of his life, with Titus Pomponius Atticus, to whom he would address some of his best-known letters.

In 77 B.C., Cicero returned to Rome and married Terentia, the daughter of a well-to-do and socially prominent family. He was old enough to campaign for quaestor (financial officer), the first rung of the public-office ladder. Elected at the minimum age of thirty in 76 B.C., Cicero served in Sicily and distinguished himself in office by sending large supplies of grain to the capital in a time of near famine. In gratitude, the senate admitted him to membership.

Meanwhile, Cicero continued to offer his services as orator and advocate, since Roman law prescribed an interim between terms of service as a magistrate. In 70 came another noteworthy event in his career: his impeachment of Gaius Verres, Governor of Sicily from 73 to 71. Most provincial governors pursued a policy of extortion to enrich themselves, but Verres had been uncommonly greedy and cruel. Having spent two months preparing a painstakingly well-documented case, Cicero

prosecuted Verres so vigorously that the defendant's legal adviser—the same Hortensius whose primacy Cicero had challenged ten years earlier—gave up the defense, and Verres went into voluntary exile.

Cicero's skill as a speaker in public trials was an important factor in his election to public office, especially since he was not from one of Rome's leading aristocratic families. He won by a landslide the office of aedile (roughly, superintendent of public works) in 69 B.C. Two years later, he was chosen praetor, or judicial officer, and in 63 came the supreme honor: election as consul, Rome's chief executive. Two consuls were elected each year, and Cicero's colleague in office, Gaius Antonius Hybrida, was politically insignificant. Essentially, he allowed Cicero complete control during what became a year of crisis.

First, Cicero felt compelled to oppose a bill that ordered the distribution of state-owned land to the poor. The real significance of this particular bill lay in the powers it accorded to a commission that would be appointed to implement it. Sponsoring the bill were two wealthy aristocrats, Crassus and

Caesar. Cicero, a professed "man of the people," soundly defeated the measure, but at the cost of appearing to be an ally of the moneyed, landowning classes, while Caesar seemed a champion of the masses.

An aristocrat was similarly responsible for the next crisis, the Catilinarian conspiracy. After losing several bids for high office, Lucius Sergius Catilina (Catiline), in desperation, began plotting a coup. He recruited popular support by promising to cancel all debts and proscribe the wealthy if he came to power. When Catiline tried to enlist a group of tribal delegates from Roman Gaul, however, they informed Cicero, who arranged that they should be arrested while carrying incriminating letters from the plotters. The evidence was incontrovertible, and Cicero called for summary execution.

This bold move proved a serious mistake that almost destroyed Cicero's political career. Roman law provided that no citizen should be put to death without the privilege of final appeal to the people. Cicero, in his fourth Catilinarian oration, held that those who had plotted against their country were no longer citizens and thus had lost the right of final appeal. Despite the danger to the Republic—Catiline's supporters outside Rome were virtually in a state of rebellion—Cicero pressed for an arbitrary interpretation of the law. He had the power to do so, for in October, because of the crisis, the senate had practically given him dictatorial power. Catiline himself escaped but was soon killed in the battle that finally ended the conspiracy. Cicero prevailed upon the senate to pass the death sentence on the other ringleaders. Thereafter, he was hailed as a "savior" and "father of the fatherland." Nevertheless, there were to be reprisals.

Publius Clodius Pulcher, a favorite of Caesar's and a private enemy of Cicero's, introduced a bill to exile anyone who had put Roman citizens to death without the right of public appeal. Cicero was not named, but the measure was clearly aimed at him. His attempts to block it failed, and in 58 B.C., stricken with grief, he was forced to leave Rome. Clodius and his followers tore down Cicero's house in Rome and persecuted Terentia.

Cicero was recalled to the capital, however, after eighteen months. Perhaps as a reaction to Clodius' excesses, the people gave Cicero a hero's welcome. His house and wealth were restored, and Julius Caesar courted him as a potential ally. Cicero's dream at this time, however, was to save the Republic by detaching Pompey the Great from the Triumvirate. Caesar and Pompey did indeed fall out, but the breakup of the Triumvirate did not save the Republic. During the years between 57 and 51 B.C., Cicero lived in retirement and concentrated on philosophical and rhetorical studies and the writing of treatises in these fields, works in which he articulated the political and moral philosophy he had tried to exemplify in his life. In 51, sick of living in ignominious luxury, he leaped at the opportunity to govern the province of Cilicia as proconsul. Unlike most provincial governors, he was a just, sympathetic administrator, sincerely desirous of improving the lot of the Cilicians, who had been severely exploited by his predecessors.

Cicero never forgave Caesar for putting an end to the Republic, though he took no part in Caesar's assassination in 44 B.C. Afterward, he expected to see the Republic restored, but he soon came to fear Antony as a second Caesar. When the Second Triumvirate was formed by Antony, Octavian (later Augustus), and Marcus Aemilius Lepidus, Cicero and other defenders of the old Republic were proscribed. Antony's supporters hunted Cicero down and killed him in Formiae, Latium, on December 7, 43 B.C. To disgrace him, Antony had his head and hands mounted on the Rostra at Rome.

Summary

It was for his political acts than Marcus Tullius Cicero most wanted to be remembered, and, having acted courageously and decisively at certain critical moments—notably during the Catilinarian conspiracy—he was viewed in his own time as the savior of Rome. Nevertheless, Rome as Cicero knew it—the Republic—could not be saved. Though Cicero did often set an example of personal courage for his contemporaries, his more lasting value is in having articulated the political and moral ideals of the Roman Republic at the very moment when their realization was no longer possible. Through his writings, Cicero also helped to shape the form and style of a literature that was just coming into its own. In his orations and philosophical essays, he showed that the Latin language could be employed with the same grace and elegance as Greek. Though his philosophical reasoning was seldom profound, it adequately served his avowed practical purpose—in literature as in life—of helping humanity find a way of life and a consistent purpose. By recording the ideals of Republican Rome, Cicero may have ensured their availability in other times when their realization may be more feasible.

Bibliography

Balsdon, J.V.P.D., ed. *Roman Civilization*. Baltimore, Md.: Penguin, 1965; London: Penguin, 1969. Includes chapters by various specialists on early Roman history, law, architecture, and engineering. The chapter on education and oratory focuses on Cicero.

Cicero. *Letters of Cicero: A Selection in Translation*. Compiled and translated by L. P. Wilkinson. New York: Norton, and London: Hutchinson, 1966. Provides translations of Cicero's important letters from the year after his consulship to the end of his life, with an informative introduction.

Cowell, F. R. *Cicero and the Roman Republic*. 5th ed. London: Penguin Books, 1972. Contains detailed chapters on Roman history, culture, and commerce, as well as discussions of Cicero's political relationships.

Fuhrmann, Manfred. *Cicero and the Roman Republic*. Oxford and Cambridge, Mass.: Blackwell, 1992. A chronological account of Cicero's political life. The author sees Cicero's consulship as a turning point in that it solidified Cicero's political beliefs but weakened his power in the state. Contains discussions of many of Cicero's works.

Habicht, Christian. *Cicero the Politician*. Baltimore and London: Johns Hopkins University Press, 1990. A brief re-evaluation of Cicero's political activities with the aim of securing for him "a prominent place among the political leaders of the time." Though ultimately unsuccessful, Cicero was not, Habicht claims, negligible or despicable. Provides a useful overview of the political situation in the last two decades of the republic.

Mackail, J.W. *Latin Literature*. Edited with an introduction by Harry C. Schnur. Rev. ed. London: Murray, 1896; New York: Scribner, 1899. Contains a chapter with literary evaluations of Cicero's forensic oratory, political philosophy, philosophy, and epistolary prose. Includes a bibliography.

Powell, J. G. F., ed. *Cicero the Philosopher: Twelve Papers*. Oxford and New York: Clarendon Press, 1995. The essays in this collection treat specific topics in Cicero's philosophical works. On the whole they stress the need to take seriously Cicero's understanding of and contribution to philosophy. Includes papers on *De Finibus, Tusculan Disputations, De Re Publica*, as well as articles on topics relevant to the whole philosophical corpus.

Shackleton Bailey, D.R. *Cicero*. New York: Scribner, and London: Duckworth, 1971. Provides a detailed biography of Cicero and discusses his writings in the context of his life. Part of the Classical Life and Letters series.

Sihler, Ernest G. *Cicero of Arpinum: A Political and Literary Biography*. 2d ed. New York: Stechert, 1933. A classicist's approach to the study of Cicero's life and character. Special emphasis is placed on Cicero's writings.

Thomas Rankin

CIMON

Born: c. 510 B.C.; place unknown

Died: c. 451 B.C.; near Citium (modern Larnaca), Cyprus

Areas of Achievement: Politics and warfare

Contribution: Through skillful military leadership and diplomacy, Cimon became an important force behind the establishment of the Delian League—a Greek alliance against the Persians— and its later transformation into the Athenian Empire. Domestically, he struggled unsuccessfully against the further extension of democracy in ancient Athens.

Early Life

As the oldest child of Miltiades the Younger, the victor of the Battle of Marathon, and Hegesipyle, the daughter of King Olorus of Thrace, Cimon inherited the political leadership and influence of one of the most ancient and respected aristocratic families in Athens, the Philaidae clan. He received a traditional Athenian education, emphasizing simple literacy skills and athletic prowess, as opposed to the stress upon rhetoric and speculative philosophy which would prevail in later generations. As a youth, however, Cimon disappointed his fellow clan members and other Philaidae supporters by his dissolute behavior. His riotous living and heavy drinking recalled to Athenian minds the infamous conduct of his grandfather and namesake, Cimon, nicknamed *koalemos* (the "nincompoop"). The younger Cimon's irresponsible attitudes threatened to cast the Philaidae clan into obscurity in an Athenian political arena where familial relationships and alliances counted for much in the competition for power.

Although Cimon possessed the personal assets essential to successful political leadership—high intelligence and an impressive physical appearance—he also entered manhood in the 480's with crippling liabilities. His father's conviction in 489 for "deceiving the people" had cast disrepute upon the Philaidae, while responsibility for the enormous fine imposed at the trial impoverished Cimon for several years after Miltiades' death. Inability to provide a dowry for his beautiful sister, Elpinice, forced him to support her in his own household under circumstances which incited rumors of incestuous relations. (Ancient and modern historians have debated the nature of Cimon's relationship with Elpinice. Many believe that she was his half sister, and thereby, appropriately married to Cimon under Athenian law and custom, which allowed such unions.) Cimon's hopes for a successful political career appeared dim.

Persia's invasion of Greece in 480 thrust Cimon into the limelight and decidedly reversed his political fortunes. When the Persian King Xerxes I invaded Attica and threatened Athens, the city's leaders had difficulty persuading the populace to adhere to the previously agreed-upon strategy: evacuation of noncombatants and concentration of military resources and personnel with the fleet in the Bay of Salamis. Cimon resolved to set an example for the young aristocrats who traditionally formed the small, Athenian cavalry contingent. He led his comrades up to the Acropolis, where he was the first to dedicate his horse's bridle on the altar of Athena. Seizing a shield from the wall of the sanctuary, he then joined the fleet at Salamis as a simple hoplite. His actions inspired his fellow Athenians. After fighting courageously at the subsequent Battle of Salamis, Cimon emerged a

hero from the Great Persian War. He was not slow to utilize his refurbished reputation.

Life's Work

About 480, Cimon was married to Isodice, an Athenian woman from the Alcmaeonidae clan. This marriage produced at least three sons: twins, Lakedaimonios and Oulios, and Thettalos. According to some ancient sources, Cimon also had three other sons—Cimon, Miltiades, and Peisianax—although most modern historians are skeptical of the existence of these children. Marriage to Isodice promised important political advantages, yet Cimon also loved her passionately, and the depth of his devotion to her was unusual enough to induce comment from contemporary observers and ancient historians.

Shortly after his own marriage, Cimon was able to find a husband for Elpinice. She was betrothed to Callias of Alopeke, a member of the Hipponikos clan and the richest man in Athens. This new brother-in-law assisted Cimon in paying his father's fine and recouping the Philaidae clan's finances. More important, the marriages of Cimon and Elpinice forged an alliance between three of the most politically important clan-factions in Athens: the Philaidae, Alcmaeonidae, and Hipponikos. This coalition may have been directed against Themistocles, who had emerged from the Great Persian War as the leading Athenian politician; his skilled courting of the populace engendered defensive reactions from fellow aristocrats.

Although Cleisthenes of Athens had instituted democratic reforms to the Athenian constitution, aristocratic clan-factions, especially those based in Athens itself, still exerted considerable influence over the city's political life. Because payment for public officials was as yet unknown in Athens, only men of independent financial means could spare the time and energy necessary to state service. Ordinary Athenian voters tended to coalesce around aristocratic leaders, who could assist them with financial and judicial problems. In the 470's and 460's, Cimon was especially renowned for his skillful use of this "politics of largesse," that is, the disbursement of monetary and commodity gratuities in the hope of securing votes.

Changes in Athenian constitutional practices during the 480's strengthened aristocratic influences on government. The prestige of the Areopagus—a judicial-administrative body composed of former archons drawn from the upper classes—increased during the Persian War because of its skilled handling of the crisis. Moreover, the decision in 488/487 to select archons by lot actually enhanced the ability of the aristocracy to direct Athenian politics, because consequently the *strategoi* (board of generals) increasingly assumed leadership of the Assembly and the Council of Five Hundred. Unlike the archons, the *strategoi* could be elected to office consecutively and as many times as possible. During the 470's and 460's, aristocratic defenders of the status quo, such as Cimon and Aristides, served as *strategoi* for years, dominating Athenian foreign policy and influencing domestic developments.

These years also witnessed the establishment of the Delian League, an alliance between Athens and numerous Ionian and Aegean city-states, by which continuous war was vigorously pursued against the Persian Empire. In the 470's, Cimon's fair treatment of Athens' allies in the League spread his fame over the Greek world and ensured for him perennial command of major military expeditions. Between 476 and 469, he expelled the renegade Spartan commander Pausanias from Byzantium, seized Eion on the Strymon River from the Persians, and conquered Scyros from Dolopian pirates and colonized it with Athenians. During the latter expedition, Cimon discovered and transported to Athens the supposed bones of Theseus, the mythical founder of the Athenian state, an act which fulfilled an ancient oracle and won for him great applause.

Cimon's finest military achievement, however, took place at the mouth of the Eurymedon River around 468. There, utilizing a self-designed trireme which accommodated a greater number of hoplites, Cimon destroyed a large Persian fleet and defeated an accompanying army on land. A Phoenician fleet sailing to reinforce the Persians was similarly devastated by the new triremes. Cimon had brought Athens and the League to the pinnacle of success. Persian presence in the Aegean, in Ionia, and on the shores of southern Asia Minor had been obliterated. Cimon's foreign policy—peace with Sparta and other Greeks and concentration on the traditional Persian enemy—had proved its value.

The leader of the Philaidae, nevertheless, teetered dangerously on the brink of political disaster, as his tremendous success had aroused the jealousies of aristocratic rivals. Following Cimon's successful siege of Thasos—a city-state which had attempted to secede from the Delian League—and his conquest of the Persian-occupied Chersonese, he was brought to trial for allegedly accepting a bribe from Alexander I of Macedon not to attack his territory. Although Cimon was acquitted, the charge was an ominous portent of difficulties to come: The accusation had been brought by a young Pericles and other aristocrats, intent upon further democratizing the Athenian state to their own political advantage.

During the trial, Cimon had convincingly pleaded his incorruptibility by citing his long tenure as *proxenos* (a Greek who officially represented the interests of another city-state to his fellow citizens) for Sparta, whose citizens were known for their self-imposed poverty and inability to provide large monetary rewards for services rendered. Cimon's admiration for Spartan culture and military institutions was well known to his fellow Athenians, but previously his loyalty to his own city-state had gone unquestioned. Worsening relations between Athens and Sparta would soon cast suspicion upon Cimon and his pro-Spartan foreign policy and thereby wreck his political career.

By the late 460's, an earlier spirit of cooperation and friendship between Athens and Sparta, proceeding from the Persian War, had been replaced by fear and hostility. The tremendous growth of Athens' power—realized through the gradual conversion of the Delian League into an Athenian Empire—was largely responsible for this change. The Spartans so greatly resented Athenian usurpation of their traditional leadership role in Greece that they promised Thasos an invasion of Attica to support the Thasian secession attempt. Before the Spartans were able to execute their plan, however, Laconia was struck by a severe earthquake and a widespread helot (serf) rebellion. Sparta was forced to call upon other Greek cities, including Athens, for aid.

Among the Athenians, the debate over aid to Sparta grew acrimonious. The so-called democratic party, led by Ephialtes, strongly opposed assisting the Spartans, regarding them as dangerous rivals. Cimon, on the other hand, argued that abandoning the Spartans would weaken all Greece, while he referred to Sparta as Athens' "yoke-fellow." In the end, his position prevailed, because the Athenians had not yet learned of Spartan complicity in the Thasian revolt. In 462, Cimon led a large Athenian army into Laconia to assist in the suppression of the helots.

With Cimon away on this expedition, Ephialtes and Pericles moved to weaken the foundations of conservative rule in Athens. They began by bringing forth accusations of malfeasance against prominent members of the Areopagus. Meanwhile, in Laconia, Cimon and his army suffered the ignominy of a curt dismissal by the Spartans, who probably feared that progressive Athenian political ideas would exacerbate Sparta's current problems with subject peoples. When Cimon returned to Athens, he faced the wrath of prideful Athenians, distrustful of Sparta and humiliated by the recent events in Laconia. With emotions running high against the Spartans, Cimon's admiration for them appeared treasonous to many Athenians. In 461, he was ostracized, a formal, political procedure by which leaders considered dangerous to Athens were exiled for ten years. In Cimon's absence, Ephialtes and Pericles stripped the Areopagus of nearly all of its judicial and administrative powers and strengthened those of the Assembly, the Council of Five Hundred, and the law courts. Athens had entered the final, radical phase of democratization.

With Cimon in exile and his pro-Spartan policies thoroughly discredited, relations between Athens and Sparta deteriorated. In 459, war broke out between the two cities and their allies. This conflict, known as the First Peloponnesian War, lasted until 445. Initially, the Athenians enjoyed success, despite the fact that the war with Persia continued in Cyprus and Egypt, and necessitated the dispersal of Athens' resources over several theaters of action. In 457, however, the Spartans and their allies counterattacked by invading central Greece and directly threatening to invade Attica.

The Athenians, Spartans, and their respective allies met at Tanagra, a small city in southern Boeotia. Athenian morale was low because of pervasive rumors of a pro-Spartan conspiracy by Cimon's supporters and other clan-factions against the new democratic state. Nevertheless, before the battle began, Cimon appeared fully armed and offered his services to the Athenian generals. Although suspicion of Cimon's motives caused his offer to be spurned, the leader of the Philaidae exhorted his friends and relatives along the Athenian battleline to give their greatest efforts to demonstrate their loyalty to Athens. In the subsequent battle, the Philaidae faction fought courageously, making up a disproportionate number of the Athenian dead. Sympathy for Cimon revived in Athens.

While Cimon's gift for political theatrics rejuvenated his public image, events elsewhere set the stage for his return to Athens. In 454, the large Athenian expeditionary force in Egypt was annihilated by the Persians. This reversal of fortunes incited several revolts against Athenian rule in Ionia and the Aegean. Cimon was recalled from exile as the statesman who could best attenuate Athens' overextended military commitments by making peace with Sparta. In 451, he returned to Athens and negotiated a five-year truce with the Spartans. In the next year, serving again as *strategos,* Cimon led an expedition to Cyprus, where he died while besieging Citium, fighting once again the Persians.

Summary

Although as fiercely competitive as any Greek aristocrat, Cimon was extraordinary in his dedication to principle and a loyalty to his city-state. By adhering to three policies—aristocratic predominance in Athenian democracy, peace and fair-dealing with fellow Greeks, and war against the Persians—he remained unusually consistent over a long career. His political style transcended the personal and clan rivalries which had structured Athenian politics for centuries and presaged a reshaping of political competition along ideological lines in the latter fifth and fourth centuries.

Bibliography

Burn, A. R. *Pericles and Athens.* London: English Universities Press, 1948; New York: Macmillan, 1949. Contains useful material on the relationship between Cimon and Pericles. Burn's depiction of Cimon as a myopic, obtuse conservative is overdrawn. It was Cimon, after all, not Pericles, who stressed Greek unity against the Persians, in anticipation of similar fourth century visions.

Kagan, Donald. *The Outbreak of the Peloponnesian War.* Ithaca, N.Y.: Cornell University Press, 1969. Serves well as an introduction to interstate relations in the Aegean and eastern Mediterranean worlds during the period of Cimon's career. Important chapters on Spartan and Athenian internal politics show the relationships between domestic developments in these city-states and the growth of hostility between them. May also be used as a guide to the ancient sources on Cimon and his times.

Laistner, M. L. W. *A History of the Greek World from 479 to 323 B.C.* 3d ed. London: Methuen,

and New York: Barnes and Noble, 1957. This introductory book should be consulted first by those unfamiliar with Cimon's era. It is also useful as a broad outline of ideological interpretations of Athenian politics after the Great Persian War.

McGregor, Malcolm F. *The Athenians and Their Empire.* Vancouver: University of British Columbia Press, 1987. Written especially for students and nonprofessional historians, this is a very useful introduction to its subject. Although lacking footnotes, the information is highly reliable. Numerous maps, appendices, charts, and a glossary of Greek political terminology make this volume required reading for beginners.

Meiggs, Russell. *The Athenian Empire.* Oxford: Clarendon Press, 1972; New York: Oxford University Press, 1979. This is the standard, scholarly work on its subject, replete with footnotes which can be used to guide the reader to ancient sources. Also contains detailed discussions of the controversial issues surrounding the Athenian Empire.

Plutarch. *Life of Kimon.* Edited and translated by A. Blamire. *Bulletin of the Institute of Classical Studies* 56, Classical Handbook 2. London: Institute of Classical Studies, 1989. A historical commentary on Plutarch's *Life* that brings to it the results of recent scholarship on the 5th century.

Plutarch. *The Rise and Fall of Athens: Nine Greek Lives.* Translated by Ian Scott-Kilvert. Baltimore, Md., and London: Penguin Books, 1960. An adaptation of Plutarch's famous *Bioi paralleloi* (c. A.D. 105-115; *Parallel Lives*), this volume contains the biographies of nine important Athenians. Plutarch's "Life of Cimon," contained herein, is the most significant source of information on him and the place to start serious research. Use Plutarch only in conjunction with modern histories, however, because his love of a good story often led him to errors, which later historians have corrected.

Sealey, Raphael. *A History of the Greek City-States, c. 700-338 B.C.* Berkeley: University of California Press, 1976. Written by a prominent proponent of the prosopographical approach to Greek politics, that is, the concept that personal and familial relations overrode ideological issues in shaping events. Includes discussion of major aspects of Cimon's life and times, with ancient sources referenced. Most historians have not found Sealey's interpretation of Athenian politics in the era 480 to 450 to be persuasive, because ideology does seem to have structured political behavior much more clearly after the Great Persian War than before.

Thucydides. *The Peloponnesian War.* Translated and edited by Rex Warner. Rev. ed. Baltimore, Md. and London: Penguin Books, 1972. Book 1 contains Thucydides' famous account of the period between the Great Persian War and the outbreak of the Second Peloponnesian War. While recounting the development of hostility between Athens and Sparta, Thucydides reveals much about the Athenian Empire and Cimon's role in its establishment and expansion.

Michael S. Fitzgerald

CLAUDIUS I

Born: August 1, 10 B.C.; Lugdunum, Gaul
Died: October 13, A.D. 54; Rome, Italy
Area of Achievement: Government
Contribution: Coming to power after the politically and financially devastating reign of Caligula, Claudius I completed the centralizing tendencies of Roman imperial government by creating a bureaucracy that was totally professional in training and totally loyal in its devotion to the imperial concept of government.

Early Life

Tiberius Claudius Drusus Nero Germanicus was born in Lugdunum, Gaul (modern Lyons, France), the youngest son of the Elder Drusus and Antonia Minor. Claudius' father was the stepson of the emperor Augustus and his mother was Augustus' niece. Despite such illustrious parentage, Claudius was never expected to hold any important government office or military post. Although his elder brother Germanicus was adopted into the imperial family by his uncle, the future emperor Tiberius, Claudius was not considered to be in line for the throne because he was physically handicapped. In an age when physical beauty and perfection were admired, he was an embarrassment to the imperial family.

Claudius' multiple handicaps and infirmities were readily apparent. He had weak knees, trembling hands, and a wobbly head; he dragged his right foot, walked with a limp, stuttered when he spoke, and drooled uncontrollably. Desiring to preserve an image of power and authority in the eyes of the Roman people, the imperial family kept Claudius' public appearances to a minimum. Although not permitted a career in government service, Claudius received an excellent education. As he grew older, he became more and more interested in historical studies and wrote numerous scholarly works on Roman, Etruscan, and Carthaginian history. In addition, he wrote an apology for Cicero and composed an autobiography. Not content to limit himself to historical work, Claudius studied philological problems of Latin and introduced three new letters into the Latin alphabet.

During the reigns of Augustus and Tiberius, Claudius continued to have little role in affairs of state. When his nephew Caligula ascended the throne, however, Claudius' life changed dramatically. In July, A.D. 37, Claudius became consul along with Caligula. Although consuls lacked any real power, they enjoyed considerable prestige. Still, such public recognition only made life more difficult for Claudius. Even though he was related to the reigning emperor, Claudius was the frequent butt of cruel jokes and insults, the ever-present, easy target for court jesters and practical jokers. Indeed, this was probably the most difficult and dangerous time of his life. To protect himself from the murderous whims of his mad nephew, Claudius endured the insults and played the fool. People were all too ready to believe him mentally as well as physically handicapped. The role of the simpleton was a convenient ruse which saved Claudius' life on more than one occasion.

Life's Work

When Caligula became so autocratic as to attempt the establishment of a Hellenistic-style monarchy, assassins killed him along with his wife and daughter. While searching the imperial palace, a soldier of the Praetorian Guard discovered Claudius hiding behind a curtain. After dragging Claudius to the Praetorian camp, the soldiers quickly realized the advantage to them of perpetuating the imperial system. Thus, the Praetorian Guard hailed Claudius emperor on January 25, A.D. 41, while the senate was still trying to decide what to do.

Despite the unusual circumstances of his coming to the throne, Claudius was not a revolutionary. He wasted no time in capturing and punishing the assassins of Caligula while simultaneously distancing himself from his predecessor's policies. As emperor, Claudius looked upon Augustus as his role model, following his lead in attempting to revive the traditional religious practices and political institutions of the Roman Republic. Despite his amicable overtures toward the senate, Claudius learned what Augustus had learned: The senate, never having renounced its claim to state leadership, was resentful of being dominated by an emperor. Claudius tried to show respect for the senate by giving back provinces that Tiberius had made imperial (Achaea and Macedonia), appointing imperial legates of senatorial rank, allowing the senate to issue copper coinage in the provinces, and enforcing senatorial resolutions. Despite all of his efforts at cooperation, the senate was not very receptive. Eventually, this lack of response led Claudius to work against the senate and to concentrate all the power of the government in his own hands.

After a lapse of sixty-eight years during which the office of censor had gone unoccupied, Claudius temporarily restored and held it for eighteen months in 47-48. As a result of his censorship, numerous old senatorial families were discredited and expelled from the senate, while many new provincial families were admitted. Imperial oversight of the senate also extended to those aspects of government which had been traditionally controlled by the senate. The *aerarium Saturni* and the *fiscus* were both brought under close imperial supervision through the imperial appointment or nomination of the officials who ran these treasuries.

Not able to rely upon the old senatorial aristocracy for administrative support, Claudius set himself the task of creating an executive staff manned by freedmen who were to be obedient only to the emperor. While freedmen had been used in government since the reign of Augustus, Claudius made more extensive use of them by placing them in charge of government departments and entrusting them with confidential tasks. This practice guaranteed the emperor's independence from the senate and antagonized the aristocratic elite of Rome. The freedmen Narcissus and Pallas became rich and powerful as Claudius' closest and most trusted advisers. With the establishment of a centralized administration directly under the emperor's control, Claudius was able to extend his jurisdiction into senatorial provinces.

At the same time, Claudius sought uniformity of administration and equal status for the provinces. Historically, Rome and Italy had enjoyed privileged positions within the empire, while the provinces' status had been inferior. Claudius tried to eliminate this inequality by extending citizenship rights to various provincial communities and by establishing Roman colonies, particularly in the newer imperial provinces such as Britain and Mauretania. This policy, while politically and militarily motivated, had the effect of quickening the pace of provincial Romanization.

Claudius was as aware as Augustus had been that the army was the real power base of the Roman government. Although he lacked military experience, Claudius needed to assume the image of a military leader and so was hailed *imperator* twenty-seven times. While not known in history for his military exploits, Claudius did expand the empire. Under Claudius, Rome conquered Mauretania in 41, Britain in 43, and Thrace in 46. In addition, Claudius established the province of Lycia in 43 and the province of Judaea in 44.

In an effort to improve communications and the movement of troops, Claudius instituted a great road-building program. Not only did these roads tie the provinces closer to Rome, but they also stimulated trade between and among the provinces. Whenever Claudius saw an opportunity to expand trade and commerce, he immediately improved area roads and port facilities and built warehouses. The level of trade within the empire and with foreign lands increased dramatically under Claudius.

Despite his emphasis on improving the economic condition of the provinces, Claudius did not neglect Italy, in general, or Rome, in particular. In central Italy, Claudius employed thirty thousand men for eleven years to drain the Fucine Marsh and reclaim much-needed arable land. What Julius Caesar and Augustus had only planned, Claudius accomplished. To increase the water supply of the capital, Claudius completed an aqueduct, begun by Caligula, which brought water to Rome from a distance of sixty-two miles; he also built the Aqua Claudia, which brought water from forty-five miles away. To guarantee Rome a secure supply of grain all year round, Claudius insured grain shippers against any loss so that they would continue to sail in the winter months. If a ship owner put his ships in the service of the grain trade for six years, he was granted full Roman citizenship. In order to handle the increased volume of trade, Claudius rebuilt the port of Ostia and built the new port of Portus, outfitting both ports with appropriate warehouses.

Keeping true to his Augustan ideals, Claudius tried to rekindle the old republican virtues through a religious restoration. By reviving ancient religious rites and linking them to Rome's glorious past, he tried to instill in the Romans of the empire both the patriotism and the religious belief of an earlier generation. Claudius founded a College of Haruspices and held the Secular Games for Rome's eight hundredth birthday. To keep the religion of Rome focused on the traditional gods, Claudius extended the *pomerium* (religious boundary) and expelled Jews from the city. Religion as practiced outside Rome, however, was a different matter. With the exception of Druidism (because of its practice of human sacrifice), religious practices indigenous to the provinces were allowed to flourish.

If Claudius had a failing, it was in his relationships with his wives. Despite marrying four times, Claudius was unable to achieve happiness with his wives. His first two marriages, to Plautia Urgulanilla and Aelia Paetina, ended in divorce. His marriage to Valeria Messalina produced two children, Octavia (who later married Nero) and Britannicus. Messalina was executed in 48 as a result of the intrigues of Narcissus. Claudius' fourth marriage was to his niece Agrippina, whose cause was championed by Pallas. Agrippina succeeded, in 50, in getting Claudius to adopt her son Nero (from an earlier marriage) as his heir and the guardian of his own son, Britannicus.

Having lived his early life as a scholarly historian, Claudius ended his days as a very involved ruler of one of the greatest empires in history. A dish of poisoned mushrooms offered to him by Agrippina was the cause of his death. Although Claudius had pulled Rome from the brink of chaos after the disastrous reign of Caligula, he did not show the same acumen in leaving Rome in the hands of Nero. While Nero was not as outrageous as Caligula, he proved to be such a major disappointment to the Romans that he was the last of the Julio-Claudians to rule.

Summary

Claudius, a man never intended to assume control of Rome, a man having symptoms of what may have been cerebral palsy, a man more comfortable in a scholar's library than in an emperor's palace, ruled and profoundly changed the Roman Empire. While trying to maintain an empire-wide approach to the administration of the empire, Claudius was, nevertheless, a major contributor to the evolution of a highly centralized and autocratic governmental administration.

Claudius' reforming tendencies and his emphasis on equality and justice show a basic contradiction in thinking. In trying to bring about equality by admitting provincials to the senate, Claudius was perpetuating the inequality of the old republican class structure. While honoring the senate in various ways, he actively worked to undermine it by creating an executive staff that guaranteed that all would be under the emperor's control. Thus, even though Claudius was attempting new approaches to old problems, he was bound too closely to Augustan tradition to be a strong champion of the new ideals of his age.

Bibliography

Levick, B. M. "Antiquarian or Revolutionary? Claudius Caesar's Conception of his Principate." *American Journal of Philology* 99 (1978): 79-105. The author maintains that Claudius was not a disinterested observer of contemporary events before his accession to the throne. As a historian, Claudius developed his own ideas on how the imperial government should be organized. Levick believes that Claudius used Julius Caesar as his role model rather than Augustus.

———. *Claudius*. New Haven, Conn.: Yale University Press, and London: Batsford, 1990. This book is less a biography focused on the emperor's life and character than a study of the larger historical setting of Claudius' reign. Written primarily for the advanced scholar, the book is scrupulous about evaluating and citing the ancient sources.

Momigliano, Arnaldo D. *Claudius: The Emperor and His Achievement*. Rev. ed. Cambridge: W. Heffer and Sons, and New York: Barnes and Noble, 1961. Momigliano believes that Claudius modeled himself on Augustus and tried to find some common ground with the senate. The centralization of the imperial administration was the direct result of the senate's rejection of Claudius' offer of cooperation. Despite its brevity, this book is one of the seminal works on Claudius.

Scramuzza, Vincent M. *The Emperor Claudius*. Cambridge, Mass.: Harvard University Press, and London: Oxford University Press, 1940. The first and only full-scale biography of Claudius to appear in English. The author has gathered and analyzed all the available archaeological, epigraphic, and literary evidence on the life of Claudius and has presented it in a most readable form. The coverage is comprehensive, thorough, and sound.

Scullard, H. H. *From the Gracchi to Nero: A History of Rome from 133 B.C. to A.D. 68*. 5th ed. London and New York: Methuen, 1982. Gives a straightforward account of Roman history during the last century of the Roman Republic and the first century of the Roman Empire. Scullard shows the financial and administrative problems caused by Gaius (Caligula) and the important changes that occurred under Claudius.

Suetonius. *The Twelve Caesars*. Revised and translated by Robert Graves. Rev. ed. London and New York: Penguin Books, 1979. Contains a chapter on Claudius, together with other chapters on his predecessors and successors. While Suetonius is one of the most important sources of information on Claudius, he is not always reliable. Still, he is useful because he preserves much contemporary detail which otherwise would be lost.

Peter L. Viscusi

CLEISTHENES OF ATHENS

Born: c. 570 B.C.; place unknown
Died: After 510 B.C.; place unknown
Areas of Achievement: Government and law
Contribution: The famous lawgiver and reformer Cleisthenes was the real architect of Athenian democracy. His statesmanship created radical innovations in the constitution: the representative principle and the idea of political equality.

Early Life

Cleisthenes was a son of the Athenian Megacles, a member of the illustrious Alcmaeonid family, and a non-Athenian, Agariste, daughter of Cleisthenes of Sicyon. Little is known of his personal life.

The Alcmaeonidae had been in exile during the tyranny of Peisistratus but regained favor by their generosity in the rebuilding of the temples, and the oracle of Delphi pressed upon the Spartan king, Cleomenes I, for their reinstatement. Hippias, the tyrant leader of Athens, was overthrown by the Spartans in 510 B.C., leaving Athens at the mercy of the powerful families.

Cleisthenes returned to Athens and realized that he would not be accepted as a leader of another oligarchy, nor would the people tolerate another tyranny. Cleisthenes did not covet personal power but wanted to benefit the city. Although the way seemed open for Athenian self-government, the problem of competing families or clans would have to be overcome. His initial attempt at reform met with aristocratic resistance. Cleisthenes had to retreat but returned after the opposition, Cleomenes and Isagoras, were forced out by the *demos*, that is, "the people."

Life's Work

Unlike Solon and Peisistratus, Cleisthenes did not work within the existing system but introduced a completely new scheme which he thought out in detail. He did not abolish or destroy existing institutions; instead, he insisted that the government function within the new plan. He systematically introduced into the constitution a well-coordinated and harmonic operation of government founded upon political equality of all the citizens and the representation and participation of all.

The age-old division of Attica into four tribes, each with three brotherhoods and ninety clans, based on blood, led to many conflicts of loyalties. Cleisthenes' objective was to direct Athenian loy-

alty to the community. A long period of time would seem necessary for this transfer of loyalty, but Cleisthenes brought the transfer very quickly. He developed an artificial plan for public loyalty.

Cleisthenes' basic plan abolished the four ancient tribes and created ten new ones in their place. He also persuaded the god Apollo to tell him after what legendary heroes he was to name them. The new tribes represented national, not local, interests and unity. The marketplace of Athens had a statue of each tribal hero. Each tribe also had its own shrine and its own hero cult but was not controlled by a particular family or local group.

Cleisthenes was able to destroy the old territorial loyalties of the Coast, the Plain, and the Hill. Before Cleisthenes' reform, the adult citizen population was 10,800. After the changes introduced by Cleisthenes, fifth century Athens numbered between twenty thousand and thirty thousand citizens.

To take the place of the old ship districts, Cleisthenes created a new unit of local government called the *deme*, or village. More than one hundred such villages were established, divided into ten groups to correspond with the ten tribes. Membership in the *deme* was made hereditary, and a family maintained its name wherever it moved. Blood ties were weakened, because one was now recognized as "Cleisthenes of Athens," for example, rather than as "son of Megacles." This artificial arrangement separated and weakened the authority of strong families and encouraged the enrollment of new citizens. The old, established aristocracy, with its agricultural concerns, would gradually have to share its influence with the seafaring commercial population of the coast.

Each of the ten tribes was made up of three *trittyes* (thirds), and the *trittyes* of *demes*. The *deme* corresponded geographically to a district of the city and was the local administrative unit. Membership in the *deme* guaranteed citizenship. The *trittyes* were divided into three geographical groups—coastal, inland, and city—and each tribe contained one from each group. The city itself had six *demes* in five different tribes, and the other five tribes were in the suburbs and the coast.

The Athenians were mistrustful of entrenched representatives or experts; they preferred that the government be run by intelligent amateurs. According to Athenians, the person of ordinary intelligence was capable of political responsibility. Thus, the people were the supreme authority and gave in the Assembly their vote to all acts. All business was discussed prior to the assembly in the Boule, or Council, and passed on to the Assembly for ratification. The Council was composed of five hundred members elected annually, fifty from each tribe. Each *deme*, according to the number of citizens on its rolls, elected candidates for the Council, and from these candidates, Council members were elected by lot, fifty being selected from each tribe. The Council was divided into ten committees, one of which was on duty for the tenth part of each year. This committee of fifty members, called a *prytany*, held office for a tenth of the year under a chairman who sat for one day and was chosen by lot. He was acting head of the government and had the keys to the Acropolis, the state seal, and the archives. He could not be reelected. Part of the prytany remained on duty day and night, eating and sleeping in the Tholos, a round building provided for this purpose. The Council prepared matters for the Assembly and was also responsible for fiscal policy, receiving an account from all civil officials leaving office.

Cleisthenes established ostracism in a systematic manner as a safeguard against conflict. The Assembly voted once a year whether to have an ostracism. An affirmative vote meant that each member would write on a piece of pottery, *ostrakon*, the member he would like to see exiled. The person who received the most votes, six thousand or more, went into honorable exile for a period of ten years without loss of property. This measure may well have been a deterrent in neutralizing opposition; there is no record of its being used until 487 B.C., after Cleisthenes' time.

Legislative powers were in the *ecclesia*, or assembly that discussed and passed laws. Judicial authority was with the *heliaea*, the court of popular representatives, elected by the tribes in the same manner as the council. Judicial functions were controlled by people's juries, selected from an annual panel of six thousand citizens chosen by lot from the same units.

The magistrates, the nine archons, and the *colacietae* and *strategoi* were elected from among the wealthier citizens. The former were concerned with finance; the latter commanded ten companies of militia. This organization may have been reasonable, since the state did not pay citizens in discharging their public duties.

Each tribe supported a regiment of infantry and a squadron of cavalry who were commanded by elective officers, called *taxiarchi* and *hipparchi*. Each of the ten *strategoi* commanded the army in turn. The army was similar to a national militia. Cleisthenes, however, did not reform the navy.

Summary

The constitution of Cleisthenes of Athens was put into effect in 502 B.C. While it did not end the conflict between parties or the unequal distribution of wealth, it did mitigate many of the problems. The government was no longer something external or alien but identified with the life and goals of each citizen. At the time of Cleisthenes' death, the *demes* were the real rulers of Athens, although they were led by the aristocracy. Cleisthenes created a strong and well-organized state and constitution. At the end of the Peloponnesian War there was a brief oligarchic reaction, but Cleisthenes' reforms were restored in 403 B.C.

Cleisthenes is credited with the complete breakdown of the patriarchal idea of the state as a corporation. It was never restored in Athens. He established new tribes, enrolled aliens as new citizens, and contributed to the idea of free communication and interchange between different peoples. This idea, together with the principles of representation and of political equality, strengthened democracy.

Bibliography

Aristotle. *The Athenian Constitution.* Translated by P. J. Rhodes. London and New York: Penguin, 1984. Contains the great philosopher's brief history and description of the Athenian state with a helpful commentary. This 208-page work is an essential source for the workings of Cleisthenes' constitution. Aristotle provides a good introduction to study of Cleisthenes.

Davies, J. K. *Democracy and Classical Greece.* 2d ed. Cambridge, Mass.: Harvard University Press, and London: Fontana, 1993. This study was the clearest reexamination of the present state of knowledge about democratic ideas in Athens. It emphasizes archaeological evidence in social and political history.

Ehrenberg, Victor. *From Solon to Socrates: Greek History and Civilization During the Sixth and Fifth Centuries B.C.* 2d ed. London: Methuen, 1973; New York: Routledge, 1989. An excellent illustrated political textbook on the central period of Greek history during the sixth and fifth centuries B.C. Contains good references to primary and secondary sources.

Forrest, William G. *The Emergence of Greek Democracy, 800-400 B.C.* New York: McGraw-Hill, and London: Weidenfeld and Nicolson, 1966. This work is a clear, lively interpretation of the reforms of Cleisthenes and provides a general account of his time. It is written in an interesting style and describes the social and political developments and the transition from aristocracy to democracy in Athens. The notes are especially good.

Hignett, Charles. *A History of the Athenian Constitution to the End of the Fifth Century B.C.* Oxford: Clarendon Press, 1952. Scholarly treatment of the development of the Athenian constitution, discussing its successive phases of growth from the early monarchy and aristocracy to the decline of the Athenian empire. An important and thought-provoking analysis of the beginnings of Athenian democracy.

Larsen, Jakob A. O. "Cleisthenes and the Development of the Theory of Democracy at Athens." In *Essays in Political Theory Presented to George H. Sabine*, edited by Milton R. Konvitz and Arthur E. Murphy. Ithaca, N.Y.: Cornell University Press, 1948; London: Kennikat, 1972. A discussion of the early characteristics of Athenian democracy. Particularly good for insights into the Greek political mind.

O'Neil, James L. *The Origins and Development of Ancient Greek Democracy.* London and Lanham, Md.: Rowman and Littlefield, 1995. The author places Athenian democracy (which is normally treated independently) within the larger context of other Greek democracies (e.g. at Megara, Chios, Elis, etc). The activities of Cleisthenes are treated in the first chapter.

Staveley, E. S. *Greek and Roman Voting and Elections.* Ithaca, N.Y.: Cornell University Press, and London: Thames and Hudson, 1972. This study illuminates many practices in the Athenian government and the spirit of public service over several centuries.

Thorley, John. *Athenian Democracy.* Lancaster Pamphlets. London and New York: Routledge, 1996. A brief introduction to the development of Athenian democracy and a description of its structures from the time of Solon to the end of the Peloponnesian War. An appendix lists the Cleisthenic tribes.

Zimmern, Alfred. *The Greek Commonwealth: Politics and Economics in Fifth Century Athens.* 5th ed. Oxford and New York: Oxford University Press, 1931. This classic work presents an interesting analysis of fifth century Athens but lacks an adequate bibliography. Important aspects of Cleisthenes' career and the cultural background of this period are discussed.

Peter F. Macaluso

CLEMENT I

Born: Date unknown; perhaps Rome

Died: c. 99; perhaps in the Crimea

Area of Achievement: Religion

Contribution: Clement was the first of the Apostolic Fathers about whom anything is known and, according to tradition, was the third successor to Peter as Bishop of Rome. Clement was also the author of the earliest and most valuable surviving example of Christian literature not included in the New Testament.

Early Life

Of the life of Clement very little is known with absolute certainty. He is called Clement of Rome (Clemens Romanus) to distinguish him from the later Clement of Alexandria (Clemens Alexandrinus). No reliable source gives even the approximate date or place of his birth. An early Christian work attributed to him entitled *Recognitions* (third century) states that he was born in the city of Rome and that he was from his early youth given to meditating and sober reflection on such serious subjects as the nature of life, whether there was a preexistence, and the possibility of immortality. According to that work, he was converted to Christianity by the disciple Barnabas, who came to Rome to preach and thereafter introduced him to Peter, who received him with great joy.

Such a story is not inconsistent with other information now known about Clement. Nevertheless, true authorship of *Recognitions* cannot be ascribed to Clement himself, since most scholars believe that it was penned more than a century after his time. Despite this doubt, however, the work is not completely without value; indeed, it seems to preserve traditions which contain some kernels of truth.

Undoubtedly, Clement was a younger contemporary of Peter and Paul. The early church scholars and theologians Origen (c. 185-254), Eusebius of Caesarea (c. 260-339), Epiphanius (c. 315-403), and Jerome (331-420) all identify Clement of Rome as the Clement spoken of in Philippians 4:3. This Scripture calls him Paul's fellow laborer. Similarly, Irenaeus (c. 120-202) states that Clement saw the Apostles and talked with them, that their preaching was so fresh in his mind at the time he rose to prominence that it still rang in his ears, and that many of Clement's generation had been taught personally by the Apostles. Clement himself intimates that he was closely associated with Peter and Paul.

Clement was probably of Jewish descent. His close association with the Apostles, who were all Jewish, and his wide use of and familiarity with the Old Testament, as demonstrated in the one surviving authentic Clementine work, lend support to this inference. Clement's style of writing is colored with Hebraisms but he probably possessed no real understanding of Hebrew, knowing only the Septuagint (Greek) translation of the Old Testament as many Jews of the day did.

An ancient tradition identifies Clement with a certain Flavius Clemens, a distinguished Roman nobleman who held the office of consul in 95 and was the nephew of the emperor Vespasian. It is difficult to believe that the same man held both the consulship and the bishopric, since these times were difficult ones for the Church because of Roman antagonism.

It is also unlikely that the Hellenistic Jewish style of Clement's epistle would be as prominent if Clement came from the Roman classical culture of

CLEMENS ·I· PP ·ROMANUS

a court circle. It is more likely, then, that the future church leader was a freedman or former slave belonging to the house of Clemens and that in accordance with custom he assumed the name of his patron when fully liberated.

Life's Work

At some point in his life, Clement became a leader in the Roman church and was ultimately ordained bishop of that Christian community about the year 90. While Tertullian, writing about 199, says that Clement was ordained by Peter before the Apostle's death (c. 64), other ancient, reliable authorities state that Clement was preceded by two other successors to Peter (Linus and Anacletus) and thus was the fourth Bishop of Rome. Clement's fame rests on both his designation as the first known Apostolic Father and his authorship of the epistle to the Corinthian church.

The expression "Apostolic Fathers" seems to have been used first by Severus of Antioch, Patriarch of Alexandria in the sixth century and scholar of early Christian literature. The phrase referred to those who were not Apostles but disciples of the Apostles and who authored writings contemporaneous with or prior to those of Irenaeus in the second century. The Apostolic Fathers, then, were the earliest orthodox writers outside the New Testament. Clement was the first, chronologically, of this group, which includes Ignatius of Antioch, Polycarp, Barnabas, and Hermas. *Klementos pros Korinthious epistola prōtē* (first century A.D.; *The First Epistle of Clement to the Corinthians,* also known as *First Clement*) is the earliest extant Christian document outside the New Testament.

The epistle to the Corinthians was Clement's most important achievement. Although Clement's name is not mentioned in the letter, he seems to have been from the first recognized as its author. About 170, Dionysius, Bishop of Corinth, while acknowledging another letter written from the church of Rome to the church of Corinth, mentions that the letter written by Clement was still read from time to time in their Sunday assemblies. Eusebius also speaks of the epistle to the Corinthians as being Clement's, as do Irenaeus, Origen, and Clement of Alexandria.

Clement wrote his epistle sometime after he became Bishop of Rome, though the exact date of its composition is not known. The second century Christian historian Hegesippus, who visited the Corinthian church on a trip to Rome, learned that the letter was written during the reign of Domitian (81-96). If one considers an allusion which Clement makes in the epistle to the persecutions of Christians which took place at Rome under Domitian in 93, the date of the epistle can be narrowed down to between the years 93 and 96.

Clement's main objective in writing *The First Epistle of Clement to the Corinthians* was to restore peace and unity to that Greek branch of the Church. The Corinthians had been led by some young, rebellious individuals to rise up against their lawfully appointed presbyters. The significance of Clement's epistle is twofold. First, it outlines the organization or structure of the apostolic church. Second, it seems to have helped lay the foundation for the birth of the Roman Catholic Papacy and papal theory.

Clement states that the action taken by the seditious persons at Corinth was inexcusable. He declares that Christ was sent forth by God, the Apostles were sent by Christ, and the Apostles, preaching throughout the known world, appointed the first fruits of their proselytizing activity to be bishops after having proved them by the Spirit. Clement also says that the Apostles gave instructions that when these bishops appointed by them should die, other approved men should succeed them in their ministry by appointment from the Apostles or other eminent men with the consent of the whole church. He urges the schismatics at Corinth to return to the true order of the church, to put away strife, disorder, jealousy, and pride.

While no claim is made by the Roman church leader to interfere with another on any grounds of superior rank, the unmistakably authoritative tone of the letter gives its author more than merely a peacemaker's role. Using Clement's epistle as a precedent, Roman bishops of the second century began to assume preeminent authority to resolve general Christian disputes. By the mid-third century, the practice had arisen of reckoning Peter not only as chief Apostle but also as first Bishop of Rome. Gradually, the term "pope" or "father" (Latin *papa*), which had been used for any bishop in Western Europe, began to be directed toward the Bishop of Rome exclusively.

Clement served as Bishop of Rome about nine years. Besides writing his epistle, Clement's time as head of one of Christianity's most important communities was taken up with duties centering on proselytism, exhortation, keeping the Church unified, and helping it to survive attacks and persecutions such as the one promoted by Domitian.

Concerning the death of Clement there are conflicting tales. According to Eusebius and Jerome, he died a natural death in the third year of the reign of the emperor Trajan. Other traditions, however, reckon him among the martyrs.

The apocryphal *Acts of the Martyrs* relates how, toward the end of his life and tenure of office, Clement converted more than four hundred Romans of rank; as a result, Trajan banished the bishop to the Chersonese Peninsula in the Black Sea area. There Clement set to work converting the people of the country (two thousand in number), who built seventy-five churches. Trajan then had Clement thrown into the sea with an iron anchor around his neck. This story circulated for many years until around 868 when Saint Cyril, Apostle to the Slavs, dug up some bones and an anchor in the Crimea. Hailed as the relics of Clement, these remains were carried back to Rome and deposited by Pope Adrian II with the relics of Ignatius of Antioch in the Basilica of Saint Clement in Rome.

Summary

Next to the Apostles themselves, Clement was for many generations the most esteemed figure in the Church. Clement of Alexandria called him an Apostle. Jerome referred to him as an apostolic man, and Rufinus said that he was almost an Apostle.

Clement's letter to the church at Corinth was for centuries considered canonical by many and on a par with the epistles of Paul. Eusebius speaks of the public reading of Clement's letter as the ancient custom of many churches down to his own time. The list of ancient Christian authorities and leaders who quoted *The First Epistle of Clement to the Corinthians* includes Polycarp and Ignatius, themselves Apostolic Fathers.

Numerous spurious writings have been attributed to Clement. The most celebrated among these was probably the second century *The Second Epistle of Clement to the Corinthians,* purporting to supplement the first. This second letter was also held in great respect by early Christians. It is interesting to note that the two epistles disappeared from the Western Church in the sixth century. They were rediscovered in the year 1628, when an ancient manuscript of the Greek Bible was presented to King Charles I of England by the Patriarch Cyril Lukaris.

Much is not known about Clement. What is known, however, sheds a glimmer of light on a very poorly illumined but critical period in the history of one of Western civilization's most significant institutions—the Church.

Bibliography

Clement I, Pope. *The Apostolic Fathers*. Vol. 2, *First and Second Clement*. Robert M. Grant and Holt H. Graham, eds. New York and London: Nelson, 1965. A companion volume to the introductory volume above, this work includes a translation (in idiomatic English) of, and commentary on, the two epistles ascribed to Clement. Its value lies in the numerous and detailed annotations and cross-references for virtually every verse of the two epistles. Though not a long book, its detail reflects a depth of scholarship on the part of the translators which may, at first, overwhelm the newcomer. Its strength is its correlation and analysis of literature and motifs similar to the two letters.

Clement I, Pope. *The First Epistle of Clement to the Corinthians*. Edited by W. K. Lowther Clarke. London: Society for the Promotion of Christian Knowledge, and New York: Macmillan, 1937. Prepared by a British scholar, this concise volume contains introductory notes and a translation of Clement's authentic epistle. The translation is rendered in the style of the Revised Standard Version of the Bible. The explanations of the text illuminate Clement's life and the historical context of the letter.

Grant, Robert M. *The Apostolic Fathers*. Vol. 1, *An Introduction*. New York: Nelson, 1964. This is, perhaps, the best and most accessible single volume on the Apostolic Fathers and their world. It discusses who the Apostolic Fathers were and their historical circumstances, theological outlook, and writings. It also presents the place and significance of Clement and his epistle within the context of early Christianity and Hellenistic Judaism. The relationship between Clement and the other Apostolic Fathers is also discussed. Though the volume contains no index or bibliography, a detailed and well-organized table of contents greatly aids the reader.

Lightfoot, J. B. *The Apostolic Fathers, Part I: S. Clement of Rome*. 2 vols. 2d ed. London and New York: Macmillan, 1890. This is the most extensive and most authoritative work ever done on Clement and his writing. It presents a facsimile of the actual Greek texts of the two epistles along with translations, notes, and commentaries on the texts. Lightfoot synthesizes and distills all the references to Clement in ancient literature and history to attempt to fill in the gaps concerning his life.

Meeks, Wayne A. *The Origins of Christian Morality: The First Two Centuries*. New Haven, Conn. and London: Yale University Press, 1993. This account of early Christian moral beliefs deals with Clement in a number of places.

Richardson, Cyril C., ed. *The Library of Christian Classics*. Vol. 1, *Early Christian Fathers*. Philadelphia: Westminster Press, 1943; London: SCM Press, 1953. This first volume in a series on the classic documents of Christianity contains a fine translation of both epistles, as well as a brief but thorough introduction to Clement and his writing. Its greatest value is the extensive bibliography on Clement and his work.

Staniforth, Maxwell. *Early Christian Writings*. Baltimore, Md. and London: Penguin Books, 1968. Available in paperback, this work is a very readable introduction to the Apostolic Fathers and their writings. The section on Clement contains an introduction to the man and his work and a translation of the two epistles. It is valuable because of the informative footnotes it presents and the way the introduction discusses the significance of Clement's bishopric for the Church.

Andrew C. Skinner

CLEOMENES
Cleomenes I

Born: Date unknown; Sparta, Greece
Died: c. 490 B.C.; Sparta, Greece
Area of Achievement: Warfare and conquest
Contribution: Through a number of military victories and even in defeat, Cleomenes I strengthened Sparta as no ruler had before him.

Cleomenes I succeeded his father, King Anaxandridas, to the throne around 519 B.C. Initially, his half-brother Dorieus challenged his ascendancy, but Cleomenes was planted firmly in power when Dorieus left Sparta to establish a colony elsewhere. Cleomenes I wanted to fight against Athens' tyranny and to expand Sparta's boundaries and influence outward, even into Greece. After a naval failure, he led a land expedition against Athens that succeeded in trapping the Athenian dictator, Hippias, and members of his government on the Acropolis. Spartans captured Hippias's children as they were being smuggled out of Athens and ransomed them to force Hippias to accede to the Spartans' demands and leave the city.

Overseen by Cleomenes I, Kleisthenes and Isagoras ruled Athens. Years later when a struggle between them threatened civil war, Cleomenes ordered Kleisthenes out of Athens. He exiled seven hundred supporting Athenian families and threatened to replace Kleisthenes's council of five hundred with a three-hundred-member council supportive of Isagoras. Isagoras was Cleomenes's protege, and Athenians did not appreciate his efforts to install him on their throne. Struggles continued until Isagoras's entire party was executed. Isagoras was able to escape.

Kleisthenes and his seven hundred supporting families returned to Athens and began negotiations with Darius of Persia for a possible alliance. Upon hearing of Athens' deceit, Cleomenes gathered an army to attack the city. Cleomenes's co-monarch, Demaratus, joined the military forces to demonstrate unanimous Spartan support for the campaign. Cleomenes's main goal for the attack on Athens was to return Isagoras to the throne, not to punish it for its recent negotiations with Persia as many thought. When Demaratus discovered the true nature of the campaign, the two monarchs argued. Corinthian forces who had joined the Spartans refused to participate and went home. The campaign failed.

Early in the fifth century, Sparta's ancient enemy, Argos, refused to pay tribute. Cleomenes led his armies northward to Argosian territory to re-establish Sparta's authority. Before crossing the Erasinos River, Spartans offered sacrifices to the gods for support. Believing the sacrifices did not satisfy the gods, Cleomenes boarded his men on ships and instead attacked the Argosians at Sepeia. He won complete victory in c. 494 B.C., but in a controversial move, Cleomenes pursued a number of Argosians to a grove where they had taken refuge. Calling them out under the pretense of arranging for their ransom, Cleomenes executed fifty of Argos's leading citizens. Again citing religious reasons, he decided not to attack Argos and went home.

Three years later, a Persian invasion of Athens seemed imminent. Cleomenes received word that a number of local islands were paying homage to King Darius of Persia, in particular the strategically located Aegina. Athens appealed to Cleomenes for support. Cleomenes led military forces to Aegi-

na in 491 B.C. to arrest leading members of the offending parties. He was met by Krio, known as "the Ram." Krio refused to acknowledge Cleomenes's power to arrest, stating that he did not have Spartan governmental support for his campaign. If Sparta supported his cause, Krio asserted, both Spartan kings would have come to Aegina. Because of arguments between the monarchs in the struggle against Athens, Spartan law forbade any two rulers from participating together in the same campaign.

Cleomenes believed his co-king, Demaratus, was behind Krio's words and decided to try to remove him from office. He revived old rumors that Demaratus was illegitimate and therefore had no claim to the Spartan throne. When the prophetess at Delphi was consulted as to his paternity, she affirmed his illegitimate status, and Spartans replaced Demaratus with his enemy Leotychides. Rumors began that Cleomenes had bribed the prophetess.

For a few months, Cleomenes and Leotychides worked well together. They further strengthened the Peloponnese against the Persian threat and managed to arrest Aeginetan leaders who opposed them. However, reports of Cleomenes's bribery of the Delphi oracle grew. Cleomenes became so unpopular that he was forced to flee to Thessaly and later Arcadia. While in Arcadia, Cleomenes I put together a military force to retake his own city. He was recalled to Sparta where, upon his return, his own family had him arrested. Cleomenes I reportedly stabbed himself to death; however, it is also possible that his Ephorian enemies killed him.

Though some historians claim that Cleomenes I suffered from intermittent madness, his actions in office and on the military front show him to have been a capable strategist. Rumors of madness may have been spread by his enemies to justify forcing him out of Sparta. Though he may not have spread Spartan rule as far as he desired, Cleomenes I increased Sparta's power more than any ruler before him.

Cleomenes II

Born: Date unknown; Sparta, Greece
Died: c. 309 B.C.; Sparta, Greece
Area of Achievement: Government and politics
Contribution: Cleomenes II ruled Sparta during a difficult and trying time. He managed to hold a beaten city-state together and ally it with neighboring powers. Cleomenes II's rule gave Sparta time to rebuild without threatening its confidence.

A year before Cleomenes II ascended to the throne in 370 B.C., the great city-state of Sparta was brutally defeated at the battle of Leuctra in Boeotia. What was once the most feared of cities had been reduced to a seemingly benign town. Under Cleomenes II, Sparta did not try to expand so much as to defend the territory it still had.

In 362 B.C., Thebes threatened the peninsula. After some initial successes in relieving Sparta of some of her possessions, the Theban threat encouraged Spartans to form a new coalition with her neighbors to fight their common enemy. Sparta was defeated during the ensuing battle, but Theban armies lost their leader and, with him, the will to continue.

Afterward, negotiations over the reunification of the peninsula continued. After years of arguing and contending for power, Sparta rejoined the Achaean League in 332 B.C. Cleomenes II reigned during a time of great trouble, and perhaps his greatest accomplishment was to have held the defeated city together and thus prepare it for a resurgence of power.

Cleomenes III

Born: Date unknown; Sparta, Greece
Died: 219 B.C.; Alexandria
Area of Achievement: Government and politics
Contribution: Cleomenes III instituted social reforms in Sparta that canceled debt, registered hundreds of new citizens, and redistributed lands.

Cleomenes III was the son of Leonidas II, who ruled Sparta from 254 to 235 B.C. Leonidas and his co-monarch, Agis IV, ascended to the Spartan throne during a time of financial crisis. Agis IV attempted to institute a program of social reform in Sparta. He believed that returning to a Lycurgian form of government would help Sparta regain its former glory. He proposed land redistribution so that every freeman would share equally in the city. To reform the financial situation, Agis called for the cancellation of all debts, a measure supported by many Spartans who owed creditors and by landowners who had mortgaged their properties.

While Agis was away at war, his support diminished in Sparta. Leonidas believed part of Agis's reform strategy included removing him from office. With Leonidas's consent, Agis was tried and executed. Though Leonidas was banished and forced into exile, he later returned and regained the throne. In an effort to bring unity to the city, Leonidas induced Agis's widow, Agiatis, to marry his son, Cleomenes. Though the marriage was arranged, Cleomenes III fell in love with his wife and was swayed by her former husband's political ideas.

When Cleomenes III ascended to the throne in 235 B.C., he rededicated himself to instituting Agis IV's social reforms and restoring a Lycurgan constitution. The people of Sparta were calling for change. Most of Sparta's land was held by only one hundred families. Fewer and fewer people in the city could declare themselves full citizens (only about seven hundred men). As years passed, increasing numbers of poor called for more equitable land distributions and cancellation of debts.

By conducting a few successful military skirmishes, Cleomenes III strengthened Sparta's position in the Achaean League and gained support from the military. His reform ideas and relatively austere lifestyle gained him support from the people; however, his reforms were strongly opposed by rich landowners. The Gerousia, the governing body of Sparta, refused to pass his measures. In 237 B.C., Cleomenes III staged a governmental coup and rearranged Sparta's government. He abolished the Gerousia on the grounds that Lycurgean never sanctioned its creation. In addition, Cleomenes killed and exiled many of those who opposed him. He liberated thousands of serfs by allowing them to purchase their freedom for a fee, thus increasing the treasury as well. He succeeded in canceling debts and redistributing four thousand lots of land. At the same time, Cleomenes attracted and registered thousands of new citizens.

After the liberation of the serfs, three thousand men joined Cleomenes's phalanx of soldiers. He reintroduced traditional discipline into the military, preparing them to extend Sparta's influence throughout the Peloponnese. Agis IV had strengthened Sparta's position in the Achaean League by joining Aratus of Sicyon in a joint Peloponnesian defense against the Aetolians. However, when Cleomenes III wanted to be named commander-in-chief of the Achaean forces, Aratus refused to acquiesce to his demands. Cleomenes quarreled with the Achaean League and then set out to break it up. The same Aratus who had assisted Agis IV against the Aetolians called on Antigonus Doson of Macedon to help the league in the impending attack from Sparta.

In the meantime, Cleomenes gained support for his cause from various Peloponnesian cities. He succeeded in taking Corinth, Hermione, Troezen, Pellene, Argos, Epidaurus, Philius, and Aratus. Commoners in these cities hoped that Cleomenes III would bring his social reforms with him and redistribute land as he had in Sparta. Many saw Cleomenes as a liberator from their oppressive rulers and surrendered without a fight.

In 222 B.C., Cleomenes met Doson at Sellasia in the hills of north Sparta. Doson defeated the Spartan forces and forced Cleomenes to flee to Alexandria, where he hoped to find refuge with Egyptian ruler Ptolemy III. Cleomenes, though, failed to win support among the Egyptian people. He was reportedly killed in 219 B.C. during the palace purges that surrounded the accession of Ptolemy IV. In Cleomenes' absence, the oligarchic regime was reinstated in Sparta. Doson and his armies later occupied Sparta and revoked Cleomenes' social-reform projects.

Bibliography

Boardman, John, Jasper Griffin, and Oswyn Murray, eds. *The Oxford History of the Classical World.* Oxford and New York: Oxford University Press, 1986. Chapter 1 discusses the Persian Wars and the involvement of Cleomenes I. Other chapters discuss art, life, religion, and politics of the Hellenistic Age.

Forrest, W.G. *A History of Sparta 950-192 B.C..* New York: Norton, and London: Hutchinson, 1968. Chapter 8 discusses the life and times of Cleomenes I and Cleomenes III (referred to as "Kleomenes I" and "Kleomenes III").

Grimal, Pierre. *Hellenism and the Rise of Rome.* London: Weidenfeld and Nicolson, and New York: Delacorte Press, 1968. Chapter 3 describes some of the social reforms instituted by Cleomenes III and discusses his motivations.

Huxley, George L. *Early Sparta*. Cambridge, Mass.: Harvard University Press, and London: Faber and Faber, 1962. Chapters 6 and 7 describe the military campaigns, career, and ultimate fall from power of Cleomenes I and the history of Sparta to 490 B.C.

Tarn, W. W., and G. T. Griffith. *Hellenistic Civilization*. 3d ed. London: Edward Arnold, and New York: New American Library, 1952. Tarn and Griffith discuss Cleomenes III's rise to power and successful military campaigns.

Walbank, F. W. *The Hellenistic World*. 2d ed. Cambridge and New York: Cambridge University Press, 1984. Discusses how Cleomenes III came to power and the influences of his wife, the former wife of Agis IV, on his political views.

Leslie A. Stricker

CLEOPATRA VII

Born: 69 B.C.; Alexandria, Egypt
Died: 30 B.C.; Alexandria, Egypt
Area of Achievement: Government
Contribution: Cleopatra VII, as the last of the Ptolemaic Greek rulers of an independent Egypt, tried to come to terms with the ceaseless expansion of the Roman Empire throughout the Mediterranean and at her death left behind a rich, imperial province which continued to flourish as a center of commerce, science, and learning under Roman rule.

Early Life

Cleopatra VII was the daughter of Ptolemy XII Auletes and (possibly) of his sister and wife, Cleopatra Tryphaena. Such brother-sister marriages were common among the members of the Egyptian ruling house. It is believed that Cleopatra had three sisters, two older and one younger, and two younger brothers. Her representation with Negroid features by Michelangelo and her depiction as an Egyptian in cult paintings conceal her Macedonian ancestry; her family traced its lineage back to the Macedonian house of the Lagid Ptolemies, which had succeeded to the Egyptian throne after the untimely death of Alexander the Great in the early fourth century B.C. The Ptolemaic rule of Egypt was centered in Alexandria, the beautiful and populous city Alexander had founded to the west of the delta of the Nile when he invaded Egypt in 332.

Cleopatra was reared in a court beset by violence, murder, and corruption and dominated by the reality of Roman military might—all of which had played an important role in her father's accession to the throne. In 80, upon the death of Ptolemy Soter II, the only legitimate male Ptolemaic heir came to the throne as Ptolemy Alexander II. He was confirmed in power by the Romans but after murdering his wife, Berenice III, was himself murdered. Two illegitimate sons of Ptolemy Soter II were now claimants to the kingship.

The Romans put one brother in control of Cyprus. The other, Cleopatra's father, Ptolemy Theos Philopator Philadelphos Neos Dionysos or, as he was known to the Alexandrians, Ptolemy XII Auletes (the Flute Player), succeeded to the throne of Egypt. His relations with his subjects were difficult, in part because he recognized, unlike them, the growing power of Rome throughout the Mediterranean and realized that the only way to secure

his position was to maintain close contact with the rulers of the world. During a visit to Rome, when he was hoping by means of massive bribes to secure the aid of the Roman army, his daughter, Berenice, in alliance with Archilaus, son of Mithridates, seized the throne, only to be put to death by her father upon his return.

When Ptolemy XII Auletes died in 51, after nearly thirty stormy years in office, he willed the kingdom of Egypt to his seventeen-year-old daughter and his ten-year-old son, who ruled jointly as Cleopatra VII and Ptolemy XIII Philopator. The young Ptolemy, however, soon fell under the influence of his advisers—Pothinus, a eunuch; Theodotus, a rhetorician; and Achillas the army commander—who must have found the boy king far more manipulable than his older sister, the intelligent, headstrong, energetic Cleopatra. As a result, Cleopatra was driven from Alexandria. When Julius Caesar arrived in Egypt, in pursuit of Pompey, after the Battle of Pharsalus in 48, Cleopatra was in Pelusium, on the eastern frontier of Egypt, with her newly acquired army preparing to attack her brother and his associates.

Caesar, as Rome's official representative, was in a position to arbitrate between the siblings, and his plan to reconcile Cleopatra and Ptolemy might have worked had not Ptolemy's advisers decided that power should remain in their own grasp. In the resulting showdown, known as the Alexandrian War, Caesar was victorious—but not without a struggle. Pothinus, Achillas, and Ptolemy were all killed, and Cleopatra was restored by Caesar to the throne, this time with Ptolemy XIV, her younger brother, as consort. By 48, Cleopatra was in control of Egypt.

Life's Work

From this point onward, Cleopatra's future is inexorably intertwined with that of Rome and her leaders. In their writings, Plutarch and Suetonius dwell on the love affair that developed between Julius Caesar, then in his fifties, and the twenty-one-year-old Cleopatra. In spite of the arguments to the contrary, the child born to Cleopatra shortly after Caesar left Egypt on his eastern campaign was probably Caesar's son. At any rate, Cleopatra, by naming the child Caesarion, was claiming that her son was indeed the son of the Roman conqueror. Moreover, young Octavian, Caesar's heir, who had most to

fear if Julius Caesar had a genuine son, had Caesarion put to death in 30, immediately after the death of Cleopatra.

Little is known about Cleopatra's rule of Egypt, although there is evidence that she tried to win the favor of the farmers by reducing their taxes. From 46, she was living in Rome with Caesarion and Ptolemy XIV. The reason stated for her visit was that she had come to ask the senate for confirmation of her father's treaty of friendship; yet she was lodged by Caesar, along with Caesarion and Ptolemy XIV, in his villa in Trastevere, where she attempted to cultivate good relations with as many influential Romans as possible. Caesar also put a golden statue of Cleopatra in the temple of Venus Genetrix at Rome, thus associating her with the goddess who was in legend the mother of Aeneas and thus of the Julian line. He may have planned to gain special permission from the Roman people to contract a legal marriage with her, since his Roman wife was childless. The plans were frustrated by Caesar's assassination in 44, and Cleopatra probably left Rome shortly afterward.

Egypt's wealth did not pass unnoticed by the Romans, so it is not surprising that during Marc Antony's eastern campaign after the Battle of Philippi in 42 he saw the chance of subsidizing his wars by taxing Cleopatra's subjects. Cleopatra was shrewd enough to realize that her personal charms would be far more effective in preserving her kingdom than would open confrontation. Plutarch's account of the meeting between Antony and Cleopatra brilliantly describes both the fabulous wealth of the monarch and her grace. Just as Cleopatra had captivated Julius Caesar in her "salad days" when she "was green in judgment," she now in her maturity set out to win the heart of Antony.

After the formation of the so-called Second Triumvirate between Antony, Octavian, and Lepidus, which was sealed by Antony's marriage to Octavian's half sister Octavia, Cleopatra was left to rule Egypt. In 37, however, Antony's march eastward led to renewed friendship and an understanding between the two, which made available to Antony the resources of Egypt. From this time onward, Cleopatra's influence over Antony grew. She also now assumed Egyptian dress that represented the goddess Isis and is reported to have adopted the following oath: "As surely as I shall one day dispense judgment in the Roman Capitol." When Antony arranged for Caesarion and his own three children by Cleopatra to share in ruling both Egypt and Roman provinces in Asia Minor and formally divorced Octavia, Octavian declared war not against his fellow Roman Antony but against Cleopatra. He must have realized that Antony could not help but join Cleopatra.

At the Battle of Actium in 31, Cleopatra's Egyptian forces, together with Antony's Roman forces, faced Octavian's fleet, commanded by Marcus Vipsanius Agrippa. When Cleopatra retreated, she was quickly followed by Antony. Cleopatra's suicide in 30 marked the end of Ptolemaic rule and the beginning of direct Roman rule in what was now an imperial province.

Summary

The historical picture of Cleopatra VII is one-sided. Very little is known of her apart from her association with the two Roman generals, Julius Caesar and Marc Antony. As one might expect, the Roman writers do little to enhance her reputation. In the work of Augustan poets, she is never mentioned by name, but merely as "the queen," "the woman," or "that one." She is chiefly seen as a crazy drunkard, surrounded by wrinkled eunuchs. Horace also pays tribute to her courage, but he, Vergil, and Sextus Propertius, whose livelihood depended upon Octavian's bounty, quite clearly toe the party line in suggesting that she received no more than she deserved. William Shakespeare's depiction of her as high-spirited, shrewd, sensuous, and fickle is based on that found in Plutarch, a Greek biographer, who mentions her only in association with his two heroes, Caesar and Antony. Yet Plutarch also depicts her as a highly intelligent woman who, unlike her Ptolemaic predecessors, actually went to the trouble of learning the language of her subjects. He reports, moreover, that she could converse easily with "Ethiopians, Troglodytes, Hebrews, Arabians, Syrians, Medes, or Parthians" in their own languages.

Although Cleopatra is often imagined as a ravishing beauty because of the ease with which she seduced experienced and mature soldiers such as Caesar and Antony, a few coins survive depicting her as large-nosed, sharp-chinned, and determined. She was also ruthless. After the Alexandrian War, Caesar thought it sufficient to expel Cleopatra's sister, Arsinoe, for her part in the uprising; Cleopatra later had her put to death.

Plutarch in fact describes not so much her beauty as her charm, humor, and ability to amuse and delight her company. She probably also made a powerful impression on the Romans by her intelligence and political ambition. The Roman political system was in a period of transition. Republican government had proved inadequate. Egypt in Cleopatra's time and afterward was essential as a source of wheat for the Roman populace, and its master, if properly armed, could dictate his terms to Italy and the Roman senate. As the creation of Alexander the Great and the place where he was buried, Alexandria provided an obvious starting point for the revival of his empire and its extension even as far as India. The capital of the Roman Empire would eventually be shifted to the east anyway, by Diocletian and Constantine the Great. Legend related that the Romans' ancestor Aeneas originated from Troy in Asia Minor. There may well be some truth in the stories that Caesar intended, if he had lived, to remove the capital to the old site of Troy, and Antony may have been captivated by his dead commander's vision. Cleopatra gambled that, with the aid of such Roman generals, she could make her dynasty a partner in a new eastern empire that would reduce Rome to second place. Like Caesar and Antony, she failed because she was ahead of her time. Her failure has fascinated many throughout the centuries—including Shakespeare and George Bernard Shaw—who have felt the romance and energy of her ambitions.

Bibliography

Bevan, Edwyn. *The House of Ptolemy: A History of Egypt Under the Ptolemaic Dynasty.* Rev. ed. Chicago: Argonaut, 1968. In chapter 13, Bevan offers a brief account of the final days of Ptolemaic rule. Includes illustrations of coins depicting Cleopatra.

Fraser, P.M. *Ptolemaic Alexandria.* 3 vols. Oxford: Clarendon Press, 1972. The most comprehensive and scholarly treatment of the entire period of Ptolemaic rule. Especially valuable for the massively detailed citation of primary sources.

Hamer, Mary. *Signs of Cleopatra: History, Politics, Representation.* London and New York: Routledge, 1993. In spite of some factual errors, a useful source for the image of Cleopatra from antiquity through the Renaissance, 19th century Paris, and the 20th century.

Lindsay, Jack. *Cleopatra.* New York: Coward-McCann, and London: Constable, 1971. A complete treatment of Cleopatra's aspirations and influence. Many details of political events of the period help to place Cleopatra's defeat in a Roman context. Lindsay includes full notes citing an-

cient sources and provides a bibliography.

Marlowe, John. *The Golden Age of Alexandria.* London: Victor Gollancz, 1971. A popular treatment of one of the most famous cities, from antiquity to its capture in the sixth century A.D. Includes a discussion of Cleopatra.

Plutarch. "Caesar." In *Fall of the Roman Republic,* translated by Rex Warner. Rev. ed. London: Penguin, 1972; Baltimore: Penguin, 1980. The meeting of Caesar and Cleopatra is recounted in chapters 48 and 49. Plutarch accepts Caesar's paternity of Caesarion.

———. "Mark Antony." In *Makers of Rome,* translated by Ian Scott-Kilvert. London and Baltimore, Md.: Penguin, 1965. Offers by far the best depiction of the intelligence, vivaciousness, shrewdness, cunning, and ruthlessness of Cleopatra. This life of Antony was used to great effect by Shakespeare in his famous play.

Pomeroy, Sarah B. *Women in Hellenistic Egypt: From Alexander to Cleopatra.* New York: Schocken Books, 1984. Chapter 1, which discusses the queens of Ptolemaic Egypt, places Cleopatra in a historical context. Pomeroy's discussion of married women, slaves, and women of the capital city of Alexandria in Cleopatra's time brilliantly depicts the female subjects of this great queen.

Volkmann, H. *Cleopatra: A Study in Politics and Propaganda.* Translated by T.J. Cadoux. New York: Sagamore Press, and London: Elek, 1958. Volkmann provides a full account of all periods of Cleopatra's life and reign and her influence on world history. His appendix gives a brief survey of modern and ancient literature, and his genealogical tables and maps are helpful.

Weigall, Arthur. *The Life and Times of Cleopatra Queen of Egypt.* Rev. ed. London and New York: Putnam, 1923. Although dated, this book gives a shrewd assessment of Cleopatra's relationship with Caesar and Antony. Weigall argues that Caesar was quite clearly intending to move the center of Roman power to the east and that in Cleopatra he had found an ally uniquely qualified to help him realize his plans.

Whitehorne, John, ed. *Cleopatras.* London and New York: Routledge, 1994. An interesting, if somewhat unusual, survey treatment of the numerous ancient women who bore the name "Cleopatra." Chapters 15 and 16 discuss the most famous one.

Frances Stickney Newman

CONFUCIUS
K'ung Ch'iu

Born: 551 B.C.; state of Lu, China

Died: 479 B.C.; Ch'u-fu, state of Lu, China

Areas of Achievement: Philosophy, education, and ethics

Contribution: Confucius' teachings had little impact on his own times, but through his disciples and followers Confucianism became the official state philosophy in the second century B.C., while its texts became the basis of formal education. Confucianism, modified and developed by succeeding centuries of interpreters, remained the dominant philosophy of China until the early twentieth century and still has a major influence on people throughout East Asia.

Early Life

The name Confucius is the latinized version of a formal title, K'ung Futzu, meaning "The Master K'ung." He was born as K'ung Ch'iu somewhere in the state of Lu (in the present-day province of Shantung), into a family that was part of the official class but had fallen on hard times. It is said that his great-grandparents had emigrated from the neighboring state of Sung. Confucius is believed to have lost his father when still a small child and to have been reared in poverty by his mother.

Nevertheless, Confucius learned the arts of a courtier, including archery and charioteering; at age fifteen, he began to study ancient texts. In his mid-twenties, Confucius held minor posts in Lu, first as a bookkeeper and later as a supervisor of royal herds. His approach to the problems of statecraft may have begun in his thirties, but he is best known for the period after the age of fifty when he was an established teacher or philosopher-master to young men. The actual teachings that have been handed down are contained in epigraphic and somewhat disjointed form in the *Lun-yü* (*Analects*). The book is a compilation of moral teachings, usually in the form of brief dialogues between Confucius and a questioner, who might be either a high feudal lord or one of Confucius' own disciples. Tradition holds that Confucius had an ungainly personal appearance, but nothing is actually known about his looks. He was married and had a son.

During Confucius' lifetime, China was divided into contending states under the nominal rule of the Chou Dynasty. By the eighth century B.C., the Chou rulers had lost all effective control over their subordinate lords, who became independent rulers. By Confucius' day, these rulers often were themselves figureheads, controlled by powerful individuals or families close to the throne. Murder, intrigue, and double-dealing had become the common coin of political exchange. Moreover, established authority and traditional social distinctions were violated in daily life. In this atmosphere of treachery and uncertainty, Confucius emerged as a teacher who valued constancy, trustworthiness, and the reestablishment of the rational feudal order contained in the codes of the Chou Dynasty.

Life's Work

Confucius was already known as a teacher, but desired to become an adviser or government minister, when sometime before his fiftieth year he went to live in the powerful neighboring state of Ch'i. The

222

Duke of Ch'i honored Confucius as a moral teacher but did not give him an important position in the government; eventually, Confucius returned to Lu.

When the ruler of Ch'i asked Confucius the best way to govern, he replied, "Let the ruler be a ruler, the subject a subject, the father a father, and the son a son." The ideas contained in this moral maxim are central to Confucius' teaching. He taught that social order and stability could be achieved at a societal and a personal level if individuals studied and followed the proper standards of behavior. Confucius taught that if one acted properly in terms of one's own social role, others would be influenced positively by the good example. That worked for a ruler in state and for an individual in his or her daily life. Thus, Confucianism, from its earliest teachings, contained an approach useful for both practical living and governing.

Virtue (*te*) displayed by living properly brought one into harmony with the correct human order, called "the Way" (*tao*). Confucius acknowledged the existence of an overarching force in life called "Heaven" (*t'ien*) but did not accept any concept of a God or gods. He specifically opposed the belief in spirits and was not interested in the immortality of the soul.

For Confucius, the human order and human character are fundamentally good, but there is a tendency to slip away from proper behavior through laxity and lack of understanding. A primary responsibility of leaders and elders is to uphold the social ideals through positive demonstration in their own lives. In Confucianism, the most complete statement of this approach is called the doctrine of the Rectification of Names (*cheng-ming*). One begins with study to establish the original meaning of the Chou feudal order. Once that understanding is gained, individuals should alter their behavior in order to fulfill completely and sincerely the social roles they are assigned, such as minister, father, or brother. This entire process constitutes the Rectification of Names, which Confucius believed would restore the ideal social order.

Upon his return to Lu around the year 500, Confucius took up an official position under the sponsorship of Chi Huan-tzu, the head of the Chi clan, who were the real power holders. His post was not an important one, and Confucius resigned shortly over a question of improper conduct of ritual sacrifices. Ritual (*li*) plays a central role in Confucius' teachings. He downplayed the supernatural or religious aspects of ritual but taught that meticulous and sincere observance of rituals imparted moral improvement.

The state of Lu where Confucius lived derived from a collateral line of the Chou Dynasty and was known for careful preservation of Chou ritual practices. Confucius used this tradition as a proof of the importance of rituals. In addition to the moral training acquired by the mastery of ritual, Confucius taught ritual as a means to acquire the practical skills needed to carry out the functions of high office.

In 497, after his resignation over the ritual issue, Confucius set out, with a few disciples, as a wandering philosopher-teacher, looking for a ruler who would try his methods of governing. This long trek, which lasted from 497 to 484, led to his enhanced reputation for uprightness and wisdom, but he never obtained a significant office. In his mid-sixties, he was called back to Lu, possibly through the influence of his disciple Jan Ch'iu, who had become the chief steward of the Chi family. Upon his return, however, Confucius denounced Jan Ch'iu's tax policies as exploitative of the common people.

Confucius' approach to government stressed that the ruler should be benevolent and sincerely concerned about the well-being of his subjects. In Confucius' hierarchical conception of the social order, the ruler's concern for his subjects would be repaid by obedience and support. Confucius believed that the same hierarchical yet reciprocal principles applied to all social relationships.

Although later Confucius came to be deified as a sage of infinite powers, in the *Analects* he appears as a dignified, austere, but gentle man who suffered ordinary human disappointments. Significantly, his ideas are colored by a strong humanism. His teachings as recorded in the *Analects* emphasize benevolence (*jen*), meaning a love of one's fellowman, as the key virtue of the ideal man, whom he referred to as a "gentleman" (*chün-tzu*). Benevolence begins with straightforwardness (*chih*) of character and then is trained or modified through practice of the rituals. Ritual and music impart the inner character needed by a gentleman. Confucius taught that a gentleman would have other virtues as well, such as loyalty (*chung*), righteousness (*i*), altruism (*shu*), and filial piety (*hsiao*). This last virtue—the love and concern of a child for his parents which expresses itself in dutiful and sincere concern for their well-being—became particularly important in Chinese and East Asian civilization. All Confucius' teachings about social relationships demand the subordination of the individual; thus, Confucius was neither an egalitarian nor a libertarian.

During his last years, Confucius lived in Lu and was often consulted by the titular ruler, Duke Ai, and the new head of the dominant Chi clan, Chi K'ang-tzu, but still was never an important minister. Many of his statements from this period are preserved in summary form and enhance the elliptical tone of the *Analects*.

Confucius, before his death at the age of seventy-two, completed the editing of several ancient texts. Both tradition and modern scholarship connect him with three classical texts. These are the *Shu-ching* (*Book of Documents*), which contains pronouncements by the founders of the Chou Dynasty, the *Shih Ching* (*Book of Songs*), which preserves 305 songs from the time before 600 B.C., and the *Ch'un-ch'iu* (*Spring and Autumn Annals*). The last is a terse chronicle of events in the state of Lu from 722 to 481 B.C. and has been closely studied through the centuries, for it was believed that Confucius edited it with the intent of transmitting moral messages about good government. Confucius also studied the *I Ching* (*Book of Changes*), but the tradition that he edited that cryptic ancient book of divination is not widely accepted today.

Confucius' concern to compile correct versions of ancient texts fits the image of him that survives in the *Analects*. There Confucius stressed his own role as simply a transmitter of the knowledge and ways from the past. Confucius' model from history was the Duke of Chou, who acted as regent for the infant King Ch'eng, "The Completed King," who reigned from 1104 to 1067. Confucius taught that the Duke of Chou was the perfect minister who served his ruler and carried out his duties in complete accord with the feudal codes of the Chou. The story of the Duke of Chou, as a good regent and loyal minister, emphasizes the exercise of power in accord with the established social codes. Much of the appeal of Confucianism to later dynasties can be found in Confucius' emphasis on loyalty to proper authority.

At the same time, Confucius' teachings have been seen as democratic, in that what he valued in others was their good character, benevolence, humanity, and learning rather than their social position, cunning, or strength of will. His teaching that anyone may become a gentleman, or good person, with proper training and devotion established the important Chinese social ideal of personal cultivation through study.

Summary

Confucius died in 479, disappointed in his own career, upset at some disciples for their inability to follow his own high standards of conduct, and saddened by the deaths of both his own son and his favorite disciple, Yen Hui. Like Socrates, Confucius became known primarily as a teacher through the preservation of his teachings by his disciples. Some of those disciples went on to government service and others took up their master's calling as teachers.

By the second century B.C., the study of Confucian texts had become the norm for those aspiring to official posts. Young men were trained to memorize a set group of Confucian texts. That educational regime remained the heart of learning in China until the early twentieth century. The flourishing of his pedagogical approach is eloquent testimony to Confucius' genius. His concepts of the goodness of man and the importance of benevolence and humanity in political and personal affairs were developed by Mencius and given a more practical and realistic interpretation by the philosopher Hsün-tzu. By the second century B.C., students of Confucian teachings were highly valued for their skills in ritual, knowledge of ancient texts, and mastery of other learning that rulers needed to regulate their courts and administer their states. During the Former Han Dynasty (206 B.C.-A.D. 8), Confucianism became the official court philosophy and then was elevated to a state cult. Confucianism continues to be a powerful philosophy in China, Japan, and other states of East Asia.

Bibliography

Confucius. *The Analects*. Translated by D. C. Lau. New York: Penguin, 1979. The best available translation of the *Lun-yü*, with an outstanding introduction to Confucius' ideas and his life.

———. *The Analects of Confucius*. Translated by Arthur Waley. New York: Vintage Books, and London: Allen and Unwin, 1938. Another version of the *Lun-yü*, rendered into elegant English by a British poet and scholar of Chinese. Contains only limited material to help the reader understand the often elusive context of the *Analects*.

Creel, H. G. *Chinese Thought from Confucius to Mao Tsê-tung*. Chicago: University of Chicago

Press, 1953; London: Eyre and Spottiswoode, 1954. A readable, nontechnical summary that puts Confucius in the overall context of Chinese philosophy.

Dawson, Raymond. *Confucius*. Oxford: Oxford University Press, 1982; New York: Hill and Wang, 1982. A short, general introduction and biography of Confucius written for a series on great individuals. Stresses Confucius' ethical and moral influence.

Fingarette, Herbert. *Confucius: The Secular as Sacred*. New York: Harper and Row, 1972. An interpretive essay that attempts to explain Confucius' attention to ritual (*li*) and to show how this can be reconciled with his humanism.

Schwartz, Benjamin I. *The World of Thought in Ancient China*. Cambridge, Mass.: Harvard University Press, 1985. Contains a long chapter on Confucius that includes extensive comparisons with ancient Western philosophers. Schwartz emphasizes Confucius' role as a teacher who was both a perpetuator of tradition and an innovator.

Ssu-ma Ch'ien. *Records of the Historian*. Translated by Yang Hsien-yi and Gladys Yang. Hong Kong: Commercial Press, 1974. Contains a translation of the biography of Confucius written c. 90 B.C. for inclusion in the monumental *Shih chi* (*Records of the Historian*). Modern scholars do not accept many of the details about Confucius' life and career recorded by Ssu-ma Ch'ien, but his characterization of Confucius is still important.

David D. Buck

CONSTANTINE THE GREAT

Born: February 17 or 27, c. 272-285; Naissus (in modern Yugoslavia)

Died: May 22, 337; Nicomedia

Areas of Achievement: Warfare, government, and religion

Contribution: As the result of a series of successful wars, Constantine became ruler of Rome and its empire. As the first Christian emperor of Rome, he was primarily responsible for initiating the great changes which in a few decades turned the pagan empire into a Christian one. Finally, Constantine refounded the old Greek city of Byzantium as the New Rome, which, as Constantinople, became Europe's greatest city during the next millennium.

Early Life

Flavius Valerius Constantinus (Constantine) was born at a crucial time in the long history of Rome. According to the eighteenth century English historian, Edward Gibbon, the second century A.D. had been a golden age, but the third century saw economic decline, barbarian invasions, and political instability, the latter often brought about by the ambitions of Rome's many generals and their armies. Constantine's father, Flavius Valerius Constantius, born in the militarily crucial Danubian provinces, was a successful general who rose to high political position. Constantine's mother, Helena, came from a lower-class background and was probably not married to Constantius, who himself later married a daughter of Marcus Aurelius Valerius Maximianus (Maximian), by whom he had several additional children. Little is known of Constantine's early life; even the year of his birth is unknown, but it was probably between A.D. 272 and 285.

In 293, the emperor Gaius Aurelius Valerius Diocletianus (Diocletian), in a continuing attempt to stem the long imperial decline, created a tetrarchy for administrative and defensive reasons. He retained the position of augustus in the east and appointed Maximian as augustus in the west. Constantius became Maximian's caesar, or assistant, and Gaius Galerius Valerius Maximianus (Galerius) was caesar to Diocletian. During the years which followed, young Constantine remained in the east at Diocletian's imperial court, possibly as a guarantee of good behavior by Constantius.

What type of formal education Constantine received is unknown, and historians have long argued over his intellectual abilities. There is, however, no question that he successfully learned the military arts.

Diocletian abdicated his throne in 305, forcing Maximian to do the same. Galerius became augustus in the east, as did Constantius in the west. When the latter requested that Constantine be allowed to join him, Galerius was reluctant, but in 306, Constantine was reunited with Constantius in Britain and when Constantius died later that year in York, Constantine was acclaimed the new western augustus by his army. Galerius, however, only reluctantly granted Constantine the lesser rank of caesar, the position of the western augustus going to one of Galerius' own favorites.

Conflict dominated the next several years, as a result of the ambitions of the empire's many leaders. Maximian's son, Marcus Aurelius Valerius Maxentius, seized power in Rome with the help of his father. They joined forces with Constantine and resisted attempts at deposition by Galerius. Maximian, who had earlier given his daughter, Fausta, in marriage to Constantine, then attempted to seize power himself, first from his son and then from his son-in-law, Constantine, but the latter forced him to commit suicide. In the east, Galerius still ruled, joined by Valerius Licinianus (Licinius), who had also become an augustus. In the west, Maxentius and Constantine survived as rivals, each also claiming the rank of augustus. Diocletian's tetrarchy no longer had subordinate caesars, only ambitious and warring augusti.

Life's Work

Despite his important role in furthering Christianity, Constantine's religious beliefs remain uncertain. During the previous century the worship of the sun, Sol Invictus, had spread throughout the empire, and that religion seemed more important to Constantius and Constantine than the traditional pantheon of Roman gods. Christianity had also taken root in parts of the empire, although it was still a movement which lacked general acceptability. After several decades of toleration, Diocletian instituted a period of Christian persecution, but in the west, Constantius apparently refused to pursue that policy. The connection, or the confusion, be-

tween the Christian God and Sol Invictus is still unclear as regards Constantine's beliefs.

Whatever his religious convictions were, they soon became inextricably tied to his political ambitions. After Galerius died in 311, Constantine invaded Italy in early 312, hoping to unite the empire under his rule. Constantine and Licinius became allies through Licinius' marriage to Constantine's sister, and Maxentius seemed reluctant to face Constantine on the battlefield. Favorable omens from the gods eventually encouraged Maxentius, and on October 28, 312, he led his army out of the city gates of Rome and across the Tiber River on the Milvian Bridge. Constantine's army fought with the sign of the Christian cross on their shields and banners, and at battle's end, Maxentius lay drowned in the Tiber, leaving Constantine sole ruler in the west. When Constantine and Licinius met at Milan in 313, just prior to Licinius' struggle against the other eastern augustus, Galerius, they granted religious toleration to all sects. This edict especially benefited the Christian minority, the primary victims of persecution during the past decade. In his subsequent victory against

Galerius, Licinius upheld the cause of monotheism against the traditional Roman gods. It had become impossible to divide politics and war from religion.

There is considerable difficulty when it comes to determining Constantine's own religious beliefs at the battle of the Milvian Bridge. In the first biography of Constantine, the *Vita Constantini* (339; *Life of Constantine,* 1845) by Bishop Eusebius of Caesarea, written after the emperor's death, Eusebius recalls that Constantine told him of a vision he had on his journey from Gaul to Italy in 312. He saw a cross in the sky, an apparition visible to his entire army. Later he said that he had a dream in which Christ appeared with the cross. Another version, by Lactantius, writing only a few years after 312, tells that Constantine, on the very eve of the battle at Milvian Bridge, had a dream in which he was told to put the sign of the cross on the shields of his soldiers. Some later historians have accepted those stories as sufficient evidence of Constantine's Christian commitment before his conquest of Rome, and they have argued that he was a sincere believer. Others have expressed doubts, contending instead that he was always primarily a hypocritical opportunist. Also, the depth of Constantine's perception of the Christian beliefs is still in question. Did he have a fundamental knowledge of the doctrines of Christianity in 312, or were his actions merely a superstitious adoption of a new god of battle against other, older gods?

What is not in question is that in the years which followed, Constantine favored more and more the Christian religion and its adherents. Property seized during the persecutions was returned, Christian bishops were freed from taxes and certain public obligations in order to pursue their religious calling, and Christian advisers at court became commonplace. Other religions and their followers were not immediately discriminated against or proscribed. In Rome, in particular, where the old religion was so much a part of the political and social fabric of the city, the upper classes remained generally in favor of the traditional gods. Many of the soldiers in Constantine's armies probably remained pagan, and he never dispensed entirely, even among his close advisers, with some who opposed, peacefully, the new religion.

Two continuing disputes between Christian factions, the Donatist and the Arian heresies, posed the greatest problems to Constantine in the years which followed his victory. In North Africa, the Donatists, who believed that the efficacy of Christianity depended on the sanctity of the priest or bishop, argued that those Christian clerics who had surrendered holy writings during the period of persecution were unfit either to consecrate other clergy or to distribute the sacraments to believers. The opposition claimed that the institution of the church itself was sufficient, not the personal holiness of the individual cleric. Constantine sided against the Donatists, for he believed that the church should be inclusive, or catholic, an attitude largely based on his belief that both his well-being and that of the empire depended upon a unified church. The issue remained unresolved.

Meanwhile, in the east, in a dispute over the relationship between Christ and God, the Arians argued that the Son was subordinate to the Father. Constantine participated at the first general church council in Nicaea in 325, which issued the Nicene Creed and condemned the Arian position as a heresy. Until the end of his reign, however, Constantine was to waver between the two positions, often depending upon which advocate last caught his ear. Constantine was the first Christian emperor of Rome, but it was often easier to win victories on the battlefield than over one's fellow believers.

Licinius, who still ruled the eastern part of the empire, acknowledged Constantine's position as senior Augustus, but Constantine refused to accept permanently such a division, even with his brother-in-law. The friction continued for many years, sometimes resulting in war, usually at Constantine's instigation. When Licinius began to persecute Christians, possibly in reaction to Constantine's active support of Christianity, Constantine found justification for a final confrontation, from which he emerged victorious. In 324, Licinius was allowed to abdicate, but within a short time he was executed. Constantine stood alone as ruler of the empire.

Following Licinius' defeat, Constantine, as befitting a great conqueror, founded a New Rome in the east. For more than a century, Rome had not been the effective capital of the empire; a government positioned closer to the Rhine and Danube rivers was better able to defend against the ever-threatening barbarian tribes. In addition, Rome had proved to be less tractable to Constantine's rule and religion. The site picked for the New Rome was the old Greek city of Byzantium, a natural crossroads between Europe and Asia Minor and between the Mediterranean and the Black Sea, rededicated as Constantinople in 330. Unlike Rome, Constantinople was much more a Christian city, and the emperor spent lavishly on his new creation, as he had in constructing churches throughout the empire, particularly in Jerusalem, where basilicas were erected to commemorate Christian holy places. Constantine's New Rome became in time the greatest city in Europe.

Initially, Constantine intended to be buried in Rome, but after the founding of Constantinople he made the decision to be buried there, and he directed the building of his own tomb in the Church of the Holy Apostles in Constantinople. As was usual in his era, he was only baptized a Christian on the eve of his death. He had hoped to have that ceremony performed in the Jordan River, but in the spring of 337, his health began to fail. He left Constantinople in order to seek a cure at the springs of Helenopolis, named after his mother, who on a pilgrimage to the Holy Land had purportedly discovered the cross on which Christ had been crucified. On his return to Constantinople, Constantine worsened in Nicomedia, was baptized there, and died on May 22.

Summary

The empire under Constantine's rule was prosperous and secure, at least in comparison to the previous century, if not to Gibbon's golden age of the second century A.D. By the time he died, Constantine had eliminated his rivals, so that there were only members of his family, sons and nephews, to inherit the empire; heredity was to determine once again the ruler, or rulers, of Rome. In 326, he had ordered the execution of his eldest son, Crispus, and then his own wife, Fausta, in reaction to an unknown scandal. After Constantine's death, his nephews were summarily executed, leaving the empire divided among his three surviving sons. Constantine II was killed by his brother, Constans, in 340, who in turn was killed in 350. The last brother, Constantius II, died while suppressing a rebellion by Julian, the son of one of Constantine's half brothers.

At the time of his death, the force of Constantine's influence was yet to be realized. Militarily, he had created a reserve force, more mobile, supposedly better able to respond to the barbarian threat than the less mobile legions. Perhaps more ominously, increasing numbers of German barbarians were enlisted in the empire's armies. This was not new, but it was a portent for the future. Constantinople was still a secondary city, whose ultimate importance would arrive only after the sack of Rome in 410, the fall of the western empire in 476, and the consolidation of the eastern empire under Justinian in the sixth century. Julian, who succeeded Constantius II, followed the old gods of Rome, and the various heretical movements within the Church continued long after 337. Julian, however, was the last of the pagan emperors, and the empire, governed from Constantine's New Rome, survived to protect the west and to preserve the ancient heritage for the next thousand years before falling to Islam in 1453. As the first Christian emperor of the Roman Empire, Constantine became, for better or worse, one of the founders of the medieval world.

Bibliography

Barnes, Timothy D. *Constantine and Eusebius.* Cambridge, Mass.: Harvard University Press, 1981. The author accepts the reality and the sincerity of Constantine's religious commitments and his desire to create a Christian empire. Concentrates particularly upon religious issues, using as a focus Constantine's contemporary biographer, Eusebius of Caesarea, and the various issues, doctrinal and otherwise, which affected the church and empire, especially in the east.

Baynes, Norman H. *Constantine the Great and the Christian Church.* London: Milford, 1930; New York: Haskell House, 1972. The author argues that Constantine was a sincere Christian who believed that he had a mission to maintain unity in the church and convert the nonbelievers to his new faith, in part because of his belief that his future and that of Rome depended upon the Christian God.

Burckhardt, Jacob. *The Age of Constantine the Great.* London: Routledge, and New York: Doubleday, 1949. This classic was first published in 1852. Burckhardt portrays Constantine, not as a sincere Christian, but rather as a worldly and accomplished politician who aimed only at success and whose religious beliefs were a combination of superstition and opportunism.

Cameron, Averil. *The Later Roman Empire, A.D. 284-430.* London: Fontana, and Cambridge, Mass.: Harvard University Press, 1993. An up-to-date and excellent history. The author is careful with sources, and she believes that the period was marked more by continuity than by radical change.

Eadie, John W., ed. *The Conversion of Constantine.* New York: Holt, Rinehart and Winston, 1971. The author has collected and edited a number of historical works, from the fourth century onward, which discuss the question of the meaning and importance of Constantine's religious beliefs. An excellent summary of different viewpoints on one of the central issues of his reign.

Elliott, T. G. *The Christianity of Constantine the Great.* Scranton, Penn.: University of Scranton Press, 1996. This study argues the need to get behind the mythical, miraculous account of Constantine's conversion in 312 and envision instead a more gradual process. Full attention is given to the narrative of Constantine's life and to the religious controversies (especially those argued at Nicaea) of his reign. The emperor emerges as one who followed a consistent "Christianizing mission."

Gibbon, Edward. *History of the Decline and Fall of the Roman Empire.* London: T. Cadell, 1776; New York: Virtue, 1800. Vol. 1. This elegantly written work by the eighteenth century historian is one of the literary classics of Western civilization. Gibbon's writings have posed questions about the fall of empires that historians have been pursuing ever since. Reflecting the Enlightenment era, Gibbon has little empathy with any religious movement, thus Constantine is pictured finally in negative terms.

Grant, Robert M. *Augustus to Constantine: The Thrust of the Christian Movement into the Roman World*. New York: Harper and Row, 1970; London: Collins, 1971. Traces the development of Christianity from its beginnings to the fourth century, and argues that Constantine was a sincere Christian, in whose era Christianity finally triumphed.

Jones, A. H. M. *Constantine and the Conversion of Europe*. Rev. ed. New York: Collier, 1962; London: English Universities Press, 1965. This work, by an eminent scholar, was written for the general reader. Jones argues that Constantine was not a great ruler, that he was too emotional and easily distracted. His major abilities were military, but his impact upon religion and politics was profound because of his control over both church and state as the first Christian emperor.

Jordan, David P. *Gibbon and His Roman Empire*. Urbana: University of Illinois Press, 1971. This is a study of Gibbon and his great work. The author, in a chapter on Constantine, notes that Gibbon believed that Constantine was the central figure, and thus the villain, in the decline and fall of the empire, because he turned away from the religion which had created the empire.

Lieu, S. N. C. and Dominic Montserrat. *From Constantine to Julian: Pagan and Byzantine Views. A Source History*. London and New York: Routledge, 1996. A good collection of ancient sources translated into English.

MacMullen, Ramsay. *Christianizing the Roman Empire, A.D. 100-400*. New Haven, Conn.: Yale University Press, 1984; London: Yale University Press, 1986. This brief volume is a sensitive and complex essay on the appeal, and lack of appeal, of Christianity during its early centuries, what groups were most likely to respond to the Christian message, what approach would succeed, and the major difference that Constantine made as an emperor who was a convert himself.

———. *Constantine*. New York: Dial Press, 1969; London: Weidenfeld and Nicolson, 1970. This well-written biography of Constantine by a serious scholar is written for the general reader. An excellent summary of the various aspects of the life of the emperor, including war, politics, and religion. The author sees Constantine in many ways as a traditional Roman emperor, but of great significance because he was the first Christian emperor.

Pelikan, Jaroslav. *The Excellent Empire: The Fall of Rome and the Triumph of the Church*. San Francisco: Harper and Row, 1987. In this provocative series of lectures, Constantine's establishment of Christianity is perceived as the key to both fall and triumph. The author particularly focuses upon the ideas and writings of Saint Augustine of Hippo and Edward Gibbon.

Pohlsander, Hans A. *The Emperor Constantine*. Lancaster Pamphlets. London and New York: Routledge, 1996. A short introduction to the history of Constantine and his era and to the questions about them that are still subject to debate. Pohlsander provides background information for the decades prior to Constantine's reign and analyzes the emperor's relations with Christianity.

Eugene S. Larson

CTESIBIUS OF ALEXANDRIA

Born: fl. c. 270 B.C.; Alexandria, Egypt
Died: Probably after 250 B.C.; Alexandria, Egypt
Areas of Achievement: Invention and technology
Contribution: One of the great mechanical geniuses and inventors of antiquity, Ctesibius was the father of pneumatics, the first to employ compressed air to run his devices. He is credited with a number of inventions, including a water pump, a water organ, a more precise water clock, and bronze spring and pneumatic catapults.

Early Life

Biographical details about Ctesibius are scarce. He was from Alexandria in Egypt and would have grown up during the reign of Ptolemy I, who, following the death of Alexander the Great, founded the Ptolemaic dynasty in Egypt in 322. Ctesibius' father was a barber, a trade he apparently taught his son. Ctesibius is said to have married a woman named Thais.

Vitruvius, the first century B.C. architect and military engineer who utilized Ctesibius' lost treatise on pneumatics, describes him as an industrious youth endowed with great natural ability who occupied much of his time amusing himself with the ingenious devices he routinely fashioned. The most famous anecdote about Ctesibius has him devising a counterweight system to raise and lower a mirror in his father's barbershop. As the counterweight moved rapidly through a narrow channel, it compressed trapped air which escaped with a loud noise. The sounds and tones created supposedly gave Ctesibius the idea for his water organ, for which he used pipes of different lengths to vary pitch and water to pressurize the air.

The same barbershop experiment apparently also inspired Ctesibius' water pump, which consisted of two vertical cylinders, each with a plunger worked reciprocally by a rocker arm. Water was drawn into a cylinder chamber through a valve connected to a water source when its plunger was raised and then was forced out in the direction desired through another valve when its plunger was lowered. Continuous pumping on the rocker arm handle guaranteed a steady flow of water.

Life's Work

Much of Ctesibius' adult life was spent during the reign of Ptolemy II, for whom he fashioned a singing cornucopia for a statue of Arsinoe, the king's deified wife, about 270. Because of his mechanical skills, it can be safely assumed that he was often employed by Ptolemy to produce other machines, both serious and amusing (for example, singing birds to grace water clocks and call out the hour).

Alexandria at that time had become the cultural center of the Hellenistic world. The Ptolemaic court was never more brilliant than under Ptolemy II, who, while expanding Egyptian power overseas, was responsible for the Great Library and Museum and one of the Seven Wonders of the Ancient World, the lighthouse on the island of Pharos at the entrance to Alexandria's harbor. This was almost certainly the period of Ctesibius' greatest achievements, which, because his own work is lost, are known primarily through three later technical writers—Vitruvius (*De architectura*, c. 25 B.C.; *The Ten Books on Architecture*, 1914), Philon of Byzantium (*Mechanikē syntaxis*, third century B.C.), and Hero of Alexandria (*Pneumatica*, c. A.D. 62).

In addition to inventing the water organ and pump, Ctesibius also perfected the first accurate water clock. Previous water clocks did not keep precise time because the flow of water to the clock could not be correctly regulated. Ctesibius first fashioned orifices of gold or other substances which would not be worn by the action of water and did not collect dirt. Having guaranteed an uninterrupted water flow into the first chamber of the clock, Ctesibius then devised a way to keep the water level in that chamber constant. An automatic valve, worked by a float, shut off the supply when the water in the chamber rose too high and opened it again as soon as enough water had drained into the clock's second chamber. The flow of water from the first chamber to the second, consequently, was always the same, and the passage of a certain amount of water represented the passage of so much time. On the simplest of water clocks, elapsed time could be determined by noting the markings on the side of the second chamber. More elaborate water clocks had complex and imaginative ways of denoting the time.

Summary

While perhaps not as familiar today as some of his famous scientific and technological contemporaries, Ctesibius of Alexandria was one of the greatest Hellenistic inventors and the founder of pneumatics. Primarily a craftsman, Ctesibius had little interest in theoretical issues, but was a mechanical genius of the first rank. He was influenced by and contributed to the cultural and intellectual atmosphere characterizing the reigns of Ptolemy I and especially Ptolemy II, by whom he was employed. Over his lifetime, he produced several important devices which would have lasting value, among them a water pump, a water organ, the first accurate water clocks, and improvements to artillery.

Bibliography

Cohen, M. R., and I. E. Drabkin. *A Source Book in Greek Science*. New York: McGraw-Hill, 1948. A compilation of passages from ancient writers about science and technology, including references to Ctesibius.

Drachmann, A. G. *The Mechanical Technology of Greek and Roman Antiquity*. Madison: University of Wisconsin Press, 1963. The standard study of the literary sources for Greek and Roman technology, particularly Hero of Alexandria's *Mechanica* (c. A.D. 62; *Mechanics*).

Landels, J. G. *Engineering in the Ancient World*. Berkeley: University of California Press, and London: Chatto and Windus, 1978. The best recent survey of ancient engineering. Includes discussion of Ctesibius' contributions, some illustrated.

Lloyd, G. E. R. *Greek Science After Aristotle*. New York: Norton, and London: Chatto and Windus, 1973. A good brief survey of ancient science, beginning with the Hellenistic period. Discusses Ctesibius' work, with some illustrations.

Sarton, George. *A History of Science*. Vol. 2. New York: Norton, and London: Oxford University Press, 1959. A standard survey of the history of Hellenistic science and culture. Ctesibius' achievements are considered.

Vitruvius. *The Ten Books on Architecture*. Translated by Morris Hicky Morgan. Cambridge, Mass.: Harvard University Press, 1914; London: Oxford University Press, 1926. In books 9 and 10, Vitruvius provides more details about Ctesibius and his work than any other ancient writer.

Robert B. Kebric

CYRUS THE GREAT

Born: c. 601-590 B.C.; Media (modern northern Iran)

Died: c. 530 B.C.; Scythia (southern Russia)

Areas of Achievement: Warfare and government

Contribution: Cyrus conquered Media and brought Persia into the arena of world leadership by defeating the Neo-Babylonians (Chaldeans) in Babylon (c. 539 B.C.). He created a Persian Empire—the Achaemenian dynastic empire—stretching from Turkey to India. His unusually beneficent treatment of conquered peoples was widely praised throughout the Ancient Near East as well as the later Greco-Roman world.

Early Life

The most lengthy accounts of Cyrus' early life are found in the Greek historians Xenophon and Herodotus. Xenophon's *Cyropaedia* (fourth century B.C.), however, is not so much a biography of Cyrus as a "historical romance," that is, largely fiction, with only a few bits of factual information. Most of the valuable information in Xenophon is that dealing with Cyrus' conquest of Babylon. Information dealing with Cyrus' early life is of little value or interest. In like manner, the information in Herodotus' *Historiai Herodotou* (c. 425 B.C.; *The History of Herodotus,* 1709) contains very speculative legends dealing with the birth and youth of Cyrus that were most likely borrowed from earlier legends, such as those surrounding the birth of Sargon of Akkad from the twenty-fourth century B.C., and there is even some similarity with the legends dealing with Romulus, the founder of Rome in the eighth century B.C. Therefore, little confidence can be placed in the information dealing with Cyrus' early life. That Cyrus was half Median and half Persian, however, seems to be quite likely, and he probably spent part of his youth in Media with his grandfather, Astyages. Cyrus' father was a Persian named Cambyses, and his mother, Mandane, was a Median.

Life's Work

Most of Herodotus and Xenophon's accounts of Cyrus deal with his military campaigns, which were widespread throughout Media, Lydia (western Turkey), former provinces of the Neo-Assyrian and Neo-Babylonian empires, including Babylon itself, and later the unsuccessful campaign against the Massagetae, a nomadic tribe in Scythia.

Cyrus began his military rule over the Persians about 559, and by 550, he had taken over neighboring Media and added it to his kingdom. The decisive battle over the Medes was probably at Pasargadae, the city that was to become Cyrus' own capital. He also conquered the capital city of Media, Ecbatana.

Of considerable interest to Herodotus was Cyrus' first contact with the Greek world when he defeated Croesus, King of Sardis, in Lydia in 546. Shortly afterward the Greeks of the regions of Aeolia and Ionia (also in western Turkey) submitted to the rule of Cyrus. A revolt in the city of Miletus in 499 was to bring on the famous conflict between the Greeks of the mainland and the Persian Empire.

Between 546 and 540, Cyrus campaigned primarily in the Near East. The famous Behistun Inscription of the Persian Darius the Great mentions that by 520 several areas were already under Persian rule, many of which were probably added while Cyrus was still alive, including Parthia, Bactria, and Sogdiana.

The most famous conquest of Cyrus was that of Babylon in 539. Considerable information dealing with this battle is known from the Bible, Babylonian cuneiform, and the writings of Xenophon and Herodotus.

Isaiah 45:13 records the prediction that Cyrus would set the Jews free from their slavery in Babylon. The same theme of Jewish return was mentioned by other biblical prophets, including Jeremiah (16:14-15; 23:7-8; 25:12-14; 50:8-10), Ezekiel (11:14-21; 28:24-26; 34:11-16; 37:1-39:29), Daniel (6:28; 10:1), and the apocryphal work Bel and the Dragon (1-2).

The Judeo-Roman historian Flavius Josephus of the first century A.D. said that Cyrus was so impressed with these predictions that he decided to free the Jews on the basis of them (*Antiquitates Judaicae,* c. A.D. 93; *The Antiquities of the Jews*). For whatever reason Cyrus made his decision, one should not assume that the treatment of the Jews was unique. One of the most notable features of Cyrus' reign was his benevolent treatment of former captive peoples who had served as provincial servants of the Neo-Assyrians and later of the Neo-Babylonians. Their former plight was in marked contrast under Cyrus' rule. Little wonder, then, that Cyrus was admired by many of his new subjects as being a benevolent ruler.

The benevolent rule of Cyrus in the biblical texts is correlated in the cuneiform sources called the "Nabonidus Chronicle," the "Cyrus Cylinder," and the "Verse Account." These sources mention that Nabonidus, the last of the Neo-Babylonian rulers, was so preoccupied with the worship of the moon god Sin that he neglected the worship and state-cult of Marduk. This infuriated the priests of Marduk and much of the population of Babylon. Therefore, when Cyrus and his generals attacked that great city, they probably had assistance from defectors of the city of Babylon. In fact, the "Cyrus Cylinder" mentions that Marduk specifically chose Cyrus as a champion of the rights of the Babylonian people.

In the classical Greek sources, Herodotus and Xenophon, Cyrus was described as an ideal general, politician, and diplomat. In later times, Cicero and Scipio Africanus expressed admiration for the military exploits of Cyrus.

In spite of all the great military victories of Cyrus, his death was at the hands of a nomadic tribe, the Massagetae of Scythia. To make matters more embarrassing for the great king of Persia, the Massagetae were led in battle by a woman, Queen Tomyris. According to Herodotus, Tomyris decapitated Cyrus, dipped his head in a skin full of human blood and gore, and said that Cyrus could now have his fill of blood.

Summary

The remarkable interest in the life and influence of Cyrus the Great exhibited by the Hebrews, Babylonians, and later the Greek historians can be explained most easily by understanding the harshness of earlier rule by the Assyrians and Babylonians. Both the Assyrians and the Babylonians were oppressive in their collection of tribute, taxes, and gifts in honor of state events, and, on occasion, quotas of military men were required of conquered provinces. In addition to these humiliating aspects of their rule, they sometimes destroyed temples and shrines of the subjected provinces and forced the people to make an oath of allegiance, under "divine" penalty if the oath was broken.

Therefore, Cyrus' popularity arose from his restoration of native religious observances; his tolerance of their cults was a welcome relief from earlier oppression. The famous biblical example of such tolerance found in the "Cyrus Decree" in Ezra 1:1-4, which mentions that the Jews (former captives of the Babylonians) could return home to Jerusalem in Judah and rebuild their temple, is typical of Cyrus' policies.

Cyrus' burial monument in Pasargadae was humble by ancient standards. It was inscribed with words to the effect that he wanted to be remembered as founder of the Persian Empire and master of Asia.

Bibliography

Bickermann, Elias J. "The Edict of Cyrus in Ezra 1." *Journal of Biblical Literature* 65 (September, 1946): 249-275. Provides an able defense of the probable historicity of the decree of Cyrus authorizing the Jews to return to their homeland and rebuild their temple.

Dougherty, Raymond Philip. *Nabonidus and Belshazzar: A Study of the Closing Events of the Neo-Babylonian Empire.* New Haven, Conn.: Yale University Press, and London: Oxford University Press, 1929. In volume 15 of the Yale Oriental Studies series, Dougherty arranges the cuneiform evidence in probable chronological order, showing the sequence of events leading to Cyrus' capture of Babylon.

Drews, Robert. "Sargon, Cyrus, and Mesopotamian Folk History." *Journal of Near Eastern Studies* 33 (October, 1974): 387-393. Compares the legendary birth accounts of Sargon and Cyrus, and concludes that the Greek historians borrowed oral legends about Cyrus' birth and early life.

Harmatta, J. "The Rise of the Old Persian Empire: Cyrus the Great." *Acta Antiqua* 19 (1971): 3-15. Tries to make sense of the early birth legends, and also describes Cyrus' military conquest over Media and consolidation of rule in Persia.

Lawrence, John M. "Cyrus: Messiah, Politician, and General." *Near East Archaeological Society Bulletin,* n.s. 25 (1985): 5-28. An attempted comparison and harmonization of the accounts of Cyrus from the biblical, cuneiform, and classical sources.

————. "Neo-Assyrian and Neo-Babylonian Attitudes Towards Foreigners and Their Religion." *Near East Archaeological Society Bulletin,* n.s. 19 (1982): 27-40. Describes the cruelty and oppression of the Assyrians and Babylonians prior to Cyrus' freeing of countless provinces of their former captives and the stark contrast of Cyrus' benevolent rule.

Mallowan, Max. "Cyrus the Great (558-529 B.C.)." *Iran* 10 (1972): 1-17. Provides a chronology of the conquests of Cyrus and a linguistic-historical analysis of some of the cuneiform inscriptions that mention Cyrus.

Vogelsang, W. J. *Studies in the History of the Ancient Near East.* Vol. 3, *The Rise and Organisation of the Achaemenid Empire: The Eastern Iranian Evidence.* Leiden and New York: Brill, 1992. A specialized study that argues that the development of the Persian Empire was affected not only by the example of Mesopotamian civilizations, but also by contacts with the steppes of central Asia. Archaeological, epigraphic, and literary evidence are brought in to support the argument.

Wiesehöfer, Josef. *Ancient Persia from 550 B.C. to 650 A.D.* Azizeh Azodi, trans. London and New York: Tauris, 1996. The first four chapters discuss political and cultural events of the reigns of Cyrus, Darius, and Xerxes. The author uses Persian sources as much as possible and suspects the reliability of Herodotus and other Greek writers.

Wiseman, Donald J. *The Chronicles of the Chaldaean Kings (626-556 B.C.) in the British Museum.* London: Trustees of the British Museum, 1956. Includes historical background for the struggle between the Assyrian and Babylonian empires shortly before Cyrus conquered Babylon.

John M. Lawrence

DARIUS THE GREAT

Born: 550 B.C.; place unknown

Died: 486 B.C.; Persepolis, Persia

Areas of Achievement: Government and law

Contribution: Darius consolidated and expanded the Persian Empire through humane, wise, and judicious administration. He respected the languages, religions, and cultures of his subject nations, and in return they fought his battles, built lavish palaces for him, and brought him precious gifts.

Early Life

According to his own account in the Behistun friezes, somewhat different from that of Herodotus in *Historiai Herodotou* (c. 425; *The History,* 1709), Darius was the son of Hystaspes, grandson of Arsames, and great-grandson of Ariaramnes. This genealogy is important: Ariaramnes and Cyrus I were grandsons of Achaemenes, the eponymous ancestor of the Achaemenian dynasty.

Upon the death of their father, Teispes, Cyrus I became the ruler of Anshan; Ariaramnes inherited the principality of Parsua. By the time of Cyrus the Great, Ariaramnes' son, Arsames, ruled Parsua. Cyrus the Great deposed Arsames and annexed Parsua to his own share of the inheritance, calling himself the King of Anshan and Parsua. A charismatic leader, Cyrus expanded his small kingdom to imperial heights within a short time by defeating Media (which included Assyria) and capturing Sardis in Asia Minor. Babylonia, his neighbor and ally, capitulated to his rule soon after. Cyrus' star rose in power and prestige, while that of Ariaramnes fell.

Before his death, Cyrus made plans to capture Egypt and Ethiopia. Grain from Egypt and ivory from Ethiopia were necessary commodities for the upkeep of the empire that Cyrus envisaged. After Cyrus' death, Cambyses II continued his father's plans for expansion. He captured Egypt and remained there in the hope of adding Ethiopia, the oasis of Ammon, and Carthage to the empire. He succeeded, however, only in subjugating the Greeks of Libya.

The king's long absence prompted a severe sociopolitical upheaval in Persia and Media. A usurper—either the king's brother Smerdis (also called Bardiya) or a pretender—assumed rulership and gained public sanction. When Cambyses, returning hastily to Persia, died in Syria from a self-inflicted wound, Darius appeared in Media to claim his own Achaemenian divine right. With the help of six Persian noblemen, his father-in-law Gobryas among them, he invaded the palace of the pretender and ended his rule after seven months. It is not clear who the pretender was; according to Darius, he was Gaumata, a Magian. Smerdis, Darius explained, had already been slain by Cambyses in secret.

Thus, ten years after the death of Cyrus, the twenty-eight-year-old son of Hystespes returned the Achaemenian throne to the house of Ariaramnes. There is no information on Darius' childhood and early youth. It is assumed that, as the son of a satrap, he was educated in the basic disciplines and in the martial arts. As a youth, he was ambitious; Cyrus suspected him of treason. After Cyrus' death, Darius commanded the prestigious ten thousand Immortals and served as the new king's spear bearer and bodyguard in Egypt. Tall, with long, curly hair and a long beard, he cut an impressive figure.

Darius' claim to legitimacy was slender. As descendants of Achaemenes, his immediate ancestors had lost the *farr* (divine sanction), and both Arsames and Hystespes were still living. During the reign of Cambyses II, Darius' father, Hystespes, had been the satrap of Parthia and Hyrcania. Darius had to create legitimacy; he had to provide visible proof that the god Ahura Mazda favored him and his family. During the first year of his rule, he married Atossa, the daughter of Cyrus the Great, and he fought nineteen battles and captured nine rebel leaders. A gigantic bas-relief commemorating the end of his ordeal depicts the nine rulers standing crestfallen before the king. The king has his foot on the slain Gaumata. Ahura Mazda, the king's helper and embodiment of legitimacy, hovers above the assembly. Columns of cuneiform writing inform the spectator that the rebellious provinces included Persia, Elam, Media, Assyria, Egypt, Parthia, Margiana, and Scythia, and that the strategically important provinces were brought within the fold quickly, while the subjugation of Scythia and Egypt took a while longer. Some provinces did not give up after the first defeat. Susa, for example, rose up three times before it was completely crushed. When the resistance finally ran its course and tranquillity returned to the land, Darius became convinced that his rulership was undisputed and set his sights on expansion of his empire.

Life's Work

Subjugation of the unruly elements in the empire had taken about three years. After tranquillity had returned, the only threat Darius could envisage was an external threat: an invasion of the northern provinces of the empire by the Scythian tribes who had fought and killed Cyrus II. To prevent this, Darius attacked the Scythians to the east of the Caspian Sea and pushed them far back into Soghdia. He also captured the fertile Indus Valley, adding this region to the empire for the first time.

By 518, the empire was tranquil enough for Darius to visit Egypt as king. The visit to this ancient and important land fulfilled two objectives: adding to the king's prestige at home and consolidating Persian rule in Egypt, the empire's southwestern flank, which had been neglected since the death of Cambyses.

Darius lived at a time when men thought it possible to unify the world and to rule it with justice. Darius, duty-bound to expand Zoroastrianism, also considered himself obliged to subjugate the Greeks

and to put an end to their intrigue in lands under Persian domination in Asia Minor. In 513, therefore, he crossed the Bosporus and the Danube and pushed the Scythians so far into Europe that he eventually had to abandon the campaign for lack of provisions. Thrace and Macedonia were subjugated by Persian satraps.

With the lifeline of the Greek islands in his hands, Darius decided to postpone any further campaigns in Europe and return to Persia. His return, however, did not preclude a systematic invasion of Attica at a later date. While he knew that he had shown enough might to intimidate Greece for the present, he also knew that the Greeks would continue to incite riots in Persia's Greek settlements in Asia Minor and force him to return to the battlefield.

Darius' decision to return to Persia, rather than engage his troops in a new European theater, was wise. He lacked sufficient information to formulate a coherent strategy. Intelligence on the naval capability of Greece was especially crucial, because without it, Darius could not address the question of logistics or establish a stable supply line between his land army and his navy. Furthermore, to take on Greece and her neighbors, he needed a better-equipped and stronger military and naval force than Persia could afford at the time. In addition, he was not sure that his subjects would be able to withstand the trauma of a prolonged war. After all, the young empire comprised diverse religious and cultural entities, some of which, such as Egypt and Babylonia, had enjoyed a glorious past.

Darius' forte was administration. He now brought this strength to bear on the problem of bringing Europe under Persian rule. Following Cyrus' lead, he had allowed his subjects to retain their languages, religions, and cultures. He now instituted the rule of justice under the divine right of kings throughout the empire. This rule of justice would require numerous changes in the makeup of the empire. These changes were implemented with a reform of the tax system—the amount of tax was measured by ability and by the yield of the land—and the introduction of a monetary system based on the darik to replace payment in kind.

The introduction of currency led not only to further utilization of the mineral wealth of Persia but also to the institution of a simple system of banking. The guardianship of wealth, hitherto the sole privilege of the royal court and of the priests, was gradually turned over to the people. More money in the hands of the populace meant better *qanats* (subterranean water conduits) and canals for agriculture, better roads for trade, and overall a more unified kingdom. To free the weak from the bondage of the strong further, Darius instituted a fixed system of wages. Tablets discovered at Persepolis indicate the rates at which men, women, and children were paid for their labor.

The vast empire of Darius stretched from Macedonia and Egypt to the Jaxartes River and the Indus Valley. It could not be managed by one man. His three long years of struggle to establish his credibility had proved to Darius that he needed trustworthy men to help him rule. Toward this end, he revamped the satrap system introduced by Cyrus, increasing the number of satraps to twenty. The satraps were chosen from among the Persians of royal blood and appointed to the provinces. Each satrapy had a governor (the satrap) and a secretary to organize the affairs of the state. The secretary had a small army attached to his office. When necessary, the secretary could mobilize this army to unseat an ambitious satrap. The satrapy was also assigned a tax collector and a military general, both of whom reported to the king.

In order to safeguard his position further, Darius appointed a fifth person, an individual referred to as the "eyes and ears" of the king, to each satrapy. This officer kept the king abreast of events in his part of the empire and reported on abuses of power and activities that bordered on treason. An inspector would arrive unannounced to examine the satrapy's books and file a report at court.

Such an elaborate administrative machine could not function without a similarly elaborate communications system. Darius therefore built a royal road, 1,677 miles in length, to connect Sardis to Susa. A similar road connected Babylon to the Indus Valley. Royal *chapars* (messengers) carried the king's messages on fresh horses provided at 111 stations. In addition, Darius completed the construction of the 125-mile canal in the Nile Delta, a project that had been abandoned by the pharaoh Necos.

In 499, incited by Greece and Eretria, the Ionians of Asia Minor revolted against Darius and set the city of Sardis on fire. The insurrection was quickly suppressed. Seven years later, Darius' son-in-law, Mardonius, was sent on an expedition to subjugate Eretria and Athens. When Mardonius' fleet was destroyed in a storm near Mount Athos, Darius sent another expedition under Datis, a Mede. Datis conquered Eretria but failed to impress its population. His maltreatment of the Eretrians convinced the Greeks that they should prevent any further Persian advance in Europe. Datis' actions thus roused the Greek states to join forces and defeat the Persians.

After a defeat at Marathon, Darius could no longer focus his efforts on a final assault on Europe. Internal problems plagued the empire. Chief among them were two: the question of succession and a revolt in Egypt. The competition regarding succession had pitted Xerxes, Darius' son by Atossa, against Artabazanes, his eldest son by the daughter of Gobryas. Darius chose Xerxes to succeed him. Yet the more pressing problem of Greek infiltration in the uppermost stratum of Persian administration, infiltration that had resulted in revolt in Egypt, remained unresolved. Darius died, after thirty-six years as the King of Kings of Persia, in 486.

Darius had worn the Achaemenian crown and the royal robes very well. As a king, he was wise, determined, and a good judge of human character. More than anything, he was a builder in both the physical and the abstract senses of the word. The foundation of his empire survived not only Alexander's invasion but also the Arab invasion of Iran.

Summary

Because of the dubious validity of his claim to the throne, Darius had to impose his rule by force. Once his credibility was established and order was restored, he launched a series of reforms that improved agriculture and trade. These reforms provided a solid foundation for notable military triumphs and expansion of the Persian Empire.

Darius had a deep concern for the welfare of the individual. He studied the most reliable literature available at his time, the civil law code of Hammurabi, and devised his own set of rules for the Persian Empire. In the satrapies, such as Egypt, he provided guidance for the priests who wrote the local codes.

Though according to some sources Darius was the ruler who imposed the Zoroastrian religion on the Persians, he did not force his subject nations to follow the dictates of Ahura Mazda. On the contrary, in Egypt he built a temple to Ammon and endowed another. In 519, following Cyrus' long-neglected decree, he ordered that work be resumed on rebuilding the temple at Jerusalem.

Darius was fond of massive building projects. Indeed, he used these projects as a means to unify the country. For example, in building Persepolis, the palace wherein he received foreign dignitaries on the occasion of the Now Ruz (Persian new year), he employed the full spectrum of human and mineral resources of the empire so that everyone could have a share in the product. Babylonian bricklayers, Median and Egyptian goldsmiths and designers, Ionian and Carian carpenters, and others cooperated. They gathered a wealth of material—ivory from Ethiopia, cedar from Lebanon, turquoise from Khorazmia, and gold from Lydia—and constructed Persepolis as a genuinely cosmopolitan landmark.

Darius, however, failed to do for his nation-states what he did for his individual subjects. He did not allow subject nations such as Egypt and Babylonia to participate in the administration of the empire. In time, this policy drove the frustrated elites of those societies to conspiracy and revolt. Furthermore, Darius underestimated Greece, which, making capital use of the king's vulnerability, had sown discord in Asia Minor and Egypt before the burning of Sardis, which incited Darius to march on its territories. Greek policy, therefore, should be credited for both the defeat of Darius' military might at Marathon and the establishment of Western superiority over the empire of the East.

Bibliography

Burn, A. R. *Persia and the Greeks: The Defense of the West c. 546-478 B.C.* 2d ed. London: Duckworth, and Stanford, Calif.: Stanford University Press, 1984. Contains detailed discussion of the campaigns of Darius in Europe. The book includes maps, charts illustrating battle formations, and genealogies for the major figures.

Cook, J. M. "The Rise of the Achaemenids and Establishment of Their Empire." In *The Cambridge History of Iran,* vol. 2, edited by Ilya Gershevitch. Cambridge: Cambridge University Press, 1985. This article examines the principal sources on ancient Iran and the extent and composition of the empire. Toward the end, an assessment is made of the leadership that raised Persia to the head of the world's first empire.

Frye, Richard N. *The Heritage of Persia.* 2d ed. London: Cardinal, 1976; Costa Mesa, Calif.: Mazda, 1993. Frye's account of ancient Iran is unique. It focuses on the eastern provinces of the ancient kingdom but, unlike other accounts, it draws on cultural, religious, and literary sources. The book is illustrated; it includes an index, maps, genealogies, and an informative bibliography.

Ghirshman, Roman. *The Arts of Ancient Iran from Its Origins to the Time of Alexander the Great.* New York: Golden Press, 1964. This massive volume, with incomparable illustrations in color and black and white, deals with Iranian art, especially Achaemenian art, and its influence on the art of the Western world and of India. The book also includes a comprehensive list of illustrations, a glossary, and good maps.

———. *Iran from the Earliest Times to the Islamic Conquest.* London and Baltimore, Md.: Penguin, 1954. In this account of prehistory to Islamic times in Iran, Ghirshman juxtaposes textual information and archaeological data to place ancient Iran in proper perspective. The book is illustrated with text figures as well as with plates. It includes an index and a selected bibliography.

Herodotus. *The Histories.* Translated by Aubrey de Sélincourt; revised with an introduction and notes by A. R. Burn. Rev. ed. London and New York: Penguin, 1972. This, the most comprehensive classical account of the rise of Darius to kingship, also includes information on his administrative reforms, campaigns in Europe, and defeat at Marathon. This book should be read alongside other authoritative sources. The Penguin edition features poor maps but a good index.

Kent, Roland G. *Old Persian: Grammar, Texts, Lexicon.* Rev. ed. New Haven, Conn.: American Oriental Society, 1953. Although set forth as a textbook, this volume provides an English translation of the most important Old Persian texts left for posterity by the Achaemenian kings, especially by King Darius.

Olmstead, Albert T. *History of the Persian Empire, Achaemenid Period.* Chicago: University of Chicago Press, 1948. This detailed history of the Achaemenid period remains the chief secondary source for the study of ancient Iran. The book includes a topographical index, maps, and many carefully selected illustrations.

Vogelsang, W. J. *Studies in the History of the Ancient Near East.* Vol. 3, *The Rise and Organisation of the Achaemenid Empire: The Eastern Iranian Evidence.* Leiden and New York: Brill, 1992. A specialized study that argues that the development of the Persian Empire was affected not only by the example of Mesopotamian civilizations, but also by contacts with the steppes of central Asia. Archaeological, epigraphic, and literary evidence are brought in to support the argument.

Warner, Arthur G., et al. *The Shahnama of Firdausi.* London: Kegan Paul, Trench, Trübner and Co., vol. 1-7, 1905; vol. 8-9, 1925. This nine-volume versified translation of Iran's major epic provides a wealth of information on ancient Iranian religion, social hierarchy, and military organization. It especially underscores the role of the king—an absolute ruler carrying out a divine decree.

Wiesehöfer, Josef. *Ancient Persia from 550 B.C. to 650 A.D.* Azizeh Azodi, trans. London and New York: Tauris, 1996. The first four chapters discuss political and cultural events of the reigns of Cyrus, Darius, and Xerxes. The author uses Persian sources as much as possible and suspects the reliability of Herodotus and other Greek writers.

Wilber, Donald N. *Persepolis: The Archaeology of Parsa, Seat of the Persian Kings.* Rev. ed. Princeton, N.J.: Darwin Press, 1989. Wilber provides an account of Achaemenian history and of the monuments at Persepolis built by Darius and his successors. He discusses the layout of the palaces and their division into the *apadana,* harem, and throne hall.

Iraj Bashiri

DAVID

Born: c. 1030 B.C.; Bethlehem, Judah

Died: c. 962 B.C.; Jerusalem, Israel

Area of Achievement: Religion

Contribution: According to Hebrew tradition and the biblical record, David was the greatest king of Israel. It was prophesied of him that through his lineage the promise of a latter-day Messiah and other spiritual blessings would be fulfilled, making him a key monarch in the history of Israel and of importance to the development of both Christianity and later Judaism.

Early Life

The record of the life of David is found in the Bible in the historical writings of 1 Samuel 16 through 1 Kings 2, with some material repeated in 1 Chronicles 2-29 and in selected psalms attributed to him in the Old Testament. The early story of David's life is contained in 1 Samuel 18-19, though there are references to his life scattered throughout the rest of the Old Testament and in the New Testament. In the latter book, the birth of Jesus of Nazareth is specifically linked with the line of David and serves as one of the criteria Jesus and his later followers used to proclaim him the Messiah and King of the Jews. Most modern scholars accept the substantial historicity of these narratives.

The dating of David's birth and early life is primarily informed guesswork, but archaeological consensus is that David was born sometime around the second half of the eleventh century B.C. The great-grandson of Ruth and Boaz, David was the youngest of eight sons of Jesse, evidently a wealthy man who owned property and livestock and faithfully worshiped Yahweh, the God of Abraham, Isaac, and Jacob. As part of the lineage of Judah, David was qualified by Jewish tribal tradition for rulership in Israel. In the Bible, he alone is named David, symbolic of his prominence and importance in sacred history to both Jews and Christians.

David's early fame and preparation for kingship arose from his humble shepherding and his affinity for music; he was said to be a boy who could tame both beasts and the belligerent with his sweet tones. When Saul, the King of Israel, was to be deposed as a result of his lack of obedience to God, the prophet Samuel was commissioned by God to anoint the young David, much to the jealous chagrin of his elder brothers. There ensued from this

set of events much intrigue between David and Saul, as the rejected king's fall from the throne was accompanied by an apparent madness or manic-depressive state that affected his ability to govern even himself, a malady which the young shepherd-musician was called upon to soothe with his music.

After David was put to the test in his legendary confrontation with the giant Philistine, Goliath, his stature as a leader began to overshadow that of Saul. In this familiar tale, David kills the taunting adversary with his slingshot and then beheads him, giving the glory of the victory to God. As the reputation of David spread from this heroic exploit, Saul became less enamored of the young shepherd boy who had befriended his son Jonathan, and he began to see David as a bitter rival, ignorant of the fact that God had already chosen David to be his successor. Soon David was under siege, as attempts were made upon his life. He was saved from one plot against him by the ingenuity of his wife Michal, one of Saul's daughters. (An irony of these court intrigues was the support David received from Saul's household through Jonathan and Michal.) The next stages in the life of David were marked by finding refuge from Saul, awaiting the former king's demise and his own coronation as king. During this time, David wrote many of the psalms attributed to him in the Book of Psalms, autobiographical poems and songs that reveal the inner conflict he experienced while trying to evade the plots on his life that were initiated by Saul and his followers.

Life's Work

As the reign of Saul came to an end, David had two opportunities to assassinate Saul and assume the throne immediately, but he chose to spare the king's life. In battle against the Philistines, Jonathan and Saul's other two sons were killed. Himself mortally wounded, Saul committed suicide rather than fall into the hands of the enemy. When David learned of their deaths, he tore his clothes and wept. David was eventually anointed by his own tribesmen and established his reign in Hebron at the age of thirty. He remained in Hebron for seven and a half years; eventually after a fierce but brief civil war between supporters of David and the remaining followers of Saul, he moved the capital to Jerusalem. David's reign in Jerusalem lasted more than thirty-three years, and the early decades

of it were quite successful and blessed by God. With David's skillful military leadership, Israel conquered many of its enemies, including the ever-threatening Philistines and neighboring rivals Moab, Ammon, and Edom. During David's reign, Israel's dominance grew from the Egyptian boundaries to the upper Euphrates River. Major highways were built for travel and trade, and the kingdom prospered mightily. David was motivated, however, by more than a desire for military conquest and social prosperity for his people. At the center of his commitment was a religious devotion to God, who he believed had brought him to power.

In response to his devotional impulses, David won back from the Philistines the ark of the covenant, a sacred vessel that housed the tablets for the Ten Commandments and other sacred relics of Israel's history. It was then returned to a special tabernacle prepared for it in Jerusalem. This acquisition gave Jerusalem even more prominence in a time when Israel was just coming to maturity as a nation-state and looking for a center of influence. The irony of David's laudable motivations to restore these important religious artifacts to Israel, and thus to inspire Israel to greater faith and devotion, is that his adultery with Bathsheba and the arranged murder of her husband occurred in this time period. The biblical record suggests that while gazing from his palace, David saw below the figure of Bathsheba, who bathed seductively in open view. Acting upon his lust, David committed adultery, and a child was conceived. David then ordered her soldier-husband, Uriah, to the front lines, where he was killed. The prophet Nathan, commissioned by God to confront David with his sins, told the king a parable of a rich man who stole a lamb from a poor man. David was crushed by the weight of his sin and the subsequent death of the child born to Bathsheba. Bathsheba gave birth to another child of David's, Solomon, who later succeeded his father upon the throne. David's reign, however, never quite recovered from this defiant act, and it symbolized the turning point in his kingship. Absalom, David's son by his wife Maacah, began to plot against his father to take over the throne but was defeated by David's loyal commander, Joab. David's last days as king were marred by the internecine warfare between Adonijah and Solomon for his throne.

The one triumph of his career that would have meant most to David was the construction of a temple of worship to Yahweh in Jerusalem. This privilege, however, was ironically denied to David, the master of ode, music, and song, "the sweet psalmist of Israel" (2 Sam. 23:1), and left for his son Solomon. David was denied this honor because he had been a man of war. David died, however, with the reassuring words of the prophet Nathan on his heart: "When your days are fulfilled and you lie down with your fathers, I will raise up your offspring after you, who shall come forth from your body, and I will establish his kingdom. He shall build a house for my name, and I will establish the throne of his kingdom for ever" (2 Sam. 7:12-13). Many later Christian writers interpret this prophecy as messianic, as pointing to the coming of Jesus. In the Book of Acts, the Apostle Peter, in his first message after the ascension of Christ, refers to many of David's deeds and words as being fulfilled in the life of Jesus.

Summary

David is clearly a pivotal figure in the history of ancient Israel and in the development of Christianity. In regard to the latter, he is mentioned fifty-eight times as an ancestor, forerunner, and foreshadower of Jesus Christ. David's impact and influence can be directly related to his personality, at once winsome and capable. His understanding of military strategy and administrative decision making allowed him to achieve innumerable successes. He was also clearly a flawed character, however, one given to momentary flights of wild misjudgment, including lust, that magnified the instability of his family life. In a time of polygamy, David fared no better than most men in maintaining multiple households, often engendering much strife among his sets of children and in his notorious relationship with Bathsheba.

Nevertheless, it was to David and the city he built, Jerusalem, to which Israel's people repeatedly turned for inspiration. When later generations sought relief from foreign domination or unwise kings, they longed for a king like David and looked forward to a time when the Messiah, promised to David himself, would sit upon his throne and reign over Israel.

No summary of David's life would be complete without a discussion of the many psalms that are attributed to him in the Old Testament's Book of Psalms. While it is difficult to determine how many of the psalms were actually composed by him, a number of them can be seen as true reflections of a man of many triumphs and sorrows. Perhaps the two most famous psalms attributed to David are Psalm 23 and Psalm 51. The former is the famous "shepherd psalm," in which David compares his relationship to God with that of a sheep to a shepherd. The latter psalm is an intensely autobiographical poem that details David's adultery with Bathsheba and his confession of that sin. In this most personal, psychologically complex psalm, the writer calls out desperately for mercy, recognizing that what is needed is not another animal sacrifice but a "broken spirit." Many generations of Jewish and Christian believers have been enriched by the psalmic literature attributed to David. The psalms have formed the basis for many Christian hymnals and prayer books since their compilation in the late centuries B.C. The confessional nature of many of these psalms also has inspired religious writers from Saint Augustine to Anne Bradstreet to John Bunyan to create autobiographical narratives detailing their estrangement from and reconciliation with God.

Bibliography

Albright, William Foxwell. *The Archaeology of Palestine*. Rev. ed. London and Baltimore, Md.: Penguin Books, 1954. This standard work on the archaeology of the ancient world remains the most comprehensive and informed overview of the historical data gleaned from that time. Overall, it provides the reader with an authentic sense of the civilization from which David originated and the one in which he became a prominent ruler.

Alexander, David, and Pat Alexander, eds. *Eerdmans' Handbook to the Bible*. Rev. ed. Grand Rapids, Mich.: Eerdmans, 1983. A comprehensive handbook to biblical history and geography with helpful historical interpretations that trace David's rise to power in the Kingdom of Israel and illuminate for the lay reader the specific episodes in his life drawn from the biblical text.

Bright, John. *A History of Israel*. 3d ed. London: SCM Press, and Philadelphia: Westminster Press, 1981. Probably the most thorough and compelling nontheological treatment available of the history of Israel. Sections on the world of the kingdoms and civilizations contemporary with the rule of David shed light on the story of his life and sustain the interest of both the common reader and the scholar with helpful anecdotal commentary on life in ancient times.

Bruce, F.F. *Israel and the Nations*. Grand Rapids, Mich.: Eerdmans, and Exeter, England: Paternoster Press, 1963. A comprehensive historical analysis of the kings of Israel beginning with Saul and David and continuing through the Davidic line. Provides a clear and succinct overview of the reign of David and the impact of David's rule throughout Israeli history.

Finegan, Jack. *Light from the Ancient Past: The Archeological Background of Judaism and Christianity*. 2d ed. Princeton, N.J.: Princeton University Press, 1959. A serious historical and archaeological work that concentrates primarily on corroborating the historicity and historical accuracy of the Old Testament accounts of the exploits, wars, and founding of nations that occurred during the rise and reign of David.

Harrison, R.K. *An Introduction to the Old Testament*. Grand Rapids, Mich.: Eerdmans, 1969; London: Tyndale, 1970. A complete overview of the origin, message, and impact of each book of the Old Testament, speaking directly to the issues of the chronology and authenticity of the biblical narrative of David's life and discussing his influence both in ancient Israel and in the present. A massive, comprehensive scholarly work with extensive documentation.

Kidner, Derek. *The Psalms*. 2 vols. Downers Grove, Ill. and London: Inter-Varsity Press, 1973-1975. Comprehensive overview and interpretation of the psalms written by David. Illuminates and authenticates much of the life of David by revealing the private thoughts of the greatest king of Israel in ancient times.

Kitchen, K.A. *The Bible in Its World*. Downers Grove, Ill.: Inter-Varsity Press, and Exeter, England: Paternoster Press, 1977. An insider's look at the world of archaeology and how it functions in validating ancient records and narratives. It is particularly helpful in its extensive examination of antiquity's cultural artifacts and social conditions against the backdrop of the age of Saul, David, and Solomon, and the remainder of David's lineage.

Noll, K. L. *The Faces of David*. Journal for the Study of the Old Testament, supplemental vol. 242. Sheffield: Sheffield Academic Press, 1997. A literary study that investigates the characterization of David in the book of Samuel.

Schultz, Samuel J. *The Old Testament Speaks*. 4th ed. San Francisco: Harper, 1990. Written for the lay reader, this cogent and lucidly written volume presents an objective, historical analysis of the lives of the patriarchs, including a major section on David and the kings of Israel and their role in the evolution of ancient Israel.

Thompson, J.A. *Handbook of Life in Bible Times.* Leicester and Downers Grove, Ill.: Inter-Varsity Press, 1986. A colorful, lavishly illustrated reference tool with key sections on the domestic life, travel, family customs, and cultural preoccupations of the biblical world. Illuminates the life and times of Israel and its kings in the period between 1400 and 1000 B.C., and thus is a helpful contextualizing volume for a study of David.

Bruce L. Edwards

DEBORAH

Born: c. 1200 B.C.-1125 B.C.; central Israel
Died: c. 1200 B.C.-1124 B.C.; central Israel
Areas of Achievement: Biblical figures; literature; religion; warfare and conquest
Contribution: A Joan of Arc of the Bible, Deborah rallied Israelite tribes to defeat oppressors as she had prophesied; her victory poem is considered one of Scripture's most ancient texts.

Early Life

The biblical figure named Deborah is believed to have lived between 1125 B.C. and 1200 B.C. These years, falling between the death of Joshua and the institution of the monarchy in ancient Israel, are recounted in the biblical book of Judges. Tradition assigns Joshua as Moses's successor, charged with leading the loose federation of Hebrew tribes that were resettling ancestral lands in the area then known as Canaan. Whether or not the initial stage of resettlement proceeded as a unified military effort under Joshua, instability marked the years chronicled in Judges. Archaeological evidence supports a scenario of periods of war and crisis alternating with peaceful intervals during the twelfth and eleventh centuries B.C. Most towns in the region apparently suffered destruction, indicating a time of turmoil and uncertainty.

The Bible views the era as a cycle of lapses into idolatry punished by Yahweh through the agency of outside aggressors, followed by repentance and subsequent deliverance by divinely appointed leaders, or "judges." In Deborah's lifetime, the Israelites had become enslaved to Jabin, the king of Canaan. Scripture states that following the death of the judge Ehud, the people had fallen under the sway of gods other than Yahweh, who in turn, had given them up to their Canaanite oppressors.

The vulnerability of the Israelite population during Deborah's formative years would have highlighted her role as childbearer, particularly in a patriarchal society in which a man could sell his daughter as payment for debts. Yet the primacy of survival also required that women labor alongside men for the good of the community.

Deborah's development may have been affected by her tribal affiliation. Residing in the hill country in what is now central Israel, she was most likely a member of the tribe of Ephraim. The central position of their area of settlement, along with the fact that the religious center of Shiloh was located in their territory, engendered in the Ephraimites a proud and even militant spirit.

Life's Work

The fourth chapter of the biblical book of Judges introduces Deborah as a prophet to whom people came to settle controversies. She is described as bestowing her counsel under a palm tree, apparently a sacred site popularly associated with the burial place of Deborah, the nurse of the matriarch Rebecca.

Some see in this image the kahin (or *kahina*), known from nomadic Arabic tribes as a kind of magician or fortune-teller holding court and dispensing judgments in a sanctified place. A common phenomenon in antiquity, prophecy was essentially oracular; that is, it involved communication of the divine will regarding a specific matter. The prophet thus played a prominent role in the political life of a community by delivering messages in the name of a god. Nothing in the biblical account indicates that Deborah as a female functioned in the role of prophet any differently than a male. Nevertheless, it has been suggested that, as a woman whose priority was childrearing, her calling was at best part-time during her childbearing years and may not even have begun until later in life.

As one to whom they came with their troubles and concerns, Deborah was no doubt keenly aware of her people's suffering under Jabin. Headed by Jabin's field commander, Sisera, the Canaanite army was equipped with iron chariots, giving them considerable military superiority over the Israelites, who were still technologically in the Bronze Age. This advantage enabled the Canaanites to control the passage through the valleys that separated the mountain tribes in the center of the land—including Ephraim, where Deborah resided—and those in the north, in Galilee, thus ensuring their subjugation of the Israelites.

Despite this obstacle, after twenty years of domination, Deborah initiated a war of liberation by summoning a military commander, a man named Barak, out of Kedesh-naphtali in the northern reaches of the territory. Because of the similarity of meaning between the name Barak ("lightning") and that of Deborah's apparent husband, Lapidoth ("torches"), some medieval commentators identify Barak as her spouse. Most commentators, however,

246

fail to find this identification borne out by the context. Based on the ambiguity stemming from the Hebrew word *esheth*, signifying either "woman" or "wife," and the question of whether or not *Lapidoth* is a proper noun, at least one commentator—the author of the first century *Biblical Antiquities*—interprets *esheth lapidoth* to mean "fiery woman," or "enlightener." The phrase therefore refers to Deborah herself and not her marital status, though given the social conventions of the time, it is doubtful that Deborah was unmarried, whether or not her husband is named in the biblical account.

In any event, in her role as prophet and now as judge, Deborah relayed Yahweh's command that Barak gather a force of ten thousand volunteers to Mount Tabor, at the boundary of the territories of the northern tribes of Zebulun, Naphtali and Issachar. Barak, convinced of Deborah's power and influence, refused to act unless she accompanied him. She agreed, declaring that Sisera would suffer defeat at the hand of a woman.

True to Deborah's reckoning, Sisera and his army approached Mount Tabor from the south, along the valley of the river Kishon. The strategy of the poorly armed Israelite tribes was to exploit the flooding of the riverbed and lure Sisera and his nine hundred iron chariots into the muddy river valley. The Israelites descended the mountain and engaged the enemy in Taanach, by the waters of Megiddo, a Canaanite town located near a tributary of the Kishon. As the Israelites had planned, the Canaanites' chariots sank deep in the mire, leaving their troops to be routed by the Israelites. Not one of Sisera's camp escaped, though Sisera himself fled by foot to the tent of Jael, wife of Heber, a Kenite with whom Jabin was apparently at peace. Offering Sisera hospitality, Jael then proceeded to drive a nail into his head as he slept. There Barak tracked Sisera down, defeated as Deborah had said by a woman—by herself as well as Jael, many would argue. The victory over Sisera that Deborah had inspired ushered in a forty-year span of prosperity for Israel, twice the years of their oppression.

The narrative in Judges, chapter 4, names only the tribes of Naphtali and Zebulun as fighting in the battle against Sisera. The account of the victory in poetic form that follows in chapter 5, however, cites numerous tribes, either extolling their participation (Ephraim, Benjamin, and Issachar, as well as Naphtali and Zebulun) or condemning their absence (Reuben, Dan, and Asher). This hymn of triumph is said to be sung by Deborah and Barak, though the Hebrew verb is in the feminine form. Also in support of the claim that what has become known as the "Song of Deborah" was indeed authored by a woman, commentators note the presence of many feminine images. Chief among them is Deborah as "a mother in Israel." Her bold actions are understood to be that of a mother fiercely protective of her family—metaphorically, the family of her people. Female authorship is supported as well by the fact that more of the text is devoted to the actions of Jael and Sisera's mother—imagined as anxiously awaiting her son's return—than to a recapitulation of the battle.

Summary

The defeat of Sisera, instigated by Deborah, proved decisive in the decline of the Canaanite kingdom, thus easing the resettlement of the area by the Israelites. This proved significant in the history of religion, as both Judaism and Christianity developed from the nation that formed from Israelite expansion into the territory. Deborah's poetic reconstruction of the defeat has also made a mark in literary history. The Song of Deborah is intensively studied as one of the most ancient texts in Scripture, and it also forms part of the Jewish liturgy.

Commentators have noted how unremarkable Deborah's judgeship appears in the biblical text. Yet while the Scripture portrays Deborah as a woman of power and influence, interpreters of the biblical tradition have often blunted her impact. Flavius Josephus, in his first century account of Jewish history, omits any mention of Deborah's role as military strategist or judge, displaying a discomfort with a woman exercising authority over men that appears in rabbinical commentaries as well. The rabbis actually chastise Deborah for sending for Barak rather than going to him.

"We never hear sermons pointing women to the heroic virtues of Deborah as worthy of their imitation," bemoaned nineteenth century American suffragist Elizabeth Cady Stanton. Instead, she noted, "the lessons doled out to women" exhorted "meekness and self-abnegation." In the latter half of the twentieth century, the precedent set by Deborah has taken on new significance—in large part as a result of the rise of the woman's movement and the rebirth of the state of Israel, whose fourth prime minister was a woman and whose women have, from the nation's beginning, served in its military.

Bibliography

Bird, Phyllis. "Images of Women in the Old Testament." In *Religion and Sexism: Images of Women in the Jewish and Christian Traditions*, edited by Rosemary Radford Ruether. New York: Simon & Schuster, 1974. Writing from a feminist perspective, Bird views Deborah as an exceptional women whose story is recounted in a book that portrays a man's world, that is, a world dominated by war and issues of power and control.

Brown, Cheryl Anne. *No Longer Be Silent: First Century Jewish Portraits of Biblical Women*. Gender and the Biblical Tradition Series. Louisville, Ky.: Westminster/John Knox Press, 1992. Examines references to Deborah in Pseudo-Philo's *Biblical Antiquities* and Flavius Josephus's *Jewish Antiquities*, retellings of the biblical narrative composed during Judaism's and Christianity's formative years. Brown's discussion demonstrates the variability of Deborah's image in Western religious tradition. A bibliography and index are provided, along with endnotes.

Deen, Edith. *All the Women of the Bible*. New York: Harper & Row, 1955; London: Independent, 1960. A highly reverential treatment of the biblical character, rife with speculation on her feelings and motivations. Contains a bibliography and index.

Lacks, Roslyn. *Women and Judaism: Myth, History, and Struggle*. New York: Doubleday, 1980. Concludes that Deborah's story counteracts conventional assumptions about women derived from elsewhere in the Bible as well as from rabbinic literature. Includes a bibliography, index, and endnotes.

Otwell, John H. *And Sarah Laughed: The Status of Woman in the Old Testament*. Philadelphia: Westminster Press, 1977. In two chapters, "Freedom of Action" and "Women in the Cult," Deborah's example is used to argue that women participated fully in the life of the ancient community of Israel. Provides a bibliography and index; because the index is of biblical passages, however, familiarity with Scripture is helpful.

Phipps, William E. *Assertive Biblical Women*. Contributions in Women's Studies, No. 128. Westport, Conn.: Greenwood Press, 1992. Briefly examines Deborah in her various leadership roles. Contends that ancient society practiced gender egalitarianism to a greater degree than later generations. Offers endnotes as well as an index and select bibliography.

Williams, James G. *Women Recounted: Narrative Thinking and the God of Israel*. Bible and Literature Series. Sheffield: Almond Press, 1982. Views the biblical texts from a literary perspective, so that the figure of Deborah owes less to historical accuracy than to ancient literary conventions. Contains a bibliography, endnotes, and an index of biblical passages.

Amy Allison

DEMOCRITUS

Born: c. 460 B.C.; Abdera, Thrace
Died: c. 370 B.C.; Abdera, Thrace
Area of Achievement: Philosophy
Contribution: Democritus worked out a far-reaching atomism, which he applied to science, metaphysics, and ethics. His view that the world is made up of changing combinations of unchanging atoms was addressed to one of the central questions of his age—"How is change possible?"—and provided a model of reasoning that was mechanistic, materialist, and nonsupernatural.

Early Life

Democritus was born, probably to wealthy parents, in the city of Abdera, Thrace. Although Leucippus, the philosopher who became his teacher, can properly be regarded as the founder of Greek atomism, Leucippus himself wrote very little, and very little is known about him. Democritus, however, was a prolific writer who developed a well-reasoned atomistic view and applied it to a wide variety of fields, including science, metaphysics, and ethics.

As a young man, Democritus traveled to Egypt, Persia, and Babylonia. Some ancient sources hold that he went as far south as Ethiopia and as far east as India, but modern scholars consider this doubtful. It is reported that Democritus boasted that he had visited more foreign lands and carried out more extensive inquiries and investigations than anyone else of his time. He traveled both for the "broadening" experience that falls to any inquisitive traveler and in order to receive instruction from those who were considered wise in many lands. When he returned to Greek soil, he himself earned a reputation for wisdom. He carried with him an aura of the exotic, having delved into cultures that the Greeks thought of as exotic and foreign: the cultures of Egypt, Persia, and Babylonia.

In character, Democritus is reported to have been a man of serenity, strength, and cheerfulness. The ancient Romans referred to him as "the laughing philosopher," alluding, perhaps, to his attitude toward the typically human fault of taking oneself too seriously.

As a thinker and writer, he addressed the most pressing philosophical and intellectual issues of the age in his works, which numbered at least fifty. Unfortunately, his texts have survived only in fragmentary form.

Life's Work

During the years following his travels, when Democritus began to develop his philosophical system, the Greek intellectual world was occupied with grave difficulties arising from the philosophy of Parmenides of Elea and his followers, the Eleatics. Parmenides was a practitioner of strict deductive logic. Taking premises that he thought would be generally acceptable, he argued logically to necessary conclusions. Many people admired his strong reliance on reason and thought; nevertheless, Parmenides arrived at conclusions that were deeply problematic. He concluded that there is no such thing as change and that no more than one thing exists. This clearly conflicts with common experience, which seems to show constant change and plurality. Still, Parmenides held fast to logic and reasoning as sources of knowledge that are more reliable than sense experience. If reason rules out change and plurality, he thought, then change and plurality do not exist.

The basis of his argument—an argument that Democritus and Leucippus had no choice but to

grapple with—is the idea that reason either apprehends something or it apprehends nothing. If it apprehends nothing, then it is not reason (that is, not an apprehending) after all. Thus, reason apprehends what exists, not nothing. Now if things came into existence or passed out of existence, or if things changed their qualities over time, then reason would have to think of the things or qualities as not existing at some time (that is, before coming into existence or after passing out of existence). Reason would then, however, be apprehending nothing—and this, it was said, cannot occur. Similarly, if more than one thing existed, and there was empty space between the things, reason would again have to apprehend nothing. The conclusion is that only one thing exists, and this one thing is eternal, never coming into existence, never passing out of existence, and never changing. This one thing Parmenides called "the One."

One of the great achievements of Democritus and the atomists lies in overcoming this argument—an argument that probably seemed much more convincing to the ancient Greeks than to modern thinkers—while retaining some of its logical points and, at the same time, acknowledging the reality of change, plurality, and other common-sense ideas that Parmenides apparently denied.

It is a fundamental principle of Democritean atomism that "nothing exists but the atoms and the void." The atoms (literally, in Greek, "the indivisibles" or "the uncuttables") are the smallest units of matter, the smallest pieces of "being," and cannot be further divided. The void, considered "non-being," is thought to be just as real as the atoms. It was very important for Democritus that both exist: being and non-being, the atoms and the void. In a sense, the atoms are individually much like the One of Parmenides. They do not come into existence or pass out of existence, and they do not change (internally). Nevertheless, the void—a necessary feature of atomism—makes it possible for the atoms to combine and separate and recombine in changing arrangements.

As Democritus envisioned them, atoms differ from one another only in shape, size, and position. Qualities such as color and flavor were said to arise from the particular arrangements of (inherently colorless and flavorless) atoms and their interaction with the senses of the observer.

Atoms are constantly in motion, according to Democritus' theory. They do not require any force or intelligence to put them into motion. Surrounded by the void, they are not held in any one position but move quite freely. Atoms crash into one another, become entagled with one another, and sometimes establish regular motions or streams of motion. There is no limit to the void or to the number of atoms, and Democritus thought that the universe visible to human beings was only one among countless worlds, many of which must also contain stars, planets, and living things.

The atomism of Democritus was a reaffirmation of the reality of change as experienced in everyday life, yet it agreed with Parmenides concerning the unchanging reality that lies behind observed phenomena. The theory attempted to do justice to both experience and reason, change and permanence. Democritus envisioned a world in which combinations and configurations of atoms change within the void, but the atoms themselves never undergo internal change. Thus it is the void that makes change possible. Ironically, it could be said that in the theory of Greek atomism it is really the void (and not the atoms) that is innovative and enables the theory to escape from the unpalatable conclusions of Parmenides and the Eleatics.

Democritus also addressed questions raised by an entirely new movement in Greek thought. Previous to the time of Democritus, Greek philosophers had been almost exclusively concerned with physical and metaphysical questions—for example, questions about being and change. Around the time of Democritus, however, a revolution in philosophy was brought about by the Sophists and Socrates, who raised questions about human nature, society, and morality, rather than questions that focused on the physical world.

Democritus approached all these questions through his atomism. The soul, he surmised, is made up of highly mobile spherical atoms, which disperse at death. He hypothesized that people who seem to die but who "come back to life" have actually retained their atomic integrity all the while; they did not really die and come back to life. Eventually, in a real death, the atoms in the body begin to lose their connections with one another. This process is gradual, however, so that hair and fingernails might grow for a while even after the life-breath (and the necessary spherical atoms) was gone. Then, as the atoms lose their connections, the entire body decays.

Democritus taught that people should have no fear or apprehension concerning supernatural matters or an afterlife. Since the totality of reality consists of the atoms and the void, when the atoms of a person disperse and the person dies, the person no longer exists. Therefore, according to Democritus, there is nothing to fear in death. The corollary conclusion is that people should not delay pleasures in anticipation of an afterlife. It is in this life—this arrangement of atoms—that human beings can find their only fulfillment and happiness.

The best life is one that is characterized by contentedness and cheerfulness. Democritus believed that passions are powerful, disturbing factors that tend to upset the natural harmony and balance in the arrangement of atoms in human beings. Democritus used his atomism to support traditional Greek views that strong passions can cause much trouble and that moderation is best. The key to moderation and to the achievement of happiness in life is knowledge. Knowledge determines one's proper goals and activities, while passion is a threat.

It is important, however, to distinguish Democritus' knowledge-passion polarity from that of many later Platonic thinkers. Platonic thinkers (and some Christian Neoplatonists) are dualists. They distinguish between one's spiritual or intellectual part— the seat of reason, which is divine and immortal— and one's physical or irrational part—the seat of passion, which is animal and mortal. The first is the spiritual soul and lives forever; the second is the body, which suffers death and decay. In contrast, Democritus was a thoroughgoing naturalist and materialist; he believed that all the atoms disperse at death and nothing survives. Knowledge was seen as important and passion was seen as a threat, not for religious or supernatural reasons but because of their import for human contentedness and cheerfulness.

Ancient sources agree that Democritus lived to a remarkably advanced age. Few details of his later life, however, are known. The legend that he blinded himself (in order to root out lustful desires, according to Tertullian) is denied by Plutarch. Democritus is thought to have died in Thrace around the year 370 B.C.

Summary

The theory of atomism was not favored by Plato (c. 427-347 B.C.) and Aristotle (384-322 B.C.), the two major Greek philosophers who followed Democritus, but it was adopted by the Greek Epicurus (341-270 B.C.) and the Roman Lucretius (c. 98-55 B.C.). Epicurus was attracted to the moral teaching of Democritus and held that human well-being is best achieved by eliminating pain and the painful desire for things that people cannot (or cannot easily) obtain. Consequently, he aimed to live a life of utmost simplicity. Both Epicurus and Lucretius followed Democritus in denying supernatural influences on human life and rejecting the idea of an afterlife. Moreover, all these thinkers believed that their position on these points was not only true but also useful in freeing people from superstitions that lead to pain and suffering.

Atomism, as an essentially physical and mechanical account of the world that leaves no place for "higher purposes" or "meanings," was particularly unacceptable to religious and theological writers of the Christian tradition, which dominated Western philosophy from about the fourth to the fourteenth century. In the wake of the Renaissance and the scientific revolution (that is, since about the fifteenth and sixteenth centuries), however, the influence of Democritus has again become apparent in philosophy and science. Modern science, like ancient Democritean atomism, deals with the world purely in terms of physical objects operating according to natural laws; the question of higher purposes or meanings is considered to lie beyond the scope of science. In some points of detail there is significant agreement between ancient atomism and the modern scientific view. On both accounts, for example, qualities such as the color of a book or the taste of a cup of coffee are thought to be attached not to individual atoms—there are no red atoms or coffee-flavored atoms—but to combinations of atoms in interaction with a perceiver. One obvious difference between the two forms of atomism, however, is that in the Democritean view atoms cannot be split, while the modern scientific view upholds the existence of many kinds of subatomic particles and has even led to the development of atom-splitting technology that can unleash great power.

It must be remembered, however, that the atomism of Democritus is not a scientific theory and does not pretend to be based on experiment, experience, and observation. It is basically a philosophical theory, based on argument, which was designed to refute the theory and the arguments of Parmenides and the Eleatics. Thus, interesting as it is to compare ancient and modern atomism, it is not really fair to think of the two views as competing in the same arena. Democritus and the Greek atomists succeeded in developing an attitude toward the world that enabled them to look upon it as thoroughly physical and mechanical, and it is this attitude, or significant aspects of it, that many modern scientists have shared. According to this view, observable phenomena are explainable in terms of unseen movements which occur according to natural (not supernatural) law.

Bibliography

Bailey, Cyril. *The Greek Atomists and Epicurus.* Oxford: Clarendon, and New York: Russell and Russell, 1928. Contains a thorough historical account of the origins of Greek atomism, the contributions and elaborations that derive specifically from Democritus, and the further adaptation of the view at the hands of Epicurus. Bailey stresses the differences between Leucippus, Democritus, and Epicurus.

Brumbaugh, Robert S. *The Philosophers of Greece.* New York: Crowell, 1964; London: Allen and Unwin, 1966. Chapter 11 covers Democritus, atomism, and the development of materialism. Brumbaugh compares Greek, Roman, and modern atomisms. The chapter is brief, but Brumbaugh shows the place of Democritus and the atomists within Greek philosophical history.

Burnet, John. *Greek Philosophy: Thales to Plato.* London: Macmillan, and New York: St. Martin's, 1914. A classic work that has been reprinted many times. Burnet's chapter 11 is entitled "Demokritos," but refers to the philosopher generally known as Democritus. Burnet's strictly Greek spelling here is evidence of his overall carefulness. This is a scholarly work, with indexes of both English and Greek terms.

Freeman, Kathleen. *Ancilla to the Pre-Socratic Philosophers.* Cambridge, Mass.: Harvard University Press, and Oxford: Blackwell, 1948. A complete translation of all the Greek philosophical fragments that were first collected and translated (into German) by the German scholar Hermann Diels. About thirty pages are given to fragments of works and titles of works by Democritus. Most of the fragments relate to the ethics of atomism rather than to its physics.

Guthrie, W. K. C. *A History of Greek Philosophy.* Vol. 2. Cambridge: Cambridge University Press, 1962; New York: Cambridge University Press, 1978. A very useful volume that contains more than one hundred pages on Democritus, an appendix on atomism, a long bibliography, and three indexes. Democritus has been called an encyclopedic thinker, and Guthrie shows the truth of this remark by exploring a great number of areas with which Democritus was concerned.

Kirk, G. S., and J. E. Raven. *The Presocratic Philosophers.* 2d ed. Cambridge and New York: Cambridge University Press, 1983. Chapter 17 covers Leucippus, Democritus, and the theory of atomism. This book contains the actual Greek texts of the philosophers, always accompanied by English translations and explanations. Kirk and Raven concentrate on the physics of atomism; the ethics of atomism is treated very briefly.

Sandywell, Barry. *Presocratic Reflexivity: The Construction of Philosophical Discourse, c. 600-450 B.C.* Volume 3. London and New York: Routledge, 1996. A difficult, wide-ranging book that tries to evaluate pre-Socratic thinkers in terms of the "cultural discourse" in which they participated and to which they in turn contributed. Chapter 8 deals with Democritus.

Vlastos, Gregory. "Ethics and Physics in Democritus," in *Philosophical Review* 54/55 (1945/1946): 578-592, 53-64. This long article, printed in two parts in two volumes of the same journal, argues, against Cyril Bailey (cited above), that the ethics and the physics of Democritus are indeed linked. Vlastos stresses the relationship between the naturalism (nonsupernaturalism) of the physical worldview of atomism and the naturalism of the ethics of atomism.

Wright, M. R. *Cosmology in Antiquity.* London and New York: Routledge, 1995. A general account, designed for the non-specialist reader, of ancient cosmology. Extensive coverage given to the pre-Socratics. Arrangement is not chronological but topical.

Stephen Satris

DEMOSTHENES

Born: 384 B.C.; Athens, Greece
Died: 322 B.C.; Calauria, Greee
Areas of Achievement: Law and politics
Contribution: Demosthenes' life and career as an orator were consumed by his titanic struggle with Philip II of Macedonia and by his efforts to recall Athenian spirit and vigor to its former greatness. The single-mindedness, sincerity, and intense patriotism of Demosthenes—combined with his consummate genius and mastery of oratorical technique—make him one of the most notable personalities of antiquity.

Early Life

Demosthenes was born in Athens in 384 B.C., the son of Demosthenes, an Athenian citizen of the deme of Paeania, and Cleobule, the daughter of Gylon. The elder Demosthenes, the owner of a lucrative weapons workshop, died when his son was only seven, bequeathing him a substantial fortune. Most of this patrimony, however, was embezzled by the child's three guardians, Aphobus, Demophon, and Theryppides, who handed over to the young Demosthenes, when he came of age, only a fraction of his inheritance. As a boy, Demosthenes had witnessed the orator Callistratus win a stunning victory in the courtroom and had thereupon vowed to become an orator himself. He had turned his attention to the art of oratory and studied with Isaeus, an orator known for his acumen in cases involving questions of inheritance. This early training was now to bear fruit: Demosthenes, at only eighteen years of age, brought a series of actions against his guardians and secured a decisive victory; it is unlikely, however, that he recovered more than a little of what was owed him.

Employing his knowledge of the law and oratory, Demosthenes turned to professional speech writing (logography) and enjoyed success as a composer of orations for others. His own speaking debut before the Assembly, however, met with little approval from the people, for he was short of breath, weak in voice, and hampered by some sort of speech impediment. Chagrined, Demosthenes then began the legendary regimen of oratorical training that has become for subsequent generations a paradigm of the efficacy of hard work and perseverance in overcoming the defects or shortcomings of nature: He pronounced periods with pebbles in his mouth, declaimed to the waves over the roar of the sea, spoke while running up hill, and shaved one side of his head so that his humiliating appearance would confine him to his underground practice studio for several months at a time.

By the age of thirty, with physical impediments overcome and oratorical skills honed to near perfection, Demosthenes found himself increasingly involved in legal cases whose character was essentially political in nature. In 354, he delivered his first major speech before the Assembly, wherein he countered the rumored threat of war against Athens by the King of Persia, cautioned against rash action, and proposed an elaborate revision of the method for outfitting the navy. In this speech, as well as others written and delivered during this period, Demosthenes tended to support the conservative program of Eubulus, leader of the dominant party in Athens at the time, who advocated peace abroad and financial security at home. The impact of these orations thrust Demosthenes dramatically into the arena of politics and statesmanship, from which he retired only at his death.

Life's Work

It was to the north that Demosthenes now directed his attention, troubled, like many of the Greeks, by the startling and unexpected ascendancy of Philip II of Macedonia in Thrace and Thessaly. Henceforth the story of Demosthenes' life was to be the drama of his all-consuming struggle to persuade the Athenians and the rest of the Greeks to oppose the Macedonian threat to their freedom. Encroaching southward, Philip had run roughshod over Athenian interests and sources of supply in Amphipolis and the Thermaicus Sinus. Alarmed by these acts of aggression, Demosthenes delivered the impassioned "First Philippic" in 351, rousing his fellow citizens to take notice of the threat posed by Philip and calling them to military preparedness. This speech, injected with a newfound vigor and intensity, made clear his volte-face from the policy of Eubulus and established the orator as leader of the opposition to Macedonia's infringement upon Athenian and Greek liberty.

Philip's subsequent advance on Olynthus spurred the orator to respond with three stirring speeches, known as the "Olynthiacs," in 349, aimed at securing aid for Olynthus. Demosthenes urged the Athenians to resist the onslaught of Philip with all of their physical and financial resources,

going so far as to propose that the Theoric Fund (the public dole that paid for the poor's admission to the theater) be made available for the necessities of war. The Athenians did respond—but too late and with too little assistance: Olynthus and several of the confederate towns were razed by Philip in 348.

Seeing that Athens was weak, vulnerable, and in need of time to collect its resources and strength, Demosthenes acceded to peace talks with Philip. In February of 346, he, along with several other ambassadors, including Aeschines and Philocrates, was sent to negotiate a treaty. Demosthenes' rhetorical collapse before Philip proved to be one of the most embarrassing ordeals in the orator's life and marked the beginning of enmity between him and Aeschines, to whom Philip apparently directed his reply. Nevertheless, it was Demosthenes who had been able to detect Philip's real intentions; thus, he condemned the terms of the treaty to his fellow citizens. Aeschines, on the other hand, rashly assured the Athenians of Philip's goodwill. Demosthenes' worst fears were realized when Philip, dallying before taking the final oath of rati-

fication, secured more territory, crushed Phocis, assumed a place on the Amphictionic Council, and took from Athens the right of precedence in consulting the oracle at Delphi.

In response to the growing bitterness of the Athenians over Philip's continued successes and perhaps to deflect criticism aimed at his conduct during the peace negotiations, Demosthenes impeached his rival Aeschines in 343. Charged with having caused grave injury to Athens by delaying the embassy, rendering false reports, giving bad advice, disobeying orders, and opening himself to bribery, Aeschines counterattacked with a speech and, with the support of Eubulus and other pro-Macedonians in Athens, was narrowly acquitted. Yet it was clear that the pro-Macedonian party had lost ground and that Demosthenes' hard-line anti-Macedonian stance was finally beginning to win support among the Athenians.

By 342, Philip had firmly incorporated Thrace in his kingdom and was now turning his eye toward the Chersonese, an area vital to Athens because of its geographically strategic location on the supply route from the Black Sea. In his speech "On the Chersonese" (341), Demosthenes countered Philip's complaints about Athenian supported activity in this area. Shortly thereafter he reiterated his plea for support of the Chersonese; in the "Third Philippic" Demosthenes was at his oratorical best, arguing that Philip's actions had already amounted to a violation of the peace and a declaration of war and passionately insisting on a union of all Greeks under the leadership of Athens.

The years immediately following were certainly Demosthenes' "finest hour" and represent the high point in his career. The naval reforms that he had earlier proposed were effected, and his eloquence and indefatigable energy finally prevailed to secure an alliance of almost all Greek states with Athens at its head. After Philip's declaration of war in 340, Demosthenes moved to suspend the allocation of surplus funds to the Theoric Fund and managed at length to secure an alliance between Athens and her traditional enemy, Thebes. For his actions during this time, the Athenians honored him, now their recognized leader, with two golden crowns, one in 340 and another in 339.

Demosthenes' dream of a unified Greek front, temporarily realized, was short-lived. In 338, Philip crushed the Greek allied forces on the battlefield of Chaeronea. Demosthenes, who took part in the battle, was said by his enemies to have fled disgracefully, but back in Athens it was Demosthenes who organized the city's defenses and who, in fact, was called upon by the citizens to deliver the funeral oration over those who had fallen in the fray.

To the surprise of some, Philip treated his enemies graciously in victory and refrained from occupying Athens. Nevertheless, such clemency failed to secure the goodwill or cooperation of Demosthenes. On the contrary, after Philip's assassination in 336, Demosthenes once again urged his countrymen to rally their support against Macedonia, reassured by rumors about the demise of Alexander (known later as Alexander the Great), Philip's son and successor. When Alexander's quick and decisive action against a rebellious Thebes (335) proved him to be as formidable a foe as his father, it was only through the agency of a special embassy that Demosthenes and other anti-Macedonian statesmen were spared.

In 336, a man named Ctesiphon proposed that Demosthenes should be awarded a crown at the festival of the Greater Dionysia because, in service to the state, "he continually speaks and does what is best for the people." Aeschines, bent on prolonging his feud with the orator, immediately charged Ctesiphon with an illegal action, thereby preventing the award of the crown. After several delays the case finally came to trial in 330 in what was, perhaps, the most celebrated oratorical contest of all time. Demosthenes' defense of Ctesiphon ("On the Crown"), in reality an apologia for himself and his entire political career, is not only the orator's masterpiece but also, in the judgment of many scholars throughout the centuries, the most sublime oratorical work of antiquity. To Demosthenes' repeated question, "What else could I have done?" the Athenian jury answered resoundingly with an overwhelming verdict in his favor; Aeschines, who received less than one-fifth of the votes, was forced into exile.

Some six years later, in 324, Demosthenes' shining victory was tarnished by charges of having accepted a bribe from Alexander's fugitive treasurer, Harpalus. Although the precise details of the case are obscure, Demosthenes was convicted of the charge and fined fifty talents. Unable to pay, he escaped from prison and fled into exile. In the following year, however, Alexander's death occasioned a dramatic reversal for the orator: He was recalled to Athens in triumph, and his fine was paid by the citizens who offered him fifty talents for preparing and adorning the altar for the sacrifice to Zeus the Savior. Macedonian power seemed broken once again, but once again Demosthenes and the Athenians were deluded: Antipater, Alexander's successor, defeated the Greeks in the Lamian War and demanded that Demosthenes be handed over to him. The orator fled to the island of Calauria off the coast of Argolis and there, on the approach of Antipater's minions in 322, committed suicide by drinking poison concealed in his stylus.

Summary

To the ancients, Demosthenes was simply "the orator," in much the same way Homer had always been "the poet." His singleness of purpose, the compelling vehemence and force of his argumentation, his sincerity and intensity, and the lucidity, rapidity, flexibility, and variety of his style established him as the model for subsequent speakers, including the great Roman orator Cicero. For many he has symbolized the patriot par excellence, the champion of a lost cause, fighting to preserve the Athenian democracy in its death throes, a tragic hero and an eloquent spokesman battling for political freedom against the tyrannical threats and designs of the Macedonian aggressor. Others have had little sympathy for his policies, sharing Aeschines' view of him as a humorless "water-bibber" among wine drinkers, a stiff-necked politician whose stubbornness in the face of a new order and a powerful, inevitable force brought destruction upon himself and his homeland.

In the final analysis, no matter what judgment is rendered regarding his policies as a statesman, Demosthenes' ability to persuade is unquestionable. In his life and career he accomplished what few orators have ever been able to approach. Although a consummate master of every rule and artifice of rhetoric, Demosthenes rejected their use as ends in themselves in a mere show of rhetorical relativism; rather, the entire force of his oratorical talent was directed as a means to greater ends, namely the recovery of the public spirit, the restoration of public vigor, the preservation of the Athenian democracy and its institutions, and the reestablishment of Athens' preeminent influence and reputation among the Greek cities. In pursuit of that goal, Demosthenes lived, spoke, and died.

Bibliography

Adams, Charles Darwin. *Demosthenes and His Influence*. New York: Longmans, Green, and London: Harrap, 1927. In addition to chapters on the life and oratory of Demosthenes, Adams includes important chapters on the influence of Demosthenes in antiquity, modern Europe, and on English and American oratory. Adams' apologia on behalf of Demosthenes is slightly overstated, but in general the volume is an excellent introduction.

Jaeger, Werner W. *Demosthenes: The Origin and Growth of His Policy.* Berkeley: University of California Press, 1938. Systematic attempt to reconstruct the origin and growth of Demosthenes' policy, considering his youth, education, early career, turn to politics, and the development of his political thought. A balanced presentation that offers a corrective to the nineteenth century notion that Demosthenes stood only as an obstacle to the inevitable progress of Panhellenism.

Kennedy, George A. *Art of Persuasion in Greece.* Princeton, N.J.: Princeton University Press, and London: Routledge, 1963. Standard handbook on Greek rhetorical theory and practice that offers perceptive analyses of Demosthenes' major orations and places them in their proper historical and rhetorical context.

Murphy, James J., ed. *Demosthenes' "On the Crown": A Critical Case Study of a Masterpiece of Ancient Oratory.* New York: Random House, 1967. Includes Plutarch's biography of Demosthenes, an analysis of Demosthenes' oratorical career by George Kennedy, John J. Keaney's excellent translation of "On the Crown," and an examination of the background, style, and argument of the speech.

Pearson, Lionel. *The Art of Demosthenes.* Chico, Calif.: Scholars Press, 1981. Concerned with Demosthenes the orator, Pearson attempts to provide analysis and exposition of the speaker's technique, including his command of argumentation and his skill in narrative. Both forensic and deliberative speeches are examined.

Pickard-Cambridge, A. W. *Demosthenes and the Last Days of Greek Freedom.* New York and London: Putnam, 1914. A sympathetic but balanced and reliable view of Demosthenes' life and career set in its historical and political context. Contains a chronological table (404-322 B.C.), several illustrations, maps, and diagrams of battles. An authoritative, sound introduction to Demosthenes.

Sealey, Raphael. *Demosthenes and His Time: A Study in Defeat.* New York and Oxford: Oxford University Press, 1993. This work is less a biography than a description and analysis of fourth-century history and the decline of Athens. Demosthenes is important, however, as a source for and participant in these events. Sealey forebears to pass judgment on Demosthenes' political policies but laments the rise of Macedon and the defeat of Athens.

James M. May

SAINT DENIS

Born: Date unknown; Italy
Died: c. A.D. 250; near Paris
Area of Achievement: Religion and saints
Contribution Saint Denis (pronounced Deh-NEE), a third century bishop and missionary from Italy, converted the Gauls to Christianity around the area of Paris, thereby establishing the foundation of what would later become one of the leading centers of the Christian faith in Europe. Legend has attributed much about his origins and deeds that is misleading and erroneous.

Early Life

Saint Denis was originally named Dionysius. He was a Christian bishop in Italy and a citizen of the Roman Empire. The name "Dionysius" is related to the Greek god Dionysus, known as Bacchus in Roman mythology. The use of such a name among early Christians is an example of how some pagan nomenclature continued in Christian culture and would be passed on in variant forms in many European languages.

Saint Denis lived during the first half of the third century. This period was dominated by increasing instability in the government of the empire. Emperors of the time had very short reigns. More and more frequently, their reigns ended with their assassinations by military guards who precariously succeeded them. After two centuries of growth, Christianity was an increasingly strong, even aggressive, element within the empire. Christianity existed throughout the eastern Mediterranean and in northern Africa, had advanced in Italy, and was entering into the furthest European reaches of the realm.

To the imperial government, this growth and spread were very dangerous. Christians would not worship the emperor as a god. They were, therefore, contributing to the decline of Roman society and government, which was already enfeebled and threatened. During the third century, in unstable fits and starts, Roman officials became more desperate to stamp out Christianity. Bishops, the leaders of Christian communities, were especially the target of government persecution.

Such persecution, however, was strengthening Christianity, creating a powerful corps of heroic Christian martyrs and saints. Many popes, who were the bishops of Rome, were martyred. In this atmosphere, Saint Denis and several other bishops set out in the middle of the third century on an evangelizing mission to the Gauls along the northwestern edge of the empire.

Life's Work

In Gaul, the name "Dionysius" was transformed into "Denis." (The name was also rendered as "Denys," "Dennis," and "Dionis.") In addition, Saint Denis was later sometimes referred to as "Dionysius of Paris." Along with several colleagues, he evangelized in and around the Roman outpost of Lutetia, which later became Paris. The city was then a village on an island (today the Isle de la Cité, the center of Paris) in the Seine River. The area was inhabited by members of the Parisii tribe. With its bridges connecting to the mainland, Lutetia was convenient as a location where Roman troops and traders could move on their way up and down Gaul, and it could be defended from barbarian invaders. To Christians, it was a strategic frontier point.

Lutetia was located in Middle Gaul, one of the three provinces of Gaul that Julius Caesar conquered and described. The outpost was administered from the Roman capital of the province, the city of Lugdunum (later Lyons). The first Christians are thought to have appeared in the province in the latter half of the second century.

When Saint Denis and his colleagues arrived in Lutetia, they were under direct Roman scrutiny. They engaged in missionary activities, attempting to increase the Christian population. Saint Denis was a successful preacher and leader of the Christian community, and he engaged in extensive pastoral activities. He was the first bishop of Paris, and he came to be considered the founder of Christianity in France. He not only he enlarged the community of lay Christians but also ordained new members of the clergy.

His success attracted Roman retaliation. During the reign of the emperors Decius (249-251) and Valerian (253-260), renewed brutal attempts were made to eliminate Christianity throughout the empire. It was at some time during these reigns that Saint Denis and two of his assistants, the priest Rusticus and the deacon Eleutherius, were imprisoned. Refusing in spite of torture to deny their Christianity, they were beheaded on October 9 at Martyrs' Hill, which is today the Montmartre district of Paris. In the third century, Montmartre was a separate district just north of Lutetia.

The bodies of the three martyrs were retrieved by the faithful and buried in a chapel, which became the site of the Benedictine Abbey of Saint Denis in Montmartre. The abbey church later became the burial site of the kings of France. As was customary at the time, Christians immediately venerated martyrs as saints. In later history, the Church would initiate a formal bureaucratic process for the canonization of saints.

The burial site of Saint Denis became a place of worship and intercession and over the centuries became the center of powerful cult. The date of the deaths of Saint Denis, Saint Rusticus, and Saint Eleutherius became a feast day of the Church.

While there is no reliable visual evidence of what Saint Denis looked like, he is usually portrayed as a bearded man in the vestments of a Catholic bishop. These clothes are sometimes etched with the fleur-de-lis, the stylized lily or iris that is a symbol of France and French royalty. As a beheaded martyr, he is often depicted holding his head, still wearing a mitre, the peaked ritual headpiece of a bishop. He is portrayed in this manner in paintings and stained-glass windows in many French and English churches, including Canterbury Cathedral.

Christian legend sometimes related that beheaded martyrs walked to their grave sites bearing their heads. Imagined scenes of Saint Denis's martyrdom were portrayed in murals at the English Benedictine Abbey of Wilton. Considerable veneration of Saint Denis occurred in England in the Benedictine monasteries founded there after the French Norman Conquest in the eleventh century. The English name Dennis and its feminine variant, Denise, also became popular.

As French history developed and Paris became the residence of the king and the political and religious center of the country, Saint Denis came to be considered the patron saint of France. He shares this honor with, among others, Saint Joan of Arc and Saint Martin of Tours. Medieval French armies appealed to Saint Denis for support in battle, much as the English did to Saint George. Saint Denis came also to be considered protector of the French Crown.

There is sparse factual data about Saint Denis. The most reliable source comes from the sixth century French historian Saint Gregory, who was bishop of Tours, France. Much other inaccurate infor-

mation about Saint Denis has resulted from the confusion of him with religious figures of other periods having the same name. For example, several centuries after he died, Saint Denis began to be confused with Saint Dionysius the Aeropagite, a disciple of Saint Paul in the mid-first century who is mentioned in the Acts of the Apostles ("Aeropagite" refers to a small hill near the Acropolis in Athens, Greece where Saint Paul preached.)

Thus confused with Dionysius the Aeropagite, Saint Denis was sometimes thought to have been sent to Gaul by Pope Clement I at the end of the first century A.D., near the end of apostolic times. Because Dionysius the Aeropagite was considered the first Christian bishop of Athens, Saint Denis is sometimes portrayed, even in France, in the vestments of an Orthodox bishop.

Further confusion about the life of Saint Denis occurred when he was identified as the author of certain writings of Dionysius the Aeropagite that appeared in the fifth century. These writings were treatises and letters dealing with mysticism and religion that became widely popular in the medieval period. Long after their appearance, it was proved that they were not actually written by Dionysius the Aeropagite. However, their early attribution to Saint Denis greatly contributed to his fame and further enhanced the reputation of the abbey named after him. The actual author came to be identified as "Pseudo-Dionysius."

In the high Middle Ages, Saint Denis was the subject of several religious plays. In these works, he was always viewed as the combined character of Dionysius the Aeropagite and the historical Saint Denis. A striking feature of the plays was the extent to which they focused on the sequence of tortures he endured before his martyrdom. In these plays, he and his companions valiantly resist torment, affirming the strength of their faith. Such a sequence was the standard script for recounting the life and death of martyrs.

Summary

The life of Saint Denis provides a telling example of the difficulties inherent in attempting to understand the lives of even the most significant figures of ancient times. His case illustrates a common problem that complicates efforts to study and write about such individuals: Names often have several variations, and one or more of these can be easily mistaken with those of another person or other persons. Furthermore, certain mistakes sometimes become entrenched because they are advantageous for later individuals and institutions associated with a historical figure. In the case of Saint Denis, his followers benefited from the belief that he was an associate of the apostles and that he was the author of widely influential religious writings. French kings, especially, benefited from these distinctions of their patron, and they thereby encouraged belief in them. The problem of understanding the life of Saint Denis—and that of so many other saints and heroic figures—is complicated by the need to separate layers of legend or myth from kernels of fact.

Despite the limited facts available about him, and despite the confusion and ambiguity that surround his memory, several things are quite apparent about Saint Denis. He confronted difficult, unknown, and dangerous circumstances, and he was resolute and effective in following his beliefs. Moreover, his life and work had great significance in the advance of Christianity and in the historical development of France and of Europe as a whole.

Bibliography

Brogan, Olden. *Roman Gaul*. London: G. Bell and Sons, 1953. This description of Gaul as a part of the Roman Empire sheds light on the world in which Saint Denis lived and worked. Includes illustrations.

Drinkwater, J. F. *The Gallic Empire: Separatism and Continuity in the Northwestern Provinces of the Roman Empire, A.D. 260-274*. Stuttgart, Germany: Franz Steiner Verlag, 1987. This work focuses on the immediate social, political, and military conditions in which Saint Denis lived. Includes maps. This author has also written *Roman Gaul: The Three Provinces, 58 B.C.-A.D.260* (London: Croom Helm, 1983).

King, Anthony. *Roman Gaul and Germany*. London: British Museum, and Berkeley: University of California Press, 1990. An examination of the Roman provincial, colonial environment before and after the time of Saint Denis, based on archeological excavations.

Saint Gregory of Tours. *Glory of the Martyrs*. Liverpool: Liverpool University Press, 1988. Relates stories of saintly miracles in the early Church, especially in France, some of which were associated with Saint Denis.

Lacaze, Charlotte. *The "Vie de Saint Denis" Manuscript*. New York: Garland, 1979. An annotated translation of a manuscript in the French National Library that makes up the most extensive narrative on, and pictorial representation of, Saint Denis and his era. Numerous illustrations.

Van Dam, Raymond. *Leadership and Community in Late Antique Gaul*. Berkeley: University of California Press, 1985; Oxford: University of California Press, 1992. Outlines the social and political environment in which Saint Denis operated and functioned. Includes maps and a bibliography.

Edward A. Riedinger

DIOCLES OF CARYSTUS

Born: c. 375 B.C.; Carystus, Greece
Died: c. 295 B.C.; Athens?, Greece
Area of Achievement: Medicine
Contribution: Diocles was a fourth century B.C.
Greek physician who was regarded in antiquity
as second only to Hippocrates. He wrote several
medical works, including the first separate treatise on anatomy and the first herbal. His best-
known contributions to medicine are in the area
of hygiene.

Early Life

Not much is known of Diocles' early life. His father's name was Archidamos and he was a native of
Carystus, a small town on the southern tip of the island of Euboea, off the eastern coast of mainland
Greece. According to the Roman writer Pliny, Diocles was second in age and fame to the famous
physician Hippocrates (probably 460-377 B.C.). He
has traditionally been placed in the first half of the
fourth century B.C. It has been observed, however,
that the language of his extant writings points to
the latter rather than to the earlier half of the fourth
century B.C. It is likely that he was a younger contemporary of Aristotle (384-322 B.C.) and thus was
active until 300 or perhaps later. Diocles is the only
physician between Hippocrates and the Hellenistic
period about whom very much is known.

Diocles probably learned his trade from his father, who was a physician, for medicine in the ancient world was a craft that was often passed from
father to son. The ordinary physician acquired his
skill and knowledge through an apprenticeship
where he learned the elements of traditional practice. Diocles wrote a work entitled *Arkhidamos*
(date unknown), dedicated to his father's memory,
in which he argued against his father's condemnation of the practice of rubbing the body down with
oil because he believed that it overheated the body.
Diocles suggested instead that in the summer a
mixture of oil and water be employed, while in the
winter only oil be used. There is good evidence, on
the basis of Diocles' language and thought, that he
was a pupil of the philosopher Aristotle, who
founded his philosophical school, the Lyceum, in
Athens in 335. Whether Diocles came to Athens
specifically to study at the Lyceum or had earlier
established residence there is not known. He was
the first Greek to write medical treatises in Attic
Greek rather than in Ionic, which was the dialect

normally employed by medical writers. He seems
to have belonged to the same generation of Aristotle's pupils as Theophrastus and Strato, who provide the earliest evidence for Diocles' work.

Diocles employs Aristotelian terminology and
shows the influence of Aristotle's ethics, for example, in his use of the ideas of proportion and suitability in his theory of diet. On the other hand, it is
quite possible that Diocles in turn influenced his
master, perhaps as a source for Aristotle's zoologi-
cal works. Although Diocles was apparently closely associated with the Peripatetic school, which
was the chief center of scientific research in the
Greek world until the founding of the Museum at
Alexandria, Aristotle was not the only source of his
ideas. He apparently had access to a collection of
Hippocratic treatises and may, in fact, have been
the first medical writer to assemble such a collection. His indebtedness to Hippocratic medicine is
indicated by his treatises, some of which resemble
Hippocratic works in title and subject matter. Diocles' thought also shows a debt to the Sicilian
school of medicine, which was dominated by the
philosopher and physician Empedocles (c. 490-430
B.C.). A later member of the school, Philistion of
Locri (427-347 B.C.), who was a contemporary of
Plato, also influenced him. Nevertheless, Diocles
was no slavish follower of Aristotle or of any medical or philosophical system. He borrowed elements from Hippocratic medicine, from the Sicilian school, and from Aristotle, all the while
maintaining his own independence and making
original contributions.

Life's Work

Diocles was a prolific writer. The titles of seventeen of his medical treatises are known, including
Peri puros kai aeros (on fire and air), *Anatomē*
(anatomy), *Hugieina pros Pleistarkhon* (directions
on health for Plistarchus), *Peri pepeseōs* (on digestion), *Peri puretōn* (on fevers), *Peri gunaikeiōn* (on
women's diseases), *Peri epideomōn* (on bandages),
Peri tōn kat iētreion (on the equipment of a surgery), *Prognōstikon* (prognostic), *Peri therapeiōn*
(on treatment), *Pathos aitia therapeia* (sickness,
causes, and treatment), *Rhizotomika, Peri lakha-
nōn* (on vegetables), *Peri thanasimōn pharmakōn*
(on lethal drugs), *Arkhidamos*, and *Dioklēs epistolē
prophulaktikē* (a letter to King Antigonus on preserving health). Of these works, more than 190

fragments have been preserved by later medical writers. Diocles' style is polished, with some literary pretensions, and shows the influence of rhetorical devices (for example, the avoidance of hiatus), while maintaining a deliberately simple style that reflects the influence of Aristotle.

According to the physician Galen (A.D. 129-199), Diocles' *Anatomy* was the first book written on that subject. In it he described the heart, lungs, gall bladder, ureters, ovaries, fallopian tubes, and ileocecal valve. Diocles' *Anatomy* was based on the observation of animals and not human beings (he is said to have dissected animals). Nevertheless, his work marked a significant turning point in the study of human anatomy, and other writers after him began to produce treatises on the subject. Diocles was indebted to Empedocles for his views on embryology. He believed that both the male and the female contributed seed, which originated in the brain and spinal marrow, to the embryo. The embryo, he believed, required forty days to develop fully; boys, who developed on the warmer, right side of the uterus, grew more quickly than girls. Diocles was interested in the problem of sterility and dissected mules to determine the causes of infertility. He also wrote on gynecology. From Empedocles he adopted the view that menstruation began at fourteen and lasted until sixty in all women. He also described signs of expected miscarriage and suggested causes of difficult birth.

In physiology, Diocles was also indebted to Empedocles, perhaps by way of Philistion. Like Empedocles, he believed that there were four elements (fire, air, water, and earth), which he equated with the four qualities (heat, cold, moisture, and dryness) that were responsible for the processes of the body. The body, possessing an innate heat, altered food that was consumed, producing the four humors (blood, phlegm, yellow bile, and black bile). Health was the result of an equilibrium of the four qualities, while disease was the result of an excess or deficiency of one of them. Diocles wrote that health and disease also depended on external factors (for example, wounds, nourishment, or sores) and on pneuma (air), inhaled or absorbed into the body through the pores in the skin. Pneuma then went to the heart, the central organ, from which it was distributed throughout the body by means of veins. Pneuma was essential to life, and if its passage was blocked, a humor disease or death would result. The heart was believed to be the chief organ of sensation and thought and the source of blood in the body. Diocles' theory of pneuma was also taken over from Empedocles and came to exercise much influence in Greek medical thought. Diocles recognized that fever was not itself a disease but rather the symptom of a disease. He also distinguished between pneumonia, which is a disease of the lungs, and pleurisy, which is an inflammation of the pleura (the lining over the lung).

Diocles wrote as well on botany and pharmacology. He compiled the first Greek herbal, *Rhizotomika*, which described the nutritional and medical value of plants. This treatise was widely used by later writers on the subject until replaced in the first century A.D. by the definitive work of Pedanius Dioscorides. While herbal drugs had been mentioned in the Hippocratic treatises, before Diocles no descriptions had been given of the plants themselves. Diocles' work on botany was no doubt influenced by his teacher's interest in the subject, and his work was apparently known to Theophrastus, a fellow student at the Lyceum and Aristotle's successor, who founded scientific botany.

It was in dietetics and hygiene that Diocles made his greatest contribution to Greek medicine. In the late fifth century, dietetic medicine had become a means of maintaining health rather than (as it had been earlier) a method of treating disease by restoring the proper balance to the body. Treatises appeared on hygiene containing detailed instructions for a daily regimen that regulated food and drink, rest and sleep, swimming, massage, gymnastic exercise, physical cleanliness, and sexual activity. Diocles treated the subject of hygiene in several partially extant works. In *Directions on Health for Pleistarchos* (written after 300), addressed to a Macedonian prince who was the son of Antipater, a general of Alexander the Great, Diocles reproduced (with some variations) the recommendations of earlier Hippocratic works on the subject of regimen. In an earlier work, *Dioklēs epistolē prophulaktikē* (c. 305-301), addressed to King Antigonus, another of Alexander's generals (which is quoted by the Byzantine writer Paul of Aegina), Diocles discussed, among other subjects, the matter of diet, advising that food and drink be adjusted to the seasons in order to counteract the effects of seasonal variation.

Diocles also wrote a treatise on diet that is preserved in fragments quoted by Oribasius, who was the physician to the Roman Emperor Julian from A.D. 361 to 363. The treatise describes a complete routine, from rising to bedtime, for one typical day of each of the four seasons of the year. Gymnastic exercise in both morning and evening plays an important part in Diocles' regimen. This work reveals the influence of Aristotle's concepts of the mean and suitability to the individual and his circumstances. Although Diocles prescribes an ideal regimen, chiefly intended for a man of means and leisure, it is one that can be adapted to the needs of those who have less time as well as to those of different ages.

Summary

Diocles was an important medical figure in his own day, as his reputation as a "second Hippocrates" indicates, and he forms a significant link between Hippocratic and Hellenistic medicine. He was indebted to the Sicilian school, particularly in his pneumatic pathology, but his work also shows the influence of Hippocratic medicine in hygiene and therapeutics. No mere compiler, he synthesized and improved upon the work of his predecessors. Like the Hippocratics, he realized the importance of prognosis. Some later writers considered Diocles to have been a leading member of the dogmatic sect, which sought "hidden causes" in medicine and supplemented experience with reason and speculation. He lived too early to be labeled a dogmatic, however, and his independent and synthetic approach to medicine would in any event seem to rule out this possibility.

Diocles wrote on a number of medical subjects: dietetics, embryology, anatomy, botany, pharmacology, and gynecology. He also invented a device, called the "spoon of Diocles," for extracting barbed arrows. He influenced subsequent medical writers, beginning with his own pupil, Praxagoras of Cos, who became head of the Hippocratic school, and he is quoted by Galen, Oribasius, Caelius Aurelianus, and Paul of Aegina. Galen praises him as a "physician and rhetorician" and credits him with having arranged Hippocratic medicine in a more logical form. Diocles appears as well to have been, like many of the early Peripatetics, something of a Renaissance man, whose interests extended beyond medicine to botany, meteorology, zoology, and even mineralogy.

Bibliography

Edelstein, Ludwig. *Ancient Medicine: Selected Papers of Ludwig Edelstein.* Edited by Owsei Temkin and C. Lilian Temkin. Translated by C. Lilian Temkin. Baltimore: Johns Hopkins University Press, 1967. This work includes discussions of the dates of Diocles and the importance of dietetics to Greek ideas of health and medicine.

Jaeger, Werner. *Aristotle: Fundamentals of the History of His Development.* 2d ed. Oxford: Oxford University Press, 1948. A detailed argument for dating Diocles in the late fourth and early third centuries and a discussion of Aristotle's influence on Diocles.

————. *Paideia: The Ideals of Greek Culture.* Vol. 3, *The Conflict of Cultural Ideals in the Age of Plato.* Translated by Gilbert Highet. 2d ed. New York: Oxford University Press, 1945; Oxford: Blackwell, 1946. A fine discussion of the Greek ideal of health and the place of Diocles and his views on dietetic medicine in the context of the Greek emphasis on health.

Phillips, E. D. *Aspects of Greek Medicine.* New York: St. Martin's Press, and London: Thames and Hudson: 1973. A summary of Diocles' medical doctrines that includes a list of the titles of his known works.

Sigerist, Henry. *A History of Medicine.* Vol. 2, *Early Greek, Hindu, and Persian Medicine.* New York: Oxford University Press, 1961. A summary of Diocles' views on diet and hygiene against the background of Greek views of hygiene.

von Staden, Heinrich. "Jaeger's 'Skandalon der historischen Vernunft': Diocles, Aristotle, and Theophrastus." In *Illinois Studies in the History of Classical Scholarship.* Vol. 2, *Werner Jaeger Reconsidered.* William M. Calder III, ed. Atlanta, Ga.: Scholars Press, 1992. Von Staden summarizes and critiques the most important book on Diocles, Werner Jaeger's *Diokles von Karystos* (published in German in Berlin in 1938). Jaeger's work had been based on the contention that Diocles was influenced by the thinking of Aristotle and the Peripatetic school. Von Staden looks closely at Jaeger's evidence and finds much of it inadequate and partial. He also agrees with other scholars that Diocles' lifetime should be placed "considerably earlier" than the 340-260 B.C. advocated by Jaeger.

Gary B. Ferngren

DIOCLETIAN

Born: c.245; possibly Salona
Died: December 3, 316; Salona
Area of Achievement: Government
Contribution: Diocletian put an end to the disastrous phase of Roman history known as the Military Anarchy or the Imperial Crisis and laid the foundation for the later Roman Empire known as the Byzantine Empire. His reforms ensured the continuity of the Roman Empire in the East for more than a thousand years.

Early Life

Little is known for certain about Diocletian's early life. He was a native of the Dalmatian coast, and was of very humble birth, and was originally named Diocles. He was either the son of a freedman or a slave by birth who was later set free. His father may have been a scribe. He grew up in the household of the senator Anullinus, and it is unlikely that he received much education beyond the elementary literacy he may have learned from his father. The scanty evidence suggests that he was deeply imbued with religious piety. Later coin portraits give an impression of his appearance: They show a close-cropped beard in the current Illyrian style, a wide forehead, and eyes spaced far apart. He had a wife, Prisca, and a daughter, Valeria, both of whom reputedly were Christians.

During Diocletian's early life, the Roman Empire was in the midst of turmoil. In the early years of the third century, emperors increasingly insecure on their thrones had granted inflationary pay raises to the soldiers. The additional costs could be met only by debasing the silver coinage, which soon became worthless, causing the ruin of the Roman economy. The only meaningful income the soldiers now received was in the form of gold donatives granted by other leaders. This practice served to encourage emperor-making. Beginning in 235, armies throughout the empire began to set up their generals as rival emperors.

The resultant civil wars opened up the empire to invasion in both the north, by the Franks, Alemanni, and Goths, and the east, by the Sassanid Persians. Another reason for the unrest in the army was the great gap between the social background of the common soldiers, who were recruited from the more backward provinces of the empire, such as Illyria, and the officer corps, made up largely of

cultured senators. As of the 250's, however, this situation began to change. Many legionaries made their way to high rank. Beginning in 268, some even were acclaimed emperors themselves. These individuals, the so-called Illyrian or soldier emperors, gradually were able to bring the army back under control, even though their newfound status aroused enmity against them from the senators.

Like many of his countrymen, Diocletian sought his fortune in the army. He showed himself to be a shrewd, able, and ambitious individual. He soon rose to high rank. He is first attested as Duke of Moesia (an area on the banks of the lower Danube River), with responsibility for border defense. He was a prudent and methodical officer, a seeker of victory rather than glory. In 282, the legions of the upper Danube proclaimed the praetorian prefect Carus emperor. Diocletian found favor under the new emperor and was promoted to Count of the Domestics, the commander of the cavalry arm of the imperial bodyguard. In 283 he was granted the honor of a consulate.

In 284, in the midst of a campaign against the Persians, Carus was killed, struck by a bolt of lightning which one writer noted might have been forged in a legionary armory. That left the empire in the hands of his two young sons, Numerian in the east and Carinus in the west. Soon thereafter, Numerian died under mysterious circumstances near Nicomedia, and Diocletian—he had, by this time changed his name from Diocles to Diocletian—was acclaimed emperor in his place. In 285, Carinus was killed in a battle near Belgrade, and Diocletian gained control of the entire empire.

Life's Work

As emperor, Diocletian was faced with many problems. His most immediate concerns were to bring the mutinous and increasingly barbarized Roman armies back under control and to make the frontiers once again secure from invasion. His long-term goals were to restore effective government and economic prosperity to the empire. Diocletian concluded that stern measures were necessary if these problems were to be solved. More than earlier emperors, he believed that it was the responsibility of the imperial government to take whatever steps were necessary, no matter how harsh or unor-

thodox, to bring the empire back under control. Earlier emperors, with typical Roman conservatism, by and large had attempted to apply the methods instituted by the first emperor, Augustus (who reigned from 27 B.C. to A.D. 14), even if they no longer were appropriate for the times. Diocletian believed that contemporary needs required him to abandon the Augustan "Principate" and to strike out on his own.

Diocletian was able to bring the army back under control by making several changes. He subdivided the roughly fifty existing provinces into approximately one hundred. That would put less authority into the hands of each governor. The provinces also were apportioned among twelve "dioceses," each under a "vicar," and later also among four "prefectures," each under a "praetorian prefect." As a result, the imperial bureaucracy became increasingly bloated. He institutionalized the policy of separating civil and military careers, so that provincial governors would not also be the commanders of armies. He divided the army itself into so-called border troops, actually an ineffective citizen militia, and palace troops, the real field army, which often were led by the emperor in person.

Following the precedent of Aurelian (reigned 270 to 275), Diocletian transformed the emperorship into an out-and-out oriental monarchy. The emperor now became a truly august, godlike figure, removed from the rest of society. He wore gold and purple robes and a pearl diadem. Access to him became restricted; he now was addressed not as "princeps" (first citizen) or the soldierly "imperator" (general), but as "dominus noster" (lord and master). Those in audience were required to prostrate themselves on the ground before him.

Diocletian also concluded that the empire was too large and complex to be ruled by only a single emperor. Therefore, in order to provide an imperial presence throughout the empire, he introduced the Tetrarchy, or Rule by Four. In 285, he named his lieutenant Maximianus "caesar," or "junior emperor," and assigned him the western half of the empire. This practice began the process which would culminate with the de facto split of the empire in 395. Both Diocletian and Maximianus adopted divine attributes. Diocletian was identified with Jupiter and Maximianus with Hercules. In 286, Diocletian promoted Maximianus to the rank of augustus, "senior emperor," and in 293 he appointed two new caesars, Constantius (the father of Constantine I), who was given Gaul and Britain in

the west, and Galerius, who was assigned the Balkans in the east.

By instituting his Tetrarchy, Diocletian also hoped to solve another problem. In the Augustan Principate, there had been no constitutional method for choosing new emperors. The result of this, especially in the third century, had been civil wars when different armies named their own generals as the next emperor. According to Diocletian's plan, the successor of each Augustus would be the respective caesar, who then would name a new caesar. Initially, the Tetrarchy operated smoothly and effectively. Even though Diocletian and Maximianus technically were of equal rank, it always was clear that Diocletian really was in charge.

Once the army was under control, Diocletian could turn his attention to other problems. The borders were restored and strengthened. In the early years of his reign, Diocletian and his subordinates were able to defeat foreign enemies such as Alamanni, Sarmatians, Saracens, Franks, and Persians, and to put down rebellions in Britain and Egypt. The eastern frontier was actually expanded.

Another problem was the economy, which was in an especially sorry state. The coinage had become so debased as to be virtually worthless. Diocletian's attempt to reissue good gold and silver coins failed because there simply was not enough gold and silver available to restore confidence in the currency. A Maximum Price Edict issued in 301, intended to curb inflation, served only to drive goods onto the black market. Diocletian finally accepted the ruin of the money economy and revised the tax system so that it was based on payments in kind (the "annona") rather than in the now-worthless money. The annona came to be recalculated in periodic reassessments (indications) every fifteen years. The soldiers, too, came to be paid in kind. Their only salary of value eventually became donatives issued at five-year intervals in gold and silver.

In order to assure the long-term survival of the empire, Diocletian identified certain occupations which he believed would have to be performed. These were known as the "compulsory services." They included such occupations as soldiers, bakers, members of town councils (the "decurions"), and tenant farmers (the "coloni," who evolved into the serfs of the Middle Ages). These functions became hereditary, and those engaging in them were inhibited from changing their careers. The repetitious nature of these laws, however, suggests that they were not widely obeyed. Diocletian also expanded the policy of third century emperors of restricting the entry of senators into high-ranking governmental posts, especially military ones.

Like Augustus and Decius (249-251), Diocletian attempted to use the state religion as a unifying element. Encouraged by the caesar Galerius, Diocletian in 303 issued a series of four increasingly harsh decrees designed to compel the Christians to take part in the imperial cult, the traditional means by which allegiance was pledged to the empire. This began the so-called Great Persecution.

On May 1, 305, wearied by his twenty years in office and determined to implement his method for the imperial succession, Diocletian abdicated. He compelled his co-regent, Maximianus, to do the same. Constantius and Galerius then became the new augusti, and two new caesars were selected, Maximinus (305-313) in the east and Severus (305-307) in the west. Diocletian then retired to his palace at Split on the Yugoslavian coast. In 308 he declined an offer to resume the purple, and the aged former emperor died in 316.

Summary

Diocletian recognized that the empire as it had been established by Augustus simply did not meet the needs of his own time. He therefore instituted many administrative reforms. Not all of them, however, were completely successful. His Tetrarchy, for example, in the choice of new emperors, bypassed obvious dynastic choices. As a result, another round of civil wars swept the empire. Constantine, the son of Constantius, emerged as the victor. Diocletian's retention of the ineffective border troops created a great drain on the treasury, and his abandonment of the money economy meant the ruin of much of the private business in the empire. The Great Persecution ended in failure in 311, and soon after Constantine identified Christianity itself as a more viable unifying factor.

Diocletian's successes, however, greatly outweighed his failures. He was much more skilled as an administrator than as a general, but an administrator was just what the empire needed at that time. The pattern he established was maintained, and expanded, after his death. Emperors continued to claim absolute authority in all matters, and to try to solve problems by legislative decree. Diocletian's reforms brought the empire back from the brink of extinction and laid the foundation for the Byzantine Empire.

Bibliography

Arnheim, M. T. W. *The Senatorial Aristocracy in the Later Roman Empire.* Oxford: Clarendon Press, 1972. A detailed discussion of the evolution of the ruling class of the empire under Diocletian and his successors. Uses the methodology known as "prosopography," or "collective biography."

Barnes, Timothy D. *The New Empire of Diocletian and Constantine.* Cambridge, Mass.: Harvard University Press, 1982. An investigation of the administrative restructuring of the empire which occurred under Diocletian.

Brauer, George C. *The Age of the Soldier Emperors: Imperial Rome, A.D. 244-284.* Park Ridge, N.J.: Noyes Press, 1975. A clear discussion of the Illyrian emperors of the third century, culminating in the reign of Diocletian. Particular use is made of the numismatic evidence.

Brown, Peter. *The World of Late Antiquity: From Marcus Aurelius to Mohammed.* London: Thames and Hudson, and New York: Harcourt, 1971. A very broad and well-illustrated discussion of the social and cultural background of the new age which began in the later part of the third century.

Cameron, Averil. *The Later Roman Empire, A.D. 284-430.* London: Fontana, and Cambridge, Mass.: Harvard University Press, 1993. An up-to-date and excellent history. The author is careful with sources, and she believes that the period was marked more by continuity than by radical change.

Corcoran, Simon J. J. *The Empire of the Tetrarchs: Imperial Pronouncements and Government, A.D. 284-324.* Oxford: Clarendon Press, and New York: Oxford University Press, 1996. A technical study that uses legal records to explore and describe the patterns of interaction among Diocletian and his imperial colleagues in the divided empire.

Jones, Arnold H. M. *The Later Roman Empire, 284-602: A Social, Economic, and Administrative Survey.* Oxford: Blackwell, and Norman: University of Oklahoma Press, 1964. The standard scholarly discussion of the Roman world beginning with the restructuring which occurred during the time of Diocletian. Places Diocletian's reforms in their broader context. Very fully annotated, with many citations from original sources.

Sutherland, C. H. V. "The State of the Imperial Treasury at the Death of Diocletian," in *Journal of Roman Studies* 25 (1935).

———. "Diocletian's Reform of the Coinage," in *Journal of Roman Studies* 45 (1955).

———. "The Denarius and Sestertius in Diocletian's Coinage Reform," in *Journal of Roman Studies* 51 (1961). In this series of articles Sutherland discusses the Roman economy and attempts at economic reform under Diocletian, paying particular attention to the coinage.

Williams, Stephen. *Diocletian and the Roman Recovery*. New York: Methuen, and London: Batsford, 1985. A detailed, chronological biography of Diocletian. Includes an extensive bibliography of other scholarship on Diocletian, as well as some illustrations.

Ralph W. Mathisen

DIOGENES

Born: c. 412 B.C.; Sinope, modern Turkey

Died: c. 323 B.C.; probably Corinth, Greece

Areas of Achievement: Philosophy, religion, and theology

Contribution: The most famous and colorful of the Cynic philosophers, Diogenes lived in extreme poverty and shunned all comforts in his quest for a virtuous life.

Early Life

Diogenes was born in Sinope, an ancient Milesian community on the southern coast of the Black Sea. The colony of Miletus was ruled by Persian kings from 495 B.C. until Alexander's conquest in 331 B.C. Diogenes himself was probably Greek, of Milesian roots. Little is known about his early life, although it is probable that he came from an educated and well-to-do family. His father, Hicesias, was a banker in charge of issuing the city's currency; coins minted between 360 and 320 B.C. and bearing what is presumed to be Hicesias' name have been found in Sinopean archeological digs.

The first known accounts of Diogenes all relate to his exile from Sinope, an event that was somehow related to an episode of tampering with the Sinopean currency. Several versions of the story exist, variously incriminating Diogenes, his father, or both. How they were involved and what exactly they did—whether defacing coins, counterfeiting currency, or altering the stamping process of coins— is not certain; in any case, it was an illegal activity resulting in exile.

This event is linked to another important story in Diogenes' life that is much less probable but that is recounted in various sources. Diogenes supposedly traveled to Delphi or Delos to consult an oracle, a place where visitors in search of guidance or answers to difficult questions came to receive answers or prophecies from people considered to be divinely inspired. The reply to Diogenes' query was "falsify (a word that can also be translated as "counterfeit," "deface," or "alter") the currency." One idea supposes that Diogenes heard this, went back to Sinope, and literally did what he was told. Another suggests that this event occurred after his exile and that Diogenes took the command allegorically. In any event, Diogenes' exile was a key event in his becoming a philosopher and adopting a life of asceticism. It seems that by the time he appeared in Athens, he was already leading an ascetic life.

Life's Work

Diogenes' main goal was to "deface the currency" or to "put false currency out of circulation." The Greek word for "currency" can also be translated to mean "social rules of conduct." In "defacing the currency," then, Diogenes sought to rebel against conventional norms that he felt to be false and contrived and to encourage people to live a life adhering to the rules of nature. Unlike other philosophers, he did not teach a group of students (although he did have students at various times) or engage in intellectual study; rather, he taught by the example of his lifestyle. He believed that virtue produced happiness. Self-sufficiency was the key to virtue, and self-sufficiency was attained by ridding oneself of money, possessions, physical comforts, traditional values, associations, and internal emotions and desires. These were all unnecessary creations of humanity that kept people from being self-sufficient and, therefore, happy; only by breaking these bonds could one return to a natural life. Diogenes thus lived a bare-minimum, instinctive existence, focusing on complete mastery of his only possession, his soul.

Diogenes looked to animals and their ways of life for inspiration; one story, for example, says that Diogenes was converted after watching a mouse darting about, not having any sure place to sleep or any guaranteed source of food or warmth. Diogenes earned the nickname "the Dog" soon after his arrival in Athens, and much of his behavior was doglike in its disregard for social norms. He practiced indifference to criticism and therefore felt free to say or do as he pleased. He slept in an earthenware barrel, had a ragged appearance, and acquired food wherever he could. He relieved himself wherever he felt the need and was known to eat raw meat. He was biting in his criticism and actions toward most other people, finding them loathsome. He also belittled other philosophers, finding fault with them all. He continually sought to change people's values by criticizing them and shouting at them.

Diogenes also carried a great disdain for the state and civic responsibility. Many stories depict him suffering through self-inflicted physical hardships such as rolling in hot sand, walking on snow,

or embracing a bronze statue in the cold of winter. These acts were designed to test the mind and body and achieve mastery over them, for through this training, he believed, virtue could be achieved.

On first glance, it appears that Diogenes had an intense hatred for people; however, he supposedly claimed that it was because of his love of his fellow humans that he sought to change their ways to something he felt was far superior. His standards for a "good man" were extremely high, and probably few could ever hope to meet them.

Though Cynicism is most commonly associated with Diogenes, he was preceded by an earlier Cynic, Antisthenes (c. 444 B.C.-c. 365 B.C.) Antisthenes, who was influenced by Socrates, is considered the founder of Cynicism, while Diogenes brought the essence of classical Cynicism to fruition. Antisthenes taught that traditional intellectual training and discourse did not necessarily produce enlightenment. For enlightenment to occur, one needed to live a virtuous life, and by self-sufficiency of mind, one could become wise. This idea of virtue is central to Cynicism, and the lifestyle traits associated with it all center on the quest for virtue. Antisthenes showed indifference to material possessions, had no particular ties to society, and criticized many of the standards of his day.

Some sources claim that Diogenes was a pupil of Antisthenes, though others argue that this is a chronological impossibility. It is more likely that Diogenes read or heard about Antisthenes' ideas. Diogenes' lifestyle and actions were Antisthenes' carried to extremes; indeed, Diogenes was critical of his predecessor, whose writings drew on various philosophical and metaphysical ideas, who lived a life of simplicity but not abject poverty, and who derived his living from teaching. Diogenes advocated complete asceticism and uncompromising contempt for intellectualism. It is possible that Cynicism derives its name from Diogenes' nickname, "the Dog." *Cynos* is the Greek word for "dog," and the Cynics were in many respects dog-like in their lifestyles and attitudes.

Understanding Diogenes' life is difficult for several reasons. First, none of his writings still exist, only quotes and paraphrases by other writers and philosophers. Whether these writings were actually written by him is another question; opinion varies. Moreover, the legend that grew around the man after his death has probably obscured accurate factual data about him. Diogenes is referenced and described by a plethora of authors, but the information often conflicts. Many of the accounts attribute wise sayings and amazing anecdotes to him, and his eccentric nature perhaps encouraged some authors to exaggerate. It is therefore difficult to separate fact from fiction, but one can assume that the accounts point to the general essence of who Diogenes truly was.

One well-known story involves his walking around in daylight with a lantern looking for true human being—or, as has been added in modern times, "an honest man." In another story, Alexander the Great encounters Diogenes and offers him anything he desires; Diogenes asks Alexander to step aside, as he is blocking the sunshine. Another account claims that Diogenes was captured by pirates and sold as a slave to a Corinthian named Xeniades. Diogenes asked the slave auctioneer to announce his skill as "governing men." When Xeniades bought him, Diogenes told his new master that he would have to obey Diogenes. Diogenes lived in Xeniades' house for several years and taught his sons his ideas. All these stories, whether entirely truthful in their accounts, portray Diogenes as self-sufficient, a slave to no person or land, and an overseer of others.

Despite his ascetic life, Diogenes is portrayed in a small minority of writings as more of a hedonist than an ascetic. This view points to Diogenes living as a professional beggar, denouncing wealth but accepting comforts so long as they were given to him and he was not forced to work for them. It is also clear that some people thought him to be psychopathic. His assuredness that he was always right and everyone else wrong, his extreme indifference to others' opinions, and his disregard for social norms such as work and dress proved him crazy to some, including the philosopher Plato.

Diogenes is believed to have traveled extensively, but Athens and Corinth were his two main residences. He lived to a relatively old age and most likely died in Corinth, where he was living in a gymnasium called the *Craneum*. The cause of death has been variously reported as natural death, suicide by holding his breath, illness brought on by eating raw octopus, fever, and dog bite. Most reports state that the citizens of Corinth buried Diogenes in a tomb marked with an inscription and a marble effigy of a dog.

Summary

Marking a departure from the philosophical and moral standards of the time, Diogenes sought to promote a radical and rebellious return to a "natural" world by the example of his own lifestyle. By clinging to what he felt was virtuous (though it involved hardship and suffering) and condemning what he felt to be pretentious and worthless, he showed his commitment to honesty amid an often-hostile environment. Diogenes became a legend as much after his death as in his own time, and he set the stage for many important Cynics who succeeded him, such as his disciple Crates.

Bibliography

Brehier, Emile. *The History of Philosophy.* Volume 2. Chicago: University of Chicago Press, 1963. A short yet clear and revealing portrait of Diogenes and Cynicism. The volume contains many quotations from primary sources.

Dudley, D. R. *A History of Cynicism from Diogenes to the 6th Century.* London: Methuen, 1937; New York: Gordon, 1974. A detailed history of Cynicism. The chapter on Diogenes cites primary source accounts of his life. Diogenes' disciples are also described.

Gomperz, Theodor. *Greek Thinkers: A History of Ancient Philosophy.* London: J. Murray, and New York: Scribner, 1901-1912. A concise account of Diogenes' life in the perspective of other concurrent events.

Navia, Luis E. *Classical Cynicism: A Critical Study.* Westport, Conn.: Greenwood Press, 1996. A comprehensive study of Cynicism that features a long and exhaustive study of Diogenes. Other chapters compare and contrast Diogenes with predecessors and successors, placing him in a historical and philosophical framework. His life is explored in detail, and every attempt is made to distinguish between fact and supposition.

Sayre, Farrand. *Diogenes of Sinope: A Study of Greek Cynicism.* Baltimore: J. H. Furst, 1938. Contains extensive writing on Diogenes' life and spends one chapter exploring the legends and myths surrounding him.

Michelle C. K. McKowen

DIOPHANTUS

Born: fl. c. A.D. 250; place unknown
Died: Date unknown; place unknown
Area of Achievement: Mathematics
Contribution: Diophantus wrote a treatise on arithmetic which represents the most complete collection of problems dating from Greek times involving solutions of determinate and indeterminate equations. This work was the basis of much medieval Arabic and European Renaissance algebra.

Early Life

Almost nothing is known about Diophantus' life, and there is no mention of him by any of his contemporaries. A reference to the mathematician Hypsicles (active around 170 B.C.) in his tract on polygonal numbers and a mention of him by Theon of Alexandria (fl. A.D. 365-390) give respectively a lower and an upper bound for the period in which Diophantus lived. There is also evidence that points to the middle of the third century A.D. as the flourishing period of Diophantus. Indeed, the Byzantine Michael Psellus (latter part of the eleventh century) asserts in a letter that Anatolius, Bishop of Laodicea around 280, wrote a brief work on the Diophantine art of reckoning. Psellus' remark seems to fit well with the dedication of Diophantus' masterpiece *Arithmētika* (*Arithmetica*) to a certain Dionysius, who might possibly be identified with Saint Dionysius, Bishop of Alexandria after 247. The only dates known about Diophantus' life are obtained as a solution to an arithmetical riddle contained in the *Greek Anthology,* which gives thirty-three for his wedding age, thirty-eight for when he became a father, and eighty-four for the age of his death. The trustworthiness of the riddle is hard to determine. During his life, Diophantus wrote the *Arithmetica,* the *Porismata,* the *Moriastica,* and the tract on polygonal numbers.

Life's Work

Diophantus' main achievement was the *Arithmetica,* a collection of arithmetical problems involving the solution of determinate and indeterminate equations. A determinate equation is an equation with a fixed number of solutions, such as the equation $x^2 - 2x + 1 = 0$, which admits only 1 as a solution. An indeterminate equation usually contains more than one variable, as for example the equation $x + 2y = 8$. The name indeterminate is motivated by the fact that such equations often admit an infinite number of solutions. The degree of an equation is the degree of its highest degree term; a term in several variables has degree equal to the sum of the exponents of its variables. For example, $x^2 + x = 0$ is of degree two, and $x^3 + x^2y^4 + 3 = 0$ is of degree six but of degree three in x and degree four in y.

Although Diophantus presents solutions to arithmetic problems employing methods of varying degrees of generality, his work cannot be fairly described as a systematic exposition of the theory of solution of determinate and indeterminate equations. The *Arithmetica* is in fact merely a collection of problems and lacks any deductive structure whatsoever. Moreover, it is extremely hard to pinpoint exactly which general methods may constitute a key for reading the *Arithmetica*. This observation, however, by no means diminishes Diophantus' achievements. The *Arithmetica* represents the first systematic collection of such problems in Greek mathematics and thus by itself must be considered a major step toward recognizing the unity of the field of mathematics dealing with determinate and indeterminate equations and their solutions, in short, the field of Diophantine problems.

The *Arithmetica* was originally divided into thirteen books. Only six of them were known until 1971, when the discovery of four lost books in Arabic translation greatly increased knowledge of the work. The six books which were known before the recent discovery were transmitted to the West through Greek manuscripts dating from the thirteenth century (these will be referred to as books IG-VIG). The four books in Arabic translation (hence-forth IVA-VIIA) represent a translation from the Greek attributed to Qusta ibn Luqa (fl. mid-ninth century). The Arabic books present themselves as books 4 through 7 of the *Arithmetica*. Since none of the Greek books overlaps with the Arabic books, a reorganization of the Diophantine corpus is necessary.

Scholars agree that the four Arabic books should probably be spliced between IIIG and IVG on grounds of internal coherence: The techniques used to solve the problems in IVA-VIIA presuppose only the knowledge of IG-IIIG, whereas the techniques used in IVG through VIG are radically different and more complicated than those found in IVA-VIIA. There is also compelling external evidence that this is the right order. The organization of problems in al-Karaji's *Fakhri* (c. 1010), an Islamic textbook of algebra heavily dependent on Diophantus, shows that the problems taken from IG-IIIG are immediately followed by problems found in IVA. The most interesting difference between IG-VIG and IVA-VIIA consists in the fact that in the Greek books, after having found the sought solutions (analysis), Diophantus never checks the correctness of the results obtained; in the Arabic books, the analysis is always followed by a computation establishing the correctness of the solution obtained (synthesis).

Before delving into some of the contents of the *Arithmetica,* the reader must remember that in Diophantus' work the term "arithmetic" takes a whole new meaning. The Greek tradition sharply distinguished between arithmetic and logistics. Arithmetic dealt with abstract properties of numbers, whereas logistics meant the computational techniques of reckoning. Diophantus dropped this distinction since he realized that although he was working with numerical examples, the techniques he used were quite general. Diophantus has often been called "the father of algebra," but this is inaccurate: Diophantus merely uses definitional abbreviations and not a system of notation which is completely symbolic. At the outset of the *Arithmetica,* Diophantus gives his notation for powers of the unknown x, called *arithmoi* (and indicated by the symbol σ), and for their reciprocals. (For example, x^2 is denoted by Δ^v and x^3 by K^v.) Diophantus has no signs for addition and multiplication although he has a special sign for minus and a special word for "divided by."

It is impossible to summarize here the rich content of the 290 problems of the *Arithmetica* (189 in the Greek and 101 in the Arabic books), but from the technical point of view a very rough description of the books can be given as follows: IG deals mainly with determinate equations of the first and second degree; IIG and IIIG address many problems which involve determinate and indeterminate equations of degree no higher than two; IVA to VIIA are mainly devoted to consolidating the knowledge acquired in IG-IIIG; and IVG to VIG address problems involving the use of indeterminate equations of degree higher than two.

Throughout the *Arithmetica,* Diophantus admits only positive rational solutions (that is, solutions of the form p/q where p and q are natural numbers). Although negative numbers are used in his work,

he seems to make sense of them only with respect to some positive quantity and not as having a meaning on their own. For example, in VG.2 (where 2 refers to problem 2 of VG), the equation $4 = 4x + 20$ is considered absurd since the only solution is -4.

In IG are found many problems involving pure determinate equations, such as equations in which the unknown is present only in one power. The solution to IG.30, for example, requires solution of the equation $100 - x^2 = 96$, which gives $x = 2$. Note that Diophantus is not interested in the solution $x = -2$. Diophantus gives a general rule for solving pure equations:

> Next, if there results from a problem an equation in which certain terms are equal to terms of the same species, but with different coefficients, it will be necessary to subtract like from like on both sides until one term is found equal to one term. If perchance there be on either side or on both sides any negative terms, it will be necessary to add the negative terms on both sides, until the terms on both sides become positive, and again to subtract like from like until on each side only one term is left.

In other words, Diophantus reduces the equation to the normal form $ax^m = c$. If the result were a mixed quadratic, however, such as $ax^2 + bx + c = 0$, Diophantus might have solved it by using a general method of solution similar to the one commonly learned in high school. As an example, problem VIG.9 can be reduced to finding the solution of $630x^2 - 73x = 6$, for which Diophantus merely states the solution to be $x = 6/35$. Although the possibility that Diophantus might have solved these problems by trial and error is open, internal evidence strongly suggests that he knew more than is relayed in the *Arithmetica.* In fact, the passage immediately following the above quote reads, "we will show you afterwards how, in the case also when two terms are left equal to a single term, such an equation can be solved." The promised solution may be in the lost three books.

Diophantus also solves problems involving equations (or systems of equations) of the form

(a) $a_n x^n + a_{n-1} x^{n-1} + \ldots + a_1 x - a_0 = y^2$
(where n is at most 6)
(b) $a_n x^n + a_{n-1} x^{n-1} + \ldots + a_1 x - a_0 = y^2$
(where n is at most 3)

The methods are seldom general, however, and rely on special cases of the above equations as found in VIG.19, where one finds the system given by the two equations $4x + 2 = y^3$ and $2x + 1 = z^2$. (The reader is reminded that Diophantus always works with numerical cases and so equations in abstract form are not to be found in his work.)

In many problems, Diophantus needs to find solutions which are subject to certain limits imposed by a condition of the problem at hand. He often uses some very interesting techniques to deal with such situations (so-called methods of limits and approximation to limits).

The tract on polygonal numbers has been transmitted in incomplete form. Whereas the *Arithmetica* used methods which could be called algebraic, the treatise on polygonal numbers follows the geometrical method, in which numbers are represented by geometrical objects.

Of the other two works, *Porismata* and *Moriastica,* virtually nothing is known. The *Moriastica* was mentioned by Iamblichus (fourth century A.D.) and seems to have been merely a compendium of rules for computing with fractions similar (or identical) to the one found in IG. The *Porismata* is referred to often by Diophantus himself. In the *Arithmetica,* he often appeals to some results of number theoretic nature and refers to the *Porismata* for their proofs. It is unclear, as in the case of the *Moriastica,* whether the *Porismata* was part of the *Arithmetica* or a different work. There are other number theoretic statements which are used by Diophantus in the *Arithmetica* and which might have been part of the *Porismata.* They concern the expressibility of numbers as sums of two, three, or four squares. For example, Diophantus certainly knew that numbers of the form $4n + 3$ cannot be odd and that numbers of the form $8n + 7$ cannot be written as sums of three squares. It was in commenting on these insights of Diophantus that the distinguished mathematician Pierre de Fermat (1601-1665) gave some of his most famous number theoretic statements.

Summary

Diophantus' *Arithmetica* represents the most extensive treatment of arithmetic problems involving determinate and indeterminate equations from Greek times. It is clear from the sources that Diophantus did not create the field anew but was heavily dependent on the older Greek tradition. Although it is difficult to assess how much he improved on his predecessors' results, his creativeness in solving so many problems by exploiting

new stratagems to supplement the few general techniques at his disposal was impressive.

The *Arithmetica* was instrumental in the development of algebra in the medieval Islamic world and Renaissance Europe. The Arabic writers al-Khazin (c. 940), Abul Wefa (940-998), and al-Karaji (c. 1010), among others, were deeply influenced by Diophantus' work and incorporated many of his problems in their algebra textbooks. The Greek books have come to the West through Byzantium. The Byzantine monk Maximus Planudes (c. 1260-c. 1310) wrote a commentary on the first two Greek books and collected several extant manuscripts of Diophantus which where brought to Italy by Cardinal Bessarion. Apart from a few sporadic quotations, there was no extensive work on the *Arithmetica* until the Italian algebraist Rafael Bombelli ventured into a translation (with Antonio Maria Pazzi), which was never published, and used most of the problems found in IG-VIG in his *Algebra,* published in 1572. François Viète, the famous French algebraist, also made use of several problems from Diophantus in his *Zetetica* (1593). In 1575, the first Latin translation, by Wilhelm Holtzmann (who Grecized his name as Xylander), appeared with a commentary. In 1621, the Greek text was published with a Latin translation by Claude-Gaspar Bachet. This volume became the standard edition until the end of the nineteenth century, when Paul Tannery's edition became available. A new French-Greek edition of the Greek books is planned since the Tannery edition is long outdated.

Bibliography

Bulmer-Thomas, Ivor, ed. *Selections Illustrating the History of Greek Mathematics.* 2 vols. London: Heinemann, and Cambridge, Mass.: Harvard University Press, 1939-1940. Volume 2 of this work contains selections from the *Arithmetica* and the quotations from the *Greek Anthology,* Psellus, and Theon of Alexandria which are relevant for Diophantus' dates. Greek texts with English translation.

Diophantus. *Les Arithmétiques.* Edited by Rushdi Rashid. Vols. 2/3. Paris: Société d'Édition "Les belles lettres," 1984. An edition with French translation of the Arabic books IV to VII with a mathematical commentary and a discussion of the Arabic tradition of Diophantus. (These are part of a projected four-volume series which will include a new edition with translation of the

Greek books.) The same author prepared an edition of the Arabic text in 1975 in Arabic.

Heath, Thomas L. *Diophantos of Alexandria: A Study in the History of Greek Algebra.* 2d ed. Cambridge: Cambridge University Press, 1910. This volume is still the major reference work on Diophantus in English. It gives an extensive treatment of the sources, the works, and the influence of Diophantus. The appendix contains translations and a good sample of problems from IG-VIG of the *Arithmetica* and translations from the tract on polygonal numbers. The second edition also contains a supplement dealing with some of Pierre de Fermat's and Leonhard Euler's work on Diophantine analysis.

———. *A History of Greek Mathematics.* 2 vols. Oxford: Clarendon Press, 1921; New York: Dover Press, 1981. The second volume of this classic study contains a very thorough exposition of Diophantus' work with a rich analysis of types of problems from the *Arithmetica.* It is probably the best secondary source for the reader who wants to know more about Diophantus.

Sesiano, Jacques. *Books IV to VII of Diophantus' Arithmetica: In the Arabic Translation Attributed to Qusta Ibn Luqa.* New York: Springer-Verlag, 1982. A detailed analysis of the Arabic books with a translation and a commentary on the text. The introduction presents a summary of the textual history of arithmetic theory in Greek and Arabic. The English translation and the commentary are followed by an edition of the Arabic text. Other features include an Arabic index, an appendix which gives a conspectus of the problems in the *Arithmetica,* and an extensive bibliography. (The same author offers a brief overview of the contents of the Arabic books in "Diophantus of Alexandria," *Dictionary of Scientific Biography,* volume 15, supplement 1, 1981.)

Vogel, Kurt. "Diophantus of Alexandria." In *Dictionary of Scientific Biography,* vol. 4. New York: Scribner, 1970. A survey of Diophantus' life and works with an extensive selection of types of problems and solutions found in the *Arithmetica.*

Wilbur R. Knorr
Paolo Mancuso

PEDANIUS DIOSCORIDES

Born: c. A.D. 40; Anazarbus, Roman Cilicia (modern Turkey)

Died: c. A.D. 90; place unknown

Area of Achievement: Medicine

Contribution: Through wide travel and much observation, Dioscorides compiled, organized, and published the most comprehensive pharmacological text produced in the ancient world. The work, *De materia medica,* remained a standard reference work for herbalists and physicians for some sixteen hundred years.

Early Life

Pedanius Dioscorides came from the city of Anazarbus, located along the banks of the Pyramus River in Roman Cilicia, in the far southeastern corner of Asia Minor. In his day, Anazarbus considered itself a worthy rival to its more famous neighbor Tarsus for preeminence in this province. Other than for Dioscorides, Anazarbus is most famous for its red stone buildings and for having produced the poet Oppian in the second century A.D.

Dioscorides probably received his early education and medical training in Tarsus, a city famous for its pharmacologists (experts in the preparation, administration, and effects of drugs). Scholars have inferred that Dioscorides was schooled in Tarsus, not only because of Tarsus' reputation but also because Dioscorides dedicated his *De materia medica* (c. 78; *The Greek Herbal of Dioscorides,* 1934, best known as *De materia medica*) to the physician Arius of Tarsus, from whom he seems to have received his medical training. It is also worth noting that Galen, the most famous of all Greek medical writers, referred to Dioscorides as Dioscorides of Tarsus, rather than of Anazarbus, indicating that Dioscorides was closely associated with the medical traditions of Tarsus in the minds of later scholars.

It may also have been in Tarsus that Dioscorides acquired his Roman name, or nomen, Pedanius. Even after the Romans had made the entire Mediterranean area part of their vast empire, it remained common for Greeks to have only one name. Yet it was also common for provincials who were granted Roman citizenship to recognize their Roman patrons by adopting their names. Most likely, Dioscorides took his name from a connection with a member of the gens, or family, of the Pedanii (one of whom, Pedanius Secundus, had served as governor in the neighboring Roman province of Asia in the 50's).

There is some debate over whether—and in what capacity and for what duration—Dioscorides served in the Roman military. It is quite possible that Dioscorides did serve in the military; if he did, it would account for some of his wide travels and would likely have brought him into contact with people from distant parts of the Roman world. Yet his military experience does not account for his genius, and his later work does not greatly reflect the most pressing concerns of a field surgeon: treating wounds. It will suffice to say that his military experience was not an obstacle to his later career.

Life's Work

Virtually all that is known about Dioscorides comes from the single source of his lasting fame, his great book on the medical properties of plants and other natural agents, *De materia medica,* which he wrote in Greek. In this book, a pharmacological text which describes hundreds of plants—as well as animals and minerals—and their properties when employed as drugs, Dioscorides reveals himself to be high-minded and genuinely concerned with the physician's essential task of healing his fellowman. Although Dioscorides may have been associated with the empirical school of medicine, his writing shows no trace of the contentious spirit or rancor so prevalent elsewhere in the ancient medical corpus. He was, almost without question, a physician himself rather than, as has sometimes been suggested, a traveling drug dealer. Selling drugs was a highly lucrative profession during Dioscorides' time and quackery was a serious problem, as pharmacists and so-called root-cutters competed for business with physicians. There were no licensing boards to protect patients from malpractice or fraud in the ancient world, and the motto of the day was *caveat emptor,* "let the buyer beware." Dioscorides, by producing his encyclopedic reference book on pharmacy, did much to alleviate this problem.

Dioscorides' system of classifying plants based on their pharmaceutical properties is an original one. He divided his study into five books, each concerned with a different broad group of medicinal agents. Within these books, he then discussed each plant, animal, or mineral in its own chapter. He methodically lists the plant's name (including common variants or synonyms), presents a drawing of it, gives its habitat and a botanical description, and then discusses its properties as a drug. He not only discusses positive qualities of these drugs but also warns of dangerous side effects. He instructs his readers on how and when to harvest, prepare, and store each plant or compound. He hastens to add in most cases that he has traveled extensively through the eastern Mediterranean and as far afield as India, Arabia, North Africa, Spain, and Gaul to examine these plants personally.

Book 1 of *De materia medica* deals with aromatics, oils, salves, trees, and shrubs. Book 2 covers animals, their parts and products, cereals, pot herbs, and sharp herbs. Book 3 is devoted to roots, juices, herbs, and seeds, while book 4 continues with more roots and herbs. Finally, in book 5, Dioscorides deals with wines and minerals. Throughout his work, Dioscorides stresses the importance of observation. Plants are living organisms, and they have different properties in youth and decay, when flowering and in seed, and they are affected by both the changing weather of the seasons and the local environment. A physician cannot expect plants gathered at different stages of growth and in different seasons to have the same effect on patients. Naturally, he also stresses the importance of observing the action of these medicaments on each and every patient. The body of medical knowledge must constantly be updated.

Dioscorides is notable for two characteristics. One is simply his excellence. Because he was a gifted empirical observer, his work was particularly valuable. Beyond that, he was moving toward a systematic classification of drugs based on their actions. If Dioscorides is compared, for example, to his near contemporary Scribonius Largus, the difference in outlook is immediately evident. Scribonius organized his book of drugs, called the *Compositiones* (c. A.D. 43-50), based on ailments. He begins with compounds useful for headaches and proceeds downward to the patient's feet. Dioscorides, on the other hand, is concerned with what effect a particular drug has. Much as a modern physician's reference book classifies drugs into categories such as analgesics, anesthetics, antibiotics, decongestants, and so on, Dioscorides was concerned with whether a particular drug had a warming effect, was an astringent, was a laxative, and so on. Once its properties were established, its

medical applications could be discussed. Thus, plants are organized not so much by botanical similarity—as many later writers supposed—as by similar pharmacological properties.

Unfortunately, although the usefulness of Dioscorides' *De materia medica* was recognized at once, the potential medical and scientific implications of his attempt at classification were not. By the end of the Roman Empire, his work had been reissued in new editions in which the plants had been arranged alphabetically, undermining the basic principles that Dioscorides had laid out. Thus, while his work continued to receive study, it came to be seen as the culmination of a process rather than the beginning that its author intended. Had this not been the case, the progress of medical science in the next thousand years might well have been drastically different.

Summary

The medical arts in the ancient world had progressed fitfully at best. Despite the genius of individual physicians such as Hippocrates and Galen, the medical profession was often disrupted by internal disputes between rival schools. Pedanius Dioscorides is one of the few writers of his day to rise above such personal concerns and produce a reference work of use to members of all medical schools. His great herbal was a landmark achievement and an instant success.

In terms of his influence, Dioscorides can rightly be placed amid the greatest of ancient medical writers. If he is not to be classed with Hippocrates and Galen, he certainly belongs in the distinguished company of such authorities as Aulus Cornelius Celsus and Pliny the Elder. Until his classification was supplanted by that of Carolus Linnaeus in the eighteenth century, he stood as the foremost authority on pharmacy for more than sixteen hundred years. He was recognized not only by later Roman and Byzantine writers but also by Islamic scholars. Throughout the Middle Ages, his writings were a veritable gold-mine of information for herbalists, who often copied his work—in true medieval fashion—without citing their debt to him. Nevertheless, *De materia medica* was first published as a printed book in 1478, barely twenty years after Johann Gutenberg perfected the use of movable type, and by the sixteenth century, Dioscorides' writings had found a central position in the curriculum of virtually every university in Europe.

If Dioscorides' reputation was tarnished by Linnaeus and subsequent followers of "scientific medicine," it was at least in part because they did not genuinely understand his system. Moreover, it is likely that in years to come Dioscorides will once again be studied and his fame will once again be widespread. In the modern age, many doctors and scientists have become increasingly aware that traditional remedies do in fact possess medicinal properties. The plant kingdom, as Dioscorides well knew in the first century, is a giant pharmacopoeia, waiting to be used for the benefit of humankind.

Bibliography

Allbutt, T. Clifford. *Greek Medicine in Rome.* London: Macmillan, 1921; New York: Blom, 1970. Part of the FitzPatrick Lectures on the History of Medicine delivered at the Royal College of Physicians of London (1909-1910), this volume is a very readable, standard survey of Roman medicine by a pioneer in the field. Particularly valuable for an appreciation of Dioscorides is chapter 17, "Pharmacy and Toxicology."

DeFelice, Stephen. *From Oysters to Insulin: Nature and Medicine at Odds.* Secaucus, N.J.: Citadel Press, 1986. This book by one of the champions of research into natural substances by the pharmaceutical industry, advocates a return to the perspective and lessons of Dioscorides.

Dioscorides, Pedanius. *The Greek Herbal of Dioscorides.* Edited by Robert T. Gunther. Oxford: Oxford University Press, 1934; New York: Hafner, 1959. Based on the translation made by John Goodyer in 1655, this work is the only complete translation of Dioscorides' *De materia medica.* This edition is enhanced by the inclusion of some 396 illustrations taken from a sixth century A.D. Byzantine manuscript.

Hamilton, J.S. "Scribonius Largus on the Medical Profession." *Bulletin of the History of Medicine* 60 (1986): 209-216. This article is a translation of and commentary on the preface to the *Compositiones* of Scribonius Largus, a contemporary of Dioscorides, who addressed many of the same concerns as Dioscorides. He was particularly concerned with the ethical and practical issues relating to the administration of drugs by physicians and with the many internal divisions by which the medical profession of his day was riven.

Riddle, John M. "Dioscorides." In *Catalogus Translationum et Commentariorum: Medieval and Renaissance Latin Translations and Commentaries, Annotated Lists, and Guides,* edited by F. Edward Cranz and Paul Oskar Kristeller, vol. 4. Washington, D.C.: Catholic University Press, 1980. The first dozen pages of this article provide a clear and concise synopsis of Dioscorides' life, career, and influence. The following 130 pages trace his great work, *De materia medica,* through its tortuous history of subsequent editions and commentaries. This is meant for specialist scholars but will provide students of all levels with insight into the remarkable—and tenuous—process by which knowledge of the ancient world has been preserved.

————. *Dioscorides on Pharmacy and Medicine.* Austin: University of Texas Press, 1985. This book not only contains the best analysis of the work of Dioscorides available in English but also evaluates the sources of information available for the life of the distinguished pharmacologist. The book is made even more valuable by its extensive bibliography. Contains a number of instructive diagrams and illustrations.

Sadek, M.M. *The Arabic "Materia medica" of Dioscorides.* Quebec: Éditions du Sphinx, 1983. This book provides a brief illustration of the extent to which Dioscorides' writings had an impact on Arab medicine in the Middle Ages, a period in which Arab physicians equaled or excelled their Western counterparts.

Scarborough, John. *Roman Medicine.* Ithaca, N.Y.: Cornell University Press, and London: Thames and Hudson, 1969. An excellent brief overview of the development and status of the medical profession in the Roman world. The book is extensively illustrated and contains a useful appendix of very brief biographical sketches of Greek and Roman medical writers and practitioners.

Scarborough, John, and Vivian Nutton. "The Preface of Dioscorides' *De materia medica:* Introduction, Translation, Commentary." *Transactions and Studies of the College of Physicians of Philadelphia* 4 (September, 1982): 187-227. This article provides the most accurate English translation of Dioscorides' own preface to *De materia medica,* along with an extensive commentary. The preface is particularly important because, in it, Dioscorides explains his system of classifying plants and drugs and also reveals virtually all that is known of his own life and medical education.

J. S. Hamilton

DRACO

Born: Unknown; perhaps seventh century B.C.; perhaps Athens, Greece

Died: Unknown; perhaps seventh century B.C.; perhaps Athens, Greece

Areas of Achievement: Government and politics; law

Contribution: At the behest of the Athenian Council, Draco produced the first written codification of law for the ancient city-state. His effort is remembered primarily for the harshness of its penalties and for its differentiation between various homicidal acts. Draco was the first to assert that the state should be responsible for the punishment of homicide.

Early Life

Little is known about Draco the individual. He is clearly an example of a man who was made a leader by the context of the historical moment in which he found himself. To that end, it is important to understand what was happening in ancient Greece just prior to Draco's arrival on the historical scene.

Justice has not always been dispensed by judges operating under a written or common law equally applicable to all. In early Athens, justice was not a matter of applying a written standard to any situation or dispute. There were no explicitly written sentencing guides or judicial precedents upon which to call. Rather, the victims themselves were responsible for exacting retribution or compensation for any crime. If the victim was dead, the family was left to take revenge or seek compensation. These blood feuds could last for generations as families sought to avenge a loss, rarely admitting fault and always seeking absolution.

As time wore on, groups of citizens came together to consider en masse how to prevent transgressions or punish criminals from other areas and thus avoid protracted wars based on blood feuds. Popular assemblies were called for this purpose in instances where the action affected the community as a whole. Over the years, leaders within the aristocracy of Athens began issuing the rulings. This system was not without its problems, as these "chiefs" were often the recipients of bribes.

Ten years before Draco would be called upon to serve his fellow Athenians, Cylon, a member of a noble Athenian family, married the daughter of Theagenes. Theagenes was the tyrant of Megara, and his power soon infected his son-in-law. With his help, Cylon attempted to make himself the ruler of Athens. Cylon plotted to seize the Acropolis on the greatest festival day of Zeus, as he had been instructed by the oracle at Delphi. His first effort failed. A second attempt, aided by select young nobles and members of Megarian military, was successful. However, Cylon quickly lost any sympathy he might have mustered when the Athenian people witnessed the taking of the Acropolis by these foreigners.

After being blockaded in the citadel, Cylon escaped with his brother, and the remaining conspirators were forced to seek shelter in the temple of Athena Polias. In exchange for their surrender, these conspirators were promised that their lives would be spared. For whatever reason, Megacles, who was in charge at the time, betrayed the promises and ordered the conspirators killed. In line with beliefs surrounding the act of murder and in the tradition of blood feuds, Athenians deemed this act a great pollution to their city. Those who killed the surrendering conspirators were ordered into exile, and their property was confiscated.

Conditions for the lower economic classes deteriorated over the next ten years as a result of these actions and the ensuing war with Megara. In the context of an increasingly complex society, the people began to call for written laws so that they might be protected from the corruption seeping into the courts. In 621 B.C., Draco (also known historically as "Dracon") was charged with the unenviable task of sorting through traditions and "laws" to produce a written code of law.

Life's Work

Draco, a citizen and lawyer of the city-state of Athens, was thus selected to draft a comprehensive written code of law for the people of Athens. While Draco's work did not change the Greek constitution, this "extraordinary legislator" did bring some semblance of organization to the laws and prescribe punishments for their violation. His written code was built upon the premise that the state should be the primary entity responsible for the prosecution and punishment of crimes.

Draco's code mixed religious, civil, and moral ordinances. His code made no attempt to separate religion from law or morality from law. In fact, Draco emphasized in certain cases the link between human action and the glorification of the

Greek deities. Particularly in the area of homicide, Draco pointed to the defiling nature of murder to the gods and to the Athenian community. Murder was a crime not only against the victim but also against all things of religious significance to the early Greeks. Draco thus introduced the Ephetae, a council of fifty-one judges that was convened to hear cases of bloodshed. Depending upon the charge in question, the court was held in one of three places: Dephinian Apollo, Palladion of Phaleron, and Phreatto, which was reserved for the consideration of manslaughter cases originating outside of Athens.

Draco also gave considerable attention to the relationship between the debtor and the creditor. Again, his sentences against debtors in default were severe. A creditor could go so far as to lay claim to the person of an insolvent debtor. Nevertheless, establishing the expectations of this relationship was of tremendous benefit to the Athenian poor.

A conviction for many of the crimes enumerated in Draco's written code meant death for the accused. It was said by Athenians at the time that Draco's laws were so harsh that they were written not in ink but in blood. So severe were the penalties for crimes ranging from murder to the theft of vegetables that a word based upon Draco's name, "draconian," is still used to denote unreasonably harsh laws or regimes.

Despite the harshness of his code, Draco was apparently admired by his fellow Athenians. In fact, he may have been "loved to death." According to one account, a reception was held to honor Draco; as he entered the facility, the shower of hats and cloaks thrown in appreciation of his work buried him. Draco smothered before he could be rescued from the pile of clothes.

Much of Draco's work was undone by Solon, who succeeded him. Solon did, however, incorporate Draco's laws regarding homicide or murder into his own decisions. In an effort to prevent a return to the blood feuds of the previous decades, Solon left the responsibility for punishing murderers in the hands of the state.

Summary

Although only a few portions of Draco's code are extant, it is recognized for being progressive in one important aspect. Draco, for the first time, defined homicide and introduced definitions of various shades of this crime, ranging from murder with intent to accidental and justifiable homicide.

Many Western concepts of law and order originated with the efforts of Draco and his contemporaries. By establishing regular processes of law and government, the ancient Athenians contributed to the creation of a tradition to which modern governments still look for guidance in the equitable distribution of justice before the law. With the writing of this first comprehensive code of law, civilization took another step forward. Moving away from the arbitrary dispersal of justice, Athens set the stage for the creation of an independent judiciary and a state responsible for the safety and well-being of its citizens.

Bibliography

Bury, J. B. *A History of Greece to the Death of Alexander the Great*. 4th ed. London: Macmillan, and New York: St. Martin's Press, 1975. Useful for understanding the historical context into which Draco's code was introduced.

Carawan, Edwin. *Rhetoric and the Law of Draco*. Oxford: Clarendon Press, and New York: Oxford University Press, 1998. A scholarly examination of the treatment of homicide in Greek legal tradition, with particular reference to Draco's code. Bibliography, index.

Gagarin, Michael. *Drakon and Early Athenian Homicide Law*. New Haven, Conn.: Yale University Press, 1981. Part of the *Yale Classical Monographs* series. Provides a thorough discussion of Draco and his role in the evolution of homicide laws in early Greece. Bibliography, index.

Maine, Sir Henry Sumner. *Ancient Law*. Dorset Press, 1986. Examines the legal traditions of the ancient world, including those of Athens and Draco.

Stroud, Ronald S. *Drakon's Law on Homicide*. Berkeley: University of California Press, 1968. A transcription, with English translation and commentary, of a fifth century B.C. version of Draconian precepts. Taken from the inscription found on an marble stele now in the collection of the Epigraphical Musuem in Athens. Bibliography.

Donna Addkison Simmons

EMPEDOCLES

Born: c. 490 B.C.; Acragas, Sicily
Died: c. 430 B.C.; in the Peloponnese, Greece
Areas of Achievement: Philosophy, science, and natural history
Contribution: Empedocles was one of the earliest of the Greek philosophers to provide a unified theory of the nature of the world and the cosmos.

Early Life

Born c. 490 in Acragas, Empedocles was a member of the aristocracy. Much of his life has become shrouded in legend; fact is more difficult to discover. It is known that he spent some time with Zeno and Parmenides in the city of Elea; some time after that, he studied with the school of Pythagoras. Later, he left the Pythagoreans for reasons that are not completely clear and returned to Acragas.

In Acragas, he became a political figure, eventually participating in a movement to depose a tyrant, despite his aristocratic background. He made enemies, however, and they used their influence, while he was absent from Acragas, to banish him from his home. He would spend much of his life in exile.

Life's Work

Empedocles' two main works, *Peri Physeōs* (fifth century B.C.; *On Nature*) and *Katharmoi* (fifth century B.C.; *Purifications*), exist only in fragments. *On Nature* is an expression of Empedocles as a cosmic philosopher and as one of the earliest natural scientists. An essay on the ability of humans to experience the world, in general *On Nature* describes Empedocles' theory of the cosmology of the world. Parmenides believed that the world can be apprehended through the use of reason; Empedocles, however, believed that neither reason nor the senses can provide a clear picture of reality: Reason is a better instrument for dealing with abstraction, and the physical senses are best suited for the phenomenological world.

Unlike Parmenides, Empedocles assumed that the universe is in motion and that it is composed of a multitude of separate parts, but that their nature is such that the senses can perceive neither the motion nor the great plurality of living and spiritual forms that inhabit the natural world. In his conception, the basic building blocks of true reality lie in the four archaic "roots": earth, air, fire, and water. In the abstract, these four elements are also represented by spiritual beings: Aidoneus is associated with earth, Hera with air, Zeus with fire, and Nestis with water. The elements can neither be added to the natural world nor deleted from it: The universe is a closed system. The elements can be mixed with one another, however, and the mixture of these elements in various proportions constitutes the stuff of the perceived world.

Every physical entity is a composite of the four elements, in varying forms and degrees of mixture. Empedocles' own analogy was that the blending of the elements could be likened to the creation of a painting: A few basic colors on the palette could be blended in such a manner that all the colors of the rainbow could be achieved.

He saw living things as only a matter of appearance: While they live, they have control over their corporeal forms and assume that the forms of life are as they perceive them. At the time of their death, when the bonds that hold together the elements of which they are composed are loosened, they die.

Empedocles believed that two opposing principles, Love and Strife (also variously called Love and Hate, Harmony and Disharmony, Attraction and Repulsion), are engaged in a constant struggle in the universe, a process that gives rise to a continual mixing and shifting of the basic particles of earth, air, fire, and water. The two powers alternate in their dominance in a great cosmic cycle that involves the whole universe. When Love dominates, the particles of matter are brought into a homogeneous mass. When Strife is in the ascendant, the effect is to separate the mixed elements into four separate and discrete masses. These alternating states form the poles of existence; the periods when neither dominated were times of flux during which the power of one gradually increased as the power of the other waned. The human world is one where Strife is in the process of slowly overcoming Love: a place of relative disintegration.

In the beginning of the cycle, the elements are separated, under the control of Strife. As the powers of Love manifest themselves, the integrative process creates from the earth random or unattached portions of animals. These combine in various haphazard ways, creating monsters. A similar integrative process creates unattached human parts: disembodied heads, shoulderless arms, unattached eyes. Through chance wanderings, the parts begin to join, creating human monsters, such as many-

handed creatures with double faces, cattle with human faces, and people with the faces of oxen.

Nevertheless, some join in a manner which allows them to survive. As time and chance do their work, more and more improvements allow certain forms to prosper; eventually, human form, because of its relatively high survival value, becomes established and flourishes. The same process brings about the various orders of beasts.

After a relatively short period, the flux begins again. Strife becomes gradually more powerful, and the cycle is eventually completed. Empedocles may have meant his theory of Love and Strife to apply to human experience as well: These two forces, acting in the world of men, are the causes of the harmony of friendship and the disharmony of hatred.

Empedocles thought that every entity in the universe was endowed with particular consciousness. In addition to being conscious of each other, Love and Strife are aware of their effect on the elements. The elements in turn are conscious of the workings of Love and Strife. Finally, the four elements—fire, air, earth, and water—are aware of one another, both pure and in their various mixtures, and thus humans have consciousness, if only on a lower level, as well. Everything in the world constantly gives off emanations into the atmosphere, consisting of the particles of which they are made. As these particles pass through the air, humans absorb them (through their pores), transmitting them through the body by the blood.

In addition, the four elements and their combinations are aware of themselves; for example, the water in the air is conscious of the water in a human body. A particle that enters the human body is eventually transported to the heart, which is a particularly sensitive organ: It is closely associated with the creation and perception of human thought. The blood is the prime medium for this transfer, because it contains equal proportions of the four elements. The operation of the senses also is based on the awareness of the elements: The particles in the air are perceived differentially by the particles in the sense organs.

After Empedocles had completed *On Nature,* he apparently changed many of his beliefs—probably after he had studied among the Pythagoreans. Especially attractive was the Pythagorean doctrine concerning the transmigration of the soul. Earlier, Empedocles seems to have thought that the human, having been formed from the four elements, died, both body and soul. In *Purifications,* however, Empedocles seems to have adopted the Pythagorean idea that an individual's soul survives physically, going through a series of incarnations. Each soul has to pass through a cycle somewhat like the cosmic cycle of Love and Strife.

Sinfulness, as conceived in Christian thought, was not a factor in the Greek world. Nevertheless, *Purifications* reflects a concept of sin and atonement. The most likely source for such an abstraction would be the Buddhist Middle East, and Empedocles was probably aware of certain Buddhist doctrines.

Empedocles linked his cycle of incarnations with the concept of sin. The soul is initially in a state of sinlessness when it enters the world. In this stage, it is pure mind—a beatific state. As it resides in the world, the soul becomes tainted, especially, by the sin of shedding the blood of humans or animals. The sinful soul is condemned to undergo a series of physical incarnations for thirty thousand years (an indeterminate period of time; Empedocles never defined the length of a season). The soul is incarnated in bodily forms that are in turn derived from air (such as a cloud), water, earth, and fire. Empedocles recounted some of his own incarnations: He was a boy; in another life he was a girl; he was also a bird, a bush, and a fish at various times. Each successive incarnation allows the sincere soul an opportunity to better itself. Declaring that he had progressed to the company of such people as doctors, prophets, and princes, Empedocles hoped to be reborn among the gods.

One interesting facet of Empedocles' greatness is his pioneering work in the field of biology. Implicit in his observations on anatomy is the assumption that he conducted experiments on the bodies of animals and humans. He conjectured that blood circulates throughout the body in a system powered by the heart, that respiration occurs through the pores of the skin, and that some of the organs of the human body are similar in function to the organs of animals. He also observed that the embryo is clearly human in form in the seventh week of pregnancy.

Most interesting of Empedocles' theories is his concept of evolution. In *On Nature,* he assumed that the first creatures were monstrosities, crudely formed; some of these were, by chance, better adapted to survive than others. As the millennia passed, certain mutations (Empedocles did not use the word) made some forms more efficient in basic matters, such as eating and digesting and adapting their anatomy to catch and kill prey. In the passage of time, the successful body forms became nearly perfectly adapted to living in a particular environment.

Despite the great differences in the forms of various animals, Empedocles still saw unity in the whole of life. All organisms adapted safeguards against predation; all reproduced, breathed air, and drank water; and all had a particular consciousness—they rejoiced in the act of living and grieved at physical death.

Empedocles seems to have been many-faceted. According to contemporary accounts, his wardrobe was idiosyncratic, and some of his actions were bizarre. In his own works, and according to other testimony, he claimed to be a god. This claim seems to have gained credence: He boasted that crowds of people followed him, entreating him to use his magical healing powers. He claimed to be able to resurrect the dead as well as to have some control over the weather.

Several versions of Empedocles' death have survived: He hanged himself; he fell and broke his thigh; he fell from a ship and was drowned. From the second century B.C., one version superseded all others: He disappeared in a brilliant light when a voice called his name. The best-known version, however, is that made famous by Matthew Arnold in his poem *Empedocles on Etna* (1852), in which Empedocles jumped into the crater of the volcano, apparently to prove that he was immortal.

Summary

In many ways, Empedocles influenced medieval and Renaissance conceptions of science and anticipated modern theories. For example, despite some criticism, Plato and Aristotle adopted his biological theories; his conception of the four elements, probably derived from the work of Hippocrates, thus had influence until the scientific revolution in the seventeenth century. Finally, his ideas on human and animal evolution foreshadow modern theories, and his conception of a universe in which elements maintained a constant though ever-changing presence presages the law of the conservation of energy.

His accomplishments were honored by his contemporaries, and his memory was revered. Aristotle called him the father of rhetoric, and Galen considered him the founder of the medical arts. According to Lucretius, Empedocles was a master poet, and the extant fragments of his works support this claim. His main contribution was philosophical, however, and his two works were an important influence on early Greek philosophy.

Bibliography

Empedocles. *Empedocles: The Extant Fragments.* Edited by M. R. Wright. New Haven, Conn.: Yale University Press, 1981; London: Bristol, 1995. This modern critical work includes the Greek text of Empedocles' works, a translation, and a closely written and copious set of notes.

Inwood, Brad. *The Poem of Empedocles: A Text and Translation with an Introduction.* Phoenix supplements, vol. 29. Toronto and London: University of Toronto Press, 1992. This volume includes a long introduction that provides an overview of Empedocles' life and thought, followed by texts and translations of all the fragments. Inwood stresses Empedocles' interest in the interplay of love and strife in creation.

Kingsley, P. *Ancient Philosophy, Mystery and Magic: Empedocles and Pythagorean Tradition.* Oxford: Clarendon Press, and New York: Oxford University Press, 1995. A thorough and important re-examination of Empedocles and Pythagoreanism. The author ranges widely over ancient and medieval sources and proposes new interpretations of Empedocles' fragmentary writings. He argues that magic played an important role in Empedocles' Sicilian environment.

Kirk, Geoffrey S., and John E. Raven. *The Presocratic Philosophers.* 2d ed. Cambridge and New York: Cambridge University Press, 1983. Much of the material on pre-Socratic philosophers is subject to interpretation; this book presents both sides of dozens of equivocal topics. It has a useful chapter on Empedocles.

Lambridis, Helle. *Empedocles: A Philosophic Investigation.* University: University of Alabama Press, 1976. This book begins with a preface by Marshall McLuhan, entitled "Empedocles and T.S. Eliot." The book itself serves two useful purposes: It is a good and comprehensive survey, and it is the best analysis of the poetry of Empedocles. Both modern and ancient Greek criteria are brought to bear on the poetry.

O'Brien, D. *Empedocles' Cosmic Cycle.* Cambridge: Cambridge University Press, 1969. The most comprehensive and scholarly discussion of Empedocles' *On Nature.* Contains a useful section of notes, following the text, in which relatively minor but interesting topics are discussed. Its exhaustive annotated bibliography is as valuable in itself as is the text.

Smartenko, Clara E. Millerd. *On the Interpretation of Empedocles*. Chicago: University of Chicago Press, 1908. This important study discusses a number of topics concerning the intellectual background and development of Empedocles' ideas. The discussions are well written and knowledgeable. Though by no means obsolete, the book is somewhat dated.

Richard Badessa

QUINTUS ENNIUS

Born: 239 B.C.; Rudiae, Calabria
Died: c. 169 B.C.; Rome?
Area of Achievement: Literature
Contribution: Known as the father of Latin poetry, Ennius extended the Latin language into areas previously reserved for Greek, offering explanations for Roman origins. He thus paved the way for the Golden Age of Latin poetry and influenced poets as different as Lucretius and Vergil.

Early Life

Not much is known concerning Quintus Ennius' early life aside from the material he included in his own works. Because of the popularity of his writings, it is likely that this information is accurate: His contemporaries could easily have contradicted him, and that would have been, at the least, embarrassing, given the important circles in which Ennius moved after his arrival at Rome. It is clear that Ennius was born in Calabria and that his circumstances were humble. His origins were a point of personal pride which he would conscientiously maintain throughout his life. Even when established at Rome as a teacher and recognized poet, Ennius lived with somewhat awkward simplicity in the wealthy surroundings of the Aventine and employed but a single servant.

Ennius began his career as a soldier rather than as a poet and served with distinction during the Second Punic War. It was, paradoxically, his military talent rather than his skill in writing verse which first brought him to the attention of Cato the Censor, whose surname and hatred for Carthage made him a symbol of stern discipline and morality, even in his own time. It was during these years, while stationed in Sardinia, that Cato, then serving as military quaestor (a post with many of the same duties as quartermaster), tutored Ennius, his centurion, in Greek. Cato introduced Ennius to Scipio Africanus and Fulvius Nobilior; these men would further Ennius' interests after he came to Rome. Ennius subsequently served on Fulvius' staff during the Anatolian campaign, and in 184 B.C. Fulvius' son, with the approval of the Roman people, awarded Ennius a lot among the *triumviri coloniae deducendae.* This award constituted a grant of citizenship, though it brought him no personal wealth. Scipio, too, remained friends with his junior officer, and (at least according to tradition) asked that a bust of Ennius be placed next to his tomb.

Copies of this bust from the tomb of the Scipios may surprise the person who imagines Ennius as an old Roman ascetic. If this bust is, indeed, of Ennius (and some would disagree), he was full-faced, with an aquiline nose, thick lips, and generally provincial features. His hair is close-cropped in the republican mode but with straight locks rather than the "crab-claw," curled ones found in imperial sculpture. He wears the expected laurel wreath, but, again unlike imperial sculpture, the artist has made no attempt to idealize his subject. One should contrast this frank rendering of Ennius with the sensitive, idealized (also suspect) sculptures of his successor Vergil. These are products of Augustan Rome and present Vergil as an idealized poet of an idealized city.

Life's Work

At first, Ennius supported himself in Rome after his military service by teaching, armed with impressive recommendations from Cato, Scipio, and Fulvius; these were essential to attract good students, and Ennius, no doubt, attracted the best. Even so, Ennius must always have had intentions of making his mark in literature, and he wrote from his first arrival in the city.

Circumstances favored his efforts. The dramatist Livius Andronicus died in 204, and his colleague Gnaeus Naevius retired soon after, thus leaving a place to be filled. Ennius began writing dramas, primarily on mythic themes related to the Trojan War: *Achilles, Aiax (Ajax), Andromacha (Andromache), Hectoris lytra (The Ransom of Hector),* and *Hecuba.* He seems also to have chosen mythic subjects which would allow one to draw moral lessons on the folly of excess and pride: *Alexander, Andromeda, Athamas, Erechtheus, Eumenides, Iphigenia, Medea,* and *Thyestes.* Clearly, the Trojan War plays would have been very popular among republican audiences. Rome wistfully traced its uncertain origins to an amalgam of Trojan, Latin, and native Italic stock and consequently saw its history in its myth. Similarly, moralizing was popular in republican Rome; at least, high moral standards were officially privileged. The second group of subjects provided fertile ground for this. Unfortunately, these works (indeed all Ennius' writings) survive only as fragments quoted by subsequent authors. Even order of composition and dates of first performances are uncertain.

What is clear is that Ennius became popular quickly after 204 and that he was versatile. Though he continued to write drama throughout his life, he is best known as an analyst historian, that is, one who chronicled Roman history by using the *Annales Maximi,* official lists of significant events recorded year by year from the traditional date of Rome's founding, 753. His own now-fragmentary *Annales* (*Annals,* 1935) was originally written in eighteen books of verse and spanned Roman history from the legendary period of Aeneas' arrival in Italy to his own day. This work was begun sometime after his success as a playwright and occupied him throughout his middle years until his death.

Its eighteen books were originally circulated in groups of three and almost immediately became a part of the school curriculum. In part, they satisfied a need for material on Rome's past; they also were elegantly written style models and were patriotic in tone. If the content of the lost sections can be judged from extant passages such as the "Dream of Ilia" (the daughter of Aeneas) and the "Auspices of Romulus and Remus," each about ten lines, the *Annals* must have struck a responsive note in the hearts of patriotic Romans. In fact, Ennius' patriotic themes, combined with his sophisticated use of the Latin language, not only made his works subject matter studied by Roman youth but also won for him the title "father of Latin poetry." His simple manner of living, even amid the luxury of the Aventine, served to support the popularly held notion of his personal ethos and integrity.

Widespread early acceptance of his works likely encouraged Ennius to write at least one *praetexta* (a historical drama played in Roman dress), known as *Sabinae,* on the rape of the Sabine women, and perhaps another, the *Ambracia,* in praise of Fulvius, though the authorship of these works is open to question. If Ennius did indeed write *praetextae,* he would then have been trying his hand at a form to that time associated with Andronicus and Naevius. Only a few lines of these *praetextae* remain, not enough to establish his certain authorship.

Ennius' prolific writing, accomplished in his comfortable but simple quarters in Rome, kept him for the most part out of the public arena even as it made him a popular literary figure. He never possessed great wealth, though his old Roman simplicity did not prevent his living well. Personal references in his works note his longtime suffering with gout. Unfortunately for those interested in his private life during these middle years, such mundane asides in his works are rare. It is clear, however, that he was struggling at this time, with varying degrees of success, to fashion Latin epic and dramatic meters which could worthily mirror their Greek antecedents. This struggle to make the Latin tongue literary sums up the contradictory impulses of Ennius himself: distrustful of Greeks and all non-Romans, yet an admirer of Greek literature and art, in this sense a grecophile; an innovator in his use of the Latin language, yet one who consistently portrayed himself as an upholder of Roman tradition.

Despite his incontestable patriotism, Ennius was fond of saying that he "possessed three hearts" (that he could speak three languages—Greek, Latin, and Oscan—and was at home in each culture). He saw no particular difficulty in maintaining both his cosmopolitanism and his staunch Roman loyalties. Indeed, Roman audiences took pleasure in his Latin adaptations of the Greek dramatists, and his *Annals* made him the "Roman Homer."

Recognition and success in drama and historical epic allowed Ennius to devote considerable energy in the last third of his life to his *Saturae* (*Miscellanies,* 1935). This work is a collection of miscellaneous poems in various meters on everything from Pythagorean philosophy (specifically that of Epicharmus) and the Pythagorean mythology of Euhemerus to gastronomy and assorted personal reflections. It is in this work and in Ennius' epigrams that personal content is greatest, though both *Miscellanies* and the epigrams are fragmentary. What personal information survives concerns Ennius' early life.

Summary

One of the best known of Quintus Ennius' epigrams is a panegyric to the Roman military hero Scipio Africanus. Scipio is precisely the kind of personality Ennius would favor, and in a sense he sums up Ennius' ideas of well-lived Roman life. Ennius too made his mark in military affairs, but he made an easy transition to the literary world and used his considerable skills to write sophisticated Latin verse. Though he used Greek models, particularly for his plays, and prided himself on his sophistication, he nevertheless fashioned poetry appropriate to the high morality and ethical standards of the Roman Republic.

Ennius is most associated with Roman history, though *Annals* is actually a historical epic which inspired subsequent Roman poets as diverse as Lucretius (author of the philosophical epic *De Rerum Natura*, c. 69 B.C., *On the Nature of Things*) and Vergil, whose *Aeneid* (c. 29-19 B.C.) often quotes, modifies, and improves upon Ennian verse.

In the second century B.C., the critic Volcacius Sedigitus drew up a list of the ten best poets up to that time. He includes Ennius and supposedly does so only because of his early date. This action indicates that Ennius was not considered the equal of his predecessors in drama. His greatest contribution to Latin literature, recognized in his own times as well, is his historicizing of Roman myth in the *Annals*. The Roman historian Suetonius called Ennius "semi-Graecus," since origins and long residence in southern Italy had culturally made Ennius a Hellenized Roman. In spirit, however, as well as in his verse, Ennius could not have been more Roman, even if he had been born within the walls of the city.

Bibliography

Beare, W. *The Roman Stage: A Short History of Latin Drama in the Time of the Republic*. 3d ed. New York: Barnes and Noble, 1963; London: Methuen, 1964. This is a scholarly history of the development of Roman drama with chapters on playwrights and the various genres of dramatic poetry. It discusses Ennius as successor of Livius Andronicus and Naevius and considers the mechanics of drama production as well.

Duff, J. Wight, and A. M. Duff. *A Literary History of Rome in the Silver Age: From Tiberius to Hadrian*. 3d ed. New York: Barnes and Noble, and London: Benn, 1964. Chapter 3 discusses at some length Livius Andronicus, Naevius, and Ennius, and chapter 5 considers Roman tragedy after Ennius, with emphasis on Pacuvius, Accius, and the *praetextae*. Analysis of the frag-ments appears as well as what is known about the lives of the playwrights.

Ennius, Quintus. *The Tragedies of Ennius*. Edited by H. D. Jocelyn. Cambridge: Cambridge University Press, 1967. Though primarily a Latin text of the fragments, the general reader will find Jocelyn's introduction both to Ennius and to his era interesting and meaningful. Those who cannot read Latin can still use Jocelyn's English commentary against the translation of the fragments in the Loeb edition, noted below.

Goldberg, Sander M. *Epic in Republican Rome*. Oxford and New York: Oxford University Press, 1995. This is one of the few studies in English to treat Ennius and other early Latin poets as real literary artists whose works (though they exist only in fragments) are worthy of attention and appreciation. Goldberg's book contains not only close readings of the poetry, but discussion of the cultural climate of Ennius' day and of the relationship between poetry and politics.

Skutsch, Otto. *Studia Enniana*. London: Athlone Press, 1968. This is a collection, in quite readable English, of previously published articles on all areas of Ennian studies. All were written by Skutsch, and those on the *Annals* are excellent. Included as well are articles on Ennius' *Iphigenia, Medea,* and Ennian tragedy.

Warmington, E. H., trans. *Remains of Old Latin*. Vol. 1. Rev. ed. Cambridge, Mass.: Harvard University Press, 1956; London: Heinemann, 1957. This volume, one of four on the earliest Latin writers, contains all the extant Ennian fragments in its first half with English and Latin texts on facing pages. It is kept in print as part of the Loeb Classical Library, separate volumes with original texts and English translations of all the major Greek and Latin authors.

Robert J. Forman

EPAMINONDAS

Born: c. 410 B.C.; Thebes
Died: 362 B.C.; Mantinea, Greece
Areas of Achievement: Government and warfare
Contribution: The greatest military tactician of the classical Greek period, Epaminondas broke the hegemony of Sparta and made Thebes the most powerful state in Greece.

Early Life

Little is known of Epaminondas' early life. His father, Polymnis, was from a distinguished yet impoverished Theban family, and the relative poverty of his youth may explain the simple life-style for which Epaminondas was later famous. The young man displayed an intellectual bent and formed a close attachment to the Pythagorean philosopher Lysis of Tarentum, who served as his primary tutor. Another close friend was Pelopidas, with whom he would eventually share the leadership of Thebes. While the ancient writers' contrast between the rich, athletic, daring family man—Pelopidas—and the reflective, frugal bachelor—Epaminondas—is no doubt overdrawn, it may reflect something of their characters and relationship. If the story is true that the young Epaminondas saved the life of his wounded friend during battle in 385, then he was probably born about 410.

Epaminondas' city-state, the home of the legendary Cadmus and Oedipus, was the largest of the dozen or so towns in Boeotia, a district in central Greece whose inhabitants shared a distinct dialect and ethnic identity. Because its central location so often made Boeotia the arena for battles between the major Greek city-states, Epaminondas referred to his land as "the dancing floor of Ares." Although in the fifth century Thebes rose to considerable influence as head of a federation of Boeotian towns, the city remained a secondary power behind Athens and Sparta. The Thebans sided with Sparta in the Peloponnesian War (431-404 B.C.), which destroyed the Athenian empire and made Sparta supreme in Greece, but they were quickly disillusioned by Sparta's selfish settlement of the war. As Sparta aggressively exercised its hegemony and extended its area of control, Thebes led Athens and other resentful city-states against Sparta in the Corinthian War (395-386 B.C.). Sparta's superior military capabilities gave it the upper hand in the war, however, and an accommodation with the

Great King of Persia allowed Sparta to force its opponents to accept the "King's Peace" on terms favorable to Sparta.

Thebes was the worst victim of this settlement, which did not recognize the Boeotian confederacy. Thebans, among them the maturing Epaminondas, then had to watch as Sparta dismembered the federation and installed pro-Spartan oligarchies in the newly autonomous towns of Boeotia. The nadir of Theban fortunes came in 382, when a faction headed by Leontiades betrayed the city to a Spartan force. Backed by a Spartan garrison, Leontiades' pro-Spartan oligarchy ruled the city for three years, and many anti-Spartan Thebans, including Pelopidas, went into exile. Perhaps because he was not yet politically active, Epaminondas remained in Thebes without suffering harm.

Life's Work

When Pelopidas returned with other exiles in 379 to liberate the city, Epaminondas made his political debut in a decisive fashion. As the exiles entered the city at night to begin their revolt, Epaminondas came to their aid with a group of armed men whom he had recruited. The next day, he presented the exiles to the Theban assembly and rallied citizens to support the revolution. Following the liberation, the Thebans formed an alliance with Athens and, despite repeated Spartan invasions of Boeotia, gradually reconstituted the Boeotian federation on a democratic basis. By 373, citizens from practically all the Boeotian towns voted at Thebes in a common assembly and annually elected seven Boeotarchs, who had wide powers as the primary administrative, diplomatic, and military officials of the confederacy. Epaminondas' role in these developments is not clear, but it is likely that he honed his military skills in various operations with the federal army. By 371, his reputation was such that he was elected Boeotarch, a position he subsequently would hold almost every year.

As a member of the Boeotian delegation to the peace conference at Sparta in 371, Epaminondas faced a dilemma. If he acquiesced in the Spartan refusal to recognize the Boeotian Confederacy and signed the treaty for Thebes alone, the newly reconstructed federation would crumble and Sparta would again be able to dominate the individual towns of Boeotia. If, on the other hand, he refused to sign except as representing all Boeotia, he

would place Thebes in a precarious position: A Spartan army was already poised on the frontier of Boeotia, and Athens had deserted Thebes in favor of reconciliation with Sparta. Apparently Epaminondas wavered and at first signed the peace treaty for Thebes alone. Before the conference ended, however, he spoke out strongly against Spartan arrogance and infuriated Agesilaus, the Spartan king, by asserting that Thebes would dissolve its confederacy when Agesilaus made independent the many Laconian towns dominated by Sparta. Agesilaus immediately excluded Thebes from the peace agreement, and Epaminondas hastened home to prepare for the impending Spartan attack.

At Leuctra in July, 371, Epaminondas stunned the Greek world when he led a smaller Boeotian force to victory over the heretofore invincible Spartan army. By his innovative use of an unequally weighted battle line in an oblique attack, Epaminondas overwhelmed the strongest part of the enemy formation, and his troops killed four hundred Spartans, among them the junior king Cleombrotus. This victory made Epaminondas famous throughout Greece and encouraged a number of Sparta's southern allies to defect.

While some Boeotians were now content to consolidate the confederacy's position in central Greece, others, including Epaminondas, successfully argued for a more aggressive policy toward Sparta. Consequently, Boeotia joined in alliance with those southern city-states that had defected from the Spartan alliance after Leuctra, and in the winter of 370 Epaminondas took the federal army south to aid these states against Spartan retaliation. This campaign was to be a short one in defense of allies, but, upon discovering the extent of Sparta's weakness, Epaminondas seized the opportunity to strike at Sparta herself.

When his fellow Boeotarchs objected that extending the campaign would be illegal, Epaminondas promised to take full responsibility and led the army in a daring invasion of Sparta's home district of Laconia. Although he did not dare assault the city itself, he secured the defection of many Laconian towns around Sparta and ravaged a rich land that had not seen an invader in centuries. Worst of all for the future of Sparta, Epaminondas liberated Messenia, the rich agricultural district west of Sparta where the bulk of Sparta's huge slave population resided. He then organized the freed Messenians into an autonomous city-state and oversaw the construction of a marvelously fortified capital city. The freeing of Messenia impoverished Sparta and presented it with a hostile new neighbor.

By his victory at Leuctra and the invasion of Laconia Epaminondas had broken Sparta's hold over Greece, and he now undertook to establish the hegemony of Thebes in its place. Some Thebans opposed this effort, but his enormous prestige usually allowed Epaminondas to pursue his goals as he saw fit. When a political rival brought him to trial for his illegal extension of the campaign against Sparta, Epaminondas made no defense and agreed to accept the death penalty—provided his tombstone bear a list of his accomplishments, which he proudly enumerated. Upon hearing this, the judges laughed the case out of court, and Pelopidas soon obtained the banishment of Epaminondas' accuser.

The two friends shared the conduct of Boeotian foreign policy. While Pelopidas secured the northern frontier with his operations in Thessaly, Epaminondas devoted his attentions to the southern alliance. Twice he led invasions designed to force further defections from the Spartan league and strengthen the band of allies that hemmed in Sparta. One notable success of the second invasion was the founding of Megalópolis, a great fortified city in Arcadia that permanently blocked Spartan access to Messenia.

Epaminondas' efforts reached their peak of success in 365, when Sparta's most powerful traditional ally, Corinth, along with several of its neighbors, made peace with Thebes on terms that recognized the autonomy of Messenia. Athens and Sparta refused to accept Theban ascendancy, but the Persian king looked upon Thebes as the preeminent state of Greece and subsidized the construction of a Boeotian fleet with which Epaminondas hoped to disrupt Athens' revived naval league.

Within a year, however, the Theban position began to deteriorate. To be sure, Epaminondas was given warm receptions by three of Athens' most important naval allies when he sailed with the new Boeotian fleet in 364. His expedition failed to defeat the Athenian naval league, however, and the Persians suspended their subsidy of the Boeotian fleet, which never sailed again. Upon returning home, Epaminondas learned that Pelopidas had met his death in battle in Thessaly. He also discovered that in his absence the Thebans had destroyed the Boeotian town of Orchomenus. Provoked by an oligarchic conspiracy and fed by an ancient rivalry, this act of vengeance engendered suspicion and criticism from abroad. Worst of all, Epaminondas had to reckon with serious dissension among his southern allies. Resentful of Theban preeminence, the Arcadians had formed an alliance with Athens and now waged a territorial war that led Elis, the westernmost member of the anti-Spartan alliance, to renew its tie to Sparta. Complicating matters further, Arcadian democrats struggled against the resurgent Arcadian oligarchs of Mantinea, who also reestablished links with Sparta.

To prevent the complete collapse of his anti-Spartan coalition, in June of 362, Epaminondas undertook his fourth invasion of southern Greece. Aware that the combined might of his opponents would be formidable, he sought to confront and destroy them one by one before they could unite. Unfortunately, misinformation led him to abandon the ambush he had set for the Athenians near Corinth, and the treachery of a deserter barely prevented him from taking Sparta unguarded. Consequently, near Mantinea Epaminondas drew up his force for a conflict that would involve contingents from every major Greek city-state. Against the combined forces of Sparta, Athens, Mantinea, and their allies, he employed the same tactics that had brought him victory at Leuctra but on a far grander scale in this battle, which involved nearly fifty thousand men. Catching his enemy off guard, Epaminondas opened the battle with an effective attack of his excellent cavalry and then crushed the Spartan formation with an oblique strike by his massively overbalanced left wing.

Tragically, as his troops stood poised to pursue the broken enemy and complete a brilliant victory, Epaminondas himself fell, mortally wounded. At the news of their leader's fall, the stunned Boeotians immediately abandoned the fight and allowed the beaten enemy to escape. When he was informed of the seriousness of his wound, Epaminondas reportedly advised the Thebans to make a speedy peace. The loss of Epaminondas completely nullified any gains that this well-fought battle brought and marked the end of the Theban ascendancy.

Summary

A brave and resourceful general, Epaminondas was without question the outstanding tactician of the Greek classical period. His masterful use of cavalry and his oblique, unbalanced battle formation won for him two great victories and transformed the Greek art of war. He successfully employed his military skills to break the oppressive hegemony of Sparta and to make Thebes the most powerful state in Greece. The victory at Leuctra, the liberation of Messenia, and the foundation of Megalópolis ensured that Sparta would never again dominate Greece. To his credit, Epaminondas did not imitate the earlier imperial practices of Athens and Sparta: He respected the autonomy of his allies and refused to impose garrisons or levy tribute. Unfortunately, his attempt to rule Greece could not succeed without some institutional means of expressing consensus and resolving disputes among the many autonomous Greek city-states. A formal league headed by Thebes could have been a viable vehicle, but Epaminondas' simple anti-Spartan alliance inevitably required repeated armed interventions of the kind that led to the conflict at Mantinea. If he failed to envision a new political order for Greece, his achievements were nevertheless substantial. They are well expressed in the funeral verses that the Thebans inscribed on his statue:

This came from my counsel:
Sparta has cut the hair of her glory:
Messene takes her children in:
a wreath of the spears of Thebe
has crowned Megalopolis:
      Greece is free.

Bibliography

Adcock, Frank E. *The Greek and Macedonian Art of War.* Berkeley: University of California Press, 1957. This short volume provides the best brief introduction to Greek warfare, with appropriate references to Epaminondas.

Anderson, John K. *Military Theory and Practice in the Age of Xenophon.* Berkeley: University of California Press, 1970. This work provides a thorough analysis of military developments during Epaminondas' time. It includes plates and battle diagrams. See especially chapter 10 on the Battle of Leuctra, with a diagram and discussion of the sources.

Buck, R. J. *A History of Boeotia.* Edmonton: University of Alberta Press. 1979. Although this study stops short of Epaminondas' time, it provides good historical and geographical background material on Boeotia.

Buckler, John. *The Theban Hegemony, 371-362 B.C.* Cambridge, Mass.: Harvard University Press, 1980. This thorough work is the starting point for serious study of Epaminondas' career. It provides excellent analysis of the political and constitutional questions and full treatment of the diplomatic and military developments. Includes an evaluation of the sources for Boeotian history in this period and a full bibliography of modern works.

Bury, J. B., S. A. Cook, and F. E. Adcock, eds. *The Cambridge Ancient History*. Vol. 6, *Macedon, 401-301 B.C.* Cambridge: Cambridge University Press, and New York: Macmillan, 1927. Chapters 2 through 4 of volume 6 provide a detailed treatment of Spartan, Athenian, and Theban developments during Epaminondas' time.

Munn, Mark. "Thebes and Central Greece." In *The Greek World in the Fourth Century: From the Fall of the Athenian Empire to the Successors of Alexander*. Lawrence A. Tritle, ed. London and New York: Routledge, 1997. Munn provides a survey of Theban history and follows the course of Epaminondas' career. Copious references to the ancient sources support the account.

Pausanias. *Guide to Greece*. Translated by Peter Levi. 2 vols. Rev. ed. London: Penguin, 1984. In book 9 this first century traveler preserves valuable details of Epaminondas' life, probably largely derived from Plutarch's lost biography.

Plutarch. "Pelopidas." In *Plutarch's Lives*, translated by Bernadotte Perrin, vol. 5. London and Cambridge, Mass.: Harvard University Press, 1967. This brief (fifty-page) biography describes the friendship of Pelopidas and Epaminondas and provides important details of Epaminondas' early life and his role in the liberation of Thebes, as well as a description of the Battle of Leuctra.

Xenophon. *A History of My Times*. Translated by Rex Warner. London and Baltimore, Md.: Penguin, 1966. In this work, the Athenian soldier-historian provides a contemporary narrative of the entire period of Epaminondas' life, the only such account to survive complete. Xenophon participated in many of the events he describes and provides many revealing details. Unfortunately, he is biased in favor of Sparta and suppresses many of Epaminondas' accomplishments. Note especially the descriptions of the Battles of Leuctra and Mantinea.

James T. Chambers

EPICURUS

Born: 341 B.C.; Greek island of Samos
Died: 270 B.C.; Athens, Greece
Area of Achievement: Philosophy
Contribution: Epicurus founded the Garden School of Greek philosophy, which has had a significant influence on philosophers, statesmen, and literary figures throughout the history of Western culture.

Early Life

Epicurus was born on the Greek island of Samos, about two miles off the coast of Turkey. His father, Neocles, was an immigrant from an old Athenian family who had moved to the distant island for economic reasons and who made his living as an elementary school teacher. Epicurus was forever disadvantaged in the eyes of the men of Athens because of his rustic birth and the low social status of his father's occupation. To make matters worse, his mother was reputedly a fortune-teller. His experiences as her apprentice might well account for Epicurus' later criticism of all kinds of superstitions, and even for his controversial renunciation of the ancient Greek myths and stories.

Epicurus shared a happy family life with his parents and three brothers, Neocles, Chaeredemus, and Aristobulus, who would eventually become his disciples. It is recorded by Diogenes Laertius that he began to study philosophy at the age of fourteen, because he was unsatisfied with his schoolmasters' explanations of the meaning of "chaos" in Hesiod. Others contend that he was drawn to philosophy by the works of Democritus, echoes of which can be seen in Epicurus' later writings.

At eighteen, Epicurus served his two years of compulsory military duty in Athens, at an exciting time when both Xenocrates and Aristotle were lecturing. He clearly familiarized himself with the works of Aristippus, Socrates, and Pyrrhon of Elis. He served in the garrison with the future playwright Menander, with whom he established a close friendship. Many critics believe that they see the impress of Epicurus' ideas on Menander's later plays.

After his military service, Epicurus rejoined his family, who, with other Athenian colonists, had been expelled from Samos by a dictator and had subsequently moved to Colophon. Not much is known of the ten years that Epicurus spent at Colophon, but it might be surmised that he spent much of his time in study and contemplation, perhaps even visiting the intellectual center of Rhodes. At around the age of thirty he moved to Mytilene, on the island of Lesbos, to become a teacher. As he developed his own philosophy, he came into conflict with the numerous followers of Plato and Aristotle on that island, and after only a short stay, he left. He took with him, however, Hermarchus, a man who would become a lifetime friend and perhaps more important, after Epicurus' death, the head of his Athenian school.

Hermarchus and Epicurus moved to Lampsacus on the Hellespont for the fertile years between 310 and 306 B.C. At Lampsacus, Epicurus gathered around him the devoted disciples and the influential patrons who would make it possible for him, at the age of thirty-five, to move to Athens and begin the major stage of his career. They presented to him the house and the garden in the outskirts of Athens which would be both his school and his home for the rest of his life.

Life's Work

Once established in Athens, Epicurus founded his Garden School, whose name came from the practice of the resident members, who in almost monastic fashion provided for their own food by gardening. The many statues, statuettes, and engraved gems which bear the image of Epicurus' long, narrow, intelligent face, with its furrowed brows and full beard, attest the devotion of his followers and the unusually enduring influence of his ideas.

Epicurus organized his Garden School in a strict hierarchical system, at the apex of which stood only himself: The Master. One of the common slogans of the school was: "Do all things as if Epicurus were looking at you." While this motto may sound dictatorial, it represented a benevolent tyranny to which all the disciples and students of Epicurus happily adhered, and it no doubt accounts for the consistently accurate promotion of his philosophical ideas, even after his death. Three men—Metrodorus, Hermarchus, and Plyaenus—reached the rank of associate leaders in the Garden School and were understood to follow in their master's footsteps so closely that they might teach the Epicurean doctrine in its purest form. Beneath them were the many assistant leaders, unfortunately unknown to modern scholars by name, and the numerous students. It is important to mention that among Epicurus' students were women (for example, the distinguished Leontion) and slaves (Epicurus' own slave Mys was one of his favorite students). The accessibility of the Epicurean philosophy, which eschewed most classical learning, ensured a remarkably heterogeneous following.

Despite many later slanders against him, by writers who misconstrued his emphasis on pleasure as a license for sensory excess, the overwhelming evidence supports the idea that Epicurus lived in his Garden School simply and privately, following his own dictate to "live unobtrusively." His health, which was delicate and complicated by a bladder or kidney stone, would certainly not have survived the riotous living ascribed to him by his detractors.

Fortunately, both Epicurus and his closest disciples were prolific writers, and in some ways the home of Epicurus was a kind of publishing house for their works. Still, only a small portion of that original writing is extant, and an even smaller part is translated into English. Of Epicurus' three hundred or more books (it is best to think of them as scrolls), all that remains are some fragments of his central work *De natura* (c. 296 B.C.; *On Nature*), three important letters recorded by Diogenes Laertius in the early third century B.C., and some miscellaneous correspondence, which shows Epicurus' affectionate relationship with his friends. Yet, as Plato had his Socrates, Epicurus had the Roman poet Lucretius, from whose book *De rerum natura* (c. 60 B.C.; *On the Nature of Things*) most of our understanding of Epicurus' ideas comes.

Through Lucretius' works one is introduced to Epicurus' theories on matter and space, the movements and the shapes of atoms, life and the mind, sensation and sex, cosmology and sociology, and meteorology and geology. In addition to Epicurus' atomic theory, which in some interesting respects presages modern physics, the parts of Epicurus' philosophy that still have the power to move people are the simple axioms of behavior around which he organized life at the Garden School.

Rejecting much of traditional education because it did not foster happiness through tranquillity (which was the ultimate goal of life), Epicurus had a more profound respect for common sense than for classical learning. Prudence was an important virtue, and the senses were the ultimate sources of all knowledge. The highest good in life was attaining a secure and lasting pleasure. To Epicurus, pleasure was not unbridled sensuality but freedom from pain, and peace of mind. These two goods could easily be obtained by simple living, curbing one's unnecessary desires, and avoiding the stresses and compromises of a public life. It might even be profitable to avoid love, marriage, and parenting, since they usually bring more pain than pleasure. Friendship, on the other hand, was regarded as one of the highest and most secure forms of pleasure.

Epicurus thought that the great aim of philosophy was to free men of their fears. Epicurus was not an atheist, but he considered the gods to be very remote—living in Epicurean serenity—and not likely to be tampering viciously with the lives of men. For Epicureans, the soul dies with the body and, therefore, not even death was to be feared.

Perhaps the most salient criticisms of Epicurus' ethics of self-reliance and free will are that they are very negative (viewing wisdom as an escape from an active, hazardous, but possibly full life) and very selfish (placing the good of the individual above the needs of society or the state). While these criticisms may be valid, the life of Epicurus showed that there was much everyday merit in his philosophy. He was blessed with many lifelong friendships which became legendary throughout Greece. His enthusiastic followers kept his ideas alive long into the fourth century. Even on his deathbed, he exhibited that almost Eastern detachment and calm which was the major goal of his philosophy. In a letter that he wrote to friends at his last hour, he commented that the extreme pain of his abdomen was considerably relieved by the happy thoughts he had of his talks with them.

Summary

Epicurus' thought outlived most other important Greek philosophical systems, but it too was finally overwhelmed in the fourth century by Christianity, which considered it just another pagan creed. Some critics believe, however, that the writer of Ecclesiastes in the Old Testament was likely a member of the Garden School and that the Epistles of Saint Paul in the New Testament were strongly influenced by Epicurean thought.

Ironically, it was a French priest, Pierre Gassendi, who revived interest in Epicurus in the seventeenth century with his short treatise *De vita et moribus Epicuri libri octo* (1647; eight books on the life and manners of Epicurus). This interest was manifested in English by Walter Charleton and further fueled by Sir William Temple, a renowned seventeenth century English essayist. In the early nineteenth century, the United States had an avowed Epicurean as its president: Thomas Jefferson.

Discoveries of inscriptions and manuscripts in Asia Minor and Herculaneum have kept scholars debating the issues raised in the works of Epicurus up to the present day. Richard W. Hibler, for example, has studied Epicurus, focusing on what he has to teach about pedagogy. There is no question that as long as humans worry about ethics, strive after the good life, or try to make sense of the universe, the voice of Epicurus will continue to be heard.

Bibliography

Durant, Will. *The Life of Greece.* New York: Simon and Schuster, 1939. Contains an excellent chapter, "The Epicurean Escape," which places Epicurus in the context of his times and also evaluates the tenets of his philosophy.

Edwards, Paul. *The Encyclopedia of Philosophy.* 4 vols. New York: Macmillan, 1967. Contains the most lucid short explanation of Epicurus' complex theory and a definitive scholarly bibliography.

Epicurus. *The Epicurus Reader: Selected Writings and Testimonia.* Brad Inwood and L. P. Gerson, eds. Indianapolis: Hackett, 1994. This excellent volume presents in English translation the most important fragments and ancient testimonia about the thought of Epicurus.

Frischer, Bernard. *The Sculpted Word: Epicureanism and Philosophical Recruitment in Ancient Greece.* Berkeley: University of California Press, 1982. A somewhat eccentric work whose premise is that the sculptures and other images of Epicurus, which were so common in the ancient world, were used by the Epicureans as charismatic recruitment devices. The book contains an important set of plates showing many of the images of Epicurus in statues and in print.

Hibler, Richard W. *Happiness Through Tranquillity: The School of Epicurus.* New York: University Press of America, 1984. Hibler's interest in Epicurus is primarily as a great teacher; consequently, he follows his discussion of the philosopher's life and works with a summary of twenty points which are especially relevant to readers who wish to know more about Epicurus' educational methodology.

Hicks, R. D. *Stoic and Epicurean.* New York: Scribner, and London: Longmans, 1910. Hicks compares the Stoics with the Epicureans. He gives an excellent, extended account of Epicurus' theory. This book contains a useful chronological table and is well indexed.

Jones, Howard. *The Epicurean Tradition.* London and New York: Routledge, 1989. A survey of Epicurus' influence in classical Rome, medieval and Renaissance Europe, and 17th century France and England.

Laertius, Diogenes. *Lives of the Philosophers.* Edited by A. Robert Caponigri. Chicago: Henry Regnery Co., 1969. The most valuable parts of this early third century work are the many quoted extracts directly from the writings of Epicurus. Laertius' unusual focus on the ancient philosophers as living men gives an interesting view of Epicurus, who is, surprisingly, treated more extensively in this work than Socrates.

Long, A. A., and D. N. Sedley. *The Hellenistic Philosophers.* 2 vols. Cambridge and New York: Cambridge University Press, 1987-1989. The first volume provides a translation of principal sources and a philosophical commentary. The second contains the Greek and Latin texts and a bibliography.

Lucretius Carus, Titus. *On the Nature of the Universe.* Translated by Ronald Latham. London and Baltimore: Penguin, 1951. This philosophical poem forms the basis of the modern reading of Epicurus. Lucretius, in true Epicurean fashion, avoided the usual occupations of his times—war and politics—to devote himself to an extensive exposition of Epicurus' teachings.

Nussbaum, Martha C. *The Therapy of Desire: Theory and Practice in Hellenistic Ethics.* Martin Classical Lectures, new series vol. 11. Princeton, N.J.: Princeton University Press, 1994. This evaluation of Hellenistic ethics includes chapters on Epicurus and Lucretius.

Rist, J. M. *Epicurus: An Introduction.* Cambridge: Cambridge University Press, 1972. Rist describes his book as an unambitious and elementary account of the philosophy of Epicurus. It is, in fact, a fine introduction to the thought of Epicurus and takes full advantage of the most important developments in Epicurean scholarship.

Cynthia Lee Katona

ERASISTRATUS

Born: c. 325 B.C.; Iulis, Island of Chios
Died: c. 250 B.C.; possibly Mycale or, Ionia, Asia
   Minor, or Alexandria, Egypt
Area of Achievement: Medicine
Contribution: Erasistratus made numerous physiological and anatomical discoveries, perhaps using—like his contemporary Herophilus—an exceptional combination of human and animal dissection (and possibly vivisection) to explore the structure and workings of the human body. By creating illuminating alternatives to Hippocratic and Aristotelian models of physiopathological explanation, he also paved the way for the influential Asclepiades of Bithynia.

Early Life

Already during his childhood on the rocky, forested Aegean island Chios (also known as Keos or Ceos), Erasistratus was no stranger to medicine. His father, Cleombrotus, was a physician, as was his mother's brother Medius (or Medias). His brother, Cleophantus, joined this family tradition as well. Erasistratus apparently left Iulis for apprenticeships, perhaps with the doctor Metrodorus (whom one ancient source identifies as the third husband of Aristotle's daughter Pythias) and Metrodorus' teacher Chrysippus of Cnidus, whom Erasistratus regarded as his main mentor. He may also have attended lectures by Theophrastus, Aristotle's successor as leader of the Peripatetic school of philosophy in Athens, and come under the philosophical influence of Theophrastus' successor, Strato of Lampsacus, but this remains a matter of dispute.

Where Erasistratus subsequently practiced and conducted his research has become a controversial question, but the ancient evidence suggests that he was at the court of the Seleucid rulers in Syrian Antioch (founded on the Orontes River in 300 B.C.) for at least some time in the late 290's. Several ancient sources report that Erasistratus cured a mysteriously ill, suicidal Antiochus (the future King Antiochus I Soter) in Antioch. Through imaginative observation of the patient's face, demeanor, heart, and pulse, it is said, the physician correctly diagnosed that young Antiochus was in love with his stepmother Stratonice. Erasistratus subtly persuaded Antiochus' father, King Seleucus I Nicator, to give up Stratonice in order to save his son; the king promptly arranged the marriage of his wife and son.

Whether Erasistratus also practiced in Alexandria, as many modern historians have assumed, is less certain. No ancient evidence explicitly confirms his presence in Alexandria, but there is suggestive indirect evidence that he may have worked in Alexandria for at least some time during the lifetime of Herophilus.

Life's Work

Erasistratus' ingenuity as a physiologist overshadows his anatomical discoveries, but the two are closely linked. By dissecting animals—and possibly, like his brilliant contemporary Herophilus, by dissecting and vivisecting humans, as one ancient source claims—Erasistratus made major anatomical and physiological discoveries. Among his achievements, two, in particular, won high praise from later authors. First, he described the heart valves (more accurately than did Herophilus), noting the irreversibility of the flow through the valves and detailing the heart's pumping action. Second, his account of the brain includes descriptions of its four ventricles, the convolutions of the cerebrum and the cerebellum (which he linked to humans' superior intelligence), and the origin of the nervous system in the brain (or, as Erasistratus originally believed, in the dura mater, the outermost, toughest of the three membranes covering the brain and the spinal cord).

Three strikingly consistent features of Erasistratus' physiology are his use of mechanical principles rather than Aristotelian innate powers or invisible "faculties" to explain processes in the body, his willingness to verify hypotheses by means of experiments, and a teleological perspective (which he shares with Aristotle and others). In his version of the vascular system, the veins contain only blood, whereas the arteries transport only pneuma, a warm, moist, airlike substance ultimately derived from the atmosphere by respiration. From the lungs the "vein-like artery"—that is, the pulmonary vein—carries pneuma to the left ventricle of the heart, where it is refined into "vital" (life-giving) pneuma before being pumped into the arteries. If, however, the arteries contain only an airlike substance, how does Erasistratus account for the fact that blood flows from a punctured artery? Resorting to one of his favorite mechanical principles, he argues that when the artery is cut its pneuma escapes, creating an empty space into which blood instantly rushes from the adjacent veins (veins being connected to the arteries throughout by means of *synanastomōseis*, or capillarylike communications). The underlying mechanical principle—"following toward what is being emptied," later called *horror vacui*—is that if matter is removed from a contained space, other matter will inevitably enter to take its place, since a natural massed void or vacuum is impossible. It is therefore blood from the veins, not from the artery, that escapes when a lesion of an artery occurs.

Erasistratus' similarly mechanical explanation of the pulse is closer to the truth than his view of the content of the arteries. Whereas Herophilus believed that a "faculty," flowing from the heart to the arterial coats, draws or pulls a mixture of blood and pneuma from the heart into the arteries when they dilate, Erasistratus recognized that the heart functions as a pump: Every time the heart contracts, according to his account, its left ventricle pushes pneuma through a one-way valve into the aorta and the whole arterial network, causing the arteries to dilate. Since the left cardiac ventricle is empty after contraction, pneuma from the lung rushes into it again as it dilates, in accordance with the *horror vacui* principle, and thus the cycle continues, the systole of the heart always being simultaneous with the diastole of the arteries. Once in the arteries, the pneuma cannot return to or through the heart because of the one-way valves. After circulating through the arteries and providing the body with air, the pneuma apparently passes out of the body through the pores, making room for the fresh pneuma constantly being pumped into the arteries.

Erasistratus tried to prove experimentally that it is the heart, functioning as a pump, that causes pulsation, rather than some invisible "pulling" faculty in the arterial coat. After exposing an artery in a living subject, he tied a ligature around the artery. Below the ligature he made a lengthwise incision in the artery, into which he inserted a tube or hollow reed. The incised section of the artery was then ligated, with linen thread wound all around the tube and the surrounding tissue. When the ligature above the tube was undone, Erasistratus claimed, the pulse could be observed below the tube as well as above it, proving that the content of the arteries, pumped in by the heart, causes the pulse. The pulse could not, then, be attributed to a faculty in the incised, ligated, and hence "interrupted" coats of the arteries. (Galen, who reports this experiment, claims that he repeated it with opposite results.)

The central blood-making organ of the body, according to Erasistratus, is not the heart but the liver, where digested food finally is converted into blood. From the liver blood is carried as nourishment for the entire body through the veins. The largest vein in the body, the vena cava, carries blood into the right side of the heart through the tricuspid valve to nourish the heart. From the heart blood flows to the lungs through the pulmonary valve and pulmonary artery, or, as Erasistratus called it, the "arterial vein." The liver, however, cannot in and of itself account for the flow of the blood, since it has no pushing or pulling motion of its own. It is possibly for this reason that Erasistratus described the heart as the *archē* (origin, principle, or rule) not only of the arteries but also of the veins, despite his regarding the liver as the central blood factory. "The heart itself," Galen reports Erasistratus saying, after each contraction "expands like a blacksmith's bellows and draws in matter, filling itself up by its dilation." The *horror vacui* principle thus renders the heart responsible for the movement of blood into and from the heart and consequently, it would seem, for the motion of all blood through the veins, just as it is for the movement of pneuma through all the arteries (although blood is also absorbed into tissues throughout the body, thus creating space for fresh blood in the veins).

The nervous system, muscular activity, respiration, appetite, digestion, and vascular system are all united by Erasistratus in a brilliantly coherent and comprehensive physiological model. External air moves into the lungs through the windpipe and bronchial ducts when the thorax expands. While the air (pneuma) is in the lungs, the left ventricle of the heart draws some pneuma into itself by its own expansion or diastole, contributing to the cycle described above. Excess air, having absorbed some of the superfluous body heat produced by the heart, is then exhaled by the lungs as the thorax contracts, after which the thorax expands once again, drawing in fresh air. The breathing cycle of the lungs thus both cools the body and provides the arteries with the pneuma they need for the body's life and health, whereas appetite and digestion—both of which are similarly explained in terms of the *horror vacui* principle—along with the liver, provide the veins with the food-derived nourishment that the body needs.

The nerves, like the arteries, carry pneuma that is ultimately derived from respiration, but it is a more highly refined version of air. Some of the vital pneuma produced in the left ventricle of the heart is carried by the arterial system to the brain, where it is refined into "psychic" pneuma, which in turn is distributed to the body through the nerves emanating from the brain. Not unlike Herophilus, Erasistratus distinguished between sensory and motor nerves; in his system, it is presumably by means of psychic pneuma that data and impulses are transmitted through the nerves to and from the brain.

Voluntary motion takes place through the muscles, which—like the nerves and perhaps all organic structures in the body—consist of triple-braided strands of veins, arteries, and nerves. Pneuma carried to the muscles by the arteries or nerves endows them with the ability to contract or relax—that is, to increase their width while simultaneously reducing their length, or vice versa, the speed of the muscular motions standing in direct relation to the amount of pneuma in the muscle at a given time.

Erasistratus' efforts in pathology were marked by some innovation as well. He emphasized three related causes of disease which, though not entirely inconsistent with humoral and other earlier theories, introduce some new perspectives. Plethora or hyperemia is a condition marked by excessive blood-nutriment in the veins, which can cause swollen limbs, diseases of the liver and stomach, epilepsy, spleen and kidney ailments, fever, inflammation, blockage of the arteries, and mental disorders (in part because excessive blood in the veins can spill over into the arteries through the *synanastomōseis* between veins and arteries, thus impeding the flow of vital pneuma). Second, disease can result from other disturbances of the arterial flow of pneuma, such as when blood enters a punctured artery (*horror vacui*) and some of it remains trapped in the artery after the wound has healed. Third, digestive dysfunctions cause the presence of sticky, bad moistures in the body that give rise to ailments such as apoplexy and paralysis. In Erasistratus' system, all bodily malfunctions, like all functions, must be understood in terms of the actions and interactions of matter, whose ultimate constituents are solid, possibly atomlike particles.

Numerous diseases, their symptoms, and their causes were described by Erasistratus; his works, which are all lost, addressed subjects such as dropsy, diseases of the abdominal cavity, and fevers.

Summary

In his *Hoi katholou logoi* (general principles) and other lost works, Erasistratus succeeded in accounting for practically all bodily functions within a single explanatory model whose economy, coherence, and scope is unmatched in antiquity except perhaps by Aristotle and Galen. Especially striking is his amalgam of mechanical principles and teleology. The latter is expressed in his Platonic-Aristotelian view of Nature as a supreme artisan, whose providential care for living beings is revealed in the perfection and beautiful purposiveness of every part of the human body. Erasistratus' anatomical discoveries were, however, not as numerous as those of Herophilus, and there are some weak links in his system, such as his reproductive theory.

Bold in his theories, Erasistratus advocated restraint in practice. He assigned higher priority to preventive hygiene, on which he wrote a treatise, than to therapeutics, which, along with the study of symptoms, he regarded as a merely "stochastic," or conjectural, venture (in contrast to etiology and physiology). Proper treatment of patients requires the clear identification of the causes, both proximate and ultimate, of their diseases, as well as an individualized, mild therapy. Opposed to drastic cures, he also rejected the tradition of therapeutic bloodletting in all but a few cases, thereby provoking the notorious ire of Galen, who wrote an entire treatise against Erasistratus' views on bloodletting (and another against the Erasistrateans of Galen's own time, who were defending their Cean patriarch). Instead of bloodletting, Erasistratus advocated drawing off morbid substances through fasting, vomiting, inducing perspiration, urine, plasters, poultices, steam baths, fomentations, fairly conventional dietary prescriptions, and exercise.

For all of their theoretical differences, Erasistratus and Herophilus shared this combination of theoretical audacity and clinical restraint, exceptional scientific originality and pragmatic conservatism. To a greater degree than in the case of Herophilus, Erasistratus' views—as transmitted through fragments and secondhand reports, since none of his works is extant—were met with the polemics of Galen. Yet even a hostile Galen could not refrain from repeatedly acknowledging Erasistratus' significant stature in the history of medicine. Galen also recognized his enemy's scientific honesty: Even in old age, he reports, Erasistratus stood ready to correct his errors in the light of fresh observations. In his search for a better understanding of the human body, the great theorist did not allow the systematic coherence of his theories to stand in the way of his own scientific progress.

Bibliography

Brain, Peter. *Galen on Bloodletting.* Cambridge and New York: Cambridge University Press, 1986. Includes translations of Galen's works against Erasistratus and the Erasistrateans, with extensive annotations.

Fraser, P. M. "The Career of Erasistratus of Ceos." *Istituto Lombardo, Rendiconti* 103 (1969): 518-537. Argues that Antioch on Orontes (Syria), not Alexandria, was the center of Erasistratus' activity, and that he did not perform extensive dissections.

Galen. *On Respiration and the Arteries.* Edited by David J. Furley and J. S. Wilkie. Princeton, N.J.: Princeton University Press, 1984. Pages 26 to 37 offer an excellent introduction to Erasistratus' views on respiration, the heart, and the arteries. The volume also includes an annotated translation of three Galenic works that are important sources for Erasistratus' physiology.

―――. *On the Doctrines of Hippocrates and Plato.* Edited and translated with commentary by Phillip De Lacy. 3 vols. 3d ed. Berlin: Akademie-Verlag, 1984. Excellent translation of, and commentary on, an important source for Erasistratus' views on the brain, nerves, and heart.

―――. *On the Natural Faculties.* Translated by Arthur John Brock. New York: Putnam, and London: Heinemann, 1916. Translation of a polemical but vitally informative introduction to Galenic and Erasistratean physiology. Part of the Loeb Classical Library.

―――. *Three Treatises on the Nature of Science.* Translated by Michael Frede and Richard Walzer. Indianapolis, Ind.: Hackett, 1985. A useful source for aspects of Erasistratus' theory of scientific method and his epistemology.

Harris, C. R. S. *The Heart and the Vascular System in Ancient Greek Medicine.* Oxford: Clarendon Press, 1973. Chapter 4 presents the most extensive analysis available of Erasistratus' description of the vascular system, with some attention to his theories of respiration and the nerves.

Lloyd, G. E. R. "A Note on Erasistratus of Ceos." *Journal of Hellenic Studies* 95 (1975): 172-175. Argues against Fraser (see above) that Erasistratus performed human dissection, was an outstanding anatomist, and worked for at least some time in Alexandria.

Lonie, I. M. "Erasistratus, the Erasistrateans, and Aristotle." *Bulletin of the History of Medicine* 38 (1964): 426-443. A thoughtful analysis of Erasistratus' theory of the vascular system and of the expropriation of Aristotle by later Erasistrateans to justify aspects of Erasistratus' views.

Pope, Maurice. "Shakespeare's Medical Imagination." *Shakespeare Survey* 38 (1985): 175-186. Traces the influence of Erasistratus' physiology on Renaissance poetry.

Smith, W. D. "Erasistratus' Dietetic Medicine." *Bulletin of the History of Medicine* 56 (1982): 398-409. Argues that attention to Erasistratus' own words, in the literal fragments preserved by Galen and others, reveals a less revolutionary, less contentious, and more conventional Erasistratus than the one suggested by Galen's polemics. Shows that his dietetics was a conservative development of an earlier tradition.

von Staden, Heinrich. "Experiment and Experience in Hellenistic Medicine." *Bulletin of the Institute of Classical Studies* 22 (1975): 178-199. Relates the growth and decline of experimentation in Erasistratus' century to changing theories of scientific method; includes a close analysis of some of Erasistratus' experiments.

Heinrich von Staden

ERATOSTHENES OF CYRENE

Born: c. 285 B.C.; Cyrene

Died: c. 205 B.C.; Alexandria

Areas of Achievement: Literature, geography, and mathematics

Contribution: Through his energetic directorship, Eratosthenes helped make the Library of Alexandria the greatest repository of learning in the Mediterranean world, and his varied contributions made him the most versatile scholar and scientist of the third century B.C.

Early Life

Eratosthenes was born in the Greek North African city of Cyrene about 285 B.C. The only surviving ancient biographical reference places his birth in the 126th Olympiad (276-273 B.C.), but this is too late to allow his reported meeting in Athens with Zeno of Citium, founder of Stoicism, who died around 261. His subsequent career suggests, moreover, that he was about forty years of age when he was called to Alexandria in 245; a birth date in the mid-280's therefore seems accurate. Because neither his name nor that of his father, Aglaus, is otherwise mentioned in Cyrenaean records, it seems that Eratosthenes was not of an especially prominent family.

While his family was not illustrious, his mother city had achieved considerable renown. Founded by Greeks from Thera before 600, Cyrene had prospered as an independent city-state. Following the death of Alexander in 323, however, the Hellenistic Age brought a new political order in which large, bureaucratic monarchies dominated and absorbed the formerly autonomous city-states. Cyrene grudgingly accepted incorporation into the neighboring Ptolemaic kingdom of Egypt, which was ruled from Alexandria.

Founded by Alexander the Great in 331, by Eratosthenes' time this harbor city was well on the way to becoming the commercial and cultural center of the Mediterranean world. Thanks to the generous subsidies of the Ptolemies, the city boasted the great Library and its adjunct Museum, a school of advanced studies that attracted scholars in literary and scientific studies, including Callimachus of Cyrene.

The most famous poet of the early third century and compiler of the Library's first catalog, Callimachus was the latest in a long line of Cyrenaean intellectual figures. Eratosthenes thus followed in a well-established tradition of Cyrenaean learning and scholarship when he undertook his early training at home with the renowned grammarian Lysanias. One might have expected him to pursue advanced studies in nearby Alexandria in the company of his countryman Callimachus, but the young man was primarily interested in philosophy, and for philosophy one went to the city of Socrates and Plato. Therefore, at age fifteen, Eratosthenes sailed to Athens, where he would remain for twenty-five years.

Life's Work

Eratosthenes later recalled that in Athens he found more philosophers than had ever been known to exist within the walls of one city. The eager student sampled all of their offerings and came away disappointed. He studied Stoicism with the aged Zeno, founder of the school, but he spent more time with Zeno's revisionist pupil, Ariston of Chios, who became the subject of one of Eratosthenes' earliest works, a biographical sketch entitled *Ariston.* He also witnessed the flamboyant diatribes of Bion of Borysthenes, the son of a former slave and a prostitute, who preached the doctrines of Cynicism on street corners and dockside. Eratosthenes accused Ariston of not living true to his Stoic principles and Bion of adorning his philosophy to attract more attention, much like a tart in gaudy clothes.

Eratosthenes seems to have been more receptive to the Platonism that he learned from Arcesilaus, head of the Academy in this, its "middle" period. His first seriously intellectual work, the *Platōnikos* (*Platonicus*), followed the dialogue format pioneered by Plato and explored traditional Platonic cosmological and mathematical themes. He also wrote another philosophical study entitled *Peri agathōn kai kakōn* (*On Good and Evil Qualities*), which has been lost. Eratosthenes' eclectic approach to his philosophical studies together with his criticisms of established philosophers provoked some later scholars to accuse him of dilettantism.

Less than satisfied with his experiences in philosophy, Eratosthenes fared somewhat better with poetry, the field in which he first achieved a degree of recognition. Although none of his early poetic pieces survives, two poems are known by name. The hexameter *Hermes* (c. 250) recalled the birth and career of that god, while the *Erigone* employed elegiac verse to portray the legendary suicide of an Athenian maiden. Both displayed the highly polished style of Callimachus, and the latter poem was later described as completely faultless. Without a doubt it was his early reputation as a poet, not his work in philosophy, that brought Eratosthenes' name to the attention of the royal patrons in Alexandria, when the poet Apollonius of Rhodes retired from his position as librarian in 245.

Ptolemy III Euergetes must have considered other, equally famous poets for the position, but personal and political factors led him to invite Eratosthenes to Alexandria. While Eratosthenes had pursued his studies in Athens, his homeland had enjoyed a period of independence under the rule of Magas, a renegade Ptolemaic governor who had broken with the government in Alexandria and for several decades styled himself King of Cyrene. In 245, Cyrene had only recently returned to Ptolemaic rule, largely as a result of the conciliatory marriage of Ptolemy III to Berenice, the daughter of Magas. Less than a year on the throne, the young king sought a further gesture of reconciliation to Cyrenaean opinion. Many Cyrenaeans enjoyed Ptolemaic patronage in Alexandria, but none of them, not even the great Callimachus, had been offered the prestigious post of librarian. In addition, the aging Callimachus no doubt lobbied the king on behalf of his countryman Eratosthenes. Consequently, the invitation arrived in Athens, probably in 245, and Eratosthenes sailed for Alexandria to begin the greatest phase of his life.

In assuming the title Director of the Library, Eratosthenes accepted a post of huge prestige, one which brought great responsibilities as well as opportunity. In addition to serving as tutor to the royal children, he admirably fulfilled his primary obligation to maintain and develop the largest repository of learning in the world.

During his tenure, the Library acquired authentic texts of the great tragic dramas of Aeschylus, Sophocles, and Euripides and opened an entire section dedicated solely to the study of Homer. As competition for manuscripts developed with the founding of a rival institution at Pergamum, it may have been at Eratosthenes' behest that the Alexandrian harbor authorities began requiring all ships to surrender their books for inspection and possible duplication.

Despite his archival and tutorial duties, Eratosthenes found time to take advantage of the scholarly opportunities offered by his position—

full access to the immense holdings of the Library and to the circle of resident scholars at the nearby Museum. Because he refused to specialize and instead explored almost every area of learning, his admirers gave him the nickname "Pentathlos," for the all-around athletes of the Olympic pentathlon. His critics preferred to call him "Beta," that is, second-best in many endeavors but never first. That he abandoned his original interest in philosophy in favor of other fields is understandable, for the intrigue-ridden court of an authoritarian monarch was not the place to pursue moral and constitutional questions. Although none of his works survives intact, it is possible to reconstruct the main lines of his achievement.

Eratosthenes' three-volume *Geōgraphika* (*Geographica*) drew upon the work of earlier geographers, but in two ways it represented a more scientific and systematic approach to the subject. He completely rejected the commonly accepted notion that writings such as Homer's *Odyssey* (c. 800 B.C.) contained reliable geographic information. He angered many established geographical authorities when he declared: "You will find the scene of the wanderings of Odysseus when you find the cobbler who sewed up the bag of the winds." Nor was Eratosthenes content merely to describe geographical' phenomena and assign them to the various continents. Instead, by establishing distances and positions in relation to two primary axes intersecting at Rhodes, he created the first reasonably accurate map of the world. Admittedly crude, Eratosthenes' map anticipated the modern system of longitude and latitude, and it was the first to incorporate the knowledge of Eastern regions derived from Alexander the Great's expedition.

Eratosthenes' *Peri tēs avametrēoeōs tēs gēs* (*On the Measurement of the Earth*) presented his most famous geographical achievement—a calculation of Earth's circumference. By means of a novel and elegantly simple application of two of Euclid's geometric propositions, Eratosthenes reasoned that the distance from Alexandria to Syene in Upper Egypt represented one-fiftieth of Earth's circumference. Coupling this figure with the known distance between the two cities, a measurement perhaps obtained at his request by Ptolemy's royal surveyors, Eratosthenes arrived at his figure of 252,000 stades (24,662 miles). Far more accurate than the then generally accepted estimate of 300,000 stades, Eratosthenes' result falls within 1 percent of the best modern measurements.

As he attempted to systematize geography, Eratosthenes also sought to replace the myriad local chronographical schemes with a universal chronology for all Greek history. A preliminary study, the *Olympionikai,* prepared an authoritative list of Olympic victors that could serve as a chronological yardstick. In his *Chronographiai (Chronological Tables),* which covered the period from the Trojan War to the death of Alexander, Eratosthenes placed events from various local and regional traditions in one coherent chronological system based on Olympiads.

In the field of mathematics, Eratosthenes is best known for his "sieve"—a method for discovering prime numbers—and for his solution to the "Delian Problem," the long-standing problem of doubling a cube. For the latter, Eratosthenes composed a proof and designed a mechanical instrument, his "mesolabe," to demonstrate it. In Alexandria he dedicated a monument bearing a model of the instrument, the proof, and his poem in praise of his patron, Ptolemy III. His longest mathematical treatise, *On Means,* of undetermined content, formed part of the Royal Mathematical Collection. Although Eratosthenes' mathematical work did not match his outstanding achievements in geography and chronography, it is worth noting that the greatest mathematician of his day, Archimedes, valued his opinion and corresponded with him on mathematical issues.

The most important of his works on literary subjects was the *Peri archaias kōmōidias (Ancient Comedy),* in at least twelve books, which dealt with the foremost authors of that genre—Aristophanes, Cratinus, Eupolis, and Pherecrates. The few surviving fragments indicate that Eratosthenes was concerned with variations in the dialect and vocabulary of the plays, as well as the history of their revisions and stagings.

A fragment of Eratosthenes' last work, the *Arsinoē (Biography of Arsinoe III),* reveals the aging scholar's sympathy for the wife and sister of Ptolemy IV. Eratosthenes recalls that while walking with him at the palace during the rowdy "Feast of the Beakers," the queen shared with him her disgust over her husband's drunken celebrations. Shortly after the murder of this hapless queen in 205, Eratosthenes, at age eighty, met his own death, reportedly by voluntary starvation after he had gone blind. He was buried at Alexandria within sight of the Library.

Summary

In his career, Eratosthenes perfectly exemplifies the apolitical cosmopolitan culture of the Hellenistic period. Uninterested in the political affairs of his city-state, he abandoned Cyrene for the cultural attractions of Athens, just as he later accepted the patronage of the Ptolemies. His work as librarian helped make Alexandria the outstanding center of learning in the Mediterranean world. Sadly, his remarkable scholarship had limited influence on later generations, and his reputation faltered. This circumstance is explained by his failure to produce students and by the envy that his exceptional versatility engendered. The outstanding geographer and chronographer of his day, Eratosthenes also applied his powerful and independent intellect to important questions of mathematics and to literary studies. A polymath of extraordinary abilities, he definitely was no dilettante. Perhaps Eratosthenes is best recalled by the name that he coined to describe himself—*philologos,* a lover of human reason in all its various forms.

Bibliography

Bulmer-Thomas, Ivor. *Selections Illustrating the History of Greek Mathematics.* 2 vols. Cambridge, Mass.: Harvard University Press, and London: Heinemann, 1939-1940. Includes all the important sources pertaining to Eratosthenes' mathematical achievements, with notes and commentary. See chapter 3 for Eratosthenes' "sieve," chapter 9 for the duplication of the cube, and chapter 18 for the measurement of Earth.

Fraser, P. M. "Eratosthenes of Cyrene." *Proceedings of the British Academy* 56 (1970): 175-207. This fairly technical article attempts to resolve the considerable chronological and source problems associated with Eratosthenes' life. It is the best single work on Eratosthenes' career.

————. *Ptolemaic Alexandria.* 3 vols. Oxford: Clarendon Press, 1972. This monumental work provides a detailed view of Alexandrian society, politics, and intellectual life. It is especially good on the history of the Library and the Museum. Most valuable are its sensible reconstructions based on the fragments of Eratosthenes' lost works.

Freeman, Kathleen. *Greek City-States.* London: Macdonald, and New York: Norton, 1950. Chapter 6 provides a brief history of Eratosthenes' city-state of Cyrene.

Heath, Thomas L. *A Manual of Greek Mathematics*. Oxford: Clarendon Press, 1931; New York: Dover, 1963. This volume places Eratosthenes in the context of the overall development of Greek mathematics, especially chapters 7 and 11.

Lloyd, G. E. R. *Greek Science After Aristotle*. London: Chatto and Windus, and New York: Norton, 1973. Provides an excellent overview of Greek science in Eratosthenes' time but has only a brief reference to him in chapter 4. Includes a diagram of his measurement of the Earth.

Pfeiffer, Rudolf. *History of Classical Scholarship: From the Beginnings to the End of the Hellenistic Age*. Oxford: Clarendon Press, 1968. This standard study of Greek scholarship in the classical and Hellenistic periods has an excellent chapter that briefly discusses the chronological problems associated with Eratosthenes' life and provides a complete catalog of the works attributed to him.

Strabo. *The Geography of Strabo*. Translated by Horace Leonard Jones. 8 vols. London: Heinemann, and New York: Putnam, 1917. The first century historian and geographer Strabo provides important information for the reconstruction of Eratosthenes' early career and his geographical theories in books 1 and 2 of his *Geography*. He must, however, be studied with the understanding that he is hostile to Eratosthenes' rejection of Homer and presents him as a dilettante.

Tarn, W. W., and G. T. Griffith. *Hellenistic Civilisation*. 3d ed. London: Arnold, and New York: World Publishing, 1952. This classic study provides an overview of Eratosthenes' world, most notably in the chapters on Ptolemaic Egypt and Hellenistic intellectual life.

Thomson, James Oliver. *History of Ancient Geography*. Cambridge: Cambridge University Press, 1948; New York: Biblo and Tannen, 1965. This study provides an overview of the evolution of geographical knowledge and theory from early Babylonia to the later Roman period. See chapter 4 for a discussion of Eratosthenes; includes two excellent maps based on his theories.

James T. Chambers

EUCLID

Born: 335 B.C.; probably Greece
Died: 270 B.C.; Alexandria, Egypt
Area of Achievement: Mathematics
Contribution: Euclid took the geometry known in his day and presented it in a logical system. His work, the *Elements*, became the standard textbook on the subject down to modern times.

Early Life

Little is known about Euclid himself, and even the city of his birth is a mystery. Medieval authors often called him Euclid of Megara, but they were confusing him with an earlier philosopher, Eucleides of Megara, who was an associate of Socrates and Plato. It is virtually certain that Euclid came from Greece proper, and probable that he received advanced education in the Academy, the school founded by Plato in Athens. By the time Euclid arrived there, Plato and the first generation of his students had already died, but the Academy was the outstanding mathematical school of the time. The followers of Aristotle in the Lyceum included no great mathematicians. The majority of the geometers who instructed Euclid were adherents of the Academy.

Euclid traveled to Alexandria and was appointed to the faculty of the Museum, the great research institution that was being organized under the patronage of Ptolemy Soter, who ruled Egypt from 323 to 283. Ptolemy, a boyhood friend of Euclid and then lieutenant of Alexander the Great, had seized Egypt soon after the conqueror's death, became the successor of the pharaohs, and managed to make his capital, Alexandria, an intellectual center of the Hellenistic Age that outshone the waning light of Athens. Euclid presumably became the librarian, or head, of the Museum at some point in his life. He had many students, and although their names are not specifically recorded, they carried on the tradition of his approach to mathematics, and his influence can still be identified among those who followed in the closing years of the third century B.C. He was thus a member of the first generation of Alexandrian scholars, along with Demetrius of Phalerum and Strato of Lampsacus.

Two famous remarks are attributed to Euclid by ancient authors. On being asked by Ptolemy if there was any easier way to learn the subject than by struggling through the proofs in the *Stoicheia*

(*Elements*), Euclid replied that there is no "royal road" to geometry. Then when a student asked him if geometry would help him get a job, he ordered his slave to give the student a coin, "since he has to make a profit from what he learns." In spite of this rejoinder, his usual temperament is described as gentle and benign, open, and attentive to his students.

Life's Work

Euclid's reputation rests on his greatest work, the *Elements*, consisting of thirteen books of his own and two spurious books added later by Hypsicles of Alexandria and others. This work is a systematic explication of geometry in which each brief and elegant demonstration rests upon the axioms and postulates given previously. It embraces and systematizes the achievements of earlier mathematicians. Books 1 and 2 discuss the straight line, triangles, and parallelograms; books 3 and 4 examine the circle and the inscription and circumscription of triangles and regular polygons; and books 5 and 6 explain the theory of proportion and areas. Books 7, 8, and 9 introduce the reader to arithmetic and the theory of rational numbers, while book 10 treats the difficult subject of irrational numbers. The remaining three books investigate elementary solid geometry and conclude with the five regular solids (tetrahedron, cube, octahedron, dedecahedron, and icosahedron). It should be noted that the *Elements* discusses several problems which later came to belong to the field of algebra, but Euclid treats them in geometric terms.

The genius of the *Elements* lies in the beauty and compelling logic of its arrangement and presentation, not in its new discoveries. Still, Euclid showed originality in his development of a new proof for the Pythagorean theorem as well as his convincing demonstration of many principles that had been advanced less satisfactorily by others. The postulate that only one parallel to a line can be drawn through any point external to the line is Euclid's own invention. He found this assumption necessary in his system but was unable to develop a formal proof for it. Modern mathematicians have maintained that no such proof is possible, so Euclid may be excused for not providing one.

Other works by Euclid are extant in Greek. *Ta dedomena* (*Data*) is another work of elementary geometry and includes ninety-four propositions.

The *Optika* (*Optics*), by treating rays of light as straight lines, makes its subject a branch of geometry. Spherical geometry is represented by the *Phainomena* (*Phaenomena*), which is an astronomical text based in part on a work of Autolycus of Pitane, a slightly older contemporary. Euclid wrote on music, but the extant *Katatomē kanonos* (known by its Latin title, *Sectio canonis*) is at best a reworking by some later, inferior writer of a genuine text by Euclid, containing no more of his actual words than some excerpts. Discovered in Arabic translation was *Peri diaireseon* (*On Division*), for which the proofs of only four of the propositions survive.

Also discovered have been the names of several lost books by Euclid on advanced geometry: The *Pseudaria* exposed fallacies in geometrical reasoning, and *Kōnika* (*Conics*) laid some of the groundwork for the later book of the same title by Apollonius of Perga. There was a discussion of the relationships of points on surfaces entitled *Topoi pros epiphaneia* (*Surface-Loci*), and *Porismata* (*Porisms*), a work of higher geometry, treated a kind of proposition intermediate between a theorem and a problem.

In addition to the last two books of the *Elements*, there are works bearing Euclid's name that are not genuinely his. These include the *Katoptrica* (*Catoptrica*), a later work on optics, and *Eisagōgē armonikē* (*Introduction to Harmony*), which is actually by Cleonides, a student of Aristoxenus. None of Euclid's reputation, however, depends on these writings falsely attributed to him.

Summary

Euclid left as his legacy the standard textbook in geometry. There is no other ancient work of science which needs so little revision to make it current, although many modern mathematicians, beginning with Nikolay Lobachevski and Bernhard Riemann and including Albert Einstein, have developed non-Euclidean systems in reaction to the *Elements*, thus doing it a kind of honor. The influence of Euclid on later scientists such as Archimedes, Apollonius of Perga, Galileo Galilei, Sir Isaac Newton, and Christiaan Huygens was immense. Eratosthenes used his theorems to measure with surprising accuracy the size of the sphere of the Earth, and Aristarchus attempted less successfully, but in fine Euclidean style, to establish the size and distances of the moon and the sun.

Other Hellenistic mathematicians, such as Hero, Pappus, Simplicius, and most important, Proclus, produced commentaries on the *Elements*. Theon of Alexandria, father of the famous woman philosopher and mathematician Hypatia, introduced a new edition of the *Elements* in the fourth century A.D. The sixth century Italian Boethius is said to have translated the *Elements* into Latin, but that version is not extant. Many translations were made by early medieval Arabic scholars, beginning with one made for Harun al-Rashid near A.D. 800 by al-Hajjaj ibn Yusuf ibn Matar. Athelhard of Bath made the first surviving Latin translation from an Arabic text about A.D. 1120. The first printed version, a Latin translation by the thirteenth century scholar Johannes Campanus, appeared in 1482 in Venice. Bartolomeo Zamberti was the first to translate the *Elements* into Latin directly from the Greek, rather than Arabic, in 1505. The first English translation, printed in 1570, was done by Sir Henry Billingsley, later the Lord Mayor of London. The total number of editions of Euclid's *Elements* has been estimated to be more than a thousand, making it one of the most often translated and printed books in history and certainly the most successful textbook ever written.

Bibliography

DeLacy, Estelle Allen. *Euclid and Geometry.* New York: Franklin Watts, 1963. A good introduction for the general reader.

Euclid. *The Thirteen Books of Euclid's "Elements."* Translated by Thomas Little Heath. 3 vols. 2d ed. Cambridge: Cambridge University Press, 1926; New York: Dover, 1956. Translated from the text of Heiberg, with introduction and commentary. This work is the definitive English translation, with extensive commentary, of Euclid's *Elements.* This admirable work supersedes all previous translations and has not been outdated. It contains a full introduction, 151 pages in length, touching on all the major problems.

Fraser, P. M. *Ptolemaic Alexandria.* 3 vols. Oxford: Clarendon Press, 1972. Has a useful section on the intellectual background and influences of Euclid but is primarily valuable in providing a study of the cultural setting of Alexandria in Euclid's day.

Heath, Thomas Little. *A History of Greek Mathematics.* Vol. 1, *From Thales to Euclid.* Oxford: Clarendon Press, 1921; New York: Dover, 1981. Places Euclid in the context of the development of ancient mathematics and is a thoroughly dependable treatment.

Knorr, W. R. *The Evolution of the Euclidean Elements: A Study of the Theory of Incommensurable Magnitudes and Its Significance for Early Greek Geometry.* Boston: D. Reidel Publishing Co., 1975. An important, very professional and technical treatment.

Mueller, Ian. *Philosophy of Mathematics and Deductive Structure in Euclid's "Elements."* Cambridge, Mass.: MIT Press, 1981. A study of the Greek concepts of mathematics found in the *Elements,* emphasizing philosophical, foundational, and logical rather than historical questions, although the latter are not totally neglected. Attention is directed to Euclid's work, not that of his predecessors. This monograph requires mathematical literacy and the general reader may find it overly technical.

Reid, Constance. *A Long Way from Euclid.* New York: Crowell, 1963; London: Routledge, 1965. An explanation of how modern mathematical thought has progressed beyond Euclid, written for those whose introduction to mathematics consisted mainly of studying the *Elements.* Accessible to the general reader, this study takes Euclid as its starting point and shows that he did not provide the reader with all the answers, or even all the questions, with which mathematicians concern themselves.

Szabo, Arpad. *The Beginnings of Greek Mathematics.* Translated by A. M. Ungar. Boston: D. Reidel Publishing Co., 1978. Places Euclid within the context of the development of the Greek mathematical tradition.

J. Donald Hughes

EUDOXUS OF CNIDUS

Born: c. 390 B.C.; Cnidus

Died: c. 337 B.C.; Cnidus

Areas of Achievement: Mathematics and astronomy

Contribution: Eudoxus and his disciples resolved classical difficulties in the fields of geometry and geometric astronomy. Their approach became definitive for later research in these fields.

Early Life

As for so many ancient figures, little is known about the life of Eudoxus of Cnidus. If one follows the account of the ancient biographer Diogenes Laertius (c. A.D. 250), Eudoxus first visited Athens at age twenty-three to study medicine and philosophy. He soon returned home, however, and from there, joining the company of the Cnidian physician Chrysippus, he moved on to Egypt, where for more than a year he studied among the priests and engaged in astronomical investigations. Later, as he traveled and lectured in the wider Aegean area (specifically, Cyzicus and the Propontis), he built up a following and thus returned to Athens a man of considerable distinction. His main subsequent activity seems to have centered on Cnidus, where he was honored as a lawgiver. His renown extended to many areas, including astronomy, geometry, medicine, geography, and philosophy.

There is disagreement over his dates. The ancient chronologist Apollodorus sets Eudoxus' prime activity in 368-365 B.C. In general, the prime means age forty; if that holds here, Eudoxus' birth would be set circa 408. There is reason for doubt, however, since this early a date conflicts with other biographical data. G. L. Huxley favors circa 400; G. de Santillana and others argue for circa 390. Since Eudoxus is reported to have died at the age of fifty-three, the corresponding date would be 355, 347, or 337.

Life's Work

None of Eudoxus' writings survives, but fragments cited by ancient authors offer a reasonable impression of their diversity and significance. His principal efforts were in the areas of mathematics and astronomy, the former best represented in portions of *Stoicheia* (c. fourth century B.C.; *Elements*) of Euclid, the latter in astronomical discussions of the fourth-century cosmology of Aristotle and the ancient commentaries on it.

According to Archimedes (287-212 B.C.), Eudoxus was the first to set out a rigorous proof of the theorems that any pyramid equals one-third of the associated prism (that is, having the same height and base as the pyramid), and that any cone equals one-third of the associated cylinder. Eudoxus also appears to have proved two other theorems, that circles are as the squares of their diameters, and that spheres are as the cubes of their diameters. The proofs of these four theorems constitute the main part of book 17 of *Elements* and the technique used there is likely to derive from Eudoxus.

To take the circle theorem as an example, one could imagine a regular polygon having so many sides that it seems practically indistinguishable from a circle. Since two such polygons (with equally numerous sides) are proportional to the squares of their diameters, the same could be supposed for the corresponding circles. Presumably, an argument of this sort was assumed by geometers who used the circle theorem in the time before Eudoxus. In the strict sense, however, the reasoning would be invalid, for only by an infinite process can rectilinear figures eventuate in the circle.

In the Eudoxean scheme, one assumes the stated proportion to be false: If two circles are not in the ratio of the squares of their diameters, then one can construct two similar regular polygons, one inscribed in each circle, and one can make the difference between the polygon and its circle so small that the polygon is found to be simultaneously greater and less than a specified amount. Since that is clearly impossible, the stated theorem must be true. (This indirect manner for proving theorems on curved figures is often called, if somewhat misleadingly, the "method of exhaustion.")

A key move in this proof is making the polygon sufficiently close to the circle. To this end, one observes that as the number of sides is doubled, the difference between the polygon and the circle is reduced by more than half. The procedure of successively bisecting a given quantity will eventually make it less than any preassigned amount, however, as Euclid proves in *Elements*. According to Archimedes, however, it seems that Eudoxus took this bisection principle as an axiom.

The notion of proportion itself runs into a similar difficulty with the infinite. As long as quantities are related to one another in terms of whole or fractional numbers (for example, if one area is $7/5$ of another area), their ratios can be specified from these same numbers (that is, the ratio of the one area to the other will be 7 to 5). Yet what if no such numbers exist? For example, it was found, a century or so before Eudoxus, that the diagonal and side of a square cannot equal a ratio of whole numbers. (In modern terms, one calls the associated number $\sqrt{2}$ "irrational"; its decimal equivalent 1.414 . . . will be nonterminating and nonrepeating.) Only by means of some form of infinite sequence can "commensurable" quantities (those whose ratio is expressible by two integers) equal the ratio of incommensurable ones. Geometers in the generation before Eudoxus had pursued the study of incommensurables with considerable interest, but Eudoxus was the first to see how the theorems on ratios could be rigorously proved when their terms were incommensurable.

It is usually supposed that Eudoxus' approach was identical to that given by Euclid in book 5 of *Elements.* Other writers, in particular Archimedes, however, knew of a different technique of proportions that seems more like what Eudoxus would have proposed. By this technique, one first establishes the stated theorem for the case of commensurable quantities. For the incommensurable case, one uses an indirect argument: If the proportionality does not hold, one can find commensurable terms whose ratio differs by less than a specified amount from the ratio of the given incommensurable terms—this is done by successively bisecting one of the givens until it is less than the difference between two others; when the commensurable case of the theorem (already proved) is applied, a certain term will be found to be simultaneously greater and less than another. Since that is impossible, the theorem must be true.

The defining notions of the proportion theory in Euclid's book 5 can be derived as a simple modification of this technique, for the role that the intermediate commensurable terms play in it is assumed by the Euclidean definition of proportion: that A:B = C:D means that for all integers m, n, if $mA > nB$, then also $mC > nD$; the same holds true if = or < are substituted for >. Proofs in this Euclidean manner do not require a division into commensurable and incommensurable cases, nor do they make use of the bisection principle; in general, they are rather easier to set up than in the alternative technique. It is thus possible to see Euclid's approach as an intended refinement of the Eudoxean.

In either the Eudoxean or Euclidean form, this manner of proportion theory can be made to correspond to the modern definition of real number, as formulated by the German mathematician Julius Wilhelm Richard Dedekind. In each example, the real term (possibly irrational) is considered to separate all the rationals into those greater and those less than it.

It seems likely that Eudoxus also contributed to the study of incommensurable lines. His predecessor Theaetetus (died c. 369) had shown that if the squares of two lines are commensurable with each other but do not have the ratio of square integers, then the lines themselves will be incommensurable with each other; further, if two such lines A, B are taken, the lines A ± B will be incommensurable with them, not only as lines but also in square (lines of this latter type were called *alogoi,* literally, "without ratio"). The further study of the *alogoi* lines, as collected in book 10 of Euclid's *Elements,* divided into twelve classes all the *alogoi* formed as the square roots of R(A ± B), where R is a unit line, and A and B are commensurable with each other in square only. Presumably, Eudoxus and his followers played a part in this investigation.

Eudoxus' efforts are rooted in a concern for logical precision in geometry, and this interest may reflect his close association with the Platonic Academy at Athens. Two anecdotes (of questionable historicity) celebrate this connection. The first explains how Eudoxus came to be involved in seeking the cube duplication, the so-called Delian problem. To allay a plague, the citizens of Delos were commanded by the oracle to double a cube-shaped altar. When their attempts failed, they sent to Plato, who directed his mathematical associates Archytas, Menaechmus, and Eudoxus to solve it. When they did so, however, Plato criticized their efforts for being too mechanical. The solutions of a dozen different ancient geometers are known, but that of Eudoxus has not been preserved. It supposedly employed "curved lines" of some sort, and reconstructions have been proposed.

In a second story, Plato is said to have posed to Eudoxus the problem of "saving the phenomena" of planetary motion on the restriction to uniform circular motion. An account of Eudoxus' scheme is transmitted by Simplicius of Cilicia (sixth century A.D.) in his commentary on Aristotle's *De caelo* (fourth century B.C.; *On the Heavens*). From this account a reconstruction has been worked out by the Italian historian of astronomy Giovanni Virginio Schiaparelli in 1875. The Eudoxean system reproduces the apparent motion of a planet by combining the rotations of a set of homocentric spheres. The planet is set on the equator of a uniformly rotating sphere. If a second sphere is set about the first, rotating with equal speed to the first but in the opposite direction and having its axis inclined, then the planet will trace out an eight-shaped curve (which the ancients called the *hippopede,* or horse fetter), so as to complete the full double loop once for every full revolution of the spheres. One superimposes over this a third spherical rotation, corresponding to the general progress of the planet in the ecliptic, and finally over this a fourth rotation, corresponding to the daily rotation of the whole heaven. In this way, each of the five planets requires four spheres, while the Sun and the Moon each take three.

Schiaparelli's exposition thus revealed the ingenuity of Eudoxus' scheme for reproducing geometrically the seemingly erratic forward and backward (retrograde) motion of the planets. Nevertheless, the model proves unsuccessful in some respects: Since the planets do not vary in distance from the earth (the center of their spheres), Eudoxus cannot account for their variable brightness or for asymmetries in the shape of their retrograde paths. Even worse, the values that Eudoxus had to assign for the rotations of the spheres do not produce retrogrades for Mars or Venus, and the Sun and the Moon are given uniform motions, contrary to observation. Apparently, the latter two defects were recognized, for Eudoxus' follower Callippus introduced seven additional spheres (two each for Sun and Moon, one each for Mercury, Venus, and Mars) to make the needed corrections.

The Eudoxean-Callippean scheme is enshrined in Aristotle's *Metaphysica* (c. 335-323 B.C.; *Metaphysics*), where it serves as the mathematical basis of a comprehensive picture of the entire physical cosmos. Doubtless, Eudoxus proposed his geometric model without specific commitments on physical and cosmological issues. Nevertheless, it suited well the basic Aristotelian principles—for example, that the cosmos separates into two spherical realms, the celestial and, at its center, the terrestrial, and that the natural motions of matter in the central realm (for example, earthy substances moving in straight lines toward the center of the cosmos) differ from those in the outer (where motion is circular, uniform, and eternal). Ironically, these Aristotelian principles persisted in later cosmology, even after astronomers had switched from the homocentric spheres to eccentrics, epicycles, and other geometric devices.

Eudoxus also produced works of a descriptive and empirical sort in astronomy and geography. His *Phainomena* (fourth century B.C.; phenomena) and *Enoptron* (fourth century B.C.; mirror) recorded observations of the stars—the basis, one would suppose, of a systematic almanac of celestial events (for example, solstices and equinoxes, lunar phases, heliacal risings of stars). He adopted, as Diogenes and others report, an *oktaeteris,* or eight-year calendar cycle. As known to later authors, an *oktaeteris* is one of the cycles found to reconcile the solar year of 365.25 days with the period of the moon's phases (somewhat over 29.5), by parsing out the 2,922 days in eight years into ninety-nine lunar periods (fifty-one of thirty days and forty-eight of twenty-nine). Yet it is unclear whether this was the arrangement used by Eudoxus. His geographical treatise, the *Gēs periodos* (fourth century B.C.; circuit of the Earth), systematically described the lands and peoples of the known world, from Asia in the east to the western Mediterranean. A connection with his astronomical studies can be seen in the use of the ratio of longest to shortest periods of daylight for designating the latitudes of places.

Summary

However interesting Eudoxus' contributions to calendarics, geography, and philosophy may be, they are secondary to his achievement in mathematics, for he may justly be viewed as the most significant geometer in the pre-Euclidean period. He advanced the study of incommensurables, introduced a new technique for generalizing the theory of proportion, and made exact the theory of limits with his new method of "exhaustion." Remarkable for the logical precision of his proofs, Eudoxus here set the standard against which even the foremost of the later geometers, such as Euclid and Archimedes, measured their own efforts.

Eudoxus' influence on geometric astronomy is more subtle. Already, early in the third century B.C., astronomers had discarded his system of homocentric spheres in their pursuit of viable geometric models for the planetary motions. If the shortcomings of Eudoxus' model were evident, however, it nevertheless defined for later astronomers the essence of their task: to represent the planetary phenomena by means of uniform circular motion. Eudoxus' success thus remains implicit in the later development of astronomy, from Apollonius and Hipparchus to Ptolemy.

Bibliography

De Santillana, G. "Eudoxus and Plato: A Study in Chronology." In *Reflections on Men and Ideas*. Cambridge, Mass.: MIT Press, 1968. A revised chronology of Eudoxus' life is argued on the basis of a detailed examination of the ancient biographical data and collateral historical evidence.

Huxley, G. L. "Eudoxian Topics." *Greek, Roman, and Byzantine Studies* 4 (1963): 83-96. Huxley provides a survey of Eudoxus' life and work, including a discussion of the problems of dating.

Knorr, W. R. *The Ancient Tradition of Geometric Problems*. Cambridge, Mass.: Birkhäuser, 1986. Chapter 3 considers Eudoxus' studies of "exhaustion" and cube duplication, discussed in the wider context of pre-Euclidean geometry.

———. "Archimedes and the Pre-Euclidean Proportion Theory." *Archives internationales d'histoire des sciences* 28 (1978): 183-244. The Eudoxean theory of proportion is here reconstructed on the basis of materials from Archimedes and others and set in the context of the Euclidean theory (*Elements,* book 5).

Neugebauer, O. *A History of Ancient Mathematical Astronomy*. New York: Springer-Verlag, 1975. All facets of Eudoxus' contributions to astronomy are covered; particularly detailed is the discussion of his planetary models. Includes an index.

Van der Waerden, B. L. *Science Awakening*. 5th ed. Leiden: Noordhoff, 1988. The author provides a brief, insightful review of Eudoxus' mathematical work.

Wilbur R. Knorr

EUPALINUS OF MEGARA

Born: c. 575 B.C.; Megara, Greece
Died: c. 500 B.C.; place unknown
Area of Achievement: Engineering
Contribution: Eupalinus was the architect of the tunnel and aqueduct on the island of Samos that bear his name. Probably built for the tyrant Polycrates in the sixth century B.C., they still stand today as monuments to the advanced engineering skills of the Greeks of the archaic period.

Early Life

Eupalinus, the son of Naustrophos, was from the Greek city-state of Megara, in the district of Megaris, located between Athens and Corinth. No details of his life have been preserved, but much can be inferred from what is known about the history of his birthplace in the sixth century B.C. Eupalinus was born into a prosperous land. Megara had experienced much growth in the years before his birth and was the mother city of numerous colonies. The young Eupalinus doubtless heard stories from his father and grandfather about the tyrant Theagenes, who had diverted water from the mountains to the city. The waterworks were still in operation, and the youth must have observed for himself the extensive underground conduit system which the tyrant had built to provide the city with water. The Megaris area was not well endowed with water, and the management of that precious resource was a prime concern. It is possible that a fountain house built in Megara toward the end of the century could have been designed by Eupalinus. In any case, it is likely that he gained some reputation in hydraulic engineering before being called to Samos for the great tunnel project.

Education for boys of Megara in the sixth century was mostly a matter of training for military activities and of learning manners and politics from their elders during banquets and symposia (drinking parties). Eupalinus would also have observed the productions of some of the first comedies, for the Megarians were said to have invented this dramatic form during Eupalinus' youth. As a result of his upbringing, it is likely that he was cultured and comfortable in "polite company."

Eupalinus probably lived most of his life in the democracy that followed the tyranny but would have observed the many struggles between the wealthy conservative oligarchs and the poorer supporters of popular rule. The poetry of Theognis of Megara preserves many of the passions that this strife aroused. The differences between rich and poor were exacerbated by the introduction of coinage, which also took place during Eupalinus' lifetime, as did the *Palintokia,* or debt-relief measures meant to help farmers. Eupalinus had firsthand experience with siege and warfare as well. Throughout the sixth century, Megara fought a series of wars with neighboring Athens. In one incident, the Athenian Peisistratus is said to have besieged and captured the Megarian harbor Nisaea. This background points to Eupalinus' later success in his life's work: He had a worldly background in politics and culture and a good knowledge of warfare and hydraulic engineering. These elements point to his future favor in the court of Polycrates.

Life's Work

Eupalinus is known from statements by Herodotus to have been the architect of the tunnel cut through the mountain bordering the capital city of the island Samos. Herodotus says that on Samos were the three greatest constructions of all the Greeks and lists the tunnel of Eupalinus first, describing its dimensions fairly accurately. The other two marvels of construction were Polycrates' great harbor works and temple of Hera. Today, the tunnel is by far the best preserved of the three. Archaeological evidence points to a date somewhere between 540 and 530 B.C. for the beginning of the work. Scholars have inferred that the tyrant Polycrates called Eupalinus from Megara to direct the project.

The task facing Eupalinus was formidable: In order to keep the Samians supplied with water in time of siege, he was to bring water from a spring on the north side of Mount Ampelus (now called Kastro) into the walled city on the other side. His solution was ingenious, consisting of an 850-meter-long underground conduit (high enough for a man to walk) that led from the spring to the entrance of a straight tunnel cut almost one kilometer through the mountain. The conduit was circuitous, so as to make disposal of the fill easier on the hilly terrain and to make detection more difficult and thus secure the Samians' water supply. The tunnel not only had a channel for the water, but also provided a convenient escape route should the city ever be taken. The system was so efficient that it continued to be used into Byzantine times, after which it fell into disrepair. The system was so well hidden that it lay undiscovered until 1853, when some of the conduit pipes were found, but the tunnel itself was not located by archaeologists until 1882, when a German team began excavations. The results of their work are still being published.

The tunnel itself was cut through solid limestone by workmen using only hammer and chisel. It consists of two levels: an upper level where people could walk—approximately two meters in height and width—and a deeper shaft on the east side up to seven and a half meters deep, where the water flowed in a channel made of ceramic tiles.

Eupalinus instructed his workmen to divide into two teams, each of which began digging at opposite ends of the mountain. The method which he used to ensure that they met in the middle has not yet been discovered. The teams were only two meters apart when they could hear each other's chisels and abruptly turned east. The northern team then broke through into the southern tunnel at a right angle. It has been calculated that had the diggers continued digging in a straight line, they would have met head-on although the northern shaft was a bit higher than the southern one. A conduit within the town led from the south end of the tunnel, not only providing drinking water for the inhabitants, but possibly also a steady stream to operate the town's water clock.

It is not known how long Eupalinus took to complete the tunnel—estimates range from five to fifteen years—nor is it known how many men he employed; certainly the size of the shafts would have permitted only a few workers on each team. It is obvious that Eupalinus took pride in his work and was something of a perfectionist, for the quality of the carving is very high, and there are niches carved in the walls to support lamps. In addition, Eupalinus saw to it that the tunnel was well provided with fresh air, which flowed through a ventilation hole and the conduits themselves.

It is likely that the tyrant Polycrates had ulterior motives when he hired Eupalinus. In addition to wanting the citizens of Samos to have a safe water supply and full employment, the tyrant was concerned that his people be occupied with large projects so as not to have time or desire to revolt against his power. Aristotle compares Polycrates' constructions to those undertaken by tyrants at Athens and Corinth. While the tunnel on Samos is the only undisputed work of Eupalinus, the similarity of the pipes used in its construction to those found in the Peisistratean aqueduct at Athens has

led some to think that Eupalinus was the architect of that water system also, but no certain proof has yet been offered.

Summary
Eupalinus was not the first of the ancients—or the last—to engineer an underground tunnel for water transport. His contribution was not one of originality, but of quality: He proved that tunneling through a mountain for an aqueduct could be done efficiently with a simple technology. Although his northern team worked at a higher level than the southern tunnelers, and though the tunnel did not meet in a perfectly straight fashion, the work was nevertheless outstanding for its excellence: No other ancient tunnel matched its standards. Two hundred years earlier, a tunnel was constructed at Jerusalem between the Virgin's Pool and Siloam. Like Eupalinus' aqueduct, this construction was begun at both ends, but it was not as straight as the Samian tunnel. In fact, the Jerusalem tunnel wasted more than 150 meters on its winding way. A Roman tunnel project in northern Africa, at Saldae (modern Bejaïa), that used the two-team technique—more than five hundred years after Eupalinus—is also known. This project failed because the teams were unable to find each other. Their courses were so misdirected, in fact, that they dug a total distance that exceeded the mountain's width.

Eupalinus' engineering methods are not fully understood and probably combined empirical "trial and error" with some surveying techniques which have yet to be discovered. He might have aligned poles carefully up one side of the mountain and down the other or have used a method of triangulation that the engineer Hero of Alexandria described six hundred years later. It is also possible that Eupalinus kept the shafts straight by having his workmen keep their eyes on a light behind them at the end of the tunnel or shining through a hole cut in the roof. Whatever his methods were, they were effective, and the tunnel that bears his name stands as one of the most impressive engineering feats of antiquity.

Bibliography
Burns, Alfred. "The Tunnel of Eupalinus and the Tunnel Problem of Hero of Alexandria." *Isis* 62 (Summer, 1971): 172-185. An excellent analysis of Hero of Alexandria's first century A.D. treatise, *Dioptra,* in relation to the tunnel, with diagrams from Hero's work compared with the Samian to-

pography. Includes a good discussion of Pythagorean mathematics in relation to the surveying problem. This is a well-reasoned approach by a former industrial engineer. Illustrated.

Figueira, Thomas J., and Gregory Nagy, eds. *Theognis of Megara: Poetry and the Polis*. Baltimore: Johns Hopkins University Press, 1985. The best historical background of archaic Megara. Includes a chronological table with extensive annotations, a discussion of Megarian society and education during Eupalinus' lifetime, and a thorough treatment of the Theognidean elegy and the city-state of Megara.

Goodfield, June. "The Tunnel of Eupalinus." *Scientific American* 210 (June, 1964): 104-110. An account of a scientific/photographic expedition to investigate the tunnel. Contains summaries of the German excavators' findings and engineering problems, and excellent diagrams, photographs, and maps.

Goodfield, June, and S. Toulmin. "How Was the Tunnel of Eupalinus Aligned?" *Isis* 56 (Spring, 1965): 45-56. This article argues against the theory that the tunnel was planned by mathematical triangulation like that described later by Hero of Alexandria. Instead, the authors think that Eupalinus used a line of vertical posts over the mountain above the tunnel. This article should be read with Burns's corrective. Illustrated.

Legon, Ronald P. *Megara: The Political History of a Greek City-State to 336 B.C.* Ithaca, N.Y.: Cornell University Press, 1981. A good source for the historical background of Eupalinus, discussing Megarian geography, tyranny, oligarchy, democracy, and commerce. Also treats the fountain house of Theagenes and Eupalinus' possible role in its construction.

Mitchell, B. M. "Herodotus and Samos." *Journal of Hellenic Studies* 95 (1973): 75-91. In the course of discussing Herodotus' relations with Samos and information about the town, Mitchell includes a concise and well-documented discussion of the tunnel, with speculations on date, manpower, rate of work, and use.

Shipley, Graham. *A History of Samos: 800-188 B.C.* Oxford: Clarendon Press, and New York: Oxford University Press, 1987. Contains an account of the tunnel of Eupalinus with a summary of scholarship on it. Since most of the work considering the tunnel is in German, this book is useful for English readers. The author uses the tunnel to date Polycrates' accession to the tyranny.

White, K. D. *Greek and Roman Technology*. Ithaca, N.Y.: Cornell University Press, and London: Thames and Hudson, 1984. This book includes a section on hydraulic engineering with a discussion of the tunnel, comparative material from other ancient waterworks, and an extensive bibliography, as well as an explanation of Eupalinus' use of the channel on the east side of the tunnel. Discusses surveying problems and Hero of Alexandria's solution. Illustrations.

Daniel B. Levine

EURIPIDES

Born: c. 485 B.C.; Phlya, Greece

Died: 406 B.C.; Macedonia, Greece

Areas of Achievement: Theater and drama

Contribution: Ranking with Aeschylus and Sophocles as a master of Attic tragedy, Euripides was the most "modern" of the great Greek tragedians, often criticizing traditional mythology and realistically working out the logical implications of ancient legends.

Early Life

Little is known of Euripides' life, since few records were kept in his time. Philochorus, a careful annalist who lived in the early third century B.C., wrote a biography of Euripides, fragments of which have survived; it is long on anecdotes but short on dates. What is reasonably certain is that Euripides' father, Mnesarchos, was an affluent merchant and that his mother, Cleito, was of aristocratic descent. When he was four years old, the great naval battle of Salamis, in which the Greeks defeated the Persians, caused Euripides' family to flee the small town of Phlya for Athens. When the boy was eight, the ruined walls of Athens were rebuilt, after the Greeks had decisively defeated Persia on land as well as sea. Freedom had triumphed over despotism—only temporarily, as Euripides was to discover.

In 466, Euripides became officially a "youth," whereupon the state conscripted him for garrison duty in the frontier forts of Attica. Full military service ensued when he was twenty. He distinguished himself as an athlete, did some painting and sculpting, and undoubtedly participated in what may have constituted the greatest intellectual awakening in Western history. As the mother-city of the Ionian territories, Athens had become the harbor for a great influx of artists, poets, historians, philosophers, and scientists fleeing Persian repression. Euripides is known to have been involved with the Sophists, particularly Protagoras, author of the doctrine that "Man is the measure of all things" and a skeptic about the universal validity of science or religion. Euripides may also have associated with Anaxagoras, a philosopher concerned with theories of the mind; Archelaus, Anaxagoras' pupil; Diogenes of Apollonia; and Socrates. Sophocles was his contemporary; undoubtedly, the tragedians knew each other's works, but no evidence exists that they socialized with each other.

Euripides had his first play produced in 455, competing at the Great Festival of Dionysus one year after the death of Aeschylus and thirteen years after Sophocles' first victory. Titled *Peliades* (daughters of Pelias), it was a trial run of his later *Mēdeia* (431 B.C.; *Medea*); the manuscript is not extant.

Life's Work

Altogether, Euripides wrote ninety-two plays, of which eighty-eight were entered in the Dionysian contests, although he won on only four occasions. Seventeen of his plays survive, compared to seven out of eighty for Aeschylus and seven out of 123 for Sophocles.

His earliest extant play is a tragicomedy, *Alkēstis* (438 B.C.; *Alcestis*), based on a folktale. It was placed fourth in a set of Euripidean plays, in the position usually accorded a comic satyr play, but its comic elements are minor. In this play, Admetus, a Thessalian king, has his young wife Alcestis agree to die in his place. The visiting Heracles, however, wrestles with Death and forces him to

317

yield his beautiful victim. Euripides exposes the underside of this romantic legend: Admetus behaves as a warmly courteous host to Heracles and weeps over his "dead" wife, but essentially he is a coward. He lacks the courage to die at the time appointed for him, instead complacently allowing his wife to replace him; moreover, he fails to admit his selfishness even to himself.

Euripides' next surviving drama was *Medea*, his most famous work. Athenians watching the first performance would have known the drama's mythic background: Medea, a barbarian princess and sorceress related to the gods, helped Jason the Argonaut to steal the Golden Fleece and even murdered her own brother so that she and Jason could safely escape pursuit. In the play's action, Medea's beloved Jason has tired of his dangerous foreign mistress and agreed to marry the daughter of Creon so that he can succeed to the throne of Corinth. Desolate and maddened, Medea pretends reconciliation with Jason's bride and sends her a poisoned robe which fatally burns both her and Creon. Medea proceeds to kill her two children by Jason and then sails away on a magic dragon-chariot sent by her grandfather Helius, god of the sun. Euripides' treatment of Jason and Medea renders their personalities in a rather modern fashion: He is calm, self-confident, and rational, but cold; she is devoted and kind, but her rage at being rejected transforms her into an elemental incarnation of vengeful hatred. Their arguments constitute brilliant fireworks of articulated feelings and clashing temperaments.

Hippolytos (428 B.C.; *Hippolytus*) is more restrained and economical. It was his second version of the Phaedra-Theseus-Hippolytus plot; the first has been lost. Framing the drama is a prologue spoken by Aphrodite and an epilogue spoken by Artemis. The tragedy consists of the conflict between them, since Phaedra is identified with love and lust, Hippolytus with chastity and a consequent neglect of Aphrodite's charms. The scorned Aphrodite causes Phaedra, Theseus' newest wife, to fall hopelessly in love with her stepson Hippolytus. Refused by him, she writes a letter falsely accusing him of having raped her; then she commits suicide. Upon reading the letter, Theseus curses Hippolytus, and Poseidon fulfills the malediction by having a monster fatally wound the young man. It is Artemis who reveals the truth to Theseus so that father and son can at least be reconciled before Hippolytus' death. Though Euripides magnificent-

ly celebrates the frustrated passion of his heroine, he permits the play to end in rhetorical commonplaces as Hippolytus and Theseus first argue, then forgive each other.

From a structural perspective, the most innovative achievement of *Hippolytus* is the freedom Euripides grants his characters to change their minds: Phaedra first resolves not to reveal her love, then does so; the nurse gives her mistress conflicting advice; and Hippolytus first decides to reveal his stepmother's lust to his father, then chooses not to do so. In his focus on the unpredictability of his characters' wills, Euripides anticipates psychological dramas such as those of Henrik Ibsen and Luigi Pirandello.

Numerous relatively minor works were also first mounted in the 420's and 410's. Many of these reflect events of the Peloponnesian War, the decisive struggle between Athens and Sparta. While Athens had become a model of democracy under the leadership of Pericles, Sparta favored despotic oligarchies. Euripides, still subject to military service, presumably saw combat during the first years of this agonizing conflict, which eventually ended with Athens' capitulation. *Hērakleidai* (c. 430 B.C.; *The Children of Herakles*), a mutilated text, presents a humane Athens as the protector of Heracles' children, standing for fairness, mercy, and right principles. *Hekabē* (425 B.C.; *Hecuba*) is a pacifist tragedy whose heroine, like Medea, is transformed by unbearable wrongs from dignified majesty to vindictive bitterness. *Ēlektra* (413? B.C.; *Electra*) is a melodrama which presents the protagonist as a slave princess in rags, morbidly attached to her dead father and inexorably jealous of her mother. *Andromachē* (c. 426 B.C.; *Andromache*) makes the Spartan king its villain; with its direct denunciations of Sparta, the play is virtually a wartime propaganda polemic. *Hiketides* (c. 423 B.C.; *The Suppliants*) also expresses Athenian wartime feeling, centering on the ceremonial lamentations of bereaved mothers over their sons' corpses.

Trōiades (415 B.C.; *The Trojan Women*) paints an even bleaker portrait of war's havoc. Only a few years earlier, Athens had emerged from an indecisive ten year's struggle with Sparta. In the spring of 415, Athens was but weeks away from launching the Sicilian expedition, which would touch off the last, disastrous phase of the same war. The Sicilian venture had been voted when Euripides presented a trilogy of which only *The Trojan Women*, its concluding tragedy, survives. It shows the conquest of

Troy by the Achaeans degenerating into calamity: The ancient Greeks have committed *hybris* by insulting the altars of the gods, killing all Troy's male inhabitants, and defiling virgins in holy places. The Trojan princesses must be the slaves of their Greek captors: Hecuba, Priam's widow, has been allotted to Odysseus; Cassandra, the virgin priestess, will be Agamemnon's concubine; Hector's widow, Andromache, will become slave to Pyrrhus, Achilles' son; and Hector and Andromache's son, the boy Astyanax, is taken from her arms and thrown to his death. Two of the mightiest scenes in Attic drama elevate this play to heartbreaking greatness: first, the parting between Andromache and Astyanax, and second, Hecuba's lament upon receiving the boy's dead body after it has been flung from Troy's battlements. The work justifies Aristotle's designation of Euripides as "the most tragic . . . of the poets"; in this work, he is also the most nihilistic.

Euripides' later plays fall into two main divisions. One category consists of lighter, more romantic works with happy endings. These include *Iphigeneia ē en Taurois* (c. 414 B.C.; *Iphigenia in Tauris*), in which the heroine succeeds in saving her brother Orestes from the murderous Taurians; with this work, Euripides can be said to have written literature's first melodramatic thriller. *Iōn* (c. 411 B.C.; *Ion*) is Euripides' most intricately plotted and irreverent play: Apollo is treated as a selfish, mendacious rapist who is thoroughly discredited amid complex intrigues. *Helenē* (412 B.C.; *Helen*) is another melodrama, loaded with reversals: It was only Helen's ghostly double who went to Troy to start the Ten Years' War, while the substantive Helen takes refuge in Egypt and outwits its barbaric king. Her husband, Menelaus, arrives, and the two are able to escape.

An alternative line of development continues Euripides' ruthlessly probing tragedies. *Orestēs* (408 B.C.; *Orestes*) is a densely textured work focusing on Orestes' fate some days after he murdered his mother. He is intermittently mad and ill, nursed by Electra; both are imprisoned in the royal palace by an angry, rebellious populace and condemned to death for their matricide. A blazing climax—Orestes' party sets the palace on fire—leads to the intervention of Apollo, who orders Orestes to go to Athens, there obtain acquittal for his crime and then marry Menelaus and Helen's daughter, Hermione, in order to restore peace to the House of Atreus. *Iphigeneia ē en Aulidi* (405 B.C.; *Iphigenia in Aulis*) was discovered after Euripides' death in incomplete form and finished by another hand. It shows an irresolute Agamemnon preparing to sacrifice his youngest daughter, Iphigenia, but a messenger's speech predicts the ending Euripides presumably would have written had he lived longer: Artemis' last-minute substitution of a deer as the victim.

Probably Euripides' finest tragedy is a play he did finish, though it, too, was posthumously produced: *Bakchai* (405 B.C.; *The Bacchae*). The work features Dionysus playing a central role as both actor and Fate. He is described in the opening scene as "of soft, even effeminate, appearance. . . . His long blond curls ripple down over his shoulders. Throughout the play he wears a smiling mask." His identity remains elusive as well as demonic as he mingles gentleness with cruelty, flirtation with terror, coldness with passion. He presents himself as universal humanity, protean, both female-in-male and male-in-female, essentially amoral, blessing those who worship him and having no mercy on those who deny him. He personifies the bestial, primitive constituent of the psyche, free from ego constraint, at once superhuman and subhuman.

Dionysus' chief victim is the young ruler Pentheus, intemperate, self-willed, disdainful of tradition, scoffingly arrogant. Pentheus masks his primitive instincts behind authority and orderliness, only to have Dionysus crack his shell of artificial self-control, maddening him into frenzies of voyeurism and sadism. The civilized, rational ruler is transformed into a bisexual Peeping Tom who costumes himself in women's clothes so that he can spy on the Bacchantes' orgies. His frenzied mother Agave takes her son for a wild lion and, in the grip of Dionysian delusion, slaughters him. Thus, Pentheus dies as both a convert to and a victim of the instinctual life. Dionysus has ruthlessly destroyed the self that is ignorant of its nature. Euripides in this way dramatized the pitiless drive of the unconscious and the precariousness of human existence.

Legend has it that Euripides in old age was a sad man who conversed little and sat for long hours in his cave by the sea on Salamis. In 408, he exiled himself to the court of King Archelaus in Macedonia. Details of his subsequent death, in the winter of 406, are unknown. Philochorus claims that when Sophocles introduced his chorus during the 406 Dionysian festival, he brought the men onstage without their customary garlands as a sign of mourning for his great rival.

Summary

Anticipating such later playwrights as Henrik Ibsen and George Bernard Shaw, Bertolt Brecht and Jean-Paul Sartre, Euripides was an innovative, agile thinker who used the stage as a forum for his ideas about the world. The second half of the fifth century B.C. saw immense cultural convulsions involving the destruction of the Hellenic world's religious and political stability. Euripides recognized a world devoid of rational order and hence of Sophoclean notions of human responsibility and divine wisdom. He often highlighted the discrepancy between received traditions and experienced reality of human nature. Thus, his Admetus is shown as a shabby egotist, his Odysseus as a sly demagogue, his Agamemnon as an incompetent general, his Jason as an opportunistic adventurer. In contrast to the pious, conventional plays of Aeschylus and Sophocles, Euripidean drama is skeptical, rational, and diagnostic, stressing an often-difficult encounter between culture and the individual. It was this dramatic confrontation between mythic traditions and the elemental demands of the human psyche that chiefly interested Euripides.

His characters often find themselves captive to myths that strain their personalities: Euripides' Orestes murders his mother in an Argos that provides for judicial fairness; his Odysseus, Medea, Hermione, and Electra are all divorced from a culture in which their conduct was appropriate and are set instead in an alien time which distorts and misunderstands their choices. Euripidean personages tend to behave in self-contradictory and self-destructive ways, anticipating William Shakespeare's problematic Angelos, Claudios, and Lucios, August Strindberg's Miss Julie, and Eugene O'Neill's Cabots and Tyrones. Euripides' theater sabotages the conventions of ancient tragedy, replacing them with a challenging, turbulent, and revolutionary drama that bridges the gap between classical integration and contemporary chaos.

Bibliography

Conacher, D. J. *Euripidean Drama: Myth, Theme, and Structure*. London: Oxford University Press, 1967. Conacher conducts the reader on an erudite tour of Euripidean treatments of myths, beginning with such conventional texts as *Hippolytus* and ending with romantic melodramas such as *Alcestis*.

Croally, N. T. *Euripidean Polemic: The Trojan Women and the Function of Tragedy*. Cambridge and New York: Cambridge University Press, 1994. This well-written book draws together much recent scholarship on Euripides and Greek tragedy in an analysis of *The Trojan Women*. Croally shows how the context of war allows the playwright to engage in penetrating criticism of received truths of Athenian civic ideology, questioning such distinctions as man/woman, slave/free, Greek/barbarian.

Euripides. *Euripides: A Collection of Critical Essays*. Segal, Erich, ed. Englewood Cliffs, N.J.: Prentice-Hall, 1968. An anthology of ten essays by distinguished classical scholar/critics. Part of the Twentieth Century Views series. All the essays are worth reading; long studies by Bernard Knox of the *Hippolytus* and Thomas Rosenmeyer of *The Bacchae* are particularly rewarding.

Gregory, Justina. *Euripides and the Instruction of the Athenians*. Ann Arbor: University of Michigan Press, 1991. Discussions of several plays (*Hecuba, Heracles, Alcestis, Hippolytus, The Trojan Women*) unified by the view that Euripides was engaged in civic instruction designed to "reconcile traditional aristocratic values with the democratic order."

Kitto, H. D. F. *Greek Tragedy: A Literary Study*. 3d ed. New York: Barnes and Noble, 1959; London: Methuen, 1961. This is a paperback reprint of a distinguished study first published in 1939. Kitto devotes five of his thirteen chapters to Euripidean tragedy.

Murray, Gilbert. *Euripides and His Age*. 2d ed. London and New York: Oxford University Press, 1946. The great British Hellenist's work remains vivid, vigorous, and lucid. His perspective is that of an Enlightenment liberal for whom religion is a form of superstition.

Powell, Anton, ed. *Euripides, Women, and Sexuality*. London and New York: Routledge, 1990. Seven essays by various hands, concentrating on sex and gender and Euripides. *Medea, Hippolytus*, and *The Trojan Women* are among the plays discussed.

Segal, Charles. *Euripides and the Poetics of Sorrow: Art, Gender, and Commemoration in "Alcestis," "Hippolytus," and "Hecuba."* Durham, N.C. and London: Duke University Press, 1993. A collection of previously published articles united around the common theme of Euripides' treatment of gender. Segal argues that Euripides wishes to "question traditional values and the familiar definitions of male heroism."

Segal, Erich, ed. *Greek Tragedy: Modern Essays in Criticism*. New York: Harper and Row, Publishers, 1982. Segal reprints eight of the essays from the above-cited text and includes three additional articles of merit, one of which, by Jacqueline de Romilly, compares Aeschylus' and Euripides' treatments of fear and suffering.

Webster, T. B. L. *The Tragedies of Euripides*. London: Methuen, 1967. Webster's highly detailed study contains a vast amount of information, but his style is pedestrian and his focus on metrics may deter the reader who has not mastered ancient Greek.

Gerhard Brand

EUSEBIUS OF CAESAREA

Born: c. 260; probably Caesarea, Palestine
Died: May 30, 339; Caesarea, Palestine
Areas of Achievement: Historiography and religion
Contribution: Living through both the last major Christian persecutions and the legalization of Christianity under Constantine the Great, Eusebius interpreted human history in terms of an upward process toward a divine purpose. He formulated the political philosophy of unity of church and state under the providence of God that became standard in the East.

Early Life

Relatively little is known of Eusebius' early life. He was likely born near Caesarea to peasant parents. The church historian Socrates, writing in the fifth century, states that Eusebius received Christian teaching and baptism at Caesarea and was later ordained a presbyter there.

Eusebius' mentor, a presbyter from the church at Alexandria named Pamphilus, was one of the leading biblical and theological scholars of the day, a disciple of the Christian philosopher Origen. He founded a school in Caesarea and gathered a large library of both pagan and Christian works there. Eusebius read widely under his teacher's guidance. By 303, Eusebius had completed early versions of at least two of his most important historical works, *Chronicon* (c. 300, 325; *Chronicle*) and *Historia ecclesiastica* (c. 300, 324; *Ecclesiastical History*).

Eusebius grew very close to Pamphilus, eventually adopting the surname Pamphili (son of Pamphilus). During the persecution begun by the emperor Diocletian, Pamphilus was imprisoned for two years, eventually suffering martyrdom in 309 or 310. Before his teacher's death, Eusebius assisted him in completing five volumes of a six-volume defense of Origen.

It is possible that Eusebius was jailed for his faith for a short period in Egypt following Pamphilus' death. At the 335 Synod of Tyre, which dealt with the continuing Arian controversy, Eusebius was accused by Potammon, a rival bishop from Egypt, of having sacrificed to the emperor cult to avoid torture while in prison. The charge was probably false, judging by the harsh stance the Church took toward Christians who lapsed into such actions and by the honors Eusebius received immediately after the persecution. These honors included his consecration as Bishop of Caesarea about 314,

shortly after the proclamation of peace by Constantine and Licinius.

Life's Work

Eusebius lived in a period when one of the most dramatic events in the Church's existence occurred: the transformation of the Roman Empire, under Constantine's direction, from persecutor to supporter and protector of Christianity. Eusebius' work cannot be fully understood without recognizing the importance of this apparent miracle for his thought. The first editions of his works, however, were certainly composed before Constantine's rise, probably during the first years of Diocletian's reign. A cautious optimism pervaded Christian circles at that time as a result of the lack of persecution, and Eusebius seems to have developed his idea of Christianity as the culmination of the course of human history in the first editions of his *Chronicle* and *Ecclesiastical History*.

It was when the Church again came under attack in 303 that Eusebius felt compelled to set forth his views at length, doing so primarily in the works

EVSEB: CÆSARIENSIS.

Praeparatio evangelica (c. 314-318; *Preparation for the Gospel*) and *Demonstratio evangelica* (after 314; *Proof of the Gospel*). Eusebius' notions of history and its meaning were greatly influenced by his work in and interpretation of the Scriptures. For him, the Bible was the key to a correct understanding of human history. His beliefs were deeply rooted in the study of the Old Testament, where he saw the beginning of Christianity—not in Judaism proper, but rather in the earlier era of the patriarchs.

Christianity from its earliest days had been extremely sensitive to the charge that it was of recent origin. In *Contra Celsum* (248), Origen quoted the pagan writer Aulus Cornelius Celsus as scornfully saying, "A few years ago he [Christ] began to teach." The earliest Christian apologists tied Christianity to its Jewish roots and insisted that the loftiest ideas of paganism had actually been borrowed from the Hebrews. Eusebius did not consider that explanation to be adequate; he reinterpreted the biblical accounts to show that Christianity was, in fact, the most ancient of all the religions of mankind.

Eusebius, like Origen, saw history as having begun with a fall away from God, as illustrated in the Old Testament by the sin of Adam and Eve. Human beings after the Fall were characterized by savagery and superstition. There were some, however, who were able to see that God transcended the created world. These friends of God were the patriarchs, to whom were made known divine truths by the *Logos* (Christ). The patriarchs were the original Christians, knowing both God the Father and His Son, the divine Word. The unenlightened contemporaries of the patriarchs were the original pagans.

Judaism came into Eusebius' scheme as a purely transitional phase, to prepare the way for the new covenant of Jesus which would diffuse the religion of the patriarchs to all mankind. Following the period of the Mosaic Law came the central period of history, which began with the nearly simultaneous appearance of Christ and Caesar Augustus, the foundation of church and empire. He saw the reign of Constantine as the culmination of human history, the last era before the end of the world. The whole story was a "salvation history" which set the Christian experience into a context of historical knowledge that was basically shared by all educated people in the ancient world.

The whole of Eusebius' *Ecclesiastical History* could be interpreted as the account of the Church's continual movement forward in the working out of its victory over the demoniac powers. He viewed Constantine as leading people into the way of truth, as preached by the Church. Under his influence, the Gospel could be preached everywhere, and when that was accomplished, the end of the world and the return of Christ would take place. *Oratio de laudibus Constantini* (335-336; *In Praise of Constantine*, 1976) and *Vita Constantini* (339; *Life of Constantine*, 1845) contain several passages in which Eusebius seems to express hope of seeing the end in his own time.

It is likely that Constantine first took notice of Eusebius at the Council of Nicaea in 325. This council was called by the emperor to put an end to the strife in the Church over the doctrines of Arius, a presbyter of Alexandria, who taught that Christ was a created being and therefore not eternal. Although Eusebius had at first opposed action against Arius and evidently favored his subordinationist position, Eusebius was primarily interested in preserving unity in the Church. He was the leader of a moderate group at Nicaea which attempted to steer a middle course between the position of Arius and that of his chief antagonist, Athanasius.

Eusebius had been provisionally excommunicated by an earlier council in Antioch for his refusal to sign its strongly anti-Arian creed. At Nicaea, Eusebius presented a creed used in Caesarea as proof of his orthodox beliefs and as a possible solution statement to the question of the relationship between the Father and Son in the Godhead. This Caesarean creed, however, was expanded considerably before the bishops arrived at a final form. The most notable addition was of the term *homoousios* (Greek for "of the same substance" as God) to describe Christ. Although Eusebius reluctantly subscribed to the new creed for the sake of unity, during subsequent years he was involved in various actions against Athanasius, including the Synod of Tyre in 335, which formally condemned him.

Eusebius gained the respect of Constantine because of his peacemaking attitude; he enjoyed a rather close relationship with the emperor through the rest of his life. In 336, in celebration of the thirtieth anniversary of Constantine's accession, Eusebius praised the ruler in a lengthy speech which had as its theme the resemblance of Constantine to Christ. When Constantine died in May, 337, Eusebius immediately set about writing his *Life of Constantine*, which was left unfinished at his death in 339. His successor as Bishop of Caesarea, Acacius, finished and published the book later the same year.

Summary

Eusebius' approach to historiography is unique in several ways. He was the first Christian apologist to bring the literary-historical point of view to his works. While all other early opponents of paganism and heresy wished only to enter into polemical discussion, occasionally mentioning chronological facts only when it served their argument, Eusebius fixed the dates of writers and cataloged their works, clearly grasping the concept of a Christian literature.

In the ancient world, Eusebius' *Ecclesiastical History* was so successful that no one tried to supersede it. Instead, 150 years after his death, three writers, Socrates, Sozomen, and Theodoret, continued Eusebius' history down to their own times. The approach of Eusebius was dominant in the writing of church history almost until the time of the Enlightenment in the eighteenth century. The *Ecclesiastical History* is classed as one of the four or five seminal works in Western historiography.

Eusebius' overriding theme was celebration of the success of Christianity in the Roman world. He produced the reformulation of Christian political theory necessitated by the legalization of Christianity under Constantine. In his reinterpretation, the government became a positive institution in which Christians could take a more active part and for which they began to take more responsibility. In the Eastern Empire, his idea of the Church under the jurisdiction of a Christian ruler remained the norm until the fall of Constantinople in the fifteenth century.

Eusebius' optimistic theory of the general advance of human history under God proved to be the only real alternative to the historical views that would be developed in the fifth century by Saint Augustine of Hippo. Augustine was as much influenced in his comparatively pessimistic concept by the sack of Rome in 410 as Eusebius had been by the triumph of Constantine.

Bibliography

Attridge, Harold W. and Gohei Hata, eds. *Eusebius, Christianity, and Judaism.* Leiden and New York: Brill, 1992. A huge collection of thirty scholarly papers on many aspects of Eusebius' life, background, ideas, and writings. Includes a substantial bibliography.

Barnes, Timothy D. *Constantine and Eusebius.* Cambridge, Mass.: Harvard University Press, 1981. An extremely well-documented and interesting volume which the author describes as an "interpretive essay" on Eusebius and Constantine as individuals and their relationship to each other. Of the 458 pages, more than 180 contain helpful apparatus, including copious notes to the chapters, a bibliography, a list of editions of Eusebius' works, and a chronology of his life.

Chesnut, Glenn F. *The First Christian Histories.* 2d ed. Macon, Ga.: Mercer University Press, 1986. Details the historical work of Eusebius and the historians who followed him—Socrates, Sozomen, Theodoret, and Evagrius—placing them in the context of historiography in the pagan world of their times. Shows the importance of Eusebius' work in the development of a Christian historiography. Footnotes but no bibliography.

Drake, H. A. Notes to *In Praise of Constantine: A Historical Study and New Translation of Eusebius' Tricennial Orations.* Berkeley: University of California Press, 1976. Although focusing primarily on Eusebius' laudatory speech of 336, this slender volume of 191 pages is much more than simply a critical edition of the speech. It provides a number of valuable insights into the thought and actions of Eusebius throughout his life. Sixty pages of notes and bibliography make it very valuable for a study of Eusebius.

Eusebius. *The History of the Church from Christ to Constantine.* Translated by G. A. Williamson. London and New York: Penguin Books, 1965. A popular and widely available edition of Eusebius' most famous work. An introduction by the translator, a map, and several helpful appendices of names mentioned in the text make this volume of the Penguin Classics series a must for students of Eusebius.

Grant, Michael. "Eusebius." In *The Ancient Historians.* New York: Scribner, and London: Weidenfeld and Nicolson, 1970. A chapter in Grant's monumental work, which, though only fifteen pages long, is valuable for its insights into Eusebius' place among historians of the ancient world. The book itself is lengthy and more than most students need for a study of Eusebius alone, but very valuable for a context of ancient historians. The notes and brief bibliography are of limited value.

Grant, Robert M. *Eusebius as Church Historian.* Oxford: Clarendon Press, 1980. An in-depth study of the *Ecclesiastical History* and an evaluation of Eusebius as a historian. Focusing on seven major themes (including apostolic succession, heretics, persecution, martyrdom, and the canon of Scripture), Grant points out both strengths and weaknesses of the first church historian's work. Footnotes and a brief bibliography are included.

Mosshammer, Alden A. *The Chronicle of Eusebius and Greek Chronographic Tradition.* Lewisburg, Pa.: Bucknell University Press, 1979. A critical study of Eusebius' seminal work of historical chronology which details the possible sources for the work and places it in the context of early Greek chronography. While much of the book is of a technical nature and of little use to the general student, the sections dealing with the *Chronicle* and other writings and with the sources upon which Eusebius based his work are of some value.

Valesius (Valois), Henri de. "Annotations on the Life and Writings of Eusebius Pamphilus." Translated by S. E. Parker. In *The Ecclesiastical History of Eusebius Pamphilus.* Rev. ed. Philadelphia: Davis, 1833; London: Bohn, 1858. An important early study done by the French lawyer and classical scholar Henri de Valois in 1659. Valois was quite familiar with the ancient literature known in his day and took great pains to substantiate and document all citations he made from these sources. While more recent scholarship has gone beyond Valois, his work is a very helpful compilation of information on a figure about whom relatively little is known.

Wallace-Hadrill, D. S. *Eusebius of Caesarea.* London: Mowbray, 1960; Westminster, Md.: Canterbury, 1961. While not a full-scale "life and works" of Eusebius, this volume comes closer than any other to that description. Wallace-Hadrill gives a chapter on the life of Eusebius, then treats various topics in Eusebius' intellectual life, including his views on Scripture, the work of Christ, the Arian controversy, and the purpose of God in human history. A chronological listing of the works of Eusebius following the chapter on questions of dating is valuable, but the notes and brief bibliography are far less helpful than those of Barnes or Drake.

Douglas A. Foster

EZEKIEL

Born: c. 627 B.C.; Jerusalem
Died: c. 570 B.C.; Babylonia
Area of Achievement: Religion
Contribution: As a visionary and prophetic leader, Ezekiel was one of a number of individuals who held the Jewish community together during the early years of the Babylonian Exile (586-538 B.C.). His visions and consolatory prophecies encouraged those in exile to look toward the day of the restoration of the Temple in Jerusalem.

Early Life

All knowledge about Ezekiel is drawn from direct statements in the Book of Ezekiel or inferences from it. To develop a picture of his life, one must compare this material with that gathered from other books of the Hebrew Bible and additional contemporary texts. The tendency to discount much of the Book of Ezekiel as later editorial writing, prevalent throughout much of the twentieth century, has given way to an acceptance of the bulk of the material as coming from Ezekiel; later revisions are assumed to have originated from Ezekiel himself or those close to him.

Ezekiel was born in Jerusalem around the time of the Josiah reforms (c. 627) to a priestly family of the Zadok line. His father's name is given as Buzi. Ezekiel in his writing shows great familiarity and concern with the temple cult, and it is likely that he was part of the priestly cult and an important member of the hierarchy.

Ezekiel's life and career were played out against the background of ancient Near Eastern world events. By the end of the seventh century B.C., Nebuchadnezzar II had helped his father, Nabopolassar, defeat the Assyrians and take over the southern part of that empire, including the Kingdom of Judah. As long as Judah remained a faithful ally, it was secure, but when Nebuchadnezzar succeeded his father as king, Judah, under King Jehoiakim and with the encouragement of Psammetichus II of Egypt, rebelled against Babylon (2 Kings 24:2). In 598, Nebuchadnezzar marched against Judah. Jehoiakim was assassinated by those hoping for milder treatment, and his eighteen-year-old son, Jehoiachin, also known as Coniah, was placed on the throne. Three months later, defeated, he and his court were taken into exile in Babylon, and his uncle, Zedekiah, was given control of the state.

Ezekiel was one of those taken with King Jehoiachin into exile by Nebuchadnezzar in 597. This event was sufficiently important for Ezekiel to use it as the starting point for calculating the dates of his prophecies. Those prophecies that are dated are based on the number of years from the beginning of Jehoiachin's exile.

It would be expected that Ezekiel was married and had a family. His marriage is attested by a reference to his wife's death in Babylonia. He had a residence which was sufficiently large to hold a gathering of the elders of the Israelites in Babylonia. His prophecies suggest that he was resident at Tel Aviv near Nippur in Babylonia.

Ezekiel's mystic personality and his prophetic role should not be allowed to mask his position as an important member of the priestly establishment who continued to function in a leadership role in exile. While there is no direct proof, the linguistic similarities and priestly concerns exhibited in Ezekiel's own writings are not inconsistent with his inclusion among the "priestly" writers who were responsible for the preservation of many of the Israelite traditions of history and worship, which culminated in the creation of Torah.

Life's Work

Ezekiel's call to prophecy is dramatically described in the opening phrases of his book. He was thirty years old at the time, resident in Tel Aviv and standing on the Chebar canal. Ezekiel, in his prophetic actions and utterances, is revealed to be a dramatic mystic. Some have described his condition as that of a catatonic schizophrenic, and his actions as reported by him are congruent with clinical descriptions of that condition.

After Ezekiel received his call, he apparently abandoned all normal discourse and spoke only to utter the words of the Lord, Yahweh, as revealed to him, accompanied on several occasions by graphic symbolic actions. In this first period, Ezekiel's prophecies centered on the forthcoming destruction of Jerusalem, the impious actions of Zedekiah (the regent in Jerusalem), the futility of depending on Egypt for deliverance, and the false nature of prophets who predicted such deliverance. The prophecies were written in a mixture of poetry and prose notable for their graphic imagery, dramatic vocabulary, and extensive parables. In addition to the prophecies against Jerusalem, the prophecies

against foreign nations reserved most of their invective for Tyre and Egypt, the two allies of Zedekiah against Babylon. In all these matters, Ezekiel's prophecies were paralleled by those of Jeremiah writing from Egypt to Babylonia. In both cases, their prophecies stemmed from activities taking place in Jerusalem and the importance of the homeland for the exiles.

After the final fall of Jerusalem to Nebuchadnezzar in 586 and the entrance of the second wave of exiles into Babylonia, the general tenor of Ezekiel's prophecies changed from one of denunciation to one of hope and encouragement. It is assumed that at that time Ezekiel returned to normal, everyday activity. Even in this period, however, he seems periodically to have gone into a catatonic state in which he claimed to have visionary and out-of-body experiences, which he then recorded in detail. Of these, the most famous are the vision of the valley of the dry bones and that of the restored Temple and the city of Jerusalem. This extensive passage shows the idealized Temple under priestly control.

In the period after 586 B.C., there were several overreaching problems facing the Israelite (or Jewish) community. First, and most important, was gathering the community together and encouraging it to continue the ancestral belief in the Lord and the covenant agreement. To the exile this was no small problem, for the destruction of the Temple by the Babylonians would have universally been regarded as a defeat of Yahweh by the chief Babylonian god, Marduk, through the actions of Nebuchadnezzar. With Marduk having proved himself the stronger god, there would have been no compelling reason to continue the cult of Yahweh, particularly in exile. It was uniquely Ezekiel in Babylonia and Jeremiah in Egypt who interpreted the actions of Nebuchadnezzar as directed by Yahweh against His own people for not upholding the covenant agreement. The emphasis on the position of the deity in Ezekiel is made clear by the constant use in the prophecies of the phrase "Adonai Yahweh," which emphasizes His continuing power. (Since "Adonai" is usually translated as "Lord," most translations use "Lord God," which is the normal translation of the Hebrew "Adonai Elohim." Grammatically, the form in Ezekiel is usually described as an emphatic form.)

Ezekiel's prophecies either ceased or were not recorded after 571. There was a revision to the prophecy of the destruction of Tyre which suggests an unwillingness on the part of Ezekiel or his editor to change the wording of the earlier prophecy, preferring instead to add a corrected version. He may well have continued his nonprophetic activities after that date, including the preparation of the Book of Ezekiel.

Evidence of Ezekiel's death, although recorded late and not from the most secure sources, should not be neglected. Evidence from the third century A.D. Dura Synagogue wall painting and the fourth century Christian work on the lives of the prophets suggests that Ezekiel was arrested by the authorities and executed under the orders of Jehoiachin. What brought this about is unknown, but given Ezekiel's orientation it is not hard to conclude that his words could have aroused official opposition. It has been suggested that Ezekiel had realistic expectations of the restoration of the Temple in his lifetime. Only the death of Nebuchadnezzar and the incompetence of his successors postponed that event until the reign of Cyrus, the Persian liberator of Babylon.

Summary

The personality of Ezekiel as expressed in his book is a forceful and enduring one that has become part of the religious heritage of Judaism and Christianity. He presents himself as a mixture of opposites. There is the mystic visionary and the priest concerned with minutiae of cult and religious law. He is a superb poet but at the same time can write in the most pedestrian prose. His words seem strange, even repulsive, but then reveal a sympathetic and sensitive nature. He revels in symbolic acts and elaborate allegories one moment and speaks with directness and bluntness the next. By uniting these contradictions, he has impressed himself on tradition.

Ezekiel was one of the primary architects of Judaism. Faced with a historical situation in which the abandonment of the covenant was a high probability, not only was Ezekiel one of the few who demanded that the Israelites keep the covenant, but he also outlined the procedures and methods for doing so in the exilic environment, thus laying the foundations for Judaism. In addition to emphasizing the importance of the covenant, Ezekiel was one of the first to stress the importance of individual responsibility over collective or familial responsibility. In the recognition of God working outside Judah and through non-Israelite rulers, Ezekiel developed a concept of a universal deity while still holding to particularistic practices that became basic to all subsequent Judaism.

The influences of Ezekiel on Christianity have been less obvious but are nevertheless significant. His concepts of salvation and divine grace point to the reinterpretations of the concepts by the Apostle Paul. The unique prophetic use of the term "Son of Man" (in Hebrew, *ben-adam*) to indicate Ezekiel's special position as prophet had a strong effect on early Christian writers. His general mysticism found its way into the writings of the Apostle John and the Book of Revelation. This influence is most clear in Ezekiel's prophecies on Gog and Magog as the ultimate foes before the establishment of God's kingdom.

Bibliography

Broome, Edwin C., Jr. "Ezekiel's Abnormal Personality." *Journal of Biblical Literature* 65 (September, 1946): 277-292. A fascinating and convincing account of the mental state of the prophet. Based on modern case studies, it is particularly helpful in suggesting that Ezekiel's visions and descriptions are not incompatible with his being able to remember them in detail and to function normally while not in such a condition.

Eissfeldt, Otto. *The Old Testament: An Introduction.* Translated by Peter Ackroyd. Oxford: Blackwell, and New York: Harper and Row, Publishers, 1965. This volume is still the best of the introductions, of which there are many. Skilled exposition, clear analysis, and extensive bibliographies up to 1965.

Goodenough, Erwin R. *Jewish Symbols in the Greco-Roman Period.* Vols. 9-11, *Symbolism in the Dura Synagogue.* Princeton, N.J.: Princeton University Press, 1953. The short section in this rather large work concerned with the late Roman synagogue paintings at Dura is the best available clear exposition of the traditions of the death of Ezekiel.

Gottwald, Norman K. *The Hebrew Bible: A Socio-Literary Introduction.* Philadelphia: Fortress Press, 1985. Well-written and up-to-date analysis of the Hebrew Bible. Gottwald's ideas are not always in the mainstream of critical thinking, but in this work he is more general than usual and is thus easier to read and more useful for information on the background of Ezekiel and on the prophet himself. Excellent bibliography.

Greenberg, Moshe. *Ezekiel, 1-20.* New York: Doubleday, 1983. Included in the Anchor Bible series, the most definitive translation available with extensive introduction, translation, notes on the translation and textual problems, commentary, and bibliography. The introduction is rather skimpy here, but a more extensive introduction is promised for the next volume, which will complete Ezekiel. The notes and comments are particularly extensive.

Jewish Publication Society, trans. *The Prophets, Nevi'im.* Philadelphia: Jewish Publication Society of America, 1978. Readers will differ in their choice of the translations of Ezekiel, Jeremiah, and 2 Kings they will wish to use. This new translation by the Jewish Publication Society follows the traditional text with annotations where readings can be improved from other sources. It is written in clear, modern English with particular attention to translation of poetic passages in poetic form. For more detail consult the Anchor Bible series.

Klein, Ralph W. *Ezekiel: The Prophet and His Message. Studies on Personalities of the Old Testament.* Columbia, S.C.: University of South Carolina Press, 1988. An accessible study of Ezekiel's prophecy that focuses on the prophet's "radical" theology, with its strong belief in the immediacy of God's presence.

Michael M. Eisman

EZRA

Born: Late sixth or early fifth century B.C.; southern Mesopotamia

Died: Date unknown; probably Jerusalem

Area of Achievement: Religion

Contribution: As a "scribe skilled in the law of Moses," Ezra led a religious reform movement which transformed the identity of the Jewish community which had returned from exile to Jerusalem. This new identity of the Jewish people was premised upon a return to observance of the Law (Torah).

Early Life

Nothing of substance is known about the early years of Ezra, though his genealogy is given in Ezra 7:1-5. There he is called the son of Seraiah, and he is presented in the priestly heritage, with his ancestral line traced all the way back to Aaron, the first high priest and brother of Moses. While in the Bible Ezra is never specifically called the high priest or chief priest, he is so referred to in Flavius Josephus' *Ioudaikē archaiologia* (c. A.D. 93; *The Antiquities of the Jews*).

Ezra was born, like many Jews in the fifth century, in captivity under the yoke of the great Persian Empire. It actually had been about a century earlier, under the imperialistic policies of the Neo-Babylonian Empire in the early sixth century, that the stage had been set for several generations of Jews to be born in exile. Beginning in 597, when Jerusalem fell under the onslaught of Nebuchadnezzar, the Babylonian king, a series of deportations was initiated in which large numbers of people within the Kingdom of Judah were physically transported to Babylon and other tightly controlled sectors in southern Mesopotamia.

For almost six decades after 597, the exiles lived and worked under Babylonian control. Although sources describing the daily life of the exiles are meager, there is evidence that suggests that some were put to forced labor for various building projects; perhaps the greatest numbers were relocated to agricultural communities with a relative amount of freedom. Remarkably, the once-powerful Babylonian Empire was overthrown with ease. To the east of the empire, the Persians had been a growing threat for many years. By 539, the great city of Babylon was taken, virtually without a fight. Cyrus the Great, the Persian king, embarked on a series of military campaigns with the goal of securing the bulk of territory once controlled by the Babylonians. Within a year, much of the Near East was under Persian influence. Cyrus determined to control his new empire via a novel approach: as liberator. Thus, the Assyrians and Babylonians' traditional methods of terror and deportations were cast aside in favor of very tolerant policies. It is within this framework that Ezra 1:1-4 relates how Cyrus, in 538, issued a decree which allowed and even encouraged the exiled Jews to return to their homeland. Indeed, they did return. Under the leadership of Sheshbazzar, and later his nephew Zerubbabel, those who returned resettled and even commenced rebuilding the Temple, which had been destroyed by the Babylonians. Construction began in 520, and by 515 the work had been completed. Chapter 6 of the Book of Ezra relates the events of completing and dedicating the new Temple and the observance of Passover in the spring of 515. With this accomplishment, the stage was set for the return of even more exiles and the coming of Ezra to Jerusalem. Ultimately, Ezra would provide the leadership and spiritual direction needed by the Jewish community of Jerusalem in order to restore and invigorate its once-rich religious heritage.

Life's Work

Between the close of the biblical narrative in Ezra 6 and the introduction of Ezra himself at the start of chapter 7, a substantial number of years passed. It was probably early during this period, sometime after 515, that Ezra was born. With virtually no information concerning his early years, the real story of Ezra begins with his return to Jerusalem along with groups of other Israelites, as mentioned in Ezra 7:7. It is at this point that one of the more vexing problems in biblical studies arises: the dating of Ezra's return to Jerusalem. Artaxerxes I ruled the Persian Empire from 464 to 423. The text of Ezra 7:8 states that Ezra and his retinue arrived in Jerusalem in the fifth month of the seventh year of Artaxerxes' reign; by this reckoning, Ezra came to Jerusalem in 458. This straightforward calculation would place him in Jerusalem before Nehemiah. There are, however, some murky waters surrounding the chronological relationship between Ezra and Nehemiah. For this reason, two other theories concerning the date of Ezra's return have been articulated. Some believe that a scribal error marred

the biblical text and that "the seventh year" should read "the thirty-seventh year" of Artaxerxes. This would place the return of Ezra to Jerusalem in 428. Although supported by some, this position has not met with widespread acceptance. There is a third possibility: "The seventh year of Artaxerxes" does not refer to Artaxerxes I but rather to Artaxerxes II, who ruled from 404 to 359. Accordingly, the seventh year would be 398. The thorny problem of dating Ezra's return has by no means been resolved. To deal pragmatically with the events of Ezra's life, however, the traditional date of 458 for his return to Jerusalem has been adopted here.

As a "scribe skilled in the Law of Moses" (Ezra 7:6), Ezra received a special royal commission from the Persian king Artaxerxes. The document, which was written in Aramaic, is preserved in Ezra 7:12-26. This document presented Ezra with far-reaching powers to teach and enforce measures of the Law among the members of the Jewish community residing in the Persian satraphy of Abar-nahara—thus including not only those in Palestine proper but also the Jews in the Trans-Euphrates area. The idea that the Persian king would so em-

power a man to impose the Law of Moses upon Jewish subjects within the Persian Empire might seem on the surface to be unreasonable. Yet many attested Persian documents clearly demonstrate that, indeed, most of the kings implemented such policies. There was a long-standing Persian commitment to giving official sanction to the various religious elements within the empire.

Armed with the royal decree, Ezra, upon his return to Jerusalem, initiated a program of religious reform which was designed to renew loyalty to the Law in the hearts and minds of Jews. He had been given explicit authority to appoint magistrates and judges and to teach those who had no knowledge of the laws of God. He was even granted authority to mete out punishment upon those who did not comply with the Law, as Ezra 7:26 states: "Whoever does not obey the law of your God and the law of the king must surely be punished by death, banishment, confiscation of property, or imprisonment."

There is great variance of opinion over the chronological order of the events which followed. What is clear is that Ezra initiated changes which brought about profound religious reforms and the reconstituting of the Jewish community along lines drawn within the Law. Some scholars hold that the narrative of Nehemiah 8 probably reflects the events shortly after Ezra's arrival in Jerusalem. As priest and scribe, Ezra presented the Law publicly to the people in what must have been a very solemn ceremony. Standing on a platform before an assembly of "men and women and all who were able to understand," Ezra read from the Law from dawn until noon. The next day, Ezra, along with the heads of certain families and various priests and Levites, gathered to study the precepts of the Law. They read about the Feast of Tabernacles, proclaimed in Leviticus 23. Realizing that the observance of this festival had long been neglected, Ezra immediately issued a decree throughout the country that the people were to gather materials necessary for the construction of the booths that were requisite for the celebration. The people's response was overwhelming: Nehemiah 8:17 states that "the whole company that had returned from exile built booths and lived in them. From the days of Joshua son of Nun until that day, the Israelites had not celebrated it like this. And their joy was very great." The reforms of Ezra were under way.

The public reading of the Law and the celebration of the Feast of Tabernacles made a powerful spiritual impact upon the people. They began fasting, wearing sackcloth, and confessing their sins as they came to understand the wickedness of their ancestors and their own role in Israel's recent and unfortuitous history. Yet, in this very humbling circumstance, the people were encouraged by the rehearsing of their place as God's chosen and as beneficiaries of redemptive works performed by God on their behalf throughout history. Their repentance and gratitude are articulated in a long penitential prayer recorded in Nehemiah 9. The spiritual underpinnings of the community were being reshaped as the Law began to find a central place within the lives of individuals.

As the spiritual leader of a society which was reaping the consequences of years of abuse and neglect of the Law of God, Ezra exerted remarkable influence in addressing a basic problem within Israelite culture: intermarriage. The Law strictly forbade marriages between Jews and pagans, and clearly intermarriages had created innumerable problems throughout Israelite history. Marriage to foreigners did nothing but water down the worship of Yahweh and the observance of God's ordinances. When a contingent of elders reported that intermarriage was rampant and that certain leaders and officials had, in fact, led the way in this pattern of activity, Ezra reacted with the emotion of one understanding the true nature of God's holiness and His utter hatred of sin: "When I heard this, I tore my tunic and cloak, pulled hair from my head and beard and sat down appalled." The passion of Ezra for the Law and holiness before God was further revealed as he prostrated himself and prayed:

> What has happened to us is a result of our evil deeds and our great guilt, and yet, our God, you have punished us less than our sins have deserved and have given us a remnant like this. Shall we again break your command and intermarry with the people who commit such detestable practices?

Ezra now moved in such a way as to penetrate the conscience of the entire community. Broken before God because of the calamity of intermarriage, Ezra prayed to God near the Temple. As he was praying, weeping, and confessing this great sin, the people were moved. A large crowd gathered around him, spellbound by the realization of their sin. Masses began to weep bitterly and confess their sins. It was one of those few times in history when a solitary individual touches the inner recesses of an entire nation's soul. Ezra, the scribe, by revealing his contrition and weeping in anguish before the Lord and before the people, moved the nation of Israel that day. Leaders from the community issued a declaration that all the exiles must assemble themselves in Jerusalem within three days. Anyone not complying would be removed from the ranks of Jewish community life. In what must have been an incredible scene, all the exiles gathered near the Temple in a driving rainstorm to hear Ezra's public rebuke and plea for change. The result was that the people did acknowledge their sin, and a program was established for separating themselves from the foreigners. Within three months, all mixed marriages had been dissolved. Once again, the Law became foremost in the hearts of the people.

Summary

Ezra did not become a long-standing force in the Jerusalem community. In fact, he was probably an active leader for only about a year after arriving in the city. He does not appear in any biblical narratives of later events. According to Josephus, after the accomplishment of his mission, Ezra died and was buried in the Holy City. How does one accurately judge the impact of Ezra? Certainly, his reputation in the succeeding generation suggests a level of awe and respect comparable to that afforded to Moses, the unquestioned hero of the faith. Yet reputation is not the proper criterion for judging an individual's significance. In this case, Ezra's pragmatic reforms, which reorganized and reenergized the struggling Jewish community, should serve as a measuring rod.

Undoubtedly, the elevation of the Law to a place of centrality in the Jewish community was Ezra's paramount achievement. The primacy of the Law in the lives of the people was a renewed force which enabled the Jews to survive as a separate entity. Although the stringency of the reforms concerning intermarriage may have seemed unreasonable to some, the observance of the Law aided them in realizing anew their stature as a people chosen by God. The acceptance of the Law as presented by the faithful scribe Ezra brought about a reorganization of the people which was desperately needed in the tumultuous years after the return from exile.

Bibliography

Bossman, D. "Ezra's Marriage Reform: Israel Redefined." *Biblical Theology Bulletin* 9 (1979): 32-38. The focus of this article is the intermarriage problem addressed by Ezra and the restructuring of Israel around the Law. Bossman shows that cultic aspects of the Jewish community were purified through the reforms of Ezra.

Bright, John. *A History of Israel.* 3d ed. Philadelphia: Westminster Press, and London: SCM Press, 1981. Chapter 10 of this work is a very useful overview of the Jewish community in the fifth century. A full discussion of the problems involved in the dating of Ezra's mission to Jerusalem is included in an excursus to the chapter.

Childs, Brevard S. *Introduction to the Old Testament as Scripture.* Philadelphia: Fortress Press, and London: SCM Press, 1979. Chapter 42 presents an in-depth bibliography of resources dealing with the Ezra-Nehemiah era. Although there is no focus upon the life of Ezra specifically, short summaries are presented which address, among other issues, the chronological controversies and the reforms initiated by Ezra.

Davies, Philip R. *Second Temple Studies. Journal for the Study of the Old Testament*, supplemental volumes 117, 175. Sheffield: JSOT Press, 1991 and 1994. These two volumes contain several scholarly essays on Ezra.

Fensham, F. Charles. *The Books of Ezra and Nehemiah.* Grand Rapids, Mich.: Eerdmans, 1982. This volume is part of the New International Commentary on the Old Testament. Particularly valuable is the introductory matter, which presents a clear and concise discussion of the major issues, such as sources, historical background, and theology.

Grabbe, Lester L. *Judaism from Cyrus to Hadrian.* 2 vols. Minneapolis, Minn.: Fortress Press, 1992. A reference handbook that provides bibliographies, historiographical discussion of sources, and summary accounts of important events in Jewish history.

LaSor, William, David Allan Hubbard, and Frederic William Bush. *Old Testament Survey: The Message, Form, and Background of the Old Testament.* Grand Rapids, Mich.: Eerdmans, and Cumbria, England: Paternoster, 1982. Chapter 50 of this book offers an excellent presentation of the crux of the Ezra and Nehemiah narratives. Among the gems to be discovered in this work are potent insights into the achievements and significance of Ezra.

Williamson, H. G. M. *Ezra and Nehemiah.* Waco, Tex.: Word Books, 1985; Sheffield: Sheffield Academic Press, 1987. This commentary, volume 6 in the Word Biblical Commentary series, presents full bibliographies for each literary unit within the books of Ezra and Nehemiah. It includes a fresh translation of the text along with insightful commentary on the historical aspects of the narratives about Ezra.

W. R. Brookman

FABIUS
Quintus Fabius Maximus

Born: c. 275 B.C.; place unknown

Died: 203 B.C.; possibly Rome

Areas of Achievement: Government and politics; warfare and conquest

Contribution: During the Second Punic War (218-202 B.C.) between Carthage and Rome, Fabius, nicknamed "the Delayer," using feint-and-run tactics, carried on a fairly successful war of attrition against Hannibal, the great Carthaginian general whose army ravaged the Italian peninsula and threatened Rome itself.

Early Life

Quintus Fabius Maximus was born into the patrician Fabii *gens*, or clan, in about 275 B.C. Although the Fabii traced their ancestry back to a mythic origin, to Hercules, their actual origin is obscure. However, they became an important family group with a distinguished history in Roman affairs. Fabius was the great-grandson of Fabius Rullianus (fl. c. 325-290 B.C.), the first of the Fabii to append the title *Maximus* to his surname and the most famous of Fabius's forbears.

In his youth, Fabius seemed to show little promise. He was nicknamed *Verrucosus* ("Warty") because he bore disfiguring warts on his upper lip, and also *Ovicula* ("Lambkins") because he was docile and unassuming. He readily submitted to the will of childhood friends, and to some of them seemed both slow and rather dimwitted. His apparent placidity would later mature into an admirable forbearance that served him well in the turmoil of Roman politics. In his deliberate, plodding manner, he studied and mastered military tactics and oratory, important disciplines for the public offices for which he quietly and diligently prepared himself. In time, perceptive colleagues came to see that his outward lethargy masked great inner strengths, including quiet persistence, fortitude, and a nearly inexhaustible patience.

Fabius's political career also proved slow in developing. He did not serve as consul until 234, when he was about forty, and even though he drove the Ligurians from Cisalpine Gaul in 233 and was awarded a triumph, he garnered little support from the Roman populace. He lacked the more flamboyant manner and aggressive style of many soldier-statesmen, and his cautionary counsel was often ig-

nored. In fact, his political star rose rather late, starting in 221, when, in his fifties, he was elected dictator for the first time. Thereafter, with the military failures of rivals during the Second Punic War (218-202 B.C.), he gained prominence as the conservative leader in the Roman Senate and the primary architect of a strategy designed to wear down Rome's great adversary, Hannibal of Carthage.

Life's Work

In 219, Hannibal provoked Rome by attacking its Spanish ally, Saguntum. The next year, in one of history's boldest military ventures, he crossed the Alps, invading northern Italy. Aided by Cisalpine Gauls, his army won battle after battle, including, in 217, a major engagement at Lake Trasimene, where the Roman army under Flaminius was utterly destroyed.

Flaminius had been a proponent of an aggressive military policy opposed by Fabius, and his defeat and death prompted the re-election of Fabius as dictator. To the Romans, hunkering down in anticipation of Hannibal's imminent siege of the city, Fabius's defensive tactics finally made good sense.

Fabius's strategy was to erode Hannibal's strength by denying him access to supplies and fresh troops while constantly harassing his army with hit-and-run sorties against his flanks. Fabius knew that time was on Rome's side, and he studiously avoided a general engagement that promised less than certain victory. He kept his legions in the hills, protected by the terrain from assaults by Hannibal's vaunted calvary.

Fortunately for Rome, Hannibal deferred an assault on Rome. Instead, he drove further down the Italian peninsula, hoping to capture Mediterranean ports and strengthen his army by turning or neutralizing Rome's allies. At first his strategy faltered, for Rome's allies remained steadfast.

Meanwhile, Fabius was nicknamed "Cunctator," or "the Delayer," an appellation used mockingly by his opponents. The nickname was not entirely just, however, for at one point, having Hannibal at a distinct disadvantage, Fabius was ready to risk a pitched battle. He had the Carthaginians outnumbered and trapped near Casilinum, on the Campania frontier; using a celebrated ruse, however, Hannibal escaped the snare. He had his soldiers attach burning kindling to the horns of two thousand oxen and drive the frantic animals against the bewildered Roman troops guarding his escape route. In the resulting confusion, Hannibal's army broke out of the trap and vanished.

As the threat of a siege of Rome faded, its citizens again clamored for a more aggressive policy, turning against Fabius's cautious strategy. Hannibal helped fueled the ire of Fabius's critics. By carefully protecting Fabius's provincial property from pillage and burning, he deliberately created the impression that Fabius, worse than a coward, was an out-and-out traitor in league with the enemy.

While the ever-hostile Roman tribunes fanned the flames of suspicion toward Fabius, the dictator's master of the horse, Lucius Minucius, acting against the express orders of his absent superior, sought open battle with a detachment of Hannibal's troops and achieved a minor victory. When word of Minucius's success arrived in Rome, Fabius, in the city on official business, came under vicious verbal attack from the tribune Metilius, a close friend and kinsman to Minucius. He wanted Fabius stripped of power, but the Senate instead opted to give Minucius joint control of the army.

Fabius, upon his return from Rome, rejected Minucius's demand that each of them assume command on alternate days. By then, Minucius was openly bragging of his superiority to Fabius in military strategy and leadership, and Fabius feared that his rival, when in command, would imperil the whole army through some rash venture. Fabius therefore would only agree to divide the army into two separate commands, each composed of two legions.

Minucius quickly justified Fabius's fears by leading his two legions into one of Hannibal's clever traps. Surrounded, with escape routes cut off, Minucius's army faced annihilation, but Fabius attacked and forced Hannibal's forces to retreat. Reportedly, the narrow escape from disaster humbled Minucius, who, apologizing for his imprudence, ceded supreme command of the army to Fabius alone.

In 217, momentarily assured that his defensive strategies would be followed, Fabius stepped down from his dictatorship. In 216, however, Terentius Varro, another headstrong but popular soldier, was elected consul and gained joint control of the army with his less popular co-consul, Aemilius Paulus. With the support of the Senate, which authorized

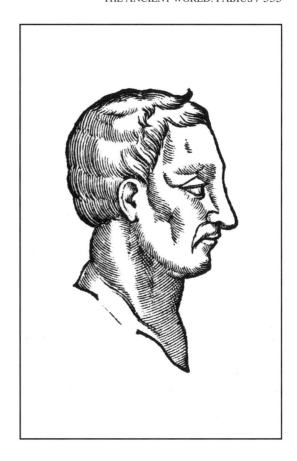

an offensive policy, he engaged Hannibal in an all-out battle at Cannae, a village located near the Aufidus River in southeastern Italy. Fabius had hoped that Paulus, whom he supported, could prevent Varro from making such a costly mistake. Because command of the army alternated between the commanders, however, Varro was able to ignore Paulus's advice. The result was the worst Roman debacle of the war, with the loss of upward of sixty thousand men. The defeat also allowed Hannibal to take Capua, the second most important city in Italy, and to roam freely through the rich provinces in the southern part of the Italian peninsula, forcing some of Rome's former allies into his camp.

The Roman Senate, again fearing an attack on the capital, once more turned to Fabius. He quickly took measures to steel the citizens' resolve to survive the expected siege, stopping a panic and flight from the city. Fortunately for Rome, against the advice of his lieutenants, Hannibal once more passed up the opportunity to take advantage of his victory. Rome took heart and again sent Fabius into the field. His cautionary tactics soon found balance in the bolder stratagems of another general, Claudius

Marcellus, who led attacks against the main body of Hannibal's army and in 211 captured Syracuse, greatly eroding the Carthaginian influence in Sicily. Marcellus and Fabius became known, respectively, as "the Sword and Shield of Rome." Marcellus was eventually led into one of Hannibal's tactical snares and killed. Fabius, meanwhile, eluded all traps that Hannibal set for him, and in 209, during his fifth consulship, won an important victory at Tarentum, one of Hannibal's important strongholds. The tide of war by that time had turned in Rome's favor.

Up until his death, Fabius remained circumspect in his policies. He vigorously opposed the plans of Cornelius Scipio, who, after winning renown by driving the Carthaginians out of Spain, was elected consul in 205. Scipio proposed an invasion of Africa and, against the strong objections and blocking maneuvers of Fabius and his faction, undertook the expedition in 204. He defeated the Punic army in 203, with the result that Carthage, in the ensuing armistice, recalled Hannibal from Italy. Fabius died before Scipio's great victory over Hannibal at Zama in 202, the battle that effectively ended Carthage's Mediterranean dominance and earned for Scipio the cognomen "Africanus."

Summary

The only blemish on Fabius's career came in his final years, when his caution and superstition led him to oppose Scipio, whose achievements would finally eclipse his own. By then, he was about seventy and securely bound to his delaying tactics by virtue of their past successes. He had sought to outlast Hannibal and to force his withdrawal from Italy when it became impossible for the invader to meet the logistical needs of his marauding army or win over Rome's unstable allies. Once shorn of him, Fabius saw little need to pursue Hannibal or attack Carthage itself.

Clearly, in his policies, Fabius placed a high value on the lives of his soldiers. He was unwilling to risk them for personal glory or political advantage. Legends concerning him relate that he also won the loyalty of his soldiers by a leniency uncharacteristic of Roman discipline. He was also generous; on one occasion, when the Senate refused to honor an obligation, he sold some of his own lands to ransom 240 soldiers held prisoner by Hannibal. Moreover, Fabius seemed remarkably free of grudges, bearing with great patience the most vituperative political attacks upon him. Although too vain for popular tastes, Fabius was an honorable man. He never abused his power by exacting revenge on his political adversaries.

Perhaps the greatest tribute to both his policies and his genius lies in the fact that it was in Fabius that Hannibal saw his greatest threat. He is said to have told his followers that Fabius was like a terrible cloud, ever hovering in the mountains, threatening to storm down on them with terrible destruction. The acknowledged fear of such an enemy as Hannibal constitutes the highest kind of praise.

Bibliography

De Beer, Sir Gavin. *Hannibal: Challenging Rome's Supremacy.* New York: Viking Press, 1969. A richly illustrated, approachable study treating its subject figure as tragic and inevitably doomed to fail in his efforts to save Carthage in the rise of Rome. Gives a solid account of the major battles and the part played by Fabius in Hannibal's Italian campaign.

Lamb, Harold. *Hannibal: One Man Against Rome.* New York: Doubleday, 1958; London: Hale, 1959. An engaging study by one of the leading writers of biographical narratives. Offers a more balanced assessment of Fabius as Hannibal's nemesis than that afforded him by Roman historians, although, as a popular biography, it lacks documentation and guides to further research.

Livy. *The War with Hannibal: Books XXI-XXX of The History of Rome from Its Foundation.* Translated by Aubrey de Sélincourt and edited by Betty Radice. London and Baltimore: Penguin Books, 1965. A full account of the Second Punic War from the vantage point of a major Roman historian who flourished at the time Rome became an empire. Although prone to romanticizing the events and major figures, Livy's narrative is both vivid and detailed. Includes maps and a chronological index.

Plutarch. *The Lives of the Noble Grecians and Romans.* Translated by John Dryden and revised by Arthur Hugh Clough. New York: Modern Library, 1932. The famous work of a major first century Roman biographer and moralist, whose "parallels" included a comparison of Fabius with Pericles of Athens. Gives a very positive assessment of Fabius's character. Includes index.

Scullard, H. H. *Roman Politics: 220-150 B.C.* 2d ed. Oxford: Clarendon Press, 1973; Westport, Conn.: Greenwood Press, 1981. An in-depth study of the various political factions in Rome at the time of the Second and Third Punic Wars. Devotes chapters to the patrician family groupings and the conservative strategies and politics of Fabius and his followers. Includes genealogical charts and year-by-year listings of consuls, censors, and praetors.

―――. *Scipio Africanus: Soldier and Politician*. London: Thames and Hudson, and Ithaca, N.Y.: Cornell University Press, 1970. A biographical study of Fabius's final rival. Useful for its analysis of Scipio's military success in Spain, leading to the final discrediting of Fabius's more timorous tactics and Scipio's expedition into Africa. Includes extensive notes, plus maps and photographs.

John W. Fiero

GALEN

Born: 129; Pergamum, the capital of Asia

Died: c. 199; possibly Rome or Pergamum

Areas of Achievement: Medicine, physiology, and philosophy

Contribution: Although not a first-rate philosopher, Galen was influential in formulating a powerful logical empiricism which took scientific axioms as self-evident rather than hypothetical. His greatest contribution was in medicine, where he made the best presentation of anatomical knowledge in the ancient world; his theories and practices remained dominant during the Middle Ages.

Early Life

Galen was born on an estate in Pergamum (also known as Pergamon), a city situated on the mainland almost opposite the island of Lesbos in Asia Minor. Pergamon lay inland in a fertile valley, and its hilltops were crowned by temples and theaters. Pergamon's library rivaled Alexandria's. Another distinguishing feature was the Asclepieion, or medical temple dedicated to Asclepius, the god of healing. This was a combination religious sanctuary, sanatorium, and place of recreation. Pergamon was one of the great seats of Christianity and held one of the seven churches mentioned by John the Apostle in Revelation (2:12-17). Because of these features, the city became one of the great pilgrimage and entertainment centers in the Roman world, and Galen grew up exposed not only to scholars but also to rhapsodists, musicians, tumblers, actors, and snake-charmers.

Galen's father, Nicon, was an architect and geometer. He was also a prosperous landowner with a farm that cultivated peas, beans, lentils, almonds, figs, olives, and grapes. Nicon himself came from a highly educated family and was able to provide his son with an education partly in the country and partly in the city. Galen (whose name derives from *galenos*, Greek for "calm" or "serene") was closer to his father than to his mother, who scolded the maids and quarreled almost incessantly with her husband. Galen compared her with Socrates' difficult wife, Xanthippe, but was able to keep his distance from her by accompanying his father to lectures in the city. His father provided or supervised Galen's education until the boy reached fourteen, then he directed his son to philosophical studies.

There were four leading philosophical systems at the time—Platonism, Aristotelianism, Stoicism, and Epicureanism—and Galen was not prodded along any single path of knowledge. He had the benefit of a liberal education, although he found confusion in philosophy and had doubts about mathematics. His father wanted a state career for the boy, but after having a dream in which Asclepius directed attention to medicine, Nicon sent Galen, then seventeen, to study under the celebrated anatomist and Sophist Satyros.

Life's Work

When Nicon died, probably in 151, Galen worked with Pelops in Smyrna and with Numisianos in Corinth and Alexandria, where he wrote a treatise in three parts on the movement of the lungs and thorax. He remained in Alexandria for roughly five years, traveling in various parts of Egypt. There were six main medical sects at the time, three ancient (the Hippocratic, Dogmatic, and Empirical) and three "modern" (the Methodist, Pneumatic, and Eclectic). Galen, like any of his colleagues,

338

was free to try combinations of these sects, and he devoted two treatises to the discussion of them.

Upon his return to Pergamon, he was appointed physician to the school of gladiators by the head priest of the Asclepieion. Galen's appointment lasted more than two years and was a useful experience. Because gladiators often received severe wounds, a physician was obliged to attend to the diet, exercise, and convalescence of these combatants in order to ensure that they were in good health and that they would recover in due course from certain injuries. Galen did not perform much surgery on the gladiators, and his knowledge of anatomy was derived exclusively from dissections on animals—particularly the Barbary ape (for which he was nicknamed the "ape doctor"). Slaves or students would prepare the cadavers of pigs, sheep, oxen, cats, dogs, horses, lions, wolves, birds, and fish by shaving and flaying them, and it is a wonder that Galen and other anatomists were not killed by infection.

Dissection led to insights about the general plan of the body, and Galen showed that this plan was essentially the same from creature to creature. He discovered that arteries contain blood and that a severed artery (even a small one) could drain all the body's blood in one-half hour or less. He showed that the right auricle outlives the rest of the heart and that there is a link between the brain and the larynx.

When a new war between the Pergamonians and the neighboring Galatians began, Galen left for Rome. His life and career coincided with the noble rule of Antoninus Pius and that of his son, Marcus Aurelius. Galen rented a large house, practiced as a physician, attended medical meetings in the Temple of Peace, and continued his interest in philosophy.

He respected the ancients, particularly Aristotle, Plato, and Hippocrates. He argued that all scientific knowledge begins with the senses, or mind, and he was opposed to the Skeptics, who taught their disciples to argue on either side of any point. Galen found it absurd to argue so freely while doubting, as the Skeptics did, the starting points of knowledge. Although somewhat "magical" or irrational in medical practice (he believed in the therapeutic value of excrement and amulets), he was a rationalist in his philosophical method, recognizing a role for syllogistic reasoning and admiring the purposiveness of all nature. He believed, with Aristotle, that nature never makes anything superfluous; he

tried in *De usu partium corporis humani (On the Usefulness of the Parts of the Body)* to justify the form and function of each organ of the body. He interpreted other philosophers (especially Plato, Aristotle, Theophrastus, Chrysippus, Epicurus), but his many ethical treatises were lost, as was a series of works on lexicographical and stylistic problems.

He held a Platonic view of the soul, recognizing the three parts (nutritive, animal, rational) distinguished in Plato's *Republic* and opposing the Stoic doctrine of a single, indivisible soul. His treatise on the subject ascribes nutrition to the liver and veins, the pneuma or spirit to the lungs and heart, and sensation and muscular movement to the brain and nerves. It is easy to see how physiology and philosophy mixed in Galen's theories, especially in his pneumatic theory which, though derived from Hippocrates and Anaximenes of Miletus, was an interesting revision of those older beliefs. According to Galen, each of the three fundamental members (liver, heart, brain) was dominated by a special pneuma or spirit: the liver by natural or physical spirit—a vapor from blood, which controlled nutrition, growth, and reproduction; the heart by vital spirit, transmitted in the veins and conveying heat and life; the brain by animal or psychical spirit, which regulated the brain, nerves, and feeling. Galen believed that the habits of the soul were influenced by bodily temperament (rather than by climate, as Hippocrates had insisted). Galen's theory of the four humors (based on the four elements earth, air, fire, and water) went back to Empedocles but was a restatement of Hippocrates' theory of four qualities (dry, wet, hot, cold) and of another version of the four humors (blood, yellow bile, black bile, phlegm). This attempted reconciliation of medicine and philosophy was consistent with his claim that the best physician was also a philosopher.

Galen became a friend of the Aristotelian philosopher Eudemos, and when the latter fell ill, Galen was consulted—much to the hostility of the patient's other physicians. A contest of invective, suspicion, and tactlessness broke out between Galen and his rivals. Galen's outspoken and contemptuous criticism of those he considered charlatans put his life in danger; he decided to return to Pergamon.

His recuperation from Rome-weariness was short. He received a letter from the two rulers, Marcus Aurelius and Lucius Verus, ordering him to join the imperial camp in Aquileia (a commercial and military center and one of the great cities of the west), where legions were gathering to march against the Barbarians. These military preparations were disrupted by plague, a form of typhus or smallpox probably brought in from Syria and stubbornly resistant to health measures. The emperors decided to leave the army, but when Verus died in 169, Marcus returned to the field after ordering Galen back to Rome to take medical charge of Marcus' eight-year-old son, Commodus.

As court physician, Galen strengthened his position. He continued in office when Commodus succeeded his father as emperor in 180. Galen remained in Rome until 192, when a fire destroyed the Temple of Peace, as well as many libraries and bookshops. Many of his writings, especially some of his philosophical treatises, which existed only in a few copies, were annihilated.

Under Commodus, the climate for scholars and philosophers became intolerable. The emperor, a superior athlete who regarded himself as a reincarnation of Hercules, placed a premium on hunting and circus games rather than on intellectual pursuits. Galen returned to Pergamon in 192, where he had yet another encounter with the plague. He was saved by letting his own blood. Most of his time was devoted to meditation and writing, and he died about 199.

Summary

Galen's writings were diverse and profuse. Although he did not have students of his own, nor did he found a school, his stature was large in his lifetime and larger after his death. His texts were translated into Syriac and Arabic as Greek culture spread throughout Syria and then into Persia and the Muhammadan world. From the eleventh century onward, Latin translations of Galen made their way into Europe, where the phenomenon of Galenism dominated the medicine of the Middle Ages, despite the plethora of other commentators and forgeries of Galen's texts.

As a medical practitioner and theorist, Galen mixed fact and speculation. Although a brilliant diagnostician, he relied on observations of "critical days," pulse, and urine for his prognoses. He had a deep distaste for surgery, except as a means to repair injuries or suppurations, and confined his operative surgery to nasal polyps, goiters, and tumors of fatty or fibrous tissues. His writing in the field, however, provides information on the use of caustics, unguents for healing wounds, and opium and other drugs for anesthesia. His anatomical knowledge suffered from the unavailability of human cadavers, so his errors were understandable. His physiology was strictly limited, but he was far ahead of his time in developing concepts of digestion, assimilation, blood formation, nerve function, and reproduction.

As a philosopher, he was hardly original, but he was useful for his commentaries on Plato and Hippocrates, and he wrote about logic, ethics, and rational psychology, arguing that "passions" were the result of unbridled energy opposed to reason, and "errors" of the soul were the result of false judgments or opinions. Galen believed that psychological troubles could be related more to the body's predisposition to disease than to disease itself, and so he recommended a daily self-examination as a preventative.

Galen erred in thinking that inadequate medical knowledge could be compensated by general knowledge. Nevertheless, he was versatile, producing works of philology (including two dictionaries) and an autobiography in addition to his more than 100 treatises on medicine. His language was often repetitive and difficult, but he never assumed literary affectations, and he continually revised his work.

Despite the fact that the Renaissance saw the overthrow of many of his theories of anatomy, physiology, and therapy, Galen can be credited for several things: setting a high ideal for the medical profession; insisting on contact with nature as a condition for treating disease; stressing the unity of an organism and the interdependence of its parts; and realizing that a living organism can be understood only in relation to its environment. His fame and theories lasted for nine centuries, before being rivaled by those of the Muslim philosopher-physician Avicenna.

Bibliography

Barton, Tamsyn S. *Power and Knowledge: Astrology, Physiognomics, and Medicine under the Roman Empire*. Ann Arbor: University of Michigan Press, 1994. This study argues that the modern distinction between science and pseudoscience does not hold good for the ancient world. The author examines the medical writers (including Galen) for the ways in which they laid claim to an elevated, authoritative status.

Brock, Arthur John, trans. *Greek Medicine, Being Extracts Illustrative of Medical Writers from Hippocrates to Galen.* London: Dent, and New York: Dutton, 1929. A good historical survey by one of the best English translators of Galen. Places Galen in historical context. Includes annotations.

Galen. *On the Therapeutic Method, Books 1 and 2.* Translated by R. J. Hankinson. Oxford: Clarendon Press, and New York: Oxford University Press, 1991. A good translation and commentary on these introductory works, in which the ancient physician contends that the good doctor must also be a philosopher.

Gilbert, N. W. *Renaissance Concepts of Method.* New York: Columbia University Press, 1960. Contains information on Galen's scientific methodology.

Jackson, R. *Doctors and Diseases in the Roman Empire.* London: British Museum Publications, and Norman: University of Oklahoma Press, 1988. A survey of medical thought in the Roman empire that includes translated selections from the major medical writers.

Kudlien, F. and R. J. Durling, eds. *Galen's Method of Healing: Proceedings of the 1982 Galen Symposium.* Leiden and New York: Brill, 1991. Scholarly essays on Galen's important, but little read, treatise *On the Method of Healing.* The book includes a number of pieces on Galen's later influence (down to the 16th century) as well as discussions of "style and context" and of Galen as a philosopher.

Lloyd, G. E. R. *Methods and Problems in Greek Science.* Cambridge and New York: Cambridge University Press, 1991. Collected papers of an eminent scholar of Greek science. Chapter 17, "Galen on Hellenistics and Hippocrateans: Contemporary Battles and Past Authorities," investigates Galen's attitudes toward his predecessors.

Sarton, George. *Galen of Pergamon.* Lawrence: University of Kansas Press, 1954. Perhaps the most accessible and readable biography of the subject. Contains interesting historical background, but the discussion of philosophy is brief and takes some knowledge for granted.

Temkin, Owsei. *Galenism: Rise and Decline of a Medical Philosophy.* Ithaca, N.Y.: Cornell University Press, 1973. An authoritative overview of the phenomenon that so influenced medieval medicine and philosophy. Also contains a description of the various forgeries of Galen's texts.

Walzer, Richard. *Galen on Jews and Christians.* London: Oxford University Press, 1949. A discussion of Galen's lack of interest in the two major religions and of his belief in the Demiurge and the purposiveness of nature.

Keith Garebian

GENSERIC

Born: c. 390; probably Slovakia

Died: 477; Carthage

Areas of Achievement: Government and politics; warfare and conquest

Contribution: One of the most important Germanic rulers, the Vandal leader Genseric invaded north Africa, sacked Rome, and hastened the fall of the Western Roman Empire.

Early Life

Born into a tumultuous era, Genseric, or Gaiseric, was the son of the Vandal king Godigisel and his freed slave wife. By the time of Genseric's birth, the Roman Empire's unity, uneasily based on the mutual recognition of several emperors, had to be renewed constantly by force. The emperors' use of Germanic troops to combat discord among Romans eventually got out of control, and barbarian peoples meant to serve as nonpolitical military resources gained control over large areas. The Franks and Goths would be the most famous of these groups, while eastern Germanic peoples included the Vandals, Suevi, and Alans.

The polygamy, love of war, unsophisticated nature worship and often brutish customs practiced by Germans left lasting bad impressions on the Romans. The Roman historian Tacitus regarded the illiterate Germans as savages incapable of knowledge. Yet the Germans were also characterized by their rejection of slavery. Their thirst for independence fostered by poverty overcame the sophisticated despotism of Rome. Militarized by the unstable situation, these peoples left an indelible mark. Many geographical names (including "France," "Burgundy," "Lombardy," and "England") originated with the Germans who conquered them. Words such as "vandal" and "frankness" became part of the English language.

Little is known of the origins of the Vandals. Tacitus used "Vandilii" as a general term for eastern Germans. Two branches of the group are later mentioned, Silings and Asdings. Driven west by the Huns, they burst into the Roman Empire on December 31, 406, when, together with the Alans, Suevi, Alamanni, and Burgundians, they crossed the ice-bound Rhine near Mainz. Genseric was in his teens when this migration marked the end of Roman power north of the Alps.

This crisis began when Emperor Theodosius died in 395 shortly after reconquering the West.

The empire was inherited by his underage sons, Arcadius in Constantinople and Honorius in Rome. Born in 384, Honorius was greatly influenced by his subordinates. Stilicho, a Vandal general who had married into the Theodosian dynasty, claimed that Theodosius had bequeathed the regency of the entire empire to him. Many refuted his claim. Ambitious warlords played the opposing courts off against each other, but no one warlord had enough power to destroy his rivals. Discredited, Stilicho was assassinated in 408. Under their able leader Alaric, the Visigoths, who had crossed Rome's borders to avoid the Huns, invaded Italy three times and sacked Rome in 410. The security and plenty that Romans had enjoyed for centuries was lost.

Barbarian bands ravaged Gaul. By 409, the Vandals, Suevi, and Alans moved into Spain, where they divided the spoils by lot. The Silings and Alans took the south, while the Asdings and Suevi occupied Galicia. In 411, they became federati, or Roman military allies. In 416, however, the Visigoths were sent by the emperor to evict the Silings and take Galicia from the Suevi. Warfare between the Suevi and the Visigoths would continue for eighty years.

Beset by barbarian warlords and hostile imperial claimants, Honorius's court went into hiding in the heavily defended city of Ravenna. The fortifications on the Danube and Rhine were abandoned. Honorius was reduced to relying on armies raised by gifts to slaves and deserters. He died heirless in 423, ending a reign afflicted by revolts and usurpations. Not until 425 did his nephew Valentinian III restore the legitimate dynasty.

After the grant of Aquitaine to the Visigoths in 418, weak governments and ambitious generals regularly turned over provinces to warlords in exchange for support in whatever crisis arose. Around 420, the Asdings moved south to rejoin the Silings, who had suffered severely under Visigothic occupation. Raiding far and wide, the united Vandals were content to plunder rather than rule. Only when they had exhausted the riches of the southern Spanish region of Andalusia (Vandalusia) did they move on.

Life's Work

In 427, the Vandals were invited to Africa by a rebellious Roman official, Bonifactius, who recruited their support against Honorius's regent. Lured by the prospect of controlling rich North African lands, Genseric and his half-brother Gunderic responded by organizing an expedition. Gunderic died before the plans were carried out, but in Genseric, the Vandals had a single leader of immense ability.

In 429, in the largest seaborne movement of Germanic peoples, some eighty thousand Vandals and Alans, including about twenty thousand warriors, landed near Tangier. Ignoring the interests of Bonifactius, Genseric laid siege to the coastal city of Hippo Regius for fourteen months; shortly before its capitulation in the summer of 430, the seventy-five-year-old bishop Augustine died inside the besieged city. Genseric overran Mauretania and Numidia (Algeria), defeating Bonifactius's troops in 431. Seven provinces that had known peace and prosperity for centuries were given over to plunder and massacre. Although the Vandals' destructiveness has been exaggerated, Genseric seldom gave quarter to opponents. Torture was employed to force captives to reveal hidden wealth. Stern policies were backed by the frequent use of execution. Yet the alleged wholesale destruction of olive trees and crops is improbable given that the Vandals intended to settle in the region.

By 435, Genseric concluded a treaty with imperial authorities who made the Vandals *federati* in Numidia. Only Carthage held out. After the city's destruction following Rome's defeat of Hannibal, the great city of Carthage had been rebuilt as the capital of Roman Africa. The surrounding region, Africa Proconsularis, became vital to Rome's grain supply. Wealthy Romans maintained vast estates, which they rarely saw, in the region. By Genseric's time, decades had passed without an emperor having visited Africa. Africa's economic and strategic importance was taken for granted by the Romans but was well known to the Vandal invaders. Foreshadowing what was to come, the Roman general Gildo had cut off Rome's grain shipments during a dispute in 397.

In a surprise attack, Genseric captured Carthage on October 19, 439, giving the Vandals a major naval base and a stranglehold on Rome's food supplies. As feared as Attila's horsemen, Vandal fleets made Genseric master of the western Mediterranean. By 442, Rome was forced to acknowledge Genseric in a second treaty that gave the Vandals North Africa.

Having spent a generation harried by stronger groups throughout Europe, Genseric was determined not to be moved again. He therefore ran a regime that was aggressive externally and harsh domestically. Although he continued to use many Roman administrators, he asserted an independent stance toward the Empire, especially terms of religion. He confiscated estates belonging to the imperial court and Roman landlords. His tyrannical regime was hated by both his Vandal subjects and the local inhabitants, who were crushed by heavy taxation. The kingship became hereditary, based on succession by the oldest living male. Consistent with his autocratic nature, he even attempted to establish a new chronological era dating from his capture of Carthage.

Meanwhile, Rome's decline continued. Like Honorius, Valentinian III had little political aptitude. His early years were beset with intrigues over succession. Spoiled, hedonistic, and overshadowed by his mother and his general Aetius, he ironically oversaw the accumulation of papal authority, particularly that of Leo the Great. Attempting to neutralize the Vandal threat, he betrothed his sister to Vandal prince Huneric. Having murdered Aetius to assert power in his own right, he himself was assassinated by members of his bodyguard in 455.

After his death, the decay of Rome accelerated. Northern Gaul fell to the Franks, the only Germans to succeed in building an enduring state. Southern Gaul and Spain were ruled by the Visigoths, and Africa by Genseric. Eventually, Ostrogoths captured Italy itself. Preserving classical civilization, Greek-speaking "Eastern Romans" ruled the eastern Mediterranean from Constantinople.

A few months after Valentinian's assassination, Genseric descended on Rome. Pope Leo was able to convince him to choose peaceful occupation over bloody massacre. Heaps of treasure were carted off to Carthage, and thousands of citizens, including the widow and daughters of the recently murdered emperor, were made captives. Genseric, though, spared the city from destruction. In 468, Genseric crowned his achievements by destroying a naval expedition sent jointly by the Eastern and Western emperors.

Vandal and Roman societies were separated by religious differences. As a sign of independence and a way of avoiding domination by the Roman clergy, most Germanic groups had converted to Arianism, which questioned Jesus Christ's divinity. Genseric brought an organized Arian clergy to Africa. Allied with the Donatists, a rival Christian sect, he and his successors instituted vengeful persecutions against Catholics. Churches were burned, and all Catholic gatherings were forbidden. Bishops and priests were deported. After two decades of persecution, Valentinian III intervened, and Genseric allowed Catholic bishops to be installed. When the bishop of Carthage died two years after Valentinian's murder, the election of a new bishop was forbidden. Genseric presided over another twenty years of repression, particularly of Catholics surviving within the administration.

Summary

After a fifty-year reign, Genseric died in 477 and was succeeded by his even more fanatical son, Huneric. After Catholic bishops refused to convert to Arianism, Huneric applied Roman laws against heretics. The bishops were exiled. Members of the Catholic laity found every trade closed to them. Huneric died within months, but forced baptisms, martyrdoms, and tortures continued. African Catholicism was left with no bishops, no churches, and hardly any priests. Persecution ended only when Hilderic, the son of Huneric and a captive daughter of Valentinian III, came to power in 523. Meanwhile, Mauritania and Numidia were abandoned to the Moors.

The pro-Catholic Hilderic was half Roman, the last descendant of the old imperial family of Theodosius. He enjoyed friendly relations with the Emperor Justinian, and he recalled bishops and restored churches. Incurring the wrath of the Arian Vandal nobility, he was overthrown and murdered in 532. Justinian intervened with a large force. On September 14, 532, the imperial general Belisarius defeated the Vandals at Ad Decimam, took Carthage, and easily subdued one district after another. By 539, Vandal rule in Africa had ended.

Unlike the Goths and Franks, the Vandals were unable to put down deep roots. They made no lasting cultural contribution and left almost no records. Those Vandals who survived became Roman slaves, intermingled with the peoples of North Africa, and disappeared from history. Nevertheless, Genseric was one of the most able, and unscrupulous, of all Germanic leaders. His conquest

of Roman Africa irreversibly weakened the empire and the North African church. A feeble Roman-Christian North Africa survived the barbarian onslaught only to succumb to seventh century Muslim invasions, which permanently destroyed the unity of the Mediterranean world.

Bibliography

Gibbon, Edward. *The History of the Decline and Fall of the Roman Empire*. Edited by J. B. Bury. 7 vols. New York: Macmillan, 1896-1902. Although inaccurate in parts, Gibbon's classic work on Rome's fall contains much valuable information and commentary on the Vandals, Alans, Germanic society in general, and imperial intrigues.

Goffart, Walter. *Barbarians and Romans*. Princeton, N.J.: Princeton University Press, 1980. A reprint of a 1928 work, Goffart's book emphasizes the ruthlessness of Genseric and the Vandals, who he argues played a key role in the collapse of the Western Roman Empire.

Gwatkin, H., and J. Whitney, eds. *The Cambridge Medieval History*. 2d ed. Cambridge and New York: Macmillan, 1957. The first volume of this standard source includes an excellent section by Ludwig Schmidt, who offers a balanced look at the social, political, and military aspects of the Vandals from Genseric to Hilderic.

O'Donnell, James J. *Augustine*. Boston: Twayne, 1985. A biography of Augustine that contains much information about religious controversy within Roman Africa, Rome's decline, and Genseric's siege of Hippo Regius.

Tacitus. *The Germania*. London and Baltimore: Penguin, 1948. Translated by H. Mattingly. Tacitus provides a representative Roman view of the society, politics, and customs of the Vandals and other Germans in the era prior to Rome's decline.

Todd, Malcolm. *The Early Germans*. Oxford and Cambridge, Mass.: Blackwell, 1992. The society, organization, migrations, customs, and conquests of the Vandals and other Germanic groups are surveyed in this useful book, which sheds much light on a confused era.

Randall Fegley

THE GRACCHI

Tiberius Sempronius Gracchus

Born: 163 B.C.; probably Rome
Died: 133 B.C.; Rome

Gaius Sempronius Gracchus

Born: 153 B.C.; probably Rome
Died: 121 B.C.; Rome
Area of Achievement: Government
Contribution: Although the Gracchi brothers were born into one of the wealthiest and most influential families in Rome, they dedicated their lives to the service of the people. In the waning years of the Roman Republic, when greed and the lust for power consumed the energies of many from the ruling class, the Gracchi tried through a series of reforms to restore the vigor of popular government; many of their ideas were later adopted by rulers such as Julius Caesar and his nephew and heir, Augustus.

Early Lives

Tiberius and Gaius Gracchus were among the twelve children born to Tiberius Sempronius Gracchus and Cornelia, the daughter of Scipio Africanus, the general who defeated the Carthaginian leader Hannibal in the Second Punic War. The elder Gracchus died when Tiberius was twelve and Gaius was barely two, but his widow reared the boys and her other surviving child, a daughter, in the traditions of their ancestors and in the virtues responsible for the greatness of the Republic. She was assisted by Diophanes of Mitylene, a noted master of rhetoric, and Blossius, the famous Stoic philosopher. Ptolemy VI, the King of Egypt, sought to marry Cornelia, but rather than deny her duty to her children, she rejected his suit. Remaining in Rome, she set an example of simplicity and frugality which both amazed and confounded her friends.

A serious youth, Tiberius was quiet, gentle, and always obedient to his elders. To test his courage and further shape his character, he was sent to Africa during the final phase of the Third Punic War to serve under his brother-in-law, Scipio the Younger. At the age of sixteen, Tiberius distinguished himself by being the first to climb the walls of Carthage when the Roman army launched its final assault on the doomed city. Shortly thereafter the war ended, and he returned to Rome, where he was betrothed to and later married Claudia, the daughter of Appius Claudius, a man with tremendous influence and great wealth. In 137, Tiberius was chosen a quaestor, and in the Numantine Wars in Spain which followed his election, he distinguished himself for his bravery and fairness in dealing with the enemies of the Republic. He was elected tribune in 133 at the age of twenty-nine.

Although Gaius Gracchus eventually proved himself to be a more effective politician than his brother, as a young man he had the reputation of being emotional, high-strung, fiery tempered, and extravagant. In his teens he, too, was sent to serve under his brother-in-law, Scipio the Younger, in Spain. When he was twenty, his brother selected him in absentia as one of the commissioners to conduct the redistribution of land under the provisions of the revised agrarian law, but the untimely murder of Tiberius rendered his appointment useless. Gaius returned to Rome, married the daughter of Publius Crassus, and assumed the character of a young man of fashion with very expensive tastes. The senators who were responsible for the death of Tiberius constantly anticipated the revenge of the younger Gracchus.

Goaded by the jibes of his family and friends, Gaius finally sought public office. Chosen a questor, he was sent to Sardinia to serve under Aurelius Orestes. Rather than considering his duty an exile, Gaius enjoyed it because at the age of twenty-seven he was not yet ready for a life in public service. Days spent on the march or in camp suited him well. The success of Gaius in Sardinia only deepened the suspicions of his enemies in the senate, and to keep him abroad they extended the term of Orestes and consequently those of his subordinates. This devious manipulation of the civil service infuriated Gaius, who returned to Rome without permission to confront his enemies. Accused of acting contrary to orders, a charge of which he was easily acquitted, Gaius began to consider seriously entering public life. Against the advice of his mother, he offered himself as a candidate for the office of tribune, and in 123 he was elected to that position.

Lives' Work

While Tiberius may have been encouraged by his mother and his former tutors to seek a tribuneship, it was the plight of the poor that really moved him to forgo the quiet of private life for the stress and uncertainty of elected office. For decades the number of small family farms had been declining, and Tiberius wanted to reverse this trend. As the Romans conquered their neighbors, thereby laying the foundations of an empire, they increased the slave population by a tremendous percentage since those who resisted the power of the Republic were condemned to perpetual servitude. Many a wealthy Roman had grown even richer by investing first in slaves and then in both public and private land which could be devoted to agriculture. These *latifundia*, great estates worked by slave labor, yielded an enormous profit. Roman farmers were forced to sell their land when they discovered that they could not compete with the cheaper slave-produced foodstuffs which flooded the market. In many instances, they sold their farms to the very men who had driven them to bankruptcy. By the thousands these dispossessed men flocked to Rome with their families hoping to find jobs, but there were none. Tiberius wanted to put this vast army of unemployed farmers back on the land, and his program of agrarian reform was designed to do exactly that.

In 376, the tribunes Licinius and Sextius had passed a law which limited the amount of public land which could be held by one individual to five hundred *iugera*, or 311 acres. This measure was ignored because no mechanism was ever created to enforce it. Tiberius now sought not only to revive it but also to form a three-man commission to see that the letter of the law was fulfilled. On the advice of some of the most respected men in Rome, he sought not to punish those who had violated the law but merely to encourage them to abandon the land they occupied illegally. To make the task easier, compensation in the form of the fair market price of each acre abandoned was offered by the government. The land-rich rejected the reforms of Tiberius and began to offer bribes to anyone they thought could help defeat the measure. Many a senator was counted among those who sold influence in exchange for gold, but an honest man, Marcus Octavius, was persuaded to stop Tiberius. Octavius was the fellow tribune of Tiberius, and he

had the obligation to veto any bill proposed by his colleague which in his opinion violated the rights of the Roman people. The founders of the Republic had created this system of checks and balances to ensure honest government, but now this safeguard of liberty was unwittingly corrupted to serve greed. Octavius was convinced that the newly revised law was illegal; thus, he vetoed it. No amount of pleading could make him change his mind. Frustrated at every turn, Tiberius resorted to measures which were ill advised, if not unlawful.

The mild law was withdrawn and a new measure with no provision for compensation was substituted. Octavius naturally opposed this measure with more energy than he had the previous one, and thus Tiberius appealed to the people to vote Marcus out of office. This was an illegal move, but once aroused, Tiberius would not heed the advice of his family or his associates. When Octavius had been recalled, Tiberius had one of his close supporters elected in his place and the agrarian law was finally passed. The three men quickly appointed to enforce the law were Appius Claudius, Gaius Gracchus, and Publius Crassus. Tiberius had originally reserved one of these places for himself, but he was persuaded to appoint his brother's father-in-law instead.

The method Tiberius used to finance his plan was ingenious. King Attalus III of Pergamum, a state in Asia Minor, had, in his will, left his kingdom and all of his treasure to the Roman people in the hope of sparing his subjects Rome's inevitable conquest. Tiberius now proposed to sell the treasures and use the profits to buy farm tools and livestock for those to receive land under the provisions of the new law. It was a very popular move with the people but not with the senate.

Just as Tiberius began to implement his plan, his term of office expired. Convinced that the success of the new agrarian law depended on him, Tiberius ignored tradition and stood for reelection. The senate responded to his challenge by goading the city mob into a frenzy. In the resulting riot, Tiberius was beaten to death and his body was thrown into the Tiber River. Three hundred of his closest followers were arrested and condemned to death without a trial.

Thus, when Gaius was elected tribune ten years after his brother, the senators who had arranged the murder of Tiberius had reason to fear for their lives. Almost immediately after his election, Gaius proposed legislation to punish Octavius and Popillius, the magistrate who had unjustly sentenced Tiberius' associates to death. Only the intervention of Cornelia saved Octavius, but Popillius fled Rome. Gaius, who craved the adoration of the people and welcomed conflict, revived his brother's agrarian law in the face of certain senatorial opposition. That controversy was only the beginning.

While serving in Sardinia, Gaius had witnessed the privation of the average Roman soldier, who was ill equipped and poorly fed. In quick succession, laws were passed to furnish each soldier with clothing proper to the season and climate at government expense. By law, boys under the age of seventeen were forbidden to enlist in the army. The market price of grain sold to the poor was lowered and the government absorbed the difference. To curtail the control of the senate over the judiciary, he expanded the number of judges and then personally recruited them from the nonsenatorial orders. Roads and public granaries were built, giving jobs to the unemployed. Then, as his first term of office ended, Gaius turned his attention to the founding of colonies as places of settlement for the landless.

When Gaius sought reelection, he met with no open opposition from his enemies in the senate, because he was too popular with the people. Unwisely, Gaius left Rome to supervise personally the laying of the foundations of a new colony on the site of Carthage. In his absence, his opponents began to undermine his policies. Returning to the capital, he found Rome on the verge of anarchy. The issue that led to the downfall of Gaius was his proposal to extend the benefits of Roman citizenship to the Italian allies. This reform would have seriously weakened the power and influence of the senate. Once again he sought the endorsement of the people, but this time he lost at the polls. At last his senatorial enemies had their chance. Gaius was declared an outlaw, and within a day the second of the remarkable Gracchi brothers was dead, the victim of a murder-suicide. Three thousand of his followers were judicially murdered, and an uneasy peace settled over Rome.

Summary

In the middle of the second century before the Christian era, the Roman Republic faced a constitutional crisis which threatened to destroy the fabric of the state. Invincible on the field of battle, Rome suddenly enjoyed unbelievable wealth as the booty from a host of countries flowed into the capital, accompanied by thousands of captives who were reduced to servitude. Condemned to endless labor on the huge farms that dotted the Italian landscape, these slaves drove free Romans from their tiny family farms when they could no longer compete. As they swelled the mob of unemployed in the capital, the Gracchi brothers, Tiberius and Gaius, arose to give them hope. In their respective programs lay the last and best chance for the Republic, and their assassinations were its death knell.

An uneasy quiet descended on Rome after the murder of the Gracchi and their supporters, but within a generation the peace was shattered as two men, Gaius Marius and Lucius Cornelius Sulla, vied for control of the state. Marius was a successful general who modernized the Roman army, transforming it from a force formed of draftees into one filled with long-term volunteers. Most of these recruits were landless peasants who received a tract of land at the end of their service; thus, one of the proposals of the Gracchi was revived and became a permanent part of the Roman system. Marius led the Populares, the party of the Gracchi, while Sulla headed the Optimates, the party composed of the senatorial enemies of Tiberius and Gaius. In the ensuing civil war, thousands of innocent victims from both sides were butchered.

A slave rebellion, countless conspiracies, and another civil war followed in the wake of Sulla's victory. Then the Romans, weary of the bloodshed, turned to Julius Caesar for deliverance. Caesar used a number of the ideas of the Gracchi to win and retain popular support, a practice continued by his imperial successors. The welfare system proposed by Gaius Gracchus thus became a political weapon and then a financial liability during the latter days of the Roman Empire. The distribution of public lands to veterans, however, settled thousands of responsible and loyal citizens on the frontiers of the Empire. Thus, the best that Rome had to offer survived despite the steady decline of the imperial system.

With the rediscovery of classical culture during the Renaissance, the Gracchi once again caught the public's imagination, but it was not until the birth of popular republics in the United States and France that they regained their places in the pantheon of democratic heroes. Their deeds have become legendary and their names are synonymous with reform and the best in the liberal tradition.

Bibliography

Badian, E. *Foreign Clientelae, 264-270 B.C.* Oxford: Clarendon Press, 1958; New York: Oxford University Press, 1984. This scholarly work is extremely valuable because it enables the student to place the Gracchi in the context of Roman history. The bibliography serves as an excellent departure point for further reading.

Bernstein, Alvin H. *Tiberius Sempronius Gracchus, Tradition and Apostasy.* Ithaca, N.Y.: Cornell University Press, 1978. The author has written an excellent, well-balanced biography of the eldest of the Gracchi. Each step in the career of Tiberius is carefully examined and evaluated. The bibliography is comprehensive.

Plutarch. *Plutarch's Lives.* Vol. 10, *Agis and Cleomenes, and Tiberius and Gaius Gracchus, Philopoemen and Titus Flaminus.* Translated by Bernadotte Perrin. Cambridge, Mass.: Harvard University Press, and London: Heinemann, 1926. Another volume in the Loeb Classical Library, this work contains the Greek original and a very fine English translation. Plutarch supplies his reader with a clear, concise, and moving portrait of the two brothers who might have saved the Roman Republic.

Scullard, H. H. *From the Gracchi to Nero: A History of Rome from 133 B.C. to A.D. 68.* 5th ed. London and New York: Methuen, 1982. This work chronicles not only the rise and fall of the Gracchi but also the aftermath of their attempts to save the Roman Republic: the tragic decline of Roman liberty from the mid-second century B.C. to the reign of Nero. The author also includes a number of chapters dealing with other aspects of Roman culture.

Stockton, David. *The Gracchi.* Oxford: Clarendon Press, and New York: Oxford University Press, 1979. For those unfamiliar with the actual mechanisms by which the Roman Republic was governed the author provides an excellent foreword. This slim volume provides a detailed treatment of the careers of the Gracchi as well as a series of useful appendices.

Clifton W. Potter, Jr.

GREGORY OF NAZIANZUS

Born: 329 or 330; Arianzus, Cappadocia

Died: 389 or 390; Arianzus, Cappadocia

Areas of Achievement: Oratory, literature, and religion

Contribution: A consummate rhetorician, Gregory produced many orations, poems, and letters which provide much information on the religious and social life of Christianity in the second half of the fourth century. As a theologian, Gregory was influential in the formulation of orthodox doctrine regarding the divinity of the Holy Spirit.

Early Life

Gregory was born on the family estate of Arianzus, near Nazianzus, the son of Bishop Gregory the Elder of Nazianzus. His mother, Nonna, a pious woman who had converted her husband to Christianity in 325, was a very formative influence on her son. Young Gregory was educated in the school of rhetoric in Caesarea in Cappadocia, then briefly in the Christian schools of Caesarea in Palestine and of Alexandria, where he became familiar with Christianized Platonism. On his sea journey from Alexandria, his ship encountered a great storm; realizing that he was not yet baptized, Gregory made a solemn vow to spend the rest of his life in the service of the Church if he survived. Finally, he went to the great secular university of Athens, where he spent nine years, becoming an outstanding student of the rhetoricians Prohaeresius and Himerius. There he became an inseparable friend of Basil of Caesarea, whom he commemorated at length in his famous autobiographical poem, *Carmen de vita sua* (c. 382; *On His Life*, 1814).

Life's Work

In 362, Gregory's father ordained him a priest against the young scholar's own will but by popular demand. Gregory subsequently fled to the desert, where he wrote a famous treatise on the priesthood, *Apology for His Flight*, but he soon rejoined his father. He preached his first sermon on Easter Sunday, 362. In this sermon, he likened his father to the patriarch Abraham and himself to Abraham's son Isaac being led forth to sacrifice. Thereafter, he helped to administer his father's diocese. His school friend, Basil, now Bishop of Caesarea, soon appointed him Bishop of Sasima, "a bewitched and miserable little place," according to Gregory, who refused to take possession of the see.

After his father's death in 374, Gregory administered the see of Nazianzus for a time. In 375, he retired to a monastery in Seleucia, Isauria, but four years later he was invited to reorganize the dwindling Nicene community in Constantinople, a city rife with Arianism. In 380, Emperor Theodosius the Great formally inducted him into the Church of the Apostles in Constantinople, which he served until the middle of 381. His Forty-second Oration is a speech announcing his resignation from the see of Constantinople, which he characterized as a place "not for priests, but for orators, not for stewards of souls, but for treasurers of money, not for pure offerers of the sacrifice, but for powerful patrons." Though still only in his early fifties, he retired, a prematurely old, sick, and very disillusioned man, to Cappadocia, where he died in 389 or 390.

Gregory's celebrated speeches defending the orthodox teaching on the Trinity against the heretical Eunomians and Macedonians, collected as the *Orationae* (362-381; *Theological Orations*, 1894),

S. GREGORI NAZIANZEN

earned for him the appellation "the Theologian." These orations represent brilliant defenses of the divinity of the Son and the Holy Spirit. *In laudem Basilii Magni* (381; *On St. Basil the Great*, 1953) is regarded as the finest piece of Greek rhetoric since the time of Demosthenes. Indeed, in Byzantine times Gregory was often called "the Christian Demosthenes." Also surviving are panegyrics on his father, his sister, his brother, and the church fathers Saint Athanasius of Alexandria and Saint Cyprian of Carthage.

Gregory's poetry, though rarely inspired, makes competent use of classical models; it deals didactically with a variety of topics, mainly theological. Some forty of the surviving four hundred poems are dogmatic, dealing with such themes as the Trinity and Divine Providence. Most of the poetry was composed in Gregory's final years of retirement.

Particularly important among his numerous letters, written in a very engaging classical style, are three—addressed to a certain Cledonius—which present a forceful refutation of the popular contemporary heresy of Apollinarianism. In writing to pagans, Gregory quoted authors such as Homer and Demosthenes as freely as he quoted from the Old and New Testaments when writing to Christians.

Summary

Gregory was a man of great sensitivity and spirituality. His was a contemplative nature, very ill-suited to the rough and tumble of ecclesiastical politics in Constantinople at the time of the Second Ecumenical Council of 381. He had great rhetorical skills, and his lasting achievement is the surviving forty-five orations, evidencing a masterful synthesis of classical rhetoric and Christianity. Gregory was particularly adept at countering the logic-chopping of the later Arians, known as Eunomians. He was obviously well trained in Aristotelian and Stoic logic and dialectic. Moreover, his wide knowledge of Scripture also enabled him to outwit his opponents in the deployment and interpretation of scriptural texts. The theological importance of the orations is especially evident in their Trinitarian and christological concerns.

Some of Gregory's autobiographical poems are as deeply spiritual and revealing as the *Confessiones* (397-400; *Confessions*) of Saint Augustine. A careful reading of the poems dealing with his brief tenure in Constantinople can contribute much to an understanding of the ecclesiastical politics of
the time, the shallowness and wiliness of some of his fellow bishops at the council, and Gregory's dissatisfaction with the compromise statement on the divinity of the Holy Spirit that emerged in 381.

The original text of his surviving works is contained in volumes 35 to 38 of J.-P. Migne's *Patrologia Graeca* (1842-1853). Gratifying progress is being made by an international committee of scholars in producing new critical texts of his individual works, some of which have been published as part of the series Sources Chrétiennes.

One of Gregory's epitaphs on his father is equally applicable to himself:

If there was one Moses privileged on the mountain
to hear the pure voice, there was also the mind of great
  Gregory,
whom once God's grace called from afar
and made a great high-priest.
Now he dwells near the holy Trinity.

Bibliography

Gregg, Robert C. *Consolation Philosophy: Greek and Christian Paideia in Basil and the Two Gregories.* Cambridge, Mass.: Philadelphia Patristic Foundation, 1975. A useful comparative study of the three great Cappadocians' consolatory letters and discourses, with a consideration of their biblical and Hellenistic background. Letters of consolation and panegyrics are examined in the light of the established rhetorical norms of Greek literature.

Gregory of Nazianzus. *Three Poems.* Translated by Denis M. Meehan, with notes by Thomas P. Halton. Washington, D.C.: Catholic University of America Press, 1987. These poems reveal Gregory's sensitivity and reflect his unrelenting quest for perfection in a world full of intrigue and corruption. A sensitive translation, with a useful introduction, bibliography, and notes. Part of the series The Fathers of the Church.

Gregory of Nazianzus and Saint Ambrose. *Funeral Orations of Saint Gregory Nazianzen and Saint Ambrose.* Translated by Leo P. McCauley and others. New York: Fathers of the Church, 1953. Particularly useful for the translation of *In laudem Basilii Magni.* Also includes the panegyrics on Gregory's father, brother, and sister.

Kennedy, George A. *Greek Rhetoric Under Christian Emperors.* Princeton, N.J.: Princeton University Press, 1983. Chapter 4, "Christianity and Rhetoric," includes a lengthy and sympathetic study of Gregory, described as "the most important figure in the synthesis of classical rhetoric and Christianity."

Lim, Richard. *Public Disputation, Power, and Social Order in Late Antiquity*. Berkeley: University of California Press, 1995. This study of the meaning of public debate in late antique Christianity deals, in its fifth chapter, with Gregory Nazianzus and John Chrysostom, who in their sermons (Lim claims) attempted to stem the tide of excessive theological disputation by mystifying and "obfuscating" contentious questions about the divine nature.

Meredith, Anthony. *The Cappadocians*. Crestwood, N.Y.: St. Vladimir's Seminary Press, and London: Geoffrey Chapman, 1995. An introductory discussion of St. Basil, St. Gregory Nazianzus, and St. Gregory of Nyssa that situates them in their historical context and discusses the salient features of their thought.

Quasten, Johannes. *Patrology*. Vol. 3, *The Golden Age of Greek Patristic Literature*. Westminster, Md.: Newman Press, 1950. Contains a well-documented and sympathetic account of one characterized as "the humanist among the theologians of the fourth century." Part of a four-volume set. Includes copious bibliographies.

Ruether, Rosemary R. *Gregory of Nazianzus, Rhetor and Philosopher*. Oxford: Clarendon Press, 1969. A careful examination of the Hellenistic influences apparent in Gregory's thought. Includes a particularly helpful examination of his early training. Ruether shows that Gregory became a master of numerous rhetorical devices taught in fourth century schools.

Thomas Halton

GREGORY OF NYSSA

Born: c. 335; Caesarea, Cappadocia
Died: c. 394; Constantinople
Areas of Achievement: Religion and theology
Contribution: A profound thinker and theologian, as well as an eloquent preacher, Gregory was one of the brilliant leaders of Christian orthodoxy in the late fourth century. His influence led to the defeat of the Arian heresy and the triumph of the orthodox Nicene position at the Council of Constantinople in 381.

Early Life

One of ten children, Gregory was born in the city of Caesarea, the capital of Cappadocia, to an important and wealthy Christian family which had suffered in the persecutions of the Roman emperor Diocletian. He was the third son and one of the youngest children of Basil the Elder and Emmelia—herself the daughter of a martyr. Gregory was left fatherless at an early age and was reared largely by his older brother, Basil (later called "the Great"), Bishop of Caesarea, and by his sister Macrina. Throughout his life, Gregory looked up to his brother with great affection and respect.

As a young man, Gregory was educated in his native city, attending secular pagan schools. His feeble constitution and natural shyness caused him to concentrate on scholarship rather than physical activities or public life. Thus, his intellectual prowess was enhanced by diligent private study.

While in his youth, Gregory became involved in church activities, but he did so without great conviction. Later in life, he recounted his reluctant, even unwilling, attendance at a ceremony given by his mother in honor of church martyrs. Wearied with his journey and the length of the service—which lasted far into the night—he fell asleep. A terrifying dream soon followed which filled him with a sense of remorse for his neglect of spiritual matters, and he became a lector, or reader of biblical passages in a Christian congregation.

Gregory's youthful years coincided with the last revival of pagan culture, which reached its peak under the emperor Julian the Apostate (reigned 361-363). Gregory was completely won over to the pagan humanistic ideal. Therefore, after a time, Gregory abandoned his church position and devoted himself to secular pursuits. Sometime after the year 360, he accepted a position as a teacher of rhetoric. This desertion from the Christian cause

gave his friends and family great pain and brought to him accusations of all kinds.

At about this same time Gregory married a woman named Theosebeia. She is believed to have been the sister of Gregory of Nazianzus, who was a family friend. In a letter written many years later, Gregory of Nazianzus, consoling his friend upon the death of Theosebeia, extolled her as a true priestess, most fair and lustrous. In fact, Gregory's final conversion to the Christian faith undoubtedly resulted in part from the pleadings and remonstrations of both his wife and his friend.

Another contributing factor which led Gregory back to the Church was the increasing distaste he felt for teaching rhetoric. He became discouraged by the results of his efforts to inspire literary tastes among youths who, he complained, were more ready and better suited to enter the army than follow rhetorical studies.

Gregory abandoned his teaching sometime before 370. He then retired to a monastery at Pontus which was presided over by his brother Basil. There he devoted himself to the study of the Scrip-

S.GREGORIVS NYSSENVS

tures and the works of Christian commentators. He was especially influenced by Origen, as is evident from Gregory's own theological works.

While he was at the monastery, an episode occurred which may reveal a flaw in Gregory's judgment. A rift had arisen between Basil and an aged uncle, also named Gregory, over doctrinal matters. Acting as a self-appointed mediator, the younger Gregory forged some letters which purported to be from his uncle to his brother Basil offering peace. The deception was exposed, and Gregory received a stern but dignified rebuke from his brother.

Life's Work

Around the year 365, Basil had been summoned by Eusebius, Metropolitan of Caesarea, to aid in repelling the assaults of the Arian faction of Christianity on the Nicene orthodox faith. During the next few years, the Arian believers were assisted and encouraged by the emperor Valens. Basil greatly helped orthodox resistance and in 370 was called, by popular voice, to succeed Eusebius upon the latter's death.

To strengthen his position and surround himself with defenders of the orthodox faith in the outposts of his diocese, Basil persuaded Gregory (in spite of his protests) to accept the bishopric of Nyssa, an obscure town of Cappadocia, about ten miles from Caesarea. It was as Bishop of Nyssa that Gregory achieved his greatest fame and realized his greatest accomplishments. When a mutual friend wrote to express his surprise at Basil's choosing such an obscure place for so distinguished a man as Gregory, Basil replied that his brother's merits did indeed make him worthy of governing the entire Church. Basil added, however, that the see should be made famous by its bishop, and not the bishop by his see.

Gregory was consecrated bishop in 372. Nevertheless, as soon as he arrived in Nyssa he faced grave difficulties. Arianism was strong in the city and was supported by the emperor. In addition, one of the emperor's courtiers had wanted the bishopric, and Gregory's appointment made for immediate hostility. A man named Demosthenes had been recently appointed governor of Pontus by the emperor and charged to do all in his power to crush the adherents of the orthodox Nicene faith. After some petty acts of persecution, a synod was summoned in 375 at Ancyra to examine charges made against Gregory, including embezzlement of church property and irregularities surrounding his consecration.

Though Gregory escaped from the band of soldiers sent to arrest him, his Arian enemies continued their persecution. Finally, in 376, another synod was summoned at Nyssa; this time the assembled bishops deposed Gregory. A successor was consecrated and Valens banished Gregory from the city. For many months he was driven from place to place to avoid his enemies. Heartsick over the apparent triumph of Arianism, Gregory nevertheless encouraged his friends to be of good cheer and trust in God. This advice proved to be well-founded. In 378 Valens died and the youthful emperor Gratian restored Gregory to his bishopric.

Soon afterward another event occurred which forever changed Gregory's life; Basil died in 379, and Gregory fell heir to his position of leadership. Basil had been a man of action and an organizer. Gregory was forced to stand on his own, carrying out the work of his brother and bringing it to completion.

From 379 onward, Gregory's activity was limitless. The next two years saw him preach tirelessly against heresies, Arianism especially. Named after Arius, a priest in Alexandria, Egypt, this doctrine denied the true divinity of Jesus Christ by maintaining that the Son of God was not eternal but created by the Father from nothing, that He, therefore, was not God by nature—being a changeable creature—and that His dignity as Son of God was conferred on Him by the Father because of His abiding righteousness. During this time Gregory preached against Eunomius (an Arian bishop); this preaching would lay the foundation for a major theological treatise entitled *Contra Eunomium* (382; against Eunomius).

The spring of 381 marked the pinnacle of Gregory's career. It was then that the emperor Theodosius I convoked the Council of Constantinople. Gregory played a major role in the council. He gave the opening address, influencing many, and witnessed the complete victory of the orthodox Christian doctrines and ideas for which he and Basil had fought. Thus, the work of the Council of Nicaea (in 325) regarding the doctrine of Christ was ratified. The council condemned all varieties of Arianism and added clauses to the Nicene Creed which were supplied by Gregory himself.

After the Council of Constantinople, Gregory became one of the leading personalities of the church in the East. The council gave him jurisdiction, together with two other church leaders, over the regions of Cappadocia and Pontus. He was also sent to Arabia to mediate a dispute between two bishops, though he met with limited success. On his return, he visited the Holy Land, including the city of Jerusalem and the places associated with the life of Christ.

By the end of 381 Gregory was back in Nyssa. The following year, he produced two of his most important theological writings, *Contra Eunomium* and *Adversus Apollinarem* (against Apollinaris), in which he responded to heretical ideas and discussed the doctrines relating to Christ and His nature.

Gregory's influence outside the Church was also at its peak during the years from 381 to 386, and he enjoyed the favor of the imperial court. When Gregory visited the Holy Land, the emperor provided a public chariot for his transportation. Following the success of the Council of Constantinople, Theodosius wanted to hold a council every year; in 383 Gregory was chosen by the emperor to give a major sermon on the divinity of the Son and the Holy Spirit at the convocation. In 385 he was chosen to deliver the funeral eulogies in honor of Empress Flacilla and her daughter Pulcheria, who had died shortly before her mother. At Constantinople, too, Gregory enjoyed the friendship of Olympias, one of the outstanding women of the age.

After 386, Gregory's influence began to decline. His ideas were called into question a number of times, and he had to defend himself against charges that his thinking was tainted with heretical notions. Finally, in Asia Minor, Gregory's prerogatives began to be restricted to his own diocese, and he increasingly came into conflict with the metropolitan, Helladius.

In the year 394, Gregory was invited to attend a synod at Constantinople which was called to decide once and for all the claims of two bishops over the see of Bostra. At the request of Nectarius, who was the presiding official there, Gregory delivered his last recorded sermon. It is very likely that he did not long survive the synod, dying in Constantinople the same year as the meeting.

Summary

Among church fathers and theologians, there is no more honored a name than Gregory of Nyssa. Besides receiving the accolades of his brothers Basil and his friend Gregory of Nazianzus, Gregory of Nyssa was praised by biblical scholar Jerome for the sanctity of his life, his theological learning, and his strenuous defense of the Nicene faith. Gregory came to be regarded as one of the three Cappadocian fathers of the Church, along with Basil the Great and Gregory of Nazianzus.

Though not considered as able an administrator as his brother, Gregory was highly appreciated for his eloquence in writing and speaking. He was chosen to deliver many discourses in the company of other theologians, and his writings show him to be well versed in the work of pagan philosophers as well as in Holy Scripture and the writings of Christian commentators. His works comprise some thirty letters, many sermons and exegetical writings, polemical treatises, including *Contra Eunomium* and *Adversus Apollinarem*, and several ascetic pieces.

Gregory's tireless championing of the Nicene faith and battle against heresies, especially Arianism, are his greatest legacy. Indeed, his efforts seem to have made prophetic the statement of his brother Basil, spoken at the time of Gregory's consecration to the bishopric: Nyssa was ennobled and made famous by its bishop, and not the other way around.

Bibliography

Brown, Peter. *The Body and Society: Men, Women, and Sexual Renunciation in Early Christianity.* New York: Columbia University Press, 1988. A fascinating exercise in the history of ideas and their impact on society. In chapter 18 Brown discusses Gregory of Nyssa's treatise *On Virginity.*

Dunstone, Alan S. *The Atonement in Gregory of Nyssa.* London: Tyndale Press, 1964. This small volume was originally a lecture delivered in Cambridge, England. It provides a succinct discussion of one of the most important themes of Gregory's christological writings and sermons. Its value lies in its concise analysis of Gregory's thinking on a complex theme.

Gregory of Nyssa, Saint. *From Glory to Glory.* Edited by Herbert Musurillo. New York: Scribner, 1961; London: Murray, 1962. This volume comprises an anthology of texts taken from Gregory's mystical and ascetical writings. It also contains a readable, well-organized, and most valuable introduction, which presents a history of Gregory's life and work as well as an analysis of some of his writing. The notes and comments on the texts by the editor are also very enlightening. The selected texts have been translated into modern idiomatic English.

————. *Gregory of Nyssa's Treatise on the Inscriptions of the Psalms*. Ronald E. Heine, ed. Oxford Early Christian Studies. Oxford: Clarendon Press, and New York: Oxford University Press, 1995. Translation of Gregory's exegetical work on the headings of the psalms. The introduction contains valuable information on the intellectual background of Gregory's theology.

————. *The Lord's Prayer, the Beatitudes*. Edited and translated by Hilda C. Graef. New York: Newman, and London: Longmans, 1954. This book is a compilation of various sermons given by Gregory on the subjects of the Lord's Prayer and the Beatitudes. They give the flavor of Gregory's style of preaching. The work contains an adequate introduction, including a sketch of the scholar's life. Gregory's sermons display his imaginative, rhetorical, and devotional talents.

Hardy, Edward Rochie, and Cyril Richardson, eds. *The Library of Christian Classics*. Vol. 3, *Christology of the Later Fathers*. London: SCM Press, and Philadelphia: Westminster Press, 1954. This volume devotes almost half of its contents to the writings of Gregory of Nyssa. It provides an excellent biographical sketch of Gregory and a summary of his work. It also contains selections, translated into English, of his more important works. Its greatest value, however, lies in the very thorough bibliography of the works of Gregory, as well as of biographies and articles on his life—a good share of the best ones being written in foreign languages.

Jaeger, Werner, ed. *Two Rediscovered Works of Ancient Christian Literature*. Leiden, Netherlands: E. J. Brill, 1954. A scholarly volume containing critical notes and commentary on two important treatises by Gregory, this book presents the relationships between Greek theologians and Greek philosophy and Gregory's thought. It contains valuable commentary on the cultural context of Gregory's work. The editor is one of the foremost authorities on Gregory.

Meredith, Anthony. *The Cappadocians*. Crestwood, N.Y.: St. Vladimir's Seminary Press, and London: Geoffrey Chapman, 1995. An introductory discussion of St. Basil, St. Gregory Nazianzus, and St. Gregory of Nyssa that situates them in their historical context and discusses the salient features of their thought.

Schaff, Philip, and Henry Wace, eds. Introduction to *Gregory of Nyssa: Dogmatic Treatises*. Vol. 5 in *A Select Library of Nicene and Post-Nicene Fathers of the Christian Church*. New York: Christian Literature Co., 1893. This is an important and informative introduction to Gregory's life and work, though the style is somewhat awkward. The selected texts from Gregory's compiled major works are supplemented by scholarly notes and references.

Andrew C. Skinner

HADRIAN

Born: January 24, 76; Italica, Spain
Died: July 10, 138; Baiae, Bay of Naples
Area of Achievement: Government
Contribution: Hadrian succeeded in bringing a relatively peaceful period to the Roman Empire, in realizing much-needed domestic and civil reforms, and in leaving, through his architectural and artistic gifts, his personal stamp on Rome, Athens, and Jerusalem.

Early Life

Hadrian was born in Italica, Spain, a Roman settlement, of Publius Aelius Hadrianus Afer, a distinguished Roman officer and civil administrator, and Domitia Paulina. Hadrian's parents, however, were not as influential in his development as Hadrian's cousin Trajan, the future Roman emperor who served as his coguardian after his father died when Hadrian was ten years old. Soon after his father's death, Hadrian was sent to Rome to further his education; during his stay in Rome, his study of Greek language, literature, and culture made him so much a Hellenist that he became known as the "Greekling." When he was fifteen, he returned to Italica, where he supposedly entered military service but actually spent his time hunting, a lifelong passion of his. As a result of the jealousy of his brother-in-law Servianus, who complained to Trajan of Hadrian's "dissipation," he was recalled to Rome in 93 and probably never saw Italica again.

In Rome, Hadrian continued his studies, laying the groundwork for a lifelong commitment not only to literature and art but also to music, architecture, astronomy, mathematics, law, and military science. In fact, few rulers have received such appropriate education and been so fortunate in their political connections; he had the support of Trajan and of Trajan's wife, Plotina, who helped to further his advancement. Since Hadrian also began his public career in 93, he added practical experience in public service and in military affairs to his extensive educational background. Through Trajan's influence with Emperor Domitian, Hadrian became a decemvir, a minor magistrate in probate court, as well as a military tribune serving at a Roman outpost on the Danube River.

When Domitian was assassinated in 96, the Roman senate chose Nerva to succeed him. Nerva, in turn, adopted Trajan in 97, and when Nerva died in 98, Trajan became emperor. With his coguardian as

emperor, Hadrian rose rapidly within the civil and military ranks, despite Servianus' interference. In 101, he was appointed quaestor and communicated Trajan's messages to the senate; in 107, he became praetor and governor of a province on the Danube; and in 108, he was elected consul and soon began writing Trajan's speeches.

As a provincial governor and as *legatus* of Syria during Trajan's Parthian campaign, Hadrian had military as well as civil responsibilities and he had already demonstrated his military talents during the second Dacian war. Moreover, since Trajan's ambitions had greatly, and precariously, extended Roman rule, Hadrian benefited from firsthand observations of a military conqueror.

On his return from the Parthian campaign in 117, Trajan died; on his deathbed, however, he apparently adopted Hadrian (there is considerable controversy about the "adoption"). The adoption practically guaranteed Hadrian's accession, and after the Syrian troops acclaimed him emperor, the senate quickly confirmed their action. At the age of forty-two, Hadrian became emperor, and his twenty-one-year rule was to be marked by policies and actions almost antithetical to those of his guardian, cousin, and mentor.

Life's Work

Hadrian commanded the largest Roman army at the time of Trajan's death and his ties to the emperor had been close, but his position was far from secure. He had many enemies among the Roman senators, some of whom considered him a provincial upstart opposed to militaristic expansion and enamored of Greek culture. In fact, Hadrian's policy of peace, retrenchment, and reform was diametrically opposed to Trajan's expansionist policy. Domestically, moderation was the order of the day as Hadrian attempted to convert his enemies by exercising restraint even in suppressing rebellious factions; in fact, when his coguardian Attianus became too zealous in his emperor's cause—he had four traitors executed—Hadrian eased him out of power. To gain the support of the Roman populace, Hadrian canceled all debts to the imperial treasury, renounced the emperor's traditional claim to the estates of executed criminals, extended the children's welfare centers, and staged spectacular entertainments for the masses. In addition to these public relations measures, Hadrian accomplished a

major overhaul of the administrative system—he created opportunities for the talented as well as the wealthy—and a thorough reform of the army. His domestic achievements culminated in the codification, under Julian's supervision, of Roman statutory law in 121.

Such reforms were necessary, since Hadrian, who never felt at home in Rome, was intent on establishing his rule before leaving to tour the provinces, a task that occupied him, for the most part, from 120 to 131. In fact, Hadrian's travel was consistent with his imperial policy of creating sister relations—with a subsequent loss of prestige for Rome—bound to him as to a patriarch. (He assumed in 128 the title *pater patriae*, "father of the fatherland.") During his extensive travels, Hadrian determined not on expanding the empire but on consolidating it, even reducing where necessary, and establishing *limes*, definite physical boundaries that could be effectively defended.

Accordingly, after visiting Roman outposts on the Rhine River, Hadrian traveled through the Netherlands to England, where rebellious tribes were unwilling to be assimilated. As there was no natural defensive barrier against northern invaders, Hadrian's Wall was constructed. This man-made fortification, parts of which survive today, also served as a seventy-three-mile road which facilitated the defense of the empire. Hadrian then traveled to Spain and Mauretania before he arrived in 124 in Ephesus, in what is now Turkey; there, Hadrian's Temple, one of the Seven Wonders of the ancient world, was constructed. Hadrian's next significant visit was to Bithynia, where he met Antinous, a young man who became his inseparable companion for the next nine years. After a trip to Athens, his intellectual and cultural homeland, Hadrian returned to Rome in 125.

Although he continued his travels, Hadrian's next four years were distinguished primarily by his architectural achievements and the rebuilding, or recreation, of Rome and Athens. The renowned Roman Pantheon is Hadrian's work, as is his mausoleum, built in imitation of the tomb built for Augustus, the emperor who always served as a model for Hadrian. When he left Rome, he stopped in his beloved Athens, where he constructed bridges, canals, and an elaborate gymnasium.

In the autumn of 129, Hadrian went south, and after literally saving the famous cedars of Lebanon, he made a fateful error involving the Jews in Palestine. An ardent supporter of Hellenism, which was in philosophical conflict with Judaism, and a xeno-

phobe who considered the Jews as foreigners, Hadrian enacted laws against circumcision and also determined to rebuild Jerusalem as a Roman city. Both actions infuriated the Jews, who were almost forced into another rebellion against Rome. After inciting the Jews, Hadrian traveled to Absandria; then, on a trip up the Nile River, he lost his beloved Antinous, who was drowned. It is not certain whether Antinous' death was an accident or suicide—the matter is controversial—but in any case it profoundly affected Hadrian. When he returned to Palestine, Hadrian found the reconstruction of Jerusalem interrupted by a Jewish uprising; although the bloody rebellion was eventually ended in 134, his punitive actions against the Jews, many of whom were sold into slavery, were decidedly uncharacteristic.

The remaining years of Hadrian's life somewhat negated the positive image he had created. Despite his rebuilding of Rome, the Romans never really accepted their provincial ruler who openly preferred Athens. Hadrian's problems were compounded by the onset of debilitating health problems which transformed the athletic emperor into a weak as well as a cruel and vindictive ruler. The man who had used moderation and patience to establish his rule actually began to order some executions, and the troublesome Servianus was finally put to death. The only notable achievement of these troubled years was the villa he had begun to build at Tibur in 126; the villa, itself of immense proportions, was an architectural blend of Roman and Greek styles.

Hadrian's problems even extended to the naming of his successor. Since his wife, Sabina, had failed to produce an heir, Hadrian named Lucius Aelius, who was perhaps his illegitimate son; Lucius, however, died before Hadrian. Hadrian adopted Antoninus Pius, a loyal and capable supporter, and then required that Antoninus in turn adopt the younger Aelius, as well as Marcus Annius Verus (the future philosopher and emperor Marcus Aurelius), Antoninus' nephew. When Hadrian died in 138, it was Antoninus, his successor, who was responsible for persuading a reluctant senate to deify the man whose last few years unfortunately clouded the real accomplishments of the early years of his reign.

Summary

Because he succeeded the militaristic Trajan, who had trained him to be an emperor, Hadrian determined to bring peace to a war-weary Rome, which was already overextended. By consolidating and precisely fixing defendable boundaries, he was able to focus his considerable energies on much-needed civil reforms, among them the law code and the civil service; as a result of his artistic training and architectural expertise, he was able to transform Rome, Athens, and Jerusalem. While he is widely known for the Pantheon and Hadrian's Wall, Hadrian left his architectural stamp on many of the cities he visited in his extensive travels.

Through his rule and his adoption and appointment of Antoninus Pius as his successor, he also was largely responsible for establishing what many historians have regarded as a golden age that lasted through the reigns of Antoninus Pius and his successor, the celebrated philosopher and emperor Marcus Aurelius. (Since he had required Antoninus to adopt his successor, Hadrian was directly involved in Marcus Aurelius' appointment as emperor, even though it occurred after his death.) When an iron age began with the ascension of Commodus, son of Marcus Aurelius, the so-called Antonine dynasty came to an end. Nevertheless, Rome had enjoyed approximately one hundred years of prosperity, greatness, and—with the exception of Trajan's reign—relative peace.

In fact, Hadrian's only significant military campaign, the suppression of the Jewish rebellion late in his reign, also became the indirect cause of an ironic development Hadrian neither intended nor desired: the spread of Christianity throughout the Roman Empire. By banishing the Jews from Jerusalem, the site of both Judaism and Christianity, Hadrian inadvertently caused Christianity to be separated from the Christian Jews who had controlled the early Christian Church. Consequently, as Stewart Perowne has suggested, Hadrian became the "unwitting forerunner of Constantine, and of the triumph of the faith in his own Rome." It seems both ironic and appropriate that Hadrian, the intellectual, artistic Hellenist and advocate of peace, should play such a role in the development of Christianity.

Bibliography

Birley, Anthony R. *Hadrian: The Restless Emperor.* London and New York: Routledge, 1997. A sober, carefully researched biography.

Gray, William Dodge. "A Study of the Life of Hadrian Prior to His Accession." *Smith College Studies in History* 4 (1919): 151-209. Gray provides a scholarly review of Hadrian's pre-accession life and concentrates on his training as Trajan's successor. After examining the evidence, he finds not much proof to support contemporary accounts of a hostile marriage between Hadrian and Sabina, of friction between Hadrian and Trajan, or of a fabricated adoption of Hadrian.

Gregorovius, Ferdinand. *The Emperor Hadrian: A Picture of the Greco-Roman World in His Time.* Translated by Mary E. Robinson with an introduction by Henry Pelham. London and New York: Macmillan, 1898. Gregorovius' work is particularly helpful in placing Hadrian within the cultural, literary, artistic, and philosophical contexts of his day, but the book, as Pelham indicates, lacks a general thesis to account for Hadrian's individual arts or his apparently contradictory nature. Pelham provides that thesis, although in condensed form.

Henderson, Bernard W. *The Life and Principate of the Emperor Hadrian, A.D. 76-138.* London: Methuen, and New York: Brentano's, 1923. The acknowledged standard work in English on Hadrian, Henderson's book is a scholarly and gracefully written biography. Henderson succeeds in rendering Hadrian as a person, not merely a public figure, and his comments on "personalia" provide a glimpse of the man and an objective corrective to those toolavish apologists for Hadrian.

Ish-Kishor, Sulamith. *Magnificent Hadrian: A Biography of Hadrian, Emperor of Rome.* New York: Minton, Balch and Co., 1935. An extremely sympathetic account of Hadrian's life, this book is also a heavy-handed psychological study designed to outline the "final tragedy of the homosexual temperament" in the relationship between Hadrian and Antinous. Ish-Kishor contrasts Trajan, the life-destroying father figure, with Hadrian, the life-building and life-restoring mother figure.

Perowne, Stewart. *Hadrian.* London: Hodder and Stoughton, 1960; New York: Norton, 1961. This comparatively short, readable biography is accompanied by a map illustrating Hadrian's travels, a bibliographical essay, appropriate illustrations, and tables outlining the Roman emperors, Hadrian's ancestors, and the problem of succession. Perowne categorizes Hadrian's travels and policies as manifestations of a political philosophy unique in its day.

Thomas L. Erskine

HAMMURABI

Born: c. 1810 B.C.; Babylon
Died: 1750 B.C.; Babylon
Areas of Achievement: Government and law
Contribution: Building upon an Amorite sheikhdom of four generations of ancestors, this long-
reigning representative of the dynasty matured
gradually in power until he was able to streatch
his control over the entire length of the Euphrates and Tigris river valleys. The literary creativity of the age brought into being the Old
Babylonian dialect, most fully exemplified in the
codification of law remembered under Hammurabi's name.

Early Life

The founder of Babylon and the creator of the first
Babylonian dynasty was a nineteenth century B.C.
Amorite chieftain named Sumu-abum. His ancestral predecessors are known by name back into the
twenty-first century B.C., when Shulgi, King of the
Third Dynasty of Ur in southern Sumer, first began
to encounter the movements of Amorite-speaking
Semitic peoples down the Euphrates. A famine began to devastate the economy of the Sumerian city-
states, weakening their defenses so that old centers
such as Larsa and Isin passed directly into the newcomers' hands.

Another family within the same tribal grouping
as Sumu-abum replaced his control, and with that
shift came into being the dynasty which Hammurabi recalled in his inscriptions. He was son of Sin-
muballit, grandson of Apil Sin, great-grandson of
Sabium, and great-great-grandson of the dynastic
founder, Sumu-la-el. The rapidity of succession
brought Hammurabi to the throne as quite a young
man.

The initial years of Hammurabi's life were lived
in the shadow of greater or longer-established
chieftains of comparable ancestry. The region to
the east along the Diyala River was centered on
Ibal-pi-El II at Eshnunna. The region to the south
was centered on Rim-Sin at Larsa. Rim-Sin's reign
was long, but there are only a few inscriptions,
mainly concerned with that piety of building for
the gods which was one of the principal ways of
proving one's greatness as a ruler in those times.
Rim-Sin's thirtieth year, during which he captured
Isin, was the year when Hammurabi assumed the
throne at Babylon.

During Hammurabi's father's reign, Babylon
was in the particular shadow of Shamshi-Adad I,
who had gained control of the capital of Assyria
and had spread his influence not only up the Tigris
but also across the steppes and tributaries to the
Euphrates itself, placing his own son on the throne
at the great trading center of Mari. Much of what is
known about this earlier period comes from the
vast archival records found in excavations at Mari
since 1929.

Life's Work

Hammurabi, upon ascending the throne in 1792,
found himself hemmed in on all sides by formidable powers. The political situation is well described
in a letter from a Mari diplomat or spy to his king:
"No one king is strong by himself. Ten to fifteen go
after Hammurapi man of Babylon, similarly after
Rim-Sin man of Larsa, similarly after Ibal-pi-el
man of Eshnunna, similarly after Amut-pi-el man
of Qatanum. Twenty go after Yarim-Lim man of
Yamhad."

Thus, the whole country was split among petty
chiefs joined together in leagues with some stronger figure nominally as head. Rather than a clear-
cut struggle between well-defined, uniformly large
states, it was a situation requiring a constant shuf-
fling of alliances among aggregations of minor rulers under some stronger chief as head. These combinations changed often. Economic issues played a
major role in the formation of alliances.

From the variety of year-names of the various
chiefs, it is possible to reconstruct an overall picture of the way Hammurabi was hemmed in at the
time of his accession. The sheikhdom of Larsa, by
conquering Isin in the south, covered almost all the
territory that had once been Sumer.

At Mari, the situation had undergone change.
In the middle of the nineteenth century, in the
days of Sabium, great-grandfather of Hammurabi, Mari had been ruled by Iaggid-Lim. When
Iaggid-Lim broke a treaty made with Ila-kabka-
bu, father of Shamshi-Adad I of Ashur, there was
retaliation. The occasion was used effectively by
Shamshi-Adad to take over rule in Mari, where
he placed his son, Iasmah-Adad, on the throne.
Mari was retained as long as Shamshi-Adad was
alive, but in the days of his successor at Ashur,
Ishme-Dagan, the old line at Mari was reinstated

under Zimri-Lim. These latter two, neither as strong as his predecessor, were the ones with whom Hammurabi had to deal. From the time of Zimri-Lim, the district of Terqa, just to the north of Mari, was entirely denuded of trees, so that the lucrative timber trade came to an end and the area received an ecological blow from which it never recovered.

When Hammurabi took over, Babylon was a small principality. In his second year, Hammurabi established "righteousness in the land." He remitted debts and other obligations, allowing land to revert to original owners. In undertaking such measures, he was following the tradition of his royal ancestors.

In 1787, Hammurabi captured Uruk and Isin, indicating that he and his allies were strong enough to challenge Rim-Sin in the latter's territory. It would appear, however, that the success was ephemeral: The cities were taken back. In 1783, Hammurabi destroyed Malgum on the Tigris, south of the Diyala. In 1782, he took Rapiqum on the Euphrates; it was close to a major caravan crossing and thus provided for him access to the west.

Mention of this achievement is the last reference to military accomplishments during this period in Hammurabi's official inscriptions, which thereafter focus on pious deeds of rebuilding walls and refurbishing temples. Their index illustrates, if not the extent of the Babylonian sheikhdom, at least the increasing strength of its economic base. From Mari, letters give account of Hammurabi's diplomatic relations; messengers went back and forth between Mari and Hammurabi's court.

In the inscriptions for 1763, the chronicle of Hammurabi's military conquests is taken up once more, beginning with his defeat of Elamite troops at the boundaries of Mahashi, Subartu, Eshnunna, Gutium, and Malgum—all to his east. He successfully opposed a concerted attack of northern and eastern principalities surrounding him, though there is no reference to his annexation of territory. Hammurabi was intent upon restoring the foundations of old "Sumer and Akkad."

These victories allowed Hammurabi to turn undivided attention to the south. In 1762, he fought successfully against the very old Rim-Sin of Larsa, who was brought alive in a cage to Babylon. With this termination of the independent dynasty of Larsa, all southern Mesopotamia passed into Hammurabi's hands.

In 1761, a core of the old coalition of enemies was against Hammurabi again. He defeated the armies of Subartu, Eshnunna, and Gutium and conquered all the territory along the Tigris as far north as the border of Assyria. In 1760, he fought with Mari on the Euphrates and Malgum, south of Eshnunna. In 1758, he destroyed the walls of both Mari and Malgum. A change in relations with Mari occurred once more. Hammurabi had previously sent troops to assist Zimri-Lim, and the latter had been instrumental in his taking over Eshnunna. Now native rule at Mari ended. In 1755, the "great waters destroyed" Eshnunna; it is not clear whether the reference is to a natural disaster or to Hammurabi's damming up and diverting a river. In any case, the inscriptions make no further mention of Eshnunna until the time of Hammurabi's son.

In 1754, Hammurabi conquered all of his enemies as far as the land of Subartu, east beyond the Tigris. With this success, he was established as the dominant figure in all Mesopotamia. No further references to warfare are made in the chronicle of his reign. To this final period belongs the monumental edition of his law code, upon which he is portrayed standing humbly before Shamash, the sun god and overseer of justice. Its prologue identifies his control over twenty-six cities, from each of whose deities, whose temples he adorned, he received powers to make justice in the land.

By intensive restructuring of the whole geographical area under his control, Hammurabi had inadvertently set in motion the forces which during the next century and a half were to terminate the dynasty and its Amorite leadership—a decline culminating in the Hittite's sacking of Babylon in 1595. The prosperity of Babylon depended upon remuneration from its conquered territories for massive construction of buildings and waterworks organized by Hammurabi with the help of appointed officials. Once a system of governors and palace dependents was created, however, this bureaucracy established itself in hereditary positions, so that the territories fed local rather than royal interests.

Already before Hammurabi's death, his son Samsuiluna reported in a letter to an official, Etil-pi-Marduk, that his father was ill and that he had to assume charge of what was by then no longer a mere sheikhdom but instead a real kingdom. Hammurabi was succeeded by Samsuiluna and his grandson Abi-eshu. There remained three further generations, Ammi-ditana, Ammi-zaduga, and Samsu-ditana, before Hammurabi's achievement was terminated by Kassite invaders, dividing the realm again into petty sheikhdoms warring on relatively equal terms.

Summary

Coming at the middle of the First Dynasty of Babylon, Hammurabi created out of a small principality not merely an imperial kingdom but a distinctive city whose name is not to be forgotten: Old "Sumer and Akkad" became thereafter Babylonia. From the many preserved Old Babylonian letters, especially those to or by Hammurabi, it is possible to understand the administrative structure of his power and that of Babylon. These letters document the lines of communication existing within the capital itself and out to the official governors appointed to administer annexed cities and territories. Two large collections are illustrative: those related to Sin-idinnam, Hammurabi's governor of Larsa after the defeat of Rim-Sin, and those related to Shamash-hazir, a lesser official, also at Larsa, who managed for the king the landholdings and the landholders.

Extensive economic records from the various cities, especially Sippar, provide details of royal involvement. At Sippar, Hammurabi's sister Iltani engaged in business transactions on behalf of the gods Lord Shamash and Lady Aja for more than fifty years, at least until 1755. She lived in that unique Old Babylonian institution, the *gaga* (cloister), as one of the many *naditu*-women, among whom she ranked the highest. *Naditu*-women were dedicated to a god, often from youth; they were usually unmarried and were always forbidden to have children, but they frequently played significant economic roles.

The period was one of great literary creativity. Epic poetry, some of it based on Sumerian-derived sources, addressed central issues and problems of human existence. Two epics of the period, for example, took up issues of life and death in their glorification of the heroes Gilgamesh and Atra-hasis. Another remembered the ancient Etana. During this time, the chief god Marduk replaced older creator gods, just as Babylon had replaced the older Sumerian city-states.

Aside from the monumental copy of Hammurabi's code, clay tablet examples demonstrate that its text was regularly copied in both Babylonia and

Assyria until the era of the Seleucid state at Uruk (third century B.C.). The great stela itself was carried off as a prize to Susa by the twelfth century B.C. Elamite king Shutruk-nakhunte I. There it remained until January, 1902, when its rediscovery changed Hammurabi from simply another ruler among many into a world-famous lawgiver with a status comparable to that of the biblical Moses or the Byzantine Justinian I.

The last great king of Assyria, the seventh century B.C. Ashurbanipal, sought texts of Hammurabi's era for his library at Nineveh. While no building attributable to Hammurabi has been excavated beneath the rubble of Babylon, it is known that its last king, Nabonidus (sixth century B.C.) knew of his work and remembered him.

Bibliography

Hammurabi. *The Babylonian Laws*. Edited by G. R. Driver and John C. Miles. 2 vols. Oxford: Clarendon Press, 1952. Volume 1 provides a detailed commentary upon all Babylonian law, with special focus upon the Code of Hammurabi. Volume 2 contains the transliterated texts with full translation, philological notes, and glossary.

Finkelstein, J. J. "The Genealogy of the Hammurabi Dynasty." *Journal of Cuneiform Studies* 20 (1966): 95-118. The discovery of a new text within the large collection of the British Museum allowed the connection of Assyrian and Babylonian royal ancestries within a common Amorite genealogy.

Leemans, W. F. *The Old Babylonian Merchant: His Business and His Social Position*. Leiden, Netherlands: E. J. Brill, 1950. Beginning from provisions in Hammurabi's code, and on the basis of texts coming from various archives, especially those of Larsa and Sippar, the nature, role, and function of the merchant class are described as independent but bound by the law of the king.

Munn-Rankin, J. M. "Diplomacy in Western Asia in the Early Second Millennium B.C." *Iraq* 18 (1956): 68-110. This major essay, working from the Mari archive, puts in perspective the historical situation and the interaction among major figures during Hammurabi's reign.

Pallis, S. A. *The Antiquity of Iraq: A Handbook of Assyriology*. Copenhagen, Denmark: Ejnar Munksgaard, 1956. This volume is a vast storehouse of information including a history of Babylon, a description of the city, an account of its rediscovery in the nineteenth century, and the subsequent excavations. Chapter 8 explains the chronological shift in dating Hammurabi, made possible by the discovery of the Mari archive and the correlation with Shamshi-Adad of Assyria. Chapter 10 provides a picture of Hammurabi and his age, with extensive discussion of the code.

Saggs, H. W. F. *The Greatness That Was Babylon: A Survey of the Ancient Civilization of the Tigris Euphrates Valley*. Rev. ed. London: Sidgwick and Jackson, 1988. A clearly written introductory history of Babylon from the earliest days to its conquest by Persia. Hammurabi is discussed in chapter 3 and appears as a vigorous leader and scrupulous administrator.

Yoffee, Norman. *The Economic Role of the Crown in the Old Babylonian Period*. Malibu, Calif.: Undena Publications, 1977. This study is significant for its close analysis of economic texts from various urban archives, shedding light on the operations of Hammurabi's palace economy and the administration of conquered realms. Extensive bibliography.

Clyde Curry Smith

HANNIBAL

Born: 247 B.C.; probably Carthage, North Africa
Died: 182 B.C.; Libyssa, Bithynia, Asia Minor
Area of Achievement: Warfare
Contribution: During the Second Punic War, Hannibal led an army of mercenaries across the Alps into Italy, where, for fifteen years, he exhibited superior generalship, defeating the Romans in one battle after another.

Early Life

Hannibal was born in 247 B.C., probably in Carthage, of an aristocratic family which claimed descent from Dido, the legendary foundress of the city. Of his mother nothing is known, but his father, Hamilcar Barca, was for nearly twenty years the supreme military commander of the Carthaginian forces. Assuming this position in the year of Hannibal's birth, Hamilcar guided his country through the last difficult years of the First Punic War and then began the construction of a new empire in Spain. After his death, in 229 B.C., Hamilcar's son-in-law, Hasdrubal, extended Carthaginian dominion northward to the Ebro River and founded New Carthage.

Little is known of Hannibal during these years. Livy, the principal source of information, notes that when Hannibal was nine years of age, he accompanied his father to Spain. Prior to their departure, Hamilcar invoked the blessings of the gods with a sacrifice at which Hannibal was compelled to swear that he would never be a friend to Rome. Such was the hostile atmosphere in which the youth was reared. Although little is known about the years of Hannibal's apprenticeship under his father and later under Hasdrubal, there can be little doubt that Hannibal would benefit immeasurably from the rigors of frontier life. When Hasdrubal was assassinated in 221, Hannibal, age twenty-six, was ready to assume command. That he had already distinguished himself as a warrior and a leader is indicated by the alacrity with which the army proclaimed him commander.

Life's Work

Hannibal was the epitome of a warrior. According to silver coins supposedly bearing his likeness, he had curly hair, a straight nose, a sloping forehead, a strong neck, and a look of determination in his eyes. A man with a mission, in his mid-twenties Hannibal was ready to carry his father's dream to completion. All that was needed was an excuse. The opportunity presented itself in 219, when Rome violated a treaty with Carthage by intervening in the political affairs of the Spanish state of Saguntum. Hannibal dismissed a Roman commission sent to investigate the matter and then laid siege to the city, which fell eight months later. Rome's failure to aid its client state probably encouraged Hannibal to extend Carthaginian dominion northward to the Pyrenees. When Carthage refused to surrender Hannibal, Rome declared war.

The Roman strategy was to end the war quickly. One army was dispatched under the leadership of the consul Publius Cornelius Scipio to confront Hannibal in Spain, while the other consul, Tiberius Sempronius Longus, was to attack Carthage. In this matter, however, the Romans greatly underestimated the military genius and determination of Hannibal. In the spring of 218, Hannibal gathered his army of Numidians and Spaniards—variously estimated at forty thousand to sixty thousand men—and, in one of the most celebrated marches in history, crossed the Pyrenees, the Rhone River,

and finally the snow-laden Alps to reach the Po River valley. It was a perilous five-month journey fraught with dangers of all sorts—hostile tribes, bad weather, impenetrable geographical barriers, and a scarcity of provisions. Thousands of Hannibal's soldiers and many of the elephants perished along the way. By journey's end, Hannibal's forces had been reduced to about twenty thousand infantry and six thousand cavalry, too few to undertake the conquest of Roman Italy. The success of the venture would depend on Hannibal's ability to lure many of Rome's disaffected allies to his side.

In the meantime, after hearing of Hannibal's departure from Spain, the two consuls rushed northward to meet the threat. Scipio, in a move of future importance, sent his army on to Spain to prevent reinforcements from joining Hannibal. In December, the two consuls joined forces to stop Hannibal's advance, but the Romans fell into an ambush in the frigid waters of the Trebia River. Approximately two-thirds of the Roman force was lost. Although Rome managed to conceal the defeat from its citizens, it was necessary to abandon the Po River valley to the Punic forces. Hannibal, to curry favor with the natives, released his Italian prisoners.

Hannibal wintered in northern Italy. During that time, his army grew with the addition of Celtic recruits to about fifty thousand in number. In the spring of 217, Hannibal moved southward into the peninsula. The Romans sent the consul Gaius Flaminius with orders to hold Hannibal at the Apennines. Hannibal, wily as ever, slipped around the Roman commander by sloshing through the marshes of the Arno River into Etruria. Along the way, Hannibal contracted malaria and lost the sight of one eye. Flaminius regained his composure and eventually caught up with Hannibal's forces, only to suffer a crushing defeat at Lake Trasimene. Flaminius and virtually all of his soldiers perished in the battle.

A second major defeat was more than Rome could endure. In desperation, Rome resurrected an old emergency procedure and appointed a dictator, Quintus Fabius Maximus, to handle the crisis. Nicknamed the "delayer," Fabius refused to meet Hannibal in open battle, preferring hit-and-run tactics. He also used a scorched-earth policy to prevent Hannibal from living off the land. While the strategy worked and restored Roman morale, public opinion favored more aggressive action. In 216, Rome felt strong enough to send the consuls Lu-

cius Aemilius Paulus and Gaius Terentius Varro with an army of about sixty thousand men to engage Hannibal in open battle at Cannae in northern Apulia. Although numerically superior, the Romans fell prey once again to Hannibal's genius. While the Romans drove hard through the middle of the Carthaginian line, they were gradually encircled and destroyed. Only a fraction of the Roman force managed to escape. Hannibal's double-envelopment maneuver has since been copied many times by other generals.

The news of defeat threw Rome into chaos. Hannibal, contrary to the advice of his generals, refused to march on the panic-stricken city. The reasons for his cautious behavior are not clear, though he probably understood that Rome was strongly fortified, and he may have continued to hope that Rome's allies would now defect. The major rebellion for which he had hoped never occurred. There were, however, encouraging signs. Much of southern Italy, including Capua, second only to Rome in importance, went over to Hannibal's side. He also gained the support of Macedonia's King Philip V, who hoped to involve Rome in a war in the east.

Hannibal was supreme for the moment, but he had not broken the indomitable Roman spirit. There were also some encouraging signs for Rome. Many of Rome's allies, especially in central Italy, had remained faithful. Property qualifications for military service were lowered and new armies were raised which returned to Fabius' successful tactics of the past. Furthermore, the decision to remain in Spain, coupled with Rome's continued mastery of the sea, made it difficult for Hannibal to receive reinforcements. While Hannibal moved his diminished, bedraggled army from one encampment to another without benefit of open battle, the Romans began to reconquer the lost cities and provinces. In 211, both Capua and Syracuse were retaken. Compounding Hannibal's problems was the fact that the alliance with Philip V had proved ineffectual.

In the meantime, Rome had gained the advantage in Spain through the efforts of the brilliant young general Publius Cornelius Scipio. In 209, New Carthage, the major city of Hannibal's Iberian empire, was captured by Scipio's forces, along with vast quantities of supplies. He could not prevent Hasdrubal, Hannibal's brother, from crossing the Pyrenees in an attempt to reach Hannibal in Italy, but the relief expedition was intercepted and defeated at the Metaurus River in 207. Nevertheless,

Hannibal and his diminished army remained a threat. In 211, he appeared before the walls of Rome, though he took no action, while he defeated and killed the consuls Gnaeus Fulvius and Marcus Claudius Marcellus in other battles. It was becoming increasingly obvious, however, that Hannibal could not win the war.

In 205, Scipio returned triumphantly from Spain to assume the consulship. Under his leadership, Rome was ready to take the offensive. In the following year, Scipio invaded Africa and after a brief campaign forced Carthage to capitulate. Hannibal and his army were recalled from Italy, ostensibly as a part of the peace agreement. Once he and his fifteen thousand veterans were on African soil, however, the Carthaginians broke off the negotiations and renewed the war. In 202, Scipio and Hannibal met at Zama in a titanic battle. Using tactics he had learned from Hannibal, Scipio was victorious.

Following Zama, a harsh treaty, termed a "Carthaginian Peace" ever since, was imposed on the defeated Carthage. Hannibal remained in the city for five years and worked hard to build a more unified and democratic state. His enemies would give him no rest, however, and in 196, he fled first to Syria and then to Bithynia, where he served briefly as commander of the army in a war with the Romans. In 182, Hannibal committed suicide rather than surrender to his enemies.

Summary

The Second Punic War was, in large part, the biography of Hannibal of Carthage. Perhaps no other man in history has so thoroughly dominated a conflict. The historian Polybius observed that Hannibal was the architect of all things, good and bad, which came to the Romans and Carthaginians. His feats, although recorded by reliable ancient historians, are almost legendary. After inheriting his father's struggle with Rome, he crossed the Alps into Italy, where for fifteen years he moved about the countryside at will. He never lost a major battle, scoring decisive victories at the Trebia River, Lake Trasimene, and Cannae. Hannibal's impact was so great that the Romans were driven at times to desperate measures—the appointment of dictators, human sacrifice to appease the gods, and what today is known as guerrilla warfare.

Roman historians, through whose eyes the conflict must be viewed, were not niggardly in their praise. Livy recounts with amazement the fact that Hannibal was able to hold his army of various nationalities and beliefs together for so long a time in hostile territory. That he succeeded was the result in large part of his courage, an element of recklessness, and an excellent rapport with his men. Yet, Livy continues, he was capable of great cruelty and had little respect for either gods or men. According to Polybius, on the other hand, while Hannibal might have been guilty of these things, he was forced by circumstances and the influence of friends to behave in this paradoxical manner.

Hannibal was, in the eyes of both his contemporaries and modern scholars, the perfect general. Yet, like Pyrrhus before him, he was fighting an unwinnable war. Rome had the advantages of terrain, command of the sea, and inexhaustible reserves of men. In the end, he lost, and Rome, from which much of Western civilization is derived, remained in the ascendant for the next six centuries. Nevertheless, Hannibal remains one of the most fascinating figures in the annals of military history.

Bibliography

Bagnall, Nigel. *The Punic Wars.* London: Hutchinson, 1990. The author, a British field marshal, provides a straight, narrative account of the wars based on Polybius and Livy. Scholarly controversy is largely avoided.

Baker, George P. *Hannibal.* New York: Dodd, Mead, 1929; London: Eveleigh Nash and Grayson, 1930. A good introductory work for the student. The author uses primary materials to good advantage, but the style more closely resembles a historical novel.

Bradford, Ernle. *Hannibal: The General from Carthage.* New York: McGraw-Hill, and London: Macmillan, 1981. One of the most recent studies, derived in large part from the accounts of Livy and Polybius. Provides excellent descriptions of the major battles at the Trebia River, Lake Trasimene, and Cannae. The author attempts to put Hannibal's career in better perspective through the use of modern examples.

Cary, M., and H. H. Scullard. *A History of Rome Down to the Reign of Constantine.* 3d ed. New York: St. Martin's Press, and London: Macmillan, 1975. For many years one of the standard texts for Roman history. Provides a very good overview of Hannibal's career. Excellent maps illustrate the disposition of troops at Lake Trasimene, Cannae, and Zama.

De Beer, Gavin. *Hannibal: Challenging Rome's Supremacy.* New York: Viking Press, 1969. A well-written and copiously illustrated biography. The author puts much emphasis on geography, especially on the march from Spain over the Alps into Italy. Excellent for the beginning student.

Livy. *The War with Hannibal.* Translated by Aubrey de Sélincourt. London and Baltimore: Penguin, 1965. Written by a patriotic Roman historian who greatly admired Hannibal's military genius. Along with Polybius' work, it is the best source of information on the Punic Wars. Useful for the more knowledgeable reader. The Penguin edition has been taken from Livy's overall history of Rome.

Polybius. *The Histories of Polybius.* Translated by Evelyn S. Shuckburgh. 2 vols. London and New York: Macmillan, 1889. A history of Rome from the onset of the First Punic War in 264 B.C. to the destruction of Carthage in 146 B.C. One of the best sources of information about Hannibal. Like Livy's account, recommended for the more advanced student.

Sinnigen, William G., and Arthur E. Boak. *A History of Rome to A.D. 565.* 6th ed. New York: Macmillan, 1977. One of the better surveys of Roman history. Includes a valuable chapter on the conflict with Carthage in which the chief events of Hannibal's career are mentioned. Useful for scholars and students alike.

Starr, Chester G. *The Ancient Romans.* New York: Oxford University Press, 1971. A well-illustrated topical history. One-fourth of the book is devoted to the Punic Wars, with particular attention to Hannibal. An excellent introduction to the subject.

Toynbee, Arnold. *Hannibal's Legacy.* 2 vols. London and New York: Oxford University Press, 1965. An expanded version of lectures delivered in 1913-1914 at Oxford. The beginning student will find it ponderous, but it is a valuable study which goes far beyond Hannibal.

Larry W. Usilton

HANNO

Born: c. 520-510 B.C.; place unknown
Died: Date unknown; place unknown
Area of Achievement: Exploration
Contribution: Hanno successfully founded the first trading colonies along the western African coast and then pushed on to explore the coast at least as far as modern Sierra Leone. His account of his journey provided the only reasonably accurate account of Africa until the time of Prince Henry the Navigator.

Early Life

Hanno belongs to that lamentably large class of ancients whose names have survived the centuries for a single history-shaping deed, but about whom little else is known. Apart from scattered, confused references to his voyage in a few ancient authors, the main source of information on the man Hanno is the text known as the *Periplus* (*The Voyage of Hanno*, 1797; best known as *Periplus*). Consisting of just under 650 words of Greek, it purports to be a translation of the public inscription Hanno erected in the temple of Kronos at Carthage to commemorate his voyage.

The introduction to the *Periplus* calls Hanno a king. The Carthaginian constitution had no kings but placed supreme power in two *suffetes*. In any case, Hanno was surely of the ruling nobility of Carthage. The dating of Hanno's life depends on the dating of his voyage. Pliny the Elder asserts twice that the voyage was undertaken when the power of Carthage was at its peak; modern scholars have suggested a date just prior to 480 B.C. Before this time, Carthage enjoyed a period of prosperity and expansion in the western Mediterranean. Just at the time the Persians were losing their war with the Greeks at Thermopylae and Salamis, however, so too the Carthaginians, led by Hamilcar, fell decisively to Gelon of Syracuse at the Battle of Himera. Subsequently, it took several decades for Carthage to regain its former strength and influence. This fact, together with philological evidence dating the Greek text to the fifth century, makes it seem best to place Hanno's exploits prior to the Carthaginian defeat at Himera.

There are two men named Hanno known from this period, one the father and the other the son of the Hamilcar who died at Himera. The birth dates given above result from adding the probable age of a magistrate and state-sponsored explorer (between thirty and forty) to the upper limit of the date of the voyage (480). With this date, evidence seems to lean toward the younger Hanno, but there is ample room for doubt.

One can easily understand what may have inspired Hanno's career. As a member of the ruling class, he viewed at first hand the cosmopolitan activity of a trading town such as Carthage. A young man could have been readily lured by the possibility of travel and exploration as he walked along the busy docks and through the hectic markets of Carthage, which traded with Etruria, Phoenicia, and countless Greek city-states and African nations. It can be assumed that Hanno received the best Punic education of his day. His inscription, translated though it is, remains the longest bit of Punic literature available to modern scholars.

Life's Work

The *Periplus* begins by stating that the Carthaginians instructed Hanno to sail "beyond the Pillars of Heracles" (Gibraltar) to found Lybyophoenician cities. Modern scholars suggest plausibly that these cities were to serve as bases for trade with inner Africa, perhaps in precious metals.

The narrative claims that he left with thirty thousand colonists and sixty fifty-oared ships. Since such ships were small fighting craft, they must have served as a convoy for the colonists in transports. Two days beyond Gibraltar, Hanno founded his first city; five others followed in rapid succession. He then pushed along the western coast of Africa, stopping at Lixus River (now Wad Dra) to recruit interpreters before sailing along the coast of the Sahara Desert. He thereupon came to an island which he named Kerne and upon which he founded his seventh colony.

From here, his colonizing done, Hanno became an explorer. The *Periplus* tells of two excursions south from Kerne. On the first, Hanno encountered wild, skin-clad savages who pelted his crew with rocks; he discovered a river, filled with crocodiles and hippopotamuses, which he called the Chretes. On the second, apparently longer exploration, he eventually came to forests from which his crew heard the sounds of pipes, cymbals, and shouting. Terrified, they fled until they came to a burning country, filled with fragrant odors and from which burning streams flowed to the sea. In the midst of it stood a towering, blazing mountain which Hanno called the Chariot of the Gods, from whose summit fire shot up almost to the stars. Three days later, he reached an island inhabited by small, hairy "wild men" who threw rocks at the Carthaginians. The nimble males escaped, but Hanno's crew managed to capture three scratching, biting females, who were promptly skinned. According to Pliny the Elder, two of these skins were on display in the temple of Juno at Carthage until its destruction by the Romans in 146 B.C. Hanno's interpreters informed him that these creatures were called "gorillae." Following the account of this incident, the *Periplus* notes rather abruptly that Hanno ran out of supplies and returned home.

There is no persuasive reason to believe that the *Periplus* is either a forgery or a literary exercise. It is exactly what it purports to be—a public version, probably abridged, of an actual voyage. Its few sentences, however, have caused rivers of ink (and no small amount of vitriol) to flow, all in an attempt to determine where Hanno went. Nineteenth century investigators tended to shorten the voyage too much, even claiming that Hanno never got beyond the Atlantic border of Morocco. A confused Pliny the Elder went to the other extreme, stating that Hanno sailed from Cádiz to the borders of Arabia. Somewhere in between lies the truth.

The solution to this problem hinges on the identification of several key places mentioned in the text, and one must first be aware of its limitations. It is at best a translation of an abridgment, and in spots the text is in question. There are no consistent indications of distance from one point to another; where measurements are given, they are in days. How many hours a day were spent in sailing? Were the explorers under sail or oars? Were they against or with the wind and currents?

Despite all these problems, a consensus seems to exist among many scholars on some matters. It is generally accepted that Hanno's first six colonies dotted the northwest Atlantic coast of Africa, all fairly close to the Pillars. The location of the seventh colony, Kerne, reached in two days after the Lixus River, is as difficult as it is crucial. When "two" is emended to "nine," as it often is, it suggests a small island named Herne, lying opposite the Río de Oro off Western Sahara. Another candidate for Kerne is the Island of Arguin, farther still to the south.

One site of Hanno's first exploration is accepted without question. The river full of crocodiles and hippopotamuses can only be the Senegal. It is the first river he could have reached with the requisite wildlife, and Pliny the Elder elsewhere remarks that the name of this river was the Bambotum, a name plausibly explained as a corruption of *behemoth*, the Semitic word for hippopotamus.

In recounting his adventures farther south, Hanno's reports seem to take on a less believable tone. Nevertheless, his descriptions of aromatic, blazing lands, of the mountain called the Chariot of the Gods, and of the wild, hairy gorillas, once scorned as fictions, can be explained in such a way as to make them plausible.

An early report from the explorer Mungo Park, for example, made clear that the fires Hanno saw sweeping the plains were the natives' annual burning of the fields to increase their fertility. Hanno's description of the "fiery streams" rushing to the sea and of the Chariot of the Gods with its fire reaching to the stars has prompted many, ancient and modern, to suppose a volcano is meant. Rather far to the south lies Mount Cameroon, a volcanic peak towering 13,353 feet over the plain and quite visible from the coast. The time given in the text for this leg of the trip, however, is clearly insufficient for Hanno to have reached this latitude. Other scholars, therefore, choose to see the Chariot of the Gods in the much closer Mount Kakulima in Guinea (on some maps called Souzos or Sagres). At 3,300 feet, it is much less spectacular, but ablaze it could perhaps resemble a volcano. There are sound arguments for and against either site, and the choice is significant in determining the southern extent of the voyage. It is safest to say that Hanno reached at least as far as Sierra Leone.

Finally, there are the much-debated gorillas. One of the few things agreed upon concerning this segment of the *Periplus* is that these are surely not gorillas in the modern sense of the word, for these animals are not found in this part of Africa. Most scholars believe that Hanno saw either chimpanzees or baboons, while a few hold to the earlier belief that they were pygmies or dwarfs. "Gorilla" in its modern sense was first used by Thomas Savage, an American missionary who happened to see some gorilla skulls and in 1847 announced to the world a new creature, locally called a *pongo*. Since this word was already in use scientifically, he recalled Hanno's hairy creatures and bestowed the name gorilla upon his new find. Any attempt to claim that Hanno saw real gorillas—and thus to extend his voyage as far south as Gabon—is undoubtedly incorrect.

Summary

Hanno's work itself seems not to have been widely acclaimed in antiquity, and his reputation could not have been helped by the fact that he was a Carthaginian. The authors who cited him were often confused, and several seem incredulous. Educated guesses about Hanno's dates and true identity are all that is possible. Yet much the same is true of Homer, and his influence is undenied. Hanno must be judged by his work.

Hanno was not the first to attempt a voyage down the western coast of Africa. Herodotus says that Pharaoh Necho II (early sixth century) engaged Phoenicians to circumnavigate Africa from east to west and that they did so in a three-year voyage. Most scholars treat the story with caution, and its lack of any precise geographical details does make it suspect. Herodotus also notes that in the fifth century King Xerxes I of Persia commuted the sentence of death by impalement of a certain Sataspes with the provision that he attempt to circumnavigate Africa from west to east. Sataspes returned a failure and, perhaps to appease the king, told a tale of dwarfish races he had seen. The ploy did not work, and Sataspes was promptly impaled. A third sailor, a Greek from Massalia named Euthymenes, claimed to have sailed south along Africa until he saw a river filled with crocodiles (the Senegal?). His date, however, is merest conjecture. These tales demonstrate at the least that the idea of such a voyage was in circulation before Hanno attempted it. Also, the fact that his charge was to establish settlements along the coast indicates that the Carthaginians knew at least the closer, northwestern shore of Africa.

These facts, however, do not detract from Hanno's accomplishments. His is the earliest believable and documented voyage of this scope. Moreover, later authors suggest that the colonies, including southern Kerne, continued to engage in trade up to the destruction of Carthage by Rome in 146. Furthermore, there are no records of any further voyages of this length along the African coast until the Middle Ages, when ships routinely turned back at the "impassable" Cape Bojador. It was not until the expeditions of Prince Henry the Navigator that ships went farther, and then it took them forty years to get as far as Hanno had done.

Thus, in one summer, Hanno traveled farther than anyone was to do for some two thousand years. Moreover, his written record of his voyages, flawed as it may be, remained the sole source for the geography of western Africa during all the intervening years. Few explorers since have had such an influence.

Bibliography

Bunbury, Edward Herbert. *A History of Ancient Geography Among the Greeks and Romans, from the Earliest Ages till the Fall of the Roman Empire*. 2d ed. London: Murray, 1883; New York: Dover, 1959. Features a reasonable discussion of the *Periplus*, with a fine map. Identifies Herne as Kerne, Kakulima with the Chariot of the Gods, and chimpanzees as the gorillas.

Carpenter, Rhys. *Beyond the Pillars of Heracles*. New York: Delacorte Press, 1966. Includes a translation of the *Periplus* and a lucid discussion of the practical problems of sailing times. Carpenter emends the text to produce a new identification of Herne with Saint-Louis at the mouth of the Senegal. Excellent source.

Cary, Max, and E. H. Warmington. *The Ancient Explorers*. Rev. ed. Baltimore: Penguin Books, 1963. Provides treatments of Euthymenes, Hanno, Necho, and Sataspes. A map of northwest Africa, with major landfalls marked, is of great use. Balanced interpretation of the evidence for Hanno's itinerary.

Hyde, Walter Woodburn. *Ancient Greek Mariners*. New York: Oxford University Press, 1947. Includes an extended discussion of the gorilla question. Good summary of Hanno's text. The maps, however, are of low quality.

Kaeppel, Carl. *Off the Beaten Track in the Classics*. New York: Melbourne University Press, 1936. This essay, entirely devoted to Hanno, is a fine example of the passionate writing the *Periplus* has evoked. Excellent discussion of all questionable locations and of the results of the voyage.

Oikonomides, Al N., and M. C. J. Miller, eds. *Hanno the Carthaginian, Periplus*. 3d ed. Chicago: Ares Publishers, 1995. A text, translation, and commentary on the *Periplus*.

Thomson, J. O. *History of Ancient Geography*. Cambridge: Cambridge University Press, 1948; New York: Biblo and Tannen, 1965. Good sections on Hanno and his predecessors. Excellent bicolored map shows various theories as to locations of Hanno's landfalls.

Kenneth F. Kitchell, Jr.

HATSHEPSUT

Born: Mid- to late sixteenth century B.C.; probably near Thebes, Egypt

Died: c. 1482 B.C.; place unknown

Area of Achievement: Government

Contribution: Governing in her own right, Hatshepsut gave to Egypt two decades of peace and prosperity and beautified Thebes with temples and monuments.

Early Life

Hatshepsut, or Hatshopsitu, was the daughter of Thutmose I and his consort (the Egyptian title was "great royal wife") Ahmose. Nothing is known of Hatshepsut's date of birth and early life. Although Thutmose I was the third king of the powerful Eighteenth Dynasty, he was probably not of royal blood on his mother's side; the princess Ahmose, however, was of the highest rank. During the period in Egyptian history known as the Empire or New Kingdom (from the Eighteenth to the Twentieth Dynasty; c. 1570-1075 B.C.), royal women began to play a more active role in political affairs. Among her titles, the pharaoh's chief wife was called the "divine consort of Amon" (Amon was one of the principal Theban deities). Being the wife of a god increased her status, and her offspring were given a certain precedence over the children of minor wives or concubines.

In addition to Princess Hatshepsut, at least two sons were born to Thutmose I and Ahmose, but both of the boys died young. The male line had to be continued through a third son, born to a minor wife, who was married to his half sister, Hatshepsut. Thutmose II's claim to the throne was strengthened by this marriage; he succeeded his father around 1512.

A daughter, Neferure, was born of this union but apparently no son was born. The ancient records are fragmentary and at times obscure, but there is evidence that Thutmose II was not very healthy and thus his reign was short, ending around 1504. Once more there was no male of pure royal blood to become pharaoh; thus, the title passed to a son of Thutmose II by a concubine named Isis. This boy, also named Thutmose, was at the time of his father's death between the ages of six and ten, and dedicated to the service of the god Amon at the temple at Karnak. Since he was underage, the logical choice as regent was his aunt Hatshepsut, now the queen mother.

Life's Work

Hatshepsut soon proved to be a woman of great ability and large ambitions. The regency was not enough for her; she wanted the glory of being called pharaoh as well as the responsibility for Egypt and the young king. To accomplish this desire, however, seemed impossible. There had never been a female pharaoh—only a man could assume that title, take a "Horus name," and become king of Upper and Lower Egypt.

For a time Hatshepsut looked for possible allies, finding them among the various court officials, the most notable being the architect and bureaucrat Senmut (or Senenmut), and among the priests of Amon. By 1503 her moment had come. Accompanied by young Thutmose, she went to Luxor to participate in one of the great feasts honoring Amon; during the ceremonies, she had herself crowned. There was no question of deposing Thutmose III, but he was in effect forced to accept a coregency in which he played a lesser part.

To justify this unique coronation, Hatshepsut asserted that she had been crowned already with the sanction of her father the pharaoh. To support this claim an account was given of her miraculous birth, which was later inscribed at her temple at Dayr el-Baḥrī on the west bank of the Nile. According to this account, Amon himself, assuming the guise of Thutmose, had fathered Hatshepsut. With the approval of both a divine and a human parent, none could oppose the new pharaoh's will, while Thutmose remained a child and the army and the priests supported her.

Hatshepsut did not merely assume the masculine titles and authority of a pharaoh; she ordered that statues be made showing her as a man. In the stylized portraiture of Egyptian royalty, the king is usually shown bare-chested and wearing a short, stiff kilt, a striped wig-cover concealing the hair, and a ceremonial beard. The number of statues commissioned by Hatshepsut is not known, but in spite of later efforts by Thutmose III to blot out the memory of his hated relative, several examples exist, showing Hatshepsut kneeling, sitting, or standing, looking, as aloof and masculine as her predecessors.

Neferure, the daughter of Hatshepsut and Thutmose II, was married to Thutmose III. This marriage served the dual purpose of strengthening the succession and binding the king closer to his aunt, now his mother-in-law. Hatshepsut then focused

her attention on domestic prosperity and foreign trade, activities more to her personal inclination than conquest. Throughout Egypt an extensive building program was begun. At Karnak four large obelisks and a shrine to Amon were built. Another temple was constructed at Beni-Hasan in Middle Egypt. Several tombs were cut for her, including one in the Valley of the Kings. Her inscriptions claim that she was the first pharaoh to repair damages caused by the Hyksos, Asian invaders who had conquered Egypt in the eighteenth through mid-sixteenth centuries with the aid of new technologies, such as war chariots pulled by horses. The usurpation of these foreign kings was an unpleasant and recent memory to the proud, self-sufficient Egyptians; Hatshepsut's restorations probably increased her popularity.

The crowning architectural triumph of her reign was her beautiful funerary temple at Dayr el-Baḥrī. Built by Senmut, her chief architect and adviser, it was constructed on three levels against the cliffs; the temple, a harmonious progression of ramps, courts, and porticoes, was decorated in the interior with scenes of the major events of the queen's reign.

Probably the most interesting of the achievements so portrayed was the expedition sent to the kingdom of Punt, located at the southern end of the Red Sea. As the story is told, in the seventh or eighth year of her reign, Hatshepsut was instructed by Amon to send forth five ships laden with goods to exchange for incense and living myrrh trees as well as such exotic imports as apes, leopard skins, greyhounds, ivory, ebony, and gold. Pictured in detail are the natives' round huts, built on stilts, and the arrival of the Prince and Princess of Punt to greet the Egyptians. The portrait of the princess is unusual, because it is one of the rare examples in Egyptian art in which a fat and deformed person is depicted.

In addition to the voyage to Punt, Hatshepsut reopened the long-unused mines of Sinai, which produced blue and green stones. Tribute was received from Asian and Libyan tribes, and she participated in a brief military expedition to Nubia. Despite the latter endeavors, Hatshepsut's primary concern was peace, not imperialistic expansion. In this regard, her actions were in sharp contrast to those of her rival and successor Thutmose III, who was very much the warrior-king.

It would not be sufficient, however, to explain Hatshepsut's less aggressive policies on the basis of her sex. Traditionally, the Egyptians had been isolationists. Convinced that their land had been blessed by the gods with almost everything necessary, the Egyptians had throughout much of their earlier history treated their neighbors as foreign barbarians, unworthy of serious consideration. Hatshepsut and her advisers seem to have chosen this conservative course.

As Hatshepsut's reign continued, unpleasant changes began to occur. Her favorite, Senmut, died around 1487. In addition to the numerous offices and titles related to agriculture, public works, and the priesthood, he had also been named a guardian and tutor to Neferure. No less than six statues show Senmut with the royal child in his arms. At the end of his life, he may have fallen from favor by presuming to include images of himself in his mistress' temple. Most were discovered and mutilated, presumably during Hatshepsut's lifetime and with her approval since her names remained undisturbed.

Princess Neferure died young, perhaps even before Senmut's death, leaving Hatshepsut to face the growing power of Thutmose III. The king had reached adulthood: He was now the leader of the army and demanded a more important role in the coregency. His presence at major festivals became more obvious, although Hatshepsut's name continued to be linked with his until 1482.

It is not known exactly where or when Hatshepsut died or whether she might have been deposed and murdered. That her relations with her nephew and son-in-law were strained is evident from the revenge Thutmose exacted after her death: Her temples and tombs were broken into and her statues destroyed. Her cartouches, carved oval or oblong figures which encased the royal name, were erased, and in many cases her name was replaced by that of her husband or even of her father. She was eliminated from the list of kings. Thutmose III ruled in her stead and did his best to see that she was forgotten both by gods and by men.

Summary

The nature and scope of Hatshepsut's achievements are still subject to debate. Traditional historians have emphasized the irregularity of her succession, the usurpation of Thutmose III's authority, and her disinterest in military success. Revisionist studies are more generous in assessing this unique woman, praising her for her promotion of peaceful trade and her extensive building program at home.

Her influence throughout Egypt, though brief and limited only to her reign, must have been profound. The considerable number of temples, tombs, and monuments constructed at her command would have provided work for many of her subjects, just as surely as the wars of her father and nephew provided employment in another capacity. Art, devotion to the gods, and propaganda were inextricably mingled in the architectural endeavors of every pharaoh. Hatshepsut's devotion to the gods, especially the Theban deity Amon, and her evident need to justify her succession and her achievements enriched her nation with some of its finest examples of New Kingdom art.

Controversial in her own lifetime and still something of a mysterious figure, Hatshepsut continues to inspire conflicting views about herself and the nature of Egyptian kingship. She was a bold figure who chose to change the role assigned to royal women, yet at the same time, she seems to have been a traditionalist leading a faction that wanted Egypt to remain self-sufficient and essentially peaceful. Perhaps that was yet another reason that she and Thutmose III were so much at odds. His vision of Egypt as a conquering empire would be that of the future. She was looking back to the past.

Bibliography

Aldred, Cyril. *The Development of Ancient Egyptian Art from 3200 to 1315 B.C.* London: A. Tiranti, 1952. The title indicates the focus of the work. There are more than fifteen plates depicting Hatshepsut, other members of her family, and her adviser Senmut. Detailed explanations accompany each picture, and there is also an index and a bibliography.

Edgerton, William F. *The Thutmosid Succession.* Chicago: University of Chicago Press, 1933. This brief work contains a considerable amount of technical information on hieroglyphs and disputes among Egyptologists, although it presumes some knowledge on the part of the reader of the period from Thutmose I to the death of Hatshepsut.

Gardiner, Sir Alan. *Egypt of the Pharaohs.* Oxford: Clarendon, 1961; New York: Oxford University Press, 1964. Although a lengthy study, Gardiner's work is pleasantly written, with balanced views of both Hatshepsut and her successor, Thutmose III. Provides a good background for the less knowledgeable reader. Includes an index, a bibliography, and a comprehensive chronological list of kings. Illustrated.

Hayes, William C. "Egypt: Internal Affairs from Thuthmosis I to the Death of Amenophis III." In *Cambridge Ancient History.* Vol. 2, *History of the Middle East and the Aegean Region, c. 1800-1380 B.C.* 3d ed. London and New York: Cambridge University Press, 1973. Much information about Hatshepsut is given, although Hayes indicates a definite preference for Thutmose III.

Maspero, Gaston. *History of Egypt, Chaldea, Syria, Babylonia, and Assyria.* 13 vols. London: Grolier Society, 1903-1906. Maspero's work, though dated in some respects, is a mine of information. Many drawings that illustrate the text, taken from on-site photographs, are beautifully detailed; they cover everything from temples and bas-reliefs to statues, weapons, and the mummies of Thutmose I and Thutmose II. The material devoted to Hatshepsut is in volume 4, and the account of her reign is generally favorable.

Nims, Charles F. *Thebes of the Pharaohs: Pattern for Every City.* New York: Stein and Day, and London: Elek, 1965. The city of Thebes was extremely important to Hatshepsut and her family as both a political and a religious center. This book is helpful because it places the queen in her environment.

Tyldesley, Joyce A. *Hatchepsut: The Female Pharaoh.* London and New York: Viking, 1996. This book provides as full a biography as the evidence allows. The author aims to give an impartial account and deprecates the excesses of praise and blame heaped on the queen by earlier writers. Accessible to the non-specialist reader.

Wenig, Steffen. *The Woman in Egyptian Art.* New York: McGraw-Hill, 1969. This book is extremely well illustrated with both color and black-and-white photographs as well as drawings. The period covered is from c. 4000 B.C. to c. A.D. 300. Contains a chronology and an extensive bibliography and is written for the general reader.

Wilson, John A. *The Burden of Egypt.* Chicago: University of Chicago Press, 1951. This extensive study is both detailed and well written; it deals with the importance of geography to Egypt. Includes maps, a bibliography, illustrations, and a chronology of rulers. Wilson's analysis of political theories and discussion of possible motivations of the pharaohs is very useful in understanding the conflict between Hatshepsut and Thutmose III.

Dorothy T. Potter

SAINT HELENA

Born: c. 248; Drepanum (modern Herkes) in Bithnyia, Asia Minor

Died: c. 328; Nicomedia

Area of Achievement: Religion and saints

Contribution: Literally the most important woman in the world during her time, Helena was the mother of Constantine the Great, the first Christian Roman emperor. Helena's elevation to sainthood was conferred, according to tradition, because she set out on pilgrimage to Palestine to discover the cross of Christ's crucifixion and, upon doing so, founded the Church of the Nativity and the Church of the Holy Sepulchre in the Holy Land.

Early Life

Historical fact and historical fiction intertwine in the writings regarding Helena's life and times. The more authentic versions are believed to be those that are oldest, those being from Eusebius, Ambrose, and Cassiodorus. Eusebius, Helena's contemporary, was bishop of Caesarea in Palestine and author of the "eulogy" *Vita Constantini*, the biography of Constantine written shortly after his death in 337. Eusebius dedicated paragraphs 42-47 of Book III of *Vita Constantini* to the eastern provinces of the Empire and Helena's stay in Palestine.

Although little is known of her early life, the commonest belief is that Helena was born of the humblest of origins and possibly started her life as a stable girl or servant at an inn. While a few accounts claim that she married Constantius Chlorus, more often the interpretation has been that she was his concubine. In the Roman Empire of that time, concubinage was an accepted form of cohabitation. The relationship, however legal it may have been, began around 270; Helena gave birth to Constantine sometime near the period from 273 to 275.

Constantius was an officer in the Roman army when Helena met him. He rose to the position of Caesar, or deputy emperor, in 293 and to the rank of Augustus from 305 until his death in 306—but not before deserting Helena. He became Caesar under Maximian in the West of the Roman Empire. Constantine's mother was cast off in order that Maximian could marry his stepdaughter Theodora to Constantius in 289. Constantius' marriage with Theodora was a prerequisite for a successful political career in Diocletian's newly introduced tetrar-chy. Helena and her son were separated, and not until 306, when Constantine was named successor of his father, did she reappear in the historical accounts in her new role as the empress-mother at Constantine's court.

A definitive interpretation of historical writings on the era is not possible, but tradition says that during his rule, Constantine was struck with incurable leprosy. Pagan priests advised him to bathe in the warm blood of three thousand boys. When the children were gathered, Constantine responded to the anguished pleas from their mothers and freed them. For this act, he was visited by two emissaries from Jesus Christ. Constantine was baptized, catechized, and cured. This story was later popularized by the famous Italian painter Raphael (1483-1520), whose interpretation of the event is captured in the painting *The Donation of Constantine*.

Helena, as the legend continues, challenged her son's conversion from pagan idolatry to Christianity, and a theological debate was established to resolve the dispute. Saint Silvester entertained the ar-

guments of eleven leading Jewish scholars who protested the Christian faith. Silvester ultimately won when he brought back to life, in the name of Jesus Christ, a bull that the Jew Zambri had caused to drop dead. As the legend recounts, Helena, the Jews, and the judges all then converted. Another popular legend regarding Constantine's conversion to Christianity tells that the Christian Saint Silvester pardoned Constantine for the murder of his son and wife and won the leader to Christianity for doing so.

Constantine gave the first impetus to the Christianization of the Roman Empire and the eventual Christianization of Europe. He became sole ruler of the Roman Empire in 324, proclaimed Helena as Augusta soon after, and summoned the Council of Nicea (from *Nike*, meaning "victory") in 325. A prominent participant in this religious council, Constantine pushed for the dogmatic unity of the Christian religion. The bishops agreed on a common dogma expressed in the Nicene Creed. Constantine's focus on Christianization led to the building of many churches, including those over Christ's purported tomb and over the cave where Christ was said to have been born in Bethlehem; both structures were credited to Helena's pilgrimage to those places.

During Constantine's reunification efforts following his victory in 324, he equated the harmonious unity of his family with the unity of the empire. This position was lethal to his political leadership when, in 326, he executed his wife, Fausta, and his eldest son, Crispus, the young man who had been born to his concubine, Minervina. The most plausible justification was that a sexual relationship had developed between Fausta and Crispus, but the truth is obscure. Various accounts relate the pain experienced by Helena at the news of her favorite grandson's murder; her pilgrimage may have been in some part a response to the sin on her son had committed in ordering the murder.

The scandal in the Constantinian family and the turmoil caused by Constantine's insistence on Christianity created unrest in the eastern parts of the Roman Empire. To appease the people of the eastern provinces, Helen set off to meet them. Her travels were marked by her piety and gracious giving to all whom she encountered. An old Anglo-Saxon poem by Cynewulf (c. eighth century) tells the legend of Saint Helena's journey to Jerusalem to search for the Cross.

Life's Work

Tradition says Helena discovered the True Cross. She discovered three crosses, and Pontius' inscription marked the True Cross, as one tradition tells. In a more symbolic interpretation, historians have written that upon finding three crosses, Helena turned to Marcarius, bishop of Jerusalem, for mediation. A mortally sick woman (in some tellings, one who had just died) was brought to the crosses. When she was touched by the first two, nothing happened; upon the touch of the third cross, she was immediately healed. Thus, the holy wood of the True Cross was identified. More important, the healing symbolized the salvation of Christianity for those who believed in Christ.

Because of her visit to the Holy Land, churches were erected at the cave where the nativity occurred in Bethlehem (the Church of the Nativity) and on the Mount of Olives, from which Christ is said to have ascended into heaven (the Church of the Assumption). The attachment of holiness (or unholiness) to something tangible was not inherent in Christianity, for nothing earthly was considered holy. The concept of churches as holy places was established by Constantine and Helena as part of the establishment of Christianity. The churches were thus structured to represent the places where earth and heaven met.

The bodies of the Three Magi, now shown at Cologne, germany, are said to have been brought by Helena from the East and given to the Church of Milan; she is also said to have given the Holy Coat, the seamless robe of Christ, to the cathedral of Trier in Germany. In some accounts, she is also credited with finding the nails that fastened Christ's body to the Cross.

Legend reports she established Stavrovouni Monastery in Cyprus, where she stayed during her return journey from Jerusalem; she is said to have presented a piece of the True Cross in establishing the monastery. The monastery occupies the easternmost summit of the Troodos range of mountains, at a height of 2,260 feet. Tradition describes the Monastery as an impregnable fortress against pagan attacks.

To the southeast of Rome, a territory called *fundus Laurentus* was an estate belonging to Helena (acquired sometime after 312). The site was one of the first areas in Rome where the new Christian convictions of the members of the imperial house were manifested.

Another historical legend, with some archaeological support, tells that Helena gave her imperial palace in Trier to Agricius, at the time priest to Antioch, for use as Trier's Cathedral. Legend also has it that she was involved in the foundation of the Abbey of Saint Maximin at Trier.

Summary

The sarcophagus of Saint Helena is in the Vatican Museum. Originally intended for Constantine, the sarcophagus is covered with reliefs celebrating military triumphs.

More than one hundred churches have been dedicated to Saint Helena in England. By the end of the Middle Ages, her feast was kept in many churches on February 8. Throughout the world, her feast day is celebrated: by the Roman Catholic church on August 18; by the Greeks on May 21; by the Ethiopians on September 15; and by the Copts on March 24 and May 4. She is the patroness of dyers, needlers, and nailsmiths.

Jan Willem Drijvers reported in his definitive book *Helena Augusta: The Mother of Constantine the Great and the Legend of Her Finding of the True Cross* (1992) that there may be two cameos depicting Helena: the so-called Ada-cameo, preserved in the Stadtbibliothek in Trier and a cameo in the Koninklijk Penningkabinet in Leiden, the Netherlands. It is difficult to identify statues of Helena with any certainty. Since Helena's coiffure was well attested, it is typically the test for images. On the coin portraits that have been identified as depicting Helena, her hair is sleekly combed and worn in a knot over the middle of her head. Yet though her image is sometimes difficult to distinguish, her impact is not. For many empresses and queens who came to the throne after her, Helena Augusta became the perfect Christian empress whose humble piety was a model for all.

Bibliography

Bietenhoiz, Peter G. *Historia and Fabula: Myths and Legends in Historical Thought from Antiquity to the Modern Age*. Vol. 59 in *Brill's Studies in Intellectual History*, edited by A. J. Vanderjagt. Leiden and New York: E. J. Brill, 1994. Establishes a perspective from which to approach the "historical" study of Saint Helena as that concerned both with things that actually happened (*historia*) and things that are merely supposed to have happened (*fabula*). Explores myths, legends, and historical thought surrounding Constantine the Great and his mother.

Burckhardt, Jacob. *The Age of Constantine the Great*. Translated by Moses Hadas. New York: Pantheon Books, and London: Routledge, 1949. Cited as the most meaningful history for the nonprofessional reader, Burckhardt's essay of nearly four hundred pages is a humanist reaction against the microscopic but less imaginative writings of scientific historians. Topical page headings and an extensive index make the book reader-friendly.

Drijvers, Jan Willem. *Helena Augusta: The Mother of Constantine the Great and the Legend of Her Finding of the True Cross*. Leiden and New York: E.J. Brill, 1992. Originally a doctoral thesis defended at the University of Groningen, this book focuses on the task of distinguishing the history of Helena from the legend. Includes identification of coins and statues of Helena and an extensive bibliography.

Firth, John B. *Constantine the Great: The Reorganization of the Empire and the Triumph of the Church*. 2d ed. London and New York: Putnam, 1923. The twenty-seven illustrations in this 356-page edition include several of depictions of Helena and others related to her. Includes a comprehensive index.

Grant, Michael. *The Emperor Constantine*. London: Weidenfeld and Nicolson, 1993; as *Constantine the Great: The Man and His Times*. New York: Scribner, 1994. A chronological table, maps, and illustrations enhance this telling of the impact of Constantine and Helena on Christianity.

Waugh, Evelyn. *Saint Helena Empress*. In *Saints for Now*, edited by Clare Boothe Luce. London and New York: Sheed and Ward, 1952. Brief but highly readable and literary interpretation of Helena's life.

Tonya Huber

HENGIST

Born: c. A.D. 420; probably Jutland

Died: c. A.D. 488; probably Kent, England, or near Knaresborough, Yorkshire

Area of Achievement: Warfare and conquest

Contribution: Hengist is reputed to have led the first Germanic invasion of Britain and to have established the first "English" kingdom in Kent.

Early Life

Information on Hengist (or Hengest) is derived from oral tradition subsequently captured in written texts. Chief amongst these is the *Historia Ecclesiastica* (*Ecclesiastical History*, 731) of Bede, which was the basis for the relevant entries in *The Anglo-Saxon Chronicle* (c. 900), the standard source for the story of Hengist. More detail will be found in the *Historia Brittonum* (*History of the Britons*, c. 830) by Nennius, who drew on an earlier document, perhaps from the sixth century, known as the *Kentish Chronicle*, though this is clearly a mixture of fact and legend. Even less reliable is *Historia Regum Britanniae* (*History of the Kings of Britain*, 1136) by Geoffrey of Monmouth. Yet Geoffrey's work cannot be dismissed out of hand, for he may have had access to sources no longer available.

A character called Hengist appears in *Beowulf* (eighth century) and in the related fragment *The Fight at Finnesburg* (perhaps seventh century). The contemporaneity of these events and the similarity of background with Bede and Nennius are strongly suggestive that the two Hengists are the same. The references in *Beowulf* and *Finnesburg* help scholars to date Hengist to the middle of the fifth century A.D., independent of Bede's *Historia*, which specifically dates Hengist's arrival in Britain to the period 449-457. Nennius also places Hengist's arrival in that period, citing it as forty years after the end of the Roman Empire in Britain, which is usually dated to A.D. 410.

Nennius provides a genealogy for Hengist, recording that he was the son of Wichtgils and grandson of Witta. Witta is recorded elsewhere as the ruler of the Swæfe or Suebi, a tribe of Angles who lived in what is now southern Denmark. *Beowulf* and the *Finnesburg* fragment reveal that Hengist was a prince in exile, no doubt driven out of his homeland by interdynastic rivalries. He was probably of mixed Anglian/Jutish descent because he was one of an army of Half-Danes, a mercenary warband. Their leader Hnæf was killed in a fight at Finnesburg against the men of Finn, king of the East Frisians. Hengist survived the battle and became the leader of the Half-Danes. He agreed to winter at Finnesburg, but in the spring, the feud erupted again. Hengist's army defeated the Frisians, and Finn was killed.

This episode, referred to by Professor J. R. R. Tolkien as the *freswæl*, or "Frisian massacre," doubtless established Hengist's reputation as a warrior. He was probably in his late twenties at this time, since he had been some years in exile and was old enough to be accepted as leader of the Half-Danes and to entreat with Finn on equal terms. It is possible that it was news of this episode that encouraged the British high king, Vortigern, to invite Hengist to Britain.

Life's Work

In the mid-fifth century, Britain was in a state of chaos, with civil wars between the native British punctuated by incursions by the Picts from the north and the Irish from the west. This disruption to the social fabric led to poor harvests and famine. In the midst of this turmoil, the Germanic invaders began to arrive, their forces peppering the eastern coastline of Britain from Bamburgh and the Forth estuary to Thanet and the Kentish coast. What marks Hengist's arrival as different is that he was invited and, in return for his services, was granted land. Whereas other Germanic colonies may have been won by conquest, Hengist's was, at least initially, authorized. Hengist was summoned at the request of Vortigern (whose real name may have been Vitalinus Vortigern, a title that means "high king"). Neither Gildas nor Bede are specific about where Hengist settled, simply saying that it was in the "east of the island." The traditional landing place was Ebbsfleet, near Richborough in Kent, but this was probably the site of a later landing. Scholars David Dumville and John Morris, while disagreeing on many points, agree that the initial settlement was almost certainly in the north, probably around Bamburgh, a logical site for fighting the Picts. Hengist arrived with his brother Horsa in three boats, or "keels." Despite this small force, they were successful in pushing back the Picts. In gratitude, Vortigern granted Hengist and his men land in Thanet. According to Nennius, Hengist convinced Vortigern that he could be of greater as-

sistance with further warriors. Nennius reports that Hengist was able to appeal to the gullible Vortigern by handing him his daughter, Reinwen, as his wife. Reinwen was probably only fifteen or so, and Hengist might have fathered her when he was about seventeen, which would place him in his early thirties, supporting the supposition that he was about thirty during the fight at Finnesburg.

Hengist brought to Britain his son Oisc or Æsc (called "Octha" by Nennius) and his nephew Ebissa (possibly Horsa's son), along with forty ships. Oisc and Ebissa focused their efforts in the north, and the ensuing fighting evidently spread over several years. The *Anglo-Saxon Chronicle* suggests it lasted from 449 to 455, though the true date was probably later. At the end, Ebissa stayed in the north, but Oisc apparently joined his father in Kent. Later references suggest that Oisc remained in the north, so it is probable that Oisc joined his father temporarily in order to provide reinforcements. The British, led by Vortigern's son Vortimer, were trying to drive the Jutes out of Britain. The sequence of events differs in the records, but all agree that there were a series of three or four battles in which the British gradually gained the upper hand. The most important of these was at Ægelesprep, or Aylesford, near Maidstone on the river Medway, where Horsa was killed. The British may have claimed the victory, though the *Anglo-Saxon Chronicle* asserts that Hengist declared himself king of Kent after the battle. Perhaps negotiations set the river Medway as the frontier, with Hengist as ruler of the territory to the east. Vortimer continued to press Hengist's forces back. A third battle took place at an unknown location conjectured to be on the Wantsum, the river that once divided Thanet from mainland Kent. The victory again went to the British, and Hengist was forced back to Thanet and subsequently expelled from the island.

Vortimer, however, died soon afterward, reputedly poisoned by Reinwen, and Vortigern was too weak a king to resist Hengist. Hengist returned with more troops, and this time their advance was decisive. This may be the time of the battle of Crayford, dated to 456 by the *Anglo-Saxon Chronicle* though it may have occurred as much as nineteen years later. Hengist's army routed the British and sent them fleeing to London. Hengist then called a peace conference. The British representatives were unarmed, but Hengist ordered his men to hide their knives in their boots. At his command, Hengist's men slaughtered the British, save only

Vortigern. Most authorities regard this episode as fiction, but it is consistent with Hengist's character. The treachery is similar to that played upon Finn and supports the argument that the two Hengists are the same and that he was the "shrewd and skilful" warrior Nennius described. Thereafter, Vortigern was forced to grant Hengist his wishes. According to the *Kentish Chronicle*, Hengist received not only Kent but also parts of what became Essex and Middlesex, including London. Hengist's triumph established his kingdom and opened up the Thames route into the British heartland for the next wave of Saxons.

The final reference to Hengist in the *Anglo-Saxon Chronicle* is to the year 473, when, it is reported, he and his son again defeated the British and gained "innumerable spoils." Oisc succeeded to the kingdom in 488, which may be the year of Hengist's death; he would have been about sixty-eight, a remarkable age for a warrior. Bede, Nennius, and the *Anglo-Saxon Chronicle* remain silent on Hengist's fate, but Geoffrey of Monmouth reveals the full story with customary flair. He states that after Vortigern's death, Hengist was defeated by Aurelius Ambrosius (known otherwise as "Ambrosius Aurelianus") at Maisbeli, from where Hengist fled to Kaerconan or Cunungeburg, identified by some as Knaresborough in Yorkshire. There, Hengist was captured, beheaded, and buried. Since Hengist's son Oisc was apparently still in the north of England, probably at York, at this time, Geoffrey's story remains within the realm of possibility, although certainly suspect.

It is because they were descended from Oisc that the members of the Kentish royal family were known as "Oiscingas." This raises the question of the relationship between Hengist and Oisc and the matter of Hengist's real name. "Hengist" means "stallion," while "Horsa" is interpreted as "wild horse." Some commentators have suggested that these were two names for the same person. However, the horse was probably an emblem of the brothers and that the names by which they were known were nicknames, not their real names. There is also some confusion in the genealogies over the name of Hengist's son. The *Kentish Chronicle* calls him "Octha" and the *Anglo-Saxon Chronicle* calls him "Æsc" or "Oisc." However, Bede states that Oisc's real name was "Oeric." It is possible that Bede's source confused these names. If Hengist's son was Oeric, then "Octha" might be Hengist's real name. This could account for Oeric's calling his own son

"Octha," in memory of his father. The epithet "Oisc" (derived from *ossa*, meaning "gods") was a later veneration based on the tradition of ancestor worship, in which the forebears of the Angles were believed to be descended from the god Woden. Hengist may have been venerated in the same way, and Oeric was recognized as *Oisc*, the son of a god.

The argument about dates is far from resolved. John Morris proposed that Hengist arrived as early as 428, while David Dumville asserts that the correct date is closer to the year 480. The latter date is in keeping with errors in the early *Anglo-Saxon Chronicle* chronology, and it makes Oisc's age more realistic. He ruled for at least twenty-four years after 488, which suggests a birthdate of no earlier than 450. Oisc's successors each ruled for around thirty years, a surprising span for those violent times. Yet this unusual stability reinforces the view that Kent had been decisively won by Hengist, allowing its rulers to exist in relative peace.

Summary

Although there were other contemporary Germanic invaders of Britain, such as Cerdic in Hampshire and Aelle in Sussex, their conquests were not decisive. The kingdom of the South Saxons was obliterated, and the West Saxons remained as a ragged series of confederate tribes for more than a century. Hengist enabled others to benefit from a strong kingdom established by conquest and treaty and free from further British retaliation. Kent was the first of the Germanic kingdoms, and its early history, after Hengist, was relatively peaceful, allowing its people to trade, prosper, and create a wealthy kingdom. Influential Frankish connections developed during the sixth century almost certainly because of the strong base that Hengist established, and this paved the way for the arrival of Augustine and the introduction of the Roman church to the English.

Bibliography

Bassett, Steven, ed. *The Origins of Anglo-Saxon Kingdoms.* London and New York: Leicester University Press, 1989. Includes a chapter that looks specifically at the creation and early structure of the kingdom of Kent.

Kirby, D. P. *The Earliest English Kings.* London and Boston: Unwin Hyman, 1991. A highly readable and remarkably integrated study of the development of Saxon kingships.

Lapidge, Michael, and David Dumville, eds. *Gildas: New Approaches.* Woodbridge, England: The Boydell Press, 1984. A series of studies of Gildas's text, with particular emphasis on chronology and context.

Morris, John. *The Age of Arthur.* Rev. ed. London: Weidenfeld and Nicolson, 1975. A creative and often challenging study of Dark Ages Britain that throws new light on the Germanic invasion.

Tolkien, J. R. R., with Alan Bliss, ed. *Finn and Hengest: The Fragment and the Episode.* London and Boston: Allen & Unwin, 1982. A detailed study of Hengist in *Beowulf* and his relationship to the Hengist of Bede. Challenging and original.

Witney, K. P. *The Kingdom of Kent.* London: Phillimore, 1982. A thorough study of the first English kingdom, with a reasoned analysis of Hengist's contribution.

Yorke, Barbara. *Kings and Kingdoms of Early Anglo-Saxon England.* London: Seaby, 1990. Includes a detailed discussion on the origin of the Kentish kingdom and the roles of Hengist and Horsa.

Mike Ashley

HERACLITUS OF EPHESUS

Born: fl. 505-500 B.C.; Ephesus, Greece

Died: Date unknown; place unknown

Area of Achievement: Philosophy

Contribution: Heraclitus formulated one of the earliest and most comprehensive theories of the nature of the world, the cosmos, and the soul. His theory that the soul pervaded all parts of the universe and its inhabitants stood in contrast to the ideas of his more mechanistic contemporaries.

Early Life

According to Diogenes Laërtius, Heraclitus was born in the city of Ephesus to an important family that had an ancient and respected reputation. Through his family he inherited public office but resigned in favor of his brother. When his friend Hermodorus was expelled from Ephesus, Heraclitus protested publicly and subsequently withdrew from public life. Heraclitus was a man of great personal integrity, whose main purpose in life was to find the truth and proclaim it for the benefit of humankind, irrespective of the consequences. He attacked the sacred festival of the Bacchanalia, condemned the worship of images of the gods, and spoke unkind words about Pythagoras, Xenophanes, Hecataeus, and Hesiod. His arrogance was legendary. Heraclitus insisted that he was the sole bearer of the truth. He thought that the multitude of common men were too weak of wit to understand the truth, claiming that his work was meant for the few who were intelligent.

To complicate the difficulty presented by this posture, his writings (those that survived) present special problems. Aristotle and Theophrastus observed that his statements were sometimes ambiguous, incomplete, and contradictory. It is no wonder that his contemporaries named him "The Riddler," "The Obscure One," and "The Dark One." Heraclitus was well aware of their criticism, but he was dedicated to his own high purposes.

Life's Work

Heraclitus' book was entitled *Peri physeos* (c. 500 B.C.; *On Nature*). He dedicated the work to Artemis and left a scroll of it in her temple, an act that was not unusual in that culture. Heraclitus would not qualify as a scientist; his talent was more that of the mystic. He had the ability to see further into the nature of things than others did. He was the first to unify the natural and the spiritual worlds, while

others saw only the discrete components of nature. Anaximander and Heraclitus were both impressed with the ceaseless change of the temporal world and formulated theories about the primal matter of the universe. Anaximander's primal matter was colorless and tasteless, and otherwise had no characteristics. For Heraclitus, however, that which underlay the world of form and matter was not substance, it was process.

Heraclitus saw the world as a place where change, at every level and every phase of existence, was the most important phenomenon. The basic element of change, and at the heart of the process, was fire. The processes governing the world involved the four elements: fire, water, air, and earth. According to Heraclitus, fire was the element from which the others devolved, and it was always in motion. It was fire in the form of body heat that kept animal forms in motion; it was also able to transform and consume the other basic elements. In essence, air was hot and wet, water was cold and wet, earth was cold and dry, and fire was hot and dry. Under certain circumstances, each of the four

elements could be transformed into another (enough water could quench fire; a hot enough fire could reduce earth to ash, or water to steam). All the possible transformations were happening at any given time somewhere in the universe, such as in the cooking of a meal, the thawing of the winter ice, the volcanism of Mount Etna—and even in phenomena known to Heraclitus, such as the atmospheric disturbances of the sunspot cycle or the explosion of a supernova.

Heraclitus described two fundamental directions of this change. In the downward path, some of the fire thickens and becomes the ocean, while part of the ocean dies and becomes land. On the upward path, moist exhalations from the ocean and the land rise and become clouds; they then ignite (perhaps in the form of lightning) and return to fire (presumably the fiery ether, which was thought to dwell in the heights of the sky). If the fiery clouds from which the lightning comes are extinguished, however, then there is a whirlwind (a waterspout, perhaps), and once again the fire returns to the sea and the cycle is complete. All this change and transformation was not, however, simply random motion. There was a cosmic master plan, the Logos. Nothing in the English language translates Logos perfectly. As it stands in the beginning of the Gospel of John, it is usually translated as the Word, which is clearly inadequate in context and requires a definition. In Heraclitus' time, Logos could mean reputation or high worth. This meaning devolved from another definition of Logos: narrative or story.

The flexibility of the word has been a source of considerable debate. The three most important meanings of the word are: (1) general rule or general principle; (2) the carrying out of a general principle; and (3) that which belongs distinctly to the realm of humanness, the faculty of reasoning. First and foremost, the Logos is the universal law, or plan, or process, that animates the whole cosmos. The Logos is the cosmos; it inhabits the cosmos. It is also what makes the difference between the sleeping human and the awakened human. It is, in humans, the wisdom to perceive that the Logos (on the highest level of abstraction) is immanent in the cosmos, that it is the universe's governing principle. That is the fountainhead of true knowledge in Heraclitus' system. All humans have the Logos in common. What they specifically have in common is the realization or perception that they are a part of the whole, which is the Logos. Without that

realization they are fundamentally asleep. Within the slumbering human, the Logos lies dormant. Even if a human is technically awake, however, he can still be subject to error if he follows his own private "truth," that is, his own inclinations, and prefers his subjectivity more than he values the Logos. The self-dependence that one would call individuality could then be considered a violation of the Logos.

Though the physical senses are not attuned to the perception of the Logos, they are important in the process that leads to wisdom. For example, the ability to see is a prerequisite that may eventually lead to the perception that there is a plan to the universe. The senses are the mediators between that which is human and that which is cosmic. They are the windows which, during waking hours, connect the human with the portion of the Logos that can be perceived. During sleeping hours those channels are closed and the direct participation in the cosmos ceases. Respiration then becomes a channel by which the direct access can be maintained; the act of breathing maintains minimal contact. The Logos can be considered the soul of the universe. Each awakened human has a portion of higher enlightenment: the soul. Logos, Soul, and Cosmic Fire are eventually different aspects of the same abstraction—the everlasting truth that directs the universe and its conscious constituents. According to Heraclitus, the enlightened soul is hot and dry, like fire, which is why it tends upward, in the direction of the fiery ether. Soul and ether are the same material.

Soul is linked to Logos, but its roots are in the human body which it inhabits. Soul is possibly the healing principle in the body: Heraclitus likened the soul to a spider which, when its web is torn, goes to the site of the injury. Soul is born from moisture and dies when it absorbs too much water. Drunkenness was to Heraclitus a truly bad habit: A moist soul had diminished faculties as its body was also diminished, in that its intellect was stunted and its physical strength lessened.

Though the body was subject to decomposition, some souls seem to have been exempted from physical death (becoming water). Certain situations, among them dying in battle, tune the soul to such a heightened state (with the soul unusually motivated and not weakened by illness and old age) that it merged directly with the world fire. After death, there seems to be no survival of personal identity, though it is likely that the soul-stuff is merged with the Logos and that the Logos is the source of souls that exist in the physical world. Evidently, soul material follows a cycling process of its own. Heraclitus saw that the world was a unity of many parts, but the unity was not immediately manifest. The oneness of the world was the result of an infinite multiplicity. Heraclitus thought that the key to understanding this multiplicity was to look upon the world in terms of the abstract concept of Harmony.

Pythagoras had previously used musical harmony in explaining the attunement and orderliness that he saw in the universe. Heraclitus, however, used the concept of Harmony in a different way. He believed that Harmony existed only where and when there was opposition. A single note struck on a lyre has no harmony of itself. Any two notes struck together, however, form a tension or a contrast between the two sounds, creating a continuum of possible notes between the two notes that have been struck. In terms of a continuum of hot and cold temperatures, not only do the extremes exist, but so also does the continuum exist, bounded by the extremes. At every point between the extremes of hot and cold there is an identifiable point which has a specific temperature that is a function of both extremes.

Similarly, every virtue has a corresponding vice. Neither extreme on this scale is especially significant in human behavior: Few people, if any, represent extremes of either virtue or vice; most live in the continuum between. Ethical considerations motivate good individuals to tend toward the good in a choice between good and evil, and the measure of a person's soul is where one stands on the continuum defined by good and evil. Heraclitus' most controversial statement on the subject was that the opposites that define the continuum are identical. Hate and love, therefore, would have to be one and the same. The absence of either defining term destroys the continuum, and without the continuum the two extremes cannot relate to each other. They define a world in which the people are passionate haters and ardent lovers, with no real people in between. The Harmony that Heraclitus discerned was dependent on the tension between two opposites. The cosmos was, for him, a carefully and beautifully balanced entity, poised between a great multiplicity of contrasting interests, engaged in continual strife. The sum total of all these contrasting interests, however, was the Harmony that no one saw except the truly enlightened souls. Only the

Logos, which was One, and which created and tuned the Harmony, was exempt from the balancing of opposites.

Perhaps the best-known of Heraclitus' observations is that everything in the universe is incessantly moving and changing. He considered all matter to be in a state of constant transformation from one form to a different form and, at the same time, from one set of physical qualities to another. Not only did he believe that the Logos bestowed life on all its parts, but he also believed that the forms of matter were intrinsically alive and that the flux was a function of the life within the matter. All life was caught up in the constant change: Everything was involved in processes of decomposition and in the reconstitution of new forms from the products of decay.

As the Greeks viewed the world, they saw only the portions of the movement that were available within the limits of their senses. Though they were not aware of the whole spectrum of movement, they were intelligent enough to extrapolate from what they could perceive. A continuous stream of water wearing away a stone was to them a good reminder of the fact that many processes of change were not perceptible in their time scale.

Heraclitus summed it up poetically in his famous analogy: "You cannot step twice into the same river, for fresh waters are flowing on." From one second to the next, the flux of things changes the world; though the river is the same river, the flux of things has moved its waters downstream, and new water from upstream has replaced the old. According to Diogenes Laërtius and others, "The cosmos is born out of fire and again resolved into fire in alternate periods for ever." One line of interpretation is that the world is periodically destroyed by a universal conflagration. More plausible, however, is the assumption that this is a restatement of Heraclitus' doctrine that fire is the one primal element from which all others derive and into which all elements are eventually transmuted by the workings of the eternal flux. In support of this argument is a phrase from the remaining fragments of Heraclitus' work: "From all things one, and from one all things." In Heraclitus' cosmology, however, there was the concept of a Great Year that occurred every 10,800 years, at which time the sun, moon, and other heavenly bodies returned to a hypothetical starting place. These bodies, though they were not exempt from the principle of constant flux, were permanent in their forms and in their heavenly paths. Beyond the measured paths of their orbits was the fiery ether of the unmoving Logos.

Summary

Heraclitus was quite unlike his contemporaries, both in terms of his personality and in the nature and scope of his thoughts. Whereas the works of his contemporaries were more in the line of primitive scientific inquiry, the endeavors of Heraclitus were more closely akin to poesy and perhaps prophecy. His aim was not to discover the material world but to seek out the governing principles within and behind the physical forms. In this respect, he was the most mystical of the Greeks.

Though the body of Heraclitus' work is faulted by time, by problems of interpretation, and by obscurity of the text (some of which was solely Heraclitus' fault), it is clear that he believed he had provided a definitive view of the processes that govern the cosmos and the workings of the human soul. His ideas were novel and daring in their time. At the center of his cosmos is the concept of constant change, which masks the concept of unity: All things are in balance, yet all things are in motion and transition, with fire playing the central role, and the Logos disposing and directing the parts. The Logos also governs human actions, reaching into the deeper parts of the personality, with the Oversoul touching the soul material within, fire outside calling to the fire within to awake, to look, to learn, to become, and to unite.

Bibliography

Burnet, John. *Early Greek Philosophy.* 4th ed. London: Black, and New York: Barnes and Noble, 1930. Chapter 3 is devoted to Heraclitus and is probably the best of the nineteenth century English works that discuss Heraclitus. It has considerable insight and is readable without being dated.

Dilcher, Roman. *Spudasmata.* Vol. 56, *Studies in Heraclitus.* Zurich and New York: Georg Olms, 1995. The author attempts to discover unifying interests (in microcosm/macrocosm and in life/death) that tie together the fragments of Heraclitus' writings. Dilcher determines that "reticence and evasiveness . . . are . . . the essential and necessary form reflecting the very content of this philosophy."

Fairbanks, Arthur. *The First Philosophers of Greece.* New York: Scribner, and London: K. Paul, Trench, Trübner, and Co., 1898. This volume has a good section on Heraclitus, including the Greek text of the fragments as well as an English translation. The discussion is short and basic and covers most of the important points.

Guthrie, W. K. C. *A History of Greek Philosophy.* Vol. 1, *The Earlier Presocratics and the Pythagoreans.* Cambridge: Cambridge University Press, 1962; New York: Cambridge University Press, 1978. This volume is one of the best works on Heraclitus' contemporaries and contains an excellent extended discussion of Heraclitus.

Heidegger, Martin, and Eugen Fink. *Heraclitus Seminar, 1966-67.* University: University of Alabama Press, 1979. This work is an extended dialogue between two important scholars, with Fink supplying more of the conversation. The subject is (in general) the relation of the one to the many in the works of Heraclitus.

Kahn, Charles H. *The Art and Thought of Heraclitus: An Edition of the Fragments with Translation and Commentary.* Cambridge and New York: Cambridge University Press, 1979. This volume is a fine and useful scholarly tool, although not comprehensive. It includes the Greek text of the fragments and an English translation, as well as a short but very provocative appendix that discusses the possibility of a link between Heraclitus and the Orient.

Kirk, G. S. *Heraclitus, the Cosmic Fragments.* Cambridge: Cambridge University Press, 1954. A deep and thorough analysis of some of the Heraclitian fragments, this volume focuses on the "Cosmic" fragments—those that are relevant to the world as a whole, the Logos, the doctrine of opposites, and the action of fire.

Kirk, G. S., and J. E. Raven. *The Pre-Socratic Philosophers: A Critical History with a Selection of Texts.* 2d ed. Cambridge and New York: Cambridge University Press, 1983. One of the chapters provides a very good short analysis of Heraclitus. The book itself is one of the very best on Greek thought and the individual Greek philosophers.

Mourelatos, Alexander. *The Pre-Socratics: A Collection of Critical Essays.* Rev. ed. Princeton, N.J. and Chichester: Princeton University Press, 1993. A collection of critical essays covering the major contemporaries of Heraclitus. Included in the book are four fine essays on Heraclitus.

Sallis, John, and Kenneth Maly, eds. *Heraclitean Fragments: A Companion Volume to the Heidegger/Fink Seminar on Heraclitus. University: University of Alabama Press, 1980. This is a companion volume to a seminar that addressed Heraclitean topics. It pursues further some aspects of the Heidegger-Fink dialogue, but it also discusses a number of other topics related to Heraclitus.

Sandywell, Barry. Presocratic Reflexivity: The Construction of Philosophical Discourse, c. 600-450 B.C. Volume 3. London and New York: Routledge, 1996. A difficult, wide-ranging book that tries to evaluate pre-Socratic thinkers in terms of the "cultural discourse" in which they participated and to which they in turn contributed. Chapter 6 deals with Heraclitus.

Schofield, Malcolm, and Martha Craven Nussbaum, eds. Language and Logos: Studies in Ancient Greek Philosophy Presented to G. E. L. Owen. Cambridge and New York: Cambridge University Press, 1982. This collection of articles includes two rather good ones on Heraclitus.

West, M. L. Early Greek Philosophy and the Orient. Oxford: Clarendon Press, 1971. Book examines the possibility between Greek thought and the ideas of the Middle East. About half of the text is relevant to Heraclitus.

Wheelwright, Philip. Heraclitus. Princeton, N.J.: Princeton University Press, 1959. An excellent and well-written volume, the text reads very well because footnotes and matter not relevant to main points are relegated to an appendix. Includes a very good bibliography.

Richard Badessa

HERO OF ALEXANDRIA

Born: fl. A.D. 62; Alexandria
Died: late first century; Alexandria
Areas of Achievement: Mathematics and science
Contribution: Hero wrote about mechanical devices and is the most important ancient authority on them. Some of these were his own inventions, including a rudimentary steam engine and windmill. He also investigated mathematics, where his most noted contribution was a method for approximating square roots.

Early Life

Virtually nothing is known about the personal life of Hero (also known as Heron) of Alexandria, other than the fact that an eclipse of the moon visible from Alexandria and mentioned in one of his books occurred in A.D. 62. Under the Roman Empire, Alexandria flourished somewhat less than it had under the Ptolemies, but the famous museum was still a center of research and learning where scientists and philosophers were active. Technology also continued to make amazing strides, so that Hero found an atmosphere conducive to his own theories and inventions. His writings show that he was an educated man, familiar with Greek, Latin, Egyptian, and even Mesopotamian sources, and reveal a wide-ranging mind unusual for his time. There is no indication that he worked for either a Roman patron or the Roman government.

Life's Work

Hero's greatest renown results from the fact that many of his writings on mechanics and mathematics are extant. The mechanical works include the two-volume *Pneumatica (The Pneumatics of Hero of Alexandria*, 1851), on devices operated by compressed air, steam, and water; *Peri automatopoietikes (Automata*, 1971), on contrivances to produce miraculous appearances in temples; the three-volume *Mechanica*, surviving in Arabic, on weight-moving machines; *Dioptra* (partial English translation, 1963), on instruments for sighting and other purposes; *Catoptrica* (surviving in Latin), on mirrors; and two artillery manuals, *Belopoeïca* (English translation, 1971) and *Cheiroballistra* (English translation, 1971), on different types of catapults. Missing are other works on weight-lifting machines (*Baroulkos*, which might be a name for part of *Mechanica*), water clocks, astrolabes, balances, and the construction of vaults.

Of his mathematical treatises, there exist the three-volume *Metrica*, on the measurement and division of surfaces and bodies, and *Definitiones*, on geometrical terms. There are other works, more or less heavily edited by later redactors, such as *Geometrica*, *Stereometrica*, and *Peri metron* (also known as *On Measures*), all treatises on measurement, as well as *Geodaesia* and *Geoponica* or *Liber geeponicus*, on the measurement of land. A commentary on Euclid is represented by extensive quotations in the Arabic work of an-Nairīzī.

The contents of Hero's mechanical works reveal the state of technological knowledge during the early Roman Empire, reflecting the heritage of the Hellenistic period and Ptolemaic Alexandria in particular. Later writers referred to him as "the mechanic" (*ho mechanikos*). In most cases, he gives the best or most complete description extant of ancient machines. In *Mechanica*, he gives attention to the simple machines—lever, pulley, wheel and axle, inclined plane, screw, and wedge—but he goes on to present others, there and in his other books, that are more complex.

Devices described by Hero include a machine for cutting screw threads on a wooden cylinder; a syringe; an apparatus for throwing water on a fire by hydraulic pressure, which is produced by a two-cylinder force pump (designed by the earlier Alexandrian mechanic, Ctesibius); and the odometer, for measuring distances by a wheeled vehicle. Of value to scholars, there was a pantograph for enlarging drawings and an automatic wick-trimmer for lamps. Hero provides a careful account of the diopter, a sighting instrument used in surveying and astronomy which contains sophisticated gears.

The automata mentioned by Hero are of fascinating variety, including singing birds, drinking animals, hissing serpents, dancing bacchants, and gods such as Dionysus and Hercules performing various actions. Some of these were activated by lighting a fire on an altar or pouring libations into a container, and their effect on worshippers when seen in temples can be imagined. Hero also described coin-operated machines to dispense holy water, a sacred wand that whistled when dipped into water, and a device powered by heated air that would open temple doors without any visible human effort. In order to invent such a device, Hero had to recognize that a vessel containing air was not empty but contained a substance which could exert force, a fact that he clearly explained in *The Pneumatics*. His demonstration depends on the observation that water will not enter a vessel filled with air unless the air is allowed to escape. He also was aware that air is compressible, which he said was the result of its being made up of particles separated by space.

The nonproductive character of some of the inventions just mentioned has led some modern critics to call Hero's technology impractical, but he also described demonstrably useful machines. Cranes, which could be used to lower actors portraying gods into theaters (the famous *deus ex machina*), also were available to help in heavy construction. There were other weight-lifting machines utilizing gears. Cogs and gears were highly developed even before Hero's day, as archaeological evidence such as the Antikythera Machine, a calendrical, mechanical analogue computer retrieved from the Aegean seafloor, demonstrates. Hero also describes a twin screw press. He knew the use of compound pulleys, winches, and cogwheels interacting with screws. Not merely theoretical, his catapults were effective in war, particularly in siege operations. There was also the *gastraphetes* or "belly shooter," a kind of crossbow.

Hero's most famous invention was a prototype steam engine called the aeolipile. A hollow sphere, free-spinning, was mounted on a pipe and bracket on the lid of a boiling vessel. Steam from the vessel came up through the pipe and escaped through open, bent pipes on the sphere's surface, causing the sphere to rotate. Less often remarked but also significant is his windmill, used to work the water pump of a musical organ. Both of these show that Hero recommended harnessing sources of power which were not actually exploited until centuries later. In the form in which he presented them, to be sure, these engines were extremely inefficient, and the industrial processes of the first century might not have allowed improvement to the point where they could have been widely used.

In mathematics, Hero emphasized pragmatic applications rather than pure theory. For example, he showed methods of approximating the values of square and cube roots. In his writings on geometry, he followed Euclid closely, making only minor original comments or improvements. The first book of *Peri metron* deals with the mensuration of plane and solid figures, and the second explains the way to calculate the volumes of various solids. The third explains problems of the division of plane and solid figures.

Summary

Hero of Alexandria looms large in the history of ancient technology because a considerable portion of his writings on mechanics still exists, and little else on the subject survives from the Greek and Roman world. He preserved much information that came to him from earlier writers whose works have been lost, and his own contribution has been downgraded by some modern scholars because it is unclear how much he owes to previous writers, including Archimedes, Strato of Lampsacus, Philon of Byzantium, and especially Ctesibius of Alexandria. This tendency is probably unfair, however, since his work reflects a systematic mind and tireless research. Moreover, some of his ideas, such as the harnessing of steam and wind power, were clearly ahead of their time.

Although he was interested in the principles of mechanics, Hero was not primarily a theoretician. His mechanics and his mathematics are presented in a way that would have made them useful to the practical engineer of his day. For example, in *Ste-*

reometrica, he shows how to calculate the number of spectators a theater would hold and the number of wine jars that could be stacked in the hold of a ship of a certain size. Both are approximations intended for utilitarian needs.

Hero's writings were prized by later authors. Both Pappus of Alexandria (fourth century A.D.) and Proclus (fifth century) quoted from his works. Some of his works were translated and preserved by learned Arabs, and an-Nairīzī commented extensively on Hero's critique of Euclid. Four of Hero's shorter books on mechanics were published in Paris in 1693. Interest in Hero accelerated with the Industrial Revolution, and he has received much attention in histories of mechanics and mathematics which have appeared in the twentieth century.

Bibliography

Drachmann, Aage Gerhardt. *The Mechanical Technology of Greek and Roman Antiquity: A Study of the Literary Sources.* Madison: University of Wisconsin Press, 1963. Contains translations of Hero's mechanical writings, with useful running commentary. Also including sections from Vitruvius and Oreibasios, this book gives a clear idea of the written evidence for ancient mechanical technology.

Heath, Thomas. *A History of Greek Mathematics.* 2 vols. Oxford: Clarendon Press, 1921; New York: Dover, 1981. Volume 2 includes an excellent, detailed chapter on Hero's mathematical achievements. Heath's comments about Hero's dates have now been superseded by good evidence that he lived in the mid-first century A.D.

Landels, John G. *Engineering in the Ancient World.* Berkeley: University of California Press, and London: Chatto and Windus, 1978. Hero is discussed in the context of the development of technology, and Landels provides a useful brief treatment of Hero and his major writings in the final chapter.

Marsden, E. W. *Greek and Roman Artillery: Technical Treatises.* Oxford: Clarendon Press, 1969. This book includes the texts and translation of Hero's two works on war machines, *Belopoïeca* and *Cheiroballistra*, with illuminating diagrams and helpful notes and commentary.

Singer, Charles Joseph, ed. *A History of Technology.* Vol. 3, *From the Renaissance to the Industrial Revolution, c. 1500-c. 1750.* Oxford: Clarendon Press, 1957. Despite its title, volume 3 contains an informative section on Hero's diopter.

J. Donald Hughes

HEROD THE GREAT

Born: 73 B.C.; probably Idumaea, Palestine

Died: Spring, 4 B.C.; Jericho

Area of Achievement: Government

Contribution: As a loyal king of Judaea under Roman administration, Herod brought peace, prosperity, and a cultural flowering to the land he ruled. Nevertheless, negative aspects of his reign—including harsh dealings with family members and the inability to placate his Jewish subjects—have tended to overshadow these positive achievements.

Early Life

Herod was born into a prominent family of Idumaeans, an Arab people whose capital was Hebron, a city south of Jerusalem. During the time of Herod's grandfather, Antipater, Idumaea had been conquered by Jewish armies and its citizens were forced to convert to Judaism. It is not clear, at that time or in subsequent periods, exactly how deeply the beliefs and practices of Judaism were ingrained into the lives of Idumaeans such as Herod's family.

At the time of the Idumaean conquest, the Jews of the Holy Land were politically independent and ruled over by a royal family known as the Hasmonaeans. They were descendants of Judas Maccabees and his brothers, who had led a successful revolt (beginning in 168 or 167 B.C.) against their Syrian overlords and for the continuance of the monotheistic faith of Israel. When the Idumaeans came under Jewish domination later in that century, Herod's grandfather served members of the Hasmonaean dynasty with some distinction. Herod's father, also named Antipater, in turn was also closely allied to some of the Hasmonaeans. By the time of Herod's birth, a rift had developed in the Jewish royal family, with two brothers, Aristobulus and Hyrcanus, vying for the throne and the religiously significant position of high priest. Herod's father supported the elder of the brothers, Hyrcanus, but the matter was still in doubt when the rival claimants both appealed for support to the Roman general Pompey the Great, then in Damascus, Syria. That was in 63, when Herod himself was about ten years old.

Antipater's maneuvers were decisive in winning Pompey's support for Hyrcanus, whose personality seemed as weak and passive as Antipater's was aggressive and active. During the years that Herod was growing up, his father continued to show support for Hyrcanus. In fact, Antipater's actions were aimed as much at bringing his own family to the favorable notice of powerful Romans. These twin concerns—family and Rome—continued to be prominent in the subsequent career of Antipater's most famous son, Herod.

In the early 40's, Julius Caesar became a force in the Near East, and Antipater provided him with significant military support. For this, he was rewarded by Caesar, who confirmed his growing prestige while not totally displacing the Hasmonaean Hyrcanus. Antipater was able to name Herod as governor of the area of Galilee and to place other of his children (he had four sons and a daughter) in positions of power. Shortly after Caesar's death, Antipater was assassinated, a murder that Herod himself avenged. In the decade that followed, the confusion in Rome was mirrored in the provinces, and local leaders such as Herod had to be resourceful to retain power—and their lives. Herod succeeded admirably.

Hyrcanus' brother had been killed, but one of his nephews joined with the Parthians (an eastern rival to the Romans) to wrest the throne from Hyrcanus. The resultant civil war forced Herod to flee. This turned out to be but a temporary setback, however, for Herod ultimately reached Rome and gained the friendship and backing of the two most powerful individuals of the day, Marc Antony and Octavian (later Augustus). In response to their urging, the senate of Rome declared that henceforth Herod was to be King of Judaea. That was in the year 40, when Herod was in his early thirties.

Life's Work

On the basis of his family background and earlier achievements, it would appear that Herod was an ideal choice to occupy the kingship of Judaea—at least from the Roman point of view. He and his family had shown themselves to be loyal subjects and deft leaders. Herod, it seemed, could give the Romans what they wanted most: steady payment of taxes and other levies, military support against common enemies, internal peace and stability within the lands he ruled. Moreover, Herod possessed physical characteristics that the Romans appreciated. He was tall, athletic, and able to enjoy and appreciate manly activities such as hunting and riding. Dressed in proper Roman garb, he looked and acted at home in the courts of the powerful Romans whom he had to please.

There is every reason to think that his Roman benefactors were very pleased indeed with Herod's initial actions. In 40, he became a king in name, but not in fact, for his capital, Jerusalem, was still in the hands of his rivals. Within three years, that is, by 37, he had regained control of his capital and the land that was now his kingdom. At this point, Herod probably looked forward to a long and relatively serene reign. Longevity he got (approximately thirty-three years); serenity was to prove far more elusive.

From the beginning, there were substantial numbers of Jewish subjects who doubted the depth of Herod's commitment to Judaism. His Idumaean ancestry led to the taunt that he was but a half Jew. His commitment to Rome, with its polytheism and philosophical pluralism, was—in the opinion of many in Jerusalem—incompatible with the relatively austere monotheistic faith of Israel. Criticisms of Herod in this regard preceded his assumption of the kingship, and they undoubtedly increased as he consolidated power. A more pressing challenge, however, soon presented itself.

Herod was a king, and there was no mistaking it. Yet the Jews still had their own royal dynasty in the surviving members of the Hasmonaean family. Hyrcanus, while essentially powerless, was still a potential rival. Herod sought to neutralize this threat, even turn it to his advantage, by marrying Hyrcanus' granddaughter, Mariamne. Now, he may have thought, people would at last tire of bringing up details of his past, for the children he and Mariamne would produce would be royal from both the Jewish and the Roman perspective. If such were his thoughts, he erred grievously. Hyrcanus was too old to pose a threat, but Mariamne's mother, Alexandra, and eventually Mariamne herself were not. Then, too, there was Mariamne's brother Aristobulus, whom Herod was forced to appoint as high priest. One by one, these Hasmonaeans were to be eliminated by Herod, for faults real and imagined. His murder of Mariamne in 29 was especially unsettling for Herod and may have pushed him to—and over—the brink of mental disorder and instability. In his anti-Hasmonaean actions, Herod was generally supported by members of his Idumaean family and in particular by his sister, Salome.

The Romans were not overly concerned about Herod's domestic problems at this time. Herod had grown very close to Antony, who was the virtual ruler of the eastern portion of the Empire that included the lands Herod governed. When Antony did intervene, it was usually at the insistence of his queen, Cleopatra VII, who, according to one account, coveted the person of Herod as much as she did his lands. The civil war of the late 30's that pitted Antony against Octavian found Herod continuing to provide vital assistance to his benefactor, Antony. It is a credit to Herod's extraordinary abilities as diplomat and as briber that Octavian allowed him to retain his position after Antony's resounding defeat.

The fifteen-year period from 28 to 13 B.C. was the high point of Herod's reign. The most visible sign of this prosperity was the ambitious building program that Herod undertook. Throughout his kingdom and beyond, he constructed temples, amphitheaters, and even an entire city (Caesarea, on the Mediterranean coast) to honor the Romans and the civilization they represented. Part of that civilization was the worship of many gods through sacrificial offerings, athletic and dramatic competitions, and a wide array of other public functions. Herod actively promoted such activities, partly because he knew that they were important to his Roman overlords and partly—it is fair to say—because he himself enjoyed them. The Romans and their gods had been good to him, and he was only giving them their due.

Herod was not without gratitude toward the God of Israel, whose people he ruled and whose favor he also solicited. Herod's rebuilding of the Temple of Jerusalem, a vast complex that stood at the very center of the Judaism of his day, was the most tangible expression of his concerns in this regard. Moreover, he sometimes was able to accommodate his own ambitions to the religious sensitivities of his subjects. For example, he generally refrained from setting up images—which would be seen as infringements of the Ten Commandments—in locations where they would attract attention. Nevertheless, most Judaean Jews were not as "broadminded" as their monarch, nor did they regularly join in the praise Herod received when he aided Jewish communities outside Judaea.

During the last ten years of his life, domestic difficulties came to overshadow and almost cancel out all else. Herod had married ten times and produced numerous offspring. As he grew older, several of his sons grew bolder in their efforts to guarantee that they would succeed him. Some of them may even have plotted to hasten the day of their father's death. The most prominent players in this deadly game were Mariamne's sons, Alexander and Aristobulus, and Antipater, the son of Herod's first wife. Mariamne's sons, as the last heirs of the Hasmonaean dynasty, were especially dangerous. They may well have been guilty of treasonous activities against the man who had killed their mother, uncle, grandmother, and great-grandfather. In this case, Augustus was unable to effect a final reconciliation between father and sons. Their execution occurred in 7 or 6 B.C. Herod was almost seventy years old, in very poor health, and in need of an heir.

For most of the period until his death, that heir was Antipater. Unwilling to wait gracefully, he persisted in meddling in his father's plans to arrange the marriages of other offspring. More important, he grew impatient, and that impatience cost him his life and the throne just prior to Herod's own gruesome death in the early spring of 4 B.C. Herod managed to identify three of his sons whom he judged to be worthy of portions of his kingdom. When Augustus, who was a prime financial beneficiary of Herod's will, confirmed these choices, Herod's legacy was, in one sense, complete and secure. In another sense, there is much about Herod's legacy that is puzzling, even troubling.

Summary

It is difficult for contemporary scholars to take the measure of Herod as a man and as a ruler. This difficulty is almost as old as Herod himself. Nearly everything that is known of Herod is contained in the works of the Jewish historian Flavius Josephus, who wrote almost a century after Herod's death. Josephus used both pro- and anti-Herod sources and was not without biases of his own. Moreover, Josephus described Herod's reign in two separate writings, *Peri tou Ioudaikou polemou* (A.D. 75-79; *Jewish War*) and *Ioudaikē archaiologia* (c. A.D. 93; *The Antiquities of the Jews*), and the accounts are often contradictory. The problem described here is not unique to Herod. It recurs, for example, in the study of Alexander the Great, Julius Caesar, and other leaders of antiquity.

In the case of Herod, it does seem possible to affirm certain definite things. His loyalty to Rome and the values it espoused is beyond question. His ability to conceive and carry out large-scale building projects cannot be doubted. His success in organizing his kingdom to produce vast revenues for Rome, himself, and his supporters was an impressive, if not always welcome, accomplishment. All of this was compatible, in Herod's view, with a devotion to the Jewish religion and to the Jewish people. Herod undoubtedly believed that loyal support for Rome was the only hope for Jewish survival. Rebellion could only lead to disaster—a judgment that the Jewish revolts of the following centuries revealed as all too true.

Balanced against Herod's achievements was, first of all, a cruelty so monstrous that it led the author of the Gospel of Matthew to write that Herod had ordered the slaughter of innocent children (see Matthew, chapter 2). Many historians do not believe that such an event ever occurred. Nevertheless, a man who would slaughter close members of his own family was certainly capable of the actions Matthew attributed to him. It was actions of this sort that led Augustus to say, in a play on words in Latin, that he would have preferred to be Herod's pig than his son—or, one might add, his wife, his mother-in-law, or brother-in-law. Even in an admittedly violent age, it must be acknowledged, Herod's cruelty, perhaps the result of some mental disorder, stands out.

Herod's view of Judaism and Jewish survival was not without value. Still, it is hard to see what sort of Judaism Herod actually had in mind. His active support for polytheistic institutions would, it seems likely, have ultimately led to a dilution of Judaism's insistence on monotheism. A Jewish people may then have survived, but without the distinctive features of their ancestral religion.

Sometime in antiquity, the epithet "the Great" was first applied to Herod. Initially, it may have served to designate him as an older son of Antipater or to distinguish him from several other individuals named Herod who followed him. At some point, it came to describe certain elements of his personality and career. In that context, it is appropriate. In an overall evaluation of Herod, however, "great" is not the word most likely to come to mind for most observers of this complex and somehow fascinating man.

Bibliography

Brandon, S. G. F. "Herod the Great: Judaea's Most Able but Most Hated King." *History Today* 12 (1962): 234-242. A brief, accessible account that presents a good overview of Herod's achievements and of the wide variety of judgments to which he has been subjected.

Grabbe, Lester L. *Judaism from Cyrus to Hadrian*. 2 vols. Minneapolis, Minn.: Fortress Press, and London: SCM Press, 1992. A reference handbook that provides bibliographies, historiographical discussion of sources, and summary accounts of important events in Jewish history.

Grant, Michael. *Herod the Great*. London: Weidenfeld and Nicolson, and New York: American Heritage Press, 1971. A straightforward account of the reign of Herod. Grant takes care to place Herod in the larger political and cultural context of first century B.C. Rome. Viewed from this perspective, Herod, while far from a saint, is not quite the total sinner that he is made out to be in many other modern accounts. Beautifully illustrated.

Hoehner, Harold W. *Herod Antipas*. Cambridge: Cambridge University Press, 1972; Grand Rapids, Mich.: Zondervan Publishing House, 1980. Originally a doctoral dissertation, this work is a detailed account of the reign of one of Herod's heirs. It is particularly valuable because of its extensive bibliography that fully covers the reign of Herod and his successors.

Josephus, Flavius. *Josephus*. Vol. 2, *The Jewish War*, translated by H. St. James Thackeray, and vols. 7 and 8, *The Jewish Antiquities*, translated by Ralph Marcus. Cambridge, Mass.: Harvard University Press, 1927-1963. As described above, these are the primary ancient sources for the personal and public life of Herod. In this Loeb Classical Library edition, the original Greek text of Josephus is printed along with an authoritative English translation and notes. This is the essential starting point for all research on Herod.

Perowne, Stewart. *The Life and Times of Herod the Great*. London: Hodder and Stoughton, and New York: Abingdon Press, 1956. A balanced and sober account. Well-illustrated. Like Grant, Perowne makes the point that Herod was largely a product of his own time and must, to a degree at least, be judged by the standards of that period. Perowne continued his narrative in a second volume entitled *The Later Herods* (London: Hodder and Stoughton, 1958).

Richardson, Peter. *Herod: King of the Jews and Friend of the Romans*. Columbia, S.C.: University of South Carolina Press, 1996. A full-scale biography that alternates chapters on Herod's life with chapters on context and environment. Religious, political, architectural, and cultural elements of the reign are described and evaluated.

Roller, Duane W. *The Building Program of Herod the Great*. Berkeley: University of California Press, 1998. This book provides a full listing and discussion of Herod's numerous building projects, arguing that he is a crucial figure in bringing the monumental style of Roman architecture to the Greek east.

Sandmel, Samuel. *Herod: Profile of a Tyrant*. Philadelphia: Lippincott, 1967. A clear and well-written account of the life and times of Herod. Sandmel attempts to re-create Herod's mental state at key moments, such as when he had Mariamne killed. The author's overall assessment of Herod is succinctly captured in the subtitle of his book.

Zeitlin, Solomon. "Herod: A Malevolent Maniac." *Jewish Quarterly Review* 54 (1963): 1-27. The title of this article leaves no doubt as to the author's overall assessment of Herod. Zeitlin is not concerned here with a retelling of Herod's entire career. Rather, he focuses on key issues such as the reliability of Josephus, details of Mariamne's execution, and Herod's relations with the Hasmonaeans Hyrcanus and Alexandra (Mariamne's mother). Zeitlin provides a fuller account in relevant sections of his *Rise and Fall of the Judaean State: A Political, Social, and Religious History of the Second Commonwealth* (Philadelphia: Jewish Publication Society of America, 1962).

Leonard J. Greenspoon

HERODOTUS

Born: c. 484 B.C.; Halicarnassus, Asia Minor
Died: c. 424 B.C.; probably Thurii, Italy
Area of Achievement: Historiography
Contribution: For having written the first work of history, Herodotus is commonly called "the father of history."

Early Life

Herodotus was born about 484 into a notable family of Halicarnassus, near the modern city of Bodrum, Turkey. He received the education available to well-born Greek men of his day. An intellectual and creative ferment was sweeping the Greek world, and Miletus, a major center of this enlightenment, was only about forty miles from Halicarnassus. Such philosopher-scientists as Anaximander and Thales and the geographer Hecataeus influenced Herodotus. He read Hesiod, Sappho, Sophocles, Aeschylus, and Pindar, and also learned from the Sophists. The writings of Homer, in particular, shaped his worldview. If the intellectual atmosphere of the Greek world encouraged Herodotus to study the affairs of humans, it was probably Homer's masterpiece on the Trojan War that caused Herodotus to recognize that the Persian invasion of Greece, which had occurred when he was a child, was the great drama of his own age.

His early surroundings also educated Herodotus. The rich diversity of cultures in Asia Minor provided the foundation for the remarkable cosmopolitan scope and tone of his writing. Travel further shaped his mind. According to tradition, he went into a brief exile to Samos after taking part in Halicarnassian political upheavals and later left his home city permanently.

His travels took him to Athens, where intellectual and artistic life was flourishing in the age of Pericles. Around 443, Herodotus joined a Greek colony at Thurii, in Italy. From there, he probably continued the travels that provided the foundation for his history. He later said that he had interviewed people from forty Greek states and thirty foreign nations. No physical descriptions of Herodotus exist, but his travels in the ancient world testify to his physical vigor and strength and to his insatiable curiosity.

Life's Work

As Homer had preserved the stories of the Trojan War by rendering them into poetry, Herodotus came to realize that during his childhood another historic confrontation had occurred between the East and the West. The Persian War embodied all the drama and tragedy of human life, and its effects reverberated through his lifetime. He captured this human drama in one of the world's first great prose works and pioneered a new form of intellectual endeavor, history.

Herodotus states his intentions in the first sentence of *Historiai Herodotou* (c. 425; *The History,* 1709):

> I, Herodotus of Halicarnassus, am here setting forth my history, that time may not draw the color from what man has brought into being, nor those great and wonderful deeds, manifested by both Greeks and barbarians, fail of their report, and, together with all this, the reason why they fought one another.

He intended to transmit to future generations the record of men and women's deeds in this dramatic era, and in so doing explore the tragedy of human existence. In Herodotus' worldview, people were subject to a cosmic order working by rules that they did not understand, an order in which fate or destiny destroyed those who aspired to excessive achievements. He would show that rationalism, a growing force in his age, could not protect against the contingencies of existence. Nevertheless, though humans could not change the cosmic order, Herodotus could combat the ravages of time by preserving the memory of their deeds. Herodotus was interested in people and in all of their diverse ways of living and acting. He used his history to contrast East and West, detailing the diversity of the peoples of the known world but finding common humanity beneath the differences.

Herodotus wrote a narrative history of his world, from the age of myth to his own time. He did not have available to him the kinds of written records on which modern historians rely, but based his history on oral accounts. He placed most trust in his own experience and others' eyewitness accounts, but used hearsay when he deemed it proper to do so. Regarding the latter, he wrote: "I must tell what is said, but I am not at all bound to believe it, and this comment of mine holds about my whole *History.*" He sometimes recorded stories that he found dubious because he realized that just as time changed the fortunes of all people, it changed truth also. At times, he recorded material that seemed

significant despite its questionable validity, because its meaning might become clear in the future. He was aware that there was a mythical element in much that people told him, but he realized as well that human myths carry a truth that makes them as important as other interpretations of reality.

Herodotus, the father of history, more than almost any of his offspring, was a master storyteller, able to hold the interest of his audience today as easily as he did thousands of years ago. He begins his story with Croesus, the last king of Lydia, who, after having begun the Asiatic incursion against the Greeks, trapped himself in the web of fate by believing himself the most blessed of humankind. Cyrus conquered Croesus and began constructing the huge and powerful Persian Empire. Through the nine books of *The History*, Herodotus follows Cyrus, Cambyses, Darius I, and finally Xerxes I, as these Persian rulers extended their power over the known world of Asia and Africa. Eventually, they turned to Europe and the Greeks.

As Herodotus follows Persian expansion, he begins his renowned "digressions" on the Lydians, Egyptians, Assyrians, Scythians, Libyans, Greeks, and others. In these digressions, which make up the bulk of *The History*, he describes the geography and economies of the various lands, the religious practices of the people, the roles of women, and the customs of everyday life. Human creations fascinated him, and he carefully described the pyramids, the walls surrounding Babylon, canal systems, and famous temples.

The so-called digressions are a carefully wrought expression of Herodotus' larger purposes in writing *The History*. A religious man, he wanted to show that all people, Greeks and Asians alike, were living in a cosmos that destroyed the excessive aspirations of even the best and greatest. Herodotus also intended to use the story of the Persian War as a backdrop to his study of the range of possibilities expressed by humans in their social, political, and spiritual lives. He seldom condemned any custom he described, but gloried in the spectacle of life and in human achievements. The digressions, then, are part of his examination of the human condition. He knew that any custom, no matter how strange, had validity and meaning for the people who observed it: "As for the stories told by the Egyptians, let whoever finds them credible use them." The Persian ruler Cambyses revealed his madness, Herodotus believed, when he stabbed the Egyptian sacred bull. If he had not been mad,

he would never have set about the mockery of what other men hold sacred and customary. For if there were a proposition put before mankind, according to which each should, after examination, choose the best customs in the world, each nation would certainly think its own customs the best. Indeed, it is natural for no one but a madman to make a mockery of such things.

Herodotus adds, "I think Pindar is right when he says, 'Custom is king of all.'"

Whether from the shadows of the pyramids or from the walls of Babylon, Herodotus' gaze always returned to the developing conflict of Greece with the steadily expanding Persian Empire. He gives attention to Darius' first probe into Europe, blocked by the Greeks at the Battle of Marathon in 490. Darius then laid careful plans to conduct a full-scale invasion, but died before he could make another foray into the Greek world. In 480, his successor, Xerxes, invaded with a huge force. The Greeks fought heroically at Thermopylae, and in such battles as Salamis and Plataea, Athens, Sparta, and other Greek city-states defeated the Persians. It is here that Herodotus' history comes to a close.

Most historians believe that *The History* was published in stages between 430 and 424, although a minority of historians believe it contains references to events as late as 421. Most scholars place Herodotus' death at about 424, in Thurii.

Summary

Herodotus has attracted extravagant admiration. He has been commonly called the father of history, and some see him as an equally great geographer, anthropologist, and folklorist. He had his detractors also, one of whom called him "the father of lies." He was too cosmopolitan to fit well with the surge of Greek patriotism of later years; some critics saw him as a detractor of the gods because he spoke so casually of religious practices that differed from the Greeks', but others, in more rational ages, regarded him as too superstitious. As the centuries passed, his admiration for the East and his breadth of sympathy for different cultures placed him out of step with the parochial West.

Herodotus always, however, had his admirers, who usually regarded him as a charming, if credulous, storyteller. His work was first translated into English in 1584, but scholars neglected him until the nineteenth century, when archaeology began to verify much of his account. Even then, his work was seen as a loose collection of moral tales of great men.

His achievement became clearer as twentieth century historians traced the evolution of historical writing and more fully understood the intellectual breakthrough Herodotus had made in separating history from other intellectual endeavors. He established the methods that historians still use: gathering evidence, weighing its credibility, selecting from it, and writing a prose narrative. He assumed a role of neutrality, of objectivity, and, while expressing personal opinions, he never dropped his stance of universal sympathy. He tried to find the rational causes and effects of events; yet he was skeptical enough to understand that rationalism could not explain everything, perhaps not even the most important things, in human life. In recent years, admiration for him has grown as scholars have used literary analysis to show how tightly integrated were the famous Herodotean anecdotes and digressions into his larger purposes. His book is a literary masterpiece and one of the greatest works of history produced in the Western world.

Bibliography

De Selincourt, Aubrey. *The World of Herodotus.* London: Secker and Warburg, 1962; Boston: Little, Brown, 1963. This work retraces Herodotus' literary journal based on twentieth century knowledge of his world. De Selincourt translated *The History* for the Penguin Classics series.

Evans, J. A. *Herodotus.* Boston: Twayne Publishers, 1982. A recent biography that covers the known facts of Herodotus' life and clearly explains the various scholarly controversies surrounding him.

———. *Herodotus: Explorer of the Past.* Princeton, N.J.: Princeton University Press, 1991. A short work that includes discussion of individual figures in the *Histories* (e.g. Croesus, Cyrus, Darius, Xerxes), and also an essay on "oral tradition" that speculates on the publication and performance of the *Histories.* Comparative material on oral tradition in contemporary Africa is introduced.

Fehling, Detlev. *Herodotus and His "Sources": Citation, Invention, and Narrative Art.* Translated by J. G. Howie. ARCA Classical and Medieval Texts, Papers, and Monographs, vol. 21. Leeds: Francis Cairns, 1989. This controversial book impugns Herodotus' veracity by arguing that his source-citations are false and that his history-writing was based more on imagination than fact.

Flory, Stewart. *The Archaic Smile of Herodotus.* Detroit: Wayne State University Press, 1987. An analysis of literary motifs in *The History*, showing the tightness of its structure and the larger purposes Herodotus had in mind, beyond chronicling the Persian War.

Gould, John. *Herodotus.* London: Weidenfeld and Nicolson, and New York: St. Martin's Press, 1989. A brief introduction that provides background on Herodotus' environment and on the composition of his *Histories.*

Herodotus. *The History.* Translated by David Grene. Chicago: University of Chicago Press, 1987. This translation by a noted classicist includes a commentary which provides an excellent introduction to Herodotus. Illustrated with helpful maps.

How, Walter W., and Joseph Wells, eds. *A Commentary on Herodotus.* 2 vols. Oxford: Clarendon Press, 1912. This is the standard commentary on Herodotus and provides almost a line-by-line analysis.

Hunter, Virginia. *Past and Process in Herodotus and Thucydides.* Princeton, N.J.: Princeton University Press, 1982. An analysis of the first two historians, finding great similarities in their worldviews.

Lateiner, Donald. *The Historical Method of Herodotus.* Phoenix supplementary vol. 23. Toronto and London: University of Toronto Press, 1989. A full and informative study of Herodotus' methods of historiography: how he selected his subjects, how he dealt with conflicting evidence, how he structured his narrative, how he defined causes. The historian emerges as a careful writer whose methods were unique in antiquity.

Myres, John L. *Herodotus: Father of History.* Oxford: Clarendon, 1953; Chicago: Henry Regnery Co., 1971. Myres reveals the tight and deliberate construction of *The History.*

William E. Pemberton

HEROPHILUS

Born: c. 335 B.C.; Chalcedon, Bithynia
Died: c. 280 B.C.; probably Alexandria, Egypt
Areas of Achievement: Medicine and physiology
Contribution: The first systematic dissector, and possibly vivisector, of the human body, the Greek physician Herophilus made numerous anatomical discoveries and significantly enriched anatomical nomenclature. His knowledge of human anatomy was superior to that of his precursors, and he laid the foundation for subsequent Western anatomy. Herophilus' analysis of the pulse and his dream theory also exercised a strong influence on medicine and psychology in later centuries.

Early Life

The sparse ancient evidence suggests that Herophilus left his native city of Chalcedon for an apprenticeship with the distinguished physician Praxagoras of Cos before settling in the recently founded North African city of Alexandria. An Athenian sojourn is implied by the report of Hyginus, a second century Roman mythographer, that a young Athenian woman, in guileful reaction against the exclusion of women from the medical profession, disguised herself as a man and completed an apprenticeship with Herophilus. As a consequence of her popularity with female patients, who alone knew that she was a woman, Herophilus' pupil was brought before an Athenian jury on charges of seducing and corrupting her women patients. In court she raised her tunic and revealed her gender. After she received assertive support from women, Hyginus relates, "the Athenians amended the law so that free-born women could learn the art of medicine." No independent evidence corroborates Hyginus' account—which formally belongs to the genre of invention fables—but it is worth noting that Herophilus' contributions to gynecology and obstetrics are richly attested.

Life's Work

The first scientist to violate the entrenched Greek taboo against cutting open a human corpse, Herophilus made spectacular discoveries in human anatomy. From classical antiquity until the early Renaissance, anatomical accounts were mainly based on comparative anatomy—Aristotle and Galen, in particular, dissected numerous animals—and on chance observations of the wounded or in-

jured. While Herophilus continued this practice of dissecting animals, he and his contemporary Erasistratus apparently were the only pre-Renaissance scientists to perform systematic dissections on humans. Furthermore, if the controversial but unequivocal evidence of several later authors is trustworthy, Herophilus also performed vivisectory experiments on convicted criminals. Herophilus was able to break the spell of the taboo because of an exceptional constellation of circumstances in Alexandria. The combination of ambitious, autocratic patrons of science (the Ptolemies), bold scientists such as Euclid and Archimedes, a new city on foreign soil in which traditional Greek values initially were not accepted as intrinsically superior, and a cosmopolitan intelligentsia committed to literary, technological, and scientific frontiersmanship made it possible for Herophilus to overcome tenacious inhibitions against opening the human body. The native Egyptian practice of mummification, sanctioned by centuries of stable religious belief, might have been invoked as a precedent, although embalming was in fact very different from scientific dissection. The Egyptian embalmers, for example, scraped and drained the brain piecemeal through the nostrils of the corpse, mangling it beyond anatomic recognition, whereas Herophilus dissected the brain meticulously enough to distinguish some of its ventricles and to identify several of its smaller parts with unprecedented accuracy.

One of Herophilus' more noteworthy discoveries was the nerves. He distinguished between sensory and "voluntary" (motor) nerves, described the paths of at least seven pairs of cranial nerves, and recognized unique features of the optic nerve. He also was the first to observe and name the calamus scriptorius, a cavity in the floor of the fourth cerebral ventricle. His careful dissection of the eye yielded the discovery not only of the optic nerve but also of several coats of the eye (probably the sclera, cornea, iris, retina, and chorioid coat), an achievement all the more remarkable in the absence of the microscope.

Like his other works, Herophilus' main anatomical work, *Anatomika* (*On Anatomy*), survives only in fragments and secondhand reports. From its second book, ancient sources have preserved the first classic description of the human liver: The shape, size, position, and texture of the liver as well as its connections with other parts are described with admirable accuracy. The pancreas and small intestine, or duodenum (a Latin version of the name Herophilus first gave it), are among the other parts in the abdominal cavity which he explored. The third book of *On Anatomy* appears to have been devoted to the reproductive organs. In the male, Herophilus distinguished between various parts of the spermatic duct system, meticulously identifying anatomical features previously unknown. As for the female, Herophilus seems to have abandoned the traditional theory of a bicameral human uterus, and, using the male analogy, to have discovered the ovaries (which he calls female twins or testicles), the Fallopian tubes (although he did not determine their true course and function), and several other features of female reproductive anatomy. In the fourth book, Herophilus dealt with the anatomy of the blood vessels. Accepting Praxagoras' distinction between veins and arteries, he provided further anatomical precision and offered some basic observations on the heart valves, the chambers of the heart, and a variety of vessels and vascular structures. The torcular Herophili, a confluence of several great venous cavities or sinuses in the skull, was first identified by Herophilus and still bears his name.

In his physiopathology, Herophilus appears to have accepted the traditional theory of a balance or imbalance between humors (or moistures) in the body as the cause of health and disease, respectively, but he insisted that all causal explanation is provisional or hypothetical. One must start from appearances, or observation, he said, and then proceed on a hypothetical basis to what is not visible, including cause. The command center of the body is located in the fourth cerebral ventricle or in the cerebellum (which is indeed the center responsible for muscular coordination and maintenance of the equilibrium of the body). From the brain and spinal marrow, nerves—sensory and motor—proceed like offshoots. Neural transmission, at least in the case of the optic nerves, apparently takes place through pneuma, a warm, moist, airlike substance flowing through the nerves and ultimately derived from external air by respiration.

Among the involuntary motions in the human body (that is, ones for which the motor nerves are not responsible), Herophilus gave novel, detailed accounts of two: respiration, which he attributed to a natural tendency of the lungs to dilate and contract through a four-part cycle, and the pulse, which he attributed to a faculty that flows to the arteries from the heart through the arterial coats, causing the arteries to dilate and contract. His treatise *Peri sphygmōn* (*On Pulses*) is the first work devoted to the subject, and it became the foundation of all ancient and of much subsequent pulse lore.

Central to Herophilus' vascular physiology is the theory that the arteries transport a mixture of blood and pneuma (similar to the modern view that the arteries carry blood and oxygen), whereas the veins contain only blood. Here he parted ways with his teacher Praxagoras and his contemporary Erasistratus, both of whom believed the arteries contain only pneuma. The arteries, Herophilus believed, pulsate in such intricate, differentiated patterns that the pulse is a major diagnostic tool. Deploying sustained analogies between musical-metrical theory and pulse rhythm, Herophilus described nature's music in the arteries as successively assuming pyrrhic, trochaic, spondaic, and iambic rhythmic relations between diastole and systole as one passes through four stages of life—from infancy (pyrrhic) through childhood and adulthood to old age (iambic). Deviations from these rhythms indicate disorders.

Herophilus had such faith in the diagnostic value of the pulse that he constructed a portable water clock, or clepsydra, to measure the frequency (rate?) of his patients' pulses. The device could be calibrated to fit the age of each patient. One example of its clinical application suggests that it also functioned as a protothermometer: "By as much as the movements of the pulse exceeded the number that is natural for filling up the clepsydra, by that much Herophilus declared the pulse too frequent, i.e., that the patient had either more or less of a fever" (quoted from the second century Marcellinus). Herophilus' pulse theory represents an unusual attempt within ancient medicine to introduce measurement and quantification into nonpharmacological contexts. Besides rhythm and frequency, he used size, strength, and perhaps speed and volume to distinguish one pulse from another.

Reproductive physiology and pathology represent other strengths of Herophilus. He accepted, in general, Aristotle's view that male seed is formed from the blood and, according to Saint Augustine's acquaintance Vindician, Herophilus characteristically tried to defend it by arguments based on dissection. He wrote the first known treatise devoted only to obstetrics, *Maiōtikon* (*Midwifery;* also known as *On Delivery*), in which he tried to demystify the uterus, arguing that it is constituted of the same material elements as the rest of the body and is regulated by the same faculties. There is no disease peculiar to women, he asserts, though he concedes that certain "affections" are experienced only by women: menstruation, conception, parturition, and lactation. The causes of difficult childbirth, embryological questions (such as, is the fetus a living being, since it possesses involuntary but not voluntary motions?), and the normal duration of pregnancy are among the other subjects apparently explored by Herophilus. The church father Tertullian implied that the Alexandrian performed abortions and charged him with having possessed an instrument known as a "fetus-slayer" (*embryosphaktes*).

In his treatise *Pros tas koinas doxas* (*Against Common Opinions*), Herophilus also dealt with gynecological and obstetrical issues, attacking the common opinion that menstruation is good for every woman's health and for childbearing, and, characteristically, adopting a more discriminating view: Menstruation is helpful to some women, harmful to others, depending on individual circumstances. For all of his emphasis on the hypothetical nature of causal explanations, Herophilus tried to determine the causes of many individual disorders, including fevers, heart diseases, and pneumonia. He also described the symptoms of several physical and mental disorders and developed a semiotic system known as a "triple-timed inference from signs," which used a combination of the patients' past signs or symptoms, the present signs, and the "future signs" (inferences from what has happened to other similarly afflicted patients) for diagnostic, prognostic, and therapeutic purposes.

In *Die Traumdeutung* (1900; *The Interpretation of Dreams*, 1915), Sigmund Freud recognized Herophilus' importance in another area: dream theory. Dreams, Herophilus believed, belong to one of three classes by origin: "godsent" dreams occur inevitably or by necessity; "natural" dreams arise when the soul forms for itself an image of what is to its advantage; and "compound" or "mixed" dreams arise when one sees what one desires. Freud acknowledged Herophilus' emphasis on the fulfillment of sexual and other wishes in dreams as an important anticipation of his own theory. With modifications, Herophilus' tripartite classification of dreams reappears in several pagan and Christian authors, thus representing another influential part of his legacy.

Summary

The frequent modern lag between scientific discovery and clinical application, between theory and therapy, also characterized Herophilus' work. Despite his brilliant discoveries in anatomy and physiology, he was a traditionalist in practice. In his works *Diaitētikon* (*Regimen*) and *Therapeutika* (*Therapeutics*), Herophilus prescribed a preventive regimen, bloodletting, various simple and compound drugs (with at least some innovative ingredients), and a limited amount of surgical intervention (with a felicitous emphasis on checking hemorrhages). He perhaps also prompted the influential Alexandrian tradition of exegesis of Hippocratic texts, to which several of Herophilus' adherents made major contributions by taking a keen, critical interest in Hippocratic works. One of Herophilus' pupils, Philinus of Cos, broke with him and became a leader of the powerful Empiricist school of medicine, but many others continued proclaiming themselves his followers. As the old taboos against human dissection reasserted themselves after Herophilus' death, the Herophileans abandoned this central part of the founder's legacy. Yet the rich history of his school, both in Alexandria and in Laodicea-on-Lycus (Turkey), can be traced for at least three centuries after Herophilus' death. Through Galen's detailed acclaim of Herophilus' dissections and of his pulse theory, the Alexandrian's fame survived the polemics of those Christians and pagans who believed that what had been concealed by God or Nature should not be revealed by humans.

Bibliography

Dean-Jones, Lesley A. *Women's Bodies in Classical Greek Science*. Rev. ed. Oxford: Clarendon Press, 1994. Argues that classical Greek science believed that women were different from men in the whole range of their physiology. Herophilus appears as a turning point, one agent behind an increased focus on anatomy and a turning away from the belief that physiological features like female "proneness" to illness were defining sex characteristics.

Fraser, P. M. *Ptolemaic Alexandria*. 3 vols. Oxford: Clarendon Press, 1972. An excellent comprehensive treatment of Alexandria at the time of Herophilus. Chapter 7 offers a good introduction to Herophilus and other Alexandrian physicians.

Lloyd, G. E. R. *Greek Science After Aristotle*. London: Chatto and Windus, and New York: Norton,

1973. Chapter 6 offers a very useful general introduction to Hellenistic biology and medicine, with a valuable assessment of Herophilus' place in the history of science.

—————. *Science, Folklore, and Ideology.* Cambridge and New York: Cambridge University Press, 1983. Excellent observations throughout, especially on Herophilus' contributions to reproductive theory and the standardization of anatomical terminology.

Longrigg, James. "Superlative Achievement and Comparative Neglect: Alexandrian Medical Science and Modern Historical Research." *History of Science* 19 (1981): 155-200. A solid overview of the scientific views of Herophilus and Erasistratus by a classicist and historian of medicine.

Potter, Paul. "Herophilus of Chalcedon: An Assessment of His Place in the History of Anatomy." *Bulletin of the History of Medicine* 50 (1976): 45-60. A physician and historian of medicine subjects Herophilus' anatomical descriptions to thoughtful, informed scrutiny.

Solmsen, Friedrich. "Greek Philosophy and the Discovery of the Nerves," *Museum Helveticum* 18 (1961): 150-197. A pioneering, now classic, analysis of Herophilus' and Erasistratus' contributions to the discovery of the nerves.

von Staden, Heinrich. "Hairesis and Heresy." In *Jewish and Christian Self-Definition.* Vol. 3, *Self-Definition in the Graeco-Roman World,* edited by Ben F. Meyer and E. P. Sanders. London: SCM Press, 1982; Philadelphia: Fortress Press, 1983. This analysis of group self-definitions includes detailed observations on the dynamic, changing character of Herophilus' school after his death.

—————. *Herophilus: The Art of Medicine in Early Alexandria.* Cambridge and New York: Cambridge University Press, 1989. A magisterial, definitive work that includes text and translations of fragments and testimonia to Herophilus' life and thought, accompanied by interpretative commentary.

Heinrich von Staden

HESIOD

Born: fl. c. 700 B.C.; Ascra, Greece
Died: Date unknown; Ozolian Locris, Greece
Area of Achievement: Literature
Contribution: Hesiod organized and interpreted the Greek myths which form the basis for European civilization and examined with moral conscience the working life of Greek society at the dawn of modern history.

Early Life

In the centuries after his death, Hellenic historians and writers added to the legend of Hesiod's life so that a moderately detailed portrait of him developed through commentary and speculation. The work of more recent classical scholars has demonstrated that most of this material cannot be substantiated through historical records. While it is not inconceivable that subsequent archaeological discoveries will provide additional information, it seems reasonable to assume that the autobiographical information provided by Hesiod himself in *Erga kai Ēmerai* (c. 700 B.C.; *Works and Days*) is the only basis for drawing an outline of his life. Like some of the work traditionally attributed to him, it is fragmentary and sketchy, but as one of Hesiod's best translators, Apostolos Athanassakis, contends, it is "better than all fanciful conjecture." Although some scholars maintain that even this work cannot be positively authenticated, without it, "there is no poet named Hesiod," as P. Walcot argues.

In *Works and Days*, four assertions about Hesiod's father are presented—that he made a living as a merchant sailor, that he came from the province of Cyme in Aeolis, that "grim poverty" drove him from Asia Minor, and that he settled in Ascra in the region known as Boeotia, an initially inhospitable but visually striking district near Mount Helicon. Considering the fact that others who followed this migration pattern moved on to establish Greek colonies in Italy when they were unable to make a living, it is reasonable to assume that Hesiod's father was comparatively prosperous, an assumption corroborated by the story of the division of his estate between Hesiod and his brother Perses in *Works and Days*. Although Boeotia was thought to be something of a backwater by scholars possibly influenced by the prejudices of its neighbors, there is convincing evidence from artistic and poet-

ic sources that it was actually more like a cultural center. Boeotian verse shared many of the traits of epic poetry associated with the Ionian region, and the region's geographic location on the trade route to the Near East provided many opportunities for cultural advancement, including an earlier adoption of the alphabet than many other parts of the Hellenic world.

In both *Works and Days* and *Theogonia* (c. 700 B.C.; *Theogony*), the crucial moment of transformation in Hesiod's life is presented as a justification for his work. While tending sheep, probably in early manhood, Hesiod was visited by the Muses, who gave him the gift of song (that is, wisdom in poetic language) and charged him with the responsibility to instruct his countrymen. Hesiod combines the perspective of the common man—the "country bumpkin," the "swag-bellied yahoo," who the Muses address—with the poet's power to create pleasure which counters the pains of human existence and the orator's eloquence, which reconciles citizens to the necessity for compromise in a social community. Thus, when Hesiod found himself in a dispute with Perses over the division of their father's estate, he took the occasion to criticize the nobles (or "kings") who presided as judges for accepting bribes and not rendering true justice. He develops *Works and Days* as a poem in which he counsels his brother and his fellow citizens about the kind of society in which, through the gods' justice, they may all have an opportunity to live relatively comfortably.

There are hints in *Works and Days* and *Theogony* that Hesiod lived much of his life as a bachelor, although he briefly speaks as if he had a son, and there is an account of a visit to Chalcis in Euboea for funeral games, in which he won a handsome prize. M. L. West argues that the poem he performed was the *Theogony*. Beyond that, a number of inferences may be made from the sensibility that emerges through his work. As West observes in explaining the style of his translation, "If I have sometimes made Hesiod sound a little quaint and stilted, that is not unintentional: He is." The obscurity that wreathes Hesiod's life is an intriguing invitation to conjecture. As long as it is based on a careful reading of the work in its known historical context, it is a kind of modern equivalent of the mentally active participation of the audience in that earlier era of oral communication.

Life's Work

Most of the poems which were originally attributed to Hesiod in the centuries after he lived have been designated the work of other writers by modern scholarship. From an original oeuvre consisting of eleven fragments and two titles, only the *Catalogue of Women*, which was appended to *Theogony*, and *Ornithomanteia (Divination by Birds)*, which was appended to *Works and Days*, may have been based on something Hesiod wrote. Athanassakis mentions that both works, which were thematically connected and impressive imitations by anonymous writers, were often amalgamated into the work of a commanding literary figure, as is the case with Homer and Hippocrates. Athanassakis observes that the *Shield of Herakles* is included in most standard editions of Hesiod, "thus paying homage to ancient tradition," but he makes a plausible case that it is a visionary poem of apocalyptic power which stands comparison with Hesiod's finest writing.

In any event, *Theogony* stands as the beginning of Hesiod's work. It carries out the Muses' injunction to "sing of the race of the blessed gods" and "tell of things to come and things past," in return for their fabulous gift. This gift, however, like most divine bounty, carries the burden of its own mystery, and *Theogony* is not only a form of thanks and worship but also an attempt to understand the import and consequence of the action of the gods in the affairs of humans. To do this, Hesiod reaches back to the creation of Time and Space from an immeasurable, primordial flux to chart the origins of cosmic history. As he describes the beginning of the known universe, the elemental aspects of the cosmos, Earth (Gaia), Sky (Ouranos), and Sea (Pontos), are not only physical components of firmament and terrain, but gods, with all the attributes of divinity (and humanity) common to the Hellenic vision of deity. This merging compels him, in composing a poem on the birth and genealogy of the gods, to create also cosmogony, or an account of the development of the shape and form of the universe through time. As a correlative, without actually identifying the precise moment of the emergence of the human race, *Theogony* also presents an early history of humanity set amid and sometimes parallel to the genealogy of the Olympian deities.

Because the eighth century B.C. was a time of rapid economic expansion and increasing mobility for Greece, with contacts with the Orient already in process for more than a hundred years, it is not surprising that elements of creation myths from the Hittite *Song of Ullikummi* (the castration motif), the Babylonian *Enuma Elish* (activity versus entropy), the Indian *Rgveda*, and even the Norse *Elder Edda* appear in *Theogony*. Hesiod was working at the apex of a tradition, but his singular contribution was to place—above the diversity of the separate families of gods, shaping the chaos of turmoil and struggle—the controlling power of Zeus's sovereignty. The argument of the poem is the rightness and justice of Zeus's reign, the intelligent ordering of what had been a saga of endless, almost random violence. The structure of the poem itself contributes to this sense of order, beginning with the world in Hesiod's time, then moving back to show the evolution from Chaos, and then concluding with a reaffirmation of Zeus's wise aegis.

The direction of cosmic evolution is from a focus on the form of the natural world to a concentration on the structure of an anthropocentric one. This is a reflection of the imposition of the will of Zeus, since, as Hesiod presents it, the first "beings"—Chaos (Void), Gaia (Earth), and Eros (immanent creative energy)—are essentially elemental impulses, unbound and undirected. Hesiod does not postulate what preceded this condition, but sees Eros as a crucial catalyst to the proceeding procreation. First, Hesiod lists the progeny of Chaos and the progeny of Earth. The birth of the Mountains and the Sea by parthenogenesis, and then the birth of the Titans through Earth's incestuous union with her son Sky, are actions apparently without purpose, more impulse than vision. The lineage of Zeus is established with the castration of Kronos (Time)—an act challenging order—who is the last of the Titans, son of Sky and father of Zeus. Parallel to this, the children of Chaos arrive, dark and gloomy, negative in impact, a plague to humankind.

The story of the ascendancy of Zeus involves a shift from the maternal line with an obscure partner to a patriarchal lineage much more in accordance with Hesiod's own society. Zeus, a male sky god, is ultimately evolved from Mother Earth, an evolutionary process directed toward male dominance, which Hesiod justifies as necessary for law and order. Zeus, "the father of gods and men," generates the seasons (emblems of regularity and predictability) by his second wife, Thetis, herself an embodiment of wisdom which he assimilates. Their children symbolize the constants of civilization: Eunomia (Law), Dike (Justice), and Eirene (Peace). Thus, the history of Zeus is also a progression from chaos to law, as Zeus stands in antithesis to his defeated but still dangerous rivals, who are expressions of wild energy. As *Theogony* concludes, Zeus divides his spoils—titles and spheres of influence—with some principles of fairness that lead gradually to a civilized order of governmental succession. The union of Zeus with noble women produced the race of heroes which drew humankind closer to the immortals, but as the children of Night remain on the scene, strife and sorrow will always be the lot of humans. For this reason, the Muses have given the poet the gift of song to provide some relief.

Works and Days is a shift of emphasis from the cosmological and eternal to the local and specific. Hesiod examines the ways in which a man might lead a reasonably satisfying life. Working within the larger pattern of the universe as presented in *Theogony* and assuming a familiarity with it, Hesiod confronted the limitations imposed by often unfathomable forces and offered a program of sorts for survival. Because the only style of literary expression available was the dactylic hexameter of the Homeric epic, the poem follows that form, but it is essentially didactic in tone and style, a series of instructions regarding the proper conduct of a man's working life in an agricultural economy controlled by not always scrupulous nobles or "kings." The form is not ideal for Hesiod's purposes, and the poem tends to ramble, but it contains fascinating lessons designed as guidance for men who were prepared to commit their lives to productive industry proscribed by moral behavior.

Works and Days is developed out of the sense of divine justice elaborated in *Theogony*. It accepts the concept of order in human existence and sees work as "the action to fulfill that order." The rationale behind the poem is that conditions have steadily deteriorated since the Golden Age. As Hesiod tells it, men have progressively weakened through the "Five Ages," their working conditions becoming harder, their physical strength diminished, and such afflictions as hunger and disease, unknown in earlier times, now plaguing humankind in the Iron Age. These banes occur as a consequence of human deviousness as expressed in the myths of Prometheus and Pandora. Hesiod sees violence and injustice emerging from Prometheus' challenge and, without being specific, names Pandora (meaning woman) as a source of increasing complexity in human affairs for the introduction of sexual and artistic matters. Bound by the thinking of his era, he describes the feminine role as one of distraction, undermining a man's clarity of purpose and, by implication, his control. A woman's "glamor" and guile encourages dissipation and waste which restricts independence. For Hesiod, woman is "the other," an outsider, who must be taught "right" ways. That is, she must eradicate the singularity in her nature that makes her different from a man. Once a similarity is achieved, she will become valuable property, because she contributes to the permanence of the home. The perspective is very male-oriented and very narrow. A larger view of the two myths suggests that Prometheus introduces the technical to the natural and Pandora introduces the beautiful or ecstatic to the rational, each complicating but also deepening human experience. In a sense, Zeus has used Pandora as a tactic in his contest with Prometheus, and both myths are part of Hesiod's explanation for the current condition of the world.

In order to overcome these unpleasant conditions, Hesiod stresses justice as the crucial virtue, the essential value in all endeavor. Focusing on his own life, he decries the local politicians, subject to bribes, who have unjustly favored his brother Perses in dividing their father's legacy. The entire poem is supposedly addressed to Perses, who is exhorted to follow a life of honest work because without it, men would scheme to gain riches and justice could not exist. The central text of the poem is a series of maxims, suggestions, folk sayings, and specific advice about how to function in a grain-growing or wine-making world. Rather than a manual, however, it is more an outline of operations framed by a reliance on the right time of the year for a particular action. The purpose is really to inculcate a sense of appropriateness and propriety in everything. Similarly, the long, expressive descriptions of the harshness of winter and the pleasures of summer are designed to reconcile human nature to the larger patterns of the natural cosmos. The "works" section is a kind of astronomical guide for plowing, planting, and harvesting, that places man in harmony with his environment, thus putting him in synchronization with the will of Zeus. The part of the poem known as the "Days" is less impressive because it is rooted in the "science" or superstition of Hesiod's world. It is a forerunner of astrological prediction—an attempt to make sense of mysterious, perplexing aspects of existence. It represents a variety of superstitions, particularly numerology, extant in Mesopotamia and Egypt. Hesiod is recording the folk wisdom of the tribe, another valid task of the didactic poet.

Summary

The fifth century judgment of Herodotus, that "Hesiod and Homer are the ones who provided the Greeks with a theogony, gave the gods their names, distinguished their attributes and functions, and defined their various types," is still valid. The mythic truth that Hesiod established is the basis for the origin of the European mind and worldview, the beginning of a definition of Western civilization. In his work, the strong thread of value and principle that distinguishes the most admirable attributes of culture can be traced back to its inception. The ultimate lessons of his philosophy, organized through reflection upon astronomical phenomena, are to live in harmony with the visible, the regular, the knowable, and to acknowledge and forbear the illusive, the abrupt, the terrible. Speaking across the gulf of time, Hesiod remains the "great teacher and civilizer," the poet as embodiment of the divine voice that offers access to universal truth which humankind ignores at its own peril.

Bibliography

Burn, Andrew Robert. *The World of Hesiod: A Study of the Greek Middle Ages, c. 900-700 B.C.* London: K. Paul, Trench, Trübner and Co., 1936; New York: Dutton, 1937. An early study that examines the poet in his historical context. Much basic background information.

Havelock, Eric. *Preface to Plato.* Oxford: Blackwell, and Cambridge, Mass.: Harvard University Press, 1963. An excellent discussion of "oral acoustic intelligence," the tradition in which Hesiod composed.

Hesiod. *Hesiod, the Homeric Hymns, and Homerica.* Hugh G. Evelyn-White, ed. and trans. Cambridge, Mass.: Harvard University Press, and London: Heinemann, 1914. The translation considered standard through most of the twentieth century.

————. *The Poems of Hesiod.* R. M. Frazer, ed. Norman: University of Oklahoma Press, 1983. A somewhat ornate but reliable recent translation with informative commentary.

————. *Theogony.* Norman O. Brown, ed. New York and London: Macmillan, 1953. A reliable translation with a detailed, interpretive introduction that contains perceptive commentary on the poem's meaning.

————. *Theogony.* M. L. West, ed. Oxford: Clarendon Press, 1966. A critical edition with an extensive, informative introduction.

————. *Theogony and Works and Days.* M. L. West, ed. Oxford and New York: Oxford University Press, 1988. An excellent translation of Hesiod's major work by one of the leading experts on Hesiod's writing. Includes a short but very enlightening introduction and notes.

————. *Theogony; Works and Days; Shield.* Apostolos N. Athanassakis, ed. Baltimore: Johns Hopkins University Press, 1983. An imaginative modern translation, combined with lucid, thorough notes and an incisive introduction. The author's familiarity with historic and contemporary Greece enables him to offer many relevant details from folk culture.

————. *Works and Days: With Prolegomena and Commentary.* M. L. West, ed. Oxford: Clarendon Press, 1978. A companion to the author's *Theogony.*

Janko, R. *Homer, Hesiod, and the Hymns: Diachronic Development in Epic Diction.* Cambridge and New York: Cambridge University Press, 1982. Solid scholarship and interesting speculation about the development of the hexameter tradition, with many theoretical assertions about dates and origins.

Lamberton, Robert. *Hesiod.* New Haven, Conn.: Yale University Press, 1988. An accessible introduction to Hesiod's works. Historical background of the poems and problems of dating them are discussed. Major subsidiary works are analyzed.

Pucci, Pietro. *Hesiod and the Language of Poetry.* Baltimore: Johns Hopkins University Press, 1977. An extremely detailed examination of the meaning of words in Hesiod. Primarily for the specialist but clear in presentation.

Thalmann, William G. *Conventions of Form and Thought in Early Greek Epic Poetry.* Baltimore: Johns Hopkins University Press, 1984. A comprehensive, carefully annotated examination of the form and structure of the poetry of Homer and Hesiod, illuminating parallel approaches in the work of both poets and providing many incisive comments on the meanings of their poems. An impressive assimilation and extension of much previous scholarship on the subject.

Walcot, P. *Hesiod and the Near East*. Cardiff: Wales University Press, 1966. The important influences of Oriental literature and thought on Hesiod are traced and explained. Good background information on life in Boeotia in Hesiod's time as well.

West, M. L. *The Hesiodic Catalogue of Women: Its Nature, Structure, and Origins*. Oxford: Clarendon, and New York: Oxford University Press, 1985. A definitive study of a work previously attributed to Hesiod.

Leon Lewis

HIPPARCHUS

Born: 190 B.C.; Nicaea, Bithynia, Asia Minor
Died: 126 B.C.; possibly Rhodes
Areas of Achievement: Astronomy, mathematics, and geography
Contribution: Hipparchus was the greatest astronomer of ancient times. He was the founder of trigonometry, which he used in a method for determining the distances from Earth to the moon and sun, and the first to use consistently the idea of latitude and longitude to describe locations on Earth and in the sky.

Early Life

Very little is known about Hipparchus' life. He was born in Nicaea, a Greek-speaking city in Bithynia (modern Iznik, Turkey), in the northwestern part of Asia Minor. Calculations in his works are based on the latitude of the city of Rhodes, on the island of the same name, so many historians believe that he spent a major portion of his life there. Rhodes was a merchant center, a convenient port from which to make voyages. At least one of Hipparchus' observations was made in Alexandria, so it seems that he visited and perhaps spent time as a student or research scholar at that great nucleus of scientific inquiry. Since he was intensely interested in geography, it is likely that he traveled to other places in the Mediterranean basin and the Near East. He seems to have been familiar with Babylonian astronomy, including eclipse records, but it is impossible to say how he came to know these.

Life's Work

Most of what is known of Hipparchus comes from the *Mathēmatikē suntaxis* (c. A.D. 150; *Almagest*) of Ptolemy, whose work depends to a considerable extent on that of the earlier scientist, and from the *Geōgraphica* (c. 7 B.C.; *Geography*) of Strabo. Of Hipparchus' own writings, only the *Tōn Araton kai Eudoxou phainomenōn exēgēsis* (*Commentary on the Phaenomena of Eudoxus and Aratus*) survives, in three books. It criticizes the less accurate placement of stars and constellations by two famous predecessors. It is certainly not one of his most important works, but it contains some information on his observations of star positions, which were the basis of his lost star catalog. Other lost works of Hipparchus include *Peri eviausiou megethous* (on

the length of the year) and *Peri tēs metabaseōs tōn tropikōn kai isēmerinōn semeiōn* (on the displacement of the solstitial and equinoctial points). He is also credited with a trigonometrical table of chords in a circle, a work on gravitational phenomena called *On Bodies Carried down by Their Weight*, an attack on the geographical work of Eratosthenes, a compilation of weather signs, and some aids to computational astrology.

A number of achievements are attributed to Hipparchus by Ptolemy and other ancient writers. A new star appeared in the constellation Scorpio in July, 133 B.C. Hipparchus realized that without an accurate star catalog, it was impossible to demonstrate that the star was indeed new, so he set about producing a complete sky map with a table of the positions of the stars, including the angle north or south of the celestial equator (latitude) and the angle east or west of the vernal equinox point (one of the two intersections between the celestial equator and the sun's path, or ecliptic). In order to do this, he needed a means of measuring celestial angles, which led him to invent many of the sighting instruments, including the diopter and possibly the armillary astrolabe, used by astronomers before the invention of the telescope in the seventeenth century. He also knew how to calibrate water clocks. Hipparchus' star catalog included about 850 stars, along with estimates of their brightness. He divided the stars into six categories, from the brightest to the dimmest, thus originating a system of stellar magnitude. He also made a celestial globe, showing the locations of the fixed stars on its surface.

In comparing his own measurements of positions of stars with those of earlier astronomers, Hipparchus discovered that there had been a systematic shift in the same direction in all of them. He noticed the phenomenon first in the case of the bright star Spica. In 283 B.C. Timocharis had observed the star to be eight degrees west of the autumnal equinoctial point, but Hipparchus found the figure to be six degrees. He found a displacement for every other star which he was able to check. These discrepancies, he established, were the result of a shift in the position of the equinoxes—and therefore of the celestial equator and poles. In modern astronomy, this shift is called the precession of the equinoxes and is known to be caused by a slow "wobble" in the orientation of Earth's axis. The spot to which the north pole points in the sky (the north

celestial pole) describes a circle in a period of more than twenty-six thousand years. Hipparchus was first to describe and to attempt to measure this phenomenon. He was, however, unable to explain its cause, since he held the geocentric theory which postulates a motionless Earth at the center of a moving universe.

From the beginning of theoretical astronomy, the geocentric theory had been the accepted one. It assumed that the sun, moon, planets, and stars were carried on vast transparent spheres that revolved at different but constant speeds around Earth. Unfortunately, in order to explain the observed motions of the planets, which vary in speed and sometimes are retrograde relative to the stars, astronomers had to postulate the existence of additional spheres, invisible and bearing no celestial bodies but interconnected with the other spheres and affecting their motions. An Alexandrian astronomer, Aristarchus, had proposed the heliocentric theory, which holds that Earth, with its satellite the moon, and all the other planets revolve around the central sun. The main appeal of this theory was its simplicity; it required fewer imaginary spheres to make it work.

Hipparchus rejected the heliocentric theory and instead adopted modifications of the geocentric theory to make it accord better with observations, perhaps following Apollonius of Perga. The main feature of the Hipparchan system is the epicycle, a smaller sphere bearing a planet, with its center on the surface of the larger, Earth-centered sphere and revolving at an independent speed. He also postulated eccentrics, that is, that the centers of the celestial spheres do not coincide with the center of Earth. The geocentric system with epicycles is often called "Ptolemaic," since Ptolemy made observations to support the theory developed by Hipparchus. Aristarchus' heliocentric theory is closer to the picture of the solar system provided by modern astronomy.

In developing his astronomical system, Hipparchus observed the period of revolution of the celestial objects that move against the background of the stars. That of the sun, which is the year, he found to be 365 1/4 days, less 1/300 of a day, a figure which was closer to the true one than that of any previous astronomer. He noticed the inequality in the lengths of the seasons, which he correctly attributed to the varying distance between Earth and the sun but incorrectly explained by assuming that the center of the sun's sphere of revolution was ec-

centric to the center of Earth. These conclusions were, perhaps, a step in the direction of recognizing that the relative motion of the two bodies describes an ellipse. He also achieved a measurement of the length of the lunar month, with an error of less than one second in comparison with the figure now accepted. The Roman scholar Pliny the Elder wrote that Hipparchus countered the popular fear of eclipses by publishing a list which demonstrated their regularity over the preceding six hundred years.

Hipparchus attempted to measure the distances of the moon and sun from Earth by observing eclipses and the phenomenon of parallax (the shift in the apparent position of the moon against the background of the stars under changing conditions). His figure for the distance of the moon (60.5 times the radius of Earth) was reasonably accurate, but his estimate of the sun's distance (2,550 times Earth's radius) was far too small. (The true ratio is about 23,452 to 1.) In fairness to Hipparchus, it should be noted that he regarded his solution to the problem of the sun's distance as open to question.

In order to make the mathematical computations required by these problems, it was necessary for Hipparchus to know the ratios of the sides of a right triangle for the various angles the sides make with the hypotenuse—in other words, the values of trigonometrical functions. He worked out tables of the sine function, thus becoming, in effect, the founder of trigonometry.

Geography also occupied Hipparchus' attention. He began the systematic use of longitude and latitude, which he had also employed in his star catalog, as a means of establishing locations on Earth's surface. Previous geographers show evidence of knowing such a method, but they did not employ it consistently. Hipparchus was able to calculate latitudes of various places on Earth's surface by learning the lengths of the days and nights recorded for different seasons of the year, although the figures given by him were often in error. As the base of longitude, he used the meridian passing through Alexandria. He was especially critical, probably too much so, of the descriptive and mathematical errors in the work of Eratosthenes. He even had some quibbles with the famous measurement of the spherical Earth, which is the latter's most brilliant achievement. It may be Hipparchus rather than Eratosthenes who first described climatic zones, bounded by parallels of latitude north and south of the equator.

Summary

Hipparchus was a careful and original astronomer whose discoveries, particularly that of precession, were of the greatest importance in the early history of the science. He was a meticulous observer who produced the first dependable star catalog and who determined the apparent periods of revolution of the moon and the sun with an exactitude never before achieved. As a mathematician, he originated the study of trigonometry, compiling a sine table and using it in an attempt to measure distances in space beyond Earth which was, at least in the case of the moon, successful. Both as astronomer and as geographer, he pioneered the systematic use of the coordinates of latitude and longitude. He devised instruments for use in these observations and measurements.

Unfortunately, almost all Hipparchus' writings have disappeared, so modern assessments of his work must depend on ancient writers who happened to mention him. His influence was important enough to cause several later scientists whose works survive to refer to and summarize him. Most notable among these were Ptolemy and Strabo. It is sometimes hard to tell when these authors, particularly Ptolemy, are following Hipparchus and when they are going beyond him to present their own conclusions. Ptolemy's work became the standard textbook on astronomy down to the time of Nicolaus Copernicus in the sixteenth century; thus Hipparchus' name was deservedly remembered. One of Hipparchus' most important mathematical successors was Menelaus of Alexandria (fl. c. A.D. 100), who developed the study of spherical trigonometry.

Bibliography

Dicks, D. R. *Early Greek Astronomy to Aristotle.* London: Thames and Hudson, and Ithaca, N.Y.: Cornell University Press, 1970. Hipparchus is not given major treatment, although he does appear as an important figure in the history of astronomy. The discussion of his criticisms of Eudoxus and Aratus is particularly good.

Dreyer, John L. E. *A History of Astronomy from Thales to Kepler.* Rev. ed. New York: Dover Publications, 1953. This fine, accessible study places Hipparchus clearly in the context of the development of astronomy. Dreyer differs from common interpretation in crediting Ptolemy, not Hipparchus, with the theory of epicycles.

Grasshoff, Gerd. *The History of Ptolemy's Star Catalogue.* Studies in the History of Mathematics and Physical Sciences. New York: Springer Verlag, 1990. The author is primarily concerned with the relationship of Ptolemy's star catalogue to the earlier work of Hipparchus. He attempts to prove the derivative nature of Ptolemy by tracing his errors back to Hipparchus.

Heath, Thomas. *A History of Greek Mathematics.* 2 vols. Oxford: Clarendon Press, 1921; New York: Dover, 1981. Includes a section on Hipparchus in the second volume, emphasizing his probable contributions to the origin of trigonometry and establishing his place in the history of mathematics.

Lloyd, G. E. R. *Greek Science After Aristotle.* London: Chatto and Windus, and New York: Norton, 1973. Rather than giving a separate treatment to the subject, this work discusses the contributions of Hipparchus as they arise in a general study of ancient science from the fourth century B.C. to the end of the second century A.D. The attention given to Hipparchus is appropriate and appreciative.

Neugebauer, Otto. *A History of Ancient Mathematical Astronomy.* 3 vols. New York: Springer-Verlag, 1975. This work contains a section on Hipparchus in volume 1, briefly discussing what little is known about his life and chronology and devoting the rest of its space to a careful consideration of his astronomical work. There are some mathematical and astronomical symbols and formulas which the layperson may find difficult.

———. "Notes on Hipparchus." In *The Aegean and the Near East: Studies Presented to Hetty Goldman,* edited by Saul S. Weinberg. Locust Valley, N.Y.: J. J. Augustin, 1956. An important discussion of the extent to which Hipparchus knew Babylonian astronomy.

Ptolemy. *Ptolemy's "Almagest."* Translated by G. J. Toomer. London: Duckworth, and New York: Springer-Verlag, 1984. Much of what is known about Hipparchus is based on Ptolemy's words. This fine translation has complete notes and a useful bibliography.

Thomson, J. Oliver. *History of Ancient Geography.* Cambridge: Cambridge University Press, 1948; New York: Biblo and Tannen, 1965. Gives adequate notice to the geographical theories and contributions of Hipparchus in various parts of a more general study.

J. Donald Hughes

HIPPOCRATES

Born: Probably 460 B.C.; Cos
Died: Probably 377 B.C.; Larissa, Thessaly
Area of Achievement: Medicine
Contribution: Hippocrates is credited with separating the practice of medicine from magic and superstition, inaugurating the modern practice of scientific observation, and setting the guidelines for high standards of ethical medical practice.

Early Life

Hippocrates was born in Cos; he lived during the period spanning the end of the fifth century and the first half of the fourth century B.C., according to two references to him in Plato's dialogues. Though little else can be thoroughly documented, many legends, possibly true in parts, have been offered by commentators regarding Hippocrates' early life. According to tradition, Hippocrates was one of several sons of Praxithea and Heracleides. He probably had the education suitable to one of his background, which would include nine years of physical education, reading, writing, spelling, music, singing, and poetry. After another two years at a gymnasium, where he would have had intensive training in athletics, it is conjectured that Hippocrates studied medicine under his father, a member of the priest-physician group known as Asclepiads. This training was a form of apprenticeship in a medical guild.

In addition to his training, which consisted of following a physician and observing his treatment of patients, Hippocrates is believed to have traveled to the nearby islands of the Aegean Sea, to the Greek mainland, and possibly to Egypt and Libya, to study the local medical traditions. He is thought to have met the philosopher Democritus and the rhetorician Gorgias.

His sons Thessalus and Draco carried on the family tradition of medical practice. As testimony to his fame, legend also has it that King Perdiccas of Macedonia asked Hippocrates and another physician, Euryphon, to examine him and that Hippocrates helped him to recover from his illness.

Hippocrates was equally renowned as a teacher, giving rise to the image of the "Tree of Hippocrates" beneath which students sat and listened to him. Plato, a younger contemporary, referred to Hippocrates the Asclepiad as the very type of the teacher of medicine. Some historical accounts suggest that Hippocrates habitually covered his head with a felt cap, though the reason for this habit is only a matter of speculation. This description did, however, help twentieth century archaeologists to identify a likeness of him.

Life's Work

That Hippocrates was a well-known Greek physician who lived in the period of golden achievements in Greek history is undisputed. The rest of his achievements remain a matter of scholarly debate, centered on the problem of *Corpus Hippocraticum* (fifth to third century B.C.; Hippocratic collection), a substantial body of writings whose authorship seems to be spread out over different historical periods.

Thus the medical views expressed in this collection are carefully referred to as the ideas of Hippocratic medicine, acknowledging the complete lack of confirmation about the identity of his actual writings. Of the approximately seventy unsigned treatises which constitute the collection, only two are definitively known to have been written by Hippocrates' son-in-law, Polybus, because another famous ancient writer, Aristotle, quoted from them.

The normal historical tendency has been to attribute those which are written with authority and good sense and which seem to be of the approximately right time period to Hippocrates and the rest to other authors. The debate over the authorship of the *Corpus Hippocraticum* itself has produced an enormous body of scholarship; one tentative point of agreement is that the earliest essays are from the fifth century B.C. and the latest about two centuries later. To cloud the matter even further, the Hippocratic writings themselves are inconsistent, suggesting that the collection incorporates the thinking of different schools of medical practice.

The collection is historically important precisely because it had more than one purpose: to establish medicine as a practice distinct from philosophy and religion and, in furtherance of this goal, to collect information about this separate discipline in writing for the future edification of patients and physicians. Part of this effort involved debate with other schools of thought, such as the Cnidian school.

The centers of medical teaching were often in the temples of healing known as Asclepieions. The

two most famous ones of the time were on Cos and Cnidus, between which there was a traditional rivalry and a fundamental difference in approach to medical practice. The Cnidus practitioners, under the guidance of the chief physician, Euryphon, seemed to have been much concerned about the classification of diseases and continued the tradition of deductive knowledge of disease derived from the practice of ancient Greece, Babylonia, and Egypt. Hippocrates was of the Coan school, which worked more inductively, concentrating on observation and treatment of the entire patient and taking into account the mental as well as the physical state.

The first important contribution of the Hippocratic writers—to separate medicine from the shackles of religion, superstition, and philosophy—is apparent in the first text of the collection, *Peri archaies ietrikes* (fifth or fourth century B.C.; *Ancient Medicine*), which is a reminder that medicine had previously been very much a matter for philosophical speculation. This essay establishes medicine as a branch of knowledge with its own rational methods and describes a practice that calls for skill and craft and art, one based on observation.

Hippocratic medicine recognized disease as a natural process and further suggested that most acute diseases are self-limited. The symptoms of fever, malaise, and other apparent sicknesses were not considered to be mysterious spiritual symptoms but merely the body's way of fighting off the poison of infection. Epilepsy, for example, much feared as a mysterious, sacred affliction, is discussed as a medical problem. The focus of Hippocratic medicine was on regulation of diet, meaning not merely nutrition but exercise as well. The adjustment of diet to the physical state of the patient was thus viewed as the original function of medicine and the importance of the kind of food and its preparation to treat sickness was recognized early.

The Hippocratic writers mention other ideas equally surprising in their modern relevance and influence, such as the notion that great changes, whether in temperature, periods of life, or diet, are most likely to lead to illness. Thus the collection of four books entitled *Peri diaites* (fifth or fourth century B.C.; *Regimen*) starts with the argument that health is affected by the totality of diet and exercise; the age, strength, and constitution of the individual; the seasonal changes; variations in wind and weather; and the location in which the patient lives. The Hippocratic idea that a local condition must be treated in conjunction with the general condition, the whole constitution (*physis*) and the complex relations to the environment, is also remarkably similar to the modern notion of holistic healing.

Though many of the other practices and theories have been discarded medically, some were influential for so long that they have been incorporated into the history of Western culture. For example, among the most influential theories set forth in the Hippocratic collection is the idea that the human body is composed of four fluid substances: blood, phlegm, yellow bile, and black bile. Perfect health results from the balance of these fluids in the body. Concomitantly, an excess or deficiency or imperfect mixture results in pain, sickness, and disease. The influence of this theory is apparent in many classics of Western literature, such as the plays of William Shakespeare and Ben Jonson.

Hippocratic medicine was also conservative, seeking primarily to help the sick when it would be beneficial. Medicine was defined by three purposes: It should relieve suffering, reduce the severity of the illness, and finally, abstain from treating that which was beyond the practice of medicine. The physician's job was to help the natural recovery process with diet and regimen, to be administered only after careful observation of the individual symptoms and the patient's constitution. The remedies recommended were mild and adapted to the various stages of the disease; drugs were relatively rare. Most important, sudden and violent measures to interrupt the natural course of the disease were forbidden. The Coan school believed in prognosis, in predicting, from the experience of long and careful observation, the course of the disease and furthermore in telling the patients and their friends, so that they could be mentally prepared for what might follow, even if it were death. This dictum prevented the physician from prescribing ineffective or expensive treatments simply to remain busy; it is thought that the Hippocratic physician would not even undertake the treatment of a hopeless case, though he probably did his best to make the patient as comfortable as possible.

The most important view in the Hippocratic collection—the most important because it is still unchanged over the course of two thousand years—is the clearly expressed concept of the medical profession as it is summed up in the Hippocratic oath. The doctor is defined as a good man, skilled at healing. Perhaps for this definition alone, the man who is thought to have written or inspired the Hippocratic writings has been called the father of medicine, a title that suggests the ideal of the philosopher-physician—similar to the ideal of the philosopher-king—a person with moral character as well as practical skills.

Summary

Hippocrates was a much-admired physician whose contemporaries were also giants in their fields: Aeschylus, Sophocles, and Euripides in tragedy; Aristophanes in comedy; Thucydides in history; Pericles in government. Leaving aside the question of authorship of the Hippocratic writings, it is clear why the figure of Hippocrates, for whom the collection is named, is so revered: The keen observations of human behavior and health recorded in these pieces remain fruitful reading.

The Hippocratic writings include a book of more than four hundred aphorisms, pithy observations which have been absorbed, though sometimes in a mutilated form, into the English language, influencing those outside the medical field. The most

famous of these, popularly remembered as "Life is short, Art long," started as

> Life is short, whereas the demands of the (medical) profession are unending, the crisis is urgent, experiment dangerous, and decision difficult. But the physician must not only do what is necessary, he must also get the patient, the attendants, and the external factors to work together to the same end.

Others reveal a common sense which has been proven over and over again: "Restricted or strict diets are dangerous; extremes must be avoided"; "People who are excessively overweight (by nature) are far more apt to die suddenly than those of average weight"; "Inebriation removes hunger (for solid foods)."

If much of the rest of the body of medical knowledge represented by Hippocrates has long since been surpassed, its spirit has not. Hippocrates and his colleagues changed the attitude toward disease, freeing medicine from magic and superstition and insisting on the importance of observation over philosophical speculation. The Hippocratic writings established medicine as a separate discipline with a scientific basis, setting down in writing the medical knowledge of the time regarding surgery, prognosis, therapeutics, principles of medical ethics, and relations between physicians and patient, thus laying the foundations and formulating the ideals of modern medicine.

Bibliography

Coulter, Harris L. *Divided Legacy: A History of the Schism in Medical Thought.* Vol. 1, *The Patterns Emerge: Hippocrates to Paracelsus.* Washington, D.C.: Weehawken Book Co., 1975. The subtitle of the first volume refers to two patterns of thought, rational and empirical, dominating medical history. The author places Hippocrates in the empirical tradition. Provides an extensive bibliography and index. Lists quotations from original writings.

Edelstein, Ludwig. *The Hippocratic Oath: Text, Translation, and Interpretation.* Baltimore: Johns Hopkins University Press, 1943. This monograph argues that the Hippocratic oath represented the opinion of a small segment of Greek medical society, was based on Pythagorean principles, and served as a voluntary oath of conscience between teacher and student.

Goldberg, Herbert S. *Hippocrates, Father of Medicine.* New York: Franklin Watts, 1963. A short, simplified overview of the life and work of Hippocrates, his times, and his relevance to modern health practice. Index.

Heidel, William Arthur. *Hippocratic Medicine: Its Spirit and Method.* New York: Columbia University Press, 1941. Heidel discusses the close connections among science, philosophy, history, and medicine in the period of Hippocratic medicine. Provides notes and sources.

Hippocrates. *Hippocrates.* Translated by W. H. S. Jones. 4 vols. Cambridge, Mass.: Harvard University Press, and London: Heinemann, 1923-1931. Among the best English translations and critical editions of Hippocratic writings, this work is part of the Loeb Classical Library edition. Greek texts face their English counterparts.

————. *Studies in Ancient Medicine.* Vol. 2, *Hippocrates: Pseudepigraphic Writings: Letters, Embassy, Speech from the Altar, Decree.* Wesley D. Smith, ed. and trans. Leiden and New York: Brill, 1990. A translation of 24 letters and three documents once ascribed to Hippocrates. The introduction discusses their dates and analyzes the mindset behind their production.

Langholf, Volker. *Medical Theories in Hippocrates: Early Texts and the "Epidemics."* Untersuchungen zur antiken Literatur und Geschichte, vol. 34. Berlin and New York: Walter de Gruyter, 1990. Concerns the "application and evolution of medical theories in the so-called Hippocratic treatises." The author chronicles the rise of medical terminology and methods of describing diseases, and explores parallels between the prognosis provided by physicians and the divination practiced by seers.

Levine, Edwin Burton. *Hippocrates.* New York: Twayne Publishers, 1971. Levine introduces the problems of scholarship in identifying authorship of the Hippocratic writings. The discussion focuses on ideas presented in various selected essays. Includes notes, an index, and an extensive annotated bibliography.

Moon, Robert Oswald. *Hippocrates and His Successors in Relation to the Philosophy of Their Time.* London and New York: Longmans, Green and Co., 1923. A series of lectures delivered by a physician to physicians, this work briefly categorizes the philosophies underlying the practice of ancient medicine before and after Hippocrates. Index.

Petersen, William F. *Hippocratic Wisdom for Him Who Wishes to Pursue Properly the Science of Medicine: A Modern Appreciation of Ancient Scientific Achievement.* Springfield, Ill.: Charles C Thomas, Publisher, 1946. A physician's discussion of Hippocratic tenets and their relevance to modern physicians. Includes a glossary, illustrations, and an index.

Phillips, E. D. *Greek Medicine.* London: Thames and Hudson, 1973; as *Aspects of Greek Medicine.* New York: St. Martin's Press, 1973. Phillips traces practical and theoretical achievements of Greek medicine up to Galen. Includes selected references to the Hippocratic collection, an appendix on the cult of Asclepius, illustrations, an extensive bibliography, and indexes.

Sargent, Frederick, II. *Hippocratic Heritage: A History of Ideas About Weather and Human Health.* New York: Pergamon Press, 1982. A history of human biometeorology, this study traces from the ancient Hindus to the twentieth century the Hippocratic idea that the atmospheric environment influences people. Includes figures, portraits, tables, appendices.

Temkin, Owsei. *Hippocrates in a World of Pagans and Christians.* Baltimore, Md.: Johns Hopkins University Press, 1991; London: Johns Hopkins University Press, 1995. An account of the vicissitudes of Hippocrates' reputation, especially among Christians in late antiquity. Connections are drawn between medical thought, philosophy, and religion.

Shakuntala Jayaswal

HIPPOLYTUS OF ROME

Born: c. 170; place unknown
Died: c. 235; Sardinia
Areas of Achievement: Religion and philosophy
Contribution: Initiating Christian commentary on the books of the Old Testament, Hippolytus also provided the first systematic handbook regulating the ordination of the ministry and the conduct of worship. In addition, he elaborated the connections among the Greco-Roman philosophical schools and popular practices and the diversity of opinions which divided the Christian communities.

Early Life

While it remains impossible to construct an early life for Hippolytus, it is possible to identify what he studied and when. It is instructive to compare his education with those of the great Alexandrians who were his contemporaries, Clement (c. 150-c. 215) and Origen (c. 185-c. 254). Hippolytus' more spirited and argumentative character does not suggest an eastern Mediterranean origin. Yet Hippolytus did write in Greek—the last Christian author in Rome to do so. He is often thought to have been a student of Saint Irenaeus in Gaul; both tackled the subject of heresy, which at that time meant simply a variety of opinions or practices. Nevertheless, Hippolytus' work *Kata pasōn haireseōn elenkhos* (*The Refutation of All Heresies*, 1885, also known as *Against All Heresies*), written before 199, took on its own character.

Two special dimensions gave focus to his thought. In order to elaborate the catalog of heresies and extend it into his own time, Hippolytus had sought the intellectual bases for that "diversity of opinions" from Greco-Roman philosophers, from what he could learn of the inner working of the "mystery religions," from the highly popular behavior of magicians, and from astrological inquiries. His quotations, extensive though disjointed, remain a principal source for studies of pre-Socratic and later ancient intellectual tendencies.

Hippolytus' study of astronomy and astrology preserved what had taken shape in the centuries near the turn of the common era. He cataloged details of horoscopes and their attempted applications as well as the calculations of the sizes of Earth and planets and their respective distances from one another. These calculations led to arithmetic consid-

erations, including the interrelationship between numbers when expressed by letters of the alphabet and words or names. The role of magicians, with their amulets and contrivances for illusion, indicated other activities competitive with Christianity.

The summary of these alternative inquiries was not Hippolytus' major concern, but he provided large enough selections that he might use their words as a basis for his theory that Christian intellectual formulations at odds with his own teaching originated in this environment. His conclusion is that the truth is found by a method of intellectual contrast: Let the other side speak and demonstrate its own inherent falsity. His books belong to his mature years; his method illustrates how and what he learned in his early life.

The other dimension of his formative years was the practice of the "Apostolic Tradition." In it were patterns for administering both the internal core of Christian worship and the external requirements necessary for church structure. Hippolytus' later account of the tradition indicated the status of developments within the expanding Christianity of the second century, in which his religious practice was grounded, and the reason that in later years he critically opposed every alternative form with such vigor.

Life's Work

Hippolytus was already a mature thinker and author when he became well known. The Roman emperor Septimus Severus (reigned 193-211) initiated a Christian persecution in 202, the tenth year after his power was secured against rivals. Hippolytus' response was a treatise on the Antichrist and a commentary on the Book of Daniel. These works illustrate how Hippolytus perceived that the imperial demand for acts of obedience (emperor worship) violated the inhabitants of the Roman world. He reflected Greek concerns that went back to the power of the *demos* (urban people in *ekklesia*, or "assembly"); he recognized that the Roman state, with "feet of clay," had usurped the divine prerogatives, in a manner analogous to the example first propounded in the Book of Daniel. His interpretation was cautioned by his own chronological considerations: Like others of his day, he affirmed the world to be not more than fifty-seven hundred years old, so that the millennium remained at least three hundred years in the future. His discussion of

the Antichrist is the most comprehensive written in antiquity.

Severus' persecution was severe in Alexandria, where it touched the life of an adolescent whose father was executed and who, but for his mother's intervention, would have followed in his father's path. That youngster was the budding biblical scholar Origen, who became in spite of his youth the director of the greatest Christian school. Origen spent considerable time in hiding. Accompanied by his principal benefactor, Ambrose, Origen came to Rome to hear Hippolytus speak. When Origen returned to Alexandria, Ambrose provided funding for secretarial staffing and encouraged Origen to emulate Hippolytus in the production of biblical commentaries and other works against critics of Christianity, especially those of greatest intellectual impact, such as Celsus.

Hippolytus is known for commentaries on many biblical books. A close examination of these studies reveals an emerging New Testament. He recognized twenty-two books as authoritative: four Gospels, thirteen of Paul's Epistles, one Acts of the Apostles, three catholic Epistles, and Revelation.

Yet he also knew and used the Gospel of the Hebrews, the Epistle to the Hebrews, Second Peter, James, Jude, Shepherd of Hermas, Revelation of Peter, and Acts of Paul. The distinction seems to be based on what was allowed to be read in "our churches" and what, while proper for private reading, could not be publicly used since such had come into being "in our own times."

In the period of Severus' persecution and the following relative prosperity for the Church, Zephyrinus was Bishop of Rome (199-217). By the early third century, urban Rome counted some million people, with thirty to forty thousand estimated to be Christian. Administratively, this number was spread throughout the metropolis and not located in any single area. The tradition of "house churches," which goes back before the Constantinian revolution in 325, provides evidence for this diversity of location, as does the development of catacomb burial grounds.

Hippolytus described Zephyrinus as "an ignorant and illiterate individual," one "unskilled in ecclesiastical definitions," "accessible to bribes and covetous," and "incapable of forming his own judgment or of discerning the designs of others." The bishop also apparently represented a theological stance, relative to the interrelationship of Father and Son within the Christian Godhead, which was at odds with Hippolytus' understanding, so that there were continual disturbances among the diverse Christians of the capital. The theoretical formulation developing during the third century that there was but one bishop for each conurbation prevented the ancient acknowledgment that Hippolytus was a rival bishop in Rome itself; in modern times, he receives the designation "first antipope."

His principal rival was Callistus, also known as Calixtus, who became Bishop of Rome on the death of Zephyrinus. The controversy began during the reign of the emperor Commodus (180-192) and his urban prefect Sejus Fuscianus. Callistus was a slave to Carcophorus, a minor official in the imperial household; both were Christian. Carcophorus handled money deposited by widows and others toward burial expenses, and Callistus was directed to make a profitable return on these deposits through banking transactions. A failure led to his flight and capture, a further confrontation with the law, scourging, and sentencing to the mines on Sardinia. While Victor was Bishop of Rome (189-199), an imperial concubine, Marcia, also a Christian, obtained release for the captives from Commodus. As a "martyr," Callistus came to the attention of Victor, who pensioned him to Antium. When Zephyrinus became bishop, he brought Callistus into his service to take charge of the clergy and of the one principal asset held by the churches—the cemetery catacombs.

At Zephyrinus' death, none of these men was any longer young. Callistus officially succeeded, but Hippolytus held a rival claim, leading directly to theological disputes; Callistus claimed that Hippolytus' view of the relation of Father and Son was "ditheistic," while Hippolytus accused Callistus of so unifying the Persons of the Godhead that the Father could be said to have suffered equally when the Son was crucified. Some of the confusion may have been the difference between the Greek of Hippolytus and his followers and the Latin of Callistus and his followers. (There was a sizable Greek-speaking population in officially Latin Rome.)

Conflict of theology moved into conflict of administration. The actual role of Hippolytus became more evident, especially in his linguistic use of the episcopal "we" for pronouncements against the decisions of Callistus. These decisions included permission for those married more than once to enter the clergy, for clergy to marry and remain in orders, for women to live in concubinage with slaves (since Roman law did not permit full marriage to occur between slaves or between them and free persons), and for second baptism of those reconciling with the Church after lapse. In Hippolytus' opinion, such decisions were bad enough, but Callistus on his own authority determined that as Bishop of Rome he could forgive any sin, including that of abortion.

Like his North African contemporary Tertullian, Hippolytus was a champion of old causes in a rapidly changing world; tradition was encountering a variety of internal opinions and external pressures. This conservatism is nowhere better illustrated than in *Apostolikē paradosis* (second or third century; *The Apostolic Tradition of Hippolytus*, 1934). This handbook contains the most ancient forms and prayers for the ordination of bishops, presbyters, and deacons; for the consecration of confessors; and for the appointment of widows and readers. It also contains instructions for catechumens for baptism and first participation in the Lord's Supper and for fasting and praying.

Callistus died naturally and was buried not in the catacomb which bears his name but in a crypt on the Via Aureliana; his feast day is October 14. Hippolytus outlived Callistus and his successors Urban and Pontian. When Maximinus became emperor in 235, severe persecution was resumed, going after the ranking leadership. Both Pontian and Hippolytus were sent to the mines of Sardinia, where they were worked to death. Anterus was bishop for three months during this upheaval, before Fabian, a layman, was elected directly into the episcopal office in 236.

Fabian was able to recover the bodies of both Pontian and Hippolytus and bring them back to Rome. Pontian was interred in the papal crypt of Saint Callistus. In 236 or 237, Hippolytus was interred in the cemetery on the Via Tiburtina that subsequently carried his name. The date of his burial, August 13, remains his feast day.

Summary

The historical testimony to Hippolytus' role within the Church, even to location, became vague. The church historian Eusebius, Bishop of Caesarea, writing less than a century later, identified Hippolytus as a bishop of "some" church; that vagueness might be excused were it not that Eusebius knew directly of Hippolytus' writings from the library at Aelia Capitolina (Roman Jerusalem) and of his contemporaneity with Zephyrinus and the Roman persecutions of that era. A century after Eusebius, the Latin biblical scholar, Jerome, in *De viris illustribus* (392-393; lives of illustrious men), repeats this vague affirmation of Hippolytus' bishopric—"the name of the city I have not been able to learn"—in spite of extending the list of publications and confirming the correlation with Origen, whom Jerome knew had called Hippolytus his "taskmaster."

In 1551 a statue of a person seated on a throne was discovered in Rome. Since the throne base had engraved upon it Hippolytus' table for computing the date of Easter and a list of his writings, the statue was reconstructed with a bearded head—as though it were Hippolytus—even though the statue in body and dress is that of a woman, probably a follower of the philosopher Epicurus.

It was not until the mid-nineteenth century—an era refueled with conflict centering on the Bishop of Rome and pronouncements of "infallibility"—that the personality and concerns of Hippolytus were rediscovered. Those of his works that had survived had in the interim been confused with the writings of others, and only a chance manuscript-discovery permitted his own works to be disentangled from the hodgepodge of other writings. Work on the recovery of Hippolytus continues, and complete editions of his principal writings are gradually appearing.

Bibliography

Brent, Allen. *Hippolytus and the Roman Church in the Third Century: Communities in Tension before the Emergence of a Monarch-bishop.* Leiden and New York: Brill, 1995. A massive and thorough study of Hippolytus and his historical background. The author claims that, while there was historical Hippolytus, his name became symbolic of a whole community and its pattern of theological thinking. The writings that survive under Hippolytus' name reveal tensions "within a community moving to a Monarch Bishop."

Eusebius. *The Ecclesiastical History and the Martyrs of Palestine.* Translated by Hugh Jackson Lawlor and John Ernest Leonard Oulton. 2 vols. London and New York: Macmillan, 1927. The text of Eusebius' history in English translation appears in the first volume. Eusebius sets in time, space, and circumstance the earliest Christian figures, including the "succession from the apostles" and the variety of alternative opinions ("haeresies") as well as the Roman imperial context with its intermittent persecutions. The second volume provides extensive notes.

Grant, Robert. *Augustus to Constantine: The Thrust of the Christian Movement into the Roman World.* New York: Harper and Row, 1970; London: Collins, 1971. By placing the history of early Christianity within its widest socioeconomic context, Grant provides the reader with an interpretation of Christianity within rather than apart from its world. Chapters 10 through 13 most concern Hippolytus, though he informs many other sections.

Hippolytus. *The Apostolic Tradition of Hippolytus.* Edited by Burton Scott Easton. New York: Macmillan, and Cambridge: Cambridge University Press, 1934. Along with a readable edition of the text concerning the earliest Christian liturgical practice, this work provides a discussion of it with an account of its rediscovery and its centrality to Hippolytus' thought.

Mansfeld, Jaap. *Heresiography in Context: Hippolytus' Elenchos as a Source for Greek Philosophy.* Leiden and New York: Brill, 1992. A technical work of scholarship that tries to situate Hippolytus' use of Greek philosophy within his larger purpose of refuting heresy and within the context of Platonic methods of interpretation.

Quasten, Johannes. *Patrology.* Vol. 2, *The Ante-Nicene Literature After Irenaeus.* Westminster, Md.: Newman, 1953. This handbook presents in chronological and geographical order those Christian authors who provide the literature and thought of the ancient Church. Hippolytus is a major figure in this volume.

Roberts, Alexander, Sir James Donaldson, and A. Cleveland Coxe, eds. *The Ante-Nicene Fathers: Translations of the Writings of the Fathers down to A.D. 325.* Vol. 5, *Hippolytus, Cyprian, Caius, Novatian.* Grand Rapids, Mich.: Eerdmans, 1971. This volume includes a nineteenth century translation of *The Refutation of All Heresies.* Regrettably, it remains almost the exclusive access to this work for anyone not reading either the original languages or a foreign translation.

Wordsworth, Christopher. *St. Hippolytus and the Church of Rome in the Early Part of the Third*

Century. 2d ed. London: Rivingtons, 1880. This first reconstruction of the life of Hippolytus is significant for the history of the Church in the mid-nineteenth century. A major feature is the

Greek text and English translation of the ninth book of *The Refutation of All Heresies*, which includes autobiographical information.

Clyde Curry Smith

HOMER

Born: early ninth century B.C.; possibly Ionia, Greece

Died: late ninth century B.C.; Greece

Area of Achievement: Literature

Contribution: Homer wrote the *Iliad* and the *Odyssey*, Greek epic poems which played a crucial role in the birth of classical Greek civilization. These works greatly influenced history, theology, and literature in Greece and the entire Western world.

Early Life

The Greeks were not sure where Homer was born, when he lived, or even if such a person actually existed. The name "Homer" may simply be a generic term denoting "one who fits a song together." Still, various sources provide some information about the provenance of the *Iliad* and the *Odyssey*. The language of the poems is Ionic and Aeolic Greek, which points to an East Greek origin. (In antiquity, East Greece included the west coast of Asia Minor and neighboring islands.) Greek tradition named either the island of Chios or the town of Smyrna, both in eastern Greece, as Homer's birthplace. Chios boasted a guild of rhapsodists who recited the Homeric epics and who claimed, without any proof, to be directly descended from Homer himself. The geographical references in the poems, particularly the *Iliad*, are most specific and correspond to the Ionian area and thus also support an East Greek origin.

Homer's precise dates are no easier to ascertain than his birthplace. At first sight, twelfth century features in the poems, the Mycenaean geography of the *Iliad*'s Catalogue of Ships and ancient weapons such as Ajax's great body shield and Odysseus' curious boar's tusk helmet, seem to suggest that the poems were composed around the time of the Trojan War. Yet archaeological discoveries have shown that certain features of weaponry and warfare described in the poems were not in use before 900 to 700 B.C. For example, the Shield of Achilles in book 18 of the *Iliad* clearly depicts the law courts and agricultural life of an eighth century city-state, not the twelfth century monarchy of Agamemnon. The internal evidence from the poems points to a poet working in the eighth century but trying to paint a picture of the Mycenaean era more than four hundred years before his own time. The fact that there are virtually no references to events

after 700 B.C. indicates that the poems must have been completed by that date.

Life's Work

The obscurity surrounding the author of the *Iliad* and the *Odyssey* is partly a product of the conventions of the epic poetic genre itself. An epic poet was expected simultaneously to create and sing a poem on a heroic subject before an audience, without the help of writing. This astonishing feat was possible because generations of epic poets had developed traditional language, phraseology, and motifs with which to tell the stories of the great Greek heroes. Such poetry placed a premium on the ability to create poems orally, not on the development of a unique individual style. Hence, any trace of the personality of the author of the *Iliad* and the *Odyssey* has vanished.

Greek epic poets may have sung their songs at the dinner gatherings of the aristocracy, as do the bards in the *Odyssey*, as well as to members of their own artisan class. How the *Iliad* and the *Odyssey* moved from oral performance to their final

written forms is not fully understood. The poems are clearly not an assemblage of stories stitched together by a collector. Since both poems develop organically around a central theme and exhibit a sophisticated handling of poetic techniques, they are most likely the creations of a single monumental composer at the end of a long poetic tradition.

In creating the *Iliad* and the *Odyssey*, Homer employed the various conventions of epic style in a skillful and flexible manner, which satisfied both aesthetic expectations and the need for fluent oral composition. The artificial dialect mixture of the poems was created for the epic and was never used by anyone in actual conversation. The mixture of dialect forms gives the language of the poems a unique "epic" quality and provides metrically convenient words for the poets to use in oral composition. Composition is also aided by ornamental epithets which are applied to divinities, people, and objects. Such adjectives not only satisfy metrical demands but also illuminate beautifully the unchanging nature of the heroic world. Thus, ships are "swift" even when standing still, and Odysseus is already "much-suffering" in the *Iliad*, before starting his ten-year trek home. Even the sequence of events in the poems is structured in a way which helps the poet compose aloud. Frequently repeated traditional scenes, such as arming for battle and sacrificing to the gods, possess a constant order of elements which is easily remembered. This regularity of events creates a strong sense that both nature and human life proceed along a carefully ordered path and makes anomalous behavior such as Achilles' seem especially jarring.

Even the major plot elements of both the *Iliad* and the *Odyssey* are very likely traditional. Both poems employ a "withdrawal-devastation-return" framework with a revenge motif at the end, a format typical of many epic poems. Scholars have found evidence for other earlier Greek epics which contained many of the thematic elements of both the *Iliad* and the *Odyssey*, but the Homeric poems are unique in their tight organization around one major theme: the *Iliad* around the wrath of Achilles, the *Odyssey* around the homecoming of Odysseus.

The action of the *Iliad* covers only fifty-three days in the last year of the ten-year siege of Troy, although the poet cleverly inserts references to the events of the previous decade which make the listeners believe they have experienced the entire war. The abduction of the Greek queen Helen by the

Trojan prince Paris forms the backdrop for the events of the *Iliad*, which takes as its subject the wrath of one individual, Achilles, the greatest Greek warrior at Troy, and the devastation it wreaks on him and all heroic society.

The leader of the Greek army, Agamemnon, has taken away Achilles' concubine after he is forced to give up his own. Achilles responds to this slight by laying down his arms, a correct response according to the heroic code of honor. Yet he errs when refusing the fabulous ransom Agamemnon offers him to return to battle. The result is devastation: Patroclus, Achilles' closest companion, dies at the hands of the Trojan hero Hector while trying to take Achilles' place. This catastrophe finally goads Achilles to return to battle. He is, however, now fighting not for the Greeks but for personal revenge, a crucial difference. He abandons the civilized humanity of the heroic code and crosses over into inhuman frenzy, which the poet likens to the uncontrollable force of nature. Although he kills Hector, the embodiment of the civilized humanity which he has left behind, he continues to rage out of control, until the gods intervene to persuade him to give Hector's body back to the aged king Priam. Thus, the *Iliad* is more than a tale of heroic exploits: It is a profound meditation on life and death, culture and nature, and individualism and society.

The *Odyssey* tells the story of the return of Odysseus to his wife, Penelope, and son, Telemachus, on the island of Ithaca after ten years of fighting at Troy. It is the only surviving story of many which narrated the experiences of the Greek heroes returning home after the Trojan War. Odysseus' return itself took ten years, but, by using a technique seen in the *Iliad*, the poet compresses the time frame of the *Odyssey* into forty days in the tenth year of the journey, while casting many backward glances over the events of the preceding decade. While the poem centers on the return of Odysseus from Troy, the content of the *Odyssey* is thematically more diverse than that of the *Iliad*, and its structure is correspondingly more complex. It contains four major themes: the journey of Odysseus on his way home, replete with fantastic monsters, beguiling sorceresses, and a trip to the underworld; a parallel journey of Telemachus, who is now twenty years old and trying to grow to adulthood despite an absent father; Odysseus' actual return to Ithaca and his winning back of home and wife; and his revenge, aided by his son and faithful retainers, on the suitors who were vying for Penelope's hand.

The amalgamation of all of these elements into a coherent whole is most skillfully accomplished. Frequent changes of scene and an exciting narrative of his adventures by Odysseus create suspense and keep the plot moving quickly.

The *Odyssey* paints a vivid picture of life in Greece. It focuses on the city-state Ithaca and, in particular, on the nuclear family represented by Odysseus, Penelope, and Telemachus—and includes moving portraits of slaves and other nonaristocratic characters. The center of attention, however, is always Odysseus, who is not a tragic hero such as Achilles or Hector. He is a survivor who lives by his wits and his tongue. He confronts death on a daily basis but is never in danger of dying before accomplishing his goals. In later Greek literature, Odysseus became a symbol of persuasion, trickery, and deceit.

The *Iliad* and the *Odyssey* thus focus intently on the role of the individual in society. This theme is rooted in the events of the eighth century, the very beginnings of classical Greek society. The great Mycenaean Greek kingdoms had collapsed by 1150 B.C. for reasons which are not understood but which probably included intense internecine warfare. The absence of the palace bureaucracies forced small separate groups of people to fend for themselves but ultimately allowed them to grow from 1150 to 800 B.C. into the city-states of classical Greece. The ninth and eighth centuries, during which the heroic epic tradition probably took shape, saw the formation of many city-states composed of individual households, much like that of Odysseus and in contrast to the extended Mycenaean family of the Trojan king Priam seen in the *Iliad*. Each member of such a household bore a great responsibility for its maintenance and, by extension, that of the city-state. Hence, the *Iliad* and the *Odyssey* devote much attention to the crucial question of the proper behavior of individuals in society.

An awareness of the common Greek heritage shared by all the city-states sprang up alongside the growth of the different separate political units. The Olympic Games, to which every city sent athletes, were founded in 776 B.C. The Panhellenic oracle at Delphi began dispensing political as well as personal advice around the same time. The Homeric epics, which record an expedition of many Greek heroes united against a common enemy, may be seen as both an affirmation of the connections between all the Greeks and support for the hero-founders of the new city-states.

Summary

Homer bequeathed to the West the beginnings of its literature. Countless works have been inspired and influenced by the epics, in which may be found the seeds of narrative, comedy, and tragedy. The sheer genius of the *Iliad* and the *Odyssey* becomes obvious in comparison with other epic poems which have survived from ancient Greece. Fragments of other epics, known collectively as the Epic Cycle, indicate that the Homeric epics were the originals around which the poems of the cycle were fashioned. These other poems were much shorter and, judging from the scanty remains, inferior in scope and style.

Homer also gave both history and religion to the ancient Greeks, and through them to Western civilization. Little has been said here about the gods mentioned in the poems, because humans are so clearly the focus of the poet's interest. The gods, who have the same emotions and social structure as the struggling mortals, appear frequently as mirrors for human activities and emotions, but there is one essential difference. The gods will never die, whereas death is the inevitable portion of every hero. Heroic life is merely a brief and shining prelude to a long and shadowy afterlife in Hades. Immortality for humans is obtainable only in heroic song. The gods' immortality underscores the mortality of the heroes, adding emphasis and pathos. The gods watch avidly the events unfolding on the Trojan plain, but they cannot rescue anyone—even their own offspring—from death when it is fated.

Bibliography

Clarke, Howard. *The Art of the Odyssey.* Englewood Cliffs, N.J.: Prentice-Hall, 1967. General introduction to the *Odyssey*, with a chapter comparing the *Iliad* and the *Odyssey*.

Ford, Andrew. *Homer: The Poetry of the Past.* Ithaca, N.Y.: Cornell University Press, 1992; London: Cornell University Press, 1994. Ford is concerned to situate the Homeric epics in their unique poetic context. In Homer poetry is viewed not as an artificial, "literary" art, but rather as the direct revelation of past events, given by the Muses through the medium of the poet. The aim of Homeric poetry is direct, immediate involvement of the audience in the poet's vision.

Homer. *The Iliad.* Translated by Richmond Lattimore. Chicago: University of Chicago Press, and London: Routledge, 1951. Literal translation of the *Iliad*, with a detailed introduction.

————. *The Odyssey.* Translated by Richmond Lattimore. New York: Harper and Row, 1967; London: Encyclopaedia Britannica, 1990. Similar to his translation of the *Iliad*, with an introduction.

Kirk, G. S. *The Songs of Homer.* Cambridge: Cambridge University Press, 1962. The standard introduction to the Homeric poems, focusing on their language and composition. Illustrated.

Nagy, Gregory. *The Best of the Achaeans.* Baltimore: Johns Hopkins University Press, 1979. Sophisticated but stimulating analysis of the hero in Greek civilization and how the language of Greek epic defines his role.

Schein, Seth. *The Mortal Hero: An Introduction to Homer's Iliad.* Berkeley: University of California Press, 1984. An introduction to a literary interpretation of the *Iliad.* Explores questions of mortality, the gods, and heroism in detail. Excellent references.

Snodgrass, Anthony. *Archaic Greece: The Age of Experiment.* Berkeley: University of California Press, and London: Dent, 1980. Economic and social history of the age in which the epics were composed, based on the archaeological evidence. Well illustrated.

Wace, Alan J. B., and Frank H. Stubbings, eds. *A Companion to Homer.* London: Macmillan, and New York: St. Martin's Press, 1962. Essays on language, transmission of the text, and especially the archaeological evidence pertaining to the Homeric poems, by authorities in each field. Slightly dated but still authoritative. Illustrated, with many references.

Julie A. Williams

HORACE
Quintus Horatius Flaccus

Born: December 8, 65 B.C.; Venusia, Italy
Died: November 27, 8 B.C.; Rome, Italy
Area of Achievement: Poetry
Contribution: The most important Roman lyric poet, Horace took an appealing, deceptively casual approach to poetry. His odes, epistles, and satires became a beloved source of proverbial wisdom and a model for Renaissance and neoclassical poets throughout Europe.

Early Life

Horace was born in Venusia, a military colony in southern Italy. Nothing is known of his mother or siblings. His father was a freed slave whose profitable post as an auctioneer's assistant enabled him to buy land and to send his son to school in Rome. There, with the sons of senators and knights, Horace was educated in the Greek classics. Horace asserts in his *Satires* (35, 30 B.C.) that he received better education from his father, who accompanied him on walks through Rome's bustling marketplace while commenting on the character, appearance, and manners of passersby.

Sometime in his late teens or early twenties, probably in 45, Horace went to the Academy in Athens to study moral philosophy. Since this education was unusual for a freedman's son, it is likely that Horace's father recognized his son's brilliance and wished to give him every chance for success. In Athens, Horace began to write Greek poetry. In 44, Marcus Brutus came to Athens after the assassination of Julius Caesar. He recruited young Romans studying there to fight with him against Caesar's successors, Marc Antony and Octavian. The call to fight for freedom and the Republic stirred Horace to join Brutus' forces in 43. Though young and inexperienced, he became military tribune (that is, an officer capable of commanding a legion) and probably rose at the same time to the social rank of knight. At the pivotal Battle of Philippi, in 42, Brutus was killed and his army defeated. Rather than continue a hopeless cause, Horace returned to Rome.

His prospects were not bright. He had chosen the losing side. His father was dead. The farm in Venusia had been confiscated for distribution to a loyal legionnaire or officer. Yet Horace still had equestrian rank and must have had some money because he soon purchased the post of scribe in the quaestor's office, where public financial records were kept. In 39, a general amnesty for Brutus' followers removed whatever stigma attached to Horace's military service.

While a scribe, Horace began writing verse again, Latin imitations of the satirical, witty Greek poet Archilochus. Horace and the poet Vergil were physical as well as poetic contrasts. Horace was ruddy-faced, short, and stout; Vergil was dark-haired, tall, and lean. A long friendship showed that these differences made them complements, not opposites.

Life's Work

What drew Horace and Vergil together was a common interest in poetry. Vergil was at work on the *Eclogues* (43-37 B.C.), idealized poems about rural life, while Horace was writing realistic, trenchant observations of urban mores. Though their topics differed, these young writers shared an interest in

the craft of poetry. Vergil was acquainted with Gaius Maecenas, one of Octavian's counselors, who acted as patron to promising poets. In 39 or 38, Vergil introduced Horace to Maecenas. At their second meeting Maecenas invited Horace to join his literary circle. Horace, still without a published poem, accepted the offer. The decision shaped the rest of his life.

In late 35 or early 34, Horace published the first book of *Satires*. It is a misleading title for most modern readers, who associate satire with ridicule and attack. To Horace, the word meant a mixture, or medley, indicating that the work lacked a narrative structure, consistent characters, and interrelated themes. Horace also referred to these poems as *sermones* (conversations), which suggests their casual tone and varied subject matter. One poem describes a trip with Vergil, another tells a ribald story about witches, a third is a fond remembrance of his father, a fourth a witty portrait of a boor. All the poems display a mastery of metrical form and reveal a good-humored and congenial persona. The poems are like conversations over dinner, and the poet is a most attractive host.

In 33, Maecenas rewarded Horace's skillful and popular poetry: He gave Horace land in the Sabine Valley. Prudently Horace leased most of it to tenant farmers and built himself a house. The so-called Sabine Farm became his beloved retreat from the world, where he lived simply but comfortably amid attentive servants and good friends, with leisure to concentrate on writing. Maecenas also gave Horace property in Rome and a house in Tibur. All the evidence indicates that Horace and Maecenas not only were mutually useful acquaintances but also possessed a deep friendship based upon a mutual love of literature.

Horace published two works in the year 30. One was a second book of *Satires*, less personal and more consciously literary in subject matter than the first book. This volume includes the famous story of the Country Mouse and the City Mouse as well as a parody of Homer's *Odyssey* (c. 800 B.C.). The second work was the *Epodes* (or "after-songs"), which was actually written ten or twelve years earlier. Shorter and more lyrical than *Satires*, these seventeen poems treat a miscellany of topics: the pains and pleasures of love, impatience with pretenders and sycophants, tribulations of the Civil War. The poems reflect a variety of moods as well as topics, but this variety does not result in incoherence. Rather, the contrasts create the sense of bal-

ance, the portrait of personality that cannot be moved from the golden mean either by life's follies or by its tragedies.

Horace himself testifies that these years were the happiest of his life. He spent most of the time at Sabine Farm, reading and composing. Maecenas' circle remained intact for more than a decade. Most educated Romans, including Octavian, who—after 27—called himself Augustus, admired Horace.

During this productive period Horace worked on the *Odes* (23, 13 B.C.) and the *Epistles* (c. 20, 13 B.C.). The *Odes* display Horace's poetic virtuosity: Eighty-eight poems in a variety of traditional and experimental meters demonstrate Horace's absolute control of language and his ability to suit expression to subject matter. Like previous works, the *Odes* treat a spectrum of political, personal, and social topics. Whatever the topic, the theme is that piety, moderation, and fellowship undergird the good life. The spirit of the *Odes* is autobiographical; the poems reflect Horace's contentment with life. Fortunately, contentment does not breed complacency or conceit in the poet. If life is good, it is not the poet's doing: Honest friends, a peaceful state, and kindly gods bestow this gift. It is somewhat surprising that Horace's contemporaries found the poems unsatisfactory, though perhaps that can be explained by the poems' unfamiliar style. Subsequent generations reversed the verdict and regarded the *Odes* as a personal and national masterpiece.

The *Epistles* return to the conversational tone of the early *Satires*. Addressed to friends, the poems engage Horace's companions one by one in reflection upon literary and philosophical topics. Perhaps the verses were a return to the atmosphere of the Academy, where the pleasurable speculation upon life's puzzles was interrupted by Brutus' politics. The *Epistles* are leisurely, intelligent poems—indeed, compliments, tributes, memorials to the discussions they record.

Ironically, the world these collections describe rapidly vanished. A plot against the life of Augustus was indirectly linked to Maecenas. He and his circle lost their privileged place near the ruler. Vergil died in 19, while Maecenas himself seems to have been distracted by a new favorite, the poet Sextus Propertius.

In 17, Augustus himself prompted Horace to begin writing again. Horace's relationship with Augustus was never easy. Though Horace admired

Augustus' efforts to reunify the country after the Civil War, he maintained his distance. Horace never flattered the emperor openly and obsequiously as other poets did, though Augustus teased him about the omission. In this year, Augustus declared that Rome, the world's capital, would hold the Secular Games. Augustus requested Horace to write a hymn for the gods' blessing. Horace's *Carmen Saeculare* (17 B.C.), sung by a chorus of twenty-seven girls and twenty-seven boys, prays that fertility, morality, tranquillity, and glory may be the gods' gifts to Rome. The final book of *Odes*, published in 13, repeats this idea of festivity and ritual as bonding devices of community and celebrates poetry as itself a festive ritual.

Horace's last work was a second book of *Epistles*, also published in 13. These three long poems discuss the art to which Horace devoted his life. The first epistle calls upon Augustus to be the patron of developing poets rather than to enshrine a set of classics. The second epistle is Horace's moving envoi to poetry: He senses that his career is done. The third epistle is the famous *Ars poetica* (*The Art of Poetry*), in which Horace advises both readers and writers on the appreciation of poetry. It contains opinions (for example, that poetry should be pleasing as well as instructive and that a poet should set a work aside for nine years before trying to publish it) that subsequent generations would take, in very un-Horatian fashion, as a consistent philosophy of criticism. Maecenas died in the year 8 B.C., without having regained Augustus' full confidence. Horace died within months of his friend and was buried beside him.

Summary

Horace was spokesman for a generation of the Roman leadership class. He expressed its fears, its hopes, its discontents, and its pleasures. Because his poems interwove autobiography, social commentary, philosophy, and politics, they provided succeeding generations with insights, precepts, and bons mots on topics of enduring interest. Horace was remembered, therefore, in fragments. Readers quoted him and poets imitated him on particular topics (love, sex, the gods, wine, friendship) which overlapped with their own concerns. Horace appealed to different audiences for different reasons: to second century Romans for patriotism, to medieval monks for piety, to seventeenth century gentlemen for rakish self-indulgence.

Beyond the classical period Horace was most influential among aristocratic writers in European countries between 1500 and 1850. He appealed to them on several levels. His character showed how a congenial, generous temperament draws together like-minded and similarly talented men. His biography showed that one could become important and yet live independent of the world's demands. His career showed that art and politics were allies in fostering a sense of national identity and culture. His secular philosophy made clear that one could live morally without religious faith—an especially important idea to educated Europeans, who, for three centuries, watched Christian countries war with one another and split into hostile denominations. Thus, Horace was a poet whose life and art illustrated universal themes. When a society made urbanity and leisured culture its goals, its poets chose Horace as their guide.

In the twentieth century, Horace attracts attention for an additional reason. Modern scholars appreciate him as a verbal craftsman; his work is valued for the scope of the whole more than for the cleverness or beauty of the parts. Criticism today tends to value poets less as seers and legislators of mankind than as fabricators, the makers of meaning out of confusion. Contemporary critics study Horace's work in search of the unity in each volume of *Odes*, *Epistles*, and *Epodes*. The diversity of subjects and moods is no longer the sign of miscellaneous disquisition but the sign of subtle coherence. Critics aim to recover the poet's reason for grouping his poems and to gauge their aesthetic impact upon the reader. Like Shakespeare, like Cervantes, like every great author, Horace is always freshest to those who encounter him again and again.

Bibliography

Commager, Steele. *The Odes of Horace*. New Haven, Conn.: Yale University Press, 1962; London: University of Oklahoma Press, 1995. Commager's book is widely regarded as the most substantial, incisive commentary on Horace's verse in English. Commager approaches Horace as a "professional poet," one committed to art as a vocation. Horace's distinctive characteristic is that he writes poetry about poetry, as if he wants to define the idea and demonstrate verbal craftmanship at the same time.

Davis, Gregson. *Polyhymnia: The Rhetoric of Horatian Lyric Discourse*. Berkeley: University of

California Press, 1991. This book approaches Horace's lyric poetry from the standpoint of rhetoric and form. Davis argues that there is a distinctively "lyric" mode of discourse, though Horace expands its purview by introducing elements of epic and elegy.

Fraenkel, Eduard. *Horace*. Oxford: Clarendon Press, 1957; New York: Oxford University Press, 1980. This important book is for the serious student. Fraenkel approaches Horace as a poet who wrote for a few highly educated men rather than for general readers. He traces the development of his poetry from the experimental epodes and satires to the mature epistles and odes.

Hadas, Moses. *A History of Latin Literature*. New York: Columbia University Press, 1952; London: Columbia University Press, 1964. The chapter on Horace demonstrates why he is the most beloved of Roman poets. It articulates the virtues of common sense, good fellowship, and literary pleasure that generations of European writers have found in the poetry.

Highet, Gilbert. *The Classical Tradition: Greek and Roman Influences on Western Literature*. Oxford: Clarendon Press, and New York: Oxford University Press, 1949. Through judicious use of the index, the curious student can survey European attitudes toward Horace's poetry since the Renaissance. Highet is an opinionated and lively critic who inspires a return to primary texts.

Horace. *The Complete Works*. Translated by Charles E. Passage. New York: Frederick Ungar Publishing Co., 1983. This volume offers an unusual translation: without rhyme, in the original meter, with notes about the context of and allusions in each poem. Passage makes Horace accessible to the new reader and offers a fresh perspective to readers familiar with other translations.

Johnson, W. R. *Cornell Studies in Classical Philology*. Vol. 53, *Horace and the Dialectic of Freedom: Readings in "Epistles 1."* Ithaca, N.Y.: Cornell University Press, 1993. Johnson offers a witty and provocative reading of Horace's Epistles, claiming that poems traditionally seen as unproblematic in fact suggests tensions concerning the quality of Horace's "freedom" in light of compromises with the Augustan regime.

Lyne, R. O. A. M. *Horace: Behind the Public Poetry*. New Haven, Conn.: Yale University Press, 1995. In a series of close readings of Horace's poetry, Lyne attempts to demonstrate the ways in which the poet subtly undermined his apparent praise for Augustus. Most attention is devoted to the *Odes*, but there is some consideration of the *Satires* and *Epistles*.

Newman, J. K. *Augustus and the New Poetry*. Brussels: Latomus, revue d'études latines, 1967. This important book discusses the literary and social background to Horace's poetry. In the light of the rivalry between the Hellenistic, Alexandrian school of poetry and the old Roman traditions, Horace seems unsure of his own poetic purposes. Sometimes heavy going because Newman frequently argues with previous commentators, this study nevertheless richly repays close reading.

Noyes, Alfred. *Horace: A Portrait*. New York: Sheed and Ward, 1947; as *A Portrait of Horace*. London: Sheed and Ward, 1947. Himself a poet, Noyes tries to re-create Horace's real experiences from the topics, persons, and places recorded in the poetry. Noyes's reading is, therefore, fascinating, idiosyncratic, and largely unreliable. Noyes detects a proto-Christian sensibility in Horace that anticipates the end of the pagan worldview.

Perret, Jacques. *Horace*. Translated by Bertha Humez. New York: New York University Press, 1964. A good work for the general reader beginning the study or reading of Horace. Perret mixes biography and literary criticism without sentimentalism or pedantry. Perret delights in Horace's complex personality and multifarious poetry. The book contains a lengthy (though dated) annotated bibliography.

Putnam, Michael C. J. *Artifices of Eternity*. Ithaca, N.Y.: Cornell University Press, 1986; London: Cornell University Press, 1996. Putnam presents a detailed analysis of Horace's last work, the final book of *Odes*. Traditionally the fourth book is considered not unified and is said to show Horace bowing to Augustus' influence. Putnam argues that Horace remakes Augustus as the poet sees him. The approach has interesting biographical implications for interpreting Horace's last years.

Reckford, Kenneth J. *Horace*. New York: Twayne Publishers, 1969. Reckford's brief, appreciative study attempts to chart the growth of Horace's imagination and thought by a survey of his poetry. The emphasis is on theme rather than poetic technique. Some of Reckford's interpretations are more impressionistic than scholarly. The author provides useful notes and bibliography.

Rudd, Niall. "Horace." In *The Cambridge History of Classical Literature*, edited by E. J. Kenney and W. V. Clausen, vol. 2. Cambridge and New York: Cambridge University Press, 1982. Rudd attacks the tendency to see linear development in Horace's poetry and consistency in his opinions. Rudd argues that Horace was exploring new genres in Latin poetry and that the poems contain contradictory opinions and values.

Rudd, Niall, ed. *Horace 2000: A Celebration. Essays for the Bimillenium*. Ann Arbor: University of Michigan Press, and London: Duckworth, 1993. A collection of seven papers on various aspects of Horace's life and art. The essays raise the question of how reliable Horace's own information about his life is. Titles include "Horace in the Thirties" and "Horace and Augustus: Poetry and Policy."

White, Peter. *Promised Verse: Poets in the Society of Augustan Rome*. Cambridge, Mass.: Harvard University Press, 1993. White offers a thorough investigation of the literary and social milieux in which Horace and other Augustan poets moved and wrote. He is primarily concerned with structures of literary patronage, and he contends that the relationship between poets and their patrons (including Augustus) should be seen not as one involving coercion and extorted praise, but in terms of mutual services and exchange of benefits.

Wilkinson, L. P. *Horace and His Lyric Poetry*. 2d ed. Cambridge: Cambridge University Press, 1951. Though this study is intended for the student who can read Latin, the first four chapters are accessible to the general reader. Wilkinson's Horace is neither the patriotic versifier of Augustus' policies nor the contented gentleman farmer addicted to ease and companionship. Wilkinson provides valuable summaries of Horace's thoughts on subjects ranging from religion to love to the state to poetry.

Robert M. Otten

HSIEH LING-YÜN

Born: 385; Commandery of Ch'en, Yang-chia, Honan Province, China
Died: 433; Kuang-chou, Nan-hai, China
Areas of Achievement: Literature and philosophy
Contribution: Ling-yün was the first and greatest of China's nature poets, the founder of the school of *shan-shui* verse. A philosophical syncretist, he blended elements of Confucianism and Taoism with Buddhism to produce a uniquely Chinese synthesis.

Early Life

A scion of one of China's most powerful and illustrious aristocratic families of the Six Dynasties (420-589), Hsieh Ling-yün was born in Honan Province. As secretary of the Imperial Library, his father was the least prepossessing member of the Hsieh clan, which had included a host of distinguished poets, calligraphers, and high-ranking imperial officials. The Liu, Hsieh Ling-yün's mother's family, was distinguished by its calligraphers, notably Wang Hsi-chih (321-379). In the light of his familial background, Ling-yün surprised no one by his precocity. As a small child, he was placed under temporary adoption in Hang-chou with Tu Ming-shih, a devout Taoist. Calligraphy was an integral part of Tu Ming-shih's Taoism, and Ling-yün proved an apt pupil. The boy remained with his foster family in the splendid aristocratic environs of Hang-chou until he was fifteen.

In 399, a rebel faction led by Sun En invaded Chekiang and Kiangsu provinces, and in the ensuing struggle Ling-yün's father was killed. His family decided to send Ling-yün to the safety of their house in the capital, Chienk'ang (now Nanking). There he came under the decisive influence of his uncle, Hsieh Hun, a handsome, aristocratic figure who was recognized as one of China's foremost poets. Married to an imperial Chin princess and secure in worldly ways, Hun had drawn together a lively, exclusive literary salon, into which Ling-yün was inducted. He was soon recognized as a stellar member. The precocious Ling-yün cut a swath around Chien-k'ang even in an age notorious for social ostentation and eccentricity. He had inherited the title of Duke of K'ang-lo; as such, he drew revenues from more than three thousand households. Hsieh Ling-yün affected foppish dress, extravagant behavior, and a languor that challenged the efforts of scores of attendants.

Dukedom also brought government appointments: He was made administrator to the grand marshal and, more important, administrator in the Redaction Office, a post that ensnared him in the political fortunes of Liu Yï. It was thus that he was forced to endure a chain of misfortunes that dramatically altered the course of his life.

Life's Work

When Ling-yün entered service with Liu Yï, Yï had emerged as the most distinguished leader of a revolt against another rebel, Huan Hsüan, who founded the abortive Ch'u Dynasty in 404. Yï's victories against Huan brought him the dukedom of Nan-p'ing as well as a military governor generalship, these posts devolving upon him from Liu Yü, the titular restorer of the Chin Dynasty in 405. Ling-yün's fortunes might have been assured if Liu Yï had accepted Liu Yü's political supremacy. He did not. Thus, between 405 and 411, a series of complex plots and inevitable military clashes between partisans of the two men resulted in Yï's defeat and disgrace. Through the course of these events, Ling-yün served on his staff, ultimately suffering the consequences of his fall. Moved to the periphery of power, Yï, with Ling-yün in tow, was obliged in 412 to establish his headquarters at Chiang-ling in Hupei Province. There, Ling-yün's life changed decisively.

While posted to Chiang-ling, Ling-yün visited the famed Buddhist center at the nearby Mount Lu. The Eastern Grove Monastery, which eventually became the most influential southern center of Chinese Buddhism, had been founded by Hui-yüan (334-416), himself the principal disciple of Tao-an (312-385), who had been the first to emphasize the basic distinctions between Indian Buddhism—essentially an alien doctrine—and the casual versions of Buddhism that had been integrated with mainstream Chinese culture. Hui-yüan devoted himself to making the Chinese aware of the foreignness of Buddhist thought, hoping to make the purer form of its teachings and practices acceptable to well-educated Chinese aristocrats. Ling-yün found that this transcendental, poeticized Buddhism, with its many concrete images, appealed to him far more than the intellectualized Buddhism common to the capital and his native region.

Moreover, Ling-yün's poetic sensibilities were overwhelmed by the beauty of the Eastern Grove's setting—craggy, forested mountain peaks enshrouded in mists, lush gorges filled with tumbled boulders and riven by pure, roaring streams—and the austere way of life of its devotees. The contrast with the corruptions and hostilities of court life was compelling. In his poetic "Dirge for Hui-yüan," Ling-yün revealed his yearning to immerse himself in Buddhist study and to accept a place even as the least of Hui-yüan's disciples.

As Ling-yün was falling under the spell of Eastern Grove Buddhism, however, the fact that he and the Hsieh family had thrown in their lot with the wrong leader was becoming all too clear. Liu Yü, having consolidated his position, crushed Liu Yï, Ling-yün's mentor, on December 31, 412; Yï eventually was killed. Liu Yü spared Ling-yün, however, and coopted him into his service in 413, first as administrator to the commander-in-chief, then as assistant director of the Imperial Library. During the time that Ling-yün held these posts, the Chinese monk Fa-Hsien, after fourteen years in Afghanistan, returned to Chien-k'ang rich in Buddhist lore. He reported having seen a gigantic image of Buddha, in a cave, shining with brilliant light and casting mysterious shadows. Hoping to replicate this image, Hui-yüan arranged a similar shrine for the Eastern Grove. Painted shades of green on silk, the Buddha image was consecrated on May 27, 412. As a noted poet and calligrapher, Ling-yün was invited to produce a poem that he entitled "Inscription on the Buddha-Shadow," one of his earliest surviving metaphysical verses.

As always, Ling-yün's fortunes were linked to political events. In 415, he was dismissed from office, and the following year Hui-yüan died. Ling-yün's fortunes improved, however, with new administrative posts. More important was Yü's liberation of Ch'ang-an, the center of Northern Buddhism. Many of its monks thereupon traveled southward, bringing about the mingling of the two schools of Buddhist thought from which a distinctive Chinese version was to emerge. Amid this intellectual and religious excitement, however, Ling-yün was held responsible for eruption of a scandal and was again dismissed. Nothing is known of him for the next eighteen months. In 419, Liu Yü strangled the imbecilic Emperor An, ending the Chin Dynasty and allowing his assumption of power as Wu-ti, first of the Sung Dynasty.

In accordance with customary treatment of aristocrats after a coup, Ling-yün was demoted to the rank of marquess over only one hundred households. Subsequently, the rise of his cousin Hui as the chief of the emperor's henchmen and the courtly influence of a number of other relatives and friends drew him into succession politics. Unhappily, Ling-yün's romanticism, imprudence, and willful personality led him to back the wrong forces. Shortly after Yi-fu's ascension to the throne, the clique with which Ling-yün associated was disgraced. Ill and impoverished, he was banished to the lowly post of grand warden to Yung-chia, a backward town in Chekiang Province.

The mournful poems written during Ling-yün's exile from the capital reveal a distressed man confronting reality in full maturity. Middle-aged, bereft of significant income, beyond the pale of elusive political power, stricken by tuberculosis, and plagued by ulcerous legs, he had only his literary talents and religious beliefs to sustain him. Indeed, in accordance with esoteric Taoist and Buddhist teachings, he thereafter sought consolation in a search for truth in the wilderness into which he was exiled. The two months of hard travel that it took him to reach Yung-chia evoked a series of fine nature poems, elegantly descriptive and brooding. Upon arrival, he also commenced his "Pien-tsung Lun" (c. 423-430; "On Distinguishing What Is Essential"), a major philosophical work.

Many earlier Chinese philosophers had wrestled with problems examined in Ling-yün's "On Distinguishing What Is Essential," and in this sense it is a work of many authors. This fact, however, does not diminish the value of Ling-yün's contribution to Chinese philosophical discourse. Two versions of truth preoccupied him: truth that was acquired gradually and truth that was revealed instantaneously. Many Buddhists believed that an arrival at truth (Nirvana) required several lengthy stages of spiritual and bodily preparation, involving faith, study, and good works. That, Ling-yün acknowledged, was the gradualism that Siddhārtha Gautama, the Buddha, had taught. Yet Buddha, he argued, had used that explanation when teaching Indians, a people with a facility for learning but with scant predilection for intuitive understanding. Had Buddha preached to the Chinese, a people who had difficulty in acquiring learning but who were masters of intuitive comprehension, his message would have been different. Ultimate enlightenment—a state of non-being, or *wu*—although doubtless assisted by learning, would have been presented by Buddha to the Chinese as attainable in a flash, by a quantum leap in faith.

As his health improved and his literary reputation increased, Ling-yün also became more intriguing because of his new character. He was neglectful of his official duties, despite some efforts to plant mulberry trees, improve local agriculture, and undertake hydraulic works. His change in priorities had to do less with an implicit criticism of the state than with an honest desire to withdraw from worldly vexations in a mystic pursuit of truth. The climbing boots with removable studs that he designed for expeditions into the mountains became fashionable at court, and a broad-brimmed peasant hat, knapsack, and staff came to be his personal hallmarks. Soon, he resigned from office. His Taoism, which promised immortality for the body as well as the soul, required a spartan regimen of yoga, breathing exercises, and preparations of drugs, herbs, and elixirs. His "Fu of the Homeward Road" and "On Leaving My District" signaled his return in 424 to the decayed family estate at Shihning. There, moving toward a richer inner life, he labored assiduously in the mountainous wilderness. During the next several years, a number of monks joined him in his idyllic anchorite life. His continuous investigations into Buddhist meanings made him the most learned layman of his day.

The regard in which Ling-yün's poetry was held, added to the renown of his family name, made him useful to Emperor Wen upon his ascension to power. Ling-yün's presence not only would grace the court with a leading poet and calligrapher but also would solidify support for the emperor among many who had wavered. Accordingly, Ling-yün was offered the directorship of the Imperial Library. Since rejection would have constituted an affront to the emperor and meant peril for his friends, he accepted reluctantly. For several years, he collected and collated documents, including major Buddhist sutras; he wrote poems and painted for the emperor. Court life wearied him, however, and in spite of an impending promotion, he begged a sick leave, which in 428 allowed a return to Shihning. He conceived of himself during this time as free from official obligations and lived healthily and actively as a result, but the emperor viewed his conduct as defiant. Eventually, Ling-yün fell afoul of conflicts among the local gentry. In serious danger, he begged Wen-ti's forgiveness, and for a time the emperor protected him while he helped translate major sutras of Mahayana Buddhism into Chinese. Even his translations, however, were offensive to sectarians; the emperor found him a liability, and he was exiled to the wilds of Kiangsi Province. There Ling-yün once again courted disaster by engaging in defiant conduct. Falsely implicated in a rebellious plot, he was called to Nanhai in 433. Philosophical, courageous, and aristocratic to the end, he was publicly executed the same year; he was buried in Kuei-chi, among the mountains he loved.

Summary

Of the thousands of Hsieh Ling-yün's writings and poems, relatively few survive. Those extant clearly confirm his repute as China's greatest nature poet. Nature poetry—descriptive, mystical, impressionistic, and simultaneously reflective and mood-stimulating—in Ling-yün's hands, was a disciplined, highly developed art form, particularly the five-word poem and the *yueh-fu*. Along with Pao Chao and T'ao Yün-ming, he was in his own time—and has continued to be—recognized as one of the greatest poets in a uniquely Chinese genre.

As the most learned Buddhist layman of his day, Hsieh Ling-yün exerted a major influence—through his poetry, calligraphy, essays, translations, associations, and later anchorite life-style—in the Sinicization of Buddhism. His profound understanding of Buddhism, always melded subtly with his Confucianism and Taoism, allowed him to translate and reinterpret main tenets of the religion for a distinctive Chinese context. Only a quintessential Chinese could have accomplished this task.

Bibliography

Bingham, Woodbridge. *The Founding of the T'ang Dynasty.* Baltimore, Md.: Waverly Press, 1941. Good background on the fall of the Sui Dynasty and early T'ang, with observations on contributions of the Sung. Lacks critical balance, but is accessible and gives the reader an accurate sense of the importance of the period. Limited bibliography; useful appendices.

Frodsham, J. D. *The Murmuring Stream: The Life and Works of the Chinese Nature Poet Hsieh Ling-yun (385-433), Duke of K'ang-Lo.* 2 vols. Kuala Lumpur and London: University of Malaya Press, 1967. Definitive scholarly study; eminently readable. Volume 1 is largely biographical; volume 2 translates and examines Ling-yün's poetry extensively. Helpful footnotes throughout. Adequate appendices and index.

Fung Yu-Lan. *A History of Chinese Philosophy.* Translated by Derk Bodde. 2 vols. Princeton,

N.J.: Princeton University Press, 1953. Chapter 7 of the second volume of this excellent scholarly work carefully examines various aspects of Buddhism and Ling-yün's role and influence in its interpretations. Splendid comparative chronological tables of the period of classical learning; informative notes throughout; superb bibliography; fine index.

Clifton K. Yearley
Kerrie L. MacPherson

HSÜN-TZU

Born: c. 313 B.C.; Chao, China
Died: After 238 B.C.; Lan-ling, China
Area of Achievement: Philosophy
Contribution: Through his development and modification of Confucian teachings, Hsün-tzu built a synthesized and more realistic foundation for Confucian ideology that was influential throughout China during the Han Dynasty.

Early Life

Although Hsün-tzu is undoubtedly a great figure in Chinese philosophy, the basic facts of his life are still controversial among scholars. According to most Chinese scholars, he was born in the northern state of Chao around 313 B.C., and the period of his activities as a philosopher and politician covers sixty years, from 298 to 238. The most reliable sources about his life are his own writings, published posthumously, and Ssu-ma Ch'ien's *Shih chi* (c. 90 B.C.). Yet almost no information about his early life, his education, or even his family background can be found in these early sources, which provide an account of his life beginning at the age of fifty, when he first visited the state of Ch'i and joined a distinguished group of scholars from various philosophical schools at the Chi-hsia Academy. This lack of information about his early life prompts some modern scholars to doubt the accuracy of the *Shih chi* and suggest that Hsün-tzu first visited the Chi-hsia Academy at the age of fifteen, not fifty. These scholars contend that either Hsün-tzu's age was erroneously recorded in the first place or the *Shih chi* text was corrupted.

Life's Work

Whether Hsün-tzu first appeared on the stage of history at fifty or fifteen does not change much of his historical role, for he did not really affect his contemporaries or his immediate environment during his lifetime. Like his predecessors in the Confucian school, Confucius and Mencius specifically, Hsün-tzu traveled from state to state, trying to persuade the rulers of Ch'i, Ch'u, Chao, and even the Legalist Ch'in to adopt his brand of Confucian statecraft. The dating of his various visits to these states is again an area of endless academic debate.

There are, however, two reliable historical dates in Hsün-tzu's public career. In 255, he was invited by Lord Ch'un-shen of Ch'u to serve as the magis-trate of Lan-ling. He was soon forced to resign the post when Lord Ch'un-shen gave credence to some slanderous rumors about the potential danger of the benevolent Confucian policy. Hsün-tzu then left for his native Chao. He stayed as an honored guest in the Chao court until Lord Ch'un-shen apologized for his suspicion and invited him to resume the magistrateship. Hsün-tzu remained in the position until 238, the year Lord Ch'un-shen was assassinated. Hsün-tzu was immediately dismissed from office, and he died in Lan-ling, probably soon after the coup.

The most immediate impact of Hsün-tzu on the political situation of the ancient Chinese world came, ironically, from his two best students, Han-fei-tzu and Li Ssu. Both men deviated from his teachings of Confucian benevolence and turned his emphasis on pragmatic sociopolitical programming into realpolitik. Han-fei-tzu became a synthesizer of Legalist thought, and Li Ssu became a prime minister who helped Emperor Cheng set up a totalitarian state after China was unified.

Hsün-tzu's greatest contribution to Chinese civilization lies in the field of philosophy, or, more generally, in the intellectual formation of Chinese sociopolitical behavior. His writings were perhaps compiled by himself in his later years but were definitely supplemented with a few chapters from his disciples. The standard edition of Hsün-tzu's works is the end product of a Han scholar, Liu Hsiang, who collated and edited the available sources into thirty-two chapters. Since Hsün-tzu lived through a period of fierce political strife, constant warfare, and tremendous social change on the eve of China's unification (also the golden age of Chinese philosophy known as the period of the Hundred Schools), his approach to the social and ethical issues of Confucian philosophy was markedly more realistic than those of Confucius and Mencius. In his defense of Confucian doctrine, he not only refuted the arguments and programs of other schools but also criticized the idealistic strain of thinking within his own camp, particularly in Mencius' philosophy. With an admirable command of scholarship and a powerful mind for critical analysis, Hsün-tzu demonstrated the Confucian way of thinking in a most systematic and pragmatic manner.

In opposition to Mencius' contention that human nature is innately good and man need only go back to his original psychological urges to achieve goodness and righteousness, Hsün-tzu states that human nature is evil and that only through education can man distinguish himself from animals. Despondent as it appears, Hsün-tzu's conception of human nature is quite complex and far removed from pessimism. For him, human nature—though evil—does not determine human destiny, for man has a capacity for reasoning and learning and for attaining a higher and more civilized order. That man has created civilization and sloughed off his barbarism is clear testimony to the possibility of a brighter future for mankind, as long as the civilizing order is maintained and continued. The whole process of education and socialization thus becomes the focus of Hsün-tzu's ethical concern.

It seems that when Hsün-tzu addresses the question of human nature, he has no preconceived illusions and deals squarely with human psychology as such. The evil of which he speaks is simply a composite body of animal drives and has no likeness to the Judeo-Christian concept of Original Sin. With such a no-nonsense and down-to-earth approach, he is interested in human nature less as an ontological issue than as an epistemological one. His particular emphasis on "artificial endeavor" for humanity also attests this interest, which some scholars describe as a "moral epistemology."

Hsün-tzu's interest in education and socialization centers on the Confucian concept of *li*, which has been translated in different contexts as propriety, decorum, rite, and etiquette. It is Hsün-tzu's belief that proper social behavior is foundational for moral gentlemen and that institutionalized rites regulate human relations for a better society. Thus, education is not only a way of acquiring external knowledge for its own sake but also a process of internalizing all the knowledge for the molding of a good and moral person. On the other hand, society is not merely a background against which one develops his intellectual faculty or moral character: Society is the main source of personality development. Through interaction between the individual self and the social norm, a functioning structure takes shape and reveals a pattern of *li* which serves as the very basis of social order.

How did *li* first come into existence? Confucius did not talk about its origin. Mencius was not interested in it. For Hsün-tzu, however, this question was of primary importance. In his treatise on *li*, Hsün-tzu offers the following explanation:

Man is born with desires. If his desires are not satisfied for him, he cannot but seek some means to satisfy them himself. If there are no limits and measures of regulation in his seeking, then he will inevitably fall to wrangling with other men. From wrangling comes disorder and from disorder comes exhaustion. The ancient kings hated such disorder, and therefore they institutionalized *li* and righteousness in order to define the relationship between men, to train men's desires and to provide for their satisfaction.

This explanation supports his argument that human nature is evil and also shows his concern for law and order.

For Confucius and Mencius, *li* is the internalized moral code that impels people to exhibit proper social behavior; it has nothing to do with the penal code, or law, imposed by government from outside to regulate social order. Hsün-tzu's practical concern for institutionalized law and order greatly transformed this Confucian concept of *li*. Confucius and Mencius could not bear to see a society's peace and order being enforced by law, while Hsün-tzu would acquiesce on this practical matter. Hsün-tzu, however, was by no means a Legalist entrusting the programming of social order entirely to the institution of law; he always placed the benevolence of the ruling class, the moral behavior maintained by a gentlemanly social elite, and the education of the people ahead of the enforcement of law, a necessary evil.

Hsün-tzu's concept of nature also complements his realistic approach to social and ethical issues. He believed that nature exists independent of human will. Heavenly matters have nothing to do with social and ethical issues, and, therefore, human beings are solely responsible for their behavior. This attitude underlies logically his idea that human nature is evil and that the good is the product of man's artificial endeavor. It also implies the unlimited potential of "evil-natured" mankind to do good and better the human world, because there is no supernatural force to hinder such a human endeavor. In this sense, Hsün-tzu should be taken seriously as an ardent optimist with regard to human progress.

Summary

During his lifetime, Hsün-tzu did not have any major effect on historical events. War, suffering, and political intrigue continued in his country. It was during this time of chaos and disintegration that Hsün-tzu developed his systematic reinterpretation of the Confucian tradition. If the unification of China and the institutionalization of the Legalist program toward the end of the third century B.C. can only be partly credited to his students Han-fei-tzu and Li Ssu, at least Hsün-tzu can claim a lion's share in the formation of the Confucian system during the Han period, after the Legalist Ch'in Dynasty collapsed. This Han Confucian system, with its strong emphasis on the blending of practical sociopolitical institutions with moral concerns, has served as the foundation of Chinese social and political norms for two millennia.

Bibliography

Cua, A. S. *Ethical Argumentation: A Study in Hsün Tzu's Moral Epistemology.* Honolulu: University of Hawaii Press, 1985. Contains a detailed and stimulating analysis of Hsün-tzu's ethical theory and the rationale and argumentative discourse in his philosophy. An in-depth study of an important but rarely touched area of Hsün-tzu's thought. With a bibliography, notes, and an index.

Dubs, Homer H. *Hsüntze: The Moulder of Ancient Confucianism.* London: A. Probsthain, 1927; New York: Paragon Book Gallery, 1966. A systematic study of Hsün-tzu's life and all aspects of his philosophy, this work is based on traditional Chinese scholarship and contains lengthy quotations from Hsün-tzu's writings. It is scholarly but quite cumbersome in explicating major Confucian concepts; it is also very disorganized. With notes and an index.

Hsün-tzu. *Basic Writings.* Translated by Burton Watson. New York: Columbia University Press, 1963. Contains a basically reliable translation of ten chapters from Hsün-tzu. With a useful outline of early Chinese history, annotative note and an index.

———. *The Works of Hsüntze.* Translated by Homer H. Dubs. London: Confucius, 1927; New York: Paragon Book Gallery, 1928. Still the most complete English translation of Hsün-tzu, it contains only nineteen chapters from the original book of thirty-two chapters. With an out-of-date introduction on ancient Chinese history, good textual notes, lexical explanations, and useful marginalia.

———. *Xunzi: A Translation and Study of the Complete Works.* Vol. 1. Translated by John Knoblock. Stanford, Calif.: Stanford University Press, 1988. This volume inaugurates a set of annotated translations and full-scale studies of the complete works of Hsün-tzu. Contains the first six chapters of Hsün-tzu. With a glossary, notes, a bibliography, and an index.

Munro, Donald J. *The Concept of Man in Early China.* Stanford, Calif.: Stanford University Press, 1969. A narrowly focused but valuable study of an important topic in early Chinese philosophy. It contains useful sections on Hsün-tzu. With a glossary, notes, a bibliography, and an index.

Schwartz, Benjamin I. *The World of Thought in Ancient China.* Cambridge, Mass.: Harvard University Press, 1985. A remarkable study in the field of ancient Chinese thought, this book is scholarly but never dull. It presents all the major issues in clear language and compares them with Western philosophical concepts without losing their original meanings. The chapter on Mencius and Hsün-tzu is informative. With a bibliography, notes, and an index.

Pei-kai Cheng

HYPATIA

Born: c. A.D. 370; probably Alexandria

Died: A.D. 415; Alexandria

Areas of Achievement: Mathematics, philosophy, and science

Contribution: The last of the great pagan scientists, Hypatia is best known to history for the manner of her death, which has caused her to be regarded as a symbol of courage in the face of an oppressive Christian Church.

Early Life

Almost nothing is known about Hypatia's early life. Ancient Rome did not have the elaborate systems of record-keeping found in the modern world, and no one in Hypatia's own time considered her—a woman and a scientist, not a warrior or politician—worthy of biographical attention. Although she made significant contributions to at least three fields of study, Hypatia has always been in the unusual position of being more famous for the way she died than for what she accomplished in life. While many legends about her early life have sprung up over the centuries, none are considered reliable sources of information about Hypatia's youth.

What is known is that she was the daughter of the pagan Theon, an important astronomer and mathematician in Alexandria. Alexandria, the third largest city in the Holy Roman Empire, had once been the intellectual center of Greece and was the home of the first university three hundred years before the time of Christ. Mathematics was taught then by Euclid, whose ideas about plane geometry are still at the foundation of basic geometry courses more than two thousand years later.

Seven hundred years after Euclid, Theon was teaching mathematics in Alexandria and writing books of commentary on ancient mathematics. He may also have written several books on the occult. At the time of Hypatia's birth, the Roman Empire was suspicious of Greek mathematics and attempted to suppress it. The life of a pagan scholar was intellectually exciting but politically dangerous.

The traditional date for Hypatia's birth is 370, although most scholars now believe that she must have been born earlier. Nothing is known of her mother. Some stories tell that Theon supervised her complete education, demanding that she discipline her mind and body. According to this version of her life, Theon developed a rigorous system of exercises Hypatia performed every day and oversaw her training in public speaking and rhetoric. Probably he taught her mathematics himself. According to legend, Hypatia was Theon's most talented student, surpassing her teacher and eventually becoming his collaborator. She apparently never married but devoted herself to her studies.

Life's Work

Eventually Hypatia became a university lecturer herself, teaching mathematics and astronomy. According to historical accounts left by Socrates Scholasticus (c. 379-450), a contemporary of Hypatia, she was a charismatic teacher who attracted the best students from Asia, Africa, and Europe. They were drawn to her intelligence, her legendary beauty, and her reputation as an oracle.

In Hypatia's time, mathematics was a different type of inquiry than it is today. Although it dealt with the relationships between geometric shapes, such as spheres, ellipses, and cones, mathematics was used to discover the composition of the universe. A series of mathematical problems might

seek to reveal such things as the locations of the planets or the location of the soul. The discipline was not far removed from astronomy, which was similar to what the modern world would consider to be astrology.

Although few of Hypatia's writings survive, much is known about her research, because descriptions of her work do survive in the form of letters and histories written by her students and followers. Her most important work was a thirteen-volume commentary on the *Arithmetica* by Diophantus, who is sometimes called the "father of algebra." Diophantus, who lived in Alexandria in the second century A.D., was interested in equations that can be solved in more than one way, which are now known as "indeterminate" or "Diophantine" equations. He also studied quadratic equations. Hypatia proposed some new problems and new solutions to complement Diophantine's work. A fragment of her commentary *On the Astronomical Canon of Diophantus* was found in the Vatican in the fifteenth century.

Her second major work was the eight-volume *On the Conics of Apollonius*. Apollonius, who lived in Alexandria in the third century B.C., was most interested in the geometry of cones, especially because conic sections such as the ellipse and the parabola could explain planetary orbits. Her commentary presents Apollonius's difficult concepts in a more accessible form, suitable for her students, and supplements the earlier work. Hypatia's text was the last important consideration of conic sections until the seventeenth century. Other writings thought to be Hypatia's include a commentary on Ptolemy's great second century compilation of all that was then known about the stars, the *Almagest*. She is also believed to have written, in collaboration with Theon, a discussion of the work of Euclid—the last important contribution to Euclidian geometry until the end of the sixteenth century.

In the late tenth century, a researcher named Suidas identified several more writings that he attributed to Hypatia, but no copies are known to exist today. According to letters written by one of her students, the philosopher Synesius, Hypatia was also skilled as an inventor. She is said to have developed a form of the astrolabe, used to measure the positions of planets and stars, and other instruments for the study of astronomy.

As a philosopher, Hypatia is identified as a member of the Neoplatonic school, a group based on the later teachings of Plato. Neoplatonism, the last major pagan philosophy, was founded by Plotinus a hundred years before Hypatia's birth; Neoplatonists saw reality as a hierarchical order with "the One" at the center, linked together by the "World Soul." During Hypatia's lifetime, Neoplatonism was, according to Greek thought, scientific and rational. Hypatia was as well-known as a philosopher as she was as a mathematician, and she was frequently consulted on matters philosophical and political. She was a celebrated figure, sweeping through the city on her chariot on her way to the university or to the homes of important people. It was this fame that ultimately led to her death.

Western mathematics had long been dominated by the Greeks and held little interest for the Romans (imagine trying to do even simple algebra using Roman numerals). The increasingly Christianized Roman Empire believed that science and mathematics were heretical and evil. The Church leaders also felt threatened by Neoplatonism, which involved a focus on rationalism that contradicted the notion of faith. During Hypatia's life, Alexandria was locked in a struggle between the ancient Greek ways and beliefs and the changing ideas of the Roman Christians who now ruled the city.

For most of Hypatia's career, Alexandria had been under the control of the Roman prefect Orestes, a secular civil authority who admired Hypatia and her work. In 412, however, he was joined by Cyril, a Christian bishop who was determined to eliminate any threats to Christian domination. Cyril began an immediate campaign to eradicate all heretical teachings in Alexandria, including Judaism and Neoplatonism. Despite being warned, Hypatia refused to convert to Christianity or to stop teaching mathematics and Neoplatonism.

Many stories have been told of how Hypatia met her death, each more vivid and gory than the next. What seems irrefutable is that Cyril continued his oppression, inciting mob violence against those he labeled heretics. The city of Alexandria was in chaos, as Alexandrians were torn between loyalty to tradition and to the new rulers, between science and faith. According to one account, Cyril came to believe that he could increase his own standing by calling for a virgin sacrifice. Other accounts explain that Cyril saw Hypatia as an obstacle to his shared power with Orestes.

Whatever his reason, he let it be known that Hypatia was a Satanist, a witch whose charisma was the result of evil powers. One day during March in 415, as she made her way through the city in her chariot, Hypatia was surrounded by a mob of Christian fanatics, dragged to a nearby church, stripped naked, tortured, and killed. Her body was taken outside the city and burned. There is no real evidence that Cyril ordered her execution, but historians for sixteen centuries have assumed he was responsible. No investigation was ever performed; Orestes was replaced, and the Christian hold on Alexandria was advanced. Cyril was later named a Roman Catholic saint.

Summary

Hypatia was a talented philosopher, mathematician, and astronomer and a gifted teacher of all three disciplines. None of her accomplishments in these areas changed the world, although her name has been held in high regard for nearly sixteen centuries. Perhaps her greatest significance is as a symbol of her age, a marker of changing times. Hypatia, often called the "Divine Pagan," is considered the last of the great pagan scientists; her death marked the end of an era. She was the last of the important Greek mathematicians; because of the fall of Alexandria shortly after her death, no important progress was made in Western mathematics for a thousand years. In the eighteenth and nineteenth centuries, with the publication of Edward Gibbon's *The History of the Decline and Fall of the Roman Empire* (1776) and Charles Kingsley's historical novel *Hypatia, or New Foes with Old Faces* (1853), she was regarded as a symbol of courage in the face of an oppressive Christian Church.

For the women's movement that came of age in the late twentieth century, she has also emerged as an important symbol, this time as a "first": the first important woman philosopher, mathematician, and astronomer. The leading journal of feminist philosophy is titled *Hypatia*, and its editors have stated, "Her name reminds us that although many of us are the first woman philosophers in our schools, we are not, after all, the first in history."

Bibliography

Alic, Margaret. *Hypatia's Heritage: A History of Women in Science from Antiquity Through the Nineteenth Century*. Boston: Beacon, and London: Women's Press, 1986. Examines biographical and scientific evidence to reveal the lives and accomplishments of women in natural and physical sciences and mathematics. The material dealing with Hypatia claims for her the roles of the last important pagan scientist in the western world and the representative of end of ancient science.

Cameron, Alan, and Jacqueline Long. *Barbarians and Politics at the Court of Arcadius*. Berkeley: University of California Press, 1993. A study of the Gothic rebellion and massacre under the reign of the Roman Emperor Arcadius in A.D. 399-400. Because one of the best contemporary accounts of these events was written by Synesius, a student of Hypatia, the book includes a clear and thorough discussion of Hypatia's philosophy and accomplishments.

Dzielska, Maria. *Hypatia of Alexandria*. Translated by F. Lyra. Cambridge, Mass.: Harvard University Press, 1995. The only book-length study of Hypatia in English. Examines Hypatia as she appears in literature of the past sixteen hundred years and traces what can be confirmed of her biography. Also discusses her students and followers. Includes a full bibliography of sources in several languages.

Kingsley, Charles. *Hypatia, or New Foes with Old Faces*. Chicago: W. B. Conkley, and London: Parker, 1853. A historical romance novel based on Hypatia's life. Kingsley was involved in the Christian Socialism movement and was strongly anti-Catholic. His interpretation of Hypatia's death places the blame squarely on Cyril, a representation of all Kingsley found objectionable in the Roman Catholic priesthood.

Molinaro, Ursule. "A Christian Martyr in Reverse: Hypatia." In *A Full Moon of Women*. New York: E.P. Dutton, 1990. Included in this volume's twenty-nine word portraits of notable women is a feminist treatment of Hypatia's brilliance, her refusal to live according to convention, and her murder at the hands of a tyrannical patriarchy. Although presented in prose-poem form, it includes useful and accurate biographical and historical information.

Osen, Lynn M. *Women in Mathematics*. Cambridge, Mass: MIT Press, 1974. A historical study of women mathematicians from Hypatia through the early twentieth century, and of the social contexts within which they worked. In addition to a chapter devoted to Hypatia's life and accomplishments, includes a chapter on "The Feminine Mathtique," which discusses uses and abuses of stories of exceptional women.

Perl, Teri. *Math Equals: Biographies of Women Mathematicians and Related Activities*. Menlo Park, Calif.: Addison-Wesley, 1978. Includes a brief biography of Hypatia and a series of activities to familiarize students with the mathematics important to some of her written commentaries: Diophantine equations and the geometry of conic sections. Also offers mathematical games to introduce an overview of women in mathematics.

Cynthia A. Bily

IGNATIUS OF ANTIOCH

Born: c. A.D. 30; Antioch, Syria
Died: December 20, A.D. 107?; Rome
Area of Achievement: Religion
Contribution: Ignatius served as Bishop of Antioch from the early 60's to the early 100's and was an important theologian and the exemplary martyr of the early Christian Church. By his writings and example, Ignatius strengthened the office of bishop in the church hierarchy, clarified many central Christian doctrines, such as the Real Presence and the Virgin Birth, and formulated the strategy and tactics of voluntary martyrdom.

Early Life

Ignatius was born to pagan parents at Antioch, the capital of Syria, during the second quarter of the first century, about A.D. 30. One of the largest cities of the Roman Empire, the terminus of both Eastern caravan routes and Mediterranean sea-lanes, Antioch was the center of commerce and Greek culture in the eastern Mediterranean region. It contained a large Jewish refugee population but was also the site of the first gentile Christian community, which became the mother church of Christian churches throughout the Roman Empire.

According to the earliest traditions, Ignatius was converted to Christianity by the Apostle John, whose theology certainly profoundly influenced him, and in the early 60's was consecrated Bishop of Antioch by Peter and Paul on their way to Rome and martyrdom under the emperor Nero. A charming but improbable story identifies Ignatius with the small child whom Jesus Christ presented to His disciples at Capernaum as a lesson in humility. It would appear that this story is a wordplay on the surname Theophorus (or "God-bearer") which Ignatius took later in life; the tradition shows that Ignatius was believed to have been born before the death of Christ. Ignatius, the eager young Christian convert, was blessed with strong faith and great abilities; these qualities brought him quickly to prominence in the Christian community at Antioch and to the attention of Saint Evodius, Bishop of Antioch, and Peter and Paul.

Life's Work

As Bishop of Antioch in the first century, Ignatius presided in dignity over the early gentile church, leading the greatest Christian community in the Roman Empire. Here he furthered Paul's work in transforming Christianity from a Jewish sect into a world religion. Ignatius was an exemplary bishop who maintained Christian order in the community and orthodoxy in doctrine; like a good shepherd, he protected his flock from the wolves during the persecution under the emperor Domitian (A.D. 81-96).

Bishop Ignatius of Antioch suffered martyrdom not then but later under the humane, progressive, and just emperor Trajan. Though a pagan, the emperor was a good man and an enlightened ruler who regarded himself as the servant and protector of his people. So admirable was Trajan that there would arise a popular legend in the Middle Ages that Pope Gregory the Great had interceded with God and secured Trajan's salvation. In *La divina commedia* (c. 1320; *The Divine Comedy*, 1802), Dante, following this legend, placed Trajan, though a pagan, in Heaven alongside certain eminently just Christian rulers.

S. IGNATIVS .

Trajan's policy toward Christianity was both moderate and legalistic. He strongly discouraged active persecution of Christians, though he allowed the legal prosecution of those who had been publicly denounced to the Roman authorities. Trajan laid down this policy explicitly in 112 in his correspondence with Pliny the Younger, the Governor of Bithynia. Roman officials were forbidden to search out Christians. Those denounced to the state were to be prosecuted by their denouncers before Roman magistrates, but these Christians were given procedural guarantees and the opportunity and encouragement to recant Christianity and conform to the state religion. Thus, under Trajan, Christians could be punished if legally proved guilty and then only if obdurate in their belief.

Allegations against Christians included treason, sedition, unspecified crimes, impiety, depravity, and membership in illegal secret societies, but ultimately their real offense was their primary allegiance to the Kingdom of God instead of to the Roman Empire. Ignatius could not in good conscience pay reverence to the imperial cult and the divinities in the Roman pantheon because he believed them to be idols and demons. To the emperor Trajan, however, respect for the state religion was an important aspect of civic duty and a mark of patriotism; thus, to him, a gesture of respect was a very reasonable demand.

Ironically, Trajan's policy was probably more destructive than Domitian's and Nero's persecutions had been. It was neither sporadic nor localized but was spread throughout the Empire. It seemed reasonable, legal, and just. Nevertheless, Trajan's policy threatened to divide and demoralize Christian communities by encouraging apostasy and discrediting Christian martyrs. The prosecution that Ignatius of Antioch faced was much more insidious than other persecutions because it appeared humane and just.

Later Christian hagiographers imagined a dramatic personal confrontation between Ignatius and Trajan. Ignatius was prosecuted at a time when Trajan's recent victory in Dacia had occasioned enthusiastic displays of loyalty to the Roman gods throughout the Empire. Ignatius' trial as described by his biographers probably never occurred, but the fictitious confrontation did capture the global conflict between the City of God and the earthly city. In fact, not Trajan himself but one of his governors condemned Ignatius; Ignatius was sent to Rome rather than executed in Antioch simply because the many celebrations of Trajan's Dacian victory had caused a scarcity of gladiators and victims for the Roman games. Moreover, the Roman mob found it especially entertaining to watch the death of an old man such as Ignatius. Although mistaken in imagining the personal confrontation between Ignatius and Trajan, the hagiographers were perceptive in personifying the conflict between two cities, two systems of belief, and two ways of life. It was not so much good versus evil as the best of the temporal—Emperor Trajan—versus the best of the spiritual—Bishop Ignatius.

The most significant historical source for the life's work of Ignatius is the collection of his seven epistles, which he wrote around 107, during his journey under guard to Rome and his martyrdom. Ignatius' journey was triumphant and even ecstatic: Along the way, his Roman guards permitted him to visit important Christian communities in Asia Minor and the Balkans, where he preached, blessed, ordained, and was received enthusiastically. Pausing at Smyrna, Ignatius wrote four epistles, to the Christians of Ephesus, Magnesia, Rome, and Tralles. Traveling on to Lystra, he paused there and wrote three more epistles, to the Christians at Philadelphia and Smyrna, and in farewell to Polycarp, the Bishop of Smyrna, who was Ignatius' protégé and later would himself suffer martyrdom. The contents of the seven epistles cover Christian beliefs and practices and stress Christian unity in doctrine and hierarchical organization. The most poignant of the letters is the epistle written to the Romans, in which Ignatius begged the Christian community at Rome not to try to have him reprieved.

Ignatius' eagerness and joy to be a martyr, that is, publicly to witness his Christian faith even unto death, appears to some modern psychoanalytical commentators "disturbed" and "self-destructive." Ignatius welcomed not self-destruction but union with his Lord Jesus Christ, humbly and faithfully identifying his own martyrdom with Christ's sacrifice.

Ignatius anticipated his martyrdom, which he perceived in almost Eucharistic imagery. He would become as "God's wheat, ground fine by the teeth of the wild beasts, that he may be found pure bread, a sacrifice to God." Across the millennia ring his triumphant words:

> Come fire and cross, and grapplings with wild beasts, cuttings and manglings, wrenchings of bones, break-

ing of limbs, crushing of my whole body, come cruel tortures of the Devil to assail me. Only be it mine to attain unto Jesus Christ.

On December 20, 107, according to Greek tradition, on the last day of the public games, Ignatius of Antioch was brought into the Flavian Amphitheater, the infamous Colosseum, and thrown to the lions. He welcomed the two ravenous lions, which immediately devoured him, leaving in the bloody sand only a few of the larger bones. Reverent Antiochenes gathered up the relics and brought them to Antioch, where they were enshrined.

Summary

Ignatius of Antioch was among the greatest of the early fathers of the Church. Admirable as the Bishop of Antioch and brilliantly imaginative as a Christian theologian, his greatest contribution was doubtless his exemplary martyrdom. His fortitude, commitment, authenticity, love, joy, and ecstasy illustrate the maxim that the blood of the martyrs is the seed of the Church. Ignatius was an Apostolic Father, having met and been associated with the Apostles Peter and John and with Paul, the Apostle of the Gentiles. Ignatius proved the continuity and catholicity of the early Christian Church by bridging the distance between Jew and Gentile and between the Age of the Apostles and the Age of the Martyrs.

Bibliography

De Ste. Croix, G. E. M. "Why Were the Early Christians Persecuted?" *Past and Present* no. 26 (November, 1963): 6-38. This important analysis discusses early Christian voluntary martyrdom, with Ignatius of Antioch considered as a precursor.

Eusebius. *The Ecclesiastical History of Eusebius Pamphilus*. Translated by Christian Frederick Cruse. London: Bohn, 1858; Grand Rapids, Mich.: Baker Book House, 1955. The standard narrative primary source for the first three centuries of Christianity, Eusebius' account includes some information on Ignatius of Antioch.

Frend, W. H. *Martyrdom and Persecution in the Early Church: A Study of a Conflict from the Maccabees to Donatus*. Oxford: Blackwell, 1965; New York: New York University Press, 1967. A penetrating examination of the social and psychological dynamics of martyrdom. Includes an insightful discussion of Ignatius of Antioch.

Ignatius of Antioch, Saint. "The Epistles of St. Ignatius." In *The Apostolic Fathers*, translated and edited by Kirsopp Lake. 2 vols. London: Heinemann, 1925-1930. Of the many usable modern editions of Ignatius' epistles, this Loeb Classical Library edition is one of the most readily available. These epistles are the principal primary source for the life of Ignatius and also are important for the history of early Christianity.

Ignatius of Antioch, Saint, and Saint Clement of Rome. *The Epistles of St. Clement of Rome and St. Ignatius of Antioch*. Translated and edited by James E. Kleist. Westminster, Md.: Newman Bookshop, 1946. Part of the Ancient Christian Writers and the Works of the Fathers in Translation series. Differences in translation and especially in commentary make this edition of the epistles an independently useful and complementary work.

Lane Fox, Robin. *Pagans and Christians*. London: Viking, 1986; New York: Alfred A. Knopf, 1987. An ambitious synthesis of scholarship about the cultural and social context of early Christianity, Lane Fox's work is important for background information.

Thurston, Herbert, and Donald Attwater, eds. *Butler's Lives of the Saints*. 4 vols. London: Burns and Oates, and Westminster, Md.: Christian Classics, 1956. The standard hagiography in English, Alban Butler's eighteenth century collection has been shortened, edited, supplemented, and revised by the editors. It is arranged according to feast days (Ignatius' day is February 1).

Terence R. Murphy

IMHOTEP

Born: Twenty-seventh century B.C.; Egypt
Died: Twenty-seventh century B.C.; Egypt
Areas of Achievement: Architecture and medicine
Contribution: Imhotep, the priest-physician who was deified as the Egyptian god of medicine, was also an architect and is credited with starting the age of pyramid building.

Early Life

Little is known about Imhotep's early life except that his father, Kanofer, is believed to have been a distinguished architect and that his mother was named Khreduonkh. He was probably born in a suburb of Memphis, and his early training was most likely influenced by his father's profession. To judge by his later reputation, he received a liberal education and was interested and skilled in many areas.

That Imhotep was a real historical figure in an influential position and that he was evidently respected for his wisdom and talent are deduced from his position as the chief vizier for one of the most famous Egyptian kings, Zoser (fl. 2686 B.C.), of Egypt's Third Dynasty. From what is known of the duties of viziers at a later period, it is likely that Imhotep had to be both efficient and extremely knowledgeable, for the vizier was in charge of the judiciary and the departments of the treasury, the army and navy, internal affairs, and agriculture. As a judge, Imhotep is reputed to have penned many wise proverbs, although unfortunately none is known to have survived.

The increasing stature of Imhotep during his lifetime is apparent in the changes in statuettes discovered. In some he appears to be an ordinary man, dressed simply; he looks like a sage, seated on a throne or chair with a roll of papyrus on his knees or under his arm and is depicted as reading or deep in thought. When he achieved full god status, he was shown standing, carrying a scepter and the ankh, with the beard typically worn by gods. His mother was then regarded as the mother of a god and his wife, Ronpe-nofret, as the wife of a god; following what appears to have been a tradition of Egyptian deities, Imhotep was considered to be the son of the god Ptah as well as the son of the mortal Kanofer.

Life's Work

Imhotep's reputation is remarkable not only be-
cause he was accomplished in so many fields but also because he is credited for his distinction in two distinct fields and in two distinct periods: his achievement as an architect during his lifetime and his high position as priest-physician, for which he was accorded a divine status several hundred years after his lifetime.

In his capacity as architect, Imhotep is credited with designing and implementing the building of the earliest large stone structure—the Step Pyramid of Saqqara—which inaugurated the age of pyramid building in Egypt.

A story much debated among scholars nevertheless reveals the reverence with which Imhotep was regarded. According to the Legend of the Seven Years' Famine, it happened that the Nile River had not risen to its usual level sufficient to irrigate the land for seven years, resulting in a shortage of food. King Zoser, distressed by the suffering of his subjects, consulted Imhotep about the birthplace of the Nile and its god. After absenting himself for a brief period of research and study, Imhotep revealed some unspecified "hidden wonders" which the king investigated; he offered prayers and oblations at the temple of the god Khnum and, promised by the god in a dream that the Nile would not fail again, endowed the temple of the god with land and gifts in gratitude.

Imhotep's achievement in the field of medicine is equally legendary. His reputation as a healer seems to be based almost entirely on his apotheosis from a wise and talented man who was a contemporary of Zoser, to a medical demigod, and then finally to a full deity of medicine in the period of Persian rule (about 525 B.C.). In the period of the Greco-Egyptian rule, he was called Imouthes and identified with Asclepios, the Greek god of medicine, resulting in a gradual assimilation of the two figures.

Imhotep's reputation as a wise healer is thus one that seems to have developed several hundred years after his death. The godlike status accorded him as a healer not only shows how he was revered but also points to the inextricable connection between medicine, magic, and religion in Egyptian medical practice. In addition to his other duties, Imhotep held an important position as the Kheri-Heb, or chief lector priest. Thus entitled to read holy religious texts which were believed to have magical powers, he served as a mediator and teacher of reli-

gious mysteries. Among the priest-physicians, two main classes predominated: the physicians who had some systematic training in medicine and the larger class of those who emphasized the power to cure with amulets and magic incantations. Because the names or achievements of other practitioners of medicine in ancient times have been discovered while the specific qualifications of Imhotep as a healer are not as clearly documented, it is thought that his duties as a priest who was regarded as a magician may have initiated his reputation as a medical man.

In all likelihood, his cumulative achievements as architect, physician, priest, sage, and magician led to the great reverence in which Imhotep was held and to his subsequent deification. The magic he was reputed to practice may well have been grounded in the considerably well-developed art of healing in ancient Egypt. A number of medical documents have survived in rolls of papyrus: the Ebers Papyrus, the Hearst Papyrus, the Berlin Medical Papyrus, the Kahun Medical Papyrus, the London Medical Papyrus, the Edwin Smith Papyrus, and another papyrus in Berlin. The Ebers Papyrus, the most important of these, was written about 1550 B.C. but appears to be a compilation of other books written centuries before; parts of it were already in existence during Imhotep's lifetime and may therefore be construed to reflect the kind of medicine and magic Imhotep practiced.

The Ebers Papyrus lists many prescriptions for a variety of ailments; approximately 250 kinds of diseases are identified in the various papyruses. The doses and modes of administration are specified, suggesting that clinical examination, diagnosis, and therapeutics were quite progressive. Drugs from herbs, vegetable products, minerals, and parts of animals were studied and administered in many forms, such as gargles, salves, lozenges, pills, and plasters. Simple surgery was performed and fractures were successfully treated. The custom of mummification, involving the dissection of bodies to remove the viscera, undoubtedly provided the Egyptians with a better working knowledge of the internal organs and practical anatomy than existed elsewhere for many centuries afterward.

While the papyruses demonstrate that empiric knowledge existed and medical treatment was widely practiced, they also reveal that such practical measures were always accompanied by magical formulas. Disease was treated primarily as a visitation of a malign spirit or god, not as a dysfunction of the body. The healer therefore had to identify the nature and the name of the evil spirit, determine how far it had invaded the body, take into account the times and seasons of the year in gauging the virulence of the attack, and then try to drive it out with every possible means—including magic, ritual, and material remedies. Some physicians would seek to differentiate between symptoms which called for drugs, magic, or temple sleep, suggesting that already in ancient times an elementary form of psychiatry was practiced.

Several legends show the importance of the Egyptian temples as a gathering place for the sick and the practice of incubation sleep as a form of cure. The writer of one of the Oxyrhynchus papyruses, written in Greek around the second century A.D., recounts two incidents involving Imhotep's power. The writer, a priest named Nechautis in the temple of Imhotep, and his mother both fell sick at different times. On both occasions, they went to the temple, where Imhotep appeared to them in dreams, suggesting a simple remedy; upon waking, both were cured. Other legends discovered by Egyptologists recount stories of infertile couples who sought help at the temple of Imhotep and conceived children afterward.

One explanation given for the demigod status of Imhotep during the New Kingdom (about 1580 B.C.) was the religious revival which increased the magnificence and wealth of the Egyptian gods to such a degree that they became inaccessible to the common people; in search of a superhuman but sympathetic friend, it is conjectured, the common people selected new demigods from the national heroes of the past—including Imhotep, who had a reputation as a wise man.

In at least three temples built to honor him, the cult of Imhotep flourished. The first one, at Memphis, was famous as a hospital and school of magic and medicine and was referred to as the Asclepieion by the Greeks. Two other temples, one at Philae and one at Thebes, and a sanatorium are believed to have been devoted to the worship of Imhotep. Stories similar to the one related above illustrate the power of the practice of incubation at Egyptian medical temples. People with all sorts of illnesses and others seeking protection from accidents went to the temples for help. During this natural or drug-induced sleep, it was believed that either the deity or a priest acting on behalf of the deity would appear and indicate a remedy. Temple sleep served as a powerful form of faith healing, the most effective for very high-strung patients.

It is thought that a practical man of affairs such as Imhotep, with his interest in astronomy and other sciences, probably leaned toward the scientific treatment of illnesses. From the records about the cult of Imhotep that grew hundreds of years after his death, it is apparent, however, that his greatest public achievements were in the capacity of a faith healer.

Summary

The name Imhotep means "he who cometh in peace"; the symbolic significance of the name is perhaps the best way to explain the enduring reputation of a person whom some scholars doubt even existed. For three thousand years, well into the Roman period, Imhotep was worshipped as the god of medicine, for a long time in temples devoted to him. This deification of a person who was not of the royal pharaohs was in itself a rare achievement, pointing to the great respect that a priest-physician could command. It is entirely conceivable, too, that the powerful fraternity of priest-physicians deliberately helped to create his reputation, spreading the word about the healing power of a man otherwise familiar to people as a wise and accomplished vizier in order to increase the contributions of the pharaohs to the temple coffers. The champions of Imhotep's reputation argue, on the other hand, that the civilization of ancient Egypt was unknown for hundreds of years, compared to the relative familiarity of scholars with Greek and Roman life and culture. According to this argument, Imhotep simply suffered the fate of the ancients, as the inexorable process of history dimmed his achievements and assimilated his fame with succeeding generations of medical practitioners.

Under the Ptolemies, six festivals were regularly held to honor the events of Imhotep's life, including his birthday on May 31 and his death on July 1, though there is no documentation to prove that these dates have any relation to real historical events. The elaborateness of the cult of Imhotep points, if not to his actual existence or achievement, to the power of his reputation as a healer. That reputation alone was worth much in terms of what could be called ancient psychotherapy. William Osler's often-quoted tribute to Imhotep, "the first figure of a physician to stand out clearly from the mists of antiquity," is a recognition of the power that people in pain and suffering are willing to attribute to a distinguishable healing authority who by virtue of that confidence in his skill is able to bring them a measure of peace.

Bibliography

Cormack, Maribelle. *Imhotep: Builder in Stone.* New York: Franklin Watts, 1965. A simply and imaginatively written account of Imhotep's development and achievements as an architect. Part of a series called Immortals of Engineering. Contains an outline of the chronology of Egyptian history from 3200 B.C. to A.D. 640 and an index.

Dawson, Warren R. *Magician and Leech: A Study in the Beginnings of Medicine with Special Reference to Ancient Egypt.* London: Methuen, 1929. A short account of Egyptian medicine, based on the study of the Egyptian papyruses relating to medicine and on the study of techniques of mummification. Contains illustrations and index.

Garry, T. Gerald. *Egypt: The Home of the Occult Sciences, with Special Reference to Imhotep, the Mysterious Wise Man and Egyptian God of Medicine.* London: John Bale, Sons and Danielsson, 1931. This study by a physician contains a substantial chapter on Imhotep. Outlines the scholarly arguments about the existence of Imhotep. Serves as a brief but useful introduction to the problems of Egyptology.

Hurry, Jamieson B. *Imhotep: The Vizier and Physician of King Zoser and Afterwards the Egyptian God of Medicine.* 2d ed. London: Oxford University Press, 1928; New York: AMS Press, 1978. The single most informative source about Imhotep, this monograph contains a short bibliography, an index, illustrations, and appendices referring to the construction and variants of the name Imhotep, his pedigree as architect, and the statuettes and murals depicting him.

Sigerist, Henry E. *A History of Medicine.* Vol. 1, *Primitive and Archaic Medicine.* New York: Oxford University Press, 1955. Written by one of the most promising historians of medicine (although he did not live to complete the series), this book includes a substantial chapter on ancient Egypt. Contains illustrations, an index, and appendices on histories of medicine, sourcebooks and medical history, museums of medical history, and literature of paleopathology since 1930.

Shakuntala Jayaswal

SAINT IRENAEUS

Born: Between 120 and 140; probably Smyrna, Asia Minor

Died: 202; Lugdunum, Gaul (modern Lyons, France)

Area of Achievement: Religion

Contribution: As the first systematic theologian of the Christian church, Irenaeus laid the foundation for the development of church doctrine and effectively ended the threat that Gnosticism might substitute mysticism for faith in the resurrection of Christ.

Early Life

All that is known of the life of Saint Irenaeus derives from the *Historia ecclesiastica* (before 300, revised 324; *Ecclesiastical History,* 1927-1928) of Eusebius, and from occasional comments made by Irenaeus himself in his works. Since Eusebius was less interested in biography than in recording the development and growth of the Church, he offers only a few tantalizing details. Irenaeus was born sometime after 120, in or near the trading city of Smyrna on the southwestern coast of Asia Minor, which was at that time part of the Roman Empire. His parents, who were probably Greeks, were also Christians.

In the century that had passed between the crucifixion of Christ and the birth of Irenaeus, the apostles of Jesus had spread His message throughout the Mediterranean world, and Peter and Paul, in particular, had transformed a minor Jewish sect into an established institution with churches, priests, and bishops throughout the Roman Empire. In fact, the rapid growth of the Church had frightened and angered the Roman authorities. Though most Christians tried to be good citizens of the empire, they refused to worship the old Roman gods; as a result, they were often regarded as traitors and were frequently persecuted. The early history of the Church is filled with heroic and miraculous tales of these martyrs. One of them was Polycarp, a renowned Christian teacher and bishop of Smyrna, who was burned at the stake in 156. As a young man, Irenaeus was apparently brought to Polycarp for instruction in the faith and was deeply influenced by him. Because Polycarp had known several of the apostles, he was able to transmit their teaching with a personal vigor. Irenaeus' belief that the books of the apostles accurately present the true message of Christ probably derived from

Polycarp. In his later years, Irenaeus' memories of his old teacher were still so sharp that he could vividly describe Polycarp and the lessons he had taught. It may have been Polycarp who sent Irenaeus as a missionary to the city of Lugdunum in the Roman province of Gaul.

Life's Work

After his arrival at Lugdunum, Irenaeus was ordained as a priest by Pothinus, the bishop, and he soon began a lifelong career of converting the pagans of southwestern Gaul to Christianity. In 161, however, the expansion of the Church was endangered by the appointment of a new Roman emperor, Marcus Aurelius. Though in many ways a very admirable man, the emperor saw the Christians as a threat to the strength and unity of the empire, and he initiated an especially cruel series of persecutions against them. In 177, it was the turn of the churches of Gaul, and it is said that the streets of Lugdunum ran with the blood of thousands of Christians who had been tortured and killed.

S. IRENÆVS

Fortunately, though, Irenaeus had been sent by the leaders of the Church on a mission to Pope Eleutherius at Rome, so he escaped the time of persecution. The purpose of the mission is somewhat unclear: Eusebius says only that Irenaeus acted as a mediator in a dispute over an issue related to Montanism, which was one of many heresies in the early Church.

Montanists, who took their name from their leader, Montanus, believed that they were under the direct influence of the Holy Spirit, and their worship services, like those of the nineteenth century Shakers, were often characterized by emotional outbursts and "speaking in tongues." Some modern authorities have stated that the Pope had become a Montanist and that Irenaeus tried to persuade Eleutherius to return to a more orthodox view; others assert the opposite—that Irenaeus tried to convince the Pope not to excommunicate the Montanists. In any case, while in Rome, Irenaeus saw that heresies were threatening to tear the Church apart, and he determined that he would do everything he could to eliminate them.

The problem of heresies had arisen, Irenaeus believed, because the Church had as yet no established body of doctrine accepted by all Christian churches. In the modern world, many Christian denominations coexist peacefully and are drawing closer together through the ecumenical movement. This degree of unity has only been possible because Christians of nearly every denomination acknowledge and share certain fundamental beliefs. In the early days of Christianity, however, these common beliefs had not yet been clearly or systematically articulated. Without an authoritative body of doctrine, Christians could be led astray by religious leaders who claimed to have a new revelation or a superior interpretation of the Gospels. While Montanism was a relatively minor, and even tolerable, deviation from orthodoxy, Christianity itself was but one of several competitors in a great theological contest occurring throughout the Roman world. Among the others were the pagan religions, such as that of the old Roman state gods. Despite attacks from Roman imperial authorities, Christianity had been making steady advances against these religions, because they offered no vision of eternal life. A much more dangerous threat to the Church came from the various sects called Gnostics.

Gnosticism comprised a vague system of ideas about the nature of the universe; these ideas predated Christianity and had spread throughout the Mediterranean world by the second century after Christ. A central feature of this system was a belief in the salvation of the soul through the acquisition of a *gnosis*, or secret knowledge. This mystical revelation of the origins and fate of the cosmos would be communicated by a "divine redeemer" to an elite group of individuals ready to receive it. Gnosticism had become popular, particularly among intellectuals, through a gradual process of absorbing elements of other religions, as well as some aspects of Greek philosophy. When Gnostics encountered Christianity, they attempted to integrate it into their system by identifying Christ as the "divine redeemer" and by accepting only those portions of the Scriptures that agreed with their views. In addition, they claimed to possess secret books that augmented and improved upon the Christian message. Often, Gnostics even called themselves Christians. Yet Christianity and Gnosticism were fundamentally opposed: For the Christian, salvation was achieved through faith in Christ's resurrection and cooperation with the will of God, rather than by gaining some body of esoteric knowledge.

Irenaeus had become especially distressed about Gnosticism during his visit to Rome because one of his childhood friends and fellow students of Polycarp, Florinus, had fallen under the influence of a Gnostic leader. Florinus had become a Roman consul and was thus in a position to do great harm to the Christians of the city. Irenaeus wrote his old friend a long letter explaining some of his objections to Gnosticism and reminding Florinus that Polycarp had taught them to adhere only to the teachings of the Church established by the apostles. Unfortunately, Irenaeus was unsuccessful in dissuading Florinus from leaving the Church.

In 178, after returning to Lugdunum, Irenaeus was elected to replace Pothinus, who had been martyred, as bishop, and he also continued his missionary work. In 190, he again acted as a mediator for a new pope, Victor I, in a dispute between the churches of the eastern and western parts of the empire over the determination of the proper date for the celebration of Easter. Irenaeus suggested that such differences were not particularly important and, in any case, would probably disappear eventually. Eusebius notes that through his efforts, Irenaeus certainly lived up to his name, which means "peacemaker."

The constant appearance of such controversies reinforced Irenaeus' belief that the Church must have a consistent body of doctrine. Throughout his career, the problem of heresy, and especially Gnosticism, continued to weigh on his mind. As a result, he wrote a large number of letters, treatises, and books, all building toward a clear exposition of orthodox Christianity and a refutation of heresy. Though most of these works have been lost, several Latin translations of Irenaeus' most important treatise, which was originally written in Greek, have been preserved. *Elenchou kai anatropes* is most commonly known by its Latin title, *Adversus haereses* (*Against Heresies*, 1869). The exact date of its composition is unknown; Irenaeus began the work as a response to a request from a friend for information, but he continued to expand on his ideas during a period of several years. It was finally completed by about 190.

Against Heresies is the most important exposition of Christian theology prior to the Council of Nicaea in 325. As the Greek title implies, it is both a detailed discussion of the doctrines and history of Gnosticism and a rigorous refutation of Gnostic theory. In the first section, Irenaeus demonstrates the inconsistencies and lack of logical coherence of Gnostic belief. The more important portion of the book, however, contains, in essence, the first complete and systematic articulation of Christian theology. This system is relatively familiar to every educated Christian, for it is, in essence, still the basis of Christian belief: There is only one God, of which Christ as the Son is a part. God created humanity in His image, and He created the world for man's use. Yet, through the sin of disobedience, humanity fell away from God into the clutches of Satan, an angel who had been envious of humanity. God therefore sent His Son so that humanity might be saved from damnation and ultimately rejoin God. Through the Holy Spirit, people are drawn into Christ's victory over Satan and can ultimately attain salvation.

To Irenaeus, the biblical tradition is the only source of faith; no additional "gnosis" is either necessary or compatible with biblical truth. The Old and New Testaments form a continuous unity with a clear purpose: The Old Testament predicts the coming of Christ, whose oral teachings were written down by the apostles to form the books of the New Testament. They, in turn, established the Church, which preserves and disseminates the pure Christian message of redemption through faith. This apostolic tradition, passed on through the succession of bishops of the Church, ensures the cor-

rect interpretation of Scripture against the perversions and distortions of the Gnostics and other heretics. Thus, Irenaeus not only refuted heresy; in doing so, he also became the first theologian to defend the Church as an institution.

It is not clear how *Against Heresies* became well-known, yet the fairly large number of Latin manuscripts containing it, a translation in Armenian made in the third or fourth century, and numerous fragments in other languages all testify to its popularity. The fact that Eusebius reproduced sizable portions of it in the *Ecclesiastical History* demonstrates that by the early fourth century it had become part of the standard canon of Christian dogma. Irenaeus' other works seem also to have been well-known to the ancients, yet he himself drops out of sight after about 190. A tradition which originated in the fourth or fifth century states that Irenaeus was martyred in 202 in the general persecution orchestrated by the emperor Septimus Severus, but there is no solid evidence for this. On the other hand, no evidence contradicts the story, and it would be entirely consistent with Irenaeus' devotion to his faith.

Summary

Irenaeus is regarded by most authorities as the most important Christian theologian of the second century, as well as the founder of Catholic doctrine. Chronologically, he stands at a critical point in the history of the Church. The apostles and their immediate disciples had founded Christian communities all over the Mediterranean world, but without any central doctrine or authority, some of these had begun to accept competing and very different theologies. The mystical-philosophical system of Gnosticism, as well as pagan religions newly arrived from the East, such as Mithraism, had begun to make inroads in Christian congregations, while Roman imperial policy sought to wipe out Christianity. Irenaeus' coherent expression of Christian belief and his justification of the Church as an institution provided exactly the impetus toward consolidation needed by Christians if their faith was to survive.

What was required was a concept of what "the Church" meant to Christians. In *Against Heresies*, Irenaeus provided such a definition. He stated, first, that the Church is guided by the "rule of faith," a statement of belief to which all Christians subscribe, and he offered a creed which differs very little from the Apostles' Creed used to this day. Because the creed was given by the apostles to the Church, it expresses a tradition descended directly from Christ's own disciples. Second, the churches were established by the apostles themselves, who appointed their successors, the bishops. Thus, an unbroken line of succession was established which guarantees the rule of faith and guards against any notions of "gnosis." If Jesus had been the "divine redeemer" of the Gnostics, surely He would have given the "gnosis" to His disciples, who would have passed it to their successors. Third, what the Church has instead of some secret knowledge is the Gospels of the apostles, who were eyewitnesses to Christ's resurrection, which itself fulfills the predictions of the Old Testament. Because many books claimed apostolic authorship, Irenaeus made an important contribution to the determination of what exactly would constitute the New Testament by limiting the Gospels to those written by Matthew, Mark, Luke, and John and using as accepted apostolic writings most of the other books now included in the New Testament.

In developing this threefold definition of the Church, Irenaeus not only debunked heresy but, much more important, also provided the average Christian with dependable means through which to attain salvation: the Church, its rule of faith, and the Scriptures. According to Irenaeus, these means may be trusted because the rule of faith is the essence of apostolic teaching, because the Church has descended directly from the apostles, and because the Scriptures were written by the apostles. With this explanation of the sources of Christian theology, Irenaeus provided the fundamental structure of Church doctrine and ended the early period of uncontrolled Christian diversity.

Bibliography

Coxe, Arthur Cleveland, ed. *The Ante-Nicene Fathers*. Vol. 1, *The Apostolic Fathers with Justin Martyr and Irenaeus*. Buffalo: The Christian Literature Company, 1885. Contains the only complete English translation of *Against Heresies* and fragments of other works by Irenaeus. Also includes a useful, if overly enthusiastic, introduction which explains the plan and ideas of *Against Heresies* and places the work in its historical context. The translations of works of the other church fathers who preceded Irenaeus also provide helpful material for comparison.

Eusebius. *The Ecclesiastical History*. Translated by Kirsopp Lake and John E. L. Oulton. 2 vols. London: Heinemann, and New York: Putnam, 1932. Eusebius is the primary source for nearly all information on the life of Irenaeus, and the *Ecclesiastical History* also reveals how other early Christian writers built upon his work. Eusebius is an essential source for early church history. For those who might also wish to read him in the original Greek, this Loeb Classical Library edition provides it on facing pages.

Hägglund, Bengt. *History of Theology*. Translated by Gene J. Lund. St. Louis, Mo.: Concordia Publishing House, 1968. Treats the history of Christian doctrine topically, within a chronological context. While possibly difficult for a reader with no background in theological or philosophical study, Hägglund is worth the effort. Provides the clearest explanation of Irenaeus' reasoning in *Against Heresies* and helps to show how it relates to that of other early theologians.

Minns, Denis. *Irenaeus*. London: Chapman, and Washington, D.C.: Georgetown University Press, 1994. A rueful and frankly sympathetic account of Irenaeus' thought. Particularly helpful in that it situates the thought in the context of the heresies that Irenaeus was trying to refute. Pays attention to possible sources of Irenaeus' ideas.

Quasten, J. *Patrology*. Vol. 1, *The Beginnings of Patristic Literature*. Westminster, Md.: Newman Press, 1960. The most complete discussion of early Christian literature, including poetry and stories, in addition to theological works. Details on texts, translations, and history of editions of each work covered. Extensive bibliographies for each section. Includes excellent discussion of *Against Heresies* and other works by Irenaeus.

Schaff, Philip. *History of the Christian Church*. Vol. 2, *Ante-Nicene Christianity A.D. 100-325*. 3d ed. Peabody, Mass.: Hendrickson, 1996. Though extremely dated in both its approach and its style, Schaff's is perhaps the most complete history of the Church in English. This volume discusses in great detail all aspects of the growth and spread of Christianity and the development of the Church in the period covered. Contains helpful sections on early Christian heresies, including Montanism and Gnosticism, and a chapter on Irenaeus.

Tyson, Joseph B. *A Study of Early Christianity*. New York: Macmillan, 1973. An excellent and very readable discussion of the historical and theological context in which Christianity developed, early Christian literature, the varieties of early Christianity, and the place of Jesus Christ in the development of the Christian tradition. Includes an evaluation of the contribution of Irenaeus.

Wolfson, Henry Austryn. *The Philosophy of the Church Fathers*. Vol. 1, *Faith, Trinity, Incarnation*. 3d ed. Cambridge, Mass.: Harvard University Press, 1970. Wolfson is considered by many authorities to be the greatest historian of Chris-

tian philosophy. This massive study of the relationship of Greek philosophy and Old Testament theology to the development of Christian philosophy is extremely thorough and may therefore be more detailed than some readers need. Organized topically; thus, references to Irenaeus and his thought are scattered through several sections.

Thomas C. Schunk

ISAIAH

Born: c. 760 B.C.; Jerusalem, Judah
Died: c. 701-680 B.C.; probably Jerusalem, Judah
Area of Achievement: Religion
Contribution: Because of his clear grasp of political reality and the power of his poetic utterances, Isaiah is generally considered to be the greatest of the Old Testament prophets.

Early Life

Although there are sixty-six chapters in the book which bears his name, Isaiah, the great prophet of the eighth century B.C., probably wrote only the first thirty-nine of them. Stylistic and historical evidence indicates that the later chapters were written in the sixth century B.C., after the people of Judah had passed into the Babylonian captivity predicted at the end of Isaiah's own works. The author of chapters 40-55 is probably a single anonymous prophet, called for want of a name "Deutero-Isaiah" or "Second Isaiah." The final chapters, called "Trito-Isaiah" or "Third Isaiah," are probably by various hands. At any rate, although these later chapters are clearly in the tradition of Hebrew prophecy, they have no other claim to the name of the great prophet Isaiah. In actuality, they may have been attached to the earlier chapters simply for the sake of convenience.

Isaiah was the son of Amoz; evidently he was a native of Jerusalem. Beyond that, very little is known about the life of Isaiah before he was called to prophesy around 742 B.C. Because he obviously had access to the inner area of the Temple, some scholars conjecture that Isaiah was a member of a priestly family and may even have studied for the priesthood himself. As a young man, he might have been a "wisdom teacher." Certainly he was familiar with the wisdom literature which was so much a part of Hebrew education.

The tone of Isaiah's poetry suggests that he was of aristocratic background. His pronouncements regarding specific rulers and councillors, his comments on statecraft, and his exposures of international intrigues all reveal the knowledge of an insider. Although the prophet Isaiah, like Amos and Hosea, forecast doom if the people of Judah did not reform, his warnings were often addressed to the ruling classes in words which evidence firsthand knowledge of their self-centered, luxurious, and corrupt way of life.

Even if Isaiah had not been an insider in court circles, he would have attracted attention because of his intellectual brilliance and his poetic genius. His social status, however, gave him an additional sense of security in his dealings with councillors and with kings. Even when God Himself spoke to him, Isaiah did not hide behind false modesty but volunteered with confidence for whatever mission God had in mind. It is undoubtedly this confidence which sustained him when God sent him out naked and barefoot, supposedly for three years, in order to attract the attention of his countrymen to the predictions which they had ignored.

Aside from this unusual episode, Isaiah seems to have lived a godly yet normal life. He was married—whether before or after his call is not clear. He had two sons, probably after he began to prophesy, since their names reveal his preoccupation with God's intentions toward his people. He maintained his court contacts, at times being called upon to advise the king.

It is clear that when Isaiah became the prophet of Judah, he did not emerge wild-eyed from the wilderness, nor did he change except in the intensity of his dedication. The rulers of Judah could not complain that God had not given them every chance to turn to Him; He had sent to them a prophet who spoke their language and understood their problems, a moderate, rational man who insisted only that private and public life should be subject to the will of God.

Life's Work

In the sixth chapter of Isaiah, the prophet describes the experience which directed his life. The moment is dated as falling within the year of King Uzziah's death (probably 742 B.C.). After seeing a vision of God enthroned, surrounded by angels, Isaiah's first reaction was the sense of his own uncleanness in the sight of God. After being forgiven, he heard God ask, "Whom shall I send? Who will go for Me?" Isaiah's immediate response was to utter the well-known words, "Here am I! Send me!"

During the next four decades, Isaiah took his advice, his satirical comments, his diatribes, and his predictions of doom to the people of Judah, later expanding his warnings to address the neighboring Jewish state of Israel, as well as pagan lands ranging from Egypt and Syria to powerful Assyria. Because so many manuscripts were lost after the fall of Jerusalem to Babylon, scholars cannot be certain of the chronology of Isaiah's thirty-nine chapters. Specific historical references date some segments, however, while others reflect themes which clearly preoccupied the prophet throughout his life.

Shortly after Isaiah began his life of prophecy, Judah was threatened by the allies Israel and Syria, who had joined forces in the hope of conquering Judah and placing a puppet on the throne and eventually defeating the powerful nation of Assyria. Isaiah was troubled by the fact that Israel's intended puppet was not of the house of David; furthermore, he was convinced that Assyria was in the ascendancy with the permission of God. Thus, on both counts Israel and Syria were defying God.

Given these convictions, it fell to Isaiah to convince King Ahaz that God would protect Judah. Taking his son Shear-jashub (whose name means "a remnant will return"), Isaiah went to meet Ahaz, carrying the reassurances that the king needed. Later, at the command of God, Isaiah fathered a second son, whom he named Maher-shalal-hash-baz (the spoil comes, the prey hurries). Isaiah then explained to the nervous king that the baby's name had been assigned by God, who thereby promised that before the child learned to speak, the defiant countries would be despoiled by Assyria.

Such messages from God, dictating specific directions which Judah's foreign policy should take in troubled times, evidently alternated with advice in domestic matters. God's protection could only be depended upon if Judah obeyed His moral laws. At court, in the streets of Jerusalem, and on the outlying estates of the wealthy, Isaiah saw the real danger to Judah. In Isaiah 5:8-24, he points out the inner rottenness of his people: the atheism and drunkenness of its men, the triviality and extravagance of its women, the smugness and greed of its elite. In the country, the great landholders extended their properties, squeezing out the poor; in Jerusalem, corrupt judges dispensed injustice; at the Temple, priests offered worthless sacrifices which could not substitute for righteousness; and at court, great officials served their own interests. Such a society, the prophet warned, would not be protected by the God to whom Judah gave lip service.

In chapters 10 and 11, Isaiah expresses his preoccupation with a later threat, that of Assyria, which was no longer threatened by alliances against it. Realizing its own vulnerable position,

Judah was fearful. Again, Isaiah warned that military might and political stratagem would be useless; only God's intervention on behalf of a righteous people could save Judah.

The power of Isaiah's God, however, was not limited to dealings with Judah or even Israel. Isaiah's warnings were addressed to Moab and Samaria, to Egypt, and even to Assyria itself, a nation which he saw as the tool of God, currently powerful but destined eventually to be destroyed. In 711, Isaiah walked naked and barefoot through the streets of Jerusalem in order to point out the approaching fall of Egypt, which had betrayed a confederate to the Assyrians (Isa. 20:1-6). Not only their unrighteous cowardice but also their defiance of the governing plan of God had doomed the Egyptians.

For a country as defenseless as Judah, Isaiah's warnings about defying Assyria made sense. In 703, he advised King Hezekiah against sending an embassy to Egypt in order to plot against Assyria, which clearly would constitute a rejection of common sense as well as of God's plan (Isa. 30:1-7). In 701, the Assyrian king Sennacherib and his army were at the gates of Jerusalem. Isaiah urged Hezekiah to depend on patience and righteousness, not the Judaeans' inferior military forces, as the appropriate defense. When Sennacherib's men suddenly began to die, perhaps because of a plague, he withdrew, and Isaiah's God was appropriately credited with having saved the city.

Isaiah's role at Hezekiah's court is illustrated in chapter 38. Sick and believing that he was about to die, Hezekiah was visited by Isaiah, who brought a message from God: Put your spiritual house in order, and you shall be spared. The repentant king turned to God and was promised another fifteen years of life. Still, death would at last come to him, as it would to Jerusalem itself. Isaiah's portion of the book concludes with a prophecy of the Babylonian conquest and captivity, with the promise—reflected in the name of Isaiah's first son—that a remnant would return.

Isaiah's thirty-nine chapters contain no specific references to events in his life after about 700 B.C. Whether he continued his work into old age, whether he ceased to prophesy, or whether there is truth to the legend that he was cut in two during the reign of Manasseh is not known. It is ironic that this man who spent his life transmitting God's directions to the heads of nations should disappear so silently from the stage of history.

Summary

Isaiah is considered the greatest of the Old Testament prophets not only because of the fact that so much of his work remains but also because of his stature as a poet and as a representative of the God he served.

Unlike prophets of a humbler station, Isaiah could speak to the aristocracy as one of them. He could rebuke the daughters of Zion for their frivolity with references to their tinkling anklets; he could rebuke the great landowners by detailing their greedy appropriation of land. No pretense, no hypocrisy was proof against his penetrating eye; no foreign intrigue was too complicated for his mind to fathom.

The exactness of Isaiah's perception is one of the qualities which makes him a great writer. It is not known whether all of his work was in poetic form or whether segments were deliberately written in prose. It is undisputed, however, that all of his work is evidence of a remarkable talent. His style is so individual that scholars have been able to sep-

arate his own words from later additions with a surprising degree of agreement.

Although Isaiah's words continue to be significant to the faiths which depend upon the Judaic tradition, they would be far less significant if they had come from a lesser person. Even more important than the intellectual brilliance and the poetic genius of Isaiah is the quality of his obedience to God. When God asked who would go as His messenger, without argument his greatest prophet answered, "Here am I. Send me."

Bibliography

Church, Brooke Peters. *The Private Lives of the Prophets and the Times in Which They Lived.* New York: Rinehart, 1953. Though admittedly conjectural, a plausible reconstruction of the life of Isaiah based on a scholarly study of the chapters generally attributed to the prophet. Church differs from other commentators in rejecting the usual division of the book into three parts and insisting that only forty-two excerpts can be attributed to Isaiah with any degree of certainty. Despite this skepticism about the text, the work is imaginative, readable, and useful.

Cohon, Beryl D. *The Prophets: Their Personalities and Teachings.* New York: Scribner, 1939. In three chapters, the author treats the three separate bodies of work into which the Book of Isaiah is usually divided. Using fairly lengthy excerpts from the text, Cohon reconstructs the historical setting of the prophecies in prose which sometimes has almost the force of fiction.

Herbert, A. S. *The Book of the Prophet Isaiah 1-39.* Cambridge: Cambridge University Press, 1973. Part of the Cambridge Bible Commentary on the New English Bible. A passage-by-passage explanation of the text. Clear and uncluttered. Contains a useful chronological table of events in the eighth century B.C., as well as a number of maps.

———. *The Book of the Prophet Isaiah 40-66.* Cambridge and New York: Cambridge University Press, 1975. This installment in the Cambridge Bible Commentary on the New English Bible deals with Deutero-Isaiah and Trito-Isaiah, the chapters attributed to writers of the sixth century B.C. Helpful maps, as well as a table of historical events from 626 B.C. to approximately 500 B.C.

Kraeling, Emil G. *The Prophets.* Chicago: Rand McNally, 1969. A scholarly work dealing with the prophets in chronological order. Each Isaiah segment is handled in the historically appropriate section of the book. The emphasis is on the prophets' response to external and internal pressures. Begins with a convenient chronology.

Miscall, Peter D. *Isaiah*. Sheffield: JSOT Press, 1993. A chapter-by-chapter literary commentary of Isaiah that assumes the unity of the text and focuses especially on its conceptions of time.

Phillips, J. B. *Four Prophets, Amos, Hosea, First Isaiah, Micha: A Modern Translation from the Hebrew*. New York: Macmillan, and London: Bles, 1963. The famous translator of the New Testament here has cast four prophetic books in modern poetic form. The translation of First Isaiah ceases after chapter 35 because of the close parallel between chapters 36-39 and 2 Kings.

Sawyer, John F. A. *The Fifth Gospel: Isaiah in the History of Christianity*. Cambridge and New York: Cambridge University Press, 1996. A learned and stimulating history of interpretation of Isaiah that takes into account literary and artistic evidence. The author considers Isaiah's role in the early church, during the Middle Ages and the Reformation, and into the 19th and 20th centuries. The prophet appears as a complex figure, used for different purposes in different ages.

Scott, R. B. Y. *The Relevance of the Prophets*. Rev. ed. London and New York: Macmillan, 1968. An excellent background study, ranging in subject matter from the definition of prophecy and the significance of prophecy in Hebrew life to the relation of the prophets to society, to history, and to conventional religious structures. The final chapter, which bears the title of the book, is a lucid argument for the importance of the Old Testament prophets in the modern world.

Smith, J. M. Powis. *The Prophets and Their Times*. 2d ed. Chicago: University of Chicago Press, 1941. An important study by a great biblical scholar. Places the prophets within their historical periods. Although no single prophet is treated at length, the book is extremely valuable as a panoramic re-creation of prophetic times.

Rosemary M. Canfield-Reisman

ISOCRATES

Born: 436 B.C.; Athens, Greece
Died: 338 B.C.; Athens, Greece
Area of Achievement: Philosophy
Contribution: One of the ten "Attic Orators," Isocrates made significant contributions to the development of rhetorical theory, philosophy, and education in Ancient Greece. Isocrates' model of education grounded in rhetoric guided educators for centuries to follow.

Early Life

Isocrates was born during the archonship of Lysimachus in 436 B.C.. His father, Theodorus, was a wealthy flutemaker. His fathers' wealth afforded Isocrates the finest education of the day. He studied under such luminaries as Protagoras, Prodicus, Gorgias, Theramenes, and Tisias and joined the circle of Socrates. In *Phaedrus* (c. 360 B.C), Plato described Isocrates as a "youth of great promise."

Isocrates desperately wanted to play an important role in Athenian politics. A powerful case of stage fright coupled with a weak voice precluded his participation in the public-oratory-driven Athenian Assembly.

In 404 B.C., during the reign of the "Thirty Tyrants," Isocrates fled to the island of Chios, where he operated a small school of rhetoric. As a result of the Peloponnesian War, Isocrates' father, Theodorus, lost most of his property and wealth. Thus, in 403 B.C. Isocrates returned to Athens, where, as a result of financial need, he became a "forensic locographer," writing speeches for others to deliver in the courts. After only six speeches, Isocrates discovered that he lacked the practical gifts for winning cases and abandoned the profession. Isocrates would later disavow his career as a locographer, scorning the profession.

In 392 B.C.,at the age of forty-four, Isocrates set himself up as a teacher of rhetoric. His academy, located near the Lyceum in Athens, became the first permanent institution of liberal arts education, preceding Plato's Academy by five years. Isocrates announced the school and his new profession while attacking his sophistic competition with his essay Against the Sophists (c. 390 B.C.).

Life's Work

Isocrates' main legacy is the impact of his teachings on future generations of oratory and education. Isocrates' Academy was the most successful of all the Grecian schools of rhetoric. Cicero holds that this was the school in which all the eloquence of Greece was perfected, and alumni of Isocrates' academy are among the greatest statesmen, historians, writers, and orators of their time. There is evidence that even Aristotle may have been a pupil of Isocrates. Cicero and Demosthenes used Isocrates' work as a model, and through their work, Isocrates shaped generations of rhetorical thought and practice. Isocrates' style was incorporated into the works of orators, writers, and historians and was been passed down for more than nine centuries.

Isocrates would only admit students who had mastered grammar and could demonstrate previous knowledge in mathematics and the sciences. He believed that this knowledge was necessary grounding for the mental gymnastics of rhetoric, philosophy, and civics. Isocrates also demanded that potential students must demonstrate promise in voice control, intellect, and confidence. He believed that there were three essential qualities necessary for learning: natural ability, training, and experience. The training included studies in composition, debate, literature, philosophy, math, and history. Isocrates was also the first educator to utilize imitation and models as educational tools. The *Panegyricus* (c. 380 B.C.) and the *Plataeicus* (c. 373 B.C.) were written as model speeches for his pupils.

Isocrates' students were always expected to write and speak about cultural issues, with particular attention to the keeping of a panhellenic Greece above all nations. While style and diction were important, for the first time content was stressed in an academic setting. This content served to train the student in Isocrates' Hellenic ideology. The model orations that his students studied were propagandistic in that they professed Isocrates' political beliefs. Isocrates taught, and wrote in *Panegyricus*, that "Greek" denoted a man's education, not his race. Isocrates was sorely troubled by the petty squabbles that kept the various city-states at odds. He longed for a Greece that could stand united, and he planted this desire in his students.

In light of Isocrates' patriotism, it is unremarkable that the primary focus of Isocrates' educational plan was the development of citizen-orators. Isocrates considered political science and rhetoric nearly one and the same. Greek society was driven by oratory, and Isocrates taught that those who are the best users of speech are the men of greatest wisdom. Isocrates held that all the great works of humankind are the result of rhetoric. As he wrote in *Antidosis* (c. 354 B.C.), "There is no institution devised by man which the power of speech has not helped to establish." Isocrates taught that proper speaking was a sign of proper thinking and that the properly educated citizen was conspicious for his eloquence.

Although Isocrates' known works contain no definition of rhetoric, he did describe the functions of rhetoric: "With this faculty we both contend against others on matters which are open to dispute and seek light for ourselves on things which are unknown." For Isocrates, rhetoric was an epistemic, or knowledge-discovering, tool that guides thought and action and that demonstrates wisdom. In *Against the Sophists*, he taught that good oratory is speech that proves appropriate for an occasion while demonstrating proper style and originality. In *Panegyricus*, he added that timeliness was also a key to good oratory.

Another function of good oratory, for Isocrates, is eloquence, and he freed Greek prose from the stiff style of earlier periods. He created and mastered a smoothly rolling style of prose and elevated oratory to a formal art. His style involved precise vocabulary, few figures of speech, and many illustrations from history and philosophy. He believed that good oratory was very polished, as demonstrated by his taking ten years to refine *Panegyricus* for release.

Isocrates also professed that rhetoric is philosophic in that it teaches morals and politics. By "philosophy," Isocrates was describing a theory of culture. He believed that "philosophy" was the study of how to be a reasonable and useful citizen. Isocrates held that one should deliberate about both one's own affairs and the affairs of the state. He believed that a philosophic education should arouse intense patriotism as well as construct a personal philosophy close to the stoic ideal.

While Isocrates did not believe that virtue could be taught, he argued in *Against the Sophists* that it could be strengthened through training and practice in oratory. He argued that moral argumentation encourages right action because argumentation produces a historical narrative that uses historic events as precedents for present action. Therefore, one gains moral knowledge by studying public address both as the art of oratory and by imitating the great speakers; for, as he wrote in *Antidosis*, the lessons made "by a man's life" are stronger than lessons furnished by words.

Isocrates also saw the relationship between morality and oratory as reciprocal. In *Antidosis*, Isocrates explained that the more one wishes to persuade one's fellow citizens, the more important it is that the orator have a favorable reputation among those citizens. This notion served as the basis for the Roman rhetorician Quintilian's definition of *ethos*, or credibility, as a good man speaking well.

The concept that rhetorical training is moral training is hinged on Isocrates' notion that the test of all virtue or truth lies in that which wins approval. For Isocrates, it is through rhetoric that one can approximate truth, or at least a consensual truth. One who is trained in rhetoric is trained in truth, and in the creation of that truth through oratory. In *Antidosis*, he writes that "thanks to speech, we educate the fools and put the wise to the test; for we consider the fact of speaking rightly as the greatest sign of correct thinking." Thus, for Isocrates, there is no absolute truth, only consensual truth created by rhetoric.

Isocrates also believed that rhetoric had a role to play in the study of history. He made the study of history an art, not a science as Aristotle would have it. Isocrates began the tendency for a writer or speaker to idolize the past and use examples of the past to guide political attitudes and actions in the present. He also promoted the practice of glorifying individual figures, heroes, as catalysts of history. The outstanding historians of the fourth century, Ephorus of Cumae and Theopompus of Chios, were both pupils of Isocrates, and they introduced Isocrates' rhetorical style into the construction of history. There is also evidence that Xenophon, the greatest of fourth century historians, was intellectually influenced by Isocrates' *Evagoras* (c. 365 B.C.). From Isocrates forward, history has been more than an objective recounting of events; history has been patriotic.

Ironically, the man that Cicero termed "the master of all rhetoricians" did not himself speak in public. In *To Philip* (c. 344 B.C.), Isocrates explained that "nature has placed me more at a disadvantage than any of my fellow-citizens for a public career: I was not given a strong enough voice nor sufficient assurance to deal with the mob, to take abuse, and bandy words with the men who haunt the rostrum." As a result, his writings were meant to be read and are considered to be the earliest political pamphlets known. Through these oratorical pamphlets, Isocrates espoused a brand of Hellenism that would unite all Greeks together against a common foe. In his later years, Isocrates urged Philip II, king of Macedonia, to unite the Greeks under his leadership in a war against Persia.

Relatively late in his life, Isocrates married the daughter of Hippias, a sophist. He died in the Archonship of Chaerondas in 338 B.C., reportedly starving himself to death at the age of ninety-eight after hearing the news of Philip's victory over Athens in the battle of Chaerona.

Summary

Isocrates was the first of a series of great teachers who equated rhetoric and education. His method of teaching students to speak well on noble subjects, *vir bonus dicendi peritus*, remained the ideal of the ancient world. The creation of this ideal kept the rhetorical practices of the Greeks alive and passed that knowledge on to the Romans. Isocrates' significance rests, then, on the influence he had on those who followed him. Isocrates' ideas were carried on through such luminaries as the Athenian general Timotheus; Nicocles, the ruler of Salamis, in Cyprus; the Roman rhetoricians Cicero and Quintilian; and the historians Ephorus, Theopompus, and Xenophon. *Against the Sophists* served as the prototype for Plato's *Gorgias* (c. 380 B.C.), and Isocrates' name is mentioned more than that of any other rhetorician in Aristotle's *Rhetoric* (c. 350 B.C.).

The tradition of Isocrates runs silently through intellectual history, in that the art of the rhetorician is manifest in all human practices that are dependent upon effective communication. The tradition of *vir bonus dicendi peritus* continues in all scholarship in the attempt to create consensual truth. Moreover Isocrates' refinement of the Greek ideal of educating the individual for an active life in the service of the state widened the bounds of education. Cicero reported Isocrates' style of teaching oratory through his writings, and it became the standard of excellence for rhetorical education in Europe until the Renaissance. Components of this broad-based "liberal arts" education remain in the curricula of many modern schools.

Bibliography

Benoit, William L. "Isocrates on Rhetorical Education." *Communication Education* 33 (1984): 109-119. Provides a thorough analysis of Isocratean rhetorical study. Examines the whole of Isocrates' body of works and the impact that these works have had through the centuries.

Bury, J. B. *A History of Greece*. London: Macmillan, and New York: Random House, 1913. The standard and most comprehensive history of Greece, providing a detailed account of Greek history from the dawn of Western civilization to the death of Alexander the Great.

Botsford, George Willis, and Charles Alexander Robinson, Jr. *Hellenic History*. 5th ed. New York: Macmillan, 1969. A comprehensive examination of Hellenic history and culture. Pays significant attention to the interaction of art, literature, and oratory.

Golden, James L., Goodwin F. Berquist, and William E. Coleman. *The Rhetoric of Western Thought*. 6th ed. Dubuque, Iowa: Kendall/Hunt, 1997. A thorough history of the development of rhetorical theory and practice; contains a chapter on Isocrates, Cicero, and Quintilian. The standard work in the field of rhetorical theory.

Grube, G. M. A.. *The Greek and Roman Critics*. London: Methuen, 1965. Complete coverage of the Greek and Roman philosophers, from Homer and Hesiod through Longinus. Delineates connections between individual thinkers and schools of thought. Clearly shows Isocrates' role in the broadening of rhetorical theory.

Romilly, Jacqueline de. *Magic and Rhetoric in Ancient Greece*. Cambridge, Mass.: Harvard University Press, 1975; London: Harvard University Press, 1976. An unusual, enlightening treatment of the intellectual development of *logos* (rhetoric) and magic. Includes a section on the works of Isocrates.

B. Keith Murphy

JEREMIAH

Born: c. 645 B.C.; Anathoth, Judaea
Died: After 587 B.C.; Egypt
Area of Achievement: Religion
Contribution: Though Jeremiah failed to win the people of Judaea to a repentance which might have averted the catastrophe which overwhelmed them, his prophecies remained to comfort later generations of the people of Judah and to stand as a symbol of renewal for all people.

Early Life

If Jeremiah was born about 645 (some authorities place the date later), he was born into a troubled world. Israel, the northern Jewish kingdom, had been utterly crushed by Assyria (though some of the people must have remained, for Jeremiah denounced their religious laxness), and Judah itself, under Manasseh, had accepted Assyrian overlordship. Perhaps with Assyrian encouragement, pagan cults had flourished alongside the worship of the Lord (Yahweh)—cults devoted to Baal and the "queen of heaven," involving temple prostitution and even human sacrifice. With the decay of Assyrian power, however, Josiah (reigned c. 639-c. 609) was able to institute drastic reforms, which were encouraged by the finding in 622 of the book of the Law (some version of Deuteronomy). The reforms involved not only the suppression of the cults but also the centralization of the Lord's worship in Jerusalem at the expense of local shrines, even those dedicated to the Lord. Presumably, Jeremiah supported these reforms, even though they meant the decline of the shrine of Anathoth, where he had been born into a priestly family, possibly descendants of Abiathar, a high priest who had been exiled from Jerusalem for an intrigue against Solomon. Jeremiah's support of Josiah would explain the plots which the men of Anathoth directed against him. The gloomy tone of his prophecies even after the reforms could have been justified by the lingering existence of the cults, but he was also saddened by the empty ritualism that he observed and by the failure of the revival to promote social justice.

It was in this atmosphere, at any rate, that Jeremiah grew up. Some authorities date his appearance as a prophet in 627 and see the cause as the threat of an invasion by Scythian barbarians. If this was so, and no invasion took place, his powers of prediction could have been called into question.

Not that a prophet such as Isaiah or Jeremiah was a mere fortune-teller: He was a preacher calling his people to abandon paganism, to worship only the Lord, and to practice social justice. Though sometimes a prophecy of disaster was unconditional, it was often a threat of a punishment which could be averted by repentance, and sometimes it was a promise of restoration, however far in the future. As for the prophet, his was a heavy burden, for he was commanded by the Lord to deliver a message which was usually unwelcome. It was perhaps for this reason that Jeremiah never married and that his prophecies express a troubled relationship to the Lord and to his fellowmen: "Why is my pain perpetual, and my wound incurable, which refuseth to be healed? Wilt thou be altogether unto me as a liar, and as waters that fail?" (This passage and subsequent quotations from Jeremiah are taken from the King James Version of the Bible, chosen partly for its literary quality and partly because some scholars believe that this translation, despite its archaisms, best reflects the style of the Hebrew text. Modern translations are sometimes preferred because they incorporate the results of recent linguistic and historical scholarship.)

Life's Work

In about 609, Josiah died in battle against the Egyptians, and Jehoiakim succeeded him as an Egyptian vassal. Jeremiah found little reason to be satisfied with the new king, who allowed the cults to return and, at a time when his subjects had to pay onerous tribute to Egypt, built a new palace with forced labor: "Woe unto him that buildeth his house by unrighteousness, and his chambers by wrong; that useth his neighbor's service without wages, and giveth him not for his work." Jeremiah's repeated denunciations of the social order (he prophesied that the king would be "buried with the burial of an ass") once brought him in danger of his life, and on another occasion he was beaten and put into the stocks overnight. Nevertheless, in 604, as the Babylonians were becoming an increasing menace to Judah, Jeremiah dictated to his disciple Baruch a kind of final warning, a scroll which Baruch read aloud in the Temple. When some of the king's advisers had it read to him, Jehoiakim took a knife and hacked off bits as it was read and burned them. Jehoiakim temporarily accepted the overlordship of Babylon, but three years later, un-

der his son Jehoiachin, Judah rebelled. After the fall of Jerusalem in 597, King Nebuchadnezzar II carried off an immense booty and a considerable number of the most prominent inhabitants. Zedekiah (597-587) was permitted to take over the throne as a Babylonian vassal. Jeremiah, who had come to regard Nebuchadnezzar as the Lord's instrument of punishment, persistently urged Judah to submit quietly to Babylonian rule. Zedekiah may have been inclined to accept Jeremiah's advice, but he could not control his ministers, and a rival prophet, Hananiah, promised the downfall of Babylon and the return of the captives. In 589, revolt broke out, and by 588 Jerusalem was under siege.

During the siege, Jeremiah was in considerable danger as a traitor and threat to morale. In spite of the hostility of the people of Anathoth, he had exercised a kinsman's right to redeem a piece of family land put up for sale there and had symbolically buried the dead against the time of restoration, when once again people should "buy fields for money, and subscribe evidences, and seal them, and take witnesses in the land of Benjamin." When, during an interlude in the siege, he tried to

go into the land of Benjamin, he was arrested and beaten as a deserter. When he urged the people to surrender, he was cast into a muddy pit and might have died if he had not been rescued by an Ethiopian eunuch, and he was thereafter kept in custody, though less rigorously, throughout the siege.

After Zedekiah, in accordance with the Law, had "proclaimed liberty" to all the Hebrew slaves in Jerusalem, and their masters pretended to let them go and then reenslaved them, Jeremiah made an especially bitter prophecy:

> Ye have not hearkened unto me, in proclaiming liberty, every one to his brother, and every man to his neighbor: behold, I proclaim a liberty for you, saith the Lord, to the sword, to the pestilence, and to the famine; and I will make you to be removed into all the kingdoms of the earth.

The end came in 587. The city fell; Zedekiah was blinded and his sons and many nobles executed; the city was utterly destroyed, and its surviving inhabitants were deported to Babylon. Nebuchadnezzar took care that Jeremiah was treated kindly, offering him a special place in Babylon. Jeremiah elected, however, to cast in his lot with Gedaliah, a native prince who had been appointed governor of the remnant "of the poor of the people, that had nothing, in the land of Judah," who had been left behind and given vineyards and fields. Some remnants of the army and the court and a number of other fugitives rallied to Gedaliah, but he was assassinated by diehards who regarded him as a turncoat. The survivors sought Jeremiah's advice, and he urged them to remain and submit themselves to Babylon, and under no circumstances to go into Egypt, where they would die "by the sword, by the famine, and by the pestilence." To Egypt they went nevertheless and carried Jeremiah with them. The last words of Jeremiah in Scripture are a report of his denunciation of some women who had sacrificed to the queen of heaven, but he had lost honor as a prophet, since the Lord had failed to save his people. According to one tradition, Jeremiah was stoned by the angry refugees.

Summary

In terms of immediate results, it would be easy to term Jeremiah's life a failure. The prophecies against foreign states, which were made without promise of renewal, did indeed come true, though it needed no prophet to foresee them; the same is true of his prophecies against the northern kingdom of Israel. The reforms of Josiah apparently gave him imperfect satisfaction, for presumably the cults revived after Josiah's death. In any case, the issue came to be overshadowed by Judah's suicidal foreign policy, and Jeremiah suffered persecution and derision for urging more prudent behavior toward Babylon. When the survivors of the consequent disaster elected to flee to Egypt, Jeremiah was powerless to deter them, and in Egypt he suffered a final humiliation when the Jewish women revived the worship of the queen of heaven, saying that as long as they had worshipped her in Judaea, they had been "well, and saw no evil." It is no wonder that "jeremiad" is a modern word for a dolorous tirade.

Yet these original jeremiads are eloquent and beautiful (much of the text is in the form of Hebrew poetry), and even more impressive (though less lengthy) are the promises of restoration:

> After those days, saith the Lord, I will put my law in their inward parts, and write it in their hearts; and will be their God, and they shall be my people. And they shall teach no more every man his neighbor, and every man his brother, saying, Know the Lord: for they shall all know me, from the least of them unto the greatest of them, saith the Lord: for I will forgive their iniquity, and I will remember their sin no more.

Perhaps inspired by these words, years later some of the exiles returned and, under Persian protection, established a state which observed the Deuteronomic code and endured until its destruction by the Romans. Still later, such passages were interpreted as announcing the coming of Jesus Christ.

Bibliography

Ackroyd, Peter R. *Exile and Restoration: A Study of Hebrew Thought in the Sixth Century B.C.* Philadelphia: Westminster Press, and London: SCM Press, 1968. Ackroyd's assumptions are that Old Testament prophecy is relevant to Christian theology, that the prophetic books should be viewed as a whole, and that this whole is unique and far-reaching in its influence.

Bright, John. Introduction to *The Anchor Bible: Jeremiah.* 2d ed. New York: Doubleday and Co., 1965. A thorough, scholarly introduction of nearly 150 pages. Topics include the prophets of Israel, the historical background, the structure and composition of the book, the life and message of Jeremiah, and the text. The volume also contains an original translation with heavy annotation and a bibliography. Strongly recommended.

Funk and Wagnalls New Standard Bible Dictionary. Edited by Melancthon W. Jacobus, Elbert C. Lane, and Andrew C. Zenos. 3d ed. New York: Funk and Wagnalls, 1936. Gives a brief but adequate account of Jeremiah's life and times, general character of the book, personal characteristics, significance of the work, and text, with a bibliography. There are separate entries on the history of Israel, prophecy, and other related topics.

Heschel, Abraham J. *The Prophets.* New York: Harper and Row, 1962. Attempts to attain an understanding of the prophet through analysis of his consciousness. This contrasts with an approach which either emphasizes supernatural truth or uses a psychological bias.

Perdue, Leo G., and Brian W. Kovacs, eds. *A Prophet to the Nations: Essays in Jeremiah Studies.* Winona Lake, Wis.: Eisenbrauns, 1984. An anthology representing the best modern scholarship on Jeremiah. Among the topics discussed are the date of the prophet's call, the identity of the enemy from the north, textual problems, and the composition and development of the book. On some points (for example, the dates of Jeremiah's birth and his first call, the identity of the "enemy from the north"), the conclusions differ from those given in the present essay.

Rosenberg, Joel. "Jeremiah and Ezekiel." In *The Literary Guide to the Bible*, edited by Robert Alter and Frank Kermode. Cambridge, Mass.: Harvard University Press, and London: Collins, 1987. Aside from comment on purely literary topics, this piece is chiefly valuable for making sense out of the confused chronology of the Book of Jeremiah. Valuable notes and bibliography.

John C. Sherwood

SAINT JEROME
Eusebius Hieronymus

Born: Between 331 and 347; Stridon, Dalmatia
(modern Yugoslavia)

Died: Probably 420; Bethlehem, Palestine

Areas of Achievement: Scholarship, monasticism,
and religion

Contribution: Because of his scholarship, commentaries on and translation of the Bible into Latin, and role as a propagandist for celibacy and the monastic life, Jerome is numbered with Saint Ambrose, Saint Augustine, and Gregory the Great as one of the Fathers of the Church.

Early Life

Saint Jerome grew up in a world in which the influence of Christianity was rapidly expanding. He was born Eusebius Hieronymus. The names of his mother and younger sister are unknown, but his father, Eusebius, was a wealthy landowner, and Jerome had a younger brother, Paulinianus. Jerome's parents were Christians, although apparently not fervent.

Jerome began his schooling in Stridon. From Stridon he was sent to Rome for his secondary education. His parents were clearly ambitious for him: Rome was the most prestigious center of learning in the Latin-speaking part of the empire, and Aelius Donatus, the most famous master of the day, was Jerome's instructor in grammar. For at least four years, Donatus provided Jerome with a fairly typical Hellenistic education, centering on grammar and the reading and analysis of classical literature. By his adult years, Jerome had an extensive knowledge of the Latin classics. He is generally considered to be the finest of all Christian writers in Latin. In Rome he probably also acquired an elementary knowledge of Greek.

From Donatus' school, Jerome went to a school of rhetoric, also in Rome. He seems to have studied some law during this period and later could cite the Roman law with great accuracy. One of his fellow students was the Christian Tyrranius Rufinus, who was later to translate many Greek Christian writings into Latin. He and Jerome were the closest of friends, although this friendship would later break down over a theological dispute. Jerome, as a young man, had already begun to acquire many books; in his subsequent journeys he carried his library with him.

Life's Work

Jerome's baptism at Rome, sometime before 366, signaled his deepening interest in Christianity. Nothing is known of his life from approximately 357 until 367. In the next five years, Jerome traveled in Gaul, Dalmatia, and northeast Italy, particularly to Aquileia, where Rufinus lived. Although this period is also very obscure, it is clear that Jerome had become interested in current theological controversy. More important, during this period, he felt called to a more serious Christian life. For many of his contemporaries, this call was to an abandonment of the world and a life of asceticism or strict discipline. Monasticism—an institutionalized form of asceticism commonly centered on the abandonment of private property, various forms of self-denial, such as fasting and celibacy, and the attempt to live a life of perpetual prayer—had existed in the eastern part of the empire for more than a half century, but had only recently appeared in the West. Jerome did not adopt this difficult life-style suddenly. Like his younger contemporary Augustine, he first renounced further secular ambitions and committed himself to a life of contemplation and study.

Apparently, Jerome's determination to follow the ascetic life, and his success in persuading his sister to follow suit, led to an estrangement from his parents. In 372, like many pilgrims of his day, Jerome left Rome for the East and Jerusalem. As it turned out, he was not to reach Jerusalem for some years. He remained a year in Antioch, Syria, plagued with illness, but used his time there to improve his Greek and familiarize himself with the current state of theological controversy on the nature of the Trinity.

Jerome was tormented by the fact that he still had not made a clean break with the world, and probably in 374 had his famous dream, in which a Judge appeared and accused him of being a disciple of Cicero rather than Christ. That was an expression of Jerome's inability to give up reading of the classical authors in favor of purely biblical studies. Jerome records that this dream ended with him swearing an oath no longer to possess or read pagan books. He was later to say that he could not be held permanently to an oath made in a dream, but the dream does seem to mark the point at which

his life's work—the study of Christian literature— came into focus. He began the first in a series of commentaries on the books of the Bible; this earliest work is not extant.

As Jerome's health returned, with it came the desire to follow through on his ascetic intentions. Many desert hermits lived near Antioch, and Jerome chose a hermit cell for himself near Chalcis. He remained in the desert two or three years, increasingly frustrated by the abuse heaped on him by the quarreling Syrian theological factions, each wishing to convert him to its position. He had his large library with him and continued his studies, learning Hebrew from a Jewish convert. Shortly after his return to Antioch, in 376 or 377, he began the second of his sustained projects, a series of translations of Greek Christian writings into Latin. His fame was growing rapidly, and he was ordained a priest by the Bishop of Antioch, although he was always to think of himself primarily as a monk.

By 379 or 380, Jerome was in Constantinople and suffering from a disease of the eyes. In 382, he was in Rome, in the service of Damasus, the Bishop of Rome, as secretary and adviser. Damasus commissioned what was to become the great labor of Jerome's life—the preparation of a standard Latin translation of the Bible. The intended scope of this project is unclear: He probably completed translations of the four Gospels and the Psalms while in Rome.

Jerome spent about three years in Rome, during which he became the spiritual guide for an extraordinary group of high-born girls and women committed to the ascetic life and led by the widows Marcella and Paula. Paula's third daughter, Julia Eustochium, was to be at Jerome's side for the rest of his life. Throughout his life, Jerome tended to create conflict with his sarcastic and combative remarks and letters. Damasus died in 384, and Jerome left Rome in 385 under pressure from both clergy and lay people whom he had offended.

Paula, Eustochium, and Jerome settled in Palestine in 386. The rest of Jerome's life was to be spent in Bethlehem and the environs of Jerusalem in a penitential life of prayer and study. Two monasteries were built at Bethlehem, one for women and one for men, and there the three friends lived until their deaths. Jerome returned to the study of Hebrew and moderated his earlier condemnation of the study of the classics. More and more, in his commentaries on and works related to the Old Tes-

tament, he relied on rabbinical interpretation and turned from the Septuagint—the Greek translation of the Old Testament commonly used in Christian circles—to the Hebrew. Jerome became convinced that a Latin translation of the Old Testament should be based directly on the Hebrew, and in about 390, he set aside the work he had done and began a new version from the original texts. Jerome's translation met with opposition and charges of Judaizing. It was not until the ninth century that his work was fully accepted; his translation of the Old Testament and Gospels, when added to translations of the remaining New Testament books by unknown scholars, became known as the Vulgate (common) Bible.

Jerome's last years were filled with tragedy. He continued to be in pain and poor health. Paula died in 404. The barbarians, who began their invasion of the empire in 375, attacked the Holy Land in 405, and Rome itself was sacked in 410. Jerome interpreted the Fall of Rome as the destruction of civilization. In 416, the monasteries at Bethlehem were burned and the monks and nuns assaulted. Jerome died in Bethlehem, probably in 420.

Summary

Saint Jerome's Christianity was a religion which at once challenged the mind of the scholar and urged those "who would be perfect" (Matthew 19:21) to detach themselves from normal worldly expectations. That a monasticism both learned and ascetic was the central cultural institution of the Middle Ages is in no small part his heritage. Although he is not, as was once thought, responsible for the entire Latin Vulgate Bible, he is responsible for the Old Testament and Gospel books of that translation. The Bible in Jerome's translation was the basis for the Wycliffe translation in the fourteenth century and the Douay version in the sixteenth century. His work was to influence Western theology and church life for centuries.

Jerome was a Latin scholar in a Greek and Hebrew-speaking world. At Bethlehem, he was one of the most important agents of crosscultural transference the world has known. Very few ancient Christians, Greek or Latin, knew Hebrew, and contacts between Jew and Christian in the ancient world regularly led to conflict. Against this backdrop, Jerome, because he saw the necessity of tracing Christianity to its most ancient Jewish roots, cultivated personal and scholarly contact with learned

Jews and offered a clearer vision than had ever existed of what united, and separated, the religions.

Bibliography

Bouyer, Louis. *The Spirituality of the New Testament and the Fathers*. Translated by Mary P. Ryan. London: Burns and Oates, 1960; New York: Desclee Co., 1963. This first volume in the History of Christian Spirituality series is a reliable survey of ancient Christian spirituality, with a good comparison of Ambrose, Jerome, and Augustine. More sympathetic to Jerome's spiritual ideals than Kelly (see below) and much better on the theological issues involved on the relation of the literal and spiritual senses of Scripture.

Brown, Peter. *The Body and Society: Men, Women, and Sexual Renunciation in Early Christianity*. New York: Columbia University Press, 1988. A fascinating exercise in the history of ideas and their impact on society. Brown treats Jerome and other church fathers from the perspective of their views about sexuality.

The Cambridge History of the Bible. 3 vols. Cambridge: Cambridge University Press, 1963-1970. Volume 1, *From the Beginnings to Jerome*, edited by P. R. Ackroyd and C. F. Evans, and volume 2, *The West, from the Fathers to the Reformation*, edited by G. W. H. Lampe, contain useful and generally well-informed sections on Jerome. This study is often provincial, without mention of some of the best of Continental scholarship.

Courcelle, Pierre. *Late Latin Writers and Their Greek Sources*. Translated by Harry E. Wedeck. Cambridge, Mass.: Harvard University Press, 1969. One of the great achievements of twentieth century scholarship, this volume traces in detail the use and knowledge of Greek works by Latin writers. Makes clear the central importance of Jerome as a translator and agent of dissemination of Greek authors.

Hagendahl, Harald. *Latin Fathers and the Classics*. Göteborg, Sweden: Almqvist and Wiksell, 1958. This is a careful, thorough, generally reliable study of Jerome's familiarity with and use of the pagan classics. Good on his dream of the Judge and its effect on his later life.

Hayward, C. T. R. *Saint Jerome's Hebrew Questions on Genesis*. Oxford Early Christian Studies. Oxford: Clarendon Press, and New York: Oxford University Press, 1995. An English translation of, with full commentary on, Jerome's commentary on Genesis.

Kamesar, Adam. *Jerome, Greek Scholarship and the Hebrew Bible: A Study of the Questiones Hebraicae in Genesim*. Oxford Classical Monographs. Oxford: Clarendon Press, and New York: Oxford University Press, 1993. A close study of Jerome as scholar and translator of the Bible. Attention is paid to Jerome's working methods and to the state of Biblical scholarship prior to Jerome. Some passages in Latin, Greek, and Hebrew are untranslated.

Kelly, J. N. D. *Jerome: His Life, Writings, and Controversies*. London: Duckworth, and New York: Harper and Row, 1975. This is the best and most complete book on Jerome in English. It may nevertheless be criticized for holding Jerome to a demanding modern standard of judgment, for a lack of sympathy for his spiritual ideals, especially when they involve celibacy, and for an insufficiently sophisticated presentation of the issues involved in the relation of the literal to the spiritual senses of Scripture.

Glenn W. Olsen

JESUS CHRIST

Born: c. 6 B.C.; Bethlehem, Judaea
Died: A.D. 30; Jerusalem
Area of Achievement: Religion
Contribution: As the basis for a religious faith that has attracted many millions of adherents, Jesus' life and teachings have exerted an enormous influence on Western civilization.

Early Life

Though his name is recognized by millions and his birthday is celebrated as a holiday across the Western world, Jesus Christ's early life is shrouded in obscurity. Neither the day nor year of his birth can be fixed with certainty. Some scholars think that Bethlehem was identified as the place of his birth merely to make his life conform to old prophecies. Objective study of his life is complicated by the fact that many people believe him to be the Son of God.

The earliest Christian writer whose works are extant, the apostle Paul (died A.D. 64), makes no reference to the historical life of Jesus, aside from quoting a few of his sayings. The four canonical Gospels are not, strictly speaking, biographies of Jesus. They were written as aids to memorizing his teachings or as arguments in favor of his divinity; they do not purport to be complete accounts (John 20:30). The earliest of them, attributed to Mark (c. A.D. 70), begins with the story of Jesus' baptism by John in the river Jordan. The two attributed to Matthew (A.D. 80?) and Luke (A.D. 90?) add a story about Jesus teaching in the Temple when he was twelve and give differing accounts of his birth and genealogy. John's Gospel (A.D. 100?) is a reflective memoir, differing in chronology and in its portrayal of Jesus as a Hellenistic teacher rather than a Jewish rabbi. Other gospels, not included in the New Testament, attempted to fill the gap in Christians' knowledge about Jesus' early life by concocting fantastic stories. There are no other historical sources for the study of his life.

Matthew and Luke agree that Herod the Great was King of Judaea at Jesus' birth. Herod died in 4 B.C. Since, in Matthew 2, he is reported to have slaughtered male children under the age of two in an effort to kill the infant Jesus, scholars conclude that Jesus may have been born as early as 6 B.C. (The error in calculation was made by a sixth century monk, who compared all the then-available chronological data to determine the time of Jesus' birth.) The date of December 25 was selected by the Bishop of Rome in the late fourth century. Having a Christian festival at that time of year enabled the Church to distract its members from popular pagan festivals which occurred then. Before that time, Jesus' nativity was celebrated at various times of the year, if at all.

Jesus grew up in Galilee, where Greek influences were stronger than in the southern territory of Judaea. Though his native language was Aramaic, which is related to Hebrew, he would have had to know Greek to conduct any business. His father, Joseph, is usually described as a carpenter. The Greek word actually means something more like "builder" or "general contractor."

Life's Work

The Jews of Galilee were less conservative than those of Judaea. Rabbinic traditions and regulations were challenged in the north by a greater interest in the prophetic side of Judaism. Jesus, while not trained as a rabbi, seems to have been familiar with the standard methods of argument. He engaged in debates over interpretation of Scripture where appropriate (Mark 12:13-34) but sometimes sidestepped hairsplitting questions (Luke 10:25-37). At some points, though, he showed flashes of originality. He is never recorded as basing his teaching on the opinions of earlier rabbis—the accepted technique of the day—but taught instead on his own authority (Matt. 7:29). Parables (story-comparisons) seem to have been the foundation of his teaching technique (Mark 4:33).

Judaism was a diverse religion in the early first century A.D. Flavius Josephus describes three sects or schools flourishing at that time: the liberal and popular Pharisees, the aristocratic and conservative Sadducees, and the monastic Essenes. The Pharisees were further subdivided into the school of Shammei, which urged resistance to Roman rule, and that of Hillel, which counseled accommodation. There were also radical fringe groups such as the Zealots, who hoped to provoke a confrontation with the Romans that would lead to divine intervention and the foundation of a new kingdom of Israel.

Jesus' sudden appearance in the "fifteenth year of the reign of Tiberius" (Luke 3:1), or A.D. 29, when he was "about thirty years of age" (Luke

3:23), fit in with the general mood of discontent which prevailed in Judaea at the time. His message that "the kingdom of God is at hand" found a receptive audience. The eschatological tone was interpreted by some as an announcement of the overthrow of Roman hegemony. Even Jesus' closest disciples did not easily give up their hope for a reestablishment of the Davidic kingship (Acts 1:6).

Jesus does not, however, seem to have envisioned himself as a political revolutionary. His aim appears to have been to reform Judaism, which had become so weighted down with minute requirements that even the most scrupulous Jews had difficulty adhering to the Torah. Jesus accused the Pharisees of imposing their own restrictions on top of the commandments of Torah (Luke 11:46) and of neglecting what he called "the weightier matters of the Law: justice, mercy, and faith" (Matt. 23:23). Such utterances link Jesus with Old Testament prophets such as Amos (Amos 5:21-24), Jeremiah (Jer. 31:31-34), and Micah (Mic. 6:7-8), who criticized the legalism of Judaism in their day and urged that obedience to the Law be a matter of inner motivation, not observance of external rituals.

Such a view was thus not a new creation of Jesus. Even his most familiar injunction, to love one's neighbor as oneself, was a quotation of Leviticus 19:18. In general, his teaching can be classed under three headings: criticism of the normative Judaism of his day (for example, Matt. 23), proposal of a new, interiorized ethic (Matt. 5-7, the Sermon on the Mount), and expectations of the imminence of the kingdom of God (Mark 13).

In addition to his teaching, the accounts of his life contain miracle stories, in which Jesus purportedly heals people with various infirmities or demonstrates his power over nature by calming storms and walking on water. The Gospels conclude with the greatest of the miracle stories, the account of Jesus' resurrection, which Paul saw as the proof of his divinity (Rom. 1:4). The other apostles also made it the center of their preaching (Acts 2:22-36).

These miracle stories are probably the major point of dispute between those who accept the divinity of Jesus and those who do not. Even those who find his ethical teachings attractive sometimes find it difficult to accept the supernatural accounts which surround them. The scientific orientation which has undergirded Western education since the mid-nineteenth century has produced an outlook on the world that makes the miracle stories seem more akin to fairy tales.

In the first century A.D., however, people were eager to believe stories of the supernatural. In Petronius Arbiter's *Satyricon* (first century A.D.), one of the characters tells a werewolf story. At the end, a listener says, "I believe every word of it," and goes on to tell a ghost story of his own. Suetonius, biographer of the first century Roman emperors, recounts as fact a story that Vespasian healed two men in Egypt in the presence of a large audience. The philosopher/mystic Apollonius of Tyana, a contemporary of Jesus, was credited with healing, resurrecting the dead, and having his birth accompanied by supernatural signs.

A major difficulty with the Gospel miracles is the inconsistency of various versions of some of the stories. For example, in Matthew 14:22-33, when Jesus walks across the waves to his disciples' boat, Peter steps out of the craft and takes a few steps before, becoming fearful, he starts to sink. Mark 6:45-51 and John 6:17-21, however, make no mention of Peter's aquatic stroll. John's is the only version which says that as soon as Jesus got into the boat, it reached the other shore.

Perhaps too much attention is devoted to the miracle stories, distracting from the more central issues of Jesus' teaching. The Gospels record his reluctance to perform miracles (Mark 8:12) because the crowds paid more attention to them than to his teachings.

Recovering Jesus' own sense of his purpose is difficult because all the documents relating to him were produced by people who believed him to be divine. Modern scholarship has concentrated on probing under the layers of interpretation which his followers added to the story in consequence of their claim that he was resurrected (see John 12:16). Jesus seems to have seen himself as a final messenger to the Jews. He claimed to have greater authority than the prophets, just as a king's son has greater authority than his servants (Mark 12:1-11).

His message was essentially a warning that the Jews had exalted ritual observance of God's Law to the point that they had lost sight of its moral implications. His criticism was directed especially against the Pharisees and scribes. They reacted predictably, by plotting to silence the troublemaker. With the collusion of one of Jesus' followers, Judas Iscariot, they seized him in a garden on the outskirts of Jerusalem.

The trial of Jesus has been a subject of much controversy as to its legality and the exact charges involved. The Romans normally left local matters in the hands of provincial officials, and the Sanhedrin had the right to try cases involving Jewish law. They do not seem to have had the power to condemn a prisoner to death. They found Jesus guilty of violating religious laws, especially those against blasphemy, but before Pontius Pilate, the Roman governor, they accused him of treason.

Pilate had been governor of Judaea for about three years at that time. According to Josephus, he had difficulty getting along with the Jews from the day of his arrival. His insensitivity to their religious traditions was a major part of the problem. His decision to crucify Jesus may have been made out of genuine concern that the man was a threat to the social order, but it was probably an effort to mollify the Jews, who had already complained to the emperor about him.

Within a few days of his death, Jesus' disciples were claiming that he had risen from the dead. Whatever one may think of that assertion, the disciples' belief in it had a remarkable effect on them. From a dispirited band of fishermen and peasants who had begun to scatter back to their homes, they were transformed into a fellowship of believers willing to undergo any difficulty or torment to proclaim their faith (Luke 24:13-35). Not even threats from the religious authorities of the day could silence them (Acts 5:27-32).

Summary

If his goal was to reform Judaism, Jesus Christ can hardly be judged successful. The Pharisees resisted his initial efforts and refused to recognize his followers as loyal Jews. Driven out of the synagogues, they founded a new faith which emphasized the spiritual values of Jesus' teachings. Jesus' assertion of the importance of love of God and fellowman—even one's enemies—and the shunning of ceremonialism and class distinctions were not original but resulted from his stress on long-neglected facets of Jewish scripture. His is the Judaism of the prophets, not of the Torah and the Talmud.

However one may regard the claims made about his divinity, Jesus' impact on Western culture has been too profound to ignore. His teaching introduced an element of humaneness that even the

Greeks and Romans found remarkable. Unlike their pagan neighbors, Christians did not procure abortions or abandon unwanted children after birth. They cared for their sick, and during plagues they cared for the sick and dying pagans who had been dumped in the streets. They did not seek vengeance on those who wronged them. Several pagan writers of the first four centuries, including Aulus Cornelius Celsus, Porphyry, and the Emperor Julian (sometimes called Julian the Apostate), grudgingly admired the despised Christians and urged pagans to live up to the Christian standards of charity and philanthropy.

In summary, then, Jesus' teachings laid the groundwork for the Western world's system of morality, however imperfectly it has been observed. If Socrates gave definition to the Western intellect, Jesus implanted in it a conscience.

Bibliography

Bornkamm, Gunther. *Jesus of Nazareth*. New York: Harper and Row, and London: Hodder and Stoughton, 1960. The book which reopened the question of how much can be known about the historical Jesus after a half century of pessimism engendered by Albert Schweitzer's *The Quest of the Historical Jesus* (see below).

Bowker, John. *Jesus and the Pharisees*. Cambridge and New York: Cambridge University Press, 1973. Comparison of the teachings of Jesus with those of the Pharisaic schools of his day. Bowker concludes that the content of much of his message was not new, but his interpretation of it was.

Brandon, S. G. F. *The Trial of Jesus of Nazareth*. New York: Stein and Day, and London: B. T. Batsford, 1968. Discusses the problem of evidence which makes the study of Jesus' trial so problematic. The Gospels cannot be studied as if they were legal transcripts; the biases of their authors must be understood first.

Bruce, F. F. *The Hard Sayings of Jesus*. Downers Grove, Ill.: Inter-Varsity Press, and London: Hodder and Stoughton, 1983. Examination of some of Jesus' sayings which modern readers find particularly difficult to understand. Many of them are explicable in terms of the social or economic context of Jesus' time.

Bultmann, Rudolf. *Jesus Christ and Mythology*. New York: Scribner, 1958; London: SCM Press, 1960. Bultmann is the foremost proponent of the school of thought which holds that virtually nothing can be known of the historical Jesus: The Gospels reflect only what his followers thought about him.

Goodspeed, Edgar J. *A Life of Jesus*. New York: Harper and Row, 1950. A biography based on the first three Gospels, assuming that they present a historically accurate account.

Grant, Michael. *Jesus: An Historian's Review of the Gospels*. New York: Scribner, 1977. A moderate, scholarly review of the problems related to using the Gospels as historical sources.

Jeremias, Joachim. *The Parables of Jesus*. 2d ed. New York: Scribner, and London: SCM Press, 1972. Regards the parables as the most accurately preserved part of the material relating to Jesus. Discusses principles and problems of interpretation, then analyzes the parables under subject headings.

Klausner, J. *Jesus of Nazareth: His Life, Times, and Teaching*. New York: Macmillan, and London: Allen and Unwin, 1925. A controversial classic by a Jewish scholar who surveys conditions in Palestine in Jesus' time and compares his teaching to what was current among the Pharisees.

Robinson, James McConkey. *A New Quest of the Historical Jesus and Other Essays*. Philadelphia: Fortress Press, 1983. Survey of the recent debate over the question of how much one can know about the historical Jesus on the basis of the Gospels. Robinson suggests that it is possible to learn something about his life, if one uses the sources advisedly.

Schweitzer, Albert. *The Quest of the Historical Jesus*. Translated by W. Montgomery. London: Black, and New York: Macmillan, 1910. Originally published in German in 1906, this study surveys nineteenth century attempts at writing a biography of Jesus and concludes that, because of the nature of the sources, it is an impossible task.

Albert A. Bell, Jr.

JOHANAN BEN ZAKKAI

Born: c. A.D. 1; Judaea
Died: c. A.D. 80; Beror Heil, west of Jerusalem, Judaea
Area of Achievement: Religion
Contribution: After the destruction of Jerusalem by the Romans in A.D. 70, when the temple cult—the center of Jewish life—lay in ruins, Johanan was responsible for reorienting Jewish life around faithful observance of the Law (Torah).

Early Life

Little is known of the early life of Johanan ben Zakkai. Of the three most important sources of information for Roman-occupied Judaea during the first century, two of them, Flavius Josephus' *Peri tou Ioudaikou polemou* (A.D. 75-79; *Jewish War*) and the New Testament, contain no reference to Johanan. The rabbinical writings from the Talmud which constitute the sole source of information regarding the life of Johanan ben Zakkai were compiled between the third and fifth centuries, and at best testify to carefully handed-down memory. (For reasons of standardization, the initials B.C. and A.D. are used here to designate the chronological divisions often referred to as B.C.E., "before the common era," and C.E., "common era.")

The Talmud pictures Johanan as a leader among the Pharisees, a group of especially devout observers of the Torah (the first five books in the Hebrew Bible) who first came to prominence in the late second or first centuries B.C. and who, after the destruction of the Temple in A.D. 70 by the Romans, became the sole shapers of what is today normative Judaism. The main tradition concerning Johanan relates that he "occupied himself in commerce forty years, served as apprentice to the sages forty years, and sustained Israel forty years." He was one of four Jewish leaders believed to have lived for 120 years, the others being Moses, Hillel the Elder, and Rabbi Akiba ben Joseph. Johanan was considered to have been the last of eighty students of Hillel, who, in similar manner, "went up from Babylonia aged forty years, served as apprentice to the sages forty years, and sustained Israel forty years."

Johanan actually was born near the beginning of the first century and died during its last quarter, probably around 80. "Johanan" means "the Lord gave graciously"; Ezra and Nehemiah record 760 sons of Zakkai ("righteous man") among nearly forty-five thousand exiles returning to Jerusalem and Judah from Babylonian exile during the sixth century B.C. Johanan was descended from commoners rather than priests; his halakhic (legal) rulings sternly criticize the conduct of the upper classes toward the poor. Some of his rulings reflect a detailed knowledge of business affairs and support the claim that he engaged in business in his early or mid-life. As a young man, he entered the rabbinic academy of Hillel in Jerusalem. Whether he studied under the Master himself is problematical; Hillel died probably around A.D. 10 or at most a few years thereafter.

What is certain is that, of the two great Pharisaic schools of Torah interpretation—those of Hillel and Shammai—Johanan was schooled in the traditions of Hillel, which are generally pictured as more irenic in approach to the Law and more patient in dealing with students, as well as more widely accepted among the middle classes. Hence Johanan developed traits of flexibility in casuistry and gentleness toward students which enabled him to make a lasting contribution to the development of Judaism.

As a student, Johanan was famed for both self-discipline and intellectual acuity. He never traveled four cubits (six feet) without words of Torah, even in winter. No one preceded him into the schoolroom, nor did he ever leave anyone behind there. "If all the heavens were parchment," said Johanan, "and all the trees pens, and all the oceans ink, they would not suffice to write down the wisdom which I have learned from my masters." One of his students later made a similar statement regarding his own education at the feet of Johanan. Tradition pictures Hillel endorsing Johanan, conferring as it were his own mantle on his young student. When he completed his studies in Jerusalem, Johanan moved to a village in the northern province of Galilee—the other end of the country from Jerusalem and far removed from its scrupulous observance of the Torah. There, with his wife and his young son, he undertook his career as a teacher, a missionary for the Torah. In the Pharisaic manner, he supported himself, probably in business, while he attempted to teach the Galileans.

Life's Work

A political event—the destruction of the Temple in A.D. 70 by the Romans—intervened in Johanan's life to thrust him, at seventy years of age, onto the center stage of Jewish history. Johanan had given his life to scholarship and teaching and was not involved in politics. His eighteen years in Galilee and the subsequent three decades which he spent as a teacher in Jerusalem together consumed his prime years. He reached the biblical "threescore and ten" offstage from history, and his decades of labor in Galilee and Jerusalem are historically noteworthy only as part of the story of a life made unexpectedly significant in the context of the destruction of the center of Judaism—the Temple—and the consequent reorientation of the Jewish religion around the Law.

There is no specific evidence that Johanan's purpose in going to Galilee was to serve as a missionary of the Torah, but it is clear that this is the significance of the years he spent there. He resided in Arav, a small village in the hill country of central Galilee, where he generally failed to make an impression on the religious life of the region. During his entire stay he had only one student, Hanina ben Dosa, and only two cases of halakhic law were brought before him for judgment. The Galileans, recent converts to the Jerusalem cult, sought a religion of miracle-working, messianic fulfillment, the piety of the Temple pilgrimage, and salvation in the next world. Johanan, by contrast, offered only the discipline of a humble life of faithful observance of the Law set forth in the Torah. A third century Talmudic source records the closing of Johanan's ministry in Galilee: "Eighteen years Rabban Yohanan ben Zakkai spent in 'Arav, and only these two cases came before him. At the end he said, 'O Galilee, Galilee! You hate the Torah! Your end will be to be besieged!' "

Disappointed, Johanan took his ailing son and wife and returned to Jerusalem. There he set up a school near the site of the Temple and spent the next three decades patiently teaching the Torah. His quiet success is demonstrated in his rise through Pharisaic ranks. Pharisaic leadership had often been shared between pairs—Shemaiah and Abtalion, Hillel and Shammai. Two halakhic rulings sent to Galilee from Jerusalem during this period bear the names of both Gamaliel I—the acknowledged leader of the Pharisees—and Johanan ben Zakkai, who probably served as his partner or deputy. Johanan, nearing his seventieth year, could look back with satisfaction upon a life of quiet scholarship, but he had accomplished nothing to earn for himself a permanent niche in history.

Just at this point in Johanan's life, an explosion occurred in the political life of Judaea. Judaean independence had been won from the Greeks in 166 B.C., but after 62 B.C., the nation had had to live in uncertain peace under Roman occupation. The Pharisees, for whom the heart of Judaism lay in personal fidelity to the Torah rather than in political sovereignty, had accepted tenuous coexistence with Rome. From 5 B.C. onward, however, there had grown among the people a Zealot movement which anticipated messianic fulfillment in the overthrow of Roman rule and the establishment of a divine monarchy in place of Caesar's. In late A.D. 65, a contingent of Zealots ambushed and defeated the twelfth Roman legion, inaugurating what is in Roman annals the famous Bellum Judaicum of 66-70. In face of the Zealot revolt and the siege of Jerusalem by the Romans, Johanan made the most critical decision of his life—one which made him for a brief moment the single most important figure in Judaism.

In 68, Johanan abandoned the war and the Zealot-controlled city of Jerusalem, fleeing for safety to the camp of Vespasian. He allowed himself to be smuggled past the Zealot watchguards and out of Jerusalem inside a coffin borne by two of his rabbinical students. Pharisaic leaders such as Gamaliel I who remained behind with the Zealots perished in the massacre which followed the fall of Jerusalem to the Romans.

The main Talmudic tradition regarding what happened next represents the following encounter when Johanan arrived at the camp of Vespasian:

> They opened the coffin, and Rabban Yohanan stood up before him. "Are you Rabban Yohanan ben Zakkai?" Vespasian inquired. "Tell me what I may give you."
>
> "I ask nothing of you," Rabban Yohanan replied, "save Yavneh, where I might go and teach my disciples and there establish a house of prayer, and perform all the commandments."
>
> "Go," Vespasian said to him.

Moreover, Johanan allegedly predicted that Vespasian would become emperor, a prophecy fulfilled three days later.

A different interpretation has suggested that Johanan was held under house arrest at Yavneh by the Romans. Whether Johanan was Vespasian's guest or his detainee, however, he spent the decade following the fall of Jerusalem in the Roman-protected town of Yavneh, instructing a contingent of

Pharisees who had survived the destruction. There he husbanded and nurtured the most important remnant of Pharisees, and in so doing patched together the torn fabric of Jewish national life and rescued Judaism as a Law-centered community now that it could no longer continue as a temple cult.

The period of Johanan's service at Yavneh was brief, no more than a decade. The manifest yield of his labors was sparse; few chose to sit at the feet of one who seemingly had turned his back on the nation in its hour of need. So difficult was his reception that he was even compelled to remove from Yavneh to the neighboring settlement of Beror Heil, where he died, probably around 80, surrounded by a very small number of students.

Succeeding generations, however, proved the permanent worth of Johanan's years at Yavneh. His small academy laid foundations which guaranteed the survival of Pharisaism. Furthermore, his tenure there afforded sufficient time for Gamaliel II, the true successor of Gamaliel I, to emerge from the political shadow of his family's support of the rebellion against Rome. The next decade at Yavneh—the 90's—was pivotal in the history of Judaism: Gamaliel II led five of Johanan's students, among others, in constructing the basis for what eventually emerged, in the vacuum remaining after the destruction of the Temple, as normative Talmudic Judaism.

Summary

According to rabbinic tradition, Johanan ben Zakkai acted out the nation's response to the fall of the Temple: It was he who rent his garments upon hearing the news. His physical appearance is undocumented; what is emphasized instead is the high rabbinical estimate of Johanan, whom the Jewish teachers ranked alongside Moses, Hillel, and Akiba ben Joseph as one who indeed "sustained all Israel." His title, "Rabban," indicates that he was considered the rabbi of primacy during his own period.

"My son," Johanan once replied to a student who despaired that the destruction of the Temple would mean that there could be no more atonement for sins, "be not grieved. We have another atonement as effective as this. And what is it? It is acts of lovingkindness, as it is said, *For I desire mercy, not sacrifice*." In accord with this principle, Johanan's halakhic rulings at Yavneh readjusted the Jewish ritual calendar to suit the demands of the new situation in which the synagogue, rather than the Temple, would be the center of Jewish life.

In the age of a Judaism beset with messianic movements such as those of the Zealots themselves, of Jesus of Nazareth, and of Simon bar Kokhba, Johanan set a standard of caution which became normative in Judaism through the succeeding nineteen centuries: "If you have a sapling in your hand, and it is said to you, 'Behold, there is the Messiah'—go on with your planting, and afterward go out and receive him."

"Do not haste to tear down [the altars of Gentiles], so that you do not have to rebuild them with your own hands. Do not destroy those of brick, that they may not say to you, 'Come and build them of stone.' " So Johanan had cautioned the Zealots. His advice became the watchword of the tradition of political restraint necessary for survival during the long centuries of persecution and statelessness of the Jewish people between the fall of the second Jewish commonwealth in A.D. 70 and the establishment of the third in 1948.

Bibliography

Alon, Gedalyahu, *Jews, Judaism, and the Classical World: Studies in Jewish History in the Times of the Second Temple and Talmud*. Jerusalem: Magnes Press of Hebrew University, 1977. A series of articles on a wide variety of critical issues dealing with the history of the Jewish people from the first century B.C. through the third century A.D. Alon argues that Johanan ben Zakkai was held under house arrest at Yavneh by Vespasian.

Ben-Sasson, H. H., ed. *A History of the Jewish People*. Cambridge, Mass.: Harvard University Press, and London: Weidenfeld and Nicolson, 1976. Written by six eminent scholars, this is the best one-volume interpretive history of the Jewish people. Places Johanan ben Zakkai in the context of the entire stream of Jewish history.

Bohrmann, Monette. *Flavius Josephus, The Zealots and Yavne: Towards a Rereading of the War of the Jews*. Translated by Janet Lloyd. Bern and New York: Peter Lang, 1994. Attempts to evaluate the events of the revolt from the perspective of the Jews. The war appears as the inevitable result of cultural conflict, although the author claims that some Jewish leaders (including Johanan ben Zakkai and Josephus) counseled peace.

Neusner, Jacob. *Development of a Legend: Studies on the Traditions Concerning Yohanan ben Zak-*

kai. Leiden, Netherlands: E. J. Brill, 1970. A detailed criticism of the Talmudic texts which are the sole source of evidence for the life of Johanan.

————. *From Politics to Piety: The Emergence of Pharisaic Judaism.* Englewood Cliffs, N.J.: Prentice-Hall, 1973. A brief popular account of Pharisaic Judaism during the era of Johanan ben Zakkai.

————. *A Life of Yohanan ben Zakkai, ca. 1-80 C.E.* 2d ed. Leiden, Netherlands: E. J. Brill, 1970; Nashville: Abingdon Press, 1975. The single scholarly biography of Johanan ben Zakkai written in English. Neusner contests Alon's view that Johanan was under house arrest at Yavneh and argues for the more widely accepted tradition that he was allowed to reside in Yavneh as a favor from Vespasian. Neusner published his text without notes in popular form in his *First Century Judaism in Crisis: Yohanan ben Zakkai and the Renaissance of Torah* (Nashville, Tenn.: Abingdon Press, 1975).

Zeitlin, Solomon. *The Rise and Fall of the Judaean State: A Political Social, and Religious History of the Second Commonwealth.* Vol. 3, *66 C.E.-120 C.E.* Philadelphia: Jewish Publication Society of America, 1978. An excellent narrative account of this period of Jewish history. One chapter treats the work of Johanan ben Zakkai at Yavneh.

Marlin Timothy Tucker

JOHN THE APOSTLE

Born: c. A.D. 10; probably Capernaum

Died: c. A.D. 100; Ephesus

Area of Achievement: Religion

Contribution: John the Apostle was one of Jesus' most trusted disciples during his lifetime; after his death, John was a leader in the early Church and by his writings made important contributions to Christian theology.

Early Life

Assuming John to have been a young man when he was called as a disciple of Jesus, he must have been born about A.D. 10, probably in Capernaum. His father was Zebedee and his mother Salome; he had a brother, James, also a disciple and presumably the elder of the two, since he is generally mentioned first and John is often identified as the "brother of James." The family occupation was fishing, and they were presumably prosperous, since they owned their own boat and employed servants; they may have been a priestly family as well. Salome figures occasionally in the Gospels; she requested that her sons be given seats of honor beside Jesus in Heaven (Matt. 20), and she was one of the women who helped to support Jesus financially (Matt. 15). James and John may have been cousins of Jesus, a fact which would explain their early call and the episode at the Cross in which Mary, Jesus' mother, was committed to the care of "the disciple whom Jesus loved," a term generally taken to refer to John the son of Zebedee. The nickname "Boanerges" (sons of thunder or perhaps anger) bestowed on James and John by Jesus suggests a certain impetuousness and aggressiveness; James's early martyrdom suggests that he had the greater share of the quality. As for John, his occupation and his besting of Peter in the race to Jesus' tomb suggest a strong, athletic man.

Life's Work

It is with the call by the Sea of Galilee that John's recorded life begins. Having called Peter and Andrew to leave their nets and become "fishers of men," Jesus immediately proceeded to James and John, who left "the boat and their father" and followed him. In general, the position of John in Jesus' ministry is clear. He appears on lists of the Twelve, and always among the first: "Simon who is called Peter and Andrew his brother; James the son

of Zebedee and John his brother." When a smaller group is named, John is always among them; it is James and John who would have called down fire on a village of the Samaritans (Luke 9). Generally, however, John is linked to Peter in a subordinate role. Thus, he was present at the healing of Peter's mother-in-law (Mark 1) and of Jairus' daughter (Mark 5); he was present with Peter and James at the Transfiguration (Matt. 17) and again at Gethsemane (Mark 14). Toward the end of the Gospel of John, there are numerous references to "the disciple whom Jesus loved," almost certainly John. He was the disciple whom Peter prompted to solicit Jesus' identification of the betrayer at the Last Supper (John 18); he was possibly the disciple who introduced Peter to the high priest's courtyard; he is the one to whose care Christ commended his mother; he is the one, along with Peter, to whom Mary Magdalene brought news of the Resurrection. Finally, "the disciple whom Jesus loved" is clearly present when the risen Jesus appeared at the Sea of Galilee, and the Gospel records a statement of Jesus which some interpreted as a prophecy that the disciple would not die before the Second Coming (John 21). John appears here, incidentally, in the same role in which Luke casts him at his first appearance: as a fishing partner with Peter.

After the Crucifixion and Resurrection, John seems to have filled much the same role as before: as a leader and spokesman for the infant Church, constantly in a subordinate role to Peter and sometimes also to his brother James, until the latter's martyrdom. John was with Peter when the lame man was healed (the first miracle performed after the death of Jesus); twice he was imprisoned, once with Peter, once with all the Apostles; he went with Peter to support the missionary effort of Philip of Samaria. Finally, he played a leading role when the Church had to decide whether Gentile converts were obliged to observe the Jewish ceremonial law, as some converted Pharisees had argued. Paul had gone to Jerusalem with Barnabas to confer on the matter and was cordially received by James (the Lord's brother) and Peter and John, "who were reputed to be pillars": at the prompting of Peter, the Gentiles were released from the law, except with respect to unchastity and meat sacrificed to idols (Acts 15; Gal. 2). It was a crucial episode in the history of the early Church, for it meant that Chris-

tianity could no longer be regarded as a Jewish sect.

This episode took place some seventeen years after Paul's conversion and is the last biblical record of John, but church tradition suggests the shape of his later life. According to this tradition (which is not beyond dispute), John spent the latter part of his life in missionary activity at Ephesus. During the reign of Domitian (81-96), he was banished to the Isle of Patmos (an association which is still advertised in tourist literature); he is thought to have returned to Ephesus and to have lived on into the reign of Trajan (98-117). It was during this period that he is thought to have written the Gospel of John, the three Epistles of John, and (possibly) the Book of Revelation. Some scholars would make John not so much the author of these works as the authority behind them; it is evident that another hand edited the manuscript of the Gospel, with John's certification "that this testimony is true" (John 21). Perhaps John should be envisioned as the respected leader of the community, whose disciples aided him in putting together his recollections of Christ; the Gospel apparently went through several editions as material was added, perhaps in accord with specific needs of the Church. The Epistles give evidence of dissension in the churches in the Ephesus area; if the heretics mentioned indeed denied that Christ came in the flesh, in "water and blood," they may have represented an early stage of Gnosticism (which is not to say, as some authorities have, that John at one stage was Gnostic). Revelation could well reflect this same troubled atmosphere; the church at Pergamos is accused of the same offenses that were discussed at the Council of Jerusalem: fornication and meat sacrificed to idols. The latter parts of Revelation, if indeed they are John's, would reflect his exile to Patmos. The manner and even the date of John's death are unknown.

Summary

From the time of his calling (or even before), John's name was constantly associated with that of Peter—sometimes when together they were called aside by Jesus for moments that were confidential and intimate, sometimes when he and Peter (usually Peter) took the initiative. His personality came to be defined in terms of Peter: Though he and his brother James were "sons of thunder," they almost always deferred to Peter as their spokesman. The

relationship continued after the Crucifixion and through the history of the early Church. Eventually, there had to be a parting: Peter went to Rome and John to Ephesus, where he became the leader of the churches in the area. Here too he developed his theology, which differed in emphasis from that of the Synoptic Gospels (Matthew, Mark, and Luke), which at least in part were based on the preaching of Peter. Specifically, John favored a higher Christology which affirmed not only that Christ was the Son of God and the Messiah but also that He was the Creator who had coexisted with God from all eternity. Apparently, some of his followers went beyond this to deny "the coming of Jesus Christ in the flesh" (2 John), like the later Gnostics. After John's death, these individuals presumably became Gnostics indeed, while John's church, which had pursued its own way apart from the "great church" of Peter and Paul, was absorbed into the greater church, taking with it the Gospel of John, which thus became canonical.

The whole issue may be summed up in the last chapters of the Gospel of John, which were apparently added in the last edition. Here John once more recalls his intimacy with Peter; there is an account of a final fishing expedition, and he records how the risen Christ charged Peter to "feed My sheep" and foretold Peter's death. Finally, as he asserted the divinity and coeternity of Christ at the opening of the Gospel, so here John asserts Christ's humanity in the striking image of his preparing a picnic breakfast for his disciples on the shore.

Bibliography

Alter, Robert, and Frank Kermode, eds. *The Literary Guide to the Bible*. Cambridge, Mass.: Harvard University Press, and London: Grafton, 1987. Contains an essay on John by Frank Kermode and another on Revelation by Bernard McGinn. Both are very fine essays, though by no means simple; they do not convey simply the author's own impressions but also contain historical surveys of past criticism.

Brown, Raymond E. *The Community of the Beloved Disciple*. New York: Paulist Press, and London: Chapman, 1979. Though it carries an imprimatur, this volume contains all sorts of improbable hypotheses concerning John and the church at Ephesus. It does offer a useful summary of the scholarship.

————. Introduction to "The Gospel According to St. John." In *The Anchor Bible*. New York: Doubleday, 1966; London: Chapman, 1971. Concludes that the combination of external and internal evidence associating the Fourth Gospel with John the son of Zebedee makes his authorship the strongest hypothesis. Brown's reasoning in this book has generally been accepted in the present essay.

Culpepper, R. Alan. *John, the Son of Zebedee: The Life of a Legend*. Columbia, S.C.: University of South Carolina Press, 1994. An accessible and full introduction to John and the Johannine community, utilizing the methods of modern historical research. The author surveys the gospel accounts, the New Testament books attributed to John, and later legends of John. The book concludes with a survey of 20th-century scholarship.

Dodd, Charles H. *Historical Tradition in the Fourth Gospel*. Cambridge: Cambridge University Press, 1963. Seeks to reopen the historical question. Dodd argues that though the "quest for the historical Jesus" came to nothing and led many to despair of the historical approach, modern critical methods can lead to conclusions which have a high degree of probability.

Funk and Wagnalls New Standard Bible Dictionary. Edited by Melancthon W. Jacobs, Elbert C. Lane, and Andrew C. Zenos. 3d rev. ed. New York: Funk and Wagnalls, 1936. Offers a rather conservative view of the controversy surrounding John. John's authorship of the Gospel is elaborately defended, although his authorship of Revelation is questioned. There is a good summary of what is known of John's life.

Pollard, T. E. *Johannine Christology and the Early Church*. Cambridge: Cambridge University Press, 1970. Analyzes early theological controversies which grew out of the Gospel of John. This monograph is part of a series put out by the Society for New Testament Studies. Includes an index and a bibliography.

John C. Sherwood

JOHN THE BAPTIST

Born: c. 7 B.C.; near Jerusalem, Israel

Died: c. A.D. 27; Jerusalem, Israel

Area of Achievement: Religion

Contribution: According to the biblical narrative, John was the cousin of Jesus and played a central role in introducing Jesus' ministry to the people of Palestine; as an austere, prophetic figure in the history of Judaism and Christianity, John was a stern moralist who addressed a generation of outwardly religious but inwardly corrupted people.

Early Life

The main historical record for the life of John the Baptist is the Bible, specifically the New Testament, revered by Christians worldwide as an authoritative complement to the Old Testament. Each of the Gospels records significant portions of the life and ministry of John, and three of them actually begin with his birth rather than that of Jesus, who is the central figure of the New Testament. Historical tradition suggests that John was born in a village four miles west of Jerusalem around 7 B.C. to elderly parents, Zacharias, a Jewish priest, and Elisabeth, a relative of Mary, the mother of Jesus. The Gospel of Luke provides the most extensive treatment of the early life of John and indicates that he was probably born about six months before his cousin. Like those of other famous Old and New Testament patriarchs and heroes, John's birth, Luke relates, was foretold by an angel, in this case Gabriel, who also appeared to Mary and prophesied the coming of Jesus. Gabriel, in fact, suggested the name John, and friends and relatives were shocked at the time of John's circumcision and dedication to learn that he would not be named for his father, Zacharias (Luke 1:63).

Luke's account goes on to suggest that John's education continued along the path one might expect: John, like his father, prepared for the priesthood. Sometime in his late adolescence, however, John traveled on a pilgrimage to the deserts for study, meditation, and further consecration (Luke 1:66, 80). During this extended period, John took on the appearance and habits of other prophets of Israel, especially Elijah—to whom he was compared by Jesus (Matt. 11:12-14). John is said to have eaten wild locusts and honey and to have worn coarse garments of camel hair and a leather girdle—clear associations with Elijah (Matt. 3:4;

Mark 1:6; 2 Kings 1:8). After this episode of ascetic discipline and study of the Scriptures, John emerged to begin his public ministry in "all the country about the Jordan River" (Luke 3:3), a ministry which began prior to that of Jesus by at least several months.

The message John presented to the people was in many ways unique to his ministry, but it was also linked thematically to that of the prophets of old. That message can be summarized as "prepare ye the way of the Lord." John believed unequivocally that he had been called to announce some cataclysmic work of God in the first century to which he would be both witness and martyr. The message was twofold in purpose: It was a call both to radical repentance and to immersion in water for the forgiveness of sins. In his preaching, John used straightforward language, referring to some in his audience as "vipers" or "hypocrites" and imploring them to repent or change their ways and act justly toward their neighbors and manifest their love for God in obedience to the Law. The insistence on full water-immersion gave John his unique label, "the

Baptist," and indicated the necessary radical break with past lackluster adherence to the Law of Moses. The repentant believer was to emerge from the water in some sense a new person, ready to behave and believe differently.

Life's Work

John's ministry attracted many followers, many more at one point than that of Jesus (Luke 7:29). In instructing his disciples, John taught them to pray and to fast (Luke 5:33, 11:1; Mark 2:18), but his work was not essentially preoccupied with personal devotion. Within and without his circle of disciples, his message was interpreted as an attack on organized religion—or the parody it had become. "The axe," he declared, "is laid at the root of the trees" (Matt. 3:10; Luke 3:9). His message focused on the necessity for a new beginning and on the emptiness of the Jews' continuing to claim some special merit as descendants of Abraham. The Coming One, or Messiah, John prophesied, would execute judgment on all but the loyal remnant of believers ready to embrace him. Late in an actually quite brief ministry, John suggested to his followers—many of whom would become Jesus' own most trusted associates—that John himself "must decrease, while [the Messiah he proclaimed] must increase." That is, as the time came closer for the Messiah to emerge, John's ministry would diminish in importance and finally come to an end.

John's ministry climaxed when Jesus himself came to be baptized by John "to fulfill all righteousness." John at first balked at baptizing "for the forgiveness of sins" the one who himself was regarded as sinless; earlier, John, upon glimpsing Jesus across a street, had told an assembled crowd, "Behold the Lamb of God who takes away the sins of the world." Jesus insisted on this act of identification with mankind and it was at this crucial event that the stunned crowd heard a voice from Heaven declare, "This is my beloved son in whom I am well pleased." This event signaled the beginning of Jesus' ministry and launched him on his itinerant preaching tours.

After this episode, John's ministry was abruptly interrupted and then ended by the antipathy he engendered in King Herod Antipas of Palestine. Herod had several motives for his displeasure with John. First, John's preaching drew large, enthusiastic crowds, a matter sure to perturb the Roman authorities at whose pleasure Herod himself served as a puppet ruler. More to the point, however, was John's radical insistence on the public morality of Israel's leaders; indeed, he had outspokenly denounced Herod for his adultery. When John refused to back down, Herod had him imprisoned, both to silence him and, in a sense, to protect him. Despite being humiliated by John, Herod was entertained by his gruff, quaint manner, much as Pontius Pilate was impressed with the sincerity and commitment of Jesus.

During his imprisonment, John sent some of his disciples to Jesus to confirm that he indeed was the coming Messiah; perhaps John wished to assure himself that his mission had been successful. Finally, during a particularly uproarious party, Herod was manipulated by his stepdaughter Salome into granting her any wish as payment for a lascivious dance she had performed (Matt. 14:6-12; Mark 6:21-28). Prompted by her mother, she requested that John be beheaded, and that his head be brought to her on a platter; Herod reluctantly acceded.

At his death, John elicited the highest praise from Jesus as the greatest of all men who lived under the Old Covenant: "The law and the prophets were until John; since that time the kingdom of God is preached" (Luke 16:16). Throughout his later ministry, Jesus continued to pay tribute to the faith and example of John. While John's baptism provided a gateway into the messianic community, the Apostles later interpreted baptism as a sacrament, a reenactment of the death, burial, and resurrection of Jesus that united the believer with the saving work of Jesus on the Cross.

Summary

The ancient Jewish historian Flavius Josephus adds historical perspective to John the Baptist's life outside the biblical account. Writing in the first century A.D., Josephus stated that John "was a good man who bade the Jews practice virtue, be just to one another, and pious toward God, and come together by means of baptism." This latter comment regarding John's teaching on baptism indicates the force and strength of John's ministry to first century Jews and to Christians. Its appearance in a secular account suggests the impact John's ministry had on Jewish culture as a whole. His call to baptism—which gave to him the name "the Baptist" or the "one who baptizes"—represented a call to radical commitment, to withdraw from a complacent, "everyday" faith to a bolder, more holy response to the God of Abraham, Isaac, and Jacob. Clearly, however, John was more dramatically an influence on the development of Christian thought and the ministry of Jesus. Jesus' appearance at John's baptisms stamped John himself as a true prophet of God in the eyes of first century Christians; later, when arguing on his own behalf, Jesus invoked the baptism of John to corroborate his own authority to command baptism and healing.

Important as it was, John's baptism is presented in the New Testament account as something that would eventually be succeeded by a peculiarly "Christian" baptism which brought believers into the kingdom of God rather than merely "preparing" them for it. The power of John's message and ministry was so strong, however, that even into the second and third decades of Christian faith, approximately A.D. 45-55, pockets of believers adhering to "John's baptism" and needing further instruction in the baptism practiced by the Apostles after the death and resurrection of Jesus could be found. For example, the New Testament Book of Acts tells how a married couple, Priscilla and Aquila, drew aside the respected teacher Apollos and instructed him in proper Christian baptism. Later, the Apostle Paul encountered a group of believers who had never heard of Christian baptism—only John's—and he instructed them further.

Contemporary scholarship has attempted to locate the origins of John's teaching in his presumed association with the Qumran community, a radical Jewish religious group whose teachings became known to biblical scholarship with the discovery of the Dead Sea Scrolls in 1945. The Qumran community stressed strict adherence to a legal code to achieve a higher degree of righteousness before God and, curiously, a water baptism, something that traditional Judaism had required of all Gentile converts. Whatever influence John's exposure to such teaching may have had, it is clear that he intended to link his own message with the prophecy of a coming redeemer, a ministry of preparation that would turn the hearts of the faithless and the faithful to a religious belief which transcended mere formalism and embraced an ongoing commitment to justice, righteousness, and peace; his mission, in his own words, was "to make ready a people prepared for the coming of the Lord."

Bibliography

Alexander, David, and Pat Alexander, eds. *Eerdmans' Handbook to the Bible*. Rev. ed. Grand Rapids, Mich.: Eerdmans Publishing Co., 1983. A helpful overview of the basic message of the New Testament, the life of Christ, and the relationship of John the Baptist to Jesus, his cousin. A succinct and very practical guide to the ministries of both John the Baptist and Jesus of Nazareth and their impact on first century culture.

Foster, R. C. *Introduction and Early Ministry: Studies in the Life of Christ*. Grand Rapids, Mich.: Baker Book House, 1966. A volume that focuses primarily on the life of Christ but which includes an insightful extended discussion of the life and work of John the Baptist. Especially useful to the reader unfamiliar with the basic New Testament message and the historical context in which it arose.

Guthrie, Donald. *New Testament Introduction*. 4th ed. Downers Grove, Ill.: Inter-Varsity Press, and Leicester: Apollos, 1990. A standard, scholarly overview of the entire New Testament that includes a thorough discussion of the life of John the Baptist and his ministry. Invaluable for providing the necessary context for an accurate assessment of John the Baptist's importance to later Christian faith and practice.

Hendriksen, William. *New Testament Commentary: Exposition of the Gospel According to Matthew*. Grand Rapids, Mich.: Baker Book House, 1973. An important scholarly discussion of the Gospel of Matthew, which contains the longest narratives about the birth and destiny of John. Hendriksen offers both the lay reader and the scholar an extended study and contextualization of the life of John the Baptist in relationship to the basic Christian gospel.

Malherbe, Abraham. *The World of the New Testament*. Austin, Tex.: Sweet Publishing Co., 1967. A brief but valuable overview of the entire New Testament period with special attention to the historical and theological events that served as the backdrop to the life and ministry of John the Baptist.

Taylor, Joan E. *The Immerser: John the Baptist within Second Temple Judaism*. Grand Rapids, Mich.: Eerdmans, 1997. An explication of John's life that draws on extra-Biblical sources to situate him and his practice of baptism within the context of Second Temple Judaism. The author rejects the idea that John was associated with the Essenes.

Thompson, J. A. *Handbook to Life in Bible Times*. Leicester and Downers Grove, Ill.: Inter-Varsity Press, 1986. A standard work on the archaeology of the first century world; it continues to be one of the most comprehensive and informed overviews of the historical data gleaned from the ancient world. Overall, it provides the reader with an authentic sense of the world to which John the Baptist came, his mission, and the circumstances in which he became both a prophet to Israel and the forerunner of the Messiah of both Jews and Christians.

Webb, Robert L. *John the Baptizer and Prophet: A Socio-Historical Study. Journal for the Study of the New Testament* supplementary series 62. Sheffield: JSOT Press, 1991. The author attempts to uncover the "historical" John by focusing on his prophetic and baptismal ministry within a Jewish, rather than a proto-Christian, context.

Bruce L. Edwards

FLAVIUS JOSEPHUS

Born: c. A.D. 37; Jerusalem, Palestine

Died: c. A.D. 100; probably Rome

Areas of Achievement: Historiography and scholarship

Contribution: Josephus' history of the Jewish revolt against Rome in 66, the fall of Jerusalem in 70, and the capture of Masada in 73 remains, despite patent exaggerations and questionable reporting, the primary source of information for this segment of world history.

Early Life

Flavius Josephus was born in Jerusalem into an influential priestly family. His Jewish name, Joseph ben Matthias, indicates that he was the son of Matthias, whom he asserts to have been of noble Hasmonaean (that is, Maccabean) lineage. He claims that he was consulted at the age of fourteen by high priests and leading citizens on the fine points of law and that, at the age of sixteen, he conducted inquiries into the relative merits of the Pharisees, Sadducees, and Essenes. Becoming a disciple of a Pharisee named Banus, he entered upon an ascetic existence, living with Banus in the desert for three years and then returning, as a Pharisee, to Jerusalem at the age of nineteen.

Seven years later, by his account, he went to Rome as an emissary to plead for the release of some Jewish priests who were being held on what Josephus considered to be trivial charges. The sea voyage to Rome ended in shipwreck in the Adriatic Sea with Josephus being one of eighty survivors out of the six hundred on board.

He reached Puteoli (modern Pozzuoli) and was befriended by a Jewish actor named Aliturius, who enjoyed Nero's favor. Aliturius secured for Josephus an audience with Poppaea, Nero's wife, and with her assistance Josephus gained the release of the priests. He returned to Palestine a year or two later.

His homeland at this time (66) was in a state of incipient rebellion against Roman occupation. Josephus was opposed to insurrection and sided with the moderate faction against the extremists. The insurgent nationalists, however, prevailed. The Roman garrison at Masada was captured and the Roman contingent was expelled from Jerusalem; the Roman Twelfth Legion, sent to put down the revolt and restore order, was decisively defeated by Jewish patriots. By the end of 66, the war between the Jews and the Romans was a military reality. Josephus was pressed into service as the commander of the region of Galilee.

Although his talents were for the priesthood and research, Josephus, like many learned men in classical antiquity, proved to be capable in military affairs. He conceived defenses and trained fighting forces but refrained from taking the initiative in attack. In the spring of 67 the Romans moved into Galilee. Josephus' main fighting unit was routed and he retreated to Jotapata, the most strongly fortified town in Galilee. Three Roman legions under Vespasian laid siege to Jotapata, captured it on the first of July in 67, and took Josephus prisoner.

Life's Work

The relationship of Josephus with Vespasian and the Roman imperial entourage marks the major stage in his life. Vespasian's prisoner of war became his adviser and, in time, favored client. It is this sustained association with the dominant enemy of the Jews that clouds the attitudes toward Josephus taken by his compatriots and their descen-

dants. In his early opposition to the Jewish revolt he had been suspected of complicity with the Romans, and in view of the perquisites accorded him by the Roman leaders after Jotapata, no apologist can effectively defend him against the charge of fraternization with the enemy. He appears to have ingratiated himself with Vespasian by accurately predicting Vespasian's installation as emperor. He assumed the name of Vespasian's family, Flavius, when he Romanized his own. His account, published between 75 and 79, of the Jewish revolt against Rome carries the Greek title *Peri tou Ioudaikou polemou*, which in Latin is *Bello Judaicum*. The significance of the title (in English, *The Jewish War*) is that it denotes the Roman, not the Jewish, perspective, just as Julius Caesar's *De bello Galileo* (52-51 B.C. *The Gallic War*, or, *The War with the Gauls*) denotes the Roman, not the Gallic, perspective. Josephus had clearly staked his lot with the victorious Romans.

A telling incident prior to the fall of Jotapata makes it difficult for anyone to admire Josephus as a patriotic Jew. The besieged had agreed upon a mass suicide pact as a means of avoiding capture by the Romans. Josephus relates his attempt to dissuade them, his failure to do so, and his alternate and subsequently accepted plan to draw lots whereby number two would kill number one, number three would kill number two, and so on until, presumably, the last person left would be the only one actually to commit suicide. Josephus concludes this story with a nod to divine providence or pure chance: He and one other were the last two alive and, making a pact of their own, remained alive.

By contrast, Josephus' account of the mass suicide in the year 73 of the 960 Jews at Masada, the last citadel of resistance to the Romans, who had conclusively ended the revolt three years earlier, includes reference to no survivors save two women and five children who had hidden in subterranean aqueducts. Comparison of the respective survivors of Jotapata and Masada lends no honor to the historian of both defeats.

After the Jewish revolt of 66-70 Josephus was granted living quarters and a regular income in Rome. Thus ensconced, he produced his history of the revolt. His claim that he wrote the work initially in Aramaic and then translated it into Greek need not be disputed, although no Aramaic text whatsoever remains in either small part or citation. The Hellenistic Greek in which this work and the other works of Josephus appear is faultlessly in character with the *lingua franca* of the time. The idiomatic perfection of Josephus' Greek may owe in large part to his employment of Greek-speaking assistants, but his own linguistic abilities were patently considerable.

The Jewish War was published between 75 and 79, the year in which Vespasian died and was succeeded as emperor by his son Titus. It covers not merely the years 66 to 73 but also much of the history of the Jews, from the desecration of the Temple at Jerusalem by Antiochus IV Epiphanes in 167 B.C. through the events culminating in the capture of Jerusalem by Titus in A.D. 70. The work is composed of seven books, the first two of which outline the Hasmonaean, or Maccabean, revolt, the reign of Herod the Great, and the Roman occupation of Palestine up to the military governorship of Galilee by Josephus.

The five books dedicated to the details of the revolt are both exciting and graphic. Josephus mars his credibility with hyperbole and distortion of fact—for example, he describes Mount Tabor, which has an altitude of thirteen hundred feet, as being twenty thousand feet high, and his crowd counts are almost invariably exaggerated, one such noting thirty thousand Jews crushed to death in a panic rush—but, if his particulars are questionable and his narrative self-serving, his general survey of times and events has not lost its value.

Although it may tend to disqualify him as a scientific historian, his creative imagination undeniably enhances the grand movement of his history. In one respect, *The Jewish War* resembles the history by the more scientific Thucydides. Both works are informed by a major theme: In Thucydides' *De bello Peloponnesiaco libri octo* (431-404 B.C.; *History of the Peloponnesian War*) that theme is Athenian hubris; in *The Jewish War* it is Jewish self-destructiveness. Josephus sees the factionalism of the Jews and their impractical unwillingness to yield to the overwhelming power of Rome as suicidal tendencies which make the Jews their own worst enemies. He underscores this theme with many images of suicidal conflict and with depictions of individual and mass suicides.

Josephus' pride in his heritage is evident in his work and transcends both his contempt for his Jewish rivals and enemies (especially Josephus of Gischala) and his deference to his Roman benefactors. His second work is a massive history of Judaism and the Jews which is entitled *Ioudaikē archaiolo-*

gia (c. A.D. 93; in Latin, *Antiquitates Judaicae*; in English, *The Antiquities of the Jews*). This work, in twenty hooks, or about three times the length of *The Jewish War*, begins with the Creation as recounted in Genesis and ends with the Palestinian war clouds of 66. The first eleven and one-half books cover Jewish history up to the tyranny of Antiochus IV Epiphanes. The latter eight and one-half books cover the same material as the first book and a half of *The Jewish War* but in greater detail and with many additions. The work is addressed to Epaphroditus, an otherwise unknown figure who seems to have succeeded the emperor Titus, dead in 81, as one of Josephus' patrons.

At the conclusion of *The Antiquities of the Jews*, Josephus claims, characteristically, that his work is accurate and that no other person, Jew or non-Jew, could have enlightened the Greeks on two millennia of Jewish history and practices so well as he. In quality, however, and in importance and readability, *The Antiquities of the Jews* is discernibly inferior to its predecessor.

It must be noted, however, that *The Antiquities of the Jews* offers passages that are of notable importance to Christians. For example:

> Jesus comes along at about this time, a wise man, if indeed one must call him a man: for he was a performer of unaccountable works, a teacher of such people as took delight in truth, and one who attracted to himself many Jews and many Greeks as well. This man was the Christ. And when Pilate sentenced him to crucifixion, after he had been indicted by our leading citizens, those who had been devoted to him from the start remained firm in their devotion, for he appeared to them alive again three days afterward, as it had been prophesied about him, along with countless other wonders, by holy men. And to our own time the host of those named, after him, Christians has not dwindled.

There is a passage on the aftermath of the execution of John the Baptist and another on the stoning of Jesus' brother James. Jesus is not mentioned in the Greek version of *The Jewish War*. There is, however, an Old Slavonic (that is, Russian) version with an independent late medieval manuscript tradition that contains references to the lives of John the Baptist and Jesus, one of them being a variation of the passage quoted above.

Josephus completed the *The Antiquities of the Jews* in 93 at the age of fifty-six. His plans, announced at the end of the work, to produce an epitome of *The Jewish War*, a continuation of the same work, and a tetrad of books on the Jewish religion

and laws appear not to have been realized. His brief autobiography is attached to the end of the *The Antiquities of the Jews* and contradicts some of the statements made in *The Jewish War*, in the interest, it seems, of obverting his early military opposition to the Romans and perhaps as a means of offsetting his rivals for the favor of the emperor Domitian.

The treatise which marks the end of Josephus' literary career is one that could warrant no complaint from his fellow Jews. It is called *Peri archaiotētos Ioudaiōn kata Apionos* (*Concerning the Antiquity of the Jews, Against Apion*) and is traditionally referred to simply as *Against Apion*. The work is an effective and stirring defense of the Jewish people and their religion and laws against scurrilous anti-Jewish writings of the past (by Manetho and Cheremon, for example) and by Josephus' older contemporary, Apion of Alexandria.

Having been favored by the emperors Vespasian and Titus and having enjoyed the patronage of Emperor Domitian and his wife, Josephus seems to have survived Domitian, who died in 96, by no more than a few years. Nothing is known of his reception by the emperors Nerva (ruled 96-98) and Trajan (98-117). It is significant that the last remaining works of Josephus are defenses—the autobiography a defense of his part in the Jewish revolt and *Against Apion* a defense of his Jewish heritage. It is not known whether these *apologiae*, also addressed to Epaphroditus, qualified him for a return to Judaea or, for that matter, for continued subsistence in Rome. His status with either Jews or Romans during his last years of life, as well as the actual place of his death, can only be conjectured.

Summary

The latter part of Josephus' autobiography includes a digressive apostrophe to Justus of Tiberias, who had also written an *Antiquities*, which covered Jewish history from Moses through the first century of this era and which related the insurrection and revolt of 66 to 70 in such a way as to challenge Josephus and attempt to discredit him. Justus, for example, accused Josephus of actively fomenting the revolt against the Romans. This charge, made during the reign of Domitian, would have eroded Josephus' credibility at court were it to have gone without answer, and may have done so in any case. The work of Justus stood in rivalry to that of Josephus as least until the ninth century, after which its readership, along with all traces of its actual text, disappeared. Josephus prevailed; the fact that he did attests his value, not as a benign and likable person or as an objective and fully credible historian, but as a writer of great erudition and talent, whose narrative scope and magnitude and whose personal association with many of the figures and events in his narrative make him perennially readable and provide a veritable drama in complement to scientific history.

Of especial value to general readers and to students of first century history are the detailed appraisals by Josephus of the zealotry, factions, and religious turmoil in Palestine, the political thrusts of the Roman aristocracy, and the complex relations between Rome and the Judaean principate.

Bibliography

Bentwich, Norman. *Josephus*. Philadelphia: Jewish Publication Society of America, 1914. A consideration of Josephus from the Jewish point of view. The writer is harsh on Josephus, not only as a general whom he calls traitorous but also as a scholar, claiming that Josephus was not so learned and erudite as he claims to have been and is credited as having been. According to Bentwich, Josephus misuses words such as "Gamala," an error that may have been understandable for a Roman but not for someone Jewish.

Bohrmann, Monette. *Flavius Josephus, The Zealots and Yavne: Towards a Rereading of the War of the Jews*. Translated by Janet Lloyd. Bern and New York: Peter Lang, 1994. Attempts to evaluate the events of the revolt from the perspective of the Jews. The war appears as the inevitable result of cultural conflict, although the author claims that some Jewish leaders (including Johanan ben Zakkai and Josephus himself) counseled peace.

Cohen, Shaye J. D. *Josephus in Galilee and Rome: His Vita and Development as a Historian*. Leiden, Netherlands: E. J. Brill, 1979. This work, volume 8 of the Columbia Studies in the Classical Tradition, is a very scholarly study of Josephus and his sources, the literary relationship of the autobiography to *The Jewish War*, the aims and methods of the autobiography, and the historicity of Josephus' activities in Galilee and Rome.

Feldman, Louis H. *Josephus and Modern Scholarship, 1937-1980*. New York: W. de Gruyter, 1984. A massive achievement in its comparative summaries of Josephan scholarship and in bibliographical research. This work is chiefly of interest, and indeed indispensable, to the Josephan scholar; it can also be very enlightening and of considerable help to the general reader. Under specific topics (for example, "The War Against the Romans") and subtopics (for example, "The Causes and Goals of the War," "Domitian"), Feldman provides extensive bibliographic references followed by comparative commentary on works listed.

Furneaux, Rupert. *The Roman Siege of Jerusalem*. New York: McKay, 1972; London: Hart-Davis, 1973. Furneaux's opening chapter, identifying Josephus as a "Quisling," is followed by chapters on a Zealot messiah named Judas, the Roman procurators, the emperor Titus, Pilate, and the messiah Jesus. This very readable book gives a graphic account of the systematic quelling of the Jewish revolt by the logistically superior Roman legions. Furneaux provides an appendix on the Slavonic text of Josephus.

Hardwick, Michael E. *Brown Judaic Studies*. Vol. 128, *Josephus as an Historical Source in Patristic Literature through Eusebius*. Atlanta, Ga.: Scholars Press, 1989. Examines the use and reception of Josephus by various ante-Nicene Christian authors.

Josephus, Flavius. *The Jewish War*. Edited by Gaalya Cornfeld, Benjamin Mazar, and Paul L. Maier. Grand Rapids, Mich.: Zondervan Publishing House, 1982. An adequate translation profusely illustrated and annotated. The photographs of sites and artifacts vary in quality from poor to very good. The maps and diagrams are excellent, and the annotations are bolstered by archaeological research and references to the Dead Sea Scrolls.

―――――. *"The Jewish War" and Other Selections from Flavius Josephus*. Edited and abridged with an introduction by Moses I. Finley. Translated by H. St. John Thackeray and Ralph Marcus. New York: Twayne Publishers, 1965; London: New English Library, 1966. Contains selections from Josephus' autobiography (including the "Polemic Against the Historian Justus"), *Against Apion, The Antiquities of the Jews*, and *The Jewish War*. Finley's eighteen-page introduction is well worth reading. For readers who have not the time to browse through the complete Josephus in the Thackeray-Marcus-Wikgren-Feldman nine-volume Loeb Library translation (1926-1965), this is a moderate guide.

————. *The Jewish War*. Translated by G. A. Williamson. Rev. ed. London and New York: Penguin Books, 1970. This, in its estimable revision by E. Mary Smallwood, is the definitive English translation. Its clarity and readability are commended by Louis H. Feldman. Its introduction, notes, maps, and appendices are edifying to both the student and the general reader. A helpful companion piece to this translation is Williamson's *The World of Josephus* (1964), although Moses I. Finley cautions that it lacks scholarly depth relevant to difficult Josephan problems; this criticism should not deter the interested reader, however, who will find in both works a superb introduction to the world and work of Flavius Josephus.

Mason, Steve. *Studia post-Biblica*. Vol. 39, *Flavius Josephus on the Pharisees: A Composition-Critical Study*. Leiden and New York: Brill, 1991. This book covers more than the title suggests. In order to make its central claim (that Josephus had firsthand knowledge of the Pharisees), the author includes extensive discussion of the historian's works.

Parente, Fausto, and Joseph Sievers, eds. *Studia post-Biblica*. Vol. 41, *Josephus and the History of the Greco-Roman Period: Essays in Memory of Morton Smith*. Leiden and New York: E. J. Brill, 1994. A collection of 19 essays offering a useful survey of current scholarship on questions such as "Josephus and the Essenes," "Josephus' description of the Jerusalem Temple," and "Josephus as Roman Citizen."

Schwartz, Seth. *Columbia Studies in Classical Tradition*. Vol. 18, *Josephus and Judaean Politics*. Leiden and New York: Brill, 1990. A thorough scholarly analysis of the part of Josephus' life after his surrender to Vespasian, concentrating on his knowledge of contemporary events in Palestine and his relationship and support for the upper-classes still resident in Jerusalem after the defeat of the revolt.

Smallwood, E. Mary. *The Jews Under Roman Rule: From Pompey to Diocletian*. Leiden, Netherlands: E. J. Brill, 1976. The first twelve chapters of this study, particularly chapters 11 and 12, provide an informative reprise of the world in which Josephus was elevated to greatness and offer an appreciable survey of his place in history.

Tcherikover, Avigdor. *Hellenistic Civilization and the Jews*. Translated by S. Applebaum. Philadelphia: Jewish Publication Society of America, 1959. Comprehensive exposition of the confluence of the Judaic and Hellenistic traditions; essential to an understanding of the cultural crucible in which the political identity of Josephus was formed.

Thackeray, H. St. John. *Josephus: The Man and the Historian*. New York: Jewish Institute of Religion Press, 1929. Six lectures given in 1928 as part of the Hilda Stich Stroock Lectures series. In its setting forth of the conspectus of Josephus (life and character; *The Jewish War; The Antiquities of the Jews*; Josephus and Judaism; Josephus and Hellenism; Josephus and Christianity) it is exemplary; Samuel Sandmel, however, who has provided the introduction to the reprint, finds the work lacking in an exposition of the significance and utility of Josephus' writings.

Whiston, William. *The Life and Works of Flavius Josephus*. New York: Holt, Rinehart and Winston, 1977. This translation of the complete works of Josephus, for all its faults and verbosity, remains an important part of the Josephan tradition in the English-speaking world. Both G. A. Williamson and M. I. Finley mention its being kept alongside the family Bible in Victorian homes.

Roy Arthur Swanson

JUVENAL

Born: c. A.D. 60; Aquinum
Died: c. A.D. 130; place unknown
Area of Achievement: Literature
Contribution: Juvenal expanded the dimensions of poetic satire in savage works that lashed out at man's vices and corruption.

Early Life

Juvenal (Decimus Junius Juvenalis) was born around A.D. 60 in the small Italian town of Aquinum. It is thought that his family was wealthy and that Juvenal entered the army to make a career in service to the emperor. Unsuccessful in his endeavors to achieve a position of responsibility, however, he turned to literature to establish or simply to express himself. He was a friend of the well-known poet Martial during this period and wrote his first satires against the flatterers and hangers-on in the imperial court. For this scathing attack, Emperor Domitian confiscated Juvenal's property and exiled him to Egypt.

Juvenal returned to Rome after the death of Domitian in 96 and wrote, recited, and published his *Saturae* (100-127; *Satires*) during the years that followed. Most of the satires written at this time do not refer to contemporary events but to the abuses of the earlier reign of Domitian. For several years, Juvenal was very poor, but eventually his financial problems were alleviated by a gift from Emperor Hadrian.

Life's Work

Juvenal's achievement can be found in the five books of satires he produced during his lifetime. There are sixteen satires in the collected works of Juvenal, and the first book contains the first five. These five satires have as their subject matter the corruption and immorality which Juvenal perceived among Roman aristocrats and leaders of his time; he considered that they were interested in wealth and sexual excess rather than the personal virtue and rectitude befitting leaders of the Roman Republic.

The first satire in book 1 is an introduction to the whole work; it is a justification for the literary mode which Juvenal created. There had been satire before Juvenal, but it did not have the tone, subject matter, or structure which Juvenal employed. Earli-

er satires, such as those of Horace, tended to laugh tolerantly at mankind's social foibles rather than rage about their vices. The tone set by Juvenal, then, was new: "Must I be listening always, and not pay them back? How they bore me,/ Authors like Cordus the crude, with the epic he calls the Theseid!" Juvenalian satire is an exasperated attack on those who have offended him; its realm is not the heroic but the low and the mean. He directs his hearers to the disgusting Roman scene and declares: "Then it is difficult NOT to write satire." He points to such absurdities as a eunuch marrying and Juvenal's former barber becoming richer than any patrician. Although his satire has the sweep of epic, covering "everything human" from the earliest times, its special province is contemporary life: "When was there ever a time more rich in abundance of vices?"

At the end of the poem, Juvenal brings up the problem of whether he will "dare name names," real names rather than invented ones. If he does, he is likely to end up "a torch in a tunic" in these corrupt times. He determines therefore to use only the names of the dead and reveal the type of vice if not the specific example.

The second satire is against not only homosexuality but also the hypocrisy of homosexuals who set themselves up as moral censors of society. The poem opens with a typical Juvenalian hyperbolic exclamation of frustration: "Off to Russia for me, or the Eskimos, hearing these fellows/ Talk—what a nerve!—about morals, pretend that their virtue/ Equals the Curian clan's, while they act like Bacchanal women." A list of odious examples follows this opening, the most important being that of Gracchus, a descendant of the republican Gracchi who defended the rights of the Plebeians. This Gracchus has given a large sum of money to a musician and married him in a bizarre ceremony; once more, the target of Juvenal's wrath is members of the aristocratic class, who should be offering models for the rest of society instead of pursuing debauchery. Even the great feats of Roman arms are mocked: "An Armenian prince, softer than all of our fairies" ends up in the arms of a Roman tribune, an act which Juvenal calls "the Intercourse Between Nations."

The third satire, against the city of Rome, is one of Juvenal's greatest works. The speaker in the poem is not Juvenal but his friend Umbricius. Umbricius is leaving Rome because he is "no good at lying" and therefore cannot possibly survive in Rome. One aspect of Roman life that he finds especially offensive is that the old republican Rome has become a "Greekized Rome," filled with subtle Greeks who can adapt to any role and thus are displacing the native aristocracy. Another target is the great value now given to wealth; poverty "makes men objects of mirth, ridiculed, humbled, embarrassed." In addition, Rome is a dangerous place; if its resident does not catch a disease, then he is likely to die in a fire or be killed by a burglar at night. The only sane course is to flee the city and relocate in a country town where civic virtue is still possible and one can live an honorable life.

The fourth satire contains two episodes. In the first, Curly the Cur spends an absurdly large sum of money for a red mullet which he devours by himself. Juvenal remarks that he could have bought the fisherman for less than he paid for the fish. This excess is paralleled by an incident involving Emperor Domitian. Domitian is given a huge turbot because his subjects fear that by purchasing it they would incur the wrath of the "baldheaded tyrant." There is no pot large enough for the fish, however, and a council of state is called to decide what to do. The councillors are all terrified of saying the wrong thing and ending up dead, so they treat the problem as a question of war. One suggests that the emperor will capture a monarch as great as the fish, while a craftier one suggests that a huge pot to cook the fish whole be created and "from henceforward, Great Caesar,/ Let potters follow your camp!" The motion is carried, and the councillors nervously depart. Juvenal adds a comment at the end of the poem to sum up the reign of Domitian: "Nobles he could kill. He was soaked in their blood, and no matter./ But when the common herd began to dread him, he perished." Once more, the Roman aristocrats are ineffectual or corrupt, and only the mob can bring down a vicious (and here ridiculous) emperor.

The fifth satire satirizes both the proud and overbearing patron and the submissive client who acquiesces to and even encourages this situation. The poem is structured as a description of a typical dinner with a patron. The patron drinks the best wines while the client is given wine that would make blotting paper shudder. The patron dines on a choice mullet, the client on an eel that looks like a blacksnake. The reason for such shameful treatment is the client's poverty; if he were rich, the daintiest morsels would be placed before him. Juvenal suggests to such clients that if they persist in seeking and accepting such treatment, "some day you'll offer your shaved-off heads to be slapped." If the client acts like a slave, the patron will surely treat him like a slave.

Book 2 of the *Satires* is composed of one long poem attacking Roman women; it is the longest and most ambitious of Juvenal's satires. His charges against women are similar to those he made against Rome's nobility: They have fallen into decadence, they care only about money, and they have forsaken old ways in favor of current fashions and modes. Women are no longer to be trusted, since so many have poisoned their husbands for wealth or convenience. Finally, even if a man were to find the perfect woman, she would not do since her perfection would be unbearable. It is an amusingly unbalanced, excessive, and effective poem.

The third book is made up of three poems. The subjects are again poverty, nobility, and ways of gaining a livelihood in first century Rome. The poor wretches in satire 7 are poets, historians, and teachers, occupations which had once been honored but are now despised. The poem piles negative example on example, but it does offer some hope for a decent life; "Caesar alone" can provide the help the public refuses to give. The eighth satire contrasts nobility of character to nobility of family; Juvenal cites examples of debased scions from famous families and declares: "Virtue alone is proof of nobility." The most telling contrast is between the noble heritage of Catiline (Lucius Sergius Catilina), who attempted to enslave the Roman people, and the relative obscurity of Cicero, who thwarted Catiline's designs and saved the Republic. The ninth satire has as a speaker, not Juvenal or one of his spokesmen but a homosexual, who is complaining about the difficulties he finds in his work as a prostitute. He is consoled at the end by a cohort who assures him that "there'll always be fairies/ While these seven hills stand." Since this is so, he can be content with a contingent of slaves, a villa of his own, and a sum of money equivalent to a thousand dollars—amenities unavailable to most poets of the time.

The highlight of book 4 of the *Satires* is "The Vanity of Human Wishes," in which Juvenal poses the question of the proper petitions of humans in their prayers to the gods. He inventories the usual requests that men make—for wealth, beauty, or power—only to find that their attainment produces dangerous results. The wealthy man, for example, has to fear the poison in the jeweled cup, while the poor man is free from such fears; the powerful man has to watch out for envy and hatred, while the weak man can be at peace. Even the desire for a long life is not appropriate, since the man to whom such a request has been granted must face burying his wife, children, and all those dear to him while he withers into a lonely old age. What then should people pray for? "A healthy mind in a healthy body, a spirit/ Unafraid of death, but reconciled to it." The rest must be left to the gods, for human beings do not know their own best interests.

The last book of satires contains only one important poem, "On an Education in Avarice." It deals not only with the dangers of the desire for great wealth but also with how the example of the parents influences the children. There is a surprising tenderness in Juvenal's tone when he speaks about the vulnerability of children. "To a child is due the greatest respect: in whatever/ Nastiness you prepare, don't despise the years of your children,/ But let your infant son dissuade you from being a sinner." Man should desire only enough to feed, clothe, and shelter himself; the rest is not only unnecessary but corrupting.

Juvenal's last book of satires was published in 127, and he died shortly after.

Summary

Juvenal's satires retain their power nearly two thousand years after they were written. Their powerful moral vision and the freshness of their language permit them to transcend the local and specific occasions which they address. Juvenal's solutions or consolations are not unusual; similar Stoic advice can be found in the writings of Horace or Sextius Propertius. No other poet of the period, however, exposed so much so fully. Some have complained that Juvenal went too far in his condemnation of mankind and that his poetic vision is unbalanced. These critics fail, however, to relate Juvenal's vision to the social and political system of the time and to take into consideration the special social role of the satirist in this period. Juvenal believed epic and lyric poetry to be entirely inappropriate forms for a corrupt age; instead, his time demanded exactly the sort of fiercely agitated satires that he produced.

Bibliography

Braund, Susanna H. *Beyond Anger: A Study of Juvenal's Third Book of Satires.* Cambridge Classical Studies. Cambridge and New York: Cambridge University Press, 1988. Braund argues that the speaker of Juvenal's satires is to be understood not as the poet himself, but as an adopted persona, one whose views may actually be the subject of covert satirizing by the poet, who writes from behind the scenes.

Duff, J. Wight. *A Literary History of Rome in the Silver Age: From Tiberius to Hadrian.* 3d ed. London: Benn, and New York: Barnes and Noble, 1964. A broad historical survey of the literature of the period, with a specific discussion of satire as a literary form in Juvenal's time.

———. *Roman Satire: Its Outlook on Social Life.* Berkeley: University of California Press, 1936; Cambridge: Cambridge University Press, 1937. Duff relates Juvenal's poems to the literary and social contexts, but he does not analyze the poems in any detail. A brief but useful introduction to the poet.

Highet, Gilbert. *Juvenal the Satirist: A Study.* Oxford: Clarendon Press, 1954; New York: Oxford University Press, 1961. Includes a cogent discussion of each of Juvenal's satires and of their influence on later literature. The book is very thorough but accessible to the general reader.

Jenkyns, Richard. *Three Classical Poets: Sappho, Catullus, Juvenal.* Cambridge, Mass.: Harvard University Press, and London: Duckworth, 1982. This very detailed study of Juvenal's style and poetic effects brings to light the satirist's techniques and methods. It is well written, but it is directed toward an academic audience.

Scott, Inez G. *The Grand Style in the Satires of Juvenal.* Northhampton, Mass.: Smith College, 1927. An early and still-valuable stylistic study of Juvenal's use of inflated language to create satiric effects. The book is appropriate for those who know something about the literary traditions of the period.

James Sullivan

KĀLIDĀSA

Born: c. 100 B.C. or c. A.D. 340; India
Died: c. 40 B.C. or c. A.D. 400; probably India
Area of Achievement: Literature
Contribution: Recognized as the author of no more than three plays and four poems, which fuse together themes of nature and love within the framework of Hinduism, Kālidāsa is generally regarded as India's greatest poet and dramatist. Sometimes characterized as the "Shakespeare of India," he is especially known in the West for his romantic play *Śakuntalā* and his metaphysical love poem *The Cloud Messenger*.

Early Life

Kālidāsa's play *Mālavikāgnimitra* (c. 70 B.C. or c. A.D. 370; English translation, 1875) has as its hero Agnimitra, a historical king of the Śunga Dynasty who reigned from 151 to 143 B.C. In addition, inscriptions found in the Deccan at Mandasor (dated A.D. 473) and Aihole (dated A.D. 634) quote from his poetry and laud his genius. These firm evidences are all that establish a chronological range for Kālidāsa's life. The rest is conjecture. Though the Śunga was an important successor to the great Maurya Dynasty and led a cultural revival, opinion holds that Hindu culture had not sufficiently developed and the times were too disturbed to accommodate a talent such as Kālidāsa's. Thus scholars suggest that the Gupta Dynasty (c. A.D. 320-c. 550), the golden age of India, marked by serenity and sophistication, was more in line with the spirit and style of Kālidāsa. It is quite possible that Kālidāsa flourished during the reign of Candra Gupta II (c. 380-c. 414), of whom a congenial relation of court poet to patron can be readily conceived. Still, students of Kālidāsa tend to attach two date ranges to his works to acknowledge the uncertainty.

Just as little is known of his dates, little is known of Kālidāsa's life—except by inference from his writings and the legends concerning him. Identified in various stories as an orphan, idiot, laborer, and shepherd, Kālidāsa may have had a difficult early life. His knowledge of religion, philosophy, the sciences, and Sanskrit probably marks him as a Brahman and a devotee of the cult of Siva. (Indeed, his name means "servant of Kali," one of the consorts of that god.) His aristocratic sensitivity, grasp of court etiquette, and familiarity with Indian geography suggest that he was not only a court poet to the Vikramaditya (Sun of Valor), his patron at

Ujjain, but also a traveler and an ambassador (possibly to Kuntala, a kingdom inland from the Malabar Coast). The erotic overtones in his works make it easy to accept the legend of a princess as his lover and spouse. It is not difficult to believe that his life ended, at sixty or eighty years of age, by foul play at the hands of a courtesan in Sri Lanka, as another legend would have it.

The order of his works (rejecting the twenty or so spurious works sometimes attributed to him) is unknown. Hypothetical reconstructions have been made, even to the degree of correlating the writings to his biography, but the writings are too impersonal to do this with any accuracy. Perhaps the two lyrics are early, the two epics somewhat later, while the plays are scattered at different phases of his life—*Abhijñānaśākuntala* (c. 45 B.C. or c. A.D. 395; *Śakuntalā: Or, The Lost Ring*, 1789) being the product of maturity.

Life's Work

Nearly all Kālidāsa's works were written in Sanskrit, a highly inflected language learned by an aristocratic elite—the word literally means "perfected." Sanskrit was written as poetry (*kavya*), either lyric or epic, according to precise rules of grammar. The poetry, combined with other factors, created the visual immediacy of drama. Kālidāsa, using twenty-six different meters, was the king of similes, drawing from religion and nature in a style distinguished by a grace and economy that made music.

The *Rtusamhāra* (c. 75 B.C. or c. A.D. 365; English translation, 1867) is a pastoral poem mirroring a newly married man's joy of nature during the six Indian seasons (summer, the rains, autumn, early winter, winter, and spring); it is composed of 140 stanzas divided into six cantos. Though popular with the young, it is regarded as a piece of juvenilia, generally neglected by the literary critics. Yet this "lover's calendar," because of its romance, may have been innovative at its first appearance.

The *Meghadūta* (c. 65 B.C. or c. A.D. 375; *The Cloud Messenger*, 1813), much adored by Johann Wolfgang von Goethe, is an elegiac monody of 111 to 127 verses, according to various recensions; it is cast in a series of seventeen-syllable quatrains in a single meter. A Yaksha, a sensual demigod, separated from his wife for a year by a curse, asks a rain cloud to transmit a love message to her. The first part of the poem contains a sweeping and detailed picture of the subcontinent via the hypostatized cloud; the second part focuses on its delivery to the wife in a celestial city of the Himalayas. The lyric plays on the pathos of love with full intensity of mood. The travels of the cloud and its detour over Ujjain lend credence to the idea of Kālidāsa as a traveler and diplomat. The poem is original and subjective; indeed, Kālidāsa pioneered a new genre. The traditional court epic (*Mahākāvya*) Kālidāsa found riddled with stereotype and convention. Yet he was able to condense, deepen, and stylize his works into epics of aristocratic appeal, combining elevated themes with emotional verity.

The epic *Kumārasambhava* (c. 60 B.C. or c. A.D. 380; *The Birth of the War-God*, 1879) is incomplete at eight cantos, covering the courtship and marriage of Siva and Pārvatī only. (The birth of their son Kumāra, and his exploits, are recounted in ten additional cantos which were found not to be Kālidāsa's work.) The material is drawn from the Puranas (the epic elaborating and expanding on the great epic *Mahābhārata*). Mount Himalaya's daughter Pārvatī falls in love with the meditative Yogi god Siva. Menaced by the demon Taraka, the gods determine that only a son by Siva and Pārvatī can defeat the demon; they send Kāma, the god of love, to bring about the union, but Siva burns Kāma with his third eye. Pārvatī then abandons sensuality for spiritualism, emaciating herself. Siva, in disguise, dissuades her from her course, and they come lovingly together. Thematically, self-abnegation leads to the highest form of love. Symbolically, Siva, who is Truth, combines with Pārvatī, Beauty, to produce Kumāra, Power. The risqué depiction of the lovers' honeymoon led to the charge that canto 8 is sacrilegious.

In the epic *Raghuvamśa* (c. 50 B.C. or c. A.D. 390; *The Dynasty of Raghu*, 1872-1895), Kālidāsa traces a line of kings descended from the sun god over nineteen cantos, dwelling on the varying aspects of the ideal king in terms of *dharma* (moral duty): Dilipa, the ascetic; Raghu, the warrior; Aja, the lover; and Rāma, the *avatāra* (incarnation) of Vishnu. Yet the line ends with Agnivarna, the consumptive voluptuary: Does this reflect the poet's tragic vision of lost ideals, or is the epic merely incomplete? Much of the poem is a brilliant summary of the classical epic *Rāmāyana*. The first nine cantos of that classic deal with Rāma's forebears, cantos 10 through 15 with Rāma, and cantos 16 through 19 with his descendants. One critic wonders

whether Kālidāsa preferred Raghu to Rāma, who shuns the pregnant Sītā as unclean after her abduction by Rāvana the demon. When one compares these epics, *The Birth of the War-God* has singleness of legend, theme, structure, and philosophy, while *The Dynasty of Raghu* is a multifaceted pageant and chronicle.

The *Mālavikāgnimitra*, a spirited, musical harem intrigue for a spring festival, involves the love of Agnimitra, a historical figure, for a princess disguised as a maiden, Mālavikā, against the opposition of his two queens, the mature Dhārinī and the accomplished Iravati. In winning her in this parallelogram of relationships, Agnimitra has the aid of a jester, a nun, and good luck, as well as an asoka tree that responds to those that touch it by flowering or not. Perhaps the key element of the plot is Dhārinī's final acceptance of Mālavikā into the harem.

Vikramorvaśiya (c. 56 B.C. or c. A.D. 384; *Vikrama and Urvaśī*, 1851), probably intended to be sung at a royal coronation, concerns the love of a semidivine hero, Purūuravas, for an immortal nymph, Urvaśī, a tale drawn from Vedic legend. Though their love is opposed by Purūravas' queen and subjected to a divine curse which separates them, the gods bring the couple together in the end. Thus, love (*kāma*), supported by wealth (*artha*), issues in progeny (*dharma*, moral duty). Act 5, when the grief-maddened king wanders in the woods apostrophizing nature, is a famous scene.

It was the eighteenth century Calcutta judge Sir William Jones, the founder of comparative philology by his "discovery" of Sanskrit, who brought Kālidāsa to the attention of the West by rendering the first English translation of *Śakuntalā* in 1789. The play remains one of the world's masterpieces. Its story of love spanning Earth and Heaven must have appealed to Europeans, as the Romantic movement was then in its infancy. Drawn from the *Mahābhārata*, the play centers on star-crossed lovers: the tender, tortured ruler Dushyanta and the natural, selfless Śakuntalā, daughter of a sage and a nymph. Their match is destroyed by a curse which erases the king's recognition of his spouse when she comes to him at his palace after a separation. Only his ring, lost and swallowed by a fish, can recover his memory of love. When the ring is found, the lovers are reunited via the aerial chariot of the god Indra, and they live happily together with their child Bharata, the first legendary emperor of India. Throughout, the play contrasts the demands of public life and the sorrow of frustrated love to the serenity of simple values and the conception of ideal love.

Summary

The drama of Kālidāsa can only be understood within its own cultural context. The theater was part of the palace complex, playing to sensitized aristocratic audiences. It combined poetry, music, dance, song, mime, and characterization in a highly stylized presentation shorn of scenery and props, with most actions occurring offstage. The absence of evil—indeed, the fusing of Heaven and Earth into a happy ending—is unique to Indian thought. The transmigration of souls, the demand of moral duty, and the consequences of fate make the cosmos ultimately moral and purposeful and eliminate the role of chance. The plays are dominated by psychological rather than plotting factors, by the power of a basic mood, or emotion (*rasa*), and the characters fill roles assigned by the cosmos rather than marked by individualism. Thus, Kālidāsa was actually a traditionalist, a believer in a finally beneficent world order (politically, he subscribed to benevolent monarchy). With such ideals as *maya* (illusion of reality), *moksa* (enlightenment), and *santa* (tranquillity) and a view of love encompassing sensual, aesthetic, and spiritual levels in different lives and worlds, Kālidāsa contributed to literature an elucidation of the cosmic pervasiveness of love.

Bibliography

Dimock, Edward C., Edwin Gerow, C. M. Naim, A. K. Ramanujan, Gordon Roadarmel, and J. A. B. van Buitenen. *The Literatures of India: An Introduction*. Chicago: University of Chicago Press, 1974. This critical study complements historical and sociological approaches of earlier Orientalists. It was a cooperative venture mostly of University of Chicago faculty for the Asia Society. Covers full sweep of Indian literature. See especially sections on the epic, drama, poetics, and the lyric. Scholarly, invaluable insights.

Horrwitz, E. P. *The Indian Theatre: A Brief Survey of the Sanskrit Drama*. London: Blackie, 1912; New York: Benjamin Blom, 1967. An old but evocative description of the Indian theater. A court theater of Ujjain and imaginary performances of Kālidāsa's plays are especially well described.

Kālidāsa. *Theater of Memory: The Plays of Kālidāsa*. Translated by Edwin Gerow, David Gitomer, and Barbara Stoler Miller. New York: Columbia University Press, 1984. Contains three brilliant chapters: "Kālidāsa's World and His Plays" (by Miller), "Sanskrit Dramatic Theory and Kālidāsa's Plays" (by Gerow), and "Theater in Kālidāsa's Art" (by Gitomer). The texts of the three plays are freshly translated and accompanied by copious annotations. Most valuable.

Krishnamoorthy, K. *Kalidasa*. New York: Twayne Publishers, 1972. Literary and scholarly introduction by an Indian scholar, written in the light of both Indian and Western criticism. The author attempts a biographical analysis based on a supposed order of the works. Comprehensive but tends toward the Romantic-Victorian school of literary appreciation and consequently suffers from Kalidasian hagiography. Includes full references to translations of all of his works.

Majumdar, R. C., ed. *History and Culture of the Indian People*. Vol. 3, *The Classical Age*. 4th ed. Bombay: Bharatiya Vidya Bhavan, 1988. Full treatment of the Gupta Dynasty by eighteen Indian scholars. Outlines the Gupta Empire, discusses the Sanskrit literature, and treats politics, law, religion, art, socioeconomic conditions, and education. Provides comprehensive backdrop to Kālidāsa's world (on the widely held assumption that he belongs to the Gupta age, when Hindu culture underwent its most glowing renaissance).

Ralph Smiley

KANISHKA

Born: First or second century A.D.; probably west-central Asia

Died: Probably second century A.D.; probably northern India

Areas of Achievement: Government, religion, and patronage of arts

Contribution: Kanishka, the greatest ruler of the Kushan Empire, administered an extensive realm that embraced much of modern India and Pakistan and parts of central Asia and China. Kanishka's patronage was responsible for the introduction of Mahayana Buddhism into China and for a remarkable flowering of Buddhist iconography.

Early Life

Considering the fame of Kanishka, remarkably little is known of his life, certainly not enough to construct a proper biography. Symbolic of this gap in history is the fact that the six-foot statue of him in the archaeological museum in Mathura, Uttar Pradesh, India, is headless. The scarcity of data is further compounded by the tangled, obscure complexities of the wider history of Inner Asia and northern India during the first centuries of the common era. What is known regarding Kanishka and his achievements has been gleaned principally from folklore and archaeological artifacts dating from this period. Inscriptions, coins, sculpture, architecture, legend, and Chinese and Iranian literary sources are the raw materials from which scholars have attempted to reconstruct an understanding of Kanishka's life and times.

Even the time frame of Kanishka's reign has been the subject of much discussion; indeed, two scholarly conferences (in 1913 and 1960) were convened in London to explore the issue. One long-accepted reckoning places it roughly between A.D. 78 and 103, but more recent scholarship (agreeing with an earlier line of thought) places it between A.D. 128 and 151. Kanishka's reign has been associated, probably mistakenly, with the Saka Era dating system, which was initiated in A.D. 78 and which ultimately became the basis of the modern Indian governmental calendar.

The precise origin of the Kushans is also an open question, since they arose out of a welter of Central Asiatic races and languages in a region of complex migrations. They could have been Turkic or Iranian or, more probably, a mixture of the two. They can be traced to the Yueh-chi (or Indo-Scythians) in Chinese Turkistan on the frontier of Han China. Displaced by the Hsiung-nu (the Huns), the Yueh-chi crossed the Jaxartes River (modern Syr Darya) and occupied Sogdiana (Transoxiana) at the expense of the Saka (Iranian nomads) by 150 B.C. Then, having crossed the Oxus River (modern Amu Darya) by 130 B.C., they conquered the Indo-Greek Bactrian kingdom. The Bactrians' developed trading economy and advanced culture had a deep influence on their nomadic conquerors. One of the five tribes among these conquerors, the Kushans, rose up to assert dominance and establish political unity under Kujula Kadphises I. For unknown reasons, the Kushans eventually gravitated to the east to the Hindu Kush region and ultimately to northwest India, a world of petty states floundering in a political vacuum since the end of the Maurya Empire.

Life's Work

Precisely how, when, and how deeply the Kushans penetrated northwest India is not entirely clear, nor are the roles of Kujula, his son Wima Kadphises II, and their successor Kanishka. Until the coming of the Muslims in the twelfth century, however, no foreign power after the prehistoric Indo-Aryans gained control over as much of India—and held it for as long—as did the Kushans. There is some suggestion that Kanishka was not in the line of the Kadphises; moreover, there is the problem of a king of unknown name, "Soter Megas," who preceded him. It is thought that Kanishka may have begun a new line of succession. He may have invaded India from the north (Khotan in Sinkiang according to one authority), or he may have been one of several chiefs in India engaged in a struggle for the succession. When Kanishka came to power, he apparently used co-optation, for he shared rule with a junior, Vashishka (either his brother or his son), who ultimately succeeded him; he may have had other corulers as well.

A statue of Kanishka at Mathura shows him in Turkic warrior garb. Images of him on gold coins of the time render him as a bearded man with large, thoughtful eyes and thin, determined lips. He seems to have had a forceful personality, yet in cultural and religious matters he was more tolerant and accommodating than rigid and austere.

The Kushan Empire reached its zenith under Kanishka. An inland realm with its capital at Purushapura (modern Peshawar, Pakistan) at the foot of the Khyber Pass leading to Kabul and the Hindu Kush region, it centered on the upper Indus and the upper Ganges valleys (in modern Iran and India). It seems in India to have embraced Pataliputra (Patna) to the east, Sanchi to the south, and Bahawalpur on the Sutlej River, but its key southern city was Mathura on the Yamuna River. To the north, beyond the Pamirs, the Kushans dominated the caravan city-states of eastern Turkistan, especially Khotan, and held Bactria; to the west, in what is now Afghanistan, they held sway over Begram and Balkh. This location enabled the Kushans to connect India with China, Persia, and the Roman Empire via the Old Silk Road opened in 106 B.C. across Central Asia, combined with the old Mauryan royal highway between Taxila and Pataliputra and then through the Ganges Delta (where a Roman ship is known to have arrived about A.D. 100). Other roads led to the Arabian Sea ports of Barbaricum and Barygaza (modern Broach). The Kushans, with their command of animal power and soldiery, held the routes together and exacted great revenues through transit dues. In this way, the Kushans maintained a network of international trade that also allowed for a wide-ranging exchange of art and ideas. Within the empire, though agriculture remained important, trade profits gave rise to an urban society of guilds and merchants.

Not surprisingly, the Kushan Empire, comprising as it did many peoples, religions, and belief systems—such as Hellenism, Mithraism, Hinduism, and Buddhism—was marked by attitudes of coexistence and syncretism. The Kushans, who had spoken Bactrian (an Iranian tongue) and then Greek, in India began to adopt Sanskrit. Kadphises I had been a Buddhist, Kadphises II a Hindu; Kanishka was a Buddhist. Such cosmopolitanism was a product not only of their history and economy but also of their role as foreigners faced with the inflexibilities of *karma* (destiny) and *jati* (caste) within the Hindu system, within which the Kushans could be treated as "fallen *Kshatriya*" (warriors). Their low position within the stratified social classes of Hinduism helps to explain the Kushan tendency to embrace Buddhism (though later rulers such as Huvishka and Vasudeva were Hindu).

Such a huge and complex empire could only be governed by a feudal system allowing for significant regional autonomy. The emperor did, however, appoint satraps (provincial governors), *meridareks* (district officers), and *strategoi* (military governors). The ruler ascribed to himself a divine origin and borrowed such appellations as "King of Kings" (from Bactria), "Great King" (from India), "Son of Heaven" (from China), and "Emperor" (probably from Rome). After death, emperors were deified and temples were dedicated to them.

Religiously eclectic, to judge by his coins bearing images of a variety of gods, Kanishka came to favor the emerging Mahayana form of Buddhism over Hinduism, probably because he found the former to be more cosmopolitan and more amenable to mercantilism. It is not clear whether he underwent a genuine conversion or simply found embracing Buddhism to be politically expedient. In any case, Kanishka gave official support to Buddhist proselytization by means of education and iconography, stimulating the spread of Buddhism through Central Asia into China. Under his auspices, the Sarvastivadins, a sect of monks who favored the nascent Mahayanist Buddhism, organized the fourth Buddhist council (a gathering that cannot be called ecumenical, for the Hinayanists in the south called a separate fourth council in Sri Lanka). Rejecting Pali (the Hinayana or Theravada language) in favor of Sanskrit, the monks spent twelve years in Kashmir (or in Punjab) writing commentaries on the Buddhist canon, in the process probably launching Mahayana Buddhism. The records of this gathering, inscribed on copper plates in stone boxes, are found today only in Chinese translation.

In old age, Kanishka may have sent an army of seventy thousand over the Pamirs to oppose Chinese military thrusts into Central Asia, a venture that failed miserably. The date and circumstances of Kanishka's death are unknown.

Summary

Kanishka's policies were responsible for generating a new style in Oriental sculpture, a style that combined Greco-Roman and Iranian elements with Indian ideology to lay the basis for a Buddhist representational art with a popular appeal. The Gandhara school (in Purushapura, Taxila, and Bamian) produced more naturalistic Buddhas mostly in schist, while the Mathura school turned out more stylized images in sandstone, suggesting a Western versus an Indian inspiration in the respective schools.

Throughout the historic Punjab and modern north-central Afghanistan east of Balkh and Kandahar, more than in the Hindustan, can be found the monumental ruins of Kanishka's building projects. He erected a 638-foot stupa to Buddha at Peshawar, a monument celebrated through Asia: a five-stage, 286-foot diameter base, surmounted by a thirteen-story carved wood structure topped by an iron column adorned with gilded copper umbrellas (*chhatras*). In decay by the seventh century, the relic casket bearing an effigy and inscription of Kanishka was found *in situ* in 1908 and now may be seen in the Peshawar Museum.

The most important Kanishka inscriptions are those found on a monolith before a temple-acropolis in Greco-Iranian style at Surkh Kotal (Baghlan) in the Kunduz River Valley of northeast Afghanistan. The structure, excavated between 1952 and 1964, suggests a dynastic Zoroastrian fire-temple. In Begram (now Kāpīsā), north of Kabul, Kanishka built a monastery (*vihara*) to house Chinese royal hostages. At Bāmiān, in the high passes at the Hindu Kush west of Kabul, two colossal rock Buddhas, though carved well after his time, may have been modeled on Kanishka. Further records of Kanishka's reign are numerous coins minted during his time, many of gold, bearing images of a variety of Greek, Iranian, and Indian gods. The first Buddha coin also dates from this period.

Not only was Kanishka another Aśoka the Great in his championship of Buddhism, but he also seems to have been a patron of scholarship and the arts. It is thought that such distinguished men as the Sanskrit poet-dramatist and Buddhist popularizer Aśvaghosa (who wrote the conciliar commentaries) and the physician and medical writer Charaka may have been at his court. Imperious in nature, Kanishka could launch an army against China and carry off Aśvaghosa from Varanasi. Yet, when demanding huge booty at Varanasi, he could accept instead a begging bowl of Buddha. Kanishka stood at a crossroads of world civilization, keeping the way open for the cross-fertilization of Eastern and Western economics and culture. His patronage of Mahayana Buddhism, however, though it brought about the introduction of Buddhism to Central Asia and China, may have weakened that religion in India, for Kanishka was regarded as a foreigner, and his religion was therefore alien as well. Hinduism correspondingly came to be accorded status as India's indigenous religious system.

Bibliography

Basham, Arthur L., ed. *Papers on the Date of Kaniska*. Leiden, Netherlands: E. J. Brill, 1969. Proceedings of a conference, held in London in 1960, that attempted to resolve the question of Kanishka's dates. The date of Kanishka's accession to power, and its implications for understanding the Vikrama and Saka calendars, is the major vexing question of Indian history.

Davids, T. W. Rhys. *Buddhist India*. New York: Putnam, and London: T. Fisher Unwin, 1903. Chapter 26 constitutes a full discussion of Kanishka's historic role. Based on the ancient sources, it examines socioeconomic, political, and religious aspects of the Buddhist ascendancy from a non-Brahmin point of view. The author was a distinguished Buddhologist who died in 1922.

Majumdar, R. C., ed. *The History and Culture of the Indian People*. Vol. 2, *The Age of Imperial Unity*. 6th ed. Bombay, India: Bhartiya Vidya Bhavan, 1990. See especially D. C. Sircar's discussion of the Kushanas, M. Dutt's section on the Buddhist councils, J. N. Banerjea's treatment of Buddhist iconography, and S. K. Saraswati's description of the stupa. N. R. Ray has a helpful discussion of Gandhara sculpture and coins, and R. C. Majumdar contributed a survey of Indian cultural expansion.

Narain, A. K. *The Indo-Greeks*. Oxford: Clarendon Press, 1957. The Kushans are actually a peripheral theme in this study, which deals at greater length with the Yavanas (Indo-Greeks in the Punjab). The book is based on a University of London doctoral dissertation. Data drawn largely from numismatics. Narain challenges the interpretation of W. W. Tarn (see below).

Rapson, E. J., ed. *The Cambridge History of India*. Vol. 1, *Ancient India*. New York: Macmillan, 1922. Chapter 23 includes a discussion of the Scythian and Parthian invaders of India. The volume contains maps and plates showing coins of ancient Indian civilizations.

Smith, Vincent A. *Early History of India: From 600 B.C. to the Muhammadan Conquest, Including the Invasion of Alexander the Great*. 4th ed. Oxford: Clarendon Press, 1924; New York: Oxford University Press, 1957. Offers general background information for the period delineated in its subtitle. Its author, however, was a British official in India, and his interpretations reflect an old-fashioned colonialist point of view.

Tarn, W. W. *The Greeks in Bactria and India*. 3d ed. Chicago: Ares, 1984. See especially chapters 7, 8, and 9. This is a seminal study of the penetration of Hellenism into Inner Asia. The author was a scholar at the University of Edinburgh.

Warder, A. K. *Indian Buddhism*. 2d ed. Delhi, India: Motilal Banarsidass, 1980. Cites ancient sources to survey the doctrines and history of Buddhism in India. The first section deals with early Buddhism through the schisms of the fourth and third centuries B.C., the second examines the eighteen schools of Indian Buddhism, and the third has to do with the Mahayana movement.

Yar-Shater, Ehsan, ed. *The Cambridge History of Iran*. Vol. 3, *The Seleucid, Parthian, and Sasanian Periods*. Cambridge: Cambridge University Press, 1983. See especially chapter 5, "The History of Eastern Iran," by A. D. H. Bivar, and chapter 26, "Buddhism Among the Iranian Peoples," by R. E. Emmerick, for fully updated scholarship and comprehensive examinations of the historical regions of Iran.

Ralph Smiley

Born: 604 B.C.; Ch'ü-jen, State of Ch'u, China
Died: Sixth century B.C.; place unknown
Area of Achievement: Philosophy
Contribution: Lao-tzu is widely recognized as the premier thinker of Taoism, the second of China's great philosophical schools.

Early Life

Lao-tzu (also known as *Tao-te Ching*) is the name of a slim volume from China's classical era that forms a principal text of the Taoist school of philosophy. The title literally means "Old Master," and the book has traditionally been ascribed to the "Old Master" himself—or, at least, it has been thought to reflect faithfully the philosophy of someone known as Lao-tzu. This Lao-tzu is, however, the most shadowy of all classical Chinese philosophers, and nothing at all can be said with any certainty about him.

The earliest attempt to write a biography of Lao-tzu was made in the first century B.C. by the great historian Ssu-ma Ch'ien (c. 145-c. 86 B.C.), but even at that early date the historian was only able to assemble a few scraps of information concerning Lao-tzu, many of which are mutually contradictory. Ssu-ma Ch'ien attempted to merge the stories of at least three different individuals into his biography of Lao-tzu, since he was uncertain which one was "the real Lao-tzu," and in the end the various stories proved impossible to reconcile. As Ssu-ma Ch'ien concluded, "Lao-tzu was a reclusive gentleman," and it is perhaps fitting that he remain forever elusive.

Among the few "facts" that are alleged about Lao-tzu are that his family name was Li, his given name Erh, and his "style" Tan. He was supposedly born in the southern state of Ch'u; indeed, Lao-tzu's thought does typify the lush, mystical, romantic, and sometimes erotic southern side of ancient Chinese culture that contrasts so starkly with the stern moralism of northern Confucianism.

Ssu-ma Ch'ien says that Lao-tzu served as Historian of the Archives in the court of the Chou Dynasty and that Confucius (551-479 B.C.) personally sought instruction from him in the rites. At age 160, or perhaps two hundred, disappointed with the decline of civilization in China, Lao-tzu departed. The Keeper of the Hsien-ku Pass detained him on his way out and required him to commit his wisdom to writing in the book that came to be known as the *Tao-te Ching*, before permitting him to continue his westward journey. According to a later legend, Lao-tzu subsequently went to India, where his teachings gave birth to Buddhism.

None of this information is historically reliable, however, and many modern scholars doubt that Lao-tzu is a historical figure at all. It seems more likely that there were several "Old Masters" in ancient China who taught ideas similar to those of the *Tao-te Ching* than that no such man ever existed at all. In either case, however, it ceases to be meaningful to say that Lao-tzu wrote the book that is sometimes called by his name.

The best evidence indicates that the *Tao-te Ching* was compiled sometime during the fourth or third century B.C., probably incorporating earlier fragments, and that it did not settle into its present form until the middle of the second century B.C. It may be that it is largely the product of one hand, but it can also be plausibly viewed as a jumble of anonymous Taoist sayings assembled by an editor or editors during this period.

Life's Work

The *Tao-te Ching* has been translated into English more often than any book except the Bible, and in China hundreds of commentaries have been written on it. The explanation for all this attention is that, aside from the great intrinsic appeal of the work, it is a very cryptic book that defies definitive interpretation. Each reader finds something different in the *Tao-te Ching*, and, despite deceptively simple grammar and vocabulary, it is often possible to argue at great length even about the meaning of individual sentences.

For example, the famous opening line of the *Tao-te Ching* could read, in English, "Any way that you can speak about is not The Constant Way." Alternatively, it could also read: "The way that can be treated as The Way is not an ordinary way," or, "The way that can be treated as The Way is an inconstant way." Multiply this kind of ambiguity by the more than five thousand Chinese characters in the book, and it becomes easy to understand why so many different translations of the *Tao-te Ching* are possible.

The work is divided into two sections and eighty-one brief chapters; more than half of it is written in rhyme, and it is suffused throughout with a distinct poetic atmosphere. There appears to be no particular order to the chapters, and even individual paragraphs may be unrelated to their context, thus reinforcing the impression of the *Tao-te Ching* as an anthology of Taoist maxims rather than a systematic treatise.

Interpretation of the *Tao-te Ching* must hinge, in part, upon the date one chooses to assign for its composition. Its pointed ridicule of Confucian sanctimoniousness, for example, is puzzling if the legend that Lao-tzu was older than Confucius is true, but would make sense if it was really compiled in the post-Confucian period. At least one scholar claims that the *Tao-te Ching* was not compiled until the late third century B.C.; he bases his argument on signs of opposition he sees in it to the Legalist school that was then developing.

More critical is the *Tao-te Ching*'s position within the chronology of the Taoist movement itself. Tradition gives the *Tao-te Ching* pride of place as the oldest Taoist work, but there are grounds for speculation that the other great Taoist text, the *Chuang-tzu*, might be older. Not knowing which book was written first makes it difficult to determine which book influenced which and seriously cripples scholars' ability to analyze the development of Taoism.

The principal philosophical difference between the *Tao-te Ching* and the *Chuang-tzu* is that the former advocates understanding the laws of change in the universe so as to conform to them and thereby harness them to work for one's benefit; *Chuang-tzu*, on the other hand, contends that a true understanding of the laws of change reveals all transformations to be equally valid and all differences to be ultimately relative. Hence the wise man does not try to manipulate the Tao, but simply accepts what it brings.

The Tao (pronounced "dow") is the central concept of all Taoist philosophy. The basic meaning of the word is "road" or "way," and by extension it came to refer to "the way" of doing various things. Philosophers of all Chinese schools of thought (even the Confucians) used this word and considered it to be important, but only the Taoists treated it as a universal absolute. For Confucians, the Tao is the moral Way of proper human behavior; to a Taoist, it is an amoral principle of nature.

The Tao is the constant law (or laws, since the Chinese language has no plurals) that governs the otherwise incessant change of the material universe. It is thus the one permanent, immutable thing in existence, the hub at the center of the wheel of life. Since the Tao is absolute, however, it is impossible to break it down for analysis. The mere act of giving it a name, such as Tao, is misleading, because it implies that the Tao is a thing which can be critically examined and labeled. The Tao actually transcends all humanly imposed conceptual models.

Since the Tao cannot be logically analyzed or described in words, it therefore can only be perceived holistically through intuition. This gives the *Tao-te Ching* its mystic tone and helps explain the frustrating statement in chapter 56 that "he who knows does not speak; he who speaks does not know." Ultimate truth is beyond the capacity of speech to convey. For this reason, one third century A.D. wag remarked that Confucius actually understood the Tao better than Lao-tzu, since Confucius was wise enough to keep silent about the subject.

Lao-tzu's favorite theme is the disparity between intention and result. "Reversal is the action of the Tao," he wrote (chapter 40). Striving to make oneself strong eventually exhausts and weakens a man; striving for wealth leads to poverty in the long run. The wise man instead conforms to the Tao and aligns himself with the weak, the humble, and the poor.

This philosophy was in large part a reaction to the highly competitive environment of the Warring States period in Chinese history (403-221 B.C.), when conflict was continuous and life itself uncertain. Amid such surroundings, *Tao-te Ching* taught that survival came through not competing. The solution to the problem of how to preserve life and happiness was simply to be content.

The *Tao-te Ching* contains wisdom for all men, but much of the book is directed in particular toward the ruler. It teaches a kind of laissez-faire approach to government: The state will function best if left to run itself naturally, and strenuous efforts on the part of the ruler can only cause greater confusion and disorder. The more the ruler acts, the more work he creates for himself, and the more impossible it becomes to do everything that is necessary. Far better to do nothing. The *Tao-te Ching* calls this form of government *wu-wei*, or "nonaction."

As a concrete application of this principle, the *Tao-te Ching* criticizes attempts to improve the state through moral codes or laws. The very existence of laws produces lawbreakers, and moral codes result in pretense, competition, and the very kinds of immorality they were intended to discourage. Far better, says Lao-tzu, to return to the child-like condition of original innocence that prevailed before the awakening of desires.

Summary

Lao-tzu the man is a will-o'-the-wisp—an insubstantial legend. Even a legend, however, can have important consequences. During the common era, religious Taoism (Tao-chiao) emerged under Buddhist influence out of earlier immortality cults. This Taoist religion adopted very little of the philosophical content of the *Tao-te Ching*, but its adherents came to venerate Lao-tzu himself as a god.

By the second century A.D., Lao-tzu was being worshipped as a progenitor of the universe, an incarnation of the Tao itself. The deified Lao-tzu became one of the most important members of the native Chinese religious pantheon, and the eighty-one earthly manifestations he was ultimately said to have taken included Siddhārtha Gautama (the Buddha) and Mani (Manes), the Persian founder of Manichaeanism.

The religious Taoist canon includes more than fourteen hundred separate titles, but the *Tao-te Ching*—often badly misunderstood, to be sure—ranks at the top. Even for Chinese who remained skeptical about this native religious movement, the *Tao-te Ching* continued to be regarded as an outstanding guide for living and a delightful work of literature.

The *Tao-te Ching* and *Chuang-tzu* represent the native Chinese tradition of true metaphysical speculation (as opposed to the political and social philosophy of Confucius and others) and as such have contributed immensely to the subsequent development of Chinese thought. Ch'an Buddhism (Japanese Zen), for example, owes much to Taoist influence. Taoist philosophy has always been the natural consolation of the Chinese gentleman in retirement or disgrace. The *Tao-te Ching*, one of the most profound and baffling books ever written, is a principal text in China's perennial "other" school of thought: the playful, mystical, Taoist alternative to staid and conventional Confucianism.

Bibliography

Creel, Herrlee G. *"What Is Taoism?" and Other Studies in Chinese Cultural History*. Chicago: University of Chicago Press, 1970; London: University of Chicago Press, 1977. Contains a definitive essay on the subject, emphasizing the distinction between philosophical and religious Taoism.

Fung, Yu-lan. *A Short History of Chinese Philosophy*. Edited by Derk Bodde. New York: Macmillan, 1959. The standard survey of Chinese philosophical schools. Accessible to the general reader.

Kaltenmark, Max. *Lao Tzu and Taoism*. Translated by Roger Greaves. Stanford, Calif.: Stanford University Press, 1965. A point-by-point explanation of various Taoist terms and ideas. Its discussion of religious Taoism is especially helpful.

Lao-tzu. *Tao te Ching*. Translated by D. C. Lau. London and New York: Penguin Books, 1963. An excellent translation, with clear and reliable introduction and supplementary materials, including an essay entitled "The Problem of Authorship."

Lao-tzu. *The Way and Its Power: A Study of the "Tao tê Ching" and Its Place in Chinese Thought*. Translated by Arthur Waley. London: Allen and Unwin, and New York: Macmillan, 1934. This work is somewhat dated, and its introduction is long and rambling. Still, it is a valuable study, and Waley's translation has been very influential.

Munro, Donald J. *The Concept of Man in Early China*. Stanford, Calif.: Stanford University Press, 1969. A rigorous analysis of early Chinese thought by a Western-trained professional philosopher.

Ronan, Colin A. *The Shorter Science and Civilisation in China: An Abridgement of Joseph Needham's Original Text*. Vol. 1. Cambridge and New York: Cambridge University Press, 1978. An eccentric view of Taoism as protoscience, tracing the development of alchemy and the study of nature.

Welch, Holmes. *The Parting of the Way: Lao Tzu and the Taoist Movement*. Boston: Beacon Press, and London: Methuen, 1957. A popular presentation of Lao-tzu's ideas, with an attempt to show their contemporary relevance. Also contains a fine—though brief—history of the Taoist movement.

Charles W. Holcombe

LEONIDAS

Born: c. 510 B.C.; Sparta, Greece

Died: August 20, 480 B.C.; Thermopylae, Thessaly, Greece

Area of Achievement: Warfare and conquest

Contribution: The bravery and supreme sacrifice of Leonidas and his men at Thermopylae sent a surge of pride through all Greece, made the Greeks aware of their heritage, and stiffened their resolve to face—and, eventually, to prevail over—what seemed to be overwhelming odds.

Early Life

When Leonidas was born, it was not expected that he would be king. Leonidas' father, King Anaxandrides, and his wife at first had no children. In order that the royal line not die out— for it was said to be directly descended from the mythical hero Hercules—the Ephors, or administrators of Sparta, asked the king to take a second wife, with whom he had a son, Cleomenes. The king's first wife then bore three sons: Dorieus, Leonidas, and Cleombrotus. When Anaxandrides died, Cleomenes was named king—to the indignation of Dorieus, who considered himself the better qualified.

Not wishing to stay in Sparta under the rule of Cleomenes, Dorieus went to Sicily to found a colony, and he died there. Cleomenes was a controversial king; some considered him insane. He forced his co-ruler Demaratus into exile; then tried to expand and consolidate his limited power to the extent of attempting to bribe the sacred Oracle at Delphi. His policies aroused so much controversy that he was forced to leave Sparta. When Cleomenes returned, Leonidas, now king, had him arrested and imprisoned. Cleomenes was later found in his cell badly mutilated, and he died soon after. It was said he had bribed his jailer to give him a knife with which to commit suicide. Others maintained that Leonidas had a hand in his half-brother's death. Leonidas subsequently married Cleomenes' daughter, Gorgo.

In appearance, Leonidas was a typical Spartan: a lean body hardened by years of gymnastics and military exercises, free of physical defects; no Spartan infant with deformities was permitted to live. A characteristic of all Spartan warriors was their long hair, which they took care to groom, especially if they were about to die on the battlefield. Like all young Spartans, and the more so because

of his royal status, Leonidas from the age of seven spent his life in military training. Leonidas became king in 490 B.C., the year of the first Persian War, in which a small Greek force defeated a much larger Persian army on the plain of Marathon. The victory belonged mainly to Athens. Sparta, Greece's most formidable military power, did not participate because its citizens were celebrating a sacred festival. Leonidas was determined, should a second Persian attack occur, that Sparta and its army would participate.

Life's Work

Leonidas' life work and short reign as king revolved around the preparation for and participation in one important battle, one of the most significant in Western history. Humiliated by the defeat of his forces by the Greeks in 490 B.C., Darius, the Persian king, ruler of one of the world's largest and richest empires, was determined to avenge the defeat, but he died in 486 B.C. His mission became that of his son Xerxes, who began assembling the largest military force known to the ancient world to defeat the Greeks. The exiled Demaratus, who was living at the court of Darius, sent a message to the Spartans, concealed under a layer of wax on a table, warning them of the danger; the message was reportedly discovered by the sharp eye of Queen Gorgo.

The Panhellenic League was formed at a military conference held in Corinth the fall of 481 by those Greek states willing to take a stand against Xerxes. Leonidas was given command of the army. Athens had the most powerful fleet, and naval activities were largely under the command of the Athenian Themistocles. Greece at the time consisted of many independent, often warring states. The Greeks, however, shared a common language and value system, and as the war was to prove, they could, if necessary, act in unison.

In the early spring of 480 B.C., Xerxes and his mighty army began the slow march to the Greek mainland. The Persians crossed the Bosphorus, the waterway between the Black and Mediterranean Seas, by constructing pontoon bridges. Skirting the Aegean Sea and marching parallel to his fleet, Xerxes sought to capture Athens in central Greece. The land through which he marched could not support such a mighty army, and Xerxes was therefore dependent on his ships to replenish supplies. Without the necessary naval support, the expedition would fail.

The Persians prepared to enter central Greece in August, again the time of the festival that had kept the Spartans home ten years before. Leonidas marched nevertheless with only three hundred Spartans, expecting to pick up allies en route and to be joined by the rest of the Spartan army once the festival was over. It was decided to try to check the Persian advance by holding the pass of Thermopylae between northern and central Greece. Only about fifty feet wide, the pass was hemmed in between high cliffs and the Malian Gulf.

By the time he reached Thermopylae, Leonidas had assembled a force of about seven thousand men. He reconnoitered the area, laid waste the valley through which the Persians would have to pass, and coordinated his activities with Themistocles and the fleet. The bodies of water bordering Thermopylae are among the most complex and dangerous in the Mediterranean. It was an area the Greeks knew well. They also knew that the Aegean in August was subject to violent, unexpected windstorms, and storms did occur with extraordinary force and frequency, destroying a significant portion of the Persian fleet. The naval battle of Artemisium, which coincided with the land battle of Thermopylae, gave the Greeks a small victory and valuable experience.

Leonidas deployed his forces to the rear of the pass and the adjoining mountains, leaving mainly the Spartans to face the Persians. The Persians called upon the Spartans to lay down their arms; Leonidas shouted back that the Persians would have to come and get them. On August 18, Xerxes gave the order to attack. Wave after wave were sent against the Greeks, but the first encounters proved how badly equipped the Persians were for close-quarter fighting. Their armor was too thin; their shields were too small and weak; their short spears were ineffective against the Greek long spears; and their arrows dashed harmlessly against the great bronze shields of the Spartans. Successive attacks only succeeded in piling up bodies in the narrow pass and made no progress in dislodging the Spartans and their allies.

At the end of the second day of fighting, Xerxes ceased his attacks in favor of another plan. A Greek traitor revealed the existence of a path through the mountains that led around and behind the Greek position. Xerxes dispatched the captain of his best troops to lead a contingent of chosen soldiers along the path and thus cut off Leonidas' forces from the rear. Leonidas, who had learned of the path soon after he reached Thermopylae, had sent an inexperienced contingent of Greek soldiers to guard it, for he could spare no Spartans. The soldiers fled as the Persians approached, and word came to Leonidas that before noon of the third day he would be trapped between enemy forces. After a hurried conference and with the road to the south still open, Leonidas sent away most of his troops, leaving only the Spartans and some hand-picked soldiers. As his men sat down to eat their last meal, Leonidas with wry humor told them to eat heartily, for they would next dine in Hades.

The little band was determined to fight to the last. In order to kill as many of the enemy as possible, Leonidas had his men leave the defensive wall behind which they had been fighting and to prepare for hand-to-hand combat. Seeing how few the defenders were in number and realizing that their resistance could at last be broken, Xerxes ordered column after column of Persians to sweep down on the Greeks. Four times the Spartans and their allies flung them back. Shouts from the rear told the Greeks that the escape route was closed, so the heroic remnant gathered for a last stand on a small knoll. Leonidas was among the first to fall, and a struggle for his body ensued. Fighting without their leader, their weapons broken, those Greeks still standing fought with their fists and even their teeth until the last of the Spartans was killed. Xerxes had his men find the body of Leonidas, cut off the head, and impale it on a pole to show his army know that the great warrior was mortal.

Summary

Why the heroic stand of Leonidas and his men? Retreat and regrouping were permitted a Spartan commander; cowardice and surrender were not. Legend has it that Leonidas willed his own death because the Delphic oracle had warned him that either a king or Sparta must fall. Closer to the truth is probably that Leonidas realized that the manner of his death would be a source of inspiration to other Greeks, enabling them to resist the Persian foe. His assessment was correct, for Leonidas almost instantly became one of Greece's greatest heroes. His sacrifice imbued the Greeks with the pride and confidence necessary foe them eventually to expel the enemy. The Greek naval forces shared in the confidence. The knowledge gained of the composition and tactics of the Persian navy enabled the smaller, more maneuverable Greek ships to ram and sink so many Persian ships in a later naval battle that the Persian navy was no longer an effective fighting force. Even the windstorms served to bolster Greek confidence, for they believed their gods of the wind and sea were supporting their cause.

The Greco-Persian War made Europe possible. It enabled Western civilization to develop its own political and economic life; its tradition of democratic government; and its emphasis on the rights of the individual, as opposed the theocratic absolutism and social orientation of the East. In its aftermath, Greece entered its golden age of art, philosophy, literature, and science, the single greatest influence on the development of Western civilization.

Bibliography

Bowra, C. M. *Classical Greece*. New York: Time-Life Books, 1965. Written by a noted authority on classical studies and available in many school libraries. Using a pictorial approach to history, the book is rich in details such as models of the Greek ships and the pontoon bridges across the Bosphorus.

Bradford, Ernle Dusgate Selby. *The Year of Thermopylae*. London: Macmillan, 1980; as *Thermopylae: The Battle for the West*. New York: McGraw-Hill, 1980. Despite its detailed and thorough research on the battle, Bradford's account is easy to read and is presented in a chronological format. Also of value is the discussion of the sequel to Artemisium and Thermopylae at the battles of Salamis and Platea, which brought an end to the Persian menace.

Durant, Will. *The Life of Greece*. New York: Simon & Schuster, 1939. A comprehensive yet easy-to-read work on Greek civilization. Chapter 4 contains an excellent description of Sparta; book 3 examines Greece's golden age.

Herodotus. *The History*. Translated by David Grene. Chicago: University of Chicago Press, 1987. Much of the knowledge of the Persian Wars, including the Battle of Thermopylae, is from Herodotus. Known as "the father of history," Herodotus, although detailed, is remarkably easy and interesting to read. Book 7 deals with the Battle of Thermopylae; book 5 contains background information on Leonidas. Includes a detailed index.

Sinnigen, William G., and Charles Alexander Robinson, Jr. *Ancient History*. New York and London: Macmillan, 1981. The time of Leonidas and the dawn of Greece's golden Age should be viewed in the context of Hellenic civilization, which this book presents very well. Part 3 begins with the Aegean age and ends with the conquests of Alexander the Great.

Nis Petersen

Born: 59 B.C.; Patavium (modern Padua), Italy
Died: c. A.D. 17; probably Patavium, Italy
Area of Achievement: Historiography
Contribution: Livy preserved many of the early legendary traditions and mythology dealing with the earliest phase of ancient Roman history. Since many of the authors and sources he used have long been lost, his work assumes a greater importance.

Early Life

Titus Livius (Livy), according to the theologian Jerome, was born in 59, in Patavium, northern Italy. Livy makes only a few brief references to his homeland, but they indicate a patriotic pride. Unfortunately, nothing certain is known regarding his youth, but the general assumption is that he was schooled in his native town. This assumption is based on a comment made by Asinius Pollio that Livy's style was provincial. This criticism, however, is largely negated by the excellent Ciceronian style of most of Livy's historical writings.

Livy's early education must have included philosophical studies, since his writings contain many allusions and direct references to traditional Stoic values. Also, his frequent comments about religion show that he was familiar with the traditions and rituals of the Roman cults.

Livy probably did not begin writing his history of Rome until he was about thirty years old. Presumably, he had had adequate time in the previous years to read and research in preparation. By the age of thirty, he had probably moved to Rome, but regarding this there is no sure evidence. By the year 5 B.C., Livy was definitely in Rome, since at this time he was criticized by Augustus Caesar for being a "Pompeian," a person who was biased in favor of the aristocratic, senatorial views. Augustus seems not to have meant this remark too seriously, for there is ample evidence to suggest that the emperor counted Livy as a friend and took an interest in his work. Indeed, it is known that about A.D. 8 Livy helped the future emperor Claudius in his own historical studies.

Life's Work

Livy's great history was written in Latin and is generally known as *Ab urbe condita libri* (c. 26 B.C.-A.D. 15; *The History of Rome*), literally meaning "from the founding of the city (of Rome)." The

work was exceptionally long, containing 142 books (scrolls); this length has been estimated to be equivalent to twenty-four or twenty-five crown-octavo volumes of three hundred pages each.

Probably as a result of the extreme length of the original work, abridgments and summaries were made in antiquity. Most of these have survived, but much of the original work has been lost. Only thirty-five of the 142 books have survived the ravages of time, including books 1-10 and 31-45. These surviving books deal chronologically with events between the years 753 and 243 B.C. and between 219 and 167 B.C. From the surviving summaries and fragments, it is clear that the work included information about Rome from its traditional foundation date in 753 through 9 B.C. The last twenty-two books were probably not published until after the death of Augustus Caesar in A.D. 14. The surmised reason for this is that Livy was fearful of publishing information about contemporaneous people and events.

Most scholars who have studied Livy's work in detail have noted certain distinctive features of his

great history: intensely personal psychological portraits of major military and political figures, speeches of uncertain origin interwoven with the chronological narrative to reflect certain political or religious perspectives of ancient Romans, lengthy discourses on cultic religion, including references to miracles and prodigies, frequent references to the virtuous morals and ethics of the early Romans in contrast to the degeneration of morals in the more recent age, a clear sympathy with Stoic views on the providential determination of history, and a patriotic bias in favor of aristocratic, republican conservatism.

Of these features, greater scholarly attention has been devoted to two aspects: Livy's use of speeches and his emphasis on religion and morals. With regard to Livy's use of speeches, it should be noted that he was not alone among ancient historians in the use of oratorical devices. The Greek historian Thucydides, like most other ancient historians, made the most of rhetoric in his accounts. In each case, the scholar must ask whether the speeches reflect the beliefs and attitudes of the author or of the one being quoted. Unfortunately, the question cannot be resolved with certainty. Most scholars have concluded that the speeches are not verbatim (though shorthand methods of taking dictation were known), but that they represent the historian's artful summary of what he assumed must have been said on the occasion. In the particular case of Livy's history, there is evidence that Cicero was used consciously with regard to style. There are 407 major speeches in Livy's extant volumes, and if indirect speeches and minor exhortations are included, the number rises to more than two thousand. These statistics, obviously, are only from the surviving books of Livy.

One of the most lengthy of his speeches deals with Livy's other chief preoccupation, religion. Marcus Furius Camillus, who has been called the second founder of Rome, was the man who prevented the Romans from abandoning the site of Rome, which had been badly damaged by warfare with the Gauls. Though the Romans had finally defeated the Gauls, many citizens of Rome wanted to migrate to the city of Veii, which had earlier been taken from the Etruscans. Camillus convinced them, however, that such a move would be a sin, a sacrilege, according to Livy's report. Most scholars believe that references to ancient religious beliefs, whether occurring in an alleged speech or in the narrative, reflect traditional views of the time more than Livy's personal beliefs. Regardless of scholarly controversy, however, Livy's history is so full of references to religion, morals, and ethical concerns that it seems difficult to believe that he simply repeated them to fill space. Instead, he probably did believe that his age had degenerated from earlier, more austere times. Examples of dramatic concern for morality include the stories of the rape of Lucretia, the execution of the vestal virgin Minucia, the debauchery of Hannibal's army at Capua, and the introduction of the worship of the Greek god of wine, Dionysus-Bacchus.

The frequent references to religion and morals in Livy have led many scholars to conclude that he had Stoic sympathies or perhaps was actually a Stoic. Evidence for this conclusion is Livy's frequent use of such terms as *fatum* (fate), *fortuna* (chance), *felicitas* (good fortune), *virtus* (virtue, bravery), *fors* (luck), and *causa* (cause), which may indicate some sympathy with the Stoic concept of the universe.

Having enjoyed years of productive work in Rome, Livy retired to his hometown, Patavium, sometime near the end of his life; an Augustan tomb inscription discovered in the modern city of Padua honors the memory of a Titus Livius. Some scholars believe that he died as early as A.D. 12, although Saint Jerome records his death as occurring in 17.

Summary

The popularity of Livy in ancient times cannot be denied. He is also customarily covered in modern scholarly accounts of great ancient historians of Greece and Rome. The fact that he did have religious and political biases does not negate the fact that he did occasionally record his sources of information and make comments about their reliability. The ancient historian Valerius Antias is mentioned by name thirty-six times, Claudius Quadrigarius twelve times, Coelius Antipater eleven, Licinius Macer seven; Calpurnius Piso, Polybius, and Fabius Pictor are mentioned six times. In most cases, Livy tried to evaluate his sources in regard to probable accuracy and truthfulness.

Livy did, however, have undeniable weaknesses as a historian: occasional anachronisms, mistaken chronology, and topographical and geographic confusions, especially in accounts of battles. Furthermore, his patriotism makes him seem a bit prejudiced against other nations and peoples, most notably the Greeks.

Bibliography

Canter, H. V. "Rhetorical Elements in Livy's Direct Speeches." *American Journal of Philology* 28/29 (April, 1917/January, 1918): 125-141, 44-64. Canter shows that Livy's practice of putting speeches in the mouths of historical personages was a device used by most ancient historians. In only a few cases should the speeches be interpreted as literal quotations; generally, they are paraphrases or summaries of ideas expressed on the occasions of interest.

Duff, John W. "Augustan Prose and Livy." In *A Literary History of Rome: From the Origins to the Close of the Golden Age*. 3d ed. London: Benn, and New York: Barnes and Noble Books, 1953. A brief but able analysis of Livy and other literary figures of the age of Augustus, with special emphasis on the Ciceronian literary style of Livy.

Frank, Tenney. "Republican Historiography and Livy." In *Life and Literature in the Roman Republic*. Berkeley: University of California Press, 1930. An excellent summary and analysis of Livy's predecessors in writing Roman history. Special emphasis is placed on archaeological discoveries which have confirmed some of the early legends about the founding of Rome mentioned by Livy.

Grant, Michael. "Livy." In *The Ancient Historians*. New York: Scribner, and London: Weidenfeld and Nicolson, 1970. Grant summarizes the contents of Livy's history and emphasizes his historiographical methods and aims, concluding that Livy deserves credit as a great historian. Grant complains, however, that Livy was an "armchair historian," not a participant in great historical events.

Hadas, Moses. "Livy as Scripture." *American Journal of Philology* 61 (October, 1940): 445-456. According to Hadas, Livy's references to miracles, prophecies, and religion are somewhat comparable to such references by biblical authors; Hadas concludes that Livy was probably sincerely religious, or at least sympathetic to Stoicism.

Laistner, M. L. W. "Livy, the Man and the Writer" and "Livy, the Historian." In *The Greater Roman Historians*. Berkeley: University of California Press, 1947. A detailed treatment of Livy as an adherent of a Stoic view of history in which religious signs were considered valid. Laistner describes Livy as a good example of a patriotic historian praising Roman virtues.

Miles, Gary B. *Livy: Reconstructing Early Rome*. Ithaca, N.Y.: Cornell University Press, 1995. An analysis of the first five books of Livy's history, concentrating on the historian's rhetorical skill, on his discussion of Roman decline and resurgence, and on his conception of truth in historiography.

Walsh, P. G. "Livy." In *Latin Historians*, edited by T. A. Dorey. London: Routledge, and New York: Basic Books, 1966. Describes Livy's themes, such as the decline of Roman morality, his political views (senatorial and conservative), and his philosophical views (Stoic). Walsh also points out Livy's weaknesses: He is too rhetorical and too concerned with individual psychological factors in history.

John M. Lawrence

LUCIAN

Born: c. 120; Samosata, Syria
Died: c. 180; probably Egypt
Area of Achievement: Literature
Contribution: Lucian turned the philosophical dialogue into a form for satirizing ideas and manners. Lucianic satire became a mainstay of European literature in the Renaissance.

Early Life

Almost nothing is recorded about Lucian's life, outside his own works. Because most of these are satires, full of topical allusions and semiautobiographical asides, readers must be cautious before accepting the claims he makes. By his own account, Lucian was born in Samosata (modern day Samsat) on the Euphrates River. It was a strategic point in the Roman province of Syria, but far from the centers of culture. His father was a middle-class citizen, poor enough to suffer the tedium of life at the edge of empire but wealthy enough to send him to school.

Lucian left school for awhile to apprentice with his uncle, a successful stonecutter and sculptor. His master beat him, however, and he thought again about the value of education. He was good at Greek, the language of learning and commerce in the eastern part of the Roman world, and he developed an elegant prose style. In conversation, he may have had a provincial accent—he may have spoken a Semitic language at home—but in writing, he showed exceptional purity.

His training qualified him to work as a public speaker—also called a *rhetor* (the Greek word) or an orator (the Latin word). Citizens who took a case to the law courts, or who had to defend themselves, would hire an orator who knew the finer points of law and who could argue their cases in memorable language with a voice that would carry in a large public gathering. As his reputation grew, Lucian began to give public performances of his oratorical skills, which included the ability to improvise on a theme, to speak eloquently, and to entertain large, paying crowds. He says he was a great success, but he made his appearances on the fringes of the Roman empire—in Ionia (modern Turkey) and Gaul (modern France) rather than Athens or Alexandria—and no other orators referred to him. Several of his early orations survive, including a speech in praise of a fly and two serio-comic defenses of a tyrant named Phalaris and the officials at the Oracle of Delphi who accepted the tyrant's bribe. When Lucian was approximately forty, he stopped traveling and began a new career as a writer of satires.

Life's Work

Having made his fortune as an orator, Lucian retired to Athens and enrolled in the school of the Stoic philosopher Demonax. He studied philosophy during a great revival of interest in ancient Greek thought known as the Second Sophistic. He became acquainted with the leading ideas of all the philosophical schools, including the Cynics and the Epicureans. He may have called himself a "philosopher," but the main thing he learned was the dialogue form developed by Plato (482-348 B.C.). In such works as the *Symposion* (c. 380 B.C.; *The Banquet*), Plato used dialogue and other dramatic devices to voice philosophical ideas—and to challenge them. In Lucian's *Symposion* (*The Carousal*), the ideas are used for comic effect. Lucian always goes for the laugh.

Lucian was not the first to adapt the philosophical dialogue for satiric purposes. A Cynic named Menippius developed the satiric dialogue a century after Plato's death. Menippius called himself a "dog," for he wrote biting satires, and Lucian used him as his alter ego or persona. The *Nekrikoi Dialogoi* (*Dialogues of the Dead*) followed Menippius into the underworld and recorded the questions he put to the gods of the dead and the heroes of old. There were conversations between the Greek and Trojan heroes Ajax and Agamemnon; between Philip of Macedon and his son, Alexander the Great; between Alexander and the general Hannibal and the Cynic philosopher Diogenes; and between Diogenes and the comic dramatist Crates.

Lucian's dialogues have survived in several collections. Much as he satirized popular views of heroes and heroism in the *Dialogues of the Dead*, he satirized religious beliefs and practices in the *Theon Dialogoi* (*Dialogues of the Gods*), calling attention to the artifices of a state-sponsored revival of the Olympian religion. Greek philosophers back to Socrates (469-399 B.C.) had questioned the morality of the Olympian gods. Lucian did not raise serious objections, though; he was too busy having fun, and he was prepared to challenge the sobersided philosophers.

EXSPECTANDO.

One of Lucian's longest dialogues, *Bion Prasis* (*Philosophies for Sale*), put the famous philosophers of Greece in the marketplace, where each one hawked his wares. Philosophers are supposed to be above all that, but in fact they competed fiercely for private students as well as for positions in the best towns and schools. If anything, the competition grew fiercer during the Second Sophistic. Lucian knew how to expose their rivalries. His philosophers in the dialogue, like the pedants in comedies, are their own worst enemies. They unwittingly reveal their human weaknesses.

Eventually, Lucian's savings gave out, and he had to perform in public to support himself. It was common for readers to perform Plato's dialogues as minidramas, and it seems likely that Lucian performed his own dialogues, perhaps doing all the voices himself. (Most dialogues are short skits that would take only five or ten minutes to perform.) He also used elements from the old Attic comedy of Aristophanes (444-388 B.C.). For example, his *Hetairikoi Dialogoi* (*Dialogues of the Courtesans*) presented comic scenes that might arise among prostitutes and their clients. Although Lucian

wrote down the dialogues—perhaps for sale to members of the audience—he probably improvised extensively. Indeed, his dialogues may remind modern readers of the sometimes improvisational comedy associated with such television shows as *Monty Python's Flying Circus* and *Saturday Night Live*.

Lucian traveled again reprising his success as a public speaker who could improvise something to say on any topic for any occasion. He also tried his hand at a new literary form, the prose romance. Two stories attributed to him are among the first forerunners of the novel. *Alethon Diegematon* (*A True Story*) tells the outrageous story of his journey to the Moon. It is the first in a series of imaginary travels that includes Sir Thomas More's *Utopia* (1516), Jonathan Swift's account of *Gulliver's Travels* (1726), and Samuel Butler's *Erewhon* (1872). *Loukios e Onos* (*Lucius, or the Ass*) is a story of a young man's transformation into an ass. It may not be Lucian's work, however, and at any rate it became famous only in the extended Latin reworking by a contemporary, Apuleius of Madura (c. 125-170).

Lucian says he married, but he says nothing about his wife, nor does he mention children. Presumably, he traveled alone. Occasionally, he sought a permanent position. Perhaps it was at this time that he applied for a post as the public-speaking teacher in a Greek-speaking city, a well-paid position in the civil service. He was not successful and lampooned the new teacher in the satiric speech, *Rhetoron Didaskalos* (*A Professor of Rhetoric*). Lucian traveled through Italy and into Egypt, where he found work as a public official in the law courts. He was still writing dialogues, and he described himself as an elder statesman. While in Egypt he died, in relative obscurity, at about the age of sixty.

Lucian's contemporaries and near-contemporaries probably thought of him as a clever entertainer who was also a bit of a braggart and clown, rather than as a serious philosopher. They probably regarded his writings as "low" exercises in prose satire and comedy rather than "high" examples of poetic epic and drama. They liked his works enough to preserve a great many of them—some eighty works attributed to Lucian survive in some twelve dozen manuscripts—but they did not mention him in histories of philosophy and literature. Ironically, the works of Lucian's model, Menippius, have not survived, though the name appeared often enough in ancient works on literature. The type of satire that Lucian wrote—the tough intellectual dialogue, full of gossip and farce—is most commonly known today as "Menippian" satire and less frequently as "Lucianic." Very occasionally, it is called "Varronian" after the Latin writer Varro (116-27 B.C.), who modeled his satires on those of Menippius.

Some scholars think that Lucian may have known other great writers of Greek, including the Roman emperor Marcus Aurelius (121-180), but the emperor was a true Stoic and would have preferred Lucian's prose style to his sense of humor. There is more reason to think that Lucian influenced the emperor Julian (331-363), who wrote a Menippian satire about the Caesars. Julian, though, attempted a last revival of the Olympian religion—for which he became known as "the Apostate"—and could not have approved of Lucian's levity in the *Dialogues of the Gods*.

Summary

With the revival of interest in Greek during the Renaissance, Lucian's writings caught the interest of such humanist scholars as Desiderius Erasmus (c.

1467-1536). Soon they were translated into Latin and the modern European languages. One of the first printed books in Germany was a Latin translation of *Lucian, or the Ass*, printed in Augsburg c. 1477. One of the favorite books of Renaissance scholars was a Latin translation of selected dialogues made by Erasmus, who imitated Lucian's style in the celebrated *Moriae Encomium* (1511; *The Praise of Folly*, 1668). Erasmus's friend Sir Thomas More (c. 1477-1535) translated four dialogues into English and showed Lucian's influence in *Utopia* (1516), which used the dialogue form to tell of an imaginary voyage. The religious reformer Martin Luther scolded Erasmus for translating such an irreligious, indeed anti-Christian, author, but Luther was in the minority.

Lucian has influenced many other writers of English, from Geoffrey Chaucer (1343-1400) to Ben Jonson (1573-1637) and Henry Fielding (1707-1754). His influence is also apparent in the works of French writers from François Rabelais (c. 1494-c. 1553) to Voltaire (1694-1778). The literary critic Northrop Frye discussed Lucian and the "Menippian" satire in *Anatomy of Criticism: Four Essays* (1957), one of the most influential books of literary theory to appear in the twentieth century. Frye saw this form of satire persisting in such unlikely places as *The Complete Angler* by Izaak Walton (1653) and *Alice's Adventures in Wonderland* by Lewis Carroll (1865). Frye suggested replacing the rather cumbersome term "Menippian satire" with the word "anatomy" and so placed his own book, with all its clever comments on the classics, within the tradition of Lucian. The writer who was almost forgotten by his contemporaries has thus become an important name in the history of European literature.

Bibliography

Anderson, Graham. *Lucian: Theme and Variation in the Second Sophistic.* Leiden: E. J. Brill, 1976. Considers the role of fantastic description and storytelling in Lucian's dialogues; explores the differences between characterization and caricature, learning and "mock-learning."

Branham, R. Bracht. *Unruly Eloquence: Lucian and the Comedy of Traditions.* Cambridge, Mass.: Harvard University Press, 1989. Discusses Lucian's relation to Epicurean philosophy and to comic traditions. Emphasizes the role of laughter in a successful life.

Frye, Northrop. *Anatomy of Criticism: Four Essays*. Princeton, N.J.: Princeton University Press, 1957. One essay discusses the "myth," or master plot, of satire, with many references to Lucian. Another discusses the "genre," or form, of prose satire, again with reference to Lucian.

Gay, Peter. *The Bridge of Criticism: Dialogues Among Lucian, Erasmus, and Voltaire on the Enlightenment*. New York: Harper, 1970. Written by an influential historian, this book shows how the satiric tradition has contributed to the freedom of thought.

Highet, Gilbert. *The Anatomy of Satire*. Princeton, N.J.: Princeton University Press, 1962. A history of satire, written by a great classicist. Offers a good introduction to the Menippian satire written by Lucian.

Jones, C. P. *Culture and Society in Lucian*. Cambridge, Mass.: Harvard University Press, 1986. A careful study of social satire in Lucian's dialogues. Discusses his historical context and his comments on the writing of history.

Lucian. *Lucian with an English Translation*. Translated and edited by A. M. Harmon and M. D. MacLeod. Loeb Classical Library. 8 vols. Oxford: Oxford University Press, and New York: Macmillan, 1913-1927. The standard translation, including works of doubtful attribution. Provides Greek and English texts on facing pages, brief introductions to individual works, and an index at the end of each volume.

Payne, F. Anne. *Chaucer and Menippean Satire*. Madison: University of Wisconsin Press, 1981. Provides background on Lucian's tradition in satire and his influence on the greatest English poet of the Middle Ages.

Robinson, Christopher. *Lucian and His Influence in Europe*. Chapel Hill: University of North Carolina Press, and London: Duckworth, 1979. A study of Lucian's times and works, with attention to his influence on the Renaissance and Enlightenment. Includes chapters on Erasmus and Fielding.

Thomas Willard

LUCRETIUS

Born: c. 98 B.C.; probably Rome

Died: October 15, 55 B.C.; Rome

Areas of Achievement: Literature, natural history, and philosophy

Contribution: Though he in no sense offered an original philosophical outlook, Lucretius' *On The Nature of Things* synthesized primary tenets of Greek Epicureanism and atomism and offered a rational, nontheological explanation for the constituents of the universe; just as remarkable is the fact that he did this in Latin hexameter verse and developed a philosophical vocabulary required for the task.

Early Life

It is much easier to show why most of what has been written about the life of Titus Lucretius Carus is incorrect, doubtful, or malicious than it is to arrive at a reliable account. Relatively little can be deduced from his poem, and there are no substantive contemporary references to him. Consequently, too much credence has been given to the jumbled biographical note written by Saint Jerome, which itself was derived from an unreliable account by the Roman historian Gaius Suetonius Tranquillus. Jerome miscalculates Lucretius' dates of birth and death; also, it is unlikely that Lucretius was driven insane by a love potion and wrote *De rerum natura* (c. 60; *On the Nature of Things*) during periods of lucidity. The latter story seems to have arisen from Lucretius' treatment of love in section 4 of the poem.

Several details of Lucretius' early life can, however, be inferred with relative certainty. His name is a strange combination which implies both servile (Carus) and noble origins (from the kinship grouping *Gens Lucretia*), but he was likely closer to the middle class of his contemporary Cicero. Though Cicero himself did not emend Lucretius' poetry, as Jerome reports, it is likely that his brother Quintus Cicero oversaw its publication. Like Cicero, Lucretius appears to have evinced an early interest in philosophy, influenced by the Alexandrian movement, though his own poetry has an old Roman spirit reflecting his readings of Quintus Ennius. Cicero considered that Lucretius had the "genius" of Ennius and the "art" of the Alexandrians.

Lucretius lived through the turmoil caused by the civil war between aristocrat Lucius Cornelius Sulla and populist Gaius Marius as well as the conspiracy of Lucius Sergius Catilina. He also witnessed the consequent decline of Roman republican government. Perhaps this political uncertainty directed him to the comfortable philosophy of Epicurus, which held that the goal of human existence should be a life of calm pleasure tempered by morality and culture. The atomism of Democritus and Leucippus, which held that the material universe could be understood as random combinations of minute particles (*atomoi*), provided a rational and scientific means of explaining the cosmos and avoiding what Lucretius came to see as the sterile superstitions of religion.

In all, the impressions one has of Lucretius at this early stage in his life are of a young man of good background and a good education, who is eager not for the political arena or personal advancement but to explain the world in a reasonable way to Romans with similar education who would read his verse. In addition, he aimed to make living in that rationally explained world as pleasant an experience as possible.

Life's Work

One can only guess how Lucretius lived during the years he was writing *On the Nature of Things* from its dedication to Gaius Memmius. Memmius held the office of praetor in 58 and fancied himself a poet, primarily of erotic verse in the style of Catullus. Memmius' shady political dealings eventually caught up with him, and he was driven into exile; nevertheless, it is reasonable to assume that Lucretius received some financial support from him. Memmius figures less importantly in the body of the poem, however, and his name is used in places only for metrical convenience.

Details of the poem show the kind of atmosphere Lucretius wished to escape, essentially that of his own city in the final years of the Republic. The world is filled with gloom, war, and decay. The poet wishes to stand on a hill, far removed from wickedness and ambition, and watch the waste and destruction. Passages such as these reveal a man who yearned for tranquil anonymity. Other writers, such as Cicero, would find themselves propelled into a political maelstrom which would ultimately destroy them; Lucretius was determined to avoid this fate.

The times in which Lucretius lived cried out for reasonableness. Educated Romans saw the obvious conflict between their elaborate mythology and their religion, which glorified deities who did everything from seducing women to causing mildew. Even so, Rome continued to fill the various priestly colleges, to take auspices as a means of determining favorable outcomes, and to celebrate public games in honor of these very deities. A century later, Rome would deify its emperors, partly to shift its religious observances to personalities who were incontestably real, and partly to curb the spread of imported cults such as Mithraism and what came to be known as Christianity.

Lucretius had solved this problem, for himself at least, and outlines his position on religion in *On the Nature of Things*. The creative force of nature is real; it is personified in the goddess Venus. The deities are simply personifications of various aspects of nature, and human beings can free themselves of superstition by seeing the world as constantly recombining *atomoi*. Death itself is nothing more than atomic dissolution, a preparation for new arrangements of atoms and new creation. If human beings can accept death in these terms, they can cast aside the fear that binds them to religious superstition. This acceptance will prepare them to see that life's purpose is to maximize pleasure and minimize pain.

Neither of these theories is new; they are derived from the atomism of Democritus and Leucippus and the teachings of Epicurus. What is new is Lucretius' synthesis and his offering it as rational scientism to educated Roman readers. One reason almost nothing is known about Lucretius' personal life is undoubtedly his determination to practice these ideas. Removing himself from the fray to seek philosophical calm necessarily results in a lack of contemporary biographical references, but it is precisely on this score that Lucretian Epicureanism is most misunderstood. It is just the opposite of egocentric gratification, because Lucretius couples it with the mechanics of atomism. Seen in this way, the individual is merely a part in the world machine; immortality exists, but only in the myriad indestructible *atomoi* which constitute each part.

One can only guess how Lucretius first encountered Epicureanism. There were Greek professors in Rome during the first century B.C. who taught the theories of Epicurus. Cicero mentions non-Greek Epicureans who wrote treatises Lucretius might easily have read. The ease with which Lucretius deals with the technical vocabulary of atomism suggests that he was accomplished in Greek. (This would be expected of any educated Roman.) He no doubt read Epicurus, Democritus, and Leucippus in the original language.

Reading Greek gave Lucretius access to other sources such as Empedocles, the philosopher-poet who wrote *Perì Phýseōs* (*On Nature*). What the modern world calls "natural selection" comes to Lucretius through Empedocles, as does the principle of attraction and repulsion, which Lucretius sees as "love" and "hate." Lucretius' hexameter meter is used by Empedocles but also by Homer. Indeed, Lucretius borrows from Homer, Euripides, Thucydides, Hippocrates, and various early Roman poets.

Though his philosophy is Greek, Lucretius maintains a very Roman insistence on the primacy of law. In *On the Nature of Things*, for example, he notes that human beings moved from primitive status to society only after they had agreed upon a social contract. Language improved upon gesture, and social order prevailed. It is worth noting that similar ideas later appear in the creation account of Ovid in *Metamorphoses*. Though Lucretius failed to convert the Roman masses, he obviously made inroads among his successors in poetry. Vergil read him, too, and while Vergil's work is more elegant, there can be little doubt that he was impressed by Lucretius' descriptions of nature; one can easily see their influence in Vergil's pastoral poems.

The random nature of the *clinamen* ("swerve") that atoms make when they recombine must have troubled Lucretius, since he is generally insistent on the orderly cycle of nature. This bothered others, too, but is the only way to explain natural differences atomically. The *membranae* ("films"), which are thrown from objects and thereby produce visual impressions, are another artificial means of describing a natural phenomenon, but *On the Nature of Things* is, on the whole, free of such difficulties.

The poem's six books show evidence of unfinished composition, but one cannot deduce Lucretius' premature death from this fact. The Victorian poet Alfred, Lord Tennyson, perpetuated Suetonius' marvelous fiction of Lucretius' insanity and death by a love potion, but the author of *On the Nature of Things* was a very sane man whose entire reason for living was to bring rationality to an irrational world.

Summary

Lucretius privileged the creative force of nature, but he in no sense resembled the English Romantic poets in their wonderment at its powers. He was the rare combination of natural scientist, philosopher, and poet, and he strove for clarity and reasonableness in what he wrote. He clearly was not the gaunt, love-crazed, mad genius of Suetonius and Jerome, but an evangelizer who appealed to an educated audience, much like twentieth century writers of popular science.

Lucretius thus became a symbol which served the purposes of those who wrote about him. Because the facts of his life remained a mystery, even to the generation which immediately followed his own, he could be portrayed by Suetonius as foreshadowing the Empire's vice, by Jerome as representing pagan degeneracy, and ultimately by Tennyson as typifying egocentric gratification. Even so, as is true of many great lives, work overshadows personality, and this is clearly what Lucretius intended, for *On the Nature of Things* opened a world of what would otherwise have remained esoteric Greek philosophy to a popular audience. What is more important, Lucretius presented these ideas as a means of dealing with his own troubled world.

Were one to cancel out Lucretius' masterly synthesis of Epicureanism and atomism, his contribution to both Roman poetry and the Latin language would remain. Nearly one hundred technical words adapted from the Greek appear within six books of hexameter verse, the epic meter of Homer and of Lucretius' fellow Roman Ennius. That Lucretius' work inspired the succeeding generation of Roman poets, which included both Vergil and Ovid, attests its immediate influence. The modern reader, armed with contemporary science and psychology, can object only to the mechanics of the natural phenomena Lucretius discusses; his plea to cast aside superstition and fear strikes a welcome note.

Bibliography

Bailey, C. "Late Republican Poetry." In *Fifty Years (and Twelve) of Classical Scholarship*, edited by Maurice Platnauer. 2d ed. New York: Barnes and Noble Books, and Oxford: Blackwell, 1968. This fine article, in an anthology which surveys all major aspects of classical studies to the mid-1960's, discusses Lucretius with special emphasis on editions and translations of his poem, possible sources, textual criticism, and Lucretian thought, philosophy, and natural science.

———. *Lucretius*. 3 vols. Oxford: Oxford University Press, 1947. This standard edition of *On the Nature of Things* presents not only the full Latin text and apparatus but also a readable and accurate translation on facing pages. A "Prolegomenon" in the first volume analyzes what little is known about Lucretius' life against the background of his poem as well as various aspects of scholarship relating to Lucretius.

Duff, J. Wight, and A. M. Duff. *A Literary History of Rome from the Origins to the Close of the Golden Age*. 3d ed. London: Benn, and New York: Barnes and Noble Books, 1953. This companion volume to the Duffs' study of Silver Age Latin literature devotes a sizable chapter to Lucretius. It records the basic meager details of Lucretius' life, analyzes his poem, and makes several interesting cross-references to English Romantic and Victorian poets.

Gale, Monica R. *Myth and Poetry in Lucretius*. Cambridge Classical Studies. Cambridge and New York: Cambridge University Press, 1994. Gale attempts to resolve the controversy regarding Lucretius' simultaneous use and condemnation of myth. She argues that "Lucretius follows consistent and comprehensive rhetorical, poetic and philosophic strategy in his use of myth," undercutting its credibility even while utilizing its expressive power.

Lucretius Carus, Titus. *T. Lucreti Cari De rerum natura*. Edited by William Ellery Leonard and Stanley Barney Smith. Madison: University of Wisconsin Press, 1942. Though this is a Latin text with full apparatus, its special feature for non-Latinists is an introductory essay by Leonard, "Lucretius: The Man, the Poet, and the Times." Virtually a book-within-a-book, this essay discusses the period in which Lucretius lived, what is known and conjectured about his life, and what impelled Lucretius to write his poem.

———. *Lucretius: On the Nature of the Universe*. Translated by R. E. Latham. Baltimore and London: Penguin Books, 1951. This accurate translation has the great virtue of an introduction which discusses what is known about Lucretius' life and, more, outlines his poem section by section with line references. It is, by far, the best introduction to Lucretius for one unable to read Latin.

Nussbaum, Martha C. *Martin Classical Lectures.* Vol. 11, *The Therapy of Desire: Theory and Practice in Hellenistic Ethics.* Princeton, N.J.: Princeton University Press, 1994. This evaluation of Hellenistic ethics includes chapters on Epicurus and Lucretius.

Segal, Charles. *Lucretius on Death and Anxiety: Poetry and Philosophy in "De rerum natura."* Princeton, N.J.: Princeton University Press, 1990. Segal explains the apparent contradiction between Lucretius' professed disregard for death and his lavish poetic portrayals of death and destruction. He argues that Lucretius uses violent images to overcome his readers' fear of dying by "displacing" (the term is psychoanalytic) their anxieties.

Robert J. Forman

LYSIPPUS

Born: c. 390 B.C.; Sicyon, Greece
Died: c. 300 B.C.; place unknown
Area of Achievement: Art
Contribution: A sculptor whose career spanned virtually the entire fourth century B.C., Lysippus was not only a major transitional figure between classical and Hellenistic styles but the most renowned portraitist of the century as well.

Early Life

Though relatively little contemporary evidence survives about the man or his life, a considerable amount is known about the era in which Lysippus produced his art and about the key events and a number of the significant individuals that helped shape his career. Lysippus was born in Sicyon, in southern Greece. His early work is said to have reflected certain values and preoccupations of the fifth century B.C., when Greek civilization, led by Athens, defined for the West the essence of the classical in art. With the work of his later career, Lysippus' artistic concerns show dramatic change, as he established himself as perhaps the most renowned portraitist of antiquity, defining forever in sculpture the essence of Alexander the Great. There is perhaps no other ancient artist whose style evolved more dramatically or whose work more clearly reflects the significant changes of an era.

Subsequent to the great wars with Persia (490-478 B.C.), the Greek city-states, though independent political units, fell generally under the influence of either Sparta or Athens. These two city-states had achieved their ascendancy chiefly by force of arms; Sparta had been the dominant military power in Greece since at least the sixth century, and Athens had converted an alliance of coastal and island states in the early fifth century into a naval empire. Although it eventually fell to Sparta in 404, Athens for the last half of the fifth century was the cultural and intellectual center of all Greece. Here was defined the classical in the arts, notably in architecture (chiefly by the Parthenon) and in sculpture.

The fourth century witnessed in its early decades a series of attempts by different city-states to repeat the fifth century achievements of Athens and Sparta. Some, such as Thebes and Athens and Sparta themselves, met with limited success, but none had the resources, economic or military, to sustain it. Internally divided and weakened by con-

stant warfare, the city-states by the mid-fourth century began to be pressured by the ambitions of outsiders, including Mausolus, dynast of Caria in Asia Minor, Jason of Pherae in Thessaly, and finally, Philip of Macedonia. Abruptly and decisively, the uncertainties of the mid-fourth century Greek world were brought to an end in 338, when Philip and his eighteen-year-old son, Alexander, overwhelmed a Greek allied army at Chaeronea in central Greece. With defeat, the states of Greece were obliged to follow the lead of Macedonia, and during the next sixteen years stood, cowed and helpless, as Alexander succeeded his father and marched east, conquering by the time of his death in 323 most of the then-known world. By the time of his death, Alexander had been formally acknowledged a god by the Greeks, though his kingdom quickly suffered irreparable division at the hands of his successors. All of this Lysippus witnessed, from the attempts early in the century to replicate the achievements of the classical era to the partitioning of Alexander's empire in the last decades of the century. What Lysippus witnessed is reflected in his art.

Life's Work

While Lysippus is said to have been especially prolific during the course of his long career—it is claimed that he produced as many as fifteen hundred pieces—none of his works is known in fact to have survived, a consequence in part of his having worked primarily in bronze. What has survived is written testimony about a number of his more important pieces—mainly in the work of the first century A.D. Roman encyclopedist, Pliny the Elder—and some stone copies, which in subject matter and manner of execution seem consistent with what is known of Lysippus' work.

Lysippus' style early in his career is said to have been influenced by the work of Polyclitus, also a southern Greek and unquestionably one of the most important sculptors of the fifth century B.C. Polyclitus in his sculpture is said to have sought to express a sense of the Good and the Beautiful; that is, he attempted to represent in sculpture abstract values. It was Polyclitus' belief that there existed an underlying order in the universe and that this order could be understood in terms of mathematical ratios, much as the order of music can be understood. Polyclitus wrote a treatise (now lost) detailing his views and executed a piece that was to embody them, entitled the *Doryphorus or Spear Bearer* (dated c. 450-440 B.C.). This statue of an athlete standing, poised with spear held over the left shoulder, of which only stone copies survive, was so sculpted that each element stood in what Polyclitus judged to be a perfect ratio to every other element. Thus it possessed a perfect order and expressed Polyclitus' ideal of the Good and the Beautiful. Such preoccupation with form, with principles of organization, and with effecting a tension between the abstract and the concrete, the universal and the individual, became central characteristics of fifth century Greek classical style.

As he matured, Lysippus moved away from conformity to the classical norms of Polyclitus. Though no copies of his earlier works survive, those that do from the middle part of his career mark a turning from the abstract and universal toward a more explicit expression of the individual, the concrete, and the momentary. Not only is the statue of the athlete scraping himself with a strigil (called the *Apoxyomenos* and dated c. 330) executed in proportions more elongated (and thus visually more realistic) than those of the *Doryphorus*, but the statue is also fully three-dimensional: The arms are outstretched and actually intrude into the viewer's space and thus make more immediate the relationship between figure and viewer. Indeed, the action of the figure, cleansing after exercise, is intimate and private. Here, then, in the uncertainty of the mid-fourth century, the confidence that had been expressed by classical form gives way to the exploration of the momentary and transient.

Exploration of the individual in sculpture is effected most naturally through portraiture; in his later career, Lysippus became the master of this medium. An example that has survived, though again only in stone copies, is the statue of the seated Socrates. There is nothing in this statue to suggest the idealization of the human form. The philosopher, balding, eyes bulging, with satyrlike features and an exposed upper torso exhibiting the physical softening brought on by old age, sits gazing ahead in reflection or in mid-dialogue. The effect of realism is genuine and remarkable, especially since Socrates had been tried and executed in Athens in 399 and thus would never have been seen by Lysippus. As illustrated by this statue, Lysippus' portraiture sought to capture the essence of the subject. Like Polyclitus, Lysippus explored beneath the surface of things, but whereas Polyclitus sought with his art to define the ideal, Lysippus sought to define the real.

Such became the reputation of Lysippus that he was retained by the Macedonian court and later in his career served as the official sculptor of Alexander the Great. So prized was Lysippus' ability to capture Alexander's character that the young Macedonian king is alleged to have allowed no one else to render a likeness of him. Again, stone copies constitute the only visual evidence, but these are suggestive. Consistently in these copies, Alexander's head is turned to the side, tilted slightly upward, eyes deep-set and gazing, and hair folded back in waves. The essence captured is of a man in search, looking longingly beyond the present—an attitude attributed to Alexander by the historian Arrian. Lysippus would have seen Alexander and thus there is reason to believe the likeness truer to the person than is the portrait of Socrates. Confirmation comes from a story told by the ancient biographer Plutarch, who notes that Alexander's former rival and successor, Cassander, while walking in the sanctuary at Delphi, encountered a statue of Alexander, presumably by Lysippus, and was seized by a shuddering and trembling from which he barely recovered.

The realism of Lysippus' work was heightened, so it seems, by the attention he devoted to detail. He was recognized throughout his career as an especially skilled craftsman. In fact, Pliny notes that Lysippus was said to have been a student of no one but originally to have been a coppersmith. Other of his works known from copies are the *Agias* of Pharsalus, the copy of which is nearly contemporary with the original, a series of works on Heracles, who, like Alexander, attained the status of a divinity as a consequence of his heroic exploits, as well as depictions of a satyr, the god Eros, and Kairos (Fortune) made a divinity. Of his other works, only written testimony survives.

Summary

With the death of Alexander the Great in 323, a new era dawned in the eastern Mediterranean. Alexander's kingdom, lacking a designated heir, quickly was divided among his generals and companions into a series of rival monarchies and remained so until absorbed by Rome in the second century B.C. With the defeat at Chaeronea, the city-states of Greece had ceased to exercise internationally significant political or military influence. Greek culture, on the other hand, during this so-called Hellenistic era was suffused throughout the entire Mediterranean. Much that was characteristic of Hellenistic visual art had been anticipated by Lysippus in the fourth century. In brief, Hellenistic sculpture explored the unique and the individual; it investigated internal emotional states and sought to extend the appreciation of form beyond the canons of the classical. Beyond the particular achievements of his own career, Lysippus may also be regarded as one of the significant transitional figures in the history of art.

Bibliography

Beazley, J. D., and Bernard Ashmole. *Greek Sculpture and Painting to the End of the Hellenistic Period.* Cambridge: Cambridge University Press, and New York: Macmillan, 1932. This is a standard, scholarly handbook on Greek sculpture and painting from the early archaic period to the Hellenistic era. The text is concise; the illustrations are numerous and of excellent quality. There is a separate chapter on the sculpture of the fourth century.

Boardman, John. *Greek Art.* 4th ed. New York: Thames and Hudson, 1996; London: Thames and Hudson, 1997. Part of The World of Art series, the volume surveys systematically and with numerous illustrations the arts of Greece, major and minor, from the post-Mycenaean through the Hellenistic eras. Lysippus is examined in two chapters, one on classical sculpture and architecture, the other on Hellenistic art.

Carpenter, Rhys. *Greek Sculpture: A Critical Review.* Chicago: University of Chicago Press, 1960; London: University of Chicago Press, 1971. Although a survey of sculpture from the archaic to Hellenistic eras, the work also focuses on the evolution of style in sculpture. Consequently, it makes no claim to completeness. The plates are excellent, though there are none of Lysippus' work.

Edwards, C. M. "Lysippus." *Yale Classical Studies: Personal Styles in Greek Sculpture* 30 (1995): 130-154. This essay is the most recent study of Lysippus' artistic style. Also discussed is the relationship of extant Roman copies to his lost originals. The black-and-white plates reproduce some of the less-known of these copies

Hammond, N. G. L. *A History of Greece to 322 B.C.* 3d ed. Oxford: Clarendon Press, and New York: Oxford University Press, 1986. This is an excellent standard survey, detailed and clearly written, of ancient Greek history: political, military, and cultural. Lysippus is noted in a chapter on the intellectual background of the fourth century.

Johnson, Franklin P. *Lysippus.* Durham, N.C.: Duke University Press, 1927. A revised doctoral dissertation, this remains the most complete work on Lysippus available, though it is somewhat dated. The appendix is especially valuable, since it preserves all the ancient notices on Lysippus with English translations. There are numerous and excellent plates.

Pliny, the Elder. *The Elder Pliny's Chapters on the History of Art.* K. Jex-Blake and Eugenie S. Strong, eds. London and New York: Macmillan, 1896. This work includes the appropriate chapters from the text of Pliny the Elder's *Historia naturalis* (A.D. 77; *The Historie of the World,* 1601, better known as *Natural History*) with a translation by Jex-Blake and a commentary and historical introduction by Sellers. In addition, there is a preface and select bibliography on Pliny by R. V. Schoder. Pliny is the principal ancient source on Lysippus.

Pollitt, J. J. *Art and Experience in Classical Greece.* Cambridge: Cambridge University Press, 1972. This is an excellent analysis of Greek classical art, chiefly sculpture and architecture, and the intellectual and cultural context in which it was produced. Lysippus is examined in some detail. The plates are numerous and of a high quality.

Richter, G. M. A. *The Sculpture and Sculptors of the Greeks.* 4th ed. New Haven, Conn.: Yale University Press, 1970. This remains the standard volume on Greek sculpture from the early archaic through the late Hellenistic eras. As the title suggests, there are two main sections, one on sculpture, the other on known sculptors, including Lysippus. There are approximately three hundred pages of plates.

Ridgway, Brunilde S. *Hellenistic Sculpture.* Vol. 1. Bristol: Bristol Classical Press, and Madison: University of Wisconsin Press, 1990. This is an up-to-date art history handbook. It gives a short account of Lysippus' career and lists all his known works. Generously illustrated.

Sjöqvist, E. "Lysippus." *University of Cincinnati Classical Studies: Lectures in Memory of Louise Taft Semple II* 2 (1973): 1-49. A succinctly and perceptively written article. Sjöqvist advances a reconsideration of the sculptor's career through a critical examination of Pliny's account of it. Further, several aspects of Lysippus' art are discussed, primarily on the example of his statues of Socrates and Heracles.

Smith, R. R. R. *Hellenistic Sculpture: A Handbook.* New York: Thames and Hudson, 1991. Contains a brief, accessibly written, and informative section on Lysippus, with good black-and-white illustrations.

Stewart, Andrew F. *Greek Sculpture: An Exploration.* 2 vols. New Haven, Conn.: Yale University Press, 1990. A very useful general handbook. The section on Lysippus discusses mainly his style and aesthetics. Lysippus' portraits of Alexander are singled out as the beginning of heroic ruler portraiture. A few of Lysippus' works are illustrated.

Edmund M. Burke

GAIUS MAECENAS

Born: April 13, c. 70 B.C.; probably Arretium

Died: September 30, 8 B.C.; Rome

Areas of Achievement: Literature and government

Contribution: Maecenas was one of the most powerful men in Rome of the first century B.C., often functioning as diplomatic arbiter and city administrator. His most significant role was as patron to a circle of writers who became known as the poets of the Golden Age of Latin literature.

Early Life

Gaius Maecenas Cilnius was born in Arretium (modern Arezzo, Italy) to a wealthy equestrian family that traced its origins to Etruscan kings. Nothing is known of the first thirty years of his life, but he must have received an aristocratic education, for he knew Greek as well as Latin. He first emerges in ancient writers as the intimate friend and financial and political supporter of Gaius Octavius (called Octavian before 27 B.C., Augustus thereafter), the heir of Gaius Julius Caesar, the junior member of the Second Triumvirate, and the future first Emperor of Rome.

Maecenas greatly preferred the life of a private citizen, but he shocked Rome. He hosted extravagant parties, drank excessively, and wore his tunic unbelted (in opposition to proper Roman fashion). Two eunuchs frequently accompanied him through the streets. Although he became notorious as self-indulgent and effeminate, Maecenas appears to have been popular with the Roman people.

Octavian also liked, and trusted, Maecenas. In the years directly following 44 B.C., the young heir found himself faced with the monumental task of avenging his adopted father's murder and making all Italy safe from disenfranchised Romans. Initially, he struck an alliance with Marcus Antonius (Mark Antony), then with Sextus Pompeius, whose bands were raiding the southern coast of Italy. Repeated setbacks with these two, however, convinced Octavian to enlist the aid of friends. Marcus Vipsanius Agrippa became his general, and Maecenas his diplomat and politician.

At Octavian's request, Maecenas arranged an engagement between Octavian and Scribonia, Sextus' sister-in-law, in the hope of allying Octavian with Sextus. When relations grew strained between Octavian and Antony, Maecenas helped arbitrate reconciliations at Brundisium, in 40, and at Tarentum, in 37 B.C. For unknown reasons, he was present at the Battle of Philippi (42 B.C.), where Octavian and Agrippa defeated the forces of Gaius Cassius Longinus and Marcus Junius Brutus, the major surviving assassins of Julius Caesar. Octavian again inexplicably summoned him to Actium (31 B.C.), where the troops of Antony and Cleopatra were defeated. He may also have been present at the campaigns against Sextus.

When Maecenas' services were not required in the field, he was governing Rome and the rest of Italy. Octavian had entrusted Maecenas in his absence with temporary administration of the city, hoping to bolster popular support for himself and quash any resurgent popularity for his opponents. Maecenas now held all the powers of City Prefect, but without the title. His power even extended to issuing official proclamations. He quelled a civil riot in 37 B.C., and in 30 B.C. he quietly crushed the assassination plot against Octavian which was led by the son of the recently deposed Triumvir, Marcus Aemilius Lepidus. Maecenas made the city streets safe after dark and may have helped rid Rome of magicians and astrologers. All these du-

MÆCENAS.

ties without benefit of public office endowed Maecenas with powers greater than those of any elected official.

Life's Work

Octavian's return to Rome in 29 B.C. ended Maecenas' role as public servant, but not his influence in Rome. While he had been acting as diplomat and administrator, Maecenas had also begun befriending at Rome a number of writers whose talents he could use to the advantage of Octavian's new political order. To this growing group of friends he had assumed the role of literary patron, a role to which he now devoted all his energy. Literary patronage frequently included gifts of money or possessions. In addition, it usually included a larger audience for a poet's writings, circulation of his poems, and their publication. Maecenas entertained certain of his friends at his mansion to provide these benefits. Scholars disagree as to what extent Maecenas actually used his patronage to foster a state propaganda literature, but the works of his poets make it clear that they realized some expectation on the part of Augustus. In several of his *Odes* written in 23 B.C. (for example, 1.20) the poet Quintus Horatius Flaccus (Horace) answers with a polite refusal (*recusatio*) a request from his patron to write on a suggested topic. Sextus Propertius (*Elegies* 2.1, c. 25-28 B.C.), does the same when Maecenas suggests a change in theme from love to state matters. Since the literary refusal was standard in Alexandrian verse, it is uncertain how strongly Maecenas actually made his requests for propaganda poems. He may have done no more than give general guidance.

Maecenas' circle included many people who have become little more than names to posterity: Gaius Melissus, Lucius Varius Rufus, Domitius Marsus, and Plotius Tucca. His three most famous poets, however, whose works have survived to modern times have immortalized Maecenas. Publius Vergilius Maro (Vergil) may have become Maecenas' protégé as early as 40. His three major works, the *Eclogues* (43-37 B.C.), the *Georgics* (c. 37-29 B.C., written in honor of Maecenas), and the *Aeneid* (c. 29-19 B.C.), all glorify ideals which Octavian was trying to reinstate in society. In 38, Vergil and his friend Varius Rufus introduced Horace to Maecenas, who invited the young man to become one of his special "friends" eight months later when he returned from a diplomatic mission to the east on Octavian's behalf. Horace's lyric poetry, while not as universally patriotic as Vergil's, does reflect his respect for Octavian and the new regime. Propertius, who was already an established elegiac poet, became one of Maecenas' circle about 25 B.C. and dedicated the first poem of his second book to Maecenas, though his poetry is least indicative of Augustan ideals.

It is a paradox that the man who sought out and encouraged the most talented group of literary artists of his day was himself an author of the worst type. Enough fragments of his works survive to reveal that his compositions were oddly expressed and affected. Augustus disliked his style and parodied it unmercifully.

From his semiretirement in 29 until about 20, Maecenas reigned as the predominant literary patron in Rome. This era saw the publication of Horace's *Odes* (books 1-3), Vergil's *Georgics*, and the second book of Propertius' *Elegies*. Thereafter, Augustus personally assumed the role of patron, and Maecenas returned completely to private life.

Ancients and moderns have speculated on this shift in literary power. Ancient historians supposed that Augustus never forgave Maecenas for telling his wife, Terentia, of the discovery of her brother's conspiracy against the emperor. Others say that Augustus' passion for his friend's wife led to the rift. Maecenas, for his part, may have wished, for personal or health reasons, to resume the life of a private citizen. Many modern scholars believe that Augustus was the real patron, Maecenas only his interim manager. Augustus, now secure in his position as princeps (first citizen) and at leisure to pursue more than war, no longer needed Maecenas as an intermediary between himself and the writers. Since Maecenas always preferred the life of a private citizen, his retirement may have been mutually desirable.

Even in retirement, however, Maecenas retained influence with the emperor in public and private matters. Several times, Maecenas' sound judgment restored Augustus to an even temper. Moreover, it was supposedly on Maecenas' advice that Augustus married his daughter, Julia, to his general, Agrippa, in 21 B.C.

The life of private citizen seems to have suited Maecenas' tastes well. Despite his years as Augustus' factotum, Maecenas chose to limit his involvement in politics, refusing all elective offices and remaining an equestrian all of his life. He erected a huge mansion on the Esquiline Hill, which he transformed from a plebeian cemetery into a magnificent residential area. The estate included a large house, a magnificent tower, lush gardens, and even a swimming pool. There he lived with his wife, Terentia, a beautiful but faithless woman from whom he may eventually have been divorced.

Despite his eccentricities, Maecenas retained his popularity with the Roman people and his intimacy with individual friends. After recovering from a serious illness, for example, Maecenas was greeted with resounding applause from the audience as he entered a theater. Whenever Augustus was ill, he slept at Maecenas' house. Vergil had a house on the Esquiline Hill very near Maecenas'. Horace, who became his personal as well as professional friend, was buried near the tomb of Maecenas on that same hill.

Maecenas' excesses, though tolerated by Augustus and the Roman people, seem to have caught up with him. He suffered from a chronic fever for the last three years of his life. When Maecenas died, he was mourned by his friends and especially by Augustus, to whom he had devoted so much of his life, talents, and energy.

Summary

Maecenas, through his lifelong friendship with Augustus and his almost fifteen years' government service, helped Augustus establish a firm foundation for a smooth transition from the Roman Republic to the Roman Empire. It is his discovery, support, and nurturing of some of the greatest poets of Latin literature, however, that accounts for Maecenas' most lasting effect on the ancient world. He provided a buffer between the emperor and the poets, a role which had advantages for both factions. On the imperial side, Augustus was protected by the figure of Maecenas from the embarrassment of being eulogized by any poet unworthy of his theme. On the other hand, poets who might have felt compelled to yield to a suggestion from Augustus as if it were a command still exercised their prerogative of saying "no" to Maecenas. In this way, the illusion of the Roman Republic which allowed freedom of choice was maintained. Maecenas' patronage supported Augustus' assertion that the Republic had been restored.

Maecenas believed in the idea of merit rather than wealth or social class. In the poets he selected he must have recognized their ability to form their own judgment and must have trusted that judgment to guide them in their writings. While he may have provided encouragement and general guidance to the poets, Maecenas shrewdly avoided demanding particular types of poems from his authors. This policy of nonintervention distinguished him from preceding centuries of literary patrons and set the standard for later generations of patrons in Europe. By fostering such poets as Vergil, Horace, and Propertius, Maecenas became identified with the Golden Age he helped Augustus establish. By giving the poets the freedom to express themselves as they saw fit, Maecenas became the model for all future literary patrons. Immortalized by the Golden Age poets, Maecenas' name has become synonymous with the term literary patron.

Bibliography

Dalzell, A. "Maecenas and the Poets." *Phoenix* 10 (1956): 151-162. Provides an interesting argument, based on the evidence of ancient texts, that Maecenas was not really Augustus' special patron of state propagandist literature. Most notes are from secondary sources (commentators), and more than half are in English.

DuQuesnay, I. M. Le M. "Horace and Maecenas: The Propaganda Value of *Sermones* I." In *Poetry and Politics in the Age of Augustus*, edited by Tony Woodman and David West. Cambridge and New York: Cambridge University Press, 1984. A look at the *Satires* in the atmosphere of 38-36 B.C. and a convincing argument for the propagandist nature of the poems dedicated to Maecenas. Copious notes and a fine bibliography are useful to readers wishing to pursue the subject of Augustan propaganda through Maecenas.

Evenepoel, H. "Maecenas: A Survey of Recent Literature." *Ancient Society* 21 (1990): 99-118. This is a useful overview of some ten books and articles, half of them in languages other than English.

Fraenkel, Eduard. *Horace.* Oxford: Clarendon Press, 1957; New York: Oxford University Press, 1980. Focuses especially on Maecenas' personal relationship to Horace, with occasional references to the public Maecenas and fewer to the person. No bibliography, and the footnotes are in general good only for readers of Latin.

Gold, Barbara K. *Literary Patronage in Greece and Rome.* Chapel Hill: University of North Carolina Press, 1987. Bibliography, index, and copious notes are useful for both the general and the experienced reader. Maecenas' role as patron is explored especially in part 3, chapter 5, "Maecenas and Horace," which carefully explores their dynamic relationship as seen through Horace's writings.

Griffin, J. "Augustus and the Poets: *Caesar Qui Cogere Posset*." In *Caesar Augustus: Seven Aspects*, edited by Fergus Millar and Erich Segal. Oxford and New York: Clarendon Press, 1984. Cites practical reasons for Maecenas, not Augustus, being the patron of the literary set. Endnotes provide little explanation but instead refer the reader to ancient works, most of which can be found in English translation. Citations of foreign texts are of limited use to the general reader.

Reckford, Kenneth J. "Horace and Maecenas." *Transactions and Proceedings of the American Philological Association* 90 (1959): 195-208. Abundant bibliographical notes on the ancient sources that recount Maecenas' life and activities. A number of citations in Latin are of limited use to the general reader, but the first part provides good background for Maecenas.

Shackleton Bailey, D. R. *Profile of Horace*. Cambridge, Mass.: Harvard University Press, and London: Duckworth, 1982. Maecenas is mentioned everywhere in this excellent literary criticism of Horace's *Epodes* and *Satires*. Gives more of a sense of who Maecenas was as a patron than actual data on his life. Latin passages are translated. Limited bibliography.

Syme, Ronald. *The Roman Revolution*. Oxford: Clarendon Press, 1939; New York: Oxford University Press, 1951. Maecenas is mentioned often as the close friend of Augustus, running personal and political errands for the leader and acting as a diplomat of invaluable skill. No straightforward biography. Minimal notes.

Joan E. Carr

MARCUS AURELIUS

Born: April 26, 121; Rome

Died: March 17, 180; Sirmium or Vindobona (modern Vienna)

Areas of Achievement: Government and literature

Contribution: Although renowned as the last of Rome's "good emperors," Marcus Aurelius is best remembered for the *Meditations.* These simply written private notes reflect the emperor's daily efforts to achieve the Platonic ideal of the philosopher-king and are the last great literary statement of Stoicism.

Early Life

Marcus Aurelius Antoninus was born Marcus Annius Verus in Rome. His father was Annius Verus, a magistrate, and his mother was Domitia Calvilla, also known as Lucilla. The emperor Antoninus Pius was by virtue of his marriage to Annia Galeria Faustina, the sister of Annius Verus, the boy's uncle. The emperor, who had himself been adopted and named successor by Hadrian, eventually adopted Marcus Annius Verus. The young man then took the name Marcus Aelius Aurelius Verus. The name Aelius came from Hadrian's family, and Aurelius was the name of Antoninus Pius. The young man took the title Caesar in 139 and, upon becoming emperor, replaced his original name of Verus with Antoninus. Hence, he is known to history as Marcus Aurelius Antoninus.

Marcus Aurelius was well brought up and well educated. Later, he would write of what a virtuous man and prudent ruler his uncle and adoptive father had been. To the fine example set by the emperor was added the dedicated teaching of excellent masters. Letters exist which attest the boy's industry and the great expectations engendered by his performance as a student. He studied eloquence and rhetoric, and he tried his hand at poetry. He was also trained in the law as a preparation for high office. Above all, Marcus Aurelius' interest was in philosophy. When only eleven years of age, he adopted the plain, coarse dress of the philosophers and undertook a spartan regimen of hard study and self-denial. In fact, he drove himself so relentlessly that for a time his health was affected. He was influenced by Stoicism, a sect founded by the Greek philosopher Zeno of Citium in the fourth century B.C.

Life's Work

Antoninus Pius became emperor upon the death of Hadrian in July, 138. He adopted not only Marcus Aurelius but also Lucius Ceionius Commodus, who came to be called Lucius Aurelius Verus. The adoptive brothers could scarcely have been more different. Verus was destined to rule alongside Marcus Aurelius for a time despite his manifest unworthiness. He was an indolent, pleasure-loving man, whereas Marcus Aurelius was proving himself worthy of more and more responsibility. The year 146 was a highly significant one, for it was at about that time that Antoninus Pius began to share with him the government of the empire. Further, the emperor gave him Faustina, his daughter and the young man's cousin, in marriage. A daughter was born to Marcus Aurelius and Faustina in 147.

At the death of Antoninus Pius in March, 161, the senate asked Marcus Aurelius to assume sole governance of the empire. Yet he chose to rule jointly with Verus, the other adopted son. For the first time in its history, Rome had two emperors. Apparently, and fortunately for the empire, Verus was not blind to his inadequacies. He deferred to Marcus Aurelius, who was in turn tolerant of him. Marcus Aurelius cemented their relationship by giving his daughter Lucilla to Verus as wife. That their joint rule lasted for eight years was really a credit to them both.

The first major problem to be faced by the joint rulers was the war with Parthia. Verus was sent to command the Roman forces but proved ineffectual. Fortunately, his generals were able, thus achieving victories in Armenia and along the Tigris and Euphrates rivers. The war was concluded in 165, but as soon as Marcus Aurelius and Verus received their triumph—a huge public ceremony honoring the victors in war—Rome was struck by a virulent pestilence. As the plague spread throughout Italy and beyond, the loss of life was great.

At this time, barbarians from beyond the Alps were threatening to invade northern Italy. Although Marcus Aurelius was able to contain them, they would periodically renew their efforts. For the rest of the emperor's life, much of his time and effort was spent in holding these warlike people at bay. Verus died suddenly in 169, and Marcus Aurelius became the sole emperor of Rome. His reign continued as it had begun, beset by difficulties on every hand. He was almost constantly in the field,

campaigning against one enemy or another. He was on the Danube River for three years, prosecuting the German wars, and by 174 he had gained a series of impressive victories.

In 175, Avidius Cassius, who commanded the Roman legions in Asia, led a revolt against the emperor. Up to that time, Cassius had been a fine general, but when he declared himself Augustus, the emperor marched east to meet the threat. Before the emperor arrived, however, Cassius was assassinated by some of his officers. Marcus Aurelius' treatment of the family and followers of Cassius was magnanimous. His letter to the senate asking mercy for them has survived. During this time, Marcus Aurelius suffered a severe personal tragedy. The empress, Faustina, who had accompanied her husband on the Asian march, abruptly died. Some historians have written that she was scandalously unfaithful and promiscuous, but their reports are contradicted by her husband's pronouncements. He was grief-stricken at her death, and his references to her are loving and laudatory.

It was during this decade of constant warfare, rebellion, and personal grief that Marcus Aurelius began to write the lofty, dignified contemplative notes that were originally known as *Tōn eis heauton* (c. 171-180) and would come to be called his *Meditations* (1634). They were meant for no eyes but the emperor's, and their survival down through the centuries is a mystery (although scholars have no doubts as to their authenticity). They reflect his sense of duty, his high-mindedness, his apparent inner peace. Two themes dominate the *Meditations*: that man, to the utmost of his ability to do so, should harmonize himself with nature and that it is not the circumstances of one's life that produce happiness, but one's perception of those circumstances. According to the emperor, happiness always comes from within, never from without. The *Meditations* are also marked by their author's common sense. He observes that when one is seduced by fame and flattered by others, one should remember their want of judgment on other occasions and remain humble. A great emperor might be expected to be self-assured, perhaps even self-centered and self-satisfied; Marcus Aurelius strikes the reader as more self-composed and self-contented.

Although the emperor's campaigns were generally successful (one victory, in which a fortuitous storm threw the enemy into a panic, was even viewed as a miracle), his reign was not unblemished. He was often forced to make concessions which allowed large numbers of barbarians to remain in Roman territory and which eventually resulted in a proliferation of barbarians within his own armies (some of his legions were already identifiably Christian in makeup). He also seems to have been blind to the vices of Commodus, his son and successor. It is the persecution of the Christians, however, which brings his record into question.

The constant state of war, aggravated by widespread pestilence, caused the populace to demand a scapegoat. The Christians were a natural target, since their repudiation of the ancient gods was thought to have brought divine retribution upon Rome. An ardent persecution was begun, especially in the provinces. At first, the persecutions seem to have progressed ad hoc. Eventually, however, a provincial governor appealed to the emperor for guidance. His directions were, by contemporary standards, severe. If the Christians would deny their faith, they should be released. Otherwise, they must be punished. Those unrepentant Christians who were Roman citizens were beheaded. The others were put to death in a variety of imaginative ways. Apologists for Marcus Aurelius have maintained that he had little to do with these persecutions, and they do seem out of character for the author of the *Meditations*. Still, in order to argue that Marcus Aurelius was in no way culpable, one must read history quite selectively.

In 180, the emperor was conducting yet another successful, though somewhat inconclusive, campaign, this time along the upper Danube. He fell ill with the plague or some other contagious malady and died on March 17 of that year.

Summary

The commemorative bust of Marcus Aurelius features a noble head indeed. Framed by a full head of curly hair and neat chin whiskers, the countenance is strong, honest, and handsome. Any idealization of the likeness is appropriate, for the emperor's demeanor as well as his words set one of the greatest examples in history. When his ashes were returned to Rome, he was honored with deification and, for long afterward, he was numbered by many Romans among their household gods. Commodus erected in his father's memory the Antonine column in Rome's Piazza Colonna. The emperor's statue was placed at the top of the column and remained there until Pope Sixtus V caused it to be replaced by a bronze statue of Saint Paul. The substitution is symbolic, as it was meant to be.

Throughout the Christian era, attempts have been made to associate the *Meditations* with Christian thought. Such efforts are understandable, for the emperor's self-admonitions to virtuous conduct for its own sake, steadfastness, magnanimity, and forbearance are congenial to the mind of the Christian apologist. The weight of evidence, however, indicates otherwise. Marcus Aurelius seems to have known little about the Christians, and what he knew he did not like. Even granting that he was not deeply involved in their persecution, he clearly regarded them as fanatical troublemakers. He should be viewed, then, not as an incipient Christian but as the voice of paganism's last great moral pronouncements.

The emperor was an able but not a great military figure. He was an intelligent but not a brilliant thinker. As a writer, he was a competent but not a formidable stylist. In short, Marcus Aurelius was great because he brought a human quality to his leadership and made optimal use of his limited talents.

Bibliography

Arnold, E. Vernon. *Roman Stoicism*. London: Routledge and Kegan Paul, and New York: Humanities, 1911. A series of lectures by a classical scholar, arranged in seventeen chapters. The thought of Marcus Aurelius receives ample treatment, as he is discussed in four chapters.

Aurelius Antoninus, Marcus. *The Meditations of Marcus Aurelius Antoninus and A Selection of the Letters of Marcus and Fronto.* Arthur S. L. Ferguson and R. B. Rutherford, trans. Oxford and New York: Oxford University Press, 1989. These new translations are supplied with a brief introduction and notes. The latter are intended for the general reader, and overall are very comprehensive.

Aurelius Antoninus, Marcus. *The "Meditations" of the Emperor Marcus Aurelius Antoninus.* Translated by R. Graves. London: Robinson, 1792. The editor's translation, reproduced in the Library of English Literature, is accompanied by a biography and notes. Graves was a clergyman and an Oxford don. His assessment of Marcus Aurelius, written toward the end of the Enlightenment, is of historical interest.

———. "The *Meditations* of Marcus Aurelius." Translated and edited by George Long. In *Plato, Epictetus, Marcus Aurelius*, edited by Charles W. Eliot. New York: P. F. Collier and Son, 1909, 2d ed. 1937. An entry in the Harvard Classics series. Long's translation of Marcus Aurelius' work is accompanied by his brief and readable life of the author. His companion essay, "The Philosophy of Antoninus," includes a very useful explanation of Stoicism and traces its progress and decline in the Roman world. Long, writing in the freewheeling academic style of the late nineteenth century, is occasionally pugnacious in making his point, but he is always lucid and direct.

Birley, Anthony R. *Marcus Aurelius: A Biography.* Rev. ed. London: Batsford, 1993. A comprehensive biographic study of the emperor, the book is mostly devoted to his political career but also includes a chapter on his philosophy. The extremely useful appendices contain overviews of the sources and of modern scholarly literature on him, as well as genealogical trees and short prosopographical notes on the Antonine family.

Grant, Michael. *The Antonines: The Roman Empire in Transition.* London and New York: Routledge, 1994. In this book on the political, social and cultural history of the period, Marcus Aurelius receives substantial treatment. The politics of his reign are examined in Part I, and the *Meditations* are discussed along other literary products of the age in Part II, Chapter 6.

Guevara, Antonio de. *Archontorologion: Or, The Diall of Princes, Containing the Golden and Famovs Booke of Marcvs Avrelivs, Sometime Emperour of Rome.* Translated by Thomas North. London: Alsop, 1619. North's translation, reproduced in the Library of English Literature, of a sixteenth century book by a Spanish bishop. The work is a sort of romance, founded on the life and character of Marcus Aurelius. A view of the emperor from the Renaissance perspective, the book was written to put before the emperor Charles V the model of antiquity's wisest and most virtuous prince. The final edition of North's translation has corrected "many grosse imperfections."

Rutherford, R. B. *The Meditations of Marcus Aurelius: A Study.* Oxford: Clarendon Press, 1989. The book is the single major study dedicated exclusively to Aurelius' text. It explores in detail its use of rhetoric and verbal imagery. The various influences upon the emperor's thought are discussed, and he is compared to other Stoic philosophers and Roman contemporaries.

Stanton, G. R. "Marcus Aurelius, Emperor and Philosopher." *Historia* 18 (1968): 570-587. The article re-examines Aurelius' legislation in the light of contemporary narrative sources (Dio Cassius, the Historia Augusta), rather than that of the Meditations. Stanton denies the influence of Stoicism upon Aurelius' policy as emperor.

Wenley, R. M. *Stoicism and Its Influence*. New York: Longmans, 1924; London: Harrap, 1925. An entry in the series called Our Debt to Greece and Rome. A defense of the importance of Stoicism against historians of philosophy who have tended to dismiss it lightly. Discussions of Marcus Aurelius are liberally sprinkled throughout the text.

Patrick Adcock

GAIUS MARIUS

Born: 157 B.C.; Cereatae
Died: January 13, 86 B.C.; Rome
Areas of Achievement: Warfare and politics
Contribution: Marius was a successful Roman general whose military innovations created the professional army of the late Roman Republic and early empire. Representing the Popular Party, he was elected consul seven times.

Early Life

Gaius Marius was born on a farm near the village of Cereatae in the district of Arpinum, about sixty miles southeast of Rome. He was the son of a middle-class farmer. Marius received little formal education and grew to manhood with a certain roughness in speech and manner which characterized him throughout his life. He first saw military service in 134 in Spain under Scipio Aemilianus in the campaign against the Numantines. Marius readily adapted to military life and was decorated for valor. For the next ten years, he served as a junior officer in Spain and the Balearic Islands.

Returning to Rome, Marius began his political career. With the help of the powerful Metelli clan, he won the election for tribune of the people in 119. During his tribuneship, he showed his independence by carrying a bill for election reform despite opposition from the Metelli and the Senatorial Party. In the next year, Marius stood for the office of aedile but was defeated. In 115, he was elected praetor but only with difficulty. In the following year, he was appointed propraetor for Further Spain. About the year 111, Marius contracted a highly favorable marriage alliance with the ancient Julian clan. His marriage to Julia, a future aunt of Julius Caesar, gave him an important link to the aristocracy.

Life's Work

The Jugurthine War soon brought Marius to a position of prominence in Roman affairs. In 109, he was appointed staff officer to Quintus Caecilius Metellus, who as consul was given command of the army in the war against Jugurtha, the King of Numidia. Bringing his army to Africa, Metellus waged war against the wily Jugurtha for two years without success. Amid growing criticism of the slowness of the campaign, Marius determined that he would seek the consulship for the year 107. If successful, he hoped to replace Metellus as commander and reap the glory of ending the war. Returning to Rome, he boldly attacked Metellus and the senate and promised to capture or kill Jugurtha if elected. He was supported by members of the business class, who desired stability in North Africa, and the plebeians, who used the war as an opportunity to criticize senatorial leadership. Marius won the consulship by a wide margin. Although the senate voted to extend the command of Metellus for an additional year, the tribal assembly passed a measure directing that the command be transferred to Marius.

In raising an army, Marius chose not to rely upon conscription, which involved a small property qualification. Instead, he called for voluntary recruits from the proletariat, promising land at the end of military service. The innovation was made by Marius out of necessity, since conscription was viewed as a burden by the small farmers, whose numbers were diminishing and who were reluctant to leave their farms. Those who joined the army were often the poorest citizens. For them, the army offered hope for the future.

After arriving in North Africa, Marius began seizing and occupying the fortified strongholds of Jugurtha. By the end of 107, most of eastern Numidia was under Roman control. Jugurtha retreated westward, joining forces with his father-in-law, Bocchus, King of Mauretania. During the year 106, Marius marched across the western half of Numidia. He reached the river Muluccha, five hundred miles west of his base of operations, and seized the war treasure of Jugurtha in a remote mountain fortress. As the Roman army returned eastward, Bocchus and Jugurtha attacked but were repelled. Convinced now that he was on the losing side, Bocchus secretly offered to make peace. Marius sent his quaestor, Lucius Cornelius Sulla, to the Mauretanian camp. Sulla persuaded Bocchus to betray Jugurtha, who was kidnapped and turned over to the Romans. With the capture of Jugurtha, the war ended. Marius took credit for the victory, overlooking the critical role played by Sulla, who was to become his bitter rival. Marius returned to Rome in triumph with Jugurtha in chains; a few days later, Jugurtha was executed.

Marius had returned from Africa at a critical time, for two Germanic tribes, the Cimbri and the Teutons, had invaded the Roman province in southern France. In 105, the Cimbri had annihilated a Roman army at Arausio (Orange) in the lower Rhone Valley. Marius was elected consul for 104 even before he returned from Africa. With Italy threatened by invasion, the Romans disregarded the law requiring a ten-year interval between consulships. The need for Marius' military ability was so great that he was elected consul repeatedly between 104 and 101. Fortunately for Rome, the Cimbri migrated to Spain and the Teutons to northern France, giving Marius time to prepare for their return. In raising an army, Marius again used voluntary recruits from the propertyless class. He increased the strength of the legion to six thousand men; each legion was divided into ten cohorts of six hundred men. Marius completed the process of making the cohort the standard tactical unit of the legion, replacing the smaller maniple. The cohort was subdivided into six centuries, led by veteran centurions who had risen through the ranks. Weapons were standardized to include the short sword and the hurling pilum. Each soldier was required to carry his own pack. Marius introduced the silver eagle as the standard for each legion; each developed its own traditions and *esprit de corps*.

In 102, the Cimbri and Teutons reappeared. The Teutons advanced toward Italy along the southern coast of France. Marius met them at Aquae Sextiae (now Aix). The battle took place in a narrow valley, with the Teutons advancing uphill against the Romans. At the height of the battle, the Teutons were attacked from the rear by a Roman force that had been concealed behind a hill. The Teutons panicked, and the battle became a rout. As many as 100,000 Teutons may have perished. The Cimbri invaded Italy through the Brenner Pass. The other consul, Quintus Lutatius Catulus, brought an army northward to intercept them but was driven back south of the Po. In the spring of 101, Marius joined Catulus with additional troops. The decisive battle was fought on the Raudine Plain near Vercellae, located between Milan and Turin. The Cimbri, facing a burning sun, advanced against the Roman center. As soon as they were overextended, Marius attacked on the flanks. The Cimbri were dealt a severe defeat from which they could not recover. With the threat of the German invasion ended, Marius and Catulus returned to Rome to celebrate a joint triumph.

After these victories, Marius began a new phase of his career as a politician, but he failed miserably. He formed a coalition with two political opportunists, Lucius Appuleius Saturninus and Gaius Glaucia. In the elections for the year 100, Marius won the consulship for the sixth time; Glaucia was elected praetor and Saturninus tribune. Soon afterward, Saturninus introduced bills to establish land grants for Marius' veterans in Transalpine Gaul and colonies in the east. Marius was to be given the right to bestow citizenship upon a select number of the settlers. When the senate objected, Saturninus took the unprecedented step of requiring all senators to take an oath supporting the bills after passage or suffer exile. The urban proletariat also protested, for they judged the measures overly generous to the Italian allies who made up a large part of the veterans. The bills were finally passed after Saturninus used Marius' veterans to drive off the opposition in the assembly.

In the elections for 99, Saturninus again won the tribuneship. Glaucia stood for consul but was defeated by Gaius Memmius. Seeking to intimidate their opponents, Saturninus and Glaucia ordered their henchmen to murder Memmius. The reaction to the slaying restored momentum to the senate, which passed a decree directing Marius to arrest Saturninus and Glaucia. After some hesitation,

Marius ordered his veterans to seize his former friends, who were encamped on the Capitoline. He placed them in the senate building for protection, but the angry mob tore off the roof and pelted the prisoners to death with tiles. Marius completed his term as consul, but his influence and prestige disappeared. Under the pretext of fulfilling a vow to the goddess Cybele, he departed for the east.

After returning to Rome, Marius remained in relative obscurity until the outbreak of the Social War. When the allies gained early victories in the war, Marius was recalled to military service in the year 90. Although serving in a subordinate status, he was responsible for inflicting two defeats on the Marsi. Despite his success, he was given no assignment for the following year. The glory of concluding the war went to Sulla. In the year 88, when Mithridates, King of Pontus, led a revolt in the east, Marius sought to gain the command for the approaching war. The senate, however, ignored him and bestowed the command on Sulla, who was consul for 88. Marius gained the support of the tribune Publius Sulpicius Rufus, who initiated a tribal assembly measure transferring the command to him. Sulla, who was with his army in Campania, marched on Rome and ordered the executions of Marius and the leaders of the assembly. Sulpicius was captured and put to the sword; Marius fled to the coast, hiding in the marshes near Minturnae. At length he found refuge on the island of Cercina off the coast of Africa.

When Sulla departed for the east in 87, Marius returned to Italy and raised a new army. He joined forces with the democratic leader Lucius Cornelius Cinna, whom the Senate had recently driven from Rome. With their combined armies, they advanced against Rome and forced its surrender. Marius now vented his anger after years of frustrations and disappointments by ordering wholesale executions of his enemies in the senate and among members of the nobility. Dispensing with the elections process, Marius and Cinna appointed themselves consuls for the year 86. Marius, now seventy-one years of age, entered his seventh consulship, but by this time he was gravely ill. He died of fever a few days after taking office in January, 86.

Summary

One of the foremost generals of his age, Marius showed his resourcefulness and capability as a military commander in his successful campaigns in North Africa, Gaul, and Italy. His innovative recruitment of troops was of major significance for the future of Rome. By relying on volunteers from the proletariat class, Marius created an army of professional soldiers who were ready to serve for extended periods of time. The new system was vastly superior to the short-term conscript militia of the past, but it also posed dangers. The soldiers of the professional army identified their interests with their general and expected to be rewarded with land following their service. They gave allegiance to their general rather than to the state. This system gave extraordinary power to any general who might desire to use the army for his own political ends. It led directly to the civil wars of the late republic, when military strength became the key to political power. Marius also introduced important reforms to improve the fighting ability of the army. His innovations in organization, weapons, and tactics produced a highly efficient fighting machine at a time when Rome was sorely pressed by its enemies. The new Marian army became the Roman army of the late republic and early empire.

Although Marius was a successful general, he failed as politician. His successive consulships are attributable not to political adroitness but to his skill as a general at a time when Rome was severely threatened. The year 100 marked a turning point in Marius' career. Elected consul for the sixth time and immensely popular after his recent victories, Marius devised no program for social reform beyond that of acquiring land for his veterans. Inept as a public speaker and vacillating in his political decisions, Marius allowed himself to be led by the demagogues Saturninus and Glaucia, whose radicalism and violence precipitated his fall. Driven by ambition, Marius spent the remaining years of his life trying to recover his former power and prestige. At his death, Rome had entered a new era of civil war and bloodshed that would last more than half a century.

Bibliography

Badian, Ernest. "From the Gracchi to Sulla." *Historia* 11 (1962): 214-228. An examination of the political career of Marius set against the background of the Roman Revolution and the accompanying contest between the Senatorial and Popular parties. Special attention is devoted to the political factions which supported and opposed Marius. Extensive notes review the progress of Marian studies. Bibliography.

Carney, Thomas F. *A Biography of C. Marius*. Chicago: Argonaut, 1970. This book is a new printing of the author's article published in the *Proceedings of the African Classical Associations*, Supplement 1, in 1962. The work is a concise, highly technical treatment of Marius' career. The notes present several new directions in research. Numerous references. Appendix with tables listing all existing and nonextant contemporary sources.

Kildahl, P. A. *Caius Marius*. New York: Twayne Publishers, 1968. Highly readable, sympathetic account of the life of Marius. This book is intended for students and the general reader but will also be useful for scholars. Preface contains an analysis of contemporary sources. Chronology, map, useful notes, and select bibliography.

Last, Hugh. "The Wars of the Age of Marius." In *The Cambridge Ancient History*. Vol. 9, *The Roman Republic*. Cambridge: Cambridge University Press, 1932; New York: Cambridge University Press, 1981. Causes and historical background for both the Jugurthine War and the Cimbrian War are discussed. Detailed accounts of military campaigns, strategy, and battle tactics. Maps with physical features, mileage scales, and Roman place-names for areas of military operations. Description of military reforms under Marius. Lengthy discussion of sources. Notes and bibliography.

Parker, H. M. D. *The Roman Legions*. Rev. ed. London: Heffer, and New York: Barnes and Noble Books, 1958. A study of the composition of the Roman army through the periods of the Republic and the Empire. The chapter on the Marian army reforms offers technical explanations and details regarding Marius' innovations and contains valuable references to contemporary sources. The introduction provides a description of the pre-Marian army.

Scullard, H. H. *From the Gracchi to Nero*. 5th ed. London and New York: Methuen, 1982. The best account for the general background of the last century of the Roman Republic. Highly readable with sound scholarly judgment. Detailed chapter on the career of Marius. Extensive notes include a discussion of sources for Marius, problems and conflicting interpretations arising from the sources, and numerous references for additional study.

Norman Sobiesk

MARTIAL

Born: March 1, c. A.D. 40; Bilbilis, Spain
Died: c. A.D. 104; Spain
Area of Achievement: Literature
Contribution: Martial perfected the epigram, the witty, sometimes salacious poem, typically of two to four lines, which points out the moral and social ills of the poet's day or lampoons prominent people.

Early Life

Everything known about Martial comes from his own poems and from one letter of Pliny the Younger, written at the time of the poet's death. Martial alludes to his Spanish origins in an early poem, but by the age of fifty-seven he had already spent thirty-four years in Rome. His parents, of whom nothing more than their names is known, provided him with the standard rhetorical education designed to equip him to be a lawyer. In one of his poems, Martial depicts them as already in the underworld. Martial seems to have been in Rome by 64, perhaps under the patronage of the powerful Seneca family, also natives of Spain.

At some point he received the status of knight and an honorary military tribunate, but he does not mention which emperor bestowed on him those privileges. By contrast, it is clear that Titus gave Martial the privileges of a father of three children and that Domitian renewed the grant. His silence about the emperor who had provided the two earlier honors leads scholars to suspect that it was Nero, who fell into disgrace upon his death in 68. It was important to Martial to have his honors known but impolitic to boast about who had given them to him.

Martial probably practiced law during Vespasian's reign (69-79), though it does not seem to have suited him. His comments about the profession are unkind, yet fairly late in his life he gibed someone who had failed to pay him for pleading his case in court.

Exactly when or why Martial turned to poetry cannot be determined. His first published effort was *Spectacula* (80; *On the Spectacles*), a collection of short poems in honor of the dedication of the Flavian Amphitheater (the Colosseum) in 80. Between 86 and 98 he published his epigrams at the rate of roughly a volume a year. Publication order is not necessarily the order of writing. Epigrams 2.59 and 5.26, for example, refer to the same incident but were published several years apart. The twelfth and final volume appeared in 101, after he had returned to Spain. There are also two volumes of incidental poems which were meant to accompany gifts given at banquets. Probably written between 80 and 85, these are sometimes numbered books 13 and 14 of his collected works, but this classification does not seem to have been Martial's intention.

One of the great puzzles about Martial's early life is how he supported himself. Many of his poems complain about his poverty and the necessity of flattering the rich in the hope of a handout or a dinner invitation. He mentions his wretched third-floor apartment, and his ragged toga is a frequent subject of lament.

In other poems, however, Martial refers to his "Nomentan farm," a suburban villa not far from Rome, and to his private home in the city. He invites guests to dine with him and boasts about his kitchen and his cook, luxuries beyond the means of the urban poor who inhabited Rome's apartment houses. He asks permission from the emperor to tap into the city water supply and pipe the water directly into his house, a privilege reserved for the ruler's wealthy friends. The image which he tries to project of a poor poet scrounging handouts from stingy patrons may be nothing more than a literary pose.

Life's Work

This problem of the poetic persona complicates enormously the study of Martial's life and work. His poems are the only source of information about his life, but there is doubt that what he says about himself is to be taken seriously. For example, in one poem he complains about his wife having a lover, while in another he objects that she is too moralistic to engage in the deviant sexual behavior which he enjoys. Can these poems be talking about the same woman? As a result, some modern scholars contend that Martial was never married and that any reference to a wife is merely a literary convention. Another possibility is that he was married several times, something that was not at all uncommon in Rome in the late first century A.D.

If one cannot be certain whether, or how many times, Martial was married, it is difficult to ascertain anything else about his life. In one poem, he refers to a daughter, but only once in passing. In another, he mourns deeply the death of the slave child Erotion, tending her grave for years and requiring the next owner of the property to observe the same rituals. Could this have been his daughter by a slave woman on his farm?

It is virtually impossible to know Martial himself from his poems, as the contradictions in his work are numerous. In some of the poems he pictures himself engaging in homosexual relations; in others he ridicules men who do the same. He praises the joys of simple country life, but he lived in Rome for thirty-five years. He claims that, although many of his poems are bawdy, his life is decent.

Every writer must please his readers, and Martial seems to have been slanting his material to the tastes of his audience; in one poem he claims that he "could write what is serious" but emphasizes entertainment value, for that is what makes people "read and hum my poems all over Rome." Most of his poetry was produced in the reign of Domitian, a cruel, self-indulgent emperor (according to the biographer Suetonius) who enjoyed brutal sex with prostitutes and initiated mixed nude bathing in Rome's public baths. After his death, the emperors Nerva and Trajan brought about a kind of Victorian reaction to the loose morality of Domitian's day. Martial found that his poetry no longer appealed to the general public, so he retired to Spain.

While he does not reveal himself to the reader, Martial does draw an intimate portrait of Roman society in the late first century. One commentator says that he "touched life closely at all levels." One of his poems describes a Roman's daily schedule and several others focus on certain daily activities.

Martial's day would begin with a visit at daybreak to his patron, a wealthy man who would give him a small daily handout in exchange for Martial's accompanying him to public meetings and generally boosting his ego. Every Roman aristocrat had as many such clients as he could reasonably support. His status was measured by the size of the throng which surrounded him as he walked through the streets. Since Rome lacked a governmental welfare system, this informal arrangement redistributed some of the wealth which was concentrated in the hands of the aristocracy, a minute percentage of the population. In addition to the daily *sportula*, clients expected to receive gifts on their birthdays and at the festival of the Saturnalia in December. Martial's poems show that the clients would complain vociferously if the gift was not as large as they had expected.

One of the client's duties was to accompany his patron to court, an obligation which the litigious Romans faced frequently. Lawyers seem to have had difficulty collecting their fees, which was perhaps one reason that Martial abandoned the calling. The speeches in court were long and often irrelevant, but the client was expected to applaud his patron's case in the hope of influencing the jury.

By midday, everyone was ready for a rest, followed by exercise and a bath. Martial frequented the baths and pointed out the flaws—the stretch marks, the sagging breasts, the brand of the former slave—which other patrons tried to hide. From the numerous poems that discuss the baths, one can conclude that they served as Rome's social center. People went there to see and to be seen, to catch up on the latest gossip, and to wangle invitations to dinner. This last function was the most important to a client such as Martial. Failure to obtain an invitation meant that he had to provide his own meal, which marked him as a social outcast.

Dinner began in the late afternoon, since the Romans did not eat much, if anything, for breakfast or lunch. The city's social life revolved around these huge meals, at which the food was often intended to impress the guests as much as to nourish them. The seating arrangement indicated the guests' social standing, with the more prominent individuals reclined on couches closest to that of the host. Many aristocrats served two meals at once: elegant food for those eating immediately around them and cheaper fare for those in the farther reaches of the dining room. That this practice was common is evidenced by Pliny the Younger, who in a letter to a friend assured him that he did not engage in such habits.

Though these dinners did not often turn into orgies, the Romans had no compunctions about promiscuous sexual activity. Martial seems to have engaged in his share of such activity and was aware of what everyone else in his social circle was doing. His language is so explicit that no one dared to translate all of his poems into idiomatic English until 1968.

Summary

Scattered through Martial's epigrams are the people of Rome, from the aristocracy to the prostitutes. He exposes their posturing and the vices they thought would remain secret. His picture of Roman society may be the most accurate available, for he does not adopt the bitterly satiric tone of Juvenal or the staid disdain of Pliny. Martial's poetry gained for him renown in his own lifetime, something which he openly pursued. What made him successful, he believed, was the shock value of his epigrams. Martial once wrote that it is the nature of the epigram, as he refined it, to jolt the reader while it amuses, just as vinegar and salt improve the flavor of food.

Martial's clearest statement of his purpose is found in epigram 6.60: "Rome praises, adores, and sings my verses./ Every pocket, every hand holds me./ Look, that fellow blushes, turns pale, is stunned, yawns, hates me./ That's what I want. Now my poems please me." Pliny's judgment on Martial's epigrams was that they were "remarkable for their combination of sincerity with pungency and wit. . . . His verses may not be immortal, but he wrote them with that intention." Later generations have agreed with Pliny's critique. Though the church fathers frowned upon him in the Middle Ages, Martial's technique was much admired and palely imitated from the Renaissance until the eighteenth century. His Erotion poems directly influenced Ben Jonson's "Epigrammes XXII on My First Daughter," and Robert Herrick's "Upon a Child That Died."

Bibliography

Adamik, T. "Martial and the *Vita Beatior.*" *Annales Universitatis Budapestinensis* 3 (1975): 55-64. Martial's personal philosophy of life seems to be closest to Epicureanism. He satirizes Cynics and Stoics especially.

Allen, Walter, Jr., et al. "Martial: Knight, Publisher, and Poet." *Classical Journal* 65, (May, 1970): 345-357. Discusses the problem of Martial's persona and concludes that he was not actually a poor, struggling poet but a reasonably successful writer and publisher.

Ascher, Leona. "Was Martial Really Unmarried?" *Classical World* 70 (April/May, 1977): 441-444. Surveys scholarly opinion on the question of Martial's marital status and finds the evidence inconclusive.

Bell, Albert A., Jr. "Martial's Daughter?" *Classical World* 78 (September/October, 1984): 21-24. Suggests that the girl Erotion, who is the subject of several of Martial's poems, was his daughter by a slave woman.

Bellinger, A. R. "Martial, the Suburbanite." *Classical Journal* 23 (February, 1928): 425-435. Depicts Martial as a "professional beggar," dependent on handouts from aristocrats to maintain himself.

Carrington, A. G. *Aspects of Martial's Epigrams.* Eton, England: Shakespeare Head Press, 1960. A nonscholarly introduction to selected poems, especially those discussing Martial's life, Roman history, and the process of creating a book in antiquity.

Semple, W. H. "The Poet Martial." *Bulletin of the John Rylands Library* 42 (1959/1960): 432-452. Discusses what can be known of Martial's life and analyzes some of the major themes or categories of his epigrams.

Spaeth, John W., Jr. "Martial and the Roman Crowd." *Classical Journal* 27 (January, 1932): 244-254. Making allowances for Martial's tendency to satirize and lampoon his contemporaries, one can gain valuable insights into the social history of the late first century.

———. "Martial Looks at His World." *Classical Journal* 24 (February, 1929): 361-373. Martial shows more interest in the lower classes than do most Roman writers, although he is not sympathetic by any means. The antilabor prejudice characteristic of his day is evident in his poems.

Sullivan, J. P. "Martial's Sexual Attitudes." *Philologus* 123 (1979): 288-302. Though graphic by modern standards, Martial was merely expressing contemporary sexual values in his poetry. His explicit language is a convention of the epigram, as seen in Catullus and earlier poets.

Albert A. Bell, Jr.

MASINISSA

Born: c. 238 B.C.; Numidia, Northern Africa

Died: 148 B.C.; Numidia, Northern Africa

Areas of Achievement: Government and politics; warfare and conquest

Contribution: Through his alliance with the Roman Republic, Masinissa helped to destroy the realm of Carthage, opening the way to Roman suzerainty over the Mediterranean.

Early Life

Masinissa was not born a king. He was the son of a minor tribal chieftain of the Massylians, a tribe of the North African group known to the Greeks and Carthaginians as the Numidia. Numidia was roughly equivalent to modern eastern Algeria (as far as present-day Constantine) and western Tunisia. The Numidians are generally considered the ancestors of the people later known as the Berbers. For at least three hundred years, the Numidians had been subjugated by the Carthaginians, colonizers from Phoenicia whose far more literate and urbane culture easily eclipsed that of the Numidians. The various Numidian tribes were used by Carthage as a source of manpower, since they were usually more warlike in nature than the commerce-minded Carthaginians.

Like many sons of Numidian nobility, young Masinissa was sent to Carthage to be educated, presumably more in warfare and in science than in high culture. It is at this point that a famous story begins, given credence by ancient historians such as Livy and Appian but suspect to more skeptical modern viewpoints. Masinissa, it is said, met and fell in love with Sophonisba, an aristocratic Carthaginian girl of the family of Gisgo. Though Numidians were subject peoples of Carthage, there were no particular racial or class differences between the two peoples, and Sophonisba's father happily encouraged Masinissa's interest in his daughter; the couple was betrothed around 216 B.C. Yet there was another suitor for Sophonisba, a man named Syphax. Syphax was the leader of a larger faction of Numidians, the Massaesylians, who co-existed in an uneasy rivalry with Masinissa's own group. While Masinissa was away in Spain serving in Carthage's war against Rome under the command of Sophonisba's father, Syphax exerted pressure on the Carthaginian leadership to proffer Sophonisba to him. Because Syphax was on hand and had a large military presence just outside Carthage, the Carthaginian leadership consented to Syphax's marriage to Sophonisba.

Masinissa was, understandably, infuriated; he also felt personally endangered, as there were rumors that Sophonisba's father was under orders from Carthage to put him to death. Though he and his family had been nothing but loyal to Carthage for several generations, he felt so betrayed by the Carthaginians that he immediately switched sides and offered his allegiance to Rome, which was engaged in a life-and-death struggle with Carthage for control of the Western Mediterranean. Masinissa would continue as a Roman ally for the rest of his long and productive life.

Life's Work

Masinissa joined the Roman side at about the time that the tide was beginning to turn in the Second Punic War. After Rome had been driven nearly to its knees after its defeat at Cannae in 216 B.C., a new, young general, Scipio, had taken command of Roman forces in Spain and was reinvigorating the Roman war effort. In 204 B.C., Masinissa began an organized offensive against Carthage in Africa. By now, Masinissa was in his early thirties, and he impressed and motivated his men by his physical energy, commanding appearance, and genius in warfare. The ascetic regimen that he mandated for his men proved perfect for the desert locale of his attacks on the Carthaginians. Lacking the heavy supply trains that encumbered the Carthaginian troops, Masinissa's mobile and maneuverable army held off the Carthaginians before Roman troops commanded by Scipio arrived in force. Eventually, Masinissa's army engaged in direct battle with that of Syphax, and the two rivals for Sophonisba's hand met each other in single combat. (It must be stressed again that the entire Sophonisba story contains many legendary elements). Masinissa prevailed over Syphax at the "Battle of the Great Plains," but there was concern in the Roman camp that Sophonisba was potentially a Carthaginian agent who would turn Masinissa against Rome. The Romans thus forced Masinissa to give up the woman he loved.

Masinissa's most important service to Rome came in 202 B.C., when Hannibal, the great Carthaginian commander who had dealt Rome stunning blows earlier in the war, returned to Africa to defend his homeland against Scipio's invasion. Scipio linked up with Masinissa at Zama, where the climactic battle occurred. Masinissa and his cavalry were stationed on Scipio's right flank. Masinissa's horsemen managed to circumvent Hannibal's front lines and, by wreaking havoc in the rear of his opponent's formation, contributed to Hannibal's defeat and that of Carthage overall.

As a reward for his participation in the victory, Rome made Masinissa king of Numidia, a position that had never before existed. Masinissa, of a formerly minor tribe, now exerted supreme authority over all the Numidians. His people's overall position in the region was also strengthened, as the peace Carthage was forced to conclude with Rome after the Battle of Zama left Carthage in a very weak position. Carthage was forced to cede to the Numidian kingdom any land that had ever belonged to Masinissa's ancestors in the past, a clause the Numidian leader was often to use as a pretext to harass Carthage over the next fifty years.

Even after Scipio's victory, Masinissa continued as an inveterate opponent of Carthage. This opposition was not ethnically or culturally motivated, as Masinissa, educated in Carthage, was an advocate of Punic (Carthaginian) culture and was far more part of the North African cultural world than the Roman. Masinissa's seemingly endless need for vengeance upon Carthage perhaps caused ancient historians to attribute so much importance to the Sophonisba legend. More plausibly, Masinissa early on diagnosed the rising power of Rome and wanted to be on the winning side. Certainly, his kingdom benefitted from Roman patronage over his career. Yet Masinissa also made material improvements in his own realm, especially in the area of agriculture, as he convinced many Numidian herdsmen to settle down as farmers. He also established a new capital at Cirta that served as an appropriate focal point for his newly unified kingdom.

While his kingdom was developing internally, Masinissa continued to press against Carthage. In 174 B.C., Masinissa accused Carthage, which as part of its peace pact with Rome had to act as a Roman ally, of receiving ambassadors from Macedonia, with which Rome was fighting a fierce war. In fact, Carthage refused Macedonian overtures; Masinissa nevertheless continued to encroach on Carthaginian territory, plundering several Carthaginian coastal outposts.

Ironically, the Carthaginians came to despise Masinissa so much for these raids that even Rome, the city's true rival, had a far larger set of sympathizers among the Carthaginian people. For Carthage to surrender to Rome, a city of equivalent stature, was one thing, but for it to potentially surrender to Masinissa, king of a people who had once been Carthaginian subjects, was unthinkable. Carthage continually appealed to Rome to rein in their client king, but their pleas went unheeded until 151 B.C., when Rome suddenly restrained Masinissa from pursuing further gains. Some historians think that Rome had finally gotten suspicious of Masinissa and feared that the Numidian king was plotting to establish an empire that would encompass all of North Africa from Mauretania to Egypt, an aspiration that would eventually conflict with Rome's plans for expansion. Yet Rome's restraint of Masinissa was probably a delaying tactic employed so that Rome's armies could be strong when the final push against Carthage came.

By now, Masinissa was in his late eighties. His sons, particularly Gulussa and Micipsa, began to take more of a role in commanding the Numidian armies. It was a Carthaginian attack upon Gulussa that enabled Masinissa not only to besiege the city of Oroscopa but also to provoke Carthage into a full-scale battle that would enable Rome, which had been looking for an excuse to destroy Carthage, to intervene. Through a brilliant set of military tactics, Masinissa appeared to pull back from Oroscopa only to engage the Carthaginians in the open. He was victorious through a combination of combat and attrition, and a massacre led by Gulussa wiped out the Carthaginian army.

The Carthaginians now switched strategies and tried to make peace with Masinissa by appointing a grandson of his, Hasdrubal, to high command. This strategy did not seem to work, though Roman callousness in not consulting Masinissa as to strategy upset the old king and made him more distant toward Rome. He never, though, showed any sign of a break with Rome and an alliance with Carthage, and he thus left no obstacle to Carthage's final destruction. He did not, however, live to see the end of his old adversary, as he died in 148 B.C. at the age of ninety. He had forty-four children, of whom ten survived him. His sons Gulussa, Micipsa, and Mastanabal all served Rome loyally in the final assault upon Carthage, which was destroyed in 146 B.C.

Summary

Masinissa saw himself as a great Numidian leader. Rome saw him as a client king who could help the

Romans gain control of Africa. Though they may have had different objectives, Rome and Masinissa worked hand in hand to subdue Carthage. Masinissa, indeed, was one of the most important and useful allies in all Roman history, and he gave major assistance to the process of Roman expansion. Although it might have seemed inevitable that the talented Masinissa would someday run afoul of his Roman patrons, there is no solid evidence of any important difference between Masinissa and Rome during the fifty years of their alliance.

Masinissa's long life, inveterate hatred of Carthage, and military skill make him a notable figure in ancient history. His enormous military achievements were complemented by his accomplishments in solidifying Numidia as a political and economic unity. By his death, Numidia was widely recognized as the preeminent realm in Mediterranean Africa. Masinissa can be seen as the first in a series of Berber leaders (the very word "nomad," according to one etymology, derives from "Numidian") to offer resistance to colonizers seeking to occupy North Africa. He is also one of the most renowned indigenous Africans to make an impact on the Greco-Roman world.

Bibliography

Armstrong, Donald. *The Reluctant Warriors*. New York: Crowell, 1966. Probably the liveliest, most informative source on Masinissa, though the author's Cold War perspective skews the general argument somewhat.

Asimov, Isaac. *The Roman Republic*. Boston: Houghton Mifflin, 1966. This entertaining general history is one of the few to perceive the individual genius of Masinissa and his role in Rome's rise.

Bagnall, Nigel. *The Punic Wars*. London: Hutchinson, 1990. A traditional military history that takes advantage of recent archaeological research. Useful for understanding the state of military practice in Masinissa's time.

Brett, Michael, with Elizabeth Fentress. *The Berbers*. Oxford and Cambridge, Mass.: Blackwell, 1996. An anthropological and historical look at the people whom Masinissa helped launch onto the historical stage.

Fentress, Elizabeth. *Numidia and the Roman Army: Social, Military, and Economic Aspects of the Frontier Zone*. Oxford: British Archaeological Review, 1979. This look at Numidia after the Roman conquest is also relevant to Masinissa's era and takes account of his achievement in agriculture.

Lancel, Serge. *Carthage: A History*. Translated by Antonio Nevill. Oxford and Cambridge, Mass.: Blackwell, 1995. This state-of-the-art history of the ancient region takes advantage of recent archaeological discoveries; also includes information on Punic culture.

Toynbee, Arnold. *Hannibal's Legacy*. London and New York: Oxford University Press, 1965. This encyclopedic and at times eccentric look at Rome in the ancient Mediterranean world shows a proper regard for Numidia's strategic importance.

Warmington, B. H. *Carthage*. Rev. ed. New York: Praeger, and London: Hale, 1969. A general history of Carthage that offers ten pages of detailed discussion of Masinissa's life and career. This book, frequently cited in subsequent scholarship, displays Masinissa in a North African context.

Wheeler, Sir Mortimer. *Roman Africa in Color*. London: Thames and Hudson, and New York: McGraw-Hill, 1966. This collection of photographs, with commentary by a famed archaeologist, gives a startlingly vivid picture of the physical and social environment in which Masinissa lived.

Nicholas Birns

MENANDER

Born: c. 342 B.C.; Athens, Greece
Died: c. 292 B.C.; Piraeus, Greece
Areas of Achievement: Theater and drama
Contribution: Noted for his careful plotting, his accurate depiction of middle-class society, and his sympathetic treatment of character, Menander is considered the finest writer of Greek New Comedy.

Early Life

Although there is some disagreement about the exact date of his birth, Menander was probably born in 342 in Athens, Greece. His father was Diopeithes of Cephisia.

Menander's family was evidently involved in both the social and the cultural life of Athens. His uncle Alexis was an important playwright in the tradition of Middle Comedy; he had some two hundred plays to his credit. Menander attended the lectures of Theophrastus, who had succeeded Aristotle as head of the Peripatetic school and who was also a notable writer, now known chiefly for his *Charactēres ethikōi* (c. 319 B.C.; *Characters*), sketches of human types, which undoubtedly influenced Menander and the other dramatists of New Comedy.

Like all Athenian men, between the ages of eighteen and twenty Menander served a year in the military. It was at that time that he became a close friend of Epicurus, whose philosophy was influential in Menander's works. Another of Menander's early friends was important in his later life: Demetrius Phalereus, a fellow student. When Menander was in his mid-twenties, Demetrius was appointed by the Macedonians as ruler of Athens. During the following decade, Demetrius constructed magnificent buildings in the city and drew the most brilliant and talented men of Athens to his court. Among them was Menander, who was already recognized as a playwright, having written his first work when he was nineteen or twenty.

The bust which has been identified as that of Menander suggests what an addition he would have been to the court of Demetrius. The classic features, well-defined profile, penetrating eyes, and strong jaw testify to strength of mind and character; the sensitive mouth and wavy hair soften the general impression. All in all, he was a strikingly handsome man.

When Demetrius fell, Menander is said to have been in some danger, and he was offered the protection of Ptolemy Soter if he would follow his friend Demetrius to Alexandria, Egypt. The playwright declined, however, as he also is said to have declined an invitation to Macedonia, and he spent the remainder of his life in Athens.

Life's Work

In somewhat more than thirty years, Menander wrote some one hundred comedies. Most of his work, however, has been lost. Until 1905, he was represented primarily by hundreds of lines quoted by other writers and by the four plays of Plautus and four others of Terence which were based on certain of his lost plays. Then, a fifth century A.D. papyrus book was discovered in Egypt; it contains one-third to one-half of three of Menander's plays, *Perikeiromenē* (314-310 B.C.; *The Girl Who Was Shorn*), *Epitrepontes* (after 304 B.C.; *The Arbitration*), and *Samia* (321-316 B.C.; *The Girl from Samos*). In 1958, another papyrus book was found in a private collection in Geneva; it holds not only a

complete play, *Dyskolos* (317 B.C.; *The Bad-Tempered Man*), but also half of *Aspis* (c. 314 B.C.; *The Shield*) and the almost complete text of *The Girl from Samos*.

Because so much of Menander's work is lost, and because the dating of those plays and fragments which have survived is very uncertain, it is difficult to analyze the playwright's development. It is known that his first work was written about 322 B.C. The only complete play which has survived, *The Bad-Tempered Man*, is an early one, performed in 317, which incidentally was the year that another of Menander's plays, now lost, won for him his first prize.

In *The Bad-Tempered Man* one can see the careful plot construction and the realistic but sympathetic treatment of characters for which Menander was noted. The title character of the play is Cnemon, a misanthrope, whose wife has left him because of his nasty temper and who lives alone with his daughter and a servant, while his virtuous stepson lives nearby. In the prologue to the play, the god Pan announces that he intends to punish Cnemon because he has offended against the principles Pan prizes, in particular good fellowship and love. It is not surprising, then, that this comedy, like Menander's other plays, must move toward suitable marriages, which symbolize reconciliation and which sometimes are accompanied by the reform of an older man who is angry, obstinate, or miserly. In this case, it must be admitted that the most interesting character, Cnemon, is not really reformed, but instead is forced into participating in the final marriage feast. Other typical Menander characters in *The Bad-Tempered Man* include the parasite who profits from his attachment to a rich young friend, a fussy chef who does not realize how stupid he really is, and various comic servants.

The Girl from Samos is based on an even more complicated plot, involving the births of two illegitimate babies, one to a poor girl, the other to a woman from Samos. When the Samian woman's baby dies, it is decided that she will pretend that the other is hers. The result is a series of misunderstandings as to who is making love to whom, who are the parents of the baby, and who is related to whom. This plot enables Menander to analyze relationships between children and their fathers, who can move from love to anger to compassion as their perceptions of the truth alter. At the end of the play, the baby's parentage is revealed, the lovers marry, and parents and children are reconciled.

In *The Girl Who Was Shorn*, too, there is a problem of identity, in this case that of twins who were separated in infancy, while in *The Shield* the confusion arises from the supposed deaths of two men, who naturally must be resurrected in the final section of the play.

Because they see a greater depth in *The Arbitration*, critics believe it to be a later play. The basis of the play is a serious situation: Pamphila was raped by a drunken reveler, and the baby to whom she later gave birth was abandoned. When she married, she concealed the truth from her young husband, and when he learned from a servant about her past, he rejected her and threw himself into a dissolute life. At this point, the play begins. As single-minded as a tragic heroine, Pamphila remains faithful to her husband throughout the play, and though there are comic scenes, such as that in which a charcoal burner argues like a lawyer, and deliberate deception, masterminded by clever slaves, finally the husband is won by his wife's nobility. The baby reappears and is revealed to be the child of Pamphila and her husband, who did not remember raping her. At that point, presented with a grandchild, even Pamphila's father is happy.

Although *The Arbitration* has many of the elements of the other plays, such as the complex plot, the love intrigue, and the stock comic characters, the profound theme elevates it above the other surviving plays of Menander and suggests the basis of his high reputation. In *The Arbitration* can be seen not only the comic confusion which was the essence of New Comedy but also the compassionate treatment of human problems for which Menander was particularly admired.

In his early fifties, Menander drowned while swimming in the harbor of Piraeus, the seaport near Athens. According to Plutarch, Menander died at the height of his dramatic powers. It is unfortunate that his literary career lasted only slightly more than thirty years and that almost all of his plays have been lost. All that remains is a name, a reputation, and an influence.

Summary

In his plot elements and stock characters Menander was probably similar to many of the other playwrights of New Comedy; his superior reputation rests upon the fact that he rejected mere Dionysian horseplay for the presentation of a real moral drama. In this may be seen the influence of his friend

Epicurus. In his penetration of character, he undoubtedly followed the tragedian Euripides.

Unfortunately, audiences of Menander's own time seem to have been less than enthusiastic about his kind of play, preferring the bawdy productions of his rivals. Of his one hundred plays, only eight won the coveted prize for comedy. After his death, however, his reputation rose rapidly. Among the Romans he was highly valued. Ovid admired him; Plutarch ranked him above Aristophanes, and others placed him just below Homer. During the period of the empire, his philosophical maxims were frequently quoted and even collected.

Menander's greatest influence, however, came through the Roman playwrights Plautus and Terence, who adapted and imitated his works, devising their own complex plots, dramatizing Roman everyday life as Menander had the life of his own people, and working toward resolutions in which folly is exposed and lovers united. Through Plautus and Terence, he survived to help establish the pattern of Renaissance drama. Menander's influence can be seen in the exaggeratedly humorous characters of Ben Jonson and the romantic lovers of William Shakespeare. Finally, his satire set in ordinary society provided the basis of the comedy of manners genre. Even though most of his work has been lost for centuries, Menander's comic vision persists in the plays of his successors.

Bibliography

Bieber, Margarete. *The History of the Greek and Roman Theater*. Rev. ed. Princeton, N.J.: Princeton University Press, and London: Oxford University Press, 1961. A lavishly illustrated volume whose text is somewhat confusing because it seems to proceed from one statue or vase to another rather than in the ordinary chronological order. Used with a more conventional history, however, extremely interesting, both for its text and for photographs of sculptures—for example, those depicting Menander at different ages.

Dover, K. J., ed. *Ancient Greek Literature*. Oxford and New York: Oxford University Press, 1980. A concise and accurate treatment of the subject. For a full understanding of Menander's place in Greek literature, it would be helpful to read the entire book, although Menander is specifically treated in the chapter headed "Comedy."

Goldberg, Sander M. *The Making of Menander's Comedy*. Berkeley: University of California Press, and London: Athlone, 1980. An outstanding scholarly discussion of Menander's work. Explains clearly his relation to Old and Middle Comedy, delineates the problems of scholarship, and then proceeds to a lucid analysis of each of the surviving works.

Menander. Introduction to *Menander: The Principal Fragments*. Translated by Francis G. Allinson. London: Heinemann, and New York: Putnam, 1921. This brief but extremely scholarly introductory essay includes a clear description of Menander's historical placement, concise comments about the playwright's use of prologue, plot, and character, and even a statement about his Greek style. Contains some material not generally available.

Pickard-Cambridge, Arthur W. *The Dramatic Festivals of Athens*. 2d ed. Oxford: Clarendon Press, 1968; New York: Oxford University Press, 1988. The authoritative account of the production of Greek drama, ranging from the descriptions of the various festivals themselves to detailed explanations of acting style, costuming, and music, even including an analysis of the composition and character of the audience. Well illustrated.

Reinhold, Meyer. *Classical Drama: Greek and Roman*. Woodbury, N.Y.: Barron's Educational Series, 1959. In outline form, an excellent guide to its subject. Chapters 5 through 11, dealing with Euripides, Old, Middle, and New Comedy, and Menander's Roman successors, are particularly recommended. Contains plot summaries, with hypothetical suggestions as to missing elements, of four of Menander's plays. With glossary and bibliography.

Sandbach, F. H. *The Comic Theatre of Greece and Rome*. New York: Norton, and London: Chatto and Windus, 1977. An excellent study of comedy from Aristophanes to Terence, with a particularly illuminating discussion of Menander's themes, in the light of the newly discovered texts. Well written. Glossary and selected bibliography included.

Rosemary M. Canfield-Reisman

MENANDER

Born: c. 210 B.C.; probably Kalasi, Afghanistan
Died: c. 135 B.C.; probably in northwest India
Areas of Achievement: Government and religion
Contribution: Menander extended the Greco-Bactrian domains in India more than any other ruler. He became a legendary figure as a great patron of Buddhism in the Pali book the *Milindapanha.*

Early Life

Menander (not to be confused with the more famous Greek dramatist of the same name) was born somewhere in the fertile area to the south of the Paropamisadae or present Hindu Kush Mountains of Afghanistan. The only reference to this location is in the semilegendary *Milindapañha* (first or second century A.D.), which says that he was born in a village called Kalasi near Alasanda, some two hundred *yojanas* (about eighteen miles) from the town of Sāgala (probably Sialkot in the Punjab). The Alasanda refers to the Alexandria in Afghanistan and not to the one in Egypt. No evidence exists on the question of whether Menander was an aristocrat or a commoner or of royal lineage. All surmises about the life of Menander are based on his coins, for information in Greek sources is very sparse indeed. All that remains of a more extensive history of the east by Apollodorus of Artemita are two sentences in Strabo's *Geography* (c. first century A.D.) that the Bactrian Greeks, especially Menander, overthrew more peoples in India than did Alexander. Strabo is dubious that Menander "really crossed the Hypanis River [Beas] toward the east and went as far as the Isamos [Imaus, or Jumna River?]." Plutarch in his *Ethica* (first century A.D.; also known as *Moralia*) calls Menander a king of Bactria who ruled with equity and who died in camp, and after his death, memorials were raised over his ashes. If Menander became a convert to Buddhism, this could mean that Buddhist stupas, covering reliquaries, were built over his remains, which were divided among different sites. The final classical source which mentions Menander, Pompeius Trogus, simply calls him a king of India together with Apollodotus.

The Pali *Milindapañha*, a series of questions put to a Buddhist sage by King Milinda, along with their answers, contains no historical data save those about Menander's birth, which may be legend, as well as moral precepts beloved to Buddhists. Another text of the period, the *Vāyū Purāna*,

only mentions him as a Greek king in India. The last reference to Menander occurs in an inscription on a relic casket dedicated in the reign of Mahārāja Minedra (Menander), which is not informative. Modern students are left with the coins, the styles and legends of which have provided the basis of hypothetical reconstructions of the life of Menander. That he was married to a certain Queen Agathocleia, daughter of Demetrius, is suggested by W. W. Tarn on the basis of the coin style of Agathocleia, especially the figure of Pallas Athena, the favored deity of Menander's coins on the reverse, and the similarity in portraits between goddess and queen. The usual epithet on Menander's coins was the Greek word *soter* (savior), but what he saved, if anything, is unknown.

From the great number of extant coins of Menander and the widespread location of find spots, one may surmise that he had a fairly long rule over a kingdom extending from the Hindu Kush Mountains into the present-day United Provinces of north India. His rule over Mathura and especially Pātaliputra on the borders of Bengal is uncertain and disputed, although the former is more likely than the latter. in any case, he obviously was that Greek king of India who made the greatest impression on the Indians, especially the Buddhists.

Life's Work

One of the two achievements which have earned for Menander a place in history books was the great extension of Greco-Bactrian rule in India, to the extent that his rule was probably the high point of Greek rule on the subcontinent. The second and equally significant factor in the life of Menander was his role in Buddhist legend. The *Milindapañha* was not popular only among Indians; a Chinese translation exists as well as the Pali version. Although it is unproven whether Menander became a convert, and there is no tradition that he propagated Buddhism as Aśoka the Great and Kanishka are supposed to have done, he holds an eminent position as an enlightened Buddhist ruler in their tradition. Whether he was considered by his Indian subjects a Chakravartin, a supreme Buddhist ruler who conquered lands by persuasion and justice rather than by the sword, is unknown. If Plutarch's statement that memorials were raised over his ashes can be interpreted as meaning Buddhist stupas containing some part or ashes of him, then it is plausible that Menander was a Buddhist. The fact that legends did grow up about him at least indicates his importance in Buddhist circles.

The suggestion of Tarn that the Pali book was modeled after a Greek original which might have had the title "Questions of Menander" is intriguing. It would imply that the Greek presence in India was neither simply a short-lived foreign military occupation nor a diluted, mixed Iranian-Indian culture with a thin Hellenistic veneer, but that it did have a strong, purely Greek content. Furthermore, that content was responsible for the introduction into India of Greek genres of literature and philosophical and other ideas, as well as the canons of Greek art, which were to flower later under the sobriquet of Gandharan art.

Summary

It may be argued not only that Menander was responsible for extending Greek arms on the Indian subcontinent to the fullest extent but also that he was much more than a conqueror. Since he has become a legend in Buddhist tradition and is praised by Plutarch as a just king, it may be further surmised that under his rule, Greek philosophy and culture met and influenced Indian civilization, which in the middle of the second century was dominated by Buddhism. Whether a hypothetical Greek "Questions of Menander" influenced not only the Buddhists in India but also Hellenistic literature in Alexandria, Egypt, and elsewhere, as Tarn suggests, is even more speculative. The flowering of Gandharan art in the second century A.D., when Hellenistic origins are overwhelmingly indicated, probably owed as much to the legacy of Menander and his many successors as it did to the influence of Roman provincial art forms. Thus, Hellenism in India and Central Asia may owe much more than is now known to Menander and his legacy.

Bibliography

Bivar, A. D. H. "The Sequence of Menander's Drachmae." *Journal of the Royal Asiatic Society*, 1970: 128-129. A basic work on the coins of Menander's reign, with historical interpretations of their presence in certain locations.

Frye, Richard N. *The Ancient History of Iran*. Munich: Verlag C. H. Beck, 1984. A summary of the milieu and events in which the life and activities of Menander may be placed.

Majumdar, N. G. "The Bajaur Casket of the Reign of Menander." *Epigraphica Indica* 24 (1937): 1-8. An analysis of the only extant inscription of Menander's reign; includes translation and commentary.

Narain, A. K. *The Indo-Greeks*. Oxford: Clarendon Press, 1957. A response to Tarn's book (below) concentrating on translations of Chinese and Indian sources. Written from the Indian perspective.

Tarn, W. W. *The Greeks in Bactria and India*. 2d ed. Cambridge: Cambridge University Press, 1951. The basic study on Menander. Includes translations and analyses of classical sources. Highly speculative, but fascinating reading.

Richard N. Frye

MENCIUS
Meng-tzu

Born: c. 372 B.C.; Tsou, China
Died: c. 289 B.C.; China
Area of Achievement: Philosophy
Contribution: Through a lifetime of reflection, Mencius clarified and expanded the wisdom embodied in Confucius' *Analects*, rendering Confucian ideas more accessible. His *Meng-tzu* eclipsed other interpretations of Confucius and gained acceptance as the orthodox version of Confucian thought.

Early Life

Mencius was born probably about 372 B.C. in the small principality of Tsou in northeastern China, not far from the birthplace of Confucius, whose work Mencius spent his life interpreting. Knowledge of Mencius' early life is scarce. What evidence exists must be extracted from his own writing, most notably the *Meng-tzu* (first transcribed in the early third century B.C.), although many biographical observations are found in the great historian Ssu-ma Ch'ien's *Shin chi* (c. 90 B.C.), a large work which has been translated in part many times and is best known by its original title.

Mencius was probably a member of the noble Meng family, whose home, like that of Confucius, was in the city-state of Lu, in what is now southwestern Shantung Province. Certainly Mencius' education was one that was common to the aristocracy, for he was thoroughly familiar with both the classical *Shih ching* (c. 500 B.C.; *Book of Odes*, 1950) and the *Shu ching* (c. 626 B.C.; *Book of Documents*, 1950), which together provided the fundamentals of his classical training. Moreover, he had a masterly grasp of Confucius' work and quoted it frequently, leading to the assumption that he studied in a Confucian school, purportedly under the tutelage of Confucius' grandson, who was himself a man of ministerial rank in the central state of Wei.

Known as Meng-tzu to his students, Mencius assumed the role of teacher early in his life and never abandoned it. Rejecting material well-being and position as ends in themselves, he, like many Confucians, nevertheless aspired to hold office inside one of the courts of the Chinese states. He did indeed become a councillor and later the Minister of State in Wei. In such positions, he tutored students, not all of them noble, in classical works: the dynastic hymns and ballads anthologized in the *Book of Odes* and state papers from archives (from 1000 to 700 B.C.) which formed the *Book of Documents*. These were works from which, by the end of the second century B.C., Confucian precepts developed. During these early years of observation and teaching, Mencius gained disciples, furthered his interpretations of Confucius, and enjoyed considerable renown in many parts of China.

Life's Work

Meng-tzu was Mencius' principal work. It appeared late in his life. Had it incorporated less wisdom than his many years of diverse experiences and reflections allowed, or a less lengthy refinement of Confucius' thoughts, it would not be likely to rank as one of the greatest philosophical and literary works of the ancient world.

Mencius garnered experience through his wanderings and temporary lodgments in various Chinese courts and kingdoms. He was fortunate to live in an age when, despite continuous political turmoil, dynastic rivalries, and incessant warfare, high levels of civility prevailed in aristocratic circles. Teacher-scholars, as a consequence, were readily hosted—that is, effectively subsidized—by princely families eager to advance their children's education and to instruct and invigorate themselves through conversation with learned men.

Some of Mencius' temporary affiliations can be dated. Between 323 and 319, Mencius was installed at the court of King Hui of Liang, in what is now China's Szechwan Province. He moved eastward about 318 to join the ruler of the state of Ch'i, King Hsuan. Prior to his sojourn to Liang (although the dates are conjectural), Mencius visited and conversed with princes, rulers, ministers, and students in several states: Lu, Wei, Ch'i, and Song.

Mencius' journeyings were not feckless. They related directly to his philosophical and historical perceptions. Like Confucius, Mencius believed that he lived in a time of troubles in which—amid rival feudatories and warring states, divided and misruled—China was in decline. Also like Confucius, Mencius looked back fondly on what he thought had been the halcyon days of Chinese government and civilization under the mythical kings (2700 B.C.-770 B.C.), when a unified China had been governed harmoniously.

Drawing on Chinese legends incorporated into literary sources familiar to him from the *Hsia* and the Shang and Chou dynasties, Mencius concluded that the ideal governments of these earlier days had been the work of hero kings—Yao, Shun, and Yu— whose successors had organized themselves into dynasties. These were the Sage kings, who, like kings Wen and Wu of the Chou family, had been responsible for China's former greatness. Their dissolute successors, however, such as the "bad" kings of the *Hsia* and the Shang Dynasty, were equally responsible for the subsequent debasement of the Sage kings' remarkable achievements and erosion of their legacy.

For Mencius, a vital part of this legacy was the concept of the Mandate of Heaven. It was an idea that he ascribed to the early Chou kings, who justified their authority by it. These kings asserted that they had received the mandate directly from the deity, who designated Chou rulers Sons of Heaven, viceroys of Heaven. Effectively, that charged them with the responsibilities of being the deity's fief holders. The Chou kings, in turn, proceeded to impose lesser feudal obligations on their own fief holders and subjects. In Mencius' view, this arrangement was more than merely an arbitrary justification for Chou authority; it was also a recognition of authority higher than man's. Because the Mandate of Heaven was not allocated in perpetuity, it was essentially a lease that was operative during good behavior. When rulers lost virtue and thereby violated the mandate, the punishment of Heaven descended upon them. Their subjects, their vassals, were constrained to replace them. It was on this basis, as Mencius knew, that the Chou kings had successfully reigned for four centuries.

Equally important in this hierarchical scheme developed around the Chou conception of the Mandate of Heaven, of Sage kings functioning in response to it, were the roles of Sage ministers. It was these ministers whom Mencius credited with the rise and harmonious rule of the Sage kings. In times when the Mandate of Heaven had obviously been forgotten or ignored, Mencius wished not only that this ideal past would be restored but also that his presence at various courts would allow him to identify, assist, and guide potential Sage kings, fulfilling the role of Sage minister himself or through his disciples.

King Hsuan of Ch'i was one of the rulers at whose court he served and for whom he envisioned greatness as the Ideal King. Hsuan, however, appeared lacking in will. King Hui of Liang also showed some promise, but Mencius despaired of Lui when he revealed his desire to rule the world by force. Briefly, Mencius saw potential in the king of T'eng, who ruled a small principality that, nevertheless, afforded a sufficient stage for a True King. That potential also went unrealized. To critics who charged that Mencius was simply unperceptive, his reply was that such rulers possessed ample ability but had not availed themselves of his services. After these encounters, despairing, he returned home to kindle his belief in the Ideal King in the hearts of his disciples.

The basis for Mencius' initial optimism lay in his interpretation of China's history, for it reassured him that great kings had appeared in cycles of about five hundred years. Half a millennium lay between the reign of T'ang, founder of the Shang Dynasty (c. 1384-1122 B.C.), and Wu, first ruler of the great Chou Dynasty (1122-221 B.C.). Consequently Heaven's dispatch of another Sage king, according to Mencius, was overdue. In this interim and in expectation of the Sage king's appearance, men such as himself—"Heavenly instruments"— had divine commissions to maintain the ideal.

There is no evidence that Mencius, any more than Confucius, was successful in the realization of such dreams. Although Mencius served briefly as a councillor, and although his knowledge was profound as well as wide-ranging, he revealed more disdain for than interest in (or understanding of) practical politics in his own highly politicized environment. Furthermore, areas of intellection such as religion, ethics, and philosophy were densely packed with rivals. A number of these, such as Micius the utilitarian or Yang Chu the hedonist, enjoyed greater recognition and higher status than he did. Nor was Mencius ranked among the leading intellectuals or scholars of his day who were inducted into the membership of the famous Chi-Hsia Academy.

Later generations would honor him, but in his own time Mencius was a relatively obscure, evangelizing teacher whose views were merely tolerated, a pedagogue who never penetrated beyond the fringes of power, a man without a substantial following. These conditions help explain his occasional haughtiness, manipulative argumentation, and assertive promulgation of Confucianism. Nevertheless, not until two centuries after his death did Confucian principles gain significant influence.

Thus, Mencius' work can be examined for its intrinsic merit, outside the context of his own lifetime. He was, foremost, a devoted follower of Confucius. As such, he never wavered in the belief that it was not enough to be virtuous; men also had to model themselves after the Sage kings. Antiquity represented the epitome of good conduct, good government, and general harmony. Consequently, the ways of old—or his interpretations of them—had to be accepted or rejected completely.

This position inevitably raised the issue of how the Sages of yesteryear had become, both as men and as governors, such ideal models. Had such gifts been divinely bestowed? Mencius believed that they were like all men. This response led him therefore into an elaboration of the central tenets of his philosophy, into an embellishment of Confucius, and ultimately into formulating his major contribution to thought.

Whereas Confucius left only one equivocal observation on human nature, Mencius—probably because the contention of his time demanded it—placed the essence of human nature at the center of his work. Discussions of humanity (jen) and of justice (yi) accordingly became his preoccupations, and, subsequently, because of Mencius, became the focus of Chinese philosophy.

In defining humanity, he declared unequivocally that all men were born sharing the same human nature and that human nature is good. Mencius sought to demonstrate this belief through his maxims and parables: All men were endowed with sympathy for those whose lives were at risk or who had suffered great misfortune; all men felt best when they were instinctively being their best. Thus, all men who cultivated jen were capable of indefinite perfectibility; they were capable of becoming Sages. Furthermore, men would find jen irresistible, for it nullified the menaces of brute physical force (pa). Writing with fewer logical inhibitions than had been displayed by Confucius, Mencius asserted that all things were complete within every man: Everyone, in microcosm, embodied the essences of everything: the macrocosm.

Consequently, men who knew their own nature also knew Heaven. In asserting this, wittingly or not, Mencius again went beyond Confucius, for knowing oneself first in order to know everything suggested meditative introspection, whereas Confucius had disparaged meditation and insisted on the superiority of observation and the use of the critical faculty. Mencius stressed the real incentives for the cultivation of one's humanity. Those who did so enjoyed wisdom, honor, and felicity. When such men became kings, the state was harmoniously governed and prospered. In turn, such kings won over the allegiance of the world—which to Mencius, as to all Chinese, meant China. Jen therefore also afforded men prestige and moral authority that constituted power (te) far greater than any physical force.

Mencius was all too aware of the extent to which his everyday world indicated just the opposite, that is, the appalling conditions men had created for themselves. He was also aware of misapplications of force, either as a result of these problems or as a result of attempts to resolve them. Yet to Mencius, the failure to cultivate one's humanity lay at the root of these difficulties. He was not naïve about some of the causes of inhumanity. Poverty and the misery of men's environments, he conceded, often left little chance for cultivating one's humanity, but that lent urgency to the search for a Sage king who could mitigate or eradicate these conditions. He was also aware that men's appetites, as well as the conditions in which they lived, left little to differentiate them from other animals. Yet, the difference that did exist was a vital one: namely, their ability to think with their hearts.

Justice (yi) was a concomitant to Mencius' concept of humanity and was also central to his teaching. By justice, Mencius meant not only doing the right thing but also seeing that others received their rights. Clearly the "right things" consisted in part of rituals and formal codes of manners and of traditional civilities. They also embraced rights which were not necessarily embodied in law: the right of peasants to gather firewood in the forests, the right to subsistence in old age, and the right to expect civilities and to live according to traditional codes of behavior. If feeling distress for the suffering of others was, according to Mencius, the first sign of humanity, then feelings of shame and disgrace were the first signs of justice.

Mencius spent his lifetime forming his maxims and parables to illustrate what humanity and justice meant to him—or what he believed they should mean to all men. Appropriately for a teacher, he provoked more questions than he answered; he never arrived at his goal, nor did his disciples. He died about 289, probably near his place of birth on the Shantung Peninsula.

Summary

A devoted Confucian, Mencius expanded and clarified Confucius' *Lun-yü* (late sixth or early fifth century B.C.; *Analects*) and the principles of his master as they were being taught and debated a century after Confucius' death. Mencius, however, went beyond Confucius by placing human nature and his belief in its essential goodness at the center of philosophical discussion. Officially ranked a Sage, he stands among the world's most respected literary and philosophical geniuses.

Bibliography

Creel, H. G. *Chinese Thought from Confucius to Mao Tse-tung*. Chicago: University of Chicago Press, 1953; London: Eyre and Spottiswoode, 1954. A very informed, bright, readable work, with a brief bibliography and selected readings. Includes a useful index.

Legge, James, trans. *The Chinese Classics*. 7 vols. Rev. ed. Oxford: Clarendon Press, 1895. The standard scholarly translation of Mencius, this set includes the works of Mencius in volume 2. With fine notes and an index.

Mencius. *Mencius*. Translated by W. A. C. H. Dobson. London: Oxford University Press, 1963; Buffalo: University of Toronto Press, 1974. Splendidly translated and arranged for general readers. Mencius' thoughts are reordered for coherence. A fine introduction is followed throughout by excellent annotations. Includes thorough notes, which more than compensate for lack of a glossary or index.

Mencius. *Mencius*. Translated by D. C. Lau. London: Penguin Books, 1970. Contains an interesting but dense introduction addressing the problems of dating events in Mencius' life. Five very informative appendices. With useful notes, glossary, and index.

Mote, Frederick W. *Intellectual Foundations of China*. 2d ed. New York: Knopf, 1989. Brief but superb for placing Mencius in context. These are brilliant, reflective, and well-crafted scholarly essays by a leading sinologist. Contains a select bibliography and an index.

Richards, I. A. *Mencius on the Mind: Experiments in Multiple Definition*. London: Kegan Paul, and New York: Harcourt, 1932. Richards concentrates on Chinese modes of meaning as revealed in Mencius. The exploration is designed to see if beneath linguistic barriers there is material for comparative understanding. Thus, though ranking Mencius among the world's great thinkers, Richards deals critically with Mencius' methods of argument.

Shun, Kwong-loi. *Mencius and Early Chinese Thought*. Stanford, Calif.: Stanford University Press, 1997. The book systematically analyzes the concepts of Mencius' ethics. His ethics are related to the major philosophical schools in early China, particularly to Confucianism (to which Mencius proclaimed himself to belong) and Mohism (which formed the major intellectual challenge to his thought).

Waley, Arthur. *Three Ways of Thought in Ancient China*. London: Allen and Unwin, 1939; New York: Macmillan, 1940. Fine basic intellectual history which for years has been standard among scholars. Readable, informative, and reflective. Contains a brief bibliography and a useful glossary and index.

Clifton K. Yearley
Kerrie L. MacPherson

MENES

Born: c. 3100 B.C.; Thinis, Egypt
Died: c. 3000 B.C.; Memphis, Egypt
Area of Achievement: Government and politics; pharaohs
Contribution: Menes is described in classical Greek and Roman sources and late-period Egyptian king lists as the ruler who was responsible for the unification of Egypt, the building of the capital city of Memphis, and the founding of the First Dynasty of Egypt.

Early Life
Virtually nothing is known about the early life of Menes, since neither the extant classical sources nor the Pharaonic period Egyptian sources make any mention about his formative period.

Life's Work
The details of Menes' life and work are few, scattered, and somewhat contradictory in some details. By classical times (c. 500 B.C.) Menes had been transformed into a culture hero whose life and accomplishments were embellished with semimythical anecdotes. He is thus at most a quasihistorical figure. According to the Egyptian historian Manetho (c. 300 B.C.), Menes, who came from the town of Thinis, about three hundred miles south of Cairo, was the first human ruler in Egypt after dynasties of demigods had ruled. He became the founder of the Egyptian state by uniting Upper and Lower Egypt; he was regarded as the first lawgiver and the leader who brought civilization to Egypt. The Greek historian Herodotus (c. 484-425 B.C.) adds that Egyptian priests told him that Min (Menes) drained the plain of Memphis by damming up the Nile, laying the foundation for Egypt's first capital.

If Menes was indeed Egypt's first unifier, then Memphis was a prime location for a capital, as it was centered between Upper and Lower Egypt. According to Manetho, Menes ruled for about sixty years (although a variant text states a mere thirty years) and was the founder of the First Dynasty of Egypt, which lasted for more than 250 years. In addition, he "made a foreign expedition and won renown." The Greek historian Diodorus of Sicily (c. 60 B.C.) adds the anecdotal statement that Menas (Menes) was pursued by his own dogs into the Lake of Moeris and was carried off by a crocodile that safely ferried him to the other river bank. In gratitude, he founded the City of Crocodiles and demanded that the locals worship them as gods. Diodorus adds that Menes built his tomb there, a four-sided pyramid (although pyramids are not attested in Egypt until centuries later). Menes is also said by Diodorus to have built a labyrinth (in another section, however, he attributes this to a king named Mendes). Manetho states that Menes was carried off by a hippopotamus and died.

Thus, the classical sources concerning Menes are in agreement concerning his position as the first king of Egypt and the founder of Memphis and the First Dynasty. The Pharaonic period Egyptian records, however, contradict the classical sources in many places. Menes is not listed as the first nondivine king and as the unifier of Egypt until king lists from the time of Thutmosis III of the Eighteenth Dynasty of the New Kingdom (c. 1435 B.C.). The Karnak list of kings commences with Menes and lists all of Egypt's monarchs who ruled over the united kingdom (omitting any kings from the Intermediate periods) down to Thutmosis III. Menes' preeminence is supported by the Turin Canon, or king list, and by a list of sixty-seven kings found inscribed on walls of a temple of Sety I at Abydos (1305-1290 B.C.). Moreover, a palette from the Nineteenth Dynasty mentions the "Ptah of Menes," presumably a reference to a cult of the Egyptian god Ptah (the god of Menes). Interestingly, the Turin Canon has the name of Meni (Menes) twice, first with a human determinative before the name and again with a divine determinative. The purpose for this repetition is unknown. However, another king list inscribed in the tomb of a scribe at Saqqara (c. 1300 B.C.) omits mention of Menes and the first five kings of the First Dynasty.

It is not certain whether the New Kingdom lists reflect some documentary material that went back to an earlier time or whether they were constructed in conformity with ideas in vogue during their own period. For example, the fragmentary Palermo Stone, a Fifth Dynasty (c. 2495-2345 B.C.) annals text, does not list Menes. It does, however, list monarchs who ruled before the unification, although the text is severely fragmented for the earliest periods. In fact, it implies that there was a unification before the First Dynasty that broke down and thus had to be reinstated.

The issue becomes further complicated when one investigates the material remains from the Predynastic and Protodynastic (First and Second Dynasty) periods. An ivory plaque from the mastaba tomb of Neithhotep at Naqada bears the name of Men (assumed to be Menes) and King Aha (likely the husband of Neithhotep). The relationship of these two is not immediately apparent. Was Menes the same person as Aha, or his father? Is one of the names a Horus name (the name a monarch took as the incarnation of the god Horus)? Some kings took as many as five different throne names. In fact, the royal tombs have different names than do the later king lists for monarchs of the first two dynasties, a fact attributed to the myriad names for the king. The name "Min," it has been argued, appears to be the Nebti name, the second name for the Egyptian king in his role as ruler over both parts of Egypt. A seal impression found at the Umm el-Qa'ab cemetery at Abydos in 1985 places Aha as the second king of the First Dynasty. The first king in this list is Narmer, presumably the father of Aha. He has also been associated with the Nebti name "Min" on jar sealings at Abydos. Thus, Min (Menes) is associated with both of these kings.

Narmer is well known from a mudstone ceremonial palette and a limestone macehead, both of which were excavated at Hierakonopolis in Upper Egypt. Both were found in poor archaeological contexts; the macehead seems to have been among a group of Predynastic items buried beneath the floor of the Hierakonopolis temple complex dated to the Old Kingdom (c. 2686-2181 B.C.), and the palette was found a few meters away. Both items have been dated stylistically to the period of the First Dynasty (c. 3100-2950 B.C.). Though the macehead is severely fragmented and the palette in good condition, both are carved with reliefs that feature Narmer. On one side, he is shown with the white crown of Upper Egypt, striking a foreigner; on the other side, he is depicted with the red crown of Lower Egypt, taking his place in a procession that is moving toward a group of decapitated prisoners. The palette has been traditionally viewed as a memorial commemorating military successes over foreigners (usually identified as Libyans and Northern Egyptians). However, recent studies have argued that the palette is a iconographic depiction of summaries of victories that occurred over the past year. If so, the palette was a votive object offered to the temple and may not express any particular historical reality.

The issue is still further complicated by the existence of a fragmentary limestone macehead containing an inscription of a king wearing the crown of Upper Egypt and identified as King "Scorpion." Like the Narmer objects, it was found at Hierakonopolis in a poor archaeological context, although it also appears to date stylistically to the Predynastic period. The king is shown excavating a ceremonial irrigation canal with the help of some subjects. More recently, a tomb at Umm el-Qa'ab at Abydos was excavated that contained many pieces of Predynastic pottery, many of which bore the scorpion hieroglyph. It is unclear whether these two items depict the same king, and his possible relationship to Menes is also uncertain.

Summary

In sum, it is impossible to identify Menes with any particular ruler from Egypt's Early Dynastic period. Some scholars, however, have argued that Menes may later have become a name given to the unifier or unifiers of Egypt and thus may represent a composite of Narmer, Aha, and perhaps King Scorpion. Conversely, there are those who argue for identifying him either with Narmer or with Aha because of Menes' association with these monarchs in various inscriptions. No doubt the later classical tradition has become garbled, since mistaken readings of the earliest cursive form of the Egyptian script were canonized by later dynasties.

Furthermore, the work of Manetho, the primary historian of ancient Egypt, is no longer extant and is known only from isolated statements in the writings of the Jewish historian Josephus (A.D. 37-100). An epitome of Manetho's work was made at an early date in the form of lists of dynasties and kingdoms, with short notes on kings and events. This was preserved in part primarily by the early Christian writers Africanus and Eusebius. The original makeup of Manetho's *Aegyptica*, however, also appears to have included narratives. If ever recovered, the *Aegyptica* may hold the key to discovering the identity of Menes.

Bibliography

Allen, J. P. "Menes the Memphite." *Göttinger Miszellen* 126 (1992): 19-22. A discussion of the difficulty of identifying Menes with any Predynastic or Protodydnastic ruler found in the ancient Egyptian record.

Arkell, A. J. "Was King Scorpion Menes?" *Antiquity* 46 (1963): 221-222. Brief discussion of King Scorpion and his possible identification as Menes.

Emery, W. B. *Archaic Egypt*. London: Penguin Books, 1961. Though dated, this work contains one of the most detailed discussions in English concerning the problem of the identification of Menes.

Foti, L. "Menes in Diodorus 1.89." *Oikumene* 2 (1978) 113-126. Contains a detailed account of the reign of Menes found in the work of Diodorus of Sicily, a classical writer of the first century B.C.

Kemp, B. "Abydos and the Tombs of the First Dynasty." *Journal of Egyptian Archaeology* 52 (1966): 13-22. A survey of the information at hand concerning the earliest royal house in Egypt and the difficulty in locating Menes in the archaeological record.

———. "The Egyptian First Dynasty Royal Cemetery." *Antiquity* 41 (1967): 22-32. A continuation of the aforementioned article by Kemp.

Lorton, David. "Why Menes?" *Varia Aegyptiaca* 3 (1987): 33-38. A discussion the placement and identification of Menes in Egyptian history.

Manetho. *Manetho*. W. G. Waddell, ed. and trans. Cambridge, Mass.: Harvard University Press, and London: Heinemann, 1940. A compilation of the extant fragments of the Egyptian historian Manetho and the relevant excerpts concerning Menes.

Millet, N. "The Narmer Macehead and Related Objects." *Journal of the American Research Center in Egypt* 27 (1991): 53-59. A recent evaluation of the evidence for Narmer's victories over Lower Egypt and Lybia. Millet argues that the Narmer palette and macehead were votive objects that have little historical value.

Redford, D. *Pharaonic King-Lists, Annals, and Day-Books: A Contribution to the Study of the Egyptian Sense of History*. Mississauga, Ontario: Benben Publications, 1986. A critical analysis of the historical value of Egyptian king lists, with a number of discussions of Menes and his identification.

Mark W. Chavalas

VALERIA MESSALLINA

Born: c. A.D. 20; probably Rome
Died: A.D.48; Rome
Area of Achievement: Government and politics
Contribution: Empress of Rome for more than seven years, Valeria Messallina was intimately involved in the highest level of Roman politics.

Early Life

Nothing is known of Valeria Messallina's childhood. By the time she is first mentioned in historical sources, she had already married the Emperor Claudius (born 10 B.C.); since their daughter Octavia was born in 40, the marriage is generally assigned to 39. The much older Claudius (born 10 B.C.) had three children by two earlier wives.

The Valerii Messallae (sometimes spelled with one "l") were among the most illustrious families of Rome, one of the five *gentes maiores*—the inner circle of the patrician elite. Prominent through the early Republic, they faded into obscurity for more than a century after 164 B.C.. An overview of the complicated family tree reveals the standing of the Valerii from the late Republic onward and goes far to explain her marriage to Claudius. Members of the high nobility often married for reasons of political advantage. This is true even of Claudius, who for fifty years was dismissed as an embarrassment to the imperial house and kept largely out of public view.

Life's Work

Messallina presents major difficulties to students, as the ancient sources are uniformly extremely hostile. According to them, her only positive accomplishment was to produce two children for Claudius: Octavia and her brother Britannicus, born in 42. According to the Roman writers, Messallina was addicted to sex and was utterly without principle, and she worked in tandem with the imperial freedmen to manipulate her imperial husband. Her scandalous life was known to everyone but Claudius. She had numerous lovers, participated in frequent orgies in the palace (on occasion compelling senators to watch their wives participate), destroyed several prominent politicians (some for refusing to have sex with her), and finally took reckless advantage of Claudius' absence to divorce him and marry her latest lover, Gaius Silius. Saved by the decisive action of the freedman Narcissus, Claudius ordered Messallina's death.

She fled to her mother's gardens but lacked the courage to commit suicide and was executed by a soldier.

There are good reasons to disbelieve accounts that characterize Messallina as a world-class nymphomaniac. The writers all lived at least two generations later and doubtless utilized stories that had grown in frequent retelling. Further, these writers were all men, and the most important of them, Tacitus, was a senator. More important, they hated women who refused to conform to Roman expectations. Women were not allowed to participate in politics; no ancient state allowed women to hold office, command troops, or vote. Men were supposed to discipline their womenfolk. In his *Annals*, Tacitus discredited individual emperors, the imperial families, and the entire imperial system; all had reduced the Senate to subservience.

In this light, the accounts of Messallina are part of a larger drama involving the ferocious females of the ruling family: Augustus' wife Livia and her allies Urgulania and Munatia Plancina; Augustus' daughter Julia; and Julia's daughters, Julia the younger and Agrippina major. The *Annals'* cast of infamous women culminates in Agrippina major's daughter, Agrippina minor, who, though Claudius' niece, became his wife after Messallina's death and who reportedly murdered the emperor by poisoning his favorite snack, mushrooms.

The ancient writers also often omitted, minimized, or distorted the sound policies of the various reigns and hurried past them to put emphasis on scandals. Claudius is no exception, appearing as a bumbling fool, timid, addicted to wine, gambling, cruelty, sex and—worst of all—unable to control either his wives or his freedmen. Messallina teamed with the powerful Narcissus to dominate the doddering quasi-cripple who became emperor almost by accident. The ancient historians give differing views of the era: Dio crams many good points into his opening survey of the reign (book 60); Suetonius categorizes events rather than proceeding chronologically; and Juvenal's *Satires* are notoriously biased and bitter. The masterful Tacitus is the best source, but his account of the period from the accession of Caligula in March, 37 to midway through 47 is lost.

Recent scholarship sees Messallina as using whatever weapons were available to her, including sex, to secure political goals. Her aim was to keep

Claudius alive and on the throne until their son Britannicus was old enough to take control. Since Claudius had many opponents who thought they had better claims and better talents to be emperor and who were prepared to act ruthlessly to achieve their ends, Messallina responded in kind. Those whom she eliminated were all powerful politicians, actual or potential enemies, or their wives. One victim was a Pompeius Magnus, married to Antonia, Claudius' daughter by an earlier wife; that combination of bloodlines was an obvious threat to Messallina's children. In several cases, she may have struck enemies only barely before they had their forces in place.

Messallina's orchestration of the downfall of D. Valerius Maximus in 47 was the beginning of the end. Her spectacular collapse remains an impenetrable mystery—her "marriage" to Gaius Silius while Claudius was at Ostia inspecting his new port facilities, Claudius' enraged return to Rome, her flight to her mother's house, and her death at the hands of the soldiers of the Praetorian Guard. Most would regard her as an adulteress to her lawful husband and as guilty of treason to the state.

Tacitus speaks of her *furor*, or madness; he too was unable to make sense of the events.

Summary

It is harsh but probably accurate to say that Messallina had relatively little significance in the long run. She was empress for a fairly short period, 41-48, and because women were excluded from office, she could not set government policies. Her influence over Claudius was limited to helping him eliminate their enemies, which she did ruthlessly. Her chief weapons were shrewd political sense and, evidently, sex. An inexplicable failure to control her political and sexual passions brought her to ruin in 48. Nero had her son Britannicus killed early in 55 and set aside her daughter Octavia a few years later, ending her bloodline. Tacitus' description of her has proved enduring; moderns will find equally compelling the fictional account in Robert Graves' 1934 novels *I, Claudius* and *Claudius the God and His Wife Messalina*. Also notable are the *Masterpiece Theater* productions of Graves' books, which introduced millions of television viewers to the intrigue and decadence of imperial Rome.

Bibliography

Balsdon, J. P. V. D. *Roman Women: Their History and Habits*. London: Blackwell, and New York: John Day, 1962. Valuable background, although many of Baldson's views now seem quaintly dated.

Barrett, Anthony A. *Caligula: The Corruption of Power*. London: Batsford, 1989; New Haven, Conn.: Yale University Press, 1990. Contains little on Messallina but much on Caligula's mother, Agrippina the elder, and his sisters.

———. *Agrippina*. New Haven, Conn.: Yale University Press, and London: Batsford, 1996. Agrippina major and minor were the dominant Roman women before and after Messallina. Agrippina major was the foe of Livia and Tiberius, while Agrippina minor probably has the worst reputation of any Roman woman: empress for only five years as Claudius' wife, but then powerful as the mother of Nero until he had her executed in 59. She may have learned much from close observation of Messallina.

Bauman, Richard. *Women and Politics in Ancient Rome*. London and New York: Routledge, 1992. A detailed study of the period from about 330 B.C. to 68 A.D.. Bauman ranks Messallina among the most powerful women of Rome, credits her with a sharp knowledge of criminal law, and dismisses some of the rumors about her sexual exploits as worthless.

Dudley, Donald R. *The World of Tacitus*. London: Secker and Warburg, and Boston: Little, Brown, 1968. A readable survey of the people who dominate Tacitus' works.

L'Hoir, Francesca Santoro. "Tacitus and Women's Usurpation of Power." *Classical World* 88 (1994): 5-25. A persuasive study of Tacitus' portrayal of women who "interfere" in politics and usurp men's place; according to Tacitus, any society that permits this "unnatural" occurrence is doomed.

Kokkinos, Nikos. *Antonia Augusta: Portrait of a Great Roman Lady*. London and New York: Routledge, 1992. A sympathetic portrait of the mother of Claudius. She and her mother Octavia were perhaps the most dignified women of the Julio-Claudian dynasty.

Levick, Barbara M. *Claudius*. London: Batsford, and New Haven, Conn.: Yale University Press, 1990. The best modern study of Claudius' reign; contains much useful information on Messallina.

Momigliano, Arnaldo. *Claudius: The Emperor and his Achievement*. Rev. ed. Oxford, England: Clarendon Press, and New York: Barnes and Noble, 1961. Though superseded by Levick's biography, this earlier study, originally published in 1934, remains valuable.

Syme, Sir Ronald. *Tacitus*. 2 vols. Oxford: Clarendon Press, 1958. A magisterial study of the greatest Roman historian; however, like all of Syme's works, it is not for beginners.

———. *The Augustan Aristocracy*. Oxford: Clarendon Press, and New York: Oxford University Press, 1986. An immensely detailed analysis of the Roman elite under the early Empire; much on the Agrippinas, Messallina, her mother Domitia Lepida, and others. Family trees in the back are invaluable for sorting out the tangled aristocratic genealogies.

Wiseman, T. P. "Calpurnius Siculus and the Claudian Civil War." *Journal of Roman Studies* 72 (1982): 57-67. Discusses a neglected poetic text that throws light on the opposition to Claudius at the beginning of his reign; the government crackdown reveals Messallina at work.

Thomas H. Watkins

MILTIADES THE YOUNGER

Born: c. 554 B.C.; probably Attica, Greece
Died: 489 B.C.; probably Athens, Greece
Areas of Achievement: Politics and warfare
Contribution: Through innovative tactics and inspired battlefield leadership, Miltiades led Athens to victory over the Persians at the Battle of Marathon. He thus helped to secure Greek civilization from engulfment by Near Eastern influences and greatly enhanced Athenian prestige in the Greek world.

Early Life

Very little is known about the first thirty years of Miltiades' life. His family and clan relationships, however, would prove to be highly influential in the shaping of his career, as was commonly the case in ancient Athens. He was born into the very old and wealthy Philaidae clan, whose members had long played an active part in Athenian politics. This family's estates were located in rural Attica (the countryside which bordered Athens). As a member of a prominent, aristocratic family, Miltiades probably enjoyed the benefits of a fine education and certainly profited from extensive political connections.

Miltiades' father, Cimon, however, was notorious for his failure to advance in the Athenian political arena, a source of considerable shame for aristocrats in Greek society. He was widely known for intellectual torpidity, a trait which earned for him the nickname *koalemos*, meaning "the nincompoop." Nevertheless, Cimon's failure to earn a prominent place in public life was probably more a result of his opposition to the Peisistratidae clan, an aristocratic family and political faction which exercised an authoritarian rule over Athens from 560 to 510 B.C., with considerable popular support.

In order to secure his own place in politics, Miltiades was forced to disavow his father's opinions and seek allies elsewhere. He did not have to search outside his own clan, because his uncle, Miltiades the Elder, and his older brother, Stesagoras, had acquiesced to Peisistratidaen rule and had been dispatched to the Chersonese (modern Gallipoli Peninsula) to conquer, colonize, and rule the region for Athens. In roughly 524 or 523, Miltiades served as archon, a judicial-administrative post which he secured through his acceptance of the Peisistratidaen tyranny.

Sometime before 514, Miltiades married an Athenian woman, about whom nothing definite is known. Some historians believe that she was a relative of the Peisistratidae. This union produced at least one child. Around 516, the Peisistratidae sent Miltiades to the Chersonese to assume the duties formerly performed by Miltiades the Elder and Stesagoras, both having recently died childless. Miltiades would utilize this opportunity to achieve renown in the Aegean world.

Life's Work

The Peisistratidae had entrusted Miltiades with an important assignment. By the latter half of the sixth century, Athens was importing unknown quantities of wheat from Black Sea regions through the Hellespontus strait to feed its burgeoning population. The Philaidae's mission was to preserve free access to the waterway by protecting the coastal regions from the depredations of pirates, Thracian tribes, and those Greek cities on the Asian side of the Hellespontus. Ancient sources tell little about the quality of Miltiades' service in the Chersonese, except that he continued the authoritarian rule over Athenian colonists and natives begun by his relations.

Miltiades' fame had its origins in the events surrounding the Scythian expedition, undertaken by Darius the Great, King of Persia. The Persians had extended their rule over the Greek cities of eastern Asia Minor (known as Ionia) in 545 and governed this region through Greek tyrants supported by their armies. From Ionia, around 513, Darius launched the first Persian invasion of Europe, utilizing the Greek fleets for logistical support. Initially, he was successful, subduing Thrace and reducing Miltiades to vassalage. His difficulties began when his army plunged into the lands of the Scythians, just north of the Danube River in modern Romania. The Persian army was doggedly harassed by the enemy and forced to retreat toward the Danubian boat-bridge maintained by the Ionians and their ships. At this crossing point, Miltiades urged the other Greeks to destroy the bridge and abandon Darius to his fate. Although his compatriots refused, Miltiades withdrew his forces to the Chersonese. His anti-Persian stand would serve him well politically in the future.

In the meantime, however, Darius' escape across the Danube left Miltiades in a precarious position.

As the Persians retreated through the Chersonese into Asia, they were pursued by the Scythians. Miltiades and his family were expelled from their small kingdom. His whereabouts during the next eighteen years are not made known by the ancient sources, but it is likely that he spent time at the court of Olorus, King of Thrace.

There, sometime between 513 and 510, he married Olorus' daughter, Hegesipyle. The fate of his first wife is unknown. This marriage produced four children: Cimon, destined to achieve greater fame than his father in the mid-fifth century as rival to Pericles and a founder of the Athenian Empire; Elpinice, a woman admired for her beauty and notorious for her free sexual behavior; and two other daughters whose names are unknown.

While Miltiades bided his time in exile, events in Ionia offered new political and military opportunities. In 499, the Ionian cities rose up in revolt against their Persian-imposed tyrants and thus began a six-year-long war in the eastern Aegean for Greek independence. Miltiades entered the fray in 495, when the inhabitants of the Chersonese invited him to return to rule over them. Installed once again in his kingdom, he utilized the Persians' preoccupation with the Ionian Revolt to seize the islands of Lemnos and Imbros, turning them over to the Athenians.

The Persian riposte was not long in coming. After suppressing Ionian resistance, their attentions focused on the Chersonese. When a Phoenician fleet in the service of the Persians closed in on Miltiades, he fled for the island of Imbros. In 493, he arrived in Athens, armed with vast political, and especially military, experience and widely admired for his consistently anti-Persian stance.

Politics in the Athens to which Miltiades returned had changed significantly since the days of his youth. Hippias, the last of the Peisistratidaen tyrants, had been expelled in 510. Around 508, Cleisthenes had introduced democratic reforms to the Athenian constitution, a political maneuver which greatly increased the strength of his clan, the Alcmaeonidae. Aristocrats seeking political power were thus forced to court the favor of the populace more strongly than ever before. It was a political culture alien to Miltiades' previous experience, but the looming Persian threat to Greek security—Athens had assisted the Ionian Revolt—made his military knowledge of the Persian Empire an important asset.

Traditionally, historians have viewed Athenian politics during the 490's as a contest between political parties supporting well-defined ideologies. Some were appeasers of the Persians, while others were decidedly in favor of resistance to them. Some favored the new democratic constitution, and others longed for a return to an era of aristocratic predominance. Recently, most historians have rejected such theories, because they do not jibe with ancient sources, which describe political rivalries largely in personal and familial terms. Modern interpretations stress the general agreement of Athenian politicians on essential issues: strong opposition to the Persian threat and a generalized acceptance—if not preference—for the democratic constitution. An exception to this rule was the Peisistratidae, still led by Hippias, who wanted to restore their tyranny with the backing of the Persians.

Miltiades' arrival on the political scene threatened to upset a delicate power balance. His appeal as a "Persian-fighter" instantly secured for him a power base, which promised to be troublesome to those clan factions which had grown used to the absence of the Philaidae. Although nearly all aristocratic politicians agreed with Miltiades' views, the essential issue in Athens in this era was not to what purposes power should be used but who should enjoy the benefits and prestige of power itself.

Shortly after Miltiades' arrival in Athens, he was brought to trial for exercising a tyranny over the Chersonese, possibly at the instigation of the Alcmaeonidae. During these proceedings, Miltiades probably strained to disassociate himself from his former affiliations to the Peisistratidae, giving rise to later legends of his youthful hostility to that clan. In any case, he was acquitted, thus foiling clever attempts to depict him as a reactionary aristocrat and to boost his enemies' popularity with the people.

In 490, with a Persian invasion imminent, Miltiades was elected to the ten-man board of generals from his tribe. Although this position was largely a command post—the Athenian army was organized tactically along tribal divisions—the board also functioned as an advisory council to the supreme commander, the polemarchos. Miltiades' expert advice was to play a crucial role in the impending campaign.

In July of 490, a Persian fleet, commanded by Datis and Artaphernes, sailed west from Ionia. King Darius' objectives were to punish Athens and another city-state, Eretria, for assisting the Ionian

Revolt and to establish a base from which all mainland Greece could later be conquered. Ancient sources give grossly exaggerated numbers for this invasion force. Modern historians have variously estimated its military strength at fifteen thousand to thirty thousand infantry, including five hundred to one thousand cavalry. After subduing the Cyclades Islands and ravaging Eretria on Euboea Island, the Persians landed on the plain of Marathon, about twenty-file miles northeast of Athens. Most Athenian strategists favored a tough defense of the city's walls as the key to victory. Miltiades, however, who had personally observed skilled Persian siegecraft during the Ionian Revolt, argued for a pitched battle in the open field. He sponsored a decree to this effect in the Assembly. On its authority, the commander Callimachus led the ten-thousand-man hoplite force out to Marathon to meet the enemy.

For several August days, the Persians and Athenians observed each other across the plain. Both sides had compelling reasons for delay. The Persians were waiting for Hippias, who had accompanied them, to rally the Peisistratidaen faction to the invasion. The Athenians were anticipating the arrival of troops from Sparta, the most militarily powerful of the city-states in Greece.

Miltiades had different ideas about how this campaign should be fought. He persuaded Callimachus at a divided meeting of the board of generals to attack the Persians in the plain immediately. Ancient sources do not give explicit reasons for this precipitate decision to engage in battle, although modern historians have generally agreed that the Athenian commanders feared the collusion of the Peisistratidae—and possibly the Alcmaeonidae—in the invasion. An immediate victory would save Athens from the treachery of these opponents.

In the ensuing battle on August 12, Miltiades' innovative tactics capitalized on Persian weaknesses: a lack of heavy armor and reliable shock weapons and an overdependence on the missile power of their archers and cavalry. As the Greek hoplites advanced toward the Persian lines, their pace accelerated. Once within missile range, they rushed headlong into contact with the enemy. The vaunted Persian archery skills were thus rendered useless. The Persians were surprised by this tactic, as Greek armies normally walked into combat to preserve the solidity of their battle lines.

To avoid being outflanked, Miltiades had deliberately extended his weaker army to match the frontage of the Persians. This formation involved weakening the center of the phalanx. As the battle developed, this emaciated center gave way before the enemy onslaught. His stronger wings, however, were triumphant. Exercising firm control over his men, Miltiades diverted these flank hoplites from pursuit in order to turn them in against the Persian center. This section of the enemy army was almost annihilated. More than six thousand Persians fell in the battle. As the Persians sailed away in retreat, Miltiades and his men could congratulate themselves on a victory which had saved Greece from tyranny.

In the aftermath of this battle, known as the Battle of Marathon, Miltiades' popularity soared. His career, nevertheless, was already very close to an ignominious end. From the Assembly, he secured funds for a secret military mission which, he promised, would enrich Athens. His subsequent assault on the island of Paros ended in failure, while Miltiades himself received a critical leg wound. Back in Athens, he was brought to trial for deceiving the people, an accusation brought forth by Xanthippus, who had married into the Alcmaeonidae clan. Miltiades was convicted and assessed an enormous fine. Jealous political rivals had triumphed. He died shortly thereafter from gangrene.

Summary

Miltiades' career provides a fine case study in the extremely competitive nature of Greek politics, a competition wherein clan and family loyalties, while very important, played a secondary role to the overpowering imperative to succeed. Aristocrats who won the political game were regarded as virtuous, while those who failed—such as Miltiades' father—were disgraced or shamed. Athenian political culture holds interesting clues to the reasons for the individual brilliance of the Greeks and their inability to achieve stable political organizations.

Bibliography

Austin, M. M. "Greek Tyrants and the Persians, 546-479 B.C." *Classical Quarterly* 40 (1990): 289-306. The article discusses Miltiades' unusual and changing relationship with both Athens and Persia. The motives behind his policy, Austin concludes, "must remain conjectural."

Burn, A. R. *Persia and the Greeks: The Defence of the West, c. 546-478 B.C.* Rev. ed. Stanford, Calif.: Stanford University Press, and London:

Duckworth, 1984. The best overall account of the titanic struggle between the Greeks and Persians, superseding the outdated, but ubiquitous, *The Great Persian War* (1901) by G. B. Grundy. Interspersed with short sections on Miltiades' activities in this era, with references to the ancient sources on him. Also includes the most precise chronology of the Battle of Marathon.

Bury, J. B., S. A. Cook, and F. E. Adcock, eds. *The Cambridge Ancient History.* Vol. 4, *The Persian Empire and the West.* London: Cambridge University Press, and New York: Macmillan, 1926. Chapter 6 contains the most accessible of the traditional interpretations of Athenian politics in the 490's. Readers are warned that J. H. Munro's reconstruction of the campaign and Battle of Marathon in this volume is no longer regarded seriously by historians.

Herodotus. *The Histories.* Translated by Aubrey de Sélincourt. New ed. London and New York: Penguin, 1996. By far the most important ancient source on Miltiades and the Battle of Marathon—the place to start for those doing research. Aspiring scholars should use this volume only in conjunction with modern accounts, because historians have discounted some of what Herodotus wrote.

Hignett, Charles. *Xerxes' Invasion of Greece.* Oxford: Clarendon Press, 1963. Despite its title, this book contains the best scholarly account of the Battle of Marathon. Provides references to nearly all the ancient sources and criticism of many of the modern attempts at reconstruction of the great event. Explains the modern tendency to regard Herodotus' writings as the most reliable of ancient sources on the Persian Wars.

Lazenby, John F. *The Defence of Greece 490-479 B.C.* Warminster, England: Aris and Phillips, 1993. The book is a narrative history of the Graeco-Persian War, provided with a chronological summary and a useful glossary. Miltiades' role in the events is amply discussed. Lazenby stresses the general lack of military experience on both sides and notes that Miltiades or Themostocles were not the military geniuses they have been made out to be.

Lloyd, Alan. *Marathon: The Story of Civilizations on Collision Course.* New York: Random House, 1973; London: Souvenir, 1974. A popular history which suffers from serious errors of interpretation and an unabashed idolization of the Greeks. Part 4, however, contains a dramatic and well-written narrative of the battle, drawn from reliable scholarly sources.

Sealey, Raphael. *A History of the Greek City States, 700-338 B.C.* Berkeley: University of California Press, 1976. Written by a prominent proponent of the prosopographical approach to Greek politics, that is, the concept that personal and familial relations overrode ideological issues in shaping events. Includes discussion of major aspects of Miltiades' life, with ancient sources referenced.

Michael S. Fitzgerald

MITHRADATES THE GREAT

Born: Probably 134 B.C.; probably Sinope, Kingdom of Pontus

Died: 63 B.C.; Panticapaeum, Crimea

Area of Achievement: Government

Contribution: Mithradates fought three wars with Rome in the first half of the first century B.C., resulting in the destruction and transformation into a Roman province of his own Kingdom of Pontus.

Early Life

Mithradates Dionysus Eupator (good father) was probably born at Sinope, the capital of the Kingdom of Pontus (in modern northern Turkey), in 134 B.C. He was the son of the Pontic king Mithradates V Euergetes (benefactor) and his wife, Laodice. When his father was assassinated in 120, Mithradates succeeded to the throne, possibly in conjunction with his brother Mithradates Chrestus (the good), under the regency of their mother. Further details of his life at this time are shrouded in mystery. According to the Latin historian Pompeius Trogus, whose work in summary form is the only literary source to describe Mithradates' activity in these years, Mithradates went to live in the wild for the next seven years to avoid falling victim to various palace conspiracies. It is clear that this story is not strictly accurate, for a series of inscriptions in honor of Mithradates and other members of the Pontic court, dated to 116, found on the island of Delos in the Aegean Sea and an inscription discovered in southern Russia show that he was a presence in the palace during these years. The Kingdom of Pontus was characterized by the difficult fusion of Greek and Iranian cultural traditions, as, indeed, was the court itself. It is therefore possible to interpret Trogus' story as a folkloric development stemming from the basic education of an Iranian noble in horsemanship and the hunt.

Whatever the case may be, it is clear from the course of his later life that Mithradates received a good education in Greek as well as in the traditional Iranian arts of war and the hunt. He was a man who truly represented the amalgam of these two powerful cultural traditions, and throughout his career there are many signs of these two sides in his upbringing. His coins suggest that he tried to model his appearance on that of Alexander the Great, for when he made war on Rome he presented himself to the cities of the Greek East as a champion against the Romans—the "common enemy"—and surrounded himself with officials of Greek descent. At the same time, he gave these officials titles such as "satrap," which evoked the memory of the ancient Persian kingdom swept away by Alexander, and he offered massive sacrifices to the high god of the Persian pantheon, Ahura Mazda. In general terms he was a man of tremendous physical and intellectual gifts, preternatural brutality, and, evidently, severe paranoia. He could speak twenty-two (or, according to another tradition, twenty-five) languages and was a patron of the arts and a lover of music. He is said to have been able to control a chariot drawn by sixteen horses and in his late sixties could still ride a hundred miles in a day. He included prophylactics against poison in his meals, murdered three of his ten sons, and, in the course of his wars, perpetrated massacres which were to become legendary in antiquity.

Life's Work

In 115 or 114 B.C., Mithradates established himself as the sole ruler of Pontus, murdering his mother and then his brother in the process. At about the same time, he began a series of campaigns to extend his control in the areas of the Crimea, in southern Russia, and along the coast of what is now Bulgaria and Romania. He appears to have undertaken these operations for several reasons. One was to increase his prestige in the Greek world as a whole, since a result of these campaigns was that he emerged as the protector of these Greek cities against neighboring barbarian tribes. Another reason was to increase the overall power of Pontus, whose natural economic base was not sufficient to support a great nation. The territories which now came under his control were extremely wealthy; they had for centuries been an important source of grain and dried fish for the Aegean world and were to become an important source of revenue for Mithradates. In the next few years, he sent his armies to establish control over the eastern shore of the Black Sea as well. The success of these operations was vital for what seems to have been Mithradates' great ambition: the establishment of Pontus as a major power in Anatolia and the Aegean world, an ambition which he could achieve only if he could match the hitherto irresistible power of Rome.

In addition to strengthening his kingdom through acquisitions along the Black Sea coast, Mithradates worked to enhance the economic base of his ancestral territories, which extended along the northern coast of modern Turkey and just across the Caucasus Mountains into the Anatolian plateau. Many parts of this realm were at the time of his accession quite backward. The settled areas south of the mountains had retained their basic political structure from the time of the Persian Empire, or, indeed, of the Hittites, while the mountainous regions had always been the preserve of wild tribes whose primary occupations were the pasturing of flocks and brigandage. Mithradates sought to encourage urbanization, founding cities in the mountain valleys and bringing the tribesmen out of the hills. He was not altogether successful in this, but the effort is a good illustration of his comprehensive planning to build up the power of Pontus.

In the final decade of the second century, Mithradates began to turn his attention to the kingdoms which lay to his south and west: Bithynia, which bordered Pontus at its western extremity in Asia Minor; Paphlagonia, to the southwest; and Cappadocia on the central Anatolian plateau to the south. All these areas were essentially under the influence of Rome, which had established a presence in what is the central portion of modern western Turkey when in 132 it had accepted this area as a bequest from the last king of Pergamon (who had ruled these areas). This land had become the Roman province of Asia. As a result of the potential might of Rome, Mithradates at first had to move against these areas through diplomacy and the promotion of domestic discord. On several occasions between 109 and 89, he sought to establish his relatives or supporters as the rulers in both Paphlagonia and Cappadocia. On each occasion, Roman embassies had ordered him to withdraw, and Mithradates, who did not believe that he could risk armed conflict, had done so.

The situation changed in 90 as a result of two events. First, a major civil war broke out in Italy between Rome and her Italian subjects, which initially went badly for Rome. Second, the incompetent Roman governor of Asia, Manius Aquillius, in conjunction with Cassius, the head of a Roman embassy which had recently ordered Mithradates out of Bithynia (from which he had expelled King Nicomedes), encouraged Nicomedes to attack the territory of Pontus. In 89, Mithradates struck with overwhelming force, thinking that he could no longer tolerate the intervention of Rome in his affairs and that Rome was now so weak that it would not be able to take effective action against him. His armies overwhelmed all resistance in Asia Minor, captured Aquillius (whom Mithradates executed by pouring molten gold down his throat) and Cassius, and began a wholesale massacre of Romans and their supporters throughout the region. In 88, at the height of his power, his forces were established in Greece while he remained to administer his newly won territories.

In the same year, after the war against the Italians had turned decisively in Rome's favor, the Roman general Lucius Cornelius Sulla, after temporarily securing his personal domination by a military occupation of the city, set out to engage Mithradates. From 87 to 86 Sulla besieged Athens, the main base of the Pontic armies in Greece; in 86, he captured Athens, defeated in two battles the two main Pontic field armies, commanded by Mithradates' lieutenants, and prepared an invasion of Asia. At the same time, a Roman army under the command of one of Sulla's rivals (Sulla's enemies had occupied Rome after heavy fighting in 87) moved directly against Mithradates. Although this army defeated him in several battles, it proved to be his salvation. When Sulla arrived in Asia Minor in 85, he was more interested in doing away with his rival and reestablishing his power in Italy than he was in destroying Pontus. Sulla struck a deal with Mithradates to restore the state of affairs before the outbreak of hostilities in return for a large indemnity, which Sulla could use to support the war that he then undertook in Italy. This deal, the Treaty of Dardanus, was signed in 85.

The treaty with Sulla saved Mithradates' kingdom and enabled him to rebuild his forces. He was able to do this rapidly enough to repulse an invasion by Murena, the officer whom Sulla had left in charge of Asia, in 82. This event is traditionally referred to as the Second Mithradatic War, even though it seems to have been no more than an unsuccessful plundering expedition. In the next several years, aided by Romans who had fled Sulla's bloody return to Italy and had continued the struggle abroad, Mithradates assembled a new army. At the same time, it is said, he offered encouragement to the pirates based in southern Asia Minor in their raids on Roman shipping.

Mithradates' third and final war with Rome began in 73 B.C. It was precipitated by the death of the King of Bithynia, who bequeathed his kingdom to the Romans. At first, Mithradates was completely successful. He defeated a Roman army, overran Bithynia, and again sent his troops into the Province of Asia. Yet his success was short-lived. At the end of the year, the Roman general Lucius Lucullus encountered Mithradates' main force as it was besieging the city of Cyzicus. At the beginning of 72, Lucullus destroyed this army and invaded Pontus itself. In 71, he drove Mithradates out of his kingdom.

Mithradates fled to Armenia, where he convinced his son-in-law, King Tigranes, to support him. Lucullus continued his invasion in 69 and defeated the combined forces of the two kings, leaving Mithradates roaming the hills with a small band of followers. Mithradates' career would have ended had it not been for a crisis of command on the Roman side. In 68, Lucullus' army mutinied and he was forced to withdraw to Asia. Mithradates was then able to defeat the Roman army which had been left behind to occupy Pontus. This defeat led to the removal of Lucullus from command, though no effective officer relieved him until 66 when Pompey the Great arrived. Mithradates used this interval in an unsuccessful effort to consolidate the defenses of his old kingdom. At the end of 66, Pompey drove him from his kingdom and he was forced to withdraw, at the head of a small army, around the coast of the Black Sea to the Crimea. It was a difficult march and its success is testimony to the enduring energy of the king.

In 63, while planning a new campaign against the Romans, which is said to have involved the grandiose scheme of marching on Italy through the Balkans, Mithradates faced a serious palace revolt. His son, Pharnaces, launched a successful coup and took command of the army. Mithradates withdrew to his palace and, after killing his harem, tried to commit suicide. His efforts to poison himself failed, as a result of the drugs he had taken against poison throughout his life, and he had to call upon one of his officers to stab him to death.

Summary

Mithradates was a man of tremendous energy and ambition. It must also be conceded, however, that this energy and ambition were fatally misdirected. No matter what steps he took, he would never have been able to match the power of Rome, and despite initial successes, he was never able to hold his own when Rome turned its superior military might against him. In fact, he was able to survive his first failure only because Sulla thought that he had more pressing business elsewhere.

Although Mithradates' determination, his refusal to admit defeat, and the broad vision he brought to the organization of his kingdom were impressive, his accomplishments were essentially negative. He initiated a series of wars which led to the expansion of Roman control in Anatolia and proved to be of great importance for Rome's subsequent organization of this area, precisely the end which he sought to avoid. Furthermore, the process involved massive devastation by both Mithradates and his enemies. There can be no doubt that the course of Roman expansion would have been very different if it had not been for Mithradates, but it can scarcely be argued that the course which Mithradates initiated was beneficial to those involved, as it resulted in the undoing of all that he had accomplished in the early part of his reign.

Bibliography

Appian of Alexandria. "The Mithridatic Wars." In *Appian's Roman History*, translated by Horace White, vol. 2. London: Heinemann, and New York: Macmillan, 1912. Appian's account of the Mithradatic Wars, written in Greek during the first half of the second century A.D., is the basic source for Mithradates' reign. This translation by White for the Loeb Classical Library is the best in English.

Green, Peter. *Alexander to Actium: The Historical Evolution of the Hellenistic Age*. Rev. ed. Berkeley: University of California Press, 1993. This is a readable general history of the period. It contains chronological and genealogical tables, as well as a large bibliography. Green makes perceptive personal characterizations of rulers, including Mithradates.

Hind, J. G. F. "Mithradates." In *The Cambridge Ancient History*. Vol. IX, *The Last Age of the Roman Republic, 146-43 B.C.* 2d ed. Cambridge and New York: Cambridge University Press, 1994. This account of Mithradates' reign, the most recent in English, is very informatively written. The book has good maps and an excellent bibliography.

Jones, Arnold H. M. *The Cities of the Eastern Roman Provinces*. 2d ed. Oxford: Clarendon Press, 1971. This work contains a useful chapter on the history of Pontus.

McGing, Brian. *The Foreign Policy of Mithridates VI Eupator King of Pontus*. Ottawa: National Library of Canada, 1984. The most detailed study of Mithradates' reign, this good, thorough treatment replaces previous studies.

Magie, David. *Roman Rule in Asia Minor to the End of the Third Century After Christ*. Princeton, N.J.: Princeton University Press, 1950. Several chapters on Mithradates, including detailed analysis of the sources in extensive notes.

Plutarch. *Fall of the Roman Republic*. Translated by Rex Warner. Rev. ed. London: Penguin Books, 1972; Baltimore: Penguin Books, 1980. This volume contains Plutarch's biographies of Sulla and Pompey, both of which provide much information about the campaigns of Mithradates. The life of Sulla is of particular interest, as it is based closely on Sulla's own autobiography.

Sherk, Robert, ed. and trans. *Rome and the Greek East to the Death of Augustus*. Cambridge and New York: Cambridge University Press, 1984. This volume contains translations of a number of documents (inscriptions, papyruses, and classical texts for which other translations are not readily available) that are relevant to the career of Mithradates. Several of these texts provide information which enables modern scholars to correct accounts preserved in other sources, chiefly those of Appian and Plutarch.

Sherwin-White, Adrian N. *Roman Foreign Policy in the East, 168 B.C. to A.D. 1*. Norman: University of Oklahoma Press, and London: Duckworth, 1984. The central portion of the book deals with the history of Mithradates' reign, including valuable studies of the military aspects.

David Potter

MOSES

Born: c. 1300 B.C.; near Memphis, Egypt
Died: c. 1200 B.C.; place unknown
Area of Achievement: Religion
Contribution: As the leader of tribal Israel who brought his people to the brink of nationhood in the thirteenth century B.C., Moses may be seen as the father of many governmental, social, and religious ideals that continue to influence the contemporary world. The codification of religious and ethical laws in the Pentateuch, the first five books of the Old Testament, is traditionally attributed to him.

Early Life

According to the biblical narrative, Moses was born to Jochebed, a Hebrew woman, during a period in which the children of Israel were under slavery to Egypt. The people of Israel had come to Egypt at the invitation of Joseph, one of Jacob's sons, who had become a prominent Egyptian leader in friendship with the pharaoh. Then, as the biblical text relates, "there arose a Pharaoh who knew not Joseph." As the Israelites grew in number and threatened the stability of Egyptian society, a more ruthless pharaoh began a policy of genocide toward newborn Hebrew males (Ex. 1:22). Immediately after Moses' birth, to spare him this fate his mother hid him in an arklike cradle and floated it down the Nile River, where it was discovered by an Egyptian princess who was bathing (Ex. 2:5-10). This princess found that Moses, whose name means "one drawn out of water," satisfied her longing for a son. Moses thus grew to manhood in the Egyptian palace, learning its language and culture, sheltered from his Hebrew heritage. Here Moses was exposed to the most sophisticated philosophies and science of the then known world, and he most likely learned how to write not only in the cuneiforms and hieroglyphics of Egyptian textuality but also in the proto-Semitic alphabetic script known to have been used near Mount Sinai even before the historical period in which Moses may be placed.

One day in his young adulthood, when visiting among the Hebrews, Moses was roused to justice on behalf of a Hebrew laborer who had been struck by an Egyptian (Ex. 2:11). In Moses' defense of his fellow Hebrew, he killed the Egyptian; he was then forced into exile in Midian. There Moses began a new life with a wife, Zipporah, and family and tended the flock of his father-in-law, Jethro. It

was evident that Moses' destiny lay in a higher calling, however, when the angel of the Lord appeared to him in a burning bush and God Himself spoke to him. Moses heard God's call to lead the Israelites out of Egyptian bondage (Ex. 3:1-17). In this divine commission, Moses was promised, on behalf of his people, a "land of milk and honey." It was during this encounter that God revealed His name to Moses as "Yahweh," or "I am that I am," the self-existing One who had chosen Israel to be His special people. Despite his initial hesitance, Moses accepted the call and was promised that his testimony would be corroborated with miracles.

Life's Work

The first part of Moses' life had been exhilarating, as he grew from infancy to adulthood in a pharaoh's house. The remainder of his life, however, was spent in turmoil, verbal and physical warfare, and continuing challenges to his authority by his own people. Upon returning to Egypt, Moses called upon his brother Aaron to accompany him and be his spokesman. In several bold and audacious audiences with the pharaoh, Moses demanded that the Egyptian leader free his people and allow them to worship Yahweh, who had called them to tabernacle at Mount Sinai. The pharaoh, amused by Moses' claim to authority and power, rejected his repeated pleas. There ensued a series of ten plagues that brought Egyptian society to its knees, including the final plague—the death of the firstborn. That plague killed many Egyptian children while sparing the Hebrews, who had spread blood over their doorposts to avert the angel of death, who "passed over" them. This event came to be celebrated on the Hebrew holy day of Passover, which commemorates the preservation of the Hebrews and their deliverance from bondage in Egypt (Ex. 12-14).

When the pharaoh finally relented, Moses led his people in a mighty throng into the Red Sea, whose waters were miraculously parted for them and then closed upon their Egyptian pursuers (Ex. 14-15). From their mountain encampment, Moses went to Mount Sinai for a momentous encounter with Yahweh, who revealed Himself so spectacularly that Moses returned from the mountain with his countenance shining. The thunder and lightning that accompanied these events caused great fear among the people, and they asked Moses to be their inter-

cessor lest they be consumed by Yahweh's omnipotence. Moses brought back to them the Covenant, a body of laws and relationships that was to bind Yahweh and the people of Israel together in a partnership (Ex. 19-20). Their task was to live in obedience to Yahweh's precepts—attributes of His holy character (justice, righteousness, peace, joy, and love)—for which He would continue to bless and protect them from their enemies. They were called upon to acknowledge Him as the only God and the surrounding civilizations as pagan and idolatrous.

Almost as soon as the people agreed to the covenant, they plunged into turmoil and rebellion. While Moses went to the mountain to receive further instruction from Yahweh, the people, impatient with Moses' absence, built a golden calf to worship, a reflection of their immaturity and naïveté and an action strictly forbidden by the covenant they had just ratified. Enraged at this apostasy, Moses returned from the mountain with vengeance, breaking the tablets on which the Ten Commandments had been written, destroying the idol, grinding it into powder, and forcing them to drink it. This lack of faith prefigured the continued disbelief and sin of the people, as the generation of Israelites who first left Egypt were destined to falter in their journey, never reaching the land promised them when Moses was called to God's service in Midian. During this time, however, Moses continued to meet with Yahweh and continued to build a record of Israel's experiences with this God who had brought them out of Egypt. Among the things that were presented to the people were the plans for building a tabernacle for worship, an elaborate ecclesiastical structure; detailed specifications for its construction and use in the corporate life and worship of the Jewish people were supplied.

The other pivotal event in the history of this first generation who left Egypt is recounted in the Book of Numbers. Moses sent spies into the land of Canaan to determine when and how the Israelites might occupy the land promised to them by Yahweh. Of the twelve spies sent out only two, Joshua and Caleb, brought a positive report. As a result, only Joshua and Caleb and their families were eventually permitted to enter Canaan. The other members of the first generation were refused entry by God as a result of their disbelief.

The Book of Deuteronomy records Moses' farewell speeches to the generation of Israel who would enter the Promised Land—a reiteration of the first covenant and an exhortation to obey the God who had called them out of bondage. In recounting the blessings and cursings that were to accrue to the Israelites, depending upon their behavior, Moses advised, "I have set before thee this day, both death and life. Choose life" (Deut. 30:19).

Moses' egotism, briefly revealed in the biblical narrative, eventually prevented Aaron and Moses themselves from entering Canaan. During one trying episode, Moses became frustrated with the Israelites' continual bickering about the availability of food and water. At one point, Moses exclaimed, "Hear now, you rebels; shall we bring forth water for you out of this rock?" (Num. 20:10), thus presumptuously attributing to himself the power to provide for Israel's needs. This sin weighed heavily on Moses toward the end of his life. Psalm 90 in the Old Testament Book of Psalms is attributed to Moses; it contains this bittersweet comment on the brevity of life: "Thou dost sweep men away; they are like a dream, like grass which is renewed in the morning: in the morning it flourishes and is renewed; in the evening it fades and withers. For we are consumed by thy anger; by thy wrath we are overwhelmed."

Near the end of his days, Moses passed the mantle of leadership over to his aging comrade, Joshua, who would lead Israel into the land that had been promised. A heroic and dutiful life was then brought to rest with a series of blessings that Moses pronounced upon the people of Israel. The concluding words of Deuteronomy offer this understated editorial judgment: "There has not arisen a prophet since in Israel like Moses, whom the Lord knew face to face" (Deut. 34:10).

Summary

The Law of Moses, his written legacy to subsequent generations, is matched only by Greek and Roman poetics and rhetoric in its impact on Western culture. Whatever editorial interventions there may have been over the centuries, it is clear that the five books of Moses—Genesis, Exodus, Leviticus, Numbers, and Deuteronomy—were intended to be histories of the Jewish people, beginning with the creation of the heavens and the earth. As a slave people fresh from redemption, this fledgling nation had few common experiences and little religious identity to bind them. Consequently, the Mosaic account of God's decision to choose the people of Israel as the blessed descendants of Abraham and to allow them to influence many civilizations can be seen as a primary attempt to solidify their nationhood during a precarious time. Moses' narrative gives the people of Israel a historical and moral vantage point from which to interpret their past and present experiences and, most important, to give praise to Yahweh, who called them out of Egypt to worship Him.

The religious foundation begun in the codification of legal and moral teaching became the scaffolding for Christianity, as Jesus Christ and his followers directly traced their heritage not only to Abraham but also to Moses. During his ministry, Jesus claimed to have come to fulfill the Law of Moses and to inaugurate a new covenant of grace that would subsume and complete the covenants made with Abraham, Isaac, and Jacob. Islam, whose sacred text is the Koran, also owes much of its message to the framework established in the works attributed to Moses. Muhammad, the Prophet of Islam, claimed Abraham and Moses as his forerunners, proclaiming that he and his message stood in the same historical and intellectual genealogy as theirs.

It is not difficult to understand the nearly universal recognition of Moses as a pivotal leader in history. He was holy and devout, a man of action and contemplation, a diplomat and military strategist, and a shrewd political adviser. In witnessing the ongoing direct and indirect influences of Mosaic thought in contemporary Judaism, Christianity, and Islam as well as the continuing political significance of the lands that he helped secure and develop for his people, one must conclude that, indeed, Moses was a man of remarkable gifts.

Bibliography

Alexander, David, and Pat Alexander, eds. *Eerdmans' Handbook to the Bible*. Rev. ed. Grand Rapids, Mich.: Eerdmans, 1983. A comprehensive handbook to biblical history and geography, with helpful interpretations that trace the history of Israel under Moses' leadership and rise to power in the ancient Middle East. Particularly useful are maps and word studies that illuminate Israel's relationships with Egypt and other Middle Eastern nations of 1400-1200 B.C.

Allis, Oswald T. *The Five Books of Moses*. 3d ed. Philadelphia: Presbyterian and Reformed Publishing Co., 1964. An older but still-valuable historical and theological defense of the Mosaic authorship of the Pentateuch, by one of the most outstanding Old Testament scholars of the twentieth century. While the archaeological data Allis supplies are clearly somewhat dated, the cogency of his arguments remains unsurpassed.

———. *God Spake by Moses*. Philadelphia: Presbyterian and Reformed Publishing Co., and London: Marshall, Morgan, and Scott, 1951. An outstanding and thorough biographical and theological analysis of the Pentateuch, the life of Moses, and his unique role as a prophet of God. The volume illuminates the life of Moses and the birth and growth of Israel as a nation.

Bright, John. *A History of Israel*. 3d ed. London: SCM Press, and Philadelphia: Westminster Press, 1981. Probably the most thorough and compelling nontheological treatment of the history of Israel available. Sections on the kingdoms and civilizations contemporary with Moses illuminate the story of his life and sustain the interest of both the common reader and the scholar.

Coats, George W. *Moses: Heroic Man, Man of God*. Sheffield: JSOT Press, 1988. The book examines the biblical tradition about Moses, focusing on several important passages and episodes in the narrative. There is an extensive review of previous scholarship on Moses, and a large bibliography.

———. *The Moses Tradition*. Sheffield: JSOT Press, 1993. This is a collection of essays, sharing a commitment to the form-critical and traditional historical methods. Among them, "The King's Loyal Opposition" explores Moses' intercession during the golden calf incident as it relates to issues of obedience and authority; "Metanoia in Ancient Israel" portrays Moses as a model for leadership; and "The Failure of the Hero" explores the interpretation of texts about Moses' failure as a leader.

Friedman, Richard Elliot. *Who Wrote the Bible?* New York: Summit Books, 1987; London: Cape, 1988. Friedman is representative of the majority of modern biblical scholars in rejecting Mosaic authorship of the Pentateuch. In this book, intended for the general reader, Friedman draws on a synthesis of current scholarship to present his own, controversial answer to the question of authorship. Includes notes and a bibliography; lightly illustrated.

Harrison, R. K. *An Introduction to the Old Testament*. Grand Rapids, Mich.: Eerdmans, 1969; London: Tyndale, 1970. A complete overview of the origin, message, and impact of each book in the Old Testament. The volume addresses directly and comprehensively the issues of the chronology, authenticity, and influence of the life of Moses on the people of Israel in ancient times and in the present. A massive, comprehensive scholarly work with extensive documentation.

Kitchen, K. A. *The Bible in Its World.* Downers Grove, Ill.: Inter-Varsity Press, and Exeter: Paternoster, 1977. An insider's look at the world of archaeology and how it functions in validating ancient records and narratives. Particularly helpful in its extensive examination of antiquity's cultural artifacts and social conditions against the backdrop of the age of Moses and his people's sojourns in Egypt and wanderings in the wilderness.

Schultz, Samuel J. *The Old Testament Speaks.* 4th ed. San Francisco: Harper and Row, 1990. Written for the lay reader, this cogent and lucidly written volume presents an objective historical analysis of the lives of the patriarchs. Includes a major section on Moses and the Pentateuch and their role in the evolution of ancient and modern Israel.

Thompson, J. A. *Handbook of Life in Bible Times.* Leicester and Downers Grove, Ill.: Inter-Varsity Press, 1986. A colorful, lavishly illustrated reference tool with key sections on the domestic life, travel, family customs, and cultural preoccupations of the biblical world. The work illuminates the birth of Israel and its development under Moses' theological and political leadership.

Wenham, John. "Moses and the Pentateuch." In *New Bible Commentary: Revised,* edited by Donald Guthrie, Alec Moyer, Alan Stibbs, and Donald Wiseman. Grand Rapids, Mich.: Eerdmans, and London: Intervarsity Press, 1970. A concise and singularly wise assessment of the career of Moses, his personality and leadership qualities, and his continuing impact on both Jewish and Christian thought.

Bruce L. Edwards

NABU-RIMANNI

Born: early first century B.C.; probably Babylonia
Died: late first century B.C.; probably Babylonia
Area of Achievement: Astronomy
Contribution: Nabu-rimanni was a Babylonian scribe who copied and preserved astronomical tables for the computation of lunar, solar, and planetary phenomena. By providing accurate numerical parameters for the prediction of astronomical phenomena, Babylonian astronomy furthered the development and success of Greek spherical astronomy, developed to its fullest in the Ptolemaic system.

Early Life

Because the nature of Babylonian sources is such that authors and authorship remain obscure, it is not possible to reconstruct for Nabu-rimanni a biography in the strict sense. The historical period with which he is associated, however, may be sketched. While the years of Nabu-rimanni's floruit were in the mid-first century B.C., one may also define this period more broadly, that is, from roughly 300 B.C. to the beginning of the common era, as the Hellenistic period. As a result of the spread of Greek political influence across the Near Eastern territories once belonging to the empires of Persia, Babylonia, and Assyria, this era produced notable cultural and intellectual change from the cities of mainland Greece to Egypt in the south and Mesopotamia in the east. In particular, science flowered in Hellenistic intellectual centers such as Alexandria, and Greek astronomy, which had already begun in the fifth century, reached its height during the Hellenistic period, in part as a result of the transmission of astronomical knowledge from Mesopotamia.

Life's Work

The Hellenistic authors Strabo (64 or 63 B.C-c. A.D. 25) and Pliny the Elder (A.D. 23-79), who traveled and produced encyclopedic compendia of the knowledge and customs of the day, mention Babylonian astronomical "schools" and a few of the Babylonian astronomers by name. Thus, one finds in book 16 of Strabo's *Geōgraphia* (*Geography*) the name Naburianos (= Nabu-rimmani), and also Kidenas, Sudines, and Seleucus, all associated with Babylonian cities such as Babylon, Uruk, and possibly Borsippa. Nabu-rimanni's particular or distinguishing role in the history of Babylonian as-

tronomy, however, cannot be determined either from the Greek account or from Babylonian cuneiform sources. Cuneiform texts yield information about the scribes only in the colophons at the end of the inscriptions. These colophons, when complete, note the names of the owner of the document and the scribe who copied it, as well as the date the tablet was written and who was king at the time. Nabu-rimanni's name is preserved on the colophon of an astronomical tablet from Babylon. The only fact, therefore, that can be established about him from Babylonian sources is that he was a scribe who copied, or possibly computed, a table of dates and positions in the sky of new and full moons for the year 49-48 B.C. This particular colophon is the source for the claim that Nabu-rimanni was the inventor of the method of astronomical computation represented in his tablet. Far from showing this scribe as an innovator of Babylonian astronomy, however, Nabu-rimanni's tablet is one of the youngest of Babylonian lunar ephemerides; the oldest such tablets stem from the third century. Nabu-rimanni can therefore be credited only with preserving the tradition of Babylonian astronomy, not inventing it.

Since Nabu-rimanni is associated with a particular method of astronomical computation, but his individual contribution cannot be determined from the sources, the focus of any examination of his life's work must be Babylonian astronomy itself. Babylonian mathematical astronomy of the last three centuries B.C. is known from only two identifiable archives, one found in Babylon and the other in Uruk. The bulk of the texts are lunar or planetary ephemerides, which are supplemented by a smaller group of procedure texts outlining the steps necessary to generate ephemeris tables. The ephemeris tables contain parallel columns of numbers in specific sequences which represent occurrences of characteristic lunar and planetary phenomena. Each column represents a different periodic phenomenon—for example, new moons, eclipses, first visibilities, stationary points. The consecutive entries in each column correspond to dates, usually months. In the case of the ephemeris for the moon, the objective is to predict the evening of the first visibility of the lunar crescent. The appearance of the new moon defines the beginning of the month in a strictly lunar calendar. Indeed, the control of the calendar seems to have provided a major motivation for the development of mathematical methods for predicting astronomical phenomena.

For calculations, the Babylonians utilized a number system of base 60; that is, numbers are represented with special digits from 1 to 59, while 60, or any power of 60, is represented by 1. These "sexagesimal" numbers were written using a place-value notation system similar to decimal notation, so that for each place a digit is moved to the left, the value is multiplied by 60. The positional system was extended for fractions, which were expressed by moving digits to the right of the "ones" place, thereby dividing each time by 60. The Babylonian sexagesimal system is still preserved in the counting of time by hours, minutes (1 hour equals 60 minutes), and seconds (1 minute equals 60 seconds).

Babylonian lunar and planetary theory comprised two separate but coexistent systems, designated A and B, which are defined according to two different arithmetical methods of describing the distance covered each month by the sun. In this way, the velocity of the sun could be measured in terms of the progress of the sun in longitude, or degrees along its apparent path through the stars, the ecliptic. In system A, the progress of the sun along the ecliptic is described as being 30° per (mean synodic) month for one part of the zodiac (from Virgo 13° to Pisces 27°) and 28° 7′ 30″ for the other part (from Pisces 27° to Virgo 13°). A mathematical model is thereby created whereby the sun moves with two separate constant velocities on two arcs of the ecliptic. If the sun's velocity, reckoned in terms of progress in longitude (degrees along the ecliptic), is plotted against time, the resulting graph represents a "step function." System A also implies a certain length of the solar year, namely 1 year equals 12;22,8 months, expressed sexagesimally. (Sexagesimal numbers are represented in modern notation with a semicolon separating integers from fractions.) This method and its complementary system B were both used during the period from c. 250 B.C. to c. 50 B.C.

System B assumes the motion of the sun to increase and decrease its speed steadily from month to month. The variation in velocity is bounded by a minimum and a maximum value, and within this range of velocities, the monthly change is always by a constant amount. To plot the progress of the sun by this model produces a graph representing a "linear zig-zag function." The name Kidenas, mentioned by Strabo, Pliny, and Vettius Valens (A.D.

second century), may be associated with System B, as a scribe by the name of Ki-di-nu (= Kidinnu) is known from colophons of system B-type ephemerides for the years 104-101 B.C. The Greeks credited him with derivation of the relation 251 synodic months = 269 anomalistic months. This numerical relation is in fact seen in system B computations.

Systems A and B constitute theoretical mathematical models of the motion of the sun that account for the varying lengths of the seasons of the year. By analogy with solar motion, the methods of systems A and B were applied to many celestial phenomena of a cyclic character. A Babylonian lunar table deals with the determination of conjunctions and oppositions of sun and moon, first and last visibilities, and eclipses, all of which are cyclic phenomena. Planetary tables for the planets Jupiter, Venus, Saturn, Mercury, and Mars predict the dates and positions in the zodiac of the cyclic appearances of planets, such as first visibilities, oppositions, stationary points, and last visibilities. The fact that each phenomenon had its own period enabled the Babylonians to compute them independently. No general theory of planetary and lunar motion was needed, since the strictly arithmetical methods of the two systems were sufficient to predict the individual appearances of the heavenly bodies. The goal of Babylonian astronomy was, therefore, to predict when the moon or planets would be visible. In contrast, the Greeks' goal was to develop a single model which would serve to describe and account for the motion of celestial bodies in a general sense, and from which the individual appearances of celestial bodies would follow as a consequence. The achievement of this goal was found in geometrical methods and kinematic models (explaining motion), developed by Apollonius of Perga (third century B.C.) and perfected by Ptolemy in *Mathēmatikē suntaxis* (c. A.D. 150; *Almagest*). Such geometrical concepts are not found in Babylonian astronomy.

The question of the identity of the Babylonian astronomers is not answered by the cuneiform astronomical texts. One scribe is hardly distinguished from another when the extent of one's information is the appearance of the scribe's name in a text colophon. Nevertheless, the question as to the significance of the scribes Nabu-rimanni and Kidinnu, whose names are remembered by later Greek and Roman authors, remains. The belief that they were the inventors of the systems A and B gains no support from the cuneiform texts. Indeed, the establishment of dates for the invention of systems A and B has proved difficult; thus, statements concerning the origins of Babylonian mathematical astronomy, in regard to both chronology and the role of individual scribes, must for the time being remain inconclusive.

Summary

Babylonian lunar and planetary theory became the foundation for the development and further refinement of astronomy by the Greek astronomers Apollonius, Hipparchus, and Ptolemy. In very general terms, one can enumerate the various Babylonian contributions to Greek astronomy and thereby to the development of science in general as follows. About 300 to 200 B.C., the Greek astronomers adopted the Babylonian sexagesimal number system for their computations and for measuring time and angles (360 degrees in a circle with degrees divisible by minutes and seconds). The use of arithmetical methods characteristic of Babylonian astronomical tables continued, particularly in the procedures used by Hellenistic astrologers. While Greek astronomical theory depended upon geometrical and kinematic models, neither of which was used in Babylonian astronomy, the parameters used in constructing those models were Babylonian. Indeed, the success of Greek astronomical theory rests upon the accuracy of the parameters established by Babylonian astronomers (such as the length of the solar year given above). The concepts related to the parameters must also have been transmitted. Such concepts were, for example, the following components of lunar motion: longitude, latitude (angular distance of the moon from the ecliptic), anomaly (irregularity in motion), and the motion from east to west of the line of nodes (the two diametrically opposed points where the moon's orbital plane intersects the plane of the ecliptic) in a nineteen-year cycle. Also of use for Greek planetary theory were the period relations essential to the determination of successive occurrences of a periodic phenomenon in Babylonian astronomy. Through the wide acceptance of the Ptolemaic tradition, as evidenced by Indian and Islamic astronomy, the direct influence of Babylonian astronomy on the Greek world had even greater impact as the ultimate impetus for the quantitative approach to celestial phenomena.

Bibliography

Aaboe, Asger. "Observation and Theory in Babylonian Astronomy." *Centaurus* 24 (1980): 14-35. Suggests a reconstruction of the process by which the Babylonian systems of computing astronomical phenomena were developed.

———. "Scientific Astronomy in Antiquity." In *The Place of Astronomy in the Ancient World*, edited by F. R. Hodson. London: Oxford University Press, 1974. Summary and explanation of the mathematical content of the Babylonian astronomical ephemerides and discussion of what constitutes a "scientific" astronomy.

Neugebauer, Otto. *Astronomical Cuneiform Texts.* London and Princeton, N.J.: Lund Humphreys, 1955. A transliteration and translation of the cuneiform astronomical texts, accompanied by an analysis.

———. *The Exact Sciences in Antiquity.* 2d ed. Providence, R.I.: Brown University Press, 1957. Concise history of mathematics and astronomy in Babylonia, Egypt, and Greece.

———. *A History of Ancient Mathematical Astronomy.* New York: Springer-Verlag, 1975. Definitive and extremely technical treatment of Babylonian, Egyptian, and Greek astronomy (pre-Ptolemaic and Ptolemaic systems).

Van der Waerden, B. L. *Science Awakening.* Vol. 2, *The Birth of Astronomy.* New York: Oxford University Press, 1974. More accessible and less technical but also less reliable than Neugebauer. Gives an overall account of the phenomena of interest in Babylonian mathematical as well as pre-mathematical astronomy.

Francesca Rochberg-Halton

NEBUCHADNEZZAR II

Born: c. 630 B.C.; place unknown
Died: 562 B.C.; Babylon
Areas of Achievement: Conquest and government
Contribution: One of the most ambitious and successful military leaders of ancient times, Nebuchadnezzar possessed excellent governing ability which made Chaldean Neo-Babylon the most powerful and feared nation in Western Asia.

Early Life

Nebuchadnezzar II, the eldest son of Nabopolassar, King of the Chaldean Neo-Babylonians, who reigned from 625 to 605, entered the world's military arena in the early 600's. As crown prince, he led Chaldean forces against the remnants of the Assyrian army and a sizable Egyptian contingent in the decisive Battle of Carchemish, fought in what is modern Syria. For the remainder of his life, Nebuchadnezzar expanded upon his father's conquests, until Babylon was the richest, most prominent, and most renowned nation in the ancient world.

Nevertheless, his exploits, considerable though they were, would not have been so well-known to later generations if he had not been the monarch who burned and looted Jerusalem, forcing its most able inhabitants into temporary exile in Babylon. By so doing, Nebuchadnezzar unwittingly fulfilled the prophecies of Jeremiah, the most noted Jewish prophet of the time. Thus, the Bible has preserved the Babylonian ruler's most notable accomplishments.

After he succeeded his father as king in 605, Nebuchadnezzar gave the city of Babylon its most famous feature, the Hanging Gardens, as well as fiery furnaces used both for commercial enterprises and for the torture and destruction of Babylon's foes; its grand celebrations of Marduk, Babylon's patron god, and the goddess Ishtar; and its huge brick outer walls, which dominated the desert for many miles. By these gifts, Nebuchadnezzar transformed Babylon from a dusty, shabby provincial city into an elegant world capital. With no remaining Assyrian enemy to engage or any significant Egyptian threat to counter, Nebuchadnezzar turned his attention not only to the rebuilding of Babylon but also to its territorial expansion. He and his architects created enormous stepped ziggurats for the glory of Marduk and Ishtar, while he planned further forays against neighboring states.

Using the Code of Hammurabi as his basis, Nebuchadnezzar created a stable, generally lawful Babylonian society. Criminals faced severe penalties ranging from torture to death. The most notorious punishments, however, were reserved for enemy rulers and their retainers; upon capture, these people were often flayed alive, partially dismembered, and cast alive into the furnaces, or were blinded and had gold clasps affixed to their tongues; with a leash attached to the clasp, the afflicted could be led around Babylon. By rigidly adhering to the Code of Hammurabi, Nebuchadnezzar reinforced his reputation for ferocity.

Life's Work

The battles which occurred after the flight of the Egyptian army brought many victories to the Chaldeans; each victory brought destruction and death to the vanquished tribe or nation. In 601, Nebuchadnezzar's forces were defeated by Necho II, the King of Egypt, an event which elevated the hopes of the kingdom of Judaea. Although Jehoiakim, appointed king of Judah by the pharaoh, had once submitted to Nebuchadnezzar, he had shortly thereafter covertly joined forces with the Egyptians in order to war against Babylon. Jeremiah, one of the principal Old Testament prophets, warned his people that God intended to punish them for their worship of foreign gods and for their allegiance to Egypt.

Nebuchadnezzar fulfilled Jeremiah's prophecy by marching on Judah and its largest city in 597. King Jehoiakim had died before the city was captured, but Nebuchadnezzar took his son Jehoiachin into Babylonian exile. Later, in 586, after an eighteen-month siege, Jerusalem was burned and its leading citizens sent into exile. As much as possible, Nebuchadnezzar attempted to erase all signs of Jewish civilization from the former kingdom. Zedekiah, the ruler of Judah-in-exile, paid for his dealings with Egypt by being blinded after witnessing the murder of his sons by Babylonian captors.

The enslavement of the Jews was nothing like the total servitude they had faced centuries before when Egyptian pharaohs forced them to make bricks for the Pyramids and treated them like

beasts of burden. Nebuchadnezzar, while never allowing them to return home, did allow them many freedoms, including the rights to work at trades and to mingle freely with the populace of Babylon. Yet the Jews were a miserable people who dreamed of one day going back to their ancestral towns and villages. In their midst was the prophet Ezekiel, Jeremiah's counterpart. Ezekiel prophesied that the Jews would be delivered from Babylonian captivity by a great king from the East, a vision that came true when Cyrus the Great of Persia invaded Babylon in the year 539.

After the destruction of Jerusalem and the capture and blinding of Zedekiah in 586, Nebuchadnezzar sent his armies against the Egyptians once again, finally capturing the important Phoenician city of Tyre in 571, thus adding considerably to the wealth, power, and authority of Babylon. With Egyptian influence flagging, Babylon became the unquestioned power of Asia Minor. Commerce with surrounding nations accompanied the empire's ascent as Babylon became the mercantile center of western Asia. A storehouse of gold, silver, and precious gems taken as tribute from vassal nations, Babylon could buy and trade virtually any commodity.

Nebuchadnezzar made certain that waterways and highways were constructed, making the city readily accessible to the heavy trade flowing into it. His earlier building program was intensified in the middle years of his reign so that Babylon would be an impregnable fortress as well as a center of commerce. The temples and ziggurats were made enormous and the city walls rose higher than they had previously, decorated with enameled figures of beasts. The Hanging Gardens were made even more elaborate so that the king and his harem could enjoy the delights of a large oasis in the middle of a desert city.

Little is known about the last years of Nebuchadnezzar. The final major event to occur before he faded from history was a battle with the Median leader Cyaxares, who had sacked Uratu and headed toward the kingdom of Lydia, which was close enough to Babylonian territory to make Nebuchadnezzar uneasy. Bitter fighting ended in May, 585, when darkness caused by a solar eclipse enveloped the Medes and the Neo-Babylonians; the event was interpreted as a sign from the gods to stop fighting. A truce was signed; nevertheless, the Medians remained a source of anxiety for Nebuchadnezzar, who ordered that a high wall be built around the city.

There is much speculation about his final days. Some scholars believe that he gradually grew weary of the burdens of kingship and retired from active life, others that he may have suffered from senility or even madness. Perhaps the best-known source for the latter theory is the biblical account of Daniel, in which the King of Babylon is depicted as an insane old man, an eater of grass. In any event, his immediate successor, his son Evil-Merodach, the man he had hoped would continue his life's work in Babylon, died in 559 (or, as some accounts have it, 560) after being overthrown. The short-lived Chaldean dynasty founded by Nebuchadnezzar's father finally ended with the death of Nabonidus in 539, when Cyrus' army swept into Babylon and established Achaemenid rule.

Summary

Nebuchadnezzar II's genius for conquering rival nations and tribes and then paralyzing them by taking their best-educated, most talented people into exile, as well as his great civic and military planning abilities, makes him one of history's most influential leaders. He took chances in his military campaigns, but such risks were shrewdly calculated. By using the punishment of exile, he placed hostile governments directly under his own surveillance and, by so doing, nipped any potential revolution before it could grow into a threat. His cruelty toward certain unrepentant foes was unrivaled in the ancient world and established him as an enemy not to be resisted. Those who did resist brought upon themselves death and destruction. A lover of pomp, he made the city of Babylon into a magnificent fortress, its gardens, palaces, courtyards, and walls the marvels of their time. Almost single-handedly, the king magnified the power and prestige of his nation. Yet the end of Babylon was soon in coming, foretold by Ezekiel and those who shared his prophetic vision; its magnificence was destroyed by enemies within and without, leaving it a warren of broken walls in the midst of a desert.

It is ironic that the Jews whom Nebuchadnezzar took into bitter exile were to portray him most memorably for later generations. To readers of the Old Testament, he is the cruel but brilliant monarch who fulfilled Jeremiah's predictions by destroying Jerusalem and creating the lengthy Diaspora as well as the man who threw Daniel into the den of lions and Shadrach, Meshach, and Abednego into a furnace. Like Daniel and his companions, the Jews survived Nebuchadnezzar's tortures, but Babylon itself, largely the creation of its king, left few traces after Cyrus made it into a wasteland. Like many empires, it had its golden age, followed by rapid decay. This golden age could not have occurred had it not been for the consummate genius of Nebuchadnezzar.

Bibliography

Kuhrt, Amelie. *The Ancient Near East c. 3000-330 B.C.* Vol. 2. London and New York: Routledge, 1995. The chapter on Nebuchadnezzar II in this up-to-date general history contains extensive quotations from primary sources. Social and administrative conditions receive equal treatment with political events.

New Catholic Edition of the Holy Bible. New York: Catholic Book Publishing Co., 1957. The books of Jeremiah, Ezekiel, and Daniel deserve special attention, although references to Nebuchadnezzar are found elsewhere in the Bible. One of the most revealing sources of information about how Nebuchadnezzar was viewed by one of his enslaved peoples.

Oates, Joan. *Babylon*. London: Thames and Hudson, 1979. Considers many aspects of life in Babylon under various kings including Nebuchadnezzar. Discusses Babylonian law, religion, social customs, festivals, and military conquests and defeats and gives a fine overview of each king's contribution to Babylon's rise and fall. An in-depth look at a sophisticated, complex society.

Oppenheim, A. Leo. *Ancient Mesopotamia: Portrait of a Dead Civilization*. Rev. ed. Chicago: University of Chicago Press, 1977. Written by one of the foremost scholars dealing with the region, this work considers the development of the nation of the Tigris and Euphrates basin. Gives much insight into relationships between strong and weak nations.

————. *Letters from Mesopotamia: Official, Business, and Private Letters on Clay Tablets from Two Millennia*. Chicago: University of Chicago Press, 1967. These letters shed light on the inner dynamics of the nations of the Near East in ancient times.

Saggs, H. W. F. *The Greatness That Was Babylon: A Survey of the Ancient Civilization of the Tigris-Euphrates Valley.* 2d ed. London: Sidgwick and Jackson, 1988. Written for both general and scholarly readers, this study covers the Babylonian monarchies. Invaluable for its lively depiction of the lives of both noble and worker. Well-illustrated; extensive bibliography.

Tabouis, G. R. *Nebuchadnezzar.* London: Routledge, and New York: McGraw-Hill, 1931. Tabouis, a member of the Académie Française, gives readers an imaginative glimpse of life in Nebuchadnezzar's court. Historical fiction at its best.

John D. Raymer

NEFERTITI

Born: c. 1366 B.C.; Thebes, Egypt

Died: c. 1336 B.C.; probably Egypt

Areas of Achievement: Diplomacy; government and politics; pharaohs; theology

Contribution: As queen of Egypt married to the iconoclastic Pharaoh Ikhnaton, Nefertiti helped in the temporary transformation of the culture's traditional religion into a monotheistic cult of sun worship. She also had an important role in ruling the empire and inspired standards of female beauty.

Early Life

Nefertiti was born in the royal city of Thebes on the Nile River in Upper Egypt; her name means "the beautiful one has come." Her origins and much about her life are unclear. Her supposed mother or stepmother, Tiy, was also described as her "nurse" and "governess." Her putative father was Aye, at first a scribe and keeper of the king's records. Eventually, Aye was to become grand vizier, or chief minister, as well as commander of the king's chariotry.

Perhaps her father's ascendancy made it possible for Nefertiti to secure an entrée to the court and to become friendly with the king's oldest son, the younger Amenhotep, a year her senior. Amenhotep happened to have her father, Aye, as tutor. Nefertiti had a younger sister, Mudnodjme, whom some scholars posit became the chief wife of King Haremhab, a view contested by others.

Given her father's presumed ambitions and the young prince's affection for her, at age eleven Nefertiti already appeared to have been groomed to be queen. It is agreed that she spent much of the her childhood in the royal palace at Thebes, a magnificent city beautified by Aye, this time in his capacity as chief architect to King Amenhotep III, the prince's father.

After the young King Amenhotep IV ascended the throne at about age sixteen upon his father's death, he married Nefertiti, then fifteen. She thus became Queen Nefertiti, empress of the Two Egypts, Upper and Lower. During the Eighteenth Dynasty, royal couples were considered the intermediaries between the people and their gods; Amenhotep and Nefertiti, according to custom, were thus ascribed near-divine attributes.

The new king, however, broke rank with his predecessors. He evinced little interest in hunting, the affairs of state, or warfare. Rather, his focus was primarily theological. In fact, the sovereign became a religious reformer and was eventually considered a heretic. In contrast to his ancestors, Amenhotep IV replaced Amen-Ra, the supreme god of all Egyptian gods, with a new paramount, powerful, and eventually sole god, Aten, whose manifestation was the sun-disk, the physical embodiment of the planet. Until then, Aten had been only a minor Theban god. Symbolically, in Year 5 of his reign, Amenhotep changed his name to Ikhnaton (commonly, Akhenaten). Because of mounting opposition to his iconoclasm and to his closure of the temples of the other gods, Ikhnaton decided to build a new capital, Akhetaten (the modern El-Amarna, on the Nile in Middle Egypt some 250 miles north of Thebes). The royal family and a good part of the court then moved there.

In the meantime, however, Meritaten and Mekitaten, two of the royal couple's six known daughters, had been born in Thebes. Four more girls—Ankhesenpaaten, Nefernefruaten the Younger, Nefernefrura, and Setepenra—were to follow. Some scholars suspect that the royal couple, or at least Ikhnaton, may also have had a son, Smenkhare, who ruled briefly either with or following his father. Indeed, under a contemporary pharaonic tradition, the king may have sired other children either with his secondary wives such as his favorite, Kiya, or even with his own daughters, of whom he married three; incestuous couplings were favored to maintain the royal line. Various reliefs show the royal couple with their daughters, often in intimate, domestic surroundings that had never been represented before.

Life's Work

The rise and fall of Egypt's new capital city, Akhetaten, with which Nefertiti became so closely associated, was little less than meteoric. In less than two decades, it was built with palaces, temples to the god Aten, monuments, residences, and burial places. A new style of art flourished during this brief "Amarna period." In the fourteenth century B.C., Egypt was still the world's most important empire. Babylonia, Assyria, Syria, Palestine, Mitanni, and the region of Asia Minor where the Hittites lived all paid tribute in the form of slaves, animals, and princesses, who were used as royal spouses or concubines to reinforce political ties.

Because her husband's interests were primarily theological, Nefertiti helped to spread the new faith as Ikhnaton's equal, participating enthusiastically in the new religious ceremonies. Unlike other chief wives, Nefertiti is shown taking part in daily worship, replicating the gestures of the king and making offerings similar to his. Yet since her husband was additionally focused on artistic innovations and poetry, not matters of state or war, Nefertiti necessarily found herself acting as a co-regent, even though such a status was never formally announced. Indeed, stelae, monuments, tomb inscriptions, and other artifacts depict the queen as assuming a major role at diplomatic receptions and in the ritual smiting of her country's foes. Even by the standards of Eighteenth Dynasty royal women, Nefertiti seems to have achieved unusual power and influence.

Whatever Nefertiti's role, and perhaps in part because of Ikhnaton's orientation as a visionary rather than a warring pharaoh, the couple's reign was not a particularly good time for Egypt. There was restlessness in the empire, which in the fourteenth century B.C. stretched from Mesopotamia (roughly modern Iraq) to Nubia (approximately the modern Sudan), with some of these dependencies being at odds with one another in petty power struggles of their own as well. Ikhnaton seems to have been unwilling to lead the traditional punitive expeditions to restore law and order.

Tragedy seems to have struck the royal family sometime after Year 11 and probably in Year 14 of Ikhnaton's seventeen-year reign. The couple's second daughter, Mekitaten, aged around thirteen, died in childbirth. Her grief-stricken parents are shown in relief mourning over her lifeless body. This was the last known record of Nefertiti. There are several theories about her abrupt disappearance from public view.

One theory assumes that Nefertiti fell out of power and retired in disgrace in the Northern Palace as another wife—perhaps Kiya or even the royal couple's oldest daughter, Meritaten—came to monopolize the king's affection. Another view holds that Nefertiti came to disagree with Ikhnaton on theological grounds; for example, he may have been shifting toward at least a partial restoration of the rival god Amen, while Nefertiti may have clung to Atenism. Still another theory has her committing suicide. Some theories stretch the imagination even further; one speculates that Smenkhare, Ikhnaton's heir, was supposedly none other than Nefertiti, appearing from that point on as a male.

However, the view that the "great royal wife" died a natural death at about age thirty—a not-unusual lifespan even among royalty at the time—is endorsed by most modern scholars. Nefertiti's mummified remains have never been discovered, nor have her husband's been positively identified. This absence of evidence may be the result of the religious counter-reformation that gathered momentum as the earlier principal god, Amen-Ra, was restored; references to Atenism and its sponsors were often obliterated and their records destroyed.

A few years after Ikhnaton's death, moreover, the court returned to the earlier royal city of Thebes, and the late capital, Akhetaten, was laid to nearly complete ruin by enemies. Vandals and thieves may also have taken their toll. Yet it should be borne in mind that archaeologists discovered the famous limestone bust of Nefertiti—among other works in what had been the workshop of the master sculptor Thutmes in Amarna—only in 1912. This may logically suggest that the final chapter about Nefertiti has not yet been written.

Summary

What is so striking about Nefertiti's life and work is that, even though her likeness—derived from Thutmes' bust of her, now located in the Egyptian Museum in Berlin, Germany—is one of the best-known and most frequently reproduced in the world, and while she lived at a time when Egypt was the most cultured and most powerful nation on earth, remarkably little is known about her. It is surmised that she must have been about four feet, six inches tall, the height of an average Egyptian woman of the time. It is known from her depictions that she often went about scantily dressed, as was customary in the warm climate. Otherwise, she appeared in the traditional garb of a clinging gown tied by a girdle with ends falling in front; at times, she is depicted coiffed with a short wig. She probably had a shaven head to improve the fit of her unusual tall blue crown. It is known that she identified with her husband's heresy and that, according to Ikhnaton's poetry, he loved her dearly. It is also known that her beauty was legendary.

Yet many other details of her life, such as her personality and character, remain unfathomed. On the whole, then, "The Heiress, Great of Favor, Lady of Graciousness, Worthy of Love, Mistress of

Upper and Lower Egypt, Great Wife of the King, Whom He Loves, Lady of the Two Lands"—as she is characterized in a contemporary inscription—though a historical figure of enormous importance, continues to be a riddle.

Bibliography

Aldred, Cyril. "The Amarna Queens." Chapter 19 in *Akhenaten: King of Egypt*. London and New York: Thames and Hudson, 1988. A foremost British Egyptologist tries to reconstruct the life and importance of Nefertiti and her controversial husband, carefully distinguishing between known facts, assumptions, and theories. Illustrated and annotated, with a selective bibliography and index.

Dodson, Aidan. *Monarchs of the Nile*. London: Rubicon, 1995. While this work on the Egyptian pharaohs incorporates late research, the scanty information on Nefertiti suggests, by implication, the enigmas surrounding the queen's life and death. Illustrated, with a good annotated bibliography and index.

Holmes, Burnham. *Nefertiti: The Mystery Queen*. New York: Contemporary Perspectives, 1977. A short first-person account written for a juvenile literature series, again emphasizing the puzzles of the subject's life and death. Illustrated.

Paglia, Camille. "The Birth of the Western Eye." Chapter 2 in *Sexual Personae: Art and Decadence from Nefertiti to Emily Dickinson*. New Haven, Conn. and London: Yale University Press, 1990. An attempt by an imaginative but iconoclastic antifeminist to "read" the world-famous Amarna face of Queen Nefertiti, concluding that it represents "a manufactured being . . . a vampire of political will." Illustrated and annotated, with a profuse index.

Redford, Donald B. *Akhenaten: The Heretic King*. Princeton, N.J.: Princeton University Press, 1984. A Canadian Egyptologist, director of the Akhenaten Temple Project excavations, theorizes about Nefertiti's "disappearance" but makes little attempt to profile the queen. Illustrated, with an excellent glossary, a selective bibliography (including works on Nefertiti), and an index.

Samson, Julia. *Nefertiti and Cleopatra: Queen Monarchs of Ancient Egypt*. London: Rubicon, 1985. A British Egyptologist tries to reconstruct, from the scanty artifacts, sites, monuments, and inscriptions contemporary with her, the life and importance of the queen. Illustrated and modestly annotated, with a short bibliography and index.

Tyldesley, Joyce. "Female Kings." Chapter 7 in *Daughters of Isis: Women of Ancient Egypt*. London and New York: Viking/Penguin, 1994. Clearly written speculations on the mysteries concerning the origins, life, death, and burial of Nefertiti. Illustrated and annotated, with a selective bibliography and index.

Wells, Evelyn. *Nefertiti*. New York: Doubleday, 1964; London: Hale, 1965. Still a widely read popular work, long on colorful atmosphere but necessarily short on hard, annotated, facts. Illustrated, with two useful glossaries, a bibliography, and a detailed index.

Peter B. Heller

NERO

Born: December 15, A.D. 37; Antium (Anzio), Italy
Died: June 9, A.D. 68; Rome, Italy
Areas of Achievement: Government and politics; patronage of the arts; Roman emperors
Contribution: As the fifth emperor of Rome, Nero continued the reign of terror of the Julio-Claudians while pursuing his own artistic career.

Early Life

Born Lucius Domitius Ahenobarbus, Nero was a member of the imperial Julio-Claudian family of Augustus through both parental lines. His formidable mother, Agrippina, was the granddaughter of Augustus' daughter Julia. His dissolute father, Cnaeus Domitius Ahenobarbus, was the grandson of Augustus' sister Octavia and Marc Antony. When Nero was two years old, his mother was banished by her mad brother, the emperor Caligula, for treason. In the following year, Nero's father died, and his estate was seized by Caligula. The orphan was reared in the house of his paternal aunt Domitia Lepida until the accession of Claudius in 41, when his mother was recalled from exile and his paternal inheritance was restored. The boy's early education was uncertain. He may have been cared for by a male dancer and a barber in his aunt's house. Later, he was given Greek tutors, including Anicetus and Beryllus, who remained advisers into his adulthood.

Nero's prospects improved significantly in 48, when the emperor Claudius married his niece Agrippina, and her son came under the tutelage of the famous statesman and Stoic philosopher Lucius Annaeus Seneca (known as "the Younger"), who supervised the boy's education. Empress Agrippina schemed tenaciously to improve Nero's place in the line of succession. In 49, she persuaded her husband to betroth Nero to his daughter Octavia. On February 25, 50, Agrippina's son was legally adopted by the emperor and renamed Nero Claudius Caesar Drusus Germanicus even though Claudius had a natural son and heir, Britannicus. On March 5, 51, Nero took the *toga virilis* and was declared an adult, six months before he was legally entitled to do so; in the absence of the emperor, he served as prefect of the city of Rome. Two years later, Nero married Octavia and gave his first public speeches. On October 12, 54, the emperor Claudius died, perhaps poisoned by Agrippina, and the sixteen-year-old Nero was declared emperor the next day.

The physical description of Nero by his ancient biographer C. Suetonius Tranquillus is supplemented by images on contemporary coins. He was of average height, with blue eyes and light blond hair that he often set in curls and grew long in the back. He had a round, prominent chin, a squat neck, a protruding stomach, and spindly legs.

Life's Work

Nero's reign was marked by lavish public displays, a dissolute personal life, and the suspicious deaths of rivals. Nero endeared himself to the Roman populace by increasing the number of days on which public games were held. In 57, he built a new wooden amphitheater for gladiatorial contests and wild-beast shows. The emperor preferred extravagant and exotic artificial displays such as mock naval battles, controlled conflagrations during dramatic performances, and reenactments of mythological events. On such public occasions, the emperor often displayed great generosity to both the performers and the audience.

Nero enjoyed an uninhibited personal life. Rumors of an incestuous relationship with his mother cannot be proven. The stories of homosexual liaisons are probably true. Nero certainly supplemented his marriage to Octavia with a long-term relationship with a Greek freedwoman named Acte.

In 55, Britannicus became the emperor's first victim, poisoned at a banquet. About the same time, Agrippina fell into disfavor. By 59, this rift had developed to such an extent that Nero ordered a bizarre assassination attempt on a barge in the Bay of Naples. When this failed, a troop of Nero's henchmen killed Agrippina in her villa.

Throughout his reign, Nero relied heavily upon others to govern the empire. At first, this dependence seemed the result of youthful inexperience; in later years, however, Nero spent much of his time composing poetry and songs that he performed publically, much to the distaste of his subjects. While Agrippina's influence was short-lived, Nero benefitted from the moderating counsel of Seneca and of Sextus Afranius Burrus, the commander of his Praetorian Guard until 62, when Seneca retired and Burrus died. Burrus was succeeded by Ofonius Tigellinus, whose heavyhanded tactics resulted in terror and bloodbaths.

The emperor had a cadre of epicurean friends on whom he could rely for help, especially in his debauchery. Marcus Salvius Otho, the future emperor, helped arrange Nero's rendezvous with Acte, and another friend, Titus Petronius Niger, the author of *Satyricon*, is often called the emperor's "arbiter of elegance."

Several competent military commanders served Nero. Gnaeus Domitius Corbulo struggled with the difficult Armenian problem on the eastern border of the empire. Gaius Suetonius Paulinus put down a dangerous revolt in the province of Britain in 60. Titus Flavius Vespasianus, the future emperor, suppressed the Jewish rebellion in Judaea in 67.

For the most part, Nero left the day-to-day management of the empire to reliable freeborn Greeks such as Phaon, his finance minister, and Doryphorus, who managed the imperial correspondence. Nero's reign was marked by few political initiatives. Rome's territory expanded modestly along the coast of the Black Sea. Some exploratory commercial expeditions were made to the Baltic and up the Nile into the present Sudan. The Armenian problem was solved, at least temporarily, with the accession to the throne of the nominal Roman vassal Tiridates.

Agrippina's death was a turning point in Nero's reign. The emperor then pursued his artistic ambitions more openly. At the end of 59, the twenty-two-year-old emperor organized religious games called *Iuvenalia* to commemorate the first shaving of his beard. While such a celebration was an ancient Roman tradition, the emperor's competition as both singer and actor was a scandalous innovation. In the next year, Nero showed his fondness for Greek culture by founding the Neronian games, modeled on the Pythian games at Delphi, with competitions in the arts (music, poetry, and oratory), in athletics, and in chariot racing. While the emperor did not compete in these games, he was awarded the prize for oratory.

By 62, Nero had fallen into a passionate relationship with a woman named Poppaea Sabina, about whom little is known except that she was the former mistress of Otho. In order to marry the pregnant Poppaea, Nero had his childless wife Octavia summarily executed on a trumped-up charge of adultery. On January 21, 63, in Antium, the emperor's beloved birthplace, Poppaea gave birth to Nero's only child, a daughter named Claudia, who died the following May.

The events surrounding the Great Fire of Rome in 64 are among the most controversial of Nero's reign. When the fire broke out on July 19, the emperor was in Antium. He quickly returned to the capital, where he opened public buildings and his gardens on the Vatican hill to refugees and arranged for emergency food supplies. Despite these relief efforts, Nero was accused of starting the fire, partly because his agents cheaply bought up the large tracts of burned property, where his infamous Golden House was later built, and partly because of the rumor that Nero callously chose the backdrop of the burning city to perform his own composition about the fall of Troy. Nero's government responded to these rumors by charging the Christian population in Rome with arson. Saint Peter and Saint Paul are traditionally considered victims of the subsequent persecution.

It is unlikely that Nero's agents actually started the fire. It is uncertain whether he actually fiddled while Rome burned. However, Nero did take advantage of the fire to change the face of Rome. He rebuilt public buildings, such as the Temple of Vesta in the Roman Forum, and erected an opulent private residence spanning at least 125 acres in the heart of Rome. This vast complex of buildings and gardens was filled with magnificent wall paintings, mechanical wonders such as a dining hall with a revolving ceiling, and great artwork, such as the Laocoön group now in the Vatican Museum. The Golden House became so closely associated with Nero's extravagance that his successors, the Flavian emperors, used part of the site to build the Colosseum.

In 65, Nero faced a major conspiracy by Roman aristocrats, who planned to make Gaius Calpurnius Piso emperor. Among those implicated in the Pisonian conspiracy were Seneca, Seneca's poet nephew Lucan (Marcus Annaeus Lucanus), and Nero's old friend Petronius. In another conspiracy, led by Annius Vinicianus in 66, Nero's general Corbulo was forced to take his own life. These incidents left a permanent scar of imperial suspicion and popular discontent on Nero's reign.

Shortly after the second celebration of the quintennial Neronian games in 65, the empress Poppaea died. While acknowledging Nero's devotion to his wife, even the ancient historian Cornelius Tacitus accepted the popular story that Nero had kicked the pregnant Poppaea after coming home late from the circus. Nero eventually married Statilia Messalina, who survived him but gave him no children.

In his final years, Nero turned increasingly to public display, and especially to personal performance, as a distraction from his political and personal troubles. Nero's reception for Tiridates, king of Armenia, in 66 was spectacular. Later in the same year, the emperor left for a tour of Greece, where he competed at a variety of festivals including the Olympic games. The emperor reportedly won 1,808 prizes, not only in artistic competitions but also in chariot racing. He also earned the enthusiastic gratitude of the Greeks by declaring the Greek province of Achaea free of Roman taxation. While in Greece, Nero also began work on an ambitious project to dig a canal across the isthmus of Corinth. Abandoned by Nero's successors, this canal was not finished until 1893.

Growing discontent led Nero to cut short his stay in the East and return to Rome in early 68, where he celebrated an extravagant triumph for his recent athletic victories. By March, Nero faced open revolt from Gaius Julius Vindex, one of his governors in Gaul (modern France). In April, Servius Suplicius Galba, governor in Spain, followed Vindex in revolt. Although Vindex's army was defeated in May by troops loyal to the emperor at Vesontio (Besançon, France), Nero lost the support of his personal Praetorian Guard in Rome and prepared for escape to Egypt. Intercepted in headlong midnight flight from the city, he committed suicide with the help of an aide. His imperial successor was Galba.

Summary

In his final hours, according to Suetonius, Nero muttered, "What an artist perishes with me." While he cherished his reputation as an artist, his work survives only in fragments. Instead, Nero's name became synonymous with incompetent government at best and despotic cruelty, debauchery, and wickedness at worst. His persecution of the Christians transformed his legend from that of a bad emperor to an antichrist whose second coming was anticipated with horror.

Nero's reign marked the end of the Julio-Claudian dynasty founded by Augustus. While the Roman Empire slipped into temporary political chaos after Nero's death, the empire was soon restabilized under new imperial dynasties that preserved the Pax Romana, built upon autocratic Julio-Claudian foundations, into the middle of the next century.

Bibliography

Bishop, John. *Nero: The Man and the Legend.* London: Hale, 1964; New York: A. S. Barnes, 1965. This scholarly biography of Nero is mostly based on the ancient historian Tacitus but offers a controversial interpretation of the role of Christians in the burning of Rome in 64. Maps and illustrations.

Grant, Michael. *Nero.* London: Weidenfeld and Nicolson, and New York: American Heritage Press, 1970. A balanced and accessible biography with useful maps, illustrations, chronological lists, genealogical tables, notes, and bibliography.

Griffin, Miriam T. *Nero: The End of a Dynasty.* London: Batsford, 1984; New Haven, Conn.: Yale University Press, 1985. A scholarly examination of the reign of Nero is followed by a detailed explanation of the reasons for his fall.

Illustrations, genealogical chart, maps, plans, and bibliography.

Henderson, Bernard W. *The Life and Principate of the Emperor Nero.* London: Methuen, 1903. Despite its publication date, Henderson's biography remains a major reference with extensive notes, maps, illustrations, genealogical table, and bibliography.

Warmington, B. H. *Nero: Reality and Legend.* London: Chatto and Windus, and New York: Norton, 1969. Emphasizes the frivolity and incompetence of Nero's reign and attributes Roman aristocratic discontent with Nero to the popularity of Stoic philosophy. Includes a select bibliography, maps, chronologies, illustrations, genealogical table, and index.

Weigall, Arthur. *Nero: The Singing Emperor of Rome.* New York and London: Putnam, 1930. This biography by a writer of popular history offers an uncritical retelling of the ancient sources. Notes and genealogical chart.

Thomas J. Sienkewicz

ORIGEN

Born: c. A.D. 185; Alexandria, Egypt

Died: c. A.D. 254; probably Tyre (modern Sur, Lebanon)

Areas of Achievement: Theology and religion

Contribution: Origen is usually considered the greatest of the early Christian thinkers; he was the first not only to write extensive commentaries on most books of the Bible but also to study the main areas and problems within theology. He did so with such intelligence that often what he wrote determined the lines of all subsequent Christian thought.

Early Life

Origen was born at the end of the period that Edward Gibbon, the eighteenth century English historian, called the happiest and most prosperous the human race had known; he died during a time of civil war, plague, economic dislocation, and persecution of the Christian Church. Alexandria, the city of his birth, was one of the great cities of the world; it used Greek as its first language and was the home of the largest library in the Mediterranean basin. There many of the best scholars of the Greek world taught and studied.

Origen was the oldest of nine children. His father, whom tradition names Leonides, was prosperous enough to provide him with a Greek literary education and concerned enough about his Christian formation to teach him the Bible. From childhood Origen was a serious Christian and a learned Greek. The Old Testament from which he studied, the Septuagint, was a Jewish translation of the Hebrew Bible into Greek. It contained, in addition to translations of those Scriptures originally written in Hebrew, books originally written in Greek. Although the canon, or list of books considered properly to be in the Bible, was not completely set in Origen's day, for most purposes his New Testament is that still used by Christians. While young, Origen memorized long passages of the Bible; thus as an adult he could associate passages from throughout the Bible on the basis of common words or themes. He, like other Christians of his day, also accepted as authoritative a body of teaching held to come from the Apostles.

Origen imbibed from his father and the Christian community the dramatic and heroic idea that he, as an individual Christian, was a participant in the drama by which the world was being redeemed.

Like many other Christians, he was uneasy about wealth and marriage and tended to see Jesus calling the Christian to poverty and celibacy (that is, to a heroic mode of existence). Although martyrdom was still relatively infrequent, it was exalted in the Christian community, and in many ways Origen saw himself throughout his life as a living martyr doing battle for the spread of Christ's kingdom. At an unknown date, thoroughly instructed in the faith, he was baptized. Around 202, when Origen was seventeen, his father was martyred and the family property was confiscated by the state. It may be argued that for the rest of his life Origen saw himself continuing his martyred father's work.

Life's Work

In the following years, Origen added to his knowledge of grammar and Greek literature a knowledge of Gnosticism, a form of dualism very common in the Greek world of his day, which condemned all things material, especially the appetites and passions of the human body, and celebrated the spiri-

S. ORIGEN.

tual, especially the human soul and spirit. Salvation was seen to lie in the separation of the soul from matter, and before Origen's day a form of Christian Gnosticism had developed. After his father's death, a Christian woman had taken Origen into her house so that he could continue his studies, and he subsequently began to teach grammar. In this woman's house Christian Gnosticism was practiced. Although Origen rejected much of what he heard there, he adopted the Gnostics' distinction between literal Christians, who understood only the literal sense of the Bible; psychic Christians, who went beyond this to consider the spiritual meaning of Scripture; and perfect Christians, who understood and followed the deepest meanings of the Bible. Origen also accepted a doctrine that was, after his death, to be condemned as heretical: He believed that ultimately all men, and even Satan himself, would be reconciled with God.

One of the second century Gnostic documents discovered at Nag Hammadi in Upper Egypt in 1945 contains many teachings similar to those found in Origen's writings and represents a form of Gnosticism more acceptable to the Christian tradition in which Origen had been formed. In this work, as in Origen's, Christ was conceived of as very similar to God the Father, although subordinate to Him in being. It also, with Origen, conceived of human existence as a long process of education, in which evil and death prepare man for union with God. Another writer, Marcion, whom Origen classified a Gnostic, provided a foil against which Origen developed the teaching that human suffering can be reconciled with God's power and goodness. Unlike Marcion, Origen held that difficult passages in the Scripture might be allegorized.

Sometime between 206 and 211, Origen added catechetical instruction (explanation of Christianity to those interested in conversion) to his duties as a grammar teacher. This period was again a time of persecution, and although he taught in secret, at one point Origen was discovered and almost killed; some of his students were martyred.

After the persecution, he gave up his work as a teacher of grammar, sold his books of Greek literature, became the chief Christian teacher in Alexandria, and gave himself totally to Bible study. He began to follow what became a lifelong practice of strictly imitating the hardest sayings of Jesus, fasting regularly, sleeping very little (the Bible had said to "pray without ceasing"), and possessing only one cloak; he also castrated himself.

In the years between 211 and 215, Origen learned much of the Platonic tradition, and that had a deep influence on him, especially the Platonists' insistence on both Divine Providence and human freedom and—against the Gnostics—on the fundamental, if limited, good of the created order. Sometime before 217 Origen traveled briefly to Rome, where he was exposed to growing controversies over the definition of the relation of Jesus Christ to God the Father. Also sometime between 215 and 222, Origen met a Hebrew-speaking convert to Christianity who had been trained as a rabbi, with whom he began to study Hebrew and Jewish biblical interpretation. He also met an Alexandrian, Ambrose, who became his lifelong patron. The first problem facing Origen as a biblical scholar was the establishment of a reliable biblical text; his response was to write first *Tetrapla* (third century) and ultimately, after he had settled in Palestine, *Hexapla* (231-c. 245), each of which contained various Greek translations in parallel columns next to a transliterated Hebrew Old Testament. In this task he revealed lifelong characteristics—painstaking interests in textual criticism and historical problems. In his mind these were completely compatible with his interest in mystical interpretation of the Bible. Origen's growing reputation is evident from an incident that occurred about 222, when he was summoned to Arabia by the Roman governor for the discussion of an unknown subject.

Most of his early writings, from between 222 and 230, have been lost, but one of his most important, *Peri archon (On First Principles*, 1869), survives. Heavily influenced by Platonism, it espoused the idea, later to be condemned, that the human soul before entering the body has existed eternally. Students were now flocking to Origen's lectures; of these he accepted only the most promising. Ambrose provided a staff of stenographers, who took down Origen's lectures in shorthand as he gave them, and of copyists, who then prepared a more finished text.

Probably in 230, after unspecified conflict with Bishop Demetrius of Alexandria, Origen moved, at first briefly, to Caesarea, in Palestine. Having returned to Alexandria, he again left in 231, summoned by the dowager empress, Julia Mamaea, to Antioch to teach her more about Christianity. After a brief return to Alexandria, he left for Greece, traveling via Caesarea, where he was ordained a priest. In 233 a final break with Bishop Demetrius took place, and Origen moved to Caesarea. Finally, works which he had long been developing, such as a commentary on the Gospel of John and *Peri eykhēs* (c. 233; *On Prayer*, 1954), the first thorough Christian examination of prayer as contemplation of God, were finished.

Even more productive were the years from 238 to 244, when he regularly preached and was consulted in matters of doctrine. Again, although most of his work has been lost, some has survived, above all more than two hundred sermons. Following an estrangement from his bishop, Theoctistus, Origen departed for Athens, where he continued his writing. In 246 or 247, he returned to Caesarea, where he set to work on commentaries on the Gospels of Luke and Matthew and on *Contra Celsum* (c.249; *Against Celsus*, 1954), a defense of Christianity. During roughly the last eight years of his life, he found himself in the midst of both theological controversy and serious persecution of the Christians by the emperor Decius. By 251, Origen, who had been imprisoned and tortured, was a broken man. The circumstances of his death are uncertain.

Summary

Origen was more important than any other early Christian thinker in assimilating the Jewish and Greek traditions to Christianity. The former he accomplished through his lifelong contact with rabbinic scholars and the latter through his lifelong devotion to the Platonic tradition. His conscious intent was always to be faithful to Christianity whenever there was a direct conflict between it and what he had inherited from the earlier traditions. Nevertheless, he also intended to be open to truth wherever it might be found. That Christians usually think of themselves as the heirs to both the Jewish and the Greek traditions is more his work than any other's. He was the first Christian to discuss at length central problems such as the nature of free will and of God's relation to the world; as the first to do so, Origen did not always arrive at conclusions deemed correct by later standards. Thus, in spite of his genius, he has often been the subject of some suspicion in later Christian tradition. Yet arguably he had as much influence in setting the terms of later Christian theology as any writer, Paul included.

Origen subjected himself to great ascetic discipline, usually surrounded by his community of scribes and students, and his mode of life may be justly described as protomonastic; indeed, it was only about forty years after his death that the monastic movement began. Finally, with his great confidence in the ability of the disciplined intellect to rise above the world of sense to the vision of God, Origen stands near the source of the Christian contemplative tradition.

Bibliography

Caspary, Gerard E. *Politics and Exegesis: Origen and the Two Swords*. Berkeley: University of California Press, 1979. Centers on Origen's thought about the relation of Christianity to the political order but has much useful information about his biblical interpretation and political thought. A structuralist interpretation which mistakenly attributes pacifism to early Christians in general before the time of Constantine the Great.

Crouzel, H. *Origen*. San Francisco: Harper and Row, 1989. Written by the leading contemporary Origen scholar, this book is an authoritative and comprehensive general study of Origen's life and thought. It contains a review of the scholarly literature and a detailed bibliography.

Daniélou, Jean. *A History of Early Christian Doctrine Before the Council of Nicaea*. Vol. 2, *Gospel Message and Hellenistic Culture*. Translated by John Austin Baker. London: Darton, Longman, and Todd, and Philadelphia: Westminster Press, 1964. Contains fine sections on Origen's catechetical teaching, biblical interpretation, Christology, anthropology, demonology, and understanding of Christian Gnosticism. Daniélou is very precise on the meaning and practice of allegory for Origen.

———. *Origen*. Translated by Walter Mitchell. New York: Sheed and Ward, 1955. Covers Origen's life and times but is especially strong on his theology, including his interpretation of the Bible, cosmology, angelology, Christology, and eschatology. This Roman Catholic reading of Origen gives a very fair account of scholarly disagreement over Origen's theology of the sacraments.

Kannengieser, C., and W. L. Petersen, eds. *Origen of Alexandria: His World and His Legacy*. Notre Dame, IN: University of Notre Dame Press, 1988. This is a collection of papers from a Colloquy on Origen, discussing the various intellectual influences he experienced and different aspects of his ideas.

Küng, H. *Great Christian Thinkers*. New York: Continuum, 1994. In this survey of the history of

Christian thought, written by a left-wing Catholic theologian, a chapter is devoted to Origen. Küng makes an assessment of Origen's place within the Christian tradition, comparing him with some of his contemporaries and with Augustine.

Origen. *Contra Celsum*. Translated by Henry Chadwick. Cambridge: Cambridge University Press, 1953; New York: Cambridge University Press, 1965. The introduction and notes of this translation of one of Origen's most important works are a mine of information. Well indexed.

Smith, J. C. *The Ancient Wisdom of Origen*. Cranbury, N.J.: Associated University Presses, 1992. This is a comprehensive study of Origen's ethical teaching and his ideas on spiritual transformation. It contains an informative appendix titled "Origen Scholarship and Textual Methodology."

Trigg, Joseph Wilson. *Origen: The Bible and Philosophy in the Third-Century Church*. Atlanta, Ga.: John Knox Press, 1983; London: SCM Press, 1985. The best general survey of Origen's life and thought in English. Daniélou's explanation (see entries above) of Origen's spiritual exegesis of the Bible is more perceptive than that of Trigg, but Trigg is consistently well-informed. A Protestant reading of Origen.

Glenn W. Olsen

OVID
Publius Ovidius Naso

Born: March 20, 43 B.C.; Sulmo, Italy
Died: A.D. 17; Tomis on the Black Sea
Area of Achievement: Literature
Contribution: While his contemporaries Vergil and Horace were glorifying the Roman Empire or harking back to sober republican virtues, Ovid wittily celebrated the senses. He also preserved for later generations many of the classical myths, although he treated the gods with the same irreverence as he did his fellow mortals.

Early Life

Publius Ovidius Naso was born in 43 B.C. in central Italy. As his family was a locally prominent one, he enjoyed the advantages of an education and preparation for an official career. Ovid's youth was a period of political chaos. Rome was still nominally a republic, but Julius Caesar had made himself dictator. When Caesar was murdered in the year before Ovid's birth, the Roman world was plunged into civil war. Peace was not truly restored until fourteen years later.

First, Octavian, great-nephew and adopted son of Julius Caesar, combined with Marc Antony and Marcus Aemilius Lepidus to defeat the chiefs of the republican party, Marcus Janius Brutus and Gaius Cassius Longinus. Then, Lepidus was shunted aside, and Octavian and Antony entered into a protracted struggle for power. In 30 B.C., the year after his disastrous naval defeat at Actium, Antony and his Egyptian ally and lover, Cleopatra VII, committed suicide. Octavian was the complete military ruler of Rome. By 27 B.C., the senate had conferred upon him the official title Imperator, or emperor, and the honorary title Caesar Augustus, or the august one.

The extent to which these wars affected Ovid's family is not known, but the eventual outcome should have proved beneficial for him. He had become a poet, and the Augustan Age was a favorable time for poets. Gaius Maecenas, a chief counselor to Augustus, was the protector and financier of poets. Yet the fun-loving Ovid was destined to squander his advantages and fall afoul of his emperor.

Life's Work

Although Ovid was born one hundred miles east of Rome, he was soon exposed to the atmosphere of the capital. As the scion of an established family, he was sent to Rome at the age of twelve to be trained in the law. His arrival at the capital roughly coincided with Augustus' final victory over Antony. The era of the Pax Romana had begun.

Ovid was twenty-two years younger than Horace and almost thirty years younger than Vergil. Since he had been a child during the civil war, his experience of those terrible times had been less immediate than that of the older poets. Vergil and Horace were conservative in temperament and viewed the emperor, despite his new title, as the embodiment of the traditional Roman virtues. Their approval of Augustus was apparently sincere as well as politically and financially expedient—Horace, who had fallen into poverty as a young man through his support of the ill-fated Brutus, received the gift of a farm from Maecenas in 33 B.C. Ovid, however, was not a member of Vergil and Horace's circle. His companions were young and less closely associated with the regime.

Ovid entered the Roman civil service but quickly abandoned the law for poetry. He was a born poet, who once wrote that whatever he tried to say came out in verse. For one element of patrician Roman society, the new era of peace and prosperity was a perfect time for pleasure seeking. Ovid was soon the darling of this brilliant society. He became a professional poet, and his social success equaled his literary success. His themes were often frivolous, but he treated them with great elegance and wit. Technically, his verse was dazzling. The tone of his work was skeptical and irreverent. He practically thumbed his nose at the official solemnity and high-mindedness of the Augustan establishment. *Gravitas* might be the prime Roman virtue, but it was not the poetic mode for Ovid.

Little is known of Ovid's appearance or personal behavior. A tradition grew up, totally unsubstantiated by evidence, that Ovid was a rake and a womanizer—a sort of ancient precursor to John Wilmot, Earl of Rochester, and George Gordon, Lord Byron. The legendary Ovid, the good-looking playboy, is largely the product of two of his poems. The first, the *Amores* (c. 20 B.C.; English translation), was also his first published work. The *Amores* unblushingly recounts the conquests of a Roman Don Juan. The second, the *Ars amatoria* (c. 2 B.C.; *Art of Love*), is a tongue-in-cheek seduction manual.

The *Art of Love* could hardly have endeared Ovid to Augustus. While the emperor's propagandists were portraying a Rome turning back to the virtuousness, dignity, and piety of its forefathers, the impudent Ovid portrayed an amoral and libertine Rome, where panting ladies were ripe for the plucking. Since generalizations must of necessity distort, both Romes probably existed simultaneously. In addition to being wickedly amusing, the poem reveals many psychologically valid insights into the gamesmanship of love. Ovid recommends the theater, the arena, dinner parties, and large festivals as the most likely sources of pliant females. He artfully plays upon the stereotypes, already centuries old in his day, of man as an unskilled dissembler and woman as a born actress. His advice to the would-be gallant is practical in nature: Bind your mistress to you through habit; it is the most potent thing in life. Never, even playfully, discuss any of her defects. Do not be so foolhardy as to demand her age; this information is not to be had. Last, if she is over thirty-five, do not be distressed; older women are more practiced, and therefore more desirable, lovers.

Ovid's passing reference to pederasty is made without apology and suggests that it was an all too common practice in his society. Perhaps the tone and theme of the poem are crystallized in one line, Ovid's assertion that after dark there are no ugly women. Yet the poem contains self-mockery too. Of the role poetry plays in wooing a woman, the poet says: Send her gold rather than verses for, even if they are perfectly written and perfectly recited, she will consider them a trifling gift at best.

Over the next seven years, Ovid worked on his masterpiece, the *Metamorphoses* (c. A.D. 8; English translation). The poem consists of fifteen books which retell the stories of classical mythology, beginning with the creation of the world. The title means "transformations," especially by supernatural means, but it is only loosely descriptive. Although many of the tales recount the transformation of human beings into animals or inanimate things, others do not. Fortunately for posterity, Ovid retold so many stories that his poem became a principal sourcebook of classical myths. One cannot read the great triumvirate of English literature—Geoffrey Chaucer, William Shakespeare, and John Milton—without noticing how often they allude to the *Metamorphoses* or choose Ovid's version of a familiar myth.

Some ancient writers later accused Ovid, with justification, of lacking a proper respect for the gods. It is clear that the author of the *Metamorphoses* did not believe the stories he was telling or in the deities who populated them. It is equally clear that he had matured artistically since the composition of the *Art of Love*. The *Metamorphoses* is, like the *Art of Love*, witty, charming, and beautifully constructed; still, it is also more comic than frivolous, often seriocomic, occasionally even tragicomic. Ovid modernized the poem in a way that should have pleased the emperor. He portrays the ascension of the murdered Julius Caesar into the heavens, where he becomes a star, and hints that Augustus himself will one day be changed into a god.

By A.D. 8, however, Ovid was in deep trouble with his emperor. Although he was by that time Rome's leading poet, he was tried before Augustus on a charge which history has not recorded and was banished from Rome. Possibly the emperor's disapproval of the *Art of Love* had finally brought about the poet's downfall. Yet that poem was completed about 1 B.C. and had been in published form since A.D. 1. Why would the emperor wait seven years before acting against Ovid? Scholars suggest that the poet's offense may have been his involvement in a scandal, possibly one associated with the emperor's daughter Julia. For whatever reason, he was banished to Tomis (located in modern-day Romania), an outpost on the Black Sea. Tomis was a cultural and intellectual backwater—and dangerous besides, since it was menaced by hostile border tribesmen.

For the next nine years, Ovid pleaded, through a series of epistles in verse known as the *Tristia* (after A.D. 8; *Sorrows*), for the lifting of his punishment. Augustus did not relent, nor did his stepson Tiberius, who succeeded him in A.D. 14. Given the excesses which were eventually to mark that reign, one wonders how corrupting the poet's presence could have been in the Rome of Tiberius. Nevertheless, Ovid died still in exile in A.D. 17.

Summary

Aeneas, Vergil's self-sacrificing Trojan prince, and the manliness and common sense of Horace's odes express one aspect of the Augustan Age. It was probably the dominant aspect, stressing as it does the patriotism of the *Aeneid* (c. 29-19 B.C.) and the traditional religious, moral, and social values of the *Odes* (23 B.C., 13 B.C.). Ovid, however, writing in the sensual tradition of Catullus, reflects another aspect of the age.

The Rome of Vergil and Horace gave to the Western world a legal system and a framework of political unity which only a serious and an industrious people could have devised. Yet there was also in the Roman nature a playfulness, a highly developed aesthetic sensibility, and a *joie de vivre*; these are the qualities found in Ovid's poetry. All men in every age are capable of excesses and base behavior, but the three great Augustan poets reflect the two faces of the Roman Empire at its best.

It is ironic that it was the skeptical Ovid who, in his *Metamorphoses*, breathed life back into the debilitated gods of Rome. Ovid lived at the dawn of the Christian era, and within a few centuries the Christians' monotheism would sweep aside the polytheism of Greece and Rome. Nothing is so dead as a dead idea, but Ovid preserved the gods as intriguing characters in dozens of charming stories told in elegant verse. His compendium of mythological tales has been so influential that few indeed are the great works of Western literature which contain no allusion to Ovid's *Metamorphoses*.

Bibliography

Barchiesi, A. *The Poet and the Prince: Ovid and Augustan Discourse.* Berkeley: University of California Press, 1997. An innovative study of Ovid's place in Roman society. Augustus' imperial propaganda and policy are discussed, with their implications for the poet's work.

Binns, J. W., ed. *Ovid.* London and Boston: Routledge, 1973. An entry in the series Greek and Latin Studies: Classical Literature and Its Influence. Composed of seven essays by British and American scholars. The first five address the poetry itself, while the last two address Ovid's influence in the Middle Ages and the sixteenth century.

Boyd, B. W. *Ovid's Literary Loves: Influence and Innovation in the Amores.* Ann Arbor: University of Michigan Press, 1997. The study concentrates exclusively on the literary qualities of Ovid's work, examined against the general background of classical Greek and Latin poetry.

Brewer, Wilmon. *Ovid's "Metamorphoses" in European Culture.* Boston: Cornhill Publishing Co., 1933. A three-volume companion work to an English translation in blank verse. Begins with a long introductory survey which includes much biographical detail. Very valuable, because every story in the poem is discussed in the light of its cultural and literary antecedents, then of later works for which it served as antecedent.

Hoffman, Richard L. *Ovid and "The Canterbury Tales."* Philadelphia: University of Pennsylvania Press, and London: Oxford University Press, 1966. Since John Dryden first compared Ovid and Chaucer in 1700, many Chaucerians have remarked that the great English poet studied, imitated, and relied on Ovid above all other authors. This study treats the *Metamorphoses* as a predecessor of *The Canterbury Tales.*

Mack, S. *Ovid.* New Haven, Conn.: Yale University Press, 1988. This short book is a good introduction to Ovid's life and writings. His works are individually discussed. There is no separate bibliography.

Rand, Edward Kennard. *Ovid and His Influence.* Boston: Marshall Jones Co., 1925; London: Harrap, 1930. Part of the series Our Debt to Greece and Rome. A professor of Latin poses the question: What does our age owe to a professed roué, a writer so subtle and rhetorical as to strike some as thoroughly insincere? His 184 pages answer that question.

Syme, Ronald. *History in Ovid*. Oxford: Clarendon Press, and New York: Oxford University Press, 1978. Concentrating on Ovid's latest poems, the author develops a kind of manual designed to cover life and letters in the last decade of Caesar Augustus. Valuable because of the relative obscurity of that period.

Thibault, John C. *The Mystery of Ovid's Exile*. Berkeley: University of California Press, 1964. The author examines various hypotheses about Ovid's exile, describes their content, and evaluates the evidence and the cogency of the arguments.

Patrick Adcock

PAN KU

Born: A.D. 32; place unknown
Died: A.D. 92; Lo-yang, China
Area of Achievement: Historiography
Contribution: Through his compilation of the *Han shu*, Pan Ku preserved a full, well-documented record for this vital period of Chinese history and set the standard for all subsequent dynastic histories of China.

Early Life

Pan Ku was a member of the illustrious Pan family of Han China (207 B.C. to A.D. 220). Since the generation of his great-great-grandfather, the Pans had distinguished themselves in scholarship, serving the Han imperial government in both court and provincial posts. His grandaunt had been a favorite concubine of Emperor Ch'eng (reigned 32-7 B.C.). Ku's twin brother, Ch'ao, assigned the title of Marquess for Establishing the Remote Regions, won for himself immortal fame by reestablishing Chinese hegemony in Central Asia. His younger sister, Chao, much respected in court circles as the tutor of imperial princesses, was one of China's foremost women scholars; she wrote the *Nü-chieh* (A.D. 106; instructions for women), the first textbook ever written for teaching Chinese women.

Life's Work

Despite having such illustrious forebears and siblings, the young Pan Ku had a hard time finding his niche in the world. The Pan family had no automatic right to high office. Ku's father, Piao, though fairly successful in his official career, died when his sons were still relatively young and unestablished. He did, however bequeath to Ku a project which was to secure to the Pan family a hallowed place in China's literary tradition: the writing of a complete history of the Former Han Dynasty, the *Han shu*. Ku's efforts in writing the history were brought to the attention of Emperor Ming (reigned 58-75), who appreciated his merits and made him a gentleman-in-waiting (*lang*). In this capacity, Ku had access to government archives which facilitated his writing efforts.

Besides writing the *Han shu*, Ku was given other writing assignments such as to report on the proceedings at the Po-hu Pavilion, in which an enclave of Confucian erudites gathered to deliberate on the correct interpretations of Confucian classics bearing on the ritual aspects of the Chinese monarchy. In addition, he found time to indulge his poetic propensities. His two *fu* (rhymed prose essays or rhapsodies) on the two capitals of the Han Dynasty established him as the foremost poet of his time.

Although other people had a hand in the compilation of the *Han shu*, notably his father Piao, his younger sister, Chao, and the scholar Ma Hsü, there is no question that the main credit has to go to Ku. He gave the book its definitive form and was personally responsible for writing most of the text. Thus, it is appropriate to credit Pan Ku as the author of the *Han shu*.

Traditionally, Pan Ku's name came to be linked to that of Ssu-ma Ch'ien (often abbreviated to read Ma-Pan) to suggest the highest standard in historiographical writing. There is no denying Ku's indebtedness to Ssu-ma Ch'ien. In fact, the *Han shu* cannot be meaningfully discussed apart from the historiographical context that Ssu-ma Ch'ien and his masterpiece, *Shih chi* (c. 90 B.C.), provided.

Before Ssu-ma Ch'ien's time (c. 145-c. 86 B.C.), historical works had not been formally or conceptually differentiated from other forms of serious literature, which all purported to be authentic words and deeds of the ancients. To the extent that conscious attempts to write history were made, the only available framework into which records of the past could be fitted was the *pien-nien* (annals), as exemplified by the *Ch'un ch'iu* (c. 480 B.C.; *Spring and Autumn Annals*), edited by Confucius. This was a strictly chronological listing of events as they transpired, recorded from the point of view of some court historian. The disadvantages of this format are obvious. In treatments of events that had to be recorded close to the time they occurred, they often appear to be abstracted from their context, unless substantial digression and background materials were incorporated. To catch the attention of the recorder, events had to be of a spectacular nature—battles, diplomatic alliances, and the accession or death of rulers. Long-term changes such as population growth or technological development occurred too slowly to be noticed. Moreover, the format could not accommodate matters such as social or cultural history that had no immediate bearing on the government.

Ssu-ma Ch'ien lived at a time when vast changes had overtaken China. The decentralized feudal China of the time of Confucius had given way to the centralized bureaucratic empire under the Ch'in (221-206 B.C.). The Ch'in Dynasty, ruling over a unified China for the first time in history, was undone by excessive tyranny and was overthrown by a universal revolt. The ensuing struggle to succeed to the throne of China ended with the triumph of the House of Han, which was to rule for more than four hundred years. Meanwhile, the quest for empire was taking the Chinese into Mongolia and Central Asia. The economy was expanding, and enormous fortunes were made. Myriad individuals had played important roles in the unfolding drama. The times called for a new historiography that would be capable of portraying these vast changes and doing justice to these individuals and their contributions.

In writing the *Shih chi*, Ssu-ma Ch'ien overcame the limitations of the old historiography by developing a composite format. The seventy chapters of the *Shih chi* are divided into five sections, each representing a distinct style of historical writing. The first section, known as "Basic Annals" (*pen-chi*), essentially follows the *pien-nien* style of the old historiography, being a chronicle of events recorded from the viewpoint of the paramount ruler of China. The longest section is the "Biographies" (*lieh-chuan*). Here, attention is given to individuals, ranging from successful generals and ministers to unconventional characters such as the would-be assassin Ch'ing K'o, as well as physicians, diviners, entertainers, and entrepreneurs. Ssu-ma Ch'ien chose people who exemplified in their words or deeds patterns of human endeavor which were to be commended. The biographical section also gave the historian the flexibility to reconcile the two moral imperatives of his profession: objectivity in reporting, and praising the worthy and castigating evildoers. Since the annals and the biographies sections together constitute the bulk of the *Shih chi*, the *shih-chi* format of historiography is often known as the *chichuan* style.

The section of hereditary houses (*shih-chia*) deals with the history of the *de facto* sovereign states during the period preceding the Ch'in unification. The section on chronological tables (*piao*) traces the genealogy of the prominent families and furnishes a convenient scheme for correlating the chronologies of the various feudal states. The most distinctive section of the *Shih chi* is the one titled "Monographs" (*shu*), which comprises eight chapters dealing with such wide-ranging matters as rites, music, pitched pipes, the calendar, astronomy, state sacrifices, rivers and canals, and the economy.

Ssu-ma Ch'ien lived during the reign of Emperor Wu-ti (140-87 B.C.), during the heyday of the Former Han Dynasty. By A.D. 9, however, Wu-ti's descendants had been edged out of the succession by the usurper Wang Mang, who founded the Hsin Dynasty (A.D. 9-22). Wang Mang, however, was unable to consolidate his regime, and his dynasty fell amid a revolt by starving peasants and disgruntled landlords, precipitating another scramble for the throne of China. The man who emerged triumphant in this contest, Liu Hsiu (reigned as Emperor Kuang-wu, A.D. 25-57), who was descended from the founder of the Former Han Dynasty, claimed that his dynasty was a continuation or restoration of the Great Han. As his capital was located at Loyang, to the east of the Former Han capital, Changan (also spelled Sian), historians refer to the restored dynasty as the Eastern or Latter Han.

To scholars living at the court of the Latter Han, the period from the founding of the first Han Dynasty to the final overthrow of the usurper Wang Mang constituted a natural unit of history. Emulating the success of Ssu-ma Ch'ien, several of them (among them Pan Piao, Ku's father) had tried to write its history. Apart from determining the overall design and collecting source materials for the project, however, Piao apparently had done little actual writing. Though Ku received the idea of writing the *Han shu* from his father, and thought he was apparently deeply moved by the Confucian value of filial piety, he saw no need to be bound by his father's design. Whereas his father had had no use for the majority of Ssu-ma Ch'ien's innovations, Ku retained almost all the sections of the *Shih chi*, with the exception of "Hereditary Houses" (for the obvious reason that in the centralized bureaucratic polity of Han China there were no authentic hereditary houses apart from that of the imperial family).

Shih chi not only was the model for Pan Ku's *Han shu* but also constituted his single most important source. Materials from the *Shih chi* pertaining to the first hundred years of the Former Han Dynasty, in which the coverage of the two works overlaps, were copied almost verbatim into the *Han shu*. Nevertheless, Ku was no mere imitator; wherever possible, he sought to develop the potentialities of the model he had inherited. Ssu-ma Ch'ien, for example, had invented the category of monographs to expand the scope of historiography to encompass ritual, social, and economic as well as political history. Pan Ku went one step further. In the section on monographs (which he renamed *chih* instead of *shu*), he retained all the *Shih chi* chapters on ritual matters but vastly expanded the scope of administrative history, adding new chapters on penal law and geography. The monograph on geography gives detailed population figures for the administrative subdivisions of the empire, thus yielding the first complete census of China, for the year A.D. 2. In addition, he ventured into the domain of intellectual history. The monograph on literature (*i-wên chih*) was more than a systematic account of Chinese intellectual history; it also contained the first complete catalog of all Chinese books extant at that time.

Although Ku's character was amiable and accommodating, he had the misfortune late in life to be caught up in the factional strife of the Han court. He joined the staff of General Tou Hsien as his confidential secretary on the eve of the latter's punitive expedition against the Hsiung-nu (Huns). Upon his return, the general was impeached for treason, and members of his retinue were also implicated. Ku was cast into prison, where he died before his friends could rescue him.

Summary

Through his *Han shu*, Pan Ku had a great impact on Chinese historiography and on Chinese political consciousness. He developed the possibilities of the *chi-chuan* format, bringing it into the mainstream of Chinese official historiography. His contribution in this regard is twofold. First, he produced a monumental work, in one hundred chapters, in the style of Ssu-ma Ch'ien's new historiography, thus helping to popularize it. Indeed, it is doubtful whether Ssu-ma Ch'ien's legacy could have survived if Pan Ku had not written the *Han shu* in support of it. There is evidence that until the T'ang period (618-907), the *Shih chi* was an extremely rare book and that it was primarily thanks to Pan Ku's *Han shu* that scholars became acquainted with the *chi-chuan* style of historiography. Second, Pan Ku was the one who arranged for the new historiography to be wedded to the salient feature of Chinese history, the dynastic cycle. Although dynasties varied in length and in the circumstances of their rise and fall, generally speaking, each dynasty marked a distinct period, an era with its own characteristics. After the time of Pan Ku, as soon as a new dynasty had consolidated its

power, one of the first things its scholars did was compile an official history of the dynasty which had preceded it, signifying in this way that that dynasty was indeed defunct. The precedent for this practice was established by Pan Ku, who also set the tone for the writing of these official dynastic histories: impersonal, objective, and dignified.

Bibliography

Hughes, E. R. *Two Chinese Poets: Vignettes of Han Life and Thought*. Princeton, N.J.: Princeton University Press, 1960. The author examines two sets of rhapsodies on the two Han capitals, by Pan Ku and Chang Heng, respectively. While the book is informative with regard to the nature of Han rhapsodies and the descriptions of the two capitals, the main purpose of the author is to highlight, through exploring the minds of the two poets, the contrasting style and ethos of the two Han dynasties. Indispensable for understanding Pan Ku's ideology and worldview.

Hulsewe, A. F. P. *China in Central Asia: The Early Stage, 125 B.C.-A.D. 23: An Annotated Translation of Chapters Sixty-one and Ninety-six of the History of the Former Han Dynasty*. Leiden, Netherlands: E. J. Brill, 1979. Particularly useful is the seventy-page introductory chapter by M. A. N. Loewe. Loewe comments on the materials on which the original copy of the *Han shu* was written (wood or bamboo slips) and discusses the relationship between the *Shih chi* and the *Han shu*. He argues, contrary to previous assumptions, that at least in one case the *Shih chi* text is not the source for the *Han shu* but indeed derivative from it.

———. "Notes on the Historiography of the Han Period." In *Historians of China and Japan*, edited by W. G. Beasley and E. G. Pulleyblank. London and New York: Oxford University Press, 1961. A general but authoritative survey on the authors of the *Shih chi* and the *Han shu* and other works of historiography of the Han period.

Knechtges, D. R. "To Praise the Han: The Eastern Capital Fu of Pan Ku and His Contemporaries." In *Thought and Law in Qin and Han China*. A. F. P. Hulsewe, W. L. Idema and E. Züchner, eds. Leiden and New York: E. J. Brill, 1990. The article examines the political and ideological background of Pan Ku's rhapsodies.

———, trans. *Wen Xuan or Selections of Refined Literature*. Vol. 1, *Rhapsodies on Metropolises and Capitals*. Vol. 3, *Rhapsodies on Natural*

Phenomena, Birds and Animals, Aspirations and Feelings, Sorrowful Laments, Literature, Music, and Passions. Princeton, N.J.: Princeton University Press, 1982-1996. Vol. 1 contains a generously annotated translation of the "Two Capitals Rhapsody," and a biographical note on Pan Ku. Vol. 3 includes an annotated translation of the "Rhapsody of Communicating with the Unseen."

Swann, Nancy Lee. *Pan Chao, Foremost Woman Scholar of China*. New York and London: Century Co., 1932. Still the most important source on Pan Ku's life. The author traces the genealogy of the Pan family, discusses the career of some of Ku's forebears, and assesses the contributions which Ku's father and younger sister and others made toward the completion of the *Han shu*. A meticulous scholar, Swann utilizes all available primary and secondary sources in arriving at her conclusions.

Watson, Burton. *Ssu-ma Ch'ien, Grand Historian of China*. New York: Columbia University Press, 1958. Not only the most authoritative study on the *Shih chi* but also indispensable for any serious work on the *Han shu*; the author often makes insightful comments on the relative merits of the *Shih chi* and the *Han shu* and their respective authors.

Winston W. Lo

PAPPUS

Born: c. 300; Alexandria, Egypt
Died: c. 350; place unknown
Area of Achievement: Mathematics
Contribution: Pappus provided a valuable compilation of the contributions of earlier mathematicians and inspired later work on algebraic solutions to geometric problems.

Early Life

Almost nothing is known about Pappus' life, including the dates of his birth and death. A note written in the margin of a text by a later Alexandrian geometer states that Pappus wrote during the time of Diocletian (284-305). The earliest biographical source is a tenth century Byzantium encyclopedia, the *Suda.* This work lists the writings of Pappus and describes him as a "philosopher," which suggests that he may have held some official position as a teacher of philosophy. Nevertheless, this reference to philosophy may be no more than an indication of his interest in natural science. The geometer had at least one child, a son, since he dedicated one of his books to him. In addition, Pappus mentions two of his contemporaries in his texts: a philosopher, Hierius, although the connection between the two is not clear; and Pandrosian, a woman who taught mathematics. Pappus addressed one of his works to her, not as a tribute, but because he found several of her students deficient in their mathematical education.

Pappus lived at a time when the main course of Greek mathematics had been in decline for more than five hundred years; although geometry continued to be studied and taught, there were few original contributions to the subject. To alleviate this lack, he attempted to compile all available sources of earlier geometry and made several significant contributions to the subject. As the first author in this new tradition, sometimes called the silver age of mathematics, Pappus provides a valuable resource for all of ancient Greek geometry.

Life's Work

Throughout his life, Pappus maintained a lively interest in a number of areas dealing with mathematics and natural science. The bulk of his surviving works can be found in the *Synagoge* (c. A.D. 340; English translation known as *Collection*). Other works either are in fragmentary form or else are no longer extant, although mentioned by other writers.

There exists part of a commentary on the mechanics of Archimedes which considers problems associated with mean proportions and constructions using straightedge and compass. There are two remaining books of a commentary on Ptolemy's *Mathēmatikē suntaxis* (c. A.D. 150; *Almagest*) explaining some of the finer points of the text to the inexperienced reader. Pappus continued his interest in the popularization of difficult texts in a work, of which only a fragment survives, on Euclid's *Stoicheia* (c. fourth century B.C.; *Elements*), in which Pappus explains the nature of irrational magnitudes to the casual reader. The lost works include a geography of the inhabited world, a description of rivers in Libya, an interpretation of dreams, several texts on spherical geometry and stereographic projection, an astrological almanac, and a text on alchemical oaths and formulas. Pappus was more than a geometer; he was a person who lived in a world where the search for new knowledge was rapidly declining and where political instability was the order of the day. Yet he expressed a continuing interest in the education of those less fortunate than himself and showed a lively interest in affairs outside his city.

Pappus' claim to historical and mathematical significance is found in a compendium of eight books on geometry. This collection covers the entire range of Greek geometry and has been described as a handbook or guide to the subject. In several of the books, when the classical texts are available, Pappus shows how the original proof is accomplished as well as alternative methods to prove the theorem. In other books, where the classical sources are not easily accessible, Pappus provides a history of the problems as well as different attempts at finding a solution. An overall assessment of these books shows few moments of great originality; rather, a capable and independent mind sifts through the entire scope of Greek geometry while demonstrating fine technique and a clear understanding of his field of study.

A summary of the contents of the eight books shows that some are of only historical interest, providing information on or elucidation of classical texts. Other books, particularly book 7, have been a source of inspiration for later mathematicians. All of book 1 and the first part of book 2 are lost. The remainder of book 2 deals with the problems of multiplying all the numbers between 1 and 800 together and expressing the product in words using the myriad (10,000) as base. Pappus refers to a lost work by Apollonius of Perga which seems to be part of the problem of expressing large numbers in words that began with Archimedes' third century B.C. *The Sand-Reckoner* (translated in 1897). Book 3 deals with construction problems using straight-edge and compass: finding a mean proportion between two given straight lines, finding basic means between two magnitudes (arithmetic, geometric, and harmonic), constructing a triangle within another triangle, and constructing solids within a sphere. Book 4 consists of a collection of theorems, including several famous problems in Greek mathematics: a generalization of Pythagoras' theorem, the squaring of the circle, and the trisection of an angle. Book 5 begins with an extensive introduction on the hexagonal cells of honeycombs and suggests that bees could acquire geometric knowledge from some divine source. This discussion leads to the question of the maximum volume that can be enclosed by a superficial area and to a sequence of theorems that prove that the circle has the greatest area of figures of equal parameter. His proof appears to follow those formulated by an earlier Hellenistic geometer named Zenodorus, whose work is lost. In a later section of this book, Pappus introduces a section on solids with a Neoplatonist statement that God chose to make the universe in a sphere because it is the noblest of figures. It has been asserted but not proved that the sphere has the greatest surface of all equal surface figures. Pappus then proceeds to examine the sphere and regular solids. Book 6 is sometimes called "Little Astronomy"; it deals with misunderstandings in mathematical technique and corrects common misrepresentations.

Book 7 is by far the most important, both because it had a direct influence on modern mathematics and because it gives an account of works in the so-called *Treasury of Analysis* or *Domain of Analysis*, of which a large number are lost. These are works by Euclid, Apollonius, and others that set up a branch of mathematics that provides equipment for the analysis of theorems and problems. Classical geometry uses the term "analysis" to mean a reversal of the normal procedure called "synthesis." Instead of taking a series of steps through valid statements about abstract objects, analysis reverses the procedure by assuming the validity of the theorem and working back to valid statements. Through the preservation of Pappus'

account of these works it is possible to reconstruct most of them.

His most original contribution to modern mathematics comes in a section dealing with Apollonius' *Kōnika* (c. 250 B.C.; *Conics*), where Pappus attempts to demonstrate that the product of three or four straight lines can be written as a series of compounded ratios and is equal to a constant. This came to be known as the "Pappus problem." Book 8 is the last of the surviving books of *Synagoge*, although there is internal evidence that four additional books existed. In this book, Pappus takes on the subject of mechanical problems, including weights on inclined planes, proportioning of gears, and the center of gravity.

There exist substantial references to various lost books of Pappus; among the lost works is a commentary on Euclid's *Elements*, although a two-part section does exist in Arabic. Several other works fit into this category, surviving only in commentary by later writers or in fragments of questionable authorship in Arabic. One of the more interesting Arabic manuscripts (discovered in 1860) shows that Pappus may have invented a volumeter similar to one invented by Joseph-Louis Gay-Lussac. Pappus was not merely a geometer; he was a conserver of classical tradition, a popularizer of Greek geometry, and an inventor as well.

Summary

The works of Pappus have provided later generations with a storehouse of ancient Greek geometry, both as an independent check against the authenticity of other known sources and as a valuable source of lost texts. For modern mathematics, Pappus offers more than merely historical interest. In 1631, Jacob Golius pointed out to René Descartes the "Pappus problem," and six years later this became the centerpiece of Descartes' *Des matières de la géométrie* (*The Geometry of Descartes*, 1925). Descartes realized that his new algebraic symbols could easily replace Pappus' more difficult geometric methods and that the product of the locus of straight lines generated from conic sections could generate equations of second, third, and higher orders. In 1687 Sir Isaac Newton found a similar inspiration in the "Pappus problem" using purely geometric methods. Nevertheless, it was Descartes' algebraic methods that would be utilized in the future. Pappus also anticipated the well-known "Guldin's theorem," dealing with figures generated by the revolution of plane figures about an axis. It can be argued that Pappus was the only geometer who possessed the ability to work out such a theorem during the silver age of Greek mathematics.

Bibliography

Bulmer-Thomas, I. "Guldin's Theorem—or Pappus's?" *Isis* 75 (1984): 348-352. There exists some question whether the Pappus text is original or if the text was corrupted at a later date. A less significant issue here is the interpretation of the Pappus manuscript—a historical problem concerned with the extent to which Pappus anticipated Guldin.

Descartes, René. *The Geometry of René Descartes.* Translated by Davis E. Smith and Marcia L. Latham. Chicago and London: Open Court, 1925. It is possible to follow from Descartes' own text the relevant passages from Pappus' work, seeing how Descartes develops his new symbols and why this method would later become the preferred method.

Heath, Sir Thomas. *A History of Greek Mathematics.* Vol. 2, *From Aristarchus to Diophantus.* Oxford: Clarendon, 1921; New York: Dover, 1981. This edition contains several long sections from the *Collection* as well as commentaries on the history and contents of these theorems.

Molland, A. G. "Shifting the Foundations: Descartes's Transformation of Ancient Geometry." *Historica Mathematica* 3 (1976): 21-49. This work focuses on how Descartes was able to shift from geometric to algebraic methods. Since Pappus plays a significant part in this transformation, it is possible for the reader to see the differences and similarities of Pappus' and Descartes' mathematical symbols.

Pappus. *Book 7 of the Collection.* Edited by Alexander Jones. 2 vols. New York: Springer-Verlag, 1986. These two volumes contain the most complete rendition of book 7; in addition, there are exhaustive commentaries and notes on every aspect of this text. Contains a detailed account of the history of various Pappus manuscripts and notes on the problems of translating ancient Greek text.

Turnbull, H. W. *The Great Mathematicians.* 4th ed. London: Methuen, 1951; New York: New York University Press, 1961. This work covers the major contributors to the history of mathematics, from the ancient Greeks to the late nineteenth century scholars. The section on Pappus is short, but it does place him in the context of the second Alexandrian school.

Victor W. Chen

PARMENIDES

Born: c. 515 B.C.; Elea (also known as Velia)
Died: Perhaps after 436 B.C.; possibly Elea
Area of Achievement: Philosophy
Contribution: By exploring the logical implications of statements which use apparently simple terms such as "one" or "is," Parmenides established metaphysics as an area of philosophy.

Early Life

In the mid-sixth century B.C., as the Persian Empire advanced through Asia Minor toward the Aegean Sea, some of the Greek city-states which were thus threatened accommodated themselves to the invaders, while others attempted to maintain their independence. In the case of one Ionian city, Phocaea, many of the inhabitants left Asia Minor entirely. They migrated to southern Italy, founding Elea around 540. Parmenides' father, Pyres, may have been one of the emigrants, or, like his son, he may have been born in Elea. At any rate, Parmenides' family background was in Ionia.

It is therefore entirely natural that Parmenides would eventually compose verse in the standard Ionic dialect which had earlier been used for Homeric epics. Philosophical influences on the young Parmenides must be more conjectural, but at least some interest in the Ionian philosophers of the sixth century, such as Thales of Miletus and Anaximander, seems entirely reasonable for someone growing up in a Phocaean settlement.

The ancient traditions about Parmenides, on the other hand, connect him with the poet and philosopher Xenophanes. Born circa 570, Xenophanes was from Colophon in Asia Minor, and like the Phocaeans, he fled before the Persians to the western Greek world. Some contact between him and Parmenides is therefore quite likely. It is not so clear, though, that one should regard Parmenides as being in any real sense Xenophanes' student. A better case can be made for a close association of Parmenides with the otherwise obscure Ameinias, to whom, after his death, Parmenides built a shrine, according to Diogenes Laërtius (c. A.D. 200). Ameinias was a Pythagorean, and thus one should add the sixth century philosopher and mystic Pythagoras to the list of early influences on Parmenides.

The date which Diogenes Laërtius gives for Parmenides' birth is around 540 B.C. Plato's dialogue

Parmenides (c. 370 B.C.), on the other hand, is inconsistent with this date. Most of the dialogue is clearly invented by Plato, since it includes details of argumentation which Plato himself developed in the fourth century. The conversation between Parmenides, Socrates, and others, therefore, can scarcely have taken place as described by Plato; still, the overall setting of the dialogue, which implies that the title character was born around 515 B.C., may be chronologically accurate. Possibly, the date given by Diogenes Laërtius arose from a reference in one of his sources to the founding of Elea around 540 B.C. as a crucial event in Parmenides' background.

Life's Work

Pondering the implications of earlier philosophy, which saw a single unifying principle—such as water, the infinite, or number—behind the various phenomena of the world, Parmenides strove to uncover a paradox residing in any such analysis. He wrote one treatise, in poetic form, in which he set forth his views. This work is generally referred to as *Peri physeos* (only fragments are translated into English), although it is not certain that Parmenides himself so entitled it. Of this poem, about 150 lines are preserved in Greek, along with another six lines in a Latin translation.

Parmenides' central concern, or at least that for which he is best known, lies in the implications of the Greek word *esti*, meaning "is." According to Parmenides, of the two predications "is" and "is not," only "is" makes sense. Merely to say "is not" gives some stamp of evidence to whatever one says "is not" and therefore involves self-contradiction. With "is not" thus rejected, all reality must somehow be single and unified, all-encompassing and unchanging. Such a view would seem to be essentially ineffable, but toward the middle of Parmenides' fragment 8, which gives the core of his argument, what "is" is compared to a well-rounded ball, perfectly poised in the middle, with nothing outside itself.

Despite this thoroughgoing monism, the opening of Parmenides' poem (fragment 1) refers to two paths of inquiry—one of *aletheia* (truth) and one of *doxa* (opinion). The argument about the primacy of "is" over "is not" follows the path of *aletheia*, while the latter part of fragment 8 follows the path of *doxa*. (These sections are generally known as the *Aletheia* and the *Doxa*.) Ancient authors did not, on the whole, find the *Doxa* so interesting. It was therefore not so much quoted in antiquity, and only about forty-five lines from it are preserved. As a result, many modern treatments of Parmenides concentrate on the better preserved *Aletheia*. Such an approach may also find a precedent in Plato's dialogue *Parmenides*. Other scholars, though, acknowledge *Doxa* as having been an integral part of the poem, and this approach is entirely supported by some of the ancient references to Parmenides. Aristotle (384-322 B.C.), for example, refers in *Metaphysica* (335-323 B.C.; *Metaphysics*) to Parmenides as having been constrained by phenomena to acknowledge change and multiplicity in the sensible world.

Aristotle's line of interpretation is probably correct. Despite the paucity of direct information about the *Doxa*, several crucial ideas in ancient science are consistently associated with Parmenides, either as originating with him or as being promulgated by him. For example, the simile which concludes the *Aletheia*—that what "is" resembles a well-rounded ball—may have a more prosaic but still-grander cosmic application to Earth as a sphere, poised in space. Fragment 14 refers to the moon's shining, not of its own accord but by reflected light. Aëtius (c. A.D. 100) and Diogenes Laërtius ascribe to Parmenides the observation that the evening and morning star are the same body (Venus) as it travels through space. Strabo (who flourished during the first century B.C.), quoting an earlier source, refers to Parmenides as having divided Earth into five zones. Such astronomical and geographic interests, along with various references to his treatment of biology, anatomy, and psychology, suggest that Parmenides had a mind more concerned with the investigation of physical phenomena than his austerely logical treatment of "is" and "is not" would suggest.

Nevertheless, Plato's contrary focus on Parmenides as primarily a metaphysician provides the earliest biographical and descriptive vignette of Parmenides. Plato's account places Parmenides in Athens in 450, at the time of a quadrennial festival to the goddess Athena. According to Plato, the Eleatic visitor to Athens was then about sixty-five years old, already white-haired but still of a forceful and commanding appearance and quite capable,

as Plato reveals in the rest of the dialogue, of engaging in a complicated philosophical discussion.

Unfortunately, there is nothing very specific in Plato's physical description of Parmenides. One might hope that the picture would be filled out by the bust from the first century A.D. found during excavations at Elea in 1966. The bust matches an inscription, "Parmenides the son of Pyres the natural philosopher," found in 1962; also, the inscription somehow connects Parmenides with Apollo as a patron of physicians. The existence of this statue obviously attests the regard in which Parmenides was held in Elea several centuries after his death. It is unlikely, however, that it actually portrays the visage of Parmenides, since it seems to be modeled on the bust of a later figure, the Epicurean Metrodorus (c. 300 B.C.), who was chosen to represent the typical philosopher.

In his account of Parmenides' visit to Athens, Plato includes the detail that Zeno of Elea, who accompanied Parmenides on that occasion, had once been his lover. Athenaeus (fl. c. A.D. 200) objects to this point as a superfluous addition which contributes nothing to Plato's narrative. Whatever the case may be, Zeno and the slightly later Melissus (born c. 480 B.C.) are often grouped with Parmenides as the founders of an Eleatic school of philosophy. In particular, the intellectual connection between Parmenides and Zeno may be especially close. Both were from Elea (while Melissus was from the Aegean island Samos), and, according to Plato, Zeno's paradoxes, purporting to show the impossibility of motion, were designed to support Parmenides' doctrine concerning the unified nature of reality.

The determination of direct influences of Parmenides beyond the Eleatic school is more tenuous. Theophrastus (c. 372-287 B.C.), however, connects two other fifth century figures with him—the philosopher-poet Empedocles and Leucippus, the founder of atomism. Also, although he is from a later generation, it is, generally agreed that Plato himself owed much to Parmenides.

Of Parmenides' life after his possible visit to Athens in 450, nothing definite is known. Theophrastus' implication that Leucippus studied with him at Elea should possibly be dated after 450. Also, Eusebius of Caesarea (who flourished during the fourth century A.D.) implies that Parmenides was still living in 436 B.C.; this information leads scholars to believe Plato's chronology over that given by Diogenes Laërtius. According to Plutarch, Parmenides was a lawgiver as well as a philosopher, and subsequent generations at Elea swore to abide by his laws.

Summary

Some critics see fundamental flaws in Parmenides' reasoning. According to the modern scholar Jonathan Barnes, for example, it is perfectly acceptable to say that it is necessarily the case that what does not exist does not exist, but Parmenides erred in holding that what does not exist necessarily does not exist. Even if this objection is valid, Parmenides' lasting influence on subsequent thought is undeniable. Often, his arguments are presented without quibble in modern treatments of the history of philosophy, as having uncovered difficulties with which any process of thinking must cope.

It is also important to keep in mind the poetic medium which Parmenides used. His sixth century predecessors, such as Anaximander and Anaximenes, had used prose for their philosophical treatises. Parmenides, however, chose verse, perhaps to give some sense of the majesty and dignity of the philosopher's quest. The ineffable quality which Parmenides claims for ultimate reality may also find an appropriate expression in poetry. Above all, the use of verse puts Parmenides in a rich verbal tradition, stretching back to the earliest extant Greek poetry, that of Homer and Hesiod, and to even earlier oral poetry. The most obvious parallels are with Homer's *Odyssey* (c. 800 B.C.). For example, the cattle of the Sun are described in the *Odyssey* as neither coming into being nor perishing, and this idea is also central to Parmenides' concept of what is. A close verbal parallel to Homer's description of the paths of night and day in the *Odyssey* is also found in Parmenides. More generally, one may note that Odysseus, after his manifold adventures in the outer reaches of the world, eventually returns home to Ithaca and to his wife, Penelope, exactly as Parmenides would both partake of and yet, somehow, eschew the realm of pure thought for the mundane world of *doxa*.

Parmenides thus emerges as a prime mediator between ancient Greek and later philosophy. While casting his thought in terms of the poetic imagery, metaphors, and formulas used by Homer and Hesiod, he still insisted emphatically on the paramount importance of reason that his contemporaries and successors, such as Zeno, Leucippus, and Plato, framed anew.

Bibliography

Barnes, Jonathan. *The Presocratic Philosophers.* Rev. ed. London and Boston: Routledge, 1982. Contains three chapters mainly on Parmenides, along with numerous other references. Barnes puts Parmenides' ideas into a modern philosophical framework, and although his use of technical jargon and symbols is sometimes a bit heavy, he nevertheless handles the ramifications of Parmenides' argument in magisterial fashion. Includes a good bibliography.

Burnet, John. *Early Greek Philosophy.* 4th ed. London: Black, and New York: Barnes and Noble, 1930. A classic work on pre-Socratic philosophy first published in 1892. Contains a clear, readable chapter on Parmenides and a chapter on Leucippus which suggests that Parmenides' reference to what "is" as a self-contained sphere may have given rise to atomism.

Finkelberg, Aryeh. "The Cosmology of Parmenides." *American Journal of Philology* 107 (1986): 303-317. Treating the *Doxa* as an important part of Parmenides' poem, this article deals principally with Aëtius' report of Parmenides as referring to various rings which comprise Earth, a fiery region within it, airy rings which are associated with the heavenly bodies, and so on.

Lombardo, Stanley, ed. *Parmenides and Empedocles: The Fragments in Verse Translation.* San Francisco: Grey Fox Press, 1982. A spirited if somewhat free translation, but the best source for getting some sense in English of the fact that Parmenides wrote in verse and that this point is important for understanding the effect he wanted to achieve.

Mackenzie, Mary Margaret. "Parmenides' Dilemma." *Phronesis* 27 (1982): 1-12. Discusses the appearance of second-person verb forms in Parmenides' poem. The use of locutions such as "you think" must inevitably lead to an acknowledgment of plurality, and Parmenides' inclusion of the *Doxa* in his poem may be explained in these terms.

Mourelatos, Alexander P. D. *The Route of Parmenides.* New Haven, Conn.: Yale University Press, 1970. The main thrust of this work is Parmenides' philosophical program, with particular attention to the way in which material in the *Doxa* parallels statements in the *Aletheia*, often through a more or less explicit appeal to paradox. There is also a good introductory chapter on Homeric prototypes for Parmenides' poetic technique. Contains Greek text of fragments of Parmenides but no translation.

Owen, G. E. L. "Eleatic Questions." *The Classical Quarterly* 10 (1960): 84-102. Rejecting Aristotle's assessment of the importance of *Doxa* in *Peri physeos*, Owen maintains that for Parmenides the preceding section of his poem, the *Aletheia*, was all that really mattered.

Parmenides. *The Fragments of Parmenides: A Critical Text with Introduction, Translation, the Ancient Testimonia, and a Commentary.* Edited by A. H. Coxon. Dover, N.H.: Van Gorcum, 1986. Greek text and English translation of the fragments of Parmenides. The extensive commentary is often hard to follow without at least some knowledge of Greek. Although somewhat technical, Coxon's introduction conveys a good sense of the textual problems which must be solved when establishing Parmenides' meaning.

―――. *Parmenides of Elea, Fragments: A Text and Translation, with an Introduction.* Edited by David Gallop. Toronto and London: University of Toronto Press, 1984. This volume consists of Greek text and English translation of the fragments of Parmenides, with English translations of the contexts in which the fragments occur. Also contains brief biographies (one to three sentences) of the ancient authors who quote or refer to Parmenides. The most convenient source for getting a general view of the ancient sources concerning Parmenides. Includes a good bibliography.

Plato. *Plato's "Parmenides": Translation and Analysis.* Translated by R. E. Allen. Rev. ed. New Haven, Conn.: Yale University Press, 1997. Primarily a translation of Plato's dialogue, with extensive commentary. Several pages deal specifically with Parmenides, however, and there are also other scattered references to his poem. Allen stresses the fundamentally fictional nature of Plato's account of Parmenides' meeting with Socrates—and the corresponding caution with which Plato must be used for biographical information concerning Parmenides.

Edwin D. Floyd

SAINT PATRICK

Born: Probably between 418 and 422; England
Died: March 17, 493; Ireland or England
Area of Achievement: Religion and saints
Contribution: Saint Patrick is a legendary figure who served as a missionary bishop to Ireland and converted large numbers of pagans to Christianity. He is the patron saint of Ireland.

Early Life

It is difficult to be certain about specific details and dates in Saint Patrick's life. The main sources for information are his very brief autobiography entitled *Confessio (Confession,* c. 489); the *Epistle to the Soldiers of Coroticus* (471), in which he excommunicated Coroticus, an Irish tyrant who had killed several Irish convers to Christianity; and a fanciful seventh century biography by Muirchu.

The first part of Muirchu's *Life of St. Patrick* is based almost exclusively on Saint Patrick's *Confession*; for this reason, historians have tried to rely almost exclusively on Saint Patrick's own autobiography in an effort to establish the major details of his life. However, Saint Patrick did not always include detailed information about specific dates and events. His main concern in writing the *Confession* was to leave a record of his spiritual transformation from a young man uninterested in Christianity into an active missionary.

Saint Patrick was born between 418 and 422 somewhere in western England. In his *Confession*, written in Latin, he wrote that his hometown was "Bannaventa Burniae," but no one has ever been able to identify this village. His father was a deacon named Calpurnius, and his grandfather was a priest named Potitus. At that time, celibacy was not required of priests in the Catholic Church, but Saint Patrick did not reveal his mother's name. In the *Confession*, Saint Patrick wrote of his indifference to religion during his early years, and he also spoke of a terrible sin that he had committed at the age of fifteen. He never explained the nature of this sin, but it still disturbed him years later when he wrote his autobiography.

When he was sixteen years old, Saint Patrick was seized by marauders and taken into slavery in western Ireland. He was sold to a landowner in County Mayo. During his six years of slavery, he became a believing Christian. In the *Confession*, he described his amazing escape. He left Mayo, walked on foot across Ireland, and escaped by boat to either Britain or Gaul (present-day France). There he was once again enslaved, but he had a series of dreams that he interpreted as meaning that God would free him from slavery so that he could return to Ireland as a missionary. After his second escape from slavery, he studied in England and became a priest. In his *Confession*, he states that when certain "senior" clergymen learned of the sin he committed at the age of fifteen, he was criticized, and another priest was appointed the bishop of Ireland, a position that Patrick would, nevertheless, eventually assume.

Life's Work

Although there is still some disagreement among historians, it is now generally assumed that Saint Patrick began his missionary work as the bishop of Ireland in 456. It is believed that he remained in Ireland until his death or until shortly before his death (when he may have retired to a monastery in England) on March 17, 493. In the *Confession*, Saint Patrick reveals himself to be a modest priest devoted to converting pagans to Christianity and to the spiritual guidance of new Christians in Ireland. Muirchu and other biographers of Saint Patrick told imaginative tales about Patrick's missionary work in Ireland. They claimed that Saint Patrick proved the superiority of Christianity over paganism by defeating pagan magicians in a wrestling contest. They also asserted that, just as Christ had fasted and prayed in the mountains for forty days, so, too, had Saint Patrick climbed Croagh Patrick, a mountain in County Connaught, where he spent forty days in prayer and direct communication with God. These legends are still popular in Ireland, and each July thousands of pilgrims climb Croagh Patrick and pray in the small chapel located at the top. However, it is not necessary to believe in such legends to recognize the significance of his central role in spreading Christianity throughout Ireland.

Ireland (or Hibernia, as it was known during Roman times) was outside the boundaries of the Roman Empire. Although earlier missionaries had made great efforts to proselytize those living under Roman domination, similar efforts had not been made outside the Roman Empire. Saint Patrick's major contribution to the spread of Christianity was his determination to consecrate his life to

bringing the word of God to people living in countries that had been long neglected by Rome.

In 431, Pope Celestine appointed Palladius the first bishop of Ireland, but he specified that Palladius was to serve as bishop to the "Irish who believe in Christ." This remark suggests quite clearly that the mission of Palladius was to serve as spiritual leader to Christians in Ireland and not to undertake missionary work. Between Palladius' appointment in 431 and Patrick's nomination twenty-five years later, another bishop had continued the pastoral work of Palladius. The name of this bishop is unknown.

Saint Patrick broke with tradition because he targeted those who were not Christian. He realized that many to whom he spoke were hostile toward Christianity. He could not coerce them to convert, as the Roman Empire had attempted after Christianity had become the state religion during the fourth century. Instead, he had to persuade men and women that they should abandon their gods and accept Christianity. Since he had lived in Ireland as a slave, he knew the local language and had no difficulty communicating in Celtic, the only language spoken by the vast majority of people in Ireland at that time. He accommodated Christianity to local traditions so that new converts would not feel threatened. He quickly realized that he needed the help of local priests so that new converts would remain faithful to their new religion. In the *Confession*, he wrote at great length of the joy he experienced each time he persuaded a pagan to accept Christianity. He did not limit his activity to one region of Ireland. He traveled extensively, and his personal missionary efforts definitely extended from the area around Dublin to as far north as Armagh and as far west as the Atlantic coast in counties Clare and Connemara. He may not have reached the southwestern and southeastern regions of Ireland, but priests whom he had ordained soon spread Christianity throughout the island.

Converting so many pagans to Christianity was a massive undertaking. Historians now believe that Christian dioceses in Britain contributed significantly to support Patrick's efforts. He did not want the Irish to believe that he was exploiting them for his own benefit. In his *Confession*, he states clearly that he refused to accept any money from them. Although celibacy was not yet required of priests, Saint Patrick never married, and he states that he returned gifts that recent converts had given him. He strove to be a spiritual leader with whom all

could identify. He demonstrated great personal courage. In one area, a local chieftain threatened to kill him, but Saint Patrick persuaded the chieftain to allow him to pay the chieftain's sons to serve as his traveling companions. After just two weeks, he states, he had converted these men to Christianity. In his *Confession*, he explains that his personal experience with poverty and slavery helped him to appreciate the dignity of all whom he encountered in Ireland. He was as proud of his conversions of family members of chieftains as he was of his conversions of impoverished peasants.

After Patrick had been working for fifteen years as a missionary in Ireland, a chieftain named Coroticus, whom he had converted to Christianity, abducted several converts and planned to sell them into slavery. Several people resisted, and Coroticus killed them. In his *Epistle to the Soldiers of Coroticus*, Saint Patrick not only excommunicated Coroticus but also instructed his soldiers that they need longer obey him, because his orders were incompatible with Christ's teaching concerning the dignity of human life. Saint Patrick showed complete disregard for the very real threat that Coroticus might attempt to kill him. His personal courage, high ethical standards, and his unrelenting efforts to spread Christianity throughout Ireland endeared him to people from all social classes.

Summary

More than fifteen hundred years after his death, Saint Patrick remains a revered figure in Ireland and elsewhere in the Catholic world. Before his arrival in Ireland in 456, there had been no systematic effort on the part of Christian missionaries to convert people who lived in countries that had not been influenced by Greco-Roman culture. Saint Patrick believed that Christianity would become a universal religion only if Christians reached out with respect and understanding to people from very different cultures. He was successful in his efforts to convert the Irish to Christianity largely because he spoke their language, respected their traditions, and did not attempt to impose his cultural values on them; instead, he simply tried to share religious values with them. He thus helped to broaden the scope of Christianity.

For the Irish, who have endured centuries of political domination and religious persecution, Saint Patrick represents a dignified man who discovered, through his own suffering, the essential dignity of each individual. Saint Patrick humbled himself to serve others, demonstrated inner courage, and remained faithful to his essential beliefs despite violent opposition from those opposed to him. Saint Patrick helped generations of Irish men and women cope with poverty, religious persecution, and economic adversity.

Bibliography

Bieler, Ludwig. *Studies on the Life and Legend of St. Patrick.* Edited by Richard Sharpe. London: Variorum Reprints, 1986. Contains nineteen essays that examine early biographies of Saint Patrick and describe the creation of the numerous legends connected with him.

Carney, James. *The Problem of St. Patrick.* Dublin: Dublin Institute for Advanced Studies, 1961. Contains a solid historical study of what is known about Saint Patrick's life. Like Bieler, Carney distinguishes carefully between fact and fiction.

Gogarty, Oliver Saint John. *I Follow St. Patrick.* London: Rich and Cowan, and New York: Reynal and Hitchcock, 1938. A lyrical book by an important Irish poet and physician who describes quite eloquently why Saint Patrick is still so highly revered by the Irish, both in Ireland and in exile.

O'Donoghue, Noel D. *Aristocracy of Soul: Patrick of Ireland.* Wilmington, Del.: Michael Glazier, and London: Darton, Longman, 1987. Examines spiritual and theological aspects of Saint Patrick's *Confession.* Contains an excellent English translation of the *Confession.*

Proudfoot, Alice Boyd, ed. *Patrick: Sixteen Centuries with Ireland's Patron Saint.* New York: Macmillan, 1983. Contains an excellent selection of literary and artistic works that evoke various aspects of the Saint Patrick legends and describe the evolving meaning of his life for generations of Irish writers.

Thompson, E. A. *Who Was St. Patrick?* Woodbridge, England: Boydell Press, 1985; New York: St. Martin's Press, 1986. Contains a reliable historical study of Saint Patrick's life as it is revealed in his *Confession* and *Epistle to the Soldiers of Croaticus.* Includes a solid bibliography of important historical studies.

Edmund J. Campion

SAINT PAUL

Born: Date unknown; Tarsus, Cilicia (now Turkey)

Died: c. A.D. 64; Rome

Area of Achievement: Religion

Contribution: Through depth of conviction and force of personality, Paul spread the teachings of an obscure Jewish sect throughout the eastern Mediterranean and eventually to Rome. As the educated apostle, he gave Christianity a measure of intellectual credibility and formulated much of what would later become doctrine.

Early Life

Saint Paul was born at Tarsus in Cilicia, a region in southeast Asia Minor, on the Mediterranean. He was a Jew, known during his early years by the name of Saul. Little documentary evidence exists concerning these years, but certain things can be inferred from Paul's status at the time that he appeared on the historical scene.

Paul was trained as a rabbi in the Pharisaic tradition. His background as a Pharisee indicates a close adherence to both the written law and the oral, or traditional, law. This stance would have been a source of constant tension between Paul and the apostles who arose out of the village culture of Palestine. In the Gospels, the term Pharisee takes on connotations of self-righteousness and sanctimony. Further, Paul was a product of the city and of the Diaspora, the settlements of those Jews who had been dispersed throughout Asia Minor. Certain awkward phrases in his writings, when he is trying to be more simple, indicate that he was never comfortable with agricultural or bucolic topics. He was exposed early in life to Greek language, mythology, and culture. In the Hellenistic synagogues where he worshipped as a youth, he would have heard the Jewish scriptures read not in Hebrew but in Greek translation. Paul is identified in the Acts of the Apostles as a Roman citizen, so rare a status for a Jew that his family must have been influential and highly connected. Finally, he was for a time a leading persecutor of the new sect, seeing the followers of Jesus as a grave threat to the Jewish legal tradition.

For all the reasons cited above, it is little wonder that after his conversion many of his fellow Jewish Christians viewed him with suspicion and even with hostility. Yet Paul's conversion was so total and the rejection of his past life so absolute that other writers have felt the need to dramatize it, even though his own letters do not describe it at all.

Life's Work

Paul's great achievement was to take Christianity from Jerusalem throughout the eastern provinces of the Roman Empire and finally to the capital itself. He possessed the vision to see that the new faith had a message and an appeal which were not limited to the Jews.

During the years preceding the conversion of Saul of Tarsus, the future of Christianity was not promising. Rome had imposed a political order upon the eastern Mediterranean and had inculcated its attitudes of tolerance (for the times) and materialism. The relative peace and prosperity of the period, however, apparently proved insufficient to meet the spiritual and psychological needs of the subject peoples. The major ancient religions had ossified and were the source of very little spiritual energy; among the Greeks and Romans, religious practice had become almost purely conventional, and the Jews awaited the great supernatural event

S. PAVLVS

which would revitalize them. In response to this state of affairs, philosophical and religious sects sprang up everywhere, including Greek syncretism, Mithraism, Zoroastrianism, and Christianity. The struggles of these and many other sects to win the minds and hearts of the people would continue for the next five hundred years (before Saint Augustine's conversion to Christianity in 386/387, he experimented with virtually all of its competitors). At the middle of the first century after the death of Jesus, Christianity—a provincial religion under the leadership of a small group of unsophisticated and unlettered men—seemed unlikely to be the winner of this great competition. Thus, it is difficult to overstate the impact of the conversion of Saul of Tarsus.

He was a most unlikely apostle of the crucified carpenter from Galilee. Far from being a man of the people, he was a member of the most learned Jewish party. He held Roman citizenship. He had not been personally associated with Jesus of Nazareth and viewed those who had been as a threat to the Jewish Law, which he uncompromisingly supported. His nature was sometimes imperious, as his writings disclose. He did not leave a description of his conversion as Saint Augustine was later to do, but something in his thinking was leading him toward the profound change which would make him history's archetypal Christian convert. He developed a sense of the frailty and corruption of the world's institutions, a disgust for the secular materialism which surrounded him, and a conviction that humanity's only hope lay in dying to all worldly things. He gave up a comfortable, settled life for that of an itinerant preacher and religious organizer. He changed from a defender of the legal tradition of Judaism to the most zealous opponent of those Jewish Christians who sought to retain any part of it.

Saul first appears in the book of the Acts of the Apostles at Jerusalem, as a witness to the stoning of Stephen, the first Christian martyr. His complicity in the execution is strongly suggested, for he is reported to have consented to the death (as if he had some say in the matter), and the witnesses laid their clothes down at his feet. His age at the time is not known, but he is described as a young man. Succeeding chapters paint him as a fierce oppressor of the Christians. His persecutions culminate in a trip to Damascus, where, under authority from the high priests, he is to harry all the Christians he can find. It is on this journey that he has his famous conversion experience: He hears the voice of Jesus challenging him, and he is struck blind. After three days, his sight is restored. He is baptized and almost immediately begins to preach in the synagogues that Christ is the Son of God. Scholars who do not subscribe to a literal interpretation of the scriptural account suggest that it results from Paul's having left no account of his own. Presented with the sudden, total, and inexplicable change in Saul's behavior, perhaps his first biographer could not resist romanticizing it.

The remainder of his story in Acts is replete with adventure and conflict. Saul is so skilled in disputation that both his Jewish and Greek opponents plot to kill him; he makes narrow and dramatic escapes. Still the Christians in Jerusalem cannot fully trust him; they remember the old Saul, and send him back to Tarsus. By chapter 13 of Acts, Saul (whose name means "asked of God" in Hebrew) has become known as Paul (meaning "small" in Greek). He has also become the missionary to the Gentiles. He travels widely: preaching, healing, organizing Christian communities, and suffering periods of hardship and imprisonment. The Scriptures hint at but give no account of his eventual martyrdom in Rome; legend would later supply one.

Much of Paul's career as a missionary can only be the object of conjecture. Some of his work and the time of its accomplishment have been verified through seven of his letters whose genuineness is generally accepted—his epistles to the various fledgling Christian communities. The first letter to the church at Thessalonica, provincial capital of Macedonia, was written from Corinth, c. 51. At that time, Paul was in the company of Silvanus (known in Acts as Silas) and Timothy. About three years later, from Ephesus in western Asia Minor, he wrote a stinging letter to the Christians in Galatia. They had been entertaining rival missionaries, who apparently argued that pagan converts were subject to the Jewish Law. In this letter, Paul defends his understanding of the gospel and his teaching authority with occasionally bitter sarcasm. The next year, near the end of his stay at Ephesus, he wrote the first of two extant letters to the church at Corinth, which he had founded c. 50. The church had developed several factions and incipient heresies (in the early church, it was largely Paul who delineated the orthodoxies and the heresies). In addition to responding to these matters, Paul offers sexual advice to husbands and wives, his famous pronouncement that the ideal Christian life is a celibate one, and his beautiful disquisition on love. A second letter to the Corinthians, written c. 56, asserts Paul's credentials and questions with heavy irony those of false prophets who have been wooing the flock. The letter addresses a number of other issues in such a curious chronology that it may well be a composite of several fragments, the work of some ancient editor. Paul's physical appearance is a mystery (early iconography seems based on little more than imagination), but in this letter he does allude to a "thorn in the flesh" from which three separate entreaties to the Lord have not relieved him. The nature of the illness is not known but has been the object of much speculation.

Around 57, during his last stay at Corinth, Paul wrote a long letter to Rome. It was both a letter of introduction and a theological treatise, written in anticipation of his preaching there. His letter to the church at Philippi was long held to have been written at Rome c. 62, during his two years of imprisonment there. Some scholars argue, however, that at least a part of it was written much earlier (c. 56) from a prison in Caesarea or Ephesus. Another letter from prison—a request that Philemon, a Colossian Christian, magnanimously take back a runaway slave whom Paul has converted—is also variously dated, depending upon whether the missionary wrote from Rome or elsewhere. Other letters (such as Timothy and Titus) bear Paul's name, but their authenticity has been disputed.

The last of Paul's many arrests occurred in Jerusalem, where he was attempting to promote unity within the Christian community (ironically, he himself had been one of the divisive factors there). As a citizen, he appealed to Rome and was transported to the capital. His lengthy period of imprisonment there is described in some detail in Acts. It is presumed that around 64 he was executed—legend has it that he was beheaded—just preceding Nero's persecution of the Roman Christians.

Summary

While Saint Peter and the other Palestinian apostles were at first content to limit Christianity to converted Jews, Saint Paul determined to take it to the Gentiles. As the other apostles moved back and forth among the villages of their native region, Paul spread the faith to the bustling cities of Asia Minor and southern Europe. He tirelessly plied the trade routes of the eastern empire, setting up church after church in the major population centers. In his second letter to the Corinthians, he catalogs his sufferings: imprisonments, beatings, floggings, a stoning, shipwreck, assassination plots, hunger, thirst, and—above all else—anxiety for the welfare of his churches.

He believed, as did the other primitive Christians, that he lived at the end of history, that the second coming of his Lord was at hand. Even so, he threw himself into every aspect of church organization—doctrine, ritual, politics. He fought lethargy here, inappropriate enthusiasm there. He constantly sought to make peace between Jewish and non-Jewish Christians. His dictates on such subjects as Christian celibacy and the lesser role of women in the church continue to provoke controversy, thousands of years after they were written.

Paul has been called the man who delivered Christianity from Judaism. He has been called the man who furnished Christianity with its intellectual content. Because of his argument that the Crucifixion represents a covenant superseding the ancient law, he has been called the father of the Reformation, and it has been suggested that Protestantism derives from him as Catholicism derives from Saint Peter. He has been called a compulsive neurotic, whose works were instances of sublimation and whose thorn in the flesh was psychosomatic. George Bernard Shaw characterized him as the fanatic who corrupted the teachings of Jesus.

It would be extravagant to claim that Christianity would not have survived without Paul. It is safe to say that it would not have survived in its present form without him.

Bibliography

Bruce, F. F. *Paul: Apostle of the Heart Set Free.* Grand Rapids, Mich.: Eerdmans, 1977; as *Paul, Apostle of the Free Spirit.* Exeter: Paternoster, 1977. Bruce is perhaps the foremost evangelical among Pauline scholars. This book, which is accessible to the general reader, focuses on Paul's life, though there is also discussion of his writings. Well illustrated, with indexes of names and places, subjects, and references.

Davies, William David. *Paul and Rabbinic Judaism: Some Rabbinic Elements in Pauline Theology.* 3d ed. London: S•P•C•K, 1970; Philadelphia: Fortress Press, 1980. The author, a professor of New Testament at Princeton, attempts to prove that Paul was in the mainstream of first century Judaism and that Hellenistic influences upon him have been overestimated. The first of ten chapters assesses the degree of difference between Palestinian and Diaspora Judaism. Chapters 5 and 6 discuss Paul as preacher and teacher.

Deissmann, Gustav Adolf. *Paul: A Study in Social and Religious History.* Translated by William E. Wilson. 2d ed. New York: Doran, and London: Hodder and Stoughton, 1926. Takes the view that primitive Christianity was more a cult marked by mysticism than a religion marked by doctrine. Interprets the Pauline Christ-mysticism.

Glover, T. R. "The Mind of St. Paul." In *Springs of Hellas and Other Essays.* Cambridge: Cambridge University Press, 1945; New York: Macmillan, 1946. A classicist's study of Paul, emphasizing the cosmopolitan nature of his world and his heroic efforts to reconcile Jew and Gentile, Greek and barbarian.

Hengel, Martin. *The Pre-Christian Paul.* London: SCM Press, and Philadelphia: Trinity Press International, 1991. This is a detailed study of the initial period of Paul's life. It examines the question of the apostle's origins and citizenship, his names, his social background and profession, and his education. It takes note of the differences between what is said in the Acts of the Apostles and Paul's own testimony. Further, the nature of 1st century Pharisianism and Paul's persecution of Christians are discussed.

Hengel, Martin, and Anna Maria Schwemer. *Paul between Damascus and Antioch: The Unknown Years.* London: SCM Press, and Louisville, KY: Westminster John Knox Press, 1997. This is a continuation of the above book, covering the years between Paul's conversion and his arrival in Antioch. The apostle's life is set against a detailed background of the early Christian world and places Paul's conversion and much of his subsequent actions in context. Hengel argues on the importance of Luke's Acts as a historical source.

Longenecker, Richard N., ed. *The Road from Damascus: The Impact of Paul's Conversion on His Life, Thought, and Ministry.* Grand Rapids, Mich.: Eerdmans, 1997. In the light of Paul's conversion experience, this collection of articles examines various aspects and concepts of his theology: christology, eschatology, justification, reconciliation, covenant, the Holy Spirit, gender, and ethics. There is also a review essay on the treatment that Paul's conversion has received in scholarly literature. Each chapter is followed by a selected bibliography.

Malina, Bruce J., and Jerome H. Neyrey. *Portraits of Paul: An Archaeology of Ancient Personality.* Louisville, KY: Westminster John Knox Press, 1996. An innovative book on Paul, who is treated as a case study on the social construction of personality in the classical world. Along with the Epistles and Acts, a large number of Graeco-Roman texts are used as sources. The characteristics of a typical personality in the 1st century A.D. are emphatically contrasted with those in modern Western culture.

Meeks, Wayne A. *The First Urban Christians: The Social World of the Apostle Paul.* New Haven, Conn.: Yale University Press, 1983. This social history begins with the admission that great diversity existed within early Christianity. The author chooses to study Paul, his coworkers, and his congregations as the best-documented segment of the early Christian movement. The book's first premise is that Paul was a man of the city and that an urban bias informed the Pauline school from the earliest period of evangelizing. The social level of Pauline Christians and the governance and rituals of their communities are discussed at length. Includes notes, indexes, and an extensive bibliography.

———, ed. *The Writings of St. Paul.* New York: Norton, 1972. A critical edition containing the Revised Standard Version of the undoubted letters of Paul and the works of the Pauline school, heavily annotated. Also contains more than two dozen essays and excerpts evaluating, from diverse points of view, Paul's thought, works, and influence on modern Christianity.

Schoeps, Hans J. *Paul: The Theology of the Apostle in the Light of Jewish History.* Translated by Harold Knight. Philadelphia: Westminster Press, and London: Lutterworth Press, 1961. The author begins by sketching the several approaches to interpretation (for example, the Hellenistic approach and the Palestinian-Judaic approach); then he treats Paul's position in the primitive church, his eschatology, his soteriology (theology of salvation), his views on the law, and his concept of history. Indexed to biblical passages and to modern authors. Heavily annotated.

Stendahl, Krister. *The Bible and the Role of Women: A Case Study in Hermeneutics.* Translated by Emilie T. Sander. Philadelphia: Fortress Press,

1966. This slim volume is composed of Stendahl's essay, a lengthy editor's introduction and author's preface, and a copious bibliography. The essay first appeared in 1958, growing out of a specific controversy over the proposed ordination of women as priests in the Church of Sweden (Lutheran). Part 2 of the essay, "The Biblical View of Male and Female," is devoted largely to an exegesis of Paul's pronouncements on the subject in his epistles.

Patrick Adcock

PERICLES

Born: c. 495 B.C.; Athens, Greece
Died: 429 B.C.; Athens, Greece
Area of Achievement: Government
Contribution: The Age of Pericles was a crucial period in the history of Athens. Pericles' transformation of the Delian League into the Athenian empire provided the financial basis for the flowering of Athenian democracy.

Early Life

Pericles was born in Athens around 495 B.C., the son of Xanthippus and Agariste (the niece of Cleisthenes). As the son of a wealthy aristocratic family in Athens and possessed of an above-average intelligence, Pericles received an excellent education from private tutors. The two men who had the greatest influence on Pericles' life were the musician Damon and the philosopher Anaxagoras. Damon taught Pericles the moral and political influence of music and Anaxagoras taught him political style, effective speech making, and analytical rationalism.

Although Pericles had prepared himself for a political life, he did not openly side with any of the factions in Athens until 463, when he joined in the prosecution of the Athenenian statesman and general Cimon. During this period, various political factions frequently brought charges against their opponents, with the goal of diminishing the prestige of the accused. Cimon, having recently returned from a two-year military campaign against the island of Thasos, which had rebelled against the Delian League, was brought to trial by the democratic faction on charges of bribery. In this instance, Cimon was acquitted.

In 462, Sparta requested military aid from Athens because of a revolt among the helots (serfs). Sparta, a city-state unfamiliar with siege warfare, needed help in trying to dislodge the helots who had fled to and fortified Mount Ithome in Messenia. Cimon urged the Athenians to cooperate with the Spartans, while the democratic faction, led by Ephialtes and Pericles, opposed any form of cooperation. On this occasion, Cimon won popular support and led an Athenian force to Mount Ithome. The Spartans, however, having reconsidered their request, dismissed Cimon and his men when they arrived. Because of this humiliation, Cimon's influence with the people declined rapidly.

With Cimon in disgrace, the democratic faction now focused its attention on the Areopagus, the council of former archons (magistrates). In 461, Ephialtes and Pericles led the people in stripping the Areopagus of any real power. Cimon, unable to rally the conservative opposition, was ostracized in the same year. Not long after, a member of the conservatives assassinated Ephialtes, and Pericles became the new leader of the democratic faction.

Life's Work

Pericles' main achievement as the leader of Athens was the conversion of the Delian League into an Athenian empire. The Delian League was originally formed in 476 as an offensive and defensive alliance against Persia. Although it was composed predominantly of Ionian maritime city-states individually bound by treaty to Athens, with all member states considered equal, only Athenians were league officials. The league collected annual tribute from its members to maintain a fleet. For all practical purposes, it was an Athenian fleet, built and manned by Athenians but paid for by the allies. Because the allies had been paying tribute every year since 476, the income of the league far exceeded its expenditures. When the league treasury was transferred from Delos to Athens in 454, it contained a vast sum of money which was essentially at the disposal of the Athenians.

Pericles, believing that the Athenians had every right to enjoy the benefits of empire, introduced numerous measures which provided pay to Athenians for their services as soldiers, magistrates, and jurors. An estimated twenty thousand Athenians were on the government payroll. In addition, so that no Athenian would be deprived of the opportunity to attend the plays of the Dionysiac Festival, even the price of admission to the theater was given to the poor.

The city of Athens itself was not to be neglected in Pericles' plans for the Delian League treasury. Pericles was building commissioner for the Parthenon and many other important building projects in Athens. The Parthenon, Propylaea, Odeum, and Erectheum are merely a few of the many temples and public buildings which were built or planned under the direction of Pericles but financed with league funds.

To increase the power of Athens, Pericles attempted to enlarge the Delian League. When the

Island of Aegina, located in the Saronic Gulf near Athens, declared war on Athens in 459, Pericles saw an opportunity to expand the league by creating an Athenian land empire which would complement the sea empire already embodied in the league. After the Athenians captured Aegina and forced it to become a member of the Delian League, the Peloponnesian coastal area of Troezen, facing Aegina, joined the league in self-defense. When Sparta tried to counter Athens by helping Thebes to dominate the Boeotian League in 457, Athens sent troops to fight the Spartans in the Battle of Tanagra. Although Athens lost the battle, Sparta soon withdrew her forces, and Athenian troops returned to rally the Boeotian League against Thebes. With the Boeotian League joined to the Delian League, the neighboring areas of Phocis and Locris joined the league, along with Achaea. By 456, the Periclean strategy of creating an Athenian land empire was a success, and the empire had reached its greatest territorial extent.

The Athenian land empire, however, disintegrated almost as quickly as it had been created. In 447, the Boeotian League revolted against Athens. As a result, Athens lost not only control of Boeotia but also the support of Phocis and Locris. When the Five-Year Truce with Sparta expired in 446, Sparta invaded Attica with a Peloponnesian army and encouraged the Athenian allied island of Euboea to revolt. Pericles quickly dealt with the two problems by bribing the Spartan commander of the Peloponnesians to leave Attica and by personally leading the Athenian reconquest of Euboea. While the Athenians were temporarily distracted, Megara broke its alliance with Athens and joined the Peloponnesian League along with Troezen and Achaea. All that remained now of the Athenian land empire was Aegina, Naupactus, and Plataea. Because Athens was in no position to reverse the situation, Athens and Sparta agreed in 445 to the Thirty Years' Peace.

Pericles successfully led the democratic faction in its control of Athenian politics from 461 until his death. He was a political genius in that he was able to provide leadership to the Athenian people without being led by them. The only surviving contemporary evidence of the opposition to Pericles is from Attic comedy. In general, the opponents of Pericles resented his oratorical skill, his family's wealth, and his political successes. Pericles was a very reserved and private individual, and his enemies interpreted these personality traits as signs of haughtiness and arrogance. Having earned the confidence of the people, however, Pericles was frequently elected *strategos* (general) in the 450's. When his chief political opponent, Thucydides, son of Melesias, was ostracized in 443, Pericles led the people virtually unopposed and was elected *strategos* every year until his death in 429.

The Peloponnesian War broke out in 431, when Athens and Sparta found that they could no longer observe the Thirty Years' Peace. Pericles believed that Athens and the Delian League had strategic advantages over Sparta and the Peloponnesian League. While the Peloponnesians had access to greater numbers of troops than the Athenians and had more agricultural land on which to produce food to support those troops, the Peloponnesians lacked a large fleet and so were more or less restricted to conducting a land war. The plan of Pericles was for the Athenians to abandon their property and homes in Attica and withdraw into the city of Athens. With its Long Walls assuring access to the port of Piraeus, Athens could withstand a siege of any length. In addition, Athens controlled the Delian League treasury and possessed a large fleet which could be used for hit-and-run raids on the Peloponnesians. As a safety precaution, however, Pericles set aside one thousand talents from the league treasury and reserved one hundred ships to be used only in the extreme emergency of defending Athens itself.

As Pericles predicted, the Peloponnesians invaded Attica in 431 and ravaged the countryside, trying to lure the Athenians from their walled city to fight a pitched battle. The Athenians, however, held firm. Instead of fighting in Attica, the Athenians, under Pericles' direction, mounted an attack on the Peloponnese. After they ravaged the territory of Epidaurus and Troezen, the Athenians sailed to Laconia to bring the war directly to the Spartans. After the Peloponnesians had withdrawn their troops from Attica, Athens prepared to bury its dead. It was the custom of the Athenians to choose their best speaker to give the funeral oration for the first men who had fallen in a war. As expected, Pericles was chosen for this honor. Pericles' funeral oration was more a speech extolling the virtues of Athens than a speech of mourning. He clearly wanted to impress upon the living Athenians the greatness of their city and the enlightened life they were privileged to lead.

In the second year of the war, the Athenians continued to follow the Periclean strategy. The people withdrew from Attica into Athens when the Peloponnesians returned to ravage the land. Athenian morale, however, was devastated by a plague which broke out in the city, killing many people. In their anger and frustration, the people blamed Pericles for their suffering and drove him from office. Though he was tried for embezzlement, convicted, and fined, he was soon elected *strategos* once again. Within six months, however, Pericles contracted the plague; he died in 429. The Athenians would have to endure the rest of the Peloponnesian War without the guidance of their greatest leader.

Summary

Pericles was the dominant political figure during the most important period in Athenian history. Rather than being a demagogue who flattered the people and pandered to their base instincts, Pericles won the people over to his policies by his forceful and energetic oratory. While some politicians sought to win a following by agreeing with whatever was currently popular, Pericles used his oratorical skill to lead the people to decisions which he thought were correct. Possessing an incorruptible character, Pericles gained the confidence of the people and knew how to keep it. By respecting their liberties and by offering the Athenians a consistent policy, Pericles prevented the people from making what he considered grave errors in judgment. What Pericles failed to understand, however, was that personal government was, in the long run, harmful to the state because it limited the ability of the people to govern themselves. In addition, while Athens enjoyed its democracy, the Athenians refused to recognize that it was based upon the political, military, and financial oppression of others in the empire.

Although Athens and Sparta did go to war in 431, Pericles had worked for peace twenty years before. In 451, Sparta and Athens agreed to a five-year truce; in 449, Persia and Athens reached an understanding in the Peace of Callias. With Athens assured of peace, Pericles called for a meeting of all Greek city-states to consider the issue of peace throughout the Greek world. According to Pericles, representatives at the proposed meeting were to discuss the rebuilding of all temples destroyed during the Persian Wars, the elimination of piracy, and the promotion of trade and commerce between and among all Greek city-states. Although because of Spartan opposition such a meeting was never held, Pericles' proposal showed that the Athenians were content with the territories they had and that they wanted peace.

Bibliography

Andrewes, A. "The Opposition to Pericles." *Journal of Hellenic Studies* 98 (1978): 1-8. While Plutarch is the main source of information on the struggle between Pericles and Thucydides, son of Melesias, Andrewes shows that he is unreliable because of his anti-imperialist bias. Although there were opponents to Pericles' building program, the argument that it was wrong to use league funds would not have been made, for Athenians viewed the empire as theirs to be enjoyed.

Bloedow, Edmund F. "Pericles' Powers in the Counter-Strategy of 431." *Historia* 36 (1987): 9-27. Bloedow tries to discover the constitutional basis for the power of Pericles through a close study of Thucydides. Although Pericles was only one of ten generals (*strategoi*) who led the state, he wielded authority that went far beyond that of a general. It was Pericles, for example, who decided if and when the assembly could meet.

Cawkwell, George. "Thucydides' Judgment of Periclean Strategy." *Yale Classical Studies* 24 (1975): 53-70. Cawkwell examines Thucydides' belief that the Athenians brought ruin upon themselves when they strayed from Periclean strategy after the death of Pericles. The author shows that, with the exception of the abandonment of Attica and withdrawal into Athens, the Athenians used the same strategies as the Spartans even during the time of Pericles.

Ehrenberg, Victor. *Sophocles and Pericles*. Oxford: Basil Blackwell, 1954. More than a third of this work directly concerns Pericles and his leadership role in Athens. The author provides an excellent analysis of all the dramatic and comedic references to Pericles and the politics of his time. The comments of the author on Plutarch's use of sources are invaluable.

Fornara, Charles W., and Loren J. Samons. *Athens from Cleisthenes to Pericles*. Berkeley: University of California Press, 1991. The book's first chapter discusses Pericles' family background and political career. The rest examines the functioning of democracy in Athens, and Athenian foreign policy in the 5th century B.C.

Hignett, C. *A History of the Athenian Constitution to the End of the Fifth Century B.C.* Oxford: Clarendon Press, 1952. Contains three chapters which cover the Athenian democracy from the revolution of 462 to the fall of the Athenian empire. The author covers all Periclean laws and their impact upon the Athenian constitution. An appendix covers Pericles' citizenship law of 451. Although a very specialized study, this work is seminal.

Kagan, Donald. *The Outbreak of the Peloponnesian War.* Ithaca, N.Y.: Cornell University Press, 1969. The author discusses the position taken by Thucydides that the Peloponnesian War was inevitable. By using all available sources, Kagan reexamines the foreign and domestic decisions made by Pericles and the Athenians and concludes that the war was not inevitable, but was the result of poor judgment and bad decisions.

———. *Pericles of Athens and the Birth of Democracy.* London: Secker and Warburg, 1990; New York: Free Press, 1991. This traditional biography is intended for a broad audience. Although certain points of chronology and details in the narrative are disputable, overall it is scholarly and well-written.

Meiggs, Russell. *The Athenian Empire.* Oxford: Clarendon Press, 1972; New York: Oxford University Press, 1979. This is an attempt to bring together all the available evidence for the Athenian empire and to evaluate it in the light of archaeological and epigraphic evidence. The coverage is comprehensive, thorough, and sound. Seventeen appendices cover controversial points of interpretation.

Plutarch. *The Rise and Fall of Athens.* Translated by Ian Scott-Kilvert. London and Boston: Penguin, 1960. Contains a chapter on Pericles, together with other chapters on some of his political rivals. Plutarch preserves much material regarding Pericles' time; the interpretations, however, are often biased. Still, the work is useful in showing the opinion of the opposition.

Ste. Croix, G. E. M. de. *The Origins of the Peloponnesian War.* London: Duckworth, and Ithaca, N.Y.: Cornell University Press, 1972. An in-depth study of the reasons for the Peloponnesian War, based upon a detailed reexamination and reevaluation of the primary sources. The author attempts to show that Thucydides is a reliable source and a keen observer of events. The work ends with forty-seven appendices and an extensive bibliography.

Thucydides. *History of the Peloponnesian War.* Translated by Charles Forster Smith. 4 vols. Cambridge, Mass.: Harvard University Press, and London: Heinemann, 1919-1923. Books 1 and 2 of the first volume of Thucydides constitute the primary source on Pericles' background, his political career, and his strategy for the transformation of the Delian League into the Athenian empire. While historians may interpret and reinterpret Thucydides, he remains the indispensable beginning point for any study of Pericles.

Peter L. Viscusi

SAINT PETER
Simon

Born: Early first century; Bethsaida of Galilee
Died: A.D. 64; Rome
Area of Achievement: Religion
Contribution: During Jesus' life, Peter was the most faithful and outspoken of the disciples; after Jesus' death he gave leadership to the early Church at Jerusalem and was active in missionary work. In Catholic tradition, he is the founder of the Christian Church and of the Papacy.

Early Life

Peter was born Simon (or Simeon), son of Jonah in Bethsaida; the date is uncertain, but it is believed that he was born in the first few years of the Christian era. The name Peter was given to him later by Jesus; the Greek word *petros* means "rock" and translates into the Aramaic Cepha or Cephas. Nothing is known of Peter's life before his call to discipleship. At the time of the call, he was working as a fisherman in partnership with his brother Andrew; according to the Gospel of Luke, he was also partners with James and John, thus beginning an intimacy with John which continued until both left Palestine.

Peter was a married man; it is recorded that Jesus cured Peter's mother-in-law of a fever. That his wife later accompanied him on missionary journeys is suggested by Paul in 1 Corinthians 9 (King James Version, the version cited throughout this article): "Have we not power to lead about a sister, a wife, as well as other apostles, and as the brethren of the Lord, and Cephas?" According to another tradition, Peter's wife was martyred at the same time as Peter. Concerning Peter's call, there are two accounts. The Synoptics (Matthew, Mark, and Luke) make Peter and Andrew the first to be called as they were fishing (or washing their nets); henceforth, they were to be "fishers of men." According to the Gospel of John, Andrew was the first to follow Jesus and afterward recruited Simon, whom Jesus immediately christened Peter (Matthew's account of the bestowal of the name will be discussed later).

Life's Work

In the accounts given of Jesus' ministry in the four Gospels, Peter plays a more prominent part than any of the other disciples, even John. When the Twelve are listed, Peter is always listed first and is even identified as "the first." He is noted as first, too, of an inner circle which includes James and John. These three were present (with Andrew) at the healing of Peter's mother-in-law and also at the healing of Jairus' daughter. Together they were present at the Transfiguration, where Peter proposed building tabernacles ("shelters" in the New English Bible) for Jesus, Moses, and Elijah (Matt. 17). Of all the Apostles, Peter was the most talkative—or the most often quoted. It was Peter who asked how often he should forgive his brother, who asked for the interpretation of a parable, who commented on the withered fig tree, and who protested that the Apostles had left all to follow Jesus. He also attempted to imitate his master by walking on the water and then lost his faith and had to be rescued. It was Peter who first realized that Jesus was indeed the Christ, "the son of the living God"

The Granger Collection, New York.

(Matt. 16). Yet it was Peter who refused to believe that Jesus had to "be killed, and the third day be raised up" (Matt. 16) and earned the rebuke "Get thee behind me, Satan."

Peter was also prominent in the events of the Passion. According to Luke 22, Jesus sent Peter and John ahead to prepare the Passover. When Jesus washed the disciples' feet, Peter alone resisted, and when Jesus insisted, Peter asked that "not my feet only, but also my hands and my head" be washed (John 13). When Jesus foretold that "one of you shall betray me," Peter prompted "the disciple whom Jesus loved" (presumably John) to ask Jesus who it was. When Peter protested that he was ready "to go both to prison and to death," Jesus answered, "Peter, the cock shall not crow this day, before that thou shalt thrice deny that thou knowest me" (Luke 22). In the Garden of Gethsemane, when Jesus went aside to pray for the last time, he took Peter, James, and John with him. Three times he found them sleeping; according to Matthew and Mark, it was to Peter that he directed his reproach: "What, would you not watch with me one hour?" (Mark 14). Yet according to John, when the officers came to arrest Jesus, again Peter alone resisted and cut off the ear of the high priest's servant. He followed Jesus to Caiaphas' house and sat in the court with the officers, warming himself by a fire; it was there that, being questioned by the servants, he denied Jesus thrice.

Though in the First Epistle of Peter, Peter calls himself a witness of Christ's sufferings (implying that he was present at the Crucifixion), he next appears in the Gospels in the aftermath of the Resurrection. According to Luke and John, Mary Magdalene, perhaps with some other women, found the tomb empty and reported the fact to Peter (and "the beloved disciple," according to John); Peter went to the tomb and found only the linen cloths in which Jesus' body had been wrapped. Luke speaks also of an appearance of the Lord "to Simon"; otherwise, aside from the appearance to Mary and to the two on the road to Emmaus, Jesus first appeared to the Eleven (or the Eleven without Thomas); neither here nor in most of the subsequent appearances was Peter particularly distinguished. An exception is John's report of an appearance by the Sea of Galilee. Peter had gone fishing with his old partners, James and John, and some others, when they became aware of a figure on the shore, whom the "beloved disciple" recognized as the Lord. It was then that Jesus gave Peter a pointed commandment, "Feed my sheep," and prophesied "by what manner of death he should glorify God."

In the period following the Resurrection appearances, one sees the Apostles gradually, and perhaps at first not intentionally, forming themselves into a church at Jerusalem, of which Peter was the natural if not the official leader. (Paul speaks of Peter and John and James, the Lord's brother, as "reputed pillars" of the Church.) Peter took the initiative in urging the appointment of a twelfth Apostle to replace Judas. When the Holy Spirit descended on the Apostles at Pentecost and they spoke in tongues, Peter spoke boldly to the astonished multitude, defending the speaking as the fulfillment of prophecy and proclaiming Jesus as the Messiah; thus he added thousands to the Church. When, in company with John, Peter healed a crippled man, he and John were for the first time arrested and brought before the high priest and the Sanhedrin, but they were released after being warned to desist from preaching in the name of Jesus. When further miracles followed, the whole body of Apostles was arrested, and although (it is said) the Apostles miraculously escaped from prison, they appeared before the high priest the next day and might have been executed except for the cautiousness of Gamaliel, a teacher of the law.

After the martyrdom of Stephen, the infant church was dispersed, and adherents carried the Gospel into the country districts. Philip preached in Samaria with such success that Peter and John were sent down to support him. This was apparently the beginning of Peter's missionary work outside Jerusalem. Tours of Lydda and Joppa, which followed, were important to the history of the Church. Peter had performed two miracles; soon afterward, he had a vision which seemed to abolish the Jewish distinction between clean and unclean food. The next day, he received a message from one Cornelius, a Roman centurion and convert to Judaism, who had had a vision urging him to send for Peter. The result was that the Holy Spirit was poured out on Gentiles, and they were baptized; Peter understood that he could no longer reject food as unclean or refuse to eat with the uncircumcised. For the time being, the disciples in Jerusalem seemed to accept Peter's position. It was about this time that Herod Agrippa I executed John's brother James. (He would have done the same with Peter if Peter had not miraculously escaped from prison.)

Meanwhile, Paul had undergone his conversion, and his missionary activity raised again the problem of the status of gentile converts. In Galatians, Paul asserts that three years after his conversion he went to Jerusalem and spent two weeks with Peter, without seeing any of the other Apostles except James, the Lord's brother. Fourteen years later, Paul went again to Jerusalem with Barnabas to discuss the problem raised by those Jewish Christians who would have imposed on gentile converts the burden of observing the Jewish ceremonial law. According to Paul, the meeting concluded amicably, with James, Peter, and John agreeing that they would minister to the Jews and Paul would minister to the Gentiles. The account in Acts (assuming that the same meeting is meant) adds that Peter spoke up on behalf of the Gentiles and was supported by James, who, however, made the condition that the Gentiles should abstain "from pollutions of idols, fornication, and from things strangled, and from blood" (Acts 15). The fragmentary evidence would suggest that by this time Peter, though apparently still the most outspoken of the group at Jerusalem, had yielded some of his authority to James. (Perhaps influence would be a better word than authority, for neither is described as holding an executive position or having any special title.) The compromise did not prevent further misunderstandings: Later, at Antioch, Peter, under pressure from James, refused any longer to eat with gentile converts and was rebuked by Paul (Gal. 2).

This, except for what can be conjectured from the Epistles of Peter, is the last that Scripture tells of Peter. The episode does not do credit to him, and yet the whole business of the controversy about the gentile converts fits with what is already known about Peter. The Gospels uniformly depict him as loyal, enthusiastic, courageous, and open to change, but he is also depicted as possessing that quality of irresolution which appeared most spectacularly in the episode of the denial.

Summary

Even though Scripture breaks off with the quarrel at Antioch, this does not mean that Peter ceased to serve the Church. Indeed, tradition has much to say about his further career, though some of the statements have proved highly controversial. It seems obvious from Scripture that Peter held a special place among the disciples. Matthew 16 elaborates on this:

> Thou art Peter, and upon this rock I will build my church; and the gates of Hades shall not prevail against it. I will give unto thee the keys of the Kingdom of Heaven: and whatsoever thou shalt bind on earth shall be bound in Heaven: and whatsoever thou shalt loose on earth shall be loosed in Heaven.

This passage can be used to support the claims of the Catholic church regarding the authority and infallibility of the Papacy. Connected with this is the question of Peter's residence and martyrdom in Rome. According to an early and persistent tradition, Peter was martyred in Rome in A.D. 64 (or a bit later), after having lived in Rome for as long as twenty-five years, serving as bishop. Tradition also asserts that Peter was in contact with Mark in Rome and furnished material for his Gospel. It is natural for Protestants to deny not only that Peter was in effect the first pope but also that he was ever in Rome at all. The controversy has of late become less intense. It seems to be agreed that Peter was in Rome, though hardly for twenty-five years, and that he was crucified there, in the vicinity of the Vatican Hill; the question of his burial is still uncertain.

Peter showed himself a leader of the Apostles even during the lifetime of Jesus, and he was also a leader of the early Church, though sharing his authority at first with John and later with James and Paul. He almost certainly was martyred in Rome. Whether he had any authority in the Roman church and whether he could transmit that authority to others are questions on which even believers are likely to remain divided.

Bibliography

Alter, Robert, and Frank Kermode, eds. *The Literary Guide to the Bible.* London: Collins, and Cambridge, Mass.: Harvard University Press, 1987. Especially relevant on the subject of Acts, which contributor James M. Robinson treats less as history than as "dramatized theology." The section "English Translations of the Bible," written by Gerald Hammond, explains the preference for the King James Version, used in this article.

Brown, Raymond E., Karl P. Donfried, and John Reumann. *Peter in the New Testament: A Col-*

laborative Assessment of Protestant and Roman Catholic Scholars. Minneapolis: Augsburg Publishing House, 1973; London: Chapman, 1974. A very learned and reasonable analysis of the evidence—but with cautious conclusions, such as "an investigation of the historical career does not necessarily settle the question of Peter's importance for the subsequent church."

Cullmann, Oscar. *Peter—Disciple, Apostle, Martyr: A Historical and Theological Study*. Translated by Floyd V. Wilson. 2d ed. Philadelphia: Westminster Press, and London: SCM Press, 1962. Although thorough and scholarly, this volume is less a biography than a Protestant criticism of Catholic claims.

Grant, Michael. *Saint Peter*. London: Weidenfeld and Nicolson, 1994. This biography of the apostle is written by a leading classical historian. It includes introductory surveys of the historical background, the problems of research and the primary sources, plus a long bibliography.

O'Connor, Daniel William. *Peter in Rome: The Literary, Liturgical, and Archeological Evidence*. New York: Columbia University Press, 1969. An exhaustive survey of the evidence. The account of the archaeological investigations (heavily illustrated) is particularly interesting.

Perkins, Pheme. *Peter: Apostle for the Whole Church*. Columbia: University of South Carolina Press, 1994. This survey of the life and ministry of Peter is based on the New Testament and some extra-canonical early Christian texts. Perkins, a theologian, stresses the modern relevance of the apostle's activity and teaching.

Reicke, Bo. Introduction and notes to *The Epistles of James, Peter, and Jude*. New York: Doubleday, 1964. Accepts that the First Epistle was written by Peter, probably with assistance from Silvanus. The First Epistle was written from "Babylon," by which Rome is almost certainly meant; there is a reference to Mark, presumably the author of the Gospel of Mark.

Smith, Terence V. *Petrine Controversies in Early Christianity: Attitudes Toward Peter in Christian Writings of the First Two Centuries*. Tübingen, West Germany: J. C. B. Mohr, 1985. In his opening statement, Smith confesses, "To talk of the Apostle Peter is to enter into a world of disaccord, polemic, and controversy." Contains an extensive bibliography.

John C. Sherwood

PHAEDRUS

Born: c. 15 B.C.; Pieria, Thessaly, Macedonia
Died: c. 55 A.D.; place unknown
Area of Achievement: Literature
Contribution: As a prolific writer of fables and reputed translator of Aesop, Phaedrus elevated the fable from a rhetorical device, used incidentally in writing and speaking, to a completely independent genre with a recognizable place in literature.

Early Life

The little that is known about Roman fabulist Phaedrus is derived either directly or by deduction from his own writings. He was born Phaeder, Gaius Julius, in Pieria, Thessaly, which was at the time part of a Roman province. He was presumably the son of a schoolteacher and was instructed by a highly educated poet and teacher of Greek. He spent part of his early youth in Italy, where he received the customary education in Latin and Greek. He studied, among others, Vergil, Euripides, Simonides, and particularly Ennius, who, together with Lucilius and Horace, had previously employed the fable in Roman literature.

During some portion of his youth, Phaedrus was attached to the retinue of L. Calpurnius Piso Frugi, who spent about three years settling disturbances in Thrace. After Piso's return to Rome, Phaedrus was brought, as a personal servant and tutor, to the house of Augustus, where he taught Greek to the emperor's grandson and heir, Lucius, while he himself attended the school of the famous scholar and philologist Verrius Flaccus. Years later, Phaedrus was granted his freedom by the emperor; however, his manumission did not confer him complete civil rights. As a freedman under Augustus, Phaedrus continued to live under the repressive tutelage and influence of the imperial rules.

Phaedrus' writing was strongly influenced by the folklore of the Aryans, as collected in the writings of Aesop (c. 600 B.C.). The fable, which originally came from the "wisdom literature" of numerous civilizations, migrated, in oral or written form, to Europe. There, Aesop, considered to be one of the wisest men of Greece, developed it and came to be known as the father of the fable. Aesop had also been a freed slave and, through his fables, he became, in scholar H. J. Blackham's words, "idealized as spokesman of the wisdom of the common man." Aesop himself explained that, in giving the use of speech to animals (actually the poet Hesiod's invention), he "laid the plan of teaching the most beautiful and useful maxims of philosophy under the veil of fables."

Aesop's influence on Phaedrus cannot be underestimated. "Where Aesop made a footpath, I have built a highway," wrote Phaedrus. He not only adopted the fable as a form of writing that he would later elevate to an independent genre but also, as a slave and later a freedman under Augustus and Tiberius, became increasingly preoccupied with the fortunes (or misfortunes) of the common man and used the fable to give a voice to those who were not allowed to speak openly. In the prologue to Book 3 of his fables, he wrote: "The slave, being liable to punishment for any offence, since he dared not say outright what he wished to say, projected his personal sentiments into fables and eluded censure under the guise of jesting with made-up stories." On more than one occasion, his allusions to the atmosphere of unfairness and injustice in which he lived got him into trouble. His audacity even brought him to the point of persecution at the hands of Sejanus, the most powerful minister of Tiberius' reign. However, it is not known which poem or poems in Books 1 and 2 offended Sejanus or what form of punishment Phaedrus received.

Life's Work

Much of Phaedrus' work is lost. His only surviving work, *Phaedri avgvsti Liberti Babvlarvm Aesopiarvm* (*The Aesopic Fables of Phaedrus, the Freedman of Augustus*), is a collection based on Aesop's fables that had been gathered in prose by Demetrius of Phalerum in about 300 B.C. Using Demetrius as his only source, Phaedrus translated Aesop's fables into Latin, cast them into verse form, and compiled them in the first collection of fables ever published as poetry and thus as literature. The five-book collection contains a total of ninety-three fables, but it is thought to be incomplete, since the length of each volume varies considerably. In particular, volumes 2 and 5 are thought to have originally contained much greater numbers of fables. Later editions include some thirty additional fables compiled by Niccolò Perotti (Archbishop of Manfredonia, A.D. 1430-80) in the *Appendix Perottina* (*Perotti's Appendix*). Except for *Perotti's Appendix*, each volume begins with a prologue in which Phaedrus stresses his independence from his source and defends his poetry from the attack of what he calls "malign critics."

The fables were written during a span of twenty years. Books 1 and 2 were published during the last years of Tiberius' reign and contain some of Phaedrus' most famous animal fables, such as "The Wolf and the Lamb," "The Wolf and the Crane," and "The Frogs Complain Against the Sun." Book 3 appeared under the reign of Caligula somewhere between A.D. 37 and 41. Book 4 differs from the previous volumes in that it includes a large number of fables composed by Phaedrus himself. This volume marked Phaedrus' return to writing after he had determined to put an end to his work. Book 5 was written without much enthusiasm under the reign of Claudius (A.D. 41-54) or during that of Nero (A.D. 54-68), when Phaedrus was at a very advanced age and probably close to death.

Phaedrus' collection of fables is far from being a mere compilation of Aesop's work. Phaedrus went beyond his source, refining and rewriting the fables in iambic senarii (a simple meter composed of lines of six iambic feet with variations that provide varying rhythms), the standard meter used by Greek and Roman dramatists. He also included some of his own fables using "the old form but with modern content." As a result, the collection includes a variety of stories, proverbs, sayings, and jests of varied length. Not all of them are animal fables. In fact, volumes 3, 4, and 5 include progressively fewer animal characters and more poets, priests, farmers, and shepherds, in conversation among themselves and sometimes even with Aesop himself (as in "The Poet," "The Thief and His Lamp," "Aesop and the Farmer," and "Aesop and the Saucy Fellow"). This difference in the form, however, does not affect their main purpose, which, following the example set by Aesop, was to "convey a moral or useful truth beneath the shadow of an allegory." Thus, "The Sheep, the Dog, and the Wolf" teaches the reader that liars are liable to lose in the end, while "Aesop and the Imprudent Fellow" instructs the reader that success dooms people to their downfall. To stress the didactic purpose of the fables, Phaedrus usually inserted a separate moral, either at the beginning (*promythion*) or at the end (*epimythion*) of each fable. It is believed that he may have derived this feature from Demetrius; it was definitely not from Aesop, who rejected such trite and wearisome additions that left little to the imagination.

Phaedrus wrote the fables in the language that characterized the early Augustan period: lucid, simple, and free from ornaments. At times, he uses a colloquial and coarse language, but it is always in agreement with his characterizations. His style, often satirical but at times serious, is defined by an extreme brevity that other fabulists both admired and envied but that most critics judged on account of the rather obscure effect some of his extremely brief sentences yielded. Only occasionally, such as in "The Poet, on Believing and Not Believing," and "The King, the Flute Player," is the language less concise, yielding a rather tedious effect. His tone has been defined sometimes as charming and humorous, other times as querulous and cantankerous, and, in one critic's opinion, embittered, particularly when commenting on the "law of the stronger."

Throughout his lifetime, Phaedrus suffered much stern criticism. Not only were his fables condemned by Sejanus, but he was also constantly ridiculed by jealous and hostile critics who underrated his writing and condemned it to a level below that of poetry. In Books 3 and 4, he asked Eutychus and Particulo, two of his patrons, to vindicate him in the eyes of the public. Their defense must not have made much of an impact, for he was rarely mentioned in classical literature. Neither Seneca the Younger nor Quintilian, both of whom wrote in the first century A.D., mentioned him in their writings, and even Flavius Avianus, himself a fabulist writing in the fourth century A.D., claims to have been influenced by Babrius (who wrote in the second half of first century A.D.) rather than Phaedrus. If, however, Phaedrus' contemporaries failed to recognize his literary merit, he regained the respect he had always sought after the fifteenth century, when his fables were rediscovered and were read by the public, paraphrased among respected fabulists, and even used for teaching Latin in school.

Summary

Phaedrus himself admitted that his ambition was to carry on, in Latin, the literary tradition of Greece, which he had inherited. He chose the fable because it combined the two traditional functions of poetry: entertainment and instruction. Some scholars suggest, however, that his main motive in adopting the fable as a literary form and Aesop as his subject was to fight against moral degradation during the reigns of Augustus and Tiberius. Since slaves were not allowed to speak outright, he chose a genre in which he was able to elude censure and thus remain immune. This may well have been true. Behind the speech of his animals and his inanimate objects such as trees, there is the constant reminder of some of his prevalent themes: the advantage of the stronger over the weak ("The Wolf and the Lamb"), the futility of protest ("The Frogs Ask for a King"), the safety found in poverty ("The Dog Carrying a Piece of Meat Across the River"), the pervasiveness of power ("The Eagle and the Crow"), and the praise of freedom ("The Wolf and the Sleek Dog"). Phaedrus was not a highly inventive fabulist nor a poet of great achievement. However, no other fabulist did for the fable what Phaedrus did: By adapting the Greek genre of the fable to Latin, he made it a subject of poetic composition and gave it a recognizable voice in literature.

Bibliography

Aesop. *Select Fables of Esop and other Fabulists.* Robert Dodsley, ed. 3 vols. Birmingham, Ala.: John Baskerville, 1761. Aesop's introduction provides an excellent account of the nature and purpose of the fable as a popular genre beforethe time of Christ.

Blackham, H. J. *The Fable as Literature.* London and Dover, N.H.: Athlone Press, 1985. Chapter 1 gives a detailed account of the fable as early popular narrative, including its Indian and Aesopic origins. Phaedrus is mentioned tangentially throughout the discussion.

Conte, Gian Biagio. *Latin Literature: A History.* Translated by Joseph B. Solodow. Baltimore: John Hopkins University Press, 1987. The section "Phaedrus: The Fable Tradition" includes a discussion of Phaedrus' merit as a man of letters and a social commentator of his time.

Duff, J. Wight. *A Literary History of Rome in the Silver Age: From Tiberius to Hadrian.* 3d ed. London: Benn, and New York: Barnes & Noble, 1964. Chapter 5, "Phaedrus and Fable: Poetry of the Time," is by far the longest discussion on Phaedrus' life and work within the Roman context.

Kenney, E. J., ed. *The Cambridge History of Classical Literature.* Vol. 2. *Latin Literature.* Cambridge and New York: Cambridge University Press, 1982. Lists Phaedrus in chapter 30 ("Minor Poetry"). Most of the discussion is restricted to Phaedrus' sources, his language, and his style.

Perry, Ben Edwin. *Babrius and Phaedrus.* London: Heinemann, and Cambridge, Mass.: Harvard University Press, 1965. The lengthy introduction covers the Aesopic fable in antiquity, its origin, and the roles of Aesop, Babrius, and Phaedrus in its development.

Phaedrus. *The Fables of Phaedrus.* Translated by P. F. Widdows. Austin: University of Texas Press, 1992. A recent translation of Phaedrus' fables. Includes a lengthy introduction discussing Phaedrus' life and work, his fables, his reputation, his use of meter, and Christopher Smart's 1764 translation of his work.

S. P. Baeza

PHEIDIPPIDES

Born: probably c. 515 B.C.; Athens, Greece

Died: perhaps 490 B.C.; perhaps Athens, Greece

Areas of Achievement: Warfare and conquest

Contribution: A courier commonly known as Pheidippides is famous for delivering a message, on foot and over a long distance, concerning the Battle of Marathon fought between Persia and Athens in 490 B.C.. Despite problems with the ancient tradition, Pheidippides' feat of running is still popularly associated with the announcement of the Athenian victory and also with the introduction of the "marathon" race in modern times.

Early Life

No information is available about Pheidippides' early life prior to his famous run, which occurred in 490 B.C. either shortly before or shortly after the Battle of Marathon, a pivotal conflict of the Greco-Persian Wars. At Marathon, located in Athenian territory to the northeast of the city of Athens, a smaller army of Athenians courageously faced and dramatically defeated a larger Persian army, and Pheidippides' run has become famous as a symbol of that victory. The Battle of Marathon showed the effectiveness of the Greek infantry soldier, and it greatly enhanced the self-confidence of the Greeks, especially the Athenians, in their military and cultural prowess. Along with the "birth of democracy" at Athens a few years earlier, the victory at Marathon marked the transition from the early Archaic Age of Greece (c. 750 B.C.-500 B.C.), a time of independent development for the Greek city-states. After Marathon, acting more in concert than ever before, Athens, Sparta, and other Greek states went on to repel an even greater Persian attack on Greece in 480 B.C.-479 B.C., and in the Classical Age of Greek glory in the fifth century B.C., the Greeks made phenomenal achievements in the areas of politics, literature, philosophy, and the arts.

The best source on Pheidippides is Herodotus of Halicarnassus, the "father of history," the fifth century B.C. author of *The Histories* (c. 430 B.C.), a work on the Persian Wars. Herodotus says that Pheidippides was an Athenian and a trained *hemerodromos*, a "day-runner," which means that he delivered messages by running long distances on foot. Clearly, he was well trained and in excellent physical shape, and he had run long distances before. Probably, but not necessarily, he was a fairly young man in 490.

Life's Work

Pheidippides' achievement was a physically impressive feat of long-distance running performed in the context of one of history's most famous battles, but details of his actions were confused and at least semilegendary even in antiquity. Even his name is a matter of debate. Some ancient manuscripts of Herodotus and some other ancient sources name the runner "Philippides," a more common name in ancient Athens. Nevertheless, the name "Pheidippides" is still popularly associated with the "messenger of Marathon," the heroic soldier who supposedly fought at the Battle of Marathon and then ran approximately twenty-five miles to Athens, delivered the message, "Rejoice! We have won," and dropped dead.

Recent studies have reexamined the ancient sources and shown that this inspirational event perhaps never happened at all, and certainly it did not happen exactly as is traditionally assumed. According to Herodotus, in 490 B.C. a Persian force landed in Athenian territory and occupied the plain of Marathon. One of the Athenian generals, Miltiades, convinced the Athenians to send out a force of heavily armed infantrymen (called "hoplites"), to meet the Persians. Before the army departed for Marathon, the Athenian generals decided to send a herald to appeal to Sparta, the leading military power in Greece, for help against Persia.

The Athenian Pheidippides (or Philippides), a courier trained at delivering messages over long distances by running, carried the appeal from Athens to Sparta, a distance of about 140 miles. Later, on his return, Pheidippides told the Athenians that while he was running over Mount Parthenion in Arcadia (a region of Greece along the route to Sparta) the god Pan (a Greek god, part human and part goat in form, associated with flocks, shepherds, and fertility) called him by name. Pan, Pheidippides claimed, told him to ask the Athenians why they had failed to worship the god with a state cult when he had been friendly to them, he had helped them in the past, and he was willing to do so in the future. Herodotus adds that, after the return to peace and prosperity, the Athenians built a shrine to Pan and established annual sacrifices and a torch race to honor the god.

According to Herodotus, on the second day after leaving Athens, the messenger arrived in Sparta. He addressed the Spartan leaders and begged them to help save Athens from slavery at the hands of the Persians. The Spartans said they wanted to help but that they were busy with an important festival, the Carnea, in honor of Apollo, and so their religion obliged them to stay at Sparta until the arrival of the full moon later in the month. As Herodotus recounts, a force of about ten thousand Greeks (mostly Athenians, with a few soldiers from Plataea, a state allied with Athens) were heavily outnumbered, perhaps by two to one, by the Persian forces. Nevertheless, the Greeks charged and defeated the Persians in an infantry battle that, Herodotus claims, cost the lives of 6,400 Persian but only 192 Athenian soldiers. Herodotus notes that immediately after the battle, the Athenian troops hurried back to the city to defend it against a possible Persian attack by sea. Troops from Sparta did arrive at Marathon, but only after the battle was over. Significantly, Herodotus, the ancient authority on the era of the Persian War, makes no mention of a post-battle run by Pheidippides. Herodotus loved stories of heroic feats and wonders, so his silence about a "Marathon run" seriously undermines the credibility of the later traditions about the runner.

The popular version of the story comes from later authors. Writing around A.D. 100, Plutarch, a Greek biographer of famous ancient leaders, stated that Herakleides of Pontus, a Greek philosopher of the fourth century B.C., had said that the messenger who brought the news from Marathon was one Thersippus of Erchia. This suggests that some story of a messenger announcing the victory at Marathon at Athens was known in the mid-fourth century B.C. but that the messenger's name was not Pheidippides. Furthermore, Plutarch says most (probably later) sources say that the messenger was a certain Eukles and that he ran directly from the battle, still in full armor, to Athens, said "Rejoice! We have won," and then died. Elsewhere, Plutarch tells a suspiciously similar story about a man named Euchidas: that in 479 B.C., after another Greek land victory against Persia, he ran from Plataea to Delphi and back to Plataea, covering the distance of about 125 miles in one day, carrying a torch burning with sacred fire, that he greeted his fellow citizens, handed them the torch, and died. The latest ancient source on the tradition is Lucian, a prolific literary figure who, around A.D. 170, wrote that the name of the messenger from Marathon was Philippides and that, with his dying words, he announced the victory to the Athenian

officials. Lucian thus is the only ancient author to combine all the now-popular details—a messenger named Philippides or Pheidippides who ran from Marathon to Athens and announced the victory with his last words before dying. In sum, since the best source, Herodotus, omits the story, and the "Marathon run" turns up only in later, less reliable sources, the popular story perhaps was a romantic invention of the type that commonly grow up around famous battles and famous figures.

Adding to the tradition and the confusion, Robert Browning's 1879 poem "Pheidippides" mixed ancient accounts with poetic creativity to produce a full-blown modern version of the tale. Browning's poem has Pheidippides run to Sparta to request help, then run back to fight at Marathon, and then run to Athens, arriving, with his heart bursting with joy, to announce the victory and die. This amounts to a truly impressive but much less credible historical accomplishment. Nevertheless, Browning's expanded, romantic version of the story inspired (or was used to suggest an ancient precedent for) the introduction of the modern marathon race in the Olympic Games held in Athens in 1896.

Despite modern misperceptions, Pheidippides' run to Sparta should not be associated with any sporting contest but rather with the abilities of ancient messengers. There simply was no marathon or ultra-long-distance running in ancient Greek athletics. At ancient Greek athletic meets, the longest footrace, the *dolichos*, was run over a distance of at most three miles. However, other ancient examples, modern studies, and the feats of modern long-distance athletes have shown that even such a lengthy run as 140 miles could have been accomplished by a well-trained runner in two days. Moreover, the story that the runner saw Pan provides a convincing detail, for long-distance runners sometimes do experience altered states of consciousness as part of the "runner's high."

Summary

Ironically, Pheidippides has not been immortalized for his historically credible and physically very impressive (though ultimately militarily futile) run from Athens to Sparta, but rather for a much shorter and historically much less credible run from Marathon to Athens, a run associated with a great military victory and his own dramatic death. Indeed, there probably was a fifth century B.C. Pheidippides (or Philippides) who carried a message from Athens to Sparta, quite conceivably covering the distance in two days. However, the popular version of the story, that a soldier running miles from the victory at Marathon to Athens and then dropping dead as he delivered the news, is surely a product of a tradition begun by later, less reliable ancient authors, amplified by Browning's 1879 poem, and memorialized by the introduction of the marathon race at the Olympics in 1896.

Although the story remains a cherished part of the folklore of ancient Greece and of modern sport, the "Marathon run" should not be associated with Pheidippides; moreover, marathon running as a sport rather than a form of messenger service is of historically recent origin. Not actually derived from ancient sport but rather invented for the Athens Olympic Games of 1896, the marathon race has nevertheless become both a symbol of the Olympic Games and an internationally popular athletic event.

Bibliography

Burn, A. R. *Persia and the Greeks: The Defence of the West, 546-478 B.C.* 2d ed. Stanford, Calif.: Stanford University Press, and London: Duckworth, 1984. A readable, traditional, but still useful military history of the conflicts between Greece and Persia.

Frost, Frank J. "The Dubious Origins of the Marathon." *American Journal of Ancient History* 4 (1979): 159-163. An important article challenging the value of sources after Herodotus on the runner, whom Frost argues was actually named "Philippides."

Herodotus. *The Histories*, translated by Aubrey De Sélincourt. Rev. ed. London and Boston: Penguin, 1996. A convenient translation of the classic ancient history of the background to and course of the Persian Wars.

Lazenby, J. F. *The Defence of Greece, 490-479 B.C.* Warminster, England: Aris & Phillips, 1993. An excellent account of the failure of the Persian invasions of Greece.

Lee, Hugh M. "Modern Ultra-Long-Distance Running and Philippides' Run from Athens to Sparta." *Ancient World* 9 (1984): 107-113. Offers modern comparisons to show that a run from Athens to Sparta in two days was possible for a trained runner.

Matthews, V. J. "The *Hemerodromoi*: Ultra-Long-Distance Running in Antiquity." *Classical World* 68 (1974): 161-167. The author, a classicist and marathon runner, thoroughly examines several ancient accounts of long-distance running.

Sweet, Waldo E. *Sport and Recreation in Ancient Greece*. New York: Oxford University Press, 1987. A sourcebook of ancient texts on sport. Includes sources on Pheidippides in a chapter on running in ancient Greece.

Donald G. Kyle

PHIDIAS

Born: c. 490 B.C.; Athens, Greece
Died: c. 430 B.C.; Elis, Greece
Area of Achievement: Art
Contribution: Phidias' work embodied the high classical ideal in sculpture; his renditions of the gods became standards to which later artists aspired. Director of the sculpture program of the Parthenon in Athens, he was best known for his cult images of Athena in Athens and of Zeus in Olympia.

Early Life

Phidias, the son of Charmides, was born just before the wars which pitted his fellow Athenians against the invading Persians in 490 and 480 B.C. This fact is of great importance in understanding his development and that of his country, for these wars proved to the Athenians that with their own resources and the gods' favor, the fledgling democracy could succeed against overwhelming odds. Phidias' sculptures came to reflect confidence in men and the gods' grace.

After the wars, Athens became the preeminent Greek state and led a confederation that continued to fight the Persians. Athenian leadership led to Athenian domination, and any city that tried to leave the league was disciplined. Pericles led the state during Phidias' adult lifetime and created a strong Athens by pursuing an expansionist policy. Phidias grew up knowing that he lived in one of the most powerful and influential of the Greek states.

Little is known of Phidias' early training beyond the fact that—like other Athenian children—he would have received his education in the gymnasium, learning athletics, music, mathematics, and poetry, including the Homeric epics. The works of Homer in particular were to have a profound impact on Phidias' vision of the gods, which expressed itself in his sculpture. Along with the sculptors Myron and Polyclitus, he received artistic training from Ageladas (also called Hageladas) of Argos, who worked mainly in bronze and is known for a great statue of Zeus which he made for the Messenians.

Phidias attended the dramatic festivals of Dionysus, where he saw performances of Aeschylus' tragedies, including *Persai* (467 B.C.; *The Persians*), a triumphant paean to Athenian success and divine favor, and the *Oresteia* trilogy (458 B.C.),

which extols the gods Zeus and Athena and ends with an encomium to justice as practiced in Athens. Phidias grew up to be proud of his land's traditions and the accomplishments of its citizens. The tragic vision revealed in Athenian drama, with the grace of the immortals contrasting with human limitations, was to have a profound effect on the sculptor's works.

Another formative influence on the sculptor was the humanistic teachings of Sophists such as Protagoras, who held that "man is the measure of all things," and Anaxagoras, who insisted on the divine supremacy of reason. With their notions of subjectivity and emphasis on the potential for human progress, these new thinkers saw people as responsible for their own advancement. Thus, they represented an anthropocentric view of life that encouraged the development of the arts, because to them civilization was advanced by *technē* (artistic skill). Phidias' work was a physical manifestation of this confidence in human accomplishment. At the same time, his statues reflected the measured relationships that Anaxagoras saw as the reflections of the divine world-reason.

Phidias was a product of his age, which was characterized by confidence in human rationality, the tragic notion of human limitation in the face of divine power, and the idea of civilization's triumph over barbarism. His sculptures both reflected his age and recalled epic notions of Homeric gods and heroes.

Life's Work

During Phidias' early years, the temples and sanctuaries which the Persians had destroyed remained untouched because the Greeks, in the Oath of Plataea, had agreed to leave the ruins as memorials to barbarian sacrilege. Consequently, Phidias' earlier sculptures were monuments to the Athenian victory over the Persians at Marathon. In fact, two of them were built with spoils from that battle. One, a colossal bronze statue of armed Athena Promachos (c. 470-460 B.C.; Athena, first in battle), stood prominently on the Acropolis at Athens; approximately fifteen meters high, its shining spear tip and helmet crest could be seen from far out at sea. The other, a bronze group containing Athena, Apollo, the legendary heroes of Athens, and the victorious Athenian general Miltiades, was dedicated at the panhellenic sanctuary at Delphi (c. 465 B.C.).

Phidias' Athena Lemnia was commissioned and dedicated by Athenian colonists settling on Lemnos around 450. This bronze stood on the Athenian Acropolis and had a reputation for extraordinary beauty. Later copies and ancient descriptions indicate that it showed the goddess contemplating her helmet in her right hand.

Pericles respected the Oath of Plataea as long as a state of belligerence with Persia—fostered by the Athenian general Cimon—kept the issue alive. When Cimon died in 449 and a peace treaty was arranged with the Persians, Pericles no longer felt the need to maintain the Athenian temples in ruins. The stage was set for a rebuilding of the sanctuaries on the Acropolis, and the next year, construction of the Parthenon began. Pericles named Phidias general supervisor for the project.

The Parthenon—the temple of Athena the Maiden—was a major synthesis of architecture and sculpture. Phidias coordinated the sculptural program, which consisted of ninety-two metopes with battle scenes (Greeks/Trojans, Greeks/Amazons, lapiths/centaurs, and gods/giants; in place by 443), a 160-meter sculptured frieze (the Panathenaic Procession; complete by 438), the cult statue of Athena Parthenos (complete by 438), and pediments (the birth of Athena and the contest of Athena and Poseidon; complete by 432). The sculpted decoration of the Parthenon was unique: No other temple had both sculpted metopes and a continuous frieze, so Phidias' genius had the maximum opportunity to show itself.

Phidias himself was completely responsible for the chryselephantine (gold and ivory) statue of Athena inside, which stood more than twelve meters high. No original pieces of this statue have survived, but later copies and descriptions give an idea of its appearance. Athena stood with a statue of Nike (victory) in her right hand, which rested lightly on a Corinthian column. She was dressed in her aegis, a magical breastplate surrounded by snakes, and wore a three-crested helmet and a belt of snakes. A spear and shield stood at her left side, the latter decorated with relief figures of gods battling giants (inside) and Greeks fighting Amazons (outside). These motifs reflected those of the Parthenon's other sculptures: the forces of order battling those of barbarity—another sign of Athenian pride in the Persian defeat. Beneath the shield rose the form of a great snake, representing the local god Erichthonius. The statue stood upon a rectangular base showing Pandora being adorned by all the gods.

After the cult image was dedicated in 438, Phidias was accused by Pericles' enemies of having stolen some of the gold from the statue. This charge was proved false when it was revealed that the gold on the statue, weighing more than one thousand kilograms, had been designed to be easily removed. When it was weighed, no gold was found missing. Upon his acquittal on that charge, Phidias was accused of sacrilege, for it was commonly believed that he had represented himself and Pericles on the shield of Athena. This charge provides the circumstances for the description of Phidias: He was shown as a bald old man lifting up a stone with both hands. Upon his conviction, Phidias had to leave Athens, probably around 437.

Fortunately for Phidias, the Elians at this time invited him to come to Olympia to make a chryselephantine cult image of Zeus for the recently completed temple of Zeus. Phidias set up a workshop behind the temple, where he worked for five years, helped by his nephew Panaenus. Pieces of the molds for the golden drapery have been found there, in addition to a cup with the inscription "I belong to Phidias."

Phidias' Zeus at Olympia represented a new conception in Greek art. Until that time, Zeus had been usually depicted striding forward with a thunderbolt in his hand. Phidias portrayed him seated on a throne in Olympian calm, seven or eight times life size (more than twelve meters), his head almost touching the roof. The throne was four-fifths of the height of the whole and was decorated with ebony, gold, and ivory. The golden cloak was decorated with lilies and glass inlay. The majesty of the statue impressed all who saw it. Quintilian asserted that it enhanced traditional religion, Dio Cocceianus (Chrysostomos) that the sight of it banished all sorrow. According to one anecdote, Phidias said that he had been inspired by the image of Zeus in Homer's *Iliad* (c. 800 B.C.), in which the god on his throne nodded and caused all Olympus to shake. Pausanias related that Phidias carved his signature beneath the god's feet and that when the statue was complete, the god sent a flash of lightning to show that he approved of the work. The men in charge of cleaning the great statue were said to be the descendants of Phidias himself.

Phidias died shortly after having completed the Olympian Zeus, probably in Elis around 430. Many other works have been attributed to him, including a bronze Apollo near the Parthenon, a marble Aphrodite in the Athenian Agora, a chryselephantine Aphrodite in Elis, and a famous Amazon in Ephesus. In addition, literary sources indicate that he was skilled in paintings, engraving, and metal embossing. None of these works survives.

Summary

Phidias' life spanned three important periods in the development of Greek art. He was born toward the end of the Archaic period, when sculpture was quite formal, orderly, and stylized, with a quality of aloofness. Phidias lived as a young man in the Early Classical period, a time of artistic transition, when statues were more representational and heavily charged with specific emotions. When he matured, Phidias worked in a style that avoided the extremes of both: the High Classical, whose statues had expressions that were neither overly remote nor involved, but simultaneously detached and aware. This attitude of idealism, congenial to Phidias' strong Homeric tendencies, colored his work and gave it its distinctive quality.

The sculpture on the Parthenon came to embody what later generations considered "classical," and Phidias' style influenced all cult images subsequent to his Athena and Zeus, setting a standard for later sculptors to follow. For example, his pupil Alcamenes was responsible for the cult images in the Hephaesteum and the temples of Dionysus Eleuthereus and Ares in Athens, as well as the Aphrodite of the Gardens. Agoracritus, another pupil, created the cult statue and base for the temple of Nemesis at Rhamnus.

The chief characteristics of Phidias' style were sublimity, precision, and an "Olympian" rendering, showing the gods as detached from the human realm yet still concerned for men. Their expressions were calm and dignified. They were so pure in their conception that stories arose that Phidias had seen the gods themselves. His works brought the divine down to earth and made heavenly forms manifest for mortals; the gods of Homer came alive under his touch.

Since so few of Phidias' works survive—the Parthenon sculptures are most likely his design, but not of his hand—scholars try to re-create his sculptures on the basis of later copies, mostly of Roman date. The Athena Lemnia, for example, has been reconstructed from ancient references, combined with a marble head now in Bologna and a torso in Dresden; the Athena Parthenos from later copies, including the Varvakeion Athena of Roman date; the Olympian Zeus from coins and gems depicting it in Roman times. Identifications of copies of Phidian originals cannot be proved for the most part, but the quest continues to exercise the ingenuity of scholars. For example, some assign to Phidias the bronze warrior statues found in 1972 in the sea off Riace in southern Italy, while others oppose the attribution.

Bibliography

Boardman, John, and David Finn. *The Parthenon and Its Sculptures*. London: Thames and Hudson, and Austin: University of Texas, 1985. The best work on the subject, with hundreds of large, clear photographs and illustrations. Excellent discussion of the history of the building, the role of Phidias, the nature of the sources, historical context, interpretation of the sculpture, and relation to religious festivals. Bibliography and index.

Harrison, Evelyn B. "The Composition of the Amazonomachy on the Shield of Athena Parthenos." *Hesperia* 35 (1966): 107-133. Exhaustive study of literary sources that describe the battle scene said to include a representation of Phidias himself, with an analysis of the ancient copies. Discussion of composition and iconography, including illustrations with discussion of each figure. Extensive bibliography, catalog of figures, and detailed reconstruction. Phidian scholarship at its best.

————. "Pheidias." *Yale Classical Studies: Personal Styles in Greek Sculpture* 30 (1995): 16-25. This discussion of Phidias' art is based mainly upon the preserved Roman copies of his works, rather than the evidence of ancient texts. The general artistic background of the period is examined, and all of Phidias' major works are discussed in detail. Questions of attribution are given great attention, and Harrison expressly states that the Kassel "Apollo" and the Dresden "Athena" cannot be copies of Pheidian statues.

Leipen, Neda. *Athena Parthenos: A Reconstruction*. Toronto: Royal Ontario Museum, 1971. Devoted to the problem of reconstructing Phidias' Parthenon cult statue, this is a photographic documentation of all relevant artifacts, with a discussion of literary descriptions, the Royal Ontario Museum's own construction of a model of the statue, and a detailed description of each part of the figure, including accessories. Extensive notes and bibliography.

Palagia, Olga. "In Defense of Furtwangler's Athena Lemnia." *American Journal of Archaeology* 91 (1987): 81-84. Discussion of a reconstruction of Phidias' most beautiful statue. Contains an illustration of the most accepted reconstruction and of other sculptures which support that interpretation. A good example of scholarly methodology used to re-create a Phidian original. Bibliography.

Pollitt, J. J. *Art and Experience in Classical Greece.* Cambridge: Cambridge University Press, 1972. The world of classical Greek art, putting Phidias in perspective. Describes the intellectual influences on the sculptor, his own influence on other media, his style and spirit, and the problems with writing his biography. Illustrations. Includes suggestions for further reading.

Richter, Gisela M. "The Pheidian Zeus at Olympia." *Hesperia* 35 (1966): 166-170. Excellent summary of what is known about the statue that was considered one of the seven wonders of the world. Includes descriptions of the statue as rendered in literature and on gems and coins. Generously illustrated and footnoted.

———. *The Sculpture and Sculptors of the Greeks.* 4th ed. New Haven, Conn.: Yale University Press, 1970. Definitive work on the lives and works of Greek sculptors. Treats anatomy, technique, composition, copies. Long and detailed section on Phidias, discussing all of his works, with extensive bibliography of ancient and modern sources. Two indexes, numerous photographs, chronological table of Greek sculptors and their works.

Schefold, Karl. *The Art of Classical Greece.* New York: Crown Publishers, and London: Methuen, 1967. Contains a significant section on the Mature Classical period, with discussion and appreciation of Phidias' genius, especially in relation to the Parthenon sculptures and statue of Olympian Zeus. Numerous small but useful illustrations.

Stewart, Andrew. *Greek Sculpture: An Exploration.* 2 vols. New Haven, Conn.: Yale University Press, 1990. This is the most up-to-date general handbook on Greek sculpture. First, Phidias' work on the Parthenon is discussed as part of the history of the High Classical style. The section titled "The Sculptors" puts together practically all available information on his personality and work, giving quotations from all major sources on him. The book has useful chronological appendices; the plates reproduce the standard works associated with Phidias.

Daniel B. Levine

PHILIP II OF MACEDONIA

Born: 382 B.C.; Macedonia

Died: 336 B.C.; Aegae, Macedonia

Areas of Achievement: Government and warfare

Contribution: Philip inherited a backward kingdom on the verge of collapse and made it a powerful state. His military innovations revolutionized warfare and created the army that would conquer the Persian Empire.

Early Life

Situated on the northern frontier of the Greek world, Philip's homeland of Macedonia long remained a kingdom without real unity. From their capitals of Aegae and Pella near the Aegean coast, Philip's ancestors had ruled the eastern area of lower Macedonia since the seventh century B.C. They exercised only a tenuous rule inland over upper Macedonia, however, and suffered repeated invasions and interference from their neighbors, barbarian and Greek alike. Philip's direct experience of these problems during the reigns of his father and two older brothers helps explain his determination as king to reverse Macedonia's precarious position.

In 393, Philip's father, Amyntas, suffered his first expulsion at the hands of the Illyrians, his neighbors to the west. Amyntas soon regained his throne, but he secured peace with the Illyrians only by paying tribute. As part of the settlement, he also married an Illyrian princess, Eurydice—the future mother of Philip. Ten years later a second Illyrian invasion forced Amyntas to entrust a portion of this kingdom to the Chalcidian Greeks, who refused to relinquish it. By 382, the year of Philip's birth, they had extended their control westward to include Amyntas' capital, Pella. An intervention by Sparta, then the most powerful of the Greek states, restored Amyntas to his capital in 379, but the Spartans demanded Macedonia's subservience to Sparta.

When Philip's older brother Alexander II assumed the throne in 370, the now-adolescent Philip went as a hostage to the Illyrians, who also demanded tribute as the price of peace. The boy returned home to find Alexander in a civil war that invited intervention by Thebes, the ascendant Greek city-state since the defeat of Sparta in 371. In 368, after the Thebans resolved the conflict in favor of Alexander, Philip and thirty other sons of Macedonian nobles were sent to Thebes as a guarantee of Macedonian obedience to Theban wishes. For three years Philip observed Thebes at the peak of its diplomatic and military power. Later accounts of the military lessons of this visit are probably exaggerated, but this experience must have influenced Philip. At the very least it allowed him to understand how the Greeks conducted their affairs, and it may explain his later severe treatment of Thebes. Following the assassination of Alexander, a second Theban intervention saved the throne for Philip's other brother, Perdiccas III, and brought more hostages to Thebes.

Back in Macedonia after 365, Philip received a district of his own and witnessed seizures of Macedonian coastal territory by the Athenians. In 359 he may have taken part in the disastrous Illyrian expedition that resulted in the death of Perdiccas and four thousand Macedonian soldiers. After the death of his brother, Philip—at age twenty-three—became the eighteenth King of Macedonia.

Life's Work

Philip inherited a kingdom on the verge of disintegration. Rival heirs challenged his right to the throne, the army threatened to collapse, and enemies menaced on all sides. Fortunately, the Illyrians did not choose to follow their victory with an invasion; to the north, however, the Paeonians began to raid Macedonian territory, while a Thracian king supported a pretender who claimed the kingship. Diplomacy and bribery forestalled these threats, while Philip dealt with a more immediate danger: Another pretender, backed by the Athenians, marched on the ancestral capital, Aegae, with three thousand mercenaries. After ensuring the loyalty of the capital, the young king trapped and disposed of his rival. Wisely, he then made conciliatory gestures to the Athenians in order to neutralize them while he returned his attention to the barbarians.

The opportune death of the Paeonian king allowed Philip to force an alliance upon his weaker successor, and by 358 Philip felt secure enough to lead a revitalized Macedonian army west against his most dangerous foes, the Illyrians. The details of his first major battle remain unclear, but Philip won a decisive victory and inflicted unusually severe casualties on his defeated enemy—three-quarters of the Illyrian army reportedly died. Followed by his marriage to an Illyrian princess, this victory secured his western frontier and allowed him to consolidate his position in Macedonia. As part of that consolidation, Philip began the transformation of Macedonia from a largely pastoral society to a more agriculturally based and urbanized state. Less visible than his military activities, these internal changes were equally important to the rise of Macedonia.

His dramatic victory over the Illyrians indicates that Philip had already begun the reorganization of the Macedonian army that would revolutionize warfare and make Macedonia the supreme military power in the Mediterranean. One year after his unfortunate brother had lost four thousand men to the Illyrians, Philip fielded a force of ten thousand foot soldiers and six hundred horsemen. (By the time of Philip's death, the Macedonian army would comprise at least twenty-four thousand infantry and four thousand cavalry, with numerous supporting troops.) As important as the increase in manpower was Philip's use of heavy cavalry as a primary instrument of attack against infantry, a tactic that explains the remarkably high rate of casualties among his foes. Equally significant was his redesign of the traditional Greek phalanx infantry formation, which he used in expert combination with his horsemen. Superbly trained to fight as a unit, Philip's phalangites used a novel fifteen-foot pike, the *sarissa*, and wore minimal defensive armor. Their success depended upon careful coordination with cavalry and lighter armed infantry. Philip's army also included specialists in siege techniques, who introduced the torsion catapult and tall siege towers. The evolution of this fighting force is obscure, but Philip clearly began his military reform early—he suffered only one defeat in his entire career.

With his kingdom more or less secure from barbarian threats, Philip abandoned his conciliatory posture toward the Athenians and moved to eliminate their presence on his eastern frontier. In 357 he seized the strategic city of Amphipolis, founded by the Athenians eighty years previously. This move gave Philip access to the rich gold and silver mines of neighboring Mount Pangaeus, which eventually rendered him an annual revenue of one thousand talents. Philip next took Pydna, one of two Athenian-controlled cities on the lower Macedonian coast. In 354 his successful siege of Methone eliminated the last Athenian base in Macedonia,

but at a considerable cost to Philip: During the assault on the city an arrow destroyed his right eye.

Once he had placed Athens on the defensive, Philip moved against two nearby Greek districts that had threatened Macedonia during his youth: Thessaly to the south, Chalcidice to the east. His venture into Thessaly in 353 produced the only serious defeat of his career, but Philip came back the next year to win the Battle of the Crocus Plain, in which six thousand enemy soldiers died. This victory, followed by his election as president of the Thessalian League and his marriage to a Thessalian princess, brought Thessaly, with its renowned supply of horses, securely under Macedonian control. In 349 Philip began his move against the thirty-odd cities of the Chalcidian League, which he subdued one by one. Olynthus, the most important city of the league and the last holdout, fell after a two-month siege in 348. Philip razed the city and enslaved its inhabitants. Having eliminated most threats in the north, Philip now turned his attention to the city-states of central and southern Greece. The former victim of Greek interventions had become the intervener.

In 346, after obtaining a peace with Athens recognizing his right to Amphipolis, Philip in a surprise move came south and forced an end to the so-called Sacred War, which had been waged for nearly a decade. By intervening against the Phocians, whose sacrilegious seizure of the international sanctuary at Delphi had brought them almost universal condemnation, he cleverly played to Greek public opinion. Moreover, his refusal to punish the Athenians, despite their aid to the Phocians, suggests that already Philip had decided to attack Persia and hoped to use the Athenian navy in that effort. Philip withdrew from Greece late in 346 to continue his work of consolidation in Macedonia.

A shattered shinbone in 345 kept Philip out of military action for a few years, but in 342 he began a systematic attack on Thrace and in 340 laid siege to the strategic cities of Perinthus and Byzantium, which overlooked the sea lane through the Bosporus. This move threatened the grain supply of the Athenians, who responded with aid to Byzantium. When the sieges of these well-fortified cities proved more difficult than expected, Philip abandoned them, declared war on Athens, and in 339 invaded Greece. At Chaeronea in August of 338 Philip faced a Greek army headed by Athens and Thebes. The battle was long, and Philip appears to have won through a controlled retreat of his right wing that created a break in the Greek line. Philip's son Alexander, who would be known later as Alexander the Great, struck through this gap with the cavalry against the Theban contingent, while Philip with his infantry crushed the Athenian wing. The elite Sacred Band of Thebes was completely destroyed, and half the Athenian participants were killed or captured. Greece lay at Philip's mercy, and many city-states anxiously expected the worst.

Philip sought their compliance, however, not their destruction, and with the exception of Thebes and Sparta he treated them leniently. He summoned representatives from all the Greek states to a congress at Corinth, where they swore to a common peace and formed what modern historians call the League of Corinth. Its members accepted Philip as their leader and agreed to provide troops for a common armed force. Early in 337, at Philip's request, the council of the league declared war on Persia and named Philip the supreme commander for the anticipated conflict.

Returning home in triumph, Philip began final preparations for the attack on Persia and took as his seventh wife a young Macedonian noblewoman named Cleopatra. His previous marriages had all shown political shrewdness, but this one was most impolitic and alienated Philip's primary wife-queen, Olympias, and her son, the crown prince Alexander. After a drunken encounter in which Philip drew his sword against Alexander, both mother and prince fled Macedonia.

With advance units of the Persian expedition already in Asia, military and political necessities forced him to arrange a reconciliation of sorts with Alexander, but Philip did not live to lead the invasion. In the summer of 336, as he attended the wedding festival of his daughter, one of his bodyguards, Pausanias, stabbed him to death. Although the murderer was almost certainly driven by a private grievance, the rift within the royal family brought suspicion on Alexander and Olympias, who were the primary beneficiaries of Philip's untimely death. Whatever the truth of this matter, Alexander succeeded Philip as King of Macedonia at a most opportune moment. Using Philip's army, he would make himself the most famous conqueror in history.

Summary

Philip II of Macedonia inherited a backward, largely pastoral kingdom on the verge of disintegration and in his twenty-three-year reign transformed it into a major power. Less visible than his military endeavors, his domestic reforms were no less important. By bringing new areas under cultivation, founding new towns, and resettling upland populations, he made Macedonia a more advanced and cohesive kingdom. His military innovations revolutionized warfare and produced the best army the world had yet seen. With it he won three major pitched battles, suffered only one significant defeat, and successfully besieged nine cities. A general of great bravery and energy, Philip also possessed good strategic sense and never lost sight of his objectives. He saw war as an instrument of policy, not an end in itself, and used it along with diplomacy to achieve realistic ends.

Unfortunately for Greece, Philip's success meant the end of Greek independence, and his victory at Chaeronea effectively ended the era of the autonomous city-state. Philip created the army that Alexander would employ to destroy the Persian Empire. Had he lived, it is likely that Philip would have used it in a more restrained and constructive fashion than did his brilliant son.

Bibliography

Adcock, Frank E. *The Greek and Macedonian Art of War.* Berkeley: University of California Press, 1957. This small volume provides the best brief introduction to Greek warfare, with appropriate references to Philip's innovations.

Bradford, Alfred S., ed. and trans. *Philip II of Macedon: A Life from the Ancient Sources.* Westport, Conn.: Praeger, 1992. The book contains selected passages from some fifty ancient sources, arranged so as to form a connected narrative. Illustrated with numerous maps, it provides a lively picture of Philip's life.

Buckler, John. *Philip II and the Sacred War.* Leiden and New York: Brill, 1989. This is a study of the events in the course of which Philip entered Greek politics. About half of the book is on Greek internal affairs, but the Macedonian involvement also receives adequate treatment.

Bury, J. B., S. A. Cook, and Frank E. Adcock, eds. *The Cambridge Ancient History.* 12 vols. Cambridge: Cambridge University Press, 1923-1939. Chapters 8 and 9 in volume 6 describe Philip's rise to power with emphasis on his relations with the Greeks, especially the Athenians.

Cawkwell, George. *Philip of Macedon.* London and Boston: Faber and Faber, 1978. An excellent—though brief—biography, with outstanding maps. References to secondary works are minimal, but the notes contain a full record of the primary sources. The discussion of Greek military practices and Philip's part in their evolution is especially good.

Chatzopoulos, Miltiades V., and Louiza D. Loukopoulos, eds. *Philip of Macedon.* London: Heinemann, 1981. A collection of thirteen essays by leading scholars of Macedonian history. Included are chapters on Philip's personality, his generalship, his coinage, his foreign policy, his achievement in Macedonia, his death, and the royal tombs at Vergina. This volume is beautifully illustrated and includes excellent maps, a chronological table, and a bibliography.

Diodorus Siculus. *Diodorus of Sicily.* Translated by C. H. Oldfather et al. 12 vols. Cambridge, Mass.: Harvard University Press, and London: Heinemann, 1935. Book 16 in volumes 7 and 8 provides the only surviving ancient narrative of Philip's reign, interspersed with descriptions of activities in other parts of the Greek world. Diodorus must be used with care, because his account is sometimes inconsistent and chronologically confused.

Ellis, J. R. *Philip II and Macedonian Imperialism.* London: Thames and Hudson, 1976. This detailed study analyzes Macedonian expansion in the light of the needs and resources of Macedonia and in the context of fourth century Greek and Aegean politics. It includes a detailed chronology of Philip's reign, an appendix on his coinage, and a full bibliography of relevant modern works.

Hammond, N. G. L., and G. T. Griffith. *A History of Macedonia.* 2 vols. Oxford: Oxford University Press, 1972-1979. Volume 2, chapter 4 (by Hammond) provides a fine picture of Macedonia's weak condition in the forty years before Philip's accession. Chapters 5 through 20 (by Griffith) form the fullest, most authoritative biography of Philip available, with complete discussion of sources and chronological problems.

Hammond, Nicholas G. L. *Philip of Macedon.* London: Duckworth, and Baltimore, Md.: Johns Hopkins University Press, 1994. Written by a leading specialist in the history of ancient Macedonia, this biography of the king is fundamental. Hammond gives a full discussion of the sources on Philip, the political conditions in 4th-century Macedonia, Greece and Thrace, Philip's reign, and his burial and posthumous cult. The text is accompanied by detailed notes and well-chosen illustrations.

Perlman, Samuel, ed. *Philip and Athens.* Cambridge: Heffer, and New York: Barnes and Noble, 1973. This volume assembles twelve important articles dealing with Philip's relations with the Greek city-states.

Plutarch. "Alexander." In *Plutarch's "Lives,"* translated by Bernadotte Perrin. 11 vols. Cambridge, Mass.: Harvard University Press, and London: Heinemann, 1959-1967. In the absence of an ancient biography of Philip, this brief (fifty-page) biography of his son provides much useful information on Philip's later career and the magnificent army that he created.

James T. Chambers

PHILO OF ALEXANDRIA

Born: c. 20 B.C.; Alexandria, Egypt
Died: c. A.D. 45; possibly outside Alexandria
Area of Achievement: Philosophy
Contribution: Philo harmonized Old Testament theology with Greek philosophy, especially Platonism and Stoicism; his thought contributed much to that of Plotinus, originator of Neoplatonism, and to the ideas of the early church fathers.

Early Life

Philo came from one of the richest and most prominent Jewish families of Alexandria. The city had a large Jewish community, with privileges granted by its founder, Alexander the Great, and confirmed by his successors, the Ptolemies. The intellectual climate was Greek, and these Jews read their Scriptures in the Greek Septuagint version. According to ancient sources, the Greek population of Alexandria showed great hostility toward Jews.

Philo's brother Alexander held the Roman post of alabarch and collected taxes from Arab communities. He also managed the financial affairs of Antonia, mother of Emperor Claudius, and supplied a loan to Herod Agrippa, Caligula's choice as Jewish king.

In A.D. 39, anti-Semitism flared in the city, touched off by the visit of Herod Agrippa. The ensuing pogrom, permitted by the Roman governor Aulus Avilius Flaccus, resulted in a mission of opposing delegations to Caligula in Rome; the delegations consisted of three Greeks, led by the famous anti-Semite Apion, and five Jews, of whom Philo was eldest and spokesman. Caligula rudely dismissed the Jews and ordered his statue placed in their temples. In 41, under Claudius, Jewish rights were restored.

Life's Work

At least sixty-four treatises attributed to Philo are known. Only four or five are spurious; a few others, whose names have survived, no longer exist. The dates of the treatises, and even the order of their composition, are not known, except when a treatise refers to a previous one or to a dated event, such as the delegation to Rome. All the treatises have been translated into English (1854-1855), but some retain their original titles.

Foremost among Philo's writings are the exegetical works on the Pentateuch. These were arranged by Philo himself. Of the cosmogonic works, *De opificis mundi* (*The Creation of the World*), an allegorical explanation of Genesis, is most important. The historical works, allegorical commentaries on various topics in Genesis, are known as *Quod Deus sit immutabilis* (*That God Is Immutable*), *De Abrahamo, De Josepho, De vita Moysis* (*On the Life of Moses*), and *De allegoriis legum* (*On the Allegorical Interpretation of the Laws*). Philo also wrote legislative works, commentaries on Mosaic legislation, such as *De Decalogo* (*On the Ten Commandments*) and *De praemiis et poenis* (*On Rewards and Punishments*). Philosophical writings, such as *De vita contemplativa* (*The Contemplative Life*), and political writings, such as *In Flaccum* (*Against Flaccus*) and *De legatione ad Gaium* (*The Embassy to Caligula*), are attributed to Philo as well.

As a devout Jew, Philo's intent was to reconcile the prevalent Alexandrian philosophical thought of Platonism and Stoicism with the Sacred Law of Israel (the Old Testament). He wanted to show the identity of the truths of philosophy and of revelation—and the priority of the latter. He thus suggests not only that Moses had been a consummate philosopher but also that the "holy assembly" of Greek philosophers (Philo includes Plato, Xenophanes, Parmenides, and Empedocles—and the Stoics Zeno and Cleanthes) had access to Holy Scripture.

Beyond the notion of the unity of God, on which the Bible, Stoicism, and Plato's *Timaeus* (360-347 B.C.) clearly agree, the Old Testament bears little relation to Greek philosophy. Philo thus adopted for the Old Testament the Stoic technique of reading the Greek myths as allegories illustrating philosophical truths. Even as a Jew he was not original in this, for the Jewish philosopher Aristobulus (fl. mid-second century B.C.) and others had employed this method. Jews, however, could not gratuitously disregard the literal sense of the Old Testament stories. Philo resolved the problem by asserting that Scripture has at least two levels of meaning: the literal, for the edification of simple folk, and a deeper spiritual meaning, of which the literal account was merely an allegory. This higher meaning was available to subtler minds capable of comprehending it. Indeed, the allegorical method seems imperative when the literal sense presents something unworthy of God or an apparent contradiction and when the text defines itself as allegorical.

Philo rejects the anthropomorphism of God in the Old Testament as a concession to weaker minds. His teaching is that Yahweh, God, is perfect existence (*to ontos on*) and absolutely transcendent, that is, outside creation, beyond comprehension, and inexpressible. One can know of His existence but nothing of His essence; one cannot predicate anything of Him, for He is unchangeable. In this Philo went beyond Plato and the Stoics. Having described God in such terms, Philo was compelled to harmonize this with the scriptural concept of Yahweh as a personal God, immanent in the world and intimate with His people.

In order to bridge the gulf between this transcendent God and the created cosmos, Philo adopted the Stoic doctrine of divine emanations, or intermediaries, as the means of God's extension to the physical world. The first emanation and—according to Philo's various terminology—God's firstborn, His mediator, administrator, instrument, or bond of unity, is the divine Logos. The Logos is, in Stoic symbolism, the nearest circle of light (fire) proceeding from God, defined as pure light shedding His beams all around. In the Old Testament, the angel of God is an allegory for the Logos. The Logos is also identified with Plato's Demiurge.

Philo varied his conception of the intermediary beings of creation, including the Logos. Sometimes they are forces, ideas, or spiritual qualities of God; sometimes they are spiritual personal beings, which Philo identifies with the biblical "powers" (*dynameis*, an order of angels). They derive from the Logos as Logos derives directly from God. God created first an invisible, spiritual world as a pattern (*paradeigma*) for the visible world. This is identified as the Logos *endiathekos* (organizer). Thus Logos is the location of Plato's Ideas. From this pattern, Logos *prophorikos* (forward-carrying) created the material world. Like the Greeks, who believed that nothing could be produced out of nothing, Philo assumed primeval lifeless and formless matter (*hyle*) as the substratum of the material world. At the same time, this matter became, for Philo, the source of the world's imperfection and evil.

God made the first preexistent, ideal man through Logos. This was man untainted by sin and truly in the divine image. His higher soul (*nous*, or *pneuma*) was an emanation of the purely spiritual Logos; it permeated man as his true, essential nature. Man's body and lower nature, or soul, with its

earthly reason, were fashioned by lower angelic powers, or Demiurges. In a flight of Platonic dualism of body and soul, Philo saw the body as the tomb of the *pneuma*. The soul's unfolding was retarded by the body's sensuous nature, which it must overcome in order to gain salvation.

Philo's ethical doctrine employs the Logos in yet another, Stoic guise: operating as man's conscience and as teacher of the virtues. Men should strive for Stoic *apatheia*, apathy—the eradication of all passions. They should cultivate the four cardinal virtues of the Stoics (justice, temperance, courage, and wisdom). As this is an interior task, public life was discouraged by Philo; man, however, will never succeed by himself in getting free of the passions. God, through His Logos, can help man build virtue in the soul. It follows that man must place himself in correct relationship to God.

For this last and most important task, the sciences—grammar, rhetoric, dialectics, mathematics, music, and astronomy—are helpful. Yet they have never been sufficient to produce the Stoic ideal man of virtue. Contemplation of God alone is true wisdom and virtue. Thus Philo forges a link between Greek philosophy and the world of the mystery religions. He advocates going beyond ordinary conceptual knowledge, which recognizes God in His works, to an immediate intuition of the ineffable Godhead. In this ecstasy, the soul sees God face-to-face. Having passed beyond the original Ideas within the Logos, already beautiful beyond words, the soul is seized by a sort of "sober intoxication." As it approaches the highest peak of the knowable (*ton noeton*), pure rays of divine light come forth with increasing brilliance, until the soul is lost to itself and understands all.

Philo says that he himself had frequently been so filled with divine inspiration but that the ecstasy was indeed available to all the "initiated." These statements lend credence to the possibility that he ended his life as a member of the sect of the Therapeutae, an Essene-like community near Alexandria which he described affectionately in *The Contemplative Life*. Eusebius of Caesarea, quoting Philo, wrote that such communities in Egypt were founded by Mark the Evangelist and that their lives epitomized Christian practice in the seminal days of the new faith.

Summary

Though Photius' remark that Philo of Alexandria was a Christian cannot be accepted, his philosophy exerted a profound influence on early Christian theology. The Logos of John's Gospel certainly seems identical with one or more senses of the Logos in Philo. Ultimately, however, the Christian Logos, meaning the incarnate Word of God, can never be traced to Philo, for whom Logos was always incorporeal. Common to both Philo and many church fathers was the belief that philosophy was a special gift from God to the Greeks, just as revelation was His gift to the Jews. The fathers also used the allegorical method in interpreting Scripture beyond its literal meaning.

Philo's importance in Christian thought is underscored by the extensive commentary on and frequent reference to him by early Christian writers. Eusebius, Jerome, and Photius all provide lists of his tractates. Philo's philosophical language regarding God's transcendence influenced Christian apologists such as Justin, Athenagoras, Clement of Alexandria, and Origen.

Philo's greatest influence extended to Plotinus, founder of Neoplatonism. Though Plotinus may have pursued philosophy in India, many of his principles echo Philo's: that the body is the prison of the soul, that politics is trivial and distracting, that God (the One) is utterly transcendent yet the source of all truth and goodness, that Creation was effected by emanations from the One, and that pure souls may hope to return to the One, though in this life it is possible to encounter the One in a mystical experience. Thus Philo had an impact on the two major theological systems of the Roman Empire.

Bibliography

Cohen, Naomi G. *Philo Judaeus: The Universe of Discourse*. New York: Peter Lang, 1995. This is an important study of Philo's relationship to Judaic and Hellenistic thought. It discusses his education, audience, vocabulary, and concepts. The introduction gives an overview of trends in modern Philonic scholarship.

Colson, F. H., and G. H. Whitaker. *Philo*. 12 vols. London: Heinemann, and Cambridge, Mass.: Harvard University Press, 1929-1962. These volumes, part of the famous Loeb Classical Library, provide the original Greek with English translation on facing pages. They supply ample introductory sections, copious footnotes, and a complete bibliography addressing all problems of Philo scholarship.

Copleston, Frederick. "Greece and Rome." In *A History of Greek Philosophy*, vol. 1. Westminster, Md.: Newman Press, 1946. Contains a short but encyclopedic survey of Philo's chief doctrines. Greek terms and references in Philo's writings are given for each specific teaching of Philo.

Philo of Alexandria. *Philonis Alexandrini: "Legatio and Gaium."* Translated by E. Mary Smallwood. 2d ed. Leiden, Netherlands: E. J. Brill, 1970. Bilingual text with commentary.

Williamson, Ronald. *Jews in the Hellenistic World: Philo*. Cambridge and New York: Cambridge University Press, 1989. An introduction to Philo's life and works is followed by chapters titled "Philo's Doctrine of God," "Philo's Logos Doctrine," "Philo's Allegorical Exegesis of Scripture," and "The Ethical Teaching of Philo." Williamson concludes that, "Hellenized Judaism in Alexandria in Philo's time was an important and powerful segment of Judaism," and that Philo's writings had a substantial influence on both Jews and Christians.

Wolfson, Harry A. "Greek Philosophy in Philo and the Church Fathers." In *The Crucible of Chris-*

tianity, edited by Arnold Toynbee. London: Thames and Hudson, and New York: World Publishing Co., 1969. Wolfson isolates the primary similarities and oppositions in the thought of the earliest Christian fathers and Philo. The chapter is fully documented for further research.

—————. *Philo: Foundations of Religious Philosophy in Judaism, Christianity, and Islam*. Cambridge, Mass.: Harvard University Press, 1947. This is the most thorough, complete, useful, and current treatment of Philo available in English.

Zeller, Eduard. *Outlines of the History of Greek Philosophy*. Translated by Wilhelm Nestle. 13th ed. London: Routledge, and New York: Humanities Press, 1931. Includes an overview of Philo's key ideas. Zeller defines major differences between Philo and Greek thought.

Daniel C. Scavone

PIANKHI

Born: c. 769 B.C.; place unknown
Died: 716 B.C.; place unknown
Areas of Achievement: Warfare and politics
Contribution: Dynamic and forceful King of Kush, Piankhi invaded a divided Egypt, conquered it, and initiated an almost century-long Kushite rule over the entire Nile Valley.

Early Life

Nothing is known of Piankhi's early life. He was the son of the Kushite chieftain, Kashta, who controlled northern Nubia, the land immediately south of Egypt. Relatively early in its history, the Kingdom of Egypt was attracted to this neighboring territory up the Nile; gold, incense, and slaves, among other things, were obtained there. Nubia also was the corridor through which Egypt traded with lands farther south in inner Africa, Nubian middlemen being essential in this commerce. Beginning in the Old Kingdom (3100-2700 B.C.), Egypt's rulers thought it necessary to control northern Nubia and therefore established permanent bases there. Gradually, as the Egyptian hold weakened through the centuries, local leadership produced a state known as the Kingdom of Kush. The nature of its relationship with the greater power to the north depended on the latter's internal stability and the successive pharaohs' ability periodically to reassert firm imperial control over this outlying territory.

By the seventeenth century B.C., Kush's rulers had their capital at Kerma, just south of the Third Cataract on the Nile River. While they looked to Egypt's impressive culture for inspiration and imported assorted luxury goods, these presumably black kings of Kush enjoyed political independence for long periods. Inevitably, however, the Egyptians took back northern areas near the Egyptian border and sometimes absorbed all of Kush. During the Second Intermediate Period (1785-1580), Egypt itself was invaded for the first time, and much of its territory was conquered by a chariot army of the Hyksos, a people from western Asia. They ruled the country for about 150 years and recognized Kush, independent once again, as an equally great power whose rule extended as far north as Elephantine (Aswan).

Kush clearly was under heavy Egyptian cultural influence from early times, borrowing religious beliefs, architectural styles, and writing from the long-established northern civilization. Not only Egyptian soldiers and merchants worked there; many craftsmen, builders, and priests are also believed to have ventured up the Nile for employment under rich Kushite kings.

Life's Work

By the time Piankhi ascended the throne in 751, Kush's royal capital was Napata, just north of the Fourth Cataract on the Nile. He inherited a strong kingship, one that had replaced an Egyptian viceroyalty lasting about four hundred years that had been imposed on Kush by pharaohs of the Eighteenth and Nineteenth dynasties (c. 1595-c. 1194). The Kushites, partly emulating Egypt's institution of divine monarchy, believed their king was the adopted son of several deities. A council composed of high priests, the queen mother, clan chiefs, and military commanders determined the royal succession, usually selecting one of the dead king's brothers. Piankhi is an obvious exception here, since he followed his father to the throne.

More than a political capital, Napata also was an important religious center. The seat of Egyptian royal power long had been the city of Thebes in Upper Egypt, which in addition was the principal center for the worship of the sun god, Amon. When the Twenty-second Dynasty of Egyptian kings moved its capital downstream to the delta region and emphasized dedication to the god Ptah rather than Amon, this alienated the latter's priests, who consequently shifted their religious headquarters to Napata, which already was the site of major temples erected by the Egyptians to honor Amon. The extensively Egyptianized Kushite population—or at least its leaders—thus became even more zealous devotees of Amon. It is likely that these newly moved religious authorities, in need of strong support in their new base, established an alliance with local chieftains who in time became the new Kushite monarchs from whom Piankhi descended. It cannot be determined, however, if this new dynasty could trace its bloodline back to the original royal lineage of Kerma.

As Kush became an increasingly centralized state under native rulers by the eighth century B.C., Egypt, in contrast, was experiencing political division. Indeed, ever since the tenth century, Egypt had been torn by dissension. By the eighth century that country was a confusing scene of about eleven major political entities, each under its own local potentate and more or less independent of the central authority of the weak Twenty-second Dynasty (c. 945-c. 730). The next dynasty returned the capital to Thebes, but evidently this did not help it overcome the political turmoil that prevailed with so many regional seats of power contending with one another. Such confusion and disunity eventually would draw Kush into Egyptian politics in a very dramatic way.

A major figure aspiring to leadership in Egypt during the mid-eighth century was Tefnakhte, lord of Sais, a principality in the western delta. He managed to extend his rule over a large part of Lower Egypt. In addition, this aggressive prince brought all the eastern- and middle-delta rulers into an alliance system dominated by him. Tefnakhte was the major power in all Lower Egypt and even a part of Middle Egypt. The man who would resist his efforts to reunify Egypt under a delta monarchy was Piankhi, who now reigned at Napata. This situation was not only one of political rivalry; Piankhi considered the northern Egyptians religiously and culturally inferior and thus unfit to govern Egypt.

When Tefnakhte sent his army south to besiege Heracleopolis, a center in Middle Egypt that had held out successfully against him earlier, the King of Kush recognized that this expanding force might be a potential threat to his own position. Still, he did not yet move against Tefnakhte. Ultimately, though, other Egyptian princes, seeing fellow rulers forced to submit to Tefnakhte's control, appealed to Piankhi to interfere, and he complied. Piankhi dispatched one of his armies, already in Egypt, to liberate the city of Hermopolis. Another force was sent to assist in that task but, having passed slightly north of Thebes, it encountered Tefnakhte's river fleet carrying many troops. The Kushites won a furious battle, inflicting heavy casualties on the enemy and taking many prisoners.

When Piankhi's two contingents joined farther northward, they fell upon Tefnakhte's forces besieging Heracleopolis. Again the men from the south were successful, and the losers were driven out of the area. The victorious Kushites then pushed on to Hermopolis, where they began their own siege of that city. When informed of his army's triumphs, King Piankhi, still in Napata, naturally was pleased. Satisfaction turned to rage, however, when he heard that his antagonist's surviving forces had been allowed to escape toward the delta. Deciding to take personal command of the campaign, Piankhi left for Egypt.

The Kushite ruler was slow to overtake his army. When he arrived in Thebes he spent some time engaged in elaborate ceremonials dedicated to Amon in the great temple complex of Karnak. This monarch was nothing if not a pious servant of his favorite god. It has been suggested that such ostentatious worship also was intended to convince Egyptians that this foreign leader enjoyed divine sanction for his impending conquest of the country. In any case, upon the completion of his devotions, Piankhi reached his army and soon ended the siege of Hermopolis by agreeing to spare its ruler's life if he surrendered. As Piankhi subsequently led his army to the north, his military strength as well as his reputation for clemency toward his enemies encouraged towns in his path to capitulate.

Tefnakhte, now concerned about the approaching Kushites, established his base at Memphis, the ancient city just south of the delta region. It was strongly defended, but Piankhi devised a shrewd plan of attack. Since the eastern side of the city was under water, its defenders thought it unnecessary to worry about an assault from that direction. Grasping the opportunity this presented, the royal commander ordered his men to seize all the enemy's boats in the harbor, which, along with the Kushite's own flotilla, were then utilized quickly to ferry his fighting men to the city walls. These were mounted easily before the opposition could react effectively. When the city fell, Piankhi characteristically gave credit to Amon.

This spectacular victory led to the submission of the surrounding country. In keeping with his religious habits, Piankhi celebrated each of his military successes by publicly worshipping in local sanctuaries, including, especially, those of Memphis. Ptah, the artificer god, was the major deity of that city and believed to be the creator of Amon. The bold conqueror from the distant south could now announce that Ptah had recognized him as the legitimate King of Egypt. All the princes of the delta eventually submitted to Piankhi's authority, demonstrating their homage by delivering their substantial treasures to him. It is interesting that Piankhi, the religious puritan, refused to meet some of these leaders personally, as he considered such "fisheaters" to be unclean.

The Kushite's principal target, however, eluded him. Even though Tefnakhte's army was destroyed, that ambitious and determined leader defied his adversary, ultimately taking refuge on an island in the northern delta. Piankhi settled for Tefnakhte's pledge of allegiance rather than continuing pursuit in the difficult, unfamiliar swampland. Thus, when the few other notable rulers of outlying territories swore obedience to him, Piankhi, the prince of a longtime colony of Egypt, was now the lord of that great imperial nation by the Nile.

Having achieved such success, the man from Napata packed his accumulated prize wealth aboard his riverboats and made his way up the river to his own desert land. Although it was short-lived, political unity had been restored to Egypt by a foreign conqueror. Nevertheless, Tefnakhte soon resumed his efforts to acquire control of Egypt himself and enjoyed considerable success in the north. Kushite dominance in Upper Egypt was secure, however, during the remainder of Piankhi's reign. That king evidently was content to have imposed his nominal authority over the entire Nile Valley without troubling to remain in Egypt in order to enforce his sovereignty over the long term. As long as Upper Egypt, particularly the holy city of Thebes, was not threatened by the "unclean" northerners, he rested easily. Piankhi's last known accomplishment, which seems fitting for a king so obsessed with pleasing the gods, was his reconstruction of and addition to the great temple of Amon at Napata (Jebel Barkal). It remained for his brother and successor, Shabako, to return to Egypt and firmly establish his dynasty's rule by residing there as pharaoh.

Summary

Piankhi's extended military effort in Egypt was the foundation for Kushite control of that country for almost a century. Although he is not officially listed as such, it is generally accepted that he initiated the Twenty-fifth Dynasty of Egyptian kings, the so-called Nubian or Ethiopian Dynasty, which reigned from about 716 to 656. His achievement, consequently, established Kush as a major power in the ancient world. If the other important states of the time had not noticed inner Africa before, they did after Piankhi's conquest. The Kushites' appearance in force in Egypt undoubtedly was feared by the proud Egyptians as the coming of barbarian hordes, but it was not the calamity they expected. Piankhi and his men represented a culture that was heavily Egyptianized. Admittedly, Kush was an African kingdom and never completely lost its unique identity under the Egyptian façade. Yet the influence of Egypt's long-established and admired civilization had brought Kush within the northern cultural orbit to a considerable extent. These were not savage barbarians but fellow residents of the Nile Valley whose leaders were literate worshippers of Egyptian gods and who expressed themselves in cultivated Egyptian terms. Piankhi, in the twenty-first year of his reign, erected a stela in Napata that recounts his Egyptian expedition. It is acknowledged as one of the most interesting and revealing documents in Egyptian and Kushite history, vividly describing the military exploits of the king and his army as well as clearly communicating details about the fiery temperament, religious piety, and generosity of Piankhi. Now exhibited in the Cairo Museum, it is a fitting memorial to one of the great figures in African history.

Bibliography

Adams, William Y. *Nubia: Corridor to Africa.* London: Allen Lane, and Princeton, N.J.: Princeton University Press, 1977. Clearly the most comprehensive account of the region from prehistoric times to the nineteenth century, it provides excellent coverage of the "heroic age" of the Nabatan kings and their rule in Egypt. It also reflects the best of recent scholarship. Extensive end notes and chapter bibliographies are included.

Arkell, A. J. *A History of the Sudan: From the Earliest Times to 1821.* 2d rev. ed. London: University of London, Athlone Press, 1961; Westport, Conn.: Greenwood Press, 1973. By an expert boasting of many years' service in the Sudan, this work is good for a description of the country and its occupation by Egypt. The chapter on Kush's conquest of Egypt is useful but inferior to that found in the Adams book.

Breasted, James Henry. *Ancient Records of Egypt.* Vol. 4, *The Twentieth to the Twenty-sixth Dynasties.* Chicago: University of Chicago Press, 1906-1907; London: Histories and Mysteries of Man, 1988. Contains a translation of the Piankhi stela as well as the editor's excellent scholarly summary of it. An essential source.

Emery, Walter B. *Egypt in Nubia.* London: Hutchinson, 1965; as *Lost Land Emerging.* New York: Scribner, 1967. A good survey, providing important background on Egyptian-Kushite relations before Piankhi's conquest.

Gardiner, Sir Alan. *Egypt of the Pharaohs: An Introduction.* Oxford: Clarendon Press, 1961; New York: Oxford University Press, 1964. An extensive chapter on Egypt under foreign rule provides a fine historical sketch as background for the Kushite conquest and includes an account of Piankhi's feat.

Hakem, A. A., with I. Hrbek and J. Vercoutter. "The Civilization of Napata and Meroe." In *General History of Africa*, edited by G. Mokhtar, vol. 2. London: Heinemann, and Berkeley: University of California Press, 1981. Provides little on Piankhi's reign but includes a good discussion of Kushite life and institutions, although the Meroitic period receives most attention. An extensive bibliography also makes the work an important resource.

Lysle E. Meyer

PONTIUS PILATE

Born: Date and place of birth unknown

Died: After 36 A.D.; place unknown

Areas of Achievement: Biblical figures; government and politics; religion

Contribution: A provincial Roman official, Pontius Pilate became infamous as the magistrate who presided over the trial of Jesus Christ.

Early Life

Nothing is known of Pontius Pilate's life before he was appointed prefect of Judaea and Samaria; even subsequent references to him, except in the New Testament and religious writings, are cursory. He belonged to none of the great Roman families and apparently left no descendants. Even known his first or given name is unknown. The name "Pontius," representing his *gens*, or tribe, would indicate that he was not Roman in ancestry but Samnite. The Samnites were an Italian people conquered by the Romans in 295 B.C.. His family name, "Pilate," means "cap," "helmet," or "spear," a fact that is of little help in tracing his lineage.

Pilate was of the equestrian class, a rank roughly equivalent to the knighthood of later European history. Because of this social rank and the fact that his patron Lucius Aelius Sejanus was commander of the Praetorian Guard, the elite troops who protected the emperor and served as the local police force, it is almost certain that Pilate gained recognition through military service, most likely in the Praetorian Guard itself.

The military background and apparent lack of any administrative or political experience would explain Pilate's mistakes in governance. One of the reasons for the success of the Roman empire was that it respected, or at least permitted, the exercise of the religions, customs, and laws of subject peoples as long as these did not interfere with Roman control. While they could be ruthless, the Romans did not impose a totalitarian regime on conquered peoples, who had their own local officials and were generally free of Roman control in their day-to-day lives. The function of a Roman governor was to maintain order and to see that taxes were collected and sent to Rome. Pilate, however, would needlessly provoke the local Jewish population; a more experienced or more competent official would probably have had a better understanding of his subjects, their religion, and their sensibilities.

Life's Work

Pilate was appointed the fifth prefect of Judaea and Samaria in A.D. 26, during the reign of the Emperor Tiberias. Pilate succeeded Valerius Gratus, who had a relatively quiet term of office and managed to avoid conflict between the Roman troops and the turbulent Jewish revolutionaries, or Zealots. Gratus resided in Caesarea; his primary concern was the acquisition of wealth, which he managed to secure through his control of appointments, especially to the office of high priest. During his tenure, he made four appointments to the office.

Upon assuming his duties, however, Pilate, took a more hands-on—and more confrontational—approach toward the Jewish people. Upon his arrival in Palestine, the new governor, in accordance with plans made beforehand with Sejanus, moved the headquarters of the Roman garrison from Caesaria to Jerusalem. Pilate himself also was to take up winter residence there.

The Roman army entered Jerusalem with their standards under cover of darkness. The standard consisted of figure of an eagle with outspread wings and a thunderbolt in the claws mounted on the end of a spear; a banner or bust with the likeness of the emperor was attached. When the city awoke to find the Roman eagles before the Herodian palace, which was to be Pilate's residence, the populace was furious. To bring the standards with their graven images almost within the precincts of Holy Temple was, to the Jews, an abomination of abominations, a gross violation of God's commandment.

Since Pilate had not yet taken up residence in Jerusalem but was still in Caesaria, a good part of the crowd together with Jews from other areas hurried to Caesaria. There, they surrounded Pilate's house demanding that the standards be removed. After five days of demonstrations, Pilate lost patience. The demonstrators were asked to move to an open area where Pilate would speak to them and respond to their grievances. This was part of a plan by Pilate to get the demonstrators in an area where they could be surrounded by his troops, who had weapons concealed under their mantles. When his troops were in position, Pilate told the crowd that unless they dispersed and left him in peace, he would order the soldiers to cut them down. To Pilate's chagrin, they reportedly answered that they would rather die than permit idolatry and disobedi-

ence to a commandment of their God; they then lay down and bared their necks, ready to die as martyrs. At this point, Pilate relented and ordered the standards removed from Jerusalem.

Another disturbance arose when Pilate ordered temple funds to be used for the construction of an aqueduct to bring water into Jerusalem. This time Pilate did not relent and ordered his troops to use force to disperse a crowd of protestors. The Roman soldiers showed no mercy, killing many Jews with blows with their cudgels; many others were killed in the stampede that followed. Other massacres are mentioned by Josephus, a Jewish historian of the period. Still others are set forth in the Talmud and in the Gospel of St. Luke (13.1), which refers to the massacre of Galilean pilgrims who were in the act of sacrificing. Galilean zealots frequently took a leading part in the insurrections. Since Galilee was not under Pilate's jurisdiction but ruled by Herod Antipas, a puppet king, the inability of Herod to control his subjects was a source of friction with Pilate.

Pilate would be little more than a footnote in history except for his role in the trial and execution of Jesus. Pilate's role and actions during the trial are set forth in the Gospel accounts of the four evangelists in the New Testament. There are no other historical accounts in existence.

Following the crucifixion of Jesus, it is almost certain that Pilate made a written report to Emperor Tiberias. Such correspondence between Roman officials and the emperor was routine. Justin Martyr, defending himself and his fellow Christians before Antonius Pius around A.D. 140, refers to reports from Pilate that were at that time in the Roman archives. This was confirmed forty years later by Tertullian, a Christian writer.

In the year 311, Emperor Maximian was engaged in persecuting the Christians. To discredit them, he caused to be circulated throughout the empire a forgery called the "Acts of Pilate." If the genuine reports and correspondence from Pilate were still in existence, they would likely have been destroyed by the emperor, as they might have been used to debunk the forgery.

In A.D. 36, Pilate was deposed by his immediate superior, Vitellius, the legate of Syria. The reason for Vitellius action was Pilate's gross mishandling of an incident involving the Samaritans, a people who were loyal and submissive to Rome. The incident arose out of a visionary's claim that Moses had hidden certain golden vessels on Mount Geriz-

im, upon which the Samaritans worshipped. This caused a large group of armed Samaritans to begin a search for the golden vessels. Pilate dispatched his troops, who surrounded the treasure seekers and killed many of them. Pilate then had several of the organizers of the treasure search beheaded.

A Samaritan delegation went to Vitellius to complain about the atrocities. After hearing the complaint, Vitellius sent one of his subordinates to relieve Pilate of his duties and ordered Pilate to return to Rome to answer the charges. By the time Pilate arrived in Rome after removal from his office, Emperor Tiberias had died and had been succeeded by Caligula. Pilate was held in prison and was ultimately banished from Rome, reportedly to Vienne in Gaul. Eusebius, an historian of the early Christian church, says that Pilate ended his life by suicide; other sources allege that he converted to Christianity. The Coptic church even honors him as a saint.

Summary

Pilate made his mark in history by presiding over the trial of Jesus Christ. The biblical account has Jesus condemned to death against Pilate's better judgment. Pilate at first seeks to save Jesus by having him scourged, thinking that this will satisfy the mob. He then gives the mob the choice of releasing either Jesus or Barrabas, a notorious murderer; the crowd chooses Barrabas. Pilate's wife then intervenes and cautions him to have no part of the blood of this innocent man. Pilate, failing in all attempts, then washes his hands and says that he is free of Christ's blood. He agrees to the crucifixion only when his loyalty to Caesar is questioned. Pilate is portrayed as a weakling unable to withstand the clamor of the crowd.

Critics of the biblical account, who became especially vocal in the 1990's, dismiss it as Christian propaganda. These critics contend that Jesus was a fanatic who posed a threat to Roman rule and that Pilate had no scruples about having such people executed. At the time the Gospels were being written, Christianity was spreading throughout the Roman empire. According to the critics, the Gospels were slanted in favor of Pilate because the Christian cause would not have been furthered by blaming Rome for Jesus' execution.

There is, however, nothing other than the biblical accounts to relate what happened at the trial. There are passing references to the event by Josephus, Eusebius, and other writers, but these are of little help. Everything written about the matter since is based on interpretation and conjecture.

Bibliography

Brown, Raymond E. *The Death of the Messiah: From Gethsemane to the Grave.* New York: Doubleday, and London: Chapman, 1994. A comprehensive and definitive two-volume work on the arrest, trial, and execution of Jesus.

Crossan, John Dominic. *Who Killed Jesus? Exposing the Roots of Anti Semitism in the Gospel Story of the Death of Jesus.* New York: HarperCollins, 1995. Crossan argues that it was the Roman government that tried and executed Jesus as a social agitator and views the Gospel accounts of the trial of Jesus as anti-Semitic and nonhistorical.

Josephus, Flavius. *Josephus: The Essential Writings.* Edited and translated by Paul L. Maier. Grand Rapids, Mich.: Kregel Publications, 1988. A condensed and illustrated edition of *Jewish Antiquities* and the *Jewish War*, written by Flavius Josephus, a Jewish historian who lived between A.D.37 and A.D.100. Covers Jewish history from its beginning to the fall of the Masada fortress in the first century. Easy reading; highly recommended for anyone who enjoys history. Contains only a few references to Pilate, but important because it is one of the few primary sources.

Latimer, Elizabeth Wormley. *Judea from Cyrus to Titus: 537 B.C. to 70 A.D..* Chicago: A. C. McClurg, 1899. Covers six centuries of Jewish history. Chapter 18 is devoted exclusively to Pontius Pilate. Written in a flowery and hortatory nineteenth century style.

Philo. *The Works of Philo.* Translated by C. D. Yonge. New ed. Peabody, Mass.: Hendrickson Publishers, 1993. Philo, Jewish scholar who lived in Alexandria, Egypt, from about 20 B.C. to about A.D. 50, makes several references to Pilate in a writing entitled "On the Embassy to Gaius." Philo is not easy reading.

Sanders, E. P. *The Historical Figure of Jesus.* London: Penguin, 1993; New York: Penguin, 1995. A comprehensive account of the life of Jesus. Sanders contends that Pilate ordered the execution of Jesus because his fanaticism posed a threat to law and order. He argues that the biblical accounts of Pilate's reluctance and weakness of will are best explained as Christian propaganda meant to lessen conflict between the Christian movement and Roman authority.

Watson, Alan. *The Trial of Jesus.* Athens: The University of Georgia Press, 1995. Argues that the Sanhedrin, or supreme Jewish court, had the authority to put Jesus to death but could not convict him because of stringent trial procedures. He was therefore handed over to Pilate, who had no scruples about ordering an execution if it served his purposes.

Gilbert T. Cave

PINDAR

Born: c. 518 B.C.; Cynoscephalae, near Thebes, Boeotia, Greece
Died: c. 438 B.C.; Argos, Greece
Areas of Achievement: Literature and music
Contribution: Pindar proved through his poetry and music that creative aspirations raise humanity to near-perfection; as the greatest lyrical poet of classical times, he influenced literature and culture for centuries.

Early Life

Pindar, the greatest of ancient Greek lyric poets, was born in Cynoscephalae, near Thebes, probably around 518 B.C. A city rich in history and legend, Thebes was located in the region known as Boeotia, north of the Gulf of Corinth. Pindar came from a noble Dorian family whose lineage went back to ancient times and included heroes whom he celebrated in his poems. His uncle was a famous flute player; Pindar, who excelled at that instrument, may have acquired his skills from him. Lyric poems were written primarily for solo or choral singing, with instrumental accompaniment, and Pindar learned his craft in writing poetry from two important lyric poets, Lasus of Hermione and Corinna of Tanagra. It is said (but disputed by some) that Corinna defeated Pindar five times in lyric competition. If the story is true, it is probable that the judges in these contests, all of whom were male, were influenced not only by Corinna's poetry but also by her remarkable beauty.

In the framing of his poetry, Pindar drew from the vast store of myths— many of them associated with Thebes—that he had learned in his youth. To him, the Olympians and other figures from ancient stories were not mythical but real. He accepted reverently, for example, the stories of the oracle of Delphi, and he devoutly worshipped Zeus (even composing a famous hymn to him) and other gods and goddesses all his life. He was also the heir to several priestly offices, which buttressed his natural inclination toward religion. In addition to being educated near Thebes, he is said to have received instruction in Athens, which was a great academic and cultural center. Studying in Athens would account for his having known the Alcmaeonids, a politically active family in Athens for which he wrote laudatory poems—probably, as was customary, under commission.

Pindar was schooled in history, philosophy, religion, music, and literature. His poetry is filled with allusions to those fields as well as to his homeland and relatives. He secured his reputation as a young man, and fabulous legends grew up around him. For example, one story explaining his talent claimed that as he slept out in the fields one day, bees had deposited honey on his lips.

Pindar received a constant flow of engagements to write poems for important figures, including the victors of athletic contests, the odes for which are the only surviving works of the poet. Usually these victory odes (*epinikia*) were performed in processionals welcoming the heroes home. Pindar's odes are named for the particular games at which they were performed—the *Olympian Odes, Pythian Odes, Nemean Odes*, and *Isthmian Odes*. This celebratory tradition was at one with the Greek belief that great deeds—including the greatest of all, the creation of the world—should be artistically remembered so as not to pass into oblivion. For a time, Hieron, tyrant of Syracuse, was a patron of Pindar and of other poets, such as Simonides, Bacchylides, and the great tragedian Aeschylus. This activity helped Syracuse to rival Athens and Thebes as an intellectual center and helped perpetuate Pindar's already considerable fame.

Life's Work

In the Alexandrian list of the nine best lyric poets, Pindar's name came first. In his own time and in later centuries he was remembered as "soaring Pindar." The fact of music is inseparable from the fact of lyric poetry in Pindar, for it is clear that his poems were written to be sung. What is not known is how to reproduce for modern performance the melody and the meter of his lyrics, all of which were written in celebration of an individual or an event, often an athletic victory. This is to speak only of the four books which have survived, for there are fragments of his other works (or allusions to them) that prove that his genius was not limited to the choral lyric. He produced thirteen books in genres other than the *epinikia*, including hymns, processionals, and dirges.

Another obstacle to the comprehension of Pindar's poetry is its allusiveness. Those people hearing the performance of a victory ode had an immediate awareness of Pindar's allusions, whether to the Olympians, the heroes of myth, the rulers of

CORWIN K. LINSON 96.

the times, the athletes or families being honored, or even autobiographical references. Only one who has read widely in Greek history, philosophy, literature, and legend can begin to understand these allusions or the stirring effect they would have had on Pindar's audience.

The poems are, then, locked into a time frame in their references and in their constructions. The themes, however, are accessible. A central theme in Pindar is the emulation of divinity. Humans are of the same race with gods but lack their powers; thus they are ever striving toward perfection, in an effort to be as much like the gods as possible. This view required the poet to overlook or disbelieve scandalous stories in mythology (which, to Pindar, was religion) which belied the perfection of the gods. Remembrance of the greatness of Zeus—Zeus unsullied by rumors about his lust, his violence, his unreasonableness—gave humanity a standard by which to live. Life is the thing of a day—another theme in Pindar—and to live it with constant reverence for the lessons taught by gods and heroes was to give reverence to oneself and to give a degree of permanence to life.

Virtue, bravery, manliness, and competitive physical activities were far more important to Pindar than was (as with Homer) intelligence, and he expressed scorn toward those who displaced these attributes with intellectual measures. The intelligent, resourceful Odysseus, for example, he found less praiseworthy than a man of physical prowess. Physical things—bodily strength and athletic skills and other things of the earth—were the things of heaven. Acquired learning paled beside innate talent, inborn greatness of soul and body.

Pindar always wrote his odes as if those they celebrated were joined with the immortals. Poets were said to have Zeus speaking through them; subjects celebrated by odes were, similarly, raised above the ordinary lot of humankind. There was a mystical link between the human being and divinity, a link that could not, to Pindar's way of thinking, be achieved by education. A basic belief of the aristocracy which Pindar represented was that qualities of goodness—humanistic ideals—could not be taught; universal edification being impossible, therefore, society depended on an aristocracy that was morally and spiritually enlightened. Pindar's place as a poet was to praise heroes in order to raise humankind.

Rooted in tradition as he was, Pindar was conservative; still, he was an innovator and a searcher. He was always seeking profound meanings from human events, ideals and nobility from everyday realities. He supported the rule of Eunomia (law, or good constitution) as a way for a moderate aristocracy to succeed tyranny. Such an aristocracy would be made up not only of those from the traditional aristocracy but also of those from the wealthy class. Those with leisure to contemplate new possibilities for humanity would most likely be those who would bring about new achievements for the betterment of humanity; the wealthy, the aristocratic, had freer minds. Large audiences listened to Pindar, audiences accustomed to hearing Homeric epics recited and therefore prepared for the exceptionally long, whirling passages of Pindar sung by an enthusiastic chorus.

Pindar's fame was even greater after his death than in his own time. His writings proved not to be locked in time; rather, they were one more link of many links in Greek literature going back to a time even before Homer, and extending through Aeschylus to Plato, which, while glorifying aristocratic tradition, pointed the way to the political principle that came to be known as democracy. The highest virtue that elitism had, in other words, was the knowledge that what was available at first to only the privileged few was ultimately accessible to all. Pindar's poetry was one of the main avenues making accessible this Greek ideal: that the commonest individuals have within them resources of divine inspiration, divine identity, divine glory.

Summary

In a chapter devoted to Pindar in *The Greek Way* (1973), Edith Hamilton says, "There never was a writer more proudly conscious of superiority." She provides arguments and examples supportive of his proud consciousness of superiority. As he felt himself superior in his poetry, so he believed that his "race," the aristocracy, could achieve for the good of all what tyranny and other kinds of rule (including democracy) could not. He could not have known that members of the aristocracy who glorified themselves as individuals of the highest order were opening the way for all human beings to see themselves as privileged and knowing aristocrats.

Pindar's complex style as preserved in the *epinikia* challenged later generations of poets to compose "Pindaric odes," in which colorful images shifted rapidly and imaginatively, like rushing water. Although the content of Pindar's surviving works is obscure for the modern reader, his inspired style remains a model of purely beautiful language.

Bibliography

Carne-Ross, D. S. *Pindar*. London and New Haven, Conn.: Yale University Press, 1985. A brief work addressed to the general reader, with a short but useful bibliography.

Crotty, Kevin. *Song and Action: The Victory Odes of Pindar*. Baltimore: Johns Hopkins University Press, 1982. Devoted to individual examinations of the performances of the odes for which Pindar is most remembered. Includes notes, bibliography, and index.

Finley, John H., Jr. *Pindar and Aeschylus*. Cambridge, Mass.: Harvard University Press, 1955. More than half the book is devoted to Pindar.

Finley, Moses I. *The Ancient Greeks*. London: Chatto and Windus, and New York: Viking Press, 1963. Gives brief but interesting and useful information on Simonides, Bacchylides, and Pindar.

Gerber, Douglas E. *A Bibliography of Pindar, 1513-1966*. Cleveland, Ohio: Case Western Reserve, 1969. A comprehensive bibliography of 160 pages, usefully divided into thirty topical sections.

Grant, Mary A. *Folktale and Hero-Tale Motifs in the Odes of Pindar*. Lawrence: University of Kansas Press, 1968. Straightforward account of the subject, with an index of motifs and an index of mythological characters.

Hamilton, Edith. *The Greek Way*. New York: Norton, 1942. The best short book on the Greek way of life; devotes a chapter to Pindar. Bridges scholarship and general readership. Seven pages of references, especially to works of ancient Greek writers.

Highet, Gilbert. *The Classical Tradition: Greek and Roman Influences on Western Literature*. Rev. ed. New York: Oxford University Press, 1951; London: Oxford University Press, 1967. The best work available on the Greco-Roman influences on Western literature. Lengthy discussion—perhaps the most accessible anywhere for general readers—on Pindar's poetical forms and on his direct influences on poetry. Extensive notes in lieu of a comprehensive bibliography.

Kurke, Leslie. *The Traffic in Praise: Pindar and the Poetics of Social Economy.* Ithaca, N.Y.: Cornell University Press, 1991. Starting from the premise that the extant texts of the odes are essentially scripts for public ceremonies, Kurke examines the social setting and functioning of Pindar's poetry. He seeks to answer the question of how traditional poetic form responded to social change. The book opens new approaches to Pindar's texts.

Norwood, Gilbert. *Pindar.* Berkeley: University of California Press, 1945. A major work based on scholarly lectures. Includes bibliography and index.

Pindar. *The Odes of Pindar.* Edited and translated by Richmond Lattimore. 2d ed. Chicago: University of Chicago Press, 1976. Translation of all the surviving odes. Contains a preface on Pindar and his poetry. Lattimore is one of the most respected modern translators of Greek.

Race, William H. *Pindar.* Boston: Twayne Publishers, 1986. As one of the volumes in Twayne's World Authors series, this work is characteristically comprehensive in biography, criticism, and bibliography. For both scholarly and general audiences.

Snell, Bruno. *Poetry and Society: The Role of Poetry in Ancient Greece.* Bloomington: Indiana University Press, 1961. Focuses on the forms, purposes, and occasions of Pindar's poetry. Snell is also the author of *The Discovery of the Mind: The Greek Origins of European Thought* (New York: Harper and Row, Publishers, 1960), which contains a valuable section on Pindar's hymn to Zeus.

David Powell

PISISTRATUS

Born: c. 612 B.C.; near Athens, Greece
Died: 527 B.C.; Athens, Greece
Areas of Achievement: Government and politics; patronage of the arts
Contribution: As benevolent tyrant of Athens, Pisistratus prepared the way for the birth of Athenian democracy by introducing social, religious, and political reforms that raised popular expectations and possibilities.

Early Life

Pisistratus' family reputedly came from Pylos on the Peloponnisos peninsula. His father, Hippocrates, claimed a family tie to Nestor, Homeric king of Pylos, and named Pisistratus for Nestor's son. Pisistratus was attractive, intelligent, and a good speaker. Athens' renowned lawgiver Solon remarked that, except for his ambition, no one would make a more virtuous man and a better citizen. The family estates of Pisistratus were at Brauron, near Marathon, in the hill country outside of Athens. Pisistratus' mother was cousin to Solon, a connection that much elevated Pisistratus' social status. During Pisistratus' youth, Solon was the genius who guided Athens to economic and political leadership among the Greek states.

In about 570 B.C., Solon won a great victory over Megara by which Athens recovered the island of Salamis. Pisistratus reportedly served Solon as commander in the capture of Nisaea, Megara's eastern port. One of Solon's reforms was the *seisachtheia*, which "shook off" the debts of Athenian farmers. These *hektemoroi* (referring to the 16 percent interest they owed) had pledged their labor as a means of repayment and had become virtual slaves to their creditors. Solon had decreed that ceding their lands to their creditors would absolve them from debt. Free but landless, they now made up the Party of the Hill (the *hyperakrioi*), and Pisistratus became their champion. The party included downtrodden miners from Laurium and people from his hometown of Brauron, to whom were added the poorest urban Athenians (the *thetes*).

In 561, Pisistratus deliberately wounded himself and blamed his political enemies. Pisistratus was given a bodyguard of fifty men. With these, he seized the Acropolis and entered his first period of tyranny. Solon, who reportedly opposed the tyranny by speeches, died the same year. By 556, Pisis-

tratus was driven out by a new coalition of the other parties. These parties, entrenched in their authority, were the Coast (*Paraloi*), led by the Alcmaeonids under Megacles, and the Plain (*Pediakoi*), under Lucurgus and later Miltiades. Megacles, though, fell out with the Plainsmen and befriended Pisistratus as a needed ally. Their families were united by Pisistratus' marriage to Megacles' daughter. In about 550, a clever plan was devised to trick the Athenians into accepting their tyrant. A tall and beautiful woman named Phya lived in the town of Paeonia. They dressed her as Athena and drove a chariot into Athens with Pisistratus at her side. The plan was completely successful.

Megacles later regretted his daughter's marriage to Pisistratus and realigned himself with the Plain. Pisistratus was again driven into exile by the coalition. Operating from Eretria in Euboea, he raised money and troops and made important friends, especially Lygdamis of Naxos, Amyntas of Macedonia, and the leaders in Thessaly, Thebes, and even Sparta.

His control of the silver mines and gold deposits of Mount Pangaeus in Thrace enabled his third ascendancy. In 540, after a ten-year exile, his army landed at Marathon. His partisans flocked to him, and his enemies were easily defeated. Pisistratus entered the city unopposed and ruled Athens for twelve years until his death in 527.

Life's Work

To secure his position in Athens, Pisistratus maintained a private army. While he did not alter Solon's laws or the government, his adherents and relations usually held the highest offices, while Pisistratus presumably ruled in the background. He took hostages from the leading families and sent them to Lygdamis on Naxos. The Alcmaeonids and his other Athenian opponents fled or were exiled, leaving their estates in the tyrant's control.

Pisistratus' expenses were now met from the Mount Laurium silver mines of Attica as well as the Pangaean mines. It is not known how he came to control the Thracian mines; perhaps it was through King Amyntas of neighboring Macedonia, who later gave a town to Pisistratus' son Hippias.

With this monetary base, Pisistratus arranged state support of citizens disabled in war. He strengthened Athenian tetradrachm coinage, guaranteeing its purity and metallic content, and thereby improved the commerce of the city. He gave land from confiscated estates to sons of *hektemoroi* for them to farm. A moderate tax was levied on all citizens to permit him to advance seed and cattle money to the new proprietors and also to refurbish the city's defenses. By colonizing the Thracian Chersonese and recovering Sigeum, he established control of the grain routes from Pontus and secured the city's grain supply.

It must be partially owing to Pisistratus that Attic pottery was traded all over the Mediterranean world, both east and west. Pisistratus thus oversaw the blossoming of the first great styles of Attic vase painting, black figure and red figure.

Pisistratus employed the urban poor in building projects. These included roads and the construction of the *enneakrounos*, or Nine-Conduit Fountain, which improved Athens' water supply. Among his public buildings were a temple of Pythian Apollo; a magnificent temple to Olympian Zeus, left unfinished (to be completed in the Corinthian style by Roman emperor Hadrian in the second century A.D.); the stately buildings of the Lyceum garden; possibly a new and larger shrine at Eleusis for the local mystery cult; and, not least, the first temple to Athena, the Hecatompedon. Its pediment held the vigorous terra-cotta statue of striding Athena, part of a gigantomachy group. Traces of once-brilliant colors can still be seen on the her skin and clothing. The Hecatompedon, predecessor of the famous Parthenon, was destroyed by the Persians in 480 B.C.

In connection with the worship of Athena, Pisistratus either instituted the Greater Panathenaea or enhanced a festival newly established about 566. Every fourth year, a new *peplos* ("shawl") was sewn by Athenian women and was borne by them as a gift to be placed upon the statue of Athena. The ceremony included a long procession of all the citizens from the agora (marketplace) to the temple, which stood close to where the present Parthenon stands on the Acropolis.

Pisistratus also initiated the Panathenaeic competitions in Homeric recitation. Each contestant memorized the texts of Homer and recited from precisely where the previous contestant had left off. Thus they were called "rhapsodists," or "stitchers of song." Pisistratus is thus credited as the first to have the texts of Homer's epics written down and preserved essentially as they exist

today. He also encouraged literature and literacy by collecting a library and allowing public access to it.

He created the city festival in honor of Dionysus. This cult was essentially a religion of the small farmer, and it harmonized with the popular stance of the tyrant. It was in association with this Dionysiac cult festival that Greek tragedy was first performed. The religious highlight of the festival was a hymn to Dionysus (the *dithyramb*) sung by a chorus of citizens. According to the Marmor Parium, a marble tablet from Paros containing a chronology of important events down to 264 B.C., it was in 534, not long after the inception of the festival, that the *choregos* ("poet" or "producer") Thespis of Icaria introduced a soloist as interlocutor with the chorus. This new "dialogue" opened the way for the creation of individual characters and for the evolution of classical Greek tragedy as best seen in the plays of Aeschylus, Sophocles, and Euripides.

Pisistratus endeared himself and his city to Apollo of Delos by carrying out the purification of that island sanctuary: This was achieved by removing all tombs visible from the vicinity of the god's temple. This is but one example of the wise and moderate foreign policy that has already been suggested by Pisistratus' cordial and peaceful relations with neighbors.

Upon Pisistratus' death in 527, his sons Hippias and Hipparchus, the *Pisistratidae*, succeeded him in the tyranny. The brothers seem to have ruled jointly and admirably. Some scholars even believe that it was Hipparchus who actually arranged the manner in which the rhapsodists recited the Homeric poems at the Panathenaea. Several poets resided in Athens at the court of the *Pisistratidae*: Simonides of Ceos, Anacreon of Teos, Lasus of Hermione, and Onomacritus, who, with the support of the brothers, introduced a new Orphic religious influence in the city, as can be seen in many parts of Greece in the sixth century.

Hippias and Hipparchus, however, brought the tyranny into disrepute. After Hipparchus' assassination, his older brother became morose, suspicious, and arbitrary in his rule. Citizens were executed, taxes were increased. The Pisistratid family was finally expelled by a force led by the rival Alcmaeonids with Spartan assistance, which was gained by trickery. The Alcmaeonids bribed the Delphic oracle to urge Sparta to free Athens from the tyranny. A Spartan army under Cleomenes drove Hippias into perpetual banishment. A monument recording the offenses of the tyrants was set up on the Acropolis.

Soon after, however, the Spartans learned of the trick and learned that the oracle had actually foretold the Athenians' enmity against them. They therefore invited Hippias to Sparta and held a congress of their allies to form an army to reinstate him in Athens, but the idea was voted down. Hippias next went to the court of King Dareius of Persia, applying for his aid. It was Hippias who led the Persians to Marathon, where the story was told that, since he was now quite old, Hippias' tooth fell out and was buried in the sand when he sneezed. This seemed to augur the failure of the Persian expedition. The Persians were defeated, and Hippias met his death on the field of Marathon. Afterward, members of Hippias' family were back at the court of Persia under Dareius' son Xerxes. There the known line of Pisistratus becomes lost in the sources.

Summary

Herodotus, a reliable historian and a major source for information on Pisistratus' life, regarded him highly. Herodotus considered tyranny to be the negation of law and order and the arbitrary rule of an individual. Pisistratus, however, gave to that title a temporary respectability that was ruined by the behavior of most other Greek tyrants. Herodotus said, "He was no revolutionary, but governed excellently without disturbing the laws or the political offices."

As if in anticipation of the Magna Carta, Pisistratus observed the laws and submitted himself before the Areopagus court. He foreshadowed Augustus, Rome's first emperor, in founding a principate (a monarchy under the guise of a republic). For the common people, Pisistratus' rule was a golden age.

Bibliography

Aristotle. *Politics*. Translated by H. Rackham. Loeb Classical Library. London: Heinemann, and New York: Putnam, 1932.

Aristotle. *Athenian Constitution*. Translated by H. Rackham. 5th ed. Loeb Classical Library. Cambridge, Mass.: Harvard University Press, and London: Heinemann, 1981. Both works of Aristotle give new details of Pisistratus' career but draw heavily from Herodotus and Thucydides. Aristotle saw tyranny as the derogatory side of monarchical rule.

Bury, J. B., and Russell Meiggs. *A History of Greece*. 4th ed. London: Macmillan, and New York: St. Martin's Press, 1975. Excellent general history.

Day, James, and Mortimer Chambers. *Aristotle's History of Athenian Democracy*. Berkeley: University of California Press, 1962. The best commentary on Aristotle's treatment of Pisistratus.

Herodotus. *The Histories*. Translated by Aubrey de Sélincourt. A. R. Burn, ed. Rev. ed. London and Boston: Penguin Books, 1996. The primary source for Pisistratus' political career. Accessible.

How, W. W., and J. Wells. *A Commentary on Herodotus*. 2 vols. Oxford: Clarendon Press, 1964. The authors disagree with P. N. Ure, arguing that too few Athenian freemen worked in the mines to serve as a power base for Pisistratus; the main struggle was between the old landed aristocracy and the rising merchant class.

Lesky, Albin. *A History of Greek Literature*. New York: Crowell, and London: Methuen, 1966. Discussion of the literary contributions of the *Pisistratidae*.

Nilsson, Martin. *The Age of Early Greek Tyrants*. Belfast: Mayne, Boyd, 1936. Assesses tyrants as social reformers.

Thucydides. *History of the Peloponnesian War*. Translated by Rex Warner. London and Baltimore, Md.: Penguin Books, 1954. Among the primary sources for Pisistratus. Accessible.

Ure, P. N. *The Origin of Tyranny*. Cambridge: Cambridge University Press, 1922; New York: Russell and Russell, 1962. Ure argues that Pisistratus was among the first Greeks to realize the political possibilities of the new conditions created by coinage, colonies, and extensive commerce in the age of tyrants and that Pisistratus' power derived from the Laurium mines and profits from trade. Excluded from a political system based on agriculture, Pisistratus seized power by force.

Daniel Scavone

PITTACUS OF MYTILENE

Born: c. 645 B.C.; Mytilene, Lesbos, Greece
Died: c. 570 B.C.; Mytilene, Lesbos, Greece
Area of Achievement: Government
Contribution: Elected tyrant by the people of Mytilene, Pittacus brought an end to his state's bitter aristocratic party struggles and established a government that remained stable for years after he had relinquished power. Though he was vilified by his political opponent Alcaeus, later Greeks considered Pittacus one of the "Seven Sages."

Early Life

Pittacus, the son of Hyrras (or Hyrrhadius), was reared in Mytilene on the island of Lesbos (famous for its wine), the richest and most powerful of the Aeolian Greek settlements in the eastern Aegean Sea. Mytilene had colonized territories on the mainland (notably Sestos, c. 670), had dealings with the nearby Lydian kingdom, and maintained commercial connections throughout the northeastern Aegean. The citizens of Mytilene were enterprising and bold in their projects and vigorous in defense of their mainland interests. Furthermore, Mytilene's citizens fought in the service of Asiatic rulers, and the city was the only one of its Aeolian neighbors to take part in the Greek trading colony at Naucratis in Egypt. In short, Pittacus was reared in a cosmopolitan city, familiar with merchants, soldiers, and colonists.

In addition to being a progressive and dynamic state, the Mytilene of Pittacus' childhood was steeped in its old Aeolian traditions. Lesbos was within sight of the territory of Troy, and heroic poetry dealing with the Trojan saga was prominent in its early literature. Pittacus' younger contemporary Alcaeus wrote a poem describing with pride a collection of armor that harked back to the heroic age.

In addition, a rich tradition of popular song on the island gave rise to the lyric monodies of Sappho and Alcaeus, performed at *symposia* (drinking parties). The Aeolians valued their descent from the house of Agamemnon, the victor of the Trojan War, and young Pittacus respected the traditions of his ancestors and the hereditary rights of his family. Although Pittacus' father's name was Thracian, there is every indication that the family was a member of the nobility.

The civic strife in the aristocracy at Mytilene is the single most important factor in Pittacus' early life. At that time, his city was involved in bitter quarrels among the nobles vying for control of the state. During his childhood, the Penthilid clan ruled at Mytilene, claiming descent from Agamemnon's son Orestes, whose own son Penthilus was said to have colonized Aeolis. The Penthilids gained a reputation for cruelty and were said to have clubbed their aristocratic rivals. Pittacus witnessed an uprising against that family, led by Megacles, followed by Smerdis' murder of Penthilus and the establishment of a tyranny by Melanchrus.

During Pittacus' youth, the aristocratic government of Mytilene functioned through a council which submitted its deliberations to an assembly for discussion and approval. As a young man, Pittacus attended the meetings of the assembly and probably became familiar with the council through his father's connections.

Life's Work

There are two main sources for Pittacus' life and work: the poetry of his political enemy Alcaeus, which is hostile, and the writings of other writers, which extol his wisdom and place him among the so-called Seven Sages of the Greeks. From the praise and blame of the two traditions a somewhat coherent picture of his life emerges.

During the forty-second Olympiad (612-608 B.C.), Pittacus and the older brothers of Alcaeus deposed Melanchrus, an aristocrat of Mytilene who had made himself tyrant and become odious to the other noble families of the city. Pittacus' role in the action is unclear, but he must have established a reputation for leadership and daring, for soon afterward the people of Mytilene put him in charge of their army in a military encounter against the Athenians in a territorial dispute over Sigeum, near Troy. One early story records that in the course of this struggle he fought and won a duel with the Athenian general and Olympic victor Phrynon (c. 607 B.C.), killing him with a trident and knife, having first caught him in a net (perhaps a reference to a popular song describing Pittacus as a fisherman hunting his prey).

In the power struggle that ensued after the fall of Melanchrus, Pittacus allied himself with the political coterie of Alcaeus against Myrsilus, another aristocratic claimant to power. After an indeterminate period of maneuvering, Pittacus forsook the coalition which he had pledged to help and gave his support to Myrsilus' party. Alcaeus and his supporters went into exile on Lesbos, where they railed against Pittacus' defection. Pittacus married into the Penthilid family probably during Myrsilus' rule, thereby gaining a larger political base. His wife, a sister of a man named Draco, was said to be the daughter of one Penthilus. Pittacus' son Tyrraeus was murdered in nearby Cyme while sitting in a barbershop. Pittacus was said to have forgiven his murderer.

Myrsilus ruled as tyrant until he died in 590. Alcaeus was overjoyed at his death and wrote a poem calling for everyone to get drunk in celebration. The poet's hopes of repatriation, however, were disappointed, for the people of Mytilene immediately chose Pittacus to succeed Myrsilus. The new tyrant maintained a policy of subduing party strife by forcing Alcaeus and his supporters to leave Lesbos altogether. Although poems of Alcaeus call for his overthrow and mention Lydian support for the rebels, there is no indication that Pittacus' rule was ever seriously threatened from without or within. One anecdote tells of Alcaeus falling into Pittacus' hands during this period. Instead of punishing his enemy for his savage attacks, the tyrant is reported to have freed him and uttered the maxim "Pardon is better than revenge." Pittacus held supreme power in Mytilene until 580, when he voluntarily gave up his post and returned to private life.

Pittacus' rule at Mytilene was benevolent and was probably the source of his excellent reputation in later years. He did not overthrow the traditional constitution but respected its institutions while adding new laws to those already in existence. His respect for the law produced his description of the best rule as one of "the painted wood" (that is, of laws written on wooden tablets). His most famous statute, aimed at curbing alcohol abuse, provided a double penalty for anyone committing a crime while drunk. This law calls to mind both the reputation of Lesbian wine and the poems of Alcaeus extolling its use.

The only physical descriptions of Pittacus come from Alcaeus' abusive poems and therefore can probably be dismissed as rhetorical excess. Alcaeus calls Pittacus flat-footed, dirty, and pot-bellied. Yet everything known about Pittacus from other sources makes doubtful the validity of these slanders. Indeed, Alcaeus also calls Pittacus "baseborn," a charge which can also be explained as simply part of the vocabulary of invective.

Several sayings of Pittacus are preserved, including "Even the gods do not fight against Necessity" and "Office reveals the man." Because of the fighting he had witnessed all of his life, Pittacus is credited with a rather un-Greek notion when he urged people to seek "victories without blood." His statement that "It is a difficult thing to be good" was the basis of a poem by Simonides and a long discussion in Plato's *Protagoras* (c. 399-390 B.C.). Numerous other quotations of his are preserved, mostly commonplace sentiments.

A number of stories tell that Pittacus had dealings with the Lydian king Croesus, and although chronology of their lives makes it unlikely that they ever met while both were in power, Croesus was the governor of the Lydian province close to Lesbos before he became king, and therefore it is possible that he could have met Pittacus at that time. It is most likely that stories relating the two are the result of an ancient attempt to create stories analogous to those which connected the Athenian sage and lawgiver Solon with the Lydian king. Pittacus' name has been identified on an inscription of his contemporary Nebuchadnezzar, King of Babylon, providing evidence that Mytilene did have important relations with the great powers to the east.

Pittacus died in 570, having lived over seventy years. He left behind a stable and prosperous city, as well as an enviable reputation—despite the protests of Alcaeus' poetry. Few ancient biographies have such happy endings. His traditional epitaph is:

With her own tears, Holy Lesbos who bore him
Bewails Pittacus who has died.

Summary

The work of Pittacus of Mytilene must have been very successful in quelling the party strife that had troubled the state for so long. He felt comfortable enough with the political situation to retire after only ten years, and there is no evidence of further civil disturbances thereafter. Indeed, Pittacus entered the ranks of the traditional Greek Seven Sages for his work. The Seven Sages were contemporaries of Pittacus who held similar positions as lawgivers and tyrants and included Periander of Corinth and Solon of Athens. More is known of them than of Pittacus, although Pittacus is admired as much as the others by later tradition.

Diodorus of Sicily said that Pittacus not only was outstanding for his wisdom but also was a citi-

zen whose like Lesbos had never before produced—nor would produce, until such time as
when it would make more and sweeter wine (that
is, never). Diodorus called Pittacus an excellent
lawgiver and a kindly man who was well-disposed
toward his fellow citizens. He released his homeland from the three greatest misfortunes: tyranny,
civil strife, and war. In addition, he was serious,
gentle, and humble, perfect in respect to every virtue. His legislation was just, public-spirited, and
thoughtful, and he himself was courageous and
outstandingly free from greed.

Encomiums such as this made up the bulk of the
later tradition dealing with Pittacus and form a
strong contrast with the poetry of his contemporary
Alcaeus. Diogenes Laertius wrote a "Life of Pittacus" in his *Peri bion dogmaton* (early third century
A.D.; *Lives of Eminent Philosophers*, 1925), which
includes numerous anecdotes illustrating his wisdom and justice. In his "Life of Thales," Diogenes
gives various ancient lists of the Seven Sages, and
Pittacus appears in each one. Plutarch provided a
similar portrait of Pittacus in his work "Banquet of
the Seven Sages," in *Moralia: Septem sapientum
convivium* (early second century; *Moralia*, 1603).
Strabo's *Geōgraphica* (c. 7 B.C.; *Geography*, 1917-
1933) twice mentions Pittacus, each time emphasizing that he was one of "The Seven Wise Men,"
and notes that Pittacus used his monarchic powers
to rid the state of dynastic struggles and to establish the city's autonomy. Aristotle wrote that Pittacus' position of elective tyrant was a distinct form
of rule called *aesymneteia*, but he gives no other
examples of it, and no others are known.

The impression made by Pittacus on his countrymen is revealed in the fact that the rich Lesbian
folk song tradition preserves his memory:

> Grind, mill, grind.
> For even Pittacus grinds,
> As he rules great Mytilene.

Historians have few details to illustrate these ancient generalizations about Pittacus' exceptional
character and achievements. Further discoveries of
ancient evidence about archaic Lesbos and its most
admired citizen would help fill in the gaps about
Pittacus' life.

Bibliography

Andrewes, Antony. *The Greek Tyrants*. London:
Hutchinson's University Library, 1956; New
York: Harper and Row, Publishers, 1963. Solid
and balanced discussion of the tyrannies at
Mytilene, Alcaeus, and Pittacus in the chapter
"Aristocratic Disorder at Mytilene." Best com-
parative material with other archaic tyrannies,
and general discussion of the phenomenon. Puts
Pittacus in perspective. Notes, index, bibliogra-
phy.

Burn, A. R. *The Lyric Age of Greece*. London: Edward Arnold, and New York: St. Martin's Press,
1960. Includes "The Lyric Age of Lesbos," with
sections on Sappho, Alcaeus, and the "Revolution at Mytilene." Good background for Pittacus'
world, explaining its politics, literature, and history. Chapters on contemporary archaic city-
states provide comparative material. Index and
notes.

Campbell, David A., ed. *Greek Lyric Poetry*. Rev.
ed. Bristol: Bristol Classical Press, 1982; Cambridge, Mass.: Harvard University Press, 1993.
Contains all fragments of Sappho and Alcaeus,
translations, and brief notes to each poem. Includes an introduction with good discussion of
how to date events in the life of Pittacus. Lists
ancient evidence for lives of Alcaeus and Pittacus. With an index.

Jeffery, L. H. *Archaic Greece: The City-States, c.
700-500 B.C.* New York: St. Martin's Press, and
London: Benn, 1976. This work provides background on all the Greek city-states during the ancient period, with a useful section on the Aeolian
Greeks and specific discussion of the political
and economic status of Lesbos and the place of
Pittacus. Comparisons made between Solon and
Pittacus. Includes notes, glossary, maps, and index.

Lefkowitz, Mary R. *The Lives of the Greek Poets*.
Baltimore: Johns Hopkins University Press, and
London: Duckworth, 1981. Includes important
perspective on ancient biography, claiming that
most material in the lives is fiction—based on
the poems, not history. Relevant to Alcaeus' information used for his life and that of Pittacus.
With a chapter on ancient lyric poets and an index and bibliography.

Murray, Oswyn. *Early Greece*. 2d ed. Cambridge,
Mass.: Harvard University Press, and London:
Fontana, 1993. Good general background on an-
cient Greece, with a short section on Alcaeus and
Pittacus and examples of Alcaeus' poems. Points
out the unique political position held by Pittacus.
With maps, illustrations, useful chronological
chart, and an annotated list of primary sources.

Page, Denys. *Sappho and Alcaeus: An Introduction to the Study of Ancient Lesbian Poetry.* Oxford: Clarendon, 1955; New York: Oxford University Press, 1959. A seminal work on the most important source for Pittacus: the poetry of Alcaeus. Complete Greek texts and translations of the political and nonpolitical poems, with detailed literary, grammatical, and historical commentary. Extensive and comprehensive.

Podlecki, Anthony J. *The Early Greek Poets and Their Times.* Vancouver: University of British Columbia Press, 1984. A substantial chapter on Alcaeus and Sappho offers chronological analysis of Pittacus and his contemporaries on Lesbos, with analysis of the use of Alcaeus' poems in creating the picture of Pittacus. A thoughtful and readable treatment, with good use of all available sources. Includes an index and bibliography.

Romer, F. E. "The *Aisymneteia:* A Problem in Aristotle's Historic Method." *American Journal of Philology* 103 (1982): 25-46. Discusses sources for the rule of Pittacus and Aristotle's definition of the *aisymneteia,* or elective tyranny. Proves that this definition originated in his own philosophical ideas about civil strife and political harmony. Well documented, with many notes and further reading.

Daniel B. Levine

PLATO

Born: 427 B.C.; Athens, Greece
Died: 347 B.C.; Athens, Greece
Area of Achievement: Philosophy
Contribution: Plato used the dialogue structure in order to pose fundamental questions about knowledge, reality, society, and human nature—questions that are still alive today. He developed his own positive philosophy, Platonism, in answer to these questions, a philosophy which has been one of the most influential thought-systems in the Western tradition.

Early Life

There is an ancient story (very likely a true one) that Plato was originally named Aristocles, but acquired the nickname Plato ("broad" or "wide" in Greek) on account of his broad shoulders. Both of Plato's parents were from distinguished aristocratic families. Plato himself, because of family connections and expectations as well as personal interest, looked forward to a life of political leadership.

Besides being born into an illustrious family, Plato was born into an illustrious city. He was born in the wake of Athens' Golden Age, the period that had witnessed Athens' emergence as the strongest Greek power (particularly through its leadership in repelling the invasions of Greece by the Persians), the birth of classical Athenian architecture, drama, and arts, and a florescence of Athenian cultural, intellectual, and political life. By the time of Plato's youth, however, the military and cultural flower that had bloomed in Athens had already begun to fade. A few years before Plato's birth, Athens and Sparta—its rival for Greek supremacy—had engaged their forces and those of their allies in the Peloponnesian War.

This long, painful, and costly war of Greek against Greek lasted until Plato was twenty-three. Thus, he grew up witnessing the decline of Athens as the Greek military and cultural center. During these formative years, he observed numerous instances of cruelty, betrayal, and deceit as some unscrupulous Greeks attempted to make the best of things for themselves at the expense of other people (supposedly their friends) and in clear violation of values that Plato thought sacred.

It was also at an early age, probably in adolescence, that Plato began to hear Socrates, who engaged a variety of people in Athens in philosophical discussion of important questions. It could

fairly be said that Plato fell under the spell (or at least the influence) of Socrates.

When, as a consequence of losing the Peloponnesian War to Sparta, an oligarchy was set up in Athens in place of the former democracy, Plato had the opportunity to join those in power, but he refused. Those in power, who later became known as the "Thirty Tyrants," soon proved to be ruthless rulers; they even attempted to implicate Socrates in their treachery, although Socrates would have no part in it.

A democratic government was soon restored, but it was under this democracy that Socrates was brought to trial, condemned to death, and executed. This was the last straw for Plato. He never lost his belief in the great importance of political action, but he had become convinced that such action must be informed by a philosophical vision of the highest truth. He continued to hold back from political life, devoting himself instead to developing the kind of training and instruction that every wise person—and political people especially, since they act on a great social stage—must pursue. Plato main-

tained that people would not be able to eliminate evil and social injustice from their communities until rulers became philosophers (lovers of wisdom)—or until philosophers became rulers.

Life's Work

In his twenties and thirties, Plato traveled widely, becoming aware of intellectual traditions and social and political conditions in various Mediterranean regions. During these years, he also began work on his earliest, and most "Socratic," dialogues.

When he was about forty years old, Plato founded the Academy, a complex of higher education and a center of communal living located approximately one mile from Athens proper. Plato's Academy was highly successful. One famous pupil who studied directly under the master was Aristotle, who remained a student at the Academy for twenty years before going on to his own independent philosophical position. The Academy continued to exist for more than nine hundred years, until it was finally forced to close in A.D. 529 by the Roman emperor Justinian I on the grounds that it was pagan and thus offensive to the Christianity he wished to promote.

In 367 B.C., Plato went to Sicily, where he had been invited to serve as tutor to Dionysius II of Syracuse. The project offered Plato the opportunity to groom a philosopher-king such as he envisioned in *Politeia* (388-368 B.C.; *Republic)*, but this ambition soon proved to be unrealizable.

One of the main tasks Plato set for himself was to keep alive the memory of Socrates by recording and perpetuating the kind of impact that Socrates had had on those with whom he conversed. Virtually all Plato's written work takes the form of dialogues in which Socrates is a major character. Reading these dialogues, readers can observe the effects that Socrates has on various interlocutors and, perhaps more important, are themselves brought into the inquiry and discussion. One of the explicit aims of a Platonic dialogue is to involve readers in philosophical questioning concerning the points and ideas under discussion. In reading essays and treatises, readers too often assume the passive role of listening to the voice of the author; dialogues encourage readers to become active participants (at least in their own minds, which, as Plato would probably agree, is precisely where active participation is required).

The written dialogue is an effective mode of writing for a philosophy with the aims of Plato, but it sometimes leaves one uncertain as to Plato's own views. It is generally agreed among scholars that the earlier works—such as *Apologia Socratis (Apology), Euthyphro,* and *Gorgias,* written between 399 and 390 B.C.—express primarily the thought and spirit of Socrates, while middle and later dialogues—such as *Meno, Symposium, Republic, Theaetetus* (all 388-366 B.C.), *Philebus,* and *Nomoi* or *Laws* (both 360-347 B.C.)—gradually give way to the views of Plato himself.

The dialogues of Plato are among the finest literary productions by any philosopher who has ever lived, yet there is evidence that Plato himself, maintaining the superiority of the spoken word over the written word, and of person-to-person instruction over "book learning," regarded the written dialogues as far less important than the lectures and discussions that took place in the Academy. There is, however, very little known about those spoken discussions, and the best evidence available for Plato's views is surely in his many dialogues.

The fundamental thesis of Plato's work is the claim that there are "forms" or "ideas" that exist outside the material realm, that are the objects of knowledge (or intellectual cognition), and that, unlike material objects, do not come into existence, change, or pass out of existence. These forms, rather than material things, actually constitute reality. This is Plato's well-known theory of forms (or theory of ideas).

The theory attempts to take two points of view into consideration and to define their proper relationship. The two points of view give the questioner access to a changing world (of sensible or material things) and an unchanging world (of intellectual objects). From the first perspective, human beings know that they live in a changing world in which things come into existence, change, and pass out of existence. If one tries to pin something down in this world and determine whether various predicates apply to it (whether it is big, or red, or hot, or good, for example), one finds that the object can be viewed from a variety of standpoints, according to some of which the predicate applies and according to some of which it does not apply. Socrates, for example, is big compared to an insect, but not big compared to a building. This train of thought leads one, however, to the other point of view. An insect, Socrates (that is, his body), and a building belong to the changing physical world in which the application of predicates is problematic or changing. In the nonphysical, or intellectual, world, however, there must be some fixed points of reference that make possible the application of predicates at all. These latter fixed points do not change. Whether one compares Socrates with the insect or with the building, when one judges which is bigger one is always looking for the same thing. Bigness or largeness itself, Plato thought, must always exist, unchanging, and it must itself be big. It is this abstract or intellectual element with which a person must be familiar if the person is to be in a position to decide whether various objects in this changing material world are big.

The forms, or objects of intellect, are quite different from (and superior to) physical objects, or objects of sense. Plato thought of knowledge as occurring only between the intellect (or reason) and its objects, the forms. The bodily senses give human beings only belief, he said, not true knowledge.

Plato considered human beings to be composed of a rational aspect and an irrational aspect. The intellect or reason, that which communes with the forms, is rational. The body, which communes with the physical world, is irrational. Plato looked down on the body, considering it merely the seat of physical appetites. Additionally, there is a third, intermediate aspect of people: passions, which may follow intellect (and thus be rational) or follow the bodily appetites (and thus be irrational).

In each person, one aspect will dominate. Reason is best, but not everyone can achieve the state in which his life is under the direction of reason. Thus, communities should be organized in such a way that those who are rational (and not led by physical appetites) will be in command. The philosopher-king is one who both attains philosophical insight into the world of the forms and holds power in the day-to-day changing world.

Summary

Plato defended the role of reason in human life, in opposition to many ancient Greek teachers who were called Sophists. The Sophists traveled from city to city and claimed to be able to teach young men how to be successful in life. They offered such services for a fee. Although the Sophists were never a unified school and did not profess a common creed, certain beliefs are characteristic of them as a group and almost diametrically opposed to the views of Plato. The Sophists mainly taught the art of speaking, so that a person could speak well in public assemblies, in a court of law, and as a leader of men. Plato thought, however, that such speakers were probably more likely to appeal to feelings and emotion than to reason. Such speakers may hold forth and sound impressive, but they tend not to be acquainted with the objects of the intellect, the ground of true knowledge. Plato argued that such speakers may, for example, be persuasive in getting a man who is ill to take his medicine, but it is only a real doctor who can prescribe the right remedy. Plato also compared the Sophist to a makeup artist, who makes only superficial changes in people's looks; the true philosopher, on the other hand, is compared to a gymnastic trainer, who is genuinely able to bring health and soundness to people's bodies.

In Plato's view, however, the stakes are really much higher, for both Sophists and philosophers actually affect people's souls or inner selves, not their bodies, and Plato followed Socrates in thinking of the cultivation of the soul as much more important than the cultivation of the body. Moreover, Plato went beyond the views of other Greek philosophers and beyond the cultural norms of ancient Athens by affirming that women and men had the same potential for philosophical wisdom and community leadership. Many writers in the twentieth century have referred to Plato as the first feminist, although it is also true that the vast majority of ancient, medieval, and modern philosophical Platonists did not follow him in this particular. The Sophists, in any case, were false teachers and false leaders, in Plato's view. True leaders must have wisdom, and the acquisition of such wisdom, he believed, could only come about in a cooperative community of inquirers who were free to follow argument, not carried away by speech making.

Throughout the history of more than two millennia of Western philosophy, Plato has been one of the most influential thinkers. One twentieth century philosopher, Alfred North Whitehead, has said that philosophy since Plato's time has consisted mainly of a series of footnotes to Plato. There have been numerous revivals of Plato's thought in Western philosophy. Platonists, Neoplatonists, and others have made their appearance, but Plato's influence is probably better gauged in terms of the importance of the questions he has raised and the problem areas he has defined, rather than in terms of the numbers of his adherents or disciples. From both dramatic and philosophical points of view,

Plato's dialogues are so well constructed that even today they serve well as a student's first encounter with the philosophical practice of inquiry and argument.

Bibliography

Crombie, I. M. *Plato: The Midwife's Apprentice.* London: Routledge, 1964; New York: Barnes and Noble, 1965. A readable examination of Plato's life, his methods, his character, and his philosophy. Well informed, yet uncluttered by footnotes and other scholarly apparatus.

Cropsey, Joseph. *Plato's World: Man's Place in the Cosmos.* Chicago: University of Chicago Press, 1995; London: University of Chicago Press, 1997. The eight dialogues of Protagoras—*Theatetus, Euthyrpo, Sophist, Statesman, Apology, Crito,* and *Phaedo*—are studies, each in an individual chapter, forming a dramatic sequence. The book is a commentary on the texts themselves, without references to other scholarly work. It attempts to reconstruct Socrates' political ethics.

Grube, George M. A. *Plato's Thought.* Boston: Beacon, and London: Methuen, 1935. Each chapter is devoted to a single topic and usefully draws quotations and ideas from the entire Platonic corpus. Topics covered are the theory of ideas, pleasure, eros, the soul, gods, art, education, and statecraft.

Guthrie, W. K. C. *A History of Greek Philosophy.* Vols. 4 and 5. Cambridge: Cambridge University Press, 1975, 1978; New York: Cambridge University Press, 1989. A very thorough and scholarly examination of Plato's life and works. Includes notes, bibliography, indexes, and references to specific passages in Plato. The Greek terms and phrases that occur are generally translated and explained.

Irwin, Terence. *Plato's Ethics.* New York and Oxford: Oxford University Press, 1994. This book discusses Plato's conception of the virtues, including his connection between virtues and happiness. It reviews his views on knowledge, belief, and inquiry, and his theory of forms, with their relevance to his ethical views. Irwin also traces Plato's moral philosophical development from the Socratic dialogues to the Republic.

Kraut, Richard. *The Cambridge Companion to Plato.* Cambridge and New York: Cambridge University Press, 1995. This volume contains fifteen new essays discussing Plato's views about a variety of topics. It also contains analyses of the intellectual and social context of his thought, his philosophical development throughout his career, alternative approaches to his work, and his writing style.

Rutherford, B. R. *The Art of Plato: Ten Essays in Platonic Interpretation.* London: Duckworth, and Cambridge, Mass.: Harvard University Press, 1995. The essays discuss the literary aspects of Plato's writing. His style and rhetoric are examined in detail.

Shorey, Paul. *What Plato Said.* Chicago: University of Chicago Press, 1933. After a review of the life of Plato, Shorey painstakingly summarizes and examines each of the dialogues of Plato (as well as some forgeries and some doubtful cases). This survey of Plato's works is followed by detailed notes and references to works of other scholars.

Taylor, Alfred E. *Plato: The Man and His Work.* Rev. ed. London: Methuen, and New York: The Dial Press, 1929. This is a classic work of scholarship that has been reprinted many times in later editions. Taylor discusses Plato's work dialogue by dialogue. He strives to convey the point of each of Plato's inquiries and the force of the arguments that are discussed.

Vlastos, Gregory, comp. *Plato: A Collection of Critical Essays.* 2 vols. New York: Anchor Books, 1970. The first volume contains essays by a variety of students of Plato on metaphysics and the theory of knowledge. The second volume focuses on Plato's theories regarding ethics, politics, eros, the soul, art, and religion. A good source for penetrating readings of Plato by modern thinkers.

Zeitlin, Irving. *Plato's Vision: The Classical Origins of Social and Political Thought.* Englewood Cliffs, N.J.: Prentice Hall, 1993. The book discusses the historical origins and the content of Plato's political philosophy. Each of his relevant writings is individually examined.

Stephen Satris

PLAUTUS

Born: c. 254 B.C.; Sarsina, Italy

Died: 184 B.C.; Rome, Italy

Areas of Achievement: Theater and drama

Contribution: Plautus' action-packed, middle-class comedies, built from a dizzyingly contrived structure of disguises, mistaken identities, and the obligatory revelatory scene, were sensationally popular in his time; they have since influenced or been adapted by such comedic dramatists as William Shakespeare, Richard Brinsley Sheridan, Molière, and Jean Giraudoux.

Early Life

The sparse details of Titus Maccius Plautus' life are drawn from historians and writers such as Livy and Cicero. From his birthplace, Sarsina, a mountainous rural region of Italy, where the native tongue was Umbrian, Plautus escaped, joining a traveling group of players (probably as an actor). He learned the technical intricacies of the profession, acquired a mastery of Latin—and perhaps some Greek—and became the unequaled practitioner of his comedic craft.

In Rome, Plautus worked in the theater, lost money in trade, and eventually became a mill worker, writing in his leisure moments. No record remains of his life except the plays that he wrote, and even some of these claim authenticity only on the basis of ascription. Plautus became so popular that dramas by other writers were attributed to him in order to gain production and popular reception. In his time, it was enough merely that a play bore his name; a generation later, it was enough that the prologue to the play *Menaechmi* (*The Twin Menaechmi*) contain the words "I bring you Plautus"—words that remain in that prologue forever as guarantors of laughter.

Life's Work

Although he may have written more than fifty plays, only twenty-one manuscripts of works attributable to Plautus survive, the oldest of these dating to the fourth or fifth century A.D. Only twenty of these are complete plays. In an age when records were shoddily kept, or not kept at all, and when aspiring contemporary playwrights did not hesitate to attach Plautus' name to their plays, a large number of comedies were attributed to him.

In an attempt to clear up the chaos of authorship, Marcus Terentius Varro, a contemporary of Cicero, compiled three lists of plays: those given universal recognition as being written by Plautus, and those identified by Varro alone as plays by Plautus, and those recognized as Plautus' work by others but not by Varro. The first list, labeled by scholars the "Varronianae fabulae," contains the twenty-one plays that succeeding generations of scholars have agreed on as belonging to Plautus. Other plays remain outside the canon.

The dates of Plautus' plays are as speculative as are the details of his life. Only two of them—*Pseudolus* (191 B.C.) and *Stichus* (200 B.C.)—are attached to specific dates, about half the remainder are unidentified chronologically, and the rest are qualified with terms such as "probably early" or "late." Like William Shakespeare nearly fifteen hundred years later, Plautus borrowed his plots and reworked Greek originals; some sources have been identified, but others remain unknown.

Among the most famous stock situations and character types associated with Plautine comedy are the vain soldier-braggart (*miles gloriosus*), which finds its most complex realization in Shakespeare's Falstaff; the farcical chaos caused by mistaken identity, a chaos to which order is eventually restored; the servant who, wiser than his superiors, extricates them from a web of near-impossible entanglements, sometimes of the master's making; and finally, a happy ending. The plays, whether serious—*Amphitruo* (*Amphitryon*)—or farcical—*The Twin Menaechmi*—are always comic in the Aristotelian definition of comedy as a play which begins in an unfortunate situation and ends fortunately.

Like the commercial playwright of modern times, Plautus wrote for a broad audience, basing his appeal on laughter and a good story, love and money forming an integral part of the story. Preceding his plays, as was the custom, with a prologue devoted to a summary of the borrowed story, he then developed his plot by highly improbable complications, witty native dialogue, slapstick scenes, and an infinite variety of jests, all kept within the limits of popular recognition. That recognition is embodied in the characters, the most famous of which in his time and, perhaps, in any time is the *miles gloriosus* figure, the Greek *alazon* or "overstater" (commonly translated as the soldier-braggart), whose vanity and consequent exposure have never failed to entertain. In Plautus' time, the Punic Wars created an audience receptive to fast-paced action and to the adventures of the returning soldier.

On a broader social scale, the element of recognition is drawn from the merchant-class milieu of his time, in which servants, wiser than their masters, extricate their superiors from entrapments of one sort or another, thereby resolving problems and bringing the play to its happy conclusion. Molière's middle-class comic heroes and villains stem from this Plautine tradition. The stories borrowed from Greek comedies became merely the scaffolding for the native Roman ribaldry, schemes, and jests that characterize the famous Plautine humor, and the upper-class characters are frequently a part of that scaffolding. In the course of the play, they give way to the servants or peasants. Thus, in the tradition of the New Comedy of Menander (as opposed to the old Aristophanic satire, which was topical), Plautus opened the comic stage to the common man. What social satire is present is a part of the more broadly based humor, concerned with the outwitting of the upper classes by their inferiors. Like death, humor becomes the great leveler.

Of the twenty-one surviving plays, the two that remain the most famous are *The Twin Menaechmi*—frequently translated as *The Two Menaechmi*—and *Miles gloriosus (The Braggart Warrior)*, the date and source of the former unknown, the latter dated about 205 B.C. Both are placed by scholars in the early or early middle of the agreed-upon chronology of his writing. Respectively, they are the direct source of Shakespeare's play *The Comedy of Errors* (c. 1592-1594) and of his most famous and complex comic figure, Falstaff. Indirectly, they have influenced both literary style and popular humor in most succeeding comedies. Both plays exude the festive spirit to which C. L. Barber attributes Shakespeare's comedies and which distinguishes Plautine humor, heavily dependent on robust and fast-moving physical actions, from that of traditional satire, invective, or other modes of comedy in which ideas are prominent.

The Twin Menaechmi, more directly imitated perhaps than any other play, builds its comedy on a set of separated twins, whose lives develop complications that, once begun, take on a life of their own in a seemingly endless web of mistaken identities and consequent misunderstandings. Only the most skillful plotting of events by the author can extricate the twins from that web created by disguises and accidental meetings.

The title figure of *The Braggart Warrior* (variously entitled *The Soldier-Braggart*), the soldier Pyrgopolynices, is considered by scholars to be Plautus' most brilliant creation. Convinced of his bravery and appeal to women and recently returned from the wars, Pyrgopolynices (who is characterized by lechery and stupidity as well as vanity) falls victim to the elaborate deceptions of a slave whose master is in love with a woman whom the braggart soldier has brought to Ephesus against her will. The slave concocts a pattern of disguises and misunderstandings that befuddle the vain soldier, and the lovers are reunited. Again, disguises, misunderstandings, and deceptions create a farcically intricate plot, delightful in its escalating complications and ingenious in its resolution.

Summary

In addition to being "the dean of Roman drama," Plautus has directly provided the plots for at least three illustrious successors: Shakespeare's *The Comedy of Errors*, based on *The Twin Menaechmi*; Molière's *L'Avare* (1668; *The Miser*, 1672), based on *Aulularia* (*The Pot of Gold*); and Jean Giraudoux's *Amphitryon 38* (1929; English translation, 1938), based on *Amphitryon*. Edmond Rostand's *Cyrano de Bergerac* (1897; English translation, 1898), Nicholas Udall's *Ralph Roister Doister* (1552), Ben Jonson's *Every Man in His Humour* (1598, 1605), and the contemporary American musicals *The Boys from Syracuse* (1938) and *A Funny Thing Happened on the Way to the Forum* (1962) are among the popular descendants of Plautus' work.

Erich Segal, writing about Plautine humor, quotes the psychiatrist Ernst Kris, who describes comedy as a "holiday for the superego." A "safety valve for repressed sentiments which otherwise might have broken their bonds more violently," Plautine comedy provides release from the conventions of a socially prescribed life. It produces a resolution of the tension between dreams and actuality, order and chaos, and finally between the vital and repressive forces in life, as it acts out that resolution for the audience. In the end, a kind of ironic equilibrium is achieved, an equilibrium that reconciles dream with reality, providing the release necessary to avoid the violence inherent in the tragic mode.

Bibliography

Anderson, William S. *Barbarian Play: Plautus' Roman Comedy*. Toronto and Buffalo: University of Toronto Press, 1993. This is a fundamental study of the playwright, discussing his use of the Greek comic tradition, plotting, construction of character, language, meter and staging, and finally, his relation to the Roman audience. The bibliography is comprehensive.

Beare, William. *The Roman Stage: A Short History of Latin Drama in the Time of the Republic*. Rev. ed. London: Methuen, 1964; New York: Barnes and Noble, 1965. A history of Roman drama with illustrations, plates, appendices, notes and sources, bibliography, and general index, as well as an index to Latin lines quoted or discussed in text.

Dorey, T. A., and Donald R. Dudley, eds. *Roman Drama*. London: Routledge, and New York: Basic Books, 1965. A collection of essays on Latin literature and its influence, focusing on Menander, Plautus, and Seneca, with illustrations and notes.

Duckworth, George E. *The Nature of Roman Comedy: A Study in Popular Entertainment*. 2d ed. Norman: University of Oklahoma Press, 1992; London: Bristol Classical Press, 1994. A historical sweep of the Golden Age, including its origins, thematic nature, and stage conventions; includes an extensive bibliography and an index.

————, ed. *The Complete Roman Drama*. New York: Random House, 1942. This volume contains four plays by Plautus and three by Terence, with an introduction contrasting the comedic qualities of their plays.

Plautus. *The Comedies*. 4 vols. D. R. Slavitt and P. Bovie, eds. Baltimore, Md. and London: John Hopkins University Press, 1995. Part of the *Complete Roman Drama in Translation* series, these volumes contain new translations of all of Plautus' works. Each play is preceded by a short introduction; the text itself is not annotated.

Plautus. *Plautus: Three Comedies*. Erich Segal, ed. and trans. New York and London: Harper and Row, Publishers, 1969. Includes Segal's translations of *The Braggart Warrior, The Twin Menaechmi*, and *Mostellaria (The Haunted House)*, with an introduction dealing with Plautus' popularity in his time as well as a pronunciation guide and a selected bibliography.

Segal, Erich. *Roman Laughter: The Comedy of Plautus*. 2d ed. New York and Oxford: Oxford University Press, 1987. A sprightly treatment of the social milieu that spawned Plautus' comedies, with extensive notes, an index of passages quoted, and a general index.

Slater, Niall W. *Plautus in Performance: The Theater of the Mind*. Princeton, N.J.: Princeton University Press, 1985. Addressed to both specialists in ancient literature and those interested in the history of drama in general, this book is an exercise in performance criticism of Plautus' plays. "Once we have a text, we can extrapolate a good deal from it about performance," Slater writes.

Susan Rusinko

PLINY THE ELDER

Born: Probably A.D. 23; probably Novum Comum, Italy

Died: August 25, A.D. 79; Stabiae, near Mount Vesuvius

Areas of Achievement: Science and natural history

Contribution: Pliny's *Natural History*, though not a work of original natural science, preserved for later times priceless information on the ancients' beliefs in countless areas. His work had great influence on later antiquity, the Middle Ages, and the early Renaissance, and he remains a major figure in the history of science.

Early Life

Gaius Plinius Secundus, or Pliny the Elder, was in his fifty-sixth year when he died during the famous eruption of Mount Vesuvius in August of A.D. 79. He therefore was probably born in late 23. His family was prominent in Novum Comum and most scholars believe that he was born there, although some prefer to use the evidence which points to Verona. Clues to his career are found in his own writing, in a life by Suetonius, and in the letters of his nephew and adopted ward Gaius Plinius Caecilius Secundus, better known as Pliny the Younger.

It can be inferred from certain remarks in his work that Pliny came to Rome at an early age to study, as befitted his status as the son of a prominent northern Italian family. He obtained the normal education of the time and thus would have been thoroughly trained in rhetoric, a discipline to which he would later return, as well as several of the fields which he would cultivate for the next thirty years until he wrote *Historian naturalis* (A.D. 77; *The Historie of the World*, 1601; better known as *Natural History*). The next natural step for a young man in his position was one of military service and therefore, at about the age of twenty-three, he went to Germany as a military officer and, in addition to holding other posts, was put in command of a cavalry troop. Later comments in the *Natural History* lead scholars to believe that he traveled throughout the area and took copious notes on what he saw during his stay there.

Although all Pliny's writings except the *Natural History* are lost, his nephew published a chronological, annotated bibliography of his uncle's works, and the titles from this early period are instructive. His first work was a single-volume book entitled *De iaculatione equestri* (on throwing the javelin from horseback), and his next was a two-volume biography of his patron Lucius Pomponius Secundus. His third book was a twenty-volume history of all the wars Rome had ever waged against Germany. Pliny claimed that he was instructed to begin this work at the behest of the ghost of Drusus Germanicus (the brother of Tiberius and the father of Claudius I), who was concerned that the memory of his deeds would be lost. Scholars also suspect a certain amount of imperial flattery in this story. It was probably also during this German campaign that Pliny became close to the future emperor Titus, to whom he dedicated the *Natural History*. A belief that he served under Titus later during the campaign in Judaea is somewhat suspect.

After a fairly lengthy stay in Germany, Pliny returned to Rome and began the second phase of his career as a writer and public servant.

Life's Work

During this time, generally thought to begin during the reign of Claudius, Pliny turned to the life of a professional pleader, a natural choice for one of his station and education. There is no record of any great successes in this regard, and none of his speeches survives, but his next book, *Studiosi* (the scholar, sometimes translated as the student), reflects again his tendency to write about matters with which he was concerned. In it, Pliny traced the training of a rhetorician from the cradle onward. The work encompassed three books in six volumes and very likely occupied Pliny during the early years of Nero's reign. It was consulted by Quintilian and earned some cautious praise from that author. The later, more turbulent, years of Nero's reign were occupied with an eight-volume study of grammar. Pliny, who later would call Nero an enemy of mankind, was clearly keeping out of the maelstrom of Neronian politics by retreating to his study. It is therefore not surprising that near the end of Nero's reign Pliny accepted a posting as procurator of Spain, perhaps to remove himself completely from the city during troubled times.

It may have been during this period that Pliny also found time to write a thirty-one-book history which continued the work of Aufidius Bassus. Bassus' history seems to have ended with the events of Claudius' reign, and Pliny began there and ended perhaps with the events of 69. It is likely that this work was published posthumously. It was also at this time that Pliny's brother-in-law died and entrusted the care of his son, Pliny's nephew, to this now-distinguished Roman figure. Pliny could not care for the lad from Spain but chose a guardian for him until he adopted him upon his return to Rome. He held his post in Spain until Vespasian emerged victorious from the turmoil which followed Nero's death in 69, a year of civil war commonly referred to as the Year of the Four Emperors.

Vespasian brought stability to a war-weary city, and for Pliny he represented political patronage as the father of Pliny's army friend Titus. After Pliny's return to Rome, he held several high-ranking posts abroad, and it can be surmised from his first-person reports in the *Natural History* that one of these trips may have taken him to Africa, where he made copious notes on what he saw. At this time, he was also made an official "friend of the court" and thus became an imperial adviser, regularly called to Vespasian's court for meetings at daybreak.

The demands of Pliny's renewed public life were thus intense, and yet he was also finishing the *Natural History* at the same time he held these offices. Pliny had been amassing information for this work for years. His nephew writes that his uncle never read without taking notes and that one of his mottoes was that no book was so bad that he could not find something of use in it. He always read or was read to whenever possible—even while bathing, eating, or sunbathing (one of his favorite pastimes). He read or dictated while riding in a sedan chair, and he once chastised his nephew for walking since it was impossible to read while one did so. He even devised a sort of glove to ensure that his slave could take notes on such trips in cold weather. To find more time for his studies, Pliny retired early and rose even earlier, reading and writing by lamplight in the early morning darkness. So diligent was he that upon his death he left his nephew 160 books of notes written in a tiny hand.

The *Natural History* became the great showcase for these notes. Its thirty-seven books cover virtually every aspect of nature's works and several of those of man. After an entertaining preface, book 1 offers a full table of contents and a list of authorities cited—a rare and welcome practice in antiquity. The remaining books range far and wide across the realms of zoology, entymology, botany, mineralogy, astronomy, geography, pharmacology, anthropology, physiology, folklore, and metallurgy. There are countless long digressions on such subjects as the history of art, the manufacture of papyrus, the growing of crops, religious practices, aphrodisiacs, and magic spells. In his preface, Pliny claims to have studied about two thousand volumes, to have emerged with twenty thousand noteworthy facts, and to have cited one hundred principal authors. In reality, the total number of authors cited by name is almost five hundred. Although it is surmised that the work was published in 77, there are certain signs that it is unfinished; Pliny may well have been revising the work when he met his death.

On August 24, 79, Pliny was on duty at Misenum as prefect of the fleet in the bay of Naples. Upon seeing the volcanic cloud from Vesuvius, he sailed across the bay both to investigate further and to help in possible evacuation plans. Once at his destination, he sought to calm his hosts by a casual attitude and even fell asleep amid the danger, a fact attested by those who overheard his characteristic loud snoring. Yet the volcano intensified, and by the next morning Pliny and his hosts had to flee to the shore with pillows tied over their head for protection.

The sea was too rough to set sail, and Pliny was exhausted from his labors, being rather obese and prone to heavy and labored breathing. He lay down for a while on a sail and requested cold water, but upon rising fell suddenly dead, the victim either of the foul air or of a heart attack. His body was found the next day, looking, according to his nephew, more like one asleep than one who had died.

Summary

It is fashionable to criticize Pliny the Elder as an uncritical encyclopedist, an assiduous notetaker with little or no discrimination. It is charged that his work is devoid of literary style and is almost completely lacking in organization. It is clear that most of his information came from late-night notetaking and not from fieldwork, a point in which he suffers by comparison to Aristotle.

Yet Pliny's sins are not as great as they may seem. In his own time, he was much consulted. One can see traces of his rhetorical and grammatical works in Quintilian and Priscian and of his histories in Tacitus, Plutarch, and Dio Cassius. The popularity of the *Natural History* is shown in the number of authors who used it as a treasure trove of facts, in its imitators such as Solinus, Martianus Capella, and Isidore of Seville, and by the great number of manuscript versions of the text, in whole or in part, which survived into the Middle Ages.

The work was much used by medieval scholars, who mined it for whatever information they needed. Several produced topical condensations, and in the early 1100's a nine-volume "reader's edition" was prepared. Its traces are frequently to be seen, often cited by name, in such authors as Thomas of Cantimpre, Bartholomaeus Anglicus, Vincent of Beauvais, and Saint Albertus Magnus. Not surprisingly, it was printed as early as 1469 and was so popular that by 1499 six more corrected editions had been printed. It was translated into Italian in 1476 and 1489.

Such popularity merits consideration and should cause the work to be judged on its own terms. In the first place, posterity owes Pliny much for preserving so many intriguing facts and the names of authors otherwise lost. Clearly, it is not meant to be read as literature. It is an old curiosity shop of antiquity, wherein a reader can wander, fascinated, at his leisure. It is a book for browsers and, as such, offers the rewards of hours of pleasurable discovery to those people who, like Pliny, believed that knowledge was inherently good.

Bibliography

Beagon, M. *Roman Nature: The Thought of Pliny the Elder*. Oxford: Clarendon, and New York: Oxford University Press: 1992. "This book is not intended to be a biography of Pliny," Beagon writes in the preface. "[It is a] testimony to the mode of thought, the outlook on life of the educated Roman citizen of the first century of our era… Early chapters deal with his [Pliny's] ideas on the cosmos, cosmic deity, and man's place in the cosmos. The second part deals with man's relation to specific areas of the natural world: the animal kingdom and the elements land and water. The final chapter looks at the use man makes of animals, minerals, but above all plants in prolonging and safeguarding his life in Nature."

Chibnall, Marjorie. "Pliny's *Natural History* and the Middle Ages." In *Empire and Aftermath: Silver Latin II*, edited by T. A. Dorey. London and Boston: Routledge, 1975. Careful and clear study of the influence of the *Natural History* from late antiquity through the Middle Ages.

French, Roger, and Frank Greenaway, eds. *Science in the Early Roman Empire: Pliny the Elder, His Sources and Influence*. London: Croom Helm, and Totowa, N.J.: Barnes and Noble, 1986. Twelve essays occasioned by a Pliny symposium, with a brief life and studies centering on such subjects as medicine, pharmacy, botany, zoology, metallurgy, and astronomy.

Isager, Jacob. *Pliny on Art and Society: The Elder Pliny's Chapters on the History of Art*. London and New York: Routledge, 1991. This is a pioneering study of Pliny as the father of art historiography. Isager emphasizes the philosophic and political overtones of Pliny's aesthetic views. The book has an extensive bibliography, and no illustrations.

Pliny the Younger. *Letters and Panegyricus*. Translated by Betty Radice. Cambridge, Mass.: Harvard University Press, and London: Heinemann, 1969. Part of the Loeb Classical Library. Letters 3.5, 6.16, and 6.20 are vivid, firsthand accounts of the elder Pliny, his writings, life-style, and death.

Thorndike, Lynn. *A History of Magic and Experimental Science*. Vol. 1, *The First Thirteen Centu-*

ries of Our Era. Rev. ed. New York: Macmillan, 1929; London: Columbia University Press, 1964. Discusses the place of Pliny in the history of science and his contributions to the belief in magic.

Wethered, H. N. *The Mind of the Ancient World: A Consideration of Pliny's "Natural History."* London and New York: Longmans, Green, 1937. An elegant defense of Pliny with seventeen chapters on various topics, accompanied by extensive quotes from Pliny, William Shakespeare, Andrew Marvell, and John Milton, among others.

Kenneth F. Kitchell, Jr.

PLOTINUS

Born: 205; possibly Lycopolis, Upper Egypt
Died: 270; Campania, Italy
Area of Achievement: Philosophy
Contribution: As the founder of Neoplatonism, Plotinus has exerted a profound influence on Western philosophical and religious thought, from his own day to the present.

Early Life

Plotinus was born in 205, but there is almost no information about his origins or his early life. His nationality, race, and family are unknown, and information about his birthplace comes from a fourth century source which may not be reliable. Plotinus told his disciples little about himself; he would not even divulge the date of his birth. Only one thing can certainly be said: Plotinus' education and intellectual background were entirely Greek. This fact can be deduced from his writings; Plotinus shows little knowledge of Egyptian religion and misinterprets Egyptian hieroglyphic symbolism. Porphyry, Plotinus' pupil and biographer, reports that Plotinus had a complete knowledge of geometry, arithmetic, mechanics, optics, and music, and he must have acquired some of this knowledge during the early years of his education.

Porphyry reports that in 232, when Plotinus was twenty-seven, he felt a strong desire to study philosophy. He consulted the best teachers in Alexandria, but they all disappointed him. Then a friend recommended a teacher named Ammonius Saccas (c. 175-242). Plotinus went to hear him and immediately declared, "This is the man I was looking for." Little is known, however, of Ammonius' philosophy; he was self-taught, wrote nothing, and made his followers promise not to divulge his teachings.

Beginning in late 232 or early 233, Plotinus studied with Ammonius for eleven years (Plotinus' long stay in Alexandria may be the only reason for the common belief that he was originally from Egypt). Following that, Plotinus wanted to learn more of the philosophy of the Persians and the Indians, and he joined the army of Emperor Gordianus III, which was marching against the Persians.

It is not known in what capacity Plotinus served; he may have been a scientific adviser, or he may have occupied a more lowly position. The expedition, however, did not achieve its objective. Gordianus was assassinated in Mesopotamia, and Ploti-

nus escaped with difficulty to Antioch. He made no attempt to return to Ammonius (nor did he ever return to the East). Instead, in 245, at the age of forty, he traveled to Rome, where he was to remain for twenty-five years, until shortly before his death. The stage was set for him to emerge as the last great pagan philosopher.

Life's Work

For the next ten years, Plotinus established himself in Rome. He accepted private students and based his teaching on that of Ammonius. During this time he wrote nothing, but by the time Porphyry joined him in 264, Plotinus no longer considered himself bound by the restrictions on publication which Ammonius had imposed (other pupils of Ammonius, such as Origen and Erennius, had already published). Plotinus had therefore written twenty-one treatises by 264, although none of them had circulated widely. Porphyry urged him to write more, and twenty-four treatises followed during the six years that Porphyry was his pupil.

Only one story survives about Plotinus' life in Rome before Porphyry's arrival. A philosopher named Olympias, from Alexandria, who was also a former pupil of Ammonius, attempted to "bring a star-stroke upon him [Plotinus] by magic." Plotinus, who apparently believed in the power of magic, felt the effects of this attack, but Olympias found his attempt recoiling on himself. He ceased his attack and confessed that "the soul of Plotinus had such great power as to be able to throw back attacks on him on to those who were seeking to do him harm."

During the time that Porphyry was his pupil, Plotinus lived comfortably in what must have been a large house, owned by a wealthy widow named Gemina. He earned a reputation for kindness and gentleness and was always generous in offering help to others. Many people entrusted their sons and daughters to his care, "considering that he would be a holy and god-like guardian." Although Plotinus was an otherworldly philosopher, he also believed in the importance of the social virtues, that the practice of them contributed to the soul's ultimate liberation. He was therefore practical, wise, and diplomatic in daily affairs, taking good care of the worldly interests of the young people in his charge. For example, they would be encouraged to give up property only if they decided to become philosophers, and even this was a decision that they would have to make for themselves. The same was true of Plotinus' attitude toward the physical body and its desires. Although he believed in self-discipline, he acknowledged that legitimate physical needs must be looked after, and he never advocated the kind of asceticism which was found in some other ancient philosophical schools.

Plotinus often acted as arbitrator in disputes, without ever incurring an enemy. The only opposition he appears ever to have aroused (apart from that of Olympias) was when some Greek philosophers accused him of stealing some of his philosophy from Numenius, a charge which modern scholars have not accepted. Plotinus was also a good judge of character, and his advice was sound. When Porphyry, for example, confessed that he was contemplating suicide, Plotinus told him that the desire was caused by physiological reasons, not by rational thought, and advised him to take a vacation. Porphyry accepted his advice.

Plotinus had a number of aristocratic friends, and members of the senate attended his lectures. One of them, Rogatianus, relinquished his property and became an ascetic after being exposed to Plotinus' teaching. The Emperor Gallienus, sole emperor from 260 to 268, and his wife, Salonia, venerated Plotinus. Plotinus once asked them to found a "city of philosophers" in Campania, to be called Platonopolis, which would serve as a monastic retreat for him and his followers. The scheme failed, however, as a result of opposition in the Roman senate. Gallienus' assassination in 268 must have been a blow to Plotinus, since Gallienus' successors showed no interest in Greek philosophy.

Plotinus' lectures were more like conversations; discussion was always encouraged. One of his pupils once complained that he would prefer to hear Plotinus expound a set treatise and was exhausted by Porphyry's continuous questions. Plotinus replied, "But if when Porphyry asks questions we do not solve his difficulties we shall not be able to say anything at all to put into the treatise." Plotinus was a thoroughly engaging teacher; when he was speaking, "his intellect visibly lit up his face: there was always a charm about his appearance. . . kindliness shone out from him."

Plotinus would never revise his written work; he complained that writing gave him eyestrain. He was careless in the formation of the letters, and he showed no interest in spelling. Porphyry comments that Plotinus would compose everything in his mind. When he came to write, the thoughts were already fully formed, and he wrote "as continuously as if he was copying from a book." Even if someone engaged him in conversation, he would continue writing and not lose his train of thought. This ability to focus on the inner life enabled him to achieve a high level of mystical experience. He attained complete mystic union four times during Porphyry's stay with him, and in a treatise written before Porphyry's arrival, Plotinus says that he had experienced it often.

In his final years he suffered from a painful illness which may have been leprosy. Although he stopped teaching and withdrew from his friends and pupils, who feared contagion, he continued to write. Nine treatises appeared in his last two years (268-270), bringing the total to fifty-four, which were collected and edited by Porphyry, at Plotinus' request. Finally, Plotinus went away to the estate of his deceased friend Zethus in Campania, where he died alone, except for the presence of his doctor, Eustochius. His last words, according to Eustochius, were "Try to bring back the god in you to the divine in the All!"

Summary

As the last great philosopher of antiquity, and the only one to rank with Plato and Aristotle, Plotinus' philosophy has exerted an enormous influence both on the thought of his own period and on that of later times. Although he probably thought of himself as no more than an interpreter of Plato, Plotinus became the founder of Neoplatonism. His thought lived on in his pupils Porphyry and Amelius, and all later Neoplatonic philosophers regarded him as a respected, although not a supreme, authority.

Plotinus' system was a comprehensive and original one. He brought to the best of Greek philosophy a dimension of mystical thought which in its force, immediacy, and beauty has rarely, if ever, been equaled in the West. The *Enneads* are not merely an ethical or metaphysical system; they are a guide to the soul's liberation, culminating in the experience and contemplation of the One. This experience is seen as the goal of the philosopher's quest, and that of all men.

Plotinus, and Neoplatonism in general, were also major influences on the development of Christian theology. Saint Augustine knew all the six *Enneads* and quotes Plotinus by name five times. The fourth century Cappadocian Fathers, especially Gregory of Nyssa, also came under his spell. His thought emerged again in the Renaissance in the work of Marsilio Ficino (who translated Plotinus into Latin) and Giovanni Pico della Mirandola. In modern thought, Plotinus' influence can be traced in the work of German Idealist philosopher Friedrich Schelling, French philosopher Henri Bergson, and English Romantic poets such as William Blake and William Butler Yeats, whose interest in Plotinus was prompted by the translations made by the English Platonist Thomas Taylor in the late eighteenth and early nineteenth centuries.

Bibliography

Armstrong, A. H. *The Cambridge History of Later Greek and Early Medieval Philosophy.* Cambridge: Cambridge University Press, 1967; New York: Cambridge University Press, 1970. This is the best introduction to Plotinus in English. Armstrong's balanced and sensible account of Plotinus' life takes into account the most recent scholarly research. One chapter discusses Plotinus' method of teaching and writing, and three additional chapters provide a concise but rich exposition of his thought. Includes a bibliography.

Bréhier, Émile. *The Philosophy of Plotinus.* Translated by Joseph Thomas. Chicago: University of Chicago Press, 1958. A concise introduction to Plotinus' thought but selective in its focus. Concentrates on Plotinus' philosophy of the three hypostases: the One, Intelligence, and Soul. Contains the best discussion in English of the possible Oriental influence on Plotinus' thought.

Dodds, E. R. *Pagan and Christian in an Age of Anxiety.* Cambridge: Cambridge University Press, 1965; New York: Norton, 1970. This brief but wide-ranging book by a renowned classical scholar discusses the historical and social background of Neoplatonism, the conflict between Neoplatonism and Christianity, and the many types of religious and psychological experience which flourished during the period. The section on Plotinus' mysticism is particularly valuable. Well written and scholarly, but accessible to the general reader.

Gerson, Lloyd P., ed. *The Cambridge Companion to Plotinus.* Cambridge and New York: Cambridge University Press, 1996. This volume presents sixteen leading scholars' explanations of the many aspects of Plotinus' complex system. Their works put Plotinus' place in the history of ancient philosophy in context and illustrate why he is known as the father of medieval philosophy.

Gurtler, Gary M. *Plotinus: The Experience of Unity.* New York: P. Lang, 1988. The book examines Plotinus' psychological teaching, and argues that it is in harmony with the basic structure of his ontology. Each term of Plotinus' rich psychological vocabulary is individually studied.

Hadot, Pierre. *Plotinus or The Simplicity of Vision.* Chicago: University of Chicago Press, 1993. Hadot is one of the greatest modern authorities on Plotinus. This short book (originally published in French in 1963) is intended as a spiritual biography of the philosopher; a chronological biography is given as an appendix. The text provides a clear and insightful introduction to Plotinus' personality and thought.

Inge, William R. *The Philosophy of Plotinus.* 3d ed. 2 vols. London: Longmans, 1941. Originally given as the Gifford Lectures at the University of St. Andrews, Scotland, in 1902-1904, this work remains a useful introduction to Plotinus' thought, gracefully written by a Christian Platonist.

O'Meara, Dominic J. *Plotinus: An Introduction to the Enneads.* Oxford: Clarendon Press, and New York: Oxford University Press, 1993. Examining the basic concepts of Plotinus' major work, the book gives an exposition of his epystemology, psychology, ontology, ethics, and aesthetics. It also addresses his life and works and his influence on Western thought.

Plotinus. *Plotinus, with an English Translation by A. H. Armstrong.* Vol. 1. Cambridge, Mass.: Harvard University Press, 1966; London: Heinemann, 1980. Contains an annotated translation of Porphyry's biography of Plotinus and an annotated bibliography of primary and secondary sources.

Rist, J. M. *Plotinus: The Road to Reality.* Cambridge: Cambridge University Press, 1967. A scholarly work which includes detailed studies of Plotinus on the One, the Logos, free will, and faith. Argues that Plotinus was aware that his philosophy differed from that of Plato. Includes a chapter on Plotinus' mysticism.

Scardigli, Barbara, ed. *Essays on Plutarch's Lives.* Oxford: Clarendon Press, and New York: Oxford University Press, 1995. These essays were originally published between the 1920s and the

1990s. Some focus on Plutarch's literary and historiographic techniques; others examine his relationship to Hellenic culture and Roman politics.

Stadter, Philip A., ed. *Plutarch and the Historical Tradition*. London and New York: Routledge, 1992. This is a collection of essays on different aspects of Plutarch's *Lives*. "The contributions of these chapters," Stadter writes, "might be summarized under two broad and interdependent categories: biographical techniques and appropriation of sources."

Wallis, R. T. *Neoplatonism*. 2d ed. London: Duckworth, and Indianapolis: Hackett, 1995. Covers Neoplatonism from its sources in Plato, Aristotle, the Stoics, and the Middle Platonists, through to Plotinus' successors, Porphyry, Iamblichus, and the fifth and sixth century schools of Athens and Alexandria. Extensive bibliography.

Bryan Aubrey

PLUTARCH

Born: c. A.D. 46; Chaeronea, Boeotia
Died: After A.D. 120; Chaeronea, Boeotia
Area of Achievement: Literature
Contribution: Plutarch was the greatest biographer of antiquity. He taught his successors how to combine depth of psychological and moral insight with a strong narrative that evokes the greatness and excitement of subjects' lives.

Early Life

Most of Plutarch's writing was not accomplished until late middle age. He was born in a Roman province to an old and wealthy Greek family. He received a comprehensive education in Athens, where he studied rhetoric, physics, mathematics, medicine, the natural sciences, philosophy, and Greek and Latin writing. His worldview was strongly influenced by Plato, and he took considerable interest in theology, serving as the head priest at Delphi in the last twenty years of his life. By the time he was twenty, he had rounded out his education by traveling throughout Greece, Asia Minor, and Egypt. Before his writing career began, Plutarch worked in Chaeronea as a teacher and was its official representative to the Roman governor. Later, he undertook diplomatic trips to Rome, where he befriended several important public servants.

The prestige of Greek learning stood very high in the Roman Empire, and Plutarch eventually was invited to lecture in various parts of Italy on moral and philosophical subjects. Sometime in his late thirties, he began to organize his notes into essays. There is evidence to suggest that by the time he was forty, Plutarch enjoyed a highly receptive audience for his lectures. This was a time in which the Roman emperors were particularly favorable to Greek influences.

Although Plutarch could easily have made a career of his Roman lecture tours, he returned to his home in Chaeronea at about the age of fifty. There, he served in many administrative posts with the evident intention of reviving Greek culture and religion. His principal great work, *Bioi parallēloi* (first transcribed c. 105-115; *Parallel Lives*), was written in these years when his sense of civic responsibility and leadership had matured and when he was able to draw on his considerable experience of political power.

Life's Work

In *Parallel Lives*, better known simply as *Lives*, Plutarch chose to write about actual historical figures. The lives were parallel in the sense that he paired his subjects, so that Alexander the Great and Julius Caesar, Demosthenes and Cicero, could be discussed in terms of each other. It was important to have a basis of comparison, to show how equally famous men had arrived at their achievements in similar and different circumstances, with personalities that could be contrasted and balanced against each other. Plutarch's aim was not merely to describe lives but to judge them, to weigh their ethical value and to measure their political effectiveness. Clearly, he believed that human beings learned by example. Thus, he would present exemplary lives, complete with his subjects' strengths and weaknesses, in order to provide a comprehensive view of the costs and the benefits of human accomplishment.

Plutarch has often been attacked for being a poor historian. What this means is that sometimes he gets his facts wrong. On occasion he is so interest-

ed in making a moral point, in teaching a lesson, that he ruins the particularity and complexity of an individual life. He has also been guilty of relying on suspect sources, of taking reports at face value because they fit a preconceived notion of his subject.

While these faults must be acknowledged and compensated for, they should not be allowed to obscure the enormous value of Plutarch's biographies. In the first place, he realized that he was not writing histories but lives and that some of his sources were questionable. Unlike the historian, he was not primarily interested in the events of the past. On the contrary, it was the personalities of his subjects that had enduring value for him. To Plutarch, there was a kind of knowledge of human beings that could not be found in the close study of events or in the narration of historical epochs. As he puts it, "a slight thing like a phrase or a jest often makes a greater revelation of character than battles where thousands fall, or the greatest armaments, or sieges of cities." Plutarch found his evidence in the seemingly trifling anecdotes about great personages. He was of the conviction that an intense scrutiny of the individual's private as well as public behavior would yield truths about human beings not commonly found in histories.

Plutarch thought of himself as an artist. He was building portraits of his subjects:

> Just as painters get the likenesses in their portraits from the face and the expression of the eyes, wherein the character shows itself, but make very little account of the other parts of the body, so I must be permitted to devote myself rather to the signs of the soul in men, and by means of these to portray the life of each, leaving to others the description of their great contests.

As the founder of modern biography, Plutarch was pursuing psychological insight. Individuals were the expressions of a society, the eyes and face of the community, so to speak. He would leave to historians the description of society, "the other parts of the body."

What makes Plutarch convincing to this day is his keen perception. No biographer has surpassed him in summing up the essence of a life—perhaps because no modern biographer has believed as intensely as Plutarch did in "the soul in men." Each line in Plutarch's best biographical essays carries the weight and significance of a whole life. It is his ability to make his readers believe that he is imagining, for example, Caesar's life from the inside,

from Caesar's point of view, that makes the biographer such an attractive source that William Shakespeare and many other great authors borrowed from him.

It has often been said that no biographer can truly penetrate his or her subject's mind. Yet Plutarch perfected a way of reading external events, of shaping them into a convincing pattern, until—like a great painting—his prose seems to emit the personality of his subject. Here, for example, is his account of Caesar's ambition:

> Caesar's successes . . . did not divert his natural spirit of enterprise and ambition to the enjoyment of what he had laboriously achieved, but served as fuel and incentive for future achievements, and begat in him plans for greater deeds and a passion for fresh glory, as though he had used up what he already had. What he felt was therefore nothing else than emulation of himself, as if he had been another man, and a sort of rivalry between what he had done and what he purposed to do.

These two long sentences, with their complex clauses, are imitative of Caesar's life itself, for they demonstrate how ambition drove him on—not satisfying him but actually stimulating more exploits. Here was a great man who had set such a high example for himself that his life had turned into a competition with itself. Plutarch manages the uncanny feat of having Caesar looking at himself and thereby gives his readers the sensation of occupying Caesar's mind.

Plutarch was by no means interested only in men of great political and military accomplishment. His pairing of Demosthenes and Cicero, for example, is his way of paying respect to mental agility and the power of the word. Both men prepared for their public careers as orators through long, careful training, but their personalities were quite different. Cicero was given to extraordinary boasting about himself, whereas Demosthenes rarely spoke in his own favor. If Cicero was sometimes undone by his penchant for joking, there was nevertheless a pleasantness in him almost entirely lacking in Demosthenes. That two such different men should have parallel careers is surely part of Plutarch's point. There is no single pathway in life to success or failure, and personal faults—far from being extraneous—may determine the fate of a career. Shakespeare realized as much when he based much of his *Coriolanus* (c. 1607-1608) on Plutarch's interpretation of the Roman leader's choleric character.

Summary

Most of the *Lives* and its companion volume, *Ethica* (*Moralia*), seem to have been written in the last twenty years of Plutarch's life—precisely at that point when he was most seriously occupied as a religious official, statesman, and diplomat. It is likely that his *Moralia*, or moral reflections on life, helped to give him the worldly perspective, tolerance, and acute judgment that are so evident in his masterpiece, the *Lives*. His studies of philosophy and religion surely gave him the confidence to assess the lives from which he would have his readers learn. He died an old man in peaceful repose, recognized for his good services by his fellow Boeotians, who dedicated an inscription to him at Delphi.

It has been suggested that Plutarch was most concerned with the education of his heroes, whose stories proceeded from their family background, education, entrance into the larger world, climax of achievement, and their fame and fortune (good and bad). He exerted a profound influence on the Roman world of his time, on the Middle Ages, and on a group of important writers—chiefly Michel Eyquem de Montaigne, Shakespeare, John Dryden, and Jean-Jacques Rousseau. If his impact is less obvious in modern times, it is probably because there is less confidence in the moral patterns Plutarch so boldly delineated. What modern biographer can speak, as Plutarch did, to the whole educated world, knowing that he had behind him the prestige and the grandeur of Greek literature and religion?

Bibliography

Barrow, Reginald Haynes. *Plutarch and His Times*. London: Chatto and Windus, and Bloomington: Indiana University Press, 1967. Includes map of central Greece. Emphasizes Plutarch's Greek background, with chapters on his role as a teacher and his relationship to the Roman Empire. The bibliography is divided between English and foreign titles.

Gianakaris, C. J. *Plutarch*. New York: Twayne Publishers, 1970. The best short introduction to Plutarch. Includes detailed chronology, discussions of all Plutarch's important works, a selected and annotated bibliography, and a useful index. Gianakaris writes with a firm grasp of the scholarship on Plutarch, corrects errors of earlier writers, and conveys great enthusiasm for his subject.

Jones, Christopher Prestige. *Plutarch and Rome*. Oxford: Clarendon, 1971. Several chapters on Plutarch's career, on his lives of the Caesars, and on the sources, methods, and purposes of the *Lives*. Concentrates on the importance of Rome in Plutarch's life and work. With an extensive bibliography and a helpful chronological table.

Russell, Donald Andrew. *Plutarch*. London: Duckworth, and New York: Scribner, 1973. Draws on the best English and French scholarship. Slightly more difficult than Gianakaris as an introduction. Chapters on language, style, and form, on the philosopher and his religion, and on Plutarch and Shakespeare. Contains several appendices, including one on editions and translations, and a general bibliography and index.

Wardman, Alan. *Plutarch's Lives*. London: Elek, and Berkeley: University of California Press, 1974. A very detailed scholarly discussion of the *Lives*. Includes chapters on the problems of historical method, politics, rhetoric, and form. The bibliography includes many foreign titles, especially from French and English scholarship.

Carl Rollyson
Lisa Paddock

POLYBIUS

Born: c. 200 B.C.; Megalopolis, Arcadia, Greece
Died: c. 118 B.C.; Greece
Area of Achievement: Historiography
Contribution: Through the advancement of sound historical methodology, Polybius contributed to the development of history as a significant area of inquiry having primarily a didactic rationale.

Early Life

Polybius was born in about 200 B.C. in Megalopolis, Arcadia, in Greece. He was the son of Lycortas, a prominent Achaean diplomat and political leader; nothing is known of Polybius' mother. His family's wealth was based on extensive and productive land holdings. During his youth Polybius developed an interest in biography, history, and military topics. He wrote a biography of Philopoenen, a legendary leader in Arcadia, and a military treatise, *Tactics*, which has not survived. As a young nobleman, Polybius complied with the expectation that he be trained as a warrior in order to support the policies of the Achaean League. At the age of twenty, Polybius was named a hipparch, a commander of cavalry, in the army of the League, and he remained in that position for a decade. Shortly after 170, the fragile tranquillity of the Greek world was disrupted by the Roman war against Perseus of Macedonia. Amid this crisis, which saw a heightened Roman distrust of the various Greek states, Polybius declared his support for the Romans and offered his cavalry to assist the Roman forces, which were under the leadership of Quintus Marcius Philippus. Not only did the Romans not accept Polybius' offer of support, which was a result of their lack of trust, but they also seized Polybius and about a thousand other Achaeans and transported them to Italy. This episode marked a transformation in the life and work of Polybius.

Life's Work

Upon arriving in Rome, Polybius came under the protection of Scipio Aemilianus, a prominent Roman general who had befriended the exiled Achaean. Polybius traveled with Scipio to Spain, Africa, and southern France; they witnessed the destruction of Carthage in 146 at the close of the Third Punic War. In the same year, Polybius was in Corinth, which had been destroyed by the Romans. Polybius exhibited effective diplomatic skills as he ar-

ranged an end to hostilities and a reasonable settlement for the Achaeans.

Throughout his travels and contacts with the Romans, Polybius developed his interest in history and formulated a plan to write a history of the emergence of Rome to a position of hegemony in the Mediterranean world. At first, Polybius intended to conclude his work in 168 with the victory of the Romans over Perseus in the Battle of Pydna. He later decided, however, to continue the history through to the fall of Carthage and Corinth in 146. It appears that his history was published in forty books; although only the first five books have survived intact, fragments and collaborative evidence provide considerable information on the remaining thirty-five books.

In *The Histories*, Polybius clarified and expanded the role of the historian and the importance of the study of history. He maintained that historians must be familiar with the geography of the regions they cover, knowledgeable about the practice of politics, and informed of the appropriate documentary sources relating to their topic. Polybius viewed history as an analysis of political developments which would better equip leaders to increase political wisdom. He advanced a philosophy of history which was based on the frequency of constitutional changes or revolutions in societies and cultures. Polybius argued that in the earliest years of a society's history, people banded together and designated a leader whose primary purpose was to provide protection for the group; the consequence of this action was the appearance of despotism. As the society expanded and the concept of law emerged, the despotism was transformed into monarchy, which eventually led to tyranny and an aristocratic reaction. The aristocratic regime yielded to oligarchy, which was then replaced by democracy. The democracy survived for a few generations until the memory of the oligarchy passed and democracy was corrupted to mob rule, during which the conditions that first resulted in the emergence of despotism were re-created. A despot would again seize power and the politically oriented and driven process would resume. Polybius argued that Rome would be exempt from the processes of decay because of the fluid nature of the constitution of the Roman Republic.

In collecting his sources, Polybius exercised a thoroughness and discrimination which were revolutionary in the study of history. He relied heavily upon the use of oral testimony; indeed, he structured the chronological limits of his study so that he could emphasize the material which he gathered from oral sources. These sources could be used as collaborative evidence and were capable of being verified. In addition to oral history, Polybius had access to and made use of a wide range of written sources. From Achaean and Roman official records to earlier histories, Polybius effectively utilized all the available sources.

The Histories constitute an apologia, an explanation for the emergence of Rome as the leader of the Mediterranean world. Polybius contended that Rome deserved its preeminent position because the Roman leaders and people had developed a progressive political system; the other Mediterranean peoples, Polybius believed, did not possess the realistic political worldview of the Romans and, as a consequence, lost their independence. In the development of this notion as well as others, Polybius demonstrated his concern with causation. On several occasions he discussed the concept of cause and effect and noted contrasts between the larger causes of a development and the immediate activities which resulted in it. It should be noted, however, that Polybius also ascribed to Tyche (the Greek goddess of chance) developments which were inexplicable. Throughout his writings Polybius repeated that history should be instructive,

> . . . for it is by applying analogies to our own circumstances that we get the means and basis for calculating the future; and for learning from the past when to act with caution, and when with greater boldness, in the present.

Polybius repudiated partisan histories, such as the writings of Timaeus, the Greek antiquarian, and warned against the worthlessness of deliberately biased works. He was interested in determining the truth and, once it was determined, learning from it.

Both in his own time and in subsequent generations, critics noted the shortcomings of Polybius' style, which in many ways appears to have been as tedious as modern bureaucratic English. Polybius was repetitious, exercised a penchant for ambiguity, and developed his arguments in such an indirect fashion that his principal points were frequently submerged. Nevertheless, Polybius, along with Herodotus and Thucydides, raised the study and writing of history to a new level of serious inquiry. Polybius' emphasis on proper methodology, his vi-

sion of a universal political historical process, and his advocacy of history as a didactic art resulted in the enhancement of the Greco-Roman historical tradition. Polybius allegedly died at about the age of eighty-two in approximately 118 B.C. in Greece, as a result of injuries suffered when he was thrown from a horse.

Summary

While Polybius was a leading Achaean during his lifetime and used his abilities and connections to develop an accommodation with Rome for his native Arcadia, his more significant legacy consisted of his contributions to the development of the study and writing of history. In the tradition of the earlier Greek historians Herodotus and Thucydides, Polybius considered the multitude of issues relating to historical methodology and developed an expanded notion of historical evidence. His use of oral history and his approach to collaborative evidence were significant contributions to his craft. Polybius' methodology and his concept of history influenced Roman historians such as Livy and Tacitus.

While much of *The Histories* of Polybius has been lost, the first five books provide the reader with more than a glimpse of Roman history at a time when the Mediterranean world was in a state of crisis. In this context, Polybius' contributions to the study of constitutions and political cycles should be emphasized; his thesis on the progression from despotism to monarchy to tyranny to aristocracy and then on to democracy and the return to despotism via mob rule not only advanced a historical analysis but also provided a framework for the discussion of constitutionalism. Twentieth century historiographers, such as Harry Elmer Barnes and Eric Breisach, have sustained Polybius' place in the first rank of ancient historians.

Bibliography

Barnes, Harry Elmer. *A History of Historical Writing.* 2d ed. New York: Dover Publications, 1962. A standard historiographical analysis which identifies Polybius as being in the tradition of Herodotus and Thucydides. Barnes credits Polybius with the advancement of historical writing during the classical period; Polybius' methodology and organizational skills are discussed in the context of Greek historiography.

Breisach, Ernst. *Historiography: Ancient, Medieval, and Modern.* 2d ed. Chicago: University of

Chicago Press, 1994. Breisach discusses Polybius' work in the context of early Roman historiography, emphasizing his concept of political history. The author also provides a schema for Polybius' cycle of constitutional revolutions. This work constitutes one of the best single-volume reviews of historiography available. Includes an excellent bibliography.

Eckstein, Arthur M. *Moral Vision in the Histories of Polybius*. Berkeley: University of California Press, 1995. The book examines the moral and political convictions which influenced Polybius' historiography, most notably his aristocratic ethos and what the author terms his "Machiavellianism." The last chapter discusses Polybius' global view of human nature and of the course of history. The book is well argued and clearly written, each chapter being followed by a short conclusion.

Magie, D. *Roman Rule in Asia Minor*. Princeton, N.J.: Princeton University Press, 1950. An excellent introduction to the expansion of Rome in the eastern Mediterranean, this volume provides a valuable insight into the world and writing of Polybius.

Robinson, Charles Alexander. *Ancient History, from Prehistoric Times to the Death of Justinian*. 3d ed. New York: Macmillan, and London: Collier-Macmillan, 1981. A somewhat dated but still excellent introduction to the study of ancient history. Polybius is presented as one of the progressives of antiquity whose contribution to the development of civilization was substantive.

Scullard, H. H. *Scipio Africanus in the Second Punic War*. Cambridge: Cambridge University Press, 1930. A classic study of the Second Punic War and the emergence of Rome as the major power in the Mediterranean region. This book provides an excellent examination of Roman policy at the end of the third century.

Walbank, Frank. *A Historical Commentary on Polybius*. 3 vols. Oxford: Clarendon Press, 1957. This is the preeminent scholarly study of Polybius by one of the major classical scholars of the twentieth century. The work includes extensive details on Polybius, textual commentary, and criticism on *The Histories*.

———. *Polybius*. Oxford: Clarendon, 1970; Berkeley: University of California Press, 1972. Walbank's volume treating the life of Polybius and his work stands as a significant contribution to biography and historiography as well as to the study of this particular historian. The work is well documented and includes a useful bibliography.

———. "Supernatural Paraphernalia in Polybius' History." In *Ventures into Greek History*. Ian Worthington, ed. Oxford: Clarendon Press, and New York: Oxford University Press, 1994. The essay examines Polybius' adducing of supernatural explanations for the course of historical events. Walbank concludes that this, along with certain arbitrariness in the construction of the narrative, detracts from *The Histories'* value as a historical source.

William T. Walker

POLYGNOTUS

Born: c. 500 B.C.; Thasos, Greece

Died: c. 440 B.C.?; Thasos, or Athens, Greece

Area of Achievement: Art

Contribution: Innovative, brash, confident in his skills, Polygnotus was the first great Greek painter. His murals at Delphi and in Athens established his reputation as the preeminent painter of the fifth century B.C. and probably the most famous in antiquity.

Early Life

Little is known about Polygnotus' early life. He was born on the Greek island of Thasos, near Thrace, and was the son and pupil of the prominent painter Aglaophon. His brother Aristophon was also an artist; a later painter named Aglaophon may have been his son or nephew. Polygnotus' family appears to have been politically active, and he may have been related to the famous seventh century poet Archilochus, whose family had colonized Thasos.

Polygnotus was already being employed as a painter, and probably also as a sculptor, for major projects on the Greek mainland during the first quarter of the fifth century. He eventually made his way to Athens, where he spent much of his life, and became the first known artistic adviser to an Athenian politician—Cimon, whom he recognized as his patron. Cimon was the dominant political figure in Athens from the late 470's to 461, and it was undoubtedly through his influence that Polygnotus became an Athenian citizen, a rare honor. Cimon's free-spirited sister, Elpinice, was Polygnotus' lover and model.

Polygnotus may have been persuaded to enter Cimon's service when the latter conquered Thasos, which had revolted from Athens and the Delian League in 465, but it is more likely that the association had begun in the previous decade. There is plausible evidence to suggest that Polygnotus helped decorate the Theseum in Athens, the shrine for the bones of the hero Theseus which Cimon had discovered and returned to the city in the mid-470's. The relationship could have begun as early as 479, when Polygnotus was painting in a shrine commemorating the Battle of Marathon, in which Cimon's father, Miltiades the Younger, had been the hero.

Life's Work

The destruction of Athens in 479 during the Second Persian War left the city in ruins; the necessity of rebuilding and beautifying the city provided an opportunity for artists such as Polygnotus. Polygnotus' friend Cimon was responsible for an extensive building program, and the artist was actively employed in decorating Cimon's structures. The most significant of these was the Stoa Poikile (painted stoa), which was funded by Cimon's brother-in-law and probably completed by 460. Polygnotus (who may have been the artistic director for the building) and other prominent artists created a "Cimonian" picture gallery in the Stoa Poikile, choosing mythological and historical themes which could call attention to Cimon's family and his accomplishments. Like many ancient murals, these paintings were executed not directly on the walls but on wooden panels which were pinned to the walls with iron pegs.

Polygnotus was responsible for the *Iliupersis*, a mural depicting Troy fallen. The theme evoked memories of Cimon's great victory at the Eurymedon River in Asia Minor in 469, where the Athenian general had inflicted so crushing a defeat upon the Persians that, at the time, it seemed as final as the legendary Greek triumph over the Trojans. Polygnotus also used the opportunity to paint the face of Elpinice on Laodice, the most prominent Trojan woman in the mural, further indication that the mural honored Cimon.

Among other works in Athens attributed to Polygnotus was a depiction of the marriage of Castor and Pollux to the daughters of Leucippus, a painting which appeared in the sanctuary of the Dioscuri, another building associated with Cimon. In the Propylaea on the Acropolis, his murals of Achilles among the virgins on Scyros and Odysseus' encounter with Nausicaa were displayed. What he painted in the Theseum cannot be determined.

Polygnotus' greatest works were not in Athens but at Delphi, in the Cnidian Lesche (clubhouse), which had been dedicated to the god Apollo by the people of Cnidus, a Greek city in Asia Minor, soon after the Battle of the Eurymedon. In that structure, the artist painted what would become the most famous murals of antiquity—the *Iliupersis* (Troy fallen), a much larger and earlier version of the painting with the same name in Athens, and the *Nekyia*, or "Odysseus' Visit to the Underworld."

The paintings were gigantic by contemporary standards and covered the interior walls of the clubhouse, which measured 55 feet long and 25 feet wide. Their dozens of mythological figures, which were arranged on at least three different levels on a surface perhaps fifteen feet tall, were almost life-sized, and the themes of the murals, like the themes of most of Polygnotus' paintings in Athens, related directly to Cimon—in this case, his victory at the Eurymedon. The Cnidians, devotees of Apollo, had themselves participated in the battle. They had been among the forces led by Cimon, whose fleet had departed for the final engagement from their harbors and whose triumph at Eurymedon guaranteed their freedom from further Persian domination. Nothing would have been more appropriate for them than to celebrate the victory by making a thank-offering to Apollo at Delphi and commissioning paintings whose symbolism would reflect favorably upon the god's agent at the battle—Cimon. The fact that Polygnotus, Cimon's close friend and client, was chosen to execute the paintings in the Cnidians' clubhouse is further evidence of the political intent of the paintings—though, politics aside, the artistic merits of the two great murals were so impressive that the artist was voted free food and lodging for life by the Amphictionic Council (the "common council" of Greece). Since Athens was a member of that council, the patriotic tradition that Polygnotus painted in the city without fee becomes understandable. He had no reason to charge, since Athens was already contributing to his upkeep, and, certainly, Cimon saw to it that his material needs were met.

Polygnotus' later life is largely a subject for conjecture. When Cimon was ostracized from Athens in 461, there is no reason to believe that the artist was adversely affected or forced to leave. He was, after all, an Athenian citizen. He may have continued to work on the Stoa Poikile; it is known that other artists who had worked on Cimonian projects or were close to Cimon were able to remain in Athens. One was the great sculptor Phidias, who became the intimate friend of Pericles, the man who had helped engineer Cimon's exile and became the single dominant politician in Athens after him. The Polygnotean paintings displayed in the Propylaea, built by Pericles in the 430's, may be indication that the artist stayed, though it is not known whether these murals were actually painted while Pericles was in power or were earlier works collected from other places and deposited there.

When and where Polygnotus died is uncertain. He held political office on Thasos sometime after 450, as did his brother Polydorus, but whether he remained there for the rest of his life cannot be determined.

Summary

Polygnotus was the first great Greek painter. A friend and client of the powerful Athenian politician Cimon, he painted murals in Athens which reflected favorably upon his patron. His *Iliupersis* and *Nekyia* at Delphi were the two most famous paintings of antiquity, and their mythological themes celebrated Cimon's crushing victory over the Persians at the Eurymedon River in 469.

Polygnotus represented a break from the conventions of earlier times, freeing painting from its archaic stiffness. He did not confine his figures to a single ground line but arranged them on several levels, scattering them about at various points in space and adding landscape elements such as rocks and trees to give an additional feeling of depth.

Among other innovations attributed to him were painting women in transparent drapery, representing their heads in multicolored headdresses, depicting the mouth open and teeth showing, and more natural treatment of the face. There was an emotional quality to his work, with figures or groups of figures reacting to events. Aristotle, at least, came close to assigning Polygnotus a didactic intent, saying that he represented men as better or more virtuous than they were and was concerned with portraying good character. Later critics maintained his greatness but considered him almost a primitive, citing his simplicity of color and lack of shading. The assertion by Cicero that Polygnotus painted in only four colors is probably erroneous. He is said to have been among the first to paint with yellow ochre.

During the early years of the Roman Empire, Quintilian averred that any serious survey of art must begin with Polygnotus, and his work was considered meritorious enough over the centuries to justify frequent restorations. Pausanias, who provides the most complete account of Polygnotus' paintings, was still impressed by them in the second century A.D., about six hundred years after they were painted. Some of Pausanius' descriptions are corroborated in the surviving work of ancient potters, who borrowed Polygnotus' themes, figure groupings, and figure poses and applied them to their own work.

Bibliography

Barron, J. P. "New Light on Old Walls: The Murals of the Theseion." *Journal of Roman Studies* 92 (1972): 20-45. A detailed discussion of the murals in the Theseum in Athens, attempting to reconstruct their content and identify who painted them. The fullest discussion of Polygnotus' role in the decoration of this building.

Jeffery, L. H. "The *Battle of Oinoe* in the Stoa Poikile: A Problem in Greek Art and History." *Annual of the British School at Athens* 60 (1965): 41-57. A discussion of the paintings in the Stoa Poikile, including Polygnotus' *Iliupersis*.

Kebric, Robert B. *The Paintings in the Cnidian Lesche at Delphi and Their Historical Context.* Leiden, Netherlands: E. J. Brill, 1983. This study is the most complete analysis of the political content of Polygnotus' major paintings and his relationship with Cimon. The major historical and chronological questions surrounding the paintings at Delphi, in particular, are discussed fully. An extensive bibliography is provided.

Meiggs, R. *The Athenian Empire.* Oxford: Clarendon Press, 1972; New York: Oxford University Press, 1979. A thorough study of the Athenian Empire which provides a detailed analysis of the period of Polygnotus' activity and of Cimonian Athens. Polygnotus himself is given a three-page treatment.

Pollitt, J. J. *The Art of Greece, 1400 B.C.-31 B.C.* Englewood Cliffs, N.J.: Prentice-Hall, 1965. An accessible sourcebook which contains relevant passages from ancient writers about Polygnotus and his work.

Robertson, Martin. *A History of Greek Art.* 2 vols. London: Cambridge University Press, 1975; New York: Cambridge University Press, 1991. This survey of ancient Greek art contains the best single introduction to Polygnotus' art and paintings.

Stansbury-O'Donnell, M. D. "Polygnotos' Iliupersis: A New Reconstruction." *American Journal of Archaeology* 93 (1989): 203-215; "Polygnotos' Nekya: A Reconstruction and Analysis." *American Journal of Archaeology* 94 (1990): 213-235. The articles suggest new reconstructions of two of Polygnotus' lost works, on the basis of a more literal reading of their descriptions by Pausanius.

Robert B. Kebric

POMPEY THE GREAT

Born: September 29, 106 B.C.; probably near Rome
Died: September 28, 48 B.C.; Pelusium, Egypt
Areas of Achievement: Government and warfare
Contribution: As a military leader and imperial proconsul, Pompey greatly extended the bounds of the Roman Empire during the late republic and, with Julius Caesar and Marcus Crassus, was one of the three leading figures whose careers and ambitions coincided with the final downfall of the Roman Republic.

Early Life

Little is known of the early years of Pompey the Great, or Gnaeus Pompeius. His family rose to prominence in Rome only during the second century B.C. and thus was not among the ancient patrician nobility. Pompey's father, Pompeius Strabo, was an ambitious and successful general during the Social War (circa 91 to 87 B.C.). As a result of his military success, Strabo extended his political influence, gaining many supporters, or *clientela*, whom he then used in advancing his own career.

The centuries-old Roman Republic was dominated by a number of ancient aristocratic families who ruled the state through the senate with individuals from the plebeian class who had achieved wealth. This government had been under tension for some time, however, as it proved to be less suitable for the great empire which Rome had become. In the resulting political instability, victorious generals and their armies often played a prominent role; Strabo, like his contemporaries Gaius Marius and Lucius Cornelius Sulla, hoped to parlay his military conquests into ruling strength. Many were relieved when he died suddenly of a plague.

Pompey had served under his father during the Social War, but after the unpopular Strabo's death, he had to forge new connections to advance his own political career. When Sulla, victorious in the east, returned to Italy at the head of his army in 83, Pompey raised an army from his own clients and took Sulla's part. After Sulla was elected dictator, Pompey divorced his first wife, Antistia, and married Sulla's stepdaughter, Aemilia. Through Sulla's influence, Pompey was given a military command to pursue opponents of the new regime. He did so, bloodily and efficiently, in Africa and Sicily. After his victories, his troops hailed him *imperator* and *magnus*, but when Sulla attempted to retire Pompey, he resisted disbanding his army. He re-turned to Rome and demanded a triumph, a recognition of his military exploits. Sulla reluctantly granted his request, and by 80 Pompey had become one of the most significant figures in the unstable landscape of republican Rome.

Because of his handsome looks, his youth, and his military accomplishments, Pompey was compared by his contemporaries to Alexander the Great, the Macedonian king who had conquered Persia and much of the known world. Yet Pompey's wars and his political machinations were directed toward placing himself among the first citizens of the Roman Republic. He was obsessively concerned with his own dignity and honor but not with absolute power for its own sake, and although he was a military hero, he often resorted to charm and tact rather than the threat of force.

Life's Work

From 80 B.C., when he was in his mid-twenties, until the end of his life, Pompey remained among the leading figures in the republic. After Sulla resigned his dictatorship, there was another period of civil

war, directed against Sulla's system of reformed oligarchy. Pompey supported the government against attack in Italy, and then he was awarded an important military command in Spain. From 76 to 72, he pursued Quintus Sertorius, who had fled Rome during the events which had brought Sulla to power and had subsequently established control over much of Spain. Pompey succeeded militarily and also added to his influence by increasing the number of his personal supporters, or clients, in Spain.

Pompey returned to find Italy in the throes of a slave uprising led by a Thracian gladiator, Spartacus. The Servile War led to several defeats of the Roman armies until Crassus took charge. Although the war was almost over when he arrived, Pompey claimed to have attained the final victory, much to the disgust of Crassus. The two rivals were elected consuls in 70 despite Pompey's youth and political inexperience; the exception was made because of his previous heroic accomplishments.

After Pompey's year as consul, he stepped down, but he remained a major figure, one of the *principes civitatis*. Then, in 67, he was granted the authority to eliminate the threat posed by pirates to Mediterranean shipping, particularly to the grain supply necessary to Roman peace and survival. Although there was considerable senate opposition to giving such power to one individual, the price of bread dropped in Rome in anticipation of Pompey's success. Beginning in the west, Pompey swept the pirates east, successfully ending the campaign in three months.

Using his still-increasing popularity and political influence, Pompey next obtained a military command against the continuing threat from Mithradates the Great, ruler of the eastern kingdom of Pontus. Again, his selection was controversial, partially because it would add to Pompey's stature and power. Turning down a peace initiative by Mithradates, Pompey pursued him ruthlessly, forcing Mithradates to retreat into the Crimea region of the Black Sea. Pompey then successfully brought the kingdom of Armenia into the Roman orbit. With the threat from Pontus and Armenia ended, Pompey turned south, into Syria, ending the Seleucid kingdom which had been founded in the aftermath of the conquests of Alexander. He conquered Jerusalem and created a client kingdom in Judaea, as he did elsewhere in the Middle East. By the time he returned to Rome in 62, Pompey had successfully extended the boundaries of the Roman Empire almost to the Euphrates River. Pompey had emulated Alexander and had justly earned the title of Pompeius Magnus, Pompey the Great.

In Rome, Pompey was awarded another triumph, during which he wore a cloak once worn by Alexander. By then, he was probably the richest individual in the empire. His conquests in the east and his wealth, however, did not easily translate into political power. The senate, led by Cato the Censor, denied his demands for rewards for his soldiers and himself. To avoid even the appearance of wishing to assume dictatorial power, Pompey disbanded his armies on reaching Italy. He divorced his wife, Mucia, on grounds of adultery, and planned to marry Cato's niece, but Cato refused to accept an alliance with someone he believed was a threat to the republic. Pompey expected honors and respect, but his return was anticlimactic.

His failure to gain senate ratification of his proposals coincided with a demand by some of Crassus' supporters for changes in the tax collection laws in the east. Pompey and Crassus had been rivals, but the senate's opposition forced the two together. Caesar, returning from campaigning in Spain, desired both a triumph in Rome and to be elected consul; his ambitions were also blocked. To gain the support of Pompey and Crassus, Caesar promised both what they had failed to receive from the senate. By the end of 60, the somewhat misleadingly named First Triumvirate had come into being; formed for practical short-term goals, it was not intended to subvert the government of the republic.

With Caesar as consul and with the public support of Pompey and Crassus, the desired legislation was passed. As a further reward, Caesar received a military command in Gaul. Yet Pompey's own popularity declined; he had returned from Asia, expecting to be accepted as Rome's principal citizen, but in order to achieve his other goals, he had been forced into an alliance with Caesar and Crassus which cast doubt on Pompey's republican patriotism. The alliance soon began to experience difficulties in Rome because of the ambitions of others, such as Clodius Pulcher. Although Pompey had to maintain the coalition for fear that his long-desired legislation might be reversed, Caesar, concerned about the possibility of Pompey's abdication, forged a new bond between them; Caesar's daughter, Julia, was married to Pompey.

Clodius soon became Pompey's chief threat. Through his own clients and his ability to manipulate the city mobs, Clodius neutralized Pompey's authority by threatening violence. Yet Pompey's successful solution to a grain shortage—perhaps the single greatest political issue in the lives of most Romans—restored much of his lost popularity by 57. When it appeared that the triumvirate might end, Pompey and Caesar met and renewed the alliance, with Pompey and Crassus becoming joint consuls for the second time in 55; they, in turn, ensured that Caesar's command in Gaul would be extended for another five years. Only with bribery and violence, however, were Pompey and Crassus able to defeat their opponents in the senate.

As a reward, Crassus gained a military command in Syria in anticipation of a war against Parthia which would add to his fame. In Rome, Pompey sponsored a large building program, culminating in the Theatrum Pompeii, Rome's first stone-built theater. The traditionalists objected to still another departure from the republican past; again, it was rumored that Pompey wished to become dictator, and again he denied it.

By 53, the triumvirate had collapsed. Julia died in childbirth, removing one bond between Pompey and Caesar, and Crassus met death in his armies' defeat by the Parthians at Carrhae. When Pompey married again, to Cornelia, daughter of Metellus Scipio, it was an alliance not with Caesar but with another ancient family. Renewed violence in Rome bolstered Pompey's position as the only person with the necessary authority who might save the state, and even Cato, defender of the republic, proposed that Pompey become sole consul in order to deal with the emergency.

In Gaul, Caesar desired a second consulship for himself, but he was unwilling to give up the military *imperium* to return to Rome in order to seek election. Pompey was not opposed to having Caesar stand for consul while still keeping his command in Gaul, but he supported legislation which might reduce the period Caesar could keep control of his province. Pompey stated that it was not directed against Caesar, but Pompey was still committed to maintaining his position as the first citizen. He had positioned himself so that Caesar depended on him for protection from the senate, and the senate depended on Pompey for protection from Caesar.

Pompey's position between Caesar and the senate was inherently unstable. In the summer of 50, Pompey suffered a serious illness, and public prayers and declarations of sympathy and gratitude at his recovery indicated to Pompey that his support was both wide and deep. When in December it was rumored that Caesar had already invaded Italy, Pompey was given the command to mobilize the necessary legions and defend the republic. He hoped that a show of strength would cause Caesar to back down, ensuring Pompey's own position of superiority. Pompey became convinced that Caesar was a threat to Rome itself, but even then Pompey hoped to avoid war; only pressure sufficient to stop Caesar, but not destroy him, would maintain Pompey's own position.

Pompey proved to be wrong on two counts: Caesar reacted more quickly than was anticipated, invading Italy in early January, 49, and Pompey's support was less than expected. In reaction to Caesar's invasion, Pompey abandoned Rome. He had not been given supreme power and continued to face the possibility of senate opposition. Both Caesar and Pompey probably wished to avoid war, but the senate, particularly Cato and his faction, opposed any compromise. In March, 49, Pompey left Italy for the east and public opinion began to turn against him. Caesar wisely pursued a policy of clemency, and some began to claim that Pompey had intended all along to establish a dictatorship on the model of Sulla.

Pompey and a majority of the senate retreated to Greece. When Caesar later arrived in Greece, Pompey had three possibilities: He could return to Italy ahead of Caesar, he could retreat and allow Caesar to exhaust his resources, or he could fight a pitched battle. Pompey's supporters demanded a confrontation, and on August 9, 48, both sides met at Pharsalus, where Caesar was victorious. Pompey fled to Egypt but on the day he landed, September 28, 48, the day before his fifty-eighth birthday, he was stabbed to death. His head was presented to Caesar, and his ashes were returned to Italy.

Summary

Two of Pompey the Great's sons continued the struggle against Caesar. After Pompey's murder, they retreated first to Africa and then to Spain, where they had much success in an area of their father's earlier conquests. The elder, Gnaeus, however, met defeat at the hands of Caesar in 45 and was executed. The younger, Sextus, continued the family's battles and survived Caesar's assassination in 44. Yet during the conflicts of the next decade, Sextus took sides against Caesar's heir, Augustus, and was eventually executed in 36.

The verdict on Pompey's career is divided between claims that both Caesar and Pompey sought the same thing—supreme power—and arguments that Pompey was the last of the republicans, a man who gave his life for the ideals of ancient Rome. Perhaps the best estimate is that Pompey was a man of his own time, reflecting the ambiguous politics of the late republic, when the institutions of the past no longer proved entirely adequate. Following the example of his father and others, he used his military conquests to influence politics. He wished to be honored as the premier citizen of Rome, but it is doubtful that he ever intended to replace the senate as the governing body of the republic. Still, Pompey's personality, his ambitions, his conquests, and his ultimate position in Roman society undoubtedly played a part in the fall of the republic.

Bibliography

Edwards, Michael. *Plutarch: The Lives of Pompey, Caesar and Cicero.* A companion to the Penguin Translation from *Fall of the Roman Republic* published in the Penguin Classics. Bristol: Bristol Classics, 1991. The book comments extensively on the major source for Pompey's life. In spite of the flattering tone of Plutarch's biography, Edwards notes, Pompey was surely cruel and vindictive in character.

Green, Peter. *Alexander to Actium: The Historical Evolution of the Hellenistic Age.* Rev. ed. Berkeley: University of California Press, 1993. This large book offers a full account of political events, including Pompey's role in them.

Greenhalgh, Peter. *Pompey: The Roman Alexander.* London: Weidenfeld and Nicolson, 1980; Columbia: University of Missouri Press, 1981. The first volume of a two-volume study of the life and times of Pompey, this work carries the subject's biography to the formation of the triple alliance between Pompey, Caesar, and Crassus. The story is presented in a theatrical style, as the author is writing for a wide audience, not simply for academic specialists.

———. *Pompey: The Republican Prince.* London: Weidenfeld and Nicolson, 1981; Columbia: University of Missouri Press, 1982. The second and concluding volume of the author's study of Pompey. Like its predecessor, it is written in dramatic form and is especially strong on Pompey's military conquests as well as on the pageant and spectacle of Rome.

Gruen, Erich S. *The Last Generation of the Roman Republic.* Berkeley: University of California Press, 1974. An important revisionist study. The author's thesis is that there was nothing inevitable about the end of the republic and that there was no predestined decline which led to the triumph of Caesar. Instead, Gruen focuses on the continuity and the traditions of the earlier republic which were still viable during Pompey's era.

Leach, John. *Pompey the Great.* London: Croom Helm, and Totowa, N.J.: Rowman and Littlefield, 1978. This brief biography praises Pompey's military abilities and accomplishments. The author also admires Pompey's political talents. Leach predicts that if Pompey had defeated Caesar, he would have more likely pursued the later path of Augustus, as *princeps*, instead of Caesar's more dangerous road to the dictatorship.

Scullard, H. H. *From the Gracchi to Nero.* 5th ed. London and New York: Methuen, 1982. One of the standard works on the late republic and the principate through Nero, this volume is scholarly but well written and naturally includes considerable information on Pompey and his peers. The author's judgment of Pompey is that he excelled in the battlefield but lacked forcefulness in the political arena, always preferring glory to power.

Seager, Robin. *Pompey: A Political Biography.* Berkeley: University of California Press, and Oxford: Blackwell, 1979. One of many biographies of Pompey, it is both brief and scholarly and concentrates primarily on the political and constitutional issues of the late republic rather than on Pompey's activities and conquests in Spain and in the east. The author maintains a balance between Pompey and Caesar in attempting to understand the motives and actions of both without praising or blaming either.

Syme, Ronald. *The Roman Revolution.* Oxford: Oxford University Press, 1939; New York: Oxford University Press, 1951. The author of this classic work on Roman history written during the twentieth century places the actions and activities of Pompey, Caesar, and Augustus in the wider context of Roman politics, including family, clan, and faction, and not simply the individual deeds and ambitions of a few at the top.

Eugene S. Larson

PORPHYRY
Malchus

Born: c. 234; Tyre, Phoenicia

Died: c. 305; probably Rome

Areas of Achievement: Philosophy and scholarship

Contribution: As the loyal and devoted disciple of Plotinus, who is credited as the founder of Neoplatonic thought, Porphyry undertook to compile and edit his master's philosophical works, the *Enneads*, and to write a unique biography of his teacher. He also wrote extensive commentaries on Greek philosophers and on the allegorical interpretation, or exegesis, of the Homeric myths.

Early Life

Porphyry was born of well-to-do Syrian parents in the Phoenician city of Tyre, where he spent most of his early years. His original name was Malchus, which in the Syro-Phoenician language signifies a king. He first Hellenized his name to Basileus, the Greek word for king. Later, at the suggestion of one of his teachers, Cassius Longinus, he changed it to Porphyry, which alludes to the royal purple color of the regal garments.

Sometime in his teens, Porphyry went to Athens to continue his education. There, he attended the lectures of the erudite critic and philosopher Cassius Longinus. From Longinus, he first learned of and was influenced by the Platonism of the time. At the age of thirty, he went to Rome to become the pupil of Plotinus. He remained with Plotinus for six years, during which time he gained his confidence and respect, enjoying prolonged private discussions with him. He was entrusted by Plotinus with the arrangement and editing of his writings. At the end of his six years with Plotinus, Porphyry suffered an acute depression and was contemplating suicide. Plotinus persuaded him to leave Rome. He traveled to Sicily and remained there for several years. He was in Sicily when Plotinus died in 270.

Life's Work

During his stay in Sicily, Porphyry wrote some of his most important philosophical works. He wrote commentaries on the Platonic and Aristotelian systems of philosophy, none of which survives. One of his works, the *Isagoge* (*The Introduction of Porphyry*, 1938), a commentary on Aristotle's *Categoriae* (fourth century B.C.; *Categories*), served as an introduction to the elementary concepts of Aristotelian logic. The *Isagoge* was translated into Latin and interpreted by the medieval philosopher and theologian Boethius. The work's views on the ontological status of universals, stated in the beginning, exercised great influence on the early medieval controversy between realism and nominalism, as well as being the subject of many commentaries. In Sicily, Porphyry also composed, in fifteen books, the polemic *Kata Christanōn* (against the Christians), written about 270. It was not a particularly philosophical work but a defensive reaction against the growing popularity of Christianity. This work was often imitated in later years, but it also provoked a number of Christian replies and brought upon Porphyry much slander and verbal abuse.

Very little is known of the remainder of Porphyry's life. He returned to Rome several years after the death of Plotinus, supposedly to take over Plotinus' school. It was in Rome that he edited the works of Plotinus, wrote his biography, and gained a reputation as teacher and public speaker by his expositions of Plotinus' thought. At the advanced age of seventy, circa 304, he married Marcella, the widow of a friend with seven children. As he states in *Pros Markellan* (*Porphyry, the Philosopher, to His Wife, Marcella*, 1896; better known as *Ad Marcellam*), the letter he sent to his wife while on a trip away from home, they married so that he could help to rear and educate her children.

Porphyry was very successful in popularizing the thought of Plotinus and in expounding it in a clear, concise, comprehensible manner. It was the Porphyrian version of Neoplatonism that influenced Western thought, both pagan and Christian, until the ninth century. His views are basically those of his master Plotinus. History does not credit Porphyry with any original views. Still, Porphyry did not follow Plotinus slavishly. The main emphasis of his thought was on the salvation, or ascent, of the individual soul, and he wanted to find a universal way of salvation that could be practiced by all individuals. Thus, he placed a greater emphasis on the moral and ascetic aspects of Neoplatonism, was much more interested in the popular religious practices than his master, and introduced the idea of theurgy into Neoplatonism. Porphyry's views on the ascent of the soul are found in the following works: *Aphormai pros ta noēta* (*Auxiliaries to the*

Perception of Intelligible Natures, 1823; better known as *Sententiae*), a disjointed collection of ideas; *Peri apochēs empsychōn* (*On Abstinence from Animal Food*, 1823; better known as *De abstinentia*), a treatise defending vegetarianism; and the *Ad Marcellam*, which deals with the practice of virtue and self-control.

Like Plotinus, Porphyry believed that the soul of an individual is of divine origin and has fallen into matter—the body. While in the body, the soul must purify itself by turning its attention from the bodily and material things to contemplation of the absolute supreme deity—the One, or God. Contemplation, or love of God, cannot be combined with concern for or love of the body. Thus, the soul must purify itself by liberating itself from the bonds of the body. This liberation is not attained by death only but by freeing the soul from its bodily concerns. The soul's purification is achieved through the practice of the virtues. Systematizing Plotinus' treatise on the virtues, Porphyry classifies them into four main types: the political (or civic), the purifying, the contemplative, and the paradigmatic. The political/civic and purifying virtues are acquired on the conscious level, while the soul is still aware of and concerned with matters of the material world, and are preparatory to the other virtues, which are acquired purely through the intellect, when the soul has entered the realm of true being or intellect.

The first and lowest class of virtues, the political/civic, produce moderation and free the soul from excessive bodily concern and indulgences, tempering the individual's behavior toward his fellow humans. Mastery of that leads to the purifying virtues. These virtues completely free the body from all bodily and material attachments and lead the soul toward contemplation of true being. Porphyry believed that the soul's purification and ascent were facilitated by the practice of asceticism. In *De abstinentia*, he stressed the abstinence from animal food, as well as from all external pleasures and desires, and the practice of celibacy. At the third stage of the ascent, the soul is directed toward the world of the intellect, is filled by it and guided by it; the soul has realized its true self, its divinity. Finally, in the fourth and last stage, the soul completely discards all the qualities of a mortal or material nature and its affection for them and becomes pure intellect, living by reason alone and becoming one with the supreme being: God.

Porphyry believed that philosophy was the best means by which the soul could achieve salvation.

Yet he realized that the discipline of philosophy as a means of salvation was not possible for all. His interest in and search for a universal way of salvation common to all nations and levels of mankind led him to accept external aids that would lead an individual to that end. He acknowledged the religious practices, rites, and superstitions of the popular polytheism of the time and accepted their gods as symbols, giving their myths an esoteric interpretation. Unlike his master, Plotinus, he upheld the worship of the national gods, claiming that it is important to show respect for the ancient religious practice of a nation.

The early centuries of the Christian era were times of increasing insecurity and anxiety that led individuals to long for salvation, a release from the misery and failure of human life. People turned to the practice of magic and the utterances of the oracles or inspired prophets for answers to their everyday concerns and solutions to their spiritual needs. Astrology and the mystery cults with their purification rites, their enthusiasm and ecstasy, and their rewards of immortality through deification enjoyed immense popularity. The Chaldaean Oracles in particular, composed about A.D. 200 in hexameter verse, were purported to be a divine revelation containing both a theology and a way of salvation communicated by the gods through an entranced medium or prophet. They presented a sure method of salvation through ritual magic, by means of which a divine force could be incarnated in a human being, resulting in a state of prophetic trance. This approach to salvation and union with the divine was known as theurgy. Porphyry acknowledged theurgy as an alternative approach to salvation. Theurgy became one of the major influences in the development of later Neoplatonism from the time of Porphyry to the eleventh century. Porphyry believed that theurgy had some validity and in some way connected the individual with the gods—but only on the lower, or conscious, level. Remaining basically loyal to the philosophy of Plotinus, Porphyry maintained that it is only philosophy that can lead the soul to final union with God.

Summary

Although Porphyry has been considered an unoriginal and uncritical thinker, his contributions to learning are far from insignificant. He had an insatiable intellectual curiosity and thirst for knowledge that led him to delve into and become well-versed in many subjects. In addition to the preservation and intelligible interpretation of Neoplatonism, his main contribution, Porphyry wrote on numerous and varied subjects: rhetoric, grammar, numbers, geometry, music, philology, and philosophy. History credits him with seventy-seven titles. Unfortunately, many of his works are either no longer extant or available only in scanty fragments. Being a detailed scholar, he quotes his authorities by name in his works and thus has preserved numerous fragments of scholarship that otherwise would not have been maintained.

His *Isagoge* became a standard medieval textbook of logic. Of his non-philosophical works, *Homērika zētēmata* (Homeric questions) is considered a milestone in the history of Homeric scholarship concerning the meaning and exegesis of the Homeric works and reveals his vast knowledge of the epics. The essay on the Homeric cave of the nymphs in the *Odyssey* (c. 800 B.C.) is an excellent example of the type of mystical allegorizing of the Homeric epics that was prevalent at the time and is the oldest surviving interpretive critical essay. In the field of religion, his polemic against the Christians is a study in biblical criticism that was not equaled until modern times, and he anticipated modern scholars in discovering the late date of the biblical Books of Daniel through sound historical scholarship. Although the text was condemned by the Christian church in 448, sufficient fragments remain to show Porphyry's expert knowledge of Hebrew and his wide and accurate knowledge of both Hebrew and Christian Scriptures. Applying the standards of historical criticism to the Scriptures, he denied the authenticity and prophetic character of the Book of Daniel, disputed the authorship of the Pentateuch, and pointed out the discrepancies within the different Gospel narratives and the Epistles of Saint Paul. He is believed to have been the first individual to apply the rules of historical criticism to the Scriptures.

Porphyry stands at the end of the creative phase of Greek philosophical thought. After him, Neoplatonism became more a religion than a philosophy. In an attempt to rescue pagan religion and culture from the overwhelming strength of Christianity, Neoplatonism sacrificed Greek rationalism for occult magico-religious practices which were meant to secure the salvation of the soul.

Bibliography

Lamberton, Robert. *Homer the Theologian.* Berkeley: University of California Press, 1986; London: University of California Press, 1989. Contains an excellent study of Porphyry's work on the Homeric epics. It analyzes in detail the surviving fragments of *Homērika zētēmata* and presents an in-depth study of Porphyry's essay on the cave of the nymphs. An unusual study, because most studies on Porphyry deal only with his philosophical work.

Porphyry. *Life of Plotinus.* Edited and translated by A. H. Armstrong. London: Heinemann, 1966. A major source of information for the life of Porphyry, this work is part of the Loeb Classical Library. Although primarily a biography of Plotinus, it contains many facts of Porphyry's own early life and discusses his association with Plotinus and with Longinus. It also presents an interesting profile of Porphyry's personality.

————. *On the Cave of the Nymphs.* Translated by Robert Lamberton. Barrytown, N.Y.: Station Hill Press, 1983. An example of Porphyry's method of allegorically interpreting the poetic mythology current at that time. The work is a mystical interpretation of the cave of the nymphs in Homer's *Odyssey.* This work is important not only because it demonstrates the mystical allegorical reading of Homer at that time but also because it is the oldest surviving commentary on a literary text.

————. *Porphyry, the Philosopher, to His Wife, Marcella.* Translated by Alice Zimmern. London: George Redway, 1896. An old work, but invaluable. It is the only translation of Porphyry's *Ad Marcellam* in English. The lengthy introduction, comprising more than half of the book, includes a summary of the development of Neoplatonism, a review of Porphyry's emphases, and a discussion of the letter to Marcella, showing its religious character and its emphasis on the practice of virtue.

Smith, Andrew. *Porphyry's Place in the Neoplatonic Tradition.* The Hague: Martinus Nijhoff, 1974. A study in post-Plotinian Neoplatonism. It presents an analysis of Porphyry's views of the soul and its means of salvation and compares them with those of Plotinus and Iamblichus, Plotinus' pupil and successor. There is an extensive bibliography of ancient and modern sources and an appendix listing the works of Porphyry relevant to the doctrine of the soul.

Antonía Tripolitis

POSIDONIUS

Born: c. 135 B.C.; Apamea of the Orontes, Syria
Died: c. 51. B.C.; Rome
Area of Achievement: Philosophy
Contribution: Though virtually none of his writings survives, it is clear that Posidonius was one of the most influential thinkers of the ancient world. He made important contributions in the fields of philosophy, history, astronomy, mathematics, natural history, and geography.

Early Life

Posidonius was born in Syria around 135 B.C. Some ancient writers refer to him as "The Apamean," from his birthplace in Syria, which, at that time, was part of the Roman Empire. This vast empire had greatly facilitated the international exchange of knowledge. The dominant philosophy which emerged under the empire was Stoicism, named for the *stoa poikile* (the "painted porch") of the building in Athens where the originators of the doctrine taught. The earliest expression of Stoic philosophy comes from Zeno of Citium (c. 335-261) in Cyprus and Cleanthes of Assos (c. 331-c. 232) in Asia Minor; they were of the Early Stoa, the first period of this doctrine, which lasted from 300 B.C. to the beginning of the second century B.C. The thinkers of the Middle Stoa introduced this philosophy to Roman culture during the second and first centuries B.C. Panaetius of Rhodes (185-109) and his prize student, Posidonius, were the most important figures of the Middle Stoa. Though Stoicism was to remain the dominant philosophy until the second century A.D., Posidonius was the last of the Greek Stoic philosophers.

Posidonius left his home country early in his life and traveled to Athens, where he studied philosophy under Panaetius. After his teacher died in 109, Posidonius traveled for several years throughout North Africa and the western Mediterranean, including Spain, Italy, and Sicily. During these travels he conducted extensive scientific research. He returned to Greece and settled in Rhodes, the largest island in the Dodecanese group, off the southwest coast of Asia Minor. In Rhodes, he was appointed head of the academy which he would later make the center of Stoic philosophy. Posidonius also became involved in local politics and influenced the course of legislation on more than one occasion. In 87, the Rhodians sent him as an envoy to Rome with the charge of appeasing Gaius Mari-

us. The result of this visit was that Posidonius developed an extreme dislike for Marius and later heavily criticized him in his historical writings.

The Stoic philosophy which Posidonius studied at Athens and taught at Rhodes consisted of three domains of concern: logic, physics, and ethics. Stoic logic included the study of grammar but emphasized the formal nature of reasoning, that is, relations between words, not between words and what they stand for. The relations in rational discourse (as studied by logic) were regarded as reflecting the processes of the cosmos (as studied by physics). The dominant theme of Stoic physical theory was that the universe is an intelligent living being. The physical theory of the Stoics was equivalent to their theology, for the rational totality was equated with God, Zeus, the logos, or the ordering principles of the universe (all these terms being synonymous within their philosophy). In the physical theory of the Stoics, matter is inert or passive and is acted upon by God, the rational active cause. All gradations of being in the universe were regarded as having been formed by this action. According to this philosophy, the action of the rational cause upon the matter is cyclical. Throughout the aeons, each cycle begins with the pure active cause organizing the four fundamental elements and ends with a universal conflagration in which all created matter is consumed and the totality reverts to its purified state. Stoic ethical doctrines were perhaps the most famous element of their philosophy and were connected to their cosmological conceptions.

The basic precept of the Stoic ethical system was to live according to the order of the universe. The ultimate goal of ethical action was to achieve self-sufficiency, the only guarantee of happiness. Happiness was regarded as possible only through that which was entirely within the individual's control, and this state was to be achieved through the practice of the virtues. The most important of the virtues were wisdom, courage, justice, and self-control. The Stoics emphasized two ways of acquiring the virtues: the imitation of exemplary lives and the study of ethics and physics.

It was in the context of these broad doctrines that Posidonius developed his conceptions of man and the universe. Though only a few fragments of Posidonius' writings have survived, he is mentioned by more than sixty ancient writers, and it is through their comments that scholars have been able to reconstruct his philosophy. He is mentioned primarily in the works of Cicero, Strabo, Seneca, and Galen.

Posidonius differed from the Stoic tradition in which he was educated in his concern with empirically oriented scientific investigations. He did, however, adhere to the Stoic division of philosophy into the branches of logic (or dialectics), ethics, and physics. His teacher, Panaetius, admired Plato, and it was with the development of Posidonius' philosophy that the influence of Plato upon Stoicism truly began. Posidonius also emphasized his agreement with the doctrines of Pythagoras, and, in general, he argued for the reconciliation of all opposing philosophies.

Life's Work

While developing his own version of Stoic philosophy at his academy in Rhodes, Posidonius became quite famous. In 78, the famous Roman orator Cicero attended his school. In fact, Cicero requested of Posidonius that he edit his account (in Greek) of the conspiracy of Catiline. Posidonius declined the request.

Posidonius' most famous visitor was the Roman general Pompey the Great, who visited Posidonius' school on two different occasions in order to attend lectures: in 72, when Pompey returned from the eastern part of the empire after action in the Mithradatic War, and again five years later, after a victorious campaign against pirates in the Mediterranean Sea. As a gesture of respect for the great philosopher, Pompey ordered his officers to lower their fasces (bundles of rods with axes in them, which were used as scepters by Roman leaders) at the door of Posidonius' school. Posidonius greatly admired Pompey and added an appendix to his *Histories*, which was devoted exclusively to Pompey's campaigns in the East.

Posidonius' history of the world began with the year 146 B.C. (the point at which the famous history of Polybius ended) and continued up to the dictatorship of Lucius Cornelius Sulla around 88 B.C. Virtually none of this work has survived, but its influence was tremendous, both at the theoretical level (that is, in the conception of history) and in terms of the sheer mass of factual information which the work contained. All the following historians were influenced by it: Sallust, Julius Caesar, Cornelius Tacitus, Plutarch, Timagenes, Pompeius Trogus, and Diodorus Siculus. Posidonius' *Histo-*

ries was noteworthy for including the histories of the Eastern and Western peoples with whom the Romans had come into contact, such as the Germans and the Gauls. His study of primitive cultures led him to hypothesize that these cultures represented the original state of the more advanced cultures. The work was written from a standpoint which favored the nobility and opposed the Gracchi and the equestrian party. It was also opposed to the independent Greeks, who were supported by Mithradates. In short, the work was strongly proRoman, and in it Posidonius attempted to show that Roman imperialism embodied the commonwealth of all mankind and ultimately reflected the commonwealth of God. To this latter commonwealth only those statesmen and philosophers who had lived worthy lives were to be admitted after their stay on earth. In addition, Posidonius argued that lesser civilizations should accept and even welcome Roman domination for the sake of their own self-betterment. This theory had a tremendous influence upon Cicero and provided the foundations for the eventual development of the doctrine of natural law.

Posidonius' conception of the history of the human race was intimately linked to his conceptions of ethics. Politics and ethics were fused within his system, since political virtue consisted in attempting to bring back the natural condition of humanity. In this condition, the philosopher-statesman apprehends the world of God (from which morality is derived) and conveys this vision to the rest of humanity living solely in the material world. Morality and religion were fused in Posidonius' view, since any moral or political duty was also a religious duty. In a work entitled *On Duty*, Posidonius argued that by adhering to duty, the philosopher-statesman gained knowledge of the spiritual world and freedom and was prepared for the superior forms of existence after death. The highest state to be achieved by a man in this life was regarded by Posidonius as contemplation of the truth and order of the universe (without distraction by the promptings of the irrational part of the soul). Posidonius parted with Stoic orthodoxy on the connection between virtue and happiness, however, and argued that the former was not a sufficient condition for the latter and that external bodily goods were also needed to achieve happiness.

Posidonius also made modifications of Stoic psychological doctrines. The most significant of these was his reaffirmation, in *On the Soul*, of the division of the soul into rational and irrational parts (the latter being the source of the emotions and appetites). Stoic tradition held to the essential unity of the soul. Posidonius claimed, in *On Emotion*, that the emotions of the irrational part of the soul have two distinct origins: the body, and judgments of good and evil. He took as evidence for this view the fact that animals, which are irrational creatures, experience emotion. This doctrine also parted from the standard Stoic conception of emotion as based solely on false judgments about good and evil. In this theory, Posidonius drew a connection between the union of the soul and the body and the external influences upon that union. He argued that some conditions of the human being are predominantly bodily, whereas others are predominantly spiritual or mental. Some influences pass from the body to the soul and others pass from the soul to the body. He based a system of character on the idea that permanent modifications of character can be caused by certain bodily organizations.

More fundamental aspects of Posidonius' psychology are contained in his metaphysical system, in which he followed the standard Stoic conception of two fundamental principles governing the universe: the passive principle (matter) and the active principle (God). God, for Posidonius, did not create the human soul, though the soul was believed to be composed of the same stuff out of which the heavenly bodies are composed. As a result, upon the death of the body the soul "escapes" and returns to the heavens. In addition, for Posidonius, God was not the creator of matter, and matter was endowed with its own form and quality. The divine principle merely shaped and modeled this matter (that is, God does not endow matter with form). As part of this cosmology, Posidonius posited, in *On Heroes and Daemones*, the existence of beings which were intermediary between God and man. These beings were regarded as immortal and were revealed to mortals in visions, divinations, and oracles. Posidonius also regarded the gap between reason and matter as bridged by mathematical forms. Of all the Stoics, only Posidonius was a realist with regard to mathematical entities. In *On the Void*, he argued that the vacuum beyond the universe was not infinite (a standard Stoic conception) but only large enough to allow for the periodic dissolution of the universe. He also argued that the end of the universe would occur not by fire but by this dissolution.

Among the scientific achievements of Posidonius which were related to his metaphysics was his construction of a model of the celestial system. This planetarium allowed the apparent motions of the sun, moon, and planets around the earth to be exhibited. An important inference he made concerning astronomy, in a work entitled *On the Sun*, was that the sun is larger than the earth because the shadow cast by the earth is conical. He rejected the heliocentric conception of the solar system in favor of a geocentric conception. He also succeeded in calculating the distance between the earth and the sun at 502 million stadia (one stadium equals approximately six hundred feet). The diameter of the sun he calculated at four million stadia, and the circumference of the earth at 180,000 stadia, figures that were generally accepted by thinkers in his day. Posidonius also considered the moon to be larger than the earth and to be composed of matter that is transparent. Because of the moon's size, light does not pass through it during eclipses. In another work on astronomy, *On Astronomical Phenomena*, Posidonius argued that the Milky Way is composed of igneous material and is intended to warm those parts of the universe which the sun cannot warm.

This view was also widely accepted by other thinkers. He had collected considerable geographical data on his various travels, and in *On the Ocean* he charted the currents of the ocean and pointed out the connection between the tides and the moons.

In about 51 B.C., Posidonius left Rhodes on another trip to Rome, where he died soon after arriving. Upon his death, the school in Rhodes was taken over by his grandson Jason.

Summary

Posidonius had an extremely influential personality—he was reported to have a good sense of humor and was known as a man of dignity. He also developed a reputation as the most learned man in the world and was especially known for his dialectical skills, shrewd powers of observation, and love of poetry. Though he was extremely influential in his own time and for two centuries afterward, his writings disappeared at some point and he is not mentioned after the second century A.D. Virtually all the important Roman philosophers and historians were influenced by Posidonius. His disciples and students included Phanias, Asclepiodotus, C. Velleins, C. Cotta, Q. Lucilius Balbus, and perhaps Marcus Junius Brutus. His influence on thought in the ancient world has been compared to that of Aristotle. He was the last compiler of the Greco-Roman heritage, furthered the development of Greek rationalism, and was influential in the development of Neoplatonism. Nevertheless from the Renaissance through the nineteenth century, Posidonius was considered to be only a minor figure in the history of Stoicism. It was not until the beginning of the twentieth century that his influence was attested and classicists began to discover references to Posidonius in many of the writers of his time.

Bibliography

Dobson, J. F. "The Posidonius Myth." *Classical Quarterly* 12 (1918): 179-191. Attacks the source criticism method of assessing Posidonius' influence, suggesting that Posidonius' achievements have been exaggerated.

Edelstein, Ludwig. "The Philosophical System of Posidonius." *American Journal of Philology* 57 (1936): 286-325. Reconstructs the philosophical system of Posidonius from the existing fragments. Written by the foremost authority on Posidonius of the twentieth century.

Kidd, I. G. "Posidonius as Philosopher-Historian." In *Philosophia Togata: Essays on Philosophy and Roman Society*. Miriam Griffin and Jonathan Barnes, eds. Oxford: Clarendon Press, and New York: Oxford University Press, 1989. Being the editor of Posidonius' Greek fragments, Kidd is a leading authority on the philosopher. This essay is on Posidonius' no longer extant *History*, a continuation of Polybius.

———. "Posidonius on Emotions." In *Problems in Stoicism*, edited by A. A. Long. London: Athlone Press, 1971; Atlantic Highlands, N.J.: Athlone Press, 1996. Contains a detailed analysis of Posidonius' modification of the standard Stoic conception of the emotions.

Mattingly, John Robert. "Cosmogony and Stereometry in Posidonian Physics." *Osiris* 3 (1937): 558-583. Contains an extensive explication of the cosmological system developed by Posidonius.

Rist, John Michael. *Stoic Philosophy*. London: Cambridge University Press, 1969; New York: Cambridge University Press, 1990. Contains a chapter devoted to the ethical system of Posidonius.

Solmsen, Friedrich. *Cleanthes or Posidonius? The Basis of Stoic Physics*. Amsterdam, Netherlands: Noord-Hollandsche Uitg. Mij., 1961. The best available discussion of the relative influence of Cleanthes and Posidonius on developments in Stoic thought concerning science and the relation between science and the cosmos.

Mark Pestana

PRAXITELES

Born: c. 390 B.C.; Athens, Greece
Died: c. 330 B.C.; place unknown
Area of Achievement: Art
Contribution: The subtle expression of personal emotions, such as tenderness and laziness, through marble statuary is the trademark of Praxiteles. His most famous work, the *Aphrodite of Knidos*, established Western civilization's standard of perfection in the female figure.

Early Life

Although very little is known of his early life, Praxiteles came from a long line of Greek sculptors. His grandfather and father were both sculptors, as were his two sons and perhaps a nephew. At least seven of the line were also named Praxiteles.

Praxiteles' father was the Athenian sculptor Kephisodotos (sometimes spelled Cephisodotus), whose most famous sculpture is entitled *Peace and Wealth*. The original statue, which was probably erected soon after Athens' victory over Sparta in 375 B.C., depicts a mother, the goddess Peace, fondly holding her infant son, Wealth. The tenderness of the mother and the playfulness of the child display a marked departure from earlier Greek statues, which expressed such public virtues as courage and honor. Also, the subject, a family scene, is very different from the usual subjects of Olympian gods and heroic humans. Praxiteles carried on and far surpassed the subtler, intimate tradition established by his father.

In addition to *Peace and Wealth*, Kephisodotos carved another statue, *Hermes Carrying the Infant Dionysus*, which had a more direct effect on the son. Kephisodotos' *Hermes* and Praxiteles' *Hermes* share both subject matter and arrangement. Although the original is lost, the fact that there are several Roman copies attests the popularity of Kephisodotos' statue. On the other hand, most historians agree that the *Hermes* found in the Olympia excavations is indeed the original work of the son. Fortunately, the condition of the statue is quite good, as it is missing only the right forearm and the two legs below the knee. Since the *Hermes* is the most muscular of Praxiteles' known statues, it is probably an early work. The smooth, sensuous young men appear to belong to a later period, during which Praxiteles was sculpting his famous female figures.

No statues of Praxiteles can be dated with absolute certainty, but his major works were carved between about 370 and 330. Early, dated works include portions of the *Altar of Artemis* at Ephesus, which was begun around 356, and the *Artemis at Brauron*, around 346.

Life's Work

Although ancient writers mention almost sixty works by Praxiteles, the surviving originals include only three heads and the major portion of one statue, the aforementioned *Hermes*. The *Hermes* was found on May 8, 1877, at the temple of Hera at Olympia. In Greek legend, Hermes, the messenger of the gods, is charged with taking young Dionysus back to the nymphs of Crete. Dionysus is a great embarrassment to Zeus, as the baby is the result of Zeus's indiscretion with a human woman. In banishing Dionysus to Crete, Zeus hopes to escape the jealousy of his wife, Hera. In Praxiteles' conception, the statue is a masterpiece of psychological complexity. Hermes, gazing tenderly at the young god, is clearly in no hurry to leave Olympus. Leaning lightly against a tree, he has placed the babe in his left arm and amuses himself by dangling in his right hand something, probably a bunch of grapes, for Dionysus. The fact that the infant Dionysus, who is eagerly grabbing at the grapes, will grow up to be the god of wine and intoxication is evidence of Praxiteles' urbane sense of humor.

Another statue which illustrates the Praxitelean sense of humor is the *Apollo Sauroctonos*, or *Lizard Slayer*. Here Praxiteles makes fun of the Greek legend in which the fierce young sun god Apollo slays Pythus, a firebreathing dragon, in order to win control of Delphi. Leaning dreamily against a tree trunk and holding an arrow in his right hand, Praxiteles' Apollo seems to have barely enough energy to swat an everyday lizard which is climbing up the trunk. While the original bronze statue is lost, reproductions occur on the coins of several city-states and in several Roman replicas, notably a marble statue in the Louvre and one in the Vatican.

Related to the *Lizard Slayer* in stance is the *Satyr*. Both statues bear Praxiteles' personal stamp. In fifth century statuary, satyrs were savage half-goat, half-man beasts with large tails and devilish eyes. Praxiteles' satyr is instead a strong and active youth with pointed ears and a small stub of a tail.

There is in his face, however, a strong sensual expression which suggests that some of the old animal instinct still lingers.

The original *Satyr* of Praxiteles, which stood in a temple of Dionysus at Athens, was a favorite collector's piece among the Romans, as more than seventy copies still exist. One of the best is the copy in the Capitol Museum in Rome. It is this statue that Nathaniel Hawthorne saw in 1858 and that inspired him to write his novel *The Marble Faun* (1860). Hawthorne, intrigued by the possibility of a real man who actually embodied all the characteristics he saw in the faun or satyr, created a character whose combination of total innocence and animalistic instincts made him unprepared to exist in the real world. The Louvre has a fragmentary version of the *Satyr*, but the execution of that statue is generally considered to be quite good. A few writers have theorized that it might be the original. Although the *Satyr* in the Capitol is complete, it is clearly a Roman copy.

Evidence that the *Satyr* was one of Praxiteles' personal favorites is related by the ancient historian Pausanias. According to the story, Phryne, Praxiteles' mistress, asked for the most beautiful of the sculptor's works. Praxiteles agreed, but he refused to say which one of his works he thought the most beautiful. Phryne secretly arranged for one of her slaves to run in and declare that Praxiteles' studio was on fire. On hearing the news, Praxiteles ran for the door, claiming that all of his labor was lost if the flames had taken the *Satyr* and *Eros*.

Phryne chose the *Eros*, god of love, and gave it to her native town of Thespiae in Boeotia. This statue made Thespiae famous. Unfortunately, the very popularity of the statue may have led to its destruction. Pausanias explains that the Roman emperor Gaius (Caligula) took it, but when Claudius assumed power, he restored the sacred statue to Thespiae. Then the Emperor Nero took it away a second time. Pausanias believes that the *Eros* eventually perished by fire in Rome. On the other hand, some art historians theorize that the *Eros* of Thespiae may survive in a headless statue which was excavated from the Palatine in Rome and is now held in the Louvre. Others have speculated that a torso in the Museum of Parma may, in fact, be the original.

What is certain is that the *Eros* once more illustrates Praxiteles' distinctive style. As Greek legend developed over the centuries, the character of Eros grew younger. In his *Theogony* (c. 700 B.C.), He-siod describes Eros as one of the oldest gods. In that version, Eros comes into existence before Aphrodite and even accompanies her at her birth form the sea to Mount Olympus. After Praxiteles, third century artists would conceive of Eros as the child of, rather than the companion to, Aphrodite. Eventually, the child becomes a mischievous, winged baby, the Cupid on a Valentine's Day card. In the Praxitelean conception, Eros stands between those surface interpretations. He is a delicate, dreamy youth, symbolizing the power of love to capture the soul, a fitting gift from the artist to his mistress.

All the works discussed have been statues depicting male figures. Yet it is Praxiteles' conception of the female form for which he is best known and most admired. His most celebrated work was the *Aphrodite of Knidos*, for which Phryne was the model. About 360, the city of Kos commissioned the sculptor to carve an *Aphrodite*, but the citizens were scandalized when they found that their statue of Aphrodite was nude. Praxiteles then made a clothed goddess of love, but the city of Knidos (sometimes spelled Knidus or Cnidus) was delighted to buy the nude *Aphrodite*. It was an enormously popular statue. Tourists came from all over the Mediterranean to see the work of Parian marble, and the elder Pliny pronounced it the finest statue yet made in Greece. King Nicomedes of Bithynia offered to buy the statue and in return excuse the city's huge public debt, but the Knidians refused. A number of ancient poets composed verses honoring the statue, the legend has it that men were crazed with desire upon viewing it.

The statue, which is thought to have been the first free-standing female nude, was put in an open shrine so that the goddess could be seen and admired from all sides. *Aphrodite* stands in a graceful pose, one hand held in front of her, the other grasping her drapery which falls on a water jar. The goddess is represented at the moment that she steps into her bath. Her gaze is turned to the left, supposedly to see an intruder. Only her right hand makes any effort to cover up and the slight smile displays a hint of welcome.

Reproductions of the *Aphrodite* are found on Roman coins of Knidos as well as in small, practically complete statuettes. The best replicas of the head are those in the Louvre and in Toulouse. Full-sized Roman copies exist in the Vatican, Brussels, and Munich museums, the most-often photographed and reprinted one being the Vatican version.

As a result of the *Aphrodite of Knidos* and other sculptures of Aphrodite by Praxiteles, the nude female figure became one of the most common forms of statuary, but the goddess was increasingly portrayed as a mortal. One example is the statue entitled *Venus of Medici*, which may have been carved by Kephisodotos and Timarchos, the sons of Praxiteles, but here the magnificent Praxitelean ideal woman has been transformed into a mere coquette.

Summary

Coming from a long line of sculptors, Praxiteles stands at the climax of a family of distinguished artists. Inspired by his father's softer, subtler treatment of subjects that the fifth century artists had treated with monumental but impersonal dignity, Praxiteles imbued statues with psychological complexities which give his work its universal appeal. The fleet-footed Hermes pauses for a moment of tenderness, the infant Dionysus turns greedy, the mature Eros becomes a sensual young man, and the heroic Apollo loses his fighting spirit so that he seems to lack the energy even to engage in lizard slaying, a popular Mediterranean boy's sport.

The crowning achievement of Praxiteles' work is his series of Aphrodites, especially the famous nude which he sold to the Knidians. The fifth century sculptors tended to carve nude males and clothed females. For example, the *Peace* by Kephisodotos is weighted down with heavy drapery. Praxiteles' female nude created a sensation and a whole new style of artistic expression. The intricately worked hair, the finely chiseled facial features with their play of emotions, and the perfectly proportioned body of the *Aphrodite of Knidos* set the standard for female beauty. Although Praxiteles did not invent the concept of a statue's standing free in order to be seen in a three-dimensional space, the success of the *Aphrodite*'s backside (her dimpled buttocks were especially admired) inspired other artists to carve free-standing nude females also.

Another Praxitelean innovation, although certainly not an invention, was the expanded employment of the S-curve or *contrapposto* for the body outline, which allows for a more natural, animated stance. The S-curve allows the *Apollo Sauroktonos* to lean casually against his tree trunk and the *Hermes* to hold the babe in one arm while he raises the other arm over his head.

Also, the surface of Praxitelean statues was technically outstanding. Ancient writers who saw the original, painted statues remarked that the body surfaces were smoothly polished and that the modeling of the hair was particularly realistic. Unfortunately, the *Hermes* is the only fairly complete work that can be taken to be an original, and many historians and archaeologists dispute even that attribution. It is so far superior to any of the Roman copies of other works by Praxiteles that the more admired original statues must have been exquisite indeed.

The many facets of Praxiteles' work meant that his work was difficult to copy accurately. While many contemporaries and the sculptors of the third and second centuries were able to capture the outward forms of the statues, they were unable to evoke the complex human emotions. The effect of the Praxitelean style in the hands of inferior artists seems to be merely mannered and elegant.

Bibliography

Ajootian, A. "Praxiteles." *Yale Classical Studies: Personal Styles in Greek Sculpture* 30 (1995): 91-129. The sculptor's known works are discussed individually. Ajootian concludes that as the attribution of the Olympian Hermes to Praxiteles remains uncertain; no clear idea of his individual artistic style can be formed.

Furtwängler, Adolf. *Masterpieces of Greek Sculpture*. Edited by A. L. N. Oikonomides. Chicago: Argonaut, 1964. Takes a close look at the original monuments in order to reevaluate generally held theories of attribution and dating.

Kjellberg, Ernst, and Gösta Säflund. *Greek and Roman Art: 3000 B.C. to A.D. 550*. Translated by Peter Fraser. London: Faber, and New York: Thomas Y. Crowell, 1968. Catalogs all the major examples of the Greek and Roman art forms. Dates, sizes, and describes included works.

Paris, Pierre. *Manual of Ancient Sculpture*. Edited by Jane E. Harrison. London: Grevel, and Philadelphia: Lippincott, 1890. Chapter on Scopas and Praxiteles discusses the works of both sculptors at length. Of particular interest is a reproduction of the *Aphrodite of Knidos* seen on a Knidian coin.

Pollitt, J. J. *Art and Experience in Classical Greece*. Cambridge: Cambridge University Press, 1972. Focuses on the period between c. 480 and 323 B.C. and seeks to integrate art styles with historical experience. Particularly useful in describing the emotional states depicted in various statues by Praxiteles.

Richter, Gisela. *A Handbook of Greek Art*. 9th ed. New York: Da Capo, and Oxford: Phaidon, 1987. For many years curator of Greek and Roman art in the Metropolitan Museum in New York, Richter presents one of the most authoritative accounts of Greek architecture and sculpture. Traces the historical evolution of Greek sculpture and adds biographical information wherever possible. Includes extensive bibliography and lucid chronology.

————. *The Sculpture and Sculptors of the Greeks*. 4th ed. New Haven, Conn.: Yale University Press, 1970. Contains a consecutive, chronological study of the human figure, drapery, and composition. Includes extensive footnotes and bibliography.

Stewart, Andrew. *Greek Sculpture: An Exploration*. 2 vols. New Haven, Conn.: Yale University Press, 1990. This is the latest general handbook on Greek sculpture. In the systematic section, Praxiteles is discussed within the context of Late Classical Athenian art. The biographical section lists all of his known works and quotes the most important passages on him by ancient authors.

Walston, Charles. "Praxiteles and the Hermes with the Infant Dionysus." In *The Art of Pheidias*. Cambridge: Cambridge University Press, and New York: The Century Co., 1885. Published only seven years after the discovery of the *Hermes*, this article contains an in-depth study of the state of the statue when it was first excavated, its importance to the Greeks for whom it was carved, and its relation to other sculptors' versions of the messenger god.

Sandra Hanby Harris

PRISCILLIAN

Born: c. 340; Spain
Died: 385; Trier
Area of Achievement: Religion
Contribution: Priscillian provides an example not only of the popularity of ascetic practices in the Christian church but also of what can happen when such activities are carried to extremes and challenge established Church beliefs and lines of authority.

Early Life

The latter half of the fourth century was a great age of Christian ascetics. These individuals withdrew from the secular world and practiced a life of fasting, deprivation, nightly vigils, and spiritual contemplation. Churchmen such as Saint Antony in Egypt, Saint Martin of Tours in Gaul, Saint Jerome in Italy and Palestine, and many others popularized this style of asceticism. In theory, these practices were merely part of the ideal Christian life. Groups of ascetics could become very influential; their members often were chosen as bishops. Extreme forms of ascetism, however, especially those which rejected established church practices and teachings, were looked upon with less favor.

Priscillian was a well-educated Spanish nobleman said to have been versed in secular and Christian literature as well as in astrology and the occult. He was possessed of a keen intellect and was an eloquent speaker. After his conversion to Christianity, he, like many others of his day, adopted an ascetic life. He also claimed to have prophetic powers. He became a wandering lay preacher and assumed the title "doctor." During the 370's, he began to teach his own peculiar brand of Christianity.

Life's Work

Insight into just what Priscillian's teachings were can be gained not only from his contemporary detractors but also from eleven treatises which were first published in 1889. Although only a few of them may have been written by Priscillian himself, or by his supporter Instantius, they do reflect Priscillian's teachings. The Priscillianists were very ascetic, recommending vegetarianism and abstinence from wine. On Sundays, they fasted. They generally walked barefoot. They also were opposed to marriage and to other aspects of the organized Church. They preferred, for example, to meet in secret, either in their own country villas or in mountain retreats. They held communion outside the established Church. At some times of the year, such as during Lent and in the days before Epiphany, which was then recognized as the day of Christ's birth, they seemed simply to disappear from sight.

As to their theological beliefs, the Priscillianists had a marked preference for the New Testament and for some of the apocryphal writings, such as the lives of the apostles Peter, John, Andrew, and Thomas. They also believed in direct, divine inspiration. Aspects of Priscillian's works do in fact seem to reflect a Manichaean dualism: He distinguished, for example, between darkness and light and saw Satan not as a fallen angel but as having an independent existence. His denial of the preexistence of Christ could have been tinged with Arianism. As a result, great controversy soon arose over Priscillian's teachings and practices. The contemporary Gallic writer Sulpicius Severus, in his chronicle, noted, "there followed portentious and dangerous times of our age, in which the churches were defiled and everything was disturbed by an unaccustomed evil."

Priscillian soon gained a large following in Galicia and Lusitania (the northern and western parts of Spain). A large number of women were attracted to him; they held meetings of their own apart from the regular church services. He also was joined by two western Spanish bishops, Instantius and Salvianus. He initially was opposed, however, by more worldly bishops such as Hyginus of Cordova and, in particular, Hydatius of Emerita. Some of his detractors accused him of Manichaeanism. It also was rumored that two of his followers, the noblewoman Agape and the rhetorician Helpidius, had infected him with the Gnostic teachings of Mark of Memphis, an Egyptian who had moved to Spain. The Priscillianists soon were joined by another bishop, Symphosius of Astorga in Lusitania (modern Portugal). Hyginus of Cordova also changed his mind and withdrew his initial objections.

In 380, a council was assembled at Saragossa to consider Priscillian's case. Ten Spanish bishops attended, as well as two Gallic bishops, Delphinus of Bordeaux and Phoebadius of Agen, the latter presiding over the meeting. Priscillian himself, however, did not attend, although he did submit a written reply. The council declined to condemn him by name, although it did denounce some Priscillianist practices, such as the speaking and teaching of women in religious "conventicles" (gatherings), the activities of lay preachers, and the absence from church during Lent. Perhaps in response to the second of these, Priscillian was consecrated shortly thereafter as Bishop of Avila in Lusitania by Salvianus and Instantius. The Priscillianists then made scandalous accusations of their own against Hydatius. In 381, Priscillian's opponents, who had been joined by Bishop Ithacius of Ossonoba, appealed to the Emperor Gratian with the help of Bishop Ambrose of Milan. Gratian then issued a decree condemning "false bishops and Manichees."

Priscillian himself realized the efficacy of such a tactic, noting, "with our names disguised [Hydatius] sought a rescript against pseudobishops and Manichees, and of course obtained it, because there is no one who does not feel hatred when he hears about pseudobishops and Manichees." The Italian writer on heresies Philastrius of Brescia made similar connections, referring to the "so-to-speak ascetics in Gaul, Spain, and Aquitania, who likewise follow the most pernicious belief of the Gnostics and Manichees," despite Priscillian's own explicit anathematization of Manichaeanism.

It was a popular tactic in ecclesiastical debates of this time, however, to attempt to associate one's opponents with some other universally detested heresy. Priscillianism was related to Origenism, for example, by the Spanish writer Paulus Orosius in his *Commonitorium de errore Priscillianistarum et Origenistarum* (c. 414; reminder about the error of the Priscillianists and Origenists). Other heresies by which the Priscillianists also were accused of being influenced included Gnosticism, Montanism, Novatianism, Ophitism, Patripassianism, Photinianism, and Sabellianism.

Priscillian, Instantius, and Salvianus, though the imperial edict had not specifically named them, left Spain seeking additional support. At Eauze in southwestern Gaul, they made many converts. After being expelled from Bordeaux by Bishop Delphinus, they were received by the noblewoman Euchrotia and Procula, the widow and daughter of the professor Attius Tiro Delphidius. They then continued on to Italy. At Rome, where Salvianus died, they were rebuffed by Pope Damasus. Thereafter, they received a similar response from Ambrose of Milan. They were successful, however, in gaining the help of Ambrose's enemies at the imperial court, and they obtained an imperial rescript of

their own authorizing them to reclaim their sees, which they then did. Ithacius even was forced to go into exile in Trier.

Soon thereafter, however, in 383, Gratian was murdered by the usurper Magnus Maximus, who subsequently was baptized as an orthodox Christian. Ithacius proceeded to place his case before the new emperor, with whom the Priscillianists had no influence. Maximus, desiring to conciliate the established Gallic and Spanish clergy, ordered a council to be convened in 384 or 385 at Bordeaux under the presidency of Priscillian's enemy Delphinus. Instantius, whose case was heard first, was declared deposed, but before Priscillian could be tried, he appealed to Maximus himself.

A hearing was therefore convened before the praetorian prefect of Gaul at Trier. Priscillian's principal accuser, Ithacius, took the lead in the prosecution. Priscillian was accused, according to Sulpicius Severus, "of witchcraft, of studying obscene teachings, of organizing nocturnal gatherings of shameful women, and of praying in the nude." Some of these crimes were capital offenses. Two other influential bishops who coincidentally happened to be in the city at the time, Martin of Tours and Ambrose of Milan, refused to take part and argued that a bishop should be tried before his fellow bishops. Other bishops, however, supported the proceedings.

In the end, Priscillian and six of his followers, including Euchrotia and the Spanish nobleman Latronianus, were condemned to death and executed. Others, such as Instantius, were sent into exile. Martin was able to prevent the sending of an imperial commission to root out the Spanish Priscillianists, but purges did take place. The aged Hyginus, for example, was sent into exile, and ascetics in general continued to be harassed.

The role of Maximus is seen especially in his letter to Bishop Siricius of Rome informing him of the affair: "Our arrival found certain matters so contaminated and polluted by the sins of the wicked that, unless foresight and attention had quickly brought aid, great disturbance and ruin immediately would have arisen, . . . but it was then disclosed how great a crime the Manichees recently had committed, not by doubtful or uncertain rhetoric or suspicions, but by their own confession." According to the emperor, the Priscillianists were Manichees: In fact, he never referred to Priscillian or Priscillianists by name at all. He may have seen no need to try to define a new heresy when Manichaeanism, a perfectly good, universally detested one, was available. An accusation of Manichaeanism would have allowed Priscillian to be tried under the statutes which made it a capital crime.

This heavy-handed secular interference in church activities led to a split in the Gallic church. Bishops such as Felix of Trier, who associated themselves with Priscillian's accusers, were seen as responsible for his execution by others, such as Martin, who had declined to participate. Thus arose the so-called Felician controversy, in which bishops of the two sides excommunicated each other.

The anti-Felicians, who had opposed the executions, came back into imperial favor in 388, when Maximus was defeated and Valentinian II, Gratian's younger brother, was restored to the throne. Both Ithacius and Hydatius were exiled and imprisoned at Naples. The remains of Priscillian and his followers were returned to Spain and buried with great ceremony. Priscillian was venerated as a martyr and saint, and his teachings continued to have many followers. Subsequently, a number of Priscillianists were chosen as bishops in Galicia, with Symphosius as one of their leaders.

The Council of Toledo in 400 was able to reconcile some of the Priscillianists, such as Symphosius, but Priscillianism continued to have many adherents. Outbreaks are attested in the 440's, mid-530's, and as late as the Councils of Braga in 561 and 572, when seventeen supposed Priscillianist teachings were condemned. Some Priscillianist practices were reflected even later in those of the medieval Albigensians (c. 1200), southern French ascetic, anticlerical dualists, and Adamites, who practiced nudity. The Priscillianist preference for clerical continence, moreover, did eventually become standard Catholic practice.

Summary

The Priscillianist controversy did not concern ecclesiastical dogma as much as it did church authority. Even in the modern day, scholars have a difficult time finding obvious heresy in Priscillian's writings. Nevertheless, his advocacy of uncontrolled scriptural interpretation, lay ministry, the participation of women, and the carrying out of the sacraments outside the established structure excited much opposition from the existing church hierarchy. His and his followers' acquisition of episcopal office, and their attempts to take over the church hierarchy themselves, only served to arouse more opposition against them. The result was a power struggle in which both sides sought assistance from the secular government. Priscillian was the loser, and paid with his life. In the future, the state would become more and more intimately involved in church activities and controversies.

Bibliography

Birley, A. R. "Magnus Maximus and the Persecution of Heresy." *Bulletin of the John Rylands Library* 66 (1983): 13-43. A detailed discussion of the part played by the emperor Magnus Maximus in the Priscillianist controversy. This incident illustrates the increasing interference of the imperial government in the operation of the Church. Includes references to recent scholarship on Priscillian and notes.

Burrus, Virginia. *The Making of a Heretic: Gender, Authority and the Priscillianist Controversy.* Berkeley: University of California Press, 1995. In the light of what is known about 4th-century conceptions of orthodoxy, asceticism, canon, creed, episcopacy, and even maleness and femaleness, Burrus examines how Priscillian was constructed as a social "other."

Chadwick, Henry. *Priscillian of Avila: The Occult and the Charismatic in the Early Church.* Oxford: Clarendon Press, 1976. The standard, English-language biography of Priscillian. Concentrates on the religious and theological aspects of Priscillian's teaching. Includes thorough documentation and bibliography, with references to many other sources, especially in foreign languages.

D'Alès, A. *Priscillien et l'Espagne chrétienne à la fin du IVᵉ siècle.* Paris: G. Beauchesne et Ses Fils, 1936. A biography of Priscillian which places him and his movement into the broader temporal and geographical context. Includes good documentation of the earlier scholarship.

De Clercq, V. C. "Ossius of Cordova and the Origins of Priscillianism." *Studia patristica* 1 (1957): 601-606. A brief discussion of the background of the Priscillianist controversy; De Clercq seeks to identify possible forerunners of Priscillian's beliefs and theology in earlier Christian teachings, especially those of Ossius of Cordova.

Schepss, G., ed. *Orosius: Commonitorium de errore Priscillianistarum et Origenistarum.* Vienna: F. Tempsky, 1889. The Latin text of Orosius' anti-Priscillianist invective. Orosius, an early fifth century Spanish writer, attempted to convict Priscillian of heresy by associating his teachings with those of the third century writer Origen. Such use of "guilt by association" was a common tactic at this time.

———. *Priscilliani quae supersunt, maximam partem nuper detexit adiectisque commentariis criticis et indicibus*. Vienna: F. Tempsky, 1889. A Latin edition of the works of Priscillian and his followers. It is still debated just how many of the works which survive under Priscillian's name actually were written by him.

Ralph W. Mathisen

PROCLUS

Born: c. 410; Constantinople, Byzantine Empire
Died: 485; Athens, Greece
Area of Achievement: Philosophy
Contribution: Proclus is known for his detailed systematization of the various theological and philosophical doctrines that he inherited from his predecessors and for his immense commentaries on the works of Plato, which consumed most of his activity.

Early Life

Proclus was born of patrician Lycian parents from the city of Xanthus. They wanted him to be educated in their city; thus, he was sent to Xanthus at a very early age. Later, he went to Alexandria to study rhetoric and Roman law in order to follow his father's profession, law. He soon became interested in philosophy and abandoned the study of law, choosing instead to attend lectures on mathematics and the philosophy of Aristotle. About the age of twenty, he went to Athens and studied under the Athenian Plutarch and his successor, Syrianus, at the Academy, the Athenian school that traced its ancestry to Plato's Academy. There, he continued his study of Aristotle and was introduced to Plato's philosophy and to mystical theology, to which he became a devotee. Proclus was such an intense, diligent student, with extraordinary powers of comprehension and memory, that by the age of twenty he had read the whole of Aristotle's *De anima* (335-323 B.C.; *On the Soul*) and Plato's *Phaedo* (388-366 B.C.), and by twenty-eight he had written several treatises as well as his commentary on Plato's *Timaeus* (360-347 B.C.).

Although a devoted disciple of Platonic thought, which he considered his main influence and inspiration, Proclus was a great enthusiast of all sorts of religious practices, beliefs, and superstitions and a champion of pagan worship against Christian imperial policy. He practiced all the Orphic and Chaldean rites of purification religiously, was a celibate, pursued a strict vegetarian diet, observed the fasts and vigils for the sacred days (more than was customary), devoutly revered the sun and moon, faithfully observed all the Egyptian holy days, and spent part of each night in prayer and in performing sacrifices. He believed that he was in complete possession of the theurgic knowledge, that he was divinely inspired, and that he was a reincarnation of the neo-Pythagorean Nichomachus.

Through the practice of theurgy, a type of ritual magic, it is claimed that he caused rainfall in a time of drought, prevented an earthquake, and was able to persuade the god Asclepius to cure the daughter of his friend Archiadas. Proclus had a vast and comprehensive knowledge of philosophy, mythology, religious practices, and cults, and he attempted to harmonize all these elements into a comprehensive system.

Marinus, his biographer, who was also his pupil and successor, describes Proclus as having lived the perfect life of a philosopher, a model of all the virtues, both social and intellectual, the life of a divine man. His only shortcomings were a quick temper and a fiercely competitive nature. Upon the death of Syrianus, Proclus succeeded him as the head of the Academy. Because of his position as the head of the Academy, and his devotion to Platonic thought, he has often been called "diadoches," or successor of Plato.

Life's Work

Proclus believed that his philosophy was a further and necessary development of Plato's thought. In reality, his views are a systematization of those found in other Neoplatonists' interpretations of Plotinian thought, and most can be traced to the teachings of Iamblichus, a follower of Plotinus. Of the many works that Proclus wrote, the most important and the one that best displays his schematization of Neoplatonic thought is *Stoikheiōsis theologikē* (*The Elements of Theology*, 1933). This work, which anticipates Benedictus de Spinoza's expositions of Cartesianism, is basically a doctrine of categories. It consists of a series of 211 propositions with deductive proofs. Each succeeding proposition follows on the basis of the preceding one, following the Euclidean procedure in geometry.

At the head of Proclus' system is the One, the ultimate First Principle existing beyond being and knowledge, ineffable and incomprehensible. Proclus often identifies God with the First Principle or One. From the One emanates or radiates innumerable lesser independent realities, reflecting the multiplicity of the world order, which strive to return to union with it. Unlike Plotinus, who held that the process of emanation was continuous and equal in degree, Proclus believed that all things emanate by triads and return to the One by triads. Every emanation is less than that from which it evolves but has a similarity or partial identity to its cause. In its emergence from its cause, the derived is also different. Yet, because of its relation to and dependence on its cause, it attempts to imitate its cause on a lower plane and return to and unite itself with it. It is only through the intermediate existences in triadic aspects that an existence can return to the highest reality, the One.

Although not original with him, Proclus was the first to emphasize and apply throughout his system the principle of universal sympathy, the view that everything is in everything else, each according to its proper nature. According to this, every reality in the universe is mirrored in everything else, but appropriately, in accordance with its nature. Eternal things exist in temporal existences temporally, and temporal things exist in eternal things eternally. This principle unifies and interweaves every part of the universe with every other part, from the One to the last stage of being or matter. In his attempt to unify the totality of the universe, Proclus also effects a total synthesis of religion with philosophy. His system is a chain of many carefully constructed links which include the traditional pagan gods, heroes, and other supernatural beings of late pagan syncretistic mythology and cult, as well as the divine principles of Greek philosophy.

Similar to his Neoplatonic predecessors, Proclus believed that the ultimate goal of the individual soul was to lose its identity and return to union with the One, or God. Although he accepted the Neoplatonic view that philosophy was important in the attainment of this goal, he added that theurgy provided an even better avenue. Philosophy is intellectual activity, is discursive and, as such, divided. Thus, it is impossible to achieve union with the undivided One through philosophy alone. Philosophy serves only as a preparation. Union with God is best achieved through the method of theurgy, or, as Proclus calls it, the sacred art, a collection of magical practices based on the principle of universal sympathy, a common sympathy existing between all earthly and divine things. According to this, there can exist in herbs, stones, and other material substances a magical or divine property. On a higher level, divinity could also be found in the names of gods, certain symbols, and even numbers. A skilled theurgist, by placing together the materials that possess divine properties and effacing others, could set forth a chain reaction of sympathies proceeding upward through a whole series of things to a divine being. The result would be a di-

vine illumination, by means of which an individual could come into external communion with a god. Thus, theurgy was considered by Proclus superior to philosophy, for, unlike philosophy, theurgy can lead an individual to the gods themselves.

Proclus posited two types of theurgy, a lower and a higher. The lower uses the unities found in specific material things to stimulate the soul toward self-knowledge, an understanding of its unity and divinity. Union with God, Himself, however, is attained only through a higher theurgy, the power of faith. Faith, according to Proclus, is when the individual goes beyond words, ritual actions, and conceptual thought and arrives at a state of simplicity, or self-unity. That leads to an unexplainable and incomprehensible belief in and love of God. When that occurs, the soul finds itself in a mystical silence before the incomprehensible and ineffable Supreme Being, and to the degree that a soul can, it becomes God.

In its later years, Neoplatonism came to be more a religion than a philosophy in order to compete with Christianity, which was becoming increasingly popular. Neoplatonism's followers were concerned with matters similar to those of their Christian counterparts: constructing a theology and interpreting and reconciling sacred texts. They also adopted some of the tenets fundamental to Christianity and other religions. Since faith is indispensable for salvation in any religion, it became for the later Neoplatonists a basic requirement for salvation or union with God. Proclus understood the problem of combating Christianity and attempted to construct a system that would bring into harmony elements of religion and Greek thought.

Summary

Proclus is considered the last of the major pagan Greek philosophers. His works represent the culminating point of Neoplatonic philosophers and the final form of its doctrines. It is in the Proclian form that Neoplatonic doctrines had considerable influence on Byzantine, Arabic, and early medieval Latin Christian thought. Proclus exerted the greatest influence, indirectly, on Latin Christendom through the writings of Dionysius, or Pseudo-Dionysius, as he is now called. It is not known who Dionysius was or when he lived. All that is known is that sometime in the late fifth or early sixth century a Christian follower of Proclus adopted his philosophy in toto, disguised it as apostolic teaching, and claimed it to be that of Dionysius the Areopagite, Saint Paul's first Athenian convert and disciple. Despite the fact that they were fraudulent, the works of Dionysius were highly regarded in the West, and beginning in the early sixth century to the eighth, elaborate commentaries were written defending both their orthodoxy and their genuineness. They soon acquired authority second only to those of Saint Augustine. Through the Dionysian corpus, Proclus' Neoplatonism influenced the thought of Western theologians for many centuries.

In the Byzantine world, the Dionysian theology had influence on the eighth century Eastern theologian Saint John of Damascus, but in general the works of Proclus were not as widely accepted as in the West, although they were well-known and often refuted. The main reason for their nonacceptance was that the Christian East considered Proclus' views on the eternity of the world heretical. It was not until the eleventh century, with the revival of Platonism, that Proclus' philosophy became widely known, studied, quoted, and commented upon in the East. The Muslim world was also influenced by Proclus. His works were translated into Arabic and influenced the thought of Arabic thinkers, especially those mystically inclined, such as al-Ghazzali and the Sufis, Ibn Gabirol and the Cabalists.

Proclus' influence on both the East and the West continued down to the eighteenth century and was especially prominent during the Middle Ages and the Renaissance, when he was considered the great pagan master. His works were translated into many languages, and his influence can be found in the philosophies of John Scotus Erigena (c. 810-c. 877), Thomas Aquinas (1225-1274), Meister Johannes Eckhart (c. 1260-1327), Nicholas of Cusa (1401-1464), René Descartes (1596-1650), Gottfried Wilhelm von Leibniz (1646-1716), and others. Traces of Proclus' philosophy can also be found in many modern works, literary and philosophical.

Bibliography

Bos, Egbert P., and P. A. Meijer, eds. *On Proclus and His Influence in Medieval Philosophy.* Leiden and New York: Brill, 1992. The collection includes four essays on special aspects of Proclus' philosophy, and another three discussing its reception in medieval scholasticism.

Lowry, J. M. P. *The Logical Principles of Proclus' "Elements of Theology" as Systematic Ground of the Cosmos.* Amsterdam: Rodopi, 1980. A study of the development of a logical structure of the cosmos as set forth in the logical systematic construction of the 211 propositions in Proclus' *The Elements of Theology.* It contains a good introductory chapter that includes a synopsis of Greek philosophy, Proclus' place in the history of philosophy, his relation to Iamblichus and Plotinus, and his influence on medieval and Renaissance thought.

Proclus. *The Elements of Theology.* Translated by E. R. Dodds. 2d ed. Oxford: Clarendon Press, 1963; New York: Oxford University Press, 1992. Greek text and English translation, with an excellent introduction and commentary on *The Elements of Theology.* The introduction includes a general description of the work, its place in the philosophical works of Proclus, a summary of Proclus' place among his Neoplatonic predecessors, and his influence during the Middle Ages. The commentary is a detailed critical discussion and historical study of each of the 211 propositions in *The Elements of Theology.* There is also a complete index of Greek terms.

Rosán, Laurence Jay. *The Philosophy of Proclus: The Final Phase of Ancient Thought.* New York: Cosmos, 1949. A compendium of Proclus' writings, with a detailed discussion and annotated bibliography. It also includes a translation of Marinus' life of Proclus, an analysis of Proclus' philosophy, and an annotated list of books, articles, and chapters on Proclus' thought or writings. A valuable book, but somewhat outdated.

Siorvanes, Lucas. *Proclus: Neo-Platonic Philosophy and Science.* New Haven, Conn.: Yale University Press, 1996. This is a major new study of Proclus. A chapter titled "Proclus' Life, Time and Influence" is followed by a systematic analysis of his metaphysics and natural philosophy.

Wallis, R. T. *Neoplatonism.* 2d ed. London: Duckworth, and Indianapolis: Hackett, 1995. The study is intended as an updated account of Neoplatonism. It is a summary of Neoplatonic thought from Plotinus to the end of the Athenian Academy, but it also includes two brief but informative chapters on the aims and sources of Neoplatonism and a lengthier chapter on the influence of Neoplatonism through the years. A chapter on the Athenian School contains a good summary of the development of Proclus' thought and its basic tenets. With an extensive bibliography.

Whittaker, Thomas. *The Neo-Platonists.* 4th ed. New York: Olms Verlag, 1987. A study in the history of Hellenism, with emphasis on Neoplatonic philosophy, from Plotinus to Proclus, and its influence. Chapter 9 contains a study of Proclus' life and a descriptive account of many of the propositions found in *The Elements of Theology*. At the end of the book, there is a supplementary section of summaries on Proclus' extant commentaries. The work is largely outdated, but it is still valuable for its supplement on Proclus' commentaries.

Antonía Tripolitis

SEXTUS PROPERTIUS

Born: c. 57-48 B.C.; Assisi?, Umbria
Died: c. 16 B.C.-A.D. 2; place unknown
Area of Achievement: Literature
Contribution: Propertius expanded the scope and power of the Roman love poem in the passionate poems to and about Cynthia.

Early Life

Sextus Propertius was born between 57 and 48 B.C. in Umbria, perhaps in the small town of Assisi. He was the son of a knight who was a well-off land-owner. Propertius' father died while Propertius was still a child, and his world was further dislocated by the appropriation of land in Umbria to settle the soldiers of Marc Antony and Octavian (later, Augustus).

Propertius grew up under the shadow of the continuing civil wars among Antony, Octavian, and Pompey the Younger—and the early consolidation of power by Augustus. His first book of poems was published about 30 B.C., and it attracted the attention of Gaius Maecenas, the patron of Vergil and Horace. This support improved Propertius' financial situation, but he continued to refuse to write poems in celebration of Augustus.

Life's Work

Propertius' poetry came at the end of the great period of the Roman love poem. His work does not have the passion of Catullus or the polish of Horace, but it does have a complexity and an intensity not found in the poetry of his predecessors. Some critics have complained about Propertius' heavy use of myth, but the allusions in his poetry are well employed—especially the contrasting of the distant gods to the immediate relationship with a woman he called Cynthia.

Propertius' poetry survives in four books. At the heart of the poems are those on Cynthia, and while commentators have been unsuccessful in discovering an autobiographical sequence the poems do give one of the fullest portrayals of an intense relationship in all literature. The first poem (book 1, elegy 1) immediately evokes this intensity: "She was the one to enslave me, and she did it with her eyes;/ till then I'd never felt love's poison arrows." Love is not a pleasant or a sentimental state but a terrible visitation and a loss of control. Propertius contrasts his subject state to mythic figures and urges the powers of love to visit his mistress with the same poison. The poem shifts at the end, as Propertius becomes adviser rather than victim and warns his friends to avoid this sorry state of unrequited love by sticking "to your own love."

In the poems that follow, Propertius frequently complains about Cynthia's mistreatment, yet in book 1, elegy 7, the poet defends his choice of the love poem over the more traditional and valued epic. Propertius' poems are his "life's work" and come from bitter and joyful experience, while the epic of one Ponticus—according to Propertius—is straight out of books. Propertius writes that when Ponticus falls in love, in vain he will try to turn his hand to love poems, while Propertius will be celebrated as "the greatest poet of them all."

In book 1, elegies 21 and 22, Propertius addresses war, not love. The speaker in elegy 21 is a dead man who advises a fleeing soldier. The dead man urges the soldier not to be brave but to "Save yourself/ and bring your parents joy." He also asks the soldier to bring a message of "tears" to his sister. The poem ends ironically, for the dead man was also a soldier and had escaped "the swords of Caesar" only to fall to robbers. It is a personal and a political poem; it evokes the sorrow of the dead soldier and points unmistakably to its cause, the wars of Antony and Octavian.

Elegy 22 is also a political poem. It begins with a question from a man named Tullus about Propertius' origins. The answer is that he comes from "the graveyard of our fatherland/ when civil war set Roman against Roman. . . ." Once more he evokes a landscape littered with "my kinsman's bones" but ends with an opposite image, life and birth: "where the fertile plain touches the foothills/ Umbria gave me birth."

The first poem in book 2 is not addressed to Cynthia but to Propertius' patron, Maecenas. Once more, he contrasts the supposedly trivial love poem to the great epic, but since Cynthia is his inspiration "each trivial incident begets/ a mighty saga." Even if he had the power to write an epic, he would avoid the usual subjects, since they are all clichés. If he had the power he would write about "your Caesar's wars" (another example of the distancing of the poet from the emperor). Yet he has no such power or ability; he can only write "of the battles I fight in bed." The poem ends in an amusing fashion, as Propertius asks Maecenas to visit his obscure tomb, drop a tear, observe the burial rites, and say, "Here lies one for whom destiny/ Was a Cruel mistress." As the poems show, Propertius' destiny was a cruel mistress, Cynthia.

Most of the poems in book 2 complain about Cynthia's ways or lack of faithfulness. Elegy 5 is the most interesting of these. It begins with a series of accusations as Cynthia is called a "whore" and the poet looks forward to following her example and acquiring a new love. The focus of the poem shifts, however, as Propertius looks not to the future but to past moments they shared like "tender sacraments." He then lists all the brutal things he will not do to her; he will, instead, "mark" her with his poetic curse that will last to her dying day.

Book 2, elegy 7, speaks of a more tender relationship between the poet and Cynthia, as well as of the complex relationship he has with Augustus. It begins with relief that some "law" was not put into operation by Augustus that would separate the poet and his beloved. The relief is tinged with defiance, as the poet declares that "mighty Caesar cannot conquer love." Nor is the poet a fit candidate to be a husband or a breeder of sons for Rome; the only war he will fight is in the name of his mistress. The last lines of the poem are an affirmation of the poet's love, "which is greater to me than the name of father."

In book 2, elegy 10, Propertius seems to have reversed his earlier position and now wishes to sing of "war and war's alarms," since "Cynthia's song is sung." By the end of the poem, however, he sees poems about war as beyond his reach, like a statue that "towers too high." He will, instead, write of and from the lower strain of love. Propertius is very clever in praising Augustus, but, finally, he relocates his art in a private rather than a public arena.

Elegy 34, the last poem in book 2, brings together many of the themes of the earlier poems. It is addressed to another poet, Lynceus, who has attempted to steal the poet's beloved. Lynceus is identified as a student of the "Socratic books," but they will be of no help to a man in love—nor will the usual epic themes. Lynceus must make himself into a love poet in the manner of Propertius if he wishes to succeed. The second section contrasts Propertius' poems with the political and nationalistic ones of Vergil and the pastoral ones of Lynceus. In the end, however, the epic and pastoral poets are left behind, as Propertius places himself in the line of Catullus and Calvus. If he is allowed to join that company, both he and Cynthia will live forever. So

the poem is both a disguised love poem that praises Cynthia and a defense of lyric poetry against the epic and the pastoral.

Book 3 continues the themes of Cynthia and the championing of the love poem over the epic. Elegy 4, however, seems to be a surrender to the claims of Rome. The poem praises the new victories of Augustus against the Parthians. Propertius even prays to see "the wheels of Caesar heaped with the spoils of war." Yet where will the poet be while this triumph is celebrated? He will be lying in his "sweetheart's arms watching the sights" rather than taking an active role or even writing about war. The last two lines define the difference between the two areas: "Let those who earned it bear the spoil away,/ and leave me to stand and cheer on the Sacred Way." The role of the poet is to sing and cheer rather than to take part in public life.

Elegy 11 deals with the power that women have over men. It begins with Propertius speaking of his bondage to Cynthia and asserting that it should be no "surprise." He cites Medea and others as examples of this same situation, but the main comparison is to Cleopatra VII. She has "brought into disrepute" the "walls of Rome" and made senators slaves. According to Propertius, however, Augustus was not awed by this woman and has recently defeated and destroyed her; the poet sings out "your triumph, Rome" over these forces. The subjection to women that seemed to be universal at the beginning is now broken and the poet tells the reader to "remember Caesar."

Elegy 22 also discusses Rome, but from a more personal perspective. It is addressed to Tullus, who has been roaming among the various wonders of the world. After listing those exotic sights, however, the poet reminds Tullus that "all the wonders of the world/ are not a patch on Rome." Not only is Rome victorious, but also it is free from the crimes and vices common in other places. So Tullus is welcomed back to a Rome that is "worthy of your eloquence," where children and "a wife to match your love" await. It is clearly a Rome in which there is no mention of Cynthia and her destructive passion.

Book 4 also begins with a celebration of Rome, in the first elegy. A "stranger" is invited to look around at "the grandeur of Rome." He is reminded of Roman history and myth from Romulus and Remus through the founding of Rome by the Trojans, as the poet offers up his song "to the service of my country." He imagines his homeland, Umbria, now proud as the birthplace of "Rome's Callimachus." In the second part of the poem, however, Horus, a god of time and an astrologer, appears and criticizes Propertius' new project. He tells him that he should be fashioning love poems to "provide a model for the scribbling mob," since Apollo "banned you from thundering in the frantic forum." Propertius' fate is Cynthia and the creation of poems about her: "It's she who tells you whether it's day or night; your teardrops fall at her command."

In book 4, elegy 6, however, Propertius returns to the subject of Augustus' wars. After listing the triumphs of his emperor, the poet focuses on the victory over Cleopatra which has made Augustus into a god.

There is one more poem on Cynthia in book 4. It speaks of her as a ghost who is "very much alive," snapping her fingers at the poet and ordering him around. She accuses him of not attending her funeral and of sleeping soon after her death. She has come, however, not to accuse but to bring information about the underworld and to instruct the poet. She tells him, first, to "burn" all the poems he has written about her and to place "this poem" on her tombstone: "Here in the fields of Tivoli/ Lies golden Cynthia/ Adding a new glory/ To the banks of the Anio." She then leaves him to other women until they can be reunited in the afterlife. It is a fitting end to the sequence.

Summary

The poems of Sextus Propertius portray the growth, flowering, decay, and death of an intense love relationship with the elusive Cynthia. From the very first, it is seen as an unconquerable obsession. There are moments of union between the two, but, for the most part, he complains about her neglect and unfaithfulness. The Cynthia sequence can be compared to the one dealing with Lesbia in the poems of Catullus. Catullus goes through a similar wrenching experience of hate and love that defines his existence.

There is, however, another side to the poetry of Propertius. He accepted the patronage of Maecenas, but he did not become an official spokesman for Augustus as Vergil and Horace did. Instead, he defended his right to a private life and a private art, the love poem. The tension created by the struggle to remain free without insulting the emperor gives another dimension to the passionate love poems and adds subtlety to their structure.

Bibliography

Benediktson, D. T. *Propertius: Modernist Poet of Antiquity.* Carbondale: Southern Illinois University Press, 1989. This is a somewhat technical but highly competent study of Propertius' metrics, style, and poetic imagery.

Highet, Gilbert. *Poets in a Landscape.* London: Hamish Hamilton, and New York: Alfred A. Knopf, 1957. Contains an evocative discussion of Propertius and other Roman poets that concentrates on the poets' biographies and societies. Well written, providing background information but no interpretation.

Luck, G. *The Latin Love Elegy.* 2d ed. London: Methuen, 1969; Totowa, N.J.: Rowman and Littlefield, 1979. A useful early study of some of the techniques and concerns of the Roman love poem. It is quite good on the literary tradition but not much of a guide to individual poems.

Propertius, Sextus. *The Poems.* Guy Lee, trans. Oxford: Clarendon Press, and New York: Oxford University Press, 1994. The introduction is informative, there is a chronology of Propertius' life, and the explanatory notes are numerous and detailed.

―――. *The Poems of Propertius.* Edited by Ronald Musker. London: Dent, 1972. A brief and adequate introduction to the poetry of Propertius with an excellent translation. A good introduction to Propertius for readers without knowledge of Latin.

Stahl, Hans-Peter. *Propertius: Love and War, Individual and State Under Augustus.* Berkeley: University of California Press, 1985. A superb study of Propertius' ambiguous relationship with Augustus and the themes of love and war. It is written primarily for an academic audience, but other readers will find it clear and informative.

Williams, Gordon. *Tradition and Originality in Roman Poetry.* New York: Oxford University Press, and Oxford: Clarendon, 1968. A scholarly treatment of many aspects of Propertius' thought and interests. The book is very good on the background and tradition of the poems but assumes knowledge of Latin.

James Sullivan

PROTAGORAS

Born: c. 485 B.C.; Abdera, Greece

Died: c. 410 B.C.; place unknown

Areas of Achievement: Philosophy and education

Contribution: Protagoras was among the first and was possibly the greatest of the Greek Sophists, itinerant teachers who professed to be able to teach men virtue for a fee. His ideas on learning, morality, and the history of human society have influenced the system of education since the fifth century B.C.

Early Life

Most of what is known of Protagoras comes from select writings of Plato, Aristotle, Aristophanes, and certain later authors. Protagoras was born about 485 B.C. in Abdera, a coastal town of Thrace to the east of Macedonia. The town was remarkable for producing several famous philosophers, including Democritus, and as the third richest city in the Delian League, a fifth century alliance established to expel the Persians from Greece.

Protagoras' father, Maeandrius (or by some accounts, Artemon), was said to have been one of the most affluent citizens of Abdera and was thus able to obtain a good education for his son. When Xerxes I, King of the Persians, stopped in the town with his army prior to invading Greece, Maeandrius supposedly gained permission for his son to be educated by the magi who were part of Xerxes' retinue. The magi were supposed to have been the source of Protagoras' well-known agnosticism. No trace of their influence, however, can be seen in his work, so the story is largely discounted.

A story arose that Protagoras invented the shoulder pad that porters used, because he himself had been a porter in his youth. A longer version of the tale claims that his fellow citizen, the philosopher Democritus, saw him working at a menial task and was so impressed by his methodical arrangement of firewood that he first made the boy his secretary, then trained him in philosophy and rhetoric. Since Democritus was actually younger than Protagoras, this story must also be rejected. Yet he may have been a "hearer" of Democritus, as some accounts claim.

The numerous stories from ancient times which have largely been discounted by later generations prove that nothing certain can be said about Protagoras' early life. It is stated authoritatively, however, that at the age of thirty Protagoras began his career as a Sophist, traveling up and down the peninsula of Greece, and into Sicily and southern Italy, giving lessons to wealthy young men for a fee.

Life's Work

Prior to the mid-400's no schools or professional teachers existed, yet the city-states experienced an increasing need for well-educated, informed leaders. The older Sophists, Protagoras, Prodicus, Hippias, and Gorgias, filled this need by teaching upper-class young men how to acquire political and personal success. They held similar views on education and had similar aversions to the objective scientific doctrines of their day. They claimed superiority in wisdom, the ability to teach that wisdom, and the right to charge a fee for their lessons. In this atmosphere Protagoras gained fame by lecturing and by writing books.

Many disapproved of the Sophists' methods, especially Socrates and Plato. Socrates argued that wisdom was a quality which could not be taught. Plato, who disparaged the rhetorical tricks used specifically by Protagoras, brought ill repute to all the Sophists. A generation later, Aristotle branded their teaching as the furthering of the appearance of wisdom without the reality, and the Sophists as men who made money on this pretense.

Still, Protagoras was clearly more than a specious philosopher. Plato consistently portrayed him as witty, intellectual, moral, and sincere in his praise of Socrates—and thought Protagoras' ideas important enough to refute in several dialogues. Aristotle's extensive refutation of Protagoras' beliefs attests the fact that he, too, took Protagoras seriously.

Protagoras' instruction was practical. He emphasized skill in persuasive speaking and effective debating. He taught his students the importance of words by the study of grammar, diction, and poetic analysis. He may have been the first to emphasize the importance of proper timing. Armed with these skills, Protagoras believed, his students would excel as civic leaders and political advisers. The Athenian orator Isocrates and Protagoras' fellow Sophist Prodicus were two of his most famous students. He also influenced Aristophanes and Euripides.

On his journeys, Protagoras no doubt stayed with influential families and read his speeches to select audiences. His most famous visits were to

Athens, which he first saw in 444 B.C., when the Athenian ruler Pericles asked him to write the constitution for the new Panhellenic colony of Thurii in southern Italy. This assignment probably required him to live in Italy for some years. He spent enough time in Sicily to have won fame as a teacher. He returned to Athens about 432, when he engaged in the debate with Socrates described in Plato's dialogue *Protagoras* (399-390 B.C.). He may have visited the city once more in 422 or 421.

Protagoras' high fee of one hundred minae was notorious; according to Plato, Protagoras earned more money in his forty years of teaching than did the famous sculptor Phidias and ten other sculptors combined. Protagoras claimed that a student was not compelled to pay the fee if he did not think the instruction worth the price.

Protagoras was known to have written at least two books, though many more titles have survived. *Aletheia* (*The Truth*) was an early, and his most important, composition. He wrote another titled *Antilogion* (*Contrary Arguments*) and may also have written a third called *Peri theon* (*On the Gods*).

Only two substantial fragments of his writing remain. In conjunction with numerous shorter fragments, they reflect the two main philosophies of Protagoras' life and portray him as a person interested in philosophy, rhetoric, grammar and syntax, and literary criticism. The statement for which he is most famous introduces *The Truth*: "Man is the measure of all things, of the things that are, that they are, of the things that are not, that they are not." The saying, perhaps a reply to the mathematicians, has been interpreted since Plato to mean that what a man perceives to be true for him is true for him. A new fragment discovered in 1968 expounds further on the remark.

Protagoras' subjectivism, as it was called, was not well received by philosophers. Aristotle declared the statement absurd. Plato argued that a pig or a baboon was equally capable of being the measure. The flaw in Protagoras' argument was that if others believed the maxim to be false, then by that very maxim their perceptions must be true for them and his maxim was false for them. Despite these objections, the dictum represented an original contribution to fifth century philosophy.

On the Gods is said to have opened with the following statement:

> With regard to the gods, I cannot know whether they exist or do not exist, nor what they are like in form; for

the factors preventing knowledge are many: the obscurity of the subject, and the shortness of human life.

Such agnosticism shocked Protagoras' contemporaries. The Athenians reportedly expelled him from the city for impiety. Nearly seven hundred years later, Sextus Empiricus labeled Protagoras an atheist for this remark, as did Diogenes Laërtius.

In *Contrary Arguments*, Protagoras stated that two contradictory propositions existed for every issue. Aristotle rejected the saying as contradicting Protagoras' own belief that all views were equally true, and Aristophanes lampooned the idea in his comedy *Nephelai* (c. 423 B.C.; *The Clouds*). Modern views of sophistry stem from the comic playwright's portrayal of these rhetorical tricks.

Minor fragments reveal Protagoras' interest in speech, grammar, and education in general. He wrote on existence, he refuted mathematics, and he discussed such varied topics as wrestling, ambition, virtues, laws, human error, and the underworld. Protagoras' influence on his contemporaries is apparent from later authorities. Porphyry claims that Plato plagiarized substantial passages from the *Contrary Arguments* for his work, the *Politeia* (388-366 B.C.; *Republic*). Protagoras' personal friend Pericles may have chosen him to draft laws for Thurii, partly because he respected the Sophist and partly because Protagoras was already familiar to Western Greeks. The drafting of the laws may have brought him into contact with the historian Herodotus, who was also involved in founding Thurii. Protagorean influence has been noted in part of Herodotus' *Historiai Herodotou* (c. 425 B.C.; *The History of Herodotus*, 1709).

The circumstances of Protagoras' death remain shrouded in mystery. By one account, he died in a shipwreck. Diogenes believed he died fleeing Athens when he was banished for impiety. Probably closest to fact is Plato's statement that he died after forty years of teaching, that is, about 410 B.C.

Summary

Protagoras' importance in the realm of Greek philosophy has been largely underrated because of the refutations of Plato and Aristotle and the lampoons of Aristophanes. He and his fellow Sophists initiated the practice of instructing students. Before this time young men had had to rely on the dramatists and their plays for lessons in how to be good citizens. After the Persian War, this brand of instruction was inadequate for the demands of the city-states, especially Athens. The Sophists provided a necessary service by establishing a definite curriculum.

Yet the system was not without flaws. The aim from the beginning was to educate only the leaders of society, not the general populace. Protagoras' claim to teach virtue was too weak an assertion to support, as Plato, Aristotle, and others clearly saw. Still, it is interesting that after the death of Socrates, who vehemently protested that he taught nothing and never charged a fee, his student Plato founded the Academy, where he lectured to paying students in the area of philosophy. In this respect, Plato much more closely resembled Protagoras than Socrates.

Protagoras' influence has spanned generations. He was known in the Middle Ages and early Renaissance through the writings of Cicero, Seneca, and Aulus Gellius—and in the Latin translations of Aristotle. Some scholars have seen evidence for sophistic origins of Renaissance Humanism. Greek Sophists founded the type of intellectual movement with which the Italian humanists are identified. There seems to have been a Humanist character to the Sophists, a character that arguably makes the Sophists, through Cicero and his knowledge of them, the progenitors of the thoughts and ideas expressed in Italian Humanism of the 1400's. Protagoras' myth on the origin of human society corresponds to the Humanists' concepts of their own moral and educational role in society.

As W. K. C. Guthrie so aptly claims:

> Protagoras' innovation was to achieve a reputation as a political and moral thinker without supporting any political party, attempting political reform, or seeking power for himself, but simply by lecturing and speaking and offering himself as a professional adviser and educator. . . .

Protagoras made men think about their lives in relation to society and sparked some very strong objections from philosophers regarding the direction of learning. In this way, he helped advance education.

Bibliography

Barnes, Jonathan. *The Presocratic Philosophers.* Vol. 2, *Empedocles to Democritus.* Rev. ed. London and Boston: Routledge, 1982. The author's special contribution is interpreting Protagoras' sayings according to ancient commentators. The extensive bibliography, endnotes, and index will be helpful to general and advanced readers.

Freeman, Kathleen. *Ancilla to the Pre-Socratic Philosophers: A Complete Translation of the Fragments in "Diels, Fragmente der Vorsokratiker."* Cambridge, Mass.: Harvard University Press, and London: Blackwell, 1948. This volume provides a translation of all the existing fragments written by Protagoras. One could have wished that the author had also translated the fragments from ancient authors about Protagoras.

———. *The Pre-Socratic Philosophers.* Cambridge, Mass.: Harvard University Press, and Oxford: Blackwell, 1946. Still the best discussion in English of all the fragments of Protagoras, fact and fiction. Freeman puts him in historical perspective with his predecessors, contemporaries, and successors. Clear and concise for general readers.

Guthrie, W. K. C. *A History of Greek Philosophy.* Vol. 3, *The Fifth-Century Enlightenment.* Cambridge: Cambridge University Press, 1962. Compiles all the ancient evidence on Protagoras and presents it in a clear, straightforward manner. Also provides a good historical background to the Sophists and a discussion of their importance. Citations of ancient authors are in the footnotes.

Jaeger, Werner. *Paideia: The Ideals of Greek Culture.* Vol. 1, *Archaic Greece: The Mind of Athens.* Translated by Gilbert Highet. New York: Oxford University Press, and Oxford: Blackwell, 1939. Jaeger's evaluation of the role and importance of the Sophists and of Protagoras' role in one of the best critical accounts. Includes extensive endnotes.

Plato. *Plato's "Protagoras": A Socratic Commentary.* Edited by B. A. F. Hubbard and E. S. Karnofsky. London: Duckworth, 1982; Chicago: University of Chicago Press, 1984. This translation of Plato's dialogue provides a clear portrayal of Protagoras as Sophist and as intellectual. In the commentary, the translators refer to sections of the dialogue which reveal bits of Protagoras' life, and a succinct biography appears in one of the indexes. Includes a short bibliography.

Schiappa, Edward. *Protagoras and Logos: A Study of Greek Philosophy and Rhetoric.* Columbia: University of South Carolina Press, 1991. Divided in three parts of almost equal length, the book begins with a general examination of early Greek rhetorical theory, moves to an analysis of Protagoras' most important preserved fragments, and ends with an assessment of his contribution to rhetoric and philosophy. It also contains a chronology of Protagoras' life and a sizeable bibliography.

Joan E. Carr

PSAMTIK I

Born: c. 684 B.C.; place unknown
Died: 610 B.C.; place unknown
Area of Achievement: Government
Contribution: Psamtik carved out political independence for Egypt after almost a century of foreign rule, inaugurating a renewal of its society and culture.

Early Life

Little is known about the early life of Psamtik I (also known as Psammetichus I); even the date of his birth is based on conjecture. He was the son of Necho I, a local Egyptian ruler in the western Delta region. For nearly a century, after the kingdom of Egypt had fragmented into several small principalities, Cushite invaders had held the Nile Valley, calling themselves the Twenty-fifth Dynasty. Assyria was beginning to expand westward; under Assarhaddon and Ashurbanipal, it vied for control of the valley, which led to confrontations with the Cushites.

Psamtik's ancestors, especially his great-grandfather Tefnachte, had unsuccessfully tried to reunite the land. Necho, his father, pursued a precarious course between the Assyrians and Cushites, trying to carve out a maximum of independence for himself and the principality of Sais, which he controlled. This political game would prove fatal: He later died on the battlefield in 664.

Life's Work

A year earlier, Psamtik had participated in a mission to Nineveh together with his father; at that time, Ashurbanipal appointed the two his vassals in Egypt. Necho became King of Memphis and Sais, while Psamtik (in the Assyrian records called "Nabu-shezibanni") was to rule Athribis in the central Delta. Upon the death of his father, Psamtik became ruler of Memphis and Sais. An invasion of the Delta by the Cushites forced him to flee to the Assyrians.

He returned in 664 when Ashurbanipal conducted a campaign against Tanatami, a Cushite ruler, which led to the expulsion of the latter and the sacking of Thebes by the Assyrians. Psamtik was reinstated and had to pay tribute to his Assyrian overlord. With both great powers removed, Psamtik craftily worked to consolidate his position and to expand his rule. A major step toward this goal was the reorganization of his army; with the help of Gyges of Lydia, he hired Carian and Ionian mercenaries—the "bronze men who would make their appearance from the sea" of the Greek historian Herodotus' romantic account. For these soldiers, the first coins were struck in Egypt.

By 657, Psamtik had gained full control over the various principalities of the Delta and Middle Egypt. How he accomplished this is not known in detail. Herodotus relates a fictitious tradition: An oracle had foretold that the one who would perform the divine libation from a bronze helmet would become king of all Egypt. At a ceremony in the temple of Ptah-Hepaistos—so the story goes—the golden cups for the ritual libation were one short and Psamtik quickly took his helmet to perform for the god.

The final unification of Egypt under Psamtik was completed in 656, when Thebes peacefully accepted him. This development was negotiated for Thebes by a local dignitary named Menthuemhet and was formalized by the appointment of Psamtik's daughter Nitocris as "Wife of Amon," the priestess who controlled the economic resources of the temple of the Theban god Amon at this time. With great pomp and lavish gifts, the young Nitocris, probably in her teens at the time, sailed to Thebes. Since Psamtik refrained from any interference in prevailing political situations, he did not stir up any opposition; Thebes remained an integral part of Egypt for the next 130 years.

Following the expansion into Thebes, Psamtik was faced with an attack from Libya; some of the invaders were former Delta princes who had fled there. In 655 he repelled this last challenge to his rule. To prevent any recurrence of outside attacks, he set up garrisons at Egypt's borders, such as Elephantine in the South and Daphne in the Northeast. The troops stationed there were foreign mercenaries, including Greeks, Hebrews, and Carians.

By 655 Psamtik not only had consolidated his rule over Egypt but also was able to shed his dependence on an Assyria exhausted from years of incessant warfare and growing internal tensions. A period of peace and economic renewal was inaugurated for Egypt. Memories of Egypt's former greatness were carefully cultivated, leading to a conscious antiquarianism which found its most visible expression in the arts, where the style of the Old Kingdom, the Pyramid age, served as model. This interest in the past also had its impact on the ad-

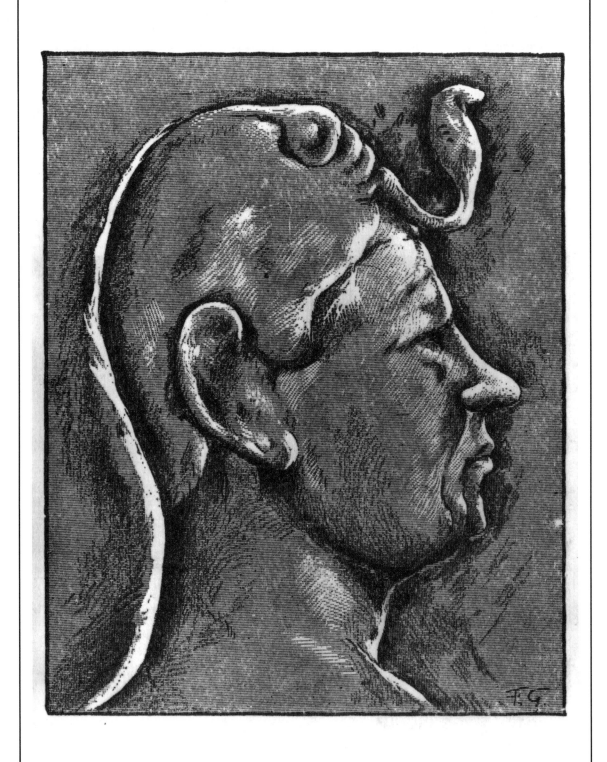

ministration of the country, as indicated by the reappearance of official titles after an absence of fifteen hundred years. The motive seems to have been a desire to emulate the achievements of the past, an illusion sustained by the prosperity following half a millennium of internal strife, political insignificance, and economic stagnation. Despite the antiquarian mold, there were numerous intellectual impulses. The traditional way of writing became increasingly replaced by a smoother, more cursive script called demotic. Medicine flourished, especially in Sais. There was religious fervor, and the cults of Isis and Amon, among others, profited.

The long reign of Psamtik coincided with major shifts in the balance of power in the eastern Mediterranean basin. Assyria, which at the beginning of his reign had been the dominant nation, was losing its importance. Following years of external and internal strife, it was no longer able to exercise influence in Syria and Palestine. In return for military assistance to Assyria, Psamtik was able to expand Egypt's political might northward, filling the vacuum which developed in the Levant as a result of Assyria's withdrawal. By 612 Egypt's control over parts of Lebanon and Palestine was reestablished, while Psamtik joined the Assyrians in their fight against the Babylonians under Nabopalassar in 616 and 610. Ashdod was seized by Psamtik, but the Egyptian did not concern himself with the affairs of Judah, which under Josiah was concentrating on religious reforms. Being landlocked at the time, Judah did not fall into the overall political plan Psamtik followed at this time in the Levant.

Unlike any of his predecessors on the throne, Psamtik was interested in making Egypt into a naval power on the Mediterranean and later also on the Red Sea. It is not clear from where the technical expertise came, but some Greek participation is feasible. These naval plans coincided with the political expansion into Palestine. Psamtik prepared the basis for Egypt's subsequent role as a truly international power, not only in its traditional land-based form but also as a naval force, culminating in the construction of a canal linking the Mediterranean—via the Nile system—to the Red Sea and the first known circumnavigation of Africa, which took place under his son and successor Necho II.

Summary

When Psamtik I died in 610, he left an entirely different Egypt from the one with which he began his reign fifty-four years earlier. Caught between the Cushites and the Assyrians, the political ambitions of the local ruler of Memphis and Sais faced considerable odds, which were overcome. Since the unification of Egypt was achieved peacefully, however, it did not generate new tensions; instead, it marked the beginning of a period of political, cultural, and economic flowering, known as the Saite Renaissance, which lasted until the Persian invasion in 525. Marked by a reawakened national spirit, which took the glorious past, especially the Pyramid age, as its model, Egypt's last fully indigenous period was a time when the land of the pharaohs exerted considerable cultural influence, on the Greeks especially. Egypt developed its Hellenic contacts, in the process entering the Mediterranean theater. A void in the international political structure not only gave Egypt the opportunity to consolidate its newly attained national identity but also offered the country the chance to become once more a major power, bringing the coastal regions of part of Syria and Palestine under Egyptian authority.

Bibliography

Gardiner, Alan, Sir. *Egypt of the Pharaohs.* Oxford: Clarendon, and New York: Oxford University Press, 1961. This volume is a fine general account of the history of ancient Egypt. Includes a short bibliography, some illustrations, and an index.

James, T. G. H. "Egypt: the Twenty-fifth and Twenty-sixth Dynasties." In *The Cambridge Ancient History.* Vol. VIII, *Rome and the Mediterranean to 133 B.C.* 2d ed. Cambridge and New York: Cambridge University Press, 1991. This chapter offers the most recent scholarly treatment of Psamtik's reign, with separate sections on foreign and domestic policy.

Kitchen, K. A. *The Third Intermediate Period in Egypt, 1100-650 B.C.* 2d ed. Warminster, England: Aris and Phillips, 1986. A well-documented, authoritative study; discusses the Twenty-sixth Dynasty, beginning with Psamtik, extensively. General bibliography.

Spalinger, Anthony. "Psammetichus, King of Egypt: I." *Journal of the American Research Center in Egypt* 13 (1976): 133-147. The only scholarly treatment of Psamtik written in English. Includes citations.

Hans Goedicke

PTOLEMY

Born: c. 100; possibly Ptolemais Hermii, Egypt
Died: c. 178; place unknown, possibly Egypt
Areas of Achievement: Astronomy, mathematics, and geography
Contribution: Ptolemy's scientific work in astronomy, mathematics, geography, and optics influenced other practitioners for almost fifteen hundred years.

Early Life

Very little is known about the life of Ptolemy. He was born in Egypt at the end of the first century A.D., but his birth date and birth place and his life thereafter are subjects of speculation. It is thought that he might have been born in the Grecian city of Ptolemais Hermii in Upper Egypt and that he might have lived to the age of seventy-eight. It has been suggested that he studied and made astronomical observations, staying for more than half of his life among the elevated terraces at the temple of Serapis in Canopus near Alexandria, where pillars were erected with the results of his astronomical discoveries engraved upon them. He was probably the descendant of Greek or Hellenized ancestors and obtained Roman citizenship as a legacy from them.

Much more is known about the age in which Ptolemy lived. It was a century during which Rome ruled the Mediterranean world and during which four successive Roman emperors, Trajan, Hadrian, Antoninus Pius, and Marcus Aurelius, built roads and bridges, opened libraries and colleges, and maintained Rome's power and peace. It was a time when educated men spoke Greek as well as Latin, when Athens was still honored for its cultural traditions, when Marcus Aurelius wrote his *Meditations* in Greek, and Greek was still the language of science and the arts.

Ptolemy, who probably used the libraries at Alexandria, was strongly influenced by a Greek scientist, Hipparchus (fl. 146-127 B.C.), who propounded the geocentric theory of the universe. As far back as the fourth century B.C., the leading view of the nature of the universe had the sun, moon, and planets revolving around the fixed Earth in concentric spheres. The competing theory was first advocated by Aristarchus of Samos (fl. c. 270 B.C.). Aristarchus discovered that the sun was much larger than Earth, and this discovery was the basis for his argument that Earth and all other planets revolved around a fixed sun and stars in circles. Yet the heliocentric theory could not be demonstrated by observable phenomena as long as it was thought that the sun was the center of a circle rather than of an ellipse. Hipparchus rejected the contention of Aristarchus, insisting on "saving the phenomena," that is, adhering to the observations. His further scientific speculations founded on the geocentric theory were the legacy to Ptolemy some two centuries later.

Life's Work

Some historians maintain that Ptolemy merely plagiarized from Hipparchus; others have said that Ptolemy superseded Hipparchus and made the work of the earlier scientist superfluous. In fact, it could be said that Ptolemy immortalized Hipparchus by acknowledging the debt he owed to his distant predecessor and by frequently quoting from him.

Whatever historical assessment is more correct, there is no doubt that Ptolemy's work in astronomy alone lasted for more than fourteen hundred years, until the great scientific achievements of Nicholaus Copernicus and Johannes Kepler. Ptolemy used new instruments or improved upon old ones to make his observations. In the *Mathēmatikē suntaxis* (c. 150; *Almagest*), one of his most significant books, he utilized the mathematical methods of trigonometry to prove that Earth was a sphere and went on to postulate that the heavens were also spheres and moved around an immobile Earth in the center of the solar system. He dealt with the length of the months and the year—and the motion of the sun; he covered the theory of the moon; and he figured out the distance of the sun, and the order and distances of the planets from Earth. Much of this was not new, not original; the *Almagest* was essentially a restatement of astronomical knowledge available three hundred years earlier. Yet Ptolemy was able to synthesize that scientific information into a system and to expound it in a clear and understandable manner. He was a teacher, and he taught well.

Ptolemy's contribution to mathematics was even more significant. Hipparchus had invented spherical and plane trigonometry for the use of astronomers. Ptolemy then perfected this branch of mathematics so that, unlike his astronomical system, which was finally discredited, the theorems that he and Hipparchus devised form the permanent basis of trigonometry.

The *Almagest*, in which trigonometry was utilized to measure the positions of the sun, Earth, moon, and planets, was later translated into Arabic and then Latin, and so also was Ptolemy's *Geōgraphikē hyphēgēsis* (*Geography*). Ptolemy attempted with considerable success to place the study of geography on a scientific foundation. His book, written after the *Almagest*, was modeled after the work of Marinus of Tyre, but Ptolemy added a unique dimension by placing his predecessor's information into a scientific structure. He assumed that Earth was round, that its surface was divided into five parallel zones, and that there were other circles from the equator to the poles. He was the first geographer to write of "parallels of latitude" and "meridians of longitude." Ptolemy, however, did make one crucial mistake. Along with other ancient geographers, he underestimated the circumference of Earth, and as a consequence few latitudes were established correctly (and, since the means were not available, no longitudes were established).

What most attracted the interest and attention of earlier geographers and of Ptolemy was the size of the inhabited world: in the north, Thule (the present Shetland Islands); in the west, the Fortunate Islands (the Canary Islands and Madeira); and in the south and east, the vast continents of Africa and Asia. Although they overestimated the size of both the eastern and southern continents, Ptolemy's findings, and Marinus' before him, were based on new knowledge derived from travelers' accounts of the silk trade with China and from sea voyages in the Indian Ocean. Ptolemy revised some of Marinus' estimates of the length and breadth of Asia and Africa, extending Asia eastward and Europe westward. More than a thousand years later, Christopher Columbus, who relied on Ptolemy's *Geography*, was led to believe that it was possible to reach Asia by a direct route across the Atlantic Ocean.

Ptolemy's *Geography* is restricted to mathematical calculations; he did not write about the physical attributes of the countries he charted or the people who inhabited them. His tables, stating the location of places in terms of latitude and longitude, gave a false impression of precision; he made frequent errors because of his basic misestimate of the size of Earth. Still, Ptolemy's objective to draw a world

map was noteworthy. His educated guess as to the location of the sources of the Nile River was remarkable, and his use of the terms "latitude" and "longitude" was a distinct contribution to the advancement of geographical knowledge.

While Ptolemy is well-known among historians of science for his volumes on astronomy and geography, it is also necessary to consider his writings on astrology, which in the ancient world was the "science" of religions. His volume *Apotelesmatika* (*Tetrabiblos*, which means "four books") is important partly because it was more famous than the *Almagest* and partly because it reflects the popular thinking of his age. The *Tetrabiblos* is a summary of Egyptian, Chaldean, and Greek ideas. It attributes human characteristics to the planets, such as masculine and feminine, beneficent and malevolent. It predicts the future of races, of countries and cities, and speaks of catastrophes, natural and human: wars, famine, plagues, earthquakes, and floods. It also expounds on such subjects as marriage, children, the periods of life, and the quality of death. Translated into Arabic, Latin, Spanish, and English, it influenced generations of Europeans (and, later, Americans) and formed the basis of modern astrological beliefs.

There are many historians of science who deplore the superstitions that pervade the *Tetrabiblos* and dismiss it as an unfortunate effort. The great historian George Sarton believes, however, that "we should be indulgent to Ptolemy, who had innocently accepted the prejudices endemic in his age and could not foresee their evil consequences. . . ."

Summary

It would be unreasonable to expect great scientific breakthroughs during the second century A.D., and they did not happen. What did occur was the gradual advancement of knowledge to which Ptolemy contributed. Not only did Ptolemy write the *Almagest* and the *Geography*, adding new and significant materials to that of his predecessors, but he also attempted to illuminate the science of optics and the art of music. In the first case, although little was known about the anatomical and physiological structure of the eye, he devised a table of refraction, and his book reveals that he understood that a ray of light deviates when it passes from one medium into another of a different density. He addressed the role of light and color in vision, with various kinds of optical illusions and with reflection. Ptolemy's volume on music theory, known as the *Harmonica*, covers the mathematical intervals between notes and their classification. He propounded a theory that steered a middle ground between mathematical calculations and the evidence of the ear. Observation was again a guiding principle of his art as well as his science.

Other work on mechanics, dimensions, and the elements was done but has not survived. What did survive had great influence on the Arabic science of astronomy, led to the rise of European astronomy, and influenced the work of Copernicus himself in the fifteenth century. The *Geography*, also translated into Arabic in the ninth century, was amended to describe more accurately the territories under Islamic rule; in the West, where the work became known in the fifteenth century, it was a catalyst of cartography and to the work of the Flemish cartographer Gerardus Mercator. Ptolemy's work on optics inspired the great improvements made by the Arabic scientist Ibn al-Haytham (died 1039), and his work became the foundation of the *Perspectiva* of Witelo (c. 1274), the standard optical treatise of the late Middle Ages.

Just as there is no exact knowledge of Ptolemy's birth date, there is no reliable information about when and where he died and under what circumstances. Yet those biographical facts are not that important; what is significant is the scientific legacy which was transmitted through the centuries. Ptolemy was not, as one expert has argued, an "original genius"; his forte was to take existing knowledge and to shape it into clear and careful prose.

Bibliography

Barker, Andrew, ed. *Greek Musical Writings*. Vol. 2, *Harmonic and Acoustic Theory*. Cambridge and New York: Cambridge University Press, 1989. Pp. 270-391 of the book contain an English translation of Ptolemy's *Harmonics*, supplied with a short introduction and very detailed explanatory notes.

Britton, John P. *Models and Precision: The Quality of Ptolemy's Observations and Parameters*. New York: Garland, 1992. This is a highly technical and detailed study that traces the errors in Ptolemy's recorded observations of the sun and the moon.

Neugebauer, Otto. *The Exact Sciences in Antiquity*. 2d ed. Providence, R.I.: Brown University Press, 1957. A study of Babylonian and Egyptian mathematics and astronomy, with a chapter describing the Ptolemaic system and comparing it with modern astronomical theory. The book was also issued in a paperback edition by Dover Press in New York in 1969.

Newton, Robert R. *The Crime of Claudius Ptolemy*. Baltimore: The Johns Hopkins University Press, 1977. The "crime," according to the author, is that Ptolemy fabricated observations to confirm his theories and that his work in astronomy is basically fraudulent. Newton concludes that Ptolemy was not a first-rate astronomer, even in terms of the period in which he lived.

North, John. *The Fontana History of Astronomy and Cosmology*. London: Fontana Press, 1994; as *The Norton History of Astronomy and Cosmology*. Roy Porter, ed. New York: Norton, 1995. The section on Ptolemy is very clearly written, successively examining his observations on each of the heavenly bodies. In general, the book, the latest of the few general histories of astronomy available, helps to see Ptolemy within the contexts of that science's development.

Ptolemy. *Ptolemy's "Almagest."* Translated by G. J. Toomer. London: Duckworth, and New York: Springer Verlag, 1984. For students and readers who may want to sample the scientific work of Ptolemy in one of the most recent English translations of his mathematical astronomy. The translator has also provided a twenty-six-page introduction and lengthy annotations.

————. *Ptolemy's Theory of Visual Perception.* A. M. Smith, trans. Philadelphia: American Philosophical Society, 1996. The long introduction comprises a biographical sketch on Ptolemy, a history of the textual transmission of the optics, an overview of its contents, and a survey of its historical influence. The notes are quite detailed, there are Latin-English and English-Latin indices to the text.

Sarton, George. *Ancient Science and Modern Civilization.* London: Edward Arnold, and Lincoln: University of Nebraska Press, 1954. The great Montgomery lecture on "Ptolemy and His Time" takes up thirty-six pages of this book. The paper describes Ptolemy's work in astronomy, geography, astrology, and optics but does not help place Ptolemy in historical context.

Taub, Liba C. *Ptolemy's Universe: The Natural Philosophical and Ethical Foundations of Ptolemy's Astronomy.* Chicago: Open Court, 1993. Rather than being simply a technical study of Ptolemy's astronomy, this book offers a broad analysis of his world view. It moves from a short chapter on his life, through an exposition of his cosmology, to an examination of the ethical motivation to study astronomy.

Toomer, G. J. "Ptolemy." In *Dictionary of Scientific Biography*, edited by Charles C. Gillispie, vol. 11. New York: Scribner, 1980. A careful dissection of Ptolemy's contributions, an assessment of his importance as a scientist, and a tracing of the transmission of his work to Islam and to Western Europe. The article includes an extensive bibliography.

David L. Sterling

PTOLEMY PHILADELPHUS

Born: February, 308 B.C.; Cos
Died: 246 B.C.; Alexandria, Egypt
Area of Achievement: Government
Contribution: Under Ptolemy, the domestic institutions and the foreign policy characteristic of Hellenistic Egypt matured. His patronage of the arts and sciences established Alexandria as the most important cultural center of the Greek world.

Early Life

In 308, Ptolemy Soter (fighting to secure his place among the Macedonian dynasts eager to claim their share of Alexander the Great's legacy) personally led an expedition into the Aegean in order to anchor his influence in the region through alliances and a series of naval bases. Along with Ptolemy Soter went his third wife, Berenice, who gave birth to Ptolemy Philadelphus on the island of Cos. Berenice was the least well connected of the polygamous Ptolemy's three wives. She had come to Egypt in the retinue of Eurydice, when that daughter of Antipater came as Ptolemy's bride. Despite her political insignificance, Berenice was Ptolemy's favorite spouse, and her son Ptolemy Philadelphus became heir to Egypt over the claims of an older son of Eurydice, Ptolemy Ceraunus, meaning "thunderbolt."

Ptolemy Philadelphus was not to be the man of action his father had been. Reared at an urbane court in the greatest city of the Greek world, he was a devotee of a softer, if more culturally inclined, life. He had the best of educations under the likes of the Aristotelian Straton and became a king who preferred to rule from his capital, rather than personally oversee his varied foreign interests.

In order to facilitate the transfer of authority to his chosen son, Ptolemy Soter elevated Ptolemy Philadelphus to the throne in 284, and they ruled jointly until Ptolemy Soter died about two years later. On the accession of his half brother, Ptolemy Ceraunus fled Egypt to the court of Lysimachus in Thrace, when his sister, Lysandra, was married to the son of Lysimachus named Agathocles. Also in Thrace, however, was Arsinoe II, the sister of Ptolemy Philadelphus and the wife of the much older Lysimachus. Probably to foster the inheritance of her own young sons, Arsinoe II convinced her husband that Agathocles was engaged in treason. Lysimachus subsequently had Agathocles executed, and, as a result, both Lysandra and Ceraunus

fled to the Asian court of Seleucus. When Seleucus defeated and killed Lysimachus in 281, Ceraunus fought for the victor.

The true nature of Ceraunus' loyalty, however, revealed itself when he soon after assassinated Seleucus and seized Thrace. Arsinoe II fled to Macedonia on the death of Lysimachus, to secure it for her children. Not satisfied with the murder of Seleucus, Ceraunus aspired to add Macedonia to his realm, which he surprisingly accomplished by marrying Arsinoe II. For reasons which are not entirely clear, Ceraunus eventually butchered two of Arsinoe's three sons. Perhaps Ceraunus limited his wife's freedom, but she remained in Macedonia until he was killed fighting Gauls in 279. With Macedonia overrun by barbarians, Arsinoe II and her surviving son, Ptolemy, again fled, this time home to Egypt.

Ptolemy Philadelphus' queen was another woman named Arsinoe (a daughter of Lysimachus), by whom he already had three children. Nevertheless, not long after Arsinoe II came to his court, Ptolemy exiled his first wife, and sometime before 274, he married his sister. It was this union which later earned for Ptolemy the name "Philadelphus." (Arsinoe II alone bore the title in life.) The marriage scandalized many of Ptolemy's Greco-Macedonian subjects, but royal brother-sister unions were known in Egypt, and its consummation had the effect of drawing the Europeans in Egypt closer to native tradition.

Life's Work

Ptolemy ruled Egypt at the height of its Hellenistic power, but before the return of Arsinoe II to Egypt, little is known of Ptolemy's foreign ambitions. In the early 270's he was interested in fostering a regular spice trade with Arabia and as a result recut a neglected ancient canal from the Nile's delta to the Gulf of Suez. Ptolemy subsequently patronized the exploration of the Red Sea (complete with colonies along the African coast) and voyages to India. His desire to tap the exotic luxuries of the East found a counterpart in his interests in sub-Saharan Africa. In fact, the only known foreign expedition personally led by Ptolemy went to Ethiopia in order to strengthen trade to the south. Perhaps Ptolemy's most interesting foreign policy initiative came in 273, when he sent an embassy to Rome and became the first Hellenistic monarch to establish friendly relations with the Republic, which had only recently unified peninsular Italy.

Arsinoe II's holdings in the Aegean (a legacy from her days as Macedonian queen) expanded the interests of Egypt in that region and eventually pitted Ptolemy against Antigonus I Gonatas, whose victories over the Gauls won for him Macedonia. Perhaps prompted by his wife's more assertive personality, in the 270's Ptolemy initiated an aggressive foreign policy which challenged not only Antigonus Gonatas, but the Seleucids as well.

His first conflict of note, the First Syrian War (circa 276 to 271), was fought against the Seleucid Antiochus I over the Phoenician coast. This land not only lay astride the best approach to Egypt but also was an important terminus for trade which stretched eastward along several routes. In this war, Antiochus secured Damascus and successfully incited Magas (Ptolemy's half brother and governor of Cyrene) to rebellion, but Ptolemy's superior fleet was a scourge to Seleucid coastal settlements and eventually won the war for him. By its end, Ptolemy had regained Cyrene and extended his control of the coast northward into Syria. Arsinoe II was probably instrumental in planning the war, since soon after its conclusion, Ptolemy approved worship of her under the auspices of a state-cult, the first attested worship of a living human being since Alexander the Great. Indeed, Arsinoe's political clout must have been enormous, since her portrait appeared with that of Ptolemy on Egyptian coins—an honor exclusively reserved for Hellenistic monarchs. Arsinoe died in July, 269.

In the Balkans, Ptolemy was a party to the Chremonidean War (from 266 to 261, named for an Athenian) in which Athens, expecting strong Egyptian backing, led a Greek coalition against Macedonia. Accounts of this war are extremely fragmentary, making a reconstruction of its significance difficult. The reason Ptolemy did not order his forces in the Aegean to exploit the war more effectively is not known, but by and large they remained on the fringes while Antigonus Gonatas defeated his opponents. Perhaps there is more than a grain of truth in the hypothesis that Ptolemy was an indecisive strategist when not influenced by the forceful Arsinoe II.

Whether the Egyptian success in the First Syrian War was because of Arsinoe, the Second Syrian War (circa 260 to 253) saw Ptolemaic losses. Not long after his accession, the Seleucid Antiochus II

attacked Ptolemaic possessions along the coast of Asia Minor. A complicated and elusive struggle followed, until Ptolemy conceded much of the Syrian coast under his garrison. The resulting place was fixed by the marriage which joined Ptolemy's daughter, Berenice, to Antiochus II.

At home, Ptolemy II faced a brief challenge to his authority in the 270's from a brother, Argaeus, and was forced to recognize the semi-autonomy of Magas in Cyrene. Ptolemy was very successful, however, in establishing a variety of institutions which anchored the legitimacy of his dynasty in Egypt. For example, for the Macedonians who still remembered their native land and its traditions, at the beginning of his reign, Ptolemy established a royal cemetery in Alexandria around the remains of Alexander the Great and Ptolemy Soter. This foundation re-created in Egypt an institution from the homeland and provided a focus for the loyalties of the Macedonians in Egypt. It also acted as a bridge between the legitimacy of the extinct house of Alexander and the new authority of Ptolemy's dynasty. Its political purpose is manifest: Ptolemy laid first claim to the authority of Alexander.

It was under Ptolemy that the apparatus which ruled Hellenistic Egypt matured. The native pharaonic system was too efficient a revenue producer to be abandoned, but the Ptolemies could not afford to trust their security to the loyalty of native Egyptians. As a result, the Ptolemies grafted an immigrant Greco-Macedonian ruling class onto the stock of Egyptian society and tried as much as possible to maintain the distinctiveness of the two social orders (for example, by severely limiting native Egyptian access to the city of Alexandria). Such a policy was doomed at least in the Egyptian countryside, but in the time of Ptolemy it worked. Egypt was the sole possession of the Ptolemaic kings. Except for those estates alienated by the Ptolemies to attract European settlement, it remained their private property. The geographical isolation of Egypt made it possible to sever all but officially sanctioned foreign trade, and its economy was monopolized in the interests of the dynasty. Native Egyptians were compelled to render to Ptolemy at a fixed rate a percentage of their grain, which he thereafter sold abroad at a huge profit, while the immigrants paid significant taxes for the use of their land. In turn, these profits paid not only for such things as cultural patronage and the construction of a city which was home to about one million people but also for the domestic and foreign security ensured by Ptolemy's sizable Greco-Macedonian military establishment.

Like his father before him, Ptolemy elevated his heir, Ptolemy Euergetes (a son of Arsinoe I), to royal authority before his own demise. Ptolemy Philadelphus, having no sons by Arsinoe II, seems originally to have selected as his heir Arsinoe II's only son to have survived Agathocles, but this Ptolemy apparently died in 258. Ptolemy Philadelphus died shortly after passing on the burdens of his office to his son.

Summary

The domestic and foreign policies which made Ptolemy Philadelphus' Egypt the most stable Hellenistic power of his day were very expensive and pushed Egypt to its financial limit. Although an adequate defense of Egypt proper was maintained, the rivalries with Antigonid Macedonia and Seleucid Asia drained the treasury greatly. Arsinoe II may have been responsible for unleashing an aggressive foreign policy, but without her decisiveness to carry the stratagem through, Ptolemy's remote interests languished, taking second place to Alexandrian pleasures.

Evidence suggests that Ptolemy was both intellectually curious and self-indulgent. He was a renowned cultural patron, attracting outstanding poets such as Theocritus and Callimachus to his court. Although Ptolemy patronized the greatest Hellenistic poets, perhaps his greatest cultural legacy resulted from his support of scientific and technological investigation. Ptolemy encouraged such investigation through the great museum and library in Alexandria, which were to be the cultural mainstays of the Hellenistic tradition for the rest of antiquity. The concentration of talent attracted to Alexandria by royal patronage brought the city a luster which drew intellectuals who did not directly enjoy Ptolemy's largess. Jews in large numbers took advantage of the city's resources and there produced a Greek version of their sacred texts, which was to begin the process whereby the Jewish and Hellenistic traditions would intermingle. Ptolemy personally enjoyed the artistic fruits of his patronage, but he also benefited in practical ways: Figures such as the poet Appollonius gave him political advice, and his engineers constantly improved the technological efficiency of the Ptolemaic navy, thus enabling the fleet to remain competitive while Ptolemy was occupied elsewhere.

It is unfair to describe Ptolemy as either lazy or hedonistic, for he was very much concerned with the administration of his kingdom at a time when his dynasty's hold on Egypt was anything but traditionally anchored. Nevertheless, his talents were hardly those of his Macedonian predecessors. He did not feel comfortable leading troops into battle as had Philip II, Alexander the Great, Ptolemy Soter, or even men such as his own contemporary, Pyrrhus. His style of kingship—surrounding himself with elaborate layers of court officials and a well-oiled administration—tempered the martial spirit which underscored the foundation of Alexander's Macedonian empire and its division. A new age had dawned, an age which based its legitimacy on conquest but aspired to more peaceful pursuits.

Bibliography

Bevan, Edwyn R. *The House of Ptolemy.* London: Methuen, 1927; Chicago: Argonaut, 1968. A standard account of the Ptolemaic dynasty. Includes a chapter on the reign of Ptolemy Philadelphus.

Burstein, Stanley. "Arsinoe II Philadelphos: A Revisionist View." In *Philip II, Alexander the Great, and the Macedonian Heritage*, W. Lindsay Adams and Eugene N. Borza, eds. Washington, D.C.: University Press of America, 1982. Argues that Arsinoe II should not be credited with single-handedly devising Ptolemy's foreign policy.

Cary, M. *A History of the Greek World, 323-146 B.C.* 2d ed. London: Methuen and Co., and New York: Barnes and Noble, 1951. Includes not only a useful outline of Ptolemy's domestic and foreign affairs but also a review of the cultural importance of Alexandria.

Fraser, Peter Marshall. *Ptolemaic Alexandria.* 3 vols. Oxford: Clarendon Press, 1972. The authoritative study of the Ptolemaic capital and virtually every institution associated with the Ptolemaic dynasty. An essential work for anyone interested in the development of Ptolemaic society.

Macurdy, Grace Harriet. *Hellenistic Queens.* Baltimore: Johns Hopkins University Press, and London: Oxford University Press, 1932. Includes excellent reviews of what is known of the careers of Arsinoe I and Arsinoe II and, in connection with the latter, a standard summary of her influence over her brother and husband, Ptolemy.

Turner, E. G. "Ptolemaic Egypt." In *The Cambridge Ancient History.* Vol. 7, *The Hellenistic World.* 2d ed. Cambridge and New York: Cambridge University Press, 1984. A review of the Ptolemaic system in Egypt. Includes a good discussion of the social structures harnessed and exploited by Ptolemy.

William S. Greenwalt

PTOLEMY SOTER

Born: 367 or 366 B.C.; the canton of Eordaea, Macedonia

Died: 283 or 282 B.C.; Alexandria, Egypt

Area of Achievement: Government

Contribution: A companion of Alexander the Great during the conquest of the Persian Empire, Ptolemy came to rule Egypt shortly after Alexander died—first as a satrap under Philip III and Alexander IV and after the extinction of the Argead royal family as a king in his own right. Ptolemy thereby founded the dynasty which ruled Egypt until the death of Cleopatra VII in 30 B.C.

Early Life

Ptolemy Soter's origins are obscure—and were so even in his lifetime, when jokes were made about his grandfather's lack of distinction. Ptolemy's father was named Lagus, although in order to enhance his legitimacy among the Macedonians he later ruled in Egypt, rumor maintained that he was an illegitimate son of Philip II and thus that he was the half brother of Alexander the Great. Ptolemy's mother was named Arsinoe, and she may have been distantly related to the Argead royal house. Ptolemy was born in Eordaea, a region in western Macedonia which was firmly brought within the political orbit of the Argead royal house only during the reign of Philip II.

Ptolemy probably came to live at the Argead court in the 350's (after Philip's victory over an Illyrian coalition which threatened Macedonia from the northwest), as Eordaea then fell under direct Argead rule. In order to control the newly incorporated cantons of Upper Macedonia, Philip invited the sons of aristocratic western families to his court at Pella. These youths served as royal pages, responsible for (among other things) the protection of the king's person. The honor associated with becoming a member of the pages was augmented by the educational opportunities (military, political, and cultural) available at court. The selection of royal pages, however, served not only to redirect the loyalty of young aristocrats but also to provide the king with hostages in order to secure the good behavior of their families.

Ptolemy is first mentioned in ancient sources with respect to the so-called Pixodarus Affair. In 337, as Philip was searching for political connec-

tions in Asia as a prelude to his proposed attack on the Persian Empire, he made diplomatic contact with the satrap of Caria, Pixodarus, to whose daughter he betrothed his handicapped son, Arrhidaeus. At the time of this initiative, Alexander the Great was temporarily alienated from his father as a result of Philip's last marriage and was in self-imposed exile.

When Alexander learned of Philip's move, he was afraid that Philip had jeopardized his status as heir to the throne. As a result, Alexander rashly interfered with Philip's plans by offering himself to Pixodarus in lieu of Arrhidaeus. The Carian was delighted with the proposed substitution, but Philip was not. Upon learning of Alexander's obstruction, Philip both broke off diplomatic contact with Pixodarus and severely chastised his son. In the wake of Philip's anger, several of Alexander's associates, including Ptolemy, were exiled from Macedonia.

Many have seen Ptolemy's exile as a result of his long-standing intimacy with Alexander, but such a close friendship between the two is doubtful since Ptolemy was eleven years older than Philip's heir—almost as close in age to Philip as he was to Alexander. By the 330's Philip seemed to have appointed Ptolemy as a counselor to Alexander, with a responsibility to advise the son according to the interests of the father. When Alexander embarrassed Philip in the Pixodarus Affair, the king drove out of Macedonia those who had failed him. Fortunately for Ptolemy, Philip was assassinated not long thereafter (336), and when Alexander became king, he brought home those who had suffered exile.

Life's Work

Although Ptolemy accompanied Alexander into Asia, he did so initially in a minor capacity—proving that Ptolemy had not been an intimate of Alexander. Ptolemy's first command came in 330, when he led one of several units at the battle which gave the Macedonians access to Persia proper. Ptolemy became a figure of the first rank shortly afterward, when he replaced a certain Demetrius as one of Alexander's seven eminent bodyguards, whose duty it was to wait closely on the king in matters of consequence. Ptolemy further distinguished himself in 329, when he personally brought to Alexander Bessus, Alexander's last rival for the Persian throne.

Having attained Alexander's confidence, Ptolemy's service at the side of the king alternated with independent assignments. In 328 he commanded one of five columns as Alexander drove into Sogdiana, in 327 he was instrumental in the capture of the fortress of Chorienes, and, while the Macedonians campaigned along the Indus River (327-325), Ptolemy often led both Macedonian and mercenary troops. The return of Alexander to Susa in 324 brought Ptolemy military honors, his first wife (the Persian Artacama), and additional commands in coordination with Alexander.

The death of Alexander at Babylon in 323 precipitated a constitutional crisis, since the only male Argead living was the mentally deficient Arrhidaeus. Alexander's son by Roxane, Alexander IV, would be born several months after his father's passing. Perdiccas, the officer to whom the dying Alexander had given his signet ring in a gesture of unknown significance, dominated the discussions concerning succession and advised the Macedonians to accept an interregnum until it could be determined whether Roxane would give birth to a son. Among others, Ptolemy objected to the unprecedented leadership role Perdiccas had delegated himself. Dissension infected the Macedonian army until a compromise averting civil war was adopted. It was agreed that the throne should go to Arrhidaeus (who was given the throne name of Philip III), until such time as Roxane gave birth to a son. When that eventuality occurred, a dual monarchy was established. Since neither king was competent, both were put under the protection of Perdiccas. There followed a general distribution of satrapies in which Ptolemy received Egypt.

Once in Egypt, Ptolemy asserted control over the satrapy and extended his authority to incorporate the region around Cyrene. He then used his considerable resources to challenge the authority of Perdiccas. His first open act of defiance concerned the body of Alexander the Great. Whether the Macedonians originally meant to bury Alexander in Macedonia or at the oracular shrine of Ammon located at the oasis of Siwah in the Egyptian desert, when Alexander's funeral procession reached Syria, Ptolemy diverted the remains to Memphis, where they were enshrined until the late 280's, when they were transferred to a complex in Alexandria. Perdiccas saw the appropriation of Alexander's corpse as a rejection of his own authority and in 321 led an expedition to Egypt against Ptolemy.

By this time, others had begun to question the ambitions of Perdiccas, and a coalition including especially Ptolemy, Antipater, and Antigonus formed to strip Perdiccas of his office. In the resulting war, Perdiccas failed miserably in an attempt to force his way into Egypt and was assassinated by his own men for his failure. Ptolemy thereafter successfully appealed to the Macedonians of Perdiccas' army and persuaded many of them to settle in Egypt. One option—that of replacing Perdiccas as the guardian of the kings—Ptolemy refused, preferring to retain his Egyptian base.

Although Perdiccas was dead, Eumenes, his most important ally, remained free in Asia. In response to this new situation, a redistribution of satrapies occurred at Triparadisus. Ptolemy again received Egypt, while Antipater returned to Macedonia with the kings and Antigonus waged war against Eumenes. Ptolemy anchored an expanded influence by taking Antipater's daughter, Eurydice, as a second wife. (A third—Berenice I—was culled from Eurydice's retinue. Ptolemy's polygamy had a precedent in the Argead house.)

The death of Antipater in 319 initiated a new era. The royal family split behind the claims of the two kings, and a civil war erupted. Eventually, both kings were murdered: Philip III by Olympias in 317, and Alexander IV by Cassander in 311 or 310. Through inscriptions and coins, however, it is known that Ptolemy remained loyal to the kings of the Argead house until they were no more. Despite his professed Argead loyalties, Ptolemy continued to secure Egypt at the expense of rivals. In particular, he seized the coast of Palestine in order to safeguard the only viable access to Egypt by land.

In addition to these problems, Antigonus' success and ultimate victory over Eumenes in 316 destabilized the balance of power which had been established among the Macedonian officers at Triparadisus. High-handed actions, such as Antigonus' expulsion of Seleucus from his Babylonian satrapy, created a fear of a second Perdiccas. An alliance consisting of Ptolemy, Cassander, Lysimachus, and Seleucus demanded that Antigonus surrender his authority. When Antigonus refused, war erupted anew. This conflict continued intermittently until Antigonus was killed at a battle near Ipsus in 301. Ptolemy saw action in Palestine (where he defeated Demetrius, the son of Antigonus, at a battle near Gaza in 312) and amid the confusion built the beginnings of a maritime empire in the eastern Mediterranean.

Although this period saw the expansion of Ptolemy's influence, most of his early gains beyond Egypt were tenuously held and setbacks occurred. For example, in 306, Demetrius defeated the Ptolemaic navy off the island of Cyprus in an action so decisive that both he and his father subsequently claimed the title of "king." Once Antigonus and Demetrius claimed the royal mantle from the defunct Argead house, others followed suit, including Ptolemy in 305.

After Ipsus, Ptolemy reestablished influence abroad, retaking Cyprus and actively engaging in Aegean affairs. His occupation of Palestine after 301, however, precipitated a series of wars with the Seleucids in the third century. These civil wars established a rough balance among the emerging powers of Macedonia, Egypt, and Seleucid Asia. This balance was constantly under strain and ever shifting in its precise makeup, composed as it was of infant dynasties seeking legitimacy and leverage.

Egypt also claimed Ptolemy's attention. He inherited an efficient bureaucratic apparatus of great antiquity, capable of funneling great wealth to his coffers. Nevertheless, Ptolemy could not afford to rely on the loyalty of native Egyptians. Rather, he grafted a new Greco-Macedonian aristocracy onto the existing political structure. Recruitment was a major concern, and Ptolemy made every effort to attract Greek mercenaries, military colonists, and professionals accomplished in administration. The wealth of Egypt made possible these initiatives, and each recruit was guaranteed a respectable status as long as Ptolemy remained secure.

In part to unify these enlistees of varied background, Ptolemy combined elements of the Egyptian worship of Osiris and Apis to manufacture the cult of a new deity: Serapis. Traditionally, religion helped to define the parameters of Greek political communities, and the invented Serapis successfully drew Ptolemy's immigrants together. In addition, in an age of emerging ruler cults, Ptolemy posthumously was worshipped as a god (indeed, to the Egyptians, who worshipped him as pharaoh, he was naturally considered divine), receiving the epithet "Soter" (savior) from the Rhodians for his naval protection.

Under Ptolemy, Alexandria became the foremost city of the Hellenistic world. Planned on a grand scale, it held architectural wonders and became the greatest literary and intellectual center of the age, with its focus being the great museum and library complex. In 284, after decades of molding Egypt to his liking, Ptolemy shared royal authority with a son by Berenice, Ptolemy II, better known as Ptolemy Philadelphus. Ptolemy Soter died shortly thereafter (in 283 or 282) at the age of eighty-four.

Summary

Ptolemy Soter was the one great link between Greece's classical age—characterized by its narrow geographical orientation and exclusive appreciation of the Greek cultural heritage—and the Hellenistic age, with its expanded horizons. He took advantage of the opportunities presented by the moment to rise as far as hard work could take him and was instrumental in combining Hellenistic traditions with those of the Orient—a mixture which was a hallmark of the Hellenistic period. Not the most talented of Alexander's successors in military affairs, Ptolemy nevertheless understood, even better than Alexander himself, how long-term stability depended on the careful selection of a defendable base coupled with a steady consolidation of resources. His success can be appreciated best once it is realized that he alone of the officers who received assignments in Babylon in 323 passed his legacy on to his descendants. He did more than politically anchor Egypt in a time of unprecedented change: Because of his patronage, which brought so many fertile minds to Alexandria, he was also able to shape the cultural experience which would dominate the civilized Western world for hundreds of years.

The range of Ptolemy's talents is not fully appreciated until it is realized that he was not only an active ruler and a cultural patron but also a historian of note. Late in life, he wrote an account of Alexander's conquests based not only on his own observations but also on important written sources (including a journal which detailed the king's activities on a daily basis, at least for the end of Alexander's reign). Although Ptolemy's account was slanted in his own favor, no other eyewitness account of the Macedonian conquest can claim greater objectivity. No longer extant, Ptolemy's work was one of the principal sources used in the second century of the Christian era by Arrian, whose history is the best extant account of Alexander's life. Without Ptolemy's attention to detail, present knowledge about Alexander would be considerably less accurate.

Bibliography

Bevan, Edwyn R. *The House of Ptolemy*. London: Methuen, 1927; Chicago: Argonaut, 1968. The standard English history of the Ptolemaic dynasty. The chapter devoted to Ptolemy I briefly reviews his pre-Egyptian career but concentrates on his achievements after 323.

Bowman, Alan K. *Egypt After the Pharaohs*. Berkeley: University of California Press, and London: British Museum Publications, 1986. This work is a broad introduction to Egypt between the conquests of Alexander and the Arabs. As such, it covers the Ptolemaic period, especially insofar as its political and social institutions evolved.

Ellis, Walter M. *Ptolemy of Egypt*. London and New York: Routledge, 1994. This biography mainly traces the political history of Ptolemy's reign, but also has a chapter titled "Ptolemy the Historian."

Fraser, Peter Marshall. *Ptolemaic Alexandria*. 3 vols. Oxford: Clarendon, 1972. The authoritative study of the Ptolemaic capital and virtually every institution associated with the Macedonian presence in Egypt. An essential work for anyone interested in how Ptolemy developed the infrastructure of his realm.

Pearson, Lionel. *The Lost Histories of Alexander the Great*. New York: American Philological Association, 1960. A chapter is devoted to Ptolemy's lost history of Alexander.

Tarn, W. W., and G. T. Griffith. *Hellenistic Civilization*. 3d ed. New York: New American Library, 1952. Chapter 1 provides a historical outline of the period (including Ptolemy's contributions), which is unsurpassed in its concise political and military coverage.

Turner, E. G. "Ptolemaic Egypt." In *The Cambridge Ancient History*. Vol. 7, *The Hellenistic World*. 2d ed. Cambridge and New York: Cambridge University Press, 1984. A review of Ptolemy's accomplishment in Egypt, with special attention devoted to the domestic difficulties associated with stabilization of Macedonian authority.

Walbank, R. W. *The Hellenistic World*. Rev. ed. London: Fontana, 1992; Cambridge, Mass.: Harvard University Press, 1993. One of the best introductions to the period in English, especially insofar as it traces the emergence of Hellenistic kingdoms.

William S. Greenwalt

PYRRHON OF ELIS

Born: c. 360 B.C.; Elis, Greece
Died: c. 272 B.C.; buried in village of Petra, near Elis
Area of Achievement: Philosophy
Contribution: The founder of skepticism, Pyrrhon, a companion of Alexander the Great, taught that the nature of things is inapprehensible; his attitude greatly influenced science and philosophy throughout antiquity.

Early Life

Few details about the life of Pyrrhon have been preserved. Born in Elis, Pyrrhon was the son of Pleistarchus or, by other accounts, Pleitocrates. Apparently of humble background, Pyrrhon first studied painting, no doubt influenced by the master Apelles in nearby Sikyon, then briefly turned his hand to poetry. Pyrrhon's early philosophical training must have begun soon thereafter; he studied under Bryson and Anaxarchus (a pupil of Democritus and adviser to Alexander the Great), whom he joined in the Macedonian invasion of Persia and India in 331 B.C. During that invasion, Pyrrhon gained a reputation for high moral conduct among the quarrelsome Macedonians. After returning to his native Elis, he was awarded a high priesthood and was exempted from taxes; he also received honorary Athenian citizenship and knew Aristotle, Epicurus, the Academic Arcesilaus, and Zeno of Citium. A tradition that Alexander had provided Pyrrhon with a comfortable endowment may help to account for the philosopher's high social standing. Although probably a man of some means, he was renowned for his modest and withdrawn life.

Pyrrhon's Greece witnessed a major revolution in philosophical thinking as the old political order of independent city-states yielded to the Hellenistic empires. Pyrrhonistic philosophy joined the Epicurean and the Stoic in seeking ways to achieve *ataraxia*—a personal state of freedom from worldly cares. Pyrrhon differed both from his contemporaries and from the previous skeptical trends of Xenophanes, Heraclitus, Democritus, and the Sophists, in that he held no dogmatic position concerning the nature of truth. According to Pyrrhon and his followers, the phenomena of sense experience are neither true nor false, and there is no access to any proof of reality beyond the empirical world. The wise and happy man takes an agnostic stance on the nature of reality.

Pyrrhon did not establish a formal school as did Epicurus and Zeno, though he was the mentor of Philo of Athens, Nausiphanes of Teios, and Timon of Phlius, his only true successor. In his third century A.D. *Peri biōn dogmatōn kai apophthegmatōn tōn en philosophia eudokimēsantōn (Lives and Opinions of Eminent Philosophers*, 1688), Diogenes Laërtius quotes extensively from the writings of Timon and from the life of Pyrrhon written by Antigonus of Carystus shortly after the philosopher's death. Diogenes Laërtius' account, together with Cicero's somewhat problematic references, provides an important check on the portrait presented by later skeptical thinkers, including the major work of second century A.D. skeptic Sextus Empiricus.

Life's Work

The second century A.D. Peripatetic philosopher Aristocles of Messana quotes Timon, saying that the happy man must examine three questions: What is the nature of things, what attitude should one adopt with respect to them, and what will be the result for those who adopt this attitude?

Pyrrhon held that things by nature are inapprehensible (*akatalypsias*) and indeterminate (*adiaphora*). Making use of the established distinction between appearances and reality, Pyrrhon elaborated, stating that sense experiences and beliefs are neither true nor false because the true nature of things, if one exists, cannot be known.

Pyrrhonistic skepticism is summed up in the following formula: The nature of things no more is than is not, than both is and is not, than neither is nor is not. Shortened to the phrase "no more," the indeterminability of nature leads the wise man to withhold judgment (*aprosthetein*). According to Pyrrhon, "That honey is sweet I do not grant; that it seems so, I agree." The objective world cannot be perceived, and no ultimate truth can be assigned to subjective observations.

Pyrrhon did not urge the cessation of inquiry into the natural world. On the contrary, he held that the skeptic should continue to seek truth; this position influenced the development of medicine and science in Cos and in Alexandria. A suspension of judgment for Pyrrhon was a system (*agoge*) which leads to the desired goal of mental imperturbability, *ataraxia*.

While the essential origins of Pyrrhonism clearly are to be found in a purely Greek philosophical dialogue, it is possible that Pyrrhon's epistemology had been influenced by Buddhist thought. Contemporary accounts of Alexander show that the Greeks did have access to interpretations of Indian gymnosophists (literally, "naked wise men"). Alexander and his men, presumably including the youthful Pyrrhon, watched a certain Sphines (called "Calanus" in Greek) voluntarily mount his own funeral pyre, declaring that it was better for him to die than to live. The extent to which Pyrrhon was aware of Buddhist agnosticism or the dictum that happiness was freedom from worldly desires cannot be determined. Pyrrhon's penchant for wandering in deserted places searching for knowledge and his attempt to achieve that state of mind he called "silence" (*aphasia*) may well have had their roots in the asceticism of India.

Given the dominance of ethical questions in Greek thought after Plato, it is not surprising that Pyrrhon also addressed the problem of virtue. The testimony of Timon and Cicero shows that Pyrrhon was a stern moralist who led an exemplary life. Rejecting all definitions of virtue, Pyrrhon declared that without any true guide to moral conduct, one must observe traditional laws and customs. Withdrawn from active life though he may have been, Pyrrhon nevertheless was a good citizen.

It is unfortunate that testimony on Pyrrhon reveals little else about his positions. It may be surmised that the debate between Stoics and later skeptics over possible criteria of right conduct had its origin in Pyrrhon's thought. A poem by Timon mentions a right standard (*orthon canona*) by which he can question those who hold that the nature of the divine and the good makes men live most equably. In this poem, Timon inserts the qualification "as it seems to me to be," perhaps to indicate that the Pyrrhonic standard is the incommensurability of appearance and reality.

Pyrrhon was not original in doubting the ultimate truth of sensory experiences. His true contribution to Greek philosophy lay in his denial of the possibility that true knowledge can be gained by pure reason: If the only access to the world is through phenomena, there is no way to judge these phenomena against any objective model. Pyrrhon thus turned away from the monumental intellectual systems of Plato and Aristotle and helped to usher in an age of empiricism.

Summary

Pyrrhon's empirical skepticism did not outlive his pupil Timon. Skeptical thought did persist, however, in the new Academy of the Aeolian Arcesilaus (315-240 B.C.) and of Carneades (214-129 B.C.). This Academic skepticism was more a second version of skepticism than a direct continuation of Pyrrhonism. The Academics used the Platonic dialectic as their basis for a suspension of judgment on the true nature of things. This Academic skepticism was a direct attack on the Stoic position, which held that some sense impressions were true. Unlike the Pyrrhonists, however, the Academic skeptic did maintain that sense impressions can be representative of an objective, external world.

After Carneades, the next important skeptical thinker was the enigmatic Aenesidemus, who lived sometime between the first century B.C. and the second century A.D. in Alexandria. Aenesidemus reorganized skeptical sayings into ten "tropes," a not-too-original attack on the possibility of deriving true knowledge from perceptual experiences.

The last major figure in the history of ancient skepticism was Sextus Empiricus, a Greek physician who lived sometime between A.D. 150 and 250. The large corpus of Sextus' writing that has been preserved provides the most complete statement of ancient skepticism. A true disciple of Pyrrhon, Sextus used the Pyrrhonistic suspension of judgment in his attacks on the dogmatic positions of contemporary philosophers and physicians. Through Sextus Empiricus, the original philosophy of Pyrrhon of Elis has been saved from oblivion.

Bibliography

Hankinson, R. J. *The Sceptics*. London and New York: Routledge, 1995. The book has a chapter titled "Pyrrhon and the Socratic Tradition," which examines the philosopher's intellectual ancestry and the possible influence of Buddhism on his thought, and attempts to reconstruct his method.

Long, A. A. *Hellenistic Philosophy: Stoics, Epicureans, Sceptics*. 2d ed. Berkeley: University of California Press, and London: Duckworth, 1986. A general work on the three main philosophical schools of the Hellenistic age. Includes a chapter on Pyrrhon and the later skeptics.

Patrick, Mary Mills. *The Greek Sceptics*. New York: Columbia University Press, 1929. A standard work on the skeptics. Includes a somewhat speculative account of the antecedents of Pyrrhon's philosophy.

Schofield, Malcolm, Myles Burnyeat, and Jonathan Barnes, eds. *Doubt and Dogmatism: Studies in Hellenistic Epistemology.* Oxford: Clarendon Press, and New York: Oxford University Press, 1980. This work is a collection of ten essays from a 1978 Oxford conference. Presents detailed studies on Hellenistic theories of knowledge.

Stough, Charlotte. *Greek Skepticism: A Study in Epistemology.* Berkeley: University of California Press, 1969. A thorough investigation of the epistemology of the skeptics. Stough includes a chapter on early Pyrrhonism.

Tarrant, Harold. *Scepticism or Platonism? The Philosophy of the Fourth Academy.* Cambridge and New York: Cambridge University Press, 1985. An original investigation of the first century B.C. philosophies of Philo and Charmadas. Discusses the influence of early Pyrrhonists.

Zeller, Eduard. *The Stoics, Epicureans, and Sceptics.* Translated by Oswald Reichel. Rev. ed. London: Longmans, 1880; New York: Longmans, 1892. Part of Zeller's massive nineteenth century history of Greek philosophy, this work contains a useful chapter on Pyrrhon. Includes bibliographical footnotes.

Murray C. McClellan

PYTHAGORAS

Born: c. 580 B.C.; Samos, Greece

Died: 504 B.C. or 500 B.C.; Croton or Metapontum

Areas of Achievement: Philosophy, mathematics, astronomy, and music

Contribution: Pythagoras set an inspiring example with his energetic search for knowledge of universal order. His specific discoveries and accomplishments in philosophy, mathematics, astronomy, and music theory make him an important figure in Western intellectual history.

Early Life

Pythagoras, son of Mnesarchus, probably was born about 580 B.C. (various sources offer dates ranging from 597 to 560). His birthplace was the Greek island of Samos in the Mediterranean Sea. Aside from these details, information about his early life—most of it from the third and fourth centuries B.C., up to one hundred years after he died—is extremely sketchy. On the other hand, sources roughly contemporary with him tend to contradict one another, possibly because those who had been his students developed in many different directions after his death.

Aristotle's *Metaphysica* (335-323 B.C.; *Metaphysics*), one source of information about Pythagorean philosophy, never refers to Pythagoras himself but always to "the Pythagoreans." Furthermore, it is known that many ideas attributed to Pythagoras have been filtered through Platonism. Nevertheless, certain doctrines and biographical events can be traced with reasonable certainty to Pythagoras himself. His teachers in Greece are said to have included Creophilus and Pherecydes of Syros; the latter (who is identified as history's first prose writer) probably encouraged Pythagoras' belief in the transmigration of souls, which became a major tenet of Pythagorean philosophy. A less certain but more detailed tradition has him also studying under Thales of Miletus, who built a philosophy on rational, positive integers. In fact, these integers were to prove a stumbling block to Pythagoras, but would lead to his discovery of irrational numbers such as the square root of two.

Following his studies in Greece, Pythagoras traveled extensively in Egypt, Babylonia, and other Mediterranean lands, learning the rules of thumb that, collectively, passed for geometry at that time. He was to raise geometry to the level of a true science through his pioneering work on geometric proofs and the axioms, or postulates, from which these are derived.

A bust now housed at Rome's Capitoline Museum (the sculptor is not known) portrays the philosopher as having close-cropped, wavy Greek hair and beard, his features expressing the relentlessly inquiring Ionian mind—a mind that insisted on knowing for metaphysical reasons the *exact* ratio of the side of a square to its diagonal. Pythagoras' eyes suggest an inward focus even as they gaze intently at the viewer. The furrowed forehead conveys solemnity and powerful concentration, yet deeply etched lines around the mouth, and the hint of a crinkle about the eyes, reveal that this great man was fully capable of laughter.

Life's Work

When Pythagoras returned to Samos from his studies abroad, he found his native land in the grip of the tyrant Polycrates, who had come to power about 538 B.C. In the meantime, the Greek mainland had been partially overrun by the Persians. Probably because of these developments, in 529

Pythagoras migrated to Croton, a Dorian colony in southern Italy, and entered into what became the historically important period of his life.

At Croton he founded a school of philosophy that in some ways resembled a monastic order. Its members were pledged to a pure and devout life, close friendship, and political harmony. In the immediately preceding years, southern Italy had been nearly destroyed by the strife of political factions. Modern historians speculate that Pythagoras thought that political power would give his organization an opportunity to lead others to salvation through the disciplines of nonviolence, vegetarianism, personal alignment with the mathematical laws that govern the universe, and the practice of ethics in order to earn a superior reincarnation. (Pythagoras believed in metempsychosis, the transmigration of souls from one body to another, possibly from humans to animals. Indeed, Pythagoras claimed that he could remember four previous human lifetimes in detail.)

His adherents he divided into two hierarchical groups. The first was the *akousmatikoi*, or listeners, who were enjoined to remain silent, listen to and absorb Pythagoras' spoken precepts, and practice the special way of life taught by him. The second group was the *mathematikoi* (students of theoretical subjects, or simply "those who know"), who pursued the subjects of arithmetic, the theory of music, astronomy, and cosmology. (Though *mathematikoi* later came to mean "scientists" or "mathematicians," originally it meant those who had attained advanced knowledge in a broader sense.) The *mathematikoi*, after a long period of training, could ask questions and express opinions of their own.

Despite the later divergences among his students—fostered perhaps by his having divided them into two classes—Pythagoras himself drew a close connection between his metaphysical and scientific teachings. In his time, hardly anyone conceived of a split between science and religion or metaphysics. Nevertheless, some modern historians deny any real relation between the scientific doctrines of the Pythagorean society and its spiritualism and personal disciplines. In the twentieth century, Pythagoras' findings in astronomy, mathematics, and music theory are much more widely appreciated than the metaphysical philosophy that, to him, was the logical outcome of those findings.

Pythagoras developed a philosophy of number to account for the essence of all things. This concept rested on three basic observations: the mathematical relationships of musical harmonies, the fact that any triangle whose sides are in a ratio of 3:4:5 is always a right triangle, and the fixed numerical relations among the movement of stars and planets. It was the consistency of ratios among musical harmonies and geometrical shapes in different sizes and materials that impressed Pythagoras.

His first perception (which some historians consider his greatest) was that musical intervals depend on arithmetical ratios among lengths of string on the lyre (the most widely played instrument of Pythagoras' time), provided that these strings are at the same tension. For example, a ratio of 2:1 produces an octave; that is, a string twice as long as another string, at the same tension, produces the same note an octave below the shorter string. Similarly, 3:2 produces a fifth and 4:3 produces a fourth. Using these ratios, one could assign numbers to the four fixed strings of the lyre: 6, 8, 9, and 12. Moreover, if these ratios are transferred to another instrument—such as the flute, also highly popular in that era—the same harmonies will result. Hippasus of Metapontum, a *mathematikos* living a generation after Pythagoras, extended this music theory through experiments to produce the same harmonies with empty and partly filled glass containers and metal disks of varying thicknesses.

Pythagoras himself determined that the most important musical intervals can be expressed in ratios among the numbers 1, 2, 3, and 4, and he concluded that the number 10—the sum of these first four integers—comprehends the entire nature of number. Tradition has it that the later Pythagoreans, rather than swear by the gods as most other people did, swore by the "Tetrachtys of the Decad" (the sum of 1, 2, 3, and 4). The Pythagoreans also sought the special character of each number. The tetrachtys was called a "triangular number" because its components can readily be arranged as a triangle.

By extension, the number 1 is reason because it never changes; 2 is opinion; 4 is justice (a concept surviving in the term "a square deal"). Odd numbers are masculine and even numbers are feminine; therefore, 5, the first number representing the sum of an odd and an even number (1, "unity," not being considered for this purpose), symbolizes marriage. Seven is *parthenos*, or virgin, because among the first ten integers it has neither factors nor products. Other surviving Pythagorean concepts include unlucky 13 and "the seventh son of a seventh son."

To some people in the twentieth century, these number concepts seem merely superstitious. Nevertheless, Pythagoras and his followers did important work in several branches of mathematics and exerted a lasting influence on the field. The best-known example is the Pythagorean Theorem, the statement that the square of the hypotenuse of a right triangle is equal to the sum of the squares of the other two sides. Special applications of the theorem were known in Mesopotamia as early as the eighteenth century B.C., but Pythagoras sought to generalize it for a characteristically Greek reason: This theorem measures the ratio of the side of a square to its diagonal, and he was determined to know the *precise* ratio. It cannot be expressed as a whole number, however, so Pythagoras found a common denominator by showing a relationship among the *squares* of the sides of a right triangle. The Pythagorean Theorem is set forth in book 1 of Euclid's *Stoicheia* (*Elements*), Euclid being one of several later Greek thinkers whom Pythagoras strongly influenced and who transmitted his ideas in much-modified form to posterity.

Pythagoras also is said to have discovered the theory of proportion and the arithmetic, geometric, and harmonic means. The terms of certain arithmetic and harmonic means yield the three musical intervals. In addition, the ancient historian Proclus credited Pythagoras with discovering the construction of the five regular geometrical solids, though modern scholars think it more likely that he discovered three—the pyramid, the tetrahedron, and the dodecahedron—and that Theaetetus (after whom a Platonic dialogue is named) later discovered the construction of the remaining two, the octahedron and the icosahedron.

The field of astronomy, too, is indebted to Pythagoras. He was among the first to contend that the earth and the universe are spherical. He understood that the sun, the moon, and the planets rotate on their own axes and also orbit a central point outside themselves, though he believed that this central point was the earth. Later Pythagoreans deposed the earth as the center of the universe and substituted a "central fire," which, however, they did not identify as the sun—this they saw as another planet. Nearest the central fire was the "counter-earth," which always accompanied the earth in its orbit. The Pythagoreans assumed that the earth's rotation and its revolution around the central fire took the same amount of time—twenty-four hours. According to Aristotle, the idea of a counter-earth—besides bringing the number of revolving bodies up to the mystical number of ten—helped to explain lunar eclipses, which were thought to be caused by the counter-earth's interposition between sun and moon. Two thousand years later, Nicolaus Copernicus saw the Pythagorean system as anticipating his own; he had in mind both the Pythagoreans' concept of the day-and-night cycle and their explanation of eclipses.

Like Copernicus in his time, Pythagoras and his followers in their time were highly controversial. For many years, the Pythagoreans did exert a strong political and philosophical influence throughout southern Italy. The closing years of the sixth century B.C., however, saw the rise of democratic sentiments, and a reaction set in against the Pythagoreans, whom the democrats regarded as elitist.

Indeed, this political reaction led either to Pythagoras' exile or to his death—there are two traditions surrounding it. One is that a democrat named Cylon led a revolt against the power of the Pythagorean brotherhood and forced Pythagoras to retire to Metapontum, where he died peacefully about the end of the sixth century B.C. According to the other tradition, Pythagoras perished when his adversaries set fire to his school in Croton in 504 B.C. The story is that of his vast library of scrolls, only one was brought out of the fire; it contained his most esoteric secrets, which were passed on to succeeding generations of Pythagoreans.

Whichever account is true, Pythagoras' followers continued to be powerful throughout Magna Graecia until at least the middle of the fifth century B.C., when another reaction set in against them and their meetinghouses were sacked and burned. The survivors scattered in exile and did not return to Italy until the end of the fifth century. During the ensuing decades, the leading Pythagorean was Philolaus, who wrote the first systematic exposition of Pythagorean philosophy. Philolaus' influence can be traced to Plato through their mutual friend Archytas, who ruled Taras (Tarentum) in Italy for many years. The Platonic dialogue *Timaeus* (360-347 B.C.), named for its main character, a young Pythagorean astronomer, describes Pythagorean ideas in detail.

Summary

"Of all men," said Heraclitus, "Pythagoras, the son of Mnesarchus, was the most assiduous inquirer." Pythagoras is said to have been the first person to call himself a philosopher, or lover of wisdom. He believed that the universe is a logical, symmetrical whole, which can be understood in simple terms. For Pythagoras and his students, there was no gap between the scientific or mathematical ideal and the aesthetic. The beauty of his concepts and of the universe they described lies in their simplicity and consistency.

Quite aside from any of Pythagoras' specific intellectual accomplishments, his belief in universal order, and the energy he displayed in seeking it out, provided a galvanizing example for others. Sketchy as are the details of his personal life, his ideals left their mark on later poets, artists, scientists, and philosophers from Plato and Aristotle through the Renaissance and down to the twentieth century. Indirectly, through Pythagoras' disciple Philolaus, his ideas were transmitted to Plato and Aristotle, and, through these better-known thinkers, to the entire Western world.

Among Pythagoras' specific accomplishments, his systematic exposition of mathematical principles alone would have been enough to make him an important figure in Western intellectual history, but the spiritual beliefs he espoused make him also one of the great religious teachers of ancient Greek times. Even those ideas of his that are seen as intellectually disreputable have inspired generations of poets and artists. For example, the Pythagorean concept of the harmony of the spheres, suggested by the analogy between musical ratios and those of planetary orbits, became a central metaphor of Renaissance literature.

Bibliography

Bell, Eric T. *Men of Mathematics*. New York: Simon and Schuster, and London: Gollancz, 1937. Includes a chapter on the intellectual challenges that led to Pythagoras' discovery of irrational numbers and the theorem named for him.

Burkert, Walter. *Lore and Science in Ancient Pythagoreanism*. Translated by Edwin L. Minar, Jr. Cambridge, Mass.: Harvard University Press, 1972. This study, translated from the German, attempts to disentangle Pythagoreanism from Platonism and to describe the various aspects of Pythagoreanism, from music theory to what is called shamanistic religion. Includes notes, indexes, and an extensive bibliography.

Kirk, Geoffrey S., and John E. Raven. *The Presocratic Philosophers*. 2d ed. Cambridge and New York: Cambridge University Press, 1983. Provides a good account of Pythagoras and his followers, in their historical context, from a philosopher's point of view.

Muir, Jane. *Of Men and Numbers*. New York: Dodd, Mead, 1961. Simply written for lay readers. Contains a chapter on Pythagoras' mathematical work and its influence on later scientists, especially Euclid.

Philip, J. A. *Pythagoras and Early Pythagoreanism*. Toronto: University of Toronto Press, 1966. Attempts to separate the valid information from the legends surrounding Pythagoras and his teachings. Includes notes and a selected bibliography.

Plato. *The Timaeus, and the Critias, or Atlanticus*. Translated by Thomas Taylor. Princeton, N.J.: Princeton University Press, 1944. An unusual Platonic dialogue, in that here Socrates is not a central figure but a listener. It portrays Timaeus, an energetic Pythagorean astronomer, expounding his teacher's ideas about the origin and character of the universe.

Thomas Rankin

PYTHEAS

Born: c. 350-325 B.C.; Massalia, Gaul
Died: After 300 B.C.; perhaps Massalia, Gaul
Areas of Achievement: Science and exploration
Contribution: Pytheas undertook the first lengthy voyage to the North Atlantic and may have circumnavigated England. This knowledge of the West, together with his astronomical observations, provided the basis for centuries of study.

Early Life

It is a special characteristic of the study of antiquity that the fewer facts scholars know about a figure, the more they seem to write about him. So it is that an enormous bibliography about Pytheas of Massalia, the first known man to explore the far reaches of the North Atlantic, has evolved.

The time period of Pytheas' voyage has been determined with some certainty. Pytheas seems to have used a reference work which dates to 347 B.C., but since he is not mentioned by Aristotle, perhaps the voyage had not occurred before Aristotle's death in 322 B.C. Also, according to Strabo, Pytheas is quoted by Dicaearchus, who died circa 285 B.C. Thus, the voyage most definitely occurred between 347 and 285 B.C. At this time Carthage was the leading city of the western Mediterranean and controlled all traffic in and out of the Pillars of Hercules (Gibraltar). It is, therefore, sometimes claimed that Pytheas could have escaped this blockade only while Carthage was distracted in the war with Syracuse. If these assumptions are correct, the voyage took place between 310 and 306 B.C. Further, since Pytheas was surely a mature adult when he undertook the journey, scholars place his birth roughly between 350 and 325 B.C.

The date for the voyage is important, for it is believed that Pytheas opened the world of the West to Greek exploration at the same time that the wonders of the Far East were trickling back to the Mediterranean as a result of the conquests of Alexander the Great. The cosmopolitan Hellenistic age was being born and a quest for knowledge of far-off lands and their marvels was to play a large role in it. Apart from this tenuous but probable date, only two firm facts about Pytheas' life—his financial condition and his place of origin—are known. Polybius, also quoted by Strabo, sneers at Pytheas' voyage, asking if it was likely that a private citizen, and a poor one at that, ever undertook such a venture. Although Polybius was far from impartial,

this comment may indicate that the voyage was state-sponsored.

Ancient authors are unanimous in calling him "Pytheas of Massalia," modern Marseilles. Modern texts often call him "Pytheas of Massilia," using the less accurate Roman form of the name. This place of origin is not unexpected, for Massalia, founded circa 600 B.C. by Phocaea in Asia Minor, was one of the most ambitious seafaring Greek towns. It soon controlled the coast, from its fine harbor down to modern Ampurias, seventy-five miles northeast of Barcelona. A Massaliote named Euthymenes was said to have sailed south along Africa until he saw a river filled with crocodiles (possibly the Senegal), and Massalia had early trading connections with metal-rich Tartessus in Spain. Friction with Carthage was inevitable as the two powers sought control of these rich trade routes. Into this tradition of Massaliote adventurism Pytheas was born, poor but ambitious.

Life's Work

Not a word of Pytheas' works remains. It has even been suggested that Pytheas' own works were not available to such authors as Diodorus Siculus (who wrote under Julius Caesar and Augustus), Strabo (who wrote under Augustus), and Pliny the Elder, who preserved for posterity meager fragments of Pytheas' research by quoting from or citing his works. Very often the information is secondhand, preceded by such phrases as "Polybius says that Pytheas claims that. . . ."

Nevertheless, it is clear that Pytheas was remembered fondly as an astronomical scientist. Using only a sundial, he calculated the latitude of Massalia with remarkable accuracy. He noted first that the pole star was not really at the pole and was also the first to notice a relationship between the moon and the tides. Much of the information on latitudes and geography that he brought back from his voyages was deemed sufficiently accurate to be used by such famous ancient scholars as Timaeus, Hipparchus, and Ptolemy.

Pytheas the explorer, however, had another reputation entirely, neatly summed up by Strabo's calling him "the greatest liar among mortals." The nature and name of the work which reaped such abuse are unknown. The work may have been called "On the Ocean," "The Periplus" (meaning "voyage"), or "Travels Around the World." Modern scholars generally believe that it was a single work and that it recounted Pytheas' voyage. There is much to be said, however, for the theory that it was a general work of geography in which he reported his own firsthand observations, along with the rumors and reports he heard from others. If this is so, the scorn of later antiquity, relying on a spurious text, is more understandable. One can imagine the same comments being directed at Herodotus if only the more marvelous passages of his work had survived in this fashion.

With all that as warning, it is still customary to take the scattered references to Pytheas' voyage and reconstruct his route. If this approach is valid, his travels are impressive indeed. He left the Pillars of Hercules and cruised around Spain and the coast of France to the coast of Brittany and Ushant Island. Instead of continuing his coastal route as was customary for ancient mariners, he apparently struck out across the channel to Land's End, at the southwest tip of Britain at Cornwall. Here he described local tin mining. It is often asserted that Pytheas then circumnavigated the entire island of Britain. This belief is based on the fact that he describes the shape of the island correctly, describes its relationship to the coast better than did his critic Strabo, and, although doubling their true lengths, still correctly determines the proportion of the three sides. He probably made frequent observations of native behavior, and he may have conducted investigations inland. Diodorus, probably relying on Pytheas, reported correctly that the natives' huts were primitive, that they were basically peaceful but knew the chariot used for warfare, that they threshed their grain indoors because of the wet climate, and that they brewed and consumed mead.

Pytheas undoubtedly passed by Ireland, although no specific mention of this is found. It is often claimed, however, that his observations on the island enabled subsequent ancient geographers to locate it accurately on their maps. He apparently moved on to the northern tip of Britain, where he blandly described incredible tides eighty cubits (120 feet) high. Modern scholars see in this the gale-enhanced tides of the Pentland Firth.

It is the next stop on Pytheas' voyage which causes the greatest discussion. Pytheas claims that the island of Thule lay six days to the north of Britain and only one day from the frozen sea, sometimes called the Cronian Sea. Here, he states, days have up to twenty hours of sunlight in summer and twenty hours of darkness in winter. As if that infor-

mation were not sufficiently incredible, he claims that the island lay in semicongealed waters in an area where earth, sea, and air are all mixed, suspended in a mixture resembling "sea lung" (perhaps a sort of jellyfish).

Where, if anywhere, is this Thule? Pytheas only claims that he saw the sea lung, getting the rest secondhand. Some parts of his tale ring true, such as long northerly days of light or darkness and a mixture of fog, mist, and slush so thick that one cannot tell where sea ends and sky begins. Scholars variously identify Thule as Iceland, Norway, the Shetland Islands, or the Orkney Islands, but no one solution is entirely satisfactory.

Pytheas soon turned south and completed his circumnavigation until he recrossed the channel. Here, again, there are problems, for he claims to have visited amber-rich lands as far as the Tanais River, acknowledged as the boundary between Europe and Asia. Scholars claim either that Pytheas reached the Vistula River and thus, remarkably, the heart of the Baltic Sea or that he stopped at the Elbe River. In either case, it is generally assumed that from there he retraced his steps along the European coast and returned home. Even by the most conservative estimates, he had traveled a minimum of seventy-five hundred miles in ships designed for the Mediterranean and manned by sailors unfamiliar with the rigors of the northern seas.

Summary

How can one assess a man and voyage so beset with problems of historicity? Did Pytheas in fact make a voyage at all? Was it a single voyage or were there two—one to Britain and one to the land of amber? In either case, how far did he go and how much information is from his own experience and how much is from what he learned through inquiry?

Barring the remarkable discovery of a long-lost Pytheas manuscript, these questions will never be answered. A coin from Cyrene, found on the northern coast of Brittany and dating to this time, has been cautiously set forth as evidence of Greek intrusion at this date, but the caution is well deserved.

Yet, despite the poor evidence and the hostility of the ancient authors, scholars can gauge Pytheas' importance from the impact he had on those who came after him. Pytheas opened Greek eyes to the wonders of the West, and it was his reports, for better or worse, which formed the basis for all writers on this area of the world for two centuries to come. In the same way, his scientific observations were respected and used by the best geographical minds of antiquity.

Still, it is highly likely that Pytheas did undertake a voyage himself and that he pushed fairly far to the north. Several thorny problems are solved if one believes that many of his wilder statements were not based on firsthand information but on tales he heard along the way. Much of the difficulty regarding Thule, for example, disappears when one views Pytheas' "discoveries" in this light.

The purpose of this voyage is also unclear. Some have hailed it as the first purely scientific voyage known to humankind. Yet if Pytheas was in fact a poor man and thus had public funds behind him, it is highly unlikely that the elders of Massalia would have found reports of sea lung proper repayment for their investment. It is wiser to see the voyage as primarily commercial, aimed at rivaling Carthaginian trade routes to lands rich in tin and amber, although Pytheas clearly lost no opportunity to engage in scientific enquiry along the way. (To be sure, his entire trip north of Cornwall seems guided more by a sense of adventure than of mercantilism.)

The world soon forgot about Pytheas' contribution to Massaliote trade routes. In fact, there is no evidence that an increase in trade followed his maiden voyage. Less ephemeral were Pytheas' tales of gigantic tides, sea lung, or Thule. His appeal extends into modern times, as the term "ultima Thule" remains a synonym for "the ends of the earth."

Bibliography

Bunbury, E. H. *A History of Ancient Geography Among the Greeks and Romans from the Earliest Ages Till the Fall of the Roman Empire.* 2d ed. London: Murray, 1883; Mineola, N.Y.: Dover Publications, 1959. A very sensible and cautious reconstruction of the probable circumstances surrounding Pytheas' voyage.

Carpenter, Rhys. *Beyond the Pillars of Heracles.* New York: Delacorte Press, 1966. A very lengthy section devoted to Pytheas treats several issues in great detail. An unorthodox date for Pytheas' life is to be rejected but the discussion of Thule is very well done.

Cary, Max, and E. H. Warmington. *The Ancient Explorers.* Rev. ed. Baltimore: Penguin Books, 1963. A somewhat uncritical re-creation of the voyage, with a tendency to gloss over several of the thornier questions.

Whitaker, Ian. "The Problem of Pytheas' Thule." *Classical Journal* 77 (1982): 148-164. A fine, careful study not only of Thule but also of most of the crucial problems surrounding Pytheas. Contains excellent documentation and bibliography, with translations of crucial passages from ancient authorities.

Kenneth F. Kitchell, Jr.

RAMSES II

Born: c. 1300 B.C.; probably the Eastern Delta of Egypt

Died: 1213 B.C.; probably Pi-Ramesse (Qantir), Egypt

Area of Achievement: Government

Contribution: Renowned for his statesmanship, military leadership, administrative abilities, and building activity, Ramses set a standard by which subsequent rulers of Egypt measured themselves.

Early Life

Born of Egypt's great god Amon (personified by King Seti I) and Queen Tuya, Ramses was designated "while yet in the egg" as Egypt's future king: Such is Ramses II's account of his own birth. The period into which he was born, that of the New Kingdom, was a time when Egypt was attempting to maintain control of an extensive empire which ranged from the Fourth Cataract of the Nile in the Sudan to the provinces of North Syria. Some fifty years prior to his birth, during the Eighteenth Dynasty, Egypt had undergone a period of turmoil. Akhenaton (Amenhotep IV, who reigned from 1379 to 1362 B.C.), reacting against the ever-growing power of the Amon priesthood, had abandoned the traditional religion and proclaimed the sun god, represented as the sun disk Aton, as sole god of the country. He worshipped the Aton at the virgin site of Amarna. He died without heirs; after his demise, a series of relatively ineffectual kings, including Tutankhamen, ruled for brief periods as the Amon priesthood set about reestablishing religious domination and refurbishing Amon's temples. Meanwhile, using this period of uncertainty in Egypt to best advantage, vassal states in Syria held back their tribute and fomented revolt. When Tutankhamen died without living heirs, a military man of nonroyal birth, Aye, assumed the throne. He was followed only four years later by another, the general Horemheb, who also ruled only a short period before his death, but not before designating another man with a military background, his vizier Pa-Ramessu, as his heir. Pa-Ramessu (Ramses I, first king of the Nineteenth Dynasty) had what rulers since Akhenaton had lacked: viable male descendants. Thus, when Ramses I died after only a two-year rule, his son, Seti I, assumed the throne. Immediately, Seti began an active program of military campaigns in Canaan, Syria, and Libya. During many of these excursions, his son, the young Ramses II, was at his side, learning the art of warfare.

Seti I instructed his son in civil and religious affairs as well, and Prince Ramses accompanied his father or acted as his deputy on state occasions and at religious festivals. As prince-regent, Ramses received the rights of Egyptian kingship, including his titulary (five royal names attributing to him divine power and linking him with Egypt's divine past) and a harem.

When his father died, after a rule of between fifteen and twenty years, Ramses II oversaw Seti's burial in the Valley of the Kings and assumed the throne. At that time, he was probably in his mid-twenties. He was about five and a half feet tall and had auburn hair. Many children had already been born to him and his numerous wives.

Life's Work

With great ceremony, on the twenty-seventh day of the third month of summer, 1279, Ramses II acceded to the throne of Egypt. Following an age-old tradition, the great gods of Egypt, in the persons of their high priests, placed the crowns of Upper and Lower Egypt (Nile Valley and Delta) on his head and presented him with other symbols of rulership: the divine cobra (uraeus) to protect him and smite his enemies, and the crook and flail. At the sacred city of Heliopolis, his name was inscribed on the leaves of the sacred *ished* tree, and birds flew in all directions to proclaim his names to all Egypt. With this ceremony concluded, the divine order (or balance) in the universe, a concept known as *Ma'at*, was once again in place. It would be Ramses' duty, as it had been of every king before him, to maintain *Ma'at*, thereby guaranteeing peace and prosperity for all.

Ramses II set out with determination to ensure the preservation of *Ma'at*. He was a shrewd politician from the start; one of his first acts as king was to journey south to Thebes to act as high priest in the city's most important religious event, the Opet Festival. Amid great and joyous celebration, Amon's cult image was carried from his home at Karnak to the Luxor temple. There, through a reenactment of his divine conception and birth, the ceremonies of Opet Festival assured the divinity of Ramses' kingship and promoted his association with the god Amon, whose cult image was recharged with divine energy during its stay at Luxor.

Afterward, Ramses II headed north to Abydos, restored that city's holy sites, and promoted a member of the Abydos priesthood to the position of high priest of Amon at Thebes, the highest and most powerful religious office in the land. In this way, he kept Amon's priesthood under his control and averted the power struggles that had beset earlier kings.

From Abydos, Ramses continued his northerly journey to the eastern Nile Delta. There, in his ancestral homeland near Avaris, he established a new capital, naming it Pi-Ramesse (the house of Ramses). Scribes extolled its magnificence, likening the brilliant blue glaze of its tile-covered walls to turquoise and lapis lazuli.

Not only at Pi-Ramesse but also at Memphis, Egypt's administrative capital, at Thebes, her religious capital, and at numerous other sites throughout Egypt and Nubia, Ramses II built extensively and lavishly. Indeed, few ancient Egyptian cities were untouched by his architects and artisans. Monuments which Ramses II did not build he often claimed for his own by replacing the names of his predecessors with his. Colossal statues of the king erected outside temples were considered to function as intermediaries between the villagers and the great gods inside. They also reminded every passerby of Ramses' power.

The territorial problems and general unrest which had compelled Seti I to travel to the Levant continued during Ramses II's rule. When the growing Hittite empire annexed the strategically important city of Kadesh in northern Syria, an area formerly under Egyptian sovereignty, Ramses rose to the challenge.

In April of the fifth year of Ramses' reign, he led an army of about twenty thousand men to meet about twice as many enemy soldiers. As the Egyptian army neared Kadesh, two Hittites posing as spies allowed themselves to be captured. The main Hittite army, they assured the Egyptians, was still far to the north. Thinking that he had nothing yet to fear, Ramses marched ahead, accompanied by only his personal guard. Two more captured Hittites, this time true spies, revealed, upon vigorous beating, that the Hittites were encamped just on the other side of Kadesh, a few miles away. Suddenly, the enemy attacked the Egyptian line, sending surprised soldiers fleeing in confusion and fright.

With valor and courage, Ramses succeeded virtually single-handedly in holding the Hittite attackers at bay. Relief came at a critical moment in the form of the king's advance guard arriving from the north. Gradually, the rest of Ramses' army regrouped and joined battle. The day ended with no clear victor. The second day also ended in a stalemate, and both sides disengaged.

Ramses headed home in triumph, having, after all, saved his army (and himself) from great disaster. Although during the next fifteen years Ramses returned frequently to the Levantine battlefield, no battle made as great an impact as the Battle of Kadesh. For decades following, on temple walls throughout the land, the king's artists told the story of this battle in prose, poetry, and illustration, with each telling more elaborate than the one before. What the chroniclers neglected to mention each time was the battle's outcome: The disputed city, Kadesh, remained a Hittite possession.

Sixteen years after the Battle of Kadesh had made Ramses a great military leader, at least in his own eyes, it cast him into the role of statesman as well. A new generation of leadership in the Hittite empire, the lack of military resolution with Egypt, and the rising power of Assyria made the prospect of continued warfare with Egypt unattractive to the Hittites. Accordingly, a peace treaty was proposed (by the Hittites according to Ramses and by Ramses according to the Hittites). Its terms are as timely today as they were in 1258 B.C.: mutual nonaggression, mutual defense, mutual extradition of fugitives, and rightful succession of heirs. A thousand gods of Egypt and a thousand gods of Hatti were said to have witnessed this treaty, which survives today in both the Egyptian and Hittite versions.

Former enemies became fast friends following the treaty's execution, as king wrote to king and queen to queen. In Year 34, the Hittite king even sent his daughter to Ramses. Chronicles of Ramses' reign indicate his pleasure upon his first sight of her, accompanied by her dowry of gold, silver, copper, slaves, horses, cattle, goats, and sheep.

Matnefrure, as Ramses II named his Hittite bride, joined a harem that was already quite large. In the course of his long rule, the king had at least eight great royal wives and numerous lesser wives. To Nefretari, who must have been his favorite wife, he dedicated a temple at Abu Simbel, and upon her untimely death he buried her in a tomb whose wall paintings are the finest in the Valley of the Tombs of the Queens. Ramses II fathered at least ninety children (some fifty sons and forty daughters), who were often represented in birth-order procession on temple walls or sculpted knee-height beside images of their father.

In 1213, nearly ninety years old and after more than sixty-six years of rule over the most powerful country in the world, King Ramses II died. His carefully mummified body was laid to rest in a splendidly carved tomb in the Valley of the Kings, and he was succeeded on the throne of Egypt by his thirteenth son, Merneptah.

Summary

Military leader, statesman, builder, family man, and possibly pharaoh of the biblical Exodus, Ramses II left a legacy which history never forgot. He distinguished himself in battle in the early years of his reign, and during the remainder of his lengthy rule—the second longest in Egyptian history—he maintained an interlude of peace in an increasingly tumultuous world. Egypt under his leadership was a cosmopolitan empire. Foreigners were free to come to Egypt to trade or settle; others were taken as prisoners of war and joined Egypt's labor force. It was an era of religious permissiveness, and foreign gods were worshipped beside traditional Egyptian deities. The cultural climate of Ramses' Egypt is similar to the one described in the Bible just prior to the Exodus (an event for which no archaeological record has been found).

The monuments Ramses II built to Egypt's gods (and to himself) are larger and more numerous than those of any other Egyptian king. Nine kings named themselves after him and patterned their lives after his. During his own lifetime, he promoted himself as a god, and he was worshipped as such for the next thousand years.

Greek and Roman tourists marveled at his monuments and immortalized them in their writings, just as the poet Percy Bysshe Shelley did hundreds of years later in his poem "Ozymandias." (The name Ozymandias is the Greek rendering of *User-Ma'at-Ra*, throne name of Ramses II.) When the greatest of all Ramses' monuments, Abu Simbel, was threatened by the rising waters of the Aswan High Dam in the 1960's, ninety countries around the world contributed funds and expertise to save it. In this way, they too paid homage to Ramses, as do millions of tourists who travel thousands of miles to visit his monuments.

Although his tomb was plundered and his body desecrated, Ramses II has gained the immortality he sought. His monuments and his actions bear testimony to his importance and justify the appellation Ramses the Great.

Bibliography

Bierbrier, Morris. *The Tomb Builders of the Pharaohs*. London: British Museum Publications, 1982; New York: Scribner, 1984. A delightfully written description of the community of workmen who built the tombs of the New Kingdom kings, including that of Ramses II. An intimate picture of their day-to-day lives. Includes a description of how they built the tombs.

Freed, Rita. *Ramesses the Great*. Memphis, Tenn.: City of Memphis, 1987. Profusely illustrated survey of Ramses II and the Egyptian Empire under his reign. Includes information about religion, daily life, and burial practices during Egypt's New Kingdom. The second part of the book is a catalog of the objects included in the North American showing of the Ramses the Great exhibition.

Gardiner, A. H. *The Kadesh Inscriptions of Ramesses II*. Oxford: Griffith Institute, 1960. Translation of and commentary on Ramses' own description of his most famous battle.

Kitchen, K. A. *Pharaoh Triumphant: The Life and Times of Ramesses II*. Warminster, England: Aris and Phillips, 1982. The best all-around survey of Egypt's most famous king, by a renowned scholar. Includes historical background information, a detailed report of his military career and international dealings, and a discussion of Egypt's contemporary administrative and social history. Includes an extensive bibliography.

MacQuitty, William. *Ramesses the Great: Master of the World*. London: Mitchell Beazley, and New York: Crown Publishers, 1978. Brief but well-written and well-illustrated overview of Ramses II and his monuments.

Murnane, William. *The Road to Kadesh*. 2d ed. Chicago: Oriental Institute of the University of Chicago, 1990. Background for the understanding of Egypt's farflung empire. Consideration of Egypt's relations with Syria and the Hittites through the reign of Ramses' father, Seti I, and detailed analyses of Seti's military campaigns.

O'Connor, D. "New Kingdom and Third Intermediate Period, 1552-664 B.C.," In *Ancient Egypt: A Social History*, by B. G. Trigger, B. J. Kemp, D. O'Connor, and A. B. Lloyd. Cambridge and New

York: Cambridge University Press, 1983. Insightful description of the administrative structure of Egypt at the time of Ramses II.

Schmidt, John D. *Ramesses II: Chronological Structure for His Reign.* Baltimore: Johns Hopkins University Press, 1972. Translation of and commentary on monuments of Ramses II in a chronological framework.

Steindorff, G., and K. Seele. *When Egypt Ruled the East.* 2d ed. Chicago: University of Chicago Press, 1957. Still the best overview for the general reader of the history of Egypt during the New Kingdom.

Wildung, D. *Egyptian Saints: Deification in Pharaonic Egypt.* New York: New York University Press, 1977. A discussion of the meaning of kingship in ancient Egypt and the mechanism by which a pharaoh was thought to cross the boundary from humanity to divinity. Written for the general reader by an expert in the field. Well illustrated.

Rita E. Freed

REGULUS
Marcus Atilius Regulus

Born: c. 300 B.C.; probably Rome

Died: c. 249 B.C.; probably Carthage

Area of Achievement: Warfare and conquest

Contribution: Through legendary embellishments on his actual exploits, Regulus has served as an example, variously, of moral courage and devotion to duty, of arrogance in the face of victory, and of the reversals of fortune that history records.

Early Life

Marcus Atilius Regulus was a Roman, born, in all probability, into a noble though not wealthy family in an age when Rome was consolidating its takeover of Italy. Consul in 267 B.C., Regulus participated in the conquest of southern Italy by capturing Brundisium (modern Brindisi), the most important seaport on Italy's eastern coast, and subduing the people around it. The reputation he earned in the engagement was no doubt instrumental in his selection to replace Q. Caedicus as consul in 257, when Caedicus died at a crucial moment in Rome's war against Carthage.

Life's Work

It is as replacement consul (consul suffectus) that Regulus enters the stage of history. The long cold war between Rome and Carthage, competitors for dominance in the Mediterranean world, finally exploded into hot war in 264. In 258, the year before Regulus assumed the consulship, Rome had laid siege to fortress-towns throughout Sicily, then a Carthaginian possession. Successful in conquering many of the towns, Rome was disabused of its enemy's invincibility and grew confident of its own military ability. Rome planned to use its navy in a daring attack on Africa, on Carthage itself. The Carthaginians, trusting their superiority in naval resources, resolved to meet the Roman navy at sea, defeat it, and so protect the African mainland, which was not well fortified for defense.

In 256, with Regulus and the other consul, L. Manlius Vulso Longus, in command, a Roman fleet of 330 battleships and 140,000 men met the more numerous (350 ships and 150,000 men) Carthaginians at Ecnomus. The advantage seemed to belong to the Carthaginians, whose ships were more maneuverable, as the Roman ships were weighed down with land weapons. In a battle in which the outcome was long uncertain, the Romans won the day, destroying or capturing many Carthaginian ships.

The Carthaginian navy under Hanno withdrew to Africa to protect the sea lanes to Carthage, while Hamilcar stayed with the land army in Sicily. A few months later, the Roman consuls led their invasion forces to Africa. It is said that en route, the tribune Nautius stirred up the fears of the already nervous Roman soldiers and that Regulus, learning of Nautius's cowardly speeches, threatened him with an ax. Thus Regulus used fear to inspire his soldiers with courage.

The Romans landed at Cape Hermaeum (modern Cape Bon) and proceeded to Clupea, a town they captured and established as their base of operations. The consuls sent to the Senate at Rome for further orders; when the reply came, Manlius returned to Rome with the fleet, while Regulus remained in Africa with forty ships and the land

army of fifteen thousand men. With the army, Regulus subdued three hundred fortresses and towns throughout Libya. Stories survive that Regulus had to fight "huge monster-serpents" that harassed his camp. Perhaps in this period Regulus can be faulted for his insistence on conquest and plunder. If he had enlisted the aid of the Libyans and Numidians, who hated Carthage and might have made willing allies, he could have acquired a cavalry, the lack of which would prove fatal to his plans.

Up to this point, the Carthaginians had not comprehended the scale of the Roman invasion. They now sent for Hamilcar, who was in Sicily with their land army. Immediately upon his return with five thousand men, he persuaded Carthage to engage Regulus in battle. While both sides possessed roughly the same number of infantry, the Carthaginians held an advantage in cavalry and elephants, animals unfamiliar to the Romans. Hamilcar was wary of confronting the Romans on a plain, though it was a terrain favorable to his cavalry and elephants, and occupied the high ground. Regulus seized the initiative and attacked the Carthaginian camp from two sides, causing a panic in the enemy and putting them to flight to Carthage. Regulus then advanced to Tunis nearby to set up winter quarters.

The Carthaginians were aware that they had been defeated at Ecnomus despite their superior navy. Their land army had been defeated in Africa. The Roman army was just outside their gates and plundering their territories with impunity. Even their Numidian subjects were raiding and plundering. Morale was at a low point. Now Regulus sent an overture suggesting willingness to settle on easy terms. Regulus's motives are not known, but Roman terms of office were one year; when his term as consul ended, he would lack the authority to carry on the struggle. If, however, he worked out a treaty with Carthage, he would leave to posterity a reputation as the man who ended the great Punic War. Perhaps thinking of glory, then, Regulus entered into negotiations with a delegation headed by Hamilcar's son Hanno.

It is not known with certainty what Regulus's terms of settlement were, though ancient historians agree that they were excessively severe. Perhaps Regulus wanted the Carthaginians to give up Sardinia, Sicily, and their entire fleet except for one symbolic ship, and to pay an indemnity as well. By these terms, Carthage would have become virtually a subject state to Rome, and the wealthy merchants who ruled Carthage chose to prolong the war rather than agree to Regulus's demands.

The desperation of Carthage was a source of courage to the Carthaginians, and they were preparing a fight to the death when there arrived in Carthage some Greek mercenaries, among them the Spartan Xanthippos, a man trained in the military tradition of Sparta. He examined the Carthaginian military and criticized it as inadequate. The Carthaginians were impressed and gave him the command. Confident that they had in Xanthippos a man who knew what he was doing, the Carthaginians took the field against Regulus in late spring. While the advantage perhaps lay with the Romans in infantry, the Carthaginians were again superior in cavalry and elephants. Under Xanthippos, at Tunis the Carthaginians were not reluctant to fight on a plain. Regulus, anticipating that he would defeat this nation of shopkeepers as easily as he had before, took to the field. Now, however, the outcome was quite different. The Carthaginian cavalry chased the smaller Roman cavalry from the field. Elephants trampled large numbers of Roman infantry . It is said, too, that Regulus's men were worn out from the heat and thirst and the heaviness of their weapons. Of Regulus's army, only a few escaped to Clupea. The rest were killed or captured, including Regulus.

If Regulus had died in the battle and not been captured alive, his story would not have excited the imagination of writers and schoolchildren for two millennia. It is not known what actually happened to Regulus after his capture. It may be that he simply died in captivity; it may be that some form of the tales the historians and poets tell is true. Yet no account of Regulus would be complete without these tales.

While Regulus was held captive in Carthage, the fortunes of war shifted back and forth for the next few years between Carthage and Rome. In 251, the Punic commander Hasdrubal advanced on Panormus in Sicily but met a devastating defeat. He was recalled to Carthage and impaled. Then, probably in 250, according to traditional accounts, Regulus was ordered by his Carthaginian captors to return to Rome and to negotiate either (by some accounts) an exchange of prisoners or (by other accounts) a peace on lenient terms. He was on his oath to persuade the Roman Senate or, failing to do so, to return to Carthage to meet torture and death. When he arrived in Rome, accompanied by Carthaginian ambassadors, he entered the Senate clad as a prisoner in Punic clothes. When the ambassadors had left, Regulus is said to have disclosed the full crisis of Carthage's desperation and to have advised peace on much harder terms than the Carthaginians wished—or, if Carthage did not accept such terms, a renewed aggressive war. Then, although he could have remained in Rome with his loving family, he kept his oath to Carthage and returned there, knowing that he would be punished for his failure to obtain a generous peace. There are varying accounts of his torture at Carthage. According to Cicero, he was kept awake until he died. According to the more common and more detailed account, he was confined in wooden box designed so that he was forced to remain standing. Through the planks of the box were placed iron spikes to prevent his lying down or resting; abused in this way, he eventually died.

According to some writers, the stories of his oath and torture are inventions to cover up an atrocity by Regulus's widow. According to this version, when Regulus died in captivity, his widow was so distressed that she tortured two Punic boys held captive by her family.

Summary

The story of Regulus has achieved prominence because of the moral lessons it instills. For some writers, Regulus is a lesson in the fickleness of fortune, the chief lesson that history teaches. Victorious in his battles and unyielding in his demands to Carthage, he was then defeated and forced to sue for his life. Thus he illustrates the law that fortune most likes to afflict those who enjoy extreme prosperity. For other moralists, Regulus's arrogance was his undoing. If he had not pressed excessively harsh terms on Carthage, he would have won glory for himself and peace for Rome. It was his contumelious belief in his powers and luck that struck him down.

To traditional patriotic Romans, Regulus became a symbol of Roman probity, the man who kept his oath, even unto death. The great orator and statesman Cicero holds him as a model. For Cicero, Regulus is a glorious example of a man who rejected what seemed to be his private advantage—his life and a comfortable existence at Rome as an ex-consul—for what was honorable and noble.

Bibliography

Caven, Brian. *The Punic Wars*. London: Weidenfeld and Nicolson, and New York: St. Martin's Press, 1980. Covers all the Punic Wars in annalistic form, concentrating on military history. Adorned with plates and maps that help the reader to follow the strategic plans of both sides.

Charles-Picard, Gilbert, and Colette Charles-Picard. *The Life and Death of Carthage*. Translated by Dominique Collon. New York: Taplinger, and London: Sidgwick and Jackson, 1968. A full history of Carthage, from its founding to its destruction by Rome. Illustrated with many plates and complete with a full bibliography.

Dorey, T. A., and D. R. Dudley. *Rome Against Carthage*. London: Secker and Warburg, 1971; New York: Doubleday, 1972. A history of the conflict between the two superpowers of the ancient Mediterranean, placing the conflict in the greater geopolitical context.

Polybius. *The Rise of the Roman Empire*. Translated by F. W. Walbank. London and New York: Penguin, 1979. By one of the great historians of the ancient world. Drawing from a great many earlier histories that have been lost, Polybius is the main source for the early story of Regulus.

Scullard, H. H. *The Elephant in the Greek and Roman World*. London: Thames and Hudson, and Ithaca, N.Y.: Cornell University Press, 1974. An encyclopedic description of the elephant in ancient history, art, and literature. Good treatment of the military use of elephants in Carthage's wars with Rome.

Walbank, F. W. *A Historical Commentary on Polybius*. Vol. 1. Oxford, England: Clarendon Press, 1957. An annotated commentary on the Greek text of the influential ancient historian. Carefully assesses Polybius's sources and weighs the evidence in the conflicting accounts of the story of Regulus.

Warmington, B. H. *Carthage*. Rev. ed. London: Hale, and New York: Praeger, 1969. Readable history drawing on ancient historians (with full awareness that they generally favor Rome) and modern archaeology.

James A. Arieti

SALLUST

Born: October 1, 86 B.C.; Amiternum (modern San Vittorino), Italy

Died: 35 B.C.; probably Rome

Area of Achievement: Historiography

Contribution: Sallust's most important accomplishments were influential works of history composed after his retirement from a checkered political career. The tone, style, and subject matter of his writings reflect the perils and disenchantments of his earlier career.

Early Life

Gaius Sallustius Crispus was born in 86 B.C. in the town of Amiternum in the Sabine uplands, some fifty-five miles northeast of Rome in the central Italian peninsula. Though likely a member of a locally eminent family, Sallust was in Roman terms nonaristocratic, that is, a plebeian. As a politician, he was thus a *nouus homo* (new man). Although by the first century B.C. plebeians regularly attained political office and senatorial rank, the highest offices—the praetorship and especially the consulship—remained almost exclusively the preserve of a few wealthy, aristocratic families and such men as they chose to support. To fulfill his political ambitions, the new man needed skill, sagacity, tact, perseverance, luck, and, most particularly, powerful friends. This helps to explain both Sallust's general dislike of the entrenched conservative aristocracy and his affiliation with Julius Caesar.

Sallust was elected quaestor (a junior official with financial responsibilities) around 55 and tribune of the people in 52. In the latter position, he was involved on the side of the prosecution in the murder trial of a notorious right-wing politician (defended by Cicero) who habitually used intimidation and mob violence. This involvement, along with various other anticonservative actions, gained for Sallust numerous political enemies, who retaliated by having him expelled from the senate in 50 on apparently trumped-up charges of sexual immorality.

Hoping for a restoration of status, Sallust sided with Julius Caesar against Pompey the Great in the civil war that broke out in the year 49. He was rewarded with a second quaestorship (c. 49), a praetorship (47), and various military commands. His service in these posts was undistinguished and occasionally incompetent. He failed to quell a troop mutiny, for example, and was not entrusted with a battle command during Caesar's African campaign. Caesar did, however, see fit to appoint Sallust as the first governor of the province of Africa Nova in 46, a fact that implies at least minimal faith in his administrative abilities. After his governorship, Sallust was charged with abuse of power—extortion and embezzlement—but saved himself from conviction by sharing his spoils with Caesar, who was by then dictator. Still, the scandal severely limited Sallust's political prospects and forced him into an early retirement, from which the assassination of Caesar in 44 made it impossible to return.

Life's Work

Sallust's inglorious political career was marred by factional strife, sensational scandals, sporadic ineptitude, and outright misconduct. Whatever he may have lost in public esteem, however, Sallust handsomely recouped in property and possessions. The wealth he amassed in office ensured an opulent style of retirement. Sallust purchased a palatial villa at Tivoli, said to have been owned at one time

SALUSTE.

by Caesar himself. At Rome, he began construction of the famed Horti Sallustiani (gardens of Sallust), in which an elegantly landscaped complex of parklands surrounded a fine mansion. The loveliness of this estate in the capital city later attracted the attention of Roman emperors, whose property it eventually became.

Sallust did not, however, simply settle into a genteel life of disillusioned and indolent leisure. He used his knowledge of the dynamics of Roman government as a lens through which to examine the gradual disintegration of the political system in the late republican period.

The men and events in Sallust's historical works are typical of a period of decline and fall. His first work, *Bellum Catilinae* (c. 42 B.C.; *The War with Catiline*), is a historical monograph devoted to the failed conspiracy of Lucius Sergius Catilina, a disgruntled, impoverished aristocrat who intended to make good his electoral and financial losses by resorting to armed insurrection. The planned coup d'état was quashed by the actions of Cicero during his consulship in 63. The story of the exposure of the plot and of the measures taken by consul and senate to eliminate the threat—ultimately in battle—is familiar from Cicero's four Catilinarian orations.

Sallust's telling of the Catiline story differs from Cicero's in several respects. He sees the conspiracy in the context of a general moral deterioration within the governing class in Rome. Many in the senatorial nobility placed their own advancement ahead of concern for the common weal. Catiline found supporters not only among disaffected political have-nots, but also among members of the ruling elite who—at least for a time—saw in his machinations opportunities for furthering their own selfish interests. This was not surprising in an era that had seen the bloodshed and confiscation of property that marked the dictatorship of Lucius Cornelius Sulla Felix. In *The War with Catiline*, two men of strong moral character—Marcus Porcius Cato (Cato the Younger) and Julius Caesar—stand out in contrast to the surrounding moral decay. Though representing very different political persuasions, both men are portrayed as admirable for their integrity. Sallust is sometimes accused of being an apologist for his erstwhile patron, Julius Caesar, but his favorable portrait of Cato argues a more nonpartisan outlook. Cicero, too, though not the triumphant savior paraded in his own writings, is given his due by Sallust.

Sallust's second work, *Bellum Iugurthinum* (c. 40 B.C.; *The War with Jugurtha*), recounts the war between Rome and an upstart king of Numidia (now eastern Algeria) between 111 and 105. This was an apt subject, in part because of Sallust's familiarity with North Africa and because of the many hard-fought battles, but especially because it afforded another case of mismanagement and corruption among the Roman ruling elite. In *The War with Jugurtha*, the handling of the conflict by the senate and its representatives is portrayed as ineffective, again largely because of divisions among the aristocrats who had allowed their own lust for power or money to displace their obligation to govern well. Some in the government were willing to accept bribes in return for their support of Jugurtha over other claimants to the Numidian throne. The phrase "everything at Rome has its price" rings like a death knell in the monograph. It was finally a new man—Gaius Marius—who succeeded in gaining victory for Rome. Yet Marius, too, in Sallust's account, had flaws of character: He is depicted as a demagogue who connived to damage the reputation of his predecessor in command. Furthermore, though he would have other spectacular military successes (against invading Germanic tribes on Italy's northern frontier), Marius' long career ended in civil war against Sulla.

Sallust's other major work, his *Historiae* (*Histories*), begun around 39, unfortunately survives only in fragments. It was more extensive in scope than the monographs, covering in annalistic fashion the years from 78 apparently to the early 60's; a continuation to perhaps 50 may have been envisaged, but Sallust's death in 35 prevented it.

Sallust does not meet the standards of modern historical scholarship. His chronology is sometimes awry; he neglected or suppressed relevant information, while including long digressions. He sometimes perpetuated patently distorted reports of personalities and events and, in general, did not assess available sources with sufficient care. Still, no ancient Greek or Roman historian is entirely free from such shortcomings, and Sallust's works are historically valuable despite them, particularly as a check against the record furnished by Cicero, who has so colored the modern picture of the late republic.

Sallust is most compelling and influential as a stylist and moralist. His language is deliberately patterned on the ruggedly direct and archaic syntax of the stern Cato the Censor and, among Greek precedents, on the brevity and abnormal grammatical effects of the greatest Greek historian, Thucydides. His terse sentence structure contributes to a forceful and dramatic progression of thought. This style is well suited to the moral outlook of a historian of decline and fall. Like Thucydides, Sallust wrote from the vantage point of a man of wide experience forced out of an active political life into that of an analyst of the causes of deterioration of character and commitment in the ruling elite of a great imperial power. This analysis is achieved by remarkably concise and trenchant sketches of, and judgments upon, persons and motives. The historical figures who are Sallust's subjects act out of clearly defined and exhibited passions—sometimes noble, mostly base, never lukewarm.

Summary

Sallust's qualities as stylist and moralist have always won for him readers, admirers, and imitators. In classical antiquity, he was recognized as the first great Roman historian; the eminent teacher and critic Quintilian even put him on a par with Thucydides. This judgment is a literary one. The most brilliant classical Roman historian, Cornelius Tacitus, was profoundly influenced by the Sallustian style of composition. The poet Martial concurred with Quintilian's high estimation of Sallust, and Saint Augustine's favorable opinion helped to ensure the historian's popularity in the Middle Ages. German and French translations of his work appeared by the fourteenth century, the first printed edition in the fifteenth, and the first English versions early in the sixteenth. The great Renaissance Humanist, Desiderius Erasmus, preferred Sallust to Livy and Tacitus for use in school curricula. In modern times, Sallust has appealed to many, including Marxist readers who find in him an indictment of decadence in a corrupted aristocracy.

Sallust produced the first true masterpieces of historical writing in Latin. His political career served as preparation, in the school of hard experience, for his work as a writer. In modern times, some have charged him with hypocrisy, noting the glaring inconsistency between his own quite dismal record as a public servant and the lofty moral tone he adopts in his histories. Moreover, doubts tend to arise regarding the presentation and interpretation of facts in the writings of a retired politician. Nevertheless, these considerations do not detract from the worth of Sallust's writings in and of themselves. His works are valuable inquiries into and reflections on sociopolitical developments in an exciting and critically significant period in Roman history.

Bibliography

Broughton, T. R. S. "Was Sallust Fair to Cicero?" *Transactions of the American Philological Association* 67 (1936): 34-46. Broughton answers "yes" to the question in his title. Sallust was neither so malicious nor so ironic in his references to Cicero as scholars often claim. Broughton shows that, in fact, Sallust gave Cicero his due in a generally appreciative, though sometimes backhanded, fashion.

Earl, D. C. "The Early Career of Sallust." *Historia* 15 (1966): 302-311. Speculates on the significance of Sallust's origins in the township of Amiternum for his political career at Rome. Traces the likely course of Sallust's shifting allegiance to Caesar and others during his service as an elected or appointed official.

————. *The Political Thought of Sallust*. Cambridge: Cambridge University Press, 1961; Chicago: Argonaut, 1966. Earl discusses Sallust's views of the political environment of the late Republic, in particular his attitude toward moral degeneracy (declining *virtus*) as a fatal element. Explicates the individual works as reflective of this political perspective.

Kraus, Christina S. *Latin Historians*. Oxford and New York: Oxford University Press, 1997. The chapter on Sallust surveys the results of recent scholarship.

Laistner, M. L. W. *The Greater Roman Historians*. Berkeley: University of California Press, 1947. Contains a chapter on Sallust giving a harsh assessment of his worth as a historian: "Sallust's merits as an artist have obscured, or made his readers willing to forget, his faults. As a historical authority he is at best in the second rank."

Leeman, A. D. *A Systematical Bibliography of Sallust (1879-1964)*. Rev. ed. Leiden, Netherlands: E. J. Brill, 1965. This very thorough and lucidly organized bibliography contains brief annotations and summaries and an index of authors. References to more recent studies of Sallust may be found in the annual volumes of the bibliographical reference work *L'Année philologique*.

MacKay, L. A. "Sallust's *Catiline:* Date and Purpose." *Phoenix* 16 (1962): 181-194. Argues for a first edition of Sallust's monograph in 50, after his expulsion from the senate. The attitudes Sallust evinces toward Pompey, Cicero, Caesar, and others are most consistent with an effort to regain his senatorial rank.

Marshall, B. A. "Cicero and Sallust on Crassus and Catiline." *Latomus* 33 (1974): 804-813. Argues that Sallust inherited from Cato the view of Marcus Licinius Crassus (triumvir with Caesar and Pompey beginning in 59) as having abetted the Catilinian conspirators out of enmity with Pompey the Great.

Paul, G. M. "Sallust." In *Latin Historians*, edited by T. A. Dorey. London: Routledge, and New York: Basic Books, 1966. Another brief description and assessment of the works of Sallust, more favorable than that given by Laistner.

Sallust. *The Histories*. Patrick McGushin, ed. and trans. 2 vols. Oxford: Clarendon Press, and New York: Oxford University Press, 1992. The translation includes all the extant fragments of Sallust's work. The commentary is very extensive, taking up more than half of the volumes. There is a bibliography of modern works on Sallust.

Syme, Ronald. *The Roman Revolution*. Oxford: Clarendon Press, 1939; New York: Oxford University Press, 1951. An extremely important and influential scholarly work on "the transformation of state and society at Rome between 60 B.C. and A.D. 14." Syme's "pessimistic and truculent tone" (his own words) make him the modern historian most like Sallust in style of presentation.

———. *Sallust*. Berkeley: University of California Press, 1964. The best and most authoritative work on the life, times, and writings of its subject: "Sallust, who had been a failure more times than one in his career as a senator, enjoyed luck and a supreme felicity. . . . He exploited the flaws and limitations of his own temperament, transmuting ambition into literary excellence."

Waters, K. H. "Cicero, Sallust, and Caesar," in *Historia* 19 (1970): 195-215. Sees Sallust's monograph as a valuable corrective to distortions in Cicero's version of the Catiline conspiracy. In particular, Sallust's account proves that Cicero exaggerated or invented many details regarding the actions, motives, and state of preparedness of the conspirators.

James P. Holoka

SAMUEL

Born: c. 1090 B.C.; Ramathaim-Zophim (or Ramah)
Died: c. 1020 B.C.; Ramah
Areas of Achievement: Religion and government
Contribution: Though famed as a priest and prophet, Samuel is chiefly remembered as the instrument by which the monarchy was established in Israel.

Early Life

When Samuel was born, the twelve tribes of Israel had conquered and settled the greater part of the Promised Land but had as yet no unified government. The tribes occasionally united against a common enemy and submitted their disputes to judges, but leaders such as Gideon and Jephthah brought victory in battle without establishing any office or administration.

Samuel's birth followed a pattern common in the Old Testament. He was the son of Elkanah, who had two wives. One, Hannah, was barren; though she had the love of her husband, she was mocked for her barrenness by her sister wife. When the family went to sacrifice at Shiloh, Hannah vowed that if the Lord gave her a man-child, she would dedicate the child to divine service for "all the days of his life." Thus, her son, Samuel, after he had been weaned, became servant to Eli, the priest at Shiloh.

One night Samuel thought that he heard Eli calling; after the third time, Eli realized that the Lord was calling to the boy. Samuel learned that God's favor was withdrawn from the house of Eli because of the misconduct of Eli's sons; shortly thereafter, these sons were killed in battle against the Philistines and Eli died. The ark of the covenant was captured, but it was soon restored when it occasioned plagues among the Philistines. Samuel was now the priest and was also recognized as a prophet who received direct revelations from God, as Eli had not.

Life's Work

Twenty years later, Samuel decided that aggressive action was needed against the Philistines, a people from overseas who had settled on the coast of Palestine. The Philistines were a constant threat to Israel, since they were technologically more advanced, especially in the use of iron. In order to regain divine favor, Samuel persuaded the Israel-

ites to abandon their worship of "strange gods" (the Baalim and Ashtoreth, Canaanite fertility gods). When the Israelites gathered at Mizpeh, and the Philistines attacked them, Samuel sacrificed, and

> as Samuel was offering up the burnt offering, the Philistines drew near to battle against Israel: but the Lord thundered with a great thunder that day upon the Philistines, and discomfited them; and they were smitten before Israel.

Several cities were recovered from the Philistines, and Samuel returned to his priestly and judicial duties, traveling "from year to year in circuit to Bethel, and Gilgal, and Mizpeh, and judged Israel in all those places; and his return was to Ramah; for there was his house" (1 Sam. 7).

In the Book of Judges, there are several examples of leaders, such as Gideon, who might have established a monarchy, but they either refused or behaved so badly that the Israelites repudiated them. Samuel seems almost to have been thought of as a king, but he could not have been accepted as one because his sons, like Eli's, were unworthy: They "turned aside after lucre, and took bribes, and perverted judgment." At this point, Samuel became less a judge or military leader and more a king-maker, one who as prophet communicated the Lord's intentions to make or unmake a particular monarch. (The narrative of 1 Samuel shows certain inconsistencies which are thought to be the result of combining two accounts, one friendly and one hostile to the idea of a monarchy. Note that the idea of monarchy implies not only authority in war and peace but also succession, the orderly passing of rule from father to son.)

"When Samuel was old," the elders of Israel asked him to give them a king "to judge us like all the nations," to "go out before us, and fight our battles." Samuel consulted the Lord, Who answered, "They have not rejected thee, but they have rejected me, that I should not reign over them." Nevertheless, He directed Samuel, after listing all the forms of oppression which a king might inflict, to give them a king.

Thus Samuel became involved in the tragic career of Saul. The younger son of a Benjaminite named Kish and a "choice young man and a goodly," Saul had been sent with a servant to find some lost asses. They were ready to abandon the search

SAUL ANOINTED BY SAMUEL

when the servant suggested that they consult a man of God, a seer in the city of Zulph, who might advise them about the asses for a present of one-fourth of a shekel of silver. They went to the seer, who was Samuel. Having been forewarned by the Lord, Samuel entertained Saul cordially and anointed him. This anointing did not imply that Saul would immediately become king. Instead, he was sent home; on the way, he met a company of ecstatic prophets and prophesied with them (perhaps an alternative account is again being presented). Samuel called the people to Mizpeh and by a drawing of lots again chose Saul king. Yet Saul did not begin his reign but went home to Gibeah; he could not even collect taxes, for the sons of Belial "despised him and brought him no presents."

The crisis came when the Ammonites besieged Jabesh-gilead. Saul behaved like a king at last: "And he took a yoke of oxen, and hewed them in pieces, and sent them throughout all the coasts of Israel by messengers, saying, Whosoever cometh not forth after Saul and after Samuel, so shall it be done to his oxen" (1 Sam. 11:7).

According to the phrase "after Saul and after Samuel," Samuel was still a power in Israel when Saul "slew the Ammonites until the heat of the day." Samuel's response to this victory was twofold. First, he conducted a formal coronation ceremony for Saul. Second, Samuel gave a formal abdication speech, stressing his function as judge: "Whom have I defrauded? whom have I oppressed? or of whose hand have I received any bribe?" Samuel further reminded the people of all that the Lord had done for them since He delivered them from Egypt. Emphasizing his point by calling down thunder and rain in the midst of harvest, he concluded grimly, "But if ye shall still do wickedly, ye shall be consumed, both ye and your king."

Saul's reign started auspiciously; he and his son Jonathan were victorious in their campaigns against the Philistines and other enemies of Israel. Yet there were two occasions when Saul acted in ways that caused him to forfeit divine favor. Saul had mobilized the people to meet a Philistine invasion and expected Samuel to meet him and offer sacrifices. When, after seven days, Samuel had not appeared, Saul, seeing his army melting away, offered the sacrifice himself. Immediately thereafter, Samuel arrived and told Saul that because of his disobedience to the Lord, his kingdom, which otherwise would have been established forever, would not continue but would be given to another, a man

after the Lord's own heart. Nevertheless, afterward, Samuel ordered Saul, in the name of the Lord, to attack the Amalekites, who had interfered with the Israelites during the Exodus, and massacre them, "both man and woman, infant and suckling, ox and sheep, camel and ass." Saul defeated the Amalekites, but he spared their king, Agag, and kept the best of the sheep and oxen for later sacrifice. This, to Samuel, was another sin of disobedience; the Lord, he said, repented having made Saul king. "And Samuel came no more to see Saul until the day of his death: nevertheless Samuel mourned for Saul."

The Lord had one more duty for Samuel to perform before his death; he was to go to Bethlehem and anoint David as Saul's successor. Saul, meanwhile, was troubled by an evil spirit sent from the Lord; the modern reader may recognize symptoms of paranoia and depression. The remainder of 1 Samuel has little to do with Samuel; it primarily concerns David's rise and Saul's decline. It is recorded simply that Samuel died; "all the Israelites were gathered together, and lamented him, and buried him in his house at Ramah."

Summary

Whether Samuel is considered a prophet or a judge, the Bible portrays him playing a variety of roles in Israel. He was, first, a priest, presiding over a shrine and offering sacrifices there; on special occasions, such as war, he may have offered sacrifices elsewhere. His powers as a prophet varied greatly; he was apparently not insulted at the idea of finding lost cattle for a small sum in silver. He also claimed, however, to receive divine communications regarding the public welfare: In this he resembled the classic prophets, such as Jeremiah and Isaiah. Samuel enforced the lesson that national prosperity meant obedience not merely to general moral principles but also to direct instruction from the Lord, as communicated through His prophets. One form of prophecy Samuel seems not to have practiced: He was not one of the ecstatic prophets who performed in bands and in whose performances Saul twice joined. Samuel also occasionally performed secular functions. At least once, he commanded the armies of Israel, and his function as a judge should not be forgotten.

Samuel's influence did not end with his death. The modern reader does not automatically side with Samuel but asks whether Saul's premature sacrifice was such a fatal piece of disobedience and whether it was necessary to carry out such a ruthless sacrifice of the Amalekites. In part, the Bible answers these doubts: After Samuel's death, Saul's depression deepened, and his jealousy and persecution of David must have weakened him politically. When the Philistines gathered their army once more, Saul "was afraid, and his heart greatly trembled." Unable to gain divine guidance, Saul, who had driven the witches and wizards from the land, in his desperation sought out a woman who had a familiar spirit and asked her to call up Samuel. Samuel appeared, an old man covered with a mantle, and pronounced a grim sentence: "The Lord will also deliver Israel with thee into the hand of the Philistines: and to morrow shalt thou and thy sons be with me." Thus it happened, but the author or last editor of 1 Samuel must have had compassion for Saul; he recorded that the men of Jabesh-gilead recovered Saul's body from the Philistines and gave it honorable burial.

Bibliography

Alter, Robert, and Frank Kermode, eds. *The Literary Guide to the Bible*. London: Collins, and Cambridge, Mass.: Harvard University Press, 1987. Contains an essay on 1 and 2 Samuel by Joseph Rosenberg which emphasizes Samuel's role in the establishment of the monarchy. See also Gerald Hammond's "English Translations of the Bible," which justifies the continued use of the King James Version.

Blenkinsopp, Joseph. *A History of Prophecy in Israel*. Philadelphia: Westminster Press, 1983; London: SPCK, 1984. Places Samuel in the context of Old Testament prophecy and in the context of other Near Eastern cultures.

Gordon, R. P. "Who Made the Kingmaker? Reflections on Samuel and the Institution of the Monarchy." In *Faith, Tradition and History: Old Testament Historiography in Its Near Eastern Context*. Alan R. Millard, James K. Hoffmeier, and David W. Baker, eds. Winona Lake, IN: Eisenbrauns, 1994. The paper briefly considers the historical backcloth to the emergence of the monarchy, and then covers in more detail, but still selectively, the narrative traditions associated with Samuel of Ramah.

Kuntz, J. Kenneth. *The People of Ancient Israel: An Introduction to Old Testament Literature, History, and Thought*. New York: Harper and Row, 1974. Useful for the historical context and for chronology. Extensive bibliographies.

Pfeiffer, Robert H. *Introduction to the Old Testament*. New York: Harper and Row, and London: Black, 1948. Gives an analysis of Samuel's story with an emphasis on its composite character.

Sternberg, Meir. *The Poetics of Biblical Narrative: Ideological Literature and the Drama of Reading*. Bloomington: Indiana University Press, 1985. The final chapter contains a very interesting study of the literary strategies used to handle the downfall of Saul.

John C. Sherwood

SAPPHO

Born: c. 612 B.C.; Mytilene or Eresns, Lesbos, Asia Minor
Died: c. 580 B.C.; probably Mytilene, Lesbos, Asia Minor
Area of Achievement: Literature
Contribution: Regarded by ancient commentators as the equal of Homer, Sappho has poetically expressed the human emotions with honesty, courage, and skill.

Early Life

Sappho was born about 612 in either Eresus or Mytilene on the island of Lesbos, just off the western coast of Turkey. Her father was probably a rich wine merchant named Scamandronymus, and her mother was called Cleis, as was Sappho's daughter. The poet had three brothers: Charaxus and Larichus, who served in aristocratic positions in Mytilene, and Eurygyius, of whom no information remains. Charaxus, the oldest brother, reportedly fell in love with and ransomed the courtesan Doricha, which displeased Sappho. Conversely, she often praised her other brother, Larichus, whose name, passed down in Mytilenian families, was the same as that of the father of a friend of Alexander the Great.

About 600, when the commoner Pittacus gained political power in Lesbos, Sappho reportedly went into exile in Sicily for a short time. She was already well-known. She married Cercylas, a wealthy man from Andros, by whom she bore her daughter, Cleis.

Although much of the information available regarding the Aeolian culture of seventh century Lesbos derives only from the poetry of Sappho and her contemporary Alcaeus, scholars have described the society as more sensual and free than that of the neighboring Dorians, Ionians, Spartans, and Athenians. Political unrest, freedom for women, and enjoyment of the senses appear to have characterized the aristocratic circle with which Sappho mingled.

Life's Work

Sappho's poetry, her principal life's work, consisted of nine books, which the grammarians of Alexandria arranged according to meter. The earliest surviving texts date from the third century B.C. Because the first book contained 1,320 lines, it can be surmised that Sappho left approximately twelve thousand lines, seven hundred of which have sur-

vived, pieced together from several sources. Only one complete poem remains, quoted by Dionysius of Halicarnassus, the rest ranging in completeness from several full lines to one word. Many of the lines lack beginning, middle, or end because they have survived on mummy wrapping in Egyptian tombs, the papyrus having been ripped crosswise of the roll, lengthwise of the poem. The long rolls of papyrus, made from the stalks of a water plant, also survived in battered condition in the dry Egyptian climate in garbage dumps and as stuffing in the mouths of mummified crocodiles.

Other lines remain because ancient grammarians used them to illustrate a point of grammar or comment on a text; literary critics quoted them to praise Sappho's style or talk about her metrics; and historians, orators, and philosophers used brief quotes from her work to illustrate their points. One fragment was recorded on a piece of broken pottery dating from the third century B.C. Important discoveries of eighth century manuscripts near Crocodilopolis were made in 1879, and two Englishmen made comparable finds in 1897 in an ancient Egyptian garbage dump. One nineteenth century German scholar who rescued Sappho's poetry from its battered condition lost his eyesight, and one of the English scholars temporarily lost his sanity during the arduous process of transcription.

The surviving poetry consists primarily of passionate, simple, love poems addressed in the vernacular to young women. "Ode to Aphrodite," the only remaining complete poem, pleads with the goddess to make the object of the poet's passion return her love with equal intensity, which Aphrodite promises to do. Sappho's equally famous poem, "Seizure," is usually interpreted as an objective description of the poet's extreme jealousy when she sees her beloved conversing with a man. She writes that her heart beats rapidly and "a thin flame runs under / [her] skin"; she cannot speak or see anything and hears only her "own ears/ drumming"; she sweats, trembles, and turns "paler than/ dry grass." Her jealousy can also burst into anger, as when she warns herself

Sappho, when some fool

Explodes rage
in your breast
hold back that
yapping tongue!

Or she can restrain her emotions, stating quietly, "Pain penetrates/ Me drop/ by drop." The intensity of Sappho's passion becomes clear in the brief metaphor "As a whirlwind/ swoops on an oak/ Love shakes my heart." In a quieter mood, she can reveal another facet of her feelings:

Really, Gorgo,

My disposition
is not at all
spiteful: I have
a childlike heart.

Sappho's subject matter helps explain the low survival rate of her poetry. Her reputation reached such greatness during the Golden Age of Greece that Solon of Athens reputedly remarked that he wished only to learn a certain poem by Sappho before he died, and Plato referred to her as the "Tenth Muse." The writers of the urbane and sophisticated Middle and New Comedy of Greece in the fourth and third centuries B.C., however, six of whom wrote plays they titled "Sappho," ridiculed Sappho's simplicity and openness, depicting her as an immoral, licentious courtesan. Although the Romans Theocritus, Horace, and Catullus praised and imitated her, Ovid referred to her both as a licentious woman lusting after a young man and as one who taught her audience how to love girls, characteristics which the Christian church did not value.

Consequently, in A.D. 180 the ascetic Tatian attacked her as whorish and love-crazy. Gregory of Nazianzus, Bishop of Constantinople, in about 380, ordered that Sappho's writings be burned, and eleven years later Christian fanatics partially destroyed the classical library in Alexandria, which would certainly have contained her work. In 1073, Pope Gregory VII ordered another public burning of her writings in Rome and Constantinople. The Venetian knights who pillaged Constantinople in April, 1204, further decimated her extant poetry. Thus, no single collection of her work survived the Middle Ages.

During the Renaissance, however, when Italian scholars recovered Longinus' *Peri hypsous* (first century A.D.; *Essay on the Sublime*) and Dionysius of Halicarnassus' treatise on style, they found "Hymn to Aphrodite" and "Seizure." At this point, scholars began to collect all the remaining words, lines, and stanzas by Sappho.

During the nineteenth century, English and German scholars began to idealize Sappho and her work. Many of them viewed her as a moral, chaste woman, either a priestess of a special society of girls who devoted themselves to worship of Aphrodite and the Muses, or as the principal of a type of girls' finishing school. Although they sometimes acknowledged the intensity of her passion for her "pupils," they denied that it resulted in physical expression, a sentiment which persisted in the work of Maurice Bowra in 1936, and which Denys L. Page began to challenge in 1955. Succeeding critical works have increasingly accepted and explored the existence of Sappho's physical love for her young female companions. Although Sappho's expressed lesbian feelings and/or practice have little bearing on her skill as a poet, the stance almost doomed her work to extinction in a predominantly Christian society, in which sexual values differed significantly from those accepted in the ancient world, especially in seventh century Lesbos.

Summary

The poetry of Sappho provides its reader with a direct experience of intense, stark emotions. Its unadorned honesty allows readers from various cultures and time periods a glimpse of the culture in which she lived, but, more important, into the human heart at its most vulnerable. Sappho loves and hates, feels jealousy and anger, and is able to transmit her emotions so immediately that the reader must respond to her stimuli.

Sappho defends the private sphere and shows the power of love within the individual heart. She has caused succeeding cultures to express their values in relation to her openness. To examine the history of Western civilization in reaction to Sappho's work is to stand back and observe as succeeding generations gaze into the mirror which she provides. Many have smashed the mirror, unable to confront the naked human heart. Some have seen themselves as they would like to be, and a few have learned more fully what it means to be feeling, passionate human beings.

Bibliography

Blundell, Sue. *Women in Ancient Greece.* Cambridge, Mass.: Harvard University Press, 1995. In a clear and insightful account, Blundell indicates the exceptional nature of the Greek society ies from which most evidence on women survives, and asserts that Athenian women had some power and autonomy in the domestic sphere. Provides a brief, sensitive treatment of Sappho.

Bowra, C. Maurice. *Greek Lyric Poetry: From Alcman to Simonides.* 2d ed. Oxford: Clarendon Press, 1961. A classic review of seven Greek lyric poets stressing their historical development and critiquing important works. Offers groundbreaking theories of the poets as a group and as individual writers. Views Sappho as the leader of a society of girls which excluded men and worshipped the Muses and Aphrodite.

Burnett, Anne Pippin. *Three Archaic Poets: Archilochus, Alcaeus, Sappho.* Cambridge, Mass.: Harvard University Press, and London: Duckworth, 1983. Rejects theories of ancient Greek lyrics as either passionate outpourings or occasional verse. Describes Sappho's aristocratic circle and critiques six major poems. Stresses Sappho's acceptance of sexuality and believes that the poet was providing her young female friends with ideals of beauty to sustain them during married life as second-class citizens.

DeJean, Joan E. *Fictions of Sappho, 1546-1937.* Chicago: University of Chicago Press, 1989. Although fictional, DeJean's work is a unique presentation of ideas on Sappho. She interconnects ideas of Sapphic scholarship to create sections that are relevant to serious classicists; for example, she addresses the appropriation of Sappho's voice by male authors, thus alluding to the presence of a feminine influence in the rules that have been formed by men to govern women.

DuBois, Page. *Sappho is Burning.* Chicago: University of Chicago Press, 1995. Directly addresses the aesthetic resonances of Sappho's poetry. Regards Sappho's eroticism as typical of an aristocrat of the archaic period, and as more concerned with domination than with a reciprocal view of love confined exclusively to women.

Grant, Michael, and Rachel Kitzinger, eds. *Women's History and Ancient History.* Chapel Hill: University of North Carolina Press, 1991. Acknowledges the interdisciplinary nature of women's studies by uniting 12 essays on a variety of topics. The volume pairs related essays, giving the impression that authors are engaging in dialogue with each other. Uses both traditional evidence and multidisciplinary perspectives. Essay on the writing of Sappho focuses on the interaction between women's public and private discourses.

Jenkyns, Richard. *Three Classical Poets: Sappho, Catullus, and Juvenal.* Cambridge, Mass.: Harvard University Press, and London: Duckworth, 1982. Stresses the relativistic view that no one theory can elucidate ancient poetry. Interesting observations about nineteenth century views of Sappho. Detailed analysis of principal poems and fragments, concluding that Sappho is a major poet and her body of work is unified while emphasizing that each poem must be judged individually.

Lipking, Lawrence I. *Abandoned Women and Poetic Tradition.* Chicago: University of Chicago Press, 1988. Lipking uses his own readings and translations to illustrate the use and misuse of the abandoned woman in the history of Western culture. Exposes the appropriation of Sappho's work by generations of poets, providing much insight into the history of literary divination.

Page, Denys L. *Sappho and Alcaeus: An Introduction to the Study of Ancient Lesbian Poetry.* Oxford: Clarendon Press, 1955; New York: Oxford University Press, 1959. Includes Greek text, translation, lengthy commentary, and detailed interpretation of twelve Sapphic poems. Views the poet as private, apolitical; regards her epithalamiums as a minor portion of her canon; pictures women in Aeolian Lesbos as uncommonly liberated; and regards Sappho as lesbian in feeling but not practice. Includes an appendix on meters.

Robinson, David M. *Sappho and Her Influence.* London: Harrap, and Boston: Marshall Jones, 1924. A lightweight account of Sappho's life, legends, and writings which offers unsubstantiated conclusions. Surveys her depiction by western artists and chronicles her influence on Greek, Roman Medieval, Renaissance, Italian, Spanish, French, English, and American literature. Views her as a pure, diligent teacher. Twenty-four plates showing paintings, sculpture, and coins associated with Sappho. Selected bibliography.

Sappho. *Lyrics in the Original Greek.* Willis Barnstone, trans. Garden City, N.Y.: Anchor Books, 1965. Includes Greek text with translation of 158 poems and fragments, arranged arbitrarily according to the subject and the chronology of the poems' speaker. Also contains major references from both Greek and Latin texts to Sappho and her poetry, metrical tables and metrical indexes, and concordances to three other major translations of her work.

———. *Sappho: A New Translation.* Mary Barnard, trans. Berkeley: University of California Press, 1958. Contains one hundred of Sappho's poems divided into six sections, a laudatory foreword by Dudley Fitts, and a lengthy footnote by Barnard which provides cultural background, biographical information, summaries of interpretations by Maurice Bowra and Denys L. Page, and notes on the process of translation and the ways the poems have survived the onslaught of time.

Snyder, Jane McIntosh. *The Woman and the Lyre: Women Writers in Classical Greece and Rome.* Bristol: Bristol Classical Press, and Carbondale: Southern Illinois University Press, 1989. Snyder does an excellent job of reconstructing the fragments of all the writers represented in this volume, placing them in both a historical and literary context. The work covers a vast historical span and demonstrates a thorough command of scholarly literature. Snyder puts forth a coherent reconstruction of the female tradition that many scholars would not approach because of the state of much of the evidence.

Shelley A. Thrasher

SARGON II

Born: Second half of eighth century B.C.; Assyria
Died: 705 B.C.; north of Assyrian empire
Areas of Achievement: Warfare and government
Contribution: Through incessant, successful warfare and widespread resettlement of conquered populations, Sargon II brought an embattled Assyria to a late zenith of power and reshaped the structure of its empire; the dynasty he founded would last until the fall of Assyria.

Early Life

There exists no known record of his life before Sargon II assumed the title of King of Assyria from his predecessor, Shalmaneser V, in December, 722, or January, 721. Because he never followed the royal custom of mentioning his father and grandfather by name in his annals, but simply utilized the formula of referring to his ancestors as "the kings his fathers," historians believe Sargon to have usurped the throne, although some insist that he was a son of the successful king Tukulti-apal-esharra (Tiglathpileser III). In any case, he must have been born to a noble family of some renown; after surviving infancy—no small achievement in a society plagued by high infant mortality—the young warrior most likely pursued the customary education for his class: archery, horseback riding and chariot driving, and perhaps reading and writing.

From the ninth century B.C. on, Sargon's royal predecessors had worked to reverse the decline of Assyrian power which had begun with the death of the powerful king Tukulti-Ninurta I in 1208. Their expansionist policy had given birth to the Neo-Assyrian empire, a state which found a most able leader in Tiglathpileser III from 744 to 727.

During his reign, Egypt in the southwest and Urartu in the northeast were defeated, and Palestine, Syria, and Babylonia were conquered and subjected to political reorganization. Indeed, Tiglathpileser bequeathed to Assyria a legacy which defined the direction of that country's interest and armed struggle for more than a century.

During a prolonged punitive mission in Samaria, when the absence of the king paralyzed official life and the work of justice at home, Tiglathpileser's successor, Shalmaneser V, lost his throne to Sargon. The name which the young king took for himself at his accession shows some clever political maneuvering and suggests the need to legitimize this succession, or at least to stress its rightfulness.

In its original Semitic form, Sharru-kin, Sargon's name means "established" or "true and rightful king." In addition to this literal claim, there is the implicit reference to the Mesopotamian king Sargon of Akkad, who had reigned more than a thousand years before and whose fame had given rise to popular myths.

Life's Work

Sargon's kingship placed him at the helm of an embattled empire to whose expansion he would dedicate his life. Immediately after his succession, Sargon reaped unearned fame abroad when the city of Samaria fell and 27,290 Israelites were captured and resettled eastward in Mesopotamia and Media; this event has always been well-known, since it is mentioned in the biblical book of Isaiah. At home, the new king secured his position by supporting the priesthood and the merchant class; his immediate reestablishment of tax-exempt status for Assyria's temples was the first demonstration of Sargon's lifelong policy of supporting the national religion.

During the first year of his reign, Sargon had to face opposition in the recently conquered territories. His annals, written in cuneiform on plates at his palace, record how Sargon first marched south against Marduk-apal-iddina II or "Merodach-Baladan, the foe, the perverse, who, contrary to the will of the great gods, exercised sovereign power at Babylon," a city which this local potentate had seized the moment Sargon became king. In league with Ummannish, King of the Elamites to the east of Babylon, the rebel proved able to prevent Sargon's advance through a battle in which both sides claimed victory; Merodach-Baladan remained ruler over the contested city for the next twelve years.

Turning west toward Syria and Palestine, Sargon's army defeated the usurper Ilu-bi'di (Iaubid), who had led an anti-Assyrian uprising, in the city of Karkar. Sargon's revenge was rather drastic; he burned the city and flayed Ilu-bi'di before marching against an Egyptian army at Raphia. There, Sargon decisively defeated the Egyptians and reestablished Assyrian might in Palestine. For the next ten years, neither Egypt nor local rebels would contest Assyrian power in the southwestern provinces, and Sargon began to look north toward another battlefield. There, at the northeastern boundary of the Assyrian empire around the Armenian lakes, King Urssa (Rusas I) of Urartu and King

754

Mita of Mushki (the Midas of Greek legend) habitually supported Sargon's enemies and destabilized the Assyrian border. For five years, between 719 and 714, Sargon battled various opponents in mountainous territory and waged a war of devastation and destruction on hostile kingdoms and their cities. Once they had overcome their enemies, the Assyrians plundered and burned their cities, led away the indigenous population, hacked down all trees, and destroyed dikes, canals, and other public works. In neighboring territories which Sargon intended to hold, a new population of Assyrians would follow the wave of destruction and deportation and settle in the land, and a new city with an Assyrian name would be founded at the site of the ruined old one.

In 714, Sargon finally defeated King Rusas and, upon its ready surrender, plundered the city of Musasir, the riches of which were immense. A year later, a minor campaign against his son-in-law Ambaridi, a northern chieftain, showed the extent of resistance which Assyrian officers and nobles encountered in dealing with their neighbors and the populations of their provinces. The Assyrian response was swift and successful, and after Ambaridi's defeat and the leading away of his family and supporters, a large number of Assyrians settled in the pacified country, as was the usual pattern by then.

The next year saw a new campaign in the west, where pro-Assyrian rulers had been murdered or replaced with anti-Assyrians, who sometimes commanded considerable local support. In all cases, Sargon proved successful. The siege of Ashdod, where an Egyptian contingent was captured as well, is the second of Sargon's exploits mentioned in the Bible.

After his successful conquests and campaigns of pacification in the north and the southwest, Sargon prepared himself for a new showdown with his old enemy Merodach-Baladan. Marching southward, the Assyrian king wedged the two halves of his army between Babylon and the Elamites; his strategy proved successful when Merodach-Baladan left his capital for Elam. In 710/709, Sargon triumphantly entered the open city and became *de facto* king of Babylon, where he "took the hand of Bel," the city's deity, at the New Year's celebration. Again, Sargon showed himself profoundly sympathetic to the cause of the priesthood and made large donations to the Babylonian temples; in turn, priests and influential citizens celebrated his arrival. Merodach-Baladan, in contrast, failed in his attempt at persuading the Elamites to fight Sargon and retreated south to Yakin, close to the Persian Gulf. In April, 709, Sargon defeated him in battle there but let him go in return for a large payment of tribute.

After the fall of Yakin, Sargon ruled over an empire which stretched from the Mediterranean to the mountains of Armenia and encompassed Mesopotamia up to the Persian Gulf in the east. He left the remaining military missions to his generals, made his son and heir apparent, Sennacherib, commanding general in the north, and dedicated his energy to the building of his palatial city at what is now Khorsabad in Iraq. There, besides commissioning his annals to be written on stone plates, Sargon had his artists create impressive reliefs of the Assyrian king. These reliefs show a strong, muscular man taking part in various royal ceremonies and functions, among which is the blinding of prisoners of war. Sargon's head is adorned with an elaborately dressed turban and bejeweled headband; as was the fashion among the Assyrians, he wears a golden earring and a long, waved beard which is curled at the end. On his upper arms he wears golden bands, and his wrists sport bracelets. His multilayered garment bears some resemblance to a modern sari; the cloth has a rich pattern of rosettes and ends in tassels which touch the king's sandals at his ankles.

In 705, Sargon died under circumstances which are as mysterious as is his rise to kingship. Some historians believe that he died in an ambush during a campaign in the north when he led a small reconnaissance unit, as he was wont to do; according to others, he died at the hands of an assassin in his newly built capital, Dur-Sharrukin, a city which was abandoned after his death.

Summary

For all of his aggression against neighboring states, which was the accepted mode of national survival in his times, Sargon showed statesmanship when it came to domestic politics and the treatment of the vast populace of his empire. He was a fair ruler who showed care for the material and spiritual well-being of his subjects. His annals make proud mention of how he paid fair market price for confiscated private land and strove "to fill the store houses of the broad land of Asshur with food and provisions . . . [and] not to let oil, that gives life to man and heals sores, become dear in my land, and regulate the price of sesame as well as of wheat."

Sargon was also well aware of the fact that his nation, in which resettlement of conquered people and colonization by Assyrians eradicated older national structures, possessed no real racial or religious unity. To achieve a sense of national homogeneity and coherence, he employed the Assyrian language. Dur-Sharrukin, his new capital, was the best example of Sargonian domestic policy. His annals record how he populated the new metropolis:

> People from the four quarters of the world, of foreign speech, of manifold tongues, who had dwelt in mountains and valleys . . . whom I, in the name of Asshur my lord, by the might of my arms had carried away into captivity, I commanded to speak one language [Assyrian] and settled them therein. Sons of Asshur, of wise insight in all things, I placed over them, to watch over them; learned men and scribes to teach them the fear of God and the King.

Thus, Sargon's successful wars and domestic policy firmly established the power of the Neo-Assyrian empire and left behind a great nation which would last for a century and help fight the northeastern barbarians who were beginning to threaten the ancient civilizations of the Middle East.

Bibliography

Goodspeed, George Stephen. *A History of the Babylonians and Assyrians.* London: Smith, Elder, and New York: Scribner, 1902. Chapter 5 deals with Sargon and critically discusses his reign and achievements. Special attention is given to the question of Sargon's legitimacy and to a careful reading of his annals. Good and accessible overview of Sargon's campaigns.

Luckenbill, Daniel David. *Ancient Records of Assyria and Babylonia.* 2 vols. Chicago: University of Chicago Press, 1926; London: Histories and Mysteries of Man, 1989. This work contains a fine translation of Sargon's letter to the god Ashur, in which the king reports on his northern campaign against Urartu. Sargon's text, far from dry, reveals a remarkable poetic bent.

Olmstead, Albert T. E. *History of Assyria.* New York and London: Scribner, 1923. Chapters 17 to 23 deal with Sargon in a detailed discussion which closely follows original sources and points out where Sargon's reign connects with biblical events. Richly illustrated with maps and photographs of Assyrian artifacts, ruins, and the present look of the country.

———. *Western Asia in the Days of Sargon of Assyria.* New York: Holt, 1908. Historically accurate and highly readable book on Sargon and his times which brings alive the Assyrians and their king. Illustrated and with helpful maps.

Ragozin, Zenaide A. *Assyria from the Rise of the Empire to the Fall of Nineveh.* 3d ed. London: Unwin, and New York: Putnam, 1891. Chapter 8 is a popular account of Sargon which views his reign partially in the light of corresponding biblical events. Good etchings of Assyrian artifacts, some of which show Sargon in fine detail.

Saggs, H. W. F. *The Might That Was Assyria.* London: Sidgwick and Jackson, 1984; New York: St. Martin's Press, 1990. Pages 92-97 deal directly with Sargon. An account of Assyrian history and culture by an author who enjoys his subject. Relatively short on Sargon, but invaluable for its modern insights into Assyrian life. Has maps and interesting illustrations, including representations of both kings and everyday objects. Very readable.

Reinhart Lutz

SCIPIO AEMILIANUS

Born: 185 B.C.; probably Rome
Died: 129 B.C.; Rome
Areas of Achievement: Warfare, government, and patronage of art
Contribution: Combining a genius for military conquest with an appreciation for literature and the arts, Scipio Aemilianus embodies—perhaps better than any other figure of his day—the paradoxical forces which swept through Rome during the central years of the Republic.

Early Life

Publius Cornelius Scipio Aemilianus Africanus Numantinus, also known as Scipio the Younger, was born into Roman society in 185, about the time that Cato the Elder was beginning his famous censorship. Scipio's earliest years were thus spent during one of the most interesting periods of the Roman Republic. From his vantage point as a member of the distinguished Aemilian *gens* (family), the young Scipio was in a perfect position to witness events which would shape the course of Roman history. In addition to this, because of his father Lucius Aemilius Paullus' interest in Greek culture, Scipio was surrounded almost from birth by Greek tutors, orators, and artists. Together, these two factors—the political distinction of his family and his father's philhellenism—were to inspire in Scipio his interest in a military career and his lifelong enthusiasm for Greek civilization.

Scipio's mother, Papiria, was a member of one of Rome's leading families: Her father had been a victorious general, the first general, in fact, to hold a triumphal procession on the Alban Mount because he had been denied an official triumph back in Rome. Scipio's father had also served as a general and had already been elected to the curule aedileship and the Spanish praetorship; at the time of Scipio's birth, Paullus was only a few years away from the consulship, the highest political office in Rome.

Ironically, at about the same time that Paullus' tenure as consul began, his marriage ended. He divorced Papiria, remarried, and soon had two other sons by his second wife. Perhaps as a result of conflicts between these two families, Paullus decided to allow Scipio and his brother to be adopted into other households. Scipio, as his name implies, was adopted by Publius Cornelius Scipio, the son of Scipio Africanus, who had won his greatest fame as victor over the Carthaginians at Zama during the Second Punic War. His elder brother was adopted into the household of Quintus Fabius Maximus Cunctator, perhaps by a son or grandson of the famous general himself. Yet both Scipio and his brother, now known as Quintus Fabius Maximus Aemilianus, remained close to their birth father. Indeed, they both accompanied Paullus on an important expedition against Macedon in 168, during Paullus' second consulship.

The climactic battle of this expedition, at Pydna in 168, was both the crowning glory of Paullus' career and, quite possibly, Scipio's own first battle. The Macedonians, led by King Perseus, were defeated, and Paullus, in accordance with his literary tastes, chose only one prize for himself out of the spoils: Perseus' library. This mixture of military and literary interests was also apparent in Scipio himself at this time. It was during his stay in Greece that Scipio met the future historian Polybius, an author who would come to be his lifelong friend.

Life's Work

In 151, nearly a decade after the death of his father, Scipio was finally given a chance to develop a military reputation of his own. He was offered the position of military tribune under the consul Lucius Licinius Lucullus, who was about to assume command of the Roman forces in northern Spain. Though the campaign against the Celtiberian tribesmen would nearly be over before Lucullus finally arrived, Scipio did manage to win the *corona muralis* (an honor awarded to the first soldier who scaled the wall of an enemy), and, on a mission to obtain reinforcements in Africa, he witnessed a major battle between the Numidians and the Carthaginians. Thus, in this single campaign, Scipio journeyed to both of the regions which would one day see his greatest victories: Spain and Africa. Later, in 149 and 148, during the Third Punic War, Scipio served again as military tribune. The high honors which he won during the early campaigns of this war prompted his election to the consulship of 147, though neither in age nor in magistracies already held did he meet the requirements for the office.

The task assigned to Scipio during the final campaigns of the Third Punic War was to besiege the city of Carthage itself. Despite fierce opposition from the local inhabitants, Scipio managed to breach the fortifications of the city; six days of bitter fighting from house to house ensued. The Carthaginians resisted the Romans with unexpected vigor, though they had only makeshift weapons with which to defend themselves. While the battle raged in the streets below, the Roman soldiers were surprised to discover that they were being pelted with rocks and roofing tiles cast down from the houses above. Yet, in the end, Carthage was set ablaze, and the Romans proceeded to demolish all remaining structures; as these orders were being carried out, many Carthaginians were trapped and buried alive in their own homes.

Some days later, as the final task of razing Carthage was completed, Polybius noticed tears in Scipio's eyes. When asked the reason for these tears, Scipio replied that he was afraid lest someday the same order might be given for his own city. He then quoted a famous passage of Homer's *Iliad* (c. 800 B.C.): "There will come a day when sacred Ilium shall perish/ and Priam and the people of Priam of the fine ash-spear." Scipio's sentiments notwithstanding, the site of Carthage was declared accursed and its fifty thousand survivors were sold into slavery.

The years following the destruction of Carthage brought Rome once again into conflict with an old enemy: the Celtiberian tribesmen of Spain. For nearly ten years, from 143 until 134, a succession of Roman commanders had tried unsuccessfully to capture a Celtiberian fortress located on the hill settlement of Numantia. In the end, the Romans elected Scipio to be consul for a second time with the hope that he might bring this prolonged campaign to a successful conclusion. Scipio collected a force of nearly sixty thousand men, far outnumbering the four thousand Celtiberians who still remained at Numantia. He then adopted the plan of surrounding the fortress with a ring of seven camps. The ploy was successful, although once again at an appalling cost to human life. The inhabitants were starved out, and some of them had even been reduced to cannibalism before their surrender. In any case, when Numantia finally capitulated to the Romans in 133, Scipio ordered the fortress to be destroyed and its survivors sold into slavery. Once again, this general who had been steeped in Greek culture since childhood felt compelled to resort to extreme measures in his efforts to subdue a Roman enemy. In order to understand this event, however, it is necessary to realize how formidable

an opponent Numantia must have seemed at the time: Nearly a century after the fall of the city, Cicero could still refer, without fear of contradiction, to Carthage and Numantia as having been "the two most powerful enemies of Rome."

While these military conquests were still under way, however, Scipio's reputation was also on the rise because of his support for a group of artists and intellectuals who would come to make up the most famous "salon" in Roman history. The group was later to be known as the Scipionic Circle, though it is doubtful that this title was ever used in Scipio's own lifetime. The discussions of the Scipionic Circle covered a wide range of issues, and one of these discussions was later dramatized by Cicero in his dialogue entitled *De republica* (54-51 B.C.; *On the State*). Though the membership in the Scipionic Circle varied from year to year, it eventually came to include such figures as Scipio himself, Polybius, the comic playwright Terence, the Roman legate Gaius Laelius, and the philosopher Panaetius. Membership in the group seems to have been based not only on these individuals' talents but also upon Scipio's genuine affection for those with whom he discussed the issues of the day. Indeed, Scipio's friendship with Laelius became so renowned in later generations that Cicero based his philosophical dialogue *De amicitia* (45-44 B.C.; *On Friendship*) upon Laelius' supposed recollections of Scipio shortly after his death.

In 129, Scipio, on the verge of being given an important new position in the Roman government, was found dead in his bed. He had been in perfect health, it was said, only the night before. As a result, no one knew whether he had been murdered or had died of an illness. Indeed, the question was so vexing that it was still being debated even in the time of Cicero. At first, suspicions fell upon Gaius Papirius Carbo, a keen supporter of the reformer Tiberius Gracchus and a politician well-known for his oratorical ability. Carbo had been tribune in 131 and had proposed that tribunes be eligible for reelection year after year. Scipio had opposed this measure and had led the fight against it. It is possible, therefore, that this political struggle eventually cost Scipio his life.

Summary

While his contemporaries probably believed that Scipio Aemilianus would best be remembered for his military conquests and the political reputation of his family, scholars of later ages have come to view Scipio in a different light, as the center of the Scipionic Circle more than as a conquering general. Though Scipio destroyed Carthage, it was his adoptive grandfather, the defeater of Hannibal, whose name became tied to that city. Though Scipio consolidated Roman rule in Spain, it was Cato the Elder—who had tried and failed to accomplish the same task—whose military vision for Rome has remained clearer throughout the succeeding generations.

The Scipio who is recalled today is thus the Scipio of Cicero's dialogues: the student of Greek civilization, the friend of Polybius and Laelius, the magnet for Roman intellectuals of his time. While this is not an inaccurate picture, it is a picture that is largely incomplete. It is important, therefore, that Scipio Aemilianus be remembered not only as the man who wept and quoted Homer at the fall of Carthage but also as the victorious strategist who brought about the city's destruction.

Bibliography

Astin, A. E. *Scipio Aemilianus*. Oxford: Clarendon Press, 1967. A most complete and accurate study of Scipio Aemilianus. Contains complete biographical data on Scipio, including references to all ancient sources. Family trees of the Aemilii Paulli and the Scipiones are provided. Appendices are included regarding various discrepancies between the accounts of different authors and other difficulties facing the historian who attempts to reconstruct the life of Scipio. Extensive and well-chosen bibliography.

———. "Scipio Aemilianus and Cato Censorius." *Latomus* 15 (1956): 159-180. Astin explores the possibility that an unusual friendship may have existed between these two very different personalities.

Brown, Ruth Martin. *A Study of the Scipionic Circle*. Scottdale, Pa.: Mennonite Press, 1934. Still the most complete and readable analysis of the Scipionic Circle. Includes information on the history and nature of the Scipionic Circle, its members during various periods in its development, and its influence in Roman society. Though not as systematically annotated as Astin's work, Brown's book is useful in tracking down many primary sources. The bibliography is mostly out of date, but two appendices listing the members of the Scipionic Circle in tabular and chronological form are still useful.

Earl, D. C. "Terence and Roman Politics." *Historia* 11 (1962): 469-485. Earl demonstrates that the political views—or lack thereof—of Terence can be traced directly to his participation in the Scipionic Circle and the Hellenic influence upon that body.

Scullard, H. H. "Roman Politics." *Journal of Roman Studies* 50 (1960): 59-74. Scullard examines the policies of Scipio and those in his immediate circle. The article is valuable for those interested in tracing the rise of the Roman reform movement before the time of Tiberius Gracchus.

Walbank, F. W. "Political Morality and the Friends of Scipio." *Journal of Roman Studies* 55 (1965): 1-16. A study, by the world's foremost authority on Polybius, of the political philosophies of such figures as Polybius, Panaetius, and other members of the Scipionic Circle. The work is useful for the insight it provides into political views current in the central years of the Roman Republic and the attitudes toward imperialism in the period preceding the Roman Empire.

Jeffrey L. Buller

SCIPIO AFRICANUS

Born: 236 B.C.; Rome
Died: 184 or 183 B.C.; Liternum, Campania
Areas of Achievement: Warfare and government
Contribution: Scipio's military victory over Carthaginian forces in Spain and North Africa, brought about by his genius as strategist and innovator of tactics, ended the Second Punic War and established Roman hegemony in the Western Mediterranean.

Early Life

Publius Cornelius Scipio, known as Scipio Africanus or Scipio the Elder, was born to one of the most illustrious families of the Roman Republic; his father, who gave the boy his name, and his mother, Pomponia, were respected citizens of the patrician dynasty of the gens Cornelii. At Scipio's birth, Rome had begun to show its power beyond the boundaries of Italy, and the young nation was starting to strive for hegemony west and east of the known world. Coinciding with expansion outward was Rome's still-stable inner structure; nevertheless, the influence of the Greek culture had begun a softening, or rounding, of the Roman character.

Scipio's early life clearly reflects this transition. His lifelong sympathy with Greek culture made him somewhat suspect in the eyes of his conservative opponents, who accused him of weakening the Roman spirit. On the other hand, as a patrician youth, he must have received early military training, for Scipio entered history (and legend) at the age of seventeen or eighteen, when he saved his father from an attack by hostile cavalry during a skirmish with the invading forces of Hannibal in Italy in 218.

His military career further advanced when Scipio prevented a mutiny among the few survivors of the disastrous Battle of Cannae in 216. As a military tribune, the equivalent of a modern staff colonel, he personally intervened with the deserters, placed their ringleaders under arrest, and put the defeated army under the command of the surviving consul.

In 211, another serious defeat for Rome brought Scipio an unprecedented opportunity. In Spain, two armies under the command of his father and an uncle had been defeated, and the commanders were killed. Although he was still rather young—twenty-seven according to the ancient historian Polybius—and had not served in public office with the exception of the entry-level position of *curulic aedile* (a chief of domestic police), Scipio ran unopposed in the ensuing election and became proconsul and supreme commander of the reinforcements and the Roman army in Spain.

His election attests the extraordinary popularity which he enjoyed with the people of Rome and later with his men. So great was his reputation, which also rested partly on his unbounded self-confidence and (according to Polybius) a streak of rational calculation, that people talked about his enjoying a special contact with the gods. A religious man who belonged to a college of priests of Mars, Scipio may himself have reinforced these adulatory rumors. Whether his charisma and popularity were further aided by particularly "noble" looks, however, is not known. Indeed, all the extant representations of him, no matter how idealized, do not fail to show his large nose and ears, personal features

760

which do not detract from the overall image of dignity but serve to humanize the great general.

His marriage to Aemilia, the daughter of the head of a friendly patrician family, gave Scipio at least two sons and one daughter, who would later be mother to the social reformers Gaius and Tiberius Gracchus.

Life's Work

Arriving in Spain, Scipio followed the strategic plan of continuing the offensive warfare of his father and uncle and thus trying to tear Spain, their European base, away from the Carthaginians. After he had reorganized his army, Scipio struck an unexpected blow by capturing New Carthage, the enemy's foremost port, in 209. A year later he launched an attack on one-third of the Carthaginian forces at Baecula, in south central Spain. While his light troops engaged the enemy, Scipio led the main body of Roman infantry to attack both flanks of the Carthaginians and thus win the battle. Hasdrubal Barca, the Carthaginian leader, however, managed to disengage his troops and escape to Gaul, where Scipio could not follow him, and ultimately arrived in Italy.

The decisive move followed in 206, when Scipio attacked the united armies of Hasdrubal, the son of Gisco, and Mago at Ilipa (near modern Seville). Meanwhile, his generous treatment of the Spanish tribes had given him native support. Scipio placed these still-unreliable allies in the center of his army, to hold the enemy, while Roman infantry and cavalry advanced on both sides, wheeled around, and attacked the Carthaginian war elephants and soldiers in a double enveloping maneuver which wrought total havoc.

Scipio's immediate pursuit of the fleeing enemy succeeded so completely in destroying their forces that Carthage's hold on Spain came to a de facto end. After a punitive mission against three insurgent Spanish cities, and the relatively bloodless putting down of a mutiny by some Roman troops, Scipio received the surrender of Gades (Cádiz), the last Carthaginian stronghold in Spain.

When Scipio returned to Rome, the senate did not grant him a triumph. He was elected consul for the year 205, but only his threat to proceed alone, with popular support, forced the senate to allow him to take the war to Carthage in North Africa rather than fight an embattled and ill-supported

Hannibal in Italy. In his province of Sicily, Scipio began with the training of a core army of volunteers; uncharacteristically for Roman thought, but brilliantly innovative in terms of strategy, he emphasized the formation of a strong cavalry.

In 204, Scipio landed in North Africa near the modern coast of Tunisia with roughly thirty-five thousand men and more than six hundred cavalry. He immediately joined forces with the small but well-trained cavalry detachment of the exiled King Masinissa and drew first blood in a successful encounter with Carthaginian cavalry under General Hanno.

Failing to capture the key port of Utica, Scipio built winter quarters on a peninsula east of the stubborn city. One night early the next spring, he led his army against the Carthaginian relief forces under Hasdrubal and King Syphax, who had broken an earlier treaty with Scipio. The raid was successful, and the camps of the enemy were burned; now Scipio followed the reorganized adversaries and defeated them decisively at the Great Plains. The fall of Tunis came soon after.

Beaten, Carthage sought an armistice of forty-five days, which was granted by Scipio and broken when Hannibal arrived in North Africa. Hostilities resumed and culminated in the Battle of Zama. Here, the attack of the Carthaginian war elephants failed, because Scipio had anticipated them and opened his ranks to let the animals uselessly thunder through. Now the two armies engaged in fierce battle, and, after the defeat of the Carthaginian auxiliary troops and mercenaries, Scipio attempted an out-flanking maneuver which failed against the masterful Hannibal. In a pitched battle, the decisive moment came when the Roman cavalry and that of Masinissa broke off their pursuit of the beaten Carthaginian horsemen and fell upon the rear of Hannibal's army. The enemy was crushed.

After the victory of Zama, Scipio granted Carthage a relatively mild peace and persuaded the Roman senate to ratify the treaty. When he returned to Rome, he was granted a triumph in which to show his rich booty, the prisoners of war (including Syphax), and his victorious troops, whom he treated generously. It was around this time that Scipio obtained his honorific name "Africanus."

There followed a period of rest for Scipio. In 199 he took the position of censor, an office traditionally reserved for elder statesmen, and in 194 he held his second consulship. An embassy to Masinissa brought Scipio back to Africa in 193, and in 190 he went to Greece as a legate, or general staff officer, to his brother Lucius. In Greece, the Romans had repulsed the Syrian king Antiochus the Great and prepared the invasion of Asia Minor. Because of an illness, Scipio did not see the Roman victory there.

At home, their political opponents, grouped around archconservative Cato the Censor, attacked Scipio and his brother in a series of unfounded lawsuits, known as "the processes of the Scipios," concerning alleged fiscal mismanagement and corruption in the Eastern war. Embittered, Scipio defended his brother in 187 and himself in 184, after which he left Rome, returning only when the opposition threatened to throw Lucius in jail. Going back to his small farm in Liternum in the Campania, Scipio lived a modest life as a virtual exile until his death in the same year or in 183. His great bitterness is demonstrated by his wish to be buried there instead of in the family tomb near the capital.

Summary

The military victories of Scipio Africanus brought Rome a firm grip on Spain, victory over Carthage, and dominion over the Western Mediterranean. Scipio's success rested on his great qualities as a farsighted strategist and innovative tactician who was bold enough to end the archaic Roman reliance on the brute force of its infantry; he learned the lesson of Hannibal's victory at Cannae. His newly formed cavalry and a highly mobile and more maneuverable infantry secured the success of his sweeps to envelop the enemy.

On the level of statesmanship, Scipio's gift for moderation and his ability to stabilize and pacify Spain secured power for Rome without constant blood-letting. His peace with Carthage would have enabled this city to live peacefully under the shadow of Rome and could have prevented the Third Punic War, had the senate later acted differently.

Finally, Scipio never abused his popularity to make himself autocratic ruler of Rome, although temptations to do so abounded. At the height of his influence in Spain, several tribes offered him the title of king; he firmly refused. After his triumph, the exuberant masses bestowed many titles on the victor of Zama, but he did not grasp for ultimate power. Unlike Julius Caesar, Scipio Africanus served the Roman state; he did not master it. He is perhaps the only military leader of great stature who achieved fame as a true public servant.

Bibliography

Dorey, T. A., and D. R. Dudley. *Rome Against Carthage*. London: Secker and Warburg, 1971; New York: Doubleday, 1972. Chapters 3 to 7 deal with the Second Punic War and place Scipio's conquests in context. Useful discussion of his campaigns, Roman policy toward Carthage, and the origins of the conflict. Contains many illustrations and maps and an adequate bibliography.

Eckstein, Arthur M. *Senate and General*. Berkeley: University of California Press, 1987. Generally scrutinizes who had the power to make political decisions. Chapter 8 illuminates various aspects of Scipio's struggle with the senate. Includes a good, up-to-date bibliography.

Haywood, Richard M. *Studies on Scipio Africanus*. Baltimore: Johns Hopkins University Press, 1933. Reprint. Westport, Conn.: Greenwood Press, 1973. Revises the account by Polybius, who rejected old superstitions about Scipio but made him more calculating and scheming than Haywood believes is justified. The bibliography is still useful.

Liddell-Hart, B. H. *A Greater Than Napoleon: Scipio Africanus*. London: Blackwood, 1926; Boston: Little, Brown, 1927. Popular account of Scipio's life, with emphasis on his military achievements. Scipio is judged sympathetically and praised for tactical innovations and rejection of "honest bludgeon work." Contains many helpful maps.

Scullard, Howard H. *Roman Politics 220-150 B.C.* 2d ed. Oxford: Clarendon Press, 1973; Westport, Conn.: Greenwood Press, 1981. Chapters 4 and 5 deal with Scipio's influence on Roman politics and place his career in the context of political and dynastic struggle for control in the Roman Republic. Shows where Scipio came from politically and traces his legacy. Contains appendix with diagrams of the leading Roman families.

———. *Scipio Africanus: Soldier and Politician*. Ithaca, N.Y.: Cornell University Press, and London: Thames and Hudson, 1970. General study and excellent, comprehensive biography. Carefully balanced and well-researched work. Written with a feeling for its subject, which makes it interesting to read. Contains useful maps.

—————. *Scipio Africanus in the Second Punic War.* Cambridge: Cambridge University Press, 1930.

An in-depth study of Scipio's campaigns and military achievements, highly technical but readable and with good maps. Brings alive Scipio while dealing exhaustively with its subject.

Reinhart Lutz

SCOPAS

Born: Possibly as early as 420 B.C.; Paros, Greece
Died: c. late fourth century B.C.; place unknown
Area of Achievement: Art
Contribution: A leader of the evolution in late classical sculpture away from the powerful but emotionally detached balance of fifth century art, Scopas created works of relaxed gracefulness on the one hand and strong emotion, stress, and turbulence on the other. With Praxiteles of Athens and Lysippus of Sicyon, his work dominated the art of the fourth century B.C.

Early Life
No biographical information survives. Scopas may have been the son of the Parian sculptor Aristander, who was working in 405 B.C.

Life's Work
Scopas of Paros worked as an architect and sculptor. His most celebrated works are sculptures designed to fit into a specific architectural setting. Ancient sources report that he worked on three important monuments of the early and mid-fourth century B.C.: the temple of Athena Alea at Tegea, the temple of Artemis at Ephesus, and the Mausoleum of Halicarnassus. It is indicative of his prominence that the last two of these three projects became famous as two of the Seven Wonders of the World.

Modern students of Scopas consider the temple of Athena Alea at Tegea the most important of his achievements because its fragments are the basis of whatever judgments can be made about his style. Pausanias (fl. A.D. 143-176) says that he was the architect of the building as a whole; judging from the consistent style of the surviving pieces, it is likely that the temple sculptures were executed by a team of artisans working under Scopas' supervision. The original temple, in southern Arcadia, had been destroyed by a fire in 394 B.C. The rebuilding took place about a generation later, on a scale of size and magnificence designed to overshadow all other temples in the Peloponnese. The central image of the temple, an ivory carving of Athena Alea, had been saved from the earlier temple. Everything else was for Scopas to create, and it is likely that he conceived of the temple itself as a vehicle for the display of the ornamental sculptures he designed. Pausanias, who saw the building intact, reports that

the sculptures of the front pediment represented the Calydonian boar hunt referred to in the ninth book of Homer's *Iliad*; the figure of Meleager on this pediment, though lost, is believed to survive in copies, of which the best two are in the Vatican and Berlin. The rear pediment showed the duel between Telephus (the local Arcadian hero) and Achilles which took place just before the Trojan War. Of these sculptures, only fragments of the heads and various body parts survive. Scopas also created the freestanding statues of the healer Asklepios and the health goddess Hygieia, which flanked the ivory figure of Athena that stood in the interior. A marble head of a woman which may be that of Hygieia was found by French excavators of the site in the early 1920's.

Scopas' role in the creation of the Artemisium at Ephesus is more problematical. There is only the authority of Pliny the Elder that he executed one of the thirty-six ornamented columns which were commissioned for this colossal structure, one of the Seven Wonders of the World. The sixth century B.C. temple of Artemis had burned in 356, reportedly on the night of Alexander the Great's birth, and construction began immediately on what would be (like Athena's temple at Tegea) considerably grander than its predecessor. The remains of this larger second temple are now in the British Museum. Of the three surviving ornamented column bases, one is dubiously attributed to Scopas. It shows Hermes leading the soul of Alcestis, who had offered to die in place of her husband, Admetus, toward a winged figure representing Thanatos, or death.

Scopas' third major work in architectural ornamentation was the Mausoleum of Halicarnassus, ordered by Queen Artemisia as a monumental tomb for her husband Mausolus, Satrap of Caria, who died in 353. This building, constructed entirely of white marble, stood until the fifteenth century, when it was brought down by an earthquake. It was excavated by the British in 1857, and many of its best pieces were taken to the British Museum. Though not its chief architect, Scopas was one of four famous artists brought in to decorate the four sides of the building with relief sculpture. His colleagues in this project, according to Pliny the Elder and Vitruvius, were Bryaxis, Timotheus, and Leochares. The best preserved of the three friezes found near the site by the British team represents an Amazonomachy, any of a number of legendary battles between Greeks and Amazons. Seventeen slabs, more or less defaced, represent this scene. Numerous attempts to attribute sections of the frieze to Scopas himself have been made, but they are problematical as a result of the lack of a single distinctive style which can serve as a signature of the master's work. Four slabs found near the northeast corner are commonly attributed to Scopas, but the touchstone of Scopadic style remains the fragments from Tegea.

Other works by Scopas are known through descriptions in ancient sources, which have led to the attribution of copies that seem to fit the ancient descriptions. A poem by Callistratus describes a Bacchante in ecstasy, carrying a kid she has killed. This image has been identified with a Maenad in the Dresden Sculpture Museum whose head is thrown up and back over her left shoulder. Her light dress, fastened over her right shoulder and held in place by a cord knotted above her waist, is blown by the wind, laying bare her left side, and her back is arched sharply backward as she strides, right leg forward. The Dresden Maenad, commonly attributed to Scopas, is representative of the late Classical and Hellenistic fondness for figures in action, gripped by powerful emotion. One of his most popular sculptures was a statue of Pothos (Longing), a young male nude leaning on a pillar or thyrsus with a cloak over his left arm and a goose at his feet. He stands with his weight on one foot, his left leg relaxed and crossing in front of his right. He looks upward in an abstracted way, as if thinking of an absent lover. Although the original of this masterpiece no longer survives, there are many Roman copies (and gemstone engravings) which testify to its popularity. This work represents the late classical departure from the powerfully built, erect, and concentrated figures of the earlier severe style. The body lines are gentle, the geometry of the figure is sloping rather than erect, the effect one of grace rather than power. Pausanias mentions a bronze Aphrodite Pandemos in a precinct of Aphrodite at Elis; the image has survived on Roman coins. Other works believed to show Scopas' influence are Roman reproductions of his statue of Meleager and the Lansdowne Herakles at the Getty Museum in Malibu, California, thought to be modeled on an original made for the gymnasium at Sikyon. Nearly all these derivative pieces are statues of gods and goddesses: Asklepios and Hygieia, Aphrodite, Apollo, Dionysus, Hestia, and Hermes.

Summary

Scopas must remain an enigmatic figure because no existing work of sculpture can safely be attributed to him; indeed, not much is known about the man or his work. Nevertheless, the testimony of ancient writers such as Pausanias, Pliny the Elder, and Vitruvius affirms that he was famed in the ancient world as both sculptor and architect, that his work was in great demand, and that he was widely imitated. The consensus of ancient opinion represents him as the preeminent sculptor of passion.

Modern students of ancient art are also unanimous in attributing to Scopas an individuality of manner which they perceive in works closely associated with his name. While the best authorities are reluctant to make dogmatic attributions of specific works, they agree in attributing to his style an impetuous force in the rendering of figures, delicate workmanship, and the rhythmical composition of a master sculptor.

Scopas' technical virtuosity is perhaps less important than the human content of his work, which reveals an emotional fervor and a sensitivity to the sadness of life. This interpretation was one of his great contributions to Hellenistic culture. Vergil's *sunt lacrimae rerum* (tears attend trials) is visually anticipated in the Scopadic style. Another aspect of his contribution is the representation of the human form under stress, where the body's tension symbolizes a turbulent emotional state. Hellenistic mannerism grows naturally out of this style. Scopas' unique achievement in recording the deeper recesses of human experience has been appropriately compared to that of Michelangelo in the Renaissance.

Bibliography

Ashmole, Bernard. "Skopas." In *Encyclopedia of World Art*. New York: McGraw-Hill, 1959-1987. An excellent summary in English supplemented by an extensive bibliography of books and articles in English, French, German, and Italian.

Barron, John. *An Introduction to Greek Sculpture*. London: Athlone, 1981; New York: Schocken Books, 1984. This volume is brief but well illustrated.

Bieber, Margarete. *The Sculpture of the Hellenistic Age*. Rev. ed. New York: Columbia University Press, 1961. A detailed account of the major works still surviving, those described by ancient sources, and existing sculptures in Scopas' style.

Finely illustrated and includes a bibliography and references to museum catalogs.

Lawrence, A. W. *Greek and Roman Sculpture*. New York: Harper and Row, and London: Cape, 1972. This work concentrates on the Tegea figures, with notices of several pieces attributed to Scopas. Limited bibliography.

Richter, G. M. A. *The Sculpture and Sculptors of the Greeks*. 2d ed. New Haven, Conn.: Yale University Press, 1950. Attentive to the ancient sources, which are quoted freely, and most sensitive to the problems of identification. Well documented with references to ancient and modern sources.

Stewart, Andrew F. *Skopas of Paros*. Park Ridge, N.J.: Noyes Press, 1977. The only full-length study in English, this work was developed from a 1972 University of Cambridge doctoral thesis. Detailed attention to features of style, based chiefly on the Tegea fragments. Richly illustrated, with a full set of ancient testimonia and detailed references to modern scholarship. Likely to remain the standard authority for some time.

Daniel H. Garrison

SELEUCUS I NICATOR

Born: 358 or 354 B.C.; Europus or Pella, Macedonia

Died: Summer, 281 B.C.; near Lysimachia, Thrace

Areas of Achievement: Government, warfare, and conquest

Contribution: By his courage and practical common sense, Seleucus created the Seleucid Empire, maintaining the loyalty of a heterogeneous population by fair government.

Early Life

Seleucus was born in 358 or 354 B.C. in either Europus or Pella, Macedonia. Although ancient sources do not agree on where or when he was born, no one disputes that he was the son of a man named Antiochus and his wife, Laodice. Nothing is known of Seleucus' early life, but both Diodorus Siculus and Appian indicate that he was with the army of Alexander the Great which marched against the Persians in 334. He must have distinguished himself in the following years, for by 326 he had assumed command of the royal hypaspists (elite infantry) in the Indian campaign and had gained a position on the king's staff. When Alexander crossed the Hydaspes River, he took with him in the same boat Ptolemy (later Ptolemy I Soter), Perdiccas, Lysimachus, and Seleucus.

One of Alexander's final acts was to preside over the festival at Susa during which his generals married Persian brides. His two fiercest opponents had been Oxyartes and Spitamenes. Alexander had already married Oxyartes' daughter Roxane; he gave Apama, daughter of Spitamenes, to Seleucus. It was a lifetime marriage which provided Seleucus with his son and successor, Antiochus. According to Appian, he named three cities after Apama.

When Alexander died in 323, Perdiccas took over as regent for Alexander's retarded half brother and his unborn child. The empire was divided among the generals, who were to serve as satraps (governors). Seleucus was named chiliarch (commander of the Companion cavalry), a position of extreme military importance but with no grant of land. For this reason, he played a relatively unimportant role for the next ten years, although he led the cavalry rebellion which resulted in the death of Perdiccas in 321. When a new appointment of satraps was made shortly after this, Seleucus gave up his position as chiliarch to become governor of Babylonia.

Babylonia, in the center of what had been Alexander's empire, was the perfect position from which to dominate the entire empire, but its security was threatened by the arrogant satraps of Media (Pithon) and Persia (Peucestas). Pithon seized Parthia to the east, was driven out by Peucestas, and subsequently sought an alliance with Seleucus. Meanwhile, Eumenes, the outlawed former satrap of Cappadocia, appeared in Babylonia with an elite Macedonian force far superior to Seleucus' army. Seleucus was forced to call on Antigonus I, the most powerful of the satraps, for help. Although Antigonus, Seleucus, and Pithon started the campaign together in 317, once they had taken Susiana, Seleucus was left behind to besiege the citadel of Susa while the other two pursued Eumenes. In rapid succession, Antigonus defeated and killed Eumenes, ordered the execution of Pithon, and masterminded the "disappearance" of Peucestas. When he returned to Babylonia, Seleucus tried to appease Antigonus with the treasure from Susa, but it was only a short time later, in 316, that he wisely fled Babylon and sought refuge with Ptolemy in Egypt.

Life's Work

Seleucus would seem to have lost everything at this point, but this was actually the beginning of his climb to even greater power. Antigonus was now the dominant figure among Alexander's successors, but he wanted the whole empire. The three other powerful leaders—Ptolemy in Egypt, Lysimachus in Thrace, and Cassander in Macedonia—formed a coalition against him. In the first phase of the resulting war, Seleucus served as commander in Ptolemy's navy, seeing action in both the Aegean Sea and the eastern Mediterranean around Cyprus. In the beginning of the second phase, he took part in the attack on Gaza by the Ptolemaic army. Antigonus had sent his son Demetrius to hold this strategically important fortress, and his defeat was a severe blow to Antigonus' plans. According to Diodorus (c. 40 B.C.), Ptolemy showed his gratitude to Seleucus by giving him a small army, which he then led to Babylonia.

The troops at first were fearful of their mission, but Seleucus convinced them that an oracle of Didymean Apollo had proclaimed him king. The Seleucids would eventually claim Apollo as an ancestor. Better than the oracle, however, was the fact that during his previous governorship Seleucus had ruled wisely and well. Reinforcements flocked to him as he marched into the territory, and he took the city of Babylon with little trouble. This feat launched the Seleucid Empire.

Seleucus regained Babylonia, but not without antagonizing Nicanor, the satrap of Media, who proceeded to march on Babylon. Seleucus, however, swiftly leading an army out to meet him, surprised and routed Nicanor, whose troops deserted to the victor.

The East was now open to Seleucus. He rapidly took Susiana and Persia before turning to Media, where, according to Appian, Nicanor was killed in battle. Between 311 and 302, Seleucus gained control of all Iran and the lands extending to the Indus River. At the Indus, he reestablished contact with the Indian chieftains of the region and returned home finally with 480 elephants.

Meanwhile, in the West, Alexander's family had been exterminated. In 306, Antigonus proclaimed himself king, and the other four satraps, Ptolemy, Lysimachus, Cassander, and Seleucus, followed suit. Antigonus still had designs on all of Alexander's empire, and by 302, the other kings considered his power so threatening to their own security that they formed a coalition against him.

The armies met at Ipsus in 301, where Seleucus' elephants played a major role in the defeat of Antigonus, who died in battle. In the redivision of land which followed, Seleucus gained Syria and Lysimachus was awarded Asia Minor. A new war could have started between Seleucus and Ptolemy, since the king of Egypt had previously occupied Coele-Syria (Palestine) and now refused to give it up, but Seleucus, remembering that Ptolemy had stood by him in a difficult time, decided to ignore the issue, although he did not give up his claim to the land.

Seleucus now held more land than any of the other kings, and that made them uneasy. In order to balance the power, Ptolemy and Lysimachus joined in marriage alliances; this, in turn, disturbed Seleucus. Although his marriage to Apama was still firm, Seleucus sent word to Demetrius to ask for his daughter Stratonice in marriage (Macedonian kings practiced polygamy). Demetrius agreed, and the marriage took place, but although Stratonice bore him a daughter, Seleucus eventually gave her in marriage to his eldest son, Antiochus, and sent them to Babylon to reign as king and queen in the East. Seleucus ruled in the West from his new capital city of Antioch, named for his father.

Seleucus spent most of the twenty years following the Battle of Ipsus consolidating his empire. One of his major policies was the division of the empire into East and West, with the heir to the throne ruling from Babylon; this would become a standard policy of the Seleucids. His major problem throughout most of this period was Demetrius, who had become king of Macedonia but would not be satisfied until he had regained his father's lost kingdom. Demetrius invaded Asia Minor in 287, but two years later, Seleucus held him captive. At first, Demetrius believed that he would soon be set free, but as that hope faded, so did his self-control. By 283, he had drunk himself to death.

There might have been a peaceful old age for Seleucus if it had not been for Ptolemy's disinherited eldest son, Ptolemy Keraunos. After causing the death of Lysimachus' son in Thrace, Keraunos fled to Seleucus, thus precipitating war between the two former allies. The two met at Corypedium in Asia Minor in the spring of 281. Lysimachus was killed in the battle. Seleucus, who was now in his seventies, suddenly saw himself as Alexander reuniting his empire. He pressed on to Thrace, only to meet death treacherously at the hand of Ptolemy Keraunos outside the capital city of Lysimachia in the following summer. His common sense had deserted him in the end, but he left behind an heir who was experienced in ruling and a well-established empire based on sound government.

Summary

Seleucus I Nicator ruled an empire made up of many diverse ethnic groups. He had inherited the Persian system of administration and was wise enough to realize its value. He continued the Persian policy of respecting the cultures and religions of the people he ruled at the same time that he proceeded to establish a governmental system entirely made up of Greeks. Unlike most of Alexander's generals, Seleucus retained and respected his Persian wife, but there were few, if any, non-Greeks in his administration. His son and successor, who was half-Persian, married a Macedonian woman. Seleucus spread Hellenism throughout the major parts of his empire by the typical Greek method of founding colonies. Antioch, his capital in the West, became one of the great cities of the ancient world.

The first of the Seleucids was a man of honor. He gained his position in Alexander's army through hard work and his empire in the same way. He was able to reclaim Babylonia because he had ruled well throughout his first governorship, and he refused to fight Ptolemy over Coele-Syria out of gratitude for past favors. Later, when he held Demetrius prisoner, Seleucus declined to turn him over to Lysimachus, who had offered a large sum of money in exchange. Demetrius was treated honorably during his imprisonment, but Seleucus realized that he was too troublesome ever to be released. Seleucus was loyal to his friends and treated his enemies fairly. Unfortunately, Ptolemy Keraunos had none of these attributes, and Seleucus died as the result of a cowardly attack by a man who had first called on him for help and then killed him to gain a kingdom he was not wise enough to keep.

Bibliography

Bar-Kochva, B. *The Seleucid Army: Organization and Tactics in the Great Campaigns.* Cambridge and New York: Cambridge University Press, 1976. This study addresses only military affairs, but Bar-Kochva points out Seleucus' courage and tactical ability. Part 1 concentrates on manpower and organization.

Bevan, Edwyn Robert. *The House of Seleucus.* Vol. 1. London: Edward Arnold, 1902; New York: Barnes and Noble, 1966. Analytical account of Seleucus' rise to power based on the ancient sources. Still the only comprehensive account of the Seleucids in English.

Cohen, Getzel M. *The Seleucid Colonies: Studies in Founding, Administration, and Organization.* Weisbaden, West Germany: Steiner, 1978. Contains information on the founding, administration, and organization of new colonies. Attempts to answer questions on the nature of the poorly documented Seleucid colonization program. The answers are tentative but thought-provoking.

Cook, S. A., F. E. Adcock, and M. P. Charlesworth, eds. *The Cambridge Ancient History.* Vol. 7, *The Hellenistic Monarchies and the Rise of Rome.* New York: Macmillan, and London: Cambridge University Press, 1928. Chapter 5 contains a systematic account of the organization of both the central and satrapy governments in the Seleucid Empire.

Grainger, John D. *Seleukos Nikator: Constructing a Hellenistic Kingdom.* London and New York: Routledge, 1990. A pragmatic presentation of Seleucus as a cautious planner who "only hazarded himself or his power on certainties." Indicates that his contemporaries were as puzzled by him as many modern scholars are. Provides a realistic view of the ancient sources tainted by contemporary propaganda.

Seyrig, H. "Seleucus I and the Foundation of Hellenistic Syria." In *The Role of the Phoenicians in the Interaction of Mediterranean Civilizations.* Beirut, Lebanon: American University Press, 1968. Part of a series of articles edited by W. A. Ward. (Phoenicia was a part of the satrapy of Syria claimed by Seleucus in 301 B.C.)

Linda J. Piper

SENECA THE YOUNGER

Born: c. 4 B.C.; Córdoba
Died: April, A.D. 65; Rome
Areas of Achievement: Government, philosophy, and literature
Contribution: An influential intellectual, Seneca also showed great abilities as coadministrator of the Roman Empire during the first years of Nero. In literature, Seneca's essays and tragedies were influential from the Middle Ages to the Renaissance, when English playwrights took his dramas as models.

Early Life

Although Seneca the Younger was born in Córdoba, his father, known as Seneca the Elder, was a conservative Roman knight who had achieved fame as an orator and teacher of rhetoric in Rome. His mother, Helvia, was an extraordinarily intelligent, gifted, and morally upright person whose love for philosophy had been checked only by her husband's rejection of the idea of education for women.

The familial conflict was handed down to the next generation: The oldest of the three brothers, Gallio, pursued a splendid political career, but the youngest, Mela, spent his life making money and educating himself (the poet Lucan was his son). Lucius Annaeus Seneca, the second child and bearer of his father's name, was torn between public life in the service of a corrupted state and life as philosopher and private man.

Coming to Rome at a very early age, Seneca received an education in rhetoric, which was the first step toward becoming an orator with an eye to public offices. Yet the youth also saw teachers of Stoic philosophy who taught a life of asceticism, equanimity in the face of adversity, and an evaluation of the daily work of the self, which laid the foundations of Seneca's eclectic philosophical beliefs.

In Rome, Seneca lived with an aunt; she guarded the precarious health of the thin, feeble boy. His physical deficiencies and what were perhaps lifelong bouts with pneumonia almost led the young man to suicide; only the thought of how much this act would hurt his aging father stopped him. Since intense studies distracted his mind from his sufferings, Seneca would later state that he owed his life to philosophy. In the light of his physical afflictions and his own description of himself as small, plain, and skinny, scholars doubt the veracity of the only

extant antique copy of a bust of Seneca, which shows the philosopher and statesman as a corpulent old man with sharp but full features and receding hair.

Seneca's ill health apparently caused him to spend a considerable portion of his youth and early manhood in the healthier climate of Egypt. It was not before A.D. 31 that he permanently left the East for Rome.

Life's Work

As a result of the lobbying of his aunt, Seneca successfully entered public service as quaestor (roughly, secretary of finances), in A.D. 33. Although it is no longer known which positions Seneca held during this period, it is most likely that he continued in ever more prestigious offices.

Besides serving the state under the two difficult emperors Tiberius and Caligula, Seneca began to achieve wealth and fame as a lawyer. From the later works which have survived, one can see how his witty, poignant, almost epigrammatical language fascinated Seneca's listeners and how his pithy sentences, which reflected his enormous active vocabulary, must have won for him cases in court. Further, Seneca's consciously anti-Ciceronian style, which avoided long sentences and ornamental language, established his fame as an orator. Early works (now lost) made him a celebrated writer as well. Seneca's first marriage, dating from around this time, cannot have been a very happy one; he fails to mention the name of his wife, despite the fact that they had at least two sons together, both of whom he writes about in the most affectionate terms.

Under the reign of Caligula (A.D. 37-41), Seneca's ill health proved advantageous. His oratorical success had aroused the envy of the emperor, who derogatorily likened Seneca's style to "sand without lime" (meaning that it was worthless for building), and Caligula sought to execute Seneca. Seneca was spared only because one of the imperial mistresses commented on the futility of shortening the life of a terminally ill man; later, Seneca commented tongue in cheek, "Disease has postponed many a man's death and proximity to death has resulted in salvation."

In 41, the first year of the reign of Claudius I, a struggle for power between Empress Messalina and Caligula's sisters Agrippina and Julia Livilla

brought Seneca into court on a trumped-up charge of adultery with Princess Julia. Found guilty, Seneca escaped death only because Claudius transformed the sentence into one of banishment to the barren island of Corsica. There, for the next eight years, Seneca dedicated his life to philosophy, the writing of letters, and natural philosophy; he also began to draft his first tragedies. The most powerful nonfiction works of this era are his letter of advice to his mother *Ad Helviam matrem de consolatione* (c. A.D. 41-42; *To My Mother Helvia, on Consolation*) and the philosophical treatise *De ira libri tres* (c. A.D. 41-49; *Three Essays on Anger*). Both works are deeply influenced by Stoic philosophy and argue that to deal with misfortune is to bear the adversities of life with dignified tranquillity, courage, and spiritual strength; further, violent passions must be controlled by the man who is truly wise.

The execution of Messalina for treason in 48 and the ensuing marriage of Claudius to Agrippina brought the latter into a position of power from which she could recall Seneca. Intent on using the famous orator and writer, Agrippina made Seneca the tutor of her son by a previous marriage, a young boy whom Claudius adopted under the name of Nero. Rather than being allowed to retire to Athens as a private man, Seneca was also made a member in the Roman senate and became praetor, the second highest of the Roman offices, in 50. Further, his new marriage to the wealthy and intelligent Pompeia Paulina drew Seneca into a circle of powerful friends—including the new prefect of the Praetorian Guard, Sextus Afranius Burrus.

The death of Claudius in 54 brought highest power to Seneca and Burrus. Their successful working relationship began when Burrus' guard proclaimed Nero emperor, and Seneca wrote the speech of accession for the seventeen-year-old youth. For five years, from 54 to 59, during the *Quinquennium Neronis*, the statesmen shared supreme authority and successfully governed the Roman Empire in harmony, while Nero amused himself with games and women and let them check his excesses and cruelty. Internally, the unacknowledged regency of Seneca and Burrus brought a rare period of civil justice, harmony, and political security. Seneca's Stoicism led him to fight the cruelty of gladiatorial combat and to favor laws intended to limit the absolute power of the master over his slaves. At the frontiers of the Empire, the generals of Burrus and Seneca fought victoriously against the Parthians in the East and crushed a rebellion in Britain, after which a more reformatist regime brought lasting peace to this remote island.

Seneca's fall was a direct result of Nero's awakening thirst for power. Increasingly, Seneca and Burrus lost their influence over him and in turn became involved in his morally despicable actions. In 59, Nero ordered the murder of his mother, Agrippina, and Seneca drafted the son's address to the senate, a speech which cleverly covered up the facts of the assassination.

Burrus' death and replacement by an intimate of Nero in 62 led to Seneca's request for retirement, which Nero refused; he kept Seneca in Rome, although removed from the court. Seneca's best philosophical work was written during this time; in his remaining three years, he finished *De providentia* (c. A.D. 63-64; *On Providence*) and wrote *Quaestiones naturales* (c. A.D. 62-64; *Natural Questions*) and his influential *Epistulae morales ad Lucilium* (c. A.D. 62-65; *Letters to Lucilius*), in which he treats a variety of moral questions and establishes the form of the essay.

Early in 65, a probably false accusation implicated Seneca in a conspiracy to assassinate Nero, who ordered him to commit suicide. With Stoic tranquility and in the tradition of Socrates and Cato the Younger, Seneca opened his arteries and slowly bled to death. Fully composed, and with honor, the Roman noble ended a life in the course of which he had wielded immense political power and enjoyed great status as statesman and writer.

Summary

Consideration of the life and work of Seneca the Younger remains controversial. On a professional level, critics have attacked his philosophical work as eclectic and unoriginal, but it is through Seneca that more ancient ideas were handed down before the originals became known. For example, Seneca's tragedies are easily dismissed as static, bombastic, lurid, and peopled by characters who rant and rave; still, English Renaissance works such as John Webster's *The Duchess of Malfi* (1613-1614) could not have been created without their authors' knowledge of Seneca.

The reputation of Seneca the man has suffered from his political alliance with Nero, one of the most monstrous creatures of popular history. The ancient historian Cornelius Tacitus is among the first to censure Seneca for his complicity in the cover-up of Agrippina's murder: "It was not only

Nero, whose inhuman cruelty was beyond understanding, but also Seneca who fell into discredit."

A final evaluation of Seneca cannot overlook the fact that his public service ended in moral chaos after a period of doing much good for the commonwealth. It is interesting to note, however, that Seneca's most mature writing came after his de facto resignation from political power and responsibility; it is for his brilliantly written letters to Gaius Lucilius that Seneca achieves the status of philosopher, and these words have been with Western civilization ever since.

Bibliography

Griffin, Miriam Tamara. *Seneca: A Philosopher in Politics*. Oxford: Clarendon Press, 1976. Definitive study of Seneca; a modern, informed reevaluation of the man who had so many lofty ideas and whose life is so full of nasty facts. Dramatizes the problem of public service for a corrupted state. Clearly written. Contains a good bibliography.

Gummere, Richard Mott. *Seneca, the Philosopher and His Modern Message*. Boston: Marshall Jones Co., and London: Harrap, 1922. Emphasis on Seneca's philosophical works and their relevance in modern times. Scholarly but not overly dry, this volume makes Stoic philosophy accessible.

Henry, Denis, and Elisabeth Henry. *The Mask of Power: Seneca's Tragedies and Imperial Power*. Chicago: Bolchazy-Carducci, and Warminster: Aris and Phillips, 1985. An interpretative study of Seneca's tragedies, placing them in their cultural context. Occasionally, dramatic conflicts which arise out of a time of corruption are related to the twentieth century. Includes a good, up-to-date bibliography.

Holland, Francis. *Seneca*. London: Longmans, 1920; Freeport, N.Y.: Books for Libraries Press, 1969. For a long time, this work was the only biography on Seneca available in English. Still useful and readable, Holland's study is thorough and aware of the problematic status of its subject.

Motto, Anna Lydia. *Seneca*. New York: Twayne Publishers, 1973. Introductory but complete presentation of Seneca's life and work. Written for a general audience, with a strong focus on Seneca's philosophical and dramatic work.

Rosenmeyer, Thomas G. *Senecan Drama and Stoic Cosmology*. Berkeley: University of California Press, 1989. Points out the interpenetration of stoic thought and Senecan drama, as well as the distance between Senecan tragedy and its Greek antecedents. Indicates that Seneca's original philosophies may have distanced him even from his contemporaries.

Sevenster, J. N. *Paul and Seneca*. Leiden: Brill, 1961. A theological comparison of the thoughts of the two men. Sevenster rejects the medieval myth that Seneca met or corresponded with Saint Paul and was a "closet Christian" and sees the two philosophers as contemporaries trying to answer the problems of their time.

Sorensen, Villy. *Seneca: The Humanist at the Court of Nero*. Translated by W. G. Jones. Chicago: University of Chicago Press, 1984. A well-written, scholarly work which, nevertheless, is understandable to a general audience. Brings alive the man, his time, and his political and philosophical achievements. Includes interesting illustrations.

Sutton, Dana Ferrin. *Seneca on the Stage*. Leiden, Netherlands: Brill, 1986. This volume argues against tradition that Seneca's tragedies were not merely written to be read, but crafted to be performed. Supports its claim with its discovery of stage directions which are "clues" hidden in the text of the dramas.

Reinhart Lutz

SESOSTRIS III

Born: Date unknown; place unknown

Died: 1843 B.C.; place unknown

Area of Achievement: Government

Contribution: Sesostris' egocentric nature inspired him to be the first king of ancient Egypt to pursue a truly imperialistic policy, conducting war in the Levant and extending Egypt's southern border. His lasting impact was on Egypt's social structure, where he eliminated the vestiges of the indigenous nobility.

Early Life

Sesostris III is commonly considered the son of Sesostris II, who ruled from 1897 to 1878 B.C., and Queen Nefertiti II, but his origins are not certain. The same uncertainty concerns a possible coregency with the latter, for which there is no indisputable evidence. It is assumed that he became King of Egypt in 1878 B.C. and ruled until 1843 B.C., although the latest attested year of his reign is the year 19. Sesostris adopted the official name Netjerykheperu.

Life's Work

Nothing is known about Sesostris' life prior to his ascent, or about events during the early years of his reign. The earliest preserved inscription dates from his fifth year of rule. It was found in Ezbet el-Saghira, in Egypt's northeastern delta. This find is not isolated; other material relating to Sesostris has been discovered in the same region. A seated statue of the king was found at Tell Nebesheh, in addition to material at Qantir, Bubastis, and Tanis. These finds may indicate the concern of Sesostris with Egypt's northeastern border.

Yet Sesostris' interests did not end at this border. There is a report about a military campaign by a follower of Sesostris named Khu-Sobek, leading to the capture of a region called Sekemem. This region has been identified with Shekhem (biblical Sichem), but because a deep military penetration into Palestine lacks substantiation, this identification has been disputed.

That there was a concerted political interest in the Levant during the reign of Sesostris is suggested by the considerable number of Egyptian objects found in the Levant, namely at Megiddo and Gezer, which date to Sesostris' reign. These objects probably reflect diplomatic rather than military activity. Such an evaluation is supported by a group of Egyptian texts commonly labeled "Execration Texts." These texts consist of magical incantations pronounced to influence the chiefs in a wide range of city-states in Palestine and Syria. Although their political effectiveness could be questioned, they display an astounding familiarity with the political situation in the Levant at the time. The claim in a hymn to Sesostris that "his words control the Asiatics" also points to the influence of Sesostris on the affairs of Syria and Palestine by diplomatic means rather than by military interference.

Egypt's interests in the exploration of the mineral resources of the Sinai Peninsula seem to have been a major force in the political contacts to the East. During the reign of Sesostris, mining in Serabit el-khadim on Sinai's western side was limited. Further, no addition to the local sanctuary of the goddess Hathor was constructed during his reign. During the ensuing reign of Amenemhet III, the Sinai mines were extensively explored. This exploration was probably a result of Sesostris' influence on the Levant scene.

The chief military activity of Sesostris was directed southward against Nubia and was specifically intended to gain control over the area of the Nile's Second Cataract. Four campaigns by the king are attested by inscriptions, namely in the eighth, tenth, sixteenth, and nineteenth years of his reign. There is no indication that this military activity was in response to any prior aggression or danger. Instead, it seems that Sesostris embarked on the campaigning for imperialistic goals and personal vainglory. At that time, Egyptian authority extended as far south as the northern end of the Second Cataract, where the fortress of Buhen (opposite modern Wadi Halfa) guarded the border. The very inhospitable terrain of the cataract region appears to have been scarcely populated, but south of it was an important Nubian state with Kerma as its center. Apparently, Sesostris aspired to subdue it and to incorporate it into his realm, goals which he ultimately failed to achieve.

Major preparations preceded the first campaign in the eighth year of his reign. In order to move troops and equipment southward, a canal more than two hundred feet long, seventy-five feet wide, and twenty-two feet deep was cut through the rocks forming the First Cataract. Sesostris met with fierce resistance, and the advance proved much more difficult than anticipated. Although the

king directed the campaign in person, the proclaimed goal "to overthrow the wretched Kush" turned out to be a more difficult task than the repelling of nomadic tribesmen. At least three more campaigns followed. As a result of these military efforts, Egypt's southern frontier was pushed some forty miles southward, but it did not advance into the fertile stretch beyond. At strategically dominating places, Sesostris had fortresses built on either side of the Nile River, specifically at Semna (Heh) and Kumna, to shield the dearly won frontier. An inscription there states the king's political principles:

> Southern boundary made in the Year 8 under the majesty of the King of Upper and Lower Egypt Sesostris, may he be given life forever, in order to prevent any Nubian from crossing it by water or by land, with a ship or any herd, except a Nubian who shall come to do trading at Yken or with a commission. Every good thing shall be done to them, but without allowing a ship of Nubians to pass by Heh going north—forever.

The conquest itself held hardly any advantages, except as a potential bridgehead for later operations. The resistance it encountered prevented those plans from succeeding, an indication that a state of considerable military power opposed Sesostris' expansionist efforts.

By his sixteenth year in power, Sesostris apparently realized the futility of his aspirations and decided to make the frontier permanent at Semna and Kumna. Despite his limited success, he announced it as a great personal achievement:

> Every successor of mine shall maintain this boundary which my majesty has made—he is my son born to my majesty. He who shall abandon it and shall not fight for it—he is not my son, he is not born to me.
> My majesty had a statue of my majesty set up at this boundary which my majesty made in order that one might stay with it and in order that one fight for it.

The egocentric attitude of Sesostris is clearly apparent in these lines. Indeed, Sesostris was the first king of ancient Egypt to receive worship as a god during his lifetime; this divinization, however, was limited to Nubia. Three hundred years later, Thutmose III erected a temple for him at Semna as the "god of Nubia." Sesostris' personality left its lasting mark on Egypt proper. Few monuments of him, however, are preserved; they are especially scarce in Middle Egypt. Sesostris favored the temple of Osiris at Abydos and was also active at Thebes.

During Sesostris' reign, all traces of the indigenous nobility of Egypt disappeared. There are no texts expounding a specific policy, but from the results there can be no question that Sesostris intended to be the sole Egyptian leader, eliminating any potential competition. His methods remain obscure, but the possibility of forced exile is likely. While Sesostris streamlined the social structure by enforcing one single center, the disappearance of the hereditary nobility had its dangers. As long as a strong personality occupied the throne, the affairs of Egypt prospered. When such a ruler was lacking, however, there was nobody in the society to provide the leadership necessary to keep the ship of state on course. It is fitting that fifty-seven years after Sesostris' death the political structures disintegrated rapidly.

Sesostris had a large mud-brick pyramid built at Dahshûr. Attached to it are the burial places for the members of the royal family. From these tombs come some stunning jewelry, a part of which is housed in the Metropolitan Museum of Art. Later traditions adopted Sesostris as a legendary hero, and stories about him were related by Herodotus and Diodorus. The stories conflate some of his exploits with those of other kings, especially Ramses II, to a romantic quasi history.

Summary

While Sesostris III was unquestionably an exceptionally strong personality on the throne of Egypt, his excessive ego brought not only blessings but also potential dangers. He demonstrated military determination unparalleled by any earlier king and opened the conquest of Upper Nubia. By concentrating the social structure exclusively on himself and eliminating the indigenous nobility, he initiated the transformation of Egypt from a conservative, traditional society into a politically motivated populace.

Bibliography

Adams, William Yewdale. *Nubia: Corridor to Africa.* Princeton, N.J.: Princeton University Press, and London: Allen Lane, 1977. Primarily concerns Egypt's advance into Nubia. Contains twelve pages of illustrations, bibliographic references, and an index.

Delia, Robert D. *A Study of the Reign of Senwosret III.* Ann Arbor, Mich.: University Microfilms International, 1980. This volume is the only comprehensive study of Sesostris' reign. It covers all of its aspects and discusses the available sources in detail.

Gardiner, Alan. *Egypt of the Pharaohs*. Oxford: Clarendon, 1961; New York: Oxford University Press, 1964. A fine general account of the history of ancient Egypt. Includes a short bibliography, some illustrations, and an index.

Hayes, William C. "The Middle Kingdom in Egypt." In *The Cambridge Ancient History*, edited by I. E. Edwards, C. J. Gadd, and N. G. L. Hammond. Vol. 1, *Early History of the Middle East*. 3d ed. Cambridge and New York: Cambridge University Press, 1971. A thorough discussion not only of one reign but also of the political tendencies of the time.

Lichtheim, Miriam. *Ancient Egyptian Literature: A Book of Readings*. Berkeley: University of California Press, 1973. Contains good translations of two major pieces of writing concerning Sesostris. Includes bibliographic references.

Hans Goedicke

SHAPUR II

Born: c. 309; Iran

Died: 379; Iran

Areas of Achievement: Government and warfare

Contribution: Shapur was one of the greatest rulers of the Sassanid Dynasty in pre-Islamic Iran. Succeeding to the throne after a period of internal confusion, he restored the fortunes of the Sassanid Empire and extended its frontiers in all directions.

Early Life

Shapur II was the eighth in the long line of rulers of the Sassanid Dynasty, which dominated much of the Middle East between 224 and 651. The first two Sassanid shahs (kings), Ardashir I and Shapur I, descendants of hereditary priests of the Zoroastrian fire temple at Istakhr in the southwestern Iranian province of Fars, replaced the disintegrating rule of the Parthians with an aggressive military monarchy based on domination of the Plateau of Iran and expansion outward in all directions. In the east, the Sassanids advanced deep into Afghanistan as far as the land near the upper Indus River. To the northeast, they crossed the Amu Darya River and the Hisar range. In the northwest, they claimed overlordship in Armenia, Iberia, and Albania (areas corresponding to modern Armenia, Republic of Georgia, and Azerbaijan). In the west, they disputed hegemony with the Romans over upper Mesopotamia, between the Tigris and Euphrates rivers (the conjunction of modern Turkey, Iraq, and Syria). Shapur I enjoyed spectacular successes over three Roman emperors, celebrated in his bas-reliefs at Naqsh-i Rustam and Bi-shapur: Gordianus III, who was murdered by his troops in 244 while campaigning against the Sassanids; Philip the Arabian, who was compelled to negotiate a humiliating peace; and Valerian, who was taken prisoner by Shapur after a battle near Edessa in 260 and who died in captivity.

Ardashir and Shapur I ruled over an empire of diverse races, religions, and languages; from their Parthian predecessors they inherited a situation of regional fragmentation, a society Iranologists refer to as "feudal." The first two Sassanid shahs recognized the pluralistic composition of their empire, but they were determined to crush the independence of the feudal nobility. They wanted to establish a highly centralized autocracy in which the Shahanshah (King of Kings) shone with a reful-

gence derived from his being endowed with the unique qualities of *farr* (the divine favor reserved for monarchs) and *hvarna* (the charisma of kingship).

Following Shapur I's death in 272, his immediate successors failed to maintain the momentum: A series of short-lived, unimpressive rulers allowed the army to deteriorate, and the Romans counterattacked with vigor. In 283, Emperor Carus advanced to within sight of the walls of Ctesiphon, the Sassanid metropolis near modern Baghdad. His successor, Diocletian (c. 245-316), then determined to stabilize Rome's eastern frontiers by constructing limes (a defensive line of forts and earthworks) from the great bend of the Euphrates northward into Armenia, the traditional bone of contention between Romans and Iranians. As a result, war broke out, and in the ensuing campaigns the Iranians fared badly. On one occasion, the family of Narses, the shah, fell into Roman hands, together with a large booty. By the Peace of Nisibis of 298, Narses was forced to relinquish not only upper Mesopotamia between the Tigris and Euphrates but also territory on the east bank of the Tigris; all trade between the two empires was to go through Nisibis, and Armenia passed definitively into the Roman sphere of influence, to which it tended to be drawn anyway, as a consequence of the Armenian king's adoption of Christianity around 303.

With the death of Hormizd II, a grandson of Shapur I, in 309 the imperial line appeared to have ended, but a ray of hope lay with a pregnant wife or concubine of the late ruler. Tradition has it that the future Shapur II was designated shah while still in his mother's womb by the crown being placed on her belly. In another version of the story, the high priest sat the woman upon the throne, a diadem was held over her head, and gold coins were poured into the crown. The events of Shapur's long reign are fairly well documented in Latin, Syriac, and Arabic sources, although there is a dearth of source material in Middle Persian. Moreover, later Arabic and Persian accounts, although quite detailed, have a tendency to confuse happenings in the reign of Shapur II with those in the reign of Shapur I.

Of Shapur II's early years nothing is known. The first third of his reign was probably spent learning the business of government, consolidating the royal authority, and taming the habitually turbulent nobility. Such campaigning as there was occurred on the exposed Arabian marches of the empire, where Bedouin raiders penetrated the prosperous agricultural settlements of lower Mesopotamia and perhaps even threatened Ctesiphon. One solution to the problem was to construct defensive lines similar to the Roman limes, with which the Iranians were already acquainted in upper Mesopotamia, but Shapur also resorted to a "forward policy" of punitive expeditions. There may be more than a grain of truth in late accounts of the shah leading his handpicked warriors, mounted on racing dromedaries, into the fastnesses of the Arabian Desert, but it is probable that he campaigned against the Ghassanid Arab clients of the Romans in the direction of Syria rather than, as much later traditions assert, crossing the central plateau to attack Yathrib (modern Medina) or to invade Yemen. More plausible are references to Arab piratical raids upon the coastline of Fars which prompted Shapur to send out a naval expedition to raid the island of Bahrain and the mainland behind it.

Life's Work

During the first thirty years of Shapur's life, roughly coinciding with the long reign of Constantine the Great (306-337), Rome was the dominant power on the frontier, but in 337 the accession of Constantius II, who controlled only the eastern provinces and whose future seemed uncertain, signified a change. At the same time, in Armenia, a party among the Armenian nobles opposed to the recent Christianization of the kingdom expelled their ruler and turned to Iran for assistance. Shapur took the field and, crossing the Tigris, besieged Nisibis in 338 (but without success), while the Romans forcibly reinstated the Armenian king. For the next decade or more, an undeclared peace settled on the western frontier, broken by sporadic border forays, while the shah campaigned in the East.

Since the time of Ardashir, the former Kushan territories of Bactria (north of the Hindu Kush Mountains, in Afghanistan), Sogdiana (beyond the Amu Darya River), and Gandhara (in eastern Afghanistan and the upper Indus country) had been ruled by Sassanid governors, probably a cadet line of the royal house, who used the title of Kushanshah (King of the Kushans). During the 340's, this arrangement seems to have broken down, perhaps as a result of a steady flow of nomads into these regions from the steppes to the north.

This nomadic influx diverted Shapur's attention from the West, and it may have been partly the fear of an attack from that quarter while he was preoccupied in the East that prompted him to order the systematic persecution of his Christian subjects, a campaign which had begun in 337 at the time of his first confrontation with Rome. The reason for this policy lay in Constantine's adoption of Christianity for the Roman Empire, some two decades after the Christianization of Armenia. Thus Shapur viewed the Christian communities in the Sassanid Empire as a fifth column which would rise up in support of their coreligionists in the event of the Romans' breaking into the Iranian homeland. He may also have undertaken this policy with the idea of endearing himself to the intolerant Zoroastrian priesthood. Certainly, the persecution, ferocious in the extreme, ended the notion that the Sassanid Empire was a kind of religious melting pot, for at this time, Manichaeans and Jews were also exposed to harassment (although less severe than that experienced by Christians). In the course of the persecutions, the ancient city of Susa in southwestern Iran, which sheltered a Christian see and a large Christian population, revolted. It was, therefore, razed, and several hundred war elephants were brought in to help with the demolition.

In 350, Shapur returned to the offensive in the West. Constantius was embroiled in civil wars, while in Armenia, Tigranes V had been pursuing a crooked policy of playing off Rome against Iran. Shapur, exasperated by his double-dealing, now had him seized and executed, replacing him with Tigranes' son, Arshak II. Meanwhile, the shah planned to besiege Nisibis. Once more, the prize eluded him. This time, a looming crisis in the East demanded his immediate presence there. The former penetration of the eastern provinces by nomadic bands had given way to the threat of all-out invasion by a people who appear in the sources as "Chionites." This nomadic confederacy probably consisted of a majority of people of Iranian stock led by a ruling elite of Huns, who now make their appearance in Iranian history for the first time. Several years of hard campaigning against the Chionites resulted in their defeat in 356 and, in the following year, their submission as tributaries of the empire.

With the East now pacified, Shapur turned to the West again and in 359 undertook the siege of the great fortress of Amida (modern Diyarbakir, in Turkey) on the upper Tigris. The fighting went on for seventy-three days before the final successful assault. The Roman historian Ammianus Marcellinus watched from the battlements as "the king himself, mounted upon a charger and overtopping the others, rode before the whole army, wearing in place of a diadem a golden image of a ram's head set with precious stones. . . ." Yet a leading scholar has hypothesized recently that Ammianus Marcellinus was mistaken, since Shapur wore a different headdress, and that the wearer of the ram's head was another Kushanshah, who was serving as an auxiliary to his overlord. Early in the course of the siege, the son of Grumbates, the Chionite ruler, was killed, and after his body had been burned in accordance with Hunnish custom, his father demanded vengeance. The city was then closely besieged. The Iranian contingents were deployed on every side. Of the allies, the Chionites were on the east, the Gelani (tribesmen from Gilan and Mazandaran in northern Iran) were on the south, the Albanians (from modern Azerbaijan) were on the north, and the Sakas (from Seistan in eastern Iran) were on the west. Ammianus Marcellinus wrote: "With them, making a lofty show, slowly marched the lines of elephants, frightful with their wrinkled bodies and loaded with armed men, a hideous spectacle, dreadful beyond every form of horror. . . ."

Eventually, Amida fell after heavy casualties on both sides. It was to be Shapur's supreme triumph. In the following year, more cities in upper Mesopotamia were taken by the Iranians, but thereafter the fighting seems to have entered a desultory phase which continued until Emperor Julian (361-363) resolved to restore Rome's fortunes in the East. Julian moved swiftly. He traversed Mesopotamia virtually unopposed to within sight of the walls of Ctesiphon, the Iranians preferring not to give battle and adopting a "scorched earth" strategy. Julian was killed in a skirmish, and his successor, Jovian (363-364), was eager to extract his forces at minimal cost. Shapur obtained possession of Nisibis at last, together with all upper Mesopotamia, and Rome abandoned its protectorate over Armenia. Arshak II, who had initially demonstrated commitment to the Iranian connection, had long since proved himself duplicitous, openly aligning himself with the Romans at the time of Julian's campaign. Now, he was abandoned to the wrath of his erstwhile overlord, who had him seized and held captive until his death (c. 367).

By then, however, Shapur had systematically ravaged Armenia, deporting thousands of captives, who were redistributed throughout the empire during the course of a campaign which also took him into Iberia (that is, modern Georgia), where he expelled a Roman client ruler and installed his own candidate (c. 365). The emperor Valens reacted to this humiliation by sending troops into both Armenia and Iberia to restore the status quo. In Iberia, the country was now divided between two kings, both bearing the same name—one was a puppet of Rome, the other a puppet of Iran.

In Armenia, the Romans installed Pap, the son of Arshak II, as king. As with other Armenian kings, however, Pap could not resist the temptation of seeking to play one power off against the other. At various times between 370 and 374, he seems to have entered into negotiations with Shapur which probably included some kind of submission. Getting wind of Pap's treachery, Valens summoned him to Tarsus to answer charges of treason, but he escaped and made his way back to Armenia, where he was subsequently assassinated at a banquet given by local Roman commanders.

Pap was replaced by a kinsman, Varazdat, whom a considerable section of the Armenian nobility was unwilling to acknowledge, while Shapur refused to recognize his accession and sent troops to oust him. With the Goths in the Balkans threatening Adrianople, Valens needed a speedy settlement of the eastern frontier. Thus some kind of arrangement was negotiated between the two great powers around 377, although the sources do not specify the existence of a peace treaty at that time. Armenia was *de facto*, if not *de jure*, partitioned, the greater part of the country passing under Iranian control. Thus, Shapur had attained a major objective of Sassanid rulers: Armenia and Iberia were partitioned into spheres of influence, and with Albania tributary, Iran dominated almost the entire region between the Caspian Sea and the Black Sea. After Shapur's death, a formal treaty between Iran and Rome during the reign of Shapur III (383-388) regularized the previous partition arrangements regarding Armenia. Then, when the king of Iranian Armenia died in 392, Bahram IV installed his own brother, Vramshapuh, on the throne, while Roman Armenia was formally integrated into the Roman provincial administration.

Little is known regarding the internal conditions of Iran during the time of Shapur II, but the evidence suggests that he vigorously pursued his predecessors' goals of curbing the power of the nobility. The favors which he lavished upon the

Zoroastrian priesthood (to which may be added his relentless persecution of the Christians) were probably intended to secure the support of this influential class. Yet in the course of helping to create an official Zoroastrian state church, well endowed, privileged, and powerful, he also ensured that it was firmly under the control of the Shahanshah.

Like his namesake, Shapur I, Shapur II played an active role in promoting new urban centers and in restoring older foundations which had been languishing. Thus, he enlarged the city of Gundeshapur in Khuzestan (southwestern Iran), originally built by Shapur I's Roman prisoners, where he founded the university, observatory, and medical school which were to become so famous in the early Islamic period. Having carried out the destruction of Susa around 350, he ordered an entirely new city to be constructed nearby, known as Iran-khwarra Shapur (Shapur's fortune of Iran), while another city, Iranshahr-Shapur, often referred to by its Aramaic name of Karkha de Ledan, was founded upstream from Susa. He also rebuilt Nishapur (or Niv-Shapur, meaning "the good deed of Shapur").

Summary

The reign of Shapur II marks one of the climactic phases of Sassanid rule. With the frontiers of his empire stretching from Diyarbakir in the west to Kabul in the east and from the Caucasus Mountains to the southern shores of the Persian Gulf, with his effective—if brutal—subjugation of all internal elements which seemed to challenge his autocratic exercise of power, and with his tight grip upon the Zoroastrian church, Shapur II must be rated as one of the most successful of all Sassanid monarchs. At his death, he was succeeded by Ardashir II, whose relationship to him is a matter of dispute but who was probably his son.

In the light of Shapur II's long reign, it is surprising that so few major monuments have survived from this period. One of the six bas-reliefs carved in the gorge at Bishapur in Fars known as "Bishapur VI," has been widely attributed to him, although some scholars have identified it with Shapur I. Those who believe that it dates from Shapur II's reign have variously interpreted it as commemorating a victory over Kushan, Roman, or even internal Iranian foes, while a recent study claims that it represents the submission of Pap.

The surviving sources do not allow for much speculation about the personality of Shapur II, al-though the known facts point to a ruler of great energy, ambition, and pride. Like those of most Sassanid rulers, his profile can be readily identified on coins, seals, and metal objects by virtue of a distinctive crown. Shapur's crown consists of the characteristic *korymbos* (a balloon-shaped bun of hair wrapped in a fine cloth and perhaps symbolizing the terrestrial or celestial globe) above a tiara of stepped crenellations with long ribbons billowing out behind. Several formal representations of him survive in the royal hunting scenes which decorate ceremonial silver dishes. One of the finest of these shows the shah in profile, mounted, turning about in his saddle to shoot a springing lion, while a second lion is being trampled beneath his horse's hooves. He wears a tunic and the baggy pantaloons favored by other Iranian peoples, his long, straight sword hangs loosely from his belt, and he draws the typical compound bow of the steppe peoples, the weapon so feared by the Romans and other adversaries of the Iranians. As with all Sassanid art, including a remarkable silver-overlay head attributed to Shapur II in the Metropolitan Museum of Art in New York, the expression is highly stylized but proclaims calm concentration, fearlessness, and regal dignity, attributes which fit well with what is known of Shapur II.

Bibliography

Ammianus Marcellinus. *Ammianus Marcellinus.* Translated by John C. Rolfe. 3 vols. London: Heinemann, and Cambridge, Mass.: Harvard University Press, 1935-1939. Sometimes described as the last classical historian of the Roman Empire, Ammianus Marcellinus served in the Iranian campaigns of Constantius and Julian and was an eyewitness at the siege of Amida. His history includes a topographical description of the Sassanid Empire, as well as an account of contemporary Iranian manners and customs.

Azarpay, Guitty. "Bishapur VI: An Artistic Record of an Armeno-Persian Alliance in the Fourth Century." *Artibus Asiae* 43 (1981-1982): 171-189. An absorbing discussion of the Bishapur bas-relief attributed to Shapur II, identifying the scene as representing the submission of Pap to the Sassanid shah.

Bivar, Adrian David Hugh. *Catalogue of the Western Asiatic Seals in the British Museum.* London: British Museum Publications, 1962. For the student of the Sassanid period, this book is essential for understanding Sassanid iconography.

————. "The History of Eastern Iran." In *The Cambridge History of Iran*, edited by Ehsan Yarshater, vol. 3. Cambridge and New York: Cambridge University Press, 1983. This chapter, by one of the leading authorities on the eastern Iranian lands in pre-Islamic times, is essential for elucidating the still-obscure relations of the Sassanid shahs with their Kushan, Chionite, and Ephthalite neighbors.

Frye, Richard N. "The Political History of Iran Under the Sasanians." In *The Cambridge History of Iran*, edited by Ehsan Yarshater, vol. 3. Cambridge and New York: Cambridge University Press, 1983. Recommended as the best account in English of the reign of Shapur II within the overall setting of Sassanid rule, by one of the leading scholars in the field. For an alternative, see the same author's *The History of Ancient Iran* (1984).

Ghirshman, Roman. *Iran, Parthians and Sassanians*. London: Thames and Hudson, 1962. The best general account of Sassanid art, magnificently illustrated. An additional strength of this book is that it relates artistic developments on the Iranian plateau to those in adjoining regions of Afghanistan and Central Asia.

Göbl, Robert. "Sasanian Coins." In *The Cambridge History of Iran*, edited by Ehsan Yarshater, vol. 3. Cambridge and New York: Cambridge University Press, 1983. In Göbl's own words, "this coinage is an invaluable source of information about the history, culture, and economic life of the Sasanian state." Easily the best introduction to the subject.

Harper, Prudence O. *The Royal Hunter: Art of the Sasanian Empire*. New York: Asia Society, 1978. This exhibition catalog illustrates well the range of Sassanid craftsmanship and includes a photograph of the silver-overlay head in the Metropolitan Museum of Art attributed to Shapur II.

Herrmann, Georgina. *The Making of the Past: The Iranian Revival*. Oxford: Elsevier-Phaidon, 1977. Beyond any doubt, the best general introduction to the Sassanid period, accompanied by fine illustrations. Written by an acknowledged authority on Sassanid bas-reliefs.

Whitehouse, David, and Andrew Williamson. "Sasanian Maritime Trade." *Iran: Journal of the British Institute of Persian Studies* 11 (1973): 29-49. An interesting discussion of a little known aspect of Sassanid history, prefaced by an account of Shapur II's activities in the Persian Gulf.

Gavin R. G. Hambly

SAINT SIMEON STYLITES

Born: c. 390; Sis, near Nicopolis, Syria
Died: 459; Telneshae (Telanissos), Syria
Area of Achievement: Religion
Contribution: An ascetic who spent the greater part of his career perched in prayer atop a sixty-foot pillar, Simeon was one of the most controversial figures of the fifth century. Although he left behind no works of enduring value, he was the conscience and spiritual example for Syrian Christians in the patristic period.

Early Life

Simeon Stylites was born of Christian parents in the town of Sis (in northern Syria) around 390. He was baptized in his youth by his very pious parents, who provided a home life in which religious matters were a frequent topic of conversation. Until he was about thirteen years old, Simeon spent his time shepherding his father's flocks in the neighborhood of Sis; this was a task which, according to the Syriac biography of Simeon, he discharged with great diligence and sometimes to the point of exhaustion.

The occupation of shepherd improved Simeon's strength, gentleness, speed, and endurance but had little effect upon his slight build. A dreamy boy, he would often meditate while watching the campfire flame and burn storax as a tribute to the ubiquitous God of his parents. Because of his kindly disposition, he was a favorite with the other sheperds, and to show his generosity he would often forgo food until his friends had eaten.

The turning point in Simeon's life occurred shortly after his thirteenth birthday. One Sunday, while attending church, he was deeply moved by the Gospel reading for that day, which included the Beatitudes "Blessed are they that mourn" and "Blessed are the pure of heart." Simeon asked the congregation the meaning of these words and how one might attain the blessedness referred to in the Gospels. An old man who was present suggested that the monastic life was the surest but steepest path to holiness because it was characterized by prayer, fasting, and austerities designed to mortify the flesh and purify the soul.

Upon hearing this reply, it is said, Simeon withdrew to the pasture lands with his flocks to burn storax and meditate upon what the old man had said. One day, in the course of his meditations,

Simeon had the first of the many visions described in his biographies. In it, Christ appeared to him under the disquieting visage of the apocalyptic Son of Man and commanded him to build a sound foundation upon which it would be possible to erect the superstructure of an edifice unparalleled in all human history.

Simeon took this vision to mean that it was his life which was to be the foundation of a great work which Christ would complete. The marvelous nature of this work, however, demanded a foundation of extraordinary strength and endurance. In Simeon's reckoning, that meant that special sacrifices would be required, and these would best be accomplished within the confines of a monastic community.

Life's Work

The various biographies differ about how Simeon spent his monastic period. Less reliable biographies mention an initial two-year sojourn, near Sis, at the monastery of the abbot Timothy, where Simeon is said to have learned the psalter by heart. Theodoret's biography and the Syriac biography, on the other hand, indicate that Simeon first took the tonsure at the monastery of Eusebona at Tell 'Ada, between Antioch and Aleppo. Whichever is the accurate narrative, the sources agree that Simeon's stay at Eusebona was charged with many extraordinary occurrences.

To mortify his flesh, Simeon engaged in fasts lasting many days, exposed himself to extremes of inclement weather, and humbly but steadfastly endured the jeering of envious monastics and the onslaught of demonic forces (whether real or imagined). One peculiar austerity, which Theodoret identifies as the principal cause of Simeon's eviction from Eusebona, serves as an example of this ascetic's willpower (and fanaticism). Finding a well rope made of tightly twisted, razor-sharp palm leaves, Simeon wrapped it snugly around his midriff. So tight was the wrapping that the flesh swelled on either side of the coils as they cut progressively deeper into his flesh. Finally, after Simeon had begun to show some signs of discomfort, the Abbot of Eusebona had the bindings forcibly removed, despite Simeon's protestations. So deep had the rope cut into Simeon's body that the bloody wound had matted the bindings and robes together. For three days, the monks had to apply liquids to soften Simeon's clothes in order to remove them, the result being that when the rope was finally uncoiled it brought with it pieces of Simeon's flesh and a torrent of blood.

From this last austerity, Simeon's recovery was slow, nearly leaving him an invalid. Tired of the bickering and petty jealousies which Simeon's practices had aroused among his monastic brothers—and probably not a little horrified at Simeon's fanatical zeal—the Abbot of Eusebona discharged Simeon, giving him his blessing and forty dinars for food and clothing.

Simeon's expulsion from the monastery at Eusebona was significant because it was typical of the response of abbots to ascetic practices which went beyond the bounds of good sense. Simeon's own desire to perform acts of supererogation, even at the expense of disobedience to his superior, may seem to suggest that he deserves to be classed among the Sarabaitic monks—those who were described by Saint Jerome and John Cassian as thwarting all authority. The various biographies, however, are unanimous in proclaiming Simeon's freedom from the grasping, care-ridden personality of a Sarabaite. After leaving the monastery, Simeon's life more closely resembled the lives of the anchorites, described by Cassian as hermits who were the most fruitful of the monastics and achieved greater heights of contemplation because they withdrew to the desert to face the assaults of demons directly. According to Cassian, John the Baptist was the forerunner of the anchorites. It is this group that most probably can claim Simeon as its own.

After his dismissal from the monastery at Eusebona, Simeon wandered to the foot of Mount Telneshae in northern Syria. Intent upon beginning a special set of austerities for the Lenten season, he approached an almost deserted hermitage and asked its keeper to provide a cell in which he might seclude himself. There, Simeon fasted for forty days. Not satisfied with this feat of extraordinary endurance, he determined to undertake a three-year fast. Frightened by the duration and severity of the proposed fast, the keeper of the hermitage, Bassus, convinced Simeon that such a work was imprudent and that he ought to divide the period in half, lest he kill himself. Simeon agreed.

It was the completion of the year-and-a-half fast that established a name for Simeon. News of his endurance and holiness was carried abroad. Everywhere people began to talk about the Syrian phenomenon: The backwater of Telneshae had been graced by God; a saint had come to dwell there. People began to flock to the hermitage to seek the wisdom of this holy man and his curative powers. When they returned home, they brought with them stories of his marvelous abilities, abilities which were the fruit of his extreme asceticism.

For about ten years, Simeon practiced his asceticism in an open cell on Mount Telneshae, each year repeating the particulars of his original Lenten fast.

One day, sometime around the year 422, Simeon had a vision which was to distinguish him forever as an ascetic of a special kind. Twenty-one days into his Lenten fast, Simeon beheld an apparition. He saw a man, noble in stature, dressed in a military girdle, face radiant as the sun, praying aloud. After finishing his prayer, the stranger climbed up on the pillar-shaped stone, three cubits (about four and a half feet) high, which stood near Simeon's cell and served as a makeshift altar. Standing on the stone, the stranger folded his hands behind his back, bowed toward Simeon, and looked heavenward with his hands outstretched. For three days and three nights the stranger thus prayed before vanishing.

Simeon regarded this experience as a decisive revelation. From that point onward, he was to practice his fasts standing on a column of stone, exposed to the extremes of weather. He had been called to be a stylite (from the Greek *stulos*, meaning "pillar").

At first Simeon's new practice aroused the ire of the Christian leaders in the region. It may have been the novelty of Simeon's practice which angered them or it may have been that Simeon's peculiar form of worship seemed a retrogression, a return to the adoration practiced in Syria in pre-Christian times—particularly in Hierapolis. Lucian of Antioch wrote that in Hierapolis, twice a year, a priest would ascend a tall column to commune with the goddess Attar'athae and the rest of the Syrian pantheon. It may have seemed to the local religious leaders that Simeon was reviving the form, if not the content, of this pagan worship.

Whatever the cause of the displeasure of the Christian leaders, its expression diminished as quickly as the public adulation of Simeon increased. One can imagine what a powerful sight the stylite must have been, a sight which awakened deep and elemental associations in the pilgrims (particularly the Syrians). He must have been a spectacle: an emaciated figure, arms raised in unceasing prayer, perched atop a narrow column whose diameter provided barely enough room for the saint to recline. Simeon's figure could be seen on his spindle 365 days a year, regardless of the weather, at all times of day. He could be seen silhouetted against the rising and setting sun, shining in the midday azure sky, and brilliantly illuminated against Stygian thunderclouds by stroboscopic flashes of lightning. Finally, add to the image a constant procession of pilgrims winding their way up Mount Telneshae (some nearly exhausted from the great distances traveled but still hopeful that they might be healed, find advice, or discover a holy truth) and one has some idea of the deep impression which Simeon Stylites made upon his age.

For thirty-seven years, Simeon stood atop pillars of various sizes under all conditions. Many pagans were converted by his miracles and example, and even those barbarians who remained unconverted held the saint in the highest esteem. If the biographers are to be trusted, three emperors (Theodosius, Leo I, and Marcian) sought his advice about difficult state matters. Also, two surviving, but possibly spurious, letters attributed to Simeon indicate that he intervened on the side of the Christians when Emperor Theodosius issued an edict to restore Jewish property unlawfully seized by Christians and that he wrote to Emperor Leo I to approve the opening of the Council of Chalcedon in 451.

Concerning the exact time of Simeon's death, his biographers give different accounts. They mark the date as Friday, July 24, Wednesday, September 2, or Friday, September 25, in the year 459. Whatever the precise date, the accounts agree that Simeon died in prayer surrounded by his disciples.

For four days the corpse of the saint was paraded throughout the region, and on the fifth day it was carried through the streets of the great city of Antioch to the accompaniment of chanting, the burning of incense and candles, a constant sprinkling of fine perfumes, and many miraculous cures and signs. The body of the blessed Simeon was laid to rest in the great cathedral of Constantine, an honor which had never before been awarded either saint or statesman. There it remained for a while, despite even the attempts of Emperor Leo to have it transported to his own court as a talisman against evil. Eventually, the cult of Simeon grew so significantly that a pilgrimage church, in the style of Constantine's cathedral, was built at Qual'at Saman to house Simeon's remains.

Summary

Unlike great philosophers, theologians, and statesmen, Simeon Stylites left no great works of intellect or polity behind. Of the surviving letters attributed to him, it is difficult to say which are spurious and which are original because of their contradictory doctrinal positions and obvious redactions. What, then, can be made of Simeon's life? What was its impact upon the world of the fifth century? It is possible to describe the impact of Simeon as twofold. First, he contributed a peculiar ascetic technique which was imitated and extended by other stylites, such as Daniel, Simeon Stylites the Younger, Alypius, Luke, and Lazarus. As an ascetic practice, Simeon's method was one of the most severe. Yet, if practiced in a pure spirit, it held great promise: It could transform its adherent into a channel of supernatural grace.

Second, Simeon contributed something symbolic to the world of the fifth century. Regardless of which accounts of his wisdom and his importance to the social and theological controversies are accurate, all of his biographers asserted that Simeon's chief significance was as a religious symbol. His was a life whose worth must be measured in terms of the possibilities of the human spirit, not in terms of practical results or durable goods. His actions—like the actions of many other saints in the various world religions—were a testimony to the existence of values which transcend those of the visible world. Because he demonstrated the power of these values through a concrete form of supererogatory practice, people could grasp them easily. That is the reason he was so respected: He enacted his belief.

Bibliography

Brown, Peter. *The Cult of the Saints: Its Rise and Function in Latin Christianity.* Chicago: University of Chicago Press, and London: SCM Press, 1981. Useful for its general analysis of the phenomena associated with saint devotion. Although Brown's work is about the cult of the saints in the patristic Latin West, some of his arguments can be extended by analogy to Eastern Christianity. Particularly pertinent are his discussions of saintly patronage, the gift of perseverance, and the power associated with saintly presence. The cult of devotion which developed after Simeon's death manifests these features as clearly as any Western cult.

Butler, Alban. "St. Simeon the Stylite." In *Lives of the Saints*, edited by Herbert Thurston and Donald Attwater, vol. 1. New York: Kenedy, and London: Burnes and Oates, 1956. A classic work of Roman Catholic hagiography. Nevertheless, this work provides a brief and, for the most part, accurate synthesis of Simeon's biographies. A good, succinct summary of Simeon's life.

Downey, Glanville. *Ancient Antioch*. Princeton, N.J.: Princeton University Press, 1963. The most accessible book on the history of ancient Antioch from its origins to the decline of the Roman Empire, it is a condensation of another work by Downey, cited below. Since Simeon was at the center of many political and theological controversies of his day, this book helps situate his involvement within the social, cultural, and religious history of Syria's most important city. Contains some maps and illustrations.

———. *A History of Antioch in Syria: From Seleucus to the Arab Conquest*. Princeton, N.J.: Princeton University Press, 1961. One of the most ambitious histories of Antioch from the time of the Seleucids until the Arab conquest, this work contains a wealth of historical information on ancient Christian and pre-Christian Antioch. Downey treats Simeon as one of the major forces to be reckoned with in any interpretation of fifth century Syrian history. Very useful for situating Simeon against the cultural history of his country. Contains maps and illustrations.

Lent, Frederick. "The Life of Simeon Stylites: A Translation of the Syriac Text in Bedjan's *Acta martyrum sanctorum*, Vol. IV." *Journal of the American Oriental Society* 35, no. 1 (1915): 104-198. The only translation of this Syriac life of Simeon into English. In comparison to Theodoret's biography, this work is much more episodic and contains more details which are historically questionable. It is, however, useful for capturing the spirit of the man.

Torrey, Charles C. "The Letters of Simeon the Stylite." *Journal of the American Oriental Society* 20 (1899): 251-276. This article is a translation of three Syriac letters attributed to Simeon. Because of their obvious partisan inventions, their authenticity is questionable. Yet they make an intriguing study of the way the authority of Simeon was marshaled to defend the Monophysite branch of the Syrian church.

Voobus, Arthur. *History of Asceticism in the Syrian Orient: A Contribution to the History of Culture in the Near East*. 2 vols. Stockholm: Louvain, 1965. The seminal work on Syrian asceticism and spirituality. Contains much material on the life of Simeon as well as his successors. The most useful work for anyone interested in studying the phenomenon of asceticism and the forms it assumed in the Syrian environment.

Thomas Ryba

SIMONIDES

Born: c. 556 B.C.; Iulis, Greece
Died: c. 467 B.C.; Syracuse, Sicily
Area of Achievement: Literature
Contribution: Having advanced the quality of Greek lyric poetry through his elegies and epigrams, Simonides brought the dithyramb and Epinician ode to a level of perfection comparable only to that of Pindar.

Early Life

One of Simonides' own epigrams, number 203, reveals both its author's place and year of birth; it is in this poem that he celebrates a victory prize he won at the age of eighty in the archonship of Adeimantus. Other ancient sources confirm these dates, and one can be certain that Simonides lived to the age of eighty-nine or ninety or even longer, if one believes the testimony of Lucian.

Unlike many of the Greek lyric poets, a surprisingly complete genealogy remains extant for Simonides. His father's name was Leoprepes and his maternal grandfather's name was Hyllichus. His paternal grandfather, also named Simonides, and a grandson known as Simonides Genealogus were poets as well. In addition, the dithyrambic poet Bacchylides was his nephew. It is clear that literary inclinations ran deeply in Simonides' family.

According to traditional accounts, the family of Simonides held some form of hereditary post in connection with Dionysus, and this would account for Simonides' early access to music and poetry festivals held in that god's honor. Supposedly, while still a boy, Simonides instructed the choruses and celebrated the worship of Apollo at Carthaea. Pindar, who became Simonides' bitter rival, criticized both Simonides and Bacchylides for these early involvements, castigating them both as *tous mathontas* ("the teachers"), with the implication that they were pedants.

Sometime after 528 B.C., the *tyrannos* Hipparchus invited Simonides to his court at Athens, and it was here that the poet acquired his first major celebrity. The poets Anacreon and Lasus, the teacher of Pindar, were present at Hipparchus' court at this time. Simonides appears to have had only minimal contact with Anacreon. The relationship between Simonides and Lasus appears, however, to have been contentious from the outset. They engaged in a number of poetry contests filled with personal invective, and Lasus' student Pindar would carry on this enmity to the final years of Simonides' life.

Based on encomia attributed to him, Simonides appears to have weathered the political storms that resulted from the murder of Hipparchus and the expulsion of his successor Hippias. With consummate irony, an inscription attributed to Simonides praises the tyrannicide committed by Harmodius and Aristogeiton and calls the death of his patron "a great light rising upon the Athenians." This inscription probably appeared at the base of a publicly displayed statue of Harmodius and Aristogeiton. The point at which one might consider the career of Simonides to be established, approximately 510 B.C., thus coincides with the death or expulsion of those who had helped him achieve recognition.

Life's Work

The unstable situation in Athens following the overthrow of the Peisistratids probably led Simonides to seek the patronage of the Aleuads and the Scopads in Thessaly. If the assessment of the poet Theocritus is correct, the names of these ruling families escaped oblivion only through the encomia that Simonides wrote in their honor to celebrate the victories of their horses at the sacred games. Most noteworthy among the extant works of Simonides is the substantial fragment of the Epnician ode on the victory of the four-horse chariot of Scopas. Plato preserves and comments on this poem (number 13) in his *Protagoras*. "Fragments on the Fall of the Scopads" (number 46) and "Antiochus the Aleuad" (number 48) are among Simonides' most familiar works. It is even possible that a threnody on Danae is a poem originally written for one of the Scopads.

Despite this considerable involvement with the tyrants of Thessaly, it seems that Simonides' relationship with them was never an easy one. The region was rugged, and the arts, praised as they might have been in the abstract, always took second place when it came to the granting of subventions. Cicero, in *De oratore*, cites the poet Callimachus as his authority for the story that Scopas, having heard Simonides' Castor and Pollux ode, gave the poet only one-half the agreed payment, telling Simonides that he should request the other half from the Tyndarids, since they had received half the praise in Simonides' poem. The tale assumes a somewhat fantastic character at this point. Having received a message that two young men wished to speak to him, Simonides, just humiliated by Scopas' behavior, left the hall to see the two young men supposedly waiting for him at the entrance to the banquet hall. When he left the hall, however, he could find no one, but he heard a sudden crash, and the entire hall fell upon Scopas, killing him and the other revelers who had ridiculed Simonides.

It is, of course, hardly likely that this event occurred as Cicero relates it. The tale concludes with the inference that the two young men were the Dioscuri themselves, Castor and Pollux. They made their half of the payment due Simonides, and the larger moral lesson of the tale is that those who treat artists with unkindness incur the wrath of the gods. Presumably, the legend also implies that tyrants such as Scopas fall from power because of their own hubris. Evidently, this was a popular narrative in the ancient world, since variations of it appear in a diverse number of ancient writings, including those of Callimachus, Quintilian, Valerius Maximus, Areisteides, and Phaedrus. Ironically, assuming that the part about Scopas' refusal of full payment is true, only the part of the poem that refers to his family line survives; that which refers to the Dioscuri is no longer extant.

Fantastic though the story is on the literal level, it nevertheless reflects the high esteem that cultured people of the day felt for Simonides even as it records the sudden historical demise of odious rulers such as Scopas. In this, it follows the same structure as the myth of Arion, who was saved by a dolphin, or of lbycus, who was avenged by cranes.

In any event, the period of this tale approximates the time of the Persian invasion, and it is at this juncture that Simonides must have returned to Athens, for his poems from this time celebrate Athenian bravery in the Persian Wars.

At this stage in his career, Simonides began to associate himself with the military leaders of Athens, his career again reflecting the prevailing political winds. It was Miltiades who, in 490 B.C., commissioned an epigram (number 188) for a statue of Pan, dedicated to commemorate the battle of Marathon. One measure of the incredible success Simonides had achieved since his first departure from Athens is the fact that, in the following year, he defeated no less a poet than Aeschylus in the contest to produce an elegy that would honor those who had fallen at Marathon (fragment 58).

Simonides' works written during this period include the epigrams inscribed on the tombs of those Spartans who fell at Thermopylae as well as an accompanying encomium (epigrams 150-155; fragment 9). His circle of acquaintance remained among the powerful, including the statesman Themistocles. An apocryphal story that parallels the Scopas narrative surrounds their acquaintance. In this story, cited by Plutarch in *Themistocles*, the statesman criticizes the poet for making extraordinary demands on public resources when commissioned to write commemorative verse for public occasions.

The extant works of Simonides reveal that many such commissions must have been forthcoming in the wake of the Persian Wars. The battle of Plataea provided the occasion for an elegy (fragment 59) as well as the famous epigram (198) inscribed on the tripod fabricated from Persian spoils and dedicated collectively at Delphi by the victorious Greek cities. Thucydides reported that, because this inscription too completely attributed the Greek victory to the general Pausanias, the Spartans erased Pausanias' name and substituted, as though for an epic catalogue, the names of all the Greek states that had taken part in the war. In any event, the zenith of Simonides' career was clearly his victory in the dithyrambic chorus competition held in 477 B.C. during the archonship of Adeimantus. Simonides would have been eighty years of age at this time, and this would have been, by his own reporting (epigrams 203-204) his fifty-sixth victory prize.

The final stage in Simonides' career began about 476 B.C. with his decision to accept the invitation of the tyrant Hiero to establish himself at Syracuse. Tales of his diplomatic prowess at Hiero's court describe his mediation of a peace between Hiero and Theron of Agrigentum, and the historian Xenophon records a dialogue between Simonides and Hiero on the positive and negative arguments for government by tyranny. Cicero, in *De natura deorum*, describes Simonides' evasive answer to Hiero on the nature of divinity.

Summary

It seems that Simonides' continuing dependence upon tyrants arose from practical necessity, but it also seems that he was able to consistently assemble a circle of personal friends who could support his aesthetic needs. The wife of Hiero, for example, protected his interests to some degree by interceding with her husband when necessary; she also became Simonides' interlocutor in philosophic conversations. At one time or another Pindar, Bacchylides, and Aeschylus were in residence at Hiero's court so that Simonides had little want of stimulating conversation, even when opinions differed. In all, Simonides had few wants at any time in his life and none at all in his later years. Indeed, despite his often uneasy relationship with the Syracusan tyrant and stories of Hiero's reluctance to pay for commissioned works, Simonides received such a generous allowance of daily supplies from the royal household that he often sold what he did not need and thereby provided himself with additional income.

Perhaps Simonides' distaste for opulence also led him to sell his excess supplies. His poems reveal that he held the conservative philosophic view traditional with the Greeks, in which *sophrosyne* ("genuine wisdom"), temperance, and order arose from moderation. Moreover, he reverenced traditional religion, and this appears in his treatment of the ancient myths. The polemical character of his political poems indicates that he considered one function of poetry to be educational and that those most in need of such education were often his patrons. In some sense, his works imply a kind of philosophic stoicism. One should enjoy, as much as possible, the calm reflection that literature offers despite the storms and stresses of the moment.

There is, of course, the other side of the argument. Simonides did live amid and depend upon the very excesses his philosophic outlook condemned. If inclined to view these facts cynically, one could accuse him of hypocrisy, but perhaps it is better to consider him a realist. He believed in the power of the arts to change human behavior, and if he used support from unsavory sources in order to achieve the results he desired, he was simply making use of the instruments available to him.

In any event, his reputation among the popular audience never suffered, and his patriotic poems always won immediate general acclaim. These, primarily because they reflected a Panhellenic view rather than the local perspective prevailing at the various locations in which he resided, encouraged a spirit of Greek identity not present in actuality until the Hellenistic period.

Bibliography

Bowra, C. M., and T. F. Higham. *Oxford Book of Greek Verse in Translation*. Oxford: Clarendon Press, 1930. Contains the largest selection of Greek verse in a single source readily available to English readers; more than 700 items with good notes that cite parallels, explain content, and account for divergences from the original *Oxford Book of Greek Verse*.

Barnstone, Willis. *Greek Lyric Poetry*. Rev. ed. New York: Schocken Books, 1987. Surveys the development of Greek lyric poetry with 614 specimens translated in free verse. Valuable, not so much for the translations, which often depart from close renderings of the Greek, but for the biographical sketches that proceed even minor poets and cite frequent *testimonia* for cross-reference. Also contains an almost forty-page glossary and a concordance to the numberings of poems used in the commonly used editions.

Lattimore, Richmond. *Greek Lyrics*. Rev. ed. Chicago: University of Chicago Press, 1960. Has the advantage of excellent translations and a good selection of poems as well as easy accessibility. Perhaps its small size (a mere eighty-two pages) is also an asset, since the collection does not overwhelm a reader new to Greek lyric poetry and presents only the best. Lattimore is particularly good in his treatment of the elegy, somewhat less so in the lyric proper. One defect of the book is a lack of commentary.

Lucas, F. L. *Greek Poetry*. New York: Macmillan, and London: Dent, 1951. Partially fills the void of critical material appropriate for the common reader. Comprehensively edited. The introduction sets Greek lyric verse into its proper literary context. There are four main sections that cover the full historical span of ancient Greek verse, provide notes on the poems, and present brief biographies as well as fine appendixes on the *Palatine Anthology* and Delphic verse attributed to the oracle.

Skelton, Robin. *Two Hundred Poems from the Greek Anthology*. Seattle: University of Washington Press, and London: Methuen, 1971. Generally good translations of a variety of poems. The introduction is particularly suitable for general readers new to Greek verse, though there are no notes to the individual poems.

Robert J. Forman

SAINT SIRICIUS

Born: c. 335 or 340; probably in or near Rome
Died: November 26, 399; Rome
Area of Achievement: Religion
Contribution: Siricius was the first pope to exercise his authority throughout the Roman Empire. In the process, he set precedents which were to be used to great effect by his successors.

Early Life

Siricius, who was probably born circa 335 or 340, was Roman by birth. Little of his early life is known. He was ordained by Pope Liberius as a lector and later as a deacon. Siricius would have received the standard Roman clerical education, and he may well have been classically educated also. His entire career was spent in the church of Rome.

On December 11, 384, Liberius' successor, Damasus I, died. By this time, the papacy had become increasingly politicized, and there followed intense campaigning for his office. The candidates included Siricius, Ursinus, who had also been a candidate and responsible for rioting in the election of 366, and Jerome, who seems to have been Damasus' favorite. Later that month, or perhaps early in January of 385, Siricius was elected and consecrated the next pope; a congratulatory letter from the emperor still survives. Ursinus and his partisans were then officially expelled from Rome. Jerome, perhaps believing that he was no longer welcome, also departed, settling in Palestine with several of his own protégés.

Life's Work

Siricius' activities during his pontificate are known primarily from the letters which he sent or received and from the account given in the sixth or seventh century *Liber pontificalis* (*The Book of the Popes*, 1916).

Siricius became pope at a time when the bishops of Rome were just beginning to exercise their claimed large-scale ecclesiastical authority. Several of his letters, for example, contain the first of the papal decrees later collected as canon law.

Some of Siricius' letters document his desire to formalize ecclesiastical discipline and practices. He was concerned, for example, that the proper procedures be followed in the choice of bishops and in appointments to other ranks of the clergy. On February 10, 385, he replied to a letter which

Bishop Himerius of Tarragona in Spain had written to Damasus. He discussed the proper way to deal with converted Arians and Novatians (they were not to be rebaptized); the proper times for baptism (Easter and Pentecost but not Christmas); and various classes of individuals, such as penitents, incontinent monks and nuns, and married priests. This epistle is the first of the papal decretals. Elsewhere, Siricius decreed that new bishops must have more than one consecrator, that bishops should not ordain clerics for another's church or receive those deposed by another bishop, and that a secular official, even if baptized, could not hold a clerical office.

Decrees such as these exemplify the papal role of overseer of ecclesiastical procedures throughout the Empire. Siricius and his successors portrayed themselves as the inheritors of the authority of Peter. Siricius even claimed to have something of Peter within himself: "We bear the burdens of all who are weighed down, or rather the blessed apostle Peter, who is within us, bears them for us. . . ." Siricius also claimed that the Bishop of Rome was the

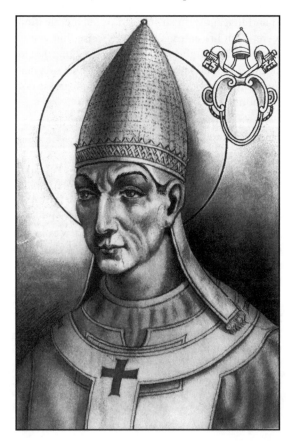

head of the college of all the bishops, and that bishops who did not obey him should be excommunicated. He asserted that his decisions, the *statuta sedis apostolicae* (the statutes of the apostolic see), should have the same authority as church councils. Like other bishops, Siricius also appropriated some of the trappings and authority of the secular government. For example, he referred to his decrees with the technical word *rescripta*, the same word used by the emperors for their responses to official queries.

At this time, however, it appeared that the authority of the Roman see was on the wane. In the east, the Council of Constantinople in 381 had assigned the Bishop of Constantinople, the capital of the eastern part of the Empire, the same honorary status as the Bishop of Rome. Nor was Siricius even the most influential bishop in Italy: He was overshadowed by Ambrose in Milan. Ambrose not only was a man of greater abilities but also was the bishop of an imperial capital. Milan, not Rome, was where emperors now tended to reside. As a result, Ambrose had the ear of the emperors. Despite his claims, Siricius was able to impose his direct authority only upon some of the local, rural bishops, whose elections he oversaw. He is said to have ordained thirty-two bishops "in diverse locations" as well as thirty-one priests and sixty deacons for the city of Rome.

In spite of these limitations, Siricius energetically tried to assert the authority of his see. In the east, he attempted to assume some administrative responsibility in Illyria by instructing Archbishop Anysius of Thessalonica to see to it that episcopal ordinations were carried out properly. The pope wished to restrict the influence not only of the see of Constantinople, which also claimed authority over Thessalonica, but also of Ambrose in Milan. Ambrose, however, had anticipated Siricius and already exercised a supervisory role in Illyria. In 381, at the emperor's request, he had assembled a council at Aquileia to investigate irregularities in the Illyrian church. As a result, Siricius made little progress there.

Siricius also belatedly became involved in a schism which had occurred at Antioch, where there were rival claimants to the bishopric. Ambrose in 391 had been instrumental in the summoning of a church council in southern Italy, at Capua, to consider the matter, and the results were forwarded to the East. Although Siricius must have been involved, the extent of his participation is uncertain.

Subsequently, according to the Eastern writer Severus of Antioch, Siricius wrote to the Antiochenes on his own initiative. He recommended that there should be only one bishop, whose election conformed with the canons of the Council of Nicaea. Shortly thereafter, the Council of Caesarea did in fact recognize the claimant who met Siricius' criteria.

In the north, Siricius became involved in other ecclesiastical controversies. In 386, he wrote to the emperor Magnus Maximus, then resident in Trier, about a priest named Agroecius, whom Siricius accused of having been wrongfully ordained. Maximus' reply survives. Noting that the matter should be dealt with by the Gallic bishops themselves, the emperor answered:

> But as regards Agroecius, whom you claim had wrongly risen to the rank of presbyter, what can I decree more reverently on behalf of our catholic religion than that catholic bishops judge on this very matter? I shall summon a council of those who dwell either in Gaul or in the Five Provinces, so it may judge with them sitting and considering the matter.

Maximus also forwarded to Siricius the results of his investigations into the Priscillianists, whom he referred to as "Manichees." Priscillian and his followers already had appealed to Ambrose and to Siricius' predecessor Damasus and been rebuffed by both. In 386, they were condemned at a synod at Trier, and Priscillian and several of his supporters were executed; others were sent into exile. This heavy-handed secular interference in ecclesiastical affairs was considered a bad precedent, and Siricius, like Ambrose and Martin of Tours, seems to have denied Communion to those bishops, such as Felix of Trier, who had supported the executions. The resultant "Felician schism" lasted until circa 400. This incident may be behind the curious account in *The Book of the Popes* of Siricius' discovery of Manichaeans in Rome and his exiling of them.

Like many of his successors, Siricius attempted to impose his authority through church councils held in Rome, attended at this time primarily by local bishops. A synod assembled on January 6, 386, dealt with matters of ecclesiastical discipline. A council of 385-386 issued nine canons concerning ecclesiastical discipline, which were sent to the African church on January 6, 386. This council met in Saint Peter's Basilica and is the first known to have met at the Vatican.

Another local concern of Siricius was a problem caused by a certain Jovinian, who, after abandoning his life as a monk, began to teach that ascetic practices such as celibacy and fasting served no useful purpose. Jovinian even went so far as to claim that Mary, by having children, had ceased to be a virgin. He also asserted that those who had been properly baptized were incapable of sin. Jovinian was denounced to Siricius, who in 390 or 392 assembled a local synod which excommunicated the former monk and eight of his followers. This news was carried to Milan, where Jovinian had fled, but Ambrose assembled another synod and excommunicated him again.

Siricius' papacy also saw the final decline of pagan worship. The emperor Theodosius I in a series of decrees formalized Christianity as the only legal religion in the Empire. As a result, this period saw the construction and expansion of the churches and sacred buildings at Rome, often at the expense of pagan temples. The Basilica of Saint Paul on the Via Ostiensis (Ostian Way) was rebuilt during Siricius' papacy in the same general shape it now has and was dedicated in 390. Siricius also rebuilt the Church of Saint Pudentiana. On November 26, 399, Siricius died, and he was buried in the cemetery of Priscilla, at the Basilica of Sylvester, on the Via Salaria. By the seventh century, his tomb was venerated by pilgrims coming to Rome.

Summary

A man of only middling talents, Siricius was more of an administrator than an innovator. In the realm of ecclesiastical politics, he had to compete with others, such as the bishops of Milan and Constantinople, who were situated in imperial capitals and who had imperial support. Nevertheless, Siricius, who had a strong view of the rights and responsibilities of the Bishop of Rome, did what he could to strengthen the position of his see. During his tenure, the pope ceased to be merely another bishop and truly began to assume an empire-wide presence.

Siricius established a secure foundation for papal authority upon which several of his fifth century successors were to build. His Italian rival Ambrose had died in 397, and with the withdrawal of the imperial administration to Ravenna, Milanese authority rapidly declined. In the fifth century, Innocent I and Leo I were successful in establishing a papal vicariate in Illyria. Leo, later called "the Great," also was able to gain the support of the imperial government in his attempts to assert his ec-clesiastical hegemony at least in the western part of the Empire.

The last years of the fourth century were a very critical period of history. Not only was the Roman Empire beginning to split into eastern and western halves, but also the "barbarian invasions" already had begun in the East, even though they had yet to affect the West. As the influence of the state weakened, the Church assumed greater authority. Even though Siricius could not foresee the fall of the Western Empire later in the fifth century, his attempts to establish the authority of the see of Rome set many precedents for the great power the popes soon were to exercise.

Bibliography

Duchesne, Louis. *Early History of the Christian Church from Its Foundation to the End of the Fifth Century.* Vol. 2. New York: Longmans, Green and Co., and London: Murray, 1909. Still one of the best histories of the early Church, it places Siricius' activities in their broader historical context. Based primarily upon the original sources.

Janini, José Cuesta. *S. Siricio y las cuatro temporas.* Valencia: Seminario Metropolitano de Valencia, 1958. The only detailed modern study of Siricius.

Loomis, Louise Ropes, trans. *The Book of the Popes.* Vol. 3. New York: Columbia University Press, 1916. This volume contains a translation of the biography of Siricius found in *Liber pontificalis,* a compilation which dates back to the sixth or seventh century. It is a mixture of tradition, myth, and solid historical fact.

MacDonald, J. "Who Instituted the Papal Vicariate of Thessalonica?" *Studia Patristica* 4 (1961): 478-482. A discussion of Siricius' role in the ecclesiastical politics of Illyria in the late fourth century, with references to other, similar studies.

Migne, Jacques Paul, ed. *Patrologiae Cursus Completus: Series Latina.* Vol. 13. Paris: J. P. Migne, 1855. A collection of Siricius' letters, written in Latin.

Pietri, Charles. *Roma christiana: Recherches sur l'Église de Rome, son organisation, sa politique, son idéologie, de Miltiade à Sixte III, 311-440.* 2 vols. Rome: École Français de Rome, 1976. The most complete modern study of the church of Rome during the times of Siricius and his contemporaries. Very extensively annotated with many references to other recent studies of the period.

Ralph W. Mathisen

SOCRATES

Born: c. 470 B.C.; Athens, Greece
Died: 399 B.C.; Athens, Greece
Area of Achievement: Philosophy
Contribution: Socrates combined his professional philosophical life with his private life in an exemplary fashion. He was a leader in the intellectual advancement that drew attention to human and social questions (in addition to physical questions) and bequeathed to posterity the Socratic method of learning by question and answers.

Early Life

The lives of many philosophers are quite undramatic: They write books, they do not lead eventful lives. Yet Socrates is a striking exception. First, he wrote no philosophy at all. He walked through the public places of Athens and engaged people of all types in philosophical discussions. In this way, he came to have many followers, especially among the young. Second, he acquired strong enemies, and eventually his enemies had him condemned to death.

Socrates—who was said to have had a broad, flat nose, bulging eyes, and a paunch—was a powerful and eccentric individual. His philosophy is intensely personal. More than any other philosopher, he successfully united his personal character with his professional career. For Socrates, there was ultimately no difference between his private life and his public career.

Socrates was the son of a stonemason (or sculptor) and a midwife. He does not appear to have spent much time in his father's line of work, although it was traditional for sons to do what their fathers did and Socrates was probably trained in stoneworking. He later claimed that he was following in his mother's footsteps, that he was an intellectual midwife. That is, he said, he assisted other people with the birth of the ideas they carried, while he himself had none. Clearly, he had ideas too; such a statement can be understood as an expression of typical Socratic irony.

Socrates was born, lived, and died in Athens. The only significant amount of time he spent outside the city was during his military service, when he earned a reputation for bravery, steadfastness in battle, and a general toughness of character. While on military campaigns in the northern parts of Greece, he reportedly went barefoot over ice and snow. In Athens, he became known for his unkempt appearance, his moral integrity, his probing questions, his self-control, his ability to outdrink anyone (while not himself becoming drunk), and his use of questions and dialogue in the pursuit of wisdom.

A friend of Socrates once asked the Delphic oracle—which was believed by the Greeks to speak with the divine authority of Apollo—whether anyone was wiser than Socrates. The answer was that no one was wiser. When Socrates heard this, he was confused. The oracle often spoke in riddles, and Socrates wondered what this saying could mean. He believed that he knew nothing and was not wise at all. He went to those who had a reputation for wisdom—to political leaders, authors, and skilled craftsmen—and questioned them. He found, to his surprise, that they really were not wise, although they thought that they were. He reasoned that since they were no wiser than he (as the oracle had said) but he knew nothing except that he was not wise, then they must know even less. Socrates' conclusion was that while others mistakenly believed that they were wise, his own wisdom consisted in knowing that he was not wise.

Life's Work

Socrates was a central figure in the revolution in fifth century Greek thought that turned attention away from the physical world (of stars and eclipses) and toward the human world (of the self, the community, the law). It has been said that Socrates brought philosophy down to earth.

Since Socrates wrote nothing himself, the evidence for his views must be somewhat indirect. Even if other sources are useful, scholars generally agree that the early, or Socratic, dialogues of Plato are the most important sources of information about Socrates' philosophy. Himself one of the foremost philosophers in the Western tradition, Plato was a personal student of Socrates. Moreover, although all the early dialogues were written after the death of Socrates, they were written while many of those who knew him were still alive, and Plato presumably would not paint a false picture of Socrates before the eyes of those who knew him.

The inquiries of Socrates, as represented dramatically in the dialogues of Plato, generally revolve around a particular concept, usually a moral con-

cept. In the dialogue called the *Laches* (399-390 B.C.), for example, Socrates inquires into the definition of courage; in the *Euthyphro* (399-390 B.C.), he asks what piety is; and in the *Theaetetus* (388-366 B.C.), he examines the nature of knowledge. Often, the dialogues follow a pattern. At first, Socrates' partners in conversation are confident of their knowledge of the subject at hand. Socrates claims to seek enlightenment and asks them seemingly simple questions, such as "What is courage?" The speaker gives an example to which the concept applies, but Socrates replies that if the item given is only an example then the speaker should know the larger concept which it represents; he says that it is precisely this relationship between the example and the concept that should be explained. The speaker then considers one definition after another, but Socrates, by a skillful use of questioning, is able to show the speaker that the definitions are unsatisfactory. The speaker often complains that Socrates has robbed him of the confidence he once had. Yet Socrates, although he had been claiming that he only wanted to learn from the speaker, has all the while been orchestrating this very result by

means of his questions. The speaker is led to see for himself that he really does not know what he thought he knew. The speaker, thus divested of false notions, is in a position to become a partner of Socrates in the quest for positive knowledge and wisdom. The ancient Greek term for this sort of question-and-answer testing of ideas is *elenchus*.

It is sometimes noted that in the dialogues Socrates refuses to suggest any positive ideas but only questions others and destroys their views (and sometimes their composure). Indeed, that is often the case. Yet there are some positive views that Socrates is willing to defend. For example, he defends the thesis that virtue is knowledge, and thus that all wrongdoing stems from ignorance, and he claims that it is far more important to care for one's soul than for one's body. These statements require some explanation, however, especially in their English and other non-Greek versions.

Socrates and other Greeks asked "What is virtue?" The Greek word that is generally translated as "virtue" is *aretē*. Another translation for this term is "excellence." (Virtue is a poor translation if it suggests ideas such as Christian charity, humility, and the like, since Socrates lived prior to Christianity and the Greeks themselves did not greatly admire charity and humility.) It was Socrates' belief, then, that human excellence consists in knowledge. If a person knew what was the best thing to do, for example, then the person would do it. Some critics have objected that this idea might be true for Socrates, who had great self-control, but that other, more ordinary people might see one course of action as superior to another and yet choose to do that which was not superior. The other side of the coin, according to Socrates, is that if a person has done something wrong, then it must be concluded that the person did not have the knowledge that what was being done was wrong. All wrongdoing, Socrates holds, is really the result of ignorance.

Socrates continually compares questions about man's nature, the purpose of life, and the nature of virtue (or excellence) to considerably more down-to-earth and sometimes humble questions. He discusses carpenters, shoemakers, horse trainers, and others. One could say that Socrates' discussions are dominated by a craft analogy. For example, the shoemaker's function is to make shoes, and he fulfills his function well when he makes good shoes. The shoemaker must know what he is doing; otherwise, he will probably produce poor shoes. Similarly, a person must know what his business in life is. "Know thyself," a Greek saying inscribed on the temple walls of Delphi, was a prominent theme of Socrates. He is also credited with saying that for a human being "the unexamined life is not worth living." A person will be an excellent human being only if that person subjects his life to examination and attains self-knowledge. Like excellence in shoemaking, excellence in human life is indeed an achievement, and it follows upon training from others and self-discipline from within.

Finally, Socrates believed that the disposition of the soul is more important than the body or any material thing. The word translated as "soul" here is the Greek *psychē*. Other translations might be "inner self" or "mind." It is the inner self that Socrates sees as inhabiting the body, just as a body can be thought of as inhabiting clothes. This *psychē*, or inner self—and not the appetites or passions or demands of the physical body—is what should give direction to one's life.

In 399, Socrates was tried in Athens on two charges: for not worshipping the Athenian gods (and introducing new divinities) and for corrupting the young. The first charge was unfair. It was a standard charge used to persecute threatening individuals, but Socrates had in fact been rather faithful in his observance of local religious customs. The only grain of truth in the charge was that he did claim to hear a voice within him—a daimon, or supernatural voice, that warned him not to do certain things. (The voice never encouraged actions, but sometimes stopped Socrates when he considered doing or saying something.) Yet Socrates and his fellow Greeks believed in many such divine signs and had little trouble accepting oracles and dreams as bearers of supernatural messages. The inner voice of Socrates did not replace the traditional gods; rather, it was supposed to be an additional source of divine messages.

The second charge was quite serious and, in some respects, plausible. As youths, Alcibiades, Critias, and Charmides had heard Socrates. As men, Alcibiades became a ruthless traitor and opportunist, and Critias and Charmides overthrew Athenian democracy (for a time) with a violent revolution, instituting a bloodthirsty regime. Moreover, Socrates himself had been a vocal critic of democracy.

It could be that this last charge was only a case of guilt by association. Socrates was not responsible for the fact that a few of his students proved troublesome. He certainly did not encourage vio-lent revolution and bloodthirstiness; he stressed argument and discussion. In fact his criticism of Athenian democracy reflects this very point. He criticized the way Athenian democracy awarded some positions by lot (as potential jurors are selected even today) and some by vote. The random lottery method is unreasonable precisely because it is not responsive to argument. In general, Socrates believed that those who know, those who are wise, should rule. Why should a community leave important social and political decisions in the hands of voters—who may well be ignorant and are likely to be swayed by their own self-interest or by smooth-talking politicians—rather than in the hands of those who have wisdom and knowledge?

At his trial, Socrates was not contrite. He asserted that he would never stop asking his questions, the questions that some Athenians found so bothersome, and refused to accept the idea that he be banished to another place. He would stay in Athens and would remain who and what he was. The jury condemned him to death by drinking hemlock.

While Socrates was being held in prison, but before he was to drink the hemlock, he was visited by a friend who proposed to get him out of prison—bribing the guards if necessary—and to arrange for him to live at some distance beyond the reach of Athenian law. Socrates investigated this option with his usual methods and concluded that there were better arguments in favor of conforming to the legal judgment and drinking the hemlock—which, when the time came, he did.

Summary

To the philosophers who came after him, Socrates not only left the example of his life but also a new sort of inquiry (that is, social inquiry) and a new way of pursuing that inquiry, namely through the use of the Socratic method of question and answer.

Several schools of philosophers claiming to follow Socrates arose after his death. One of the best known, Cynicism, took up the view that virtue is an inner knowledge that has nothing to do with externals, such as material things or even other people. Diogenes, the most prominent Cynic, rejected conventional values and is said to have lived in a tub. He claimed that the life of the dog ("Cynic" comes from a Greek word that means "like a dog"), free and unfettered by human conventions, was a good model for the natural life. The Cynics invented the concept of the cosmopolitan (citizen of the cosmos or universe) when they claimed allegiance only to the universe at large and not to particular humanly instituted and local political units—such as Athens.

The Cyrenaics, also claiming to follow Socrates, held that inner, subjective experiences were far more important for life than the existence and nature of external objects. From this view, they derived the conclusion that the best life was one that was directed by subjective feelings of pleasure and pain. This school practiced a form of hedonism that was in many respects at odds with Cynicism. The Megarics, another minor Socratic school, practiced the art of refutation, which they modeled after Socrates' destructive criticism of the views of others. In this way, several schools of thought emerged, at variance with one another but all claiming to follow Socrates. One could say that each school followed some strands of thought in Socrates but that no school was able to capture him completely.

That is one reason that Socrates remains a giant in philosophy. It is possible to go back to the stories of his life and practice many times and each time discover some new aspect or line of thought. Moreover, the Socratic method of inquiry can be used by those less wise than the giant himself. Each new generation is enabled by this method to question received opinion, alleged wisdom, and even its own values.

Socrates said that he was a gadfly who stimulated his fellows to think more clearly. This applies both to his fellow citizens in Athens and to his fellow philosophers, or seekers after wisdom. With respect to his fellow citizens, it might be said that Socrates failed, since in the end they turned on him and had him condemned to death. With respect to philosophers who have come after Socrates, however, it could well be said that his mission has proved successful, for he has had a permanent effect on the direction of philosophy, an effect that can never be undone.

Bibliography

Brickhouse, Thomas C. *Plato's Socrates*. New York: Oxford University Press, 1995. A detailed analysis of Socrates's philosophy, heavily supported by reference to Plato's early dialogues. Unabashedly discloses some of Socrates's typical philosophical inconsistencies, providing new and often convincing resolutions to them. Presents him as a sober thinker, and more conventional than usually supposed in matters of religion.

Guthrie, W. K. *Socrates*. London: Cambridge University Press, 1971. This work, which was originally published as part of volume 3 of Guthrie's *History of Greek Philosophy* (1969), is a thorough and scholarly treatment of Socrates' life, character, philosophy, and influence.

Kraut, Richard. *Socrates and the State*. Princeton, N.J.: Princeton University Press, 1984. Focuses on Socrates' rationale for not escaping from prison and from an unjust sentence. Kraut seeks to refute the contention that Socrates was a political authoritarian who believed that all laws must be obeyed without regard to consequences.

Plato. *The Last Days of Socrates*. Translated by Hugh Tredennick. London and Baltimore: Penguin, 1954. The translator provides an introduction and notes, but this work is mainly a rendering into English of four of Plato's Socratic dialogues, including Socrates' speech at his trial, his conversation in prison, and his last conversations and death.

Reeve, C.D.C. *Socrates in the Apology: An Essay on Plato's Apology of Socrates*. Indianapolis: Hackett, 1989. Convincingly reconstructs Socrates's philosophy and directly addresses some of the interpretive problems presented by the text. Presents the speech as a earnest defense aimed at his acquittal. Concise and well-reasoned, with consistent reference to recent scholarly literature.

Santas, Gerasimos X. *Socrates: Philosophy in Plato's Early Dialogues*. London: Routledge, 1978; Boston: Routledge, 1979. A contribution to the Arguments of the Philosophers series, this volume emphasizes the logical reconstruction of the arguments of Socrates and sometimes uses formal logical symbolism. The book focuses on the Socratic method and Socrates' views on ethics.

Stone, I. F. *The Trial of Socrates*. London: Cape, and Boston: Little, Brown, 1988. Stone attempts to get behind the scenes at the trial of Socrates. He aims to show that political motivations, largely stemming from Socrates' negative attitude toward democracy and his friendships with those who supported a contrary regime, were powerfully at work in the trial, even though they were not openly acknowledged.

Vlastos, Gregory, ed. *The Philosophy of Socrates: A Collection of Critical Essays*. New York: Doubleday, 1971. A wide-ranging collection of articles by scholars in Socrates' philosophy. Consideration is given to the problem of the reliability of the various ancient sources for Socrates' views, the thesis that virtue is knowledge, and problems associated with the Socratic denial that one can do wrong willingly and knowingly.

————. *Socrates, Ironist and Moral Philosopher*. Ithaca, N.Y.: Cornell University Press, 1991. Emphasizes what Vlastos calls the strangeness of Socrates. Addresses his peculiar combination of ironic detachment and erotic feeling, his intolerance of stupidity and his religious side, while still stressing the importance of his rationalism. Also illuminates his moral radicalism and his espousal of eudaimonism (the theory that right actions produce happiness).

Zeller, Eduard. *Socrates and the Socratic Schools*. 3d ed. London: Longmans, Green, 1885; New York: Russell and Russell, 1962. A reissue of a translation of the work on Socrates by Zeller, a renowned nineteenth century German scholar of Greek philosophy. A thorough investigation of the background of Socrates' life, his character, his methods of inquiry, his philosophical positions, and his influence on various ancient groups that claimed to be following in his footsteps.

Stephen Satris

SOLOMON

Born: c. 991 B.C.; Jerusalem, Israel

Died: 930 B.C.; Jerusalem, Israel

Areas of Achievement: Government and religion

Contribution: Through the application of his famous wisdom and the construction of the Temple, Solomon not only made a major contribution to the Judeo-Christian tradition but also forged the twelve tribes of Israel into a true nation, giving them an identity that would survive succeeding dispersions and persecutions.

Early Life

Solomon was the second child born to King David and Bathsheba and the fifth of David's sons. Although the sources are silent about Solomon's childhood, it is known that the prophet Nathan, who had enormous court influence, was his tutor. Accordingly, Solomon would have received a very thorough grounding in Jewish civil and religious teachings. His position at the court was enhanced by his mother, a remarkably intelligent figure with great influence over the king.

Although David had promised the throne to Solomon, David's eldest surviving son, Adonijah, harbored the ambition to be king, an ambition that to him seemed perfectly justifiable. His older brothers, Amnon, Absalom, and Chileab, had died, so should not the throne naturally devolve to the next oldest son? In order for him to secure the throne for himself, Adonijah needed allies. Through intrigue, he gained the support of his other brothers and of Joab, the commander of the army, and Abiathar, the high priest in Jerusalem. These were powerful people, but Solomon had an even more potent group backing his claim. These included Zadok, the high priest at Gilbeah, Benaiah, commander of David's mercenaries (David's "Mighty Men," who had fought with him since the king's early days and had never lost a campaign), Nathan, and Bathsheba.

To have any hope of success, Adonijah, then, had to act boldly before Solomon was consecrated king. As David lay on his sickbed, Adonijah, with an escort of fifty men and his supporters, had himself anointed king in the royal gardens at Enrogel. Nathan quickly learned of this and, alarmed, informed Bathsheba. It was vital that David reaffirm his oath concerning Solomon and have him anointed king immediately, or Solomon and his supporters would be killed. Confronted by Nathan and Bathsheba with Adonijah's acts, David ordered Benaiah and the royal troops to escort Solomon on the king's donkey and to have him anointed king by Zadok. When Adonijah and his followers realized that this had occurred, their coup attempt collapsed. His guests scattered, and Adonijah fled to the sanctuary altar and would not leave until Solomon promised not to harm him.

Solomon was now king. Shortly before David died, he advised Solomon on how to deal with his enemies, counseling him to stay true to the Lord's commandments. It was useful advice, for Adonijah quickly tried another tactic. Through Bathsheba, he asked Solomon's permission to marry Abishag, who was a member of David's harem. If this marriage were permitted, it would establish Adonijah's rightful claim to the throne. Solomon reacted swiftly. Adonijah was immediately executed, as was Joab. Abiathar was removed from his priestly office and exiled to Anathoth, fulfilling the prophecy regarding Eli's descendants (1 Sam. 2:27-37). Three years later, Shimei, an opponent whom Solomon had confined to Jerusalem, violated the terms of his punishment and was executed.

Life's Work

With his throne now secure, Solomon could concentrate on consolidating his kingdom, in order to secure the empire that his father had created. To achieve this end, Solomon initiated a sophisticated program based on three policies: There would be no further territorial conquests for the Israelite Empire, he would take advantage of the economic opportunities presented by Israel's strategic location, and he would build the Temple in Jerusalem to provide a unifying political and spiritual focal point for his people.

Although there were no significant foreign threats during his reign, Solomon realized that to attain his goals he needed to secure his borders through a combination of peaceful dealings with his neighbors and a modernized army at home. Accordingly, he launched a bold foreign policy initiative: an alliance with Egypt. After some difficult negotiations, the alliance was confirmed by Solomon's marriage to Pharaoh Siamon's daughter—a clear indication of the importance Egypt gave to the alliance, for Egyptian princesses were rarely given in marriage to foreign potentates. Solomon

received the fortified city of Gezer as a dowry after the pharaoh had taken and plundered it. The land route for the transport of goods from Phoenicia to Egypt thus secured was mutually beneficial for Egypt and Israel. The main advantage with which this alliance provided Solomon, however, was that it gave him access to Egypt's building expertise and military technology: chariots, horses, and technical advisers to train the Israelites in their proper use.

Solomon could now proceed to modernize his army. This involved creating a large chariot force of fourteen hundred chariots and twelve thousand horsemen and constructing forts with stables at strategic points around the kingdom. For example, excavations at the thirteen-acre site at Megiddo, which controlled the vital highway running through the Plain of Esdraelon between Egypt and Syria, show that this fortress could house 450 horses and 150 chariots. Similar fortresses were apparently built at Beth-horon, Baalath, Hamath-zobah, and Tadmor.

Solomon also cemented relations with Hiram of Tyre. Tyre was a vital maritime city with colonies in Cyprus, Sicily, Sardinia, and southern Spain. Hemmed in by the Lebanon Mountains, Tyre had to depend on commerce for survival. Solomon needed cedar lumber as well as skilled artisans and architects from Tyre for his building projects; in return, Hiram received food and protection for his city.

Solomon's political program required not only safe borders backed by a military force capable of protecting important trade routes but also a firm revenue base. To meet this need, Solomon divided the nation into twelve districts. The official in charge of each district had to provide the supplies for the central government for one month of the year. The rest of the time, he collected and stored the necessary provisions. The required items for a single day's supply for the king and his court are enumerated in 1 Kings 4:22-23; though the list appears excessive, it is similar to the daily victual lists for other kingdoms in Mesopotamia.

Central to Solomon's overall policy was his building program. He built not only forts and cities but also ports, mines, highways, and shipyards. Solomon is most famous, however, for two major projects completed by the middle of his reign: the construction of the royal palace and of the Temple. These two undertakings played a major role in his plan of consolidation. The palace, which in addi-

tion to the king's personal residence included the complex of buildings housing the various governmental offices, took thirteen years to complete. Cedar, gold, ivory, and silver were liberally used; the resulting grandeur would have been a source of national pride. The building that was the cornerstone of Solomon's political program, however, was the Temple.

The erection of the Temple was the most important event in the Israelites' religious history since they had left the Sinai; accordingly, Solomon must have overseen every detail of construction. With a work force of 150,000 men, the project took seven years. The Bible gives a very detailed description of the finished Temple. Though it was once thought that it was a unique structure in the ancient world, recent archaeological finds have revealed that the Temple was quite similar to other temples in Mesopotamia.

It is difficult to overstate the deep significance of the Temple for Israel. Moses had prophesied that a kingdom would be created; with the construction of the Temple, divine confirmation of the Davidic throne was established. Thus, Solomon, by the act of building the Temple, firmly cemented his mandate to rule. Further, by placing the ark in the Temple, he focused the religious fervor of his people on the Temple, making Jerusalem their holy city and their national center. Solomon also was able to control the Temple and therefore gained a reputation for piety.

While the Bible says much about the Temple, it gives little space to discussion of the commercial ventures of Solomon. These played a significant part, however, in financing his other programs, and archaeological evidence indicates that they were extensive. Solomon was the middleman in the region's lucrative horse and chariot market. His involvement in and control of the major caravan routes passing through the Negev have been well documented. Excavations at Ezion-geber have shown that Solomon was also very involved in shipping and shipbuilding. His ships carried copper and iron ore (and their related products) dug from his mines throughout the Wadi al-'Araba (biblical Arabah) as far as Yemen and Ethiopia, returning with gold, silver, ivory, and monkeys.

His shrewd commercial activities made Solomon incredibly wealthy. Anxious to meet this legendary and successful king, other rulers came to Jerusalem bearing gifts and riches to establish relations with Solomon. The Queen of Sheba may have come to learn his wisdom, but she also wanted to create trade relations with Israel.

Solomon's power and grandeur were believed to have arisen from his exceptional wisdom. The Bible states that immediately after Solomon assumed the throne, the Lord, appearing to him in a dream, granted his request for wisdom and added that he would also receive riches, honor, and long life, as long as he obeyed the Lord's commandments. Eventually, Solomon became world renowned for his sagacity. His decision regarding the two women fighting over the custody of one living child is an example of his judicial wisdom. Because Solomon's reign was a time of peace, literature and scholarship flourished; much of Israel's history, up to that point preserved orally, was set down in writing during this period. Solomon himself is credited with the authorship of the Song of Songs, the Book of Proverbs, and Ecclesiastes. While there is some question regarding Solomon's authorship of the Song of Songs, there is little doubt that he did write most of Proverbs, and the weight of evidence leans toward him as the author of Ecclesiastes. These works of genius, stamped with the character of Solomon, reveal a deep spiritual insight and have formed a vital part of the Judeo-Christian tradition.

Summary

The final years of Solomon's reign present an interesting historical problem. Chapter 11 of 1 Kings makes it clear that Solomon, King of Israel, recipient of godly wisdom, vast wealth, and international recognition, ended his reign amid predictions of failure. Indeed, immediately after his death, the kingdom was split into the kingdoms of Israel and Judah. Some of the causes that have been advanced to explain the stresses that finally fractured Solomon's empire include the increasing bureaucratization of government, the excessive taxes needed to support Solomon's programs, the use of Israelites for forced labor, the unequal distribution of wealth, and the Israelites' inability to identify fully with their king's vision of a united Israelite state. According to the biblical interpretation, however, these problems were only symptoms of the disease. The root cause was Solomon's religious apostasy.

Early in his reign Solomon had followed the Lord's commandments, but eventually he fell into disobedience in two important areas. First, he violated the command not to take foreign wives (Deut. 17:17). At the height of his power he reputedly had seven hundred wives and three hundred concubines. The wives were usually taken for diplomatic or political reasons, but concubines were given as sexual gifts that Solomon could have refused but did not. These wives and concubines were his downfall, for in his efforts to please them, Solomon fell into idolatry.

Solomon not only tolerated idolatry but indeed officially recognized it. He gave official sanction for the worship of the fertility goddess Ashtoreth (Astarte) and constructed altars near Jerusalem for the worship of Moloch and Chemosh. During his reign, a valley just outside Jerusalem became known as the site of child sacrifices to Moloch; its name, Gê Hinnom, in later years was rendered Gehenna, which became a synonym for the word "hell."

Such religious apostasy, then, clearly moved Solomon away from the sound principles of rule that had governed the first half of his reign and induced him to adopt methods that in the eyes of his people undermined the legitimacy of his vision of a permanent, unified state. As a result, Solomon suffered rebellion at home by Jeroboam, son of Nebat, and the loss of various parts of his realm, and the welfare and prosperity of the kingdom would be endangered.

Despite his failings, however, Solomon was a great king. Without his efforts, one of the great achievements of history would have been impossible: that despite unprecedented persecutions, invasions, and sufferings, the Jews would retain their distinct national identity. Furthermore, Solomon's contributions to the Old Testament have proved to be a valuable legacy to countless generations and must be counted as one of the pillars of Western civilization.

Bibliography

Barker, Kenneth, ed. *The New International Version Study Bible*. Grand Rapids, Mich.: Zondervan Bible Publishers, 1985. In this edition, each book is preceded by a detailed introduction, and there are verse-by-verse explanations on each page. There are also indexes, essays, notes, time lines, colored maps, and charts. For an excellent archaeological supplement, see the *Thompson Chain-Reference Bible*, also published by Zondervan.

Beers, V. Gilbert. *The Book of Life*. Vol. 12, *The Nation Divides*. Grand Rapids, Mich.: Zondervan Bible Publishers, 1980. Beers combines the accounts of 1 Kings and 2 Chronicles to provide a cogent picture of Solomon and his times. Excellent photographs, illustrations, and text bring the period and people alive for the reader. A superior introduction to the topic.

Maly, Eugene H. *The World of David and Solomon*. Englewood Cliffs, N.J.: Prentice-Hall, 1966. Consistently cited by later works, this book makes excellent use of twentieth century archaeological findings and interpretations. It is designed to be read by people not well acquainted with the Bible; the author's style is scholarly yet accessible. The chapter on Solomon provides valuable insights into his political program and commercial activities. Brief bibliography at the conclusion of each chapter; contains an index.

Schultz, Samuel J. *The Old Testament Speaks: Old Testament History and Literature*. 4th ed. New York: Harper and Row, Publishers, 1990. This is an outstanding book in which to begin one's research on Solomon. The author fully comprehends the deep significance of the spiritual aspect of Solomon and his reign. Makes use of other scholarly works and archaeological revelations to fill in the biblical gaps. His discussion of Solomon's decline is highly perceptive. Short bibliography at the conclusion of each chapter; indexed.

Thieberger, Friedrich. *King Solomon*. Oxford: East and West Library, 1947; New York: East and West Library, 1978. One of the few books in English that focus exclusively on Solomon. The author did not have the benefit of later archaeological discoveries, but he does depend greatly on the extensive textual research into the Old Testament that was done in Germany in the late nineteenth and the first third of the twentieth centuries. For that alone the book is worthwhile. It is well written, with excellent detail and interesting interpretations. Extensive notes and index.

Ronald F. Smith

SOLON

Born: c. 630 B.C.; probably Athens, Greece
Died: c. 560 B.C.; probably Athens, Greece
Areas of Achievement: Government, law, and literature
Contribution: Through his law code, Solon averted a civil war at Athens and established the political and social foundations for the development of classical Athenian democracy.

Early Life

The ancient sources include many details about Solon's life before 594 B.C., but most of these are probably romantic inventions about what the life of a great man ought to have been like. The fragments of Solon's own poems tell little about his early life. Plutarch, in his biography of Solon (c. A.D. 105-115), writes that Solon's mother was the cousin of the mother of Peisistratus, the tyrant of Athens who ruled between 561 and 527 B.C. This is one of many probably spurious attempts to link Solon's and Peisistratus' families. There is a stronger argument that Solon's father was Execestides, a member of one of Athens' noblest families. Execestides could trace his ancestry back to Codrus, a semilegendary king of Athens, and even to Poseidon, a wholly legendary god. Plutarch maintains that Execestides exhausted his wealth through lavish gift giving and that Solon traveled widely as a trader to recoup his fortunes, even though there were many Athenians who would have repaid his father's gifts. Another possibility mentioned by Plutarch is that Solon traveled solely to visit foreign lands.

Solon won a reputation as a poet, and several of his works are quoted at length by Plutarch and in the *Athenaiōn politeia* (c. 335-323 B.C.; *The Athenian Constitution*), attributed to Aristotle. Many early Greek statesmen were poets; poetry had an important role in politics, and Plutarch writes that Solon used his verse to catapult himself into political prominence, probably around 610. Plutarch further relates that Solon used a ruse to be put in charge of a war against Megara to win back the island of Salamis. The Athenians were so humiliated by their defeat some years before that they passed a law forbidding anyone even to mention their claim to Salamis. Solon circumvented this restriction by feigning insanity and then publicly reciting poems urging revenge. The Athenians were inspired by this act and soon won the island back. Like many

other incidents in Solon's early life, however, this story may be attributing to Solon events which really happened later in the sixth century.

According to a second story, around 600 Solon had the Alcmaeonid family put on trial for the massacre of the followers of Cylon, who staged an unsuccessful coup in Athens in the 630's. The murders had ritually polluted Athens, and Solon supposedly brought in the semilegendary seer Epimenides of Crete to help purify the state. Yet it is quite likely that this event was made up to provide a Solonian precedent for the expulsion of the Alcmaeonids during political strife around 500. A third account links Solon to the possibly fictitious First Sacred War in the 590's, fought for control of the oracle at Delphi.

Life's Work

Whatever the truth of these stories about political crises, one thing is certain: Around 600, Athens was torn by social unrest. In the words of Aristotle:

> For a long time there was strife between the rich and the poor. For the state was oligarchic in all ways, and the poor, along with their wives and children, were enslaved to the rich. And they were called "clients" and "sixth-parters," for it was at this rate that they worked the fields of the rich. All the land belonged to a few people; and if the poor did not render these dues, they and their children could be sold overseas. And before Solon, all loans were made on the security of the person; but he became the first champion of the people.

Fearing civil war, the Athenian nobles elected Solon chief magistrate (archon) in 594, to draw up new laws to avert the crisis.

Other than Solon's own poems, which are often obscure, the earliest source for his laws is Herodotus' *Historiai Herodotou* (c. 425 B.C.; *The History*), which simply mentions that "at the request of his countrymen he had made a code of laws for Athens." Yet Solon's laws were publicly displayed on wooden boards, and it is believed that these boards survived for later writers such as Aristotle to consult. The laws fall into three main groups: economic reforms, political reforms, and other laws.

In an economic reform known as the "shaking off of burdens" (*seisachtheia*), Solon cancelled all debts and forbade enslavement for debt. He said he would try to bring back to Athens all those who

had been sold as slaves overseas. He also addressed land tenure, removing from the soil certain markers called *horoi*, which probably stood on mortgaged fields. The meaning of the *horoi* is unclear, but by this act Solon claimed "I have made free the dark earth, which was enslaved." These reforms led to the disappearance of the serflike statuses of "clients" and "sixth-parters." Solon is also credited with a reform of weights, measures, and coinage, but that is probably a later fabrication (coinage only appeared at Athens circa 550 B.C.).

Solon also instituted political reforms. He divided the adult male population into four groups, based on the annual agricultural production of their land. The top class, the "five hundred bushel men" (*pentakosiomedimnoi*) monopolized the highest political offices. The next class was called the *hippeis* or "knights," who could produce three hundred to five hundred bushels, and the third class was the *zeugitai* ("infantrymen," or perhaps "yoke men"), who could produce two hundred to three hundred bushels. These two groups could hold lesser political offices. Below them were the *thetes* (usually translated as "laborers," although most of

these men probably owned some land), who could vote in the assembly and sit in the law courts but not hold office.

It is difficult to uncover the details of other political reforms because of later fabrications. In 403, the Athenians were forced by the Spartans to abandon their democracy and to return to an undefined "ancestral constitution." In the years that followed, various Athenians tried to project their own political programs back onto past statesmen, claiming that their own ideology was taken from the ancestral constitution. Solon was commonly said to have founded the democracy. According to Aristotle, Solon established the Council of Four Hundred to prepare measures to be voted on by the assembly of all citizens and set up the law courts as the central democratic organ. These institutions are uncannily like those of the fourth century B.C. and were possibly falsely attributed to Solon by propagandists at that time.

Solon is said to have legislated on all aspects of life, from mourning at funerals to the placing of trees near field boundaries and the digging of wells. While some of the laws attributed to him can be proved to have originated centuries later, the scope of his code reflects the general tendency of early Greek lawgivers to assume responsibility for every dimension of life.

According to his own notes, Solon had enough support to set himself up as a tyrant over Athens, but because of his moderation, he chose not to do so. This moderation made his position difficult after 594: The poor demanded a complete redistribution of land, which he resisted, while the rich believed that he had already relinquished too much power. It is said that he left Athens for ten years of travel, making the Athenians agree not to tamper with his laws while he was away. Similar stories are attributed to other early Greek lawgivers, however, and this story may be no more than a literary flourish.

Summary

Solon's moderation probably saved Athens from a self-destructive civil war. The greatness of his achievement was recognized in his status as one of the so-called Seven Sages of early Greece. He did not resolve all Athens' social, economic, and political troubles (unrest continued during the sixth century), but he did lay the foundations on which Athenian greatness was built. By freeing the poor from their serflike status and from the threat of bondage resulting from debt, he provided the basis of a relatively unified citizen body. His time also marked the beginning of one of the great paradoxes of Athenian society: the interdependence of democracy and slavery. Legally unable to reduce fellow Athenians to bondsmen after 594, wealthy men were forced to look elsewhere for labor to work their fields, workshops, and mines and began to import increasing numbers of non-Greeks, mainly from the Black Sea area, as chattel slaves. By the fifth century B.C., as much as one quarter of the resident population of Athens may have been slaves completely lacking civil rights.

Solon is one of the most important figures in Greek history, but also one of the most obscure, hidden beneath layers of later fabrications. Almost no detail in his biography is beyond question, but his overall contribution—averting civil war and setting Athens on the path to democratic rule—was a decisive one.

Bibliography

Andrewes, Anthony. "The Growth of the Athenian State." In *The Cambridge Ancient History.* Vol. 3, part 3, *The Prehistory of the Balkans, and the Middle East and the Aegean World, Tenth to Eighth Centuries B.C.* 2d ed. Cambridge and New York: Cambridge University Press, 1982. A concise and balanced assessment of the literary sources for the political and social development of the Athenian state, from the earliest times to the reforms of Solon. *The Cambridge Ancient History* is the standard reference work for Greek history.

Aristotle. *"The Athenian Constitution."* Translated by P. J. Rhodes. London and New York: Penguin Books, 1984. Fine translation, with excellent introduction and notes, of one of the main sources for Solon's reforms. Rhodes is the leading authority on this text, and his rendering is readable and reliable. This work was one of a collection of 158 constitutions of ancient states written by Aristotle and his students.

Edmonds, John Maxwell. *Greek Elegy and Iambus.* Vol. 1. Cambridge, Mass.: Harvard University Press, and London: Heinemann, 1931. Parallel edition of the original Greek texts with a fairly literal translation of all the surviving fragments of several early Greek poets' works, including Solon. A few new fragments have been found and new readings made, but this volume remains the most convenient collection.

Finley, Moses I. *The Ancestral Constitution.* London: Cambridge University Press, 1971. Finley's sparkling inaugural lecture at Cambridge, reprinted in his work *The Use and Abuse of History* (1975), looks at the reinterpretation and invention of Solonian laws in Athens around 400 B.C. and compares this practice to similar distortions of past politics in seventeenth century England and early twentieth century United States.

————. *Ancient Slavery and Modern Ideology.* New York: Viking Press, and London: Chatto and Windus, 1980. Reprint. Harmondsworth, England: Pelican Books, 1983. Brilliant discussion of modern attitudes toward ancient slavery and the logic of slave economies, including an analysis of the relationships between Solon's reforms and the rise of both slavery and the ideology of citizen equality in ancient Athens. Finley goes on to compare Solon's laws to similar developments in fifth century B.C. Rome.

Forrest, William George Grieve. *The Emergence of Greek Democracy: 800-400 B.C.* New York: McGraw-Hill, and London: Weidenfeld and Nicolson, 1966. Classic, beautifully written, and well-illustrated overview of the rise of democratic institutions in Athens, setting the Solonian agrarian crisis in the context of similar problems in a number of other states in seventh century Greece.

Gallant, T. W. "Agricultural Systems, Land Tenure, and the Reforms of Solon." *Annual of the British School of Archaeology at Athens* 77 (1982): 111-124. A sophisticated discussion of the archaeological data relating to Solon's economic reforms, drawing on comparative anthropological evidence from modern societies facing similar problems of agrarian debt. With an extensive bibliography.

Hignett, Charles. *A History of the Athenian Constitution.* Oxford: Clarendon, 1952. A very detailed study of constitutional developments. Hignett works within the very critical tradition of nineteenth century German scholarship and offers penetrating discussions of the sources. He is best known for his attempt to date Solon's reforms to the 570's.

Murray, Oswyn. *Early Greece.* 2d ed. London: Fontana, and Cambridge, Mass.: Harvard University Press, 1993. General and highly readable account of Greek history from 800 to 480 B.C., combining the literary and archaeological evidence with judicious use of comparative material. Highly recommended as an introductory text.

Plutarch. *The Rise and Fall of Athens.* Translated by Ian Scott-Kilvert. London and Boston: Penguin Books, 1960. Translations of nine of Plutarch's lives, including that of Solon, along with a brief introduction. Solon was of interest to Plutarch mainly as a moral example. His writing includes many clearly fictional elements but has remained popular through the ages for its lively style and content.

Woodhouse, W. J. *Solon the Liberator.* London: Oxford University Press, 1938; New York: Octagon Books, 1965. Rather dated, but still one of the best critical analyses of the ancient literary evidence for Solon's economic reforms. Particularly strong on the range of meanings of some of the obscure words (for example, *misthosis, hektemoros,* and *horos*) in Solon's poems and Aristotle's account of the unrest in seventh century Athens.

Ian Morris

SOPHOCLES

Born: c. 496 B.C.; Colonus, near Athens, Greece
Died: 406 B.C.; Athens, Greece
Area of Achievement: Literature
Contribution: One of the most important ancient Greek tragedians, Sophocles was an innovative and skilled master of character development and dramatic irony.

Early Life

Sophocles' life is known from a variety of ancient sources but especially from an Alexandrian biography included in the manuscript tradition of his plays. The playwright was born about 496 B.C. in Colonus, a suburb of Athens, which Sophocles commemorated in his last play, *Oidipous epi Kolōnōi* (401 B.C.; *Oedipus at Colonus*). His father, Sophilus, was a wealthy industrialist who owned many slaves and operated a prosperous weapons factory. The young Sophocles was given a good education. He won several prizes in school for music and wrestling, and his music teacher, Lamprus, was famous for a sobriety and restraint in composition which would later be noted in the style of his student.

The childhood of Sophocles parallels his city's long conflict with Persia, which began shortly after his birth with Darius' invasion, continued with Darius' defeat at the Battle of Marathon in 490, and climaxed in 480 with Xerxes' capture of Athens and defeat in the sea battle of Salamis. Sophocles was probably too young to have seen action at Salamis, but his family status—as well as his own personal talent and beauty—may account for his selection as a chorus leader in the public celebration which followed Athens' unexpected defeat of the Persian fleet.

Record of Sophocles' dramatic career begins in 468, when he entered an annual competition at Athens with a group of plays. It is not known if the young Sophocles was competing for the first time in this year, but his victory over the established playwright Aeschylus at this festival must have raised a sensation among the Athenians, especially if, as is recorded, the officiating public servant requested Cimon and nine other generals to replace the judges usually chosen by lot. Sophocles did not compete in the following year, but a papyrus fragment discovered in the twentieth century suggests that in 463 Sophocles was defeated by Aeschylus, who produced his Danaid trilogy.

Sophocles performed in many of his earlier plays, none of which survives. His appearance as the ball-playing heroine in one play and his lyre playing in another are recorded in his ancient biography. Later in his career, Sophocles abandoned such performances, perhaps because his voice was weakening or because the roles of actor and playwright became increasingly specialized in the second half of the fifth century.

Life's Work

The second half of Sophocles' life was dedicated to public service, both in the theater and in government. In general, the several civic offices held by the mature Sophocles are better documented than are the dates of Sophocles' extant tragedies. The most difficult extant plays to put in a chronology are probably *Aias* (*Ajax*), datable on stylistic grounds to about 448 to 445, and *Trachinai* (*The Women of Trachis*), usually placed somewhere between 435 and 429.

In 443 or 442, Sophocles served as a *Hellenotamias*, one of the financial officials in the Delian League of the Athenian empire. This appointment may have been the result of the great wealth of Sophocles' family. It may also be attributable to the well-known patriotism of Sophocles, who did not follow the example of many contemporary artists, including Aeschylus and Euripides, in leaving Athens for the court of a foreign patron.

In 441 or 440, Sophocles was elected to serve as general along with the great Athenian leader Pericles during the rebellion of Athens' ally Samos. Since the ancient *hypothesis*, or introduction, to *Antigonē* (441; *Antigone*) says that his election was encouraged by the success of this play, Sophocles' military service is often considered to have been more honorary than practical, but it is almost certain that the playwright traveled with the fleet on the campaign.

In 438, Sophocles was back in Athens, where he defeated Euripides' entry, including *Alkēstis* (438; *Alcestis*), with an unrecorded group of plays. Sometime in this decade Sophocles may also have produced a group of plays, now lost, although it is doubtful that these plays were connected thematically in the same way that the plays of Aeschylus' *Oresteia* (458 B.C.) were linked. When Euripides' *Mēdeia* (431; *Medea*) was defeated in a competition of 431 by Euphorion, the son of Aeschylus,

Sophocles received second place with unknown plays.

Shortly after the beginning of Athens' long conflict with Sparta known as the Peloponnesian War and following the Athenian plague recorded in the histories of Thucydides, Sophocles produced his most famous play, *Oidipous Tyrannos* (*Oedipus Tyrannus*), probably in 429, and was voted second place to Philocles, the nephew of Aeschylus. In the following year Sophocles made no production, and around 427 he was probably elected general again, this time with Nicias.

A combination of patriotism and piety may have again motivated Sophocles in 420 to help introduce to Athens the worship of Asclepius, the deified physician and son of Apollo. Sophocles is also known to have composed for Asclepius a paean, or hymn of praise, which survives in fragments. The playwright was also a priest of Halon, a hero connected ritually with Asclepius, and was honored after his death with Halon's epithet, *dexion*, or "receiver."

Based on comparison with Euripides' *Ēlektra* (413; *Electra*), Sophocles' extant play of the same name is variously dated by scholars between 420 and 410, except for 415, when Sophocles made no entry in the dramatic competitions. In the same decade, the octogenarian Sophocles was once again called to public office. In 413 he was one of the ten *probouloi* elected to deal with the crisis caused by the disastrous defeat of the Athenian fleet in Sicily.

In the last years of his life, Sophocles continued to produce plays. The extant *Philoktētēs* (*Philoctetes*) is known to have won first prize in 409. Three years later, Sophocles apparently again entered the competition, where he displayed a chorus in mourning for the dead Euripides. Sophocles himself died within a few months. He was certainly dead by early 405, when Aristophanes produced *Batrachoi* (*The Frogs*), in which Sophocles' death is mentioned.

The ancient biographers were not content to accept Sophocles' advanced age as sufficient cause of death—but recorded several more colorful versions, including choking on a grape, overexertion while reciting *Antigone*, and overexcitement after a dramatic victory. At the time of the dramatist's death, Spartan garrisons were in control of the road to Decelea, where the family burial plot was located, and the family had to seek special permission from the Spartan general Lysander to complete the funeral.

Like many of his contemporaries, Sophocles appears to have had two families. He had one son, Iophon, by a lawful wife, Nicostrata, and another son, Ariston, by a Sicyonian *hetaira*, or mistress, named Theoris. Iophon followed his father into the theater, where he even competed with Sophocles at least once. In *The Frogs*, Aristophanes suggests that Iophon was often helped in his career by his more famous father, but that may be an example of comic exaggeration. Of Ariston, all that is known is that he produced a son named Sophocles, who was favored by his grandfather; Ariston produced his grandfather's last play, *Oedipus at Colonus*, in 401 and won first prize.

Iophon brought a suit of senility against his elderly father, perhaps because of the attentions shown to a cherished, but illegitimate, grandson. At the trial, Sophocles is said to have told the jury, "If I am Sophocles, I am not insane; if I am insane, I am not Sophocles" and to have proven his sanity to the jury by reciting lines from his current work, perhaps *Oedipus at Colonus*.

In his long life Sophocles was associated with many of the great men of fifth century Athens. His political sentiments are difficult to verify because of strong links with both the pro-Spartan and aristocratic Cimon, who may have assured Sophocles his first dramatic victory in 468, and with the democratic champion Pericles, with whom Sophocles served as general in the early 440's. Other members of Sophocles' circle of friends included Polygnotus, an outstanding painter who produced a famous portrait of the dramatist holding a lyre; Archelaus of Miletus, the philosopher and teacher of Socrates; the dramatist Ion of Chios, whose home Sophocles is said to have visited during the Samian Revolt; and the historian Herodotus of Halicarnassus. With some of these men, Sophocles may have formed the *thiasos*, or religious guild in honor of the Muses, which is mentioned in his ancient biography.

Summary

To the ancients, Sophocles' career as civil servant, as priest of Asclepius, and, especially, as dramatist at the festival in honor of the god Dionysus, proved he was a man of great patriotism and piety, although some modern scholars have tried to find a different, more questioning Sophocles in the extant plays. Certainly this man called by his ancient biographer *philathenaiotatos*, or "a very great lover of Athens," exhibited throughout his life a high level of personal involvement in his beloved city.

During his career, Sophocles is known to have written more than 120 plays, always produced in groups of three tragedies plus one satyr play. Sophocles, therefore, competed dramatically at least thirty times, perhaps every other year during the course of his career. If his ancient biography is correct that he won first prize twenty times, second prize many times, and third prize never, then Sophocles may have won first prize in two-thirds of the competitions he entered—a great testimony to his contemporary popularity.

There is some evidence that Sophocles was interested in literary theory. Besides his book, now known as "On the Chorus," which does not survive, Sophocles' analysis of his own dramatic style is recorded in Plutarch. Here, Sophocles suggests that there were three stages in his work. The first was influenced by "the majesty and pomp of Aeschylus." The second displayed an originality in the creation of painful effects. In the third he had characters speak in languages appropriate to their personalities. Since the date of this statement is unknown and since so few of Sophocles' plays survive, it is not possible to follow these stages in Sophocles' seven extant plays.

Traditionally, in addition to abandoning the practice of a playwright acting in his own plays, Sophocles may have introduced several important innovations to the theater. He is said to have increased the size of the tragic chorus from twelve to fifteen members and to have added a third actor, scenery, and other dramatic paraphernalia. Sophocles received particularly high commendation in Aristotle's *De poetica* (c. 334-323 B.C.; *Poetics*), in which *Oedipus Tyrannus* was praised for displaying the Aristotelian ideal of tragic plot and character. In the modern world Sophocles has become known for his masterful and dramatic development of character and irony.

Bibliography

Bates, William Nickerson. *Sophocles: Poet and Dramatist*. Philadelphia: University of Pennsylvania Press, and London: Oxford University Press, 1940. A good biographical sketch. With several plates and figures depicting scenes from Sophocles' plays.

Bowra, C. M. "Sophocles on His Own Development." *American Journal of Philology* 61 (1940): 385-401. The playwright's comments about changes in his dramatic style are discussed in this article.

Helmbold, W. C. "The Mad Sophocles." *Classical Journal* 45 (April, 1950): 342. This short article argues that the trial of Sophocles for senility originated as the joke of a comic poet and has no basis in fact.

Lefkowitz, Mary. *The Lives of the Greek Poets.* Baltimore: Johns Hopkins University Press, and London: Duckworth, 1981. A translation and discussion of the Alexandrian biography of Sophocles are included in this book, which also includes a bibliography.

Lenz, F. W. "The Athenian Strategoi of the Years 441/40 and 433/32." *Transactions of the American Philological Association* 72 (1941): 226-232. While the discussion does not specifically focus on Sophocles, this article considers the evidence for the list of Athenian generals in the year 441-440, when Sophocles served with Pericles.

Lesky, Albin. *Greek Tragedy.* 3d ed. London: Benn, and New York: Barnes and Noble Books, 1979. A scholarly introduction to Aeschylus' dramaturgy, with a brief summary of his life. A bibliography is included.

———. *A History of Greek Literature.* London: Methuen, and New York: Thomas Y. Crowell, 1966. Sophocles' place in the literature of ancient Greece can be traced in this standard history, which includes biographical evidence and a bibliography.

Scodel, Ruth. *Sophocles.* Boston: Twayne Publishers, 1984. A good introduction written for the general reader, this book includes a chronological chart and a select annotated bibliography.

Webster, T. B. L. An Introduction to Sophocles. 2d ed. London: Methuen, 1969; New York: Methuen, 1979. An excellent and carefully documented life of Sophocles can be found in the first chapter of this standard study.

Thomas J. Sienkewicz

SOSIGENES

Born: c. 90 B.C.; place unknown
Died: First century B.C.; place unknown
Areas of Achievement: Astronomy and mathematics
Contribution: Sosigenes advised Julius Caesar on the development of the Julian calendar, which, with only slight modification, is still in use today.

Early Life

Virtually nothing is known about the life of Sosigenes, an Alexandrian astronomer and mathematician who flourished in the first century B.C. Even the place of his birth is disputed. Some sources maintain that he was born in the Roman-controlled Egyptian city of Alexandria; others say that he came to Alexandria from Greece. Regardless of how he got to Egypt, Sosigenes must have found it an exciting, if turbulent, place.

Since the ancient days of the pharaohs, Egypt had been besieged by foreign powers. Its people had been conquered by the Assyrians, then the Persians, and finally, in the fourth century B.C., by Alexander the Great, for whom the city of Alexandria is named. In the years just before Sosigenes' life, the Ptolemies, who ruled following the collapse of Alexander's realm, had made Alexandria into a world center for commerce and cultural development. Trading vessels arrived from lands as diverse as Britain and China. Science and art flourished. The city had several parks, a university, and a library with 750,000 volumes. It became a mecca for philosophers and scientists, producing such great scholars as Hipparchus, Ptolemy, Euclid, and Hero. It is no wonder, then, that Sosigenes ended up in Alexandria.

Interest in Alexandria was not limited, however, to intellectuals. Foreign leaders continued to see Egypt as a prize. During the century before the birth of Sosigenes, the ruler of Macedon, Philip V, conspired with the king of Syria to conquer and divide Egypt. This move attracted the attention of the great and expanding Roman Empire. Though the Romans were currently embroiled in the Second Punic War with Carthage, they managed to send an army east to punish the two rulers. After both countries had been conquered, the Romans set up a protectorate in Egypt. Thus, the Alexandria of Sosigenes' time was under profound Roman influence. The Romans did not, however, interfere with the growth and development of the city, which now held more than half a million inhabitants—more than Rome itself.

After ending a bloody civil war in 48 B.C., Julius Caesar rested a year in Egypt before returning to Rome to become dictator. Perhaps it was during this visit that he became acquainted with Sosigenes, who by that time had come to be considered an authority on astronomy. One of Caesar's goals, as ruler of the Roman Empire, was to make radical reforms to the calendar in use at that time. The Roman republican calendar was so out of synchronization with the natural year that the vernal equinox, the springtime event when the sun's path crosses the celestial equator, had occurred months later, in early summer. Caesar called on Sosigenes to advise him on this matter and to develop a new calendar to replace the problem-ridden one of old.

Life's Work

The earliest calendars were lunar in that they followed the phases of the moon. Each month was designed to chart a complete cycle of lunar phases, from new moon to full moon and then on to the next new moon. Lunar calendars were easy to use, especially since they were tied to readily observable astronomical events. Their main problem was that they were independent of important phenomena on Earth. Most notably, they did not follow the seasons. The progression of seasons follows the solar year, the time it takes Earth to complete a revolution around the sun, roughly 365 days. The phases of the moon, however, follow the synodic period (the time between successive new moons) of about thirty days. A lunar year might consist of twelve such cycles (twelve months), or 360 days. The five-day discrepancy meant that seasonal events (monsoons, river flooding, snowfall, and the like) would drift five days forward each lunar year. Thus, by the time a calendar had been in use for two decades, the cold-weather days of winter would occur three months later, in the "spring" months.

Agricultural concerns dictated a need for a calendar that would closely follow the seasons. Farmers would then know when to plant and when to harvest. Such seasonal, or solar, calendars would be based on the observed motion of the sun through the constellations of the sky (ancient astronomers did not realize that this drifting of the sun through the constellations was actually caused by the revolution of Earth). The difficulty with solar calendars was that they did not follow the phases of the moon—which were important for setting the dates of religious feasts and events.

It seemed impossible to reconcile these two demands. Egypt, at the time of Sosigenes, had no fewer than three calendars in use. The oldest calendar was actually a very good one, by modern standards. It was a lunar calendar but was corrected each year by the rising of the star Sirius (the day on which a given star rises at the moment the sun sets is a seasonal year constant). Thus, this calendar—lunar, but regulated by the solar year—accurately predicted seasonal events such as the flooding of the Nile, an important consideration for farmers. Governmental and administrative personnel, however, wanted something more: a calendar which would not vary from year to year, so that they could set predictable dates for treaties and business contracts. Therefore, a true seasonal calendar was developed. It consisted of twelve months, each of which contained exactly thirty numbered days. Since this worked out to 360 days, the Egyptians then intercalated five extra days at the end of each year. At first, this calendar worked as well as the lunar calendar. As the decades passed, however, the seasonal calendar grew out of synchronization with the seasons. Farmers went back to the Sirius-regulated lunar calendar. Astronomers tried to determine the reasons for the failure of the seasonal calendar. They developed a new lunar calendar. This one, instead of being corrected by Sirius, was tied to the civil year (the seasonal calendar). This helped the religious leaders set their events but was of no use to the farmers, who continued to use the old calendar.

Sosigenes realized that the reason for the problems that developed in the civil calendar was that the solar year did not consist of exactly 365 days. His calculations revealed that the year actually consisted of 365.25 days, so that any calendar based on a 365-day year would lose a whole day every four years. He decided that the way to solve the problem would be to intercalate an extra day every fourth year. Though the Egyptian government did not listen to his proposals, his work attracted the attention of Julius Caesar, who sought his advice on amending the Roman calendar.

This task proved quite a challenge, for the calendar of the Roman Republic was in a shambles. It consisted of twelve months, each having either twenty-nine or thirty-one days except for February,

which had twenty-eight. The year ended up having 355 days, far too few to be in step with the seasons. A Roman administrative office known as the Pontifices was assigned to intercalate whole months when necessary to reconcile the calendar with the seasons. Sosigenes must have seen this solution as a rather messy one—and it was not made any better by the actual practice of the Pontifices. It seems that these officials chose to add extra months not as needed by the solar year but instead to increase the time in office of their favorite politicians. As a result, when Sosigenes took the job, the Roman calendar was several months off the solar year.

Sosigenes' task was twofold. First, he had to correct the current year, 46 B.C., so that it would align itself with the seasons. Second, he was to develop a new calendar which would keep synchronization with the solar year. A fixed system of intercalation would also be helpful, to prevent the Pontifices from changing the calendar according to their whims. Sosigenes accomplished the first task by intercalating a full ninety days into the year 46, making that year have 445 days. Then he designed a new calendar, which was to start on the first of January in 45 B.C. For this calendar, which came to be called the Julian calendar after Caesar himself, Sosigenes used his knowledge of the problems with the Egyptian calendars. He made each standard year consist of 365 days, with each of the twelve Roman months having either thirty or thirty-one days, except for February, which he left at twenty-eight days. In order to keep the calendar in precise synchronization with the solar year, he required that every fourth year an extra day should be intercalated in February.

This calendar, with its extremely simple and fixed method for intercalation, should have finally ended all the confusion and discrepancies caused by the old calendar and the meddling Pontifices. Sosigenes and Caesar seemed to have considered everything in their new calendar. They even prescribed that the intercalary day, the *punctum temporis*, should be inserted between the twenty-third and the twenty-fourth of February (Roman custom for adding days in the past) and that persons born on the intercalary day would, for legal purposes, be considered to have been born on the twenty-fourth.

Unfortunately, both men completely overestimated the capabilities of an ignorant bureaucracy. The Pontifices managed to misinterpret the command to add the extra day every fourth year. They counted the year in which they added the day as the first year of the cycle and thus managed to insert the extra day every three years. Julius Caesar was assassinated in 44 B.C., and Sosigenes had no authority over the Pontifices. It was not until 8 B.C. that Augustus remedied the problem and enforced the correct observance of the Julian calendar. It is probable, however, that Sosigenes did not live to see this accomplished.

Summary

The Julian calendar that Sosigenes developed has survived to the present time. The names of a few months have been changed, and the extra day is now inserted at the end of February rather than after the twenty-third. Still, the basic structure of the calendar has changed little through the centuries. In fact, the only significant difference between the modern calendar and the Julian one has to do with how often the extra day is intercalated. For the most part, the four-year rule is still followed; the years of 366 days are referred to as leap years. After several centuries of using the Julian calendar, however, it was noticed that the seasonal events were again out of synchronization with the dates. This problem was traced to Sosigenes' figure of 365.25 for the length of the year. Advances in astronomy were able to determine the number more precisely, finding it to be 365.24219 days. Sosigenes was only off by eleven minutes per year, but over the centuries this error propagated into several days. It was finally corrected in 1582 by Pope Gregory XIII, who omitted ten days from the calendar that year to bring the dates back into alignment with the vernal equinox. Then he instituted the policy of making centurial years (1600, 1700, 1800, and so on) common years instead of leap years, unless they were evenly divisible by four hundred. Thus, 1900 was not a leap year, but 2000 is.

Besides his achievement with the Julian calendar, little is known of Sosigenes. The few bits of available information are intriguing. It is known that he wrote three treatises on astronomy. One of them, on "revolving spheres," was likely a primary source for Pliny the Elder's chapters on the sky in the second book of his massive *Historia naturalis* (A.D. 77; *Natural History*). Unfortunately, none of Sosigenes' texts is extant. All that has survived is a few isolated fragments. One of these fragments in-dicates that Sosigenes believed that the planet Mercury revolved about the sun—a truly remarkable insight. Hipparchus, the great Alexandrian astronomer who lived before Sosigenes, maintained that all celestial objects revolve about Earth, and Ptolemy, the great Alexandrian astronomer who lived after Sosigenes, developed a model of the solar system based on Hipparchus' data and ideas. Sosigenes' view was ignored. It would be some fourteen centuries before anyone would advance such a notion again.

Bibliography

Michels, Agnes Kirsopp. *The Calendar of the Roman Republic*. Princeton, N.J.: Princeton University Press, 1967. The best work available on the pre-Julian calendar. It includes a discussion of the peculiarities of the Roman enumeration of dates, which continued into the Julian calendar of Sosigenes.

Mommsen, Theodor. *The History of Rome*. Translated by William P. Dickson. 4 vols. New York: Scribner, 1887; London: Bentley, 1988. This work gives the political background for the calendar reform of Julius Caesar and Sosigenes.

Packer, George. *Our Calendar*. Wellsboro, Pa.: Fred R. Miller Blank Book Co., 1892. This work describes the Julian calendar and Pope Gregory's reform. Though out of date, the book is useful for anyone who seeks a mathematical examination of the calendar.

Philip, Alexander. *The Calendar: Its History, Structure, and Improvement*. Cambridge: Cambridge University Press, 1921. The best overarching discussion of Sosigenes' work with the Julian calendar. It explains, in accessible terms, both the astronomical and the anthropological concerns that influenced the development of the modern calendar.

Pliny the Elder. *Natural History*. Translated by John Bostock and Henry T. Riley. London: Henry G. Bohn, 1855; New York: Bell, 1890. Has extensive annotations; one of the most useful translations of Pliny's great work. In the second book, Pliny writes of Sosigenes' work on the planet Mercury. He discusses the calendar reform in his eighteenth book.

Greg Tomko-Pavia

SPARTACUS

Born: c. 100 B.C.; Thrace (modern Bulgaria)
Died: 71 B.C.; Lucania Province, southern Italy
Area of Achievement: Warfare and conquest
Contribution: A gladiator of great courage and capacity for leadership, Spartacus was the main leader of the largest and most violent slave insurrection in the history of Roman civilization.

Early Life

There is little reliable information about the early life of Spartacus. He grew up in Thrace, then an independent region in which various ethnic tribes were struggling against the imperialistic ambitions of the Roman Republic. For a short period, Spartacus served as a Roman soldier, but he deserted and apparently joined a group of brigands. Captured by the Romans, he was condemned to a life of slavery, a common fate of criminals, prisoners of war, and any rebels who opposed Roman hegemony. A skillful and experienced fighter, Spartacus was purchased by Lentulus Batiates, the owner of a large school of gladiators in the city of Capua, about 130 miles south of Rome on the Appian Way.

In training to become a gladiator (from the Latin word *gladius,* which means "sword"), Spartacus was entering a profession in which he would be required to fight to the death in either public arenas or private homes. These violent exhibitions had originated at Roman funerals, because many Romans believed that those who died in combat would serve as armed attendants in the afterlife. By the time of Spartacus, gladiatorial shows had long been a popular form of entertainment, and many of the larger contests would feature approximately three hundred pairs of combatants. Only a small minority of Romans expressed any concerns about the way that crowds of thousands enjoyed the savage combats; even Cicero, a sensitive moral philosopher, believed that the shows were socially useful as long as only convicted criminals killed one another.

Although a few men voluntarily chose to become gladiators for financial reasons, the vast majority, like Spartacus, were forced into the deadly work as a form of punishment. Not surprisingly, the gladiatorial schools had to maintain constant vigilance to prevent rebellion or escape. Plutarch's *The Lives of Noble Grecians and Romans* (c. A.D. 110) reports that Batiates' school in Capua had an especially bad reputation for its cruelty. Before Spartacus, there had been sporadic cases of gladiatorial uprisings in southern Italy, and the island of Sicily had experienced two large slave revolts in 136-132 B.C. and 104-100 B.C.

Life's Work

In 73 B.C., Spartacus, along with two hundred other gladiators, mostly of Thracian and Celtic background, attempted an escape from Batiates' school, and seventy-eight, including Spartacus, succeeded. Contrary to the legend of later novels, there is no documentary evidence that Spartacus ever had any idealistic vision of abolishing the institutions of slavery or gladiatorial contests. Rather, it appears that his first goal was to regain freedom for himself and his associates and to return to his home in Thrace. The historical sources also suggest that Spartacus had not entirely given up the ways of the brigand and that he wanted to steal as much wealth as he could from the Romans. Although the Romans considered Spartacus as nothing more than a ruthless criminal, Plutarch later described him as "a man not only of high spirit and valiant, but in understanding, also, and in gentleness superior to his condition."

At first, the fugitives were armed with only kitchen knives, but they had the good fortune of capturing wagons that transported gladiatorial arms. After leaving Capua, the escapees selected Spartacus as their main leader, and they also chose two Gauls, Crixus and Oenomaus, as lieutenant commanders. In desperation, the group sought refuge on Mount Vesuvius, but Roman officials soon learned of their location. One of the praetors, Clodius Glaber, pursued them with a small contingent of well-armed soldiers, and the soldiers soon blockaded the accessible parts of the mountain. The rebels, however, managed to descend a steep cliff by holding onto wild vines, and they were then able to route the Romans with a surprise attack from the rear. Shortly thereafter, the rebels also defeated small detachments of soldiers commanded by two other praetors, L. Cossinius and Publius Varinius, and Spartacus captured Varinius' horse. With each victory, the rebels captured valuable weapons that could be used in future confrontations.

As word of the initial successes of the rebellion spread, the rebels were soon joined by numerous slaves and landless laborers from the *latifundia* (or

large estates) located in the countryside of southern Italy. Eventually, the rebellion grew into a large army that included between 70,000 and 120,000 men, many accompanied by their wives and children. Plutarch, who is not always reliable in such details, wrote that Spartacus acquired a wife, but Appian, a more critical Roman historian of the second century A.D., did not provide this information.

The rebels bitterly disagreed about the best course of action. Spartacus reportedly recognized that the Romans would soon muster a large army against them and that their wisest decision would be to march north out of Italy and return to their various homelands. Crixus and several others, however, pointed out the financial advantages of plundering the estates of southern Italy, and the majority of the rebels agreed with this second option. During the winter of 73-72, therefore, there was widespread devastation throughout the south.

The Roman Senate, faced with insurgents in Itruria and Spain, was slow to realize the seriousness of the slave rebellion, but it finally commissioned the two Roman consuls of that year, Cornelius Lentulus Clodianus and L. Gellius Publicola, to pursue Spartacus with four legions (about sixteen thousand soldiers). In late 73, the Roman army managed to defeat Crixus' forces near Mount Garganus. Following the death of Crixus, Spartacus decided to head north according to his original plan; he got as far as Cisalpine Gaul, where he encountered an army led by the proconsul and governor of the region, Cassius Onginus. After Spartacus defeated Cassius' troops in the Battle of Mutina, he and his horde could have escaped north by way of the Alps but instead decided to head south, probably because the rebels preferred to continue seeking the spoils of plunder. Spartacus defeated the forces of the two consuls in Picenum, and the rebels then faced little opposition as they pillaged the southwestern provinces of Lucania and Bruttium. Spartacus entered into negotiations with some Cilician pirates for transportation to Sicily, a province known for its large numbers of discontented slaves and landless laborers.

In Rome, the Senate relieved the two disgraced consuls of their military command, and it conferred Marcus Licinius Crassus with the special command of proconsular imperium. Crassus, who had served as one of Sulla's commanders, was an extremely wealthy landowner with unbridled ambition. When one of his legates, Mummius, disobeyed orders, Crassus restored order by reviving the punishment of decimation (the execution of every tenth man). Crassus then led ten well-armed legions into Bruttium. Meanwhile, the pirates failed to keep their promise to provide Spartacus with transportation to Sicily. During the winter of 72-71, Crassus was able to construct a fortified blockade around the bulk of Spartacus' forces in the toe of Italy between the towns of Scyllaeum and Rhegium.

Spartacus' forces managed to escape the blockade in their third attempt, and the rebels went on to win two battles against relatively small Roman units in Lucania. In resources and training, however, Spartacus' rebels were clearly no match for the ten legions that Crassus commanded, and they were decisively defeated when they directly encountered these legions in a battle which was probably near the head of the Silarus river. Spartacus himself was killed in this battle, and his body was never identified. Crassus pursued the surviving rebels as they fled northward, and he ordered the crucifixion of six thousand rebels along the Appian Way from Capua to Rome. The rotting bodies were left hanging for months as a warning to anyone who might contemplate rebellion. Returning to the city of Rome, Crassus was allowed to wear a crown of laurel and received enthusiastic ovations.

During the six months that Crassus was pursuing Spartacus, the Senate had decided (probably without Crassus' knowledge) that it was necessary to recall Pompey's large army from Spain. Pompey arrived in northern Italy about the time that Crassus was concluding his successful campaign, and Pompey's army encountered and annihilated about five thousand fugitives who were trying to escape to their homes. Based on this minor engagement, Pompey sent the Senate a message claiming that it was he who had finally put the slave rebellion to an end. The competing claims of Pompey and Crassus intensified the personal animosity that the two men had for one another.

Summary

Spartacus fought courageously to end the grievous oppression experienced by himself and his colleagues, but the historical sources do not suggest that the Thracian gladiator wished to end slavery or reform the nature of Roman society. He and his followers did manage, nevertheless, to keep the Roman army at bay for almost two years, a great achievement for that period. Despite claims to the contrary, there is no evidence that the Spartacus rebellion had any humanitarian influence on the ways that the Romans treated their slaves and gladiators. From the Roman perspective, the rebellion demonstrated the need for harsh punishment as an example to dissidents, and the Romans apparently responded to the rebellion by increasing security over both slaves and gladiators. Although it would be five hundred years before the western empire would come to an end, the Romans would never again have to contend with a major slave insurrection.

Since the eighteenth century, Spartacus has often served as a mythical symbol of a courageous revolutionary, fighting for social justice and the abolition of slavery. Several historical novels and a popular film have developed this theme. The appeal of Spartacus has been especially great among communists and leftists who have endorsed violent revolt as the preferred means for social reform. During World War I, socialist militants in Germany took the name "the Spartacist League." At the time of the American Civil Rights movement, in contrast, there was a tendency to portray Spartacus as an enlightened reformer who opposed violence and oppression. Ironically, the limited nature of the ancient sources describing the persona of Spartacus has added to the protean character of the legend.

Bibliography

Bradley, Keith. *Slavery and Rebellion in the Roman World*. Bloomington: Indiana University Press, and London: Batsford, 1989. An interesting and scholarly account of the three large slave rebellions during the late Republic, with chapter 5 devoted to Spartacus. The detailed notes provide the most extensive documentation available. The best single account.

Fast, Howard. *Spartacus*. New York: Crown, 1951; London: Bodley Head, 1952. Although much of the material is fictional, this is probably the most readable and interesting of the novels devoted to Spartacus.

Grant, Michael. *Gladiators*. London: Weidenfeld and Nicolson, and New York: Delacorte Press, 1967. A concise, fascinating, and scholarly treatment of the Roman gladiators, including a short analysis of the Spartacus insurrection. Highly recommended.

Gruen, Erich. *The Last Generation of the Roman Republic*. Berkeley: University of California Press, 1974. A fascinating account of the politics and leaders of the time, with pages 20-22 giving a good summary of Spartacus' revolt.

Harris, W. V. "Spartacus." In *Past Imperfect: History According to the Movies*. Edited by Mark Carnes. New York: Henry Holt, 1995. A most interesting analysis of both the historical and fictional aspects of Stanley Kubrick's popular 1960 film.

Mitchell, James Leslie. *Spartacus*. Edited by Ian Campbell. Edinburgh, Scotland: Scottish Academic Press, 1990. Although much of this novel is fictional, Campbell's scholarly introduction discusses both the sources and the variety of perspectives in the novels about Spartacus.

Yavetz, Zvi. *Slaves and Slavery in Ancient Rome*. New Brunswick, N.J.: Transaction Books, 1988. In addition to general information about Roman slavery, pages 83-112 contain translations of almost all of the ancient sources dealing with Spartacus, including the writings of Cicero, Appian, Plutarch, and Florus.

Thomas T. Lewis

SSU-MA CH'IEN

Born: c. 145 B.C.; Lung-men, Han-ch'eng hsien, China

Died: c. 86 B.C.; China

Area of Achievement: Historiography

Contribution: As principal author of the *Shih chi*, a monumental historical work of 130 chapters which covers the history of the Chinese people from earliest times to the late first century B.C., Ch'ien is the chief source of nearly all subsequent historical knowledge of the dynasties of ancient China. For helping to fill this gap in scholarship, Ch'ien ranks with Thucydides and Herodotus as an important ancient historian.

Early Life

Ssu-ma Ch'ien was born about 145 B.C. in the county of Han-ch'eng hsien in what is modern Shensi Province, China. Nearly all information concerning his life comes from his lifework, the *Shih chi* (c. 90 B.C.), which has been partially translated in a number of editions but remains best known by its original title. As was customary, Ch'ien traced his genealogy to legendary figures of high station and high repute. In the mid-ninth century B.C., however, the family suffered a loss of position and became known by the name Ssu-ma. Ssu-ma T'an, his father, had been appointed the Grand Historian of the Emperor Wu's court early in his reign in 141 B.C. Prior to Ch'ien's birth, his father had commenced collecting materials and writing a major historical work, his motive being to ensure his immortality. Thus, on his deathbed, T'an charged his son with completion of the history.

Little is known of Ch'ien's specific training for this task. While Ch'ien was a child and before, his father was made court astrologer and historian; his family apparently earned a living farming and keeping livestock in the hills south of the Hwang River. Ch'ien's early education purportedly consisted of village schooling, which was continued after his father had been appointed to serve in the court around 140 B.C. By his tenth year, Ch'ien reportedly was reading old texts, although what texts they were is unclear.

Between his young boyhood and his twentieth year, Ch'ien traveled extensively. He reported going south to the Yangtze and the Huai rivers. He climbed Hui-chi, where the mythical Emperor Yü, a great cultural hero who had saved man and Earth from flooding, supposedly had died, and searched for a fabled cave atop the mountain. He saw the famed Nine Peaks, where the legendary Emperor Shun, whose reign had brought mankind unmatchable happiness, was interred, and then sailed down the Yuan and Hsiang rivers. Farther north, he crossed the Wen and the Ssu rivers. He traveled onward to study in Lu, Confucius' home state, and in Ch'i, the home state of Mencius, making obvious his interest in Confucianism. He also participated in an archery contest at a famed mountain near Confucius' home—an appropriate anecdote, since the role of ancient historians had been collecting arrows representing the emperor's best shots—and he encountered local toughs in Hsueh and P'eng-ch'eng. After passing through Liang and Ch'u, he returned home to Lung-men probably around 122 B.C.

There, his father's influence, careful training, and good grades brought him into government service as a Lang-chung, one of the emperor's traveling court attendants. In this capacity, he wrote of having participated in imperial expeditions—one important one, for example, that was launched in 111 B.C. to southwest China, where he became acquainted with several of the tribes of that region—as well as many other journeys, which made him one of the most widely traveled men of his era and immensely enriched his capacities as a historian.

The event critical to his career occurred in 110 B.C., as Wu prepared for the sacred Feng Sacrifice, symbolic of the divine election of the Han Dynasty. Having already reported to the authorities in Ch'ang-an, the capital, on his recent mission, Ch'ien traveled eastward to join the emperor at Lo-yang. On his way, he saw his father, who apparently had become too feeble to participate in the sacrifice. Dying, his father asked Ch'ien, for the sake of the family's glory, to succeed him as Grand Historian, thereby ensuring continuation of his historical research and writing. Ch'ien did have a family, although nothing is known of his wife and only brief mention is made of a daughter.

Life's Work

What had begun as the private initiative of Ssu-ma T'an, the court astrologer-historian whose official duties lay in divination, became in the hands of his son and successor one of the acknowledged masterworks of historical writing. Creation of most of the *Shih chi* absorbed Ch'ien for twenty years, almost until his death. In carrying out the spirit of his father's injunction, however, he produced a history that was not only monumental but also unique in the implementation of its creative perceptions. Previous "histories" had consisted essentially of genealogical records, bland chronicles of a single regime, mere cautionary tales, essays propagandizing current political morality, or, as his father had expected, work dedicated to individual or institutional glorification.

Contrary to these precedents, Ch'ien sought to depict, as far as his sources allowed, the entire past of the Chinese people—basically a universal history, but one which fortunately illuminated the presence of many non-Chinese of whom no written record would otherwise have existed. His purpose was to record what had happened—the good, the bad, and the indifferent—with judicious objectivity. While the assumption of objectivity was not novel in Ch'ien's day (objectivity had been the goal of previous chroniclers, T'an included), the degree of objectivity with which Ch'ien wrote, together with the chronological span and geopolitical range of his study, was unparalleled.

The *Shih chi* is organized into five extensive sections. The "Basic Annals" are composed of a dozen chapters relating the histories of early dynastic families—back to the mythic Yellow Emperor—and, in the instance of the Han, the lives of individual emperors. Ten "Chronological Tables," graphing and dating important events of the past, follow. Subjects such as astronomy, rites, pitch pipes, music, the calendar, religion, and political economy subsequently are discussed in eight "Treatises." In turn, there follow thirty chapters on "Hereditary Houses," which cover political and diplomatic events before the Ch'in Dynasty. The next seventy chapters relate the "Accounts," or biographies, of famous men—including invaluable information on kings, ministers, sages, rebels, Confucian scholars—as well as reports on foreign governments and "barbarian" peoples with whom the Chinese had contact. Internally, the organization of sections and chapters is chronological, although some mixing of events and biographies leads to repetition of the narrative and a dispersal of information. Such confusions notwithstanding, the singularity of the organization is undoubtedly a result of Ch'ien's research, imagination, and sheer capacity for work.

Because of losses sustained in uprisings, wars, or the Hans' wanton destruction of documents relating to their predecessors, the Ch'in, sources for early dynasties were scarce and Ch'ien's narrative was parsed out by legends. Indeed, these sections belie the fact that Ch'ien disliked superstitions. In possession of more abundant and substantiable sources in dealing with events and personalities of the Ch'in and the Han dynasties, including those of his own lifetime, he wrote fairly accurate, three-dimensional portrayals.

Yet, while evoking plausible historical personages, he rarely obtruded his own personality directly, although almost the entire work (some sections may be later emendations) bears his imprimatur. Similarly, as was the case with most Chinese historians, he avoided forthright insertion of his own opinions. He was also inclined to present the most favorable aspects of his subjects first while introducing harsher facts later in the text.

For dramatic effect, like the historians of ancient Greece and Rome, Ch'ien also composed speeches for his principal characters, though not, as was the case in the West, so that they could be declaimed publicly. He wrote of the past as a sequence of dramas; hence, the narrative portions of the *Shih chi* are actually speeches by the principal figures instead of the author's descriptions of the action. In fact, very little pure description exists in the text. The Chinese preferred the directness of speech, as readers of Thucydides, Herodotus, or Cornelius Tacitus did. The terseness of the classical Chinese language, however, lends a fluidity to the *Shih chi* that is not present in analogous Western writings.

Scholars have sought to discover the personality and beliefs of Ch'ien beneath his literary devices. Although Ch'ien may have been objective in many respects, his purpose was often didactic. Concentration on heroes, important figures, and grand events insofar as his sources allowed, was designed subtly to convey moral judgments. He doubtless believed that goodness triumphs over evil. In this respect, he was at one with Confucius, whom he admired and whose *Ch'un ch'iu* (c. 480 B.C.; *Spring and Autumn Annals)* he partly imitated. He was also Confucius' first full-length biographer in the *Shih chi*'s section on the "Hereditary House of Confucius." It seems unlikely, however, that Ch'ien extended his admiration for Confucius to all Confucianists or to Taoists.

Whether Ch'ien as a historian believed in an evolutionary process, in the inevitability of decline, in cycles, or in continuous flux, is uncertain. His selection of emperors, sages, ministers, bandits, rebels, and even nonentities (as well as his structuring of events) is too complex to suggest a firm conclusion. If, as he explained, his motive in writing was to glorify Wu, then the universal history that he produced was unnecessary. This obeisance to his emperor aside, it appears that he intended to create a new form of history.

Ch'ien was engaged in his private historical enterprise while officially attending to observance of rites, the arrangement of the calendar, and other courtly duties. He suffered as a result of a dispute with Wu over the actions of Ch'ien's friend, a general named Li Ling. Li Ling had fought brilliantly on the western frontier but, failing to receive the support essential to saving his army, went over to the enemy. For his efforts to explain Li Ling's behavior, Ch'ien was castrated in 99 B.C. and imprisoned. Contemplating suicide, he consoled himself with the past: Confucius had written a great work while in distress, Ch'u Yuan had composed a great poem while in exile, Tso-ch'iu Ming wrote while blind, and Sun Tzu produced his classic on the art of war after amputation of his feet. Persevering in order to continue his history, Ch'ien was restored to favor and completed his great work around 90 B.C. Still a minor and largely unrecognized court official, he died shortly afterward, probably in 86 B.C., presumably near the Han capital. The *Shih chi* remained unknown until the Marquess of P'ing-t'ung, Yang Yun (mid-first century B.C.), Ch'ien's grandson, succeeded in having it widely circulated.

Summary

Ssu-ma Ch'ien's *Shih chi* provides the principal written source of knowledge about ancient Chinese history and culture: its major and minor figures from many walks of life, its major events. As such, it continues to be an invaluable resource for understanding and interpreting a substantial portion of China's past. While it embodies many dramatic elements and important writings already familiar to his predecessors, it remains unique for its scope, substantive richness and literary distinction. It must also be regarded as a fresh form of historical writing. Unlike previous historians, who had been content with the production of dynastic or personal eulogies and cautionary or moralizing tales in which a recounting of the past was merely a convenient vehicle for their views, Ch'ien sought to offer an objective perspective on the whole experience of the Chinese people. Scholarly difficulties in ascertaining precisely what his final estimates of many personalities and events were and in deter-

mining what his philosophy of history might have been tend to reaffirm his objectivity. This objective cast to the *Shih chi* has lent it a timeless quality, despite Ch'ien's obvious inventions and despite later and inferior emendations. In subsequent generations, the *Shih chi* continued to be admired for its organization, execution, and objectives.

Bibliography

Gardner, Charles S. *Chinese Traditional Historiography*. Rev. ed. Cambridge, Mass.: Harvard University Press, 1961. A brief but brilliantly suggestive synthesis of the general ideas that shaped Ch'ien's intellectual environment. Intended for the fledgling sinologist but easily read, since complex technical questions are kept to the notes. Includes footnotes and a good, useful index.

Loewe, Michael. *The Cambridge History of China*. Vol. 1, *The Ch'in and Han Empires, 221 B.C.-A.D. 220*. Edited by Denis Twitchett and John K. Fairbank. New York: Cambridge University Press, 1986. An outstanding collection of scholarly syntheses that offer all the necessary background for understanding Ch'ien's work. Chapter 2, "The Former Han Dynasty," is a good place to begin; Loewe's introduction, which deals with sources for Han study, is a fine complement to that chapter. With footnotes throughout. Includes a superb forty-page bibliography, a sixty-page, double-columned glossary-index, and essential maps.

Ssu-ma Ch'ien. *Records of the Grand Historian of China*. Translated by Burton Watson. 2 vols. New York and London: Columbia University Press, 1961. The most extensive translation of Ch'ien's work in English, but it is a select translation, so portions regarded as less rewarding by the translator do not appear. Includes few but useful maps, scattered footnotes, and an excellent master index in volume 2.

Watson, Burton. *Ssu-ma Ch'ien: Grand Historian of China*. New York: Columbia University Press, 1958. The only full-length, English-language biography of Ch'ien. The author does a fine job of placing the subject in the context of his times and of examining the beginnings of Chinese historiography, the structure of his work, and the subject's thought. Includes two informative appendices, more than forty pages of detailed, instructive notes, and a brief bibliography and glossary. Unless supplemented by other works, differences between the author's interpretations and those of other scholars may be missed.

Wilhelm, Hellmut. "The Scholar's Frustrations: Notes on Type of 'Fu.'" In *Chinese Thought and Institutions*, John K. Fairbank, ed. Chicago: University of Chicago Press, 1957. A brief but provocative essay on problems of political criticism confronting Ch'ien's contemporaries and the deployment of sophisticated literary devices to overcome them. Since most Chinese soldiers were dependents of rulers, their survival depended on skill in indirect commentary. Aids an understanding of the style of the *Records*. With detailed notes at the end of the volume and an extensive general index.

Clifton K. Yearley
Kerrie L. MacPherson

SAINT STEPHEN

Born: c. A.D. 5; Samaria
Died: c. A.D. 36; Jerusalem
Area of Achievement: Religion
Contribution: By means of his innovative theology, his personal courage, and his martyrdom, Stephen helped to universalize the early Christian Church by encouraging its expansion beyond the doctrinal confines of Judaism and the political confines of Jerusalem.

Early Life

All that is known of Saint Stephen's life and thought is derived from chapters 6 and 7 of Saint Luke's Acts of the Apostles. The former chapter tells of Stephen's rise to prominence in the early Christian Church, his election to the protodiaconate (the earliest board of deacons), his theological disputations with the Jews, and his arrest on trumped-up charges of heresy. The latter chapter relates his impassioned and provocative defense before the Sanhedrin, a group of Jewish leaders who became so enraged at his ideas that they stopped his defense short and dragged him away for execution. His death at their hands made Stephen the first in a long line of Christian martyrs.

From his Greek name and the ecclesiastical task to which he was elected, on the one hand, and from his idiosyncratic theological beliefs, on the other, scholars believe that Stephen was both a Hellenist and a Samaritan prior to his conversion to Christianity. A Hellenist was not only a Greek-speaking Jew but also one who was influenced by Greek (Hellenic) culture and open to Greek ideas. That is, Hellenists had a broader outlook and a more liberal education than did those Jews whose persuasion and practice were more separatistic. That Stephen was a Hellenist is deduced from the fact that his parents gave him a Greek name (Stephanos—the other deacons also had Greek names) and that the segment of Christian people he was elected to serve were Hellenists themselves. The Samaritans, those who came from Samaria (in central Palestine, between Judea and Galilee), were known for their unorthodox religious beliefs: Though they were Jews, they deplored the temple worship conducted at Jerusalem. They opted instead for worshipping at Mount Gerizim in Samaria. Besides an intense messianism, they also had their own version of the five books of Moses, a version known as the Samaritan Pentateuch, which, though it is largely the same as the standard Pentateuch, differs in a few significant ways. Stephen's recorded defense not only contains a Samaritan-like attack on the Temple and a presentation of Jesus as Messiah, it contains allusions to numbers and events found only in the Samaritan Pentateuch. This remarkable fact underscores not only his Samaritanism but also the historical reliability of Saint Luke's account, which in all other places employs a different version of the Old Testament Scriptures. Thus, Stephen appears to have been a Hellenist and a Samaritan.

Because no record of Stephen's conversion to Christianity has been preserved, scholars are unable to date it precisely or to identify its causes. A late and unreliable ecclesiastical tradition, however, numbers Stephen among the seventy evangelists sent out by Jesus.

Life's Work

According to the second chapter of Acts, the early Church experienced periods of remarkable growth. On the day of Pentecost alone, for example, ap-

proximately three thousand people were converted to the faith. As time passed, the Church's numbers continued to swell. While desirable, this growth brought with it some knotty organizational problems, among them the problem of how the small band of twelve apostles could oversee the distribution of the Church's extensive program of charitable outreach while still devoting sufficient time and energy to teaching and preaching the Christian message, a task they considered their supreme assignment.

Especially needy among the early converts were the Hellenistic widows. Financially, they were in a precarious position. With no husbands as breadwinners, and faced with a language barrier that seems to have prevented them from making their needs known to the Church, they faced severe difficulties. In an effort, therefore, to free the apostles for teaching and preaching, and in order to relieve the Hellenistic widows' distress, the Church appointed "seven men of honest report, full of the Holy Spirit and wisdom," among whom Stephen, as the subsequent biblical narrative shows, was most prominent.

From Luke's account, it is clear that Stephen did not restrict himself to the duties attached to the care of the poor. Stephen was an impressive theological debater, one who carried his Christian message into the Hellenistic synagogues in and around Jerusalem, one whom his opponents found difficult to gainsay.

Added to his Hellenism and his Samaritanism, his Christianity aroused the ire of the established Jewish leaders. His theological adversaries, bested in argument and distressed at what they deemed his unconscionable heresies, resorted to arousing opposition to him by distorting his teachings. They raised charges against him which they not only exaggerated but also corroborated with what Luke calls "false witnesses." By prearrangement, these false witnesses testified before the Sanhedrin to Stephen's "heresies." He was accused (like Jesus before him) of advocating the destruction of the Temple and of the overthrow of the Jewish law. The former idea they extrapolated from his Samaritanism and the latter from his Christianity. That is, like the Samaritans, he opposed worship in the Jerusalem Temple, and like Saint Paul after him (who now, as Saul, was in charge of the proceedings against Stephen), he was opposed to trying to achieve salvation through observance of the Jewish ceremonial laws.

Stephen's defense before the Sanhedrin was not so much a defense of himself as a defense of the early Christian message and a counterattack against his accusers and judges. He spoke against the Temple and the system of sacrifices followed there by maintaining that, because God was not confined to buildings made by human hands, the true worship of God was not a temple-based function. Furthermore, by condemning Jesus to death, Stephen asserted, the Jews of his day had merely acted in accord with the spiritual failures of their ancestors, who had also resisted the revelation of God. In his view, the will of God had been made known by means of the prophets, and the prophets had been killed by their own people. The fate of the Messiah whose coming the prophets had predicted was no different: He too suffered at the hands of His own people. Thus, Stephen's defense chastised the Jews for what he believed to be their spiritual intransigence and wickedness. They did not grow closer to God or obey Him, even though they had the spiritual light to do so.

Quite predictably, such a speech served only to enrage his judges. In the midst of the ensuing turmoil, the council bypassed the normal procedures for passing a sentence. As they began to converge on him, Stephen offended his opponents even more by declaring that he saw, at that very moment, the heavens opened up and Christ, as if to welcome Stephen or to assist him, standing at the right of His Father. To Stephen's accusers, this was rank blasphemy. He was dragged unceremoniously out of the chambers to a place now known as Stephen's Gate, where he was stoned to death. Remarkably, in the midst of this torture, he knelt to pray aloud for his executioners. This startling sight, many believe, was the catalyst behind the conversion of Saul, soon to be the Apostle Paul, perhaps the greatest theologian and missionary of the apostolic era. As Saint Augustine later wrote, "If Stephen had not prayed, the Church would not have had Paul."

As is the case with many other notable ancient Christians, pious but unhistorical legends grew up around Saint Stephen's memory. The apocryphal apocalypse known as "The Revelation of St. Stephen" is unquestionably false and bears no genuine connection to the first Christian martyr, either by its content or by its authorship. This book purports to be a narrative of Saint Stephen's reappearance after his death; it was popular among Manichaean heretics and survives only in garbled segments. The discovery of Stephen's alleged relics occurred early in the fifth century.

Summary

Saint Stephen's not inconsiderable influence can be summarized under four important headings. First, he was the Paul before Paul. His personal conviction and courage in the face of death and his unique combination of Samaritanism and Hellenism in a dynamic system of Christian belief undoubtedly influenced the zealous Pharisee Saul of Tarsus in his pilgrimage toward a new identity as Saint Paul the Apostle. Second, Stephen's death was the immediate impetus behind the Church's leaving its nest in Jerusalem and spreading itself and its message, as Luke writes, from Jerusalem, to Judaea, to Samaria, and to "the uttermost parts of the earth." Third, Stephen's defense was the basis of an effective strategy of theological defense, one that seems to have been employed in various segments of the early Church. Fourth, Saint Stephen has served as a stimulus to piety. Christians in all ages have been strengthened by his courage and spirituality. The Roman Catholic church celebrates the feast of Saint Stephen on December 26.

Bibliography

Barnard, L. W. *Studies in the Apostolic Fathers and Their Background*. New York: Schocken Books, and Oxford: Blackwell, 1966. Chapter 6, "St. Stephen and Early Alexandrian Christianity," is a technical examination of Stephen's theology and his influence upon one segment of the early Church. Barnard argues that *Barnaba epistolē* (*The Epistle of Barnabas*, 1719) contains significant strands of Stephenic theology, especially with regard to the Temple, the Torah, and Christ. The extensive bibliography is of use primarily for biblical and theological specialists.

Bruce, F. F. *Peter, Stephen, James, and John: Studies in Non-Pauline Christianity*. Grand Rapids, Mich.: Eerdmans, 1979. Chapter 2, "Stephen and the Other Hellenists," is a well-balanced and well-documented account of the theology of Saint Stephen, especially as it is seen in the context of Jewish Hellenism. Apart from the biblical account itself, this chapter is perhaps the best and most easily accessible introduction to the man, his life, his beliefs, and his theological tradition.

Kilgallen, John. *The Stephen Speech: A Literary and Redactional Study of Acts 7, 2-53*. Rome: Biblical Institute Press, 1976. Easily the most extensive treatment of Stephen's defense before the Sanhedrin, this book is both thorough and demanding. Though specialists will benefit from its detailed analysis (and will be able to detect its weaknesses), the beginning student will quickly be overwhelmed. The bibliography is quite inclusive, but unannotated.

Munck, Johannes. *The Acts of the Apostles*. New York: Doubleday, 1964. Appendix 5, "Stephen's Samaritan Background," notes thirteen reasons why scholars identify him as a Samaritan. It also explains how the presence of these Samaritanisms in the Stephen account underscores Luke's historical reliability and clarifies Luke's use of sources.

Schmithals, Walter. *Paul and James*. Translated by Dorothea M. Barton. Naperville, Ill.: Alec R. Allenson, and London: SCM Press, 1965. Chapter 1, "Stephen," is an idiosyncratic examination, from a theologically radical point of view, of the beliefs and practices of the Jewish Hellenists. Schmithals' bibliographical citations are quite numerous and quite technical, and almost all reflect a theologically liberal stance.

Simon, Marcel. *St. Stephen and the Hellenists in the Primitive Church*. New York: Longmans, 1956; London: Longmans, 1958. Unlike Munck's book (cited above), this text emphasizes the Greek aspects of Stephen's background. Though carefully argued, Simon's conclusions are speculative and therefore open to criticism. While the documentation is extensive, no separate bibliography is given. Like most works dealing with Stephen, this book is written for specialists.

Michael E. Bauman

FLAVIUS STILICHO

Born: c. 360; Eastern Roman Empire, perhaps near
Constantinople
Died: August 22, 408; Ravenna, Italy
Area of Achievement: Warfare
Contribution: For a period of some fifteen years,
Stilicho acted as the generalissimo of the West-
ern Roman Empire (and as much of the Eastern
as he was allowed), repeatedly staving off bar-
barian assaults on Rome and on Constantinople.

Early Life

Flavius Stilicho's father was a Vandal cavalry officer, his mother a Roman. The Vandals at that time
did not have the reputation for ferocity and destruction which they were later to acquire. Nevertheless, it was never forgotten that Stilicho was a
"half-barbarian." He was never fully trusted by all
of his Greek or Roman civilian masters and colleagues. He began his career as a protector, a member of the personal bodyguard of Theodosius the
Great (c. 347-395). Following the normal course of
events, he was presumably made a tribune, attached to the imperial general staff, and sent on a
diplomatic mission to Persia in 383 or 384.

Shortly after this, an unexpected event took
place which catapulted Stilicho firmly into prominence: He married Serena, niece and adopted
daughter of Theodosius. It has been suggested that
this was a love match instigated by Serena, and
though historians have been reluctant to accept this
sentimental theory, no more plausible one exists.
Stilicho was at that time quite undistinguished, had
no important relatives, and was not a likely candidate for a diplomatic marriage. The poet Claudian
(c. 370-c. 404), who is admittedly totally biased in
favor of Stilicho, nevertheless wrote that his hero
surpassed the demigods of antiquity in strength
and size; wherever he walked, the crowds moved
out of his way. This must have some basis in fact
and could explain how the young officer attracted
the attention of the emperor's niece.

Naturally, after the marriage promotion was rapid. Stilicho was made "count of the stable," then
chief of the imperial guard. He seems to have held
independent command in a campaign in Thrace in
392, and from 393 onward he was called *magister
utriusque militiae,* meaning "master of both arms,"
that is, of the infantry and the cavalry. While still
firmly under the wing of Theodosius, he had be-

come the approximate equivalent of field marshal,
a position from which many earlier and later generals aimed at seizing imperial power. (Stilicho never
tried that.) In 394, he marched with Theodosius
from the eastern half of the Empire toward Italy, to
put down the revolt and usurpation of the general
Arbogast and his puppet emperor Eugenius, installed in 388. In early September, 394, the armies
of the Eastern and Western Empires clashed at the
Battle of the Frigidus River, and after initial failure
the easterners won a decisive victory. Both enemy
leaders were killed. Theodosius marched toward
Rome but died soon after, on January 17, 395. He
left Stilicho in charge of both the Eastern army and
the pardoned survivors of the Western army. Remote from the control of Constantinople and related by marriage to the imperial house, Stilicho was
in a position of unusual power.

Life's Work

One certainty about Stilicho's life is that he did not
use his power to the full. He never made himself
emperor, though no one was in any position to stop
him. For the rest of his life he claimed that Theodosius had appointed him guardian of both his
sons, Arcadius (c. 377-408), the Eastern Emperor,
and Flavius Honorius (384-423), declared Emperor
of the West by his father in 393. It seems that no
one else was present at Theodosius' deathbed, so
naturally people have been skeptical about Stilicho's mandate. The fact remains that Stilicho always obeyed imperial orders, even foolish ones,
and made no move against his former master's
children (although Honorius, at least, was widely
disliked).

Stilicho was left, however, with at least two
problems. One was the division now accepted between the two halves of the Empire. This was dangerous and unproductive, as neither side was willing to help the other very much, and there was
always danger of civil war—for example, over the
border province of Illyricum, the modern Balkans.
Yet neither half of the Empire could afford civil
war, for both were hard-pressed by constant waves
of barbarian invasion. In the immediate background of all events of Stilicho's life was the disaster of Adrianople, August 9, 378, when the Goths,
driven on by fear of the Huns and fury at imperial
treachery, had totally destroyed the main imperial
army and killed Emperor Valens (c. 328-378). The

barbarians then knew that the Romans were not invincible.

Stilicho had a difficult hand to play. In 395, he led his joint army out of Italy toward Constantinople, again threatened by the Goths under Alaric (c. 370-410). No decisive battle was fought, but the Goths withdrew, and Stilicho—with apparently characteristic selflessness—released the Eastern army from his control, returning it to Arcadius. The year following, he led an expedition into the West, along the Rhine River, possibly as a demonstration of force and to "show the flag." In 397, Alaric once again moved into Greece, and Stilicho launched an amphibious expedition against him. Alaric was beaten, but in some unexplained way—there were accusations of treachery—he managed to make an orderly withdrawal. Stilicho then returned to Italy, only to find that North Africa had broken its allegiance to Rome and cut off the corn supply on which Rome depended—and had done so under the pretense of authorization from the Eastern Emperor, whom Stilicho had just rescued. Stilicho dispatched a naval force against North Africa which rapidly brought the province back under control.

In late 401, Alaric invaded Italy; it was the start of a series of barbarian invasions which led to the sack of Rome itself in 410. Alaric and Stilicho fought a bloody battle at Pollenza in 402 which both sides claimed as a victory; Alaric withdrew, however, and was decisively beaten at Verona in the summer of the same year. Once again Alaric escaped; Claudian ascribes this to the poor discipline of Stilicho's auxiliaries. In early 406, a later invasion under one Radagaisus, with a mixed force of less well-disciplined barbarians, was defeated outside Florence, with very few Roman casualties (Claudian claims that there were none at all).

Matters soon worsened: The Rhine froze, Gaul was invaded by hordes of German barbarians (Vandals, Burgundians, Swabians, and Alans), the army of Britain elected the usurper Constantine as emperor and launched a cross-Channel invasion, Alaric reinvaded, and, in 408, Arcadius died, leaving the Eastern Empire insecure and leaderless. Stilicho could hardly have known which way to turn. What he did, in fact, was to leave Gaul to itself; he persuaded the bitterly resentful Roman senate to buy off Alaric with four thousand pounds of gold and dispatch him against Constantine. Stilicho then prepared to leave for Constantinople to take charge of Arcadius' seven-year-old heir, Theodosius II (401-450). Yet these measures were too pragmatic for the Roman people to accept. Thus Stilicho was accused of treachery. Honorius launched a massacre of his supporters: His Hunnish bodyguard was murdered, and Stilicho himself was arrested at Ravenna. It is clear that even then Stilicho could have fought and probably cracked Honorius' stronghold on power. Instead, he obeyed orders and surrendered to execution.

Summary

Flavius Stilicho has long proved a puzzle to historians. It is very tempting to see him as the noble upholder of an impractical and decadent imperial ruling class which rewarded his support and obedience only by murder. There is a kind of justice, in this view, in the sack of Rome by Alaric's Goths two years later. The Roman senate and emperor did not realize how much they had relied on Stilicho until they had killed him. In favor of this view is the unswerving loyalty which Stilicho himself displayed, almost to the point of quixotism.

Yet there are odd features in Stilicho's career. He hardly ever won a major battle, except against the unimportant Radagaisus. Alaric always seemed to slip away from him. Did Stilicho in fact retain a kind of alliance with the Gothic king, who had been his ally at the Frigidus River in 394? Or should Stilicho be seen as essentially a warlord, whose trade was war and whose capital was soldiers? Could it be that Stilicho would not risk casualties and did not particularly want a major victory which would only bring peace? It has also been noted that rivals of Stilicho—such as the commander of the North African expedition in 408 or Arcadius' main adviser in 395—were inclined to meet with strange accidents or be openly murdered. Stilicho was also very quick to marry his daughters to Honorius and seems to have planned to marry his son into the imperial family also. As a "half-barbarian," he could not be emperor, but his design may have been to have a grandson as ruler over a reunited empire. In this way, he was quite capable of ruthlessness.

The questions are insoluble, but one final point may be made. Stilicho may not have had as much choice as modern historians tend to suppose. Accusations of "letting people off" and military ineptitude rest on the assumption that Roman armies were competent and reliable. After Adrianople, this may not have been the case. Stilicho had continuous trouble in recruiting good Roman troops, and the barbarians he used instead were often badly disciplined and unreliable. He was fencing with a brittle weapon and may in fact have done as well as anyone could expect. Possibly his underlying weakness was something as elementary as a desperate shortage of real Roman drill sergeants.

Bibliography

Bury, John B. *A History of the Later Roman Empire from the Death of Theodosius I to the Death of Justinian (A.D. 395 toA.D. 565).* London: Macmillan, 1923; New York: Dover, 1958. This volume may be considered the nineteenth century alternative to Gibbon, cited below. It is strong on dates and events and determinedly personal in interpretation. Lacks the twentieth century awareness of social forces demonstrated, for example, by Jones, below.

Cameron, Alan D. E. *Claudian: Poetry and Propaganda at the Court of Honorius.* Oxford: Clarendon, 1970. This work attempts to distinguish truth from flattery in the work of Stilicho's greatest propagandist. Perhaps by inevitable reaction from its subject, this book takes a severely negative view of Stilicho.

Claudianus, Claudius. *Claudian.* Translated by Maurice Platnauer. London: Heinemann, and New York: Putnam, 1922. This edition and translation, in the familiar Loeb Classical Library series, makes it possible for students to see both what data can be extracted from Claudian's poems on Stilicho and how carefully data are at times concealed. The information Claudian does not mean to give is more revealing than his surface intention.

Gibbon, Edward. *The Decline and Fall of the Roman Empire.* 6 vols. London: Murray, and New York: Dutton, 1922. This set of volumes in the Everyman series is only one of innumerable reprints of Gibbon's classic work, first published from 1776 to 1788. In spite of their age, chapters 29 and 30 are well worth reading, for their style and recondite learning. Gibbon succeeded at an early stage in catching the ambiguous quality of Stilicho's achievement.

Isbell, Harold, trans. *The Last Poets of Imperial Rome.* London and Baltimore: Penguin Books, 1971. Among other poems, this volume offers Claudian's *Raptus Proserpiae* (c. A.D. 397) and the *Epithalamium* (A.D. 398) for the marriage of Honorius and Stilicho's daughter Maria. The former poem is valuable as a reminder that there was still an important pagan faction among the Roman aristocracy.

Jones, A. H. M. *The Later Roman Empire 284-602: A Social, Economic, and Administrative Survey.* 3 vols. Oxford: Blackwell, 1964; Baltimore: Johns Hopkins University Press, 1986. These volumes provide essential data for considering the complicated social, administrative, and military structures within which Stilicho functioned. This work does not make for easy reading, and careful use of the index and table of contents is advised.

O'Flynn, John M. *Generalissimos of the Western Roman Empire.* Edmonton: University of Alberta Press, 1983. The three chapters of this work devoted to Stilicho give an able summary of what is known and attempt to answer some of the riddles of his career in terms of the power structures of the time. There is some interest in the comparison with Stilicho's successors, who appear to have shed some of his inhibitions and solved some of his problems.

Randers-Pehrson, Justine D. *Barbarians and Romans.* Norman: University of Oklahoma Press, and London: Croom Helm, 1983. This work is organized geographically, but the chapters on Milan, Rome, and Ravenna all have relevance to Stilicho's career. Includes good illustrations: for example, a photograph of the monument celebrating the victory at Pollenza, with Stilicho's name carefully removed.

T. A. Shippey

STRABO

Born: 64 or 63 B.C.; Amasia, Pontus, Asia Minor
Died: After A.D. 23; probably Amasia or Rome
Areas of Achievement: Geography and history
Contribution: Building on the work of his predecessors, Strabo wrote a description of the known inhabited world, valuable for its philosophy of geography, its historical digressions, and the current scientific notions it contains. Although not always accurate in details, the seventeen books of the *Geography* stand out for their diverse subjects, encyclopedic scope, and contemporary view of the ancient world at the dawn of the Christian era.

Early Life

Strabo was born at Amasia in Pontus, about ninety kilometers inland from the southeastern shore of the Black Sea. Formerly a royal capital of Pontus, Amasia was located in a deep valley on the Iris River. It was a well-fortified place, with striking mountains towering above the town. Located there were the tombs of the kings of Pontus. Amasia controlled the river valleys and villages about itself, which doubtless contributed to its wealth. It is inferred that Strabo belonged to a rich family that could afford to give their son a good education. Although his lineage was a mixture of Asiatic and Greek, Strabo's training and language were purely Greek.

The area had been conquered by the Romans immediately before Strabo's birth. In the generation before, Mithradates the Great of Pontus had extended the kingdom's borders through Asia Minor, the islands of the Aegean Sea, and the southern and eastern shores of the Black Sea. He fought the Romans Lucius Cornelius Sulla, Lucius Licinius Murena, and Lucullus before succumbing to Pompey the Great. A most formidable foe of Rome, he died about the time Strabo was born.

Strabo thus grew up appreciating both the power of Rome and the legacy of Pontus. His mother's ancestors had been on close terms with the royal house, and one of them, the general Dorylaus Tacticus, had been a friend of King Mithradates V Euergetes. Mithradates the Great patronized Strabo's great-grandfather Lagetas and granduncle Moaphernes, appointing the latter to a governorship. The king also made Dorylaus' nephew the priest of Ma at Comana, a position that gave him power second only to Mithradates himself.

Strabo's education in grammar and rhetoric at Nysa (in southern Asia Minor) included lessons from Aristodemus, who was also the tutor of Pompey's sons. When he was nineteen or twenty years old, he went to Rome and was instructed by Tyrannio, a tutor of Cicero's sons and an expert on geography. It is likely that Strabo got his passion for the subject from this master. Also in Rome, Strabo learned from Xenarchus, who, like Tyrannio, was an Aristotelian. Nevertheless, references throughout the *Geōgraphica* (c. 7 B.C.; *Geography*, 1917-1933) indicate that Strabo himself became a follower of the Stoics, perhaps under the influence of Augustus' teacher and friend Athenodorus. In addition to his early educational trips, Strabo made other visits to Rome, most likely in 35 and 29 B.C.

As a youth, Strabo read widely and became especially enamored of Homer, as shown by his later passionate defense of the epics' historical and geographical accuracy. He also read Herodotus' *Historiai* (c. 425 B.C.; *The History*), which he did not value, and the work of Polybius, which he considered useful and accurate. He became familiar with the historical, scientific, and geographical works of Posidonius, Eratosthenes of Cyrene, Hipparchus, Artemidorus, and Ephorus. In addition, Strabo read the works of the historians of Alexander the Great, especially concerning Alexander's eastern travels.

By adulthood, Strabo had visited a good portion of Asia Minor and made several trips to Rome. He had met influential Romans and Greeks and had been introduced to the best in literature and history—all of which were to influence his later writings.

Life's Work

Probably between 25 and 19 B.C., Strabo resided in Alexandria, Egypt. At the beginning of his sojourn there, he accompanied his friend Aelius Gallus, the Roman prefect of Egypt, on a trip up the Nile River, reaching the border of Ethiopia. His time in Egypt gave him opportunity to observe the country—and perhaps to use the library at Alexandria. Afterward, he returned to Rome for an undetermined amount of time.

Strabo's travels continued through his life and reached as far west as Etruria and as far east as the border of Armenia, south to the northern edge of Ethiopia, and north to the Black Sea. Around 26, Strabo wrote a historical work, now known as *His-*

torical Memoirs, none of which has survived, although Plutarch and Flavius Josephus refer to it. It comprised forty-three books, covering the period from the destruction of Corinth and Carthage in 146 B.C. to (perhaps) the Battle of Actium in 31 B.C., thus forming a continuation of Polybius' history.

Strabo's magnum opus was the *Geography*, a work in seventeen books describing the inhabited world of the three continents Europe, Asia, and Africa. Its scope included mathematical, physical, political, and historical aspects of geography. His was a general treatise on the subject: the first ancient attempt to synthesize all known geographical knowledge.

The first two books of the *Geography* deal with the history of the discipline, including attacks on the ideas of Eratosthenes and others, whom Strabo considered to have made mistakes in their published works on geography. He discourses at length on Homer, naming him the first geographer. (Strabo was often at pains to "prove Homer right" and saw the ship catalog in the second book of the *Iliad*, transcribed c. 800 B.C., as preserving historical locales and the voyages of Odysseus and Jason's quest for the Golden Fleece as actual events.) Strabo also suggests that since the inhabited world which he knows only makes up one-third of the temperate zone, it is likely that other continents exist.

Apparently not relying on Roman writers, Strabo addresses Spain in book 3, drawing mainly on Greek sources in his description of the natural resources and physical traits of the country. This book also makes mention of the mythical island home of Geryon and the Tin Islands, which Strabo does not recognize as connected with Britain in any way.

Relying heavily on the *Commentaries* (written 52-45 B.C.) of Julius Caesar, Strabo wrote the fourth book about Britain, France, and the Alps. Although he used Caesar's description of the Gaulish tribes, for some reason Strabo ignored his descriptions of the dimensions of Britain, thereby making the island much broader and shorter than it actually is. Strabo believed that Ireland lay to the north of Britain. His description of the Alps is somewhat accurate, including discussions of trade, alpine passes, and avalanches.

Since maps of Italy and the surrounding islands were common in his day, Strabo probably had one before him while writing about this area in his fifth

and sixth books. In addition, Strabo was personally familiar with Italy and aware of several Greek and Roman writers on the subject. Impressive in this section is his description of Mount Vesuvius, which he describes as having every appearance of a volcano, although it had not erupted in living memory. His words were oddly appropriate, for Vesuvius erupted in A.D. 79. Strabo never visited Sicily, so his description is not as accurate as that of Italy proper, but his descriptions of the volcanic activity of Mount Etna and the Aeolian Islands are well done.

Northern Europe forms the bulk of the seventh book, and the lack of information handicapping Strabo is very evident in this section. It is strange that Strabo ignores things which the Romans knew about these regions: the amber trade and the testimony of Herodotus about the region. When he describes the area north of the Black Sea, however, his accuracy increases, probably because of Mithradates' recent conquests in the area.

The next three books deal with Greece and its islands and is surprisingly lacking in geographical information; Strabo probably assumed that his readers were familiar with the area, and Strabo knew little of it at first hand. In addition, his preoccupation with identifying sites mentioned in the Homeric catalog of ships skewed Strabo's account here. Finally, Greece's diminished status in the period left little outstanding to describe. Many cities lay in ruin, while others were reduced to the status of sleepy villages in Strabo's lifetime. His interest in volcanoes does not flag in this section, which describes the volcanic activity of mountains at Thera and near Methone.

Books 11 through 16 deal with Asia. Strabo's accounts of Asia Minor—especially the northern sections—are rather accurate, for he had seen much of it, his home being in Pontus. The section includes a discussion of the site of Homeric Troy. Strabo believed that the Caspian Sea connected to the northern ocean, and even describes what a sailor would see as he sailed southward into this arm of the surrounding sea. Strabo admits that he knows nothing about the extreme north of Asia, and, although he knows the name of silk producers, he does not mention the silk trade at all, although it had already become quite important. He provides an interesting account of India, derived from the lost works of those who accompanied Alexander the Great to that land. Strabo concentrates on the customs of the inhabitants there—at the expense of the actual geography of the territory. Africa, the subject of the seventeenth book, is well described along the Nile because of Strabo's personal acquaintance with the territory. He describes the antiquities of the land and gives an account of the Ethiopians. The rest of Africa is not as well delineated; in fact, Strabo reduced its size by more than two-thirds, having no idea how far to the south it actually extended. In fact, Strabo seems to have ignored or not to have known of the works of his younger contemporary Juba II, King of Mauretania, who had written extensively on North African geography and history.

Strabo died some time after completing the *Geography*, possibly in his homeland. His acquaintance with eminent Romans of his time and the admiration for the Roman Empire which he consistently shows in his writing could not ensure instant success at Rome for his work, which came to be appreciated only by later generations.

Summary

Strabo said that his work would be useful to administrators and generals calling geography a practical and philosophical science. He thus avoids tedious listings of the insignificant in favor of major points relating to places under discussion. His work is encyclopedic and comprehensive—a storehouse of information about his world.

The date and place of composition are uncertain. The latest date in it is A.D. 23, but few believe that he began his work in his eighties. It has been argued that he composed it while in his fifties, around 7 B.C., and later revised, for it lacks references to events between 3 B.C. and A.D. 19. Rome seems a likely place for its publication, but some have argued that Strabo returned to Amasia to write it, because Pliny the Elder and Ptolemy ignore the work. Had it been published in Rome, one would expect that it would have gained some attention. In fact, however, there are only a few minor references to the *Geography* before Stephanus of Byzantium made frequent use of it at the end of the fifth century A.D. Other possibilities for Strabo's residence at the end of his life include the eastern Mediterranean region or Naples.

Although Strabo boasts of his wide travels, he evidently did not make detailed studies of all the places he visited. He probably saw Cyrene in Libya only as he sailed by and likely did not even visit Athens. In Italy, he kept to the main roads leading to and from Rome.

Strabo assumed a spherical Earth at the center of the universe. An island surrounded by ocean, it was admissible of being divided into five zones, uninhabitable at the extreme north because of the cold and at the extreme south because of the heat. Aside from assuming a geocentric universe, Strabo made a number of mistakes, mainly resulting from the lack of accurate observations and reliable sources of information. Where data were available, they were often misleading. As a result, he distorted the shape of the whole of the Mediterranean and Europe. Other mistakes include the assumption that the northern coast of Africa was practically a straight line, and that a line from the Pillars of Hercules to the Strait of Messina was equidistant from Europe and Africa. Also in error are his statements that the Pyrenees form a line from north to south, that Cape St. Vincent is the most westerly point of Europe, and that eastern Crete does not extend much to the east of Sunium Promontorium (when in fact four-fifths of the entire island lie east of it). Describing Palestine, he asserted that the Jordan River flowed into the Mediterranean, being navigable for ships sailing east from the sea.

In spite of its inaccuracies, Strabo's *Geography* is the most important geographical treatise from the ancient world. Its great value lies not only in his own observations which, when firsthand, are accurate and lucid—but also in the preservation of so many previous authors whose work it summarizes, especially Eratosthenes and Posidonius.

Bibliography

Bunbury, E. H. *A History of Ancient Geography Among the Greeks and Romans from the Earliest Ages Till the Fall of the Roman Empire.* 2d ed. London: Murray, 1883; New York: Dover, 1959. Originally published in 1879, this work is the standard handbook on the subject of ancient geography. Putting Strabo in historical perspective, it has four long sections on the *Geography*, with detailed discussions of each book, commenting on Strabo's sources, errors, and value. With maps, notes, and an index.

Dilke, O. A. W. *Greek and Roman Maps.* London: Thames and Hudson, and Ithaca, N.Y.: Cornell University Press, 1985. Evidence for cartography in the ancient world, from the work in Mesopotamia to the Renaissance. Chapters on ancient Greece and geographical writers, the latter containing a section on Strabo: his cartographic terms, construction of a globe, contribution to mapmaking, use of myth, and lack of scientific accuracy. Contains numerous maps, charts, photographs, notes, appendices, and bibliography, and an index.

Keane, John. *The Evolution of Geography: A Sketch of the Rise and Progress of Geographical Knowledge from the Earliest Times to the First Circumnavigation of the Globe*. London: Edward Stanford, 1899. The chapter on ancient geography covers material from the Bible to Ptolemy. Substantial discussion of Strabo and his contribution, including his sources, life, travels, and observations. With maps and an index.

Kish, George. *A Source Book in Geography*. Cambridge, Mass.: Harvard University Press, 1978. Selections from Strabo and other ancient geographers, putting the *Geography* in context. Casts light on the geographical theory. Includes selections from Plato, Aristotle, Greek travelers' reports, Greek heliocentric theory, and selections from Strabo on geography in general, the inhabited world, changes in the earth, volcanoes, Asian lands.

Magie, David. *Roman Rule in Asian Minor to the End of the Third Century After Christ*. 2 vols. Princeton, N.J.: Princeton University Press, 1950. Exhaustive historical discussion of Strabo's homeland. Essential for understanding the geographer's background. A chapter on "The Rise of the Power of Pontus," chapters on Mithradates, Pompey, and the years of Strabo's youth. Told from the Roman perspective, it is dependent on Strabo's *Geography* as the copious notes show.

Richards, G. C. "Strabo: The Anatolian Who Failed of Roman Recognition." *Greece and Rome* 10 (1940): 79-90. Brief introductory piece about the major events of Strabo's life, including short discussions of the controversies involved. Covers his visits to Rome, dates of his works, location of his retirement, and his Roman connections. Also discusses the importance of his Stoicism and his use of sources, both scientific and poetic (Homer).

Strabo. *The "Geography" of Strabo with an English Translation*. Translated by Horace Leonard Jones. 8 vols. Cambridge, Mass.: Harvard University Press, and London: Heinemann, 1917-1933. Contains the complete Greek text and English translation, with notes and bibliography. Includes diagrams illustrating complex mathematical discussions, maps, and index. Useful introduction discusses Strabo's life and works. Identifies the sources of Strabo's many quotations, contains useful cross-references, and points out textual variations.

———. *Selections from Strabo*. Henry F. Tozer, ed. Oxford: Clarendon Press, 1893. Of great value for its fifty-page introduction on Strabo's life and works, including estimates of his style, interests, audience, defects, methods, sources, text, and date. Excellent introductions to and commentary on the most important sections of the *Geography*. With notes, maps, and an index.

Syme, Sir Ronald. *Anatolica: Studies in Strabo*. Edited by Anthony R. Birley. Oxford: Clarendon, 1995. Syme originally drafted this volume in 1944-45. He thoroughly analyzes not only Strabo's geography but practically all of the written data on the Anatolian region. In spite of Syme's low opinion of Strabo as a person, the book demonstrates the importance of Strabo's Anatolian geography studies in Roman policy. Syme adds much to the modern understanding of Strabo's methods.

Thomson, J. Oliver. *History of Ancient Geography*. Cambridge: Cambridge University Press, 1948; New York: Biblo and Tanne, 1965. Originally published in 1948 as an update to Bunbury, this work is arranged chronologically, with an emphasis on theory and regions rather than individual authors. Numerous useful maps and pertinent chapters on geography in the Roman Republic, theory in the same period, and the great days of the Roman Empire. With a brief section on Strabo. Contains an index and addenda.

Daniel B. Levine

LUCIUS CORNELIUS SULLA

Born: 138 B.C.; Rome
Died: 78 B.C.; Puteoli
Areas of Achievement: Government and warfare
Contribution: Sulla played an extremely important historical role in the transformation of the Roman Republic into the Roman Empire. While attempting to prevent others from using force to influence Roman politics, Sulla became the first Roman to use the military to gain a political end.

Early Life

Lucius Cornelius Sulla was born into an old Roman patrician family in 138 B.C. Although not much is known of his youth, Sulla did receive an excellent education in the Greek and Roman classics. He grew to be a handsome man with golden red hair and sharp piercing blue eyes. Sulla had a very pale complexion, and a severe skin condition badly scarred his face. Because his family had little wealth and his father left him nothing when he died, Sulla had to live on the income from a relatively small investment. As a consequence of his modest means, Sulla lived in a small apartment in one of the less desirable neighborhoods of Rome, a circumstance he found demeaning. To an ambitious patrician, wealth was a necessary prerequisite to participation in politics.

Sulla's life changed, however, when he inherited the estates of both his stepmother and his mistress, allowing him to pursue his dream of public service. Although Rome had been at war with Jugurtha in North Africa since 111, the Roman army had not made much progress toward victory. In 108, Gaius Marius was elected consul for the following year, and the people voted to transfer the command of the war from Quintus Caecilius Metellus to Marius. In the same election, they elected Sulla quaestor and chose him to serve under Marius.

During his years of military service in Africa, Sulla proved himself an able and courageous soldier, popular with common soldiers as well as officers. Although Marius was more successful against Jugurtha than Metellus had been, he was unable to capture the elusive enemy leader. Sulla was entrusted with the task of convincing Bocchus (King of Mauretania and father-in-law of Jugurtha) to betray Jugurtha to the Romans. Through skillful diplomacy, Sulla was able to win the friendship of Bocchus, capture Jugurtha, and end the war.

After the war, Marius returned to Rome in triumph on January 1, 104. Although Sulla captured Jugurtha, Marius claimed the triumph as his. Sulla, as a military subordinate, was in no position to dispute Marius' claim. Immediately after their victory in Africa, the Romans faced a new war against two German tribes, the Cimbri and the Teutons. Because of his recent triumph, the Romans now elected Marius consul to defend Italy. Sulla served as a legate of Marius and once again used his diplomatic skills to detach the Marsi from the German alliance.

After his latest tour of duty, Sulla returned to Rome in 99 to stand for the praetorship. Despite his military successes, Sulla failed to win office. Yet the next year, the people elected Sulla urban praetor. The senate assigned Sulla to Cilicia for his propraetorial governorship. On reaching his province, Sulla received a senatorial order to restore Ariobarzanes to the throne of Cappadocia. After his success in Cappadocia, Sulla had the opportunity to negotiate Rome's first diplomatic relations with the Parthians.

833

Life's Work

Sulla now returned to Rome to seek the consulship. When his political enemies prosecuted him in an unsuccessful campaign to discredit him, Sulla had to postpone his canvassing for office. With the failed campaign for the consulship came public notice of Sulla's feud with Marius. Many of the Roman aristocracy viewed Marius as an upstart (*novus homo*) who did not know his proper place. Sulla's capture of Jugurtha, his military successes, and his patrician background made Sulla the perfect man to challenge Marius. When Sulla received sufficient backing, he gained the consulship for 88.

Because of the territorial expansion of Mithradates the Great, King of Pontus, the senate decided to give Sulla the command of the war against Mithradates. The tribune Publius Sulpicius Rufus, however, introduced a bill in the Tribal Assembly to transfer the command to Marius. Since no public business could be conducted during a public holiday, Sulla and a consular colleague declared a public holiday to prevent the vote from taking place. Sulpicius claimed that this was illegal and incited the people to riot. To save himself from the mob, Sulla rescinded the holiday decree and pretended to accept the transfer of his command. Sulla then went to address his troops gathered in Campania for the war against Mithradates. After he explained the political developments in Rome, the troops urged Sulla to lead them to Rome to reclaim his rightful command. With the backing of his soldiers, Sulla marched on Rome and took the city by force.

Although these events marked the first time in history a Roman army had violated the *pomerium* (the sacred boundary of Rome), Sulla believed that he was defending legally constituted authority and that he was saving Rome from tyrannical demagogues. Once in control of Rome, Sulla had the senate declare Marius and Sulpicius public enemies, subject to immediate execution. Although Marius managed to escape from Rome, Sulpicius was captured and killed. After having the senate annul the laws of Sulpicius, Sulla sent his army away and allowed the election of the consuls for the next year. Gnaeus Octavius (a supporter of Sulla) and Lucius Cornelius Cinna (an enemy of Sulla) were elected consuls for the year 87. Sulla, anxious to fight the war with Mithradates, left for Greece.

With Sulla out of Italy, Cinna declared Sulla a public enemy but did nothing to hinder him in the East. After pushing the forces of Mithradates out of Greece and defeating them in Asia Minor, Sulla made peace with Mithradates. On hearing that Cinna had been murdered by his own troops, Sulla invaded Italy in the spring of 83. Within a year, Sulla defeated all the forces ranged against him. He massacred the Italians who sided with Cinna and who were still in rebellion and confiscated some of their lands.

Having Rome firmly in his control, Sulla ordered the execution of all magistrates and high military officers who had served Cinna's government. To limit the executions to those guilty, Sulla published proscription lists of those subject to the death penalty. Sulla confiscated the properties of those proscribed and auctioned them to his supporters. Motivated by greed, some Sullan supporters arranged for the proscription of certain wealthy individuals in order to acquire their money and lands. The death toll among the upper classes included seventy senators and sixteen hundred equestrians. The sons and grandsons of those proscribed were barred from holding public office in the future.

From Sulla's point of view, he meted out various punishments under his authority as proconsul. The drawback to being a proconsul, however, was that Sulla could not enter Rome. When the death of Gnaeus Papirius Carbo, Cinna's former consular colleague, became known, Sulla suggested that the dictatorship be revived after a lapse of 120 years. Although the usual term of office for a dictator in Rome was six months or less, Sulla wanted no time limit placed upon him. Accordingly, the people elected Sulla dictator and granted him complete immunity. Sulla's having the title of "Dictator for the making of laws and the settling of the Constitution" allowed his every decree to become law immediately.

As dictator in 81 Sulla instituted a constitutional reform which placed the senate in total control of the state. Sulla increased senate membership from the traditional number of three hundred to six hundred by including pro-Sullan equestrians and by automatically making all former quaestors members of the senate. The number of praetors was increased to eight and the number of quaestors to twenty. To create an orderly career ladder, Sulla established a strict *cursus honorum* in which politicians had to hold the quaestorship and praetorship before holding the consulship (the minimum age for holding this office was to be forty-two). Because tribunes had caused so much political turmoil in the past, men holding the tribuneship were now limited in the use of the veto and were barred from holding any higher office. In addition, prior senatorial approval was required before bills from a tribune could be introduced into an assembly.

At the height of his power, Sulla stepped down from the dictatorship and restored constitutional government. Sulla was elected consul for 80, after which he retired to one of his villas in Puteoli (in Campania) to write and to relax by hunting and fishing. In his extensive memoirs, Sulla minimized the humble circumstances of his early years and emphasized his career from the time of war with Jugurtha. Sulla wanted to create the image of having possessed *felicitas* (good luck) from childhood. After a lifetime spent in active service to Rome, Sulla died of liver failure in 78. His body was taken to the Forum in Rome, where it lay in state. After thousands of Sullan veterans and ordinary people passed the funeral bier to pay their respects, the body was cremated. So great was Sulla's following that the matrons of Rome mourned Sulla for a full year, just as they would have done for their own fathers.

Summary

Although Lucius Cornelius Sulla was not a talented orator, he had the ability to establish an immediate personal rapport with people. Whether commanding troops, leading the state, or managing delicate diplomatic negotiations, Sulla was always able to earn the respect of the people with whom he dealt. Sulla's contemporaries of all classes were most impressed by his personal charm and by this highly developed sense of humor. In addition, Sulla believed that he possessed a special divine gift, *felicitas*. With his natural abilities and his good luck backing him, Sulla was always confident.

Unknowingly, Sulla played an important historical role in Rome's transition from a republic to an empire. Despite his passionate belief in Rome's republican form of government, Sulla felt compelled to defend the state by being the first to use military force against it. As Roman politics became more polarized, adversaries used violence as the means to a political end. Although angered at the prospect of losing his command against Mithradates, Sulla looked upon Marius, Cinna, Carbo, and Sulpicius as men intent on violating the Roman constitution. Sulla, therefore, saw his actions in a broader context than a mere factional dispute. As a patriotic Roman, Sulla could not stand by and watch the subversion of the Republic.

When Marius allowed the Roman legions to recruit from among the urban proletariat, he made possible the rise of a man such as Sulla. Generals now recruited armies whose only loyalties were to their commanders. When Sulla's men believed their general to have been wronged, they rose to his defense, not to that of the state. Although Sulla exercised absolute power over Rome, he did not use his power to establish a Hellenistic-style monarchy. Sulla viewed the senate as representing traditional republican government: He attempted to restore it to its former central role. In short, Sulla tried to repair the Roman constitution after self-serving politicians had damaged it.

Using as many historical precedents as possible, Sulla tried to resolve Rome's problems in a constitutional manner. In reviving the dictatorship with no time limit, Sulla was harking back to 387 B.C., when Marcus Furius Camillus required more than six months to save Rome from the Gauls. Just as the Romans thought Camillus the savior of Rome, Sulla hoped for the same recognition. When the Romans needed a thorough revision of their laws in 451, they turned to the *decemviri* for leadership. In Sulla's view, the Romans needed a new constitutional reform.

Despite his great talents and his extreme patriotism, Sulla ultimately failed to accomplish what he had set out to do. The Sullan reforms were not permanent, and they did not stop the Roman constitution from changing. By 70, Sulla's own supporters, Marcus Licinius Crassus and Pompey the Great, annulled or changed much of Sulla's work. Although his efforts to preserve the Republic were well-meaning, they demonstrated that Sulla did not understand Rome's deep-seated problems. The very situation he sought to prevent, the use of force in politics, became the established norm as a result of Sulla's own march on Rome and his use of proscription lists. Rome did not achieve political stability until Augustus established the Empire in 27 B.C.

Bibliography

Appianus. *Appian's "Roman History."* Translated by Horace White. 4 vols. London: Heinemann, and New York: Macmillan, 1912-1913. Appian's "The Civil Wars," "The Mithridatic Wars," and "Numidian Affairs" cover the time periods for Sulla's participation in these events. Although

Appian lived during the late first and early second centuries A.D., he preserved some very valuable information from an unknown early imperial annalist. This work is part of the Loeb Classical Library series.

Badian E. "Waiting for Sulla." *Journal of Roman Studies* 52 (1962): 47-61. The author attempts to bring modern critical historiographical analysis to the study of the period of Sulla. Through a re-examination of the sources, Badian maintains that Sulla's ambition drove him into rebellion against lawful authority. Sulla's contemporaries did not, according to Badian, believe that Sulla was a champion of the Roman nobility.

Green, Peter. *Alexander to Actium: The Historical Evolution of the Hellenistic Age.* Berkeley: University of California Press, 1990. Green narrates, interprets, and criticizes in a lively way virtually every aspect of a vast range of kingdoms and cultures, including Sulla's activities in Roman law. Much of the narrative obviously demonstrates Green's personal views of the political and cultural history of the time. His sometimes scornful attitude occasionally eclipses the idea that in spite of much scandal, the Hellenistic Age was an important and civilized period.

Keaveney, Arthur. *Sulla: The Last Republican.* London and Dover, N.H.: Croom Helm, 1982. The first full-scale biography of Sulla to appear in English. The author gathered and analyzed all the available evidence on the life of Sulla and presents it in a most convincing manner. A very favorable interpretation of Sulla.

Plutarch. *Fall of the Roman Republic, Six Lives: Marius, Sulla, Crassus, Pompey, Caesar, Ciero.* Translated by Rex Warner. Rev. ed. London: Penguin Books, 1972; Baltimore: Penguin Books, 1980. This volume contains a chapter on Sulla together with other chapters on some of his political rivals. Because Plutarch used many sources unavailable today, he preserved much anecdotal material which may be contemporaneous with Sulla. Although Plutarch's work lacks historical perspective and is very moralistic, it portrays Sulla vividly.

Sallust. *"The Jugurthine War" and "The Conspiracy of Catiline."* Translated by S. A. Handford. London and Baltimore: Penguin, 1963. A useful and interesting but brief account of Marius and Sulla in the war against Jugurtha. Despite his prejudice against the Roman nobility and his inaccuracies in chronology and geography, Sallust is an important source of information. It is highly probable that Sallust used Sulla's memoirs as one of his sources.

Scullard, H. H. *From the Gracchi to Nero: A History of Rome from 133 B.C. to A.D. 68.* 5th ed. London and New York: Methuen, 1982. This book contains two chapters, "The Rise and Fall of Marius" and "The Rise and Fall of Sulla," which give an exceptionally clear account of this most crucial period in Roman history. Points of interpretative discussion with secondary source citations are included in the notes at the back of the book.

Peter L. Viscusi

CORNELIUS TACITUS

Born: c. A.D. 56; place unknown
Died: c. A.D. 120; probably Rome
Areas of Achievement: Government and historiography
Contribution: Combining a successful career in the Roman civil service with a lifelong interest in his nation's past, Tacitus devoted his mature years to exploring the many facets of history. His portraits of the famous and the infamous, especially during the early years of the Roman Empire, are among the most vivid and influential descriptions in all Roman literature.

Early Life

Cornelius Tacitus, considered by many scholars to be Rome's greatest historian, is an enigma. Neither the exact date of his birth nor that of his death is known. His *praenomen*, that name which distinguished each Roman from his relatives, is a mystery, as is his birthplace. Tacitus never mentioned his parents or any siblings in any of his writings. He imparts to his readers much information about his contemporaries and a number of historical personages, but he never reveals a single solid fact about himself.

Almost everything that is known about Tacitus has been gleaned from the writings of his close friend Pliny the Younger, an author in his own right and the nephew of the great scientist and historian, Pliny the Elder. The friendship seems to have been of long duration, a fact which has led authorities to speculate that Tacitus was actually the son of one Cornelius Tacitus, who served as a financial agent of the government in Gallia Belgica and was a friend of Pliny the Elder. The public career of Tacitus is a matter of record, and by carefully noting the dates of his terms of office in each position it is possible to place his birth early in the reign of Nero, probably the year 56.

Clearly, Tacitus received an excellent education with special emphasis on rhetoric, because he was recognized in later life as a fine public speaker and an outstanding lawyer. He may have studied with the great Quintilian, who taught Pliny the Younger, but Tacitus never mentions his teachers or his fellow students. The elegance of his prose and his reputation denote one of good birth who received all the advantages belonging to his class, but the actual details must remain speculation. From natural modesty, Tacitus may have thought it unnecessary to repeat facts well known to his readers or he may have done so out of caution. Most of his youth was spent during troubled times when the slightest notoriety might mean death.

In his late teens Tacitus probably had the opportunity to hold his first public offices. Usually, young men at this age were assigned minor posts in one of the four minor magistracies. During these brief terms of service it was possible to judge their preparation as well as their potential for success in government service. Having tested his mettle as a civilian, a young man then entered the military for a brief time to experience the rigor and discipline of the Roman army. This tour of duty was usually performed under a relative or close friend of the family. If a career in the military were not his choice, a young Roman of good birth reentered civilian life by selecting a wife and offering himself for a place in the civil service. Since a candidate with a wife was given priority, marriage at an early age was not unusual. In 77, Cornelius Tacitus, his military service completed, was betrothed to the daughter of the noted general Agricola.

Life's Work

Tacitus took the first step in the *cursus honorem*, or the Roman civil service, in 82, when he was chosen a quaestor. He was one of twenty young men who for a year had the opportunity to prove their potential for a political career by fulfilling the duties of the lowest regular position in the civil service. If the quaestor's command of the law earned for him the commendation of the consul under whom he served, he might be offered another year under a proconsul in one of the imperial provinces.

For Tacitus, the next rung in the ladder of preferment was probably the position of aedile. These magistrates might perform any number of duties in Rome. Some of them saw to the care of the city and supervised the repair of public buildings. Others were responsible for regulating traffic within the capital. The organization of public games or the supervision of the morals of the populace might prove more difficult than the checking of weights and measures, but all these duties could fall to an aedile during his term of office, and each was a test of his ability. Tacitus obviously succeeded, because he was elected a praetor in 88.

Originally a military title, the office of praetor was by the time of the empire essentially a legal

which he finished in 96, the year in which Domitian was assassinated.

De vita Julii Agricolae (c. 98; *Agricola*, 1793) was more than a simple biography. While recounting the various stages in the career of Agricola and imparting to the reader varied details about the Britons, their history, and their country, Tacitus began to examine a theme on which he would comment for the next twenty years: the conflict between liberty and the power of the state. He also had the opportunity to serve the state in the aftermath of the reign of terror of Domitian; in 97, he was elected consul during the first year of the reign of Nerva, a distinguished and respected senator.

In 99, Tacitus' public career reached its zenith when he and Pliny the Younger successfully prosecuted the case of Marius Priscus, who had used his government position to abuse the provincials of Africa. Both men received a special vote of thanks from the senate for their preparation of the case for the state. Tacitus also received much attention for his second book, *De origine et situ Germanorum* (98; *Germania*, 1793). Based on his observation and research while serving with the army, it was an immediate success. While Tacitus saw the Germans as a potential threat to the security of the empire, he was impressed with their love of freedom and the simplicity of their lives when contrasted to the servility and decadence of his fellow Romans. With few flaws, *Germania* is an impressive and persuasive work of scholarship.

Having embarked on the study of the past, Tacitus devoted his next work, *Dialogus de oratoribus* (c. 98-102; *Dialogue on Orators*, 1793), to the apparent decay of the art of oratory. Quintilian had addressed the problem a generation earlier, and while he may have had a strong influence on Tacitus' thoughts on the subject, it was to Cicero that Tacitus turned for stylistic inspiration. The culprit appeared to be the decline of education, but as Tacitus developed his theme using the time-honored device of the dialogue, it became apparent that the age of the Antonines was not suited to great oratory because it lacked the tension and turmoil that inspires great public speakers. The consolation for the decline of this discipline was the universal peace that had replaced the chaos of the reign of Domitian.

In 115, after serving as proconsul of the province of Asia, Tacitus finished his narration of the events between 69, when Servius Sulpicius Galba assumed the *imperium*, and the death of Domitian in

position. The experience gleaned during his term as an aedile would prepare the praetor for dealing with offenses from oppression and forgery to murder and treason. During his term as praetor, Tacitus was elected to the priesthood of one of the sacerdotal colleges, quite an honor for one so young. This election may have indicated not only his aristocratic birth but also the possession of the patronage of the influential and the powerful, including the emperor. The following year, Tacitus left for a tour of duty somewhere in the provinces.

He probably spent the next three years serving in the army, and he may have commanded a legion. During his last year abroad, Tacitus may have served as a proconsul in one of the lesser provinces of the empire. In 93, the year that he returned to Rome, his father-in-law, Agricola, died. Requesting permission to write a biography of Agricola, Tacitus was rebuffed by Domitian, who had already begun the judicial murder of anyone who he believed threatened his position or his life. While many of his friends and colleagues were slaughtered, Tacitus buried himself in his research and the subsequent writing of the forbidden biography,

96. *Historiarum libri qui supersunt* (c. 109; *Histories*, 1793) was followed the next year by *Ab excessu divi Augusti* (c. 116, *Annals*, 1698), which concentrated on the period from the beginning of the reign of Tiberius in 14 through the death of Nero in 68. As examples of historical scholarship, these works are flawed, punctuated with misinformation which might have been easily corrected had Tacitus troubled to do so. Tacitus was a student of human nature, not of politics, a moralist who sometimes reshaped history to suit his narrative. Having chosen the most turbulent period in Rome's history for his subject, Tacitus filled both works with his own prejudices, but his delineation of his characters is at times brilliant and redeems the *Histories* and the *Annals* from being mere gossip. Unfortunately, neither work exists intact. Tacitus died several years after completing the *Annals*, around 120, probably in Rome.

Summary

Reared in the tradition of sacrifice and service to Rome that had characterized the republic, Cornelius Tacitus dedicated himself to the best interests of the state, and he distinguished himself as a man of great promise from the beginning. At the age of forty, he witnessed the beginning of a three-year-long nightmare in which many of his friends and colleagues were murdered on the orders of Domitian because they espoused and publicly proclaimed many of those same principles that Tacitus held dear. For the rest of his life, Tacitus was haunted by the events of those years, and their memory runs like a dark thread through everything he wrote.

Either consciously or unconsciously, Tacitus sought to ease his fears, his guilt, and his confusion through the study and writing of history. The past held the key to Rome's gradual decay as well as the source of her possible salvation, and to reveal both was a duty Tacitus could not avoid. In his first book, *Agricola*, Tacitus not only celebrated the deeds of his father-in-law but also explored for the first time the conflict between liberty and the power of the state. The theme of freedom is also a strong element in his second book, *Germania*. Much of what is known about the early Britons and Germans is found in these two works, and while there may be some doubt about the accuracy of some facts, it would be hard to question the admiration of Tacitus for those who prized liberty above life.

His third work, *Dialogue on Orators*, seems a pleasant interlude between his earlier works and his histories of contemporary Rome, the *Histories* and the *Annals*. Tacitus was able to unleash a flood of criticism of the imperial system and question the character of a number of his fellow countrymen, because the Antonine emperors under whom he served, Nerva, Trajan, and Hadrian, were willing to tolerate free inquiry. Thus, his vivid portraits have colored the opinions of countless generations of writers and historians. They are boldly drawn to serve not only as records of past deeds but also as warnings to the future leaders of the Roman state. Tacitus accepted the imperial system as inevitable, but he believed that it could be revitalized by a return to the noble virtues that had made the republic unique. It is as a moralist more than as a historian that Tacitus has had his most positive and enduring effect.

In the years following his death, the scholars and writers who succeeded Tacitus as the guardians of the traditions of the Roman state created a vogue for everything pre-imperial, and the republic, despite its violent history, was idealized as a golden age. The emperor Marcus Claudius Tacitus, who reigned briefly at the end of the third century, sought to claim descent from the great historian. As an act of filial piety, he ordered statues of his supposed ancestor to be erected in every public library and ten copies of his works to be produced every year. The latter edict certainly was a fitting memorial to perhaps Rome's greatest historian.

Bibliography

Chilver, G. E. F. *A Historical Commentary on Tacitus' Histories I and II*. Oxford: Clarendon, and New York: Oxford University Press, 1979. Containing a wealth of information, this work will prove very helpful to students of the period, because the author takes great care to trace each source and reference used by Tacitus.

Löfstedt, Einar. "Tacitus as an Historian" and "The Style of Tacitus." In *Roman Literary Portraits*, translated by P. M. Fraser. Oxford: Clarendon, 1958; Westport, Conn.: Greenwood Press, 1978. This posthumously published collection of essays by a noted Swedish classical scholar contains two chapters which are extremely useful in understanding the personality as well as the work of Tacitus.

McDonald, A. H. "The Roman Historians." In *Fifty Years and Twelve of Classical Scholarship*, edited by Maurice Platnauer. 2d ed. Oxford: Blackwell, and New York: Barnes and Noble Books, 1968. This excellent essay compares and contrasts Tacitus with the other Roman historians and places him in the context of his time. It also contains an excellent bibliography.

Mellor, Ronald. *Tacitus*. New York: Routledge, 1993. Mellor's work challenges the notion that Tacitus was an exclusively conservative thinker, and uses frequent literary allusions and modern parallels to make the subject relevant to contemporary audiences. Mellor connects Tacitus's personal life with the course of his work to illustrate its originality. Observations are supported with readable translations, citations of ancient authors, and references to secondary works.

Syme, Ronald. *Tacitus*. 2 vols. Oxford: Clarendon Press, 1958. This superb biography is a remarkable work of scholarship which examines the life and work of Tacitus against the background of Rome in the first century. Its bibliography is an excellent resource for the student.

Tacitus, Cornelius. *Agricola*. Translated by M. Hutton and revised by R. M. Ogilvie. Cambridge, Mass.: Harvard University Press, and London: Heinemann, 1970. Part of the Loeb Classical Library, this volume also contains the *Germania*, translated by M. Hutton, and the *Dialogue on Orators*, translated by Sir W. Peterson. With the original Latin as well as line-by-line English translations. Enriched with excellent notes and scholarly essays.

———. *Annals*. Translated by John Jackson. 2 vols. Cambridge, Mass.: Harvard University Press, and London: Heinemann, 1937. Contained in these volumes are books 4 through 6 and books 11 through 14 of the *Annals*. Also included is an index to the other volumes in the Loeb Classical Library containing parts of the *Histories* and the *Annals*. With excellent maps.

———. *Histories*. Translated by Clifford H. Moore. Cambridge, Mass.: Harvard University Press, and London: Heinemann, 1925. Another volume in the Loeb series, this bilingual text contains an excellent introductory essay to the life and works of Tacitus, as well as the first three books of the *Histories*.

———. *Histories*. Translated by Clifford H. Moore. Cambridge, Mass.: Harvard University Press, and London: Heinemann, 1931. Contains fragments of the *Histories*, books 4 and 5, as well as books 1 through 3 of the *Annals*, translated by John Jackson.

Clifton W. Potter, Jr.

T'AO CH'IEN

Born: A.D. 365; Hsin-yang, China
Died: A.D. 427; Hsin-yang, China
Area of Achievement: Literature
Contribution: T'ao Ch'ien's insistence upon directness and simplicity in both form and content, although largely unappreciated during his lifetime, was in subsequent generations recognized as a major contribution to the development of Chinese poetry.

Early Life

T'ao Ch'ien was born on his parents' farm near the city of Hsin-yang in what is now the province of Kiangsi. His family had once been prominent among the local gentry, but by T'ao Ch'ien's time their property had shrunk to a few acres. In an autobiographical sketch written for his sons, he described himself as a bookish youth, fond of quiet and never happier than when observing the changing of the seasons. He received a conventional education in the Confucian Classics and upon completing his studies was awarded a minor position in the civil service.

It did not take him long, however, to become bored with this post, and he resigned to return to the life of a small farmer. He married and soon found himself with several young children to support; the unremitting toil of farming soon took its toll on his health. In 395, when he was thirty, his first wife died, and for a short time he was employed as a general's secretary. Once again, he found that he could not abide the life of an official, and he was soon back tilling his meager farm.

After remarrying and having more children, thus putting additional pressure on his already straitened circumstances, T'ao Ch'ien made one final attempt at occupying the sort of position for which his education had prepared him. In 405, an uncle with influence at court arranged for him to be appointed magistrate at P'eng-tse, not far from his home. Before long, however, he had to resign, because "my instinct is all for freedom and will not brook discipline or restraint." For the remainder of his life, he would eke out a subsistence living on his farm and refuse all further offers of government employment, while exercising the poetic gifts that would not be widely acknowledged until well after his death.

Life's Work

China was racked by dynastic warfare during much of T'ao Ch'ien's life, and some commentators have suggested that his reluctance to assume official positions was caused by an awareness of the punishments which awaited those who supported the losing side. It is far more probable, however, that it was his profound dislike of being at a superior's beck and call that made it impossible for him to take on the kinds of responsibilities society expected of him. His independent attitude was incomprehensible to most of his peers, and as a result it was commonly assumed that T'ao Ch'ien must be some sort of hermit or recluse.

This he was not, although it is true that he studiously avoided anything which carried with it formal duties or organizational affiliations. He was at one point on the verge of accepting an invitation to join the Lotus Society, an exclusive group of Buddhist intellectuals and literary men, but at the last moment he declined when he realized that no matter how convivial its members might be, it was still an organization with rules and regulations. T'ao Ch'ien was not antisocial—he was reputed to have been well liked by his neighbors, and he knew quite a few of his fellow poets—but he definitely was an advocate of the simple life, which for him meant staying close to home and nature and ignoring almost everything else.

It is this fundamental love of simplicity that distinguishes T'ao Ch'ien's verses from the works of court poets of his time, who utilized obscure allusions and complicated technical devices to fashion verses that appealed only to the highly educated. T'ao Ch'ien, by way of contrast, seldom made any literary allusions whatsoever, and he wrote for the widest possible audience. As a consequence, he was slighted by his era's critics and only fully appreciated by later generations of readers. It was more than a century after his death before a complete edition of his works appeared. The first writers to champion seriously his reputation were the T'ang Dynasty poets Meng Hao-jan (689-740) and Wang Wei (701-761), who ensured that his name would not be forgotten by honoring him as a spiritual predecessor of what would become one of the most brilliant periods in Chinese literary history.

The charms of T'ao Ch'ien's poetry are subtle. The fifth poem in his series of poems on drinking wine is perhaps as good an example as any of how simple words and thoughts can yield complex emotions:

> I built my cottage among the habitations of men,
> And yet there is no clamor of carriages and horses.
> You ask: "Sir, how can this be done?"
> "A heart that is distant creates its own solitude."
> I pluck chrysanthemums under the eastern hedge,
> Then gaze afar towards the southern hills.
> The mountain air is fresh at the dusk of day;
> The flying birds in flocks return.
> In these things there lies a deep meaning;
> I want to tell it, but have forgotten the words.

The irony resides in the concluding line's apparent confession of failure, which is superficially true— the poem's meaning has not been formally defined in words—but in a more profound sense false, since meaning has been suggestively expressed in the cumulative interaction of these direct and vivid images. Such images might strike self-consciously sophisticated readers, which was how many of the court officials of T'ao Ch'ien's time viewed themselves, as nothing more than bucolic snapshots. For those who approach them without patronizing preconceptions, however, their evident simplicity is resonant with intimations of elemental natural forces.

In order to appreciate the full impact of T'ao Ch'ien's decision to concentrate on realistic description of his humble surroundings, the reader needs to compare his approach with that of the dominant aristocratic and scholarly poets of the period. Their ideal was the mannered evocation of court life in lyrics that were rigidly controlled by parallel structures and recurring tonal patterns. A literal translation of one of Shen Yo's poems reads:

> slackening reins, dismounts carved carriage,
> changing clothes, attends jade bed.
>
> slanting hairpin, reflects autumn waters,
> opening mirror, compares spring dresses.

Each line contains two—and no more or fewer than two—parallel images, the Chinese ideograms follow a set sequence of tones, and the content is characteristically taken from upper-class life.

Compare the above to the third section of T'ao Ch'ien's "Returning to the Farm to Dwell":

> I planted beans below the southern hill
> The grasses flourished, but bean sprouts were few.
> I got up at dawn to clear away the weeds
> And come back now with the moon, hoe on shoulder.
> Tall bushes crowd the narrow path

> And evening dew soaks my clothes.
> Wet clothes are no cause for complaint
> If things will only go as hoped.

Here the conversational tone of the narrative, the way that content is restricted to the mundanities of farm life, and the *in medias res* beginning all work together to convey an impression of natural reality that is the polar opposite of Shen Yo's sort of poetry.

T'ao Ch'ien was not, however, averse to enlivening his rural existence with an overindulgence in the pleasures of wine. He was renowned for his drinking, which in the social context of his period was an acceptable way of temporarily escaping worldly preoccupations rather than a sign of moral weakness. T'ao Ch'ien's name is thus often linked with those of two other poets who were also serious imbibers: Ch'u Yuan (c. 343 B.C.-c. 289 B.C.) and Li Po (701-762). Some of his best poems were written while enjoying this favorite pastime.

T'ao Ch'ien's life ended in the same pastoral setting in which it had begun, with no dramatic anecdote to set the day of his death apart from the days that had preceded and would follow it. During his final twenty-two years, he had become both a material and a spiritual part of his natural environment. In a prose sketch written just before he died, T'ao Ch'ien described how, as was the custom, his old friends gave him a farewell banquet in honor of what he had meant to their lives. With typical unhurried deliberation, he enumerated the foods and wines that were served as he prepared "to depart from this lodging house to return for all time to his own home," where he would become one of the immortal figures of Chinese literature.

Summary

It is the high value T'ao Ch'ien set upon immediacy and immanence that has led many literary historians to see his work as pivotal in the development of Chinese poetry. Although there were advocates of simplicity who came before him and apostles of aestheticism stiil to come after him, it was his lyrics, more than any others, that served as a continuous source of inspiration for succeeding ages and would be rediscovered whenever poetry seemed in danger of becoming too mannered and removed from common experience.

In addition to his importance as a literary model, T'ao Ch'ien is admired for his decision to remain true to himself rather than subordinate his feelings to the demands of conventional life-styles. The writers and intellectuals of his day were, broadly speaking, split into the opposing camps of conformist Confucians and antiauthoritarian Taoists, and when T'ao Ch'ien rejected the former it would have been normal for him to have gravitated to the vagabond life of the latter. He chose, however, to pilot his own idiosyncratic course between these polar opposites, and he suffered much personal hardship in so doing.

Even more important than his position in literary history or his personal qualities, however, is the candid beauty of his poetry. The freshness of his images, his homespun but Heaven-aspiring morality, and his steadfast love of rural life shine through the deceptively humble words in which they are expressed, and as a consequence he has long been regarded one of China's most accomplished and accessible poets.

Bibliography

Cotterell, Yong Yap, and Arthur Cotterell. *The Early Civilization of China*. London: Weidenfeld and Nicolson, and New York: Putnam, 1975. Chapter 6, "The Age of Disunity: The So-Called 'Six Dynasties,'" gives a good general account of historical developments during T'ao Ch'ien's time. This chapter also includes useful sections on the religion and art of the period.

Hightower, James Robert. "Allusion in the Poetry of T'ao Ch'ien." *Harvard Journal of Asiatic Studies* 31 (1971): 5-27. The received view of T'ao Ch'ien is that he only rarely made use of allusion as a literary technique, an interpretation which Hightower here argues is only partially accurate. This brief discussion is much more fully elaborated in the notes to Hightower's translation of T'ao Ch'ien's poetry.

———. "T'ao Ch'ien's 'Drinking Wine' Poems." In *Wen-lin: Studies in the Chinese Humanities*, edited by Chou Tse-tsung. Madison: University of Wisconsin Press, 1968. A fuller treatment of a subject also addressed in *The Poetry of T'ao Ch'ien*. This article is more extensively documented and offers a fuller discussion of the poems' important theme of the conflict between public service and private retirement.

T'ao Ch'ien. *Poems*. Translated by Lily Pao-hu Chang and Marjorie Sinclair. Honolulu: University of Hawaii Press, 1953. This beautifully produced volume incudes original brush drawings reminiscent of a deluxe Chinese-language edition. Chang and Sinclair opt for inclusiveness in translating all the poems attributed to T'ao Ch'ien, several of which are the objects of scholarly debate. The translations themselves are reliable if not always idiomatic. A brief biography of the poet is included in an appendix.

———. *The Poetry of T'ao Ch'ien*. Translated and edited by James Robert Hightower. Oxford: Clarendon Press, 1970. The standard edition in English. The translations themselves are not noticeably superior to those of his predecessors, but Hightower's notes make the book an essential reference for anyone doing serious work on T'ao Ch'ien. It is by far the best guide to its subject's use of traditional elements of the Chinese literary tradition.

———. *T'ao the Hermit: Sixty Poems by T'ao Ch'ien (365-427)*. Translated by William Acker. London and New York: Thames and Hudson, 1952. None of the three readily available English translations of T'ao Ch'ien's poetry seems to have influenced the others. Acker's have an unassuming dignity that is quite in keeping with what is known of T'ao Ch'ien, although they can sometimes seem stiff and unidiomatic as well. The well-annotated selection he offers includes about 40 percent of T'ao Ch'ien's poetry.

Paul Stuewe

TERENCE
Publius Terentius Afer

Born: c. 190 B.C.; Carthage
Died: 159 B.C.; en route to Greece
Area of Achievement: Literature
Contribution: As a Roman comic playwright whose innovative adaptations of Greek dramas depicted in graceful Latin the social realities operating in his ancient world, Terence strongly influenced the development of sophisticated theater in the West. His psychologically accurate portraits brought integrity to his craft.

Early Life

Ancient materials reporting Terence's life frequently present contradictory information; certain facts, however, fall into the realm of probability: Publius Terentius Afer (Terence) was born at Carthage and came to Rome as the slave of Terentius Lucanus, a senator who educated him and set him free. Since Terence's life fell between the Second and Third Punic Wars, he could not have been a slave captured in combat; thus, he may have been owned and sold by a Carthaginian trader.

Of average height, medium build, and with a dark complexion, Terence was a shade of brown which could range in hue from olive to Moorish, his cognomen "Afer" further indicating his African birth. Yet one cannot be completely certain that Terence was actually ever a slave, for Roman biographers, who often wove a web of fiction around their subjects, commonly recorded playwrights as having sprung from slavery, and "Afer" need not positively establish African birth. Nevertheless, many commentators have marveled at the significant achievement of the onetime slave who learned Latin as a second language and who came to use it with such outstanding artistry and precision.

In Rome, the young man's intelligence and talent soon gained for him entry into the Scipionic circle of study, a group of patrician literati behind a philhellenic movement. So close was the involvement of Terence and particular associates in this group—including Scipio Africanus and Gaius Laelius—that rumors circulated suggesting that Terence was simply a front for these august patrons of the arts who had really authored the plays. Terence, in fact, inadvertently helped the malicious gossip along by never definitively attempting to refute the charges. Indeed, in the prologues to his plays he concentrat-

ed on stating his theories of dramatic art, trying to deflect the scurrilous accusations. Yet, unfortunately, Terence's short life came to be plagued by constant innuendo.

When Terence offered his first drama to the aediles, the officials at the public games where the performances were held, he was ordered to show his work to Caecilius Statius, a revered comic playwright of an earlier era whose successes had been, in part, a result of the abilities of noted actor Lucius Ambivius Turpio. Legend describes the youthful Terence, poorly dressed, arriving at the dramatist's home during the dinner hour, sitting himself on a bench near the old man's couch, and beginning to read from his first effort. It took only a few minutes for Caecilius to recognize the genius of his young visitor, and Terence was invited to take a seat at the table. Not only did his career as dramatist begin at that moment but also the actor Turpio, now in old age, performed in Terence's plays, giving them the same public notice and authoritative

support he had given to Caecilius. Thus promoted, Terence appeared an assured success from the beginning.

Life's Work

Terence looked to the New Comedy of Greece for his major literary resource and composed, therefore, in the tradition of *palliatae*, plays derived from Greek models, and acted in Greek dress, or *pallium*. Of the twenty-six complete plays surviving from the second century B.C. Roman stage, six are the work of Terence, whose chief model was Menander, an artist with a reputation in the ancient world superseded only by Homer and Vergil. While the Old Comedy had dealt with affairs of state, the New Comedy exemplified by Menander focused on domestic issues, particularly on wealthy youths and the tangled dilemmas of their often-complicated love lives. Filial duty, which on occasion ran counter to the young man's casual self-indulgence, and the devious machinations of crafty slaves helped generate comic situations at times to farcical extremes.

Terence found his métier in these intricate plots and, by artfully adapting the Greek models, brought with his distinctive translations a conscious artistry to the Roman stage. He developed prologues which articulated literary principles and which did not simply explain the action to follow. He developed a "doubling technique" to balance Menander's character creations. Alongside these innovations, Terence sensitively rendered the impact of behavioral fashion on the ethical values of his time. While Terence realized that in his models the characters were standard, the action was predictable, and the themes were formulaic; under his original touch the plays not only embody a vivid realism but also detail a sociological compendium of the age.

The complete works of Terence, produced over a six-year period, include the following extant plays: *Andria* (166 B.C.; *Andria*), *Hecyra* (165 B.C.; *The Mother-in-Law*), *Heautontimorumenos* (163 B.C.; *The Self-Tormentor*), *Eunuchus* (161 B.C.; *The Eunuch*), *Phormio* (161 B.C.; *Phormio*), and *Adelphoe* (160 B.C.; *The Brothers*). While the dramas themselves—all of them based on the work of either Menander or Apollodorus of Carystus—reveal the extent of Terence's achievement during his short, productive life, of greater significance to his biography are the *didascaliae* (production notes attached to the dramas) and the prologues, for these

writings candidly reveal information which chronicles the way Terence's creative life was progressing. These statements sometimes indicate his strategy for dealing with the hurtful charges of plagiarism and the jealous accusations of *contaminatio*, that is, adulterating his literary sources.

Even before the presentation of his first play, Terence was forced to defend his unorthodox, innovative literary practices. Luscius Lanuvinus, a jealous competitor who had either seen *Andria* in rehearsal or read it in manuscript, began a vendetta of slander by accusing Terence of contaminating the plays he had used in his adaptation. During the next few years, these accusations were repeated and, apparently, escalated into charges of plagiarism. Terence went about defending the legitimacy of his literary methods as well as the originality of his artistry, going so far as to point out the Roman historical precedent for adapting work from the Greek stage. On one occasion, Terence flatly charged that his accuser was simply trying to force him into early retirement, to drive a young competitor from the theater by wounding him with invective. Insisting that he would prefer to exchange compliment for compliment rather than engage in verbal skirmishes, Terence urged his audiences to enjoy his plays, to be fair in their assessments, and to disregard the gossip of an evil-tempered old man, especially one whose talent was weak.

Another difficulty in his career Terence accepted with benign amusement: the problem with presenting *The Mother-in-Law*, a drama which suffered two failures before its eventual success. The first time Terence offered the play (165 B.C.), his audience rushed out of the performance to view a prizefight and a tightrope walker. Trying again five years later, Terence watched as the audience hurriedly left to watch some gladiators. A few months later, the play was successfully performed, with Terence in his prologue requesting courteous support for his efforts and urging his audience to abstain from irreverent behavior that might expose him to more unfair criticism by his enemies.

In his plays, Terence used the stock themes—boastful soldiers, crafty slaves, kindly prostitutes, professional parasites, confused sons, all involved in innocent mistakes and switched identities—and held the mirror up for the examination of moral and ethical principles, touching such concerns as the limits of filial duty, the question of a slave's loyalty, the role of women in Roman society, and the proprieties of legal deportment. While comedy did not readily lend itself to didacticism, Terence's plays, nevertheless, were epitomes of both entertainment and instruction, especially in portraying the emotional and psychological complexities involved in all human relationships.

Summary

As Terence's brief life was filled with controversy and speculation, so were the events surrounding his death. The playwright left Rome for Greece and never returned. He had undertaken the journey possibly to study at first hand the culture from which his plays were derived or to scrutinize the work of Menander—maybe even to discover other works modeled after Menander's or to escape for a time the Roman atmosphere of jealousy and acrimony which had spawned the petulant attacks of his rivals as they jockeyed for favor among patrons of the arts and theater audiences. Terence died in 159 B.C., either of an illness in Greece or in a shipwreck which also may have destroyed more than one hundred adaptations from Menander that he was bringing home.

Terence's reputation as a master dramatist has clearly withstood the passage of centuries; his accomplishments in the development and advancement of world theater are clear. His painstaking artistry in portraying psychological motivation and social reality set benchmarks for dramatists to follow in establishing the seriousness of comedy. In eliminating the prologue as simply a means to explain plot, Terence ensured that the drama had to depend upon characterization and dialogue. When sophisticated theatrical tastes came to govern the stage, Terence became a major literary source. During the Restoration in England, when the comedy of manners reigned supreme, Terence's work influenced such masters as William Congreve and Thomas Otway. In France, Molière looked to Terence for inspiration. In addition, the expository prologue as a means for critical expression and advancement of dramatic theory came to be a mark of identity for George Bernard Shaw.

The facts of Terence's life will be forever clouded by rumor and hearsay, for speculation and gossip were often freely intermingled with fact among ancient biographers. On Terence's death, records Suetonius, he left a twenty-acre estate on the Appian Way; Licinus Porcius, however, asserts that at the end of his life Terence possessed not even a rented house where his slave might announce his master's death.

Bibliography

Beare, W. *The Roman Stage: A Short History of Latin Drama in the Time of the Republic*. 3d ed. New York: Barnes and Noble, 1963; London: Methuen, 1964. An authoritative study of the Roman stage particularly useful for revealing the stage practices, customs, and techniques of the time. Includes a detailed examination of the charge of contamination leveled against Terence. With extensive notes, bibliography, and appendices.

Duckworth, George E. *The Nature of Roman Comedy: A Study in Popular Entertainment*. 2d ed. London: Bristol Classical Press, and Norman: University of Oklahoma Press, 1994. A vital source for learning about the ancient stage and its conventions as well as for the contribution of Terence to the "Golden Age of Drama at Rome." This work is a detailed study of themes, treatments, methods, and influences of Terence, including the critical problems in studying his texts and the biographical problems in studying his life. With an extensive index and bibliography.

———, ed. *The Complete Roman Drama*. 2 vols. New York: Random House, 1942. This work includes Terence's production notes, which date the performances, describe some of the staging techniques, identify some of the actors, and generally help both in setting the Terentian ambience and establishing the plays' chronologies. A general introduction provides a sound overview of the entire era and gives important information on ancient stage discipline.

Forehand, Walter E. *Terence*. Boston: Twayne Publishers, 1985. A sound, basic work which outlines the major controversies surrounding Terence's life and productions. Contains a full account of Terence's literary career, surveying the plays and illuminating the theater background of the times. An excellent introduction to Terence and his stage. Includes a selected bibliography.

Forman, Robert J. *Classical Greek and Roman Drama: An Annotated Bibliography*. Pasadena, Calif.: Salem Press, 1989. This volume begins with an overview of Greek and Roman drama, followed by chapters covering nine playwrights of the era, including Terence. Each chapter includes three sections: one covering translations and commentaries; the other two covering recommended and general criticism.

Goldberg, Sander M. *The Making of Menander's Comedy.* Berkeley: University of California Press, and London: Athlone, 1980. A study of Menander's art important for the light it sheds upon Terence, whose adaptations came mainly from this Greek model. Terence's work in relation to Menander is discussed in detailed, analytical fashion throughout.

————. *Understanding Terence.* Princeton, N.J.: Princeton University Press, 1986. A perceptive, analytical study focusing on Terence and the Latin tradition of New Comedy rather than on Terence as an adapter of Menander; this work analyzes the prologues and the plays for their language and themes. The critical problems in dealing with Terence are studied. Contains a bibliography for the individual plays as well as for further study of ancient Greece.

Harsh, Philip Whaley. *A Handbook of Classical Drama.* Stanford, Calif.: Stanford University Press, and London: Oxford University Press, 1944. Contains an informative survey of Terence's life and work set within the context of the total range of classical drama. Extensive notes as well as full bibliographies for Terence and his peers are included.

Konstan, David. *Roman Comedy.* Ithaca, N.Y.: Cornell University Press, 1983. An examination of the New Comedy genre within contexts of the ideology and the institutions of the Roman state. With a reading of Roman plays—including Terence's—from the social and philosophical perspective to determine how the plays defined and revealed the ethical standards and moral imperatives of the age. Includes an extensive bibliography.

Norwood, Gilbert. *Plautus and Terence.* London: Harrap, and New York: Longmans, Green, 1932. Five of the nine chapters address Terence's life and work, emphasizing his style, characterizations, plot structure, and basic thought. Contains an appendix outlining specific influences of particular Terence plays on English drama. Examined also are the disputes over Terence's methods of adaptation. Includes a selective bibliography.

Terence. *The Comedies of Terence.* Frank O. Copley, trans. Indianapolis: Bobbs-Merrill Co., 1967. Translations of each play with a useful, informative introductory note on each drama. A fourteen-page essay surveys the problems encountered in attempting to reconstruct Terence's life and in trying to analyze his art.

Abe C. Ravitz

TERTULLIAN

Born: c. A.D. 155-160; at or near Carthage, North Africa

Died: After A.D. 217; probably near Carthage, North Africa

Areas of Achievement: Religion and literature

Contribution: Eloquent and aggressive, Tertullian was the most outstanding spokesman for Christianity in the Latin West before Saint Augustine; his polemical treatises set the direction for much of Western theology.

Early Life

Quintus Septimius Florens Tertullianus, though he left a strong mark on the history of Latin literature and exercised more influence than anyone but Augustine on the development of theology in the Western church, left but few scraps of biographical information. A short paragraph in Saint Jerome's *De viris illustribus* (392-393; on famous men) yields a few assertions, and several deductions can be made from Tertullian's writings, which are remarkable for their lack of self-revelation. Each item has been closely examined by scholars, and while virtually nothing can be said with certainty about the man, the following picture emerges from a cautious balancing of ancient tradition and modern skepticism.

Tertullian was certainly born and reared in Roman North Africa, in or near the proconsular capital of Carthage, to a prosperous pagan family. His father was probably a career military officer attached to the staff of the proconsul, and several relatives were active in the literary life of the city. Any birth date assigned to Tertullian (usually A.D. 155-160) is reached by subtracting from A.D. 197, the secure date of one of his earliest works, the *Apologeticus* (*Apology*), enough years—roughly forty—to account for its character as a mature masterpiece of style, argumentation, and Christian apologetics.

Tertullian received the standard education of a well-to-do Roman, culminating in extensive rhetorical training, in which he must have excelled, judging from his subsequent literary career. It is difficult to avoid identifying Tertullian of Carthage with Tertullian the jurist, whose writings are quoted in later Roman law codes. The men were contemporaries; the jurist wrote on questions of military law, and the Carthaginian had a penchant for

legalistic language and argument and was declared by Eusebius of Caesarea to have been eminent at the Roman bar. If they were indeed the same person, Tertullian of Carthage traveled to Rome, became a pupil of the great jurist Pomponius, and established among legal scholars of the Empire a reputation that was later vindicated by his apologetic works.

It was probably in early middle age, not long before 197, that Tertullian converted to Christianity. He never discusses his conversion, though he expresses repeatedly an admiration for the constancy of Christian martyrs, their steadfastness in persecution, and their stubborn defiance of Roman authority in the face of death. It was he who coined the saying "The blood of Christians is seed." He may have been ordained a priest, as Jerome claims, for some of Tertullian's works are clearly sermons. While Tertullian uses two or three turns of phrase which place him among the laity, these may be rhetorical poses—devices which he uses more frequently than any other Latin writer. He was certainly married, but though he addressed several treatises to his wife, they reveal nothing of her personality or of their relationship. This opacity is characteristic of Tertullian's writings: He turned consistently outward toward problems and enemies but seldom inward to reflect on himself or friends.

Life's Work

In the first three or four years of his career as a Christian, Tertullian devoted his rhetorical talents to apologetics—for example, in *Ad nationes* (A.D. 197; *To the Nations*) and the *Apology*—defending Christianity against pagan hostility with the aim of ending official persecution. These writings provide an invaluable window on primitive Christian belief and practice, but they are so self-righteous and vehement that they must have increased the pagans' animosity rather than diminishing it. Tertullian's strategy is often to argue that pagan Romans do not live up to their own beliefs, values, laws, and civic traditions as well as Christians do. This pose claims for the writer a privileged ability to interpret the texts and traditions of others. He denies repeatedly the right of Roman magistrates to judge Christians, on the ground that God's law is higher than man's, and he makes the claim, remarkable for a lawyer, that no law has binding force unless it is accepted by the individual's conscience. Such claims to unfettered autonomy of belief and action recur throughout Tertullian's works.

Tertullian's theological vision centered initially on the Church, seeing it as the community mediating between God and humans and thus the authoritative interpreter of Scripture and channel of God's grace. He argued against certain rigorists that post-baptismal sins could be forgiven by the Church, but his lawyer's training led him to think of sin chiefly in terms of Roman law, the categories of which he introduced into Christian theological vocabulary. He uses the term *delictum* (crime) much more often than *peccatum* (sin) and demands confession before a judge, and the imposition of a penalty, to complete the process of expiating wrongdoing. Correspondingly, penances or good deeds "hold God a debtor" and oblige Him to grant the doer forgiveness, favor, and eventually salvation.

Tertullian's logical prowess and penchant for fine distinctions served him well in dogmatic theology. He was the first to use the term "trinity" to describe the relation of Father, Son, and Spirit, and he pioneered the description of Jesus as one person with a divine and a human nature. These positions antedate the Nicene Creed by more than a century and have become standard in all the main branches of Christianity.

Not long after the year 200, Tertullian's energies turned to polemical treatises against Gnostics and other heretics, especially the ascetic Marcionites. In these contentious and angry pieces he seems to take on many of the characteristics of his opponents, sinking deep into moral rigorism and antisocial attitudes. He was forced consequently to make ever more contorted and idiosyncratic interpretations of Scripture to score points against them. By around 210, he had drifted away from the mainstream of orthodox Christianity into Montanism, a sect which claimed that its private revelations superseded those of the New Testament and which opposed a pure, invisible, "spiritual" Church to the corrupt, visible church of the bishops and clergy. Thereafter, Tertullian increasingly stressed the role of private illuminations from the Spirit and the ability of each Christian to interpret Scripture for himself, outside, or even against, the tradition of the Church.

Though he is famous for comparing classical philosophy unfavorably with Christian theology—"What . . . has Athens to do with Jerusalem?"—he does not reject the formulations and arguments of

TERTVLLIAN

philosophy, but only their claim to compel assent—so strong was his determination to be utterly unfettered in his choice of belief. In fact, he formulates his own positions much more often in philosophical than in biblical terms, quoting Scriptures more for slogans and proof texts than to develop any genuine biblical theology. His major treatise *De anima* (*On the Soul*), for example, is based on Stoic theory, affirming that the substance of the cosmos is all one, with no distinction of matter and spirit. Tertullian drew the explicit conclusion that soul-substance, as well as body-substance, is passed on from parents to children and laid thereby the foundation for the doctrine of Original Sin, unknown previously.

Having always tended toward absolutism, Tertullian became more extreme and rigorist in his Montanist phase. He reversed his earlier position that sins could be forgiven, claimed that anything which is not explicitly commanded by Scripture is forbidden, and became so confident of his own interpretations as to revoke divine commands from the Old Testament and apostolic counsels in the New. In his last writings his tone is bitterly antisocial and misanthropic; here he pictures himself as living in a world bound for damnation and gloats over the impending deaths of his enemies. Apparently he broke with Montanism in his last years to found his own sect, the Tertullianists, which survived some two centuries until the time of Augustine. His last datable writing was done in 217; according to Jerome, however, he lived to an advanced age.

Summary

Tertullian's Latin prose style is the most vehement, tortuous, and pyrotechnic ever produced, the ultimate flower of the genre of controversy, lush with innovative vocabulary and quotable phrasing. This power, however, was in the hands of a tortured spirit, a man who was hostile, suspicious, and self-righteous, alienated from the world, from others, and, ultimately, from himself. His writings exhibit many of the traits associated with the authoritarian personality. Rejecting first pagan religion, then the Roman Empire, then orthodox Christianity, and finally the Montanist heresy, he ended his days in an idiosyncratic splinter group defined solely by himself.

Though Tertullian's writings were condemned by the Church in the sixth century, his genius blazed theological paths which are followed to this day: the doctrine of Original Sin, the Trinity of Persons in God, and the dual natures of Jesus. His legalism and penchant for *quid pro quo* justice set the tone for Western Christianity's outlook on sin, forgiveness, grace, and salvation for fourteen centuries, until Martin Luther supplied a corrective. His insistence on the validity of philosophical concepts led to the Roman Catholic tradition of reasoning from natural law, as his rejection of the binding force of philosophical conclusions on his absolute God led to the primacy of scriptural authority in Protestantism. His early argument that Scripture belongs to the Church and can only be interpreted rightly by the Church in accord with its traditions is still a mainstay of Catholic and Eastern Orthodox thinking. His later emphasis on private interpretation of scriptural texts provided a strong impetus to the Protestant Reformation; combined with his moral rigorism and rejection of a visible Church in favor of a "spiritual" or personally defined one, it has exerted continuing influence on Fundamentalism.

Bibliography

Barnes, T. D. *Tertullian: A Historical and Literary Study.* Oxford: Clarendon Press, 1971; New York: Oxford University Press, 1985. This specialized work presents all the evidence ever likely to be available concerning Tertullian's life and the dates of his writings, but Barnes subjects the material to an extremely narrow and skeptical criticism, ignoring or dismissing ancient testimony. His largely negative conclusions must be taken into account, but their radical denials should be balanced by the recognition that ancient authorities had available to them more and better sources than do modern scholars.

Bray, Gerald L. *Holiness and the Will of God: Perspectives on the Theology of Tertullian.* London: Marshall, Morgan and Scott, and Atlanta: John Knox Press, 1979. This is probably the best overview of Tertullian's thought. It is particularly helpful in synthesizing his positions, which often appear fragmentarily in scattered works and which changed drastically during his writing career.

Morgan, James. *The Importance of Tertullian in the Development of Christian Dogma.* London: K. Paul, Trench, Trubner, 1928. Classic work surveying Tertullian's contributions in various areas, and thus somewhat superficial in each. Bray's work (see above) supplies more up-to-date interpretations.

Roberts, A., J. Donaldson, and Cleveland Coxe, eds. *The Ante-Nicene Fathers.* Vols. 3 and 4. Grand Rapids, Mich.: Wm. B. Eerdmans, 1956. This is a reprint of the 1925 American edition of the nineteenth century British *Ante-Nicene Christian Library.* The translation is somewhat archaic, and it is sparsely annotated, but these volumes offer the only English versions of many of Tertullian's works, including *Ad Scapulam.*

Tertullian. *Treatises on Penance.* Translated by W. P. Le Saint. Westminster, Md.: Newman Press, 1959. A modern translation of two representative works, with extensive introduction and meticulous annotation, theological, philosophical, philological, and literary. This annotation draws out well the depth and fertility of Tertullian's genius and situates him in the intellectual climate of his time.

Tertullian and Minucius Felix. *Apology: De spectaculis.* Translated by T. R. Glover and G. H. Rendall. Cambridge, Mass.: Harvard University Press, 1931; London: Heinemann, 1960. A serviceable and widely available translation of Tertullian's best-known work, with Latin text. The text of Minucius Felix is interesting since he is the only known Christian Latin writer before

Tertullian and the only author from whom Tertullian borrows extensively. "Minucius" may in fact be a pseudonym used by Tertullian for his first Christian work.

Warfield, B. B. *Studies in Tertullian and Augustine*. London and New York: Oxford University Press, 1930. This monograph-length essay on Tertullian gives the best treatment of his power and originality as a theologian, using his Trinitarian doctrine as focus for the study.

John D. Madden

THALES OF MILETUS

Born: c. 624 B.C.; Miletus, Ionia, Asia Minor
Died: c. 548 B.C.; Miletus, Ionia, Asia Minor
Areas of Achievement: Philosophy and science
Contribution: Through his various theories, Thales countered supernatural and mythical explanations of nature, attempting to replace them with empirically derived answers. He became a transitional figure between the worlds of philosophy and science.

Early Life

Few details are known about the life of the man many call "the father of philosophy." Ancient tradition often fixed a person's birth date by a major event. According to Apollodorus, an Athenian historian of the second century B.C., the major event in Thales' life was the solar eclipse of 585-584 B.C., when he was forty years old. If this is correct, then Thales was born circa 624. He was a member of a distinguished family from the port city of Miletus, Ionia, on the west coast of Asia Minor. Thales' upper-class background meant that he had the luxury of spending his life engaged in intellectual pursuits.

Although probably from Phoenicia originally, Thales' family most likely lived in Miletus for several generations. Besides his social standing, his place of birth is also significant. Miletus was the major trading center of the Aegean Sea in the sixth century B.C. The coastal city entertained merchants from Egypt, Greece, and the Persian Empire. It possessed both a frontier spirit and a cosmopolitan, intellectual environment. A thriving economic center with a rich mixture of Near Eastern and Greek cultures, Miletus had no traditional, government-imposed beliefs that it sanctioned; life in Miletus was unconventional.

The body of knowledge familiar to the young Thales came principally from two sources: the earliest Greek writers and the scholars of Egypt and Babylon. These ideas played a significant role in the philosophy of Thales, not because of their influence on him but rather because of his departure from them. Among the first ideas Thales encountered were those from the writings of Homer and Hesiod. Both these important Greeks speculated on the origins of the world and certain natural phenomena. Their answers, however, were always found within the realm of the Olympian gods. Homer and Hesiod did gather some factual data

which they incorporated into their writings, but scientific advancement was impossible as long as nature was interpreted as the supernatural caprices of the gods. Greek thinkers before Thales had some knowledge of natural occurrences but never moved toward a more rational analysis. Theirs was an anthropomorphic world. Mythology served both as science and history prior to the revolution in thought which occurred in Miletus during the mid-sixth century.

The other information common to men such as Thales came from the Near East. The ancients of Egypt and Babylon had long experimented with their own forms of science and mathematics. The wonders of the Egyptian pyramids and other structures interested the Ionians, and the Babylonians claimed the attention of scholars for their study of the stars. While the achievements of these Near Eastern civilizations were remarkable, they were also limited in their scope. The Egyptians never converted their practical knowledge of mathematics and engineering into theories and principles. The Babylonians compiled volumes of notes on the heavens and developed astrology, a discipline hardly resembling astronomy. This was the intellectual climate, complete with preconceptions and misconceptions about natural "science," into which Thales was born.

Life's Work

The philosophy Thales espoused must be gleaned from the excerpts and comments of other authors. Herodotus, Aristotle, and Diogenes are the most notable ancient writers who included Thales in their works, and Thales' contributions are represented consistently in all three accounts. Thales bridged the gap between superstition and reason. Aristotle credited Thales with being the first recorded Milesian in a line of pre-Socratic philosophers who attempted to define nature in terms of nature itself. The questions Thales asked and the assumptions he proposed changed philosophy and science and laid a rational foundation upon which others could build.

Thales searched for the "stuff," as the ancients referred to it, which composed all existing matter. He assumed that among the infinite variety of things on Earth there must be one underlying source of their existence. Though the stuff might change its form, it essentially retained its proper-

ties. Through observation, Thales concluded that the first principle of the world must be water. It was the prime substance of all things, and Earth floated on a cushion of it.

The matter of Thales' theory also possessed the quality of fluidity. It was to some degree alive and caused the change perceived in the visible world. Thales compared the inner power of water to a magnet that moves a piece of iron. This animism was typical of sixth century philosophy. It compelled Thales to conclude that all things are "full of gods." Although he used religious language, Thales did not adhere to a prevalent religious system—nor did he attempt to deify water in the traditional sense of ancient custom. To Thales, that which gave continual life must, in the vernacular of the time, be to some extent divine. Water was that life-giving substance which in one form or another composed everything and thus merited the term "god," not an anthropomorphic Olympian god but a new secular and rational god of Thales' making.

There is no extant record of the reason Thales chose water as the stuff of the world. Certainly the importance of water was not lost on ancient man. Water was central in the mythology of Greece, Egypt, and Babylon, as well as in the Hebrew creation account. Some historians suggest that these myths exerted the greatest influence on Thales. In the epics of the Near East, Earth rises out of primeval water. The principal focus of these myths, however, was the origin of the world, not a common substance underlying all things in the world; thus, Thales probably did not draw from them. Further, none of the ancient commentators on Thales mentions any influence of Near Eastern thought on Ionian philosophy developing in the sixth century B.C.

Many modern scholars have asserted that there is a rational explanation for Thales' choice of water. Since Thales' theory was founded on observation only, not experimentation, the three phases of water would have been readily apparent to him. Water, appearing in such numerous forms, fits the description of the stuff which changes but is fundamentally constant. From the sources on Thales, however, it is never established that he even understood the three states of water.

Aristotle postulated another reason which led Thales to his conclusion. It is a variation of the rational explanation fashioned by modern scholars. Given the proximity of Aristotle to Thales, this may be the closest to the latter's own thinking. As Aristotle suggested, there existed a close link in the ancient mind between water and life. There were the rivers and seas without which man could not nourish himself. Trees contained sap, and plants had liquid within their stems. Growth, and therefore change, was inextricably tied to water—and nowhere was this clearer than in the ancient world. Even the human body testified to the importance of moisture. From conception to death, water was an integral part of human existence. As Aristotle observed, when the body died two things occurred: It became cold, and it dried up. Even that which was hot and dry required water. A popular fifth century B.C. idea held that the sun drew water to itself for nourishment and then rained it back to Earth to complete the cycle. Whether myth or logic influenced Thales, his attempt to look outside the divine process for answers to the puzzles of nature was monumental. By so doing, he attributed an orderliness to the cosmos which had heretofore been regarded as the disorderly and mystical playground of the gods.

Contemporaries hailed Thales as a politician, diplomat, civil engineer, mathematician, and astronomer, but his achievements in those roles are uncertain. Among the more important feats attributed to Thales was his prediction of a solar eclipse in 585-584 B.C. During a significant battle between the Medes and Lydians, Thales is said to have forecast a solar eclipse which, when it occurred, caused such trepidation among the combatants that they ceased fighting and called a truce. The ancients certainly believed the tale, but modern scholars doubt that Thales could predict an eclipse (such a prediction requires sophisticated astronomical calculations). A more likely astronomical achievement attributed to Thales is his idea of steering ships by the constellation Ursa Minor.

Tradition also credited Thales with introducing Egyptian principles of geometry to Greece. In Egypt, Thales is said to have taken the practical knowledge of Egyptian scholars and devised a method for accurately measuring the pyramids by their shadows. Altogether, five theorems are attributed to Thales. It is impossible to know the exact contribution of Thales to mathematics; it is likely, however, that he made some fundamental discoveries that enabled later mathematicians to build a framework for a variety of theorems.

In the minds of his contemporaries, Thales was not only a philosopher but also a sage. The Greeks named him one of the Seven Wise Men, because he urged the Ionian states to unite lest they fall easy prey to the Persian Empire. Thales was so respected by his countrymen that it is difficult to determine to what extent the legends which surround him are apocryphal. In antiquity, attributing great discoveries or achievements to men with reputations for wisdom was a common practice. The ancient authors themselves often recorded conflicting accounts of the accomplishments of Thales. It seems that they chose whatever Thalesian story would substantiate the more general point they were trying to make. Whatever the veracity of the stories enveloping Thales, it seems logical that his reputation for rational thinking would spread from his cosmological interests to such fields as mathematics, astronomy, and politics.

Summary

Were all the legends surrounding Thales false, his speculations on the principal substance of the world would be enough to accord him special recognition. It is not the theory itself that is so significant but the revolution in thinking that it produced. Thales placed the study of nature on a new plane: He lifted it from the realm of the mythical to the level of empirical study. Scholars began to evaluate and analyze theories on the basis of the factual data available. Thales was the first of what has been called the Milesian group of the Ionian school of philosophy. Anaximander and Anaximenes, who followed him, produced more sophisticated philosophical systems, but they regarded Thales as the master.

To the modern scholar, the limitations of Thales' thinking are apparent. There remained elements of anthropomorphism and mythology in the work of Thales and the other pre-Socratic philosophers. While Thales rejected a universe controlled by the gods with his assertion "all things are water," he did not anticipate an atomic theory, as Democritus did. Thales attributed to nature an animism which prevented him from seeing it as a neutral agent in the world. In this sense, his ideas are less abstract than the ideas of those who came after him. Thales does not properly belong to the world of modern science, and yet he is equally misplaced when his ideas are classified with the cosmologies of Homer and Hesiod. Thales transcended, through rational analysis, the established supernatural explanations of nature, laying the foundation for major advances in philosophy and science in the following centuries.

Bibliography

Brumbaugh, Robert S. *The Philosophers of Greece*. New York: Thomas Y. Crowell, 1964; London: Allen and Unwin, 1966. Evaluation of Greek philosophy from Thales to Aristotle. Brumbaugh draws his information mainly from ancient authors themselves. Takes a "romantic" approach to the subject which depicts Thales as a Renaissance man. Includes an extensive bibliography.

Burnet, John. *Early Greek Philosophy*. 4th ed. London: Black, and New York: Barnes and Noble, 1930. An older work and somewhat out-of-date, but still considered one of the first major pieces on the subject. Emphasizes the Greeks as the earliest scientists and philosophers. The extensive use of Greek in the footnotes and to a lesser degree in the text limits the book's usefulness for less advanced scholars. Includes elaborate notes on source material.

Grant, Michael. *The Founders of the Western World: A History of Greece and Rome*. New York: Scribner, 1991. Grant places the most salient as well as the less well-known historical figures in their proper contexts. In addition to covering tactics and systems of government during each individual's period, he also covers art and philosophy.

Guthrie, William Keith Chambers. *A History of Greek Philosophy*. Vol. 1, *The Earlier Presocratics and Pythagoreans*. London: Cambridge University Press, 1962. A standard, sound, general account of the subject, beginning with Thales and continuing through to the works of Heraclitus. Concentrates on how early Greek writers of myths and theogonies influenced the early ideas of the pre-Socratic philosophers and adheres to the traditional claim of Thales as the first European philosopher. Contains a large bibliography.

Hussey, Edward. *The Pre-Socratics*. New York: Scribner, and London: Duckworth, 1972. An introduction to early Greek thought designed for the reader with no background in Greek. This volume provides a general account with less detail about historiographical controversies. Deals with philosophy and science within the political and cultural setting of the ancient world and stresses the importance of political development on the emergence of the ideas of Thales. Includes a few helpful maps and an extensive annotated bibliography.

Jones, W. T. *The History of Western Philosophy.* Vol. 1, *The Classical Mind.* 3d ed. Fort Worth, Tex.: Harcourt Brace, 1997. First volume of a four-volume work. Deals with Thales and the pre-Socratics through the late classical period of Roman philosophy. A limited coverage of Thales that places more emphasis on the philosophical and scientific foundation he laid for those who followed him than on his actual theories. Includes a small bibliography and a helpful glossary of philosophical terms.

Lindberg, David C. *The Beginnings of Western Science: The European Scientific Tradition in Philosophical, Religious, and Institutional Context, 600 B.C. to A.D. 1450.* Chicago: University of Chicago Press, 1992. Reflecting the most recent research, Lindberg's volume delineates 2000 years of science, including social, intellectual, and religious background. He shows each development within its appropriate historical context, and the book is extensively illustrated.

Nahm, Milton C., ed. *Selections from Early Greek Philosophy.* 4th ed. Englewood Cliffs, N.J.: Prentice-Hall, 1964. Short translated excerpts from the works of ancient authors on various personas in early Greek philosophy. Book spans the period from the Milesians through the atomists. Includes the commentaries on Thales by Diogenes, Aristotle, and Plutarch.

Wightman, William P. D. *The Growth of Scientific Ideas.* New Haven, Conn.: Yale University Press, 1950. Critically explores the advance of science from the Ionians through Charles Darwin. Less concerned with the philosophical aspects of the Milesian thinkers than with their contributions to science. Somewhat critical of Thales' theories, even within the context of the ancient world. Contains a limited annotated bibliography of general works, but a more specific list of sources concludes each chapter. Includes several illustrations and a helpful chronology of scientific discoveries and innovations.

Linda Perry Abrams

THEMISTOCLES

Born: c. 524 B.C.; Athens, Greece
Died: c. 460 B.C.; Magnesia, Asia Minor
Areas of Achievement: Government and military
Contribution: Themistocles engineered the naval defeat of the Persians at Salamis and thus made possible the subsequent Age of Pericles in ancient Athens.

Early Life

Themistocles was born about 524 B.C. to an Athenian father, Neocles, and a non-Athenian mother. His father's family, the Lycomidai, was respected, but his father achieved no great prominence. No details of his early life antedate Plutarch, who six centuries later related a number of anecdotes showing him to be clever, resourceful, and interested in politics from the start. In one of these stories, Themistocles was coming home from school when he saw coming toward him the tyrant Peisistratus. When the boy's tutor cautioned him to step aside, Themistocles answered, "Isn't the road wide enough for him?"

The political and military events of the final decades of the sixth century B.C. shaped the course of Themistocles' life. Even before he was born, the rapidly expanding Persian Empire had entrenched itself in Lydia, directly east from Athens across the Aegean Sea, with its countless islands available as stepping stones to the Greek mainland. In his teenage years, Themistocles would have heard older Athenians discussing the ominous Persian advance across the Bosporus into Thrace and Macedonia to the north as well as into the easternmost Greek islands.

He was growing up in an increasingly commercial culture fostered by Peisistratus and maintained by his successors until Sparta, the strongest Greek state, expelled Hippias in 510 and enrolled Athens in its Peloponnesian League. Athens found herself the focus of a struggle between the militant Spartans and the advancing Persians. It might have occurred to Themistocles early in his manhood that a strong naval force might become the key to Athenian defense.

The career of Hippias must have seemed particularly instructive. Having fled to Persia after his deposition, Hippias was first offered reinstatement as the price Athens must pay for Persian neutrality. Sparta later brought Hippias back and offered to restore him in Athens to block any increase in Per-

sian influence. Given these political realities, freedom was precarious, and Themistocles certainly would have learned how participation in such maneuvers could impair the credibility of a leader. Despite achievements much more brilliant than those of Hippias, he would eventually face both exile and suspicion himself.

Life's Work

By 493, Themistocles had attained sufficient stature to be chosen an archon in Athens, then a post of considerable authority. Nothing is known of his role in the famous Battle of Marathon in 490, which resulted in victory for the Athenian general Miltiades the Younger, and because the whereabouts of Themistocles are unknown until 483, some historians doubt the earlier archonship. In the latter year, however, he manifested his leadership by persuading the Athenians to use the proceeds of a newly discovered silver mine to modernize the navy and expand its fighting strength to two hundred vessels. Accepted as the unquestioned leader of Athens, Themistocles directed the campaign

against the great Persian commander Xerxes I. Ordering a series of strategic retreats as the Persians, fresh from their victory at Thermopylae, swept down on Athens from the north, Themistocles at length committed the newly enlarged fleet to battle at Salamis, off the Attic coast, in 480. He used deception—at which he excelled—to lull the Persian fleet into overconfidence, and he used eloquence to bolster Athenian morale. Along with its Greek allies, the Athenian navy maneuvered the larger Persian fleet into a narrow strait and decisively defeated the invaders, who fled back across the Aegean.

Themistocles being a man who needed recognition, he resented the Athenian failure to honor him sufficiently and went to Sparta, where he was given an olive crown and a chariot described by the historian Herodotus as the most beautiful in Sparta. After a shower of praise, Themistocles enjoyed an escort of three hundred Spartan soldiers who accompanied him to the border. Back in Athens, which had borne the brunt of the Persian offensive, only remnants of the city wall stood, and a massive rebuilding project loomed. A Spartan delegation tried to persuade the Athenian leaders not to reconstruct the wall, ostensibly so that no foreign invader could capture the city and hold it as the Persians had before Salamis. In reality, as Themistocles saw it, Sparta and its other allies to the south feared that with its new naval eminence, a fortified Athens itself represented too strong a potential foe. Regarding the rebuilding as essential, Themistocles persuaded his fellow Athenians to send him back to Sparta to negotiate the matter and meanwhile to put all men, women, and children to work at the reconstruction. In Sparta, Themistocles used all of his wiles to postpone the talks. He explained that he could not proceed without his colleagues, who had been unaccountably delayed. When reports came back that the wall was already rising, he labored to convince the Spartans of their falsity. Eventually he suggested that a trustworthy inspection team be sent, while at the same time he secretly sent instructions to delay the visitors in every possible way.

With the hastily constructed wall in place, Themistocles admitted the deception but defended it stoutly. The Athenians, he pointed out, had abandoned their city in the first place on their own; furthermore, they had devised the strategy that had lured the invaders to their defeat. Whenever they had consulted with their allies, the Athenians had displayed good judgment. Now it was the Athenian

judgment that without walls Athens could not contribute equally with other walled cities of the alliance. Sparta had no doubt expected such arguments from Themistocles, though not after the fact; nevertheless, he extricated himself from Sparta without drawing any overt hostility. Through his deception, he had obtained improvements which he never could have negotiated, for the workers had substantially increased both the thickness of the walls and the area they enclosed. Following Themistocles' advice, they had also fortified the "lower city," Piraeus, in accordance with his theory that as long as Athens maintained naval superiority, safety lay in the lower city, with its natural harbors on both sides of the peninsula that it straddled.

Within five years of the victory at Salamis, a reaction set in against Themistocles. He probably contributed to this reaction through boasting and heavy-handed attempts to exact payments toward the cost of his military campaign from Athenian allies. He appears to have had little to do with the ascendancy of Athens in the Delian League, formed in 477 to combat future Persian aggression. It is difficult to determine whether Themistocles' absence from leadership in this important defensive alliance springs from distrust on the part of his colleagues or his own perception that Sparta, not Persia, represented the most likely future enemy. While the new leaders, Cimon and Aristides, supported Sparta and the alliance, Themistocles opposed any extension of Spartan influence. In this respect, he showed more foresight than the men who had replaced him in power.

Themistocles had obvious faults. Herodotus depicts him as constantly seeking personal gain; even if his assiduous fund-raising went largely for the common good, suspicions to the contrary were bound to arise. He appears to have been vain and egotistical. Even his wiliness, so valuable against enemies, posed a threat. Like Homer's Odysseus, Themistocles had built his reputation not so much on valor as on duplicity. In the Athens of the 470's, it would not have been difficult to see this devious man with his unpopular anti-Spartan bias as dangerous to Athenian security.

For whatever reason, around the year 472, he was ostracized. Many prominent citizens were exiled without specific accusations or formal trials in that era, and ostracism was only temporary, but Themistocles never returned to Attic soil. He first chose anti-Spartan Argos as his refuge, but in his absence he was condemned as a traitor. He found it necessary to flee to the island of Corcyra in the Ionian Sea, but he found no welcome there and continued to Epirus in northwestern Greece. His odyssey continued in the land of the Molossians to the east and then to Pydna on the Aegean coast. Thucydides reports him to have sailed on a merchant ship to Ionia, but a storm carried the ship to Naxos, an island then under Athenian siege. Bribing the captain, Themistocles persuaded him to sail to the coast of Asia Minor, and there he applied to his old enemies the Persians for refuge. He was granted not only refuge but also honors, in fact the governorship of Magnesia, in what is now west-central Turkey, probably after the death of his old adversary Xerxes in 465. Magnesian coins bearing his imprint have survived.

One story of Themistocles' death has him committing suicide by drinking bull's blood to avoid the necessity of leading a military expedition against the Greeks, but it is much more likely that he died a natural death around 460.

Summary

An Odyssean leader, Themistocles excelled at outwitting his military and political opponents. He demonstrated the true leader's capacity to resist the popular mood and to redirect popular energy toward prudent ends. His decision to devote windfall profits from silver mines, which others wanted to divide up among the populace, to naval defense, saved Athens from almost sure defeat at the hands of the Persians and preserved Athenian autonomy in the face of Spartan ambition. Although Themistocles did nothing personally to promote Athenian democracy, its later flowering surely depended on his actions in defense of a strong and independent city-state.

Not always a good man, Themistocles was an indisputably great leader. Despite the fact that at various times he opposed all of them, the three major states of his region—Athens, Sparta, and Persia—all heaped honors on him. Thucydides reports that the Magnesians, whom he led in his last years, erected a monument to him in the marketplace. They saw him not as a former enemy but as a man whose talent for governance, frustrated in his own land, needed scope and opportunity. His brilliance and energy in public projects outweighed the devious means by which he achieved them and his penchant for boasting of them afterward. Thucydides regarded him as an intuitive genius who could operate successfully in matters for which neither his training nor his experience had prepared him. Adversity brought out the best in him and inspired him to bring out the best in the troops and citizens whom he led.

Bibliography

Forrest, W. G. "Themistokles and Argos." *The Classical Quarterly* 10 (1960): 221-241. From admittedly scanty evidence, Forrest attempts to reconstruct the period of Themistocles' exile. He summarizes succinctly the most likely causes of his ostracism and argues for a longer period in Argos than most historians have been willing to concede.

Frost, Frank J. "Themistocles' Place in Athenian Politics." *California Studies in Classical Antiquity* 1 (1968): 105-124. Frost questions the labels often applied to Themistocles of "new man," "democrat," and "radical" and suggests that they involve a misapplication of Aristotelian political theory to a period of Greek politics too little known to permit their application. He finds Themistocles working within an aristocratic culture by skillful manipulation of the powerful families that controlled Athens in the early fifth century B.C.

Gomme, A. W. *A Historical Commentary on Thucydides.* Vol. 3. Oxford: Clarendon Press, 1945. One section of Gomme's learned commentary on the work of the most respected ancient Greek historian deals with Themistocles. Gomme is particularly interested in the gap between his archonship and shipbuilding activity a decade later. Skeptical of the theories advanced to explain the gap in Themistocles' career, Gomme is inclined to doubt the archonship and places his rise to power in the 480's rather than the 490's.

Herodotus. *The Persian Wars.* Translated by George Rawlinson. New York: Modern Library, 1942. Of the two great ancient Greek historians who write of Themistocles, Herodotus is more likely than Thucydides to accept fanciful sources of information and shows less understanding of military affairs, but his subject encompasses the years of Themistocles' most notable exploits. Furthermore, Herodotus lived and wrote at a time when many witnesses of the Persian Wars were still living.

Lenardon, Robert J. *The Saga of Themistocles.* London: Thames and Hudson, 1978. This is the only true biography of book-length form for English-speaking readers. Lenardon's method is to place before the reader the full variety of evidence, with many substantial quotations from ancient sources, and encourage readers to draw their own conclusions in cases of dubious or conflicting evidence. His cautious approach can be maddening to anyone looking for an authoritative assessment of his subject, but his presentation of the facts could not be more scrupulous.

McGregor, Malcolm F. "The Pro-Persian Party at Athens from 510 to 480 B.C." In *Harvard Studies in Classical Philology*, Supp. 1. Cambridge, Mass.: Harvard University Press, 1940. McGregor emphasizes Themistocles' political cunning in his accession to power. He sees Themistocles as a "new man" who cultivated Miltiades the Younger, the hero of Marathon and an Athenian aristocrat, as a fellow hater of Persia and thus created an anti-Persian momentum in Athens.

Plutarch. *Themistocles and Aristides*. Translated by Bernadotte Perrin. New York: Scribner, 1901. Plutarch is the ancient biographer most skillful at conveying a sense of his subjects' personalities. There can be little doubt that many of his anecdotes are inventions, but others may have a basis in fact. His semi-fictionalized life of the Athenian leader makes absorbing reading.

Thucydides. *History of the Peloponnesian War*. Translated by Richard Crawley. London and New York: Dutton, 1910. Only the first of Thucydides' eight books, giving the historical background for his subject, deals with Themistocles, but this early historian's general reliability and his relative closeness to Themistocles in time (his birth came close to Themistocles' death) make his account preferable wherever, as often happens, early authorities disagree.

Robert P. Ellis

THEODORE OF MOPSUESTIA

Born: c. A.D. 350; Antioch (modern Turkey)
Died: 428; Mopsuestia, Cilicia
Area of Achievement: Religion
Contribution: The most important representative of the Antiochene school of biblical exegesis and theology, Theodore served as Bishop of Mopsuestia from 392 until his death in 428. Primarily because of alleged similarities with Pelagianism and Nestorianism, Theodore's theological views were condemned by the Emperor Justinian and by the Fifth Council of Constantinople in 553.

Early Life

Theodore, generally known by the name of his bishopric as "of Mopsuestia," was born at Antioch about 350. Little is known about his parents or family, except that his father held an official position at Antioch and the family was reportedly wealthy. Theodore's brother, Polychronius, eventually became Bishop of Apamea on the Orontes; a cousin, Paeanius, held an important civil post at Constantinople.

Since Theodore belonged to the nobility in Antioch, his early education was under the most renowned professor of rhetoric of his day, the Sophist Libanius. Theodore was an early companion, fellow student, and friend of John Chrysostom, also born in Antioch, a few years before Theodore. John, usually known simply as Chrysostom, became famous for his eloquent preaching and eventually became Patriarch of Constantinople.

Theodore and Chrysostom enjoyed an excellent philosophical education along with another friend and fellow student, Maximus, who later became Bishop of Isaurian Seleucia. It seems, however, that the three friends came to enjoy the luxurious life of polite Antioch as well. Chrysostom was the first to turn back from the pleasures of that world, and he then succeeded in winning back his fellow students, Theodore and Maximus. The three friends shortly thereafter sought a retreat in the Asketerion, a famous monastic school of Diodore (later Bishop of Tarsus) and Carterius, near Antioch.

According to Chrysostom, Theodore's conversion was sincere and fervent, and he threw himself into the monastic discipline with characteristic zeal. He may have been baptized at this time as well. His days were spent in study, his nights in prayer. He practiced almost every conceivable form of ascetic self-discipline, including lengthy fasts and sleeping on the bare ground. He is reported to have found inexpressible joy in the service of Christ as a Christian celibate until "the world" beckoned to him again.

Theodore had become fascinated by the charms of a beautiful young girl named Hermione, and he was seriously contemplating marriage and a return to the secular life. This proposal became a matter of great concern to his fellow ascetics in the monastery, with many prayers offered and various efforts made for his "recovery" from his "fall." Such efforts included the earliest known literary compositions of Chrysostom—two letters appealing to Theodore to abandon his infatuation and remain true to his monastic vows. Theodore was not yet twenty years of age, but the appeal of his friends prevailed, and he remained true to his vow of celibacy throughout his life.

From 369 to 378, Theodore remained under the spiritual leadership of Diodore, who was at that time elevated to the See of Tarsus. Theodore probably became closely acquainted with both Scripture and church doctrine during these years. He may also have developed his principles of interpretation of the Bible and his views of the person of Christ, which eventually led him into theological controversy. He subsequently came under the influence of Flavian, Bishop of Antioch, who ordained him as a priest in 383, three years before his friend Chrysostom was ordained. Chrysostom almost immediately rose to the full height of his oratorical powers in the pulpit of Antioch. Theodore may have felt himself eclipsed by his friend's greater power as a preacher, or a visit from his old master Diodore to Antioch may have caused him to move to Tarsus, where he stayed until 392, at which time he was elevated to the See of Mopsuestia, in Cilicia, where he remained for the final thirty-six years of his life.

Life's Work

Nothing is known about the physical appearance or general health of Theodore. He died in 428, at the age of seventy-eight, reportedly exhausted from more than fifty years of literary and pastoral work. Most of his later years were marked by theological controversy, but he died peacefully with a great reputation from his many books and other writings. His long episcopate was marked by no outstanding incidents, and his many friends and disciples left few personal recollections. He impressed the Emperor Theodosius I, however, who heard him preach once, and Theodosius is said to have declared that he had "never met with such a teacher." (Theodosius had also heard Saint Ambrose and Saint Gregory of Nazianzus.) A letter from Chrysostom when he was an exile also reveals that the two friends always retained a high regard for each other. Chrysostom declared that he could "never forget the love of Theodore, so genuine and warm, so sincere and guileless, a love maintained from early years, and manifested but now." He assured Theodore that, "exile as he is, he reaps no ordinary consolation from having such a treasure, such a mine of wealth within his heart as the love of so vigilant and noble a soul."

Theodore wrote widely on a great variety of topics. Active in the theological controversies of his time, he is said to have written at least fifteen books on the Incarnation of Christ before he began his serious exegetical work in 402. Unfortunately, many of Theodore's writings have not survived, and those that have do not give a true indication of the scope of his work. He began with a commentary on the Psalms and eventually wrote commentaries on practically every book of the Bible. In addition, he wrote at least thirty-seven other works on a variety of theological, ecclesiastical, and practical problems: the Incarnation, the sacraments, the Holy Spirit, exegetical method, monasticism, and other topics.

Theodore is doubtless best known today as a theologian, and in particular for his views on Christology and anthropology. Although his theological ideas were condemned by the Fifth Council of Constantinople more than a century after his death, during his lifetime he enjoyed the reputation of an orthodox teacher. It is ironic that this untiring foe of theological heresies was later condemned as a heretic himself. In his opposition to heresy, Theodore's attention was particularly directed toward the Christological views of Apollinaris of Laodicea. His fifteen-volume *On the Incarnation* was primarily directed against Apollinaris, and Theodore's (admittedly) extreme views on the "two natures" of Christ were largely by way of response to Apollinaris' teachings concerning the subordination of the human nature of Christ.

Theodore insisted on the complete manhood of Christ and roundly condemned the theory of Apollinaris that the divine Logos had taken the place of Christ's rational soul. Theodore reasoned that if the Godhead had replaced human reason, Jesus would not have experienced fear or any other human emotion. He would not have wrestled in prayer or needed the Holy Spirit's assistance; the story of the temptations of Christ, for example, would have been meaningless. Christ would have had nothing in common with humanity, which would render the Incarnation itself devoid of meaning.

Theodore also insisted that the two natures of Christ, human and divine, were perfect and always remained two. He refused to contemplate the spiritual and material as confused in any manner. His emphasis on this theological point may have been derived from a careful analysis of human personality. Since only elements of the same substance can become unified, Theodore could not conceive of any sort of union between the two natures of Christ. This view, later held in somewhat modified form by Nestorius, was condemned by the Third Ecumenical Council at Ephesus in 431.

Summary

By his insistence on maintaining the human nature of Christ along with the divine, Theodore of Mopsuestia held his own against the ontological speculations of the Alexandrian school, which were, in fact, derived primarily from philosophical abstractions. In principle, his position was vindicated by the great Council of Chalcedon in 451, which recognized in Christ two natures "without confusion, change, division, or separation in one person and subsistence." Through his emphasis on the human nature of Christ and his keen awareness of the biblical evidence, Theodore may have saved Christendom from falling into endless theological speculation.

As the greatest exegete and spiritual leader of the Antiochene school, Theodore became the acknowledged leader of numerous ecclesiastical figures of the fourth and fifth centuries. In his theological writings he also stressed the importance of free will and the human contribution to salvation. Human achievements were ascribed to free will; thus, Theodore opposed the doctrines of predestination and original sin. Because of such views Theodore was regarded by some as a forerunner to Pelagius, whose views were also condemned by the council at Ephesus in 431.

Theodore's theological views, considered orthodox during his lifetime, became controversial after his death, particularly when Nestorians and Pelagians appealed to his writings. In the end the Alexandrian school succeeded in bringing Theodore and his writings under ecclesiastical anathema. Indeed, the primary reason so few of his writings survive today is that many of them were intentionally destroyed by church authorities. Rabboula, Orthodox Syriac Bishop of Edessa from 411 to 436, vehemently attacked Theodore and his teachings and ordered all existing copies of his works confiscated and burned. It may have been Monophysite reaction to the Council of Chalcedon that first brought Theodore's theological views into question. He was condemned as a heretic by the Emperor Justinian in 544. Under imperial pressure Pope Vergilius condemned sixty propositions from Theodore's writings as heretical, and the Fifth Council of Constantinople in 553 placed his writings under anathema.

As an interpreter of Scripture, Theodore stood out among the scholars of his day. His scholarship is said to have astounded his contemporaries. In thoroughness, accuracy, and consistency of thought he had no peer, not even Chrysostom. His followers called him simply "the interpreter." He became the most remarkable and original representative of the Antiochene school of exegesis, noted for its insistence on the plain, literal meaning of Scripture and its opposition to the fanciful, allegorical interpretations so typical of Origen and the Alexandrian school.

Theodore was also a pioneer in the use of critical methods of Bible study unheard of in his day. He made careful use of scientific, critical, philological, and historical methods, thereby anticipating by more than a millennium the rise of modern historical-critical methods of Bible study. He consistently tried to take into account the historical circumstances under which biblical books were written; subsequently, he rejected several books as uncanonical, including Job, Chronicles, the Song of Songs, Ezra, Revelation, and the Catholic Epistles (except 1 Peter and 1 John). The few of his writings that survive demonstrate something of the power and authority of his work. The only commentary that survives in the original Greek is *On the Twelve Prophets*, but many of his writings were translated into Syriac very early and have been preserved, at least in part, primarily by Nestorians. His commentary on John has long been known, but recent discoveries include commentaries on the Lord's Prayer, the Nicene Creed, and the sacraments. His massive work on the Incarnation was

discovered early in the twentieth century in a codex in Seert, Turkey, but unfortunately seems to have been destroyed during World War I.

Bibliography

Dewart, Joanne McWilliam. *The Theology of Grace of Theodore of Mopsuestia*. Washington, D.C.: Catholic University of America Press, 1971. An important study of Theodore's teachings about the grace of God. Emphasizes Theodore's scriptural understanding of grace as divine benevolence, best understood against the background of the Pelagian controversy. Demonstrates Theodore's insistence on the cooperation of divine grace and the human will.

Greer, Rowan A. *Theodore of Mopsuestia: Exegete and Theologian*. London: Faith Press, 1961. A sympathetic assessment of the theology of Theodore from the point of view of biblical criticism. Greer uses Theodore's *Commentary of St. John* as representative of his critical and exegetical work and as a vantage point from which to illustrate the basic differences between the Antiochene and Alexandrian schools. He concludes that Theodore was a biblical critic first of all; his theology sprang from his study of the Bible.

Norris, Richard A. *Manhood and Christ: A Study in the Christology of Theodore of Mopsuestia*. Oxford: Clarendon Press, 1963. A thorough survey of Theodore's anthropological presuppositions and their impact on his Christological thought. This highly recommended theological analysis contains valuable appendices on fifth and sixth century discussion of Theodore as well as more recent treatment of his thought.

Patterson, Leonard. *Theodore of Mopsuestia and Modern Thought*. London: Society for Promoting Christian Knowledge, 1926. Although dated, this is an important study of Theodore's life and thought. Particularly interesting is Patterson's discussion of Theodore's relation to modern thought (for example, evolutionary theory and the mind-body relationship).

Sullivan, Francis. *The Christology of Theodore of Mopsuestia*. Rome: Apud Aedes Universitatis Gregorianae, 1956. A careful study of Theodore's thought concerning the unity of Christ. Sullivan treats some of the problems involved in making use of existing fragments of Theodore's works, mostly in Syriac translation. He concludes that Theodore was indeed, despite his orthodox intentions, the "father of Nestorianism."

Swete, Henry B. "Theodore of Mopsuestia." In *A Dictionary of Christian Biography, Literature, Sects and Doctrines During the First Eight Centuries*, edited by William Smith and Henry Wace, vol. 4. London: Murray, and Boston: Little Brown, 1887. Dated but extremely valuable and sympathetic study of Theodore's life and work. Excellent use made of primary sources, despite the fact that many of Theodore's writings had not yet been discovered when Swete prepared this article.

C. Fitzhugh Spragins

THEODORET OF CYRRHUS

Born: c. A.D. 393; Antioch, Roman Syria
Died: c. A.D. 458; Cyrrhus, Roman Syria
Area of Achievement: Religion
Contribution: Theodoret served as the Bishop of Cyrrhus for forty-one years. Aside from carrying out an effective and sensitive bishopric, he authored works on practically every aspect of Christian thought and practice. He is perhaps best remembered for his contribution to the Christological debates that led to the Council of Chalcedon.

Early Life

Theodoret was born in Antioch in the Roman province of northern Syria circa A.D. 393 to moderately wealthy Christian parents. He spent the first twenty-three years of his life in the city of Antioch, leaving in 416/417 for the monastery at Nicerte. While Theodoret wrote sparingly of these formative years in Antioch, his remarks as well as what can be deduced from his later writings reveal that he drew deeply from both the rich Greco-Roman culture of the city and the monks who lived on the fringes of Antioch. His writings reflect the education typical of the privileged population of large Greco-Roman cities in late antiquity. Such an education would have entailed training in Greek grammar, speech, and the classics of Greek literature and philosophy from Homer to Demosthenes.

From his parents, Theodoret inherited a fondness for the monks who lived in the caves and wilderness surrounding Antioch. Theodoret's mother had sought out these monks to cure an eye ailment, and his father had sought help when after thirteen years of marriage no child had been conceived. In both cases, the monks were given credit for solving the problem; from childhood, Theodoret was taken on weekly visits to them. Theodoret fondly recalled his visits to the monks Peter of Galatia and Macedonius and noted that Peter had given him a piece of linen girdle which was treasured by the family when it proved a remedy for a variety of physical afflictions.

Upon the death of his parents, Theodoret left Antioch to become a monk himself. He joined the monastic community at Nicerte near Apamea and there enjoyed some seven years of quiet seclusion. It was during his tenure at Nicerte that Theodoret composed his celebrated apology for the Christian religion, *Therapeutica* (c. 424; *A Treatise of Laws,* 1776). This apology displays the breadth of his knowledge of Greek philosophy and religion as he juxtaposes the claims of Christianity to those associated with a host of Greek philosophical schools and religious cults.

Life's Work

After seven years in the monastery at Nicerte, Theodoret was called to assume the duties of bishop of the diocese of Cyrrhus. Theodoret says he "unwillingly assumed" the office, as it meant leaving behind the beloved tranquillity of the monastery and taking on the demands of an exceptionally large and unruly diocese on the eastern edges of the Roman Empire. Theodoret's reluctance did not prevent him from fulfilling his appointed task: He served as bishop there from the year 424 until his death in 458.

The boundaries of the diocese were the same as those of Cyrrhestica, a territory of the province of Euphatensis in eastern Syria. The diocese was subject to the Metropolitan at Hierapolis and covered sixteen hundred square miles. Theodoret described

S. THEODORETVS

the diocese as mountainous and bare. This bleak landscape had not, however, discouraged the establishment and spread of Christianity; Theodoret also refers to the existence of eight hundred parishes, each with its own church. The area also contained a significant population of monks, with whom Theodoret maintained a cordial relationship.

The town of Cyrrhus, where Theodoret was to reside, was located approximately sixty-five kilometers northeast of Antioch at the confluence of the Aphreen and Saboun Souyou rivers. Cyrrhus had been an important Roman military outpost, but, like many other Roman frontier towns, it was in a state of decline by the fifth century. Theodoret called it "a solitary and ugly village." Over the course of his residence, he spent much time and energy in rebuilding and improving Cyrrhus. Using funds collected from the diocese, he constructed two bridges and public galleries, rebuilt a major aqueduct, and improved the public baths. The bishop also paid to have skilled physicians move to the town and secured the service of educators and engineers.

Theodoret's responsibilities were numerous. He describes such tasks as visiting and encouraging the monks living in the diocese, driving out heretics, playing ecclesiastical politics, and writing a number of tracts on practically every aspect of Christian life and thought. Aside from the apology mentioned earlier and the treatises on Christology to be discussed below, the extant works from Theodoret's vast corpus include historical studies, biblical commentaries, a series of sermons on Providence, and a collection of letters.

While Theodoret's interests and contributions were wide-ranging, his place in the history of Christianity has consistently been recorded in terms of his role in the Christological controversies that began with the Council of Ephesus in 431 and culminated with the Council of Chalcedon in 451. In 431, Theodoret was called upon to represent the Antiochene interpretation of Christ (the two-nature Christology) against the Alexandrian interpretation as it was put forth by Cyril of Alexandria. Theodoret's response took the form of a tract entitled *Reprehensio duodecim capitum seu anathema anathematismorum Cyrilli* (431), in which he stressed the biblical foundation for the fullness of the two natures of Christ and argued that Cyril's formula implicated the divine Christ in the passion and suffering of the Crucifixion. The Council of Ephesus was called to resolve the differences between Cyril and Theodoret; it decided in favor of Cyril.

In the years between the First Council of Ephesus and the Council of Chalcedon, Theodoret continued to be involved in the debates over the proper interpretation of the nature of Christ. In 447, he composed a work entitled *Eranistes seu Polymorphus* (*Dialogues*, 1892) as an attack on the position held by the monk Eutyches, who had succeeded Cyril as the leader of the Alexandrian one-nature school of interpretation. This work and the ensuing debate led to the Second Council of Ephesus in 449; Theodoret again lost and was deposed from his bishopric in Cyrrhus. He was apparently restored soon thereafter and the Council of Chalcedon in 451 closed the chapter on Theodoret's involvement in the Christological debates. In fact, from the end of the Council of Chalcedon till his death in 458, Theodoret must have lived a comparatively quiet and uninvolved life as bishop, as there is no record of any further writing or involvement in ecclesiastical politics.

Summary

Theodoret of Cyrrhus was one of the most prolific writers and influential voices for Christianity in the East during late antiquity. He wrote against a rich and complex background which was at once deeply indebted to the language, ideas, and ideals of the long-established, Greco-Roman culture and which at the same time increasingly felt the influence of Christianity and its otherworldly monks and theological squabbles. Theodoret labored as a bishop in the eastern provinces of the later Roman Empire to improve the life and resources for his congregation, to establish the proper interpretation of the Bible, to chronicle the history of the Church and its monks, and to clarify what the Church taught about the person and work of Christ. While in the end, Theodoret found himself on the losing side of the Christological debates, his contributions to those debates have been judged the clearest and most profound statements on the two-nature view of the person of Christ.

Bibliography

Ashby, Godfrey William Ernest Candler. *Theodoret of Cyrrhus as Exegete of the Old Testament*. Grahamstown, South Africa: Rhodes University Press, 1972. One of the few English-language studies of Theodoret, this book provides, in largely summary fashion, a guide to

Theodoret's exegesis of the Old Testament. While the author provides few critical insights, the work nevertheless proves valuable as it offers an entry into an enormous collection of biblical commentary, most of which is available only in Greek or Latin.

Chesnut, Glenn F. *The First Christian Histories.* 2d ed. Macon, Ga.: Mercer University Press, 1986. A well-researched work which compares the ecclesiastical histories of Eusebius, Socrates, Sozomen, and Theodoret. The author demonstrates how each brought to his historical studies a distinct theological and philosophical bias and shows the extent to which these early Christian historians were dependent on classical Greco-Roman models of history writing.

Grillmeier, Alois. *Christ in Christian Tradition.* Vol. 1, *From the Apostolic Age to Chalcedon.* Translated by John Bowden. Rev. ed. London: Mowbray, and Atlanta, Ga.: John Knox Press, 1975. This book provides a thorough treatment of the development of Christology in the early Church and includes a long and helpful discussion of Theodoret's contribution. The book has an extensive bibliography of works in English and European languages.

Jones, A. H. M. *The Later Roman Empire.* 4 vols. Oxford: Blackwell, and 2 vols. Norman: University of Oklahoma Press, 1964. The standard work on this period, it provides not only an account of the major events and persons but also useful insights into the contemporary social world.

Theodoret of Cyrrhus. *"The Ecclesiastical History," "Dialogues," and "Letters" of Theodoret.* Translated by B. Jackson. Grand Rapids, Mich.: Eerdmans, 1953. This English translation of the letters and two of Theodoret's works was originally published in 1892. In the case of *Ekklēsiastikē historia* (c. 449; *The Ecclesiastical History,* 1612) and *Dialogues,* new editions of the Greek text have recently been published. The translations are competent and since they are the only modern English translations of these works of Theodoret, they are invaluable for those wishing to read his words who are limited to reading publications in English. A brief historical and theological introduction has been appended to the collection.

─────. *A History of the Monks of Syria.* Translated by R. M. Price. Kalamazoo, Mich.: Cistercian Publications, 1985. One of the rare English translations of a work by Theodoret, the text and translation are based on the French edition of Pierre Canivet. The history itself offers a rare glimpse into the provocative world of Syrian monasticism. The translation is clear, and the introduction and notes do a splendid job of situating the work historically and literally.

Young, Frances M. *From Nicaea to Chalcedon: A Guide to the Literature and Its Background.* London: SCM Press, and Philadelphia: Fortress Press, 1983. This is a clearly written handbook intended as an introduction to the major figures and writings of Christianity from the period between the Council of Nicaea and the Council of Chalcedon. Many of Theodoret's works are discussed, with special attention paid to *The Ecclesiastical History* and his Christological treatises. There is a substantial bibliography.

C. Thomas McCullough

THEODOSIUS THE GREAT

Born: January 11, A.D. 346 or 347; Cauca, Gallae-cia
Died: January 17, A.D. 395; Milan
Area of Achievement: Government
Contribution: Theodosius restored peace to the Eastern Roman Empire after the Roman defeat at Adrianople and established a dynasty that held the throne for more than seventy years. His settlement of Visigoths as *federati* inside the Empire may have contributed to the fall of the western part of the Empire, and his religious policies were a major step in the development of a theocratic state in the East.

Early Life

Flavius Theodosius, known as Theodosius the Great, was the son of Count Flavius Theodosius, a Hispano-Roman nobleman whose family estates were located at Cauca in northwestern Spain. Theodosius' father distinguished himself in commands in Britain and North Africa. The younger Theodosius probably served under his father in Britain. He became military commander on the Danube River, in what is now Yugoslavia, and made a name for himself by winning victories over the Sarmatians, non-Germanic peoples who had been filtering into the Danube area from southern Russia since the first century A.D.

Theodosius' career ended suddenly in 376, when his father, who had just suppressed a revolt in North Africa, was accused on some charge and executed at Carthage. The whole incident seems to have occurred just after the death of the emperor Valentinian I, and it is assumed that Valentinian's young son Gratian, the new emperor, was persuaded to authorize the execution by a newly powerful faction at court which included enemies of Count Theodosius. The younger Theodosius may have been in danger himself; at any rate, he retired to the family estates in Spain, his official career apparently over. He married Aelia Flavia Flacilla and had a son, Arcadius, during the two years spent in Spain.

A crisis in the Eastern Empire brought Theodosius from retirement to the highest responsibility. The Germanic Visigoths had been defeated by the Huns as the latter advanced westward. The Visigoths asked for and received from the Romans permission to cross the Danube River and find refuge inside the Empire. When Roman officials sent to supervise their reception abused the Goths, they revolted and in August, 378, defeated and killed the emperor Valens in a great battle at Adrianople in Thrace. The Goths were then free to pillage the Balkans and Thrace.

Gratian, who had broken off wars with Germanic tribes in eastern Gaul to assist Valens, only to find that Valens had gone into battle without waiting for his aid, now had to find someone to restore Roman control in Thrace. The men who had accused Theodosius' father were now out of favor; a new faction made up of friends and connections of the Theodosian family had the emperor's ear. They suggested the younger Theodosius as a good candidate for emperor of the East. Gratian summoned Theodosius from Spain and apparently first gave him a military command, in which he again won victories against the Sarmatians, and then named him emperor. Theodosius officially took power on January 19, 379.

Life's Work

Theodosius' next few years were spent in campaigns against the Goths, first from headquarters at Thessalonica in northeastern Greece and then, after November, 380, from Constantinople. Very little is known about these wars, but Theodosius was unable to destroy the Goths or even to drive them out of the Empire, in part, perhaps, because of a man-power shortage caused by the losses at Adrianople. As part of an attempt to conciliate at least some of the Goths and perhaps disunite them, the emperor welcomed the Gothic chieftain Athanaric to Constantinople on January 11, 381, and, when the Gothic leader died two weeks later, gave him an elaborate state funeral. Such treatment impressed the Goths and may have disposed them to negotiate.

In October, 382, Theodosius, apparently having concluded that victory was not attainable, ordered one of his generals to make a treaty with the Goths. By its terms, they were allowed to settle in Thrace as *federati*. They owed military service to the Empire, but unlike earlier settlements of barbarians inside the Empire, the Goths were allowed to retain their arms as well as their own rulers and laws. In effect, they were a separate nation inside the imperial borders. Many contemporaries criticized this arrangement; some modern scholars have even

suggested that it was a factor in the fall of the Western Empire.

On the other hand, Theodosius reorganized the eastern armies in a way that greatly contributed to the internal security of the Eastern Empire. He set up five separate armies, each with its own commander who reported directly to the emperor. No single commander could concentrate power in his own hands as was still possible in the West.

In the same years in which he was engaged in campaigns against the Goths, Theodosius involved himself in religious affairs. He was baptized in the autumn of 380, when he was believed to be near death from illness. Many people in this period preferred to delay baptism, since it absolved sins committed before the sacrament. There is no way of knowing whether baptism on threat of death caused Theodosius to have some sort of conversion experience or whether it only intensified an already strong adherence to the Church. Certainly he took vigorous steps shortly after his recovery to demonstrate his support of the Nicene Creed (which maintained that Father and Son were of the same substance). The Arians, who were especially pow-

erful in the Eastern Empire, believed that the Son was not divine, but only a creature, and thus subordinate to the Father.

Within two days after entering Constantinople on November 24, 380, Theodosius expelled the Arian bishop Demophilus and established his own candidate, the orthodox Catholic Gregory Nazianzus, as bishop. On February 28, 380, he had issued an edict requiring everyone to accept the Trinity. Yet the new decree was enforced mainly against bishops and priests, who lost their churches if they refused to accept it. It did not, apparently, represent an attempt to force all laymen to adhere to the Nicene Creed.

Toward paganism, Theodosius adopted a more conciliatory approach, at least in the early years of his reign, even reopening a pagan temple on the Euphrates River in 382 as long as no sacrifices took place there. In January, 381, he issued another edict ordering that all churches be turned over to the Nicene Catholics, and in May through July he held the Council of Constantinople, at which about 150 eastern bishops reaffirmed the divinity of Son and Holy Spirit.

Soon Theodosius was faced with a situation in which his loyalty to the Church conflicted with the duty he owed to the man who had made him emperor. In 383, Magnus Clemens Maximus in Britain proclaimed himself emperor of the West and invaded Gaul, where Gratian's army went over to the usurper and Gratian himself was killed, perhaps by his own men. Magnus Maximus controlled Britain, Spain, Gaul, and North Africa. In Italy and the middle Danube provinces Valentinian II, Gratian's younger brother, ruled under the tutelage of his mother, Justina, an Arian. Theodosius was placed in something of a dilemma. Loyalty to Gratian would have demanded that he avenge his patron's death and restore all the western provinces to Valentinian. Religion complicated the picture, however, since Magnus Maximus was presenting himself as a champion of orthodox Catholicism. How could the defender of orthodoxy in the East put down a Catholic ruler in the West in order to put an Arian in his place?

There may also have been personal ties between Theodosius and Magnus Maximus; Maximus came from Spain, was apparently some sort of dependent of the Theodosian family, and may have served in Britain alongside Theodosius under Count Theodosius. His concern for his eastern frontier could have increased the emperor's reluctance to divert his armies to a campaign in the West. When the envoys of Magnus Maximus arrived in Constantinople to ask for official recognition, the King of Persia, Ardashir II, had just died, and it was not known whether his successor planned to attack the Romans. A revolt of tribes on the Arabian frontier, in modern Jordan, complicated the situation. Religion, personal ties, and military concerns apparently decided the issue. Theodosius not only made no attempt to get rid of Magnus Maximus but also gave him official recognition as ruler of Britain, Spain, and Gaul.

Many of the difficulties which had held Theodosius back in 383 were resolved in the next few years. In 384, the new ruler of Persia sent envoys to Constantinople with lavish gifts for the emperor, presumably to signal friendly intentions. The tribes in revolt on the eastern frontier had submitted in 385, and in 387 a treaty was signed with Persia. In an agreement similar to those made by Rome and Parthia in earlier centuries, Theodosius allowed the Persians to name a ruler for most of Armenia, a mountainous area in eastern Asia Minor which controlled the roads between Roman Asia Minor and Persia. This Persian treaty and the earlier one with the Goths gave the Eastern Empire a long period of peace in which to rebuild its forces.

Although repeated incursions by bands of Huns and other tribes kept the frontier forces on the alert, the only major wars Theodosius fought in the remainder of his reign were against usurpers in the West, the first not until about ten years after Adrianople. In those ten years, he had succeeded in rebuilding his armies to a point where they could win victories over other Roman armies. Whether Theodosius' decision to make peace with foreign enemies but to fight internal rivals was best for the whole Empire in the long run is a question fundamental to any assessment of his accomplishments as ruler.

In the same year in which the Persian treaty was signed, Maximus invaded Italy, causing Valentinian II, his mother, and his sister Galla to flee to Theodosius for help. Theodosius was now militarily in a much better position to confront Maximus, and by marrying Galla he could claim that family loyalties outweighed the claims of religion. In June, 388, he led an army from the East, defeated Maximus twice in Pannonia, at Siscia and Poetovio, and forced him to retreat to Aquileia, at the head of the Adriatic Sea. There, Maximus surrendered and was killed by Theodosius' soldiers, who feared that the emperor might pardon him. Indeed, Theodosius punished very few of Maximus' supporters and issued a general pardon for the rest. He installed Valentinian as emperor in the West under the supervision of Arbogast, an army commander of mixed Germanic and Roman parentage. Valentinian converted from Arianism to Catholicism at Theodosius' urging and established his court at Vienne in southern Gaul.

Theodosius spent considerable time in Italy between 388 and 391. On June 13, 389, he made a formal entry into Rome with his younger son Honorius. By generous gifts, reforms in the laws, and deference to powerful individuals, he cultivated the support of the senate. While in Italy, Theodosius himself came under the influence of Bishop Ambrose of Milan, one of the Fathers of the Church. If Theodosius had given orders to church officials in the East, he now found himself submitting to the demands of a western bishop. In 390, after the people of Thessalonica murdered one of the emperor's German officers, soldiers were allowed to massacre thousands of spectators in the city's stadium. Ambrose demanded that Theodosius do penance for the massacre, and after long negotiations the emperor conceded. Stripping himself of the diadem and purple cloak which symbolized his power, he knelt before the bishop in the cathedral in Milan to ask for a pardon. It was a vivid demonstration of the western Church's power in relation to the government.

Having returned to Constantinople in 391, Theodosius found himself facing another western usurper in the following year. As Valentinian II grew into his late teens, the young man realized that Arbogast meant to keep real power in his own hands. In frustration, he apparently committed suicide, although many at the time and later accused Arbogast of murdering the young emperor. Arbogast named a teacher of rhetoric, Eugenius, as the emperor of the West.

Arbogast, a pagan himself, seems to have hoped for the support of the surviving pagan aristocracy, and a number of distinguished pagan nobles did rally to Eugenius' cause. Pagan support for Eugenius allowed Theodosius to present himself as the defender of Christianity. In 394, Theodosius again led his armies westward; on September 6, 394, at the Battle of the Frigidus, a river in Yugoslavia, he defeated Arbogast and Eugenius. On the first day of the battle, ten thousand Visigoths in Theodosius' army died in a frontal assault, and the emperor's officers advised retreat. Theodosius refused to give up and on the next day won a decisive victory with the aid of a sudden windstorm. Eugenius was captured and executed; Arbogast escaped but killed himself two days later. Many consider this final defeat of the forces of paganism in the Roman Empire to have been Theodosius' greatest achievement.

The emperor, however, had only a few months to enjoy the victory; he died in Milan in January, 395. He left the Empire to his sons Arcadius and Honorius—Arcadius to rule in the East and Honorius in the West. It has been argued that this division led to the fall of the Western Empire because the wealthier East not only did not send aid when barbarians attacked the West but also diverted invaders westward to save itself, in some cases.

Summary

Theodosius the Great brought peace to the eastern empire through diplomacy, rebuilt the eastern armies, and used them to win victories against western Roman armies. He ruled the East for fifteen years in which no one successfully disputed his authority and founded a dynasty which held power in the East until 450 and in the West until 455. In his zeal for Catholic orthodoxy, he issued orders to people and bishops on matters of doctrine, conciliated the senate with high offices, and won the people's favor. He made sure that Constantinople had a secure supply of grain, extended the walls, and embellished the city with a forum and a column depicting his victories. He even managed to lower taxes.

By most of the standards applied to earlier emperors, Theodosius was successful; the Church thought he deserved the title "Great." One could argue that the Eastern Empire benefited substantially from his rule, in both the short and the long terms. Whether his settlement of the Goths and his division of the Empire between his sons did not in the long run prove disastrous to the West is a question still disputed.

Bibliography

Baynes, Norman H. "The Dynasty of Valentinian and Theodosius the Great." In *The Cambridge Medieval History*. Vol. 1, *The Christian Roman Empire and the Foundation of the Teutonic Kingdoms*, edited by H. M. Gwatkin, J. P. Whitney, and J. B. Bury. 2d ed. Cambridge: Cambridge University Press, and New York: Macmillan, 1924. This detailed account of the military and political aspects of Theodosius' reign includes an attempt to reconstruct the Gothic wars which occurred from 379 to 382.

Dudden, F. Homes. *The Life and Times of St. Ambrose*. 2 vols. Oxford: Clarendon Press, 1935. Scholarly but very readable account includes extensive material on Theodosius, emphasizing his relations with Ambrose but dealing with many other aspects of the reign as well. Contains frontispiece portrait of Ambrose, table of dates, bibliography, indexes.

Ferrill, Arthur. *The Fall of the Roman Empire: The Military Explanation*. London and New York: Thames and Hudson, 1986. Chapter 4 on Theodosius is a careful evaluation of his military accomplishments, with a description of the Roman armies in 395. With table of emperors, bibliography, and illustrations, including a sculptural portrait of Theodosius and a map of the Battle of the Frigidus.

Gibbon, Edward. *The History of the Decline and Fall of the Roman Empire*. Edited by J. B. Bury. 7 vols. London: Methuen, and New York: Macmillan, 1909-1926. This historical and literary classic includes two chapters on Theodosius. Gibbon's prejudice against religion colors his estimate of Theodosius' relations with the Church. Includes illustrations, maps, editor's appendices, bibliography of Gibbon's works and replies to it, indexes to text and appendices.

Hodgkin, Thomas. *Italy and Her Invaders.* Vol. 1, *The Visigothic Invasion,* Oxford: Clarendon Press, 1880; New York: Russell and Russell, 1967. A well-written chapter on Theodosius includes an introductory discussion of the primary sources, a chronological table of Theodosius' life, and a detailed account and evaluation of his Gothic policy, civil wars, internal administration, and religious policy. Old but still useful. With illustrations, maps, genealogical table of the Theodosian family.

Holum, Kenneth G. *Theodosian Empresses: Women and Imperial Dominion in Late Antiquity.* Berkeley: University of California Press, 1982; London: University of California Press, 1989. Part of chapter 2, "Theodosius the Great and His Women," provides a useful summary of some of the main issues of Theodosius' reign as well as a description of Theodosian Constantinople, a discussion of the position of the emperor's first wife, and an account of the implications of his second marriage for the war against Maximus. With detailed footnotes, a plan of Constantinople under Theodosius, a genealogical table of the Theodosian family, illustrations with an empha-

sis on coins, extensive bibliography, and an index.

Jones, A. H. M. *The Later Roman Empire, 284-602: A Social, Economic, and Administrative Survey.* 4 vols. Oxford: Blackwell, and 2 vols. Norman: University of Oklahoma Press, 1964. Detailed authoritative treatment of the period includes material on Theodosius' reign, his religious policy, and his laws. Third volume contains notes, three appendices, lists of collections and periodicals cited and an exhaustive list of sources with abbreviations. With seven maps in a folder.

King, N. Q. *The Emperor Theodosius and the Establishment of Christianity.* Philadelphia: Westminster Press, 1960; London: SCM Press, 1961. Scholarly treatment of the relation of church and state under Theodosius viewed in the light of modern problems in this area. King argues that Theodosius, instead of imposing his own views on the Church, never acted in church matters without the support of an important group of bishops.

Matthews, John. *Western Aristocracies and Imperial Court: A.D. 364-425.* Oxford: Clarendon Press, 1975; New York: Oxford University Press, 1990. Chapters 4 through 9 deal with Theodosius' reign in considerable detail, intermingled with extensive and occasionally digressive treatment of the social and cultural background of the aristocracies under his rule.

Carolyn Nelson

THEOPHRASTUS
Tyrtamus

Born: c. 372 B.C.; Eresus, Lesbos, Greece
Died: c. 287 B.C.; Athens?, Greece
Areas of Achievement: Science, philosophy, and literature
Contribution: Successor of Aristotle as head of his school, the Lyceum, Theophrastus became father of the sciences of botany, ecology, and mineralogy. He also wrote *Characters*, literary sketches of human psychological types.

Early Life

Theophrastus (originally named Tyrtamus) was born in Eresus, a small city-state on the Greek island of Lesbos, near the coast of Asia Minor. His father was Melantas, a cloth-fuller. He studied under the philosopher Alcippus in Eresus, later traveling to Athens to broaden his intellectual horizons. It is not known when he became Aristotle's student. It was Aristotle who called him Theophrastus, "he of godlike speech," a compliment to his polished Greek style. According to tradition, both men studied under Plato, but in Theophrastus' case this study must have been brief.

Theophrastus was in his mid-twenties when Plato died. Since Plato had not made Aristotle head of his school, the Academy, Aristotle moved to Assos at the invitation of its ruler, Hermias, and stayed three years. Theophrastus followed him there. When the Persians threatened Hermias, Theophrastus took Aristotle to the relative safety of his native island, Lesbos. The men were only twelve years apart in age, and the relationship between them was as much that of friends and colleagues as that of master and disciple. Soon Philip II, King of Macedonia, invited Aristotle to come there as tutor of his son, the future Alexander the Great. He accepted, and Theophrastus went with him, remaining until after Philip's death seven years later.

Life's Work

In 335, Aristotle returned to Athens and founded a school at the Lyceum, a cult center with a colonnade and park, where the Peripatetic philosophy flourished under his leadership for thirteen years. Theophrastus lived there, discussing, lecturing, and writing. It was a creative period. Alexander was conquering the East as far as India, and philosophers who went with him, at first including Aristotle's nephew, Callisthenes, sent back scientific specimens never seen before in Greece. Not least among these were seeds and living plants that were tended in the garden of the Lyceum and studied by Theophrastus. His books on botany thus contain descriptions of the plants of India. He traveled through Greece collecting plants and making observations of natural phenomena.

Around the time of Alexander's death in 323, Aristotle retired to Chalcis, and a few months later he also died. His choice of Theophrastus as his successor at the Lyceum proved to be a wise one. At this time Theophrastus was about fifty years old, and statues give some idea of his appearance. He was a vigorous, healthy man, but lines around his eyes and the hollows of his cheeks suggest the heavy responsibilities of leadership and the hard work of empirical research. He remained at the Lyceum as *scholarch* (senior professor) until his death in about 287. His will provided for the maintenance of the Lyceum garden, where he asked to have his body buried. He designated Strato of Lampsachus, known as "the physicist," his heir as head of the school.

Theophrastus taught some two thousand students, among them Demetrius of Phalerum, who became ruler of Athens and presented Theophrastus with the land on which the Lyceum and its garden were located. Thus the school came to possess its own real estate, instead of leasing its grounds from the city. This step was important, because many Athenians regarded Aristotle and his followers as pro-Macedonian; Theophrastus had even been charged with sacrilege in 319. He had managed to stay in the city, and the reestablishment of Macedonian power in Athens two years later had made Demetrius governor. Demetrius was not popular, and when his rule ended in 307 a law was passed forbidding the operation of philosophical schools without special permission. Theophrastus then had to leave Athens, but the law was repealed within a year, and he was able to return.

Theophrastus produced his most important writings during his years at the Lyceum. He continued to revise them until the end of his life. The titles of 227 works by Theophrastus have been recorded,

but only a small fraction have survived. They fall into three major categories: scientific, philosophical, and literary.

It is in science that Theophrastus made his most significant contributions. Here he continued the work of Aristotle, achieving important insights of his own. He pointedly repeated Aristotle's statement that "nature does nothing in vain" and added his own comment, "anything which is contrary to nature is dangerous." In describing natural objects, Theophrastus established sets of opposing characteristics, such as cold and hot, wet and dry, male and female, wild and domestic. This method is typical of the Peripatetic school and is derived from Aristotle. In some respects, however, such as his emphasis on the autonomous purposes of living things and his avoidance of the ideas of final causation and the prime mover, he rejected Aristotle's authority and marked out an independent line of investigation.

His longest extant writings are the nine books of *Peri phytikōn historiōn* (translated in *Enquiry into Plants and Minor Works on Odours and Weather Signs*, 1916; often designated by the Latin title, *De*

historia plantarum) and the six books of *Peri phytikōn aitiōn* (partial translation in *De Causis Plantarum*, 1976-   ). Aristotle had written on animals; Theophrastus' works are the first careful treatment of botanical subjects. *Enquiry into Plants* describes the parts of plants and the characteristics of more than five hundred species, arranged in four groups: trees, shrubs, sub-shrubs, and herbs. *Peri phytikōn aitiōn* discusses generation, propagation, cultivation, and diseases of plants, as well as their tastes and odors. Theophrastus originated many terms in the botanical vocabulary and distinguished some of the main divisions of the vegetable kingdom. These works are also notable for their ecological viewpoint. Theophrastus always discusses a plant in the context of its relationships to the environment: sunshine, soil, climate, water, cultivation, and other plants and animals. His conclusions are sometimes wrong—for example, he believed in spontaneous generation—but even in such cases he showed caution and skepticism.

The works of Theophrastus dealing with other sciences are extant only in fragmentary form. Only excerpts remain of his *Peri physikōn* (on physics) and *Peri pyros* (*De Igne: A Post-Aristotelian View of the Nature of Fire*, 1971). Geology is represented by *Peri lithōn* (translated in *Theophrastus's History of Stones*, 1746; also as *On Stones*), a long fragment that investigates the properties of metals, minerals, gems, and substances whose animal origin he recognized, such as pearls, coral, and ivory. Fossils are handled in *Peri ichthyōn en xera katastasei* (on fishes in dry condition). Then there are fragments on meteorology such as *Peri semeiōn hydatōn kai pneumatōn kai cheimonōn kai eudiōn* and *Peri anemōn* (translated together in *On Winds and On Weather Signs*, 1894); the treatise on winds accurately describes many of the Mediterranean winds and goes beyond Aristotle in affirming that winds are moving air. Human physiology is discussed by Theophrastus in other treatises on sense perception, odors, weariness, fainting, paralysis, and perspiration. One called *Peri hypnou kai enypniōn* (on sleep and dreams) has disappeared.

The surviving philosophical work of Theophrastus is an important section of the *Ton meta ta physika* (Metaphysics, 1929), which criticizes Aristotle's doctrine that all things have a final cause, or *telos*. Aristotle said that the final cause of all living things is the service of the higher rational nature, that is, of human beings. Rejecting his teacher's excessive teleology, Theophrastus remarked,

We must try to find a certain limit . . . both to final causation and to the impulse to the better. For this is the beginning of the inquiry about the universe, that is, of the effort to determine the conditions on which real things depend and the relations in which they stand to one another.

So he maintained that, by nature, each living thing always aims at assimilating its intake to its own goal, and the goal of a plant is not to feed humans or to give them wood, but to produce fruit containing seed for the perpetuation of its species—in other words, to produce offspring similar to itself. Aristotle would not have denied species perpetuation as a goal, but would have made it a subsidiary cause in his hierarchical organization of nature. For Theophrastus, it is the whole point.

Other authors often quoted from his now-lost reference works, *Physikon doxai* (doctrines of natural philosophers), a history of philosophical opinions about major problems, and the *Nomoi* (laws), a compilation of the statutes and traditions of Greek cities. *Charactēres ethikōi* (c. 319; *The Moral Characters of Theophrastus*, 1702, best known as *Characters*) is Theophrastus' only surviving literary work and his most famous writing. In it he sketches thirty aberrant human personality types, giving as much care to their description as he did to plant species in his botanical works. These are not objective treatises, but satirical, dryly humorous jabs at disagreeable people such as the flatterer, the faultfinder, and the miser. This genre established by Theophrastus was much imitated, particularly in Great Britain and France in the seventeenth and eighteenth centuries.

Summary

Theophrastus was, as Diogenes Laërtius wrote, "a man of remarkable intelligence and industry." His fame has suffered because he has remained in the shadow of Aristotle. Where he differed from his teacher, it was for the most part because he was more scientific, more dependent upon observation, less ready to make universal statements of principle which could not be supported by perceptible facts. Aristotle had moved away from Plato in that direction; Theophrastus went even further.

In doing so, Theophrastus anticipated some of the methods of modern science. More than Plato's or Aristotle's, his philosophical stance was congenial with scientific discovery, emphasizing as it did efficient causes, not final causes. He has been recognized as the founder of the science of botany, having made many observations about plants for the first time and having established the basic terminology in that field. In modern times, he is also recognized as the first ecologist, for he viewed species not as isolated phenomena but in interaction with their physical environment and other species. He was distinguished as a perceptive investigator of lithology and mineralogy. Many of his ideas have been corrected in the light of later work; many others have so far withstood the test of time. It is hard to criticize him too severely, since he was among the first to set out on the journey of scientific inquiry. All told, he is impressive for his rationality and good sense and for his wish to depend on observations and to criticize the reports that he received. His practical attitude may be discerned in his rejoinder to those who advised him to plant and fell trees by the moon and signs of the zodiac: "One should not in fact be governed by the celestial conditions and revolution rather than by the trees and slips and seeds."

Among those who followed him were the researchers of the Museum and Library of Alexandria in Egypt in the second and first centuries B.C. The Latin natural historian Pliny the Elder quoted him extensively, and his influence can be traced in other ancient writers on sciences such as botany and medical pharmacology. Arabic commentators studied, preserved, and translated his writings during the medieval period. When interest in the sciences was reawakened in early modern Europe, the botanical works of Theophrastus were revived and printed. A Latin translation appeared in 1483, and the Greek text was published in Venice between 1495 and 1498. An English translation of the *Peri phytikōn historiōn* was published in 1916, and of the first two books of the *Peri phytikōn aitiōn* in 1976.

Bibliography

Diogenes Laërtius. "Theophrastus." In *Lives of Eminent Philosophers*, edited by R. D. Hicks, vol. 1. Cambridge, Mass.: Harvard University Press, and London: Heinemann, 1925. Since Diogenes wrote his set of biographies about five hundred years after the death of Theophrastus, his work is not entirely reliable, but it does preserve many ancient traditions about him.

Fortenbaugh, William W., Pamela M. Huby, and Anthony A. Long, eds. *Theophrastus of Eresus: On His Life and Work*. New Brunswick, N.J.: Transaction Books, 1985. Volume 2 in the Rutgers Studies in Classical Humanities series, this volume is the fruit of Project Theophrastus, an international undertaking to collect, edit, and translate the fragments of Theophrastus. It contains numerous scholarly essays on the major issues in literary, philosophical, scientific, and historical research on Theophrastus. Three of these deal with the Arabic tradition.

Fortenbaugh, William W., and Robert W. Sharples, eds. *Theophrastus as Natural Scientist and Other Papers*. New Brunswick, N.J.: Transaction Books, 1987. Volume 3 in the Rutgers Studies in Classical Humanities series and a companion to *Theophrastus of Eresus*, this is another collection of articles on Theophrastus' shorter scientific works, and others on botany and ecology, metaphysics, ethics, religion, and politics.

Theophrastus. *The Character Sketches*. Translated with an introduction and notes by Warren Anderson. Kent, Ohio: Kent State University Press, 1970. The best recent translation on the *Characters*, with useful explanatory notes and an introductory essay on the development of the "character" as a literary genre.

————. *De causis plantarum*. Translated with an introduction by Benedict Einarson and George K. K. Link. London: Heinemann, 1975; Cambridge, Mass.: Harvard University Press, 1990. This translation of the *Peri phytikōn aitōn* has the Greek and English texts on facing pages and includes a fine introduction on the author and the work, Theophrastus' predecessors, his calendar, and more.

————. *Enquiry into Plants and Minor Works on Odours and Weather Signs*. Translated with an introduction by Sir Arthur Hort. 2 vols. London: Heinemann, and Cambridge, Mass.: Harvard University Press, 1916. This has the Greek text and English translation on facing pages; it includes a short but useful introduction. The difficult Greek of Theophrastus is rendered accurately, but in an eccentric English style.

J. Donald Hughes

THESPIS

Born: Before 535 B.C.; probably Icarios (Icaria) or
    Athens, Greece
Died: After 501 B.C.; probably Athens, Greece
Area of Achievement: Theater and drama
Contribution: Though perhaps more legendary
    than historical, since none of his plays have sur-
    vived, Thespis is credited with introducing the
    first actor into the Dionysian festival of song and
    dance. Thus, he is the traditional originator of
    Greek drama.

Early Life

In the sixth century B.C. or earlier, the Greeks established an annual festival to honor the god Dionysus. This "God of many names," as the great
dramatist Sophocles would later call him, was also
known as Bacchus and Iacchos. He was associated
with wine and other bounty and fecundity. His festival, the City Dionysia, was celebrated in March
and featured a chorus of fifty singers and dancers
whose performance was a part of the religious
rites. Eventually, the cosmopolitan City Dionysia
was succeeded by a second, domestic festival
called the *Lenaea* ("wine press") and held in January.

A performance of song and dance is not a drama,
and it was Thespis, an Athenian of whom little is
known historically, who is said to have converted
the former into the latter. According to one tradition, Thespis's home was Icarios, or Icaria, in
northern Attica, near Marathon. Yet an extant ancient source refers to him simply as "Athenian." If
"Thespis" is the name of a real person, he may
have been born to a father who was an epic singer
or have been honored with a nickname later in life,
for the name comes from a word that means "divinely speaking" or from a similar word that means
"divinely singing."

The first evolution of the chorus produced a
leader who, presumably, would take occasional
solo turns during the performance. However, until
a performer existed apart from the chorus to ask its
members questions, to be questioned by them, and
to perhaps challenge assertions made in their lyrics, no absolute dramatic form was possible. Thespis is not known to history until he makes an appearance to introduce such a performer, the first
actor.

Scholars do not agree upon the date of Thespis's
achievement. The traditional date for the appear-

ance of tragedy as a part of the City Dionysia, or
Great Dionysia, is 534 B.C., but late in the twentieth
century some scholars argued for a later date, 501
B.C. Whatever the correct date, tragedies appear to
have been acted as a part of the festival every year
thereafter. No comedy is mentioned as having been
performed at the City Dionysia until 486 B.C. The
dramas at the Lenaea were solely comic in 442
B.C., and although tragedy was added in 432 B.C.,
comedy continued to dominate. Of course, none of
these developments would have been possible
without Thespis's innovation.

Life's Work

Thespis's career as actor-playwright is inextricably
connected with the awarding of dramatic prizes at
the Dionysian festivals. Some classical scholars
have speculated that the prize originally was a
goat, a not insignificant award in ancient Greece.
Eventually, the winning dramatist received a monetary prize that was donated by a prominent Athenian. Each donor was chosen by the city government before the competition began.

According to tradition, the first official presentation of drama at Athens occurred in 534 B.C. The
prize was won by Thespis. It is believed that at
least as late as the time of Aeschylus, the next great
Athenian playwright, who died in 456 B.C., the dramatist combined in his own person the roles of
writer, director, composer, choreographer, and lead
actor. Thus, when Thespis invented the first actor,
it may be assumed that he played the role himself.
His revolutionary contribution was the creation of
a character who established a dialogue with the
chorus. The character did not merely inquire of the
chorus what happened next. Thespis impersonated
someone interacting with the chorus, contributing
to the unfolding plot. He was both the first dramatist and the first actor. Thus, it is appropriate that
actors are still called "thespians" in his honor.

The little that is known of Thespis is filtered
through the accounts of others, accounts that may
themselves be apocryphal. For example, Solon, the
famed Athenian lawgiver, supposedly reproached
Thespis after witnessing his first play. He felt that
it was inappropriate for the playwright to tell the
assembly lies. His belief that these lies might actually be believed by the audience is a testament to
the seriousness and the persuasiveness of the artifice. Thespis responded that it was appropriate in a

play to persuade people that imaginary things are true. Solon, according to the story, was troubled by the idea that such deception might spread into the practice of politics. The problem with this amusing anecdote is that a commonly accepted date of death for Solon is c. 559 B.C., fully a quarter of a century before one of the proposed dates for Thespis's first play. If the story is true, Thespis must have exhibited in Athens before 560 B.C., as other sources suggest.

Despite the absence of historical evidence, certain features of Thespis's dramaturgy may be inferred. The identities of several of Thespis's immediate successors are known, foremost among them Phrynichus. By 499 B.C. the great Aeschylus was competing at the Festival of Dionysus. He was so popular and so critically esteemed that seven of his plays have survived. In the earliest of these, *Suppliants*, or *The Suppliant Maidens*, variously dated from 490 B.C.to as late as 463 B.C., the chorus numbers fifty members. In Aeschylus's later plays, he reduces the chorus to twelve members, and Sophocles, his younger contemporary, finally fixes the number at fifteen. Reasoning backward thus supports the inference that all of Thespis's plays employed the original fifty-member chorus, since documentary evidence attests that its reduced number was a much later innovation.

One scholarly school of thought rejects Thespis as a historical personage, viewing him instead as an effort to explain an interesting development in a mythic pattern very ancient and widespread throughout the Near East. Dionysus, through his association with spring and nature's bounty, is linked to the primitive god who dies over and over only to be reborn over and over, saving humankind by means of his resurrection. This powerful myth, incorporating the deepest mysteries of life and death, has produced countless stories in cultures ranging from Egypt to India. It also accounts, according to this theory, for the emergence of drama as a central element in the worship of Dionysus.

The Greek dramatists came to play a role in their culture very similar to the role played by the prophets in Hebrew culture. The God of the Hebrews was all-wise, all-good, the very source of order in the universe. The gods of the Greeks were willful, inconstant in their sympathies, frequently the source of disorder and strife. For the Hebrews, God was the ultimate moral arbiter. Such was not the case with the Greeks, but as a highly rational and civilized people, they realized their religious

practice must address the thorny moral issues of life. To the playwrights fell the lot of supplying this moral dimension to the worship of Dionysus. It can thus be argued that the innovation of Thespis—or whoever or whatever that legendary figure represents—made possible in the next century the works of the great Aeschylus and Sophocles, dramatizing the deepest and subtlest conflicts of humankind.

For virtually every theory about Thespis and his work, there exists a countertheory. Some scholars argue that his plays grew out of the dithyramb, a wildly emotional choric tribute to Dionysus. Others insist that his first performances were given in his native region at country festivals and later brought to Athens by him and his players and that these were rather crude representations of the doings of satyrs, lustful, mischievous goat-men. Support for this theory comes from the fact that the etymology of *tragedy* can be traced to a word meaning "song of goats." Some sources indicate that Thespis gave only the most general direction to his revelling masquers and that a later poet, Pratinas, was the first person to write words for the players to learn by heart. However, this assertion cannot be correct if, as Aristotle reportedly wrote, "Thespis invented a prologue and a (set) speech" for the chorus. Thespis is not discussed in the extant part of the *Poetics* (c. 350 B.C.), Aristotle's treatise on the drama, but other ancient authors quote from the lost portion.

The Roman poet Horace says that Thespis and his actors toured the Attic countryside in a wagon. By some accounts, Thespis, as the only one of his players to impersonate individual characters, would play one part after another in the same story. Since this activity necessitated frequent changes of mask and disguise, Thespis had a *skene*, a temporary booth, set up for the purpose. Thus, Thespis would also have invented the first traveling stock company and the first dressing room.

Still, whether the most minimal or the most extravagant view of Thespis's accomplishments prevails, his essential contribution to the drama was enormous. Without his brilliant conception of a character separate from the original chorus, the great comedies and tragedies produced during the next one hundred years would never have come to be.

Summary

Thespis is a fascinating figure, in large part because of his historical elusiveness. Scarcely two classical scholars agree in every respect about his life and work. An example noted above is the belief of some experts that Thespis was producing what were essentially plays as early as 560 B.C. Others are equally convinced that a true tragedy was not acted in Athens until thirty or even fifty years later. Were Thespis's first plays crude, bucolic representations of the antics of the half-man, half-goat satyrs? Or were they another solemn evolutionary step in the worship of the archetypal god who dies and is reborn yearly? Perhaps these jousting theories will never be reconciled. It is clear, however, that Thespis, no matter what the precise details of his accomplishment, can be favorably judged—and honored—by the fruits of his labor.

Before Thespis, there was no drama. By circa 534 B.C., a competition among tragic dramatists had become a part of the City Dionysia (with Thespis himself identified as the earliest victor). The competitions began with tragedy and were expanded to include comedy. The festival's third, fourth, and fifth days were given over to tragic and comic contests. During the period of the Peloponnesian War, 431-404 B.C., tragedies were performed in the mornings, comedies in the afternoons.

At the Lenaea, the number of comedies was reduced to three for the duration of the Peloponnesian War. Before and after the war, however, five comic poets and two tragic poets regularly competed. This explosion of dramatic activity in the sixth and fifth centuries B.C. was lit by the spark of Thespis's innovation.

Bibliography

Else, Gerald F. *The Origin and Early Form of Greek Tragedy.* Cambridge, Mass.: Harvard University Press, 1965. Volume 20 of the Martin Classical Lectures delivered at Oberlin College. References to Thespis are sprinkled throughout the 102 pages of text, and chapter 3, pages 51-77, is entitled "Thespis: The Creation of *Tragôidia*." Especially interesting is a discussion on pages 51-52 of the origin and meaning of the dramatist's name.

Flickinger, Roy C. *The Greek Theater and Its Drama.* 4th ed. Chicago: University of Chicago Press, 1961. Flickinger speculates on the manner of performances by Thespis and his company. He also suggests that the earliest productions were like the satyr plays that would conclude later tetralogies.

Gaster, Theodor H. *Thespis: Ritual, Myth, and Drama in the Ancient Near East.* Rev. ed. New York: Doubleday, 1961. A Harper Torchbook from the Academy Library. Here, Thespis is used as a metaphor for the beginnings of European literature. Gaster argues that drama everywhere derived from a religious ritual designed to ensure the rebirth of the dead world. Traces the myth through Canaanite, Hittite, and Egyptian sources, concluding with biblical and classical poetry.

Goodell, Thomas Dwight. *Athenian Tragedy: A Study in Popular Art.* New Haven, Conn.: Yale University Press, 1920. Valuable because on pages 57-58 Goodell describes specific aspects of the Thespian performance not generally found elsewhere.

Little, Alan M. G. *Myth and Society in Attic Drama.* New York: Columbia University Press, 1942. Stresses the social and political environment from which the first drama emerged.

Thomson, George. *Aeschylus and Athens: A Study in the Social Origins of Drama.* New York: Grosset & Dunlap, 1968; London: Lawrence and Wishart, 1973. Thomson infers elements of Thespian dramaturgy by reasoning backward from what is known of the plays of Aeschylus.

Patrick Adcock

SAINT THOMAS

Born: c. early first century A.D.; Galilee, Palestine
Died: Second half of the first century; possibly
  Mylapore, India
Area of Achievement: Religion
Contribution: As one of the handpicked followers
  of Jesus, Thomas played a role in the epoch-
  making spread of the Christian message in the
  first century. He continues to be venerated in
  Christendom, especially among Christians of India, who plausibly claim that Thomas first
  brought the word of Jesus Christ to their ancestors and others in the Orient.

Early Life

Little specific information is available, but the general conditions of Thomas' early life are reasonably secure. The signs point to his birth around or
slightly after the traditional date of Jesus' nativity
(c. 4 B.C.). Also like Jesus, he hailed from the area
of Galilee, a district some sixty miles north of
Jerusalem. His Jewish heritage furnished him with
knowledge of the history of his race, respect for the
religious customs of his forefathers, and familiarity
with the Hebrew scriptures, perhaps in Aramaic or
even Greek form.

Yet a Galilean Jew such as Thomas (also called
Didymus in the New Testament, a Greek word
meaning "twin") likely differed somewhat from his
countrymen in Jerusalem to the south. There are
several reasons for this. First, Galilee had long
been extensively affected by foreign cultural influences and had a large non-Jewish population. Foreign merchants and settlers were encountered everywhere. Second, the Galileans' dialect was
different from that spoken by Jews in Jerusalem
(Matt. 26:73). Third, Jews of Galilee were regarded with some disdain by their southern neighbors
for their less strict observance of the oral religious
tradition which formed the basis for faith and practice among the Pharisees, the most respected and
influential Palestinian Jewish sect of the day. Finally, Galileans would most likely have been bilingual, both Aramaic and Greek being widely used
throughout the district. A Jewish male would probably have had some command of Hebrew, the language of most of the Old Testament, as well.

Thomas' early years, then, would have been
marked not only by thorough grounding in Judaism
but also by considerable exposure to non-Jewish

language and culture. The radical separation of Jew
from Gentile practiced by some in Jerusalem
would have been most difficult in Galilee. This cultural background helps account for, though it does
not totally explain, his apparent willingness to become a disciple of Jesus of Nazareth (a village in
south-central Galilee), whose views evidently met
such forceful opposition from certain more strictly
traditional Jewish authorities based in Jerusalem.

Thomas' early years would also have instilled in
him, along with the vast majority of all Jews of his
locale and time, a profound distaste for the presence of Roman military and political power, for
Galilee was part of the Roman Empire throughout
the first century. This loathing, which eventually
erupted in the First Jewish Revolt (A.D. 66-70), was
coupled in many persons with a distinct religiopo-
litical expectation, even longing. That is, the Jews
hoped that the promises of the Hebrew Scriptures
(understood quite literally as God's very words to
his chosen people) were soon to come true in a new
and dramatic fashion. God would send his designated deliverer, the Messiah (in Greek, *Christos*),
to liberate the land from foreign domination and
mightily bless his ancient covenant people, the
Jews. The kingdom of God would one day soon arrive in tangible form.

Thomas was most likely an heir of such a theological and political outlook. His life's work as a
disciple of Jesus was a response to what he understood as God's fulfillment, as promised in the
Scriptures, of his and his nation's heartfelt longing.

Life's Work

The scanty available evidence points to Thomas'
achievement in two settings: Galilee and surrounding districts during and after the life of Jesus of
Nazareth, and areas to the east of the Roman Empire in the second half of the first century.

In his native Galilee, Thomas came into contact
with Jesus, whose influence in the mid- to late 20s
was felt from Roman Syria southward through Galilee and on to Jerusalem. Galilean Jews would
have been aware of John the Baptist's prophetic
proclamation; Jesus rode on John's coattails into
the public arena, attracting followers such as Thomas.

Thomas was, according to available evidence,
one of only a dozen persons selected by Jesus from

a much larger group of followers to receive special instruction and responsibilities (Matt. 10:3, Mark 3:18, Luke 6:15). For a period of some three years, Thomas observed and participated in a religious movement (not without political implications, however) led by Jesus and bent on intensifying, if not ushering in, the earthly reign of Israel's covenant God, Yahweh ("the kingdom of God"). Thomas was among the twelve sent out to call his countrymen to repentance (Mark 6:7-13), a recognition of personal and corporate need for moral reform in the light of impending divine judgment. In this way he and his colleagues saw their mission, like that of John the Baptist and Jesus himself, as preparation for a decisive act of God in the near future (Luke 19:11, Acts 1:6).

Thomas was as disillusioned as his comrades were when Jesus' activity culminated in his arrest and execution by local and imperial authorities in Jerusalem. Like the other disciples, he fled the scene (Matt. 26:56), presumably to avoid being incriminated himself because of association with an alleged criminal. Were this the last hint of Thomas' activity, his name would long ago have been forgotten. Ancient sources, however, afford three specific glimpses into his life and thought which have for centuries enshrined him in the memories of those whose own personal religious experience resonates with that of Thomas. These traditions, all in the Gospel of John, merit specific mention as a result of their continuing religious relevance as well as their probable historical significance.

At the crucial point in Jesus' life, when his sense of destiny beckoned him from Perea (where he was fairly safe from arrest) to Jerusalem (where he was not), it was Thomas who rallied his comrades with the declaration, "Let us go with him so that we may die with him." Scholars debate whether this evinces a fatalistic or a courageous spirit. In either case, Thomas helped to galvanize the other disciples into accompanying Jesus, against their own better judgment (Mark 10:32), to the eventual site of his death. He models a stoic, or perhaps selfless, response to perceived duty.

Some days later, according to John's gospel, Jesus sought to console his disciples on the eve of his imminent betrayal. Again Thomas focused the collective spirit of his fellows. This time, however, his words betrayed not courage but curiosity, if not incredulity. Jesus spoke enigmatically of departing in order to make ready a place for his followers: Thomas observed: "We do not know where you are going; how can we know how to get there?" Thomas demonstrates here a searching if not critical temperament which articulates the heartfelt inquisitiveness, or even frustration, of many religious persons in the first century, and others since that time.

Thomas is most remembered, however, for the independent yet ultimately pliant spirit he exhibited during the days when, according to sources preserved in the New Testament, Jesus appeared to his disciples alive following his death by crucifixion (John 20:24-31). Thomas refused to give credence to hearsay evidence, saying that unless and until he had personal, tangible proof that Jesus had indeed somehow risen from the dead—which, one surmises, Thomas doubted he would receive—he refused to set any store by his friends' astonishing claims.

One week later, Thomas' skepticism was forced to contend with the corporeal presence of the person whose existence he had so roundly questioned: Jesus. Thomas was invited to satisfy his doubt and then draw the appropriate conclusions. In John's account, Thomas becomes the first person to affirm, in the wake of Jesus' resurrection, unqualified recognition of Jesus as master and deity.

Apart from his activity in Galilee, Thomas is also connected in ancient sources with missionary activity east of the Roman Empire. Evaluation of these sources is still in its early stages, and both literary and archaeological evidence awaits further sifting. *The Acts of Thomas*, dating from about the third century, speaks of Thomas' presence in India. (The second century *Gospel of Thomas* gives little if any information on Thomas and was in any case not written by him.) Much of the material in this apocryphal book may be safely regarded as fiction. There seems, however, to be a historical core which supports the view, held by several communities of Indian Christians to this day, that the Gospel was first brought to their ancestors by Thomas in the first century. According to traditions preserved in these communities, Thomas was fatally stabbed on July 3, 72, for refusing to worship Kali, a Hindu goddess.

Other ancient sources speak somewhat vaguely of Thomas' labors in Parthia, an ancient nation southeast of the Caspian Sea. Today scholars theorize that these reports reflect not an actual visit by Thomas to Parthia but written communication between Thomas and Christians in the Parthian city of Edessa. In any case, the Parthian tradition corroborates the assertion that in the early years of

Christianity's expansion Thomas was instrumental in bearing the Gospel message to lands far to the east of his native Galilee.

Summary

Saint Thomas was hardly a pivotal figure in the history of early Christianity. It cannot even be said that he occupies a prominent place in the Gospel records where he receives direct mention. During Jesus' life he was overshadowed by Peter, James, and John, while his activity in the first decades of early church expansion is now nearly hidden.

Yet there is good evidence that he played a more integral role in the spread of Christianity to India—where thousands have revered his memory for centuries—and perhaps even farther eastward than Western Christendom and historians generally acknowledge. Thomas in his milieu may perhaps be compared to someone such as Martin Bucer in the Reformation: Both men played significant roles, but in historical perspective both are eclipsed by more dominant personages and events in which they had only tangential involvement. Still, the careful student of ancient Christianity will be as loath to overlook Thomas' place as will the student of the Reformation to overlook Bucer.

Wherever the New Testament has been read through the centuries, which is virtually everywhere in the West, Thomas has served as an example, both good and bad, for Christian faith. Commentators such as John Calvin, stressing his incredulity, have criticized his obduracy and contributed to a view of him epitomized in the expression "doubting Thomas." Augustine sees in Jesus' words to Thomas ("Blessed are they who have not seen, and yet believe," John 20:28) a commendation of those who in coming centuries and God's predestinating plan place personal trust in God through Jesus. Origen refutes the claims of Augustine's adversary Aulus Cornelius Celsus by adducing Thomas' testimony as proof of the corporeality of Jesus' resurrected body.

In these and many other cases, Thomas takes his place as a continuing witness to both the objective reality and the subjective impact of the person of Jesus in the experience of one who examines his claims. Thomas himself would perhaps affirm an assessment of his contribution to religion, and even history, which would stress not his own achievement but the merit of the one whose reality convinced his questioning mind and, as a result, his heart.

Bibliography

Barclay, William. *The Master's Men*. London: SCM Press, and New York: Abingdon Press, 1959. Popular level but learned discussion. A renowned New Testament scholar devotes a chapter to an insightful, if slightly overimaginative, character sketch which attempts to assess all significant historical references to Thomas. Also discusses Thomas traditions in works by ancient historians as well as in *The Acts of Thomas*.

Barker, Kenneth, ed. *The New International Version Study Bible*. Grand Rapids, Mich.: Zondervan Bible Publishers, 1985. Makes available, in modern English translation, all extant first century references to Thomas (indexed in a concordance). Includes explanatory comments on Thomas' remarks in the Gospel of John and other Gospel references to him. Maps aid in picturing the geographical dimensions of the world in which Thomas lived.

Brown, Raymond. *The Gospel According to John*. 2 vols. New York: Doubleday, 1966-1970; London: Chapman, 1971. The most significant primary source for information on Thomas is the New Testament, especially John's gospel. This critically acclaimed entry in the Anchor Bible series is among the most competent and thorough investigations of John, and therefore of the Thomas traditions as they occur in the New Testament.

Eusebius of Caesarea. *Ecclesiastical History*. 2 vols. Translated by K. Lake and J. E. L. Oulton. Cambridge, Mass.: Harvard University Press, and London: Heinemann, 1926-1932. The classic ancient account of the rise and development of the early Church. Contains at least six references to Thomas (see index in volume 2) and furnishes an overall context for traditional understanding of his significance and the circles in which he moved.

Farquhar, J. N. "The Apostle Thomas in North India." *Bulletin of the John Rylands Library* 10 (1926): 80-111. A dated but still-relevant examination of extra-New Testament references to Thomas. Offers a creative reconstruction, based on documentary evidence, of how Thomas traveled to India. Seeks to reconcile the conflicting testimony of *The Acts of Thomas*, on the one hand, with traditions which speak of Thomas' presence in Parthia, on the other. This article and another by Farquhar are reprinted in J. Vellian, ed., *The*

Apostle Thomas According to the "Acts of Thomas": Kottayam, India, 1971.

Finegan, J. *Hidden Records of the Life of Jesus.* Philadelphia: Pilgrim Press, 1969. Contains a valuable discussion of the Gospel of Thomas with extensive bibliography. Cites portions in the original languages, then gives translation and analysis. Concludes with the verdict that alleged sayings of Jesus in the Gospel of Thomas generally have little chance of being authentic. Implies that Jesus' disciple Thomas is not the author.

Freyne, Seán. *Galilee from Alexander the Great to Hadrian, 323 B.C.E. to 135 C.E.* Wilmington, Del.: Michael Glazier, 1980. The standard history of Galilee in the days of Thomas. Useful for general background on living conditions and social environment. Discusses the languages spoken in Galilee, the religious views of Galileans, and the political currents of the time. Useful maps and full bibliography.

Hennecke, E. *New Testament Apocrypha.* Edited by W. Schneemelcher. Translated and edited by R. M. Wilson. 2 vols. Philadelphia: Westminster Press, and London: SCM Press, 1963-1965. Volume 1 contains extensive discussion of scholarly views on the Gospel of Thomas. Volume 2 contains the standard English translation of *The Acts of Thomas*, along with full discussion of its linguistic and literary distinctives. The discussion unfortunately fails to take cognizance of work by nonbiblical scholars (see studies listed elsewhere in this bibliography) which argues in favor of the probable historical core of portions of the narrative.

Medlycott, A. E. *India and the Apostle Thomas: An Inquiry, with a Critical Analysis of the "Acta Thomae."* London: David Nutt, 1905. The seminal study in English of the ancient extra-New Testament Thomas traditions in the light of modern historical and archaeological findings. Medlycott is among the first to furnish, and at times deny, solid historical footing for certain ancient ecclesiastical traditions concerning Thomas. His observations and arguments are foundational to subsequent discussion.

Mundadan, A. M. *History of Christianity in India.* Vol. 1, *From the Beginning up to the Middle of the Sixteenth Century (up to 1542).* Bangalore, India: Theological Publications in India, 1982. Chapter 1 of this exhaustive critical history focuses primarily on the traditions which link Thomas to India. Mundadan's evaluation of both primary and secondary evidence in some respects supersedes all previous discussion in its breadth and depth of treatment. He concludes that the Indian community's ancient traditions of Saint Thomas are rooted in the historical fact of Thomas' first-century labors there. Exhaustive bibliography.

Perumalil, A. C. *The Apostles in India: Fact or Fiction?* Patna, India: Catholic Book Crusade, 1953. Elaborates on ancient traditions concerning both Thomas and Bartholomew. Not always sufficiently analytical and critical in dealing with historical evidence, but this is more than compensated for by the complete listing of all references to India in both Greek and Latin sources from the second to the thirteenth century.

Placid, Fr. "The South Indian Apostolate of St. Thomas." *Orientalia christiana periodica* 18 (1952): 229-245. This careful and informed investigation examines the claims of modern Christians in Malabar, South India, that their ancestors were converted to Christianity through the labors of Thomas in the first century. Placid argues that ancient traditions in Syrian and Arabic literature substantiate this claim, while no compelling evidence requires its denial.

Robert W. Yarbrough

THUCYDIDES

Born: c. 459 B.C.; probably Athens, Greece
Died: c. 402 B.C.; place unknown
Area of Achievement: Historiography
Contribution: For the methods he employed in his account of the Peloponnesian War, Thucydides is considered one of the founders of the discipline of history.

Early Life

Thucydides was born around 459 into a wealthy and conservative Athenian family. He grew up in Periclean Athens, an exciting place for a young, intelligent aristocrat. He followed the traditional course of education founded on the study of Homer, but leavened it with the rational skepticism of the Sophists. Thucydides could listen to the teachings of Protagoras, Socrates, Herodotus, and other major intellectual and creative figures who lived in or visited Athens.

Little is known about Thucydides' personal life. His family was politically active and opposed the democratic forces led by Pericles, but Thucydides evidently did not involve himself in political intrigues. It is known that he inherited gold mines in Thrace and had an estate there. He married a Thracian woman and had a daughter. He seems to have been a slightly detached but observant young man, studying the social and political turbulence around him. He did not break openly with his family, nor did he enter actively into Athenian politics. Though he criticized the people when they acted as a "mob," he did not approve of oligarchy. He respected the wisdom and moderation of Athenian leaders such as Nicias but was stirred by the boldness of Pericles, Themistocles, and Alcibiades.

When the Peloponnesian War began, Thucydides perhaps first intended to record for posterity the events and the deeds of men in a dramatic conflict. He soon saw that the war provided instruction in something basic about human nature and the fortunes of nations. In 431, he started collecting material for his *Historia tou Peloponnesiacou polemou* (431-404 B.C.; *History of the Peloponnesian War*, 1550), at the outbreak of the twenty-seven-year conflict.

Life's Work

The victory of the Greeks over the Persians at Plataea in 479 B.C. ushered in the golden age of Athenian history. The city's economy flourished, its government became more democratic than in the past, its art, literature, and freedom of expression attracted creative people from throughout the Greek world, and its navy established it as a power over the Aegean Islands and many coastal cities. Though Athens and Sparta had cooperated against the Persians, they soon went separate ways. The slow-moving, conservative Spartans watched Athens build an empire and, under Pericle's leadership, reach for more power and wealth. "What made war inevitable," Thucydides wrote, "was the growth of Athenian power and the fear which this caused in Sparta."

War began in 431. It opened with ten years of fighting, followed by some years of shaky truce, before fighting continued for another ten years. After Sparta established its power on land, the Athenians retreated into the city, which was joined by the Long Walls to the port of Peiraeus. The Athenians supplied themselves by sea and harassed the Spartans and their allies. The war was brutal. Besieged cities turned to cannibalism, and conquerors

sometimes put defeated males to death and enslaved their women and children.

Despite Thucydides' renowned objectivity—he was acclaimed at one time as "the father of scientific history"—later military historians have seldom matched the emotional intensity and striking visual images conveyed by his calm prose. He described trapped Plataeans counting bricks in the besieging wall to determine how high to build scaling ladders. They began a desperate dash for freedom through a dark, rainy night, each man wearing only one shoe for better traction in the mud. He gave a masterful clinical description of the plague that hit Athens and chronicled the degeneration of morale and morals as disease swept the hot, overcrowded city. People gave themselves up to lawlessness and dissipation: "No fear of god or law of man had a restraining influence. As for the gods, it seemed to be the same thing whether one worshipped them or not, when one saw the good and the bad dying indiscriminately." With the gods silent in the face of human tragedy and no one expecting to live long enough to be punished for violating society's laws, people took what pleasure they could.

Revolution also spread through the city-states, with war between democratic and oligarchic forces. Brutality within cities equaled that between them. Thucydides wrote that in times of peace and prosperity most people acted decently: "But war is a stern teacher; in depriving them of the power of easily satisfying their daily wants, it brings most people's minds down to the level of their actual circumstances." People of the turbulent twentieth century found many occasions to quote his words about fanaticism:

> What used to be described as a thoughtless act of aggression was now regarded as the courage one would expect to find in a party member; to think of the future and wait was merely another way of saying one was a coward; any idea of moderation was just an attempt to disguise one's unmanly character; ability to understand a question from all sides meant that one was totally unfitted for action.

With both sides battered by war and revolution, leaders of Athens and Sparta negotiated a shaky truce in 421, but resolved none of the larger issues. The first war had revealed something basic about human affairs, Thucydides believed. The Athenians had told the Spartans before the war opened that always the weak had been subject to the strong. When the Spartans raised questions of right and wrong, the Athenians answered: "Considerations of this kind have never yet turned people aside from the opportunities of aggrandizement offered by superior strength."

War started again. The Athenians mounted a disastrous expedition to Sicily. Soon, Thucydides wrote, the Athenians, intending to enslave, were totally defeated and themselves enslaved. Athens was in turmoil, and oligarchic leaders overthrew its democracy. Vicious bloodletting occurred as the two sides fought for control. Disaster followed disaster, and the Athenians surrendered in 404. The Spartans forced them to renounce their empire, destroy their navy, and tear down the Long Walls.

Thucydides was himself caught up in the war. In 424, Athens elected him a general but then exiled him for twenty years when he failed to prevent the brilliant Spartan general Brasidas from taking the strategically important city of Amphipolis. Exile meant withdrawing a short distance from Amphipolis to his Thracian estate, where he had time to think, write, and talk to Brasidas and other opponents and to central figures in Athenian politics, such as Alcibiades.

Unlike his older contemporary, the great historian Herodotus, Thucydides did not leave much room for the divine in human affairs; he believed that human activities could be understood in human terms. Like Herodotus, Thucydides displayed breadth of sympathy for all sides in the conflict. He weighed his oral evidence carefully, seeking accuracy and precision. He stated his purpose eloquently:

> It will be enough for me . . . if these words of mine are judged useful by those who want to understand clearly the events which happened in the past and which (human nature being what it is) will, at some time or other and in much the same ways, be repeated in the future. My work is not a piece of writing designed to meet the taste of an immediate public, but was done to last forever.

Thucydides found meaning in history, evidence of a pattern or cycle. Unless human nature changed, states would continue to overreach themselves, create defensive resistance, and then decline and fall. Even the second part of the Peloponnesian War repeated the first, with new actors making much the same mistakes for the same reasons. People could, however, use their intelligence and reason. They might not escape the cycle, but some few could at least come to understand what was happening and perhaps moderate the cycle. Thucydides did not believe that cycles were endlessly repeating series of events that allowed historians to predict the future, but he thought that people could use history to interpret their times.

It is unclear when Thucydides wrote his history. Most scholars believe that changes in style and conflicting statements about events suggest that it was written in stages; Thucydides died before putting it in final form. He probably died around 402.

Summary

Thucydides and Herodotus, the first historians, retain their rank among the very greatest. Few historians who followed would equal Herodotus' breadth of sympathy for the diversity of human culture, and seldom would they match Thucydides' clarity and precision and his emotional and intellectual power.

Thucydides found a scholarly audience more easily than did Herodotus. Thucydides' objective tone, rational skepticism, and focus on the military and on politics fit the modern temper. His writing on war and revolution seemed directed at the twentieth century. His message seemed clear, especially after World War II, when in the Cold War atmosphere it was easy for Americans to identify themselves with the free Athenians, confronting dour, warlike Spartans in the form of the totalitarian Soviets. Thucydides, viewed by some scholars as the father of realpolitik, seemed to have a clear warning: Democracies must be strong and alert in a dangerous world.

When the Vietnam War changed historians' understanding of the Cold War, Thucydides did not drop from favor among scholars, but his message came to seem different. To some scholars, he seemed to be the first revisionist, revealing Athens for what it was: an arrogant and aggressive state aimed at dominating and exploiting the weak and inciting fear of the Spartans to help keep Athenian allies in line.

Changing times will bring still another Thucydides. Like every genius, he speaks to some members of each generation, who find in him insights into human affairs that clarify their understanding of their own time.

Bibliography

Adcock, Sir Frank Ezra. *Thucydides and His History.* Cambridge: Cambridge University Press, 1963; Hamden, Conn.: Archon, 1973. A short, clear study of Thucydides' mind and personality by an admiring British historian who regards Thucydides as one of the first great adventurers in thought.

Connor, W. Robert. *Thucydides.* Princeton, N.J.: Princeton University Press, 1984. A meditation on Thucydides and an analysis of the text, especially to determine the source of Thucydides' emotional impact on his readers.

Edmunds, Lowell. *Chance and Intelligence in Thucydides.* Cambridge, Mass.: Harvard University Press, 1975. A study of Thucydides' theory of reason and chance in human affairs and of the interplay of pessimism and optimism in his work.

Hornblower, Simon. *A Commentary on Thucydides I, Books I-III.* Oxford: Clarendon, and New York: Oxford University Press, 1991. In addition to a clear and precise translation of the first three books of Thucydides's work on the Peloponnesian war, Hornblower provides an opinionated discussion of the text, mixing his own views with those of other scholars. He includes an accurate presentation of how Thucydides has been viewed in the 1970s and 1980s as well.

———. *Thucydides.* London: Duckworth, and Baltimore: Johns Hopkins University Press, 1987. Places Thucydides in the intellectual atmosphere of Periclean Athens and carefully distinguishes the various influences on his thought.

Kallet-Marx, Lisa. *Money, Expense, and Naval Power in Thucydides' History 1-5.24.* Berkeley: University of California Press, 1993. Contesting the popular notion that Thucydides paid insufficient attention to financial matters, Kallet-Marx accurately links the importance of money and naval power in his work. She examines important epigraphical material in his texts to make her point, rather than looking for financial data in terns of twentieth-century economic concepts. Provides an original and rewarding perspective.

Pouncey, Peter. *The Necessities of War: A Study of Thucydides' Pessimism.* New York: Columbia University Press, 1980. A study of Thucydides' theory of human nature and its influence on history; Pouncey finds an "essential pessimism" that holds that human nature carries within it drives that destroy human achievements.

Proctor, Dennis. *The Experience of Thucydides.* Warminster, England: Aris and Phillips, 1980. A careful analysis of the text of Thucydides to try to determine the phases of its composition.

Rawlings, Hunter R., III. *The Structure of Thucydides' History.* Princeton, N.J.: Princeton University Press, 1981. Provides insights into Thucydides based on an analysis of the structure of his work.

Thucydides. *The Peloponnesian War.* London and Baltimore: Penguin, 1954. This translation by Rex Warner, with an introduction by M. I. Finley, is highly regarded and easily accessible.

———. *The Peloponnesian War, Book II.* Jeffrey S. Rusten, ed. Cambridge and New York: Cambridge University Press, 1989. Rusten's introduction details Thucydides's family, narrative themes, speeches, language, and style. He clarifies Thucydides's notoriously tortuous sentences by giving careful attention to structural pattern and consistent usages. Rusten devotes three special sections to the funeral speech, the plague, and the so-called obituary of Pericles.

William E. Pemberton

THUTMOSE III

<blockquote>
Born: Late sixteenth century B.C.; near Thebes, Egypt?

Died: 1450 B.C.; near Thebes, Egypt?

Area of Achievement: Government

Contribution: During a reign of nearly fifty-four years, Thutmose III consolidated Egypt's position as primary power in the ancient Near East and North Africa. He laid the groundwork for some two hundred years of relative peace and prosperity in the region.
</blockquote>

Early Life

Thutmose III, son of Thutmose II and a minor wife named Isis, became the fourth king of Egypt's Eighteenth Dynasty while still a child. It is very likely that Thutmose III was not the obvious heir to Egypt's throne. According to an inscription at Karnak carved late in his reign, the young Thutmose spent his early life as an acolyte in the Temple of Amon. Thutmose III asserted that the god Amon personally chose him as successor to his father: During a ritual procession of Amon's statue through the temple, the god sought out Thutmose; an oracle revealed that he was the god's choice to be the next king. Thutmose thus became his father's legitimate heir.

The historical value of this account has been doubted. It was recorded late in Thutmose III's reign. Furthermore, it closely parallels an earlier text describing the accession of Thutmose I. Whatever the historical value of this account for determining the legitimacy of Thutmose III's claim to succeed his father, he did ascend to the Egyptian throne upon the death of Thutmose II. Contemporary inscriptions make clear, however, that during the first twenty-one years of the reign, real power was held by Hatshepsut, the chief queen or "Great King's Wife" of his father.

The relationship between Thutmose III and Hatshepsut in these early years has been the subject of scholarly controversy. By year two of Thutmose III's reign, Hatshepsut had assumed all the regalia of a reigning king. Yet it is not at all certain that she thrust Thutmose III into the background in order to usurp his royal prerogative, as early twentieth century commentators have claimed. Hatshepsut probably crowned herself coregent to obtain the authority to administrate the country while Thutmose III was still a minor. Hatshepsut's year dates are often recorded alongside dates of Thutmose III. There is also evidence that his approval was necessary for significant decisions such as installing a vizier, establishing offering endowments for gods, and authorizing expeditions to Sinai.

In any case, there is no question that Thutmose's early years were spent in preparation for his eventual assumption of sole authority. His education included study of hieroglyphic writing. Contemporaries comment on his ability to read and write like Seshat, the goddess of writing. His military training must also have occurred during this time.

When Hatshepsut died in the twenty-second year of Thutmose III's reign, he assumed sole control of the country. Whether it was at this point that an attempt was made by Thutmose III to obliterate the memory of Hatshepsut is open to doubt. It is clear that Thutmose III emphasized his descent from Thutmose II as part of the basis for his legitimate right to rule Egypt.

The mummy of Thutmose III reveals a man of medium build, almost five feet in height. (For his time, he was relatively tall.) He appears to have enjoyed good health throughout most of his life,

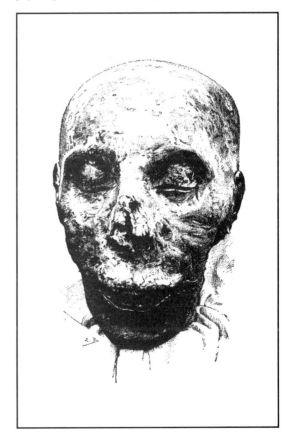

avoiding the serious dental problems common to other Egyptian kings.

Life's Work

The ancient Egyptians expected their pharaoh's career to follow a preconceived pattern which was ordained by their gods. This pattern was always followed in the historical texts which the Egyptians wrote describing the accomplishments of their kings. There is good reason to believe that Thutmose III became the prototype for a successful king. His achievements were emulated by his successors throughout most of the New Kingdom (c. 1570-1070 B.C.). The pattern included conquests abroad, feats of athletic prowess, and building projects at home.

Between the twenty-third and thirty-ninth years of his reign, Thutmose III undertook fourteen military campaigns. These campaigns are documented in a long historical text carved on the walls at the Temple of Karnak, called the Annals. Various stelae (inscriptions on upright slabs of stone) found in other Egyptian temples also provide information on his career. The most significant campaigns occurred in year twenty-three and in year thirty-three of his reign.

The campaign of year twenty-three was fought against a confederation of Syro-Palestinian states led by Kadesh, a Syrian city-state on the Orontes River. The forces allied with Kadesh had gathered at a city called Megiddo on the Plain of Esdraelan in modern Israel. The Egyptian description of the battle that took place in Megiddo follows a pattern known from other inscriptions yet contains many details that attest its basic historical value.

Thutmose III set out for Syria-Palestine with a large army. Upon reaching the town of Yehem, near Megiddo, Thutmose III consulted with his general staff on tactics and strategy. The general staff urged caution on the king, suggesting that the main road to Megiddo was too narrow and dangerous for the Egyptian army to pass safely upon it. They argued for an alternative route to Megiddo that would be longer, yet safer. Thutmose III rejected his staff's advice, judging that the bolder course was more likely to succeed. The staff acceded to the king's superior wisdom; the Egyptian army proceeded along the narrow direct path, surprised the enemy, and encircled Megiddo. The enemy emerged from the city only to be routed through Thutmose's personal valor. As the enemy retreated, however, the Egyptian forces broke ranks and fell on the weap-

ons which the enemy had abandoned. This unfortunate break in discipline allowed the leaders of the Kadesh confederation to escape back into the city of Megiddo. Thutmose was forced to besiege the city. The siege ended successfully for the Egyptians after seven months, when the defeated chieftains of the alliance approached Thutmose with gifts in token of their submission.

This total defeat of the enemy became synonymous in later times with utter disaster. The name of the Battle of Megiddo—*Har Megiddo* (Mount Megiddo) in Hebrew—entered English as Armageddon, a word that designates a final cataclysmic battle.

Thutmose was equally wise in his handling of the defeated chieftains as he had been in war. The chieftains were reinstalled on their thrones, now as allies of Egypt. Their eldest sons were taken back to Egypt as hostages to guarantee the chieftains' cooperation with Egyptian policy. As the various Syro-Palestinian rulers died, their sons would be sent home to rule as Egyptian vassals. These sons, by that time thoroughly trained in Egyptian customs and culture, proved to be generally friendly to Egypt.

Thutmose's ambitions for Egyptian imperialism extended beyond Syria-Palestine. In the thirty-third year of his reign, he campaigned against the Mitanni, who occupied northern Mesopotamia (modern Iraq), the land the Egyptians called Nahrain. This battle also demonstrated Thutmose's mastery of strategy. He realized that his major problem in attacking the Mitanni would be in crossing the Euphrates River. To that end, he built boats of cedar in Lebanon and transported them overland 250 miles on carts. Once again, the element of surprise worked in Thutmose's favor. He was easily able to cross the river, attack the enemy, and defeat them.

Thutmose demonstrated his athletic prowess on the return trip from Nahrain. He stopped in the land of Niy, in modern Syria, to hunt elephants as had his royal ancestors. His brave deeds included the single-handed slaughter of a herd of 120 elephants.

Thutmose was responsible for initiating a large number of building projects within Egypt and in its Nubian holdings. The chronology of these projects is not understood in detail, but it is clear that he either built or remodeled eight temples in Nubia and seven temples in Upper Egypt. In the Egyptian capital of Thebes, he built mortuary temples for his father and grandfather as well as for himself. He added important buildings to the complex of temples at Karnak. These projects included the site of the Annals and a temple decorated with relief sculptures showing the unusual plant life Thutmose had observed during his campaigns to Syria-Palestine and Mesopotamia. Though it is difficult to identify the plants that interested Thutmose and his artists, this unusual form of decoration for a temple illustrates the king's interest in scholarly pursuits.

Thutmose's foresight included planning for his own successor. In the fifty-second year of his reign, his son Amenhotep II was designated coregent. The custom of naming and training an heir to the throne while the father still lived had been known since at least the Middle Kingdom (c. 2040-1782 B.C.). Thutmose showed wisdom in choosing as his successor Amenhotep, a son who would largely follow his father's policies.

The last twelve years of Thutmose III's reign passed relatively peacefully. The Annals for this period record only the yearly delivery of goods for the king's and the god's use.

Little is known of Thutmose III's personal life. Scholars are in disagreement as to whether he ever married Neferure, the daughter of Hatshepsut. His earliest wife was probably Sit-iakh; she was the mother of Amenemhat, a son who probably died young. A second wife, Meryetre-Hatshepsut II, was the mother of Amenhotep II. Nothing is known of a third royal wife, Nebtu, aside from her name. Four other royal children are known.

During the fifty-fourth year of a reign largely dedicated to war, Thutmose III died peacefully. He was buried by his son Amenhotep II in the tomb which had been prepared in the Valley of the Kings.

Summary

Despite the clichés and preconceived patterns which characterize the sources available for reconstructing the life of Thutmose III, he emerges as a truly remarkable man. His conquests in Syria-Palestine and Mesopotamia laid the groundwork for at least two hundred years of peace and prosperity in the ancient Near East. Vast quantities of goods flowed into Egypt's coffers from colonial holdings during this time. The royal family, the noblemen, and the temples of the gods came to possess previously unimagined wealth. The threat of foreign domination which had haunted Thutmose's immediate ancestors was finally dissipated. Egypt looked confidently toward a future of virtually unquestioned dominance over its neighbors.

Thutmose III himself was long remembered by Egyptians as the founder of their country's prosperity and security. Succeeding kings of Dynasties Eighteen and Nineteen modeled their reigns on the historic memory of the founder of the Egyptian Empire.

Bibliography

Gardiner, Alan. *Egypt of the Pharaohs: An Introduction.* Oxford: Clarendon Press, 1961; New York: Oxford University Press, 1964. Contains a chapter on the triumph of Egyptian foreign policy under Thutmose III, emphasizing and including translations of many of the sources for modern knowledge of the period.

Grayson, A. Kirk, and Donald B. Redford, eds. *Papyrus and Tablet.* Englewood Cliffs, N.J.: Prentice-Hall, 1973. Introductory material and modern translations of Egyptian historical texts, including contemporary accounts of the campaigns of year twenty-three and year thirty-three and the elephant hunt.

Nims, Charles F. "The Date of the Dishonoring of Hatshepsut." *Zeitschrift für Ägyptische Sprache* 93 (1968): 97-100. A groundbreaking examination of the relationship between Hatshepsut and Thutmose III during the early years of his reign.

Steindorff, George, and K. C. Seele. *When Egypt Ruled the East.* 2d ed. Chicago: University of Chicago Press, 1957. An analysis of the rise and fall of the Egyptian Empire, with a chapter on the career of Thutmose III.

Wilson, John A. *The Burden of Egypt: An Interpretation of Ancient Egyptian Culture.* Chicago: University of Chicago Press, 1951. An interpretive essay on the culture of ancient Egypt which includes a chapter on the early Eighteenth Dynasty.

Edward Bleiberg

TIBERIUS

Born: November 16, 42 B.C.; Rome, Italy
Died: March 16, A.D. 37; Misenum, Italy
Area of Achievement: Government
Contribution: As the second emperor of Rome, Tiberius solidified and firmly established the new system of power—but not without devastating impact on his personal life and the Roman upper classes.

Early Life

Tiberius Claudius Nero, the second emperor of Rome, came from a very ancient family of Sabine origin, the Claudians, who had moved to Rome shortly after the foundation of the city. Among the most patrician of Rome's residents, the Claudians expressed an aristocratic disdain for the other, less ancient, less noble inhabitants of Rome.

Tiberius' father, also named Tiberius Claudius Nero, was an associate of Julius Caesar and served as a quaestor (a sort of deputy) under him. The elder Tiberius fought with Caesar during the campaign in Egypt which ended the civil war between Caesar and Pompey the Great, but after the murder of Julius Caesar in 44 B.C. he went over to the side of the republicans.

This decision made the Claudian family enemies of Octavian (later Augustus), Marc Antony, and Marcus Aemilius Lepidus, the three men who formed the so-called Second Triumvirate which succeeded Caesar in power. The triumvirs were anxious to wipe out any traces of republican sentiment, and Tiberius the elder, his wife Livia, and his young son were forced into flight, often coming close to capture and death.

When Tiberius was only four years old, even stranger events happened. Augustus imposed a divorce between Livia and her husband, and soon married Livia—although she was pregnant at the time. Despite the adverse early influences, Tiberius was reared to be a loyal and dutiful servant of Augustus, ready to serve him in civil, military, and personal capacities. For twenty-two years Tiberius was an associate of Augustus; Tiberius was to be emperor himself for an equal period of time.

He began his service early. In 26 B.C., while only a teenager, he was sent to Spain on military service. Two years later, he was made quaestor in charge of the grain supply in Rome. Later, he served primarily in military positions, commanding armies in the east and in Europe. During several hard-fought campaigns, Tiberius subdued Illyricum and Pannonia (modern Yugoslavia and Hungary) and helped secure the empire's northern border with the dangerous German tribes. For these efforts, he was awarded a triumph, the highest honor bestowed upon a victorious general.

His personal life was less triumphant. He was forced by Augustus to divorce his beloved wife, Agrippina, and marry Julia, the daughter of Augustus. The match was arranged to strengthen the chance of succession of a descendant of Augustus to power; it failed, for Tiberius and Julia were incompatible and soon lived apart. For this reason, because Augustus was advancing his grandsons, and perhaps because of simple fatigue with his exhausting duties, Tiberius retired to the island of Rhodes in 6 B.C. He remained there for eight years, until the premature deaths of Augustus' grandsons forced his return, and he was adopted by the emperor as his son and heir.

There followed more campaigns in the north, interspersed with time at Rome. During the latter years of Augustus' reign, Tiberius seems to have

been virtual co-emperor, and in A.D. 14, when Augustus died, Tiberius assumed sole power of the whole Roman world.

Tiberius was a large, strong man, well above average height. He had a fair complexion, which was sometimes marred by outbreaks of skin disease. According to the ancient historian Suetonius, he wore his hair long in back, an old-fashioned style perhaps adopted in memory of his distinguished ancestry.

For most of his life, Tiberius enjoyed excellent health, although he was reported to have indulged in excessive drinking and an astounding number and variety of sexual pleasures. He was stiff and formal in manner and seemed ill at ease in the senate chambers. He was quite well educated in Latin and Greek literature and was devoted to astrology.

Life's Work

Tiberius came to the throne at the age of fifty-six. He had served Augustus all of his adult life, helping to establish the political system of the Roman Empire, also known as the principate (after one of Augustus' titles, *princeps*, or first citizen). The new system was a delicate and highly personal one, in which Augustus balanced traditional Roman republican forms with the new reality of one-man rule; the creation and maintenance of this balance required considerable skill and tact.

Because of his nature, Tiberius found it impossible to adopt his predecessor's role completely. Although he assumed actual power, he seemed to do so unwillingly and refused most of the titles which the senate offered him. Many, including the eminent Roman historian Cornelius Tacitus, have seen this as hypocrisy; others believe that Tiberius was genuinely reluctant to become an autocrat. During the early years of his rule, he made a great show of consulting the senate on all matters, great and small. After years of Augustus' rule, however, the old methods were simply inadequate to govern a worldwide empire, and increasingly Tiberius was forced to assume and exercise absolute powers.

At first, these powers were used for the common good. In matters of religion and morals, Tiberius took firm steps against foreign beliefs which he believed threatened traditional Roman virtues: He expelled adherents of the Egyptian and Jewish religions from Rome and banished astrologers on pain of death—although he firmly believed in the practice himself. Perhaps he was protecting himself against possible conspiracies inspired by favorable

horoscopes; such things were taken very seriously in ancient Rome.

Tiberius was also firm in his suppression of riots and other civil disturbances, which often afflicted Rome and the other large cities of the empire. Many of these problems were caused by an excessively large unemployed population, which was fed by the public dole and amused by public games; with little to lose, this group was easily incited to violence. As one measure against this violence, Tiberius established a central camp for the Praetorian guard in Rome, so this elite military unit could be called out to quell civil violence. At the same time, this concentration of troops gave enormous potential power to its commander, and soon that man, Lucius Aelius Sejanus, made a bold play for power.

Sejanus came from the equestrian order, the group below the senate in social standing and generally ineligible to hold the higher offices of the state. From about A.D. 23, however, Sejanus worked on the psychological and political insecurities of Tiberius, increasing his own hold over the emperor. It seems possible that Sejanus may even have aimed at the imperial power for himself—or, at least, as regent over Tiberius' successor. Sejanus aspired to marry Livia Julia, Tiberius' daughter, and worked to increase the emperor's fear and distrust of other members of his family. At the instigation of Sejanus, many senators (and others) were accused and condemned on charges of treason.

During this time, Tiberius left Rome, never to return. He settled on the island of Capri, off the coast of Naples. It was a spot well chosen for a man grown increasingly paranoid: No boat could approach it without being seen, and there were only two landing places, both easy to defend. By A.D. 31, Sejanus was named to a shared consulship with Tiberius and was at the height of his powers.

That same year saw the abrupt fall of Sejanus. Tiberius had become convinced that the Praetorian commander was aiming to become ruler of the state, and in a carefully worded letter to the senate, read while the unsuspecting Sejanus sat in the chamber, Tiberius bitterly denounced him. Sejanus' former lieutenants and others privy to the plot quickly acted, and Sejanus and his family were brutally executed, and his aspirations ended.

After this incident, Tiberius continued to rule Rome and the empire from the isolation of Capri. Important appointments were left unmade or, if made, were not allowed to be filled: Provincial governors sometimes spent their entire terms in Rome, having been denied permission to leave for their posts. Governing by letters, Tiberius often confused and mystified the senate, which was often unable to decipher his enigmatic messages.

His fears were clear enough, however, and resulted in an endless series of treason trials. During the latter years, a virtual reign of terror descended on the Roman upper classes, as they were accused of the vague but heinous crime of *maiestas* (roughly, treason). Executions of prominent Romans became commonplace, and many of those accused by professional informers chose not to wait for the show of a trial, committing suicide instead.

Meanwhile in Capri, Tiberius is reported by Suetonius to have engaged in a series of gaudy vices and perversions. His character, weakened first by years of hard work and worry and then the intense pressures of solitary rule, gave way to tyranny, debauchery, and paranoid suspicion. Having outlived his own sons, he settled the succession on his nephew Gaius (later the emperor Caligula). Tiberius died on March 16, A.D. 37; there was widespread rejoicing, instead of mourning, in Rome, and it was not until April 3 that his body was cremated and his remains interred in the imperial city he had vacated for so many years.

Summary

When Augustus adopted Tiberius as his son and heir, he took a formal oath that he did so only for the good of the Roman state and people. Historians have puzzled over this statement ever since. Some have argued that Augustus meant it as a sincere compliment, underscoring Tiberius' high qualifications for rule and indicating Augustus' confidence in his abilities. Others, however, have perceived a darker meaning in the words: that the action was one Augustus would have preferred not to take but was forced to by the lack of other, more preferable candidates.

Assessments of Tiberius as emperor similarly take two differing views. There are those who believe that on the whole he was a fairly good emperor, maintaining peace at home and security along the borders. While there is little doubt that after the fall of Sejanus Tiberius turned increasingly suspicious and vengeful, these dark elements cloud only the latter part of his rule, and the so-called reign of terror affected only a handful of the empire's inhabitants. It was only the senatorial and equestrian orders in Rome itself which felt the weight of the treason trials, and their hostility to Tiberius and the imperial system was to a large extent responsible for these events.

On the other hand, there are those who believe that from the first Tiberius was a cruel and tyrannical ruler, one who delighted in the suffering of his victims and whose life was given over to vice and debauchery. Foremost of these critics is the celebrated Roman historian Tacitus, whose brilliant writings paint a vivid portrait of Tiberius as a completely evil despot, a ruler who used his unlimited powers to destroy his supposed enemies. So great is Tacitus' genius that his version of history and his view of Tiberius seem almost irrefutable. Yet it must be remembered that Tacitus was a firm believer in the virtues of the vanished republic and hated the empire which replaced it. In a sense, he used Tiberius as a symbol of an entire system which he believed to be evil and unjust.

Those with a more balanced view maintain that Tiberius was a man of considerable abilities, both military and political. While serving under Augustus, Tiberius used these abilities to the benefit of Rome and, following his own succession to power, continued for many years to provide effective, proper rule for the empire. A series of causes—plots against him, the hostility of the upper classes, mental and physical exhaustion caused by overwork—wrought profound and disastrous changes in his personality. In the end, the task of ruling the Roman Empire proved too great a burden for one man to bear alone.

Bibliography

Grant, Michael. *The Roman Emperors: A Biographical Guide to the Rulers of Imperial Rome.* New York: Scribner, and London: Weidenfeld and Nicolson, 1985. For a fast-paced yet comprehensive introduction to Tiberius and his reign, the relevant section in this volume is unsurpassed. Grant, an outstanding historian of Rome, combines information and explanation in a narrative that provides as much pleasure as knowledge.

———. *The Twelve Caesars.* New York: Scribner, and London: Weidenfeld and Nicolson, 1975. Working from the base of Suetonius' historical scholarship, Grant approaches Tiberius from a combination of psychology, power politics, and common sense. He asks intriguing questions about what it must have been like to be the sole ruler of the vast Roman Empire, and his answers are thought-provoking. An excellent place to start a study of this enigmatic emperor.

Marsh, Frank Burr. *The Reign of Tiberius*. New York: Barnes and Noble, and London: Oxford University Press, 1931. Still the definitive modern biography of Tiberius, this volume brings together an impressive amount of scholarship in a generally readable and often entertaining fashion. Especially good in its knowledge of the detail and connections of ancient Roman political life.

Seager, Robin. *Tiberius*. London: Methuen, and Berkeley: University of California Press, 1972. A balanced and scholarly (but not pedantic) biography which shows how, under the early Roman Empire, the personality of the ruler had a profound impact on the state. Seager is careful to place Tiberius within the context of his times and his position, both of which were unique and difficult.

Smith, Charles E. *Tiberius and the Roman Empire*. Baton Rouge: Louisiana State University Press, 1942. Reprint. Port Washington, N.Y.: Kennikat Press, 1972. A work more concerned with Tiberius the ruler than Tiberius the man or tyrant, this book is strong on events and happenings outside the arena of Rome itself and is thus useful to counteract the popular image of that time created by Tacitus, that of unrelieved terror.

Suetonius. *Lives of the Twelve Caesars*. New York: Modern Library, 1959. This is one of the enduring classics of the ancient world, and it combines shrewd personal insight, revealing anecdotes, and a contemporary point of view. The section on Tiberius also has a long-famous description of his alleged sexual escapades on the isle of Capri; readers unfamiliar with Latin should be careful to choose an unexpurgated version, such as this one.

Tacitus, Cornelius. *The Complete Works of Tacitus*. Translated by Alfred Church and William Brodribb. New York: Modern Library, 1942. The *Annals* of Tacitus covers the period of Tiberius' reign, and this work is perhaps the most impressive production of classical history. Tacitus has fashioned a Tiberius who is a monster of deceit, hypocrisy, tyranny, and cruelty. This view may be distorted, but its impact has profoundly influenced history and historians ever since its conception.

Michael Witkoski

TIGRANES THE GREAT

Born: c. 140 B.C.; Armenia
Died: c. 55 B.C.; Armenia
Area of Achievement: Government
Contribution: As King of Armenia between 95 and 55 B.C., Tigranes the Great defied the growing power of Rome and carved out a vast but short-lived empire which stretched from upper Mesopotamia to the Mediterranean.

Early Life

The Armenia of Tigranes the Great consisted of the uplands that run from the Black Sea to the Caspian Sea and from the Caucasus Mountains south to the upper Tigris and Euphrates rivers. Armenia had long been politically and culturally related, on the one hand, to the great civilizations of Mesopotamia and the Iranian Plateau and, on the other, to those of Asia Minor and the eastern Mediterranean. Centered on the fertile plain of the Araxes River between the alkaline Lake Van and Lake Sevan, Armenia had maintained a large measure of autonomy despite its status as a satrapy of the Persian Empire and, following the Macedonian conquest of Persia, a nominal part of the Seleucid Empire. After the Roman victory over Antiochus the Great at Magnesia in 190 B.C., the Seleucid Empire was stripped of its possessions north of the Taurus Mountains. In the resulting political vacuum, independent kingdoms were established in Lesser Armenia (known in antiquity as Sophene) and in Greater Armenia by the former governors of these regions, Zariadris and Artaxias, the ancestor of Tigranes the Great.

Practically nothing is known about the early life of Tigranes. Although the second century Greek writer Appian stated that Tigranes' father was also named Tigranes, the majority of scholarly opinion holds that Tigranes was the son of Artavasdes. Tigranes' birth date of circa 140 B.C. is deduced from the tradition that he was eighty-five years old at the time of his death in 55 B.C. It is known that, at some point in his early years, Tigranes was taken hostage by Mithradates the Great of Parthia when that king besieged Armenia. In 95 B.C. Mithradates placed Tigranes on the Armenian throne, having made Tigranes cede to Parthia seventy fertile valleys of eastern Armenia.

Tigranes came to power at a time which was ripe for the expansion of the Armenian kingdom. The apparently inexorable growth of Roman power in the east had been severely hampered by Rome's internal social problems and by the transformation of the Black Sea kingdom of Pontus into a significant military threat under the leadership of Mithradates VI Eupator. The Seleucid Empire had continued to disintegrate and was on the verge of total collapse.

Life's Work

Upon his accession to the throne of Greater Armenia in 95 B.C., Tigranes began immediately to enlarge his dominion. His first act as king was to invade Sophene and depose its ruler, thus uniting all Armenia under his rule. That same year, Tigranes made an extremely important political alliance by marrying Cleopatra, a daughter of Mithradates VI Eupator. For the next thirty years, the political and military fortunes of Tigranes and Mithradates were to be closely linked in their joint struggle against Rome.

The first conflict between Rome and the alliance of Tigranes and Mithradates was precipitated by Mithradates' struggle with Nicomedes III of Bithynia for the control of Cappadocia. To forestall a Roman attempt to intervene and appoint a pro-Roman king over Cappadocia, Tigranes overran the country with his Armenian army and secured it for his father-in-law. In 92 B.C., the Roman senate dispatched an army under the command of Lucius Cornelius Sulla, who cleared Cappadocia and installed the Roman candidate, Ariobarzanes I, as king. As soon as Sulla withdrew from Asia, however, Mithradates deposed both Ariobarzanes and the new Bithynian king, Nicomedes IV, from their thrones. In 89 B.C., with the support of another Roman army, both kings were reinstated, and Nicomedes, urged on by the Roman legates, provoked a full-scale war by invading Mithradates' Pontic homeland.

In 88 B.C., Mithradates the Great died, and Tigranes used the opportunity to recover the Armenian territory he had ceded to the Parthians in 95 B.C. Tigranes followed this success by invading northern Parthia, taking the important regions of Gordyene and Adiabene and the city of Nisibis. Tigranes then turned his attention to the east and annexed a large tract of Media Atropatene into his growing Armenian empire. Tigranes now called himself by the archaic title of "King of Kings" and had vassal kings wait upon him in his court.

At the same time, Tigranes' ally Mithradates responded to the provocation of Nicomedes IV and, taking advantage of the disruption of the Roman Social War, launched a major attack on the Roman province of Asia. After more than eighty thousand Roman officials and citizens were massacred in the Greek cities of Asia Minor, Mithradates invaded the Aegean. In 87 B.C., Sulla once again responded to this threat and swept Mithradates out of Roman territory. As a result of political troubles back in Rome, Sulla was unable to capitalize on his victory, and in 86 B.C. a peace between Mithradates and Rome was arranged.

With Mithradates in temporary retirement from active campaigning and with Asia Minor temporarily quiet, Tigranes moved against the tottering Seleucid dynasty. In 83 B.C., the Armenian army defeated the last Seleucid king, Antiochus Eusebius, and the entire eastern Mediterranean coast from Cilicia to the borders of Egypt became a part of Tigranes' empire. Tigranes was now at the height of his power. He divided his empire into 120 satrapies, following the old Persian model, and set an Armenian feudal lord as governor over each. As the evidence of his silver coinage shows, Tigranes now added the traditional Seleucid title "Divine" to the eastern "King of Kings."

With his kingdom stretching from the Caspian to the Mediterranean, the old Armenian capital of Artaxas on the Araxes River was far removed from the center of Tigranes' empire. Thus, Tigranes set about building a new capital in the west, near the head of the Tigris River, and named it Tigranocerta, for himself. Tigranes populated his city by forcibly displacing Greeks and natives from Syria (and later from Cappadocia), in addition to encouraging Jewish and Arab merchants to settle there.

For the next decade, Tigranes apparently was able to govern his massive empire without major incident. When trouble arose, it was once again caused by Mithradates, who dragged Tigranes into his struggle against Rome. In 74 B.C., Nicomedes IV died and willed his Bithynian kingdom to Rome. Mithradates responded by invading Bithynia, and Tigranes again invaded Cappadocia. Rome then sent out Lucius Licinius Lucullus, who, in a series of engagements from 74 to 72 B.C., was able to drive Mithradates out of Pontus.

When Mithradates fled to the safety of Armenia, Lucullus sent his brother-in-law, Appius Claudius, to Tigranes to ask him to turn over Mithradates. Initially, Tigranes employed a delaying tactic by refusing to give an audience to either Appius Claudius or his father-in-law, who was kept under virtual house arrest in an Armenian castle. When the Roman envoy finally did speak to Tigranes, Appius' haughty and preemptory tone so infuriated the king that he refused the Roman request. In 69 B.C., Lucullus invaded Armenia, with a force that Tigranes is said to have described as "too large for an embassy, too small for an army." Nevertheless, Lucullus was able to besiege Tigranocerta and, after Tigranes had fled into the Armenian hills and joined forces with Mithradates, to inflict a serious defeat on the combined Armenian and Pontic armies. Lucullus' army was unwilling, however, to fight further, and when the Roman garrison that had been left in Pontus revolted, Lucullus was forced to retire. Both Tigranes and Mithradates were able to recover much of the territory that had been seized, though Tigranes had lost Syria forever.

The final blow to Tigranes' imperial rule was soon to follow. In 67 B.C. Pompey the Great cleared the Mediterranean of pirates by destroying their bases in Cilicia; in the following year, he was awarded the command against Mithradates VI. When Pompey quickly moved against Pontus, Mithradates once again tried to seek refuge in Armenia. In the meantime, however, Tigranes was facing a new enemy. His third son, also named Tigranes, had married into the family of Phraates III, King of Parthia, and, urged on by his father-in-law, raised a revolt against his father.

As Pompey marched into Armenia, the elder Tigranes banished Mithradates from his kingdom and made overtures of submission to the Roman general. Perceiving that a weakened Tigranes would serve Roman interests, Pompey switched his support from Phraates to Tigranes, though he did set Tigranes' son on the throne of Lesser Armenia. The younger Tigranes soon intrigued again against his father, and Pompey thereupon took him prisoner and brought him back to Rome, where he perished. The next two years witnessed intermittent hostilities between Tigranes and Phraates until Pompey finally negotiated a peace between Armenia and Parthia. Tigranes the Great continued to rule as King of Armenia, albeit a king completely subservient to Rome, until his death.

Summary

The ancient Armenians themselves left no historical records, and the earliest extant Armenian history, written sometime between the fifth and eighth centuries A.D. by Moses of Khorene, presents only a very unreliable legendary account of the reign of Tigranes. Except for a single reference to Tigranes in a Parthian document and the evidence of Tigranes' coinage, all that is known about this king is what is preserved in the writings of a handful of Greek and Latin authors, who wrote from a Roman perspective; the main sources for the life of Tigranes are Strabo, Plutarch, Dio Cassius, Appian of Alexandria, and Justin. It is hardly surprising, therefore, that the Tigranes portrayed by these authors is an arrogant tyrant who through his own stupidity and hubris was unable to maintain his empire. In large part, this negative picture of Tigranes simply reflects a general Greco-Roman hostility toward absolute monarchs. In spite of his sincere philhellenism, which was shared by most of the eastern aristocracy of the Hellenistic age, Tigranes was above all an Oriental ruler.

After the death of Tigranes the Great, his descendants continued to rule as client-kings of Rome until 1 B.C., when Augustus attempted to put his own grandson, Gaius, on the throne. When Gaius was killed during an Armenian uprising in A.D. 4, the kingship was reinstated, and the Armenian throne continued to be a matter of contention between Rome and Parthia for another century. Finally, by A.D. 114, the usefulness of Armenia as a buffer state had ended, and Trajan annexed it as a Roman province.

Bibliography

Foss, Clive. "The Coinage of Tigranes the Great: Problems, Suggestions, and a New Find." *Numismatic Chronicle* 146 (1986): 19-66. A major reclassification of the silver and bronze coinage of Tigranes based on metrology, iconography, and style. Identifies mints and reassigns one type to Tigranes the Younger.

Lang, David M. *Armenia: Cradle of Civilization.* 3d ed. London and Boston: Allen and Unwin, 1980. Presents a general overview of Armenia from the Neolithic to the present. In general, the chapters on early Armenia are marred by historical errors and a strong pro-Armenian bias.

McGing, B. C. "The Date of the Outbreak of the Third Mithridatic War." *Phoenix* 38 (1984): 12-18. Suggests that the beginning of the war should be downdated from 74 B.C. to 73 B.C.

Musti, D. "Syria and the East." In *The Hellenistic World*, vol. 7 in *The Cambridge Ancient History*, edited by F. W. Walbank and A. E. Astin. 2d ed. Cambridge: Cambridge University Press, 1984. The best general account available on the relations between the Seleucids and the Eastern kingdoms.

Ormerod, H. A., and M. Cary. "Rome and the East." In *The Roman Republic, 133-44 B.C.*, vol. 9 in *The Cambridge Ancient History*, edited by S. A. Cook, F. E. Adcock, and M. P. Charlesworth. 2d. ed. New York: Cambridge University Press, 1994. Still the best narrative on the Third Mithradatic War and Tigranes' battles against Lucullus.

Peters, F. E. *The Harvest of Hellenism.* New York: Simon and Schuster, 1970; London: Allen and Unwin, 1972. In this massive history of the Hellenistic East, chapter 8, "The Romans in the Near East," presents a solid general account of the conflicts between Rome and the Eastern kingdoms from Cynoscephalae to Carrhae.

Murray C. McClellan

TRAJAN

Born: c. A.D. 53; Italica, Baetica

Died: c. August 8, A.D. 117; Selinus, Cilicia

Areas of Achievement: Government and warfare

Contribution: The first of the adoptive emperors of Rome, Trajan became one of the most successful, in both war and politics. During his reign, the Roman Empire reached its maximum territorial extent.

Early Life

Marcus Ulpius Traianus (Trajan) was born in Baetica, in what is now southern Spain, an area of Roman conquests and Latin influences for more than a century. By the time of Trajan's birth, circa A.D. 53, much of the population spoke Latin rather than the native Iberian language. Trajan's father, also Marcus Ulpius Traianus, was a native of Baetica who came from an Italian family that had been long established in Spain. The senior Traianus had a significant military and political career; he served as governor of Baetica and commanded a legion in the war Vespasian conducted against the Jews, then became a consul and a member of the patrician class before acting as governor of Syria and, ultimately, as imperial proconsul in the East. His attainments showed that most positions in the imperial hierarchy during the first century A.D. were open to non-Italians. His son, Trajan, would become the first provincial to become emperor.

Little is known of Trajan's early life. He served as a military tribune and accompanied his father to Syria during the latter's term as governor. Typically for one of his class, he held various judicial and political positions, but his primary experience was military. He held command in Spain, then in Germany, becoming governor of Upper Germany. Physically imposing, tall, and serious in manner, he was popular and successful in the military and also among the senators in Rome.

In 97, probably as a result of political pressure, Marcus Cocceius Nerva, emperor since the murder of Domitian the previous year, adopted Trajan as his successor. Nerva was a politician, not a warrior, who hoped to end the autocratic abuses of Domitian's reign. He was ill and had no children of his own, and his adoption of Trajan satisfied both the military and civilian powers. Four months after Trajan's adoption Nerva died, in January, 98, and Trajan, despite his provincial birth, became Emperor of Rome.

Life's Work

At the time of Nerva's death, Trajan was at Cologne, in Lower Germany. Before returning to Rome, he fought a series of engagements against nearby foes, both to impress upon them the might of Roman power and to establish plans for subsequent military action. His belated arrival in Rome, in the summer of 99, suggests the unchallenged position he had already achieved.

Like his predecessors, Trajan continued to wear the mantle woven by Augustus more than a century earlier. In reality he was an autocrat, but in theory he was merely the first citizen, the princeps. His power was nearly absolute, yet, unlike many of Augustus' successors, Trajan masked his powers so as to reassure rather than intimidate the former ruling body, the senate, and the aristocratic patricians who had governed during the era of the Republic. Republican sentiment still ran high, in spite of the many changes since the Republic's end, as reflected in the historical works of two of Trajan's contemporaries, Cornelius Tacitus and Suetonius. Trajan reconciled the reality of order with the appearance of freedom in a way that satisfied most people; the equilibrium sought by Nerva but established by Trajan ushered in an era which the English historian Edward Gibbon described as one of the golden ages of human history.

Trajan stressed moderation and reinforced the values of an earlier Rome. His family's upright reputation, his public generosity and private frugality, his lack of interest in excessive ceremonies glorifying himself, and his accessibility all contributed to the general popularity of his rule. As an administrator, Trajan was conscientious and hardworking rather than radically innovative; he was willing merely to improve existing practices inherited from his predecessors. If the senate remained powerless collectively, Trajan made good use of the abilities of individual senators. He created new patricians and made greater use of the class known as the knights rather than the services of freedmen, who often had attained considerable responsibility during the first century of the Empire. His judicial decisions favored the rights of slave owners rather than those of the slaves, although there is considerable evidence that Trajan's own sympathies were generally humanitarian. In his actions and demeanor, he conveyed the ruling-class virtues of the Republic.

As the Empire reached its maximum extent and its most notable era, public works projects continued to be of great importance. Roads were built or improved, particularly in the eastern part of the Empire, and road milestones from Trajan's reign have been discovered far south in Egypt. Aqueducts constructed around Rome greatly increased water supply to the city's populace. Harbors were improved, including Ostia, the port for Rome. New public baths were developed, and temples, libraries, and business facilities enhanced the city. Plans for many of the projects existed before Trajan became emperor, but he fulfilled and often expanded them. The Empire continued to become more urbanized, particularly in the East, and local municipalities also experienced considerable construction.

Trajan oversaw the reorganization of the traditional importation of grain so important to the Romans and increased the number of people qualified to receive it free. Public shows and games, a major part of urban life during his reign, were especially notable after his military victories. Trajan's interests in the plight of the lower classes possibly re-

flected his humanitarian concerns, but those actions were also simply good politics. He was fortunate to be able to reduce taxes—partially because of administrative dedication, but also because of the economic benefits which resulted from his military victories. Personally popular with the legions, Trajan successfully controlled his armies. He created a new mounted bodyguard, primarily made up of non-Italians, thus moving toward parity between Italians and those from the provinces. Concern for his personal security, given the record of violent deaths suffered by several of his predecessors, led to the development of a new secret service.

Trajan's religious beliefs, orthodox for members of his class and time, reflected his traditional and patriotic nature rather than a deep theological concern. He built and restored temples throughout the Empire, and like Augustus, he accepted the fact of emperor worship in the eastern part of the Empire but resisted its development in the West. Nevertheless, new religions, such as Christianity, were spreading throughout the Empire, and, although only a small minority of the population were

Christians, questions arose about the new movement.

Pliny the Younger, a Roman aristocrat appointed by Trajan as governor of the province of Bithynia-Pontus, wrote often to ask for solutions to problems he faced, including how Christians were to be treated. Trajan seriously considered all such difficulties; he did not allow his subordinates to decide the many matters of governance. Given the intimate tie between the Roman gods and the Roman state, Trajan's instructions to Pliny were moderate and sensible. Fearing subversive threats which might affect the tranquillity of the Empire, Trajan ordered that Christians who would not recant should be punished according to the requirements of the laws, but Christians should not be sought out for special persecution, and anonymous accusations by others against them should not be accepted. Trajan's response was typical of his nature; he was not a religious fanatic, but he understood the necessity to uphold the laws which had traditionally been accepted by the society and which had been responsible for Roman well-being.

Predictably, war and military conquest, the enterprises that had led to his adoption by Nerva, became an important theme of Trajan's reign. In eastern Europe, the great rivers of the Rhine and the Danube had long served as the natural boundaries of the Empire. Yet, because of a great inward curve of the Danube, a portion of southeastern Europe, known as Dacia, had remained a dangerous enclave which threatened the security of the Empire. The Dacians had adopted at least part of the Greco-Roman culture, including certain military techniques; although the Romans considered them barbarians, they were not primitives, and periodically they aggressively raided Roman territory across the Danube.

Trajan waged two wars against the Dacians and their formidable king, Decebalus. The first war, lasting from 101 to 102, resulted in Trajan leading the legions to victory over the Dacians, but Decebalus refused to abide by the terms of peace, and a second Dacian war was fought in 105. Again, Trajan was victorious, and Decebalus committed suicide. Most of the population of Dacia was removed and the area was colonized by Roman soldiers and civilians. The province became an important part of the Empire, until it was abandoned in the late third century after the invasion of the Germanic Goths. Trajan's conquest was celebrated by coins and inscriptions throughout the Empire, but the most famous monument stood in Rome. A hundred-foot-high column was constructed which portrayed the course of the Dacian wars; running counterclockwise from bottom to top, twenty-five hundred carved figures decorated the column, which was crowned with a statue of Trajan. It was dedicated in 113 and remains one of the most impressive remains of the Roman Empire at the time of its greatest power.

After the victory against Decebalus, Trajan spent the next several years in Rome before responding to another threat to Rome's supremacy, this time in the East, from Parthia, whose ancient borders spread at times from the Euphrates River to India. Rome and Parthia had been adversaries as far back as the late Republic, when Pompey the Great had extended the boundaries of the Empire into the area south of the Black Sea. Trajan, in 113, decided to annex Armenia to Rome, claiming that the Parthians had upset the existing arrangements in that territory. Trajan's motives have been variously interpreted; he may have acted for economic reasons, to secure the overland trade routes from the Persian Gulf and beyond, or because of ambitions for personal fame (although even the wars against Dacia resulted more from Dacian incursions than Roman aggression). Trajan was sixty years old when the war against Parthia began, and in 114 his armies easily conquered Armenia, making it a Roman province, with client kingdoms extending even father to the east.

The Roman advance continued south the following year into Mesopotamia. Behind the Roman lines, however, there was unrest; businessmen were upset by the uncertain changes brought by the new Roman regime, and many Jewish communities in the East again rose up against Roman authority. At the same time the Parthians, previously disunited, came together, forcing the Romans back. The military situation stabilized, but Trajan's health declined; there were matters at Rome that needed his presence, and he turned west toward home. Before reaching Rome, he died at Selinus in Cilicia, in southern Asia Minor, probably on August 8, 117. His ashes were deposited in a golden urn at the base of his famous column in Rome.

Summary

Before he died, Trajan apparently adopted as his successor Publius Aelius Hadrianus (Hadrian), a distant relative who had been reared in Trajan's household. Trajan had no children of his own, and his wife, Pompeia Plotina, favored Hadrian's accession. One of the first acts of the new emperor was to reach an agreement with Parthia to have Rome withdraw from the advanced positions attained by Trajan. Hadrian's decision was both strategic and political. It is possible that under Trajan the Empire was overextended, that it lacked the resources necessary to hold the new territories, and for his own success Hadrian desired peace rather than a resumption of his predecessor's forward policy. Under Hadrian, and under his successors, the Roman Empire would never again reach the limits achieved by Trajan.

The adjustment made between the ruler as princeps and the ruler as tyrant distinguished Trajan's reign. Power resided solely in the emperor's hands, but he used that power responsibly. The practice of adopting one's successor, first established by Nerva, continued until 180, and during that period the Empire was governed by men of ability and much vision. It was not, however, a golden age; even under Trajan, increased centralization took place, Italy began to fall relatively behind other parts of the Empire, and the borders were never totally secure. The traditional governing classes of Rome turned more toward the literary life than toward politics and public service, while the Empire depended in large part on the labor of slaves for its prosperity.

Nevertheless, Trajan was one of the greatest of the emperors, both because of his military and territorial conquests and because of the standards he set as governor and statesman. Early in his reign he was hailed as *Optimus*, the best. Along with Augustus, Trajan was the standard by which later Romans measured the leadership of the Empire; their expressed hope, rarely attained, was that later emperors would be *felicior Augusto, melior Traiano*, or more fortunate than Augustus and better than Trajan.

Bibliography

Garzetti, Albino. *From Tiberius to the Antonines: A History of the Roman Empire, A.D. 14-192*. Translated by J. F. Foster. London: Methuen, 1974. Until a full biography in English of Trajan is written, Garzetti's volume partially fills the vacuum. Trajan is one of the major figures and is the subject of a long chapter in the work. The author argues that Trajan was one of the best of all the emperors of Rome and that he successfully remained primarily princeps rather than dictator.

Gibbon, Edward. *The History of the Decline and Fall of the Roman Empire*. 7 vols. London: Methuen, and New York: Macmillan, 1909-1926. For Gibbon, the second century of the common era was one of humanity's golden ages. Trajan was one of the best of the emperors, whose only personal weakness was his military ambitions. Gibbon's own biases, however, were in favor of the Republic, not the Empire, and he would probably have agreed with Lord Acton's later dictum regarding the corrupting influences of power.

Grant, Michael. *The Army of the Caesars*. New York: Scribner, and London: Weidenfeld and Nicolson, 1974. The author, one of the most prolific historians of ancient Rome, has produced a well-written study of the armies of Rome from the late Republic through the fall of the Western Empire in 476. Grant discusses the military conquests of Trajan in Dacia and against Parthia and argues that the latter was ultimately beyond the resources of the Empire.

———. *The Roman Emperors: A Biographical Guide to the Rulers of Imperial Rome, 31 B.C.-A.D. 476*. London: Weidenfeld and Nicolson, and New York: Scribner, 1985. The sketch on Trajan is brief but comprehensive of the subject's accomplishments and characteristics.

Harris, B. F. *Bithynia Under Trajan*. Auckland, New Zealand: University of Auckland, 1964. This brief monograph discusses the different but complementary views of the position and powers of the Roman emperor at the time of Trajan as expressed by the Roman governor in Bithynia, Pliny the Younger, and the Greek Dio Chrysostom.

Lepper, F. A. *Trajan's Parthian War*. London: Oxford University Press, 1948; Westport, Conn.: Greenwood Press, 1979. The author discusses the last, and most controversial, of Trajan's activities and suggests the hypothesis that illness during the emperor's last years at least partially explains his excessive imperial exploits.

Millar, Fergus. *The Emperor in the Roman World*. 2d ed. Ithaca, N.Y.: Cornell University Press, and London: Duckworth, 1992. This study of the emperors of Rome from Augustus to Constantine is one of the major works on the powers and responsibilities of the many rulers of the Empire. Long and not easily digested, it is still worth the effort because of its comprehensiveness and its insights. Although there is no single chapter on Trajan, he is frequently mentioned.

Rossi, Lino. *Trajan's Column and the Dacian Wars*. Translated by J. M. C. Toynbee. London: Thames and Hudson, and Ithaca, N. Y.: Cornell University Press, 1971. The author's historical interest is in warfare, Roman and modern. In this study, in the absence of written records, he uses one of the most famous monuments of the Roman Empire in order to dissect the course of Trajan's victorious wars against the Dacians, which represented one of the most important accomplishments of his reign.

Wilken, Robert L. *The Christians as the Romans Saw Them*. New Haven, Conn.: Yale University Press, 1984; London: Yale University Press, 1986. Because of the lack of contemporary biographical works about Trajan, Pliny the Younger's letters to the emperor have continued to be one of the major sources for the era. Among other topics, Pliny wrote to Trajan regarding Christians in Bithynia. The author places that correspondence in historical context from the Roman perspective.

Eugene S. Larson

TUTANKHAMEN

Born: c. 1370 B.C.; probably Tell el-Amarna, Egypt
Died: c. 1352 B.C.; place unknown
Area of Achievement: Government and politics; pharaohs
Contribution: Tutankhamen is one of the best-known and most studied of the Egyptian pharaohs because his tomb lay undisturbed and intact until its discovery in the early twentieth century. Although he was a relatively minor figure in the course of Egyptian history, the gold-laden contents of his tomb have captured the imagination of the world and contributed much to the knowledge of ancient Egyptian life, culture, and religion.

Early Life

Tutankhamen's lineage is uncertain, and despite the vast assortment of riches discovered in his tomb, the exact dates and events of his rule remain shrouded in mystery. Presumably born in Tell el-Amarna during the reign of Akhenaten, he was most likely the son of either Amenophis III or Akhenaten. The identity of Tutankhamen's mother is less certain. She was likely one of the secondary wives or concubines of the king. Kiya, a secondary wife of Akhenaten, is the most logical candidate, since she was referred to in numerous inscriptions as the "Greatly Beloved Wife." She was probably a relative of his father, as it was the practice of Egyptian nobility of the time to marry another member of the royal family and thus ensure the purity of royal blood.

The son-in-law of Akhenaten and queen Nerfertiti by marriage to their third daughter, Tutankhamen was only nine years old when he succeeded his brother Smenkhkare. Tutankhamen's queen, Ankhesenpaaten, was also very young at the time of their marriage. The royal couple produced no known heirs. Two fetuses, however, were buried in the tomb of Tutankhamen and are assumed to be their offspring. He ascending the throne during the period of transition that followed the death of Akhenaten, who had promoted the cult of the solar disk, Aton; at such a time, the rule of Egypt would have been difficult for even the most adept of statesmen. Akhenaton had angered many by moving the capitol from Thebes to Tell el-Amarna. Akhenaton's fervent monotheism, neglect of foreign affairs, and the decline of Egyptian power abroad, especially in Syria and Palestine, had cre-

ated considerable unrest. During the final years of his reign, however, and during the brief reign of his co-regent and successor, Semenkhare, the priesthood of Amon reemerged. When Tutankhamen succeeded his brother, Smenkhkare, he initially embraced the priesthood of Aton. It was the only cult he had ever known.

Life's Work

Although the new king originally took the name Tutankhaton, meaning "gracious of life is Aton," less than three years later he changed his name to Tutankhamen, meaning "gracious of life is Amon." It is likely that the achievements of Tutankhamen's reign were actually envisioned and carried out by the vizier Ay and the general Haremhab. Tutankhamen was probably no more than a puppet ruler who, because of his youth, was easily manipulated by others for much of his reign. Ay, possibly the father of Nefertiti, was the power behind the throne and was likely responsible for the return of polytheism. The transfer of the administrative capital of Egypt back to Memphis and the re-establishment of Thebes as the religious center should probably be credited to Ay as well. Meanwhile, Hasemhab, the commander of the Egyptian armies, reasserted Egyptian authority in Asia by halting Hittite advances. Tutankhamen was thus credited with successfully halting Hittite advances on the Egyptian empire in northern Syria.

Although several objects in his tomb depict the five-foot-six-inch Tutankhamen defeating enemies in battle, there is no evidence he ever actually participated in a campaign. It is not an impossibility, however, since some other pharaohs did engage the enemy at about the age of eighteen; most scholars, though, believe that the depictions represent the king's armies as an extension of his power. It is known that Tutankhamen was a trained archer. Inscriptions on the fans found in his tomb state that the ostrich plumes they contained were taken from trophies of the king's hunts. When Tutankhamen died at about the age of eighteen, he was succeeded by Ay, who married Tutankhamen's widow. The cause of his death is unknown. There is evidence from skull damage that he may have been killed in battle or assassinated.

Whatever the cause of his demise, he had prepared for death. Tutankhamen was buried in the Valley of the Kings in a tomb that had been origi-

nally prepared for someone else. The tomb of Tutankhamen was not one typically prepared for persons of such status. It has been estimated that it took the artisans working on his tomb about ten weeks to complete the coffin and shrines that protected him. The mummification process took about the same amount of time. Before his burial, all of his internal organs, except the heart, were removed and placed in containers called "Canopic jars." The body was then placed in a dry mineral, natron, for dehydration. Other substances known only to the ancients were also used to embalm the body before it was wrapped in linen bandages and placed in the solid-gold coffin. Although the entrance of the tomb was pillaged by grave robbers some years after his death, it was later resealed and buried under the debris of the tomb of Ramses VI, which was built literally on top of his tomb. Tutankhamen was all but forgotten, both by his successors and by historians, until the discovery of his tomb by Howard Carter more than three thousand years after his death.

In 1909, Theodore Davis, a noted archaeologist, uncovered what he believed to be the tomb of Tutankhamen. Howard Carter, a self-trained Egyptolo-

gist, disagreed with Davis and vowed to continue the search. He eventually convinced George Herbert, the fifth earl of Carnarvon, to purchase Davis' concession to work the Valley of the Kings. For the next eighteen years, the two men spent half of each year in the Egyptian desert searching for the tomb of Tutankhamen or some other rare antiquity. In 1922, Carter, whose work since 1909 had been financed by Carnarvon at a cost of more than $250,000, discovered the set of steps leading down to the entrance of Tutankhamen's tomb. Within days, news of the discovery of the massive golden treasures unearthed in the tomb captured the imagination of the world.

The tomb was stocked with everything the young king might need in the afterlife. Clothing, jewelry, musical instruments, chairs, lamps, weapons, chariots, jars, and baskets containing wine and food filled the rooms. The sepulchral chamber contained his throne, covered with gold, silver, and jewels. The sarcophage contained three coffins placed one within the other. The innermost, made of solid gold and weighing 2,500 pounds, was of human shape and bore the likeness of Tutankhamen.

Carter spent more than ten years extracting and documenting every artifact removed from the tomb. He maintained meticulous field notes on every aspect of the discovery and excavation. Carter's notes and drawings, and related photographs taken during the excavation by Harry Burton of New York's Metropolitan Museum of Art, were later donated to the University of Oxford. Carnarvon, on the other hand, died as the result of a mysterious infection soon after discovering the tomb. He was only one of a series of victims— including Carter's pet canary, which was eaten by a cobra—whose deaths were attributed to the "mummy's curse." The strange circumstances surrounding their deaths, however, only served to heighten the interest in the phenomenal discovery.

Summary

Tutankhamen was a relatively minor Egyptian ruler. As a result of the discoveries of Carter and Carnarvon, however, the world became obsessed with Tutankhamen and all things Egyptian during the 1920's. Egypt greatly benefitted from the publicity surrounding the discovery, as thousands of tourists flocked to the Valley of the Kings. Although the local economy was completely unprepared for the deluge, industrious entrepreneurs soon found ways to accommodate the visitors. The "Egyptian look" became the epitome of women's fashion, and when the British Empire Exhibition of 1924 featured a replica of the tomb, it attracted more than 200,000 visitors on the opening day.

The fascination with things Egyptian created by the discovery of Tutankhamen's tomb persists today in popular culture. Many of the contents of Tutankhamen's tomb remain on display in the Cairo Museum, but several exhibitions have been conducted abroad. In 1972, to commemorate the fiftieth anniversary of the tomb's discovery, an exhibit was held in the British Museum in London. A similar exhibit toured the United States in 1976. Thousands waited in line to catch a rare glimpse of the wealth and splendor of Egyptian antiquity. Tutankhamen's greatest legacy as ruler of Egypt was not political or military but rather the knowledge of the society in which he lived that has been gleaned from the contents of his tomb.

Bibliography

Brackman, Arnold C. *The Search for the Gold of Tutankhamen*. New York: Mason and Charter, 1976. An excellent and easy-to-read narrative of the search for Tutankhamen's tomb that provides a wealth of information of interest to the casual reader. No photographs or illustrations.

Budge, Sir Ernest A. Wallis. *Tutankhamen: Amenism, Atenism, and Egyptian Monothesim*. New York: Dodd, Mead, and London: M. Hopkinson, 1923. Contains considerable information about the religious beliefs of Egypt at the time of Tutankhamen. The illustrations of Egyptian hieroglyphs are well researched and documented. The author's knowledge of Egyptian antiquities is evident.

Carter, Howard. *The Tomb of Tutankhamen: Discovered by the Late Earl of Carnarvon and Howard Carter*. New York: Doran, and London: Cassell, 1923. In this three-volume set, Carter describes the events of his discovery in detail. The photographs are of great interest.

Dersin, Denise, ed. *What Life Was Like on the Banks of the Nile: Egypt, 3050-3030 B.C.*. Alexandria, Va.: Time-Life Books, 1996. Almost every aspect of Egyptian life, including the role of women in society, is addressed in this well-written volume. The timeline is extremely helpful for the novice Egyptologist, and the bibliography is excellent.

Desroches-Noblecourt, Christiane. *Tutankhamen: Life and Death of a Pharaoh*. New York: Little Brown, and London: M. Joseph, 1963. The text is complimented by more than seventy color photographs and numerous illustrations related to the life and death of Tutankhamen. The list of principal characters of his life is invaluable. The notes on the color photographs are an excellent resource.

Gilbert, Katharine Stoddert, Joan K. Holt, and Sarah Hudson, eds. *Treasures of Tutankhamun*. New York: Metropolitan Museum of Art, 1976. Published for use with the 1970's U.S. traveling exhibition, this book is available in most libraries. Contains a brief description of the discovery and many photographs of pieces shown during the exhibition.

Reeves, Nicholas. *The Complete Tutankhamun: The King, The Tomb, The Treasure*. London and New York: Thames and Hudson, 1990. Outlines the events of the discovery of the now-famous tomb. Includes easy-to-read biographical information about the most important participants in the expedition, including often overlooked members of the excavation team. Also contains excellent photographs.

Vandenberg, Philipp. *The Curse of the Pharaohs.* Philadelphia: J. B. Lippincott, and London: Hodder and Stoughton, 1975. Discusses the alleged "curse" that was said to have ben responsible for the curious deaths of some of the people present at the excavation of Tutankhamen's tomb. The author explores several scientifically plausible explanations

Donald C. Simmons, Jr.

ULFILAS

Born: 311; the region of modern Rumania

Died: 383; Constantinople

Area of Achievement: Religion

Contribution: An apostle to the Goths, Ulfilas developed an alphabet for the Gothic language and made the first Gothic translation of the Bible. He was also instrumental in converting the Goths to Arianism, leading to conflicts once these peoples settled inside the predominately Nicene Roman Empire.

Early Life

Not much is known of Ulfilas' early life. Tradition has it that his grandparents were taken as slaves from Cappadocia into the Gothic settlements north of the Danube. This same tradition suggests that his father was a Goth. "Ulfilas" itself is a term Gothic meaning "little wolf."

Ulfilas was fluent in three languages: Greek, Latin, and Gothic. He must have learned something of all three in his youth, for in 332 he was sent to Constantinople, perhaps as an emissary of the Goths to the Romans, or perhaps as a hostage to the court of the Emperor Constantine. While there, Ulfilas either acquired or further developed his mastery of Greek and Latin. By the time he was thirty, he had risen to the position of lector, which required that he be able to read and speak in all three languages to the Gothic Christians inside the Empire.

The adult Ulfilas was an Arian rather than a Nicene Christian. When he embraced this position has been debated since antiquity. Orthodox and Arian historians alike tended to advance dates more important for their partisan positions than for their historical accuracy; modern scholars are convinced that it was around 330, during his time at the court of Constantine, since Arianism was the predominate theological position there. Whatever the accurate date, in 341, during the reign of the Emperor Constantius II, Ulfilas was consecrated a bishop by the Arian Bishop Eusebius. He would spend the remaining forty years of his life as an apostle to the Goths.

Life's Work

The Visigoths were a tribal people who, though nominally under a king, usually vested local control in the hands of "judges." In the region where Ulfilas began his preaching, the local judge, Atha-

naric, was a pagan. After Ulfilas had been preaching for seven years, Athanaric began to persecute both Arian and Nicene Christians. The danger became so great that Ulfilas sought refuge inside the Empire on the near side of the Danube. The emperor at the time, Constantius, also an Arian, granted his request for asylum, and Ulfilas and his band of followers settled in Moetia, in modern Bulgaria.

A second, more severe persecution followed, lasting from 369 to 373. Many more Arians fled to Ulfilas' community . Apparently, Athanaric feared that Christianity was undermining the tribal nature of his society and threatening the old religion. If Ulfilas' community is any example, this would certainly have been the case. They remained steadfastly loyal to Rome and devoutly Arian Christian even in the following century, when they refused to join the whole remaining body of the Visigoths who, fleeing the Huns, entered and subsequently looted the falling Roman Empire. Indeed, the community Ulfilas had founded in Moetia was still there in the middle of the sixth century when Jordanes, a Gothic historian, distinguished them from the other, more warlike Goths.

In the midst of the persecution of 368, a civil war erupted between Athanaric and another chieftain, Fritigern. Fritigern, at first defeated, sought imperial assistance. The Emperor Valens, an Arian, was prepared to assist; Fritigern, in return, was prepared to convert to Arian Christianity along with all of his followers. With Valens' help, Athanaric was defeated. From his location on the imperial side of the mountains, Ulfilas seems to have attempted to convert both peoples. In 376, when Fritigern's Visigoths entered the Empire fleeing the Huns, Ulfilas is said to have accompanied his embassy to the emperor in order to plead their case.

Ulfilas' specific activities in the remainder of his life are not well documented. That he was preaching and teaching the Goths and Romans in Moetia, and perhaps beyond, seems clear. Additionally, he must have devoted much of his time to developing the Gothic alphabet, which he used for his translation of the Gothic Bible. He also must have instructed his followers in the use of the alphabet. Subsequently, his text was copied and disseminated among other Gothic groups. The only remaining copy of Ulfilas's translation, a fragment of some 118 pages of the New Testament preserved at the University of Uppsala in Sweden, was made in Ostrogothic Italy about a century after Ulfilas' death. It is known as the *Codex Argenteus* because its uncial letters are of silver on blue velum. A few additional manuscript fragments exist that bear a striking resemblance to the work of Ulfilas, but it not possible to say with certainty that they are his. Finally, there are later references to the text that include quotations from the Psalms as well as passages from Genesis. It was his intention to translate the entire Bible with the possible exception of the Book of Kings, which he said was too much about war for the Goths's own good. In all likelihood, he completed the major portion of his work.

He was also a tireless participant in the Trinitarian controversy of his day. His disciple Bishop Auxentius records that Ulfilas attended many councils and wrote much on the controversy. Independent sources mention him only at two councils, but Auxentius' own work speaks at length of Ulfilas' polemical writings.

Ulfilas occupied something of a moderate position in the controversy. He was Arian because he subordinated Jesus the Son to God the Father. On his deathbed, he repeated his creed in a form that would become synonymous with that of other Arians who subsequently converted to this version of Christianity. He stated that he believed in one eternal God who existed alone from the beginning. It was this God who created the Son, "the only begotten God." The Son, in turn, was the creator of all things and regarded the Father as superior to himself. Finally, it was the Father through the Son who created the Holy Spirit before anything else was created . His creed was "Homoean" because it refers to Christ as being "like" the Father rather than being in any sense "of the same substance" with the Father, as the "Homousian" formula from the Nicene Council of 325 had decreed.

This debate was very important for subsequent Gothic history. Ulfilas, the apostle to the Goths, and his disciples doubtless worked tirelessly among them teaching an Arian gospel. Further, his Gothic Bible was influential in providing them with a written language and also with access to other writings, many of which would have been Arian in outlook. The Nicene community worked only in Latin and Greek. Some scholars, indeed, have suggested that Ulfilas would have served the Goths better if he had taught his priests Greek or Latin instead of the language of the Goths. Others point out that, given the hostility between Roman and Goth in this period, Latin is not a language the

Goths would have readily learned to read; their own language, though, was another matter.

It has been noted that Ulfilas' version of the Trinity was more compatible with the culture of the Goths than was the Nicene version. It was a society in which hierarchy of social rank was not only very significant but also very much threatened by the influence of Rome. A creed that made a clear subordination of Son to Father and Holy Spirit to both would have been more acceptable than the highly abstract notions of equality and co-eternity of the Nicene Creed. Finally, the centralizing tendencies of the Nicene tradition would have further weakened the traditional structures of Gothic society, making Christianity into a more threatening, less inviting religious creed.

There is a certain amount of conjecture in all these arguments. However, it is certain that in 376, when the remaining Goths crossed the Danube seeking the safety of the Empire, they embraced Arian Christianity, which they retained until their disappearance as independent successor states during the Gothic Wars of the Emperor Justinian in the sixth century.

Near the end of Ulfilas' life, the Nicene faction regained control of the imperial court, and the Arians found their position under attack. In 380, the Emperor Theodosius convened a synod at Constantinople, ostensibly to deal with the matter. Ulfilas was among those summoned; that he was personally summoned by the Emperor attests to his continuing importance among the Arian bishops of the era. In any event, he went and even testified; before the council completed its work, however, he died, in either 382 or 383.

Summary

Ulfilas' position was ultimately rejected at the Synod of Constantinople, which, following the Second Ecumenical Council, condemned Arianism. Yet the Goths did gain the recognition that, in their churches at least, the people would be governed in accordance with the manner of their forebears. In effect, Goths would be free to pursue their own beliefs. In this way, an opportunity was created for Arianism to spread. In the decades following 395, when large numbers of Huns crossed the Danube into the Empire, Ulfilas' Arian Gauls with their Gothic Bibles were prepared to convert the Gothic newcomers, who now included not only the few remaining Visigoths but the Ostrogoths, Vandals, and Gepids as well. Arianism would be a force to be reckoned with for centuries to come.

Finally, Ulfilas translation of the Bible has been of inestimable value to scholars interested in the languages and practices of the Gothic peoples of the late Empire. By comparing the Gothic words Ulfilas used to translate the biblical text, it is possible to gain insights into the social, political, and theological ideas of the Goths. Scholars frequently refer to Gothic words gleaned from the *Codex Argenteus* when describing the cultural and social structure of the early Goths. Without Ulfilas' work, scholars would know far less about them.

Ulfilas was on the losing side of the Trinitarian argument, and almost all that he himself wrote was destroyed. Yet he helped to make possible the first step in the absorption of the Gothic peoples into the West; moreover, through his translation of the Bible, he provided modern scholars with invaluable insights into the lives of peoples who, though long vanished as political and ethnic communities, continue to survive in their descendants among the populations of Southern France, Spain, and Italy.

Bibliography

Böhmer, H. "Ulfilas." In vol. 12 of *The New Schaff-Herzog Encyclopedia of Religious Knowledge*. Grand Rapids, Mich.: Baker, 1949. A lengthy article on Ulfilas as well as a helpful bibliography. A useful source helpful in organizing the major events of Ulfilas' life.

Bradley, Henry. *The Story of the Goths*. New York and London: Putnam, 1888. Although dated in some respects, still useful for its discussion of Ulfilas' Gothic alphabet and his biblical translation.

The Nicene and Post-Nicene Fathers. Second Series, vols. 2 and 3. Boston: Christian Literature, 1890. An English source for the works of Greek Church historians of Ulfilas and the Trinitarian controversy; however, they are all partisans of the Nicene position. Available in most college libraries.

Scott, Charles A. Anderson. *Ulfilas, Apostle of the Goths*. Cambridge: Macmillan and Bowes, 1885. An older work that seeks to do justice to the Arian Goths at the hands of earlier partisan Nicene Christian writers. The author presents Ulfilas as a "monument to the Goths." Checked against more recent sources, it is still quite valuable.

Thompson, E. A. *Romans and Barbarians: The Decline of the Western Empire*. Madison: University of Wisconsin Press, 1982. Presents the story of the end of the Western Roman Empire from the vantage point of the Goths. While the work contains little information on Ulfilas, it provides valuable insights into the culture of his people.

Thompson, E. A. *The Visigoths in the Time of Ulfila*. Oxford: Clarendon Press, 1966. As much about the Visigoths as Ulfilas, this work provides valuable insights into the working of Visigothic society. Helps explain Ulfilas' work and significance among the Visigoths.

Wolfram, Herwig. *History of the Goths*. Berkeley and London: University of California Press, 1988. A comparatively recent source on Ulfilas and his place in Gothic history; also the most complete work on the Goths as a whole. Covers all the Gothic peoples from their shadowy beginnings to their catastrophic end in the sixth century Gothic Wars.

Terry R. Morris

Born: Probably early second century; Lower Egypt
Died: c. 165; Cyprus or Rome
Areas of Achievement: Religion and philosophy
Contribution: A second century religious genius, Valentinus synthesized concepts drawn from such disparate sources as Christian theology, rabbinic mysticism, Neopythagoreanism, Neoplatonism, Hellenistic mystery religions, and theosophy into an elaborate system of Gnostic thought that attracted large numbers of converts in the patristic period. His influence was so great that the patristic heresiologists singled him out as one of the most formidable enemies of orthodox Christianity.

Early Life

Very little is known of Valentinus' early life, except that he probably was born in Lower Egypt and obtained a Greek education in Alexandria. During his stay in Alexandria, he became a Christian; according to Irenaeus and others, he was taught by Theodas, one of the Apostle Paul's students.

Some authors have suggested that Gnosticism influenced Valentinus even during these early days in Alexandria and that Theodas himself may have preached a Christian gnosis. The Gnostic stress on salvation through a secret gnosis, or transcendental knowledge, must have appealed to Valentinus, whose teachings, to the extent that they can be reconstructed from the scattered information found in writings of the church fathers who came to oppose him (and perhaps also from the Nag Hammadi papyruses), reflect an exceptionally creative mind with a strong aesthetic bent.

Life's Work

Valentinus apparently taught in Alexandria before going to Rome during the bishopric of Hyginus (c. 136-c. 140). Tertullian states that Valentinus himself almost became Bishop of Rome but withdrew in favor of a man who was later martyred (probably Pius I). In fact, Valentinus also withdrew from the Christian community, for he had become a Gnostic; soon, the Church branded him a heretic. Subsequently, Valentinus gained a considerable following—he probably established his own school—and he remained in Rome for another twenty years, after which he may have gone to Cyprus; it is possible that he stayed in Rome until his death after 160.

Valentinus' move into Gnosticism may have been the result of a desire to go beyond the exclusivist teachings of Christianity and to integrate Jesus Christ's teachings with contemporary Hellenistic philosophies. Valentinus' teaching was done in the form of sermons, hymns, and psalms, as well as more formally through writing and lecturing.

Valentinian Gnosticism evolved so rapidly that it is difficult to disentangle the original Valentinian teachings from those of his disciples. Still, the Nag Hammadi works, combined with the heresiologies of the patristic writers, make it possible to describe the outlines of the Valentinian system.

As its core, it had a mythical cosmogony, offered as an explanation of the human predicament. This cosmogony was structured around "aeons": Everything that exists is an emanation of a perfect, primordially existent aeon, which is the origin and source of being for all subsequent aeons. The term "aeon" in the Valentinian system suggests eternal existence (*aei on*, "always being"). This means that in terms of temporal sequence there is no difference between the One and its progeny. The differ-

ence between them is, instead, ontological: All subsequent aeons are less perfect outpourings of the One's substance. The One is also called Proarche (First Principle), Propator (Forefather), and Buthos (Primeval Depth). The One is beyond conceptualization and is the storehouse of all perfections. In Buthos there is no difference of gender; it contains all the qualities of masculinity and femininity without distinction.

According to its inscrutable purpose, Buthos brings into being a sequence of secondary aeons. Unlike Buthos, this chain of beings is differentiated into gender pairs, or syzygies, arranged according to ontological perfection (relative perfection of being). Of these fifteen pairs, which together constitute the Pleroma (Fullness or Completion), only the first four and the last have significance in the Valentinian exposition of the ontological corruption of the universe.

The first syzygy is somewhat problematic, since Buthos transcends the qualities of masculinity and femininity yet is paired with Sige (Silence). From this first syzygy emanate Nous (Understanding) and Aletheia (Truth). From their union are produced Logos (Word) and Zoe (Life), and from the union of Logos and Zoe are produced Anthropos (Man) and Ekklesia (Church). Together, these four pairs (or two tetrads) form the Ogdoad (the Eight), from which issue the remaining eleven syzygies and, indeed, all the rest of reality.

According to the Valentinians, disharmony was introduced into reality in the following way. Of all the aeons, it was Nous who was best proportioned to understand the One and who took the greatest pleasure in this contemplation. Nous, in the abundance of his generosity, wished to share his knowledge with the other aeons, and the aeons themselves demonstrated a willingness to seek out and become more directly acquainted with the primacy and fullness of the One. Yet Nous was restrained from prematurely sharing this knowledge, for it was the desire of Buthos to lead the aeons to this awareness gradually, through steady application which might prove their worthiness. Buthos also was aware that the aeons had different capacities and therefore would have to be brought to this knowledge at different rates. The knowledge of Buthos' purpose was passed down through the successive aeons, and all except the malcontent Sophia (Wisdom) acceded to his will.

Sophia's desire could not be satisfied by either her station or her mate, Theletos (Will). She craved knowledge beyond her capacity: She wanted to comprehend the perfect wisdom of the Forefather. In her desire to grasp supernatural perfection, Sophia abandoned her station and stretched herself heavenward, nearly losing her distinctive character by being reabsorbed into the plentitude of the One, against its will. Alarmed by the hubris of Sophia, Buthos, in conjunction with Nous, generated Horos, the principle of limitation, who is also called Savior, One-Who-Imposes-Limitation, One-Who-Brings-Back-After-Conflict, and Cross. Horos was generated by Buthos for the purpose of restraining Sophia and stripping her of her presumptuousness. This was accomplished when Horos separated her from her passion and *enthumesis* (esteem, glory) and rejoined the purged Sophia to Theletos, while casting her passion in the abyss outside the Pleroma.

After the rebelliousness of Sophia was cast out, Buthos and Nous gave rise to another syzygy designed to perfect and strengthen the Pleroma. This syzygy is that of Christ and the Holy Spirit. Christ was sent to the aeons as a teacher to instruct them in the purpose of Buthos, leading them to be satisfied with the knowledge they possess by convincing them that only Nous can comprehend the One in its perfection. The aeon Christ thus was sent as a mediator of consoling knowledge concerning their stations and purpose. The Holy Spirit's function was to lead the aeons to give thanks for the knowledge revealed by Christ. Through contrition and thankfulness they were all brought into harmony.

The work of Christ, however, was not yet complete. The *enthumesis* and passion of Sophia had been banished from the Pleroma to smolder, a chaotic, self-consuming power without form and without purpose. The aeon Christ, seeing her state, did not forsake her but instead took pity on her. He extended himself beyond the limit of the Pleroma and imposed a substantial form upon her, to give her a definite nature; he withdrew, however, before providing transcendental wisdom. The dim reflection of Sophia was thus given character and definition as Achamoth (Hebrew for "wisdom"). The form Christ provided resulted in a regretful awareness of Achamoth's severance from the Pleroma and made her aspire to immortality with her limited intelligence. From the confusion of passions that boiled in Achamoth, the matter of the world issued, and from the desire to return to unity with the One, all souls (including that of the Demiurge) sprang into being.

From her own psychic substance, Achamoth formed the Demiurge, but she concealed herself from him. The Demiurge, not recognizing another greater than himself, deluded himself into believing that he was the only creator god, and he immediately began to make corporeal substances and to populate the realm below Horos with all manner of things. It is he who is responsible for the creation of the seven heavens and everything in or under them. All the while he was creating, however, he was unaware that Achamoth was working through him and was adding spiritual substances to the psychic beings (animals) he created. Humans are therefore composites of matter, psyche, and spirit, although the Demiurge is ignorant of their spiritual dimension.

Achamoth, feeling pity and responsibility for the spiritual beings she had generated, decided to bring them to knowledge of the aeons. To give this knowledge to the Demiurge and his creation, she imitated the production of the Christ aeon and contributed a spiritual substance to a body prepared by the Demiurge in ignorance. The resulting composite being was Jesus the Savior. Jesus' mission thus was primarily a ministry of teaching; his mission was to teach the gnosis of the aeonic hierarchy. His mission will be accomplished when all worthy creations below the Pleroma are brought to perfection in knowledge. Then Achamoth and her perfected children will ascend to places above the Horos. The Demiurge will ascend to the eighth heaven along with those beings of a purely psychic nature, and the purely corporeal humans will be consumed in a final conflagration.

From complicated cosmological speculations such as these, the Valentinians wove a fabric of doctrines that resembled Christianity but that were, in every instance, of a much higher speculative order. Like the traditional Christians, the Valentinians had a distinctive Christology. Whereas the former emphasized the sacrificial death of Jesus as the means of remission of sins, the Valentinians thought that the spirit of Jesus ascended before he could suffer, a belief consistent with their understanding of his aeonic mission of teaching.

Anthropologically, traditional Christianity interpreted all humans as being equally capable of finding salvation in Jesus, since he had died for all. The Valentinians, however, worked out a doctrine of election that in some ways anticipated Calvinist teachings. They believed that the salvation of a given individual depended upon whether Achamoth had implanted a bit of spiritual substance, a seed of light, in that individual. Those who are spiritual have the potential (if not certainty) of achieving gnosis and thus being raptured and carried aloft to the Pleroma. The best that other humans may hope for is either a place in the eighth heaven or to be burned as garbage at the end of time.

Ecclesiologically, Valentinians construed the body of Gnostics on earth as a dim reflection of the aeon Ekklesia. Basing their speculation upon certain passages in Saint Paul and upon obscure rabbinic doctrines, they saw the syzygy of Anthropos and Ekklesia as the Platonic archetype of the relationship which eventually will exist between Achamoth and the pneumatics. In the final rapture, Achamoth will be conjoined to her seeds of light in the nuptial chamber of the Pleroma. At that point, symmetry will be restored to the chain of aeons and the universe will exist in harmony, with the lower syzygies mirroring their higher paradigms and beings of all levels finding perfect satisfaction.

On the basis of this rich and intricate mythology and its resultant theology, the Valentinians taught a form of Christian theosophy which gained large numbers of converts in the second and third centuries. Of all the forms of Gnosticism it attracted the most followers. How such a complicated and seemingly arbitrary religious cosmology could have inspired droves to seek this brand of salvation is puzzling, but there are a few features which likely made it attractive.

First, it offered a kind of salvation that placed a premium upon knowledge and de-emphasized the moral rigor that was typical of the Christianity of the period. This, no doubt, appealed to the classes that Gnosticism attracted: the plebeians and the intellectual elite, who had no strong political or religious alliances but rather identified with their plebeian followers.

Second, although the Valentinians shunned the sacramentalism of many of the other Christian sects, they apparently practiced rituals of purification and made use of hymns and prayers, all of which were designed to culminate in a powerful ecstatic experience in which the individual would achieve spiritual intercourse with Achamoth in her nuptial chamber. In this way, Valentinian Gnosticism offered an experience which at least rivaled the charismatic experiences of the more traditional Christian groups.

Finally, a large part of the appeal of Valentinian theosophy was that it was continuous with other religious phenomena of the time. In that turbulent period when religious curiosity ran rampant and when contact with magicians, astrologers, and itinerant preachers of wisdom was the norm, Valentinian theosophy offered a model of the universe which allowed for the retention of a magical worldview. Unlike traditional Christianity, which was extremely strict in its rejection of alien gods and magic, the Valentinian system was syncretistic. It allowed its adepts to move freely between its sphere of concepts and other systems of theosophy and magic.

Summary

Valentinus had a very large following and probably was the most influential of the Gnostics. There is no doubt that his teaching affected orthodox Christianity. Many Christian theologians were forced to sharpen their rhetorical and theological skills as they undertook to refute the Valentinians, and, as they engaged in this dialogue, they began to formulate explicit orthodox Christian doctrines and creeds. Valentinus, as a representative of Gnosticism, spurred Christians toward the establishment of a canon of inspired Scriptures so that they might be able to avoid syncretism and heresy.

Valentinus was very much a man of the second century in his tendency toward religious syncretism, evidenced by his application of Neoplatonic and Neopythagorean concepts to Christian theology. Thus, Valentinus' thought was a representative form of the prototheology which developed dialectically in the early Christian milieu.

Bibliography

Dawson, David. *Allegorical Readers and Cultural Revision in Ancient Alexandria.* Berkeley: University of California Press, 1992. In his study of allegorical exegesis, Dawson demonstrates how the practice of allegory is purposefully engaged to challenge competing world views and ways of life. He discusses the mystical, visionary language of Valentinus in the second century as well as Valentinus's orthodox critic, Clement of Alexandria, in the next generation.

Jonas, Hans. *The Gnostic Religion: The Message of the Alien God and the Beginnings of Christianity.* 2d ed. Boston: Beacon Press, 1963. A classic (although somewhat dated) and thorough introduction to the nature of Gnosticism. Useful because it describes the Gnostic categories and discusses various Gnostic systems. Shows how Gnosticism is both an interruption and a continuation of classic Greek thought. Chapter 5 constitutes a helpful treatment of Valentinus' system. Thorough, multilanguage bibliography.

Lacarrière, Jacques. *The Gnostics.* London: Owen, and New York: E. P. Dutton, 1977. Phenomeno-logical treatment of Gnosticism, but only partly successful since the author regards Gnostics as Promethean heroes rebelling against established religion, and his bias is evident throughout. Valuable as a lively interpretation of the Gnostic mind-set. Chapter 6 deals with Valentinus in some detail. Contains a somewhat quirky bibliography.

Pagels, Elaine. *The Gnostic Gospels.* New York: Random House, 1979; London: Weidenfeld and Nicolson, 1980. Popular treatment, readable and interesting, but unsystematic. The feminist views of the author are evident. Tends to discuss the individualism of Gnostics in a manner inappropriate to the period and to impose twentieth century values on the second century. Valentinus is treated throughout rather than in a separate chapter. No bibliography.

Perkins, Pheme. *The Gnostic Dialogue.* New York: Paulist Press, 1980. In part a response and corrective to some extremes in Pagels' work, this is a scholarly attempt to contextualize Gnosticism in setting of particular scriptural traditions, with research based on texts. Investigates Gnosticism in dialogue with Christianity and other religions. Valentinus is treated throughout. Good selected multilanguage bibliography; especially helpful are the references to the Nag Hammadi, the New Testament, and patristic sources.

Robinson, James M., ed. *The Nag Hammadi Library.* 3d ed. New York: Brill, 1988. The single most revealing collection of Gnostic scriptures available in English translation. Particularly useful because it contains fragments of second century treatises of probable or certain Gnostic origin such as the *Gospel of Truth*, the *Treatise on Resurrection*, the *Tripartite Tractate*, the *Apocalypse of Paul, A Valentinian Exposition, On the Anointing, On Baptism*, and *On the Eucharist.*

Rudolph, Kurt. *Gnosis: The Nature and History of Gnosticism.* San Francisco: Harper and Row, 1983. A comprehensive treatment by a specialist in Mandaean religion. Valentinus is cited frequently throughout, and the treatment of the Valentinian system is extensive. Extremely sensitive to all sources in all their complexity, though some Marxist bias is evident. Illustrations, photographs, maps, chronological table, and a multilanguage bibliography of original texts and secondary sources.

Thomas Ryba
Ruth van der Maas

VARDHAMĀNA

Born: c. 599 B.C.; Kundagrama, Bihar, India
Died: 527 B.C.; Papa, Bihar, India
Areas of Achievement: Religion and monasticism
Contribution: By the example of his ascetic life and his charismatic leadership, Vardhamana revived and systematized the religious tradition of Jainism.

Early Life

While the two sects of the Jains (Digambara and Svetambara) have differing traditions regarding the life of Vardhamāna, they are in agreement on the most essential features. Vardhamāna was born to Siddhartha, chieftain of a warrior (*ksatriya*) clan, whose wife Trisala was the sister of the king of Vaisali. Vardhamāna's conception was foretold to his mother in a series of dreams which are often described in Jain literature and represented artistically. About his youth virtually nothing is recorded, but probably he was trained in archery, horsemanship, and writing, as were other princes of his era. The two Jain sects disagree regarding one point concerning his adult life, the Svetambaras saying that Vardhamāna married and fathered one daughter, while the Digambaras say that he neither married nor had offspring.

By the age of thirty, Vardhamāna's parents had died. With the consent of his elder brother, he decided to abandon his royal position and become a wandering ascetic. He distributed his possessions, plucked out his hair, and renounced the life of the householder to pursue enlightenment. The most significant disagreement between the two sects of Jainism is highlighted by this incident in Vardhamāna's life, known as the Great Renunciation. Digambara ("sky-clad") Jains depict Vardhamāna as renouncing clothing as well as other possessions, choosing to remain nude and requiring this practice of his followers when they renounced the world. Svetambara ("white-clad") Jains depict Vardhamāna as wearing a single white cloth for thirteen months after the Great Renunciation, at which time he adopted nudity but did not require it of his followers after their renunciation. This difference in monastic practice has kept the two sects separate since about 300 B.C.

Life's Work

In the era in which Vardhamāna lived, dissatisfaction was growing with the then dominant religious tradition of Brahmanism, which was based on performance of sacrificial rituals and recitation of the sacred words of the Vedas. Asceticism—including endurance of hunger, thirst, pain, exposure to the elements, and celibacy—was an alternative way of being religious, by means of which individuals sought to accumulate power. It was widely believed that the actions (Karma) of one's life would cause one to be reincarnated but that the power accumulated through asceticism could enable one to destroy one's Karma and escape the otherwise endless cycle of rebirth.

Like a number of his contemporaries (such as the Buddha and ascetics of the Brahmanic Upanishads), Vardhamāna left his family to live as a homeless wanderer in the hope of escaping rebirth. For twelve years, subjecting himself to great hardship, including extended fasts, and engaged in deep meditation on the nature of the self, Vardhamāna single-mindedly persevered. Finally, after a fast of two and a half days during which he meditated continuously, he attained enlightenment accompanied by omniscience and was freed from the bondage of his Karma. According to the scriptures, following his enlightenment Vardhamāna taught large assemblies of listeners and organized the community of monks, nuns, laymen, and laywomen. He was acclaimed as Mahāvīra (Great Hero), a title by which he is best known.

Vardhamāna Mahāvīra taught others the means of attaining what he had attained. The ultimate objective was and is escape from the cycle of rebirth, with its suffering a result of the inevitability of disease, old age, and death. The infinite bliss of the cessation of such suffering was not to be attained by following the path of enjoyment of pleasures but by forsaking the finite pleasures and performing rigorous austerities. Restraint of body, speech, and mind and the performance of ascetic practices will destroy the effects of one's Karma, thereby freeing one from rebirth.

In Vardhamāna's view, Karma is a material substance which becomes attached to one's soul as a result of actions performed; Jainism is unique in its assertion of the material nature of Karma. The souls of individuals who are subject to the passions (desire and hatred) will be further defiled by the adherence of Karmic material, while the souls of those few individuals who are free from the passions will not be affected at all; Karma will not adhere to such a soul.

Absolutely necessary to the successful escape from rebirth is the avoidance of causing injury to living beings, a practice known as *ahimsa*. As a consequence of this strongly held belief, Jains are strict vegetarians. For the same reason, they have traditionally avoided occupations involving injury to living beings, including farming, and have instead often engaged in commerce. Avoidance of injury to life in all of its forms is the first vow of the Jains, ascetics and lay followers alike.

The path of the devout layman or laywoman differs from that of the monk or nun only in the extent to which ascetic self-denial is practiced. For the lay follower, eleven stages of spiritual progress are prescribed by which one is purified and prepares oneself for the ascetic life of the monk or nun. By passing through all eleven stages, the lay follower demonstrates that he or she has overcome the passions and is ready to become a monk or nun. As a result of the severity of the rules of conduct for the Jain lay follower, relatively few individuals in reality are willing or able to adhere to this ideal. Most lay followers support the monks and nuns through donations.

All Jains regard Vardhamāna Mahāvīra as the twenty-fourth and last Jina (Conqueror) or Tirthamkara (Crossing-Maker) to have lived and taught in this world. His immediate predecessor, Parsva, apparently lived in Benares, India, in the ninth century B.C.; Western scholars, however, regard the other twenty-two saintly teachers in the Jain tradition as figures of myth rather than history. The parents of Vardhamāna are described as followers of Parsva's doctrine, and there are clear references in Buddhist scriptures to the existence of an established order of Jain ascetics. This information suggests the existence of a Jain community composed of ascetics and lay followers, a community older than that of the Buddhists and predating Vardhamāna himself. Vardhamāna's teachings are presented as eternal truths and the same path as has been taught by all the Jinas. Thus, Vardhamāna's contribution was the reviving and reactualization of this ancient tradition. As one who has "crossed over" the ocean of suffering and reached the other side, Vardhamāna has demonstrated the efficacy of the spiritual discipline of the Jinas.

At the age of seventy-two, Vardhamāna died, passing into the eternal peace of Nirvana. Although the Jain scriptures repeatedly state that the Jina was a human being, lay followers often have regarded him as superhuman and endowed with marvelous attributes. The exemplary life of Vardhamāna Mahāvīra has greatly influenced the Jain community, which continues to revere his memory.

Summary

Vardhamāna Mahāvīra was both a very able organizer and a thinker of striking originality. The social organization of Jain monks and nuns may well have been the world's first monastic orders. Thanks to the support of some Indian rulers and sympathetic lay followers, the monastic orders have been able to follow the example of Vardhamāna Mahāvīra for twenty-five centuries. Vardhamāna was one of the first to oppose the Brahmanic orthodoxy, a tradition of sacrificial ritual which was dominated by priests and aristocrats. In its place he offered a systematic explanation of the laws of the universe and humanity's place within it. Vardhamāna's teachings presented to everyone the possibility of attaining the ultimate state, whether female or male, regardless of social class.

The Jain insistence on *ahimsa*, refraining from injuring living beings, has influenced the whole of India and even some who are unfamiliar with Jainism. Vegetarianism, uncommon in India during Vardhamāna's lifetime, is now a way of life for many Hindus, and Jainism's uncompromising position is in part responsible for this change. The leader of India's independence movement in the first half of the twentieth century, Mahatma Gandhi, was profoundly influenced by a Jain layman named Raychandbhai Mehta, with whom he corresponded. He helped Gandhi realize the power of nonviolence, and Gandhi began to use nonviolent civil disobedience as a political weapon, agitating for India's independence from the British Empire. A generation later, Martin Luther King, Jr., with Gandhi as his inspiration, led similar nonviolent protests for civil rights in the United States. Vardhamāna's teachings, whether regarded as the ancient doctrine of all the Jinas or as his own unique contribution, are the core of a still-vital religious tradition.

Bibliography

Bhavadevasuri. *The Life and Stories of the Jaina Savior Parsvanatha*. Maurice Bloomfield, ed. Baltimore: Johns Hopkins University Press,

1919. An excellent collection of mythic and historical data on the predecessor of Vardhamāna within the Jain tradition and its probable founder in the ninth century B.C.

Jacobi, Hermann, trans. *Sacred Books of the East.* Vols. 22 and 44, *Jaina Sutras*, parts 1 and 2. Oxford: Clarendon, 1884, 1895; New York: Scribner, 1901. A fine translation of selected scriptures of the Jain religious tradition, with an introduction by the translator which includes a brief treatment of the life of Vardhamāna. Volume 22 in the series contains Jain scriptures on the life of Vardhamāna, and volume 44 contains his teachings.

Jaini, Padmanabh S. *The Jaina Path of Purification.* Berkeley: University of California Press, 1979. An excellent treatment of the Jain religious tradition, both ancient and modern, including the life of Vardhamāna. Includes an extensive bibliography, illustrations, and thirty-two photographs.

Law, Bimala C. *Mahāvīra: His Life and Teachings.* London: Luzac and Co., 1937. A brief work with a wealth of references to Jain scriptures and other Indian literature, documenting the exemplary life and influential ideas of Vardhamāna Mahāvīra.

Schubring, Walther. *The Doctrine of the Jainas, Described After the Old Sources.* Translated by Wolfgang Beurlen. Delhi: Motilal Banarsidass, 1962. A clear and concise presentation of Vardhamāna's teachings and the subsequent Jain scholastic traditions on cosmology, ethics, rebirth, and related topics.

Williams, Robert H. B. *Jaina Yoga: A Survey of the Mediaeval Sravakacaras.* London and New York: Oxford University Press, 1963. This work presents the teachings of Jainism for lay followers, as found in the numerous texts specifically written as guides for laymen. The strict code of conduct reveals that Jainism's ascetic orientation applies even to the lay follower.

Bruce M. Sullivan

MARCUS TERENTIUS VARRO

Born: 116 B.C.; Reate
Died: 27 B.C.; Rome
Area of Achievement: Scholarship
Contribution: Varro contributed to every field of abstract and practical knowledge extant in his day, established the worthiness of intellectual pursuits such as linguistic study and encyclopedism, and left a body of knowledge that, directly or indirectly, has informed and influenced writers and scholars ever since.

Early Life

Marcus Terentius Varro was sometimes called Marcus Terentius Varro Reatinus because he was born in Reate, in the Sabine region of modern Italy. His family, which owned vast estates there, was considered to be of equestrian, or knightly, rank, although certain ancestors had attained noble rank by holding office in the senate. Varro's parents had the means to obtain for him the best education available at the time. This included a long sojourn in the capital, where he studied under the Stoic Stilo Praeconinus (who taught Cicero ten years later), and afterward a period in Athens during which he studied philosophy with Antiochus of Ascalon, the Academic. Stilo Praeconinus, the first Roman grammarian and philologist, was also a learned historian of Roman antiquity, and under his tutelage Varro soon showed an extraordinary aptitude for these pursuits.

Life's Work

As a gifted scholar, Varro could have kept himself apart from public life had he so chosen. Until he was nearly seventy, however, he remained deeply involved in both politics and the military. To people of his own era, this was not contradictory, for few of Varro's contemporaries were inclined to draw a strict boundary between intellectual and public life. Julius Caesar, during his march through the Alps to Gaul, composed a treatise on Latin grammatical inflections which he dedicated to Cicero. Indeed, political leaders such as Cicero and Caesar spent many adult years studying philosophy and ancient history, trying to draw lessons that would help them govern justly and wisely.

Varro's political and military career was closely allied with that of Pompey the Great. In 76, he served under Pompey in a military campaign against the rebel Quintus Sertorius in Spain. Afterward, Varro entered public office, serving first as tribune (a magistrate of the people with veto power over senate actions), then as curule aedile (roughly, superintendent of public works), and finally as praetor, or judicial officer. In 67, he held a naval command under Pompey in the war against the Cilician pirates, who, for a time, had virtually controlled the Mediterranean. From 66 to 63, Varro served, again under Pompey, in the third war against Mithradates the Great, King of Pontus. From 52 to 48, during the civil war between Pompey and Caesar, Varro commanded two legions for Pompey in Spain. On August 2, 48, two other Pompeian commanders in Spain capitulated to Caesar, and Varro, probably under pressure from his soldiers, was forced to follow suit. Afterward, like Cicero and Cato the Younger, he went to Dyrrachium, a sort of neutral corner, to await the outcome of the Battle of Pharsalus, which decided the entire conflict in Caesar's favor.

Varro and Caesar had remained on friendly terms during even the bitterest conflict between Caesar and Pompey. In 48, Pompey was murdered by agents of the Egyptian king, and the following year the victorious Caesar pardoned Varro and restored to him lands that had been seized by Marc Antony. Caesar also appointed Varro head of the great public library that was then being planned. Thus began the period of the works and accomplishments for which Varro is best remembered and which earned for him the title (bestowed by Quintilian in the first century A.D.) of "the most learned of Romans."

A profile of Varro, bearded and wearing a woolen, Greek-style cap, appears on an ancient coin now housed in the Museo Nazionale Romano. Most Roman men did not grow beards, although Greek men did, and Varro may have worn one along with the cap as a sign of his intellectual vocation, which was commonly associated with Greece rather than with Rome. Alternatively, regardless of Varro's actual appearance, the designer of the coin may have simply portrayed him in this fashion for symbolic purposes.

Varro is remembered, among many other reasons, for compiling in Rome what was to be the first library for public use. He concentrated on three types of prose works: the writings of the antiquarians, treatises by grammarians and philologists (by this time Stilo Praeconinus' new disciplines had come into their own), and works on practical subjects such as husbandry and domestic economy. His collection served as a kind of stylistic barometer for the times: The Ciceronian style dominated the prose of theoretical works, especially in philosophy, rhetoric, and history, while the sparser, more direct expression of Cato the Censor set the standard for practical treatises. In addition to Latin works in these genres, Varro acquired for his collection many volumes in Greek.

Although he seems generally to have ignored poetry (which was then in temporary eclipse), he is credited with establishing the canon of dramatic verse certifiably written by Plautus—some twenty-one plays, constituting what is called the *Fabulae Varronianae*—and, according to Aulus Gellius, Varro also wrote literary and dramatic criticism of Plautus.

Varro's unprecedented collection of books for public use proved of enormous benefit to contemporary scholars. As Rome passed from a republican to an imperial form of government, interest in Roman antiquity grew rapidly, and there developed a new fraternity of researchers and historians who made whatever use they could of the early records and works by the pioneering annalists of Rome. Yet before the formation of Varro's public library—as in Great Britain and the United States at comparable periods of their development—a literary worker had to depend upon the generosity of private library owners for a look at such rare works and records.

Though he now was devoted to the pursuits of scholarship and librarianship that were his forte, Varro had one remaining practical challenge to face. In 47, nearly seventy years old, he had retired altogether from political life when he accepted Caesar's appointment as librarian. Nevertheless, after Caesar was assassinated in 44 and Octavian, Marc Antony, and Marcus Aemilius Lepidus formed the Second Triumvirate, Antony declared Varro an enemy of the state and had him proscribed, that is, banished from the vicinity of Rome. Varro's home near the capital was destroyed, as was his private library, containing not only thousands of works by other writers but also many of the hundreds of volumes he himself had written up to his seventy-third year, when he was banished. If not for the proscription, with its destructive aftermath—an all-too-common occurrence in that period of Roman history—more

might be known about the exact contents of the famous public library, for which Varro probably had earmarked many volumes in his private collection. Undoubtedly, too, many more of Varro's own works would have survived down to the present day.

Indeed, Varro nearly lost his life during Antony's proscription—the same proscription that actually did lead to the death of Cicero in 43 B.C. Yet with the help of friends, led by Quintus Fufius Calenus, Varro received a pardon from Octavian and spent the rest of his days peacefully in Rome.

The vigorous, hardworking old man now turned most of his energies to his own writing. Varro claimed to have composed, over his entire career, seventy-four works comprising more than six hundred volumes. This assertion is supported by commentators such as Aulus Gellius, Macrobius, and Nonius Marcellus, who all lived and worked within a few centuries after Varro. His work spanned virtually all areas of learning and all genres of writing then known to Rome: poetry, philosophy, history, literary criticism, grammar, philology, science and mathematics, practical handbooks, and the like. Among his lost books are a work on geometry, one on mensuration, and a nine-volume encyclopedia that helped form the basis for what became the medieval program of education.

On the other hand, what Varro did for his contemporaries, in the way of preserving and concentrating sources for antiquarian research, many later scholars have done for certain of his works. For example, it is thanks in large part to quotations by Nonius Marcellus (fl. fourth century A.D.) that some six hundred lines and ninety titles of Varro's 150 books which form the *Saturae Menippiae* (c. 81-67 B.C.; *Menippean Satires*) are preserved for the twentieth century. (According to Cicero, Varro himself composed much verse, although Varro allowed little room for poetry in his library collection.)

Actually, the satires were an intermixture of prose and verse in the style of Menippus, a Greek Cynic of the third century B.C. The extant titles are greatly varied, some named after gods or persons, some quoting Latin or Greek proverbs—for example, *Nescis quid vesper serus vehat* (You know not what the evening may bring forth) and the famous Socratic dictum "Know thyself." The subject matter also varies: eating and drinking, literature, philosophy, politics, and the "good old days." The general themes are the absurdity of much Greek philosophy and the preoccupation among Romans of Varro's day with luxury and leisure. Varro expressed his disapproval for the First Triumvirate in a satire he called *Trikaranos* (the three-headed).

Modern opinion, based on the surviving fragments, varies as to the literary merit of the *Menippean Satires*. The ancients, however, quoted them so frequently as to make quite evident their popularity with Varro's contemporaries. In addition to his own poetic compositions, Varro wrote several treatises on literature and literary history, including *De poematis* (of poetry), *De compositione saturarum* (on the composition of satire), and *De poetis* (about poets).

He also made many lasting contributions to science and education, chief of which was to introduce the Greek concept of the encyclopedia, meaning "general education," into Roman thought. This he did by way of his now-lost *De forma philosophiae libri III* (on philosophical forms) and *Disciplinarum libri IX* (liberal arts). The latter set forth all the known liberal arts gathered from Greek sources. It was the Greeks who had originally divided the liberal arts into a trivium (grammar, logic, and rhetoric) and a quadrivium (geometry, arithmetic, astronomy, and music), and the *Disciplinarum libri IX* contained a chapter on each, as well as on architecture and medicine. Later scholars removed these last two from the scheme and made them professional studies, retaining the others as the basic program of education in the Middle Ages. Meanwhile, the encyclopedia, incorporating excerpts from and synopses of writings by earlier authors, became a respectable genre among the Romans, particularly in scientific circles. Other scientific contributions included two works on geography, *De ora maritima* (of the seashore) and *De aestuariis* (of estuaries), as well as numerous works on meteorology and almanacs for farmers and sailors.

Varro brought innovation in yet another area: His fifteen-volume *Imagines*, also known as *Hebdomades*, published about 39 B.C., introduced the illustrated biography to Romans. (Crateuas, the physician of Mithradates the Great, had earlier published an illustrated book on plants written in Greek.) Varro's *Imagines* contained brief life histories of seven hundred famous Greeks and Romans, accompanied by a likeness of each. Varro's choice of precisely seven hundred biographies is also interesting: He had a powerful attachment to the number seven, and Aulus Gellius quoted him as saying that the virtues of that number are many and various.

By ancient estimates, Varro's greatest work was one of which no trace now remains: the forty-one volume *Antiquitates rerum humanarum et divinarum libri XLI* (of matters human and divine). Its importance lay in the complete account it gave of Roman political and religious life from the earliest times. Because the book displayed immense knowledge of the Roman past, the church fathers used it as a source of information about official Roman religion. Although this work is lost, much information from it is preserved in Gellius, Servius, Macrobius, and Saint Augustine.

Of those works by Varro that are preserved in the original, one, *De lingua Latina* (*On the Latin Language*), has come down in mutilated form. Only five of its twenty-five volumes survive, and even these are incomplete. Varro composed the work between 47 and 45 and published it before the death of Cicero, to whom it is dedicated. It has value not only as an early study of linguistic origins and development but also as a source of quotations from early Roman poets. Although some of the etymologies are a bit fanciful, many more evince true wit and insight. Perhaps most important, this work is a pioneering systematic treatment—starting with word origins and the evolution of meanings, moving to a defense of etymology as a branch of learning, treating abstract concepts such as ideas of time and the rare and difficult words that poets often use, then introducing the debate over "anomaly" versus "analogy" (a controversy that survives to modern times). Varro's approach, the product of independent thought despite its heavy debt to his teacher Stilo Praeconinus, made the subject worthy of attention from other scholars.

His other surviving work, *De re rustica* (36 B.C.; *On Agriculture*), has come down to the twentieth century almost completely intact. *On Agriculture* is a practical handbook rather than a theoretical treatise; Varro based it on his actual experience of running his family's three Sabine farms, as well as on lore and science drawn from ancient sources.

On Agriculture is important for several reasons: as an instance of the dialogue form, as a revelation of Roman agricultural ideas, as a source for Vergil's *Georgics* (c. 37-29 B.C.), and as a harbinger of at least one discovery of modern science. In this work, Varro cautioned farmers to choose a healthy site for their farmhouse and to avoid building near swamps because, as he wrote, "certain minute animals, invisible to the eye, breed there and, borne by the air, reach inside the body by way of the mouth and nose and cause diseases that are difficult to get rid of." Cicero and his circle, though friendly to Varro, apparently considered this theory of his absurd. Varro was possibly the only Roman who approached the germ theory of disease, which Louis Pasteur would fully develop more than eighteen hundred years later.

Summary

Even the briefest survey of his work reveals how pervasive Marcus Terentius Varro's influence was—not only on his own age but also on posterity. Cicero praised Varro with the words, "When we were foreigners and wanderers—strangers, as it were, in our own land—your books led us home and made it possible for us at length to learn who we were as Romans and where we lived." Through the sheer range of his undertakings, he influenced later authors and scholars as diverse as Vergil, Petronius, Gellius, Augustine, and Boethius.

Despite the enormous scope of his abstract knowledge, Varro was primarily a shrewd, practical thinker, and, because the Roman mind looked for the practical significance of all things intellectual, he attempted to absorb and then pass on to his fellow citizens all that could be learned. So intent was he on transmitting what was knowable that he summarized some of his longer works so that less-educated Romans could comprehend them more easily. In this capacity, he became perhaps the world's first intellectual popularizer.

Bibliography

Duff, J. Wight. *A Literary History of Rome in the Silver Age from Tiberius to Hadrian*. 3d ed. London: Benn, and New York: Barnes and Noble, 1964. Contains a discussion of Varro's place in Roman literature.

———. *Roman Satire: Its Outlook on Social Life*. Berkeley: University of California Press, 1936; Cambridge: Cambridge University Press, 1937. Includes a discussion specifically focusing on Varro's *Menippean Satires*, of which only fragments remain but which is thought by some scholars to have great literary merit.

Skydsgaard, Jens Erik. *Varro the Scholar: Studies in the First Book of Varro's "De re rustica."* Copenhagen, Denmark: Munksgaard, 1968. A lucid discussion of the first part of Varro's *On Agriculture*. Written by a respected scholar.

Stahl, William H. *Roman Science: Origins, Development, and Influence to the Later Middle Ages*. Madison: University of Wisconsin Press, 1962. Includes a discussion of Varro's contributions to agriculture, mathematics, linguistic studies, geography, and encyclopedism.

Varro, Marcus Terentius. *On Agriculture*. Translated by William Davis Hooper and Harrison Boyd Ash. Cambridge, Mass.: Harvard University Press, and London: Heinemann, 1934. Varro's only complete surviving work. Written in dialogue form, with great descriptive and dramatic power. Cato's *De agri cultura* (c. 160 B.C.; *On Agriculture*, 1913) is printed in the same volume.

———. *On the Latin Language*. Translated by Roland G. Kent. 2 vols. Cambridge, Mass.: Harvard University Press, and London: Heinemann, 1938. Contains the surviving fragments of Varro's twenty-five-volume work on the derivation, grammar, and popular usage of the Latin language. With the Latin original opposite each page of translation.

Thomas Rankin

VERCINGETORIX

Born: Probably c. 75 B.C.; central Gaul (modern France)

Died: Possibly c. 46 B.C.; Rome

Areas of Achievement: Diplomacy; government and politics; warfare and conquest

Contribution: As leader of the Arverni, a Celtic tribe in Gaul, Vercingetorix fashioned a coalition of Gallic tribes to expel their Roman conquerors. Although he was captured at his capital of Alesia by Julius Caesar and more than likely executed in Rome, Vercingetorix has long been identified as an early French national hero.

Early Life

The Celts were a nonliterate society prior to the Roman era, so there are no written sources regarding the Roman conquest of Gaul from the Gallic point of view. From the Roman side, Julius Caesar's *De Bello Gallico* (43 B.C., *The Conquest of Gaul*, 1911) is primarily a narration of his successes during his eight-year war against the tribes of Gaul. It is also one of the few surviving written accounts of Celtic political structures and culture. The Gallic Revolt of 52 B.C., which is described in Book 7 of *De Bello Gallico*, provides the only source of information for the life of Vercingetorix. Caesar's work must be considered self-serving, for he was interested only in narrating his interpretation of his victories; moreover, his analysis and descriptions of the Gallic chief are limited to the revolt of 52 B.C..

According to Caesar, Vercingetorix was the son of Celtillus, chief of the Arverni, a Celtic tribe in central Gaul. The father had once claimed over-lordship over the whole of Gaul but had been executed, probably by a conspiracy of his nobles and other Gallic tribal chiefs, for having sought to make himself king. Caesar, then about fifty years old, refers to Vercingetorix as a young man, which would mean that the Gaul was probably about thirty at the time of the revolt. Caesar credited Vercingetorix with numerous talents, including great strength of character, boundless energy, and the ability to lead a fractious society. It is clear from his writing that, of all of his Gallic opponents, Vercingetorix was the leader Caesar respected most.

Other aspects of the early life of Vercingetorix can only be inferred. He was a Gallic Celt of noble birth, and societal traditions would have demanded that he be schooled in the Druidical traditions. Celtic culture placed a premium upon skill in warfare by adult males, and the youth would have been rigorously trained in Celtic battle tactics and weaponry. Celtic oral traditions of the period, which almost always focused upon military virtues such as courage and bravery, were assuredly an integral part of his learning. Additionally, he was clearly an intelligent leader who learned quickly. He had watched and learned from the Roman conquests of Gallic tribes by the Romans, which had been accomplished over a six-year period (58-53 B.C.).

Life's Work

The Gaul into which Vercingetorix had been born was divided into dozens, perhaps hundreds, of tribal groupings of various Celtic peoples. Although Celts spoke similar dialects and shared many cultural traits, they were in no way a unified people. The Druids were especially significant in this society, and it was they who passed on Celtic traditions and beliefs. It was also they who resisted the spread of Roman hegemony in Celtic areas and who orchestrated resistance to Roman conquest. Celtic warriors were fiercely independent and high-spirited, according to Roman accounts. The Romans considered them to be brave but undisciplined warriors who could not, or would not, unite against a common danger.

When Caesar was appointed governor of the province of Cisalpine Gaul, in northwestern Italy, in 59 B.C., it had been at his own request. The Celts of Transalpine Gaul across the Alps had long been viewed as dangerous enemies, and Caesar viewed the position as an opportunity to enhance his military reputation. In 58 B.C., his legions conquered first the Suevi of southeastern Gaul and then the Helvetii, from the area of modern Switzerland, thereby extending Roman influence. He moved northward, down the Rhine River, against the Belgii of northwestern Gaul; then conquered the Veneti of western Gaul, and finally subdued the Aquitani in southwestern Gaul. Celtic Britain was attacked in 55-54 B.C., and his army raided the Germans in 55 and 53 B.C.. Most of 54-53 B.C. was devoted to the brutal suppression of several Celtic uprisings in northern Gaul.

Roman success had been largely the result of to the inability of the Celtic tribes to unite in the face of the Roman danger. Caesar had also avoided cen-

tral Gaul, wherein lay the most formidable of his potential Gallic enemies. Militarily, central Gaul had been isolated and surrounded, a fact not unnoticed by the Gallic tribes there. When the whole of Gaul was treated as if it were a subservient province, it was clear that it was only a matter of time before central Gaul was attacked. During the winter of 53-52 B.C., when it was learned that Caesar had left his army in garrison in north Gaul while he returned to Rome, a coalition of tribes from central Gaul began plotting to expel the Romans. At Cenabum (modern Orleans), Roman officials and traders were slaughtered. The conspiracy turned quickly to the youthful Vercingetorix as commander-in-chief, showing that he was already held in high esteem by his peers. That they turned to the son of the chief who had been killed for having had the same pretensions is clear evidence that the Gallic tribes recognized the Roman threat for what it was.

Vercingetorix swiftly welded a confederacy of Celtic tribes upon whom he could count in the coming war. As commander-in-chief, he demanded and received hostages as pledge of a willingness to fight with him. Allies were given quotas of troops to arm and prepare, and he himself set about extending the alliance to areas already conquered by the Romans. Vercingetorix hoped to smash the Roman presence in Gaul before Caesar could return, and he moved his forces against the Roman legions wintering in northern garrisons. Despite severe weather, and with his path blocked by mountains and deep snow, Caesar effected a crossing into Gaul. His first action was to harry the rebellious tribes of southeastern Gaul, forcing Vercingetorix to move southward to face the threat. Caesar then moved rapidly northward to rejoin his troops.

The war of the next few months was that of parry and thrust. Initially, each side attacked the *oppida*, or hillforts, loyal to the other. Each side also resorted to a scorched-earth policy to deprive the enemy of needed supplies. Vercingetorix besieged Gorgobina (moern St. Parize-le-Chatel), the capital of the pro-Roman Boii; Caesar retaliated by first attacking Vallaunodunum (modern Montargis) and then retaking Cenabum. One of the most brutal battles during this phase was the Roman siege of Avaricum (modern Bourges), during which Vercingetorix attempted and failed to relieve the siege. Caesar claimed to have killed all but eight hundred of the forty thousand inhabitants when he successfully stormed the city, although these numbers are surely inflated. Interestingly, his praise of Verc-

ingetorix following this stunning defeat for the Gauls was high indeed, for he noted that it took a man of great ability to retain, let alone expand, his power after such a disaster.

In the spring of 52 B.C., Caesar moved to attack the *oppidum* of Gergovia (near modern Clermont), which Vercingetorix swiftly moved to protect. The two sides built camps facing each other, with neither willing to force an open battle. The Romans attempted to take the town by storm but failed, a disaster that prompted more Gallic tribes to join the rebellion. Caesar, though, stunned Vercingetorix by leaving the Gauls behind, marching northward towards Lutetia (modern Paris), all the while laying waste to the countryside. Vercingetorix was forced to leave his strong position and to advance against the Roman army. When Caesar moved against him, Vercingetorix attacked the Roman column with his cavalry. In this battle, the Gaulish cavalry, upon which the rebellion had placed much hope, was defeated by the Roman cavalry.

Vercingetorix was forced to withdraw to Alesia, a strong *oppidum* located upon a massif at the confluence of two streams. Although Alesia provided Vercingetorix with an excellent defensive position, he was swiftly besieged by Caesar. Within weeks, the Romans had completed their circumvallation of Alesia, with eight strong camps connected by redoubts and walls. An outer wall was also constructed to protect the Romans from the Gauls who would come to the aid of Vercingetorix. This relieving army, estimated at a hyperbolic 250,000 by Caesar, soon besieged the besiegers. Sadly for Vercingetorix and for Alesia, disunity among the Gallic forces sealed their fate, for attacks on the Roman lines were uncoordinated and failed at great cost. Even when Vercingetorix attacked from the inner side and Vercassivellaunus, a cousin of Vercingetorix, led a simultaneous attack from the outer side, the Roman lines remained unbroken. Realizing the futility of further fighting, the outer host departed; Vercingetorix submitted to Caesar, who took him to Rome and paraded him through the streets on display. According to Dion Cassius, the only extant Roman source to discuss the death of Vercingetorix, the Arverni leader was allowed to live for six more years and then publicly executed as part of a Roman spectacle.

Summary

In life, Vercingetorix warranted little more than a footnote. His entire career spanned less than a year, and his success against the Romans was minimal. He won no major battles, and his capture meant the end of Gallic aspirations of expelling the Romans from Gaul. The greatness of Vercingetorix lay in his ability to form an alliance where one had never existed before. Through force of will and persuasiveness, he manipulated and cajoled many tribes into working together for the common good. Yet he never had the full support of all Gallic tribes, for many remained loyal to the Romans; nor did he have total commitment from his own confederates. Even had he succeeded in defeating the Romans, he would have quickly found his united Gaul to have been a chimera. It should not be considered his fault that other Gallic leaders were not as perceptive as he and that, ultimately, his efforts failed.

His legacy, however, is far greater than that of a failed military leader. Caesar ascribed to him the goal of "freedom of Gaul," an intent Vercingetorix surely promoted but which probably was a cover for his own personal goals. Still, in death, Vercingetorix became a symbol of resistance to foreign aggression and domination. Nineteenth century France rediscovered Vercingetorix and made him into a national hero. Statues were erected, with the portraits stamped upon coins issued during the rebellion providing the image of his face. The lost cause of the Gaul had become the quest for national unity and the ideal state.

Bibliography

Caesar, Julius. *The Battle for Gaul*. Translated by Anne Wiseman and Peter Wiseman. Boston: D. R. Godine, 1980. A newer translation of Caesar's work. The introduction includes perspectival information as well as interpretations based upon recently discovered evidence.

————. *The Conquest of Gaul*. Translated by S. Hartford. London and New York: Penguin Books, 1951. Although there are numerous translations, this version is readily accessible. The introduction serves to place the Gallic War within the dynamics of late republican Rome and of Roman imperial expansion. It also outlines the nature of Gaul and of the Roman army of Caesar.

Holmes, Thomas Rice Edward. *Caesar's Conquest of Gaul*. 2d ed. Oxford: Oxford University Press, and New York: AMS Press, 1911. Holmes is still considered to be one of the finest interpreters of Caesar's military history of the war. Of particular value are his footnotes and references, which clarify and elucidate Caesar's narrative. Holmes also provides information about other Roman sources of the period.

Hignett, Charles. *The Roman Republic, 133-44 B.C.* Vol. 9 in *The Cambridge Ancient History*. Rev. ed. Cambridge and New York: Cambridge University Press, 1951. Hignett outlines the progress of the revolt in Chapter 13, part 6. Caesar is used extensively as the source, but Hignett provides details on geography and modern place names along with interpretations of events.

King, Anthony. *Roman Gaul and Germany*. Berkeley: University of California Press, and London: British Museum, 1990. Although only a small portion of this work deals with Vercingetorix, it places the rebellion of 52 B.C. within the context of the times. The discussion of archaeological work done at Celtic sites in Gaul is most illuminating, for it demonstrates how historical insights can be inferred without written evidence.

William S. Brockington, Jr.

VERGIL

Born: October 15, 70 B.C.; Andes, Cisalpine Gaul
Died: September 21, 19 B.C.; Brundisium
Area of Achievement: Literature
Contribution: Author of an epic poem celebrating the beginnings of the Roman race (the *Aeneid*), pastoral poems (the *Eclogues*), and a poem about the farmer's life (the *Georgics*), Vergil is among the greatest poets of all time.

Early Life

Publius Vergilius Maro (Vergil) was born in Andes, a village near Mantua in Cisalpine Gaul, in 70 B.C., a generation before the death of the Roman Republic. His origins were humble; his father eked out a living by keeping bees on the family's small farm. Though no record of his father's name remains, it is known that his mother's name was Magia Polla. It also seems likely that Vergil received his early education at Cremona and Mediolanum (Milan) and that he received the *toga virilis* (the toga of manhood) in 55 B.C., on his fifteenth birthday. Wearing the *toga virilis* would signify full rights and privileges of citizenship.

Vergil is said to have learned Greek at Neapolis (Naples) from Parthenius, a Bithynian captive brought to Rome during the war with Mithradates the Great. Supposedly, Vergil based one of his own poems, the *Moretum*, on a Greek model by Parthenius. The young poet also received instruction in Epicurean philosophy from Siron and training in rhetoric from Epidius. Most scholars believe that Vergil studied with Epidius at the same time as Octavian, the future emperor Augustus who would later become Vergil's champion and patron. In short, Vergil received a first-rate education in literature, philosophy, and rhetoric, and critics have discerned his broad learning in his *Georgics* (c. 37-29 B.C.), which deals with all elements relating to the farmer's work during the year. There is no indication that Vergil served in the military or engaged in politics. He was probably excused from these duties because of his fragile health and general bookishness.

About the year 45, upon completing his education, Vergil returned to his family's property near Mantua, but in 42, after victory at Philippi, Octavian, in assigning grants of land to his veterans, allowed his aide, Octavius Musa, to determine boundaries of lands assigned in the Cremona district, and Vergil's paternal estate was deeded to a centurion named Arrius. Vergil's influential friends Asinius Pollio and Cornelius Gallus advised Vergil to appeal directly to Octavian; that he did, and the family farm was restored. Vergil would celebrate Octavian's understanding and kindness in this matter in eclogue 1 of the *Eclogues* (43-37 B.C.). Unfortunately, a second attempt to appropriate the family's estate, led by a certain Milienus Toro, was successful several years later. (Vergil was almost killed by a ruffian named Clodius in the violence which ensued.)

Paradoxically, some good came from this sordid affair. Vergil took temporary refuge in a farmhouse owned by a neighbor named Siro but immediately thereafter moved to Rome, where he wrote the two collections of verse which attracted the notice of his first sponsor, Gaius Maecenas. The incident is referred to in section 10 of *Catalepton*, an ancient collection of poetry.

Life's Work

After Vergil's pastorals, the *Eclogues* (sometimes called the *Bucolics* and probably written with the countryside near Tarentum in mind), appeared, Maecenas became interested in Vergil's work. Maecenas led a literary circle, was influential in matters of state, and had the ear of Octavian, soon to be known as Augustus. Although Vergil did not recover his family's farm, Augustus saw to it that he was compensated with another estate, probably the one located near Nola in Campania to which Aulus Gellius refers in *Noctes Atticae* (c. A.D. 143; *Attic Nights*). Vergil also knew the poet Horace well by this time and was instrumental in admitting him to Maecenas' circle and securing a patron for him. Horace mentions his acquaintance with Vergil in the *Satires* (35, 30 B.C.), a description of a journey from Rome to Brundisium.

The *Georgics*, completed when its author had been fully accepted as a member of Maecenas' circle, is clearly the poem of which Vergil was most proud. It appears that he undertook its composition at Maecenas' suggestion and completed it at Naples sometime after the Battle of Actium (31 B.C.). Justifiably, the *Georgics* was compared with the idylls of Theocritus (c. 308-260 B.C.) and the *Works and Days* (c. 700 B.C.) of Hesiod, was found worthy of their Greek predecessors, and catapulted Vergil to prominence.

It is likely that for some time Vergil had considered writing the *Aeneid* (c. 29-19 B.C.), the epic poem for which he is best known. As early as 27, while Augustus was on military campaign in Spain, he wrote to Vergil suggesting composition of an epic which would celebrate Aeneas' founding of a so-called New Troy in Italy and set forth the ancient origins of the Roman people. It is likely that Vergil began the *Aeneid* soon thereafter. Dating composition of specific sections is difficult, but Vergil mentions the death of Marcellus, son of Octavia (the sister of Julius Caesar), in the *Aeneid*. Since it is known that Marcellus died in 23, one can assume that Vergil had outlined the entire poem by this time, the reference appearing almost exactly at the epic's midpoint. Octavia, supposedly present at Vergil's reading of this passage, is said to have fainted upon hearing the poet's allusion to her son as a young man of promise who died too young.

It is known that Vergil met Augustus in Athens late in the year 20. Possibly Vergil had intended to continue his tour of Greece, but his health, never strong, was rapidly declining, so he accompanied Augustus first to Megara, a district between the Corinthian and Saronic gulfs, then to Brundisium, on the tip of the Italian peninsula; he died there, at the age of fifty. His body was brought first to Naples, his summer residence, and supposedly interred in a tomb on a road between Naples and Puteoli (Pozzuoli), where, indeed, a tomb still stands. An epitaph, supposedly dating from Vergil's burial, reads: "Mantua me genuit, Calabri rapuere, tenet nunc Parthenope. Cecini pascua, rura, duces," meaning "Mantua bore me, Calabria ravished me, now Parthenope (the ancient name of Naples after the Siren of that name) holds me. I have nourished flocks, fields, generals." There is no evidence that Vergil himself composed this epitaph or even that it was on his tomb at the time of his death; nevertheless, the inscription is very old and has always been attributed to the poet.

One of the most dramatic events ensuing upon Vergil's death concerns his will. He left half his property to his half brother Valerius Proculus and named Augustus, Maecenas, and his friends Lucius Varius and Plotius Tucca as other legatees. His final request, however, was that Varius and Tucca burn the *Aeneid*, which he did not consider in its finished state. Tradition has it that Augustus himself intervened to save the poem and that it was published with the revisions of Varius and Tucca.

Vergil died a wealthy man, thanks primarily to the generosity of Augustus and Maecenas. His residence on the Esquiline Hill included a garden located next to that of Maecenas. Generous grants from his patrons had enabled Vergil to find the security and leisure he needed for writing his verse and enjoying the friendship of amiable fellow artists, such as Horace. Vergil was also fortunate in finding acceptance for his works, which, even during his lifetime, became an essential part of the school curriculum.

One wonders what this most celebrated of Roman poets might have looked like. Though many ancient renderings of Vergil survive, none dates to his own time and all are idealized. Artists, focusing on the certain frailty of Vergil's health, inevitably portray him as a youthful, frail, and sensitive man with hair covering the ears, longer than the close-cropped imperial style. In Renaissance paintings, he wears fillets or the poet's laurel crown and is often shown declaiming a passage from his works to an appreciative Augustus or Maecenas.

Summary

During his lifetime and even more so after his death, the *Eclogues*, the *Georgics*, and the *Aeneid* became classics, known well by every patriotic Roman. They were memorized, recited, and used for rhetorical training. Soon after Vergil's death, the poet's works were credited with every variety of mystical allusion. The fourth eclogue, for example, was taken as prophecy of the birth of Jesus Christ, though the boy whose birth will signal a new golden age is more likely the emperor Augustus. Others regularly consulted the *Aeneid* and collected its "hidden meanings" as the so-called *Sortes Vergilianae* (Vergilian allotments). This practice began as early as the period immediately after Vergil's death, becoming an obsession in the Middle Ages. The unusual *praenomen* (first name) of Magia Polla, Vergil's mother, implied for many that the poet was a gifted sorcerer as well. The alternate spelling of Vergil's name (Virgil) itself probably derives from the magician's *virga* (wand). That so many were able to see so much beyond the literal in Vergil's poems is testimony to their enduring value as masterpieces.

There is much information on Vergil's life, although much of it is embroidered with legend. Aelius Donatus' fourth century biography, appended to his commentary on Vergil's poems, is the most important ancient source, although it was derived in part from the rather random remarks in the *De viris illustribus* (second century A.D.; on famous men) of Suetonius. Suetonius is said to have derived his information from now-lost accounts by Varius (one of Vergil's literary executors) and from Melissus, a freedman of Maecenas. Other ancient biographies, less reliable, were written by Valerius Probus (first century A.D.) and Saint Jerome (c. A.D. 331-420). An unattributed life of Vergil is also attached to the Vergil commentaries of Servius (late fourth century A.D.).

Bibliography

Broch, Hermann. *The Death of Virgil*. New York: Pantheon, 1945; London: Routledge, 1946. This exceptional novel captures the drama of Vergil's last hours and describes his frustration at being unable to complete his revision of the *Aeneid*. Read symbolically, this work is a record of all human strivings against the limitations imposed by physical circumstances. It was originally written in German during World War II by an author thwarted by his own surroundings and first published in English in 1945.

Commager, Steele, ed. *Virgil: A Collection of Critical Essays*. Englewood Cliffs, N.J.: Prentice-Hall, 1966. This book of essays by well-known critics discusses everything from the landscape which gave Vergil his inspiration to important imagery in Vergil's poems. It is part of the Twentieth Century Views series and includes contributions by Bruno Snell, Jacques Perret, Brooks Otis, Adam Parry, Bernard Knox, and Viktor Pöschl, as well as a chronology of Vergil's life and a short bibliography. All essays which had been written in French or German appear in English translation.

Comparetti, Domenico. *Vergil in the Middle Ages*. Translated by E. F. M. Benecke. London: Sonnenschein, and New York: Macmillan, 1895. This book remains the classic treatment of Vergil's literary legacy showing how it influenced both education and literature for centuries. It is still the best discussion of Vergilian bibliography available. A respected scholarly source.

Conway, Robert Seymour. *Harvard Lectures on the Vergilian Age*. Cambridge, Mass.: Harvard

University Press, 1928. This study relates references in Vergil's poetry to locations which influenced him. In essence, it is an orthographic biography, accompanied by photographs. Fascinating and reliable despite its age.

Farrell, Joseph. *Vergil's Georgics and the Traditions of Ancient Epic: The Art of Allusion in Literary History.* New York: Oxford University Press, 1991. A lucid and occasionally humorous argument about one aspect of the Georgic's literary technique. Farrell offers a useful survey of explicit allusion to antecedent poetry from Pindar on.

Frank, Tenney. *Vergil: A Biography.* New York: Henry Holt, and Oxford: Blackwell, 1922. This standard biography discusses the poet's life through references to his works. Particularly interesting is Frank's use of the pseudo-Vergilian poems *Culex* and *Cirus*, the influence of Epicureanism, and his discussion of the circle of Maecenas.

Heinze, Richard. *Virgil's Epic Technique.* London: Bristol Classical Press, and Berkeley: University of California Press, 1993. Heinze's book is divided into two sections: in the first, he submits long passages from the *Aeneid* and analyzes them; in the second, he summarizes his results and probes the essence of Virgil's art. He clarifies the familiarity of many of the book's central theses, demonstrating that virtually every proceeding work in the study of Virgil can be seen as a direct literary descendant. Heinze provides abundant scholarly detail and references to support his generalizations about the literary theory.

Knight, W. F. Jackson. *Roman Vergil.* Rev. ed. London: Penguin, 1966; New York: Barnes and Noble, 1971. How Vergil changed the literary world and how Augustus changed the political world are two important concerns in this biographical and literary study. There is also good discussion of Vergilian style, meter, and language, as well as appendices on how Vergil's poetry advanced Latin as a literary language and on the allegorical and symbolic applications of Vergil's poems.

Tilly, Bertha. *Vergil's Latium.* Oxford: Blackwell, 1947. This small volume, with accompanying photographs, examines the landscape of Vergil's Italy and notes its influences on Vergil's poetry. A generalist reader or a traveler to Italy will find it worthwhile.

Ziolkowski, Theodore. *Virgil and the Moderns.* Princeton, N.J.: Princeton University Press, 1993. Ziolkowski covers a substantial amount of detailed responses to Virgil in literature from the end of the nineteenth century to the present day. He emphasizes Virgil's darker side in his doubts concerning the achievements of Roman imperium. Ziolowski addresses Virgil's reception in various nations, and portrays him as the prototype of a literary man in a time of social and political turmoil.

Robert J. Forman

MARCUS VERRIUS FLACCUS

Born: c. 60 B.C.; place unknown

Died: c. A.D. 22; place unknown

Area of Achievement: Education

Contribution: Emerging from a slave background, Verrius established at Rome an innovative method for the teaching of Latin language and literature and, through his studies of Roman antiquities, contributed to modern understanding of Latin literature and Roman history.

Early Life

The biographer Suetonius supplies the basic biographical information about Marcus Verrius Flaccus in his essay *De grammaticis et rhetoribus* (c. A.D. 120; *Lives of the Grammarians*). This work by Suetonius, a discussion of teachers active in Rome during the last half of the first century B.C., includes the statement "Marcus Verrius Flaccus the freedman was especially renowned for his method of teaching." Nothing of Verrius' background is known except for his freedman's status and the probable name of his former master, Marcus Verrius. (Manumitted Roman slaves normally took the first and family names of their former owner.)

The name Verrius points to the region about Naples, where others with precisely the same nomenclature and many of the same family name are known. Scholarly work which Verrius did late in his life for the Roman town of Praeneste (modern Palestrina), however, has suggested to some that Verrius may have had an early connection with this town twenty-three miles east and south of Rome.

Life's Work

During Verrius' time, several men of letters with similar backgrounds established private schools in Rome for the instruction of Latin language and literature. These schools normally took children at the age of eleven for several years of training in the reading, recitation, and writing of Latin, while other schoolmasters might also have trained the same students in Greek language and literature. Verrius' school was notable because he forced his students to compete in writing and recitation, with prizes of rare literary editions for the victors. Verrius thus attracted the attention of the emperor Augustus, who invited Verrius to move his school to the imperial palace and tutor—at a salary equal to that of a senior administrator—the emperor's young grand-

sons, Gaius and Lucius. The appointment of Verrius as imperial tutor must have occurred between 8 and 11 B.C. and is no doubt the reason for Saint Jerome's assertion that Verrius "flourished" in 8 B.C.

Verrius wrote on a variety of subjects. *Rerum memoria dignarum* (things worth remembering), to judge from references to this work by Pliny the Elder and other ancient scholars, ranged from elephants to Roman religious lore and rituals. Other writings touched on the Etruscans and on Roman traditions. Several important works treated the Latin language: *De orthographia* (on correct spelling) apparently urged a return to old-fashioned ways of spelling (and pronouncing) Latin words; *De obscuris Catonis* (difficult works in Cato) explained unusual words in the orations and writings of Cato the Censor (who died in 149 B.C.). Verrius' most influential work was his dictionary, *De verborum significatu* (on the meaning of words). This work, the first Latin lexicon, was an alphabetical list of Latin words with definitions, etymologies, and frequent quotations of examples of usage drawn from archaic Latin texts (c. 250-100 B.C.) otherwise unknown. For example, the dictionary's entry under *quartarios* reads:

> Romans used to call muleskinners hired on contract "fourth-parters" [*quartarios*] because the muleskinners customarily charged for their services a fourth part of the profit. Thus Lucilius [a Roman satirist who wrote at the end of the second century B.C.]: "And then the unspeakable men, like a bad fourth-partner, crashed against all of the tombstones."

None of Verrius' works has survived intact.

Suetonius also reports that the town of Praeneste dedicated a statue of Verrius to honor his work on a great calendar inscribed on marble and set up prominently in a public area of the town. Enough fragments of this calendar have been discovered at Praeneste to indicate its size (six feet high and more than sixteen feet wide) and the scope of Verrius' work. The calendar listed the days of each month, with remarks on the religious and legal nature of each day and with notes on the pertinent religious festivals and historical and legendary events associated with each day. For example, he included this information for January 30:

> A day on which legal business may be transacted, a day for religious rites. Festival decreed by the senate, because on this date the Altar of the Augustan Peace

was dedicated in Mars' Field [at Rome], when Drusus and Crispinus were consuls [9 B.C.].

The calendar has been dated to between A.D. 6 and 9 and therefore would have been the fruit of Verrius' later years.

Verrius died sometime during the reign of the emperor Tiberius (A.D. 14-37). His rise from slave to acclaimed teacher and scholar illustrates well the social mobility possible for talented freedmen in ancient Rome.

Summary

Of Marcus Verrius Flaccus' teaching methods nothing more is known, although his practice of forcing his students to compete for literary prizes has clearly had a long (if unacknowledged) history.

Suetonius observed that Verrius' work on spelling was criticized by a fellow freedman and contemporary rival in teaching, one Scribonius Aphrodisius, who attacked Verrius' morals as well as his scholarship. Yet Verrius' writings, especially his dictionary and his treatise on Cato's vocabulary, were widely consulted and discussed in the second century A.D., when Roman literary scholars took a particular interest in Cato and other early writers of Latin. About the year A.D. 200, an otherwise unknown Latin scholar, Sextus Pompeius Festus, made an abridged edition of Verrius' dictionary. The first half of Festus' edition is lost, but a further abridgment of all Festus' work was made by Paul the Deacon, a historian and teacher of Latin at the court of Charlemagne (c. A.D. 800). Modern scholars, by studying what has survived of Festus' edition and Paul's condensed version of Festus, are thus able to judge the quality and content of Verrius' dictionary.

As Verrius' annotations to the Praenestine calendar have proved to be of significant value for those who study Roman history, so also Verrius' dictionary, even in the abridged editions in which it has survived, is a major source for students of the Latin language and early Roman literature.

Bibliography

Baldwin, Barry. *Studies in Aulus Gellius.* Lawrence, Kans.: Coronado Press, 1975. Chapter 4 ("Scholarly Interests") offers a lively discussion of Roman and Greek scholarship of the second century A.D. and of how students of Latin literature exploited previous studies, including the works of Verrius. Includes adequate notes citing the ancient and modern sources.

Bonner, S. F. *Education in Ancient Rome.* London: Methuen, and Berkeley: University of California Press, 1977. The standard discussion of education in the ancient Roman world. Chapters 5 and 6 provide a general discussion of the schools of literature, language, and rhetoric in Rome. Includes sparse notes, but a good bibliography.

Marrou, H. I. *A History of Education in Antiquity.* New York: Sheed and Ward, 1956; London: Sheed and Ward, 1977. A broader and more detailed study than Bonner's, this volume is arranged along chronological lines. In part 3, chapters 2 through 7 discuss the emergence and development of schools at Rome; chapter 5, in particular, covers what is known of schools of the type that Verrius established. Includes complete bibliographic notes.

Michels, A. K. *The Calendar of the Roman Republic.* Princeton, N.J.: Princeton University Press, 1967. A technical discussion of calendars in ancient Rome, with particular attention to inscribed wall calendars such as that created by Verrius at Praeneste. Includes notes and fine schematic drawings of ancient wall calendars.

Rawson, E. *Intellectual Life in the Late Roman Republic.* London: Duckworth, and Baltimore: Johns Hopkins University Press, 1985. Offers a concise discussion of the personalities associated with literary and language studies in ancient Italy in the time of Verrius and earlier generations. Contains detailed notes and a complete bibliography.

Scullard, H. H. *Festivals and Ceremonies of the Roman Republic.* London: Thames and Hudson, and Ithaca, N.Y.: Cornell University Press, 1981. A good general introduction to the official religious holidays of ancient Rome. Scullard includes a brief discussion of Roman calendars and surveys the various types of calendars used in ancient Rome. A more general work than that by Michels, whose study should be consulted for specific details. Contains complete notes.

Suetonius Tranquillus, G. *Suetonius.* Translated by John Carew Rolfe. 2 vols. London: Heinemann, and New York: Macmillan, 1914. These two volumes (often reprinted) contain a Latin text and the standard English translation of Suetonius' works. Volume 2 contains the text and translation of Suetonius' essay *De grammaticis et rhetoribus.* The bibliography and notes are now outdated.

Treggiari, S. *Roman Freedmen During the Late Republic.* Oxford: Clarendon, and New York: Oxford University Press, 1969. The standard discussion in English of the social and legal circumstances of manumitted slaves in Roman history before circa 30 B.C. Discusses the prominence in Roman life of freedmen in education and other learned professions. Includes notes and a bibliography.

Wallace-Hadrill, J. M. *Suetonius.* 2d ed. London: Bristol Classical Press, 1995. The best study in English of the ancient biographer. Treats Suetonius' essay on ancient teachers of literature and rhetoric. The author discusses fully the history of the profession of teachers and literary men such as Verrius and Suetonius himself in Rome. Includes generous notes and a bibliography.

Paul B. Harvey, Jr.

VESPASIAN

Born: A.D. 9; Reate (modern Rieti, Italy)

Died: June 23, A.D. 79; Aquae Cutilae (modern Bagni di Paterno, Italy)

Area of Achievement: Government

Contribution: After the chaos and civil war which followed the downfall of Nero, Vespasian restored peace and order to the Roman Empire and secured its survival as an enduring political and cultural institution.

Early Life

Titus Flavius Vespasianus, better known as Vespasian, came from a family whose origins were probably humble and certainly obscure. The Flavians were of Sabine stock, and Vespasian's grandfather and father were both tax collectors and moneylenders. His father never advanced above the equestrian order (the rank below the senate) but was an associate of several influential members of the court of the emperor Claudius; through them, he obtained a military commission for his son.

Vespasian was appointed a tribune of soldiers in Thrace and demonstrated his considerable abilities within a short period of time. He advanced fairly rapidly for a man of his position and won the office of quaestor, which meant that provinces could be assigned to him; he was given Crete and Cyrene.

He married Flavia Domitilla, and they had three children. The two sons, Titus and Domitian, would succeed their father as emperors; the daughter died at a young age. After the death of his wife, Vespasian resumed a relationship with a woman named Caenis, a former slave who had been secretary to the mother of the emperor Claudius. Vespasian lived with Caenis as his wife in all but official ceremony until her death.

During 43 and 44, Vespasian was in command of Roman troops in Germany, and then in Britain, where he distinguished himself through vigorous military actions, including the defeat of several powerful tribes and the conquest of the Isle of Wight. For these accomplishments he was awarded a consulship. He next served as governor of the Roman province of Africa (modern Tunisia) but was so honest that he left office without amassing the usual wealth. His career under Claudius' successor, Nero, took a disastrous turn in 66 when Vespasian fell asleep at one of the emperor's singing performances. For this heinous offense Vespasian narrowly escaped death and was instead banished from the court. Not until the outbreak of a serious revolt in Judaea, when an experienced general was required, was Vespasian rescued from oblivion.

Vespasian was strongly built, with a broad, sturdy frame. Throughout his life he enjoyed excellent health, partly because of his temperate habits and partly because of his active and energetic life. The coins and portrait busts of the period show a face that is humorous yet shrewd, with an expression that caused the ancient biographer Suetonius to compare it to a man straining to complete a bowel movement. Vespasian had a rough, often coarse humor, which was often directed at himself—in particular, at his well-known reputation for stinginess. His outstanding characteristics were hard work, administrative genius, and a profound fund of common sense.

Life's Work

In 67, Vespasian was recalled from exile to lead Roman forces against the Jewish revolt, which was a serious threat to Rome's eastern borders and a danger to the vital grain supply from Egypt. By the summer of 68, Vespasian had regained most of Judaea, and the remnants of the rebel forces were detained in Jerusalem, which he put under siege. It was at this point that Vespasian learned of the uprising in Rome and the death of Nero.

"The year of the four emperors" followed, as Servius Sulpicius Galba, Marcus Salvius Otho, and Aulus Vitellius successively aspired to and gained the throne. While seeming to accept each in turn as the legitimate ruler, Vespasian was secretly establishing contacts and making plans with other influential governors and generals in the east; most notable were those of the two key provinces of Syria and Egypt. In 68, the troops of Vespasian's army declared him emperor; troops throughout the region quickly followed, and soon the forces pledged to him were advancing upon Rome.

Vespasian himself reached Rome sometime in the fall of 70; his son, Titus, remained in Judaea to complete the reconquest of that territory. Later, the two would celebrate a splendid double triumph, which indicated that Titus was not only Vespasian's heir but also an important part of the government.

The disastrous end of Nero's reign and the fierce civil war and struggle over the imperial power had left their harmful mark on Roman life and society, and it was Vespasian's first and most constant task to repair this damage. He reintroduced strict discipline and order into the military, hoping to remove the threat of another emperor being created far from Rome by a discontented army. He began an extensive series of construction and renovation projects throughout the empire, especially in Rome, restoring years of neglect and destruction. At the rebuilding of the Forum in Rome, Vespasian himself carried away the first load of rubble.

A parallel effort was effected in the government and administration, as Vespasian assumed the title of censor and thoroughly revised the rolls of the senate and the equestrian orders. It was in his naming of new senators that Vespasian made one of his most innovative and lasting contributions to the Empire, for he included not only many Italians from outside Rome but also men from the provinces. Through this strategy Vespasian enlarged not only the senate but also the entire concept of the Empire itself, making it less a collection of territories conquered by Rome and more a unified, organic whole. It is impossible to determine if Vespasian was working from a coherent, deliberate plan or merely responding to the situation in a sensible, practical fashion; either interpretation is possible. The result, however, was to create a broader and more lasting base for Roman power.

This reconstruction of Roman life demanded much effort from Vespasian, and he proved to be an outstandingly diligent administrator. The work also required vast amounts of money, and it was in search of these funds that Vespasian acquired the reputation for greed. He was quite open and shameless in obtaining funds, buying and selling on the commodity market and placing a tax on the public restrooms. When his son Titus found this last measure distasteful and protested to his father, Vespasian held up a coin and asked if the smell was offensive. When Titus said that it was not, Vespasian answered, "And yet it comes from urine." Even today, public rest rooms in Italy are called *vespasianos*.

Although Vespasian was quick and crafty in gathering money, he was willing to spend it freely for worthwhile purposes. In addition to his extensive building projects, he was the first emperor to give grants and stipends to those who contributed to the liberal and practical arts: Teachers of rhetoric, poets, artists, and engineers received funds during his reign.

The years of Vespasian were marked by no major conquests or expansions of the Empire's boundaries. Even if he had aspired to such glories, the situation made the option highly dubious. Internally there was simply too much restoration to be done, as Rome was depleted from the recent succession of rival emperors and from the revolt in Judaea. Peace at home, rather than glory abroad, was the theme of Vespasian's reign.

This peace and the restoration it made possible were accomplished largely through Vespasian's abilities and innate common sense. Unlike the rulers who preceded him, he had little fear of conspiracies or plots, launched no treason trials, and encouraged no informers. Historians have generally accorded him a high place, naming him one of Rome's best emperors.

From the time of Julius Caesar it had become a tradition that rulers of the Empire were deified upon their deaths. When Vespasian was in his final hours, he took note of this practice and with rough good humor made his last remark: "Dear me, I seem to be turning into a god."

Summary

Vespasian's great achievements were the restoration of peace and political sanity to the Roman Empire and the enlargement of its imperial rather than strictly Roman foundations. After the disaster of Nero's final years and the almost fatal chaos of the struggle for power which followed, Vespasian was able to provide for domestic tranquillity, reassert military discipline, and establish a political framework which prevented, at least for a time, renewed outbreaks of self-destructive civil war.

At first glance, Vespasian might have seemed unlikely to be capable of such tremendous tasks: His origins were humble, his manner was common, even coarse, and his abilities, although genuine, seemed limited. Yet it is evident that these apparent defects, when allied with a solid basis of traditional Roman common sense and a broad view of the Empire, were in fact the very qualities needed to undo years of social uncertainty and internecine violence.

As an administrator Vespasian was diligent; his major concern was to ensure the proper functioning of those operations necessary to any state: tax collections, public works, defense, and commerce. Having achieved the imperial position, he was more concerned to execute it conscientiously for the state than to defend it obsessively for himself. Ancient historians are unanimous in their view that he displayed none of the crippling suspicions and paranoid actions of earlier rulers. Cornelius Tacitus, that bleak and perceptive observer of imperial Rome, gave Vespasian the rarest of praise when he wrote that he was the only ruler who became better, rather than worse, as time went on.

Vespasian's common origins were perhaps one reason that he could form a larger view of the Empire, including more of its population as citizens and senators. He was not trapped by the old views of patrician families seeking to retain their privileged status and their time-honored, yet ineffectual, control of the state. His wide-ranging experiences, from Britain to Judaea, also helped give him this expanded perspective; there was not much doubt that this new direction enabled later emperors to maintain one of the world's most lasting political systems.

In this view, Vespasian certainly ranks as one of the best of the Roman emperors. This judgment is based upon many factors, but focuses on Vespasian's renewal and expansion of the Empire, an expansion less in geographical territory than in political unity.

Bibliography

Grant, Michael. *The Roman Emperors*. London: Weidenfeld and Nicolson, and New York: Scribner, 1985. Vespasian's rule is best judged not alone but as counterpoint to the disorder which preceded it. The brief selections in this volume provide an overview of the decline of the Empire during the last years of Nero and the near-fatal chaos that followed. Vespasian's accomplishments are viewed as the more outstanding in the comparison.

————. *The Twelve Caesars*. London: Weidenfeld and Nicolson, and New York: Scribner, 1975. Grant continues where Suetonius' *Lives of the Twelve Caesars* (see below) leaves off in using anecdotes of character and personality to establish underlying psychological and political motives. By placing Vespasian within the tenor of his times, Grant not only makes the emperor more human but also shows the impressive nature of his achievements.

Greenhalgh, P. A. L. *The Year of the Four Emperors*. London: Weidenfeld and Nicolson, and New York: Barnes and Noble, 1975. A large part of Vespasian's reputation is linked to the restoration of order to the Roman world after an intense period of chaos. This study concentrates on the events which brought him to power and reveals the extensive task of reconstruction he had to undertake.

Marsh, Henry. *The Caesars: The Roman Empire and Its Rulers*. New York: St. Martin's Press, 1971. A brisk narrative in this popular collection of biographical portraits shows Vespasian in his roles as soldier, administrator, emperor, and rough-edged individual. The nonscholarly style is admirably suited to the character of Vespasian, with his practical common sense and coarse humor.

Suetonius. *Lives of the Twelve Caesars*. Joseph Gavorse, ed. New York: Modern Library, 1931. True to the standards of ancient biography, Suetonius shows the caesars less as actors on the grand political stage than as particular individuals with quirks and characteristics. This presentation, while missing much of importance, is still excellent for revealing the unmistakable individuality of a man such as Vespasian.

Michael Witkoski

SAINT VINCENT OF LÉRINS

Born: Late fourth century; probably in or near Toul
Died: c. 450; Lérins, Marseilles, or Troyes
Area of Achievement: Religion
Contribution: In his own time, Vincent was one of the leaders in the Gallic opposition to the concept of Augustinian predestination. After his death, Vincent came to be known primarily for his formula for distinguishing orthodoxy from heresy.

Early Life

Vincent was probably a native of Toul in northern Gaul and belonged to a well-to-do family. He and his brother, Lupus, would have received a classical education. Vincent also was learned in ecclesiastical literature: In the 490's, Gennadius of Marseilles described him as "a man learned in the holy scriptures and sufficiently instructed in the knowledge of ecclesiastical dogma." Sometime during his youth, Vincent held an unspecified civil or military secular office. Around 425-426, however, he and his brother, like many other young aristocrats, adopted the monastic life, going to the island of Lérins, near Nice. The abbot there, Honoratus, was another northerner; he perhaps came from near Dijon. Another monk who entered the monastery at about this same time was Honoratus' younger relative Hilary, whose sister Pimeniola had married Lupus.

Unlike many of the monks, who remained laymen, Vincent was ordained a priest. He was active in the quasi-familial atmosphere of the monastery. Along with Honoratus, Hilary, and the priest Salvian, later of Marseilles, he assisted in the education of Salonius and Veranus, the young sons of the monk Eucherius. Many of these monks went on to become bishops in their own right, Honoratus and Hilary at Arles, Eucherius at Lyons, and Lupus at Troyes. Vincent, however, remained a monk and may have spent time also at Marseilles as well as with his brother in the north: "Avoiding the turmoil and crowds of cities, I inhabit a little dwelling on a remote farmstead and within it the retreat of a monastery."

Life's Work

Vincent is known primarily for his involvement in ecclesiastical debates, especially in the controversy in Gaul surrounding some of the teachings of Saint Augustine. Augustine was much respected in Gaul,

and every fifth century Gallic theologian cited him, at least on occasion, as an authority. Vincent himself compiled some *excerpta* from Augustine on the Trinity and the Incarnation. Augustine's opposition to Pelagianism, which denied original sin and the need for grace, was consistent with the prevalent Gallic orthodoxy. For example, according to a Gallic chronicler writing in 452, in 400 "the insane Pelagius attempts to befoul the churches with his execrable teaching."

The sticking point, however, was Augustine's concept of predestination, and according to that same source in the entry for the year 418, "the heresy of the predestinarians, which is said to have received its impetus from Augustine, once arisen creeps along." Predestination, which taught that only certain individuals were "predestined" for salvation, was seen as denying free will and as related to fatalism, Priscillianism, or Manichaean dualism.

The Gallic ambivalence toward Augustine ended in the mid-420's with the publication of his *De correptione et gratia* (426; *On Admonition and Grace,* 1873). In 426, John Cassian published an attack upon both Pelagianism and unconditional predestination. At about that same time, two of Augustine's supporters, the laymen Prosper of Aquitane and Hilarius, wrote letters to him, still extant, decrying the situation in Gaul. According to Prosper,

> Many of the servants of Christ who live in Marseilles think that, in the writings which Your Sanctity composed against the Pelagian heretics, whatever you said in them about the choice of the elect according to the fixed purpose of God is contrary to the opinion of the fathers and to ecclesiastical feeling.

In order to strengthen his case against the Gallic antipredestinarians, Prosper went so far as to accuse them of being Pelagians, referring to their "spirit of Pelagianism" and describing some of their teachings as the "remnants of the Pelagian depravity." Prosper's accusation has gained sufficient credence that the antipredestinarian party in Gaul has been given the misleading designation "Semi-Pelagian," in spite of the fact that all known influential Gallic theologians, including the Semi-Pelagians, condemned Pelagianism as heartily as did Augustine himself.

A more accurate depiction of Gallic sentiments is given by Prosper in the same letter to Augustine, when he reported on the short-lived Bishop Helladius of Arles: "Your Beatitude should know that he is an admirer and follower of your teaching in all other things, and with regard to that which he calls into question [predestination], he already wished to convey his own thoughts to Your Sanctity through correspondence. . . ."

In 430, Augustine died. Shortly thereafter, Prosper, seeing himself as the defender of Augustine in the struggle against the Gallic antipredestinarians, returned to the attack in three tracts, including the *Pro Augustino responsiones ad capitula objectionum Vincentianarum* (c. 431-434; *The Defense of Saint Augustine*, 1963). As a result, the Gauls also entered the pamphlet war; one of their most important writers was Vincent of Lérins. Although none of these anti-Augustinian works survives, Prosper's responses to them give a good idea of Vincent's objections. Augustine was accused of fatalism, of denying that all share the chance for salvation, and even of asserting that predestination compelled some to sin. The Gauls denounced Augustine for teaching that those predestined to salvation had no need to lead a Christian life, to be baptized, or to have free will.

It soon appeared to Prosper, however, that he was unable to sway his Gallic opponents with his rhetoric. He and Hilarius then exercised the increasingly popular last resort of so many disgruntled Gallic ecclesiastics: They went to Rome and appealed to the pope. As a result, Pope Celestine I, probably in 431, addressed a letter to several Gallic bishops, rebuking them for allowing the teaching of improper beliefs. Celestine, however, had been led to believe that the Gauls were infected with Pelagianism and on this basis were questioning the Augustinian interpretation of free will. Scholars have searched Celestine's letter in vain for any reference to the real reason that the Gauls opposed Augustine.

The definitive Gallic response to Celestine and Prosper came in 434, when Vincent, under the pseudonym Peregrinus (the pilgrim), wrote *Commonitoria* (*The Commonitory of Vincent of Lérins*, 1554), also known as *Adversus haereticos*, a tract ostensibly issued as a general guide for discerning heresy from orthodoxy. Vincent, stating that "the fraudulence of new heretics demands great care and attention," issued what would become the standard definition of orthodoxy, the so-called Vincentian canon: Orthodox belief was "quod ubique, quod semper, quod ab omnibus creditum est" (that

which has been believed everywhere, always, and by all). Vincent therefore espoused a triple test—ecumenicity, antiquity, and universal consent.

Although Vincent taught that the true basis for orthodox belief lay in the Scriptures, he also placed great emphasis upon church tradition, because the Scriptures were capable of many different interpretations. How was one to distinguish between legitimate doctrinal evolution, which came with greater maturity and understanding, and heretical innovation? In Vincent's view, the established Church and all the orthodox church fathers were collectively the holders of dogmatic truth and stood as the guarantors of the proper interpretation.

Vincent soon, however, narrowed his discussion down to a consideration of "novelty" and "recent heresies, when they first arise." Vincent's particular concerns were to respond to Celestine's letter and to defend the Gallic antipredestinarian position even though, as usual, Augustine was not mentioned by name. In his final argument against novelty, Vincent turned Celestine's own arguments against him: "Let [Celestine] speak himself, let him destroy the doubts of our readers himself. He said 'let novelty cease to assault tradition.' " The "inventors of novelty," whoever they might be, should be condemned.

Vincent concluded by arguing that because Pelagius, Coelestius (another Pelagian), and Nestorius, who had separated the human and divine natures of Christ, all had been condemned, it was necessary for Christians "to detest, pursue, and persecute the profane novelties of the profane." The doctrine of predestination also was novelty, and as such was to be condemned. By using Celestine's own arguments, Vincent rejected Celestine's and Prosper's claims that the Gallic antipredestinarians were guilty of wrongdoing. Vincent and the Gauls showed that, however much they might respect authorities such as Augustine and the Bishop of Rome, they reserved final judgment for themselves. For the rest of the century, the Gallic theological establishment continued to reject predestination and to define ever more carefully its own conception of the interaction among grace, effort, and free will.

Vincent's treatise is the last extant evidence for the predestination controversy for nearly forty years. Prosper apparently gave up his efforts to influence the Gauls, admitted defeat, and permanently moved to Rome. His move did not mean, however, that there did not continue to be predestinarians in Gaul or that everyone agreed with the views expressed by Vincent. Gennadius of Marseilles reported that the reason the second book of *The Commonitory of Vincent of Lérins* survived only in outline form was that the complete version had been stolen. Vincent himself is not heard from again, and Gennadius states that he was dead by the year 450.

Summary

Vincent of Lérins wrote and taught at a time when the Western Church was in theological ferment. There was a growing concern with various kinds of heretical beliefs, their identification and suppression. One previously popular view, Pelagianism, had just been condemned. Another, more recent theory of Augustine, predestination, although accepted in other parts of the Roman Empire, in Gaul was considered heretical. This Gallic rejection of foreign influence was reflected in other spheres of the Church as well. Throughout the fifth century, for example, the Gauls, especially the monks of Lérins, refused to acknowledge any direct papal authority in Gaul.

Vincent was one of the primary figures in the Gallic theological discussions of the 420's and 430's. His articulate condemnation of predestination was accepted in Gaul for nearly a century. In the sixth century, however, after the fall of the Roman Empire in the West and the division of Gaul into barbarian kingdoms, the Gallic church no longer was able to maintain its independence. In 529, at the Second Council of Orange, the southern Gallic bishops, now under the influence of the pope and the Italian court, condemned the earlier rejection of strict predestination. Vincent's method for distinguishing orthodox from heretical beliefs, however, continued to be applied; it still provides the standard definition.

Bibliography

Brunetière, Ferdinand, and P. de Labriolle. *Saint Vincent de Lérins*. Paris: Bloud, 1906. Although rather dated, this work is one of the few biographies of Vincent ever written. In French.

Cooper-Marsdin, Arthur Cooper. *The History of the Islands of the Lérins*. Cambridge: Cambridge University Press, 1913. The only English-language account devoted to the monastery where Vincent lived and worked. Includes an index.

Mathisen, R. W. *Ecclesiastical Factionalism and Religious Controversy in Fifth-Century Gaul*. Washington, D.C.: Catholic University of America Press, 1989. A detailed account of Vincent's ecclesiastical environment, including descriptions of the monastery at Lérins, Vincent's life and works, and the theological controversies in which Vincent became involved. Includes a detailed bibliography.

Nicetas of Remesiana, Saint. *Vincent of Lérins: Commonitories*. Translated by Rudolph E. Morris. Vol. 7 in *Niceta of Remesiana*. New York: Fathers of the Church, 1949. An English translation of Vincent's most influential work. Includes critical commentary.

Severus, Sulpicius. *Vincent of Lérins*. Translated by John Cassian. Vol. 11 in *A Select Library of Nicene and Post-Nicene Church Fathers*. New York: Christian Literature Company, and Oxford: Parker and Company, 1894. This English translation of Vincent's work includes a scholarly preface which discusses the background and context of Vincent's literary efforts in detail.

Vincentius Lerinensis, Saint. *The Commonitorium of Vincentius of Lérins*. Edited by Reginald Stewart Moxon. Cambridge: Cambridge University Press, 1915. This volume is considered by scholars to be the standard edition of Vincent's best-known work. In Latin.

Ralph W. Mathisen

VIRGIN MARY

Born: 22 B.C.; unknown
Died: unknown; probably Israel, perhaps Ephesus
Areas of Achievement: Biblical figures and religion
Contribution: Though little is known about the historical Mary, the virgin mother of Jesus Christ has been revered throughout the ages.

Early Life

According to tradition, Mary's parents were Joachim and Anna, from the city of Nazareth in Galilee in present-day Israel. About five hundred years later, Saint Augustine declared that the sin of Adam and Eve infects all humanity and is passed down from generation to generation through biological conception. Mary was declared to have been exempt from this sin in preparation for her role as the mother of Jesus. This exemption became known and is still celebrated as the Immaculate Conception. The event is commemorated each year on December 8, nine months before her birthday, which is celebrated on September 8.

Life's Work

Almost nothing is known about the historical personage of the woman known as the Blessed Virgin Mary. She was the mother of the man Jesus, whom Christians worship as the Son of God. In the Christian Scriptures, only two of the four gospels, Matthew and Luke, feature Mary at the birth of Jesus. Matthew traces the ancestry of Jesus through Mary's husband, Joseph, and then immediately proceeds to create an image of Jesus as a new Moses. As in Moses' life, the king is threatened by this new birth and promises to kill all Hebrew baby boys. The Holy Family escapes into Egypt to await the death of the dreaded king. After Jesus' baptism, which takes place when Jesus is approximately thirty years old, he is followed by crowds up to the mountain, where Matthew depicts him, again like a new Moses, giving a new law to the people. Scholars agree that Matthew's narrative of Jesus' birth was written later than the rest of the gospel and that its purpose was not to relate a historical fact but to convince his readers that Jesus was the Messiah for whom they were waiting.

In Luke's gospel, an angel appears to Mary and asks her to accept the privilege of being the mother of the savior. After questioning how this might happen, since she is not yet married, the angel as-sures her that the child will be born by the power of the Holy Spirit. It is thought that Mary was probably between the ages of twelve and fourteen at this time. Mary then immediately goes to the town of Ain Kerim to visit her cousin Elizabeth, who is pregnant with John the Baptist. Luke took excerpts from the song of Hannah, mother of Sampson, and put them into the mouth of Mary: "My heart extols the Lord. My spirit exults in God my savior." As soon as the child is born, an angel goes out to some shepherds and announces to them that a savior has been born. Luke recalls that Mary pondered all these things in her heart. Unlike Matthew's account, Luke's does not include a visit from the Magi or a flight into Egypt.

Outside of these infancy narratives, Mary is mentioned only a few more times in the Scriptures. Her next appearance is at a wedding in Cana, where the party runs out of wine. Mary relates this fact to her son Jesus, who, because of her request, changes water into wine. In Mark 3:20-35, Jesus' relatives are suspicious of him and think that he may be somewhat insane. They go to the place where he is preaching, and when they ask for him, the crowd yells out, "Your mother and brothers are outside asking for you." Jesus answers, "Who are my mother and my brothers? . . . Whoever does the will of God is my brother and sister and mother." At first, this answer seems to be a rebuke of his mother and his immediate family, perhaps because they do not understand what he is about. Yet Mark's purpose is to distinguish between Jesus' natural family and his followers. He is claiming that all people can be related to Jesus, not through blood ties, but by doing the will of God.

In Luke 11:27-28, a similar incident takes place. A woman calls out from the crowd, "Blessed is the mother who bore you and nursed you!" Jesus answers, "You might better say, 'Blessed are those who hear God's message and observe it!'" Again, this seems to be a rebuke of his mother, but it can be interpreted to mean that kinship has no special claim on Jesus' friends.

John's gospel is the only one that puts Mary at the foot of the cross. Mary, her sister Mary (the wife of Clopas), Mary Magdalene, and John himself are present when Jesus looks down from the cross and says to his mother, "Woman, behold your son," and to the beloved disciple John, "Son, behold your mother," thus giving Mary into the care

of John. According to later tradition, Jesus is taken from the cross and laid in the arms of his mother. This scene has inspired many artistic sculptures and paintings, the most famous of which is the *Pieta* by Michelangelo, which now stands in the Vatican in Rome.

Whether Mary stayed in Jerusalem or went to Ephesus is not known. Ephesus boasts of a house in which Mary lived and died, but most scholars think she probably stayed in Jerusalem, where there is also a place honored as the site of her "falling asleep." There is a strong tradition in the Catholic Church that Mary did not die but only fell asleep and that she was assumed into heaven, body and soul. This "Assumption" was officially declared in 1950 and is celebrated each year on August 15. In 1954, Pope Pius XII officially proclaimed her "Queen of Heaven."

Before the fifth century A.D., references to Mary were rare. In about the year A.D. 100, Justin Martyr contrasted her with Eve, a theme later developed by Irenaeus. She came into prominence until the 400's, when church councils debated whether Jesus was God. In 428, Nestorius, a Syrian, became bishop of Constantinople, the eastern capital of the Roman Empire. He preferred the term *christotokos* (mother of Christ) for Jesus' mother rather than the more popular *theotokos* (mother of God) because, he said, *theotokos* implies that Mary gave birth to God. Nestorius was quickly challenged by Cyril of Alexandria, and in 430, the bishops condemned Nestorius as a heretic. Since then, Mary has oten been referred to as the "Mother of God." In popular piety, however, this title resulted in Mary's being referred to as a goddess; in 787, therefore, the Council of Nicea clearly distinguished between worship of God alone and the lesser reverence due Mary and the saints.

The Middle Ages saw a proliferation of devotions and artistic works in honor of the Virgin and Mother Mary. She can be seen at the Annunciation, often reading a book of Scripture as the angel appears to her, a dove over her head representing the Holy Spirit. In one painting, the tiny baby can be seen flying through the window of the chapel to be implanted in her womb. Other favorite poses include the birth of Jesus in the stable, the Madonna and child, the crucifixion, and the pieta. At the time of the Reformation, Protestants deemphasized devotion to Mary. However, Martin Luther referred to her as the foremost example of God's grace and of proper humility.

In the nineteenth and twentieth centuries, Mary is reported to have appeared to various people: in Lourdes, France, in 1858; in Fatima, Portugal, in 1917; and since 1981 in Medjugorje, Bosnia. Some of the bishops at the Second Vatican Council in 1965 moved to declare her "corredemptrix" with Christ; that is, the co-redeemer of the world along with her son. The council did not approve of this, but it did include a chapter on Mary in the document *Lumen Gentium*. In his speech at the council, Pope Paul VI proclaimed Mary "Mother of the Church."

Summary

After the Vatican Council, there was more activity in Roman Catholic Mariology. At first, women did not wish to venerate Mary, because she had always been idealized strictly for her biological function as the mother of Jesus. They saw her as weak, a woman who was always submissive to others, one who did not make her own decisions about her life. Feminist theologians, however, have begun to point out Mary's strengths. In the story of the annunciation, she questions the angel who wants her to be the mother of Jesus, and, after she understands what God wants, she decides on her own to go ahead, even though she realizes that she will be criticized by those who will not understand. In her prayer, quoted from Hannah of the Hebrew Scriptures, Mary speaks of how she, along with others who had been considered humble and lowly, were lifted up by God: "He has satisfied the hungry with good things, and has sent the rich away empty-handed." Mary is seen here as a symbol for all women who traditionally have been seen as insignificant but are now seen as equal to men and are highly regarded not only for their ability to reproduce but also for other strengths of intellect, will, and determination. Women throughout the ages have been able to relate to Mary in her difficult life, especially in the loss of her son. Virginity is no longer seen simply as sexual celibacy but as a sign of autonomy and strength.

Bibliography

Brown, Raymond, Karl P. Donfried, Joseph A. Fitzmyer, and John Reumann, eds. *Mary in the New Testament: A Collaborative Assessment by Protestant and Roman Catholic Scholars*. London: Chapman, and Philadelphia, Pa.: Fortress Press, 1978. The role that Mary plays in salvation is one that has divided Protestants, Anglicans, and Roman Catholics over the centuries. This book is an effort to open the way for agreement.

Coll, Regina. "Mary, the Mother of Jesus." In *Christianity and Feminism in Conversation*. Mystic, Conn.: Twenty-Third Publications, 1994. In this brief chapter, Coll speaks of how the Virgin Mary relates to the modern woman. Feminists now say that virginity is not simply a biological phenomenon but also connotes a person who is whole in herself, one whose being was not owned by a man.

Cunneen, Sally. *In Search of Mary: The Woman and the Symbol*. New York: Ballantine Books, 1996. This book reviews the New Testament references to Mary and then traces her cult through the ages into contemporary time. The author enters into the human aspects of Mary's life (her pregnancy, for example) and discusses how, very often, she did not understand what her son was doing. Cunneen quotes many different theologians, poets, and ordinary people to bring out the humanity of Mary as a person, a mother, and a model for the church.

Kung, Hans, and Jurgen Moltmann, eds. *Mary in the Churches*. New York: Seabury Press, 1983. An ecumenical inquiry with contributions by Or-thodox, Protestant, Jewish, and Catholic scholars. For the most part, Mariology has been anti- rather than pro-ecumenical and has been largely excluded from ecumenical dialogue. The authors wish to present Mary as an essential figure in the gospel of Christ.

Macquarrie, John. *Mary for All Christians*. Grand Rapids, Mich.: William B. Eerdmans, and London: HarperCollins, 1990. John Macquarrie, a British theologian, takes up the questions of the Immaculate Conception, the Assumption, and Mary as corredemptrix. He states that Mary should not separate Christians from one another but should be seen in a wider context of Christian faith as a person who can point toward God.

Warner, Marina. *Alone of All Her Sex: The Myth and the Cult of the Blessed Virgin Mary*. New York: Knopf, and London: Weidenfeld and Nicolson, 1976. This book relates the history of the titles of the Virgin Mary such as the second Eve, queen, madonna, sorrowful mother, Immaculate Conception, and the Virgin among the moon and the stars. It also contains eight color and fifty-two black and white plates depicting scenes from the life of the Virgin.

Winifred Whelan

WANG CH'UNG

Born: 27; Shang-yü, K'uai-chi, China
Died: c. 100; Shang-yü, K'uai-chi, China
Area of Achievement: Philosophy
Contribution: During the later Han Dynasty, apocryphal literature became popular, supplementing humanistic and rationalistic Confucianism and supporting the belief in portents and prophecies. Amid this change, Wang Ch'ung became a rationalistic, naturalistic, and materialistic thinker; his philosophy subsequently contributed to clearing the atmosphere of superstition and occultism and to enhancing the spirit of skepticism, rationalism, and naturalism, which later bloomed in the form of Neo-Taoism during the Wei-Chin period.

Early Life

Wang Ch'ung was born in Shang-yü, K'uai-chi (now Chekiang Province), China, in 27; he lived during the period of transition from orthodox Confucianism to popular Neo-Taoism. During that time, China suffered a series of crop failures which resulted in widespread famine, and the country suffered from rebellions arising from the government's inability to find a solution to its people's problems. As a result, Confucianism, upon whose training advancement in the civil service was based, declined in popularity; the country began to search for another ideology. Without such a cohesive philosophy, the Chinese state and society would fragment and crumble.

While the country was going through this upheaval, Wang Ch'ung suffered his own difficulties, having been born into a family whose fortunes were already on the decline. His rebellious grandfather and father had less-than-successful careers in government service. Eventually, both were forced into an erratic life-style, moving from one job to the next. To compound matters, Wang Ch'ung was orphaned when he was very young.

Nevertheless, he always expressed an interest in learning. He continued to read, even in the most difficult of circumstances, in the local bookstores, going on to study at the national university in the capital city of Loyang. There he met Pan Piao, an eminent scholar and the father of Pan Ku, a noted historian. Much of Wang Ch'ung's education, however, was informal and irregular. In addition to teaching himself, he did not follow any of the traditional scholastic methods or values. Thus he has

been classified as a member of the Miscellaneous school.

Like his grandfather and father before him, Wang Ch'ung worked as a government official, coming into conflict with his superiors as a result of his uncompromising personality. During the course of his career, he held a few minor official positions on the local level, serving without distinction. In 88 he retired from circuit government, a job he had obtained as a favor from Tung Ch'in, a provincial official. He returned to his hometown and devoted the remainder of his life to teaching and writing.

Life's Work

The intellectual situation in Wang Ch'ung's lifetime was complex. Confucianism was supreme, yet it was being debased into a mysterious and superstitious doctrine. In addition, the belief in the unity of man and nature was changing: Man and nature were seen as mutually influencing each other, and these influences were thought to be exerted through strange phenomena and calamities. Heaven, though not anthropomorphic, was purposeful, asserting its will through prodigies which it used to warn mortals; on a smaller scale, spiritual beings exercised a similar influence.

Wang Ch'ung rejected these beliefs, declaring that Heaven takes no action; that natural events, including prodigies, occur spontaneously; that there is no such thing as teleology; that fortune and misfortune occur by chance; and that man does not become a ghost after death. In addition, he insisted that theories must be tested and supported by concrete evidence. He did not believe that the past is any sure guide with regard to the present, saying that there is no evidence that the past is better than the present, or vice versa. In short, he believed in human logic and nature's spontaneous manifestation.

Wang Ch'ung also wrote the following three books: the *Chi-su chieh-yi* (ridiculing custom and decorum), in which he discussed the vagaries of politics and power. When he himself was out of power, he wrote the *Cheng-wu* (political affairs), in which he discusses the defects of the political system, and the *Lun-hêng* (c. 85; English translation, 1907-1911), in which he calls for a logic based on tangible evidence and rejects superstition and speculation without foundation. Only the *Lun-hêng* has survived.

In the *Lun-hêng*, Wang Ch'ung presented a variety of views on human nature. In it, he first quoted Confucius, "By nature men are alike. Through practice they have become far apart," then turned to Mencius, one of Confucius' disciples, who saw mankind's nature as originally good, especially during childhood, and explained evil in terms of the circumstances of their lives. He also quoted Kao Tzu, Mencius' contemporary, who said that human nature is neither good nor evil: It is like the willow tree. Hsün-tzu, however, opposed Mencius, saying that "the nature of man is evil"; that is, just as a stone is hard as soon as it is produced, men are bad even in childhood. Tung Chung-shu read the works of both Mencius and Hsün-tzu and proposed eclectic theories of human nature and feelings: "Nature is born of yang and feelings are born of yin. The force of yin results in greed and that of yang results in humanity." He meant that human nature and feelings are both good and evil, for they are products of yin and yang. Liu Tzu-cheng concurred, saying that human nature is inborn and not expressed, but feelings are what come into contact with things; thus, human nature is yin (evil) and human feelings are yang (good).

Wang Ch'ung dealt with these theories eclectically. He considered that Mencius' doctrine of the goodness of human nature referred only to people above the average, that Hsün-tzu's doctrine of the evil of human nature applied to people below the average, and that the doctrine of Yang Hsiung—human nature is a mixture of good and evil—referred to average people. Although his statements seemingly indicate that Wang Ch'ung believed in three grades of human nature, he actually took this approach because he believed that human nature is neither good nor evil.

Nature and its spontaneity Wang Ch'ung explained in terms of skepticism and rationalism. He did not believe that nature (or heaven and earth) produces anything purposely; instead, all things are spontaneously created when the material force (*ch'i*) of heaven and earth come together. Specifically, the calamities and changes produced unexpectedly by nature are not for the purpose of reprimanding or rewarding humanity. Their occurrence is nothing but a spontaneous, natural manifestation, known as nonaction (*wu-wei*). Discussing this subject, he said, "What do we mean when we say that Heaven is spontaneous and takes no action? It is a matter of material force. It is tranquil, without desire, and is engaged in neither action nor business." Thus he rejected the teleological and anthropomorphic view of Heaven then popular among his contemporary Confucianists.

He developed his view of fate similarly. He believed that human nature and fate have nothing to do with a good or bad life: A good-natured man can be unlucky, and an evil-natured man can be lucky. He concluded that nature dictates its own course in and of itself.

Death he explained again in terms of skepticism and rationalism. First, he did not believe in the existence of spirits or ghosts because after people die they are not conscious and thus are not capable of doing anything for themselves, saying, "How can the dead be spiritual beings if such is the case?" He then continued, "When other creatures die, they do not become spiritual beings. Why should man alone become a spiritual being when he dies?" He gave further reason in terms of naturalism and rationalism: "Man can live because of his vital forces. At death his vital forces are extinct. What makes the vital forces possible is the blood. When a person dies, his blood becomes exhausted. With this his vital forces are extinct, and his body decays and becomes ashes and dust." In short, he believed in nothing after death. Human death, according to Wang Ch'ung, is like the extinction of fire: When a fire is extinguished, its light shines no longer, and when a man dies, his consciousness has no more understanding. Here Wang Ch'ung equated man (life) and matter (fire) in terms of material force (*ch'i*), which in turn is explained by nonaction (*wu-wei*). Thus he can be identified as a materialist and naturalist.

Wang Ch'ung also rejected the Confucian view that antiquity was a golden period in Chinese history. He believed in the equality of past and present, saying that the world was and is well governed because of sages and that it was and is ill governed because of unrighteous people; thus, good and bad governments, whether past or present, are not distinct. At times, however, he contradicted himself, saying that the present is better than the past. He came to this conclusion especially when the later Han Dynasty began. The Han empire's power and glory reached its pinnacle when it gained territorial expansion and political stability throughout the country; credit for these achievements was ascribed to the virtue of Han Dynasty rulers. Wang Ch'ung was neither anti-Confucian nor pro-Confucian. Although he gave the impression that he was no follower of Confucianism, he actually buttressed Confucianism through his rational skepticism and criticism.

Summary

Wang Ch'ung believed in the power of nature and its spontaneity and stressed the importance of skepticism and rationalism. Yet he did not propose any new ideas. Instead, he attacked and accommodated the old ideas in an eclectic fashion. As a result, he is generally credited with ushering in the era of Neo-Taoism which emphasized both the spontaneous power of nature (naturalism) and the critical ability of man (rationalism) during the Wei-Chin period. Orthodox Confucianism was severely challenged by such emergent unorthodox ideologies as Neo-Taoism; Wang Ch'ung, a typical Confucian scholar at heart, defended the basic Confucian tenets in his own unique way.

Bibliography

Chan, Wing-tsit. *A Source Book in Chinese Philosophy*. Princeton, N.J.: Princeton University Press, 1963. This book contains a chapter on Wang Ch'ung's life, together with extensive excerpts of his philosophical writings taken from the *Lun-hêng*.

De Bary, William T., Wing-tsit Chan, and Burton Watson, eds. *Sources of Chinese Tradition*. New York: Columbia University Press, 1960. A brief introduction to Wang Ch'ung's writings in relation to theories of the structure of the universe.

Fêng, Yu-lan. *A History of Chinese Philosophy*. Vol. 2, *The Period of Classical Learning*. Derk Bodde, trans. Princeton, N.J.: Princeton University Press, and London: Allen and Unwin, 1953. An interpretative work on Wang Ch'ung's philosophy.

———. *A Short History of Chinese Philosophy*. New York: Macmillan, 1948. A brief version of Wang Ch'ung's Confucianism is discussed in relation to yin-yang thought, Taoism, and Buddhism.

Forke, Alfred, trans. *Lun-hêng*. 2 vols. Leipzig; Harrassowitz, 1907-1911. An excellent, annotated translation of the *Lun-hêng*, the major result of Wang Ch'ung's philosophy.

———. "Wang Ch'ung and Plato on Death and Immortality." *Journal of the North China Branch Royal Asiatic Society* 31 (1896-1897): 40-60. A critical comparative study of the two philosophers on life and death.

Li, Shi-yi. "Wang Ch'ung." *Tien Hsia Monthly* 5 (1937): 162-184, 209-307. Wang Ch'ung's life and philosophy are discussed, together with his contributions.

Needham, Joseph. *Science and Civilisation in China: History of Scientific Thought*. Vol. 2. Cambridge: Cambridge University Press, 1956. The scientific aspect of Wang Ch'ung's philosophy is discussed.

Key Ray Chong

Born: c. A.D. 307; Lang-ye, Lin-hsi, Shantung Province, China

Died: c. A.D. 379; near Shan-yin, Chekiang Province, China

Area of Achievement: Art

Contribution: By refining the styles of earlier calligraphers and developing new ones, Wang Hsi-chih, through his innovative brushwork, set the aesthetic standards for all subsequent calligraphers in China, Korea, and Japan.

Early Life

In 317, because of military onslaughts by non-Chinese "barbarians," the Western Chin (Tsin) Dynasty was forced to evacuate southward, reestablishing itself in refuge as the Eastern Chin (317-420). Wang Hsi-chih (Yi-shao was another given name he used) was born some years before this move in what is today the Province of Shantung, where the Wangs enjoyed the status of a leading aristocratic family. His father, Wang K'uang, was the cousin of Wang Tao, a prominent minister of the Western Chin, who advocated moving to the south. Both Wang K'uang and Wang Tao were praised for helping save the Chin through this fortuitous move.

Many of Wang Hsi-chih's relatives, besides being active in politics, were literati well versed in philosophy, literature, and the arts, especially calligraphy, the technique of writing characters with brush and ink. Chinese characters, the oldest continuous form of writing in the world, evolved from primitive markings on neolithic pottery, to first millennium B.C. graphs carved on tortoise shells and scapulae used in divination, and later to a complex script preserved on cast bronze ritual vessels and stone tablets. By the second century B.C., characters were being written on silk and bamboo slips using bamboo brushes with animal hair tips dipped in ink made from molded lampblack hardened with glue and dissolved in water on an ink slab.

As writing changed from carving, casting, and etching to a means of expressing through a flexible brush nuances of aesthetic feeling on a receptive surface such as silk or paper, the art of beautiful writing emerged. Writing had become not only a means of communication but indeed an expression of sentiment made manifest in ink. The ability to use the brush as both an artist's and a calligrapher's tool was a hallmark of the cultured gentleman. "A person's true character is revealed in one's calligraphy" according to a Chinese maxim; the facility to write Chinese characters in an elegant hand was judged to be a sign of talent and breeding.

Calligraphy is a discipline learned through practice and imitation. Wang was introduced to the "four treasures of the scholar's studio"—the brush, the ink stick, the ink stone, and paper or silk—in his youth by his father, who was adept in the "clerical" (*li*) style of writing, and an uncle, Wang Yi, a master of the "running" (*hsing*) style. These styles of writing had evolved from earlier calligraphers' experiments with character forms and the movement of writing implements over the ages. Beginning with the Shang period "oracle bone script" (*chia-gu-wen*), calligraphic styles progressed through the inscribed "ancient script" (*ku-wen*) on bronze implements, the "large seal script" (*ta-chuan*) on Warring States-era ritual vessels, and the "official" or "clerical" (*li*) style on Han Dynasty bamboo slips to the "block" script (*k'ai-shu*) of the first century or so. By Wang's time, the "running" style, aptly named since the strokes run together, along with "official grass" (*chang-ts'ao*), were new styles emerging out of these historical predecessors.

As a teenager, Wang became a disciple of the noted calligrapher Lady Wei. She was impressed with his talent, reportedly saying, "This child is destined to surpass my fame as a calligrapher." Later, to broaden his knowledge of past masters' brushwork, Wang traveled the land examining inscriptions preserved on stone stelae. In the south, he encountered specimens of Li Ssu, the Legalist prime minister of the Ch'in Dynasty (221-206 B.C.), whose decrees unified the scripts of the rival feudal states into a single one based on Ch'in models. He was also impressed by the "regular" script (*chen-shu*) works of Chung Yao, a Wei premier, and Liang Hu, noted for his large characters. The masterpieces of Ts'ao Hsi, Ts'ai Yung, and Chang Ch'ang also had an effect on him. From their examples he learned the theoretical and technical essences of calligraphy to enable him to go beyond imitation to creativity.

Awakened to new inspirations, he reportedly lamented that he had wasted years in studying under Lady Wei. "I [then] changed my master," he wrote, "and have been taking lessons from the monuments." He absorbed all the styles that he encountered, adapting them to create new versions. Besides the "running" style, he was especially proficient in the "grass" (*ts'ao*) style, an abstract, cursive form of writing whereby individual strokes of a character are effortlessly blended together while the brush rapidly moves across the writing surface, producing characters as flowing as "grass undulating in the breeze."

Life's Work

Wang Hsi-chih held several government positions, including Censor of K'uai-chi and "General of the Right Army" (*Yu-chün*), a title frequently affixed to his surname (Wang Yu-chün). He held posts in the provinces of Hupei and Chekiang, but he was far better known as a calligrapher than as a government official.

Many anecdotes, perhaps apocryphal, but repeated nevertheless in most Chinese biographies of Wang, attest his brilliance and dedication to his art. One such legend relates that he would practice writing from morning until dusk beside a pond at the Chieh-chu Temple in Shao-hsing. Forgetting even to eat, he would copy characters repeatedly until he was satisfied. He washed out his brush and rinsed off the ink slab so frequently in the pond that its waters eventually turned black, and it became known as "Ink Pond."

Wang would practice even when he did not have paper, using his sleeve as a substitute. His writing was extremely forceful. Once, at Fen-yang, he asked a craftsman to carve out the characters he had written on a board; the worker reported that the power of his brush strokes had been impressed through three-quarters of the wood, giving rise to the phrase "penetrating three-fourths of the wood" as a metaphor for profundity and keenness. His wife, a noted calligrapher in her own right, often could not get him to stop writing even to eat; once she found him absorbed in his work, munching on sticks of ink which he absentmindedly had mistaken for food.

On another occasion, a Taoist monk, taking advantage of Wang's love of geese, connived to induce him to write out a Taoist text for him by arranging for a particularly fine gaggle to swim near the artist's boat. Instead of selling the geese to Wang, who wanted them badly and was willing to pay a high price, the monk asked him to write out the *Huang-t'ing ching* (Yellow Court Classic) in exchange for the fowl. Wang promptly obliged and sailed off with his beloved geese in tow, leaving the clever monk with an invaluable treasure. Wang's

fascination with geese was rooted in his admiration of their gliding movement in the water and their bearing, traits he studied to improve his use of the brush.

On another occasion, Wang supposedly encountered an old lady selling fans beside a bridge in Shao-hsing. When she asked him to purchase one, he inquired as to how many she was able to sell each day. Admitting that her fans were out of fashion, the woman grumbled that she could barely make ends meet. Taking pity on her, Wang offered to write some poems on the fans and urged her to sell them at a high price. Though skeptical and thinking that her fans were spoiled by his writing, she followed his advice, and within a short period of time all the fans were sold. Now realizing the value of his calligraphy on her wares, she hounded Wang to decorate more, even pursuing him to his home. In desperation, he hid behind a stone grotto in the garden; later generations referred to this site as the "Old Woman Evading Stone." The bridge where the fans were reportedly inscribed is still popularly called the "Fan Writing Bridge."

The best-known event in Wang's life happened in 353. On the third day of the third lunar month, he joined a group of some forty men of letters, including Sun T'ung and Hsieh An, to celebrate the spring festival at a scenic spot near Shao-sing, famous for the rare orchids supposedly planted there by a king of the fifth century B.C. There, at the Orchid Pavilion, they drank, challenged one another with word games, played chess, and composed poems. To commemorate the occasion, Wang wrote a preface to a collection of poetry created there by himself and his friends. This 324-character, twenty-eight-line masterpiece, the *Lan-t'ing hsu* (Orchid Pavilion preface), became treasured as one of Wang's greatest accomplishments.

This scroll's brushwork and composition were likened to "fairies flying among the clouds and dancing on the waves." Each character displayed his genius, and even where several characters, such as *chih* (repeated twenty times) and *pu* (used in seven places), were duplicated in the composition, calligraphic variations were employed to prevent any single character from being exactly like another. Wang later tried to duplicate this success by making copies, but he was forced to admit that even he could not surpass his original in beauty.

Eventually, he became dissatisfied with court intrigue and corruption, preferring to retire to a reclusive life in order to devote himself exclusively to study and calligraphy. His last days were spent secluded in the picturesque hills of Chekiang Province at the Jade Curtain Spring near Shan-yin, where he died, probably around 379 (some sources say 361).

Summary

Wang Hsi-chih is celebrated by connoisseurs of Chinese writing as the "Sage Calligrapher." His writing style was immortalized by the phrase "dragons leaping at the gate of heaven and tigers crouching before the phoenix hall," the words used by the sixth century Emperor Wu of the Liang Dynasty upon being shown Wang's works. Several of his seven sons, particularly Wang Hsien-chih (nicknamed the "Little Sage") carried on their father's legacy, becoming important calligraphers in their own right and producing equally talented progeny.

Wang Hsi-chih's holographs were greatly coveted. The *Lan-t'ing hsu*, for example, was passed on as a Wang family heirloom for seven generations, ending up in the possession of Chih Yung, a monk who was also well-known as a calligrapher. When Chih Yung died, the scroll was entrusted to his disciple, Pien Ts'ai. Emperor T'ang T'ai-tsung (reigned 626-649) wanted this scroll in order to complete his collection of Wang originals. Thrice the monk refused to give it up. Wei Cheng, the prime minister, then devised a scheme whereby a confidant named Hsiao Yi, pretending to be a kind host, disarmed the monk's suspicion by plying him with wine; taking advantage of his drunken stupor, Hsiao Yi was able to steal away the scroll, which had been hidden in a wooden temple beam. The emperor was overjoyed and ordered Chao Mu and Feng Ch'eng-su to make copies for distribution to his ministers for their enjoyment and study. On his death, T'ai-tsung ordered this scroll and all other original writings by Wang entombed with him so that he could enjoy them in the afterworld. The consensus of most experts is that none of Wang's originals exists today. Fortunately, many of his writings were carved in stone so that rubbings could be made for study, and other artists traced his originals to learn and to imitate his stroke style, thus preserving samples of Wang's genius for posterity.

Bibliography

Driscoll, Lucy, and Kenji Toda. *Chinese Calligraphy*. Chicago: University of Chicago Press, 1935. Has some references to Wang's theories on calligraphy and his studies under Lady Wei.

Froncek, Thomas, ed. *The Horizon Book of the Arts of China*. New York: American Heritage Publishing Co., 1969. A concise biography of Wang is included under the heading "Wine, Weather, and Wang." Preceding page has a picture of Wang entitled "Wang Hsi-chi Writing on a Fan," painted by Liang K'ai (c. 1140-c. 1210).

Li, Dun J., ed. *The Essence of Chinese Civilization*. Princeton, N.J.: D. Van Nostrand Co., 1967. A partial translation of Wang's biography (supposedly written by Emperor T'ang T'ai-tsung) from the *Chin shu* (265-420; *History of the Chin*).

Li, Hsing-tsun. *The Story of Chinese Culture*. Taiwan: H. T. Lee, 1964. Contains an impressionistic essay, "Wang Hsi-chih and Chinese Calligraphy," giving anecdotal highlights of Wang's life.

Nakata, Yujiro. *Chinese Calligraphy*. New York: Weather Hill/Tankosha, 1983. Historical overview of Chinese calligraphy originally published in Japanese. Chapter 6, "The Masterpieces of Wang Xizhi [Wang Hsi-chih] and Wang Xianzhi [Wang Hsien-chih]," gives a short biographical account. Numerous examples of Wang's work are illustrated and analyzed. Appendix contains a chronology of calligraphers and their works.

Willetts, William. *Chinese Calligraphy: Its History and Aesthetic Motivation*. New York and Oxford: Oxford University Press, 1981. Contains a short account of the writing of the *Lan-t'ing hsu* and reproduces a section of the scroll taken from a stone rubbing. Good bibliography on Chinese calligraphy in general.

William M. Zanella

WANG PI

Born: 226; possibly in modern Shantung Province, China

Died: 249; China

Area of Achievement: Philosophy

Contribution: Wang was a major creative force behind the most important philosophical school of his day, and his commentaries on some of the most revered Chinese classics still help shape their interpretation.

Early Life

Wang Pi (in Chinese fashion the family name, Wang, is given first) died at the age of twenty-three. It is therefore difficult to separate the story of his early life from that of his mature period of productivity. A further handicap to the student of Wang Pi is the fact that very little is actually known about the details of his life. In an uncharacteristic omission, the Chinese dynastic histories do not even contain a biography for him. Most of what is known about Wang Pi comes from a few short paragraphs appended as footnotes to the biography of another man and incorporated into a history called the *San-kuo chih* (third century; chronicles of the three kingdoms). Wang Pi's thought, however, survives in the commentaries he wrote to three Chinese classics: the *I Ching* (before the sixth century B.C.; *Book of Changes*), the *Tao-te Ching* (c. eighth to third century B.C.; also known as the *Lao-tzu*), and Confucius' *Lun-yü* (late sixth or early fifth century B.C.; *Analects*).

Wang Pi was a precocious child, and he soon proved himself remarkably adept at conversation—a skill that was much in vogue among the elite of third century China and which accounts for much of his contemporary reputation. He was a thorough master of the polite arts of the day, but, in keeping with his image as *enfant terrible*, he also was not quite sensitive enough to others' feelings and offended many of his acquaintances with his overly clever manner. He served in the relatively minor post of departmental secretary, which had also been his father's job, but failed to reach higher office because his patron, Ho Yen (190-249), was outmaneuvered at court in his efforts to have Wang appointed. Wang was not really interested in administration anyway, however, and preferred to devote his time and energy to philosophical speculation.

Wang flourished in the era of the Cheng-shih reign (240-249), which is often cited as the high point of the so-called Neo-Taoist movement in China. This period came to an abrupt end in 249, when a *coup d'état* stripped real power away from the ruling family of the Wei state in north China, where Wang lived, and placed it in the hands of a military dictator. Ho Yen perished in the wake of this coup, and Wang himself was dismissed from office, although his death later that same year came as a result of unknown natural causes.

Life's Work

Wang Pi and his patron, Ho Yen, are traditionally credited with founding the movement known in the West as Neo-Taoism. This name is misleading, however, since the movement really grew as much out of Confucianism as it did out of Taoism. It began with studies of the Confucian classic the *I Ching*, was enthusiastically discussed with reference to the Taoist *Tao-te Ching* and *Chuang-tzu* in the later third century, and in the fourth century finally merged into a newly triumphant Mahayana Buddhism. The movement is probably most accurately known by its Chinese name: *hsüan-hsüeh* (mysterious learning).

Wang himself stands accused of trying to interpret a Confucian classic, the *I Ching*, in Taoist terms, and, in the single most famous episode in Wang's life, of praising Confucius as the supreme Taoist because he knew better than to try and say anything about the ineffable Tao. The truth is that Wang was not much concerned with—indeed, he completely rejected—labels such as "Confucian" and "Taoist" and instead strove to unearth the ultimate truths concealed in each.

During the waning years of the Han Dynasty (207 B.C. to A.D. 220), various thinkers, notably the great Wang Ch'ung (27-c. 100), had become increasingly disillusioned with standard Confucian metaphysics, which in the mid-Han era had emphasized elaborate systems of correspondences between Heaven, Earth, and Man, cycles of the so-called Five Elements, and attempts to predict the future based on these. The desire to understand the basic principles of the universe was not lost, nor were the basic ideas entirely rejected, but the simplistic excesses—the teleology and the easy belief that Heaven was regular, purposeful, and concerned with humankind—were shaved away. At the same time, the so-called New Text versions of the Confucian classics which had supported the elaborate Han cosmological systems lost their standing and gradually were replaced by versions of the texts purporting to be older. These "Old Texts" did not fit neatly into vast cosmological systems and left a cosmological void in Confucian thought. By the end of the Han, the great pattern of the universe had seemingly dissolved into chaos.

In the third century, *hsüan-hsüeh* emerged to fill this metaphysical vacuum. *Hsüan-hsüeh* is predicated on the belief that the infinite phenomena of this universe are random, transitory, and without any meaningful pattern. Yet they all must, it was reasoned, be generated by one single, eternal verity. That was the "original nothingness" (*pen-wu*), or "nonbeing" (*wu*), the origin of all being.

Because of this emphasis on nonbeing as the root of all things, *hsüan-hsüeh* thinkers have sometimes been dismissed as nihilistic. This casual dismissal is reinforced by the explanation that they were escapist Neo-Taoists, who turned from the traditional social concerns of Confucianism because of political repression, the collapse of the established Han world order, or aristocratic indifference. In fact, *hsüan-hsüeh* was far more than mere escapism and represents an impassioned search for meaning in the universe by highly refined and critical intellects. The idea that nonbeing is the ontological foundation of the universe is similarly more than mere nihilism, since, in *hsüan-hsüeh* thought, nonbeing becomes the positive principle that renders the universe intelligible.

Being and nonbeing coexist and are fundamentally indivisible. This great unity of being and nonbeing is "The Mystery" (*hsüan*), also known as Tao, or the Way. It is the unifying principle of the universe, called a "mystery" because any name would be inadequate: It is absolute, and even to call it a mystery is to impose false and misleading limitations on it—better not to call it anything (but to call it "nothing" is not quite satisfactory either).

Wang's thought focused on this critical *hsüan-hsüeh* relationship between being and nonbeing. His work took the form of exegesis, an attempt to achieve an understanding of the classics of China's formative age. Wang's scholarship was solidly in the tradition of the Ching-chou school, a place in central China that had been a late Han center for Old Text scholarship and which was particularly famous for its study of the *T'ai-hsüan Ching* (contemporary with Jesus Christ; the classic of the

great mystery). This book, in turn, was largely just an amplification of ideas to be found in the more venerable *I Ching*, and it was to the *I Ching* that Wang turned his principal interest.

Working with an Old Text edition of the *I Ching*, Wang rejected the Han tradition of interpreting it in terms of astrological symbols and numerology and sought instead to return to what he thought was the original meaning of the text. The *I Ching* consists of the set of all sixty-four possible combinations of six broken and unbroken lines; the resulting hexagrams were then assigned oracular values and used in divination. Later, a set of "wings," or commentaries, was added that recast this fortune-teller's manual into a kind of cosmological blueprint of the universe. Although Wang rejected the neat teleology of Han Confucianism, he was still searching for some abstract principle that would reconcile the apparent diversity and disorder of the material universe, and he found in the *I Ching* exactly the kind of cosmic diagram for which he was looking.

The *I Ching* spoke of a Great Ultimate (*t'ai-chi*) which gives rise to the twin poles, *yin* and *yang*, which in turn generate the multitude of phenomena in the world. This schema is the primordial unity which in the third century was called The Mystery. Unlike the elaborate systems and cycles of earlier Han cosmology, this principle is spontaneous and unpremeditated. Heaven and Earth move without obvious purpose, yet naturally accord with the Tao. This system is a truth beyond words which must be looked at holistically; any attempt at analytical description violates its absolute quality. Consequently, in a typically Taoist paradox, the subject of Wang's intense investigations was beyond the power of his words to describe.

Wang belonged to the side of a raging third century debate which believed in the inadequacy of language. Characteristically, this idea harked back to a passage in the *I Ching* which said that "words cannot exhaustively [convey] meaning" (*yen pu chin i*). Wang argued, therefore, that one should pay attention not to symbols or words but to their underlying, and more abstract, meanings. When you understand the meaning of a passage, you should forget the words.

Although the cosmic principle, or Tao, is unitary, it also has a binary extension—the dialectic between being and nonbeing. From these two, then, come the many. Wang liked to view the universe in terms of the interaction between a fundamental "substance" (*t'i*), and its "applications" (*yung*) in the phenomenal world. This schema is reminiscent of Plato's famous duality between ideals and physical appearances, but, more important, it also resembles the later Neo-Confucian duality between "principle" (*li*) and "matter" (*ch'i*). Wang, in fact, appears to have been one of the first Chinese thinkers to use *li* ("principle") in essentially this sense, and, although he cannot be given credit for fully conceiving these ideas, he clearly contributed to the ongoing development of an important theme in later Chinese thought.

Summary

In his short life, Wang Pi exerted a tremendous impact on philosophy. *Hsüan-hsüeh* was the dominant mode of thought for some two centuries, and Wang's commentaries on the *I Ching* and the *Tao-te Ching*, together with the commentary on the *Chuang-tzu* by Kuo Hsiang (died 312) and Hsiang Hsiu (c. 230-c. 280), were the central texts of *hsüan-hsüeh*. Later *hsüan-hsüeh* thinkers and conversationalists measured themselves against Wang.

Wang's scholarship, if not *hsüan-hsüeh* thought itself, also affects scholars even in the twentieth century. It is well-known that the *Tao-te Ching* has been the most translated of all Chinese books, and, of the literally hundreds of Chinese commentaries to the *Tao-te Ching* Wang's is considered to be the very best that still remains. Most translations of the *Tao-te Ching* are therefore based on Wang's edition of the text and commentary. To be sure, Wang profoundly influenced his own time, but he also exerts an influence on modern scholarship, as the *Tao-te Ching*, one of the most important books of all time, continues to be viewed partly through his eyes.

Bibliography

Balazs, Étienne. "Nihilistic Revolt or Mystical Escapism." In *Chinese Civilization and Bureaucracy: Variations on a Theme*, edited by Arthur F. Wright. New Haven, Conn.: Yale University Press, 1964. A brilliant, although highly unflattering, depiction of third century thought and society.

Fêng, Yu-lan. *A History of Chinese Philosophy.* Vol. 2, *The Period of Classical Learning.* Derk Bodde, trans. Princeton, N.J.: Princeton University Press, and London: Allen and Unwin, 1953. Although somewhat dated, and not without flaws, this work remains a classic. It is also virtually the only English language study of some of the lesser known Chinese thinkers, such as Wang Pi.

Hsiao, Kung-chuan. *A History of Chinese Political Thought.* F. W. Mote, trans. Princeton, N.J.: Princeton University Press, 1979. This work contains a somewhat unsympathetic account of the political implications of Neo-Taoist thought.

Lao-tzu and Wang Pi. *A Translation of Lao Tzu's "Tao-te Ching" and Wang Pi's Commentary.* Paul Lin, trans. Ann Arbor: Center for Chinese Studies, University of Michigan, 1977. This book examines Wang's contribution to the study of the *Tao-te Ching.* It includes a complete translation of a brief third century biography of Wang.

Liu, I-ch'ing. *Shih-shuo Hsin-yü: A New Account of Tales of the World.* Richard B. Mather, trans. Minneapolis: University of Minnesota Press, 1976. A fifth century collection of anecdotes, this book is one of the principal sources of information about Wang Pi. Mather has added an introduction and invaluable biographical sketches of all 626 persons mentioned in the text.

T'ang, Yung-t'ung. "Wang Pi's New Interpretation of the *I'ching* and *Lun-yü.*" *Harvard Journal of Asiatic Studies* 10 (September, 1947): 124-161. An important essay by the foremost Chinese expert on the intellectual history of the period. This work may, however, be too technical for beginners, while experts would be better advised to consult the original Chinese text.

Yü, Ying-shih. "Individualism and the Neo-Taoist Movement in Wei-Chin China." In *Individualism and Holism: The Confucian and Taoist Philosophical Perspectives*, edited by Donald Munro. Ann Arbor: Center for Chinese Studies, University of Michigan, 1985. A fine scholarly description of Neo-Taoism viewed as an expression of Chinese individualism. The essay is marred somewhat by an insistence on the opposition between Neo-Taoism and Confucianism.

Zürcher, Erik. *The Buddhist Conquest of China: The Spread and Adaptation of Buddhism in Early Medieval China.* New York: Humanities Press, 1959. While the focus of this authoritative study is on Buddhism, it also provides an overview of intellectual developments in the period and an excellent discussion of *hsüan-hsüeh.*

Charles W. Holcombe

XANTHIPPE

Born: c. 445 B.C.; Athens, Greece

Died: Early to middle fourth century B.C.; probably Athens, Greece

Area of Achievement: Women's rights

Contribution: Through her aggressive behavior, Xanthippe forced men to reflect upon and reconsider conventional assumptions about women's nature and social roles.

Early Life

Xanthippe is known not as a mere name discovered through archeological research but as a meaningful figure in ancient literature. Since almost no contemporary Athenian women thus are recognized, the implication is that Xanthippe was unusual. She was not a "normal" woman, of whom the Greek philosopher Aristotle (384-322 B.C.) (quoting the fifth century B.C. poet Sophocles) wrote, "Silence lends decorum to a woman." Xanthippe's concern was not male notions of decorum. She spoke, often shrilly, and her voice helped to create philosophical echoes across the centuries.

Nothing certain is known of Xanthippe's childhood and youth. Her date of birth can be estimated as 445 B.C., since she was the mother of one son in his late teens and two much younger sons when her husband, the Athenian political philosopher Socrates (469-399 B.C.), was executed. Several pieces of circumstantial evidence suggest that Xanthippe was born into a noble, or at least wealthy, Athenian family. Her name, meaning "Golden Horse," was of the sort traditionally favored by the aristocracy. The biographer Diogenes Laertius (late second-early third century A.D.) mentions that Xanthippe brought a dowry into her marriage. Athenian dowries were quite sizable and often included a large sum of money. At some point, Socrates virtually abandoned his early profession of stonecutting, perhaps living on the proceeds of invested money. Given that Socrates was not from a wealthy family, the money may have come from Xanthippe. Diogenes Laertius also mentions that Xanthippe felt ashamed of a dinner that Socrates gave for some rich men, suggesting her awareness of upper-class standards. The contemporary novelist John Gardner's *The Wreckage of Agathon* (1972), based loosely on the life of Socrates, supposes that Agathon's wife Tuka ("battle-ax") is of aristocratic background.

Xanthippe was an exception to the rule that Athenian daughters, especially those of aristocratic lineage, married very young, often in their mid-teens. Socrates' eldest son Lamprocles was born when the philosopher was in his early fifties, his youngest when Socrates was about sixty-five. If Xanthippe was twenty-four years younger than Socrates, she would have borne Lamprocles at twenty-eight and her youngest son at about forty-one. These figures suggest that Xanthippe married about ten years later than was customary.

There are two probable reasons why Xanthippe married late, perhaps below her social status, and to a notoriously ugly and unproductive man: She was difficult temperamentally, and she was physically unattractive. Her temper was infamous; her looks may be inferred from some Socratic advice reported by the historian Xenophon (c. 430-c. 354 B.C.). Socrates advises his companions to avoid sexual relations with beautiful people and to restrict their sexual activity to those who would be shunned unless there existed an overwhelming physical need. Whether or not he took his own advice in marrying Xanthippe, there is not the slightest hint that she was physically attractive.

Life's Work

The marriage of Xanthippe and Socrates would seem to be a match made in hell, between an overage, unattractive, difficult woman and an even older, ugly, underemployed frequenter of the Athenian streets. Many must have seen it this way: Socrates was put to death for his disturbing activities, and Xanthippe's name became synonymous with "shrew." This view, however, is superficial, ignoring the deep moral bond between the two.

That bond is suggested by the fact that the activities of Xanthippe and Socrates were both orthodox and unorthodox. In a number of important ways, each was a conventional Athenian of the time. Xanthippe married, reared children, managed a household, and stayed clear of political life; Socrates, in addition to establishing a family, served in military campaigns and took his turn in holding public office. Neither challenged practically the genderized Athenian division of functions.

This extraordinary couple's challenge to authority was verbal. This is thoroughly familiar in Socrates' case. He questioned and criticized powerful Athenians, comparing himself to a gadfly stinging that noble but complacent horse Athens. Antagonizing many, he was indicted for impiety, tried, convicted, and executed. In the process, Socrates became a hero of free speech and moral integrity. What is not so obvious is that Xanthippe's life may be understood in roughly the same terms, once the necessary revisions in perspective are made.

Athenian males ruled the city (and much of their known world), not only politically but with their public presence. Athenian women, especially those of the upper classes, were secluded and were segregated from men. Xanthippe appears to have responded to these restrictions complexly. On the one hand, denied wider public access, she "stung" most frequently members of her own family. Xenophon tells the story of Socrates arguing Lamprocles out of his anger with his mother. Xanthippe has been abusing her son, not physically but verbally; Lamprocles protests that this is unjust, since he has done nothing wrong. Socrates induces his son to acknowledge that Xanthippe's scolding is not only not malicious but is also motivated by special concern for Lamprocles. This implies that while Lamprocles may have done nothing wrong, he may also have done nothing right, and that his mother's words were needed to get him moving. There is a glimpse here of the power of women to shape men morally through daily "encouragement."

However, Xanthippe's activities probably were not confined to the household. She appears to have known most of Socrates' friends and companions. There are a number of instances of Xanthippe appearing in public, as related by Diogenes Laertius and in Plato's *Phaedo*. In her house, in the streets, in the marketplace, in Socrates' jail cell, Xanthippe was a presence. She was not silent; she did not defer to or flatter men; she did not conceal her anger. In short, she frequently behaved like a man, being as visible, as outspoken, and as courageous—or at any rate as rash—as a man was expected to be. This presumption of equality amused but also unnerved Socrates' companions, to whom any outspoken, critical woman was abnormal and therefore a "shrew."

Xanthippe's attitude toward Socrates was straightforward. Anecdotes about her verbal and physical abuse of him have become legendary and form most of the traditional image of Xanthippe. No doubt, there is a basis in fact for these anecdotes; Socrates must have been a better philosopher than husband, father, and provider, and

Xanthippe may well have been a frequent critic. Yet Xanthippe is also shown to have admired Socrates, especially for his justice, and to have been considerably more accepting of his friends than they were of her. Overall, she seems to have had few illusions about, but considerable affection for, Socrates. It is Plato, not Xanthippe, who portrays Socrates as "young and fair."

Socrates' experience with Xanthippe may have been of major importance for his political philosophy. Contemporary scholars have noted that Socrates was unusually well-disposed toward women. This seems paradoxical, given the horrific reputation of the woman he was closest to. Yet Xenophon makes it clear that Socrates very much appreciated Xanthippe. In part, this was because he believed her to be a very good mother, painstaking and selfless, if not especially patient, with her sons.

Beyond this, however, Socrates was clear-eyed about Xanthippe's nature, and he was unbiased by the prevailing antifemale prejudice. He understood that Xanthippe was high-spirited; perhaps punning on her name, he compared her to a horse. He was not interested in changing her nature by attempting to break her. Instead of forcing Xanthippe to conform to convention, Socrates conformed to her, believing that learning to live with Xanthippe would be excellent training for getting along with all others. Socrates' acknowledgment of Xanthippe's active, high-spirited nature is reflected in the imaginary "best city" of Plato's *Republic*. There, Socrates proposes that naturally gifted women as well as men be educated as the guardian-rulers of the city.

Summary

Xanthippe disappeared from historical view following Socrates' execution in 399 B.C.. It is easy to believe that her notoriety depended entirely on her relationship with a famous man—that she was a "mere appendage" to him, and an obnoxious one at that. Yet to believe this is to misunderstand the historical significance of both Socrates and Xanthippe.

It is clear that Xanthippe had an unusual degree of freedom in her relationship with Socrates. This is not because Socrates was an ideological "feminist," but because he was observant enough and honest enough to take each person as he or she was. He believed that persons were not merely "male" and "female" in a simple anatomical sense but also had "souls" significantly independent of gender. Xanthippe had a nobly rambunctious soul, and Socrates accorded it due respect.

Very likely, Xanthippe recognized this independence of mind and sense of justice in Socrates and chose him as fully as he chose her. Nevertheless, both Athenian conventions and Socrates' own freedom-loving nature made it impossible for Xanthippe to be simply his equal and companion. The philosopher's wife was, after all, a wife; Socrates and Xanthippe were not fellow guardians in his imagined city. It is easy to believe that Xanthippe, acutely attuned to justice by nature and circumstances, felt the injustice in both her situation and that of Athenian women generally. According to Socratic doctrine, the response of the high-spirited person to injustice is anger.

Xanthippe's "shrewishness," then, may be seen in two sympathetic ways. First, to view a woman as a shrew was the common male reaction to any female who was not sufficiently deferential. Second, shrewishness was the only form contextually available to Xanthippe to express her sense of injustice. Xanthippe was in a classic double-bind: She could not remain silent, but neither could she join her husband's circle of refined, sustained moral discourse. "Conversing daily about virtue" was not an option for Xanthippe; she was too busy rearing Socrates' children and keeping his house. Instead, she shouted occasionally about virtue, and she was misunderstood. Xanthippe's life thus serves as a reminder of both the demands of and constraints upon perfect justice.

Bibliography

Blundell, Sue. *Women in Ancient Greece*. London: British Museum Press, and Cambridge, Mass: Harvard University Press, 1995. A well-illustrated survey of the topic, based on thorough scholarship and engagingly written. Part 2 covers the period of Xanthippe's life.

Cantarella, Eva. *Pandora's Daughters*. Translated by Maureen B. Fant. Baltimore: Johns Hopkins University Press, 1987. This influential interpretation of the position of women in antiquity stresses the breadth and depth of antifemale bias.

Socrates is understood as an important dissenter, but his inspiration is seen as the courtesan Aspasia, not Xanthippe.

Caputi, Jane. *Gossips, Gorgons, and Crones*. Santa Fe, N.M.: Bear & Company, 1993. An interesting, spirited interpretation of the role of "resistant women," written from an ecofeminist perspective. Xanthippe would be included under the category "Gorgon."

Diogenes Laertius. *Lives of Eminent Philosophers*. Vol. 1. Translated by R. D. Hicks. Cambridge, Mass.: Harvard University Press, and London: Heinemann, 1920. Diogenes Laertius's biography of Socrates (in book 2, chapter 5) is the principal source of the colorful, "shrewish" anecdotes about Xanthippe.

Gardner, John. *The Wreckage of Agathon*. New York: Harper, 1970. This novel gives controversial historical life to Xanthippe ("Tuka") and Socrates ("Agathon"). The fictional pair are far more involved with one another (and with heterosexual relations generally) than historical scholarship would concede.

Plato. *Phaedo*. In *The Collected Dialogues of Plato*, edited by Edith Hamilton and Huntington Cairns. New York: Pantheon, 1961. Provocative glimpses of Xanthippe begin and end Plato's treatment of Socrates' last day of life.

Shakespeare, William. *The Taming of the Shrew*. Edited by Brian Morris. London and New York: Methuen, 1981. William Shakespeare's classic comedy is an important source of the perception of Xanthippe as a shrew (see especially Act I, Scene II). In contrast to Socrates' acceptance of Xanthippe's nature, Petruchio manipulates and intimidates Katherina into submission. This Arden edition contains important introductory material on the "shrewish" tradition.

Xenophon. *Conversations of Socrates*. Translated by Hugh Tredennick and Robin Waterfield. London and New York: Penguin Books, 1990. Xanthippe as a real-world example of woman, wife, and mother is present, explicitly and implicitly, throughout Xenophon's Socratic writings.

John F. Wilson

XENOPHANES

Born: c. 570 B.C.; Colophon, near the coast of Asia
Minor

Died: c. 478 B.C.; western Greece

Areas of Achievement: Philosophy, literature, and
religion

Contribution: Xenophanes' critique of the Homeric gods marks the beginning of both systematic
theology and the rational interpretation of myth
in ancient Greek society.

Early Life

The childhood of Xenophanes, like that of most
early Greek philosophers, is shrouded in mystery.
By the time that Xenophanes himself appears in
the literary record of ancient Greece, he is already
a grown man, traveling from town to town as a professional poet. Scholars cannot even be certain of
his father's name, since several ancient authorities
have listed it as Dexius, others as Dexinus, and still
others as Orthomenes. Scholars are certain, however, that Xenophanes was born in the city of Colophon (near the coast of Asia Minor) sometime during the middle of the sixth century B.C. Moreover,
it is likely that he left this area in his youth, probably as the result of Persia's policy of imperial expansion. It was, then, during the very period of Xenophanes' youth that the Persian conquest of new
territories began to lead, inevitably, to war between
Persia and Greece.

Xenophanes himself would later allude to this
stage of his life with these ambiguous words, taken
from what is known as fragment 8:

> Already there have been seven and sixty years tossing
> my thoughts up and down the land of Greece. And
> from my birth there were another twenty-five in addi-
> tion to these, if indeed I know how to speak truly of
> such things.

Since in another fragment Xenophanes had mentioned "the coming of the Mede," it seems probable that he left Colophon at about the time that this
city fell to Harpagus the Mede in 546. For the rest
of his life, Xenophanes would support himself
through his poetry. He became a traveling rhapso-
dist, composing songs on various topics as he journeyed throughout the Greek world. Unlike many
other archaic rhapsodists, however, Xenophanes
used only his own compositions in his performances. It is probably from these works that the extant
fragments are derived.

Diogenes Laërtius states that Xenophanes spent
much of his life in Sicily. Other authorities support
this view, maintaining that Xenophanes had participated in founding the city of Elea, in what is modern Italy. Xenophanes, according to these scholars,
is thus the spiritual forebear of the philosophers
known as the Eleatics and one of the actual
founders of Elea itself. The accuracy of this claim
seems questionable, however, and the belief that
Xenophanes was instrumental in founding Elea
may have arisen solely because the philosopher
had written a poem commemorating the event. In
fact, Xenophanes seems unlikely to have had any
permanent residence; he must have spent most of
his life traveling extensively throughout Greece
and Sicily, pausing in each community only for
brief periods.

Xenophanes' lifelong travels had a profound influence on his thought. For example, after he had
observed fossils in a quarry near Syracuse, Xenophanes developed the theory that life on earth is
cyclic: Those creatures who had lived in earlier
eras, he believed, were repeatedly "dissolved" by
the encroaching seas, and life had to develop all
over again. Yet even more important than what Xenophanes observed during these travels was his
contact with the intellectual revolution in Greek
philosophy, which, by this time, was well under
way. For example, Thales of Miletus, whose views
about the composition of matter are regarded as the
origin of Greek philosophy, had by then been active for more than forty years. Anaximander, who
was Thales' successor and who had originated the
notion of the *apeiron* (the "unbounded" or "unlimited" as the source of all creation), died in about
the same year that Colophon fell. Anaximenes of
Miletus, who had believed that all matter was composed of rarefied or contracted air, is also likely to
have lived in roughly the same period as Xenophanes.

The ideas of these philosophers were of great
importance in the Greek world where Xenophanes
traveled, lived, and wrote his poetry. The young
philosopher seems to have listened to the theories
of his predecessors, considered them, and then
combined their views with his own thought to create the subjects of his songs. Unlike many other
pre-Socratics, however, Xenophanes has left the
modern world substantial portions of his poetry,
written down either by himself or by those who

studied with him. It is from these surviving words of Xenophanes—about 120 lines in all—that modern readers are able to form their clearest picture of the philosopher and of his life's work.

Life's Work

As was common among the pre-Socratic philosophers, Xenophanes devoted a substantial portion of his thought to considering the nature of the physical universe. Although it is uncertain whether he actually wrote the work entitled *Peri phuseos* (on nature), which Stobaeus and Pollux attributed to him, a large number of Xenophanes' surviving fragments are concerned with matters of astronomy and the weather. In these passages, Xenophanes reveals that he was strongly influenced by Anaximenes, who had argued that clouds were merely condensed, or "thickened," masses of air. Xenophanes expressed a similar view, substituting only the notion of "sea" or "water" for that of air. In Xenophanes' theory, the sea gives rise to the clouds, winds, and rivers; the sun and heavenly bodies are created from thickened, or "ignited," bits of cloud. Rainbows, too, are said to be nothing more than colored fragments of cloud.

In two other passages, Xenophanes says that everything in the universe is made of earth and water. This theory is apparently an attempt to combine Thales' recognition that water is necessary to life and, as ice or steam, can change its shape with Anaximenes' belief that there must be some general process (condensation or rarefaction) which accounts for this change. That same general line of thought may also lie behind Xenophanes' belief that each day the sun is created anew, arising from fiery bits of dilated cloud.

Yet far more influential than these physical theories of Xenophanes were the philosopher's theological views and his statements about the nature of God. Xenophanes disagreed with earlier authors such as Homer and Hesiod who had presented the gods as immoral and had endowed them with the same physical traits and limitations as ordinary men. In two famous fragments, Xenophanes criticized the common assumption that the gods were merely immortal creatures similar in most ways to ordinary human beings:

> The Ethiopians claim that their gods are snub-nosed and black, the Thracians that theirs have blue eyes and blond hair. . . . But if cows and horses or lions had hands or could draw and do all the other things that men do, then horses would draw images of the gods which look like horses, and cows like cows, and they would depict the bodies of their gods in the same form as they had themselves.

The argument here is that all people wrongly assume the gods to be like themselves, in form and (it is suggested) in their vices and faults.

Xenophanes' own understanding of divinity was quite different. To begin with, Xenophanes was a monotheist, believing that there exists only a single god who is unlike humankind both in form and in character. Second, Xenophanes said that this deity perceives the universe differently from mankind, using all of its "body" simultaneously to think, to hear, and to see. Finally, in two important fragments, Xenophanes anticipated Aristotle's theory of the Prime Mover, asserting that this one god remains in a single place and guides the universe without movement, relying solely on the power of Mind.

Yet, by Xenophanes' own admission, even these statements about divinity are subject to debate. For "no man," he says, "either has known or will know the clear truth about the gods. . . . Belief [and not certain knowledge] is produced for all men." While not as general in focus as the skepticism of Plato's Academy, Xenophanes' remarks here do anticipate some of the views which would arise in later periods of Greek philosophy. His distinction between "believing" and "knowing," for example, was to have a crucial influence on the work of Plato himself. Moreover, Xenophanes' theory that human knowledge is necessarily limited would reappear in the works of many later Platonic scholars.

Summary

If Xenophanes' statements about his life in fragment 8 are to be believed, he had already reached the age of ninety-two when those words were written. Xenophanes' lifetime would have encompassed a period of Greek history which witnessed the birth of both tragedy and philosophy in the Western world. At the time of his death, the Persian Wars were drawing to a close and the classical period of Greek history was about to begin.

The picture of Xenophanes which emerges from his writings is thus that of a man who was representative of his day: diverse in his interests, immensely curious, and unwilling to remain content with the dogma of the past. These are traits which characterize many of the other pre-Socratic philosophers as well.

Yet Xenophanes was also important for the impact which he would have on later scholars. His perception of divinity would influence Aristotle and, ultimately, Saint Thomas Aquinas. His belief that human knowledge was inherently limited was to reemerge in the skepticism of the Academy. Xenophanes was, in other words, a pivotal figure who helped to transform the empirical philosophy of antiquity into the more metaphysical philosophy of the classical age.

Bibliography

Fraenkel, H. "Xenophanes' Empiricism and His Critique of Knowledge," in *The Pre-Socratics*, edited by Alexander P. D. Mourelatos. Rev. ed. Princeton, N.J. and Chichester: Princeton University Press, 1993. Fraenkel uses Xenophanes' theory of knowledge, and his rejection of early beliefs about the gods, as the basis for an exploration of the philosopher's worldview. Perhaps the best short summary available on the thought and contribution of Xenophanes to Greek philosophy.

Freeman, Kathleen. *Ancilla to the Pre-Socratic Philosophers*. Cambridge, Mass.: Harvard University Press, and Oxford: Blackwell, 1948. The most convenient source of information for anyone who is interested in examining the surviving texts of the pre-Socratics. Freeman translates, without commentary or interpretation, all the fragments included in Diels's exhaustive edition of the pre-Socratics.

————. *The Pre-Socratic Philosophers*. Cambridge, Mass.: Harvard University Press, and Oxford: Blackwell, 1946. In this excellent survey, Freeman, taking each historical figure in turn, digests and summarizes all that is known about the philosophical views of the pre-Socratics. The fragments upon which she has based her information are all listed in concise footnotes. A very thorough summary of the philosopher's life begins each entry. At the end of the work is an invaluable list which presents, in a sentence or two, an encapsulated view of what is known about the authors who are the sources for the fragments.

Jaeger, W. W. "Xenophanes' Doctrine of God." In *The Theology of the Early Greek Philosophers*, translated by Edward S. Robinson. London and New York: Oxford University Press, 1947. The premise of Jaeger's book is that the pre-Socratics are important for their theological views as well as for their (more famous) doctrines on the physical universe. Xenophanes, as arguably the most theological of the pre-Socratics, naturally plays a central role in this work.

Jaspers, Karl. *The Great Philosophers*. New York: Harcourt Brace, 1993. Actually a compilation of notes left by Jaspers (a philosophy teacher for 60 years in Germany and Switzerland) at his death, this work provides a broad discussion of the teachings of ancient history's most prominent philosophers, including Xenophanes.

Kirk, Geoffrey S., and John E. Raven. *The Presocratic Philosophers*. 2d ed. Cambridge and New York: Cambridge University Press, 1983. A useful summary of pre-Socratic philosophers and their philosophy, containing both the major texts of the philosophers and reliable commentary on those texts. The extant fragments are grouped by topic rather than by number (as in many other editions). The 1983 edition contains more recent interpretations and a much-improved format: Translations follow Greek passages immediately, rather than in footnotes. Includes a short but important bibliography on each author.

Lesher, J. H. "Xenophanes' Scepticism." *Phronesis* 23 (1978): 1-21. A clear account of Xenophanes' views concerning the limitations of human knowledge. Lesher argues that it is Xenophanes' theological point of view—rejecting, for example, such traditional sources of knowledge about the gods as divination—which is revolutionary, not his skepticism per se.

Jeffrey L. Buller

XENOPHON

Born: c. 431 B.C.; near Athens
Died: c. 354 B.C.; probably Corinth or Athens
Areas of Achievement: Literature and philosophy
Contribution: Through his writings on subjects ranging from the practical to the philosophical, Xenophon, a pupil of Socrates, sought in the fourth century B.C. to instruct and improve Greek society. His works provide the modern reader with a clearer picture of the ancient world.

Early Life

Xenophon was born in or near Athens around 431 B.C. His father, Gryllus, was a wealthy Athenian aristocrat. Little is known of Xenophon's early life, but he would have come of age during the latter years of the Peloponnesian War (431-404), the great conflict between Athens and Sparta. He probably served in one of the crack Athenian cavalry units.

As a youth, Xenophon became a pupil of Socrates, joining an intellectual circle that included at various times such diverse personalities as Alcibiades and Plato. Socrates' teaching was frequently conducted out of doors and in an informal manner. No citizen was barred from listening to him or taking part in the discussions, and in a sense his pupils taught themselves. Each student thus developed his own concepts of who Socrates was and what he was saying; therefore, Xenophon should not be faulted because his views of Socrates were not those of Plato, who was gifted with an entirely different quality of mind.

Socrates' belief in moral purposes and his emphasis on the essential goodness of humankind would have appealed to Xenophon's sense of conventional morality. He was not a clever or brilliant pupil but a solid, practical person; probably he took some notes during Socrates' conversations, which would become in later years part of his *Apomnēmoneumata* (c. 381-355; *Memorabilia of Socrates*, 1712) and the *Apologia Sōcratous* (c. 384; *The Defense of Socrates*, 1832). The latter work was thought at one time to be by another author, but it is most likely genuine. Another brief work, the *Symposiou* (*The Banquet*, 1832), whose date, like much of Xenophon's writing, is unknown, places Socrates at an Athenian dinner party, where he discusses a variety of subjects, including the nature of love.

Athens was slipping beyond her golden age as the fifth century waned; Sparta's triumph and the political infighting between the parties of the right and left had tarnished the Athenian democracy. Socrates was increasingly viewed as a suspicious and even dangerous person, for he asked too many questions.

Xenophon was uncertain as to what career he should pursue. In 401, a friend and professional soldier, Proxenus, suggested that he join a band of mercenaries commanded by Prince Cyrus, son of King Darius II of Persia, on an expedition against his brother, Artaxerxes II. The lure of adventure, riches, and military glory was strong, but Xenophon hesitated and consulted Socrates, who advised him to seek counsel of the oracle at Delphi.

Xenophon went to Delphi but apparently had already made a decision before his arrival, since he asked Apollo not whether he should take service with the Persians, but how best the journey might be made. Returning home, he bade Socrates farewell, and the old man advised him to do the will of the god. They were never to meet again.

Life's Work

The high point of Xenophon's life was his military adventures in the Persian Empire, which he vividly describes in the *Kurou anabasis* (between 394 and 371; *The March up Country*, 1623, best known as *Anabasis*). In March, 401, Prince Cyrus led his mixed force of Greeks, Persians, and other troops from the city of Sardis in western Asia Minor to the Euphrates River and on toward Babylon. At Cunaxa on September 3 of that same year, a battle was fought between his and Artaxerxes' forces, and Cyrus was killed. Leaderless and isolated in hostile country, the Greeks were further devastated by the murder of their officers, who had been negotiating after the conflict with the Persians, under a flag of truce. Among the slain was Xenophon's friend Proxenus.

There could be no time for mourning; the ten thousand Greeks who survived elected new commanders, Xenophon being one, and hastily retreated northward into the mountains of Kurdistan and Armenia and fought their way back to civilization, the Greek colony of Trapezus on the Black Sea. The March of the Ten Thousand took approximately five months, and Xenophon undoubtedly played a vital role in its success. He kept a journal which he would use in writing the *Anabasis* decades later.

As Julius Caesar would later do, Xenophon told his story in the third person. Indeed, for reasons now unknown it was originally published under an assumed name. There is, however, no question of authorship; the writing style is Xenophon's, and several ancient authors, Plutarch being one, list the *Anabasis* among his works.

Lively and well written, the *Anabasis* is filled with details of army life, scenes of the countrysides through which the Greeks were passing, descriptions of strange animals and birds (such as ostriches, which ran too fast for the soldiers to catch), and the savage tribes which harassed the "Ten Thousand" on their long march to the sea. The *Anabasis* is Xenophon's most popular work.

The conclusion of these five months of danger and hardship was not as Xenophon had hoped. Denied the opportunity of enrichment and glory serving Prince Cyrus, he considered founding a colony on the Black Sea. Omens from the gods were unfavorable, however, and the Greeks were now divided in their aims. He and some of his friends were obliged to return to military life, first under the command of a petty Thracian king and then with a force of Spartans who had arrived in Asia Minor to defend the Ionian cities against a new Persian attack. During this latter campaign (399), Xenophon captured a wealthy Persian family and managed at last to make his fortune with the large ransom paid for their release.

The year 399 also saw the trial, condemnation, and execution of Socrates. Xenophon's initial reaction to this injustice is not known, but the death of his old teacher must have hastened his rejection of current Athenian democracy. To a professional military man, the order and discipline of the Spartans was more appealing.

During the campaign against the Persians and later in a war among the city-states which pitted Sparta against Athens and Thebes (395-391), Xenophon served on the staff of the Spartan king Agesilaus. In return, the Athenians banished him as a traitor. The Spartans then provided him with an estate at Scillus, near Olympia. Now married and with two sons, Xenophon had the leisure to pursue the life of a country gentleman, devoting his energies to hunting and entertaining his friends and guests, writing, and building a shrine to Artemis, the goddess of the hunt. It was probably during this period that his practical essays *Cynēgetikos* (394-371; *On Hunting*, c. 1832), *Peri hippikēs* (c. 380; *On Horsemanship*, c. 1832), and *Hipparchikos* (c. 357; *The Duties of a Cavalry Officer*, 1832) were composed.

An altogether different sort of work is the *Kyrou paideia* (after 371?; *The Institution and Life of Cyrus*, 1560-1567), a historical novel which treats not only the life and training of Cyrus the Great (not Prince Cyrus of the *Anabasis*) but also the history of the Persian Empire and Xenophon's views on what education and government should be. That the *The Institution and Life of Cyrus* is a complex work is evidenced by the fact that scholars still dispute what Xenophon hoped to accomplish. His contacts with Persians had given him a unique view of non-Greeks, whom many of his countrymen tended to dismiss as barbarians. Xenophon was both better informed and more appreciative of life outside Hellas than were most Greeks.

Local feeling against the Spartans and their allies after Sparta was defeated by Thebes at the Battle of Leuctra (371) obliged Xenophon and his family to leave Scillus and reside in Corinth. There is some question as to whether Xenophon returned to Athens after his banishment was revoked (369-365), but his sons were educated there, and the elder, Gryllus, enlisted in the cavalry as his father had done and died fighting for Athens at the Battle of Mantinea in 362.

In 361 or 360, King Agesilaus died, and Xenophon wrote the *Agēsilaos* as a tribute to him. Another of his major works was probably completed in Corinth at about this time. *Hellēnica* (411-362 B.C.; English translation, 1685) was intended to complement and complete Thucydides' unfinished history of the Peloponnesian War and carry the narrative into contemporary times, ending with the Battle of Mantinea. The *Hellēnica* is generally considered to be inferior to its predecessor, however, because of Xenophon's open expressions of admiration for Sparta and dislike of Thebes.

The *Peri porōn* (c. 355-353; *Ways and Means*, 1832) is probably Xenophon's last work; most scholars believe that he died within five years of its completion. This essay addressing the financial difficulties of Athens in the mid-fourth century offers various remedies to aid in the city's recovery, including such practical suggestions as ownership by the state of a merchant fleet, more efficient working of the silver mines, and improvement in the status of resident aliens. Xenophon eloquently cites the benefits of peace, suggesting that a board of guardians be set up to help maintain peace. In conclusion, he advises the Athenians to consult the gods, an echo of the counsel Socrates had given the young aristocratic cavalryman about to seek his fortune in Persia.

Summary

Although Xenophon was a staff officer of considerable talent and wrote several essays relative to his profession, his most lasting achievements were in the field of historical writing. One of the pleasures of Xenophon, quite apart from the readability of his prose, is his variety; he was genuinely interested in many things and eager to impart to his audience as much information as possible.

Socrates had taught his students to seek out and learn the good, and this advice is reflected throughout Xenophon's works, whether he is discussing the management of horses or a household (*Oikonomiko*, c. 361-362; *Estate Management*, 1532), describing constitutions, or exploring the nature of tyranny (*Hierōn*, date unknown; *Hiero*, 1832). At various times, it has been fashionable among scholars to dwell upon Xenophon's limitations and to compare him unfavorably to Thucydides or Plato. Such comparisons are unwise, how-ever, and further study impresses one with his versatility.

It is of interest that writers discussing Xenophon seem to fall naturally into one of two camps: those who concentrate on his military career and his more practical works and those who focus on his more philosophical writings. It is a measure of his complexity that the definitive biography of Xenophon has yet to be written.

Bibliography

Anderson, J. K. *Military Theory and Practice in the Age of Xenophon*. Berkeley: University of California Press, 1970. The title gives the focus of the work. This lengthy study (more than four hundred pages, including index and bibliography) is enhanced by diagrams of formations and battle plans, as well as nineteen black-and-white plates illustrating military costumes and weapons.

Dillery, John. *Xenophon and the History of His Times*. London and New York: Routledge, 1995. Dillery follows the recent trend of assessing Xenophon according to the goals he set for himself, instead of according to a comparison with his contemporaries such as Thucydides and Plato. Dillery demonstrates that Xenophon's deep religious sense as well as his firm belief in strong leadership strongly influenced his historical vision.

Gray, Vivienne. *The Character of Xenophon's "Hellenica."* Baltimore, Md.: Johns Hopkins University Press, and London: Duckworth, 1989. Gray demonstrates that the *Hellenica* is more interesting than is usually thought, and that Xenophon exerted greater control over his work than he is often given credit for. She divides the literary and philosophic character of the work under three headings: Conversationalized Narrative; Public Speeches; and Narrative. Gray concludes that the main concern of the *Hellenica* is moral achievement and that it is a united work, with uniform aims and techniques.

Higgins, W. E. *Xenophon the Athenian: The Problem of the Individual and the Polis*. Albany: State University of New York Press, 1977. This sympathetic study deals with Xenophon as a writer and a pupil of Socrates. The style is pleasant and clear. In addition to the index, the author's notes are extensive and impressive.

Hirsch, Steven W. "1001 Iranian Nights: History and Fiction in Xenophon's *Cyropaedia*." In *The*

Greek Historians, Literature and History: Papers Presented to A. E. Raubitschek. Saratoga, Calif.: ANMA Libri, 1985. The focus of this study is on *The Institution and Life of Cyrus* and how the author thinks that it has been misunderstood by scholars unfamiliar with Persian history and traditions.

Jacks, L. V. *Xenophon, Soldier of Fortune.* New York and London: Scribner, 1930. Xenophon's life is covered in its entirety in this accessible work, beginning with his initial meeting with Socrates. There is no real effort at analysis of Xenophon's works, and the scholarship is somewhat dated. Jacks concentrates on the *Anabasis* and is primarily interested in Xenophon's military adventures, which he treats in considerable detail.

Richter, Gisela M. A. *The Portraits of the Greeks.* Vol. 2. London: Phaidon Press, 1965; Ithaca, N.Y.: Cornell University Press, 1984. This book is useful for its illustrations, notably the one of two pillars, each topped with a portrait bust of Xenophon, who was described by several ancient writers as a very handsome man.

Strauss, Leo. *On Tyranny.* Rev. ed. London: Collier-Macmillan, and Ithaca, N.Y.: Cornell University Press, 1963. Xenophon's *Hiero* (sometimes spelled *Hierōn*) is interpreted in detail, with an analysis of the text as well as a translation. Also included is an essay by another scholar, Alexandre Kojève, not only on Xenophon and his views on tyranny but also on Strauss' own interpretations. This volume is for the serious student on Xenophon.

———. *Xenophon's Socrates.* Ithaca, N.Y.: Cornell University Press, 1972. In this study, Strauss continues his interpretation of Xenophon as a man who wrote well and with wisdom, an important author who adds to the understanding of his teacher, Socrates. The book contains an appendix and an index and is intended for a scholarly audience.

———. *Xenophon's Socratic Discourse: An Interpretation of the "Oeconomicus."* Ithaca, N.Y.: Cornell University Press, 1970. Xenophon's *Oikonomiko*, although in the form of a Socratic dialogue, is sometimes dismissed as an enjoyable essay on estate management, complete with a description of the character of the dutiful wife. Strauss writes that its purpose is misunderstood. As with previous references, this work is intended for the better understanding of Socrates as well as Xenophon.

Dorothy T. Potter

XERXES I

Born: c. 519 B.C.; place unknown
Died: 465 B.C.; Persepolis
Areas of Achievement: Warfare and architecture
Contribution: Xerxes mobilized the largest army ever assembled in ancient times and marched against Greece; he crossed Thessaly and annexed Attica to the Persian Empire. Posterity remembers him for capturing Athens and burning the Acropolis and for building the magnificent Palace of Xerxes at Persepolis.

Early Life

Among Darius the Great's seven sons, Xerxes was the youngest of two claimants to the throne of Persia. He was the eldest among the four children born to Atossa, the daughter of Cyrus the Great, whom Darius had married upon accession to the throne. The other claimant, Artabazanes, was Darius' eldest son by the daughter of Gobryas, born when Darius was still a private individual. Of the two, Xerxes had a stronger claim for succession, not only because he had been born into the royal house and his line continued that of Cyrus the Great but also because he was an able individual. In his mid-twenties, he was assigned the governorship of Babylonia in preference to Artabazanes. By the time the question of succession arose, he had already governed this kingdom for twelve years.

A bas-relief in the Archaeological Museum in Tehran depicts Xerxes as the heir apparent: He stands behind his father's throne. The father and son occupy the pinnacle of a symbolic pyramid; below them are the nobles, priests, generals, and dignitaries. The bas-relief, two versions of which are in existence, is part of a larger picture in which the king gives audience to his subject nations on the occasion of the Now Ruz (Persian new year). The participation of Xerxes in the ceremony signifies Darius' attempt to create a mutual bond between the prince and the representatives of many nations bringing gifts to the court at Persepolis.

Xerxes was about thirty-seven years old when he became king upon Darius' death in 486. His assumption of power did not represent an easy transition: His own brother, Aryamen the satrap of Bactria, rose up against him and had to be brought within the fold. Following that revolt, Xerxes marched on Egypt, where a usurper had been ruling since 484—two years prior to the death of Darius. The Persian army defeated the pretender and devastated the Nile Delta. After destroying all Egyptian fortifications, Xerxes appointed one of his brothers, Achaemenes, satrap and then left Egypt. As a result of this revolt, Egypt lost its autonomy within the empire; Egyptian citizens, however, continued to enjoy their previous rights and privileges.

While still in Egypt, Xerxes was informed of a revolt in Babylonia; by then the revolt of a first leader had given way to that of a second, Shamash-eriba. Xerxes marched on Babylonia, defeated Shamash-eriba, and then treated the kingdom in the same way as he had Egypt. He went so far as to break with Achaemenian tradition—he removed the statue of Marduk, the god who had welcomed Cyrus to Babylon, and took it to Persia. Removal of the much-adored golden statue was tantamount to the demotion of Babylonia to the rank of a satrapy. Under Xerxes, therefore, both Egypt and Babylonia lost their status as autonomous kingdoms in the empire. After his return from Babylon, Xerxes no longer called himself "Lord of Nations." He was now "King of the Persians and the Medes."

Life's Work

After his conquests in Egypt and Babylonia, Xerxes intended to live a tranquil life and attend to matters of state. Exiled Greeks and other ambitious individuals holding prominent positions in Persia, Lydia, and Athens recognized a Persian victory in Europe as the avenue to their own success. Their efforts, therefore, were expended upon convincing the king that Persia, ruled by a divine king, was superior and could easily defeat Greece. After giving the matter thought and keeping in mind his father's defeat at Marathon in 490, Xerxes assembled the notables of the empire and announced his intention to invade Greece. He proposed to build a bridge of boats across the Hellespont for the army to cross and further announced that he intended to set fire to the city of Athens in retaliation for the burning of the temple and sacred woods of Sardis by the Ionians.

The nobles, except for the king's uncle, Artabanus, agreed with the king and praised his foresight and might. Artabanus, speaking from experience, reminded the assembly of Darius' fruitless pursuit of the European Scythians in the steppes beyond the Danube. He reminded Xerxes of the enormous loss of life that had resulted from that

XERXES VIEWING THE SEA-FIGHT AT SALAMIS, FROM THE COAST OF ATTICA

futile endeavor. He further disagreed with those who claimed that the Persians could defeat the Athenians at sea. His advice to the king was to adjourn the meeting and continue with his plans to unify the empire.

Artabanus' words angered Xerxes. He shouted at the aged warrior that no Persian should sit idle while foreigners infringed upon his domain and set fire to his cities. He recounted the great deeds of his ancestors and pledged to surpass them. The assembly agreed with the king's views that war with Greece was inevitable and compromise impossible. Either Persia had to rule Greece or Greece would rule Persia. Over the next few days, Xerxes won Artabanus' agreement and began preparations for a major invasion of Europe. The king's next four years were devoted to military preparations and to diplomatic negotiations before the invasion. These preparations included marshaling forces, digging a major canal at Athos to prevent the kind of disaster experienced by Darius, and dispatching envoys to certain Greek cities to demand "water and soil," that is, recognition of Persian suzerainty without recourse to war. Drawing on the satrap system, a

system of government initially installed by Cyrus and later expanded by Darius, Xerxes assembled an army the likes of which, according to Herodotus, no one had seen or remembered. This army gathered at Sardis in the spring of 480 and from there, led by the king himself, set out for Europe.

Among the obstacles that barred access to Europe, the most awesome was the formidable Hellespont. Ten years before, in his invasion of Europe, Darius had bypassed the Hellespont and built a bridge on the Bosporus. Xerxes, however, had decided to cross the Hellespont on a bridge made up of warships. The first array of boats was easily washed away by stormy seas. For the lost ships and the wasted time, Xerxes had the two engineers responsible beheaded. He also ordered the sea to be whipped three hundred lashes to calm it. The second bridge, built with reinforced materials and heavy ropes, held for the seven days that it took the Persian army (estimated as anywhere from 360,000 to two million) to cross. The bridge was not disassembled so that, in the event of a Persian defeat, the king could return to Asia and not be stranded in Europe.

From Thrace, Xerxes circled the Aegean Sea. He crossed Macedonia and Thessaly, where he stayed while the army deforested the land and built roads. He then headed for Attica, accompanied by his fleet, which remained a short distance offshore.

The Greek states, knowing of the enormity of the invading land army, set their internal squabbles aside so that they could put up a united front against the Persians. The alliance, led by Sparta, chose the narrow pass at Thermopylae for the initial meeting with Xerxes. The Greek navy at nearby Artemisium was in constant contact with the land force.

Initially, the battle at Thermopylae did not go well for the Persians. Xerxes sent in a contingent of Medes for the first day and fielded his ten thousand Immortals the second day. Both failed to turn the tide. Worse yet, a significant part of the Persian fleet was destroyed in a storm. Undaunted, however, Xerxes continued to fight. After the third day, a large contingent of Persians, guided through a hidden path the previous night by a Greek defector, appeared on the mountain overlooking the pass. Its defenders found themselves trapped. Leonidas, the Spartan king in charge of the Greek contingent, marshaled the troops of Sparta, Thespiae, and Thebes to continue the defense of the pass. He sent the rest of his men to reinforce the allied army that would fight Xerxes beyond Thermopylae. Leonidas and his three hundred men fought bravely and died to the last man, allowing their compatriots time to withdraw to the narrow strait of Salamis. Attica, and consequently Athens, was left defenseless.

The Persian army, having lost four of Darius' sons at Thermopylae, entered Athens. Most of the inhabitants had already been evacuated. Those who remained took refuge in the Acropolis, the home of Athena, the patron goddess of the city. Xerxes, as he had vowed, burned the city and celebrated his conquest. He was now the only Persian ruler, indeed the only Asian ruler up until that time, to have set foot in Athens as a victor. He dispatched a messenger to Susa to apprise Artabanus, his vice-regent, of the victory.

Xerxes' celebration, however, was premature. He had won the battle at Thermopylae, but the war raged on. Artabanus had been right. The devastated Persian fleet was no match for the Athenian navy, especially when the latter was led by Themistocles, a general who had fought Darius at Marathon and who had spent his life building a formidable navy to match Persia's land army.

At Salamis, what had remained of the Persian fleet was dragged into narrow straits, outmaneuvered, and rammed by stout Greek ships. Witnessing the destruction of their fleet, the Persians fled the scene. Xerxes feared that he might become stranded in Europe. He immediately withdrew to Thessaly and from there to Asia. His hasty departure left the outcome of the war uncertain, especially when Mardonius, whom Xerxes had left in charge of the European campaign, was killed at Platae.

Henceforth, Xerxes became absolutely disinterested in the war and its outcome. Approaching forty, he returned to his palaces at Susa and Persepolis and watched from the sidelines as his appointees fought the war. The hostilities continued for another thirteen years.

At Persepolis, Xerxes devoted his time to the completion of Darius' Apadana and to the construction of his own palace, a magnificent complex erected southeast of Darius' palace. He also became involved in domestic politics and in the affairs of the court. A partial history of these involvements, especially in relation to the Jews of Persia, is found in the Book of Esther. Xerxes also became involved in harem intrigue. This latter involvement resulted in his death: Xerxes was murdered by his courtiers, among them Artabanus, his minister, in 465. He was fifty-four years old.

Summary

Xerxes stayed in the wings for twelve years, administering the affairs of the kingdom of Babylonia. He watched his father's rise in power and prestige and his fall at Marathon. As king, he found himself on the horns of a dilemma. He had to choose between witnessing the demise of a disunited empire and attempting to rejuvenate it through war. In addition, he needed to show his people that he was the son of Darius and that he could surpass the deeds of kings of the past. Having already decided on a course of action, he revealed his plans and spent much time and energy preparing to bring them to fruition.

The goal of his European campaign was the capture of Athens and the destruction of that city in retaliation for the burning of Sardis. This goal, however, was in conflict with a larger goal nurtured by Greece—the replacement of the absolutism of the East with the free institutions of the West. Thus the victory in Athens had a bittersweet taste for Xerxes, who was compelled by circumstances to fight at Salamis against his wishes. His defeat at Salamis demoralized him to the point that he no longer recognized the potential of his enormous land army and the possibility of an eventual victory.

Against this background, it is doubtful whether Xerxes, on his own, could have prepared the army so that it could capture and burn Athens. Behind Xerxes was the formidable war machine of Darius, a machine created for the single purpose of reducing Europe to a Persian colony. Xerxes merely guided this instrument to its destined end and then into the ground.

Furthermore, Xerxes greatly underestimated the seriousness of the fragmentation that had occurred during the final year of Darius' reign. The defeat at Marathon was closely related to the unhappiness of the peoples of such well-established kingdoms as Egypt and Babylonia. Yet Xerxes took it upon himself to further belittle these nations by reducing them to the rank of satrapies.

Rather than trying his hand at world conquest, Xerxes could have drawn on his forte, administration. Instead, he made the same mistake that his father had made: He took on Greece in Europe. Under Xerxes, therefore, the empire continued to disintegrate. Lack of leadership and squabbles among the future claimants further weakened the empire and caused its eventual demise.

Xerxes' view of himself was different. Like Darius, he attributed his success as king to Ahura Mazda, his god. He could do no wrong. Although he exercised great restraint in judgment, he allowed himself to be influenced and used by others. His inflexibility and self-confidence, both deriving from the incredible numbers he commanded rather than from the strength of his policies or that of his allies, played a major role in his demoralization and downfall. After Salamis, the man who had considered himself a good warrior, excelling in horsemanship, archery, and javelin throwing, became a womanizer and a manipulator of lowly lives at his own court.

Bibliography

Burn, A. R. *Persia and the Greeks: The Defense of the West, 546-478 B.C.* 2d ed. London: Duckworth, and Stanford, Calif.: Stanford University Press, 1984. This book contains detailed discussions of the various aspects of Xerxes' rule and an especially informative section on his campaign in Europe. Includes maps, charts illustrating battle formations, and genealogies for the major figures.

Cook, J. M. "The Rise of the Achaemenids and Establishment of Their Empire." In *The Cambridge History of Iran.* Vol. 2, *The Median and Achaemenian Periods.* Cambridge: Cambridge University Press, 1985. This article examines the principal sources on ancient Iran and the extent and composition of the empire. Toward the end, Cook assesses the leadership that enabled the Persians to form a great empire.

Firdawsi. *The Shahnama of Firdausi.* Translated by Arthur George Warner and Edward Warner. 9 vols. London: Paul, Trench, Trübner, 1905. This translation of Iran's major epic provides a wealth of information on ancient Iranian religion, social hierarchy, and military organization. It especially underscores the role of the king—an absolute ruler carrying out a divine decree.

Frye, Richard N. *The Heritage of Persia.* London: Weidenfeld and Nicolson, 1962; New York: New American Library, 1963. Frye's account of ancient Iran is unique. It focuses on the eastern provinces of the ancient kingdom, but, unlike similar accounts, it is based on cultural, religious, and literary sources. The book is illustrated; it includes an index, maps, genealogies, and an informative bibliography.

Ghirshman, Roman. *Iran From the Earliest Times to the Islamic Conquest.* Baltimore and London: Penguin Books, 1961. In this account of Iran's prehistory to Islamic times, Ghirshman juxtaposes textual information and archaeological data to place ancient Iran in its proper perspective. The book is illustrated with text figures as well as with plates. It includes an index and a selected bibliography.

Green, Peter. *Xerxes at Salamis.* New York: Praeger Publishers, 1970. This is a unique, though somewhat biased, account of the logistics of Xerxes' campaigns in Europe; it focuses on the leadership of Themistocles and on the divergent ideologies of the belligerents. The book has poor maps, an index, and a bibliography; it is sparsely illustrated.

Herodotus. *The Histories.* Translated by Aubrey de Sélincourt. Rev. ed. London and New York: Penguin, 1972. In this comprehensive classical account, Herodotus discusses Xerxes' planned invasion of Europe, his long march in Asia and Europe, his capture and burning of Athens, and his retreat to Asia. This book should be read alongside other authoritative sources. It includes poor maps but has a good index.

Hignett, Charles. *Xerxes' Invasion of Greece*. Oxford: Clarendon Press, 1963. This work deals exclusively with Xerxes and his campaigns against Greece. It critically examines previous research on Xerxes and discusses Xerxes' fleet, the number of infantry the king commanded, and the topography of Thermopylae and Salamis. The book includes a bibliography, a good index, and eight maps.

Olmstead, Arthur T. *History of the Persian Empire*. Chicago: University of Chicago Press, 1948. This detailed history of the Achaemenid period remains the chief secondary source for the study of ancient Iran. The book includes a topographical index, maps, and many carefully selected illustrations.

Iraj Bashiri

ZENO OF CITIUM

Born: c. 335 B.C.; Citium (modern Larnaca), Cyprus
Died: Probably fall, 261 B.C.; Athens
Area of Achievement: Philosophy
Contribution: Zeno founded Stoicism, the leading Hellenistic school of philosophy. Though not the school's greatest thinker, he created its unified, systematic teaching and guided it to prominence.

Early Life

While a full biography of Zeno of Citium cannot be written from the anecdotes and sayings collected in late antiquity, principally available in the work of Diogenes Laërtius, much can be learned from a critical reading of them. Diogenes quotes the honorific inscription that dates Zeno's death as well as the statement of Zeno's disciple Persaeus of Citium that the master lived to be seventy-two, which dates his birth. Nevertheless, there is no information about his childhood; even the name of his mother no longer survives. Mnaseas, his father, has a name ambiguously meaningful both in Phoenician (equivalent to the Hebrew Manasseh, "one causing to forget") and in Greek ("mindful," a strong opposition). Mnaseas, contemporary with Citium's last Phoenician king, under whom the town was besieged and burned by Ptolemy Soter of Egypt in 312 B.C., may have initiated the family's break from Phoenician and commercial to Greek and philosophical culture: The name he gave his son has no Semitic meaning but refers to the Greek god Zeus and was celebrated in a famous syncretic hymn by Zeno's disciple Cleanthes. In one story, Mnaseas brought many books by Socratic writers back from Athens for Zeno. In another story, Zeno himself, shipwrecked on a commercial trip to Athens, consoled himself in a bookstore with Xenophon's *Apomnēmoneumata* (c. 381-355 B.C.; *Memorabilia*) and rushed to follow the Cynic philosopher Crates of Thebes, when Crates was pointed out as a living Socratic teacher. Persaeus said that Zeno was twenty-two when he came to Athens; he never seems to have left. His arrival would have been in 311, the year after Citium fell to Ptolemy.

The failure of the records to mention close relationships with his parents or others may be significant: Stoicism was to teach, as Cynicism had, individual self-sufficiency and rational discipline of the emotions. Socrates was the type of this life: Personally ugly but desirable, ethically committed but unwilling to be called a teacher or to write anything, sealing his commitment to philosophy with his death at the hands of democratic Athens, Socrates was publicized by his followers, including Plato and Xenophon, and became the personal inspiration of all the fourth century schools of philosophy. Plato's Academy was almost a formal alternative to the city-state which had killed its greatest thinker, and Aristotle's Lyceum was modeled on it. The Cynics, on the other hand, avoided institutional encumbrances, living and teaching in public to a scandalous degree: Their name means "doglike." In a symbolic story, Zeno, soon after he became Crates' follower, modestly covered his teacher and Crates' student-bride Hipparchia with a cloak as they consummated their "dog-wedding" in public in the Stoa Poikile. Cynics, including the young Zeno, maintained the ill-dressed, voluntarily poor, and combatively questioning, even anti-intellectual stance they claimed to derive from Socrates' teachings.

Zeno's Cynic period culminated before 300 in the publication of his most notorious book, *Politeia* (the republic), a short work denouncing then current methods of education and calling for a city of wise men and women without temples, courts, or gymnasiums, with the god Eros to be honored by friendship and polymorphous, unrestricted sex. Zeno also studied and perhaps enrolled in the Academy (studying Plato's dialogues, dialectical method, and metaphysics—including incorporeal ideas as causes for physical events, which he rejected) and followed the dialectical teachers Diodorus Cronus and Stilpo, who arrived from Megara about 307. Their advanced modal logic, however, proved a form of determinism Zeno found unacceptable. By about 300, Zeno, in his early thirties, was able to declare his independence from other teachers and begin his regular strolls up and down the Stoa Poikile with his own students.

Life's Work

The professional career of a philosopher is rich not so much in public as in internal events, and Zeno's development is hard to follow in the absence of extensive or datable writings. *Politeia* came early, and it was widely enough quoted that a dozen or more of the extant fragments of his writings can be identified as belonging to it; none of the other

twenty-four titles of his canon allows for as definite a reconstruction. He was a powerful teacher, famous for an epistemological demonstration in which he closed one extended hand by stages and then steadied the fist with his other hand while he named the corresponding stages of knowledge: "An impression is like this; assent is like this; cognitive grasp is like this; and science is like this; and only the wise man has it." He established, for all Stoics except his unorthodox pupil Aristo of Chios, the three-part division of philosophy into logic (philosophy of language and meaning), physics (philosophy of nature—including theology, since spirit as breath and *logos* as creative word are bodies and also divine), and ethics (the famous division of things into good, bad, and indifferent; the development of the Cynic's "life according to nature" as the only virtuous and happy way of life). To a degree not approached by Plato, by Aristotle, or by his contemporaries the Cynics, Megarians, Epicureans, and Skeptics, Zeno made of these subjects a single, unified whole, giving priority neither to metaphysics—as with Plato and Aristotle—nor to ethics—as with the Epicureans. The system was seen as dogmatic, and debate with Stoicism played a large part in the Academy's move into skepticism from the 270's. The dogmatic system was not perfected by Zeno himself: He left his logic rudimentary, to be developed by his successor's successor, Chrysippus; among other changes, later Stoics softened the antisocial side of his ethics toward a propriety more acceptable to dignified Roman adherents such as the Gracchi, Seneca the Younger, and Marcus Aurelius.

Zeno was remembered for his pithy comments about and to his students; these observations were perhaps made more pointed by his Phoenician accent and manners, which he never tried to overcome. During his thirty-nine years leading the school, his oval face hardened into the philosophic persona visible in surviving portraits. It is not a handsome face: The forehead recedes, the frown lines are pronounced, the expression seems severe or even morose; the neck bends forward, and Diogenes says that it crooked also to one side, adding that Zeno was rather tall, thin but flabby, and dark-complected. Self-control was the main attribute he projected. He lived on bread, water, and "a little wine of good bouquet"—coming from a commercial family, he seems never to have been really in want—avoiding dinners and drinking parties except when his pupil and patron, the Macedonian

prince Antigonus Gonatas, the future King of Macedon, insisted. Zeno is said to have had a weak constitution—justifying his abstemiousness—but also to have been in good health until his death, which was voluntary and in response to a trivial fall that he took as a divine sign. As for his pleasures, they included green figs and sunbaths and boy slave-prostitutes, whom he "used sparingly." He did, to be sure, state in *Politeia* that Eros is a god of constructive political friendship, and he is recorded to have been in love with Chremonides, later the instigator of Athens' last, ill-starred war against the dominion of Macedon.

Zeno's school had a different sort of corporate existence from the more settled Academy, Lyceum, and Epicurean "Garden," of which the first two were technically sodalities of the Muses and Apollo meeting in public gymnasiums (religiously consecrated exercise grounds particularly used by Athenian *ephebes* in their compulsory military and civic-religious training), the last Epicurus' private house and garden, later inherited by the school's leaders. Zeno, barred as a foreigner from owning property and perhaps drawn to the Stoa Poikile from his studies with Crates, chose that public facility for his lessons. The Stoa Poikile was a sizable building (accommodating meetings of at least five hundred people) on the northwest corner of the Athenian civic center (Agora), with an open colonnade facing south across the Agora toward the Acropolis temple complex; the structure was roofed, with walls on three sides hung with paintings (hence the name Poikile, "decorated"), by Polygnotus and other masters, of great historical and mythic battles, which often suggested reason defeating emotion. It was fitting that this should be the scene for what amounted to a radical shift of the city from historical, civic excellence to philosophy. Since the building did not belong to them in any sense, the Stoics (as they came to be called in preference to "Zenoneans") must have done their administrative and library work elsewhere. In Zeno's time, given his Cynic background, administration must have been slight, though books were always important to this scholarly sect.

One sort of student was easy to find at the Stoa Poikile: The years after 307 marked the end of the compulsory *ephebeia*, and eighteen- to twenty-year-olds would have found themselves drawn to public lounging areas such as the Stoa Poikile. As a philosophical organization, however, the Stoa was formidably professional, and Zeno seems, according to remarks such as his threat to charge passers-by for listening, to have discouraged random crowds. Most of his known disciples came from abroad—including non-Greek places such as Citium, Zeno's own home—drawn, as Zeno had been, by published books and Athens' educational reputation. The most illustrious of these people was Antigonus Gonatas, who was in Athens as overlord but who thought of himself as a Stoic and employed Zeno's fellow Citiote, housemate, and disciple Persaeus as a tutor for his son and even as a general. Of the more modest sort were Persaeus himself (sometimes rumored to have been Zeno's slave); Cleanthes of Assos, who made a living at the waterworks so as to be in Athens to hear Zeno lecture and who inherited Zeno's position as leader of the school; Aristo of Chios, who set up a rival school teaching ethics; and Sphaerus, the specialist in definition who advised Sparta's revolutionary, land-reforming king, Cleomenes III.

Summary

Athens, during Zeno of Citium's fifty years there, passed through upheavals that largely left him untouched: Demetrius Eukairos, the philosopher-tyrant, was succeeded by a rivalry of democrats (who initially illegalized philosophy schools), oligarchs, and moderates, while the port of Piraeus was constantly garrisoned by Macedon. William Scott Ferguson counts seven changes of government and four of constitution, three bloody uprisings, and four sieges during this period—with Zeno, though the teacher of a major warlord, never taking any prominent part. The turmoil may already have had for him the unreal quality it acquires in retrospect; the impassive Stoic (and stoic) remains.

Zeno did influence Hellenistic politics, however, contributing some enlightenment to what would in any case have been despotisms. It is important that he did not solve all the questions he addressed but left the school with room for future development over several generations: Forward-looking, even arrogant, thinkers liked the dynamic and the sense that human action is cosmically purposeful and significant, though Epicureans and Skeptics demurred. The detailed contributions of the Stoic thought that Zeno either began or left for great successors to begin are great. Finally, Athens honored him after his death with statues in the Academy and Lyceum, a public tomb, and a resolution praising him as a teacher of virtue and temperance who had lived the morality he taught.

Bibliography

Arnold, E. Vernon. *Roman Stoicism: Being Lectures on the History of the Stoic Philosophy with Special Reference to Its Development Within the Roman Empire*. Cambridge and New York: Cambridge University Press, 1911. The fourteen pages on Zeno are nearly the longest essay on him in English, and the book—in spite of its title—is a classic treatment of Greek Stoicism in a religious context that was deemphasized in later English philosophical treatments. The chronology needs to be revised from later works.

Camp, John M. *The Athenian Agora: Excavations in the Heart of Classical Athens*. London and New York: Thames and Hudson, 1986. Photographs and discussion of the Stoa Poikile, where excavation began in 1981, in the context of extended archaeological presentation of the city center. A good background for the narratives of Ferguson, Tarn, and Walbank.

Diogenes Laërtius. *Lives of Eminent Philosophers*. Translated by R. D. Hicks. Cambridge, Mass.: Harvard University Press, and London: Heinemann, 1925. The only English translation in print of the main source of information on Zeno. Includes symbolic anecdotes and apothegms in the same relation to Zeno as the Gospels are to Jesus. Hicks's terminology is not always philosophically sophisticated and should be compared to that of Long and Sedley.

Dudley, Donald R. *A History of Cynicism from Diogenes to the Sixth Century A.D.* London: Methuen, 1937; New York: Gordon, 1974. The most vivid historical presentation in English of the philosophical environment in which Zeno studied. Includes bibliographical notes and appendices.

Ferguson, William Scott. *Hellenistic Athens: An Historical Essay*. London: Macmillan, 1911; New York: Fertig, 1969. A classic narrative, never superseded though Walbank and others have improved the chronology and updated the bibliography. Chapters 2 through 4 constitute the history of Athens in Zeno's time and pointedly end with his death. In the absence of a modern biography of Zeno, this work and Tarn's study are the two most extensive substitutes.

Hunt, H. A. K. *A Physical Interpretation of the Universe: The Doctrines of Zeno the Stoic*. Melbourne, Australia: Melbourne University Press, 1976. Though philosophically and historically naïve, this is the only English monograph on Zeno. Not a biography, it presents 105 of the fragments of his teaching in acceptable translations, with commentary and a limited bibliography.

Karageorghis, Vassos. *Kition: Mycenaean and Phoenician Discoveries in Cyprus*. London: Thames and Hudson, 1976. The dean of Cypriot archaeologists surveys Zeno's hometown with photographs, references, and bibliography. Useful as background, although no treatment of Zeno himself.

Long, A. A., and D. N. Sedley. *The Hellenistic Philosophers*. Vol. 1, *Translation and Principal Sources with Philosophical Commentary*. Cambridge and New York: Cambridge University Press, 1987. The results of a generation's study of Stoicism are presented in the central 280 pages. Philosophically illuminating, not concentrating on the philosophers' personality or history. Contains a good glossary of technical terms, lists of philosophers and ancient sources, and a panorama of Athens showing the locations of the schools. Short bibliography.

Reesor, Margaret E. *The Nature of Man in Early Stoic Philosophy*. New York: St. Martin's Press, and London: Duckworth, 1989. In this work, which includes discussion of Cleanthes of Assos, Chrysippus of Soli, Diogenes of Babylon, and Antipater of Tarsus as well as Zeno of Citium, Reesor discusses the Stoics' metaphysics and philosophy of logic and language. In addition, she addresses their theories of knowledge and moral psychology.

Richter, Gisela M. A. *The Portraits of the Greeks*. 3 vols. London: Phaidon Press, 1965; Ithaca, N.Y.: Cornell University Press, 1984. Volume 2 presents the known ancient portraits of Zeno (except for a group of carved gems) and supports the author's detailed description of Zeno's physiognomy, which, absent further data, must stand for his character to some extent.

Sandbach, F. H. *The Stoics*. London: Chatto and Windus, and New York: Norton, 1975. The short opening chapter mentions most of the data, though the death date should be brought down probably to 261. The volume is competent, though not as vivid as Dudley's (whose coverage it does not duplicate).

Tarn, William Woodthorpe. *Antigonos Gonatas*. Oxford: Clarendon, 1913; Chicago: Argonaut, 1969. A classic biography by an admirer of Alexander the Great and Hellenism, fitting Antigonus into the mold of adventurous, enlightened prince and featuring Zeno as one of his teachers and a member of his circle. Chronology and bibliography to be supplemented from Walbank.

Walbank, F. W., A. E. Astin, M. W. Frederiksen, and R. M. Ogilvie, eds. *The Cambridge Ancient History*. Vol. 7, *The Hellenistic World*. 2d ed. Cambridge and New York: Cambridge University Press, 1984. A useful, long chapter on the period of Antigonus places Zeno's adopted home in perspective with his princely student. Includes chronological improvements on Tarn's and Ferguson's works. Chronological chart, immense bibliography.

Owen C. Cramer

ZENO OF ELEA

Born: c. 490 B.C.; Elea
Died: c. 440 B.C.; Elea
Area of Achievement: Philosophy
Contribution: Although Zeno cannot be said to have succeeded in defending Paramenides' doctrine of the one, his paradoxes are still remembered, and his method of argument influenced all later philosophy.

Early Life

Little is known of Zeno's life. In the early fifth century, when he was young, Greek philosophy was still in its cruder, experimental form, sometimes mythological, even borrowing from Oriental lore, sometimes resembling primitive science by trying to explain the physical world and basing its conclusions on observation if not on experiment. One tendency was to try to explain all material phenomena as variations on one particular element. Thus, Thales of Miletus taught that all material things were derived from water; Anaximenes of Miletus taught that all things were derived from air; and Heraclitus of Ephesus, though his philosophy was by no means as simple as those of his predecessors, thought that all things were derived from fire. Empedocles, on the other hand, rejected the idea of any single element as the source of all and saw the material world as the result of the mixture and separation of four elements: earth, air, fire, and water.

Zeno's master, Parmenides, rejected this notion of multiplicity in favor of a fundamental unity. His arguments, which were placed in a mythological setting and expressed in hexameter verse, have survived only in fragments; they are exceedingly involved and hard to follow but perhaps can best be summarized as saying that multiplicity is illogical, self-contradictory, or merely unthinkable. This leaves the one, which is not water or air or fire but simply is "being"—"individual, changeless, featureless, motionless, rock-solid being." Multiplicity, however, if contrary to logic, is nevertheless a fact of experience, and Parmenides apparently undertook to give a systematic account of it. A modern thinker might say that the world of reason and the world of experience were mutually exclusive and could never be reconciled.

Life's Work

Despite the paucity of biographical information about Zeno, Plato's dialogue *Parmenides* (c. 360 B.C.) reports the conversation of Socrates—then a young man—and the visiting Parmenides and Zeno. In that account, Zeno is described as "nearly forty years of age, tall and fair to look upon; in the days of his youth he was reported to have been beloved by Parmenides." In the dialogue, having finished reading aloud from his works, written in his youth, Zeno frankly explains their origin and his motive:

> The truth is, that these writings of mine were meant to protect the arguments of Parmenides against those who make fun of him and seek to show the many ridiculous and contradictory results which they suppose to follow from the affirmation of the one. My answer is addressed to partisans of the many, whose attack I return with interest by retorting upon them that their hypothesis of the being of many, if carried out, appears to be still more ridiculous than the hypothesis of the being of one.

After Zeno confesses that his arguments were motivated not by "the ambition of an older man, but the pugnacity of a young one," Socrates endeavors to sum up Zeno's arguments:

> Do you maintain that if being is many, it must be both like and unlike, and that this is impossible, for neither can the like be unlike, nor the unlike like. . . And if the unlike cannot be like, or the like unlike, then according to you, being could not be many, for this would involve an impossibility. In all that you say have you any other purpose except to disprove the being of the many? And is not each division of your treatise intended to furnish a separate proof of this, there being as many proofs of the not-being of the many, as you have composed arguments?

In the dialogue, Zeno acknowledges that Socrates has correctly understood him. Zeno's defense of Parmenides thus consists not of evidence supporting Parmenides' position nor even of positive arguments; rather, Zeno demonstrates that the opposite position is self-contradictory.

These proofs of the being of the one by proving the not-being of the many might not seem relevant in a scientific age, but some have survived and are known to those who are not otherwise learned in pre-Socratic philosophy. The most famous of Zeno's arguments, called the "Achilles," is summed up by Aristotle: "In a race, the quickest runner can never overtake the slowest, since the pursuer must first reach the point where the pursued started, so that the slower must always hold a lead." Almost as famous is the paradox of the arrow, which can never reach its target. According to Zeno's argument, at each point of its flight, the arrow must be at that point and at rest at that point. Thus, all motion, and therefore all change, is illusory.

Zeno's famed pugnacity was not limited to philosophy. After a plot in which he was involved against the tyrant Nearchus of Elea was discovered, the philosopher died under torture, and his death became the subject of various anecdotes. Some claim that he revealed the names of the tyrant's own friends as conspirators. Another story states that Zeno bit off his tongue and spit it out at the tyrant; in another, he bit off the tyrant's ear or nose.

Summary

Plato recognized in *Sophist* (after 360 B.C.) that there is something futile about such arguments as those of Zeno and that those who make them may simply be showing off:

> Thus we provide a rich feast for tyros, whether young or old; for there is nothing easier than to argue that the one cannot be many, or the many one: and great is their delight in denying that a man is good; for man, they insist, is man and good is good. I dare say that you have met with persons who take an interest in such matters—they are often elderly men, whose meagre sense is thrown into amazement by these discoveries of theirs, which they believe to be the height of wisdom.

Zeno can be defended in a number of ways. One could argue that his motives were good—that he wanted only to defend Parmenides. In doing so, he simply showed that trait of loyalty which brought about his death. More seriously, one could argue that his position in the history of philosophy excuses his failures and could praise him for raising issues and developing methods of argument which Aristotle took seriously. In Zeno's arguments a recurring theme in philosophy can be seen: the conflict of reason and common sense. Periodically in philosophy, thinkers prove by logic things that ordinary people cannot accept. The British empiricists—John Locke, George Berkeley, and David Hume—did this by stripping away the qualities of objects until the real world had to be defended as an illusion. More recently, the poststructuralists have denounced the logocentric view of the world and have written *sous rature*—the world may be described rationally, but that analysis must be void-

ed, since any logocentric analysis of the world by definition must be faulty. Periodically, it seems, logic and common sense must be at odds.

Nevertheless, in the twentieth century, Zeno has found one eminent and eloquent defender, Bertrand Russell. Zeno, he says, for two thousand years had been pronounced an ingenious juggler and his arguments had been considered sophisms, when "these sophisms were reinstated, and made the foundations of a mathematical renaissance, by a German professor," Karl Weierstrass. Russell concludes, "The only point where Zeno probably erred was in inferring (if he did infer) that, because there is no change, therefore the world must be in the same state at one time as at another." Thus, at the dawn of philosophy, when philosophers sometimes wrote in hexameters and were executed for their politics, Zeno expressed certain philosophical problems in a form which still amuses ordinary people and which still occasions profound debates among professional philosophers.

Bibliography

Aristotle. *The Physics*. Translated by Phillip H. Wicksteed and Francis Macdonald Cornford. 2 vols. London: Heinemann, and New York: Putnam, 1929. The sixth book contains an analysis of Zeno's arguments. Important because Zeno's extant texts are so fragmentary. This translation is part of the Loeb Classical Library series.

Freeman, Kathleen. *The Pre-Socratic Philosophers*. Cambridge, Mass.: Harvard University Press, and Oxford: Blackwell, 1946. Freeman's work contains translations of the extant fragments of Zeno's work, interspersed with analysis and commentary.

Fuller, B. A. G. *A History of Philosophy*. 3d ed. New York: Henry Holt, 1955. Fuller gives a brief but helpful summary of Zeno's philosophy. Includes an extensive bibliography.

Hussey, Edward. *The Presocratics*. London: Duckworth, and New York: Scribner, 1972. This volume contains a sympathetic analysis of Parmenides and Zeno. According to Hussey, "What is historically most important here is the logical analysis of such concepts as *time, change, diversity, separation, completeness*."

Plato. *Parmenides*. In *Plato and Parmenides*, translated by Francis Macdonald Cornford. London: Routledge, and New York: Humanities Press, 1939. Plato provides a glimpse of Zeno as a person as well as some idea of the thought of

Parmenides. It is not certain that the dialogue form Plato favors was actually employed by Zeno. An "Eleatic stranger," said to be a disciple of Parmenides and Zeno, takes part in two of the dialogues, but it is not certain whether he expresses their thoughts.

West, Martin. "Early Greek Philosophy." In *The Oxford History of the Classical World*, edited by John Boardman, Jasper Griffin, and Oswyn Murray. Oxford: Oxford University Press, 1986. Although this essay does not give much detail on Zeno, it is nevertheless useful in placing him in his historical and cultural context. The volume itself is illustrated and includes an index and bibliographies.

John C. Sherwood

ZOROASTER

Born: c. 628 B.C.; probably Rhages, northeastern Iran

Died: c. 551 B.C.; probably northern Iran

Area of Achievement: Religion

Contribution: The founder of one of the great ethical religions of the ancient world, Zoroaster exerted direct and indirect influence on the development of three other great religions: Judaism, Christianity, and Islam.

Early Life

Zoroaster (the corrupt Greek from of the Persian name Zarathustra) was one of the most important religious reformers of the ancient world and the founder of a new religion which took his name: Zoroastrianism. Since very little is known about his life, the dates of his birth and death are disputed. According to tradition, he "lived 258 years before Alexander" the Great. This has been interpreted as 258 years before Alexander's conquest of Persia in 330 B.C. The date has also been interpreted not as a birth date but as the date of one of three principal events in his life: his vision and revelation at the age of thirty, the beginning of his preaching at age forty, or the conversion of King Vishtaspa (or Hystapas) two years later. Since, according to tradition, Zoroaster lived for seventy-seven years, he lived between 630 and 553, 628 and 551, or 618 and 541.

Although he was never deified, legends and pious embellishments began to grow about Zoroaster after his death. Such legends have both clarified and obscured modern knowledge about him. It was said that he was the product of a miraculous birth and that at birth he laughed aloud, thus driving away evil spirits. As an adult, he became a great lover of wisdom and righteousness, withdrawing to an isolated mountain wilderness, where he survived on cheese and wild fruit. There he was tempted by the Devil but successfully resisted. He was then subjected to intense physical torture, which he endured by clinging to his faith in Ahura Mazda, the true god and the Lord of Light. He received a revelation from Ahura Mazda in the form of the *Avesta*, the holy book of his religion, and was commissioned to preach to mankind. After suffering ridicule and persecution for many years, he at last found a convert and patron in King Vishtaspa. Married and a father of a daughter and two sons, Zoroaster appears to have enjoyed a degree of local prominence at his patron's court. His daughter apparently married a leading minister of the king.

Life's Work

Like the other great ethical religions, Zoroastrianism had its origins in its founder's reaction to the religious beliefs and practices of his people. The religion of the pre-Zoroastrian Persians displays many features in common with Hinduism. This is understandable, because the ancient settlers of Persia and India came from the same Aryan tribes which had invaded Persia and India a millennium before Zoroaster's birth. Persian religion before Zoroaster was polytheistic, with specific deities attached to the three major classes of society: chiefs and priests, warriors, and farmers and cattle breeders. The deities known as *asuras* (lords), who alone were endowed with an ethical character, were attached exclusively to the first class. Two forms of sacrifice were practiced: animal sacrifice, apparently to propitiate the gods, and the drinking of the fermented juice of the sacred *haoma* plant, which, through the intoxication it induced, supplied a foretaste of immortality. To perform the sacrifices and the other rituals, a priestly class, the *magi*, rose to a position of great power in early Persian society.

Basing his teaching on the *Avesta*, a book of revelations from Ahura Mazda, Zoroaster conceived it as his mission to purify the traditional beliefs of his people by eradicating polytheism, animal sacrifice, and magic and to establish a new, more ethical and spiritual religion. Ultimately, Zoroastrianism succeeded because of its founder's and early followers' ability to accommodate their teachings with certain features of traditional Persian religion.

It is impossible to determine how many of the teachings of Zoroastrianism originated with its founder. The *Avesta*, as it has come down to the present, is composed of several divisions, including two liturgical texts, prayers, and two sets of hymns, only one of which, the *Gathas*, is definitely ascribed to Zoroaster. Much of the *Avesta* has been destroyed or lost. Zoroaster probably made additional contributions, as did his later followers. There is, however, general agreement that it was Zoroaster who provided the central teaching of his religion.

According to Zoroaster, the history of the world was the ongoing conflict between the forces of good and evil. God, Ahura Mazda, represented the former; the Devil, Ahriman, the latter. Ahura Mazda, one of several of the *asuras* of traditional Persian religion, was elevated by Zoroaster to the place of the one high god; Zoroastrianism was originally a distinctly monotheistic religion, although later it absorbed polytheistic features. Zoroaster divided history into four three-thousand-year periods, during which Ahura Mazda and Ahriman competed for men's souls and the ultimate victory of their respective causes. At the end of the final stage, which some Zoroastrians interpreted as beginning with the birth of Zoroaster, Ahura Mazda would overpower Ahriman and his minions in a great conflagration and cast them into the abyss. This would be followed by a resurrection of the dead, a last judgment, and the beginning of a new life for all good souls (believers in Ahura Mazda) in a world free of evil, darkness, pain, and death. Zoroastrianism included concepts of a hell and purgatory as well as a paradise. At death, all souls would have to cross the narrow Sifting Bridge (also known as the Bridge of the Requiter), which was like a long sword. The good would be offered the broad (flat) side of the bridge and would be welcomed into Paradise by a beautiful young maiden. There they would reside with Ahura Mazda throughout eternity. The evil souls—the followers of Ahriman—would be forced to walk along the razor's edge of the sword-bridge and would fall into a hell which would be their abode of darkness and terror forever. For the souls who had sinned but whose good works outweighed their bad, there would be a short period of temporary punishment to cleanse them in preparation for entrance into Paradise. For sinners of greater degree, who had nevertheless performed some good works, suffering in Hell would last until God's final victory and the last judgment, when they also would be welcomed into Paradise. Those who subscribed to Zoroaster's teachings, therefore, could face death unafraid in anticipation of a blissful afterlife, if not immediately at least ultimately.

The religion of Zoraster was ethical. Man's duty was threefold: to befriend his enemy, to lead the wicked to righteousness, and to educate the ignorant. The greatest virtue toward which the believer must strive was piety, followed by honor and honesty in both word and deed. The worst sin was unbelief, which was not only a denial of Ahura Mazda but also a rejection of his ethical code of conduct and an acceptance of evil. Since piety was the greatest virtue, the first obligation of the believer was to worship God through purification, sacrifice, and prayer. Although Zoroaster rejected blood sacrifices, he retained the sacrifice of fire, which was a symbol of Ahura Mazda and thus of purity and truth. Although Zoroaster decried the drinking of the fermented juice of the *haoma* plant for its intoxicating qualities, it was retained as a medium of Holy Communion. Historically, the fire ritual became the central feature of Zoroastrian worship. Sacred fires are tended and preserved by priests in fire temples, where the king of fires, Bahram, is crowned and enthroned. Modern Zoroastrians (Parsees) have also retained the practices of wearing the *sadre*, the shirt which symbolizes their religion, and the daily untying and reknotting of the *kushti*, the sacred thread whose seventy-two strands symbolize the chapters of the *Yasna*, one of the sacred liturgical texts. The final act of piety is proper provision for the disposition of one's body after death. The corpse is neither cremated nor buried, since the first method would defile fire and the second method the earth, both of which are regarded as good creations of God. Instead, the dead are exposed to the elements, where their flesh is consumed by vultures. This practice survives today in the famous Towers of Silence in Bombay among the Parsees (Persians), virtually the last significant surviving community of Zoroastrians.

Although Zoroaster was a monotheist, he nevertheless sought to accommodate his religious traditions. Surrounding Ahura Mazda are the six "Beneficent (or Holy) Immortal Ones" and the *yazads* (the worshipped ones), who probably had their origins in the deities worshipped by the lesser orders of ancient Persian society. These beings have been compared to the archangels and angels of Christianity. Because of the exalted nature of Ahura Mazda, it came to be believed that he should be approached indirectly through these servants, who came to personify certain facets of God's creation and qualities. The *yazad* Mithra, keeper of the sacred fire (the fire temples came to be called the courts of Mithra), who represented justice and friendship and who was Ahura Mazda's chief lieutenant in the struggle against evil, was himself to become the deity in a religious offshoot of Zoroastrianism, Mithraism, which was one of Christianity's chief competitors in the Roman Empire. Opposed to the servants of God were Ahriman and his hordes of demons, who were also associated with lesser ancient Persian demigods. They brought evil into the world in its various forms and worked to deny humans their blissful afterlife with Ahura Mazda and his servants.

Zoroaster is thought to have died at the age of seventy-seven; legend states that he was murdered.

Summary

The history of Zoroastrianism following the death of its founder was characterized by change, accommodation, decline, and revival. The most notable changes were the emergence of dualism, with the deification of Ahriman and the conception of history as the struggle between separate gods of good and evil, and the emergence of an increasingly powerful priestly class, the *magi*, who introduced elements of magic, astrology, and blood sacrifice in a perversion of Zoroaster's ideals. Following the Muslim conquest of Persia in the seventh century, Zoroastrians were alternately tolerated, persecuted, and forcibly converted to Islam. In the eleventh century, all but a small remnant left Persia and emigrated to India, where most of them settled in the area around Bombay. There they have remained, and, known as the Parsees, they have become among the wealthiest, best-educated, and most charitable members of Indian society, all the while holding fast to their religious beliefs and practices. In the nineteenth century, they reestablished contact with the remaining Zoroastrians in Iran, the Gabars.

There are significant parallels between Zoroastrianism and three of the world's great religions, Judaism, Christianity, and Islam, although the extent of Zoroastrianism's direct influence remains a subject of debate. Perhaps Zoroaster's greatest contribution, both to his own age and to later civilizations, was the elevation of religion from debasement, magic, blood sacrifice, and pessimism to a scheme which optimistically promises rewards to those who conform in word and deed to a high, but realizable, code of ethical conduct.

Bibliography

Duchesne-Guillemin, Jacques. *The Western Response to Zoroaster*. Oxford: Oxford University Press, 1958; Westport, Conn.: Greenwood Press, 1973. This is a valuable introduction to scholarship on Zoroaster and Zoroastrianism by one of the leading twentieth century scholars on the subject.

Durant, Will. *Our Oriental Heritage*. New York: Simon and Schuster, 1935. This first volume in the Durants' multivolume popular classic, The Story of Civilization, contains an especially helpful and perceptive account of Zoroaster and Zoroastrianism. Durant considers the subject both in its ancient Persian context and as a powerful influence on later religions.

Masani, Rustom. *The Religion of the Good Life*. London: Allen and Unwin, and New York: Collier, 1938. This is a useful account by a Parsee of the teachings and practices of Zoroastrianism.

Olmstead, A. T. *History of the Persian Empire*. Chicago: University of Chicago Press, 1948. This classic history of ancient Persia is useful in placing Zoroaster in his historical context.

Parrinder, Geoffrey, ed. *World Religions from Ancient History to the Present*. New York: Facts on File Publications, 1983. In this revised and enlarged edition of a book first published in 1971 as *Man and His Gods* in Great Britain and as *Religions of the World* in the United States, Zoroastrianism is traced from its origins to the present, including material on its most important offshoots, Mithraism and Manichaeanism.

Zoroaster. *The Hymns of Zarathustra*. Translated with an introduction by Jacques Duchesne-Guillemin. London: Murray, 1952; New York: Beacon, 1963. This translation of the *Gathas*, which contains the only teachings of Zoroastrianism which can definitely be attributed to its founder, is indispensable to serious study of the subject.

J. Stewart Alverson

ZOSER

Born: c. 2700 B.C.; probably Memphis, Egypt

Died: c. 2650 B.C.; Memphis, Egypt

Areas of Achievement: Government and architecture

Contribution: Zoser was the first great king of the epoch known as the Old Kingdom, Third through Sixth dynasties. His outstanding achievement was the construction of the Step Pyramid at Saqqara near Memphis, the earliest of the great pyramids.

Early Life

Zoser's brother Sanekht preceded him to the throne as the first king of the Third Dynasty. Since both Sanekht and Zoser were sons of Khasekhemwy, the last king of the Second Dynasty, it is not clear why Sanekht's accession should have caused a change of dynasties. It may be that their mother, Nymaathap, was not a legitimate wife but a concubine of Khasekhemwy and the only one to produce suitable male offspring for the king. Upon his brother's death, Zoser assumed the throne and ruled for nineteen years.

Zoser's physical description is known from several reliefs found in the Step Pyramid complex and from a seated limestone statue, thought to be the oldest life-sized statue found in Egypt. This portrayal of the king was discovered in a small, doorless room near his pyramid, positioned to look out of two eyeholes in the wall so that the king could view food offerings brought to him by his funerary priests each day. Although the inlaid eyes have been gouged out and the nose has been damaged, the massive head, with its high cheekbones and prominent mouth, has lost none of its intimidating majesty. This is no idealized portrait, but the likeness of Zoser himself.

Apart from the members of his immediate family, only a few others can be linked to Zoser by name. Hesyra and Khabausokar have left impressive funerary monuments which testify to their importance in Zoser's court. Although his tomb remains to be discovered, there is one man, Imhotep, whose name must rank with that of the great king. In later antiquity he was credited with every kind of wisdom and was even accorded divine status as a god of healing. It is as Zoser's chief architect, however, that Imhotep has ensured his place in history, for the king entrusted to this innovative genius the construction of the Step Pyramid.

Life's Work

The ancient Egyptian believed that his king was a god, the incarnation of the falcon god Horus, source of all goods and prosperity for the entire land. During his life on earth, the king displayed his effectiveness as a ruler by the wealth and beauty of his royal residence; after his death, he proclaimed his ability to continue to perform good services for his subjects by the magnificence of his tomb. When the king departed this life he became one with his father, Osiris, god of the land's fertility, and continued to bestow prosperity on his subjects through the new incarnation of the god Horus, that is, the king's son and successor.

From the very beginning, royal tombs were built on the analogy of the royal residence, for the king's tomb was his "house of eternity," in the common Egyptian expression. Thus, in very early times when the king lived in a circular hut, his tomb was circular; when the royal residence became rectangular in shape, the royal tomb became rectangular. The royal tomb, despite some changes, remained essentially the same until the time of Zoser. It consisted of a subterranean structure where the dead king was buried with his most valuable possessions, topped by a brick superstructure in the form of a rectangular platform, which Egyptologists refer to as a mastaba (Arabic for "bench").

When Zoser came to the throne, he had the same assumptions about his role as his predecessors. He was the god Horus, or rather a temporary incarnation of that god, whose special name for this particular incarnation was Netjerykhet (divine of body). It was by this name that the king identified himself everywhere in the Step Pyramid complex and not by the familiar Zoser (found only in later writings together with the name Netjerykhet). Like his predecessors, Zoser assumed that one of his most important duties as king was to undertake the preparation of his "house of eternity." Fortunately, he had in his service the brilliant Imhotep.

Zoser's decision to construct a mastaba for his monument was dictated by tradition, but instead of employing the usual rectangular shape, he directed Imhotep to build it as a square, with each side facing the four cardinal points and measuring approximately 207 feet. In addition, he ordered that the monument be constructed of limestone and not brick, the material used in all previous constructions of this sort. Rising to a height of twenty-six feet, this square stone mastaba was enclosed in a rectangular area by a wall thirty-three feet high and more than a mile long.

Even as it stood, Zoser's monument displayed a number of bold innovations. Simply in point of size, it dwarfed anything in Egyptian experience, since the area enclosed by the girdle wall was more than sixty times larger than any built so far. Almost immediately, however, Zoser began to rethink the plan of his monument. In the end, the original mastaba underwent six major reconstructions and eventually emerged as a white stone pyramid rising in six unequal steps to a height of 204 feet and measuring at the base 411 by 358 feet. Instead of viewing his tomb simply as his royal residence in death, Zoser had come to think of it also as a colossal staircase by which his transfigured body might climb up into the sky and join the sun god Re in his solar barge as he passed through the sky each day (this according to information discovered in pyramids of the Fifth Dynasty).

Not until after the pyramid was finished did Zoser complete the numerous other temples and courts which he considered essential to the complex, for he envisioned it as a true necropolis, a city of the dead. Except for the Mortuary Temple and the smaller building in which Zoser's statue was found, none of the other buildings surrounding the Step Pyramid has any known precedent or parallel, and the purpose that many were intended to serve remains obscure. One group of buildings, partially restored, whose function is reasonably clear, relates to the celebration of the Sed or Jubilee Festival and requires special attention.

In earlier times, when the king's physical vigor was observed to weaken he was put to death and replaced by a younger man, since nature's bounty was thought to depend on the king's virility. In later times, this custom was supplanted by the Sed Festival, which enabled the aging king to renew his power through magic and thus ensure the welfare of his kingdom. Zoser most likely had celebrated this festival during his life and had intended that the complex of buildings south of his pyramid should provide him with the setting necessary for repeating this ceremony throughout eternity. One of the most important rites was the reenactment of the king's double coronation as King of Upper and Lower Egypt, during which he was presented with the white crown of the south and the red crown of the north. In another rite, which is depicted in a fine relief, the king is shown running a fixed course, apparently to display his renewed strength to his subjects. An area was set aside for Zoser's eternal run.

Archaeologists have carefully examined the subterranean part of Zoser's tomb, where he was buried with his most valuable possessions. Despite having been plundered by tomb robbers over the course of some four thousand years, the storage rooms have yielded to excavators some ninety tons of stone vessels made of such costly stones as alabaster, porphyry, and quartz. It is clear that Zoser was lavishly equipped for eternity, on a scale never attempted before.

Summary

Menes, the legendary first king of the First Dynasty, unified Upper and Lower Egypt in approximately 3200 B.C. An Egypt with a strong central government was able to undertake large hydraulic projects to control the annual inundations of the Nile. Under one king, the obedient army and conscribed peasants could increase the amount of arable land by draining swamps and irrigating the desert margins. During the first two dynasties, despite periods of civil strife, a unified Egypt was able to make enormous strides forward in every way. The invention of writing made it possible to conduct censuses of people and animals, make records of more complicated data, and communicate easily over long distances. Leisure provided the intelligentsia with an opportunity for speculative thought and for the fine arts as well as the practical.

Roughly five hundred years of progress culminated in Zoser's reign. Although written documents are generally lacking for this period, the Step Pyramid itself is very reliable testimony to the great prosperity and self-confidence which characterized Zoser's tenure. The size of his funerary monument alone implies much about the economic and political status of Egypt during this period. More important than mere size, however, are the architectural innovations, especially Zoser's decision to build his monument in the revolutionary shape of a pyramid and to use quarried stone for its material, the first large structure to be so raised. The Step Pyramid represents Zoser's vision of himself as king, able literally to ascend into the heavens by a stairway that would never perish. Zoser's vision was fully realized about one hundred years later in the Great Pyramid of Cheops, still a wonder to the world.

Bibliography

Aldred, Cyril. *Egyptian Art in the Days of the Pharaohs, 3100-320 B.C.* London: Thames and Hudson, and New York: Oxford University Press, 1980. Primarily trained as an art historian, Aldred has produced perhaps the most elegant and lucid descriptions of Egypt's art treasures available in any language. The chapter on the Third Dynasty is particularly informative on the precise nature and significance of the architectural innovations of Zoser's reign.

Edwards, I. E. S. *The Pyramids of Egypt.* Rev. ed. London and Baltimore: Penguin, 1961. Edwards has written the classic account of the pyramids. His chapter on Zoser's Step Pyramid includes a very helpful discussion of the king's successors, who tried to follow Zoser's example in building their tombs in step-pyramid form. The pyramid of Sekhemkhet, Zoser's son, was planned on a more lavish scale than his father's, but it was never finished.

Firth, C. M., and J. E. Quibell. *Excavations at Saqqara, the Step Pyramid.* Architectural plans by J. Ph. Lauer. 2 vols. Cairo: L'Institut Français d'Archéologie Orientale, 1935. Serious excavations around the Step Pyramid did not begin until after World War I, when Firth took charge of the work from 1920 until his death in 1931. Lauer joined Firth in 1927 as architect and is responsible for the extensive restoration work on the pyramid and surrounding buildings which is still in progress. This book is the fundamental work on the Step Pyramid complex.

Lichtheim, Miriam. *Ancient Egyptian Literature: A Book of Readings.* Vol. 3, *The Late Period.* Berkeley: University of California Press, 1975. Lichtheim translates and comments on the famous rock inscription called the "Famine Stela." It purports to be the record of an order given by Zoser himself during a time of famine to appease the god Khnum, who controlled the floodwaters of the Nile. Many scholars doubt the authenticity of the inscription.

Smith, W. S. *The Art and Architecture of Ancient Egypt.* Rev. ed. New Haven, Conn.: Yale University Press, 1981; London: Penguin Books, 1983. The chapter on the Third Dynasty is generously illustrated with black-and-white photographs. Although the bibliography cited for the chapter is much less extensive than that cited in *The Cambridge Ancient History*, it is quite sufficient for practical purposes. Smith provides a compendious and serviceable account of the major art forms of Zoser's time, excluding pottery, for which no adequate account has yet been written.

―――. "The Old Kingdom in Egypt." In *The Cambridge Ancient History*, vol. 1, edited by I. E. S. Edwards, C. J. Gadd, and N. G. L. Hammond. 3d ed. Cambridge: Cambridge University Press, 1971. Smith's discussion of the Third Dynasty includes all the minutiae pertaining to Zoser's lineage and the chief monuments of officials of his court. In general, this admirable series of volumes is written by scholars for scholars, and Smith's account is no exception. Each chapter is furnished with an extensive bibliography, an indispensable guide to further study.

H. J. Shey

Dictionary of World Biography

The Ancient World

Indices

AREA OF ACHIEVEMENT

STATECRAFT. *See* **GOVERNMENT AND POLITICS and WARFARE AND CONQUEST**

TECHNOLOGY. *See* **INVENTION AND TECHNOLOGY**

THEATER AND DRAMA. *See also* **MUSIC**

THEOLOGY. *See also* **PHILOSOPHY and RELIGION**

WARFARE AND CONQUEST. *See also* **GOVERNMENT AND POLITICS**

GEOGRAPHICAL LOCATION

NAME INDEX

PHOTO CREDITS

Unless individually credited, all photos in this volume are courtesy of the Library of Congress except for the following.

Courtesy of Archive Photos: 184, 264, 291, 322, 331, 349, 352, 375, 379, 387, 408, 440, 447, 464, 476, 504, 519, 538, 581, 717, 739, 742, 747, 775, 804, 849, 865, 923, 963, 968

Courtesy of the Chicago Public Library: 20, 31, 70, 128, 133, 219, 254, 269